A NATURE
CONSERVATION REVIEW

VOLUME 2: SITE ACCOUNTS

A NATURE CONSERVATION REVIEW

The selection of biological sites of national importance to
nature conservation in Britain

EDITOR

DEREK RATCLIFFE

CHIEF SCIENTIST, THE NATURE CONSERVANCY COUNCIL

VOLUME 2

SITE ACCOUNTS

CAMBRIDGE UNIVERSITY PRESS

CAMBRIDGE

LONDON · NEW YORK · MELBOURNE

Published by the Syndics of the Cambridge University Press
The Pitt Building, Trumpington Street, Cambridge CB2 1RP
Bentley House, 200 Euston Road, London NW1 2DB
32 East 57th Street, New York, NY 10022, USA
296 Beaconsfield Parade, Middle Park, Melbourne 3206, Australia

First published 1977

Printed in Great Britain at the
University Press, Cambridge

Library of Congress Cataloguing in Publication Data

Main entry under title:

A Nature conservation review.

Published on behalf of the Nature Conservancy Council and the
Natural Environment Research Council.

Bibliography: v. 1, p.

Includes index.

1.   Natural areas – Great Britain.   2.   Nature conservation –
Great Britain.
I.   Ratcliffe, Derek A.
II.   Great Britain. Nature Conservancy Council.
III.   Great Britain. Natural Environment Research Council.

QH77.G7N39   333.9'5'0941   76–11065

ISBN 0521 21403 3

CONTENTS

Contents   vii

PREFACE

Volume 1 of *A Nature Conservation Review* provides an outline description of the wildlife resource of Britain, in terms of the wild plants and animals, in relation to their habitats and ecological requirements. The distribution and abundance of the vascular plants, vertebrates and certain groups of invertebrates are considered, but plant communities are regarded as the most useful biological basis for the characterisation of sites. The key site concept of nature conservation is discussed and a rationale given for the selection of the most important wildlife areas within the total range of variation, grouped into the major formations of coastlands; woodlands; lowland grasslands, heaths and scrub; open waters; peatlands; and upland grasslands and heaths. The actual choice of key sites is summarised in a geographical account for each formation. Volume 2 gives a detailed account of the important biological and environmental features of each site, insofar as these are known, and with emphasis on vegetation. These site accounts are not wholly meaningful without reference to Volume 1, since they assume a knowledge of certain definitions, base-line criteria, concepts, qualifications, sources and other background information presented there.

The site accounts aim to give a concise description of the principal features by which the nature conservation value of the site is assessed. They thus tend to be comparative between sites of similar type within any formation, which may lead to different stress – and sometimes perhaps apparent inconsistency of treatment – when descriptions of dissimilar sites are compared. For instance, a species rare in one district may receive special mention, but may not be mentioned at all in places where it is common, unless it there becomes a community dominant. Moreover, different formations may require different treatment, e.g. peatland sites tend to be less extensive and diverse than upland grassland and heath complexes, so that botanical descriptions for the former are generally more detailed than for the latter. To give a full and standardised account of each site has been impossible in the present often incomplete or highly fragmentary state of knowledge, and the natural tendency has been to highlight known features of special interest. For many sites it is highly probable that further survey will disclose many other interesting features to which attention should be drawn.

A standardised format was thus rejected for, although this achieves greater consistency of treatment, it is wasteful of space and not necessarily a significant improvement when survey knowledge is incomplete. It tends, moreover, to give rather arid reading, and does not lend itself to economical emphasis of special features.

The site accounts are largely, and in many instances exclusively, botanical, for zoological knowledge is in general even more incomplete and haphazard. The presence of the more common vertebrates can usually be inferred by noting the habitat/vegetation of a site and referring to the ecological accounts of animal distribution under each formation in Vol. 1. With birds in particular, it has often been necessary to omit mention of rare or even local species because of the risks of drawing unwelcome attention to their presence. For instance, many upland sites with cliffs contain nesting places of the peregrine and (in Scotland) golden eagle, but it was judged wiser not to say which ones. Where there is a risk of the collection of rare plants and invertebrates, mention of these has also been omitted, unless the occurrence is already well known or the area so large that discovery is difficult. Knowledge of invertebrates is often scanty or totally lacking, and the mention of these is confined to sites which have been well studied, or to presence of interesting species which chance to be known in the most familiar groups of insect.

Knowledge of fungi is usually totally lacking, but the algal floras of some fresh waters are well known and receive due mention. Bryophytes and lichens are adequately surveyed for many sites (the latter especially as a result of the assiduous field work of Francis Rose and his colleagues), but lack of space often precludes mention of all except especially interesting species and communities.

Many site accounts are 'dated' in that the records of occurrence and abundance of some species, vegetational features, and habitat conditions, refer to a particular point in time, and may require future revision because of probable changes. Statements about many of the rarer species are based on the last-known records, which in some instances were many years ago; but these are regarded as acceptable when there have been no known changes to make disappearance likely.

14 COASTLANDS

SOUTH-EAST ENGLAND

C.1. CUCKMERE HAVEN–BEACHY HEAD, SUSSEX
TV 491978–604966. *c.* 840 ha   Grade 1

Alluvial grassland (c. 160 ha)

Grasslands on the alluvial soils of the River Cuckmere valley are now rarely flooded and the river meanders have been virtually isolated from tidal influence by an artificial channel cut direct to the sea. Higher than average tides allow some salt water to penetrate the meanders and adjacent ditches, however, creating a range of brackish conditions.

The grassland is irregularly grazed by cattle and sheep; the commonest species in the sward are *Dactylis glomerata, Festuca ovina, Holcus lanatus, Cirsium arvense* and *Hordeum marinum. Ophioglossum vulgatum* and *Althaea officinalis* occur more rarely. The bush cricket *Tettigona viridissima* is abundant on pasture near the sea.

Salt marsh (c. 20 ha)

There is a small area of salt marsh in a tidal range of 6 m on clay and silt with marked lime-rich influences. Species include *Puccinellia maritima, Aster tripolium, Crithmum maritimum, Suaeda maritima. Spergularia media* and *Spartina anglica* with *Agropyron pungens* form a turf on slightly higher ground.

Shingle (c. 20 ha)

There are shingle banks on both sides of the river mouth, that on the east side being the most extensive. The vegetation is sparse with scattered plants of *Rumex crispus, Crambe maritima, Beta vulgaris* ssp. *maritima, Tripleurospermum maritimum* and *Glaucium flavum. Calystegia soldanella* is found on the west bank.

Chalk grassland (c. 500 ha)

The best examples of chalk grassland are found on the tops of the cliffs known as the Seven Sisters and Beachy Head. These are the highest chalk cliffs in Britain reaching 160 m. The grassland is still subject to rabbit-grazing and is further influenced by direct exposure to south-west winds from the sea. It contains southern elements of the British flora and includes *Seseli libanotis, Bupleurum baldense, Lactuca saligna, Limonium binervosum, Senecio integrifolius, Orchis ustulata, Phyteuma tenerum* and *Raphanus maritimus.* The site is of phytogeographical interest as the eastern limit on the south coast of many south western species.

The estuary (140 ha) provides a winter feeding and roost-ing area for several species of wildfowl, while scrub on the downs provides food and cover for migrating birds especially passerines. The chalk cliffs were formerly a noted haunt of peregrines with up to three or four pairs nesting in a 1-km stretch, but there have been no nesting records since the onset of the population 'crash' around 1956.

C.2. FOLKESTONE WARREN, KENT
TR 237363–312398. 480 ha   Grade 1

Folkestone Warren is an area of landslips on the Gault and Chalk. There are extensive areas of undercliff forming steep, broken slopes above the shore and with typical development of a luxuriant, ungrazed vegetation mainly of tall herbs and shrubs. The range of habitats is diverse, with bare ground at various angles. The Warren includes areas of chalk grassland dominated by *Festuca ovina* and *Brachypodium pinnatum*; bare cliffs sparsely colonised by species of open chalk and coastal habitats; and at the bottom of the cliffs, hawthorn scrub and damp hollows with miniature fen communities containing species such as *Juncus subnodulosus. Crambe maritima* occurs on the shore. Orchids recorded from the short chalk turf areas include *Ophrys fuciflora, O. sphegodes, O. apifera* and *Coeloglossum viride.* The flora of the broken Chalk landslips and steeper cliff sections is rich, especially at the eastern end, and the following have been recorded: *Frankenia laevis, Orobanche maritima, O. caryophyllacea, Silene nutans* var. *smithiana, Inula crithmoides, Phyllitis scolopendrium, Euphrasia occidentalis, Glaucium flavum, Brassica oleracea, Crithmum maritimum, Limonium binervosum, Senecio erucifolius* and *Solidago virgaurea.* There is also extensive privet scrub with *Rubia peregrina* and *Iris foetidissima.*

The Warren also supports a remarkably rich insect fauna, especially of Lepidoptera. Four species of moth are extreme rarities: Morris's wainscot, rest harrow, sub-angled wave and fiery clearwing. The Warren is also rich in typical species of chalk downland, including the local straw belle *Aspitates gilvaria,* and is one of the best south coast sites for migrant Lepidoptera, including Blair's mocha *Cyclophora puppillaria* which was first recorded in Britain in 1946.

The Hemiptera–Heteroptera of Folkestone Warren are rich in species and several rarities occur, e.g. *Eurgaster maura* and *Ischnodemus quadratus.*

Ground-living bugs of the families Corcidae, Lygaeidae and others are particularly abundant on the warm, dry, south-facing slopes. The Coleoptera include some notable species, particularly among the curculionids. *Platystomos*

Coastlands

albinus, a rare anthribid, has been recorded. *Apion limonii* occurs in association with *Limonium binervosum* on cliffs, being much more usually taken on other *Limonium* spp. in salt marshes. *Liparus coronatus* and *L. germanus* (the latter restricted in Britain to Kent) both occur and other local species include *Tychinum schneideri*, *Phytonomus pastinacae* (rare), *Epipolaeus caligniosus*, *Ceuthorhynchus picitersis*, *C. resedae*, *C. trimaculatus* and *Ceuthorhynchidius hornidus*. *Baris laticollis* is particularly abundant here (in stems of *Brassica oleracea*).

Peregrines formerly bred on the steeper cliffs of this site.

C.3. DUNGENESS, KENT
TR 0418.   2500 ha   Grade 1*

Dungeness is a huge shingle beach system, but with other well-developed habitats such as salt marsh, freshwater marsh, open water and dunes. Floristically it is extremely rich, with about 600 species of plant.

Coastal lagoon and marsh (465 ha – split into three distinct areas)

Both natural and artificial, saline and fresh, medium-size bodies of water occur with mud over shingle bottoms carrying fringing submerged aquatic vegetation and emergent marsh. The latter includes beds of *Phragmites communis* and *Scirpus maritimus* up to 40 ha in extent. There is a great variety of plants and invertebrates, including many species with continental and southern affinities.

Shingle (2035 ha)

Dungeness carries the most extensive shingle ridge and low flora in Britain (and possibly in Europe), and contains the only complete and relatively undisturbed sere from bare shingle to woodland. Acidophilous heath or prostrate scrub has developed on the ridges, and the lichen and bryophyte flora is rich, especially that associated with blackthorn. There are the largest populations of dwarf broom, *Festuca tenuifolia* and *Crambe maritima* in Britain. Notable populations of many other shingle species include *Crepis foetida* and *Silene nutans*. The Oppen Pits (OW.1), four small water-bodies, are described under Open Waters. On Holmstone Beach is an open scrubland, mainly of holly, with a small proportion of elder, yew, gorse, broom and blackthorn. This climax 'wood' is known to have survived for at least 430 years virtually unchanged and it may have existed since Saxon times. It has been much disturbed by use of the land as an army range and earlier attempts at clearance, but still retains its essential features, including growth forms induced by exposure, and probably has no counterpart in Europe.

Entomology

In addition to being notable as a landfall for migrants Dungeness has several nationally rare and local Lepidoptera, including the toadflax brocade, pigmy footman, scarce black arches, and Sussex emerald. These four species probably only occur in one or two other neighbouring localities. Other interesting local species are the Kent black arches, white spot, feathered brindle, Webb's wainscot, grass eggar, water ermine, brown tail, and yarrow pug.

Ornithology

Dungeness is famous as a landfall for migrating birds in spring and autumn, especially the autumn passage of black terns, whitethroats, lesser whitethroats and firecrests. The lagoons now support the largest winter populations of mallard in Kent (up to 3000 birds) and good numbers of other duck species. Other notable wintering species include hen harrier, short-eared owl, merlin and snow bunting. This was the last reported breeding haunt of the Kentish plover in Britain, and stone curlews nested until recently. Dungeness is a long-established nesting site for the common gull, and about 12 pairs breed on the shingle. There are about 60 pairs of nesting little terns, one of the largest British colonies, and 150–200 pairs of common tern.

C.4. SANDWICH/PEGWELL BAY, KENT
TR 373542–352644.   1500 ha   Grade 1

Flats (670 ha)

This area of mud flats is broadest in Pegwell Bay and carries moderate numbers of waders, terns, gulls and wildfowl.

Marsh (120 ha)

Salt marsh is developed on either side of the Stour estuary, but has mainly bonus value.

Dune (710 ha)

There is a fairly extensive sand-dune system which is much disturbed and used as golf courses, and is of little importance physiographically, but has an exceedingly rich flora and fauna. The numerous rare and local vascular plants include *Himantoglossum hircinum*, *Orobanche caryophyllacea*, *O. maritima*, *Trifolium suffocatum*, *T. subterraneum*, *T. glomeratum*, *T. ornithopodioides*, *Silene conica*, *Erodium glutinosum*, *Parentucellia viscosa*, *Asparagus officinalis*, *Euphorbia paralias*, *Juncus acutus*, *Festuca juncifolia*, *Poa bulbosa*, *Bromus ferronii*, *Vulpia membranacea* and *V. ambigua*.

The invertebrate fauna is large and contains many rare species, such as the moths, bright wave *Idaea ochrata*, rest harrow and pigmy footman. The fauna of Hemiptera–Heteroptera is rich, particularly in ground-living species, of which many are probably associated with warm, dry conditions. The more notable species include *Schirus biguttatus*, *Odontascelis dorsalis* and *O. fuliginosa*, *Enoplops scapha*, *Spathocera dahlmanni*, *Arenocoris waltli*, *Ceraleptus lividus* and *Peritrechus gracilicornis*. Curiously similar disjunct distributions are shown by two Lygaeidae, *Pionosomus varius* and *Emblethis verbasci*; both occur here and in Cornwall and Glamorgan. Some species of Heteroptera (and Coleoptera) are apparently restricted to the area between the sea and the Royal Cinque Ports golf course, e.g. *Micranthia marginalis*, while others have been found only north of the Sandwich Bay Estate. There are several nineteenth-century records of rare species apparently not now

British: *Jalla dumosa, Stictopleurus pictus* and *Prostemma guttula.*

The Coleoptera are also outstanding. Among the Carabidae at least seven species of *Dyschirius* occur, including the very rare *D. extensus* near Sandown Castle. *Thalassophilus longicornis* is usually a species of northern Britain. The rare *Diachromus germanus* has not been recorded recently. Also notable are *Panagaeus bipustuiatus, Harpalus cordatus, Amara infima* and *Masoreus wetterhalii.* Several species of *Bledius* (Staphylinidae) occur in damp hollows, especially near Sandown Castle, and the rare elaterid *Adrastus rachifer* is found here. A number of notable Curculionidae occur, although *Lixus vilis*, is probably extinct. Other rare and local curculionids include *Cossonus planatus, Caulotropis aeneopiceus, Phytonomus dauci, P. pastinacae, Limobius mixtus, Ceuthorhynchus verrucatus* and *C. hirtulus.*

C.5. CHICHESTER/LANGSTONE HARBOURS, SUSSEX, HAMPSHIRE

SU 7601, SU 8004, SU 8302   Grade 1*

These two large estuarine basins lie immediately east of Portsmouth on the south coast. Their upper, northern ends interconnect but they are otherwise separated by the T-shaped Hayling Island, which widens towards its southern end, so that the narrow mouths of the two inlets are 6.5 km apart. Each estuary has large areas of mud flat of great importance to wintering wildfowl and waders.

(a) Chichester Harbour
2400 ha

Flats (1600 ha)

This tidal basin has two main, broad arms (Emsworth and Thorney), with two narrower channels (Bosham and Chichester) entering Thorney from the east. These arms and the main basin are mainly filled by lime-rich clay-silt flats, in a medium tide range (4 m), and some subsurface chalk springs. There are extensive *Enteromorpha* beds and rather small amounts of *Zostera* sp., while the invertebrate fauna is diverse and abundant. These food resources support a large population of dark-bellied brent geese, up to 3000 birds, and shelduck (3200). There are also considerable numbers of wigeon, mallard, teal and pintail, and a variety of other ducks and swans. The most important area for these wildfowl is Thorney Deep. Wader populations in winter number up to 25000 birds, with 20000 dunlin, 2000 redshank, 2000 curlew and 1000 bar-tailed godwit, and this is an important passage haunt of black-tailed godwit. These birds congregate at one or two major high-tide roosts, the largest of which is at Pilsey Island.

Marsh (730 ha)

There is a good deal of *Spartina anglica* meadow on the mud flats, but areas of true salt marsh with a more varied community are rather local, and occur mainly in the more sheltered areas. Towards the seaward end of the harbour off East Head and Pilsey Island there are species-rich salt marsh communities behind a dune and spit system, and here

over 100 species are recorded, including *Frankenia laevis.* At the head of Fishbourne channel, salt marsh grades through a *Phragmites* zone into fresh marsh influenced by a substantial chalk spring with *Carex paniculata* and a small willow carr. Thorney Deep is a reclaimed salt marsh in which the freshwater marsh vegetation has become modified subsequently by salt water intrusion.

Shingle (70 ha)

A small shingle spit is important for a colony of 40 pairs of little terns, breeding alongside about 30 pairs of common terns.

There are two small woodlands: Tournerbury Wood to the west of the Emsworth Channel is a mixture of oak and elm, and has a small heronry with about 10 nests. Old Park Wood on the west side of the Chichester Channel has a small hazel coppice with a comparatively rich ground flora. Oak scrub faces the channel and grows down to the water's edge. There is a heronry in this wood with about 25 nests.

(b) Langstone Harbour
1750 ha

Flats (1600 ha)

This large tidal basin, which has two main arms and only a narrow outlet to the open sea, has extensive lime-rich silt and sand flats in a tidal range of 5 m. There are profuse growths of *Enteromorpha* and extensive meadows of all three species of *Zostera*, supporting another major concentration of dark-bellied brent geese, distinct from that in Chichester Harbour, but with similar numbers (about 3000 birds). There are also usually about 3000 shelduck, and these two inlets together form probably the most important wintering grounds for this species in Britain. The numbers of dabbling ducks are considerable, with teal (1500), wigeon (1000) and mallard (300) as the most numerous. Pintail, goldeneye and red-breasted merganser occur regularly, and a variety of seaducks and grebes appears during winter.

Langstone Harbour has another major concentration of waders (22000), with dunlin and curlew again the most numerous species, and a noteworthy population of grey plover (450). Of about 40 species of wader recorded since 1954, 27 are seen regularly and in substantial numbers.

Marshes (150 ha)

Large areas of the upper flats consist of *Spartina anglica* meadow, which now shows quite extensive die-back. Between the two main channels, in the northern third of the harbour, lie four main islands consisting largely of high-level salt marsh, and an intruding tongue of brackish and reclaimed marsh known as Farlington Marshes. The higher salt marshes show all stages in succession from open growths of *Salicornia* to consolidated swards dominated by *Puccinellia maritima*, but with a range of other halophytes, including much *Inula crithmoides*. Farlington Marshes are mainly *Agrostis stolonifera* sward with many brackish and freshwater pools, and an extensive area of *Phragmites* along the bed of a former tidal creek and the margins of a moderate-sized lagoon. This area was embanked and reclaimed, but there has been much infiltration by sea water to give brackish conditions. This, in combination with chalk drainage water internally, gives a wide range of soil conditions, and there is a rich flora, with some 280 vascular species, including a good range of oceanic and continental European elements, and 14 comparatively rare plants. About one-third of the British grass species occur here. These marshes form an important roost for the wildfowl and wader populations at high tide.

C.6. THE SWALE (ISLE OF SHEPPEY), KENT
TQ 9966. 3100 ha   Grade 1

Flats (1130 ha)

This is a medium sized area of mid- to high-level lime-rich clay/silt mud flats in a tide range of 4 m. *Zostera angustifolia* and to a lesser extent *Z. noltii* have expanded over several hectares in the Faversham area in recent years and the site is relatively unpolluted. Together with the adjoining marshes it has a very high carrying capacity for ducks, geese and waders. The more important species are mallard (1500), teal (700), wigeon (2500), pintail (50), shoveler (100), pochard, common scoter (1200), eider, red-breasted merganser, shelduck (2000), white-fronted goose (400), brent goose (600), oystercatcher (3000+), grey plover (1000+), golden plover (3300), turnstone (300), curlew (3500), bar-tailed godwit (1000), redshank (1300), knot (10000), dunlin (5000). Average annual wader figures are, however, in the region of 20000 birds.

The most extensive flats are on the south side of the Swale where the inter-tidal fauna is among the richest known in south-east England. Over 350 invertebrate species have been recorded, including rarities such as the polychaete worm *Clymenella torquata* and the hemichordate *Saccoglossus*.

Coastal lagoon (40 ha)

Of exceptional interest are the extensive shallow fleets (e.g. Capel Fleet) formed by blocked-off creeks in reclaimed marsh. They carry some of the largest continuous populations of *Scirpus maritimus* in Britain and, adjoining them, local species such as *Carex divisa*, *Chenopodium botryodes*, and *Puccinellia fasciculata* occur, while both species of *Ruppia* have also been recorded in this area. A rich invertebrate fauna is also indicated.

Marsh (280 ha)

A fine series of species-rich ungrazed salt marshes occurs on the north shore of the Swale, backed by several hundred hectares of sheep-grazed, reclaimed marsh intersected by brackish freshwater ditches carrying many additional species of plants and animals. These reclaimed marshes are, however, likely to be subjected to extensive conversion to arable land. The salt marsh communities are fine examples of those characteristic of the fine sediments of the low-lying marshes of south-east England. All species of *Puccinellia* (except the northern *P. capillaris*) and most *Salicornia* spp. occur together with many other local plants, including *Spartina maritima*, *Inula crithmoides*, *Torilis nodosa*, and

Peucedanum officinale. The largest British staphylinid beetle *Emus hirtus*, the very rare chrysomelid *Macroplea mutica* and ground lackey moth all have their best British populations on these marshes. Work on marsh grasshopper populations is in progress at Shellness.

Shell spit (15 ha)

The small cockle shell spit at Shellness carries many species additional to those of the marshes. These include *Polygonum raii*, *Glaucium flavum*, *Eryngium maritimum*, *Euphorbia paralias* and *Tetragonolobus maritimus*. On the south side of the Swale at Castle Coot is the only known locality in the Thames estuary for *Crambe maritima*.

Maritime grassland/grazing marsh (1635 ha)

The marshes at the southern tip of the Isle of Harty are backed by undisturbed grassland on rising ground which carries much *Lathyrus nissolia* and *Ononis spinosa* and one of the largest continuous populations of *Trifolium squamosum* near the junction with the shore. *Bupleurum tenuissimum* and *Hordeum marinum* also occur. Natural transitions from marsh to lowland grassland are rare in southern England and the invertebrate fauna of this area is likely to be of particular interest.

Ornithology

Breeding wildfowl include mallard, teal, pochard, tufted duck, shoveler, garganey, shelduck, gadwall and mute swan. Ruff occur each spring on passage, but so far breeding has not been confirmed. There are small breeding colonies of black-headed gull, common tern and little tern.

Passage migrants include ringed plover, black-tailed godwit (550), ruff, avocet, spotted redshank, little stint, whimbrel and curlew-sandpiper.

C.7. BURNTWICK ISLAND/CHETNEY MARSHES (MEDWAY MARSHES), KENT
TQ 8871. 670 ha   Grade 1

This site on the south shore of the Medway estuary covers Burntwick and Deadman's Islands and the northern part of the Chetney peninsula. In some respects it is similar to the Swale and the High Halstow areas with a complex of mud flats, salt marsh, and reclaimed grazing marsh. The area is of lower botanical value than the Swale, for the salt marsh tends to be dominated by *Spartina anglica* and *Halimione portulacoides*.

Zostera is colonising some of the mud flats and there are also rich growths of *Enteromorpha* in some areas. The salt marshes support a number of *Salicornia* spp., *Suaeda maritima*, *Puccinellia maritima*, *Atriplex hastata*, *Inula crithmoides*, *Spergularia marina*, *Juncus gerardii* and *Limonium vulgare*. The dykes of the Chetney Marshes contain brackish-to-freshwater communities, where *Potamogeton pectinatus*, *Ceratophyllum submersum*, *Myriophyllum spicatum* and species of water crowfoot, *Ranunculus aquatilis*, are common aquatic plants. *Phragmites communis*, *Scirpus maritimus* and the rare *Chenopodium botryodes* occur in the emergent vegetation.

The Chetney peninsula is one of the most important wildfowl breeding areas in Kent. Breeding species include mallard, shelduck, shoveler, pochard, mute swan, garganey, tufted duck, teal and gadwall. In 1969, a combined total of 153 breeding pairs of these species was recorded on about 490 ha of Chetney Marshes, which also support large breeding populations of skylark, meadow pipit, lapwing, yellow wagtail and redshank. In the Medway complex as a whole, breeding birds in recent years have included black-headed gull, short-eared owl, ringed plover, little tern, and common tern. The Medway estuary is also the most important area in north Kent for breeding oystercatchers, and a high proportion of these birds breed on Burntwick Island.

The Medway is now believed to be the most important area in north Kent for wintering wildfowl. Such species in the south Medway include mallard (2000), teal (4000), wigeon (8000), pintail (900), shoveler (100+), pochard (150), regular occurrences of goldeneye, shelduck (3000), white-fronted goose (250), dark-bellied brent goose (400). Wader species include ringed plover (1000), grey plover (500), golden plover (500), curlew (2000), bar-tailed godwit (170), redshank (1500), knot (2500) and dunlin (4000). The two most important passage migrants are black-tailed godwit (350) and spotted redshank (200).

C.8. HIGH HALSTOW/CLIFFE MARSHES, KENT
TQ 7778. 1350 ha   Grade 2

This area of flats and reclaimed salt marsh borders the Thames estuary on its southern side, and forms a complex similar to that of the Swale farther east. However, there is much less unreclaimed salt marsh, and halophytic vegetation is found mainly along the fleets and dykes still influenced by tidal water. These lie behind the newly reconstructed sea wall and are probably freshening rapidly. The fleets are dominated by *Phragmites* and the dykes by *Scirpus maritimus*. *Rumex maritimus* and *Chenopodium botryodes* also occur at the edges of the dykes. The sea wall effectively seals off the marsh interior, which has been converted to extensive areas of neutral grassland used as pasture for cattle and sheep. The area is of more limited botanical interest than the Swale/Sheppey area.

The woodland on Northward Hill consists of old hawthorn scrub and damp oakwood invaded by English elm and sycamore, which formed dense stands, though much of the elm has been killed by Dutch elm disease. The understorey and shrub layer of elder and hawthorn is locally dense. Situated on base-poor London Clay, the ground flora is dominated by ivy, bramble, bluebell and locally dog's mercury and bracken.

In winter, the Halstow Marshes support large populations of wildfowl and waders: mallard (2000), wigeon (1500), pintail (225), shoveler (100), shelduck (2500; 2% of north-west European population), white-fronted goose (800; 10% of UK population). Wader figures have reached the following peaks: lapwing (10000), grey plover (1200), golden plover (1000), curlew (6000), redshank (3000), knot (1200) and dunlin (5000), but average populations are probably in the region of 10000–12000 birds.

Breeding wildfowl include mallard, pochard, shoveler, shelduck, teal, garganey, pintail, mute swan and gadwall, and the fresh marshes and fleets are important habitats for breeding waders and other birds. The marshes are one of the main feeding areas for the Northward Hill heronry (157 pairs in 1971).

C.9. ALLHALLOWS MARSHES/YANTLET CREEK, KENT
TQ 8677. 580 ha   Grade 2

The major part of the area is non-saline grazing marsh, primarily of ornithological interest, with dykes and fleets. There are small areas of salt marsh, shingle beach, and dune vegetation on the Thames shoreline where many plants of the shore reach their highest point in the Thames estuary. Species recorded include *Eryngium maritimum*, *Honkenya peploides*, *Calystegia soldanella*, *Crithmum maritimum*, *Salsola kali*, *Cakile maritima* and *Inula crithmoides*. The area is the chief locality in the country for *Polypogon monspeliensis* which hybridises with *Agrostis stolonifera*. *Bupleurum tenuissimum* and *Lathyrus nissolia* grow on the sea walls which have rich associations of clovers, including *Trifolium glomeratum*, *T. suffocatum*, *T. ornithopodioides*, *T. scabrum*, *T. subterraneum*, *T. striatum* and *T. arvense*. *Chenopodium botryodes* is common along the muddy margins of the salt marsh.

Breeding birds of the grazing marsh include mallard, shoveler, pochard, shelduck, garganey, redshank and lapwing. In most years Stoke Lagoon has breeding pairs of tufted duck and water rail. Passage migrants include ruff, whimbrel, avocet and black-tailed godwit. Little tern, black-headed gull and ringed plover attempt to breed on Grain Beach, and in winter it is an important high-tide roost for waders. Wintering ducks and waders include wigeon, shelduck, pochard, tufted duck, curlew, redshank, dunlin, golden plover and grey plover. Bewick's swans occur on Stoke Lagoon.

Large numbers of species of Coleoptera and Hemiptera have been recorded from the area.

SOUTH ENGLAND

C.5. CHICHESTER/LANGSTONE HARBOURS (PART), HAMPSHIRE   Grade 1*
See under South-east England (p. 3).

C.10. NEEDLES–ST CATHERINE'S POINT, ISLE OF WIGHT, HAMPSHIRE
SZ 290849–500753. 480 ha   Grade 1

This site consists of approximately 26 km of eroding coastline. At its western extremity it is formed of Chalk cliffs rising to 120 m, terminating in the series of isolated chalk stacks known as the Needles. Farther east steep slopes and cliffs have been formed in Wealden Beds and Lower Greensand and show numerous examples of slipping and undercliff formation resulting from differing strength and permeability of the various marl, clay, shale and sandstone strata.

The chalk cliffs support a highly specialised flora which,

though not fully investigated, is known to include *Anthyllis vulneraria, Arenaria serpyllifolia, Brassica oleracea, Cheiranthus cheiri, Cochlearia anglica, C. danica, Lobularia maritima, Matthiola incana, Parietaria diffusa, Sedum acre* and *S. anglicum*. The cliff tops have yielded over 60 species of flowering plants. The softer coastline farther east has yielded over 90 species of flowering plants in the varied and extensive stretches of well-vegetated undercliff, which includes marshy areas with *Dactylorchis* spp. Several local continental southern plants such as *Catapodium rigidum, Dipsacus fullonum* and *Glaucium flavum* occur here, with the rare oceanic southern species *Trifolium subterraneum*, and *Marrubium vulgare* in one of its few native stations in Britain. At the extreme eastern end, the steep slopes between and below tiers of cliff give mainly base-rich habitats with willow scrub and herb-rich grassland with local species such as *Astragalus glycyphyllos* and *Serratula tinctoria* and southern rock crevice species such as *Matthiola incana*, probably here in its only British locality. These landslips are known to carry about 200 species of flowering plants. The great botanical variety and warm, sheltered, southern aspect also provides conditions suitable for a rich invertebrate fauna which includes the Glanville fritillary butterfly and the Isle of Wight wave moth, both confined to the south coast of the Isle of Wight.

The Chalk cliffs support substantial colonies of cormorants and herring gulls, with smaller populations of shags, fulmars and kittiwakes, the last two species having only recently colonised this site. The formerly large breeding colonies of guillemots, razorbills and puffins are now represented by a few pairs of each species. The cliffs have the most easterly breeding ravens in southern England and formerly held up to three pairs of peregrines.

Two areas of paramaritime chalk vegetation above the western cliffs, Tennyson Down (L.37) and Compton Down (L.23), are of grade 1 quality and described under Lowland Grasslands, Heaths and Scrub.

C.11. NORTH SOLENT MARSHES, HAMPSHIRE

SZ 420980. *c.* 2250 ha   Grade 2

This site forms the undeveloped north-west shore of the Solent, between Stone Point and Hurst Beach, and consists of the estuaries of the Beaulieu and Lymington Rivers, their flanking salt marshes, and the shingle spit of Hurst Castle.

Flats (c. 1200 ha)

The areas of silt and sand flat, which occur in a small tide range of 2 m, are not large, but they have a good deal of *Enteromorpha* and *Zostera noltii* and carry moderate populations of wildfowl and waders in winter, including dark-bellied brent geese, wigeon, mallard and teal.

Marsh (c. 900 ha)

There are fairly extensive salt marshes in the estuaries of the two rivers, and along the more open coast adjoining them. *Spartina anglica* has invaded the flats on a large scale, but locally shows much die-back. More typical salt marsh communities, ranging from open *Salicornia* growths to closed *Puccinellia maritima, Halimione portulacoides, Aster tripolium* swards, are well developed, and there is a rich flora of halophytes and species of brackish habitats, including *Inula crithmoides, Althaea officinalis, Carex divisa* and *Eleocharis parvula*.

From these communities are various transitions to brackish and paramaritime types behind sea walls. Between Hurst Spit and the Lymington River, Keyhaven, Pennington and Oxey Marshes form a series of brackish grazing marshes. Former salt pans are relatively wet and carry a range of halophytic vegetation, from luxuriant *Zostera noltii* in saline lagoons, through typical mixed middle salt marsh swards to extensive *Juncus maritimus* stands, and finally *Agrostis stolonifera* swards of the fresh marsh. The Beaulieu estuary has reclaimed areas with a similar range of saline to fresh marsh, and there is a transition to alder–willow scrub; whilst the Lymington River has large *Phragmites* beds in places. The reclaimed marshes are important breeding habitats for redshank, lapwing and oystercatcher, and Keyhaven Marshes have a noteworthy overwintering flock of ruff. Needs Ore Point at the west side of the mouth of the Beaulieu River has a vast colony of black-headed gulls, numbering 15000 pairs in 1969, and about 180 pairs of Sandwich terns. (See Appendix.)

Shingle (150 ha)

Hurst Castle spit is the most important area, but there are smaller spits at the mouth of the Beaulieu estuary. There are transitions from salt marsh to shingle, marked by an abundance of *Inula crithmoides*, and 'lows' between the shingle ridges have either salt marsh species or others associated with less maritime conditions, such as *Eleogiton fluitans*. There are grasslands on some ridges with *Festuca rubra* and *Agropyron junceiforme*, and a range of succession from sparse strand communities to gorse–hawthorn–oak scrub. The Hurst spit is an important breeding habitat for gulls and terns, including the decreasing little tern.

C.12. NEWTOWN HARBOUR, ISLE OF WIGHT, HAMPSHIRE

SZ 4291. 320 ha   Grade 2

Flats (200 ha)

Newtown Harbour is the shallow drowned estuary of the Newtown River and its tributaries. Two main tidal arms drain northward and make a common exit into the Solent between projecting, recurved shingle spits. The mud flats lying between the two arms were reclaimed in the seventeenth century and were rough grazings (Newtown Main Marsh) until the sea wall was breached in 1954. Since that date part of the area has gradually reverted to salt marsh, the remainder forming an extensive uniform mud flat, densely colonised by *Enteromorpha*. This area of flats falls within a minimum tidal range of 2 m and is subject to double tides.

Marsh (90 ha)

Near the upper limit of the tidal range *Spartina anglica* meadows and other salt marshes flank the tidal arms of the

Harbour. There is a small area of *S. anglica* marsh, and notable populations of *Limonium vulgare, Salicornia* spp., *Althaea officinalis*, etc., are actively colonising the higher levels of the muds within the former Newtown Main Marsh. Subsurface lime-rich drainage occurs here.

Shingle (8 ha)

The shingle spits at the Harbour entrance, though covering only a small area, carry a good representative flora including an abundance of *Frankenia laevis* and *Inula crithmoides*.

Earth cliff and embankments (22 ha)

These provide further diversity of habitat and support notable populations of *Lathyrus nissolia* on Oligocene strata cliff.

Approximately 300 species of flowering plants have been recorded from this site and the invertebrate fauna contains local southern elements.

Maximum winter populations of wildfowl (including mallard, teal, wigeon, pintail, shoveler and shelduck) and waders in recent years have achieved totals of 2500 and 4000, respectively. Of particular interest is the small but increasing winter population of dark-bellied brent geese, which has exceeded 300 in recent winters. Bird breeding populations include substantial numbers of redshank, small colonies of common and little terns, and large colonies of black-headed gulls.

EAST ANGLIA

C.13. FOULNESS AND MAPLIN SANDS, ESSEX
TR 0090. *c.* 13 200 ha   Grade 1*

Flats and salt marsh (12 100 ha)

This is one of the three largest continuous sand–silt flats in Britain. It has a 4.5-m tidal range, lime-rich drainage influences and carries probably the largest surviving continuous population of *Zostera noltii* (325 ha) in Europe. The site is also remarkable for the best population of the very local *Spartina maritima*, known growing in its pioneer form only on these flats. The saltings also carry notable populations of *Limonium humile, Inula crithmoides* and *Suaeda fruticosa*. The salt marsh succession is virtually identical with that described for the south side of the Thames estuary and the Blackwater area to the north.

The flats are of international importance as winter feeding grounds for at least one-fifth of the total world population of the dark-bellied brent goose (more than 10 000 in recent years). Many geese congregate on the Foulness and Maplin Sands after their migration from north Russia, then disperse to the smaller estuaries of Essex, north Kent and the South Coast once the *Zostera* stocks are depleted. The flats are of importance for wigeon, mallard and shelduck and are frequented by up to 30 000–40 000 waders during the winter months, notably up to 2000 bar-tailed godwit, 13 000 knot and 19 500 dunlin.

The upper parts of the inter-tidal flats are typical of much of the Essex coast with an abundance of invertebrate species such as *Hydrobia* and *Corophium*, but on the main area of flats the fauna differs somewhat with Mollusca such as *Cardium* and *Tellina*, Crustacea such as *Urothöe bathyporiea* and Polychaetes such as *Scoloplos* and *Nepthys*.

Marshes (1100 ha)

The grass embankments and reclaimed marshes (all flooded in 1953 by sea water) contain over 200 species of flowering plants including most of the local southern species characteristic of lime-rich marshes such as *Bupleurum tenuissimum, Lotus tenuis, Puccinellia fasciculata* and *Trifolium squamosum*. Several Coleoptera typical of brackish conditions have been recorded, including *Bledius* spp., *Heterocerus* spp. and *Dyschirius* spp.

The flora of the borrow dykes and drainage ditches includes *Ruppia spiralis, R. maritima* and *Ranunculus baudotii*. The rough grassland is of importance for nesting short-eared owls.

Shell beaches (20 ha)

The most extensive shell beach accumulations in Britain occur off Foulness Point and classic studies on the development of these and subfossil accumulations in reclaimed marsh to landward have shed light on the oscillatory development of salt marshes characteristic of south-east England.

The shell banks are the site of one of the largest British breeding colonies of the little tern (75 pairs, formerly over 100), a rare species decreasing nationally largely through disturbance, and of common tern (150 pairs). The banks also form an important high-tide roost for waders and are used by birds from not only the Foulness and Maplin Sands but also by those from the Crouch estuary and Dengie flats. The older shell banks support a shingle flora including *Glaucium flavum*.

C.14. BLACKWATER FLATS AND MARSHES, ESSEX
c. 10 000 ha   Grade 1*
(*a*) *Dengie Peninsula*
TM 0403
(*b*) *Blackwater Estuary*
TL 9407
(*c*) *Colne Estuary*
TM 0717

The Blackwater is the largest of the main estuaries on the Essex coast north of the Thames, and at its mouth on the north side is joined by the smaller estuary of the Colne. Both estuaries have systems of mud flats, fringing salt marshes, and reclaimed marshes behind sea walls, and where the Blackwater becomes open sea on the south side, this range of habitats runs along the end of the Dengie Peninsula to the mouth of the River Crouch. Three sections are recognised, as above, and (*b*) includes Osea Island.

Flats (6160 ha)

The extensive flats of this area vary from fine clay to silt and sand in different places, and tend to be muddier (finer) in upper bays away from the main tidal flow. *Enteromorpha* is locally extensive and there are good colonies of *Zostera angustifolia* and *Z. noltii*, especially in the Blackwater. These attract dark-bellied brent geese, and there is an average population of around 4000 birds. The area is important for other wildfowl, and there are large numbers of shelduck (2500), mallard (900), teal (400), goldeneye (325), wigeon (2000), mute swans (150) and pintail (100).

Recent studies have shown an abundance of certain invertebrates such as *Hydrobia ulvae*, *Cardium edule*, *Nephthys hombergi*, *Arenicola marina*, *Littorina* spp., *Nereis diversicolor*, *Ampharete grubei* and *Macoma balthica*, though crustaceans were relatively few. The invertebrate fauna of the flats varies considerably from place to place, especially in relation to particle size. The total biomass is sufficient to support a very large winter population of waders, numbering well over 20000 birds, with over 20 species, and a special abundance of dunlin, knot, curlew, grey plover, golden plover and bar-tailed godwit.

Marsh (3800 ha)

The most extensive area of unreclaimed salt marsh is the strip bordering the Dengie Peninsula, though there are also quite large areas either side of the Colne mouth and south of Osea Island. *Spartina anglica* is an abundant pioneer and persists into the more mature marsh, but there is also a good deal of the rather rare *S. maritima* in some of these marshes. *Salicornia perennis* occurs plentifully in places. The usual species of south-eastern saltings are prominent: *Puccinellia maritima*, *Halimione portulacoides*, *Aster tripolium* var. *discoideus*, *Limonium vulgare*, *Suaeda maritima* and *Triglochin maritima*. More local species include *Inula crithmoides* and *Limonium binervosum*. Some saltings have an abundance of *Enteromorpha* and dwarf fucoids, and the rare *Ascophyllum nodosum* var. *scorpioides* is also found. Older marshes often have an abundance of *Armeria maritima*, *Festuca rubra*, *Juncus gerardii* and *J. maritimus*. An interesting area of older marsh at Tollesbury has *Limonium humile*, *Puccinellia distans*, *P. rupestris*, *Bupleurum tenuissimum* and *Myosurus minimus*. This area also appears to be the only salt marsh high enough to support regularly breeding waders and wildfowl – redshank, lapwing, oystercatcher, snipe, ringed plover, shelduck, garganey, shoveler and teal.

Until recently, the Blackwater area had a very large system of reclaimed grazing marsh with neutral grassland, but this has been converted almost entirely to arable land during the last decade. Permanently wet ditches (fleets) remain, and their water is often brackish, typically supporting beds of *Scirpus maritimus*, *Phragmites* and aquatics such as *Ceratophyllum demersum* and *Ruppia maritima*. As elsewhere, the salt marshes and reclaimed land are part of the habitat of the estuarine birds, especially as roosting places for waders at high tide, and to some degree as feeding places for certain species.

Shingle (40 ha)

A number of linear banks of shells, stones and sand occur at Bradwell-on-Sea, and there is a transition from salt marsh to sand and shingle at Colne Point. The intermediate zone of the latter is the habitat of *Frankenia laevis*, *Agropyron pungens*, *A. junceiforme* and *A. caninum*. Sand and shingle have *Suaeda fruticosa*, *Glaucium flavum*, *Calystegia soldanella*, *Anchusa arvensis*, *Honkenya peploides*, *Salsola kali* and *Beta vulgaris* ssp. *maritima* (abundant also on sea walls). Little terns and ringed plover nest here.

Insects and spiders

These salt marshes and associated habitats of the Blackwater area are the haunt of local or rare Lepidoptera such as the Essex skipper butterfly, and ground lackey, Essex emerald, *Idaea ochrata* and *Scopula emutaria* moths. This is also a notable locality for rare migrant Lepidoptera. Rare or local beetles include *Dolichosoma lineare*, *Apion limonii* and *Polydrusus chrysomela*, and the spiders *Sitticus rupicola*, *Tricoptema cito* and *Hellophanus auratus* are recorded.

C.15. HAMFORD WATER, ESSEX
TM 2326.   *c.* 2200 ha   Grade 1

Flats (940 ha)

This is a small, locally sheltered area of medium- to low-level clay and silt flats with lime-rich drainage influences in a tidal range of 3.5 m, carrying notable populations of *Enteromorpha*, *Zostera angustifolia* and *Z. noltii*. Their bird populations are to some extent interchangeable with those of the Stour; the wildfowl include 500+ dark-bellied brent geese and 1000 shelduck, with moderate numbers of teal, wigeon, red-breasted merganser and mallard, and the waders include up to 300 black-tailed godwit.

Locally, particularly on the seaward side, the London Clay bedrock is exposed, and with the soft recent muds provides contrasting substrates for littoral algae and invertebrates.

Commercial oyster lays are managed in the tidal channels.

Marsh (1200 ha)

There is a salt marsh fringe of varying width outside the sea wall around most of Hamford Water, and the islands, notably Horsey, Skippers, Hedge-End and Pewit, have substantial salt marsh on their margins or, locally, within their breached sea walls. Much of the high-level salt marsh was formerly grazed. The pioneer species at lower levels include *Spartina anglica*, *Aster tripolium* var. *discoideus* and *Salicornia* spp. (at least five species are known from the area). Small patches of *Spartina maritima* grow within the established marsh with *Limonium vulgare* and *L. humile*. The marshes carry notable populations of nearly all southern lime-rich salt marsh species, e.g. *Carex divisa*, *Inula crithmoides*, *Trifolium squamosum* and nine other *Trifolium* spp., *Puccinellia maritima*, *P. distans*, *P. fasciculata*, *Ranunculus baudotii*, *R. sardous*, *Ruppia maritima* and the very local *R. spiralis*. In addition *Peucedanum officinale*, one of the rarest coastal plants in Britain, has its headquarters here. A number of local moth species have been recorded on Hamford Water, and at least one species is confined to the site.

There is a large colony (*c.* 2000 pairs) of black-headed

gulls breeding on Horsey Island, and there are breeding colonies of common tern.

Sand and shingle (60 ha)

There are two separate areas, both terminating seawards as recurved spits, and forming the most extensive examples of this habitat in Essex. One runs southward from Dovercourt to Crabknowe Spit and the other northwards from The Naze to Stone Point. They are narrow (*c.* 30 m max.) strips topped by low dunes lying between the sea and the salt marsh, and both are gradually spreading inland over salt marsh owing to the effects of wind and storm waves. The flora on the lime-rich sand and small-pebbled shingle is well developed though nowhere dense. *Ammophila arenaria* and *Elymus arenarius* occur with large populations of *Eryngium maritimum*. Other plant species include *Suaeda fruticosa*, *Lathyrus japonicus*, *Crithmum maritimum*, *Calystegia soldanella* and other representatives of the southern sand-and-shingle flora.

The shingle areas, particularly in the Stone Point area, are breeding sites for little terns (20–50 pairs), ringed plovers and oystercatchers.

Hamford Water as a whole is of considerable physiographic interest.

C.16. STOUR ESTUARY, ESSEX
TM 1833.   2200 ha   Grade 1

Flats (2000 ha)

The Estuary has an indented shoreline on both sides, with four bays on the north and three on the south. Save for small areas of salt marsh in Erwarton Bay and Copperas Bay, the whole of the inter-tidal zone is taken up by sand, silt and mud flats. Extensive areas of *Zostera* spp. occur in Erwarton Bay and Holbrook Bay and smaller areas elsewhere. *Enteromorpha* is found throughout the middle and lower estuary. Invertebrates, particularly *Hydrobia*, are abundant. The large quantities of food for wildfowl attract up to 1000 mute swans, 500 dark-bellied brent geese, 10000 wigeon, 4000 shelduck, 460 pintail and significant numbers of mallard, goldeneye and teal. The Estuary is an important autumn arrival point for these wildfowl. Waders include up to 800 black-tailed godwit.

Marsh (200 ha)

The margin of the Estuary is marked by sharply rising land or even boulder clay cliffs for most of its length and there is little room for salt marsh accretion. This contrasts with the estuaries further south on the Essex coast, where gentle slopes on the London Clay come down and merge with the wide zones of reclaimed salt marsh. The Stour has about 80 ha of reclaimed marsh and about 120 ha of tidal salt marsh. The flora is typical of this coast and contains *Limonium vulgare* and *L. humile* (and their hybrids), *Suaeda maritima*, *Triglochin maritima* and *Ranunculus sceleratus*.

Little is known of the insect populations of these marshes, but if the vegetation is a guide, they are likely to include many of the typical Essex coast species.

C.17. ORFORDNESS/HAVERGATE, SUFFOLK
TM 4348.   1050 ha   Grade 1

This area consists of Orford Beach and Shingle Street, which are of outstanding physiographic and botanical interest; and Havergate Island and the shores of the River Ore and Butley Creek, which are of ornithological importance.

The mud flats bordering the River Ore, Havergate Island and Butley Creek are of mixed clay, silt and shingle, not markedly rich in lime, and in a tide range of 2 m. They are of special importance as feeding and roosting areas for wildfowl and waders. Bare, muddy lagoons on Havergate Island have the largest breeding avocet population in Britain, and there are sometimes good colonies of breeding Sandwich terns. Wildfowl have decreased in recent years, but moderate numbers still occur on occasions. Teal (600), pintail (230) and shoveler (100), also mallard, wigeon and shelduck occur regularly.

Very large areas of *Limonium* and *Halimione* salt marsh (minimal grazing) on silt over shingle border Havergate Island, Butley Creek and parts of Orford Beach and Shingle Street. There are large patches of *Spartina maritima* up to 100 m² in size. *Puccinellia maritima*, *Aster tripolium*, *Atriplex littoralis*, *Plantago maritima*, *Armeria maritima* and *Salicornia perennis* also occur. Differences in the salinity of the tidal lagoons at Shingle Street provide an interesting succession of salt marsh forms. Extensive *Agropyron pungens* marsh occurs on embankments together with *Artemisia maritima*.

Orford Beach and Shingle Street constitute the second largest vegetated shingle area in Britain. Though disturbed locally by Ministry of Defence activities, the flora in general is more stable than that of any other mainland shingle area in East Anglia. The complicated pattern of movement of material between North Weir Point, the southern end of Orford Beach, and Shingle Street, on the mainland, results in the accretion of new shingle deposits at North Weir Point and the colonisation of these new deposits is of interest. *Lathyrus japonicus*, *Vicia lutea*, *Crambe maritima* and *Glaucium flavum* occur together with most other shingle beach species characteristic of the region. A colony of lesser black-backed and herring gulls is the only one of any size in East Anglia.

The semi-marine spider *Praestigia duffeyi* was discovered on the Havergate marshes in 1953, and the spiders *Lycosa arenicola*, *Sitticus rupicola*, and *Euophrys browninge* were discovered at Shingle Street. *L. arenicola* and *E. browninge*, together with *Trichoncus offinis*, have not been recorded in any other locality in East Anglia.

C.18. WINTERTON DUNES, NORFOLK
TG 4921.   395 ha   Grade 1

Dune (c. 325 ha)

The site extends from Horsey Warren in the north to Winterton Great Valley in the south. The sand dunes at Winterton have been formed by accretion in front of an earlier coastline, a cliffed section of which is seen to the south at Winterton Great Valley. The physiographical interest is outstanding and there are rapid changes in plant communities from dry heath, through slacks, to dunes. The wet heath communities of the slacks are of special interest.

Winterton has a medium-sized, lime-deficient dune system with well-developed slacks, notable for the continental affinities of its flora and fauna. *Calluna vulgaris*, *Erica tetralix* and *E. cinerea* are all widespread, frequently associated with *Carex arenaria*, *Ammophila arenaria* and other dune grasses. There is the best population in Britain of the hybrid *Ammocalamagrostis baltica*, and among the largest populations of the very local dune grass *Corynephorus canescens*. The site is notable for acidic facies bryophyte and lichen flora, its fern meadow associes with distinctive association of the hybrid *A. baltica*, *Dryopteris dilatata*, *D. carthusiana* and *D. cristata*, and transitions to incipient birch woodland.

The vertebrates include natterjack toads and adders, and little terns nest on the beach. The scrub on the landward side of the dunes is an important resting point for migrant passerines, and a few uncommon birds regularly nest in the area.

C.19. NORTH NORFOLK COAST, NORFOLK   Grade 1*

(a) *Holme–Brancaster*
TF 697441–797452.   1620 ha

(b) *Scolt Head Island*
TF 788466–848460.   740 ha

(c) *Overy–Holkham*
TF 848460–912456.   1620 ha

(d) *Wells–Morston*
TF 916445–TG 027449.   2820 ha

(e) *Blakeney Point*
TF 991460–048453.   580 ha

(f) *Cley–Salthouse*
TG 046446–081440.   320 ha

The whole of this stretch of the North Norfolk Coast is of great importance to coastal physiography, and classic studies of the processes of formation of shingle, sand-dune and salt marsh systems have been made here. Mobile shingle ridges become fixed by vegetation and wind-blown sand into fringing dunes, behind which salt marsh has formed. Pioneer studies of vegetational aspects of salt marsh development have also been made. The site includes some 530 ha of reclaimed marshland in agricultural use between Burnham Overy and Wells.

Flats (*c.* 4050 ha)

These are a highly varied area of clay, silt, sand, shell and shingle, moderately rich in free lime, within a tide range of some 6 m. There is a good representative flora and fauna of this type of coast. Relatively small areas of *Zostera marina* occur and locally patches of *Z. noltii*, utilised by brent geese (1200 birds).

The flats are the resort of other wildfowl (mallard, teal, wigeon, gadwall, shoveler, goldeneye, eider and shelduck) and waders.

Marsh (2020 ha total, with largest continuous area *c.* 1200 ha)

These are among the 10 largest salt marshes in Britain and probably the most varied in floristic composition. They are of international interest for the distinctive age series of marshes enclosed by shingle spit recurves, together with a great variety of marsh development in both exposed and partially protected open coast sites on varied mixtures of clay, silt, sand and shingle. *Salicornia* species are well represented, with *S. perennis*, *S. dolichostachya*, *S. stricta*, *S. ramosissima* and *S. disarticulata*. *Frankenia laevis* is near its northern British limit on this coast and *Spartina maritima* occurs on marshes east of Wells. There is also some invasion by *S. anglica*. The best British populations of *Limonium bellidifolium*, *L. humile* and *L. vulgare* are here, and free-living *Fucus* and *Pelvetia* occur in the marshes. Brackish marshes at Cley and Holme have large beds of *Phragmites*. Within the Holme section, the Broadwater is a natural brackish lagoon and there are three artificial pools for waders.

Dune (800 ha in a series of sites up to 120 ha maximum)

A series of small moderately lime-rich dunes grading to lime-deficient dunes has developed over shingle or marsh, and is of known age sequence. Corsican pine (*Pinus nigra* var. *calabrica*) was planted on Holkham Dunes in the mid nineteenth century and has regenerated naturally. Sand dunes, such as those at Holme, are floristically rich, with a variety of orchids, including *Anacamptis pyramidalis*, *Ophrys apifera*, *Dactylorchis fuchsii* and *Epipactis palustris*.

Shingle (*c.* 300 ha in three main sites up to 160 ha maximum)

Medium-large areas of relatively undisturbed shingle have developed as mainland-attached (Blakeney) and island (Scolt Head and Thornham West Islands) spits with recurves of known age. They carry probably the largest populations of *Suaeda fruticosa* and *Limonium binervosum* on shingle in Britain and have a notable lichen flora. The strandline flora also includes an abundance of *Glaucium flavum* and *Calystegia soldanella*, whilst rare species are *Polygonum raii*, *Lathyrus japonicus*, *Juncus acutus*, *Trifolium suffocatum* and *T. subterraneum*.

There is the largest breeding colony of Sandwich terns in the country on this coast, but the birds move between Scolt Head, Blakeney Point, Stiffkey shore and perhaps elsewhere according to disturbance. There are important populations of common and little terns at these sites. At Cley, breeding birds of the brackish marshes include bitterns, bearded tits, a variety of waders and wildfowl and, formerly, Montagu's harriers. This coast is also of great ornithological interest for its spring and autumn passage migrants, and for wintering waders, wildfowl (mallard, teal, wigeon, goldeneye, shelduck, eider, gadwall and shoveler) and passerines such as shore lark, snow bunting, Lapland bunting and twite. Natterjack toads occur in small numbers at Holkham.

C.20. THE WASH FLATS AND MARSHES, NORFOLK–LINCOLNSHIRE   Grade 1*

(a) *Gibraltar Point–Wrangle*
TF 570608–440470.   6000 ha

(b) *Wrangle–Welland*
TF 440470–350340.   4000 ha

(c) *Welland–Nene*
TF 350340–490260.   5700 ha

(d) *Nene–Ouse*
TF 490260–600230.   5300 ha

(e) *Ouse–Hunstanton*
TF 600230–690440.   5300 ha

This great area of sand–silt flats and their fringing salt marshes is sealed off from the low-lying Fenlands behind by a long series of sea walls bounding the whole inlet, but receives the drainage of the three main Fenland rivers, the Welland, Nene and Ouse, and exerts a tidal influence on these for some distance inland. It has been divided into five sections, mainly between these river mouths, but the long western shore has been arbitrarily separated into two, midway between the dune and shingle peninsula of Gibraltar Point and the Welland mouth.

Flats (23 700 ha)
The Wash is one of the two largest areas of estuarine flats in Britain, the only other system of comparable size being that of Morecambe Bay, where the sediment is coarser in general and less lime-rich. Although the occurrence of *Zostera* (*Z. noltii*) appears to be limited to the lime-rich flats of the Welland estuary, the Wash Flats have large populations of *Enteromorpha*, other algae, and invertebrates which provide a rich food source for wildfowl and waders. The Wrangle flats of section (a) are one of the main haunts of the dark-bellied brent goose in Britain (3000 birds – distinct from those of the Essex coast), which here feeds mainly on *Enteromorpha*. The area also carries a flock of 2000 pink-footed geese and probably a similar number of wigeon. This is the most important part of the Wash for geese, though smaller numbers of these birds occur in other parts, notably the Welland estuary, which also has the largest population of duck (wigeon – 7500; shelduck – 1500; mallard – 750; and teal – 300). The sea off the north-east shore has valuable populations of seaducks (common scoter – 2000; velvet scoter – 100; scaup and eider – several hundred). The former Wash population of up to 15 000 pink-footed geese has declined, but shelduck have increased and this is now an important wintering haunt of the species.

The Wash Flats also carry the second largest wintering population of waders in Britain, with a total population of over 180 000 birds. There are especially large flocks of knot (85 000), dunlin (45 000), curlew (12 000) and oyster-catcher (10 000), and considerable numbers of redshank, sanderling, bar-tailed godwit, grey plover (half of the British population) and ringed plover. This is also an important area for waders on migration, and some species complete an interrupted moult on the Wash.

The sandbanks of the Wash support populations of both species of seals native to Britain. The number of grey seals is small: groups of 10 to 20 are to be seen on Dogs Head Sand in the northern part of the Wash. By contrast, the Wash is by far the most important breeding area for the common seal, which is to be found in large numbers (c. 3000–5000). Most of the sandbanks on which these seals haul out are located around the mouths of the rivers Nene, Welland and Ouse.

Marsh (2600 ha)
The marshes bordering the Wash are probably, in aggregate, the most extensive in Britain, but they have not been properly surveyed. Virtually all of them have developed outside sea walls, and vary in width from a few metres to about 1.5 km. In floristics they appear to be characteristic of the south-east England marshes on fine sediment, with *Salicornia* spp., *Puccinellia maritima* and *Spartina anglica* as usual pioneers, and an abundance of *Halimione portulacoides*, *Aster tripolium* var. *discoideus*, *Limonium* spp., *Suaeda maritima* and *Triglochin maritima*. The vegetation appears to be rather uniform, and diversity is limited by the sea walls, since most of the older marsh behind has been converted to grazing marsh and, more recently, this has been turned mainly into arable land. Ditches here have brackish conditions with a typical flora, similar to those of the north Kent fleets, but there tends to be a steady loss of interest as this reclaimed land becomes more intensively used.

The marshes are valuable as the feeding and roosting places of waders, though some of these birds (especially dunlin) rest on arable land when they are displaced by high tides in the estuary. Exceptional tides may force all the waders to resting places behind the sea wall. The main roosts are on the marshes at Snettisham/Wolferton, Terrington, Holbeach/Dawsmere and at Gibraltar Point. It thus seems likely that, while the botanical interest of the Wash salt marshes is probably well represented by those of the North Norfolk Coast, these saltings represent an integral part of the ornithological habitat which gives the Wash its international importance. Frampton/Kirkton marsh, lying immediately north of the Welland estuary, is the only remaining area of unreclaimed high saltings in the south-west Wash, and has a vast colony of black-headed gulls and some common terns.

C.21. SALTFLEETBY/THEDDLETHORPE DUNES, LINCOLNSHIRE
TF 499873–480933.   900 ha   Grade 1

This site has a complex of soft coast habitats including flats, dunes, salt and freshwater marsh. The dunes and salt marsh are rapidly accreting and the area is regarded as an important research site for studying processes of coastal development.

Flats (730 ha)

The foreshore of the nature reserve area is sandy and supports little vegetation. It is, however, an important feeding and roosting ground for waders and wildfowl.

Marsh (60 ha)

Several noteworthy vegetation types occur on the salt marsh. The seaward side consists of communities formed of *Salicornia* spp. and green algae with large areas of bare mud between the plants. On its landward side the *Salicornia* community merges with an area dominated by tussocks of *Puccinellia maritima*. A salt marsh community with *P. maritima*, *Limonium vulgare*, *Plantago maritima* and *Armeria maritima* as the most frequently occurring species is present above the main Puccinellietum. At the landward side both *Carex extensa* and *C. distans* occur. The northern end of the reserve, in the vicinity of Saltfleet Haven, has considerable areas which are dominated by *Halimione portulacoides*. Salt marsh communities of the landward margin are dominated largely by *Juncus maritimus*, though *Scirpus maritimus* is dominant over one small area.

Dune (110 ha)

The dunes are highly calcareous and support a rich flora. The seaward edge of the foredunes is covered by *Agropyron pungens* with *Atriplex* spp. where they merge with the upper edge of the salt marsh. Farther back from the limit of influence of spring tides the foredunes become dominated by *Ammophila arenaria* with *Senecio jacobaea* and *Elymus arenarius*. The older dunes support grassland rich in plant species, in which the most abundant are *Arrhenatherum elatius* and *Rubus caesius*. Where grazing by rabbits or trampling by people occurs there is a shorter grassland turf with *Hieracium pilosella*. A large part of the dunes is covered by dense scrub of *Hippophaë rhamnoides*, *Crataegus monogyna* and *Ligustrum vulgare*. The scrub forms a suitable habitat for large mammals such as badgers and foxes, whilst the berries of the *Hippophaë* are an important winter food for birds. An extensive freshwater marsh, almost a lagoon, is formed in the depression between the two lines of dunes. There are three distinct types of vegetation in this very large slack: (i) considerable areas dominated by plant communities of a rich-fen type with *Carex riparia*, *Rumex hydrolapathum*, *Lycopus europaeus* and *Scutellaria galericulata*; (ii) parts of this area with brackish conditions have *Juncus maritimus*, *J. gerardii* and *Samolus valerandi* and where this community merges with the dune grassland *Dactylorchis praetermissa* and *D. incarnata* occur; (iii) reed-beds dominated by *Phragmites communis*. These slacks are important faunally, particularly for their population of natterjack toad.

C.62. HUMBER FLATS AND MARSHES (PART), LINCOLNSHIRE   Grade 1*

See under North England, p. 27.

C.22. LEIGH MARSH, ESSEX
TQ 8384.   *c.* 1200 ha   Grade 2

Flats (880 ha)

The Flats are wide (up to 3000 m) and have a very shallow gradient; they are subdivided by a number of creeks. Very large populations of *Zostera noltii* and *Z. angustifolia* grow on these flats along with dense patches of *Enteromorpha*. In addition, there are good invertebrate populations, notably of *Nereis*, *Corophium volutator*, *C. arenaria*, *Hydrobia* and *Cardium edule*; the last form extensive beds at the lower tidal limit. Early in the winter, dark-bellied brent geese feed here in flocks totalling up to 6000, and this is one of their chief feeding grounds in Britain. There is, however, an almost daily interchange of birds between here and the main centre on the Foulness/Maplin Sands, which suggests that these sites are interdependent.

Marsh (320 ha)

Much of the marsh has been enclosed and reclaimed by embankments, but at Canvey and Leigh there are *c.* 80 ha of excellent marsh with at least five *Salicornia* spp., *Limonium vulgare*, *Armeria maritima* and *Triglochin maritima*.

The reclaimed marsh and its associated dykes have a rich flora including *Ceratophyllum submersum*, *C. demersum*, *Ruppia maritima*, *Zannichellia palustris*, *Ranunculus sardous* and *Juncus gerardii*. The invertebrate fauna includes a number of local moths: *Malacosoma castrensis*, *Polypogon cribrumalis*, *Spilosoma urticae* and *Mythimna favicolor*, and the marbled white (in its only station in Essex) and Essex skipper butterflies.

Recent work has shown that the Diptera are particularly interesting.

Shell, sand and shingle (c. 16 ha)

Canvey Point has a small area of shell, sand and shingle, but there are no records to suggest a distinctive flora or fauna.

SOUTH-WEST ENGLAND

C.23. POOLE HARBOUR, DORSET
SZ 0089.   2200 ha   Grade 1

Flats (970 ha)

The harbour has a large area of clay and silt and there is a small area of sand flat outside, both being generally deficient in lime. The tide-range of 2 m is minimal and there are distinctive double tides. There is a moderately diverse algal and invertebrate fauna, and small populations of *Zostera marina* occur (in and outside the harbour) on sandy silt. Winter wildfowl populations are of moderate size – shelduck (1340), teal (810), pintail (175), mallard, wigeon, shoveler, pochard, tufted duck, goldeneye and merganser. Brownsea Island is particularly important as a daytime retreat for dabbling ducks. Wader populations are *c.* 10000 and the area is important as a wintering ground for some 400 black-tailed godwit.

Marsh (1010 ha)

The marsh system has a minimum vertical range, a large area, and both embayed and estuarine marshes, with some of the oldest and most extensive *Spartina anglica* marshes in Britain. *Phragmites* beds occur and those greater than 100 m across are sufficient for marsh harrier to breed in, though this raptor has not nested for several years. Grazing is slight and relatively undisturbed transitions to freshwater marsh and mire provide minor habitats for a great variety of species. Many local oceanic southern species occur in the flora (e.g. *Alopecurus bulbosus*).

Dune (160 ha)

A small–medium dune system on acidic sand with heather heath is extensively developed from the coast dune landwards and there are fine examples of *Betula pubescens/Salix cinerea* ssp. *atrocinerea/Myrica gale* shrub communities on acidic slack soils. The transitions to salt marsh, freshwater marsh, mire, heath and man-made habitats provide an exceptional amount and variety of 'edge' which supports great diversity of plants with oceanic southern elements (e.g. *Carex punctata*), invertebrates and all six British reptiles. The *Phragmites* marsh locally contains exceptionally fine populations of *Osmunda regalis*. The site has been studied extensively in the past and is widely used by research workers and for teaching purposes.

Shingle (20 ha)

A small area, with a sparse flora.

Cliff (40 ha)

Short lengths of soft sand/earth, and unstable, low cliffs occur, but have few plants.

This site should be considered in conjunction with sites L.88, L.89 and OW.21.

C.24. DURLSTON HEAD–RINGSTEAD BAY, DORSET
SZ 034779–SY 760814. *c.* 600 ha   Grade 1

This stretch of coast is internationally famous for geological reasons; its outstanding flora and fauna reflect the great variety of rock formations and soil types. It is the only area in Britain in which quite large areas of chalk grassland and Jurassic limestone grassland occur together, both showing a complete range of maritime influence. Areas of Wealden sands, Gault and Kimmeridge Clay interdigitate with Chalk and limestone.

There are interesting differences between different parts of the Chalk, e.g. between the flora of the thin soils of Ballard Down in the east, where *Silene nutans* occurs, and the flora of the deeper soils between Durdle Door and White Nothe in the west where *Serratula tinctoria* occurs with *Brachypodium pinnatum*. The Jurassic limestone grasslands also show considerable variation: the area between Durlston Head and St Aldhelm's Head is an outstanding site with a very rich flora and fauna. *Ophrys sphegodes*, *Polygala calcarea* and *Arum italicum* are characteristic species. *Iris foetidissima* is unusually abundant along the same coast. *Brassica oleracea* is extremely abundant on the

clay cliffs near Kimmeridge, and one of the best national populations of this species occurs on St Aldhelm's Head.

The coastal grasslands on Chalk and limestone support interesting butterfly populations especially of Adonis blue, chalk-hill blue, small blue, marbled white and dark green fritillary. The Lulworth skipper is abundant in *Brachypodium pinnatum* grassland on the cliff tops, but is virtually confined to this area in Britain. The whole coast and particularly the small sheltered valley near Tilly Whim Caves are well known for migrant insects.

The Purbeck coast is an outstanding locality for Orthoptera, including *Platcyleis denticulata*, *Conocephalus discolor* and *Tetrix ceperoi*.

There is a small colony of guillemots on a Chalk cliff near Durdle Door, and a larger colony (about 500 pairs) on the cliffs near Tilly Whim Caves near Swanage. There are also small colonies of razorbills, puffins, kittiwakes, shags, cormorants and fulmars. Those of razorbills and puffins used to be much larger than at present; the kittiwake and fulmar are fairly recent colonists. The limestone cliffs between St Aldhelm's Head and Durlston Head have been much quarried; their bat populations include *Myotis bechsteini* and, formerly, *M. myotis*. Formerly, about eight pairs of peregrines nested on the cliffs on this stretch of coast. There is still at least one pair of ravens.

The extensive landslips under the cliffs at Chapman's Pool, Gad Cliff and between White Nothe and Ringstead have extremely variable habitats including scrub woodland which has developed spontaneously. Common buzzards, badgers, fallow deer and adders occur in these areas, and small marshes on the landslips provide a habitat for two of the rarer Orthoptera.

C.25. CHESIL BEACH/THE FLEET, DORSET
SY 487890–683733. 800 ha   Grade 1*

Coastal lagoon (480 ha)

This is the largest regularly tidal lagoon in Britain with claybottom deposits and has unusual transitional habitats with shingle. There is also the most extensive mixed population of all three *Zostera* spp. and *Ruppia maritima* in Britain, and these carry an invertebrate fauna extinct in many parts of Europe since the *Zostera* decline of the 1930s. For these features alone it is of international interest. It is notable for the diversity of waders and wildfowl in winter (wigeon – 4500; mallard, teal, pintail, shoveler, pochard, tufted duck and goldeneye) and has the largest resident mute swan population in Britain (650 birds) supported by the *Zostera* food resources.

Shingle (320 ha)

Chesil Beach is one of the five largest shingle beaches in Britain and is of international interest both as a rare habitat in Europe as a whole and for its particularly unusual linear form, with small pebbled shingle in the west which is well vegetated in parts. It is notable for very large populations of local species such as *Crambe maritima*, *Glaucium flavum*, *Lathyrus japonicus*, *Suaeda fruticosa* and *Trifolium scabrum*, all characterististic plants of shingle. It is also the only

British locality for the wingless cricket *Mogoplistes squamiger* and supports about 15% of the British breeding population of little terns (200 pairs).

C.26. AXMOUTH–LYME REGIS UNDERCLIFFS, DEVON
SY 3090.   320 ha   Grade 1*

This assemblage of Triassic, Rhaetic, Jurassic and Cretaceous rocks forms an unusually wide and diverse area of coastal cliffs and broken slopes as a result of landslips. It is of international geological importance and particular ecological interest for the exceptional degree of isolation (because of the difficult terrain), so far as the south coast of Britain is concerned, so that plant and animal communities have developed virtually untouched by man. In particular, a species-rich, ungrazed, coastal ashwood has developed on the landslip, and is regarded as a grade 1 woodland (W.67); it represents one of the best recent examples of plant succession to be found in Britain.

The abrupt transition to inter-tidal, unvegetated shingle at the cliff base prevents establishment of maritime communities and the flora and fauna of the cliff base are predominantly paramaritime. Large populations of many local species representative of south-western Britain occur and there is great variety of most terrestrial groups of plants and animals. This is one of the very few key sites with the wood white butterfly.

C.27. THE LIZARD, CORNWALL
sw 665179–795192.   240 ha   Grade 1*

The Lizard is of international interest for its distinctive south-western flora on Serpentine, a rock found elsewhere in Britain only in a few smaller areas in Anglesey and Scotland. There are the best, and in some cases the only, British populations of several local flowering plants (e.g. *Herniaria ciliolata*, *Juncus capitatus*, *J. mutabilis*, *Trifolium bocconei*, *T. incarnatum* ssp. *molinerii*), together with rare ecotypes of common species. In addition, large populations of many more generally distributed, but still local, species of flowering plants, bryophytes, lichens and algae occur on sea cliffs and in coastal flushes and there are transitions to the distinctive paramaritime *Erica vagans* heath, characteristic of this region.

See also L.95.

C.28. ISLES OF SCILLY, CORNWALL
SV 9013.   *c.* 320 ha   Grade 1*

Flats (80 ha, disjunct with largest area 10 ha and most much smaller)

These are small areas of mainly steeply sloping sand flats, poor in lime, but with local shell accumulations in a tidal range of about 5 m. *Zostera marina* is said to be abundant at and below low-water mark spring tides, but *Z. angustifolia* less so.

Coastal lagoon (2 ha of brackish lagoon)

Small pools with *Ruppia maritima* and fringing *Scirpus maritimus* or *Juncus maritimus* occur, also some with *Phragmites* and scattered *Salix cinerea*.

Dune (20 ha, disjunct with largest area about 4 ha)

Small bay-fringing dunes on lime-deficient sand have notable populations of *Viola kitaibeliana* (which is confined in Britain to the Isles of Scilly and Channel Isles) and locally a great variety of naturalised aliens (e.g. *Allium triquetrum*, *Agapanthus orientalis*, *Ipheion uniflorum*, *Oxalis* spp. and *Carpobrotus edulis*).

Shingle (10 ha, disjunct with largest areas only 1 ha)

Small bay-fringing storm beaches have small populations of *Crambe maritima*, *Glaucium flavum* and other characteristic shingle beach species, and a varied assortment of aliens locally.

Cliff and rock shores (*c.* 210 ha in terms of coastal cliff strip)

The vegetation of these granite rock islands is modified generally by salt spray, and wind-pruned *Calluna–Erica cinerea* heath on headlands gives way to *Festuca rubra* grassland with *Armeria maritima* under increasing spray near the coast. The heathlands are regarded as grade 1 in their own right and are described under Lowland Grasslands, Heaths and Scrub (L.93). Over 250 species of lichens are recorded, including many rare southern oceanic species. The best British populations of *Rumex rupestris*, *Lavatera cretica*, *Ornithopus pinnatus* and many established aliens occur on these cliffs and beaches, and the islands are of additional international interest for the variety of marine biological life on rocky shores, breeding colonies of seabirds (including Manx shearwaters, storm petrels, puffins and roseate terns), and the Scilly shrew and grey seals. This is also an important bird migration landfall that is of considerable interest for the number of North American bird vagrants which occur in autumn.

C.29. CAPE CORNWALL–CLODGY POINT, CORNWALL
sw 508412–508413.   345 ha   Grade 1

The cliffs of this coast rise to 90 m, and are notable for their extreme exposure to wind and spray. Hornfelsed dolerite and Mylor Series sediments form much of this coast, but some stretches are cut in granite.

All groups of plants (marine algae, lichens, bryophytes and flowering plants) are known to have good representation of local south-western species on this coast. Among the more notable vascular plants are *Asplenium marinum*, *Inula crithmoides*, *Lotus hispidus*, *Ornithopus perpusillus*, *Sagina subulata*, *Spergularia rupicola* and *Trifolium occidentale*, and this is also one of the very few localities in Britain (and the only Cornish one) for the very rare *Carex montana*. The Mediterranean fern *Adiantum capillus-veneris* grows on calcareous rocks and the Atlantic liverworts *Frullania microphylla*, *F. germana*, *Lophocolea fragrans*, *Riccia crozalsii* and *Scapania gracilis* occur. The more interesting mosses include *Pottia crinita*, *Pterogonium gracile*, *Scleropodium tourretii* and *Schistostega pennata*.

There are notable breeding colonies of seabirds and grey seals at present well protected from landward disturbance on this relatively inaccessible coastline.

C.30. GODREVY POINT–ST AGNES, CORNWALL
SW 582422–710518. 520 ha   Grade 1

This section of cliff coast is representative of Lower Devonian rocks, with cliffs rising to 137 m. There are notable populations of southern plants such as *Genista pilosa*, *Lotus angustissimus*, *Orobanche maritima* and *Rumex rupestris*. Good examples of maritime dwarf-shrub heath occur on the sloping tops of the cliffs, and the Chapel Porth–St Agnes grade 1 lowland acidic heathland site (L.94) is included here. The littoral zone (tide range 6 m) is of marine biological interest; there are moderate colonies of nesting seabirds on the cliffs and grey seals breed locally.

C.31. BOSCASTLE–WIDEMOUTH, CORNWALL
SX 093915–SS 195019. 345 ha   Grade 1

This is an extensive range of Culm Measure (Carboniferous) sea cliffs with extensively vegetated and wide areas of undercliff, parts of which show a base-rich influence in the soil.

The boulder-strewn foreshore contains fine examples of rock pool fauna and flora and inter-tidal algal populations typical of exposed shores. Much of the coastal cliff is actively eroding and for this reason the lichen flora is sparse near high-water mark.

Dense tracts of wind-pruned oakwood occupy much of the undercliff, with local areas of *Festuca rubra* grassland and *Ulex gallii–Calluna* heath especially near the seaward limit of growth. Among the 120 flowering plants and ferns so far recorded are locally distributed species such as *Rubia peregrina*, *Sagina subulata*, *Isolepis cernua*, *Vicia sylvatica* and *Osmunda regalis*. The wind-pruned oakwood at Dizzard is regarded as grade 1 (W.62) and has other oceanic features such as a varied corticolous lichen flora, and the Atlantic fern *Dryopteris aemula*.

The invertebrate fauna has not been studied, but the area is believed to contain a haunt of the large blue butterfly. Beeny Cliff is an important site for grey seals.

C.32. STEEPLE POINT–BLACKCHURCH ROCK,
        CORNWALL–DEVON
SS 198116–299266. *c.* 800 ha   Grade 1

This long section of rocky coast, which includes Hartland Point, is cut in Culm Measures, with alternating sandstones and shales. These are exposed as sheer cliffs, reaching a height of 137 m at Henna Cliff near Morwenstow. The diversity of cliff form is considerable, and differential erosion has produced buttresses and rugged ridges projecting into the sea, as well as off-shore stacks and skerries. The cliffs are cut in several places by a series of short rivers and streams running from the coastal watershed to the sea. Some of the deep valleys they have formed are cut right down to sea-level, as at Marsland and Welcombe, whereas others end abruptly with waterfalls which drop 15 m or more to rocky, stony beaches. The valleys themselves are steep-sided, with bottoms generally about 60–90 m below the high points of the cliff tops.

This section has an extremely wide range of coastal habitats within a small area: strand and foreshore, shingle beach and small patches of dune; rocks and cliffs within reach of sea spray; streams with pools and small marshes; and the valley sides with a range of grassland, heath, scrub and woodland from maritime to paramaritime. As the valleys mostly run east–west, they have markedly different conditions between their shaded north and sun-exposed south aspects.

There is a varied flora, with good representation of oceanic species, though no particular rarities are known. *Genista tinctoria* occurs as a prostrate form, and *Anthyllis vulneraria* shows an unusual range of colour forms. The special importance of the area, however, is its fauna. A large number of insect species, including many different butterflies, occurs here. Local butterflies are the grayling, marbled white, the marsh, pearl-bordered, small-pearl bordered, high brown, dark green and silver-washed fritillaries, brown and green hairstreaks, dingy and grizzled skippers. By far the most important insect, however, is the very rare large blue butterfly, which maintains a precarious foothold on this part of the south-west English coast. Always a very local butterfly, it has declined markedly during this century and only a handful of extant localities is known. The habitats of this and other butterflies are paramaritime communities which can also be regarded as lowland grassland and heath.

This Hartland coast also has a wide variety of breeding birds and mammals, especially when the valleys and their habitats are included. Ravens and common buzzards are relatively numerous on the cliffs, and adders occur frequently in the valleys. Grey seals visit this coast regularly but are not known to breed.

C.33. BRAUNTON BURROWS, DEVON
SS 4632. 1350 ha   Grade 1*

Flats (400 ha)

This is an area of high and medium level lime-rich sand flats with some inter-tidal shingle grading to silt in the adjoining estuary, in a tide range of 7 m.

Dune (950 ha)

Braunton Burrows is one of the 10 largest dune systems in Britain with lime-rich dunes up to 300 m high and an extensive system of slacks providing a varied habitat for some 375 flowering plants, and notable lichen and bryophyte floras. It is of international value for its large populations of very local species (e.g. *Holoschoenus vulgaris*, *Teucrium scordium*, *Matthiola sinuata*, *Juncus acutus*) and is one of the best-documented dune systems in Europe. The area is distinctive also in having some 30 flowering plant species at their southern British limits on the west coast and only two species at their northern limit. This is one of the very few British dune systems showing the full succession to hawthorn–blackthorn scrub.

Shingle (traces)

Most of the shingle is inter-tidal, but some vegetated shingle occurs. *Polygonum maritimum* has been recorded here in the past but is now believed to be extinct, as elsewhere in Britain.

C.34. BRIDGWATER BAY, SOMERSET
ST 2848. *c.* 4250 ha   Grade 1*

Flats (3880 ha)

These are one of the largest areas in Britain of medium-level clay and silt (some sand) flats with lime-rich influences, in the maximum tidal range for Europe of 12 m. They are notable as a wildfowl and wader feeding and roosting area and are of international interest (apart from the tide range) as the second European, and only British, moulting grounds for shelduck (3000 birds). The wader populations in winter average over 5000 birds and there is an autumn peak of some 1500 black-tailed godwits. The area is also of interest for its appreciable numbers of other wildfowl such as teal, pintail and shoveler and several species of wader. This is an important British site for mallard (1500) and wigeon (2000+), both of which have been increasing in numbers in recent years. European white-fronted geese also occur regularly.

Marsh (150 ha)

The marsh is notable as one of the most rapidly accreting *Spartina anglica* marshes in Europe on lime-rich silt, and is of particular interest for its contrasting grazed and non-grazed sectors. Higher-level sheep-grazed marshes carry notable populations of *Alopecurus bulbosus*, *Bupleurum tenuissimum* and *Hordeum marinum*. *Azolla filiculoides* occurs in brackish and freshwater ditches.

Shingle (120 ha)

There is one of the largest, large-pebbled shingle beach series in Britain with a rich lichen flora and full succession from pioneer *Geranium robertianum* stages to blackthorn scrub. There is an abundance of local plants such as *Hyoscyamus niger* and *Trifolium striatum*.

Cliff and stone embankment (100 ha)

A representative flora occurs on Lower Lias limestone cliffs (the source of the shingle) to the west and rather barren exposed-shore, wave-cut platforms below them. Notable populations of *Trifolium squamosum* occur on stone embankments of the Parrett estuary, and of *Trinia glauca* in grassland adjoining them. The marsh is atypical geomorphologically because of the high tidal regime, but the area is of importance as mud and shingle can be studied in close juxtaposition on the large scale. In addition, the off-shore conditions which vary from deep to shallow water permit a very wide range and variety of processes to be studied in a comparatively small area.

C.35. NEW GROUNDS, SLIMBRIDGE, GLOUCESTERSHIRE
SO 7206. *c.* 1800 ha   Grade 1

This area, made up of flats and salt marsh on the sides of the Severn Estuary and near its head, is important as a wintering haunt of wildfowl, especially European white-fronted geese which average 7000 birds ($9\frac{1}{2}\%$ of the north-west European population – over 50% of UK population) and as the head-quarters of the Wildfowl Trust. The wildfowl populations also include Bewick's swan (400), mallard (2000), wigeon (1500), pintail (150), shoveler (100), gadwall (40), teal and shelduck.

C.36. EXE ESTUARY, DEVON
SX 9884. 1100 ha   Grade 2

Flats (820 ha)

This is a medium-sized area of locally high-level sand, silt and mud flats in a tide range of 3.5 m, carrying substantial food resources for waders and wildfowl, including beds of *Enteromorpha*, *Zostera angustifolia* and *Z. noltii*. It forms an important cold-weather refuge and has a high carrying capacity for birds, especially waders, which average 22000 birds in the winter. The most numerous wildfowl species is the wigeon (5100), and there are fair numbers of mallard, teal, pintail, shoveler, goldeneye, red-breasted merganser, dark-bellied brent geese, mute swan and shelduck.

Marsh (240 ha)

There is a range of marshes from *Spartina anglica* on sandy silt to upper estuarine *Phragmites* marsh on clay silt with local areas of brackish reclaimed marsh. It is a site of particular interest for the detailed work on estuarine marsh algae and flowering plant zonation studies made by Gillham (1957), and for marine biological studies of the mud fauna by Allen & Todd (1902), and more recently by Holme (1949), which make it one of the best studied estuaries in Britain, biologically.

Dune (40 ha)

The small, moderately lime-rich dune system is again of particular interest and has been studied in detail. It is subject to rapid erosion and tourist disturbance. This is the only British site for *Romulea columnae*.

C.37. LYNHER ESTUARY AND ST JOHN'S LAKE, CORNWALL
SX 3756. 570 ha   Grade 2

This mud flat–salt marsh system is of interest chiefly for its winter wildfowl populations and the concentration of wigeon (5300) is one of the largest in south-west England. Other species include mallard, teal, pintail, shelduck and mute swan.

C.38. FAL-RUAN ESTUARY, CORNWALL
SW 8740. 200 ha   Grade 2

Flats (180 ha)

Although only a small area, these flats are of special interest as they consist of white micaceous Kaolin clays derived from outwashings of the china clay workings in the catchment. They are unusually productive for *Nereis* spp. and this together with the exceptionally sheltered conditions attracts remarkably large numbers and diversity of waders especially in hard winters when birds are driven into southern refuges.

Salt marsh and tidal woodland (20 ha)

Because of the high turbidity caused by Kaolin wastes, salt marsh development is truncated at the seaward limit and pioneers include such species as *Triglochin maritima* normally found within main marsh zones. Reduced salinity also enables *Scirpus maritimus* and *Agrostis stolonifera* to occur on open mud in the upper reaches of the estuary.

The most outstanding interest of this small marsh is, however, its fine natural transition to alder–willow woodland still tidal at the equinoxes, a habitat type now almost extinct in Europe through reclamation or grazing. The salt marsh to woodland zone carries at least 120 species of flowering plants and ferns, many not normally associated with the inter-tidal zone. Mature oak trees survive occasional flooding with water showing as much as one-tenth sea water salinity (see also W.61).

The invertebrate fauna has been surveyed and is mainly of terrestrial origin migrating from the marsh to higher-lying refuges during equinoctial flooding.

C.39. PORTHGWARRA–PORDENACK POINT, CORNWALL
SW 371217–345241.   40 ha   Grade 2

Cliff (40 ha)

This section is an excellent granite site with full south-west exposure, ungrazed, and generally undisturbed by man. It shows a nearly complete cliff top zonation with almost all the typical Cornish cliff plant associes and especially good examples of *Ulex gallii* heath. In addition there are breeding colonies of seabirds including kittiwakes and fulmars.

C.40. SEVERN ESTUARY: ABER HAFREN,
          SOMERSET–GLOUCESTERSHIRE–
          MONMOUTHSHIRE
ST 5080.   16 000 ha   Grade 2

The extensive systems of sand and silt flats which border both sides of the Severn Estuary, between its head and a line from Cardiff to Weston-super-Mare, are of national importance for their wintering wader populations, which average 45 000 birds. These numbers are, however, dispersed over a large area, and density is less than on some other important wader estuaries (e.g. the Burry Inlet, not far to the west). The New Grounds (C.35) are distinguished as the most valuable, grade 1, part of the Severn Estuary.

SOUTH WALES

C.41. SOUTH GOWER COAST: GLANNAU DE GŴYR,
          GLAMORGAN
c. 830 ha   Grade 1

(*a*) *Worms Head–Porteynon Point*
SS 383877–473842.   10.5 km

(*b*) *Oxwich Point–Crawley Cliff*
SS 491853–526878.   6.5 km

(*c*) *Pwll-du Head–Bishopston Valley*
SS 564865–579871.   3 km

Flats (130 ha)

This small area of sand flat in Oxwich Bay is in a tide range of *c.* 8 m and is integral to the growth of Oxwich and Crawley dunes but subject to heavy seasonal tourist use.

Marsh (20 ha)

This small ungrazed sandy marsh adjacent to Oxwich dunes is notable for its complex transitional communities with brackish pools, dune slack, and flowing fresh water. *Althaea officinalis* is abundant and unusually large quantities of woody tidal litter are found. In spite of reclamation activities in the eighteenth century, tidal seepage through sluices has resulted in regrowth of brackish *Phragmites* marsh and transition to alder–willow scrub liable to tidal influence are found

Dune (75 ha)

Oxwich and Crawley dunes are lime-rich with calcareous freshwater streams meandering through slacks; they are notable for their varied flora and insect fauna and local development of scrub with alder, *Betula pubescens*, *Salix cinerea*, *Thelycrania sanguinea* and *Sambucus nigra* scrub on dunes. Plant species of special note include *Gentianella uliginosa*, *Dactylorchis incarnata*, *D. praetermissa*, *Epipactis palustris*, *Equisetum variegatum* and *Carex serotina*. There is a heavy tourist use locally, but this is mainly seasonal. As at Studland there is great structural variety and length of edge providing a varied complex of habitats for plants and animals. The inner part of the dune system passes in one place to a flood-plain mire with rich fen, and this is a grade 1 peatland site (P.32).

Cliff (300 ha)

These are discontinuous in three lengths: Pwll-du Head, Oxwich Point and Worms Head to Porteynon. They are composed of Carboniferous Limestone and support maritime, lowland grassland and woodland habitats. More than 100 species of flowering plants and ferns and at least 20 species of moss have been recorded from the ungrazed maritime grassland of the Worms Head peninsula. Tall *Festuca rubra* grassland with abundant *Dactylis glomerata* and *Rumex acetosa* occupies the summit plateau and more humid north-facing slopes, which, in addition, carry *Cotyledon umbilicus* and *Heracleum sphondylium*. These tall-grass communities occur on deep (60 cm) neutral to acidic soils, and, though damaged by fire in 1957 (which resulted in some soil loss by erosion), they are re-establishing satisfactorily.

The broken limestone cliffs running east from Worms Head support calcicolous grasslands and calcareous rocks with a paramaritime or submaritime character, and these habitats on the Gower coast give a bonus lowland grassland interest. On the shallower, drier soils of south-facing mainland slopes, short mixed *Festuca rubra–Festuca ovina* turf carries a rich herb flora including *Asperula cynanchica*, *Carlina vulgaris*, *Helianthemum chamaecistus* and *Poterium sanguisorba*, with maritime elements such as *Armeria maritima*, *Euphorbia paralias*, *Geranium sanguineum* and *Scilla verna*. This is a notable area for certain disjunct calcicolous plants which have a mainly western distribution in Britain and include *Veronica spicata* ssp. *hybrida*, *Aster linosyris*, *Ononis reclinata* and *Helianthemum canum*. There is locally an abundance of *Potentilla tabernaemontani*, *Geranium sanguineum* and *Hornungia petraea*. *Draba aizoides* occurs here as a native in several places, but nowhere else in Britain. Local south-western bryophytes (e.g. *Eurhynchium circinatum*) occur on rock outcrops. Patches of *Pteridium aquilinum*, *Ulex gallii* and *Rosa pimpinellifolia* occur locally. Interesting calcareous heath with mixtures of shallow-rooted calcifuge species such as *Erica cinerea* and *Galium saxatile* occurs with deeper-rooted calcicolous species such as *Helianthemum chamaecistus* and *Poterium sanguisorba* on flatter ground near the coast. There are also areas of wind-pruned coastal scrub composed mainly of *Ulex gallii*, *U. europaeus*, *Ligustrum vulgare*, *Prunus spinosa*, *Juniperus communis* and, rarely, *Sorbus rupicola*.

There are small seabird colonies, including one of auks at Worms Head.

Shingle
Pwll-du Bay and traces at Oxwich.

Rocky foreshore (265 ha)
Woodland (40 ha)
The Oxwich National Nature Reserve (NNR) includes areas of alder carr and mixed deciduous wood and a series of limestone buttresses and gulleys with an intermixture of grassland, scrub and woodland (Crawley Wood). A few ash, elm and small-leaved lime occur, but oak (mainly *Quercus petraea*) is dominant, and on an exposed point the canopy is only 2.5–4.5 m high. A large range of native woody species is present, this includes dogwood, privet and, of great interest, *Sorbus rupicola*. *Mercurialis perennis* and *Rubus fruticosus* grow beneath the trees but the flora of the rock outcrops and grassland bears a number of typical calcicolous species such as *Ceterach officinarum*, *Origanum vulgare*, *Helianthemum chamaecistus*, *Poterium sanguisorba*, *Blackstonia perfoliata* and *Geranium sanguineum*.

Oxwich Wood and Coastguard Wood, on the eastern side of Oxwich Point, comprise a woodland of oak with ash, elm, hazel and hawthorn which was coppiced in the past. Towards the exposed southern end *Rhamnus catharticus* is abundant. The ground layer under the densest canopy is predominantly *Mercurialis perennis*, *Dryopteris dilatata* and *Hedera helix*, with extensive *Sanicula europaea*, *Galium odoratum*, *Rubus fruticosus* agg. Landslide sites appear as profusely vegetated chasms and the woodland stretches to the splash zone.

The exposed edge of Oxwich Point headland bears large patches of dense canopied scrub about 2 m high. Black-thorn, dogwood and privet are common with hazel and emergent ash. The floor is strewn with limestone blocks, between which *Mercurialis perennis* and *Phyllitis scolopendrium* grow abundantly, with *Euphorbia amygdaloides*, *Circaea lutetiana* and *Geranium robertianum*.

Bishopston Wood is in a sheltered, steep-sided, partially-wooded valley in limestone some 5 km east of Oxwich. The tree cover is predominantly ash with pedunculate oak, maple and elm. *Tilia cordata* is locally abundant, particularly on the lower edge. The shrub layer includes hazel, spindle, privet, dogwood and guelder rose. The ground flora varies from *Lonicera–Oxalis* associations through *Primula–Mercurialis* to *Filipendula*, *Allium* and *Chrysosplenium* in flushes.

The South Gower Coast is particularly outstanding for its habitat diversity, with its wide range of sea cliff, dune, marsh, woodland, scrub, calcareous grassland and wetland, and the easy access to most of this makes it an important educational site.

C.42. BURRY INLET, GLAMORGAN
SS 419938–560975.   *c.* 5000 ha   Grade 1
Flats (3250 ha)
Llanrhidian Sands are one of the larger examples in Britain of medium-level, lime-rich sand flats grading to silt at higher levels, and have a large tidal range (8 m). They form an important wader feeding and roosting area with over 10 000 oystercatchers and a total population of 45 000 birds, and one of the most important wildfowl centres in south Wales with pintail (560), wigeon, and formerly shoveler.

Marsh (1520 ha, disjunct with largest block about 700 ha)
Llanrhidian Marsh is one of the largest examples in Britain of moderately sheep-grazed and pony-grazed salt marsh areas with lime-rich influences. A good sequence occurs from panned marsh on silt over sand down the estuary to continuous marsh on deeper silt up the estuary. Pioneer *Puccinellia maritima* growth is being replaced by *Spartina anglica* on a large scale. *Althaea officinalis* and *Isolepis cernua* are plentiful in the upper marsh with transitions to alderwood (introduced) at the salt marsh/dune slack transition.

Dune (220 ha)
Whiteford Burrows contain one of the largest and least disturbed systems of calcareous dune slacks. Substantial populations of many local species (notably *Anacamptis pyramidalis*, the national rarity *Liparis loeselii*, *Rumex maritimus*, *Dactylorchis incarnata*, *D. praetermissa*, *Epipactis palustris*, *Equisetum variegatum* and *Carex serotina*) occur among the 250 species of flowering plants recorded and *Mibora minima* has recently been discovered. Local populations of introduced *Hippophaë* and *Pinus* are considered controllable. The invertebrate fauna includes 146 species of Arachnida and 130 species of Coleoptera including the strandline beetle *Eurynebria complanata*, known from only four other British localities.

Shingle (traces)
Traces of shingle with local accumulations of shell (*Cardium edule*) occur with a vestigial flora.

Cliff (10 ha)
This is a limestone, north-facing, old cliff line on the southern boundary of Whiteford NNR. It rises 90 m from

the marshes and the high-water spring tides reach the bottom of the cliff. The vegetation is a mosaic of grassland, scrub, and open ash woodland over old quarry workings. Hawthorn, blackthorn and hazel as well as young ash form the understorey with gorse, guelder rose, *Rosa* and *Rubus fruticosus* agg. in the shrub layer. Under the canopy the ground flora is mainly of *Brachypodium sylvaticum*, *Teucrium scorodonia* and *Phyllitis scolopendrium*. The grassland is species-rich with *Helianthemum chamaecistus*, *Thymus drucei*, *Poterium sanguisorba*, *Briza media* and *Blackstonia perfoliata*. The boulder-strewn slopes are rich in bryophytes. This range of paramaritime habitats is included within the Burry site for its bonus interest.

C.43. STACKPOLE HEAD–CASTLEMARTIN CLIFFS: STACPOL–CLOGWYNI CASTELL MARTYN, PEMBROKESHIRE

SS 020972–SR 883957. *c.* 650 ha   Grade 1

This site, which incorporates the Flimston Stacks, extends from Linney Head in the west along approximately 18 km of coast to Trewent Point near Freshwater East. Apart from a short length of Old Red Sandstone in the east it consists for the most part of steep Carboniferous Limestone cliffs, with dunes at Broad Haven and Barafundle.

The limestone cliffs between Linney Head and the Wash have a broad rocky cliff top zone with an incomplete plant cover of *Armeria maritima*, *Plantago coronopus*, *Cerastium atrovirens*, *Catapodium marinum*, *Limonium binervosum* and *Spergularia rupicola*. This is followed inland by dense *Festuca rubra* turf with *Armeria*, *Plantago maritima*, *Cochlearia* and *Sagina maritima*, and then a thick, damp turf with *Carex flacca*, *Thymus drucei*, *Plantago lanceolata*, *Lotus corniculatus*, *Potentilla erecta*, *Scilla verna* and scattered *Calluna* which is dominant inland. Farther east between the Wash and St Govan's Head the cliffs are high and the vegetation shows less maritime influence. Limestone grassland dominated by *Festuca ovina* and *F. rubra* grades inland into damp heather heath with conspicuous patches of *Pedicularis sylvatica*. The limestone cliffs between Broad Haven Bay and Stackpole Quay exhibit considerable variety of vegetation from the exposed cliff top communities on Stackpole Head to more sheltered grassland nearer Stackpole Quay. Species of note in the grassland communities include *Asperula cynanchica*, *Inula crithmoides*, *Koeleria cristata* and *Listera ovata*. A strong population of the rare *Ononis reclinata* occurs on one headland near Stackpole Quay.

This piece of coast is especially notable for breeding birds, including chough, wheatear, raven, peregrine (formerly), common buzzard, fulmar, razorbill, guillemot, kittiwake, shag, and rock dove. Throughout this entire length of coast a large number of geological features and landforms can be seen, including fault structures in Carboniferous Limestone, Triassic gash breccia, pipes filled with presumed Tertiary deposits, a non-glaciated marine platform, caves, stacks, natural arches, and an enclosed shaft 155 m in diameter formed from the multiple collapse of blow-hole caves

The cliffs skirt one of the best open water sites in south Wales – Bosherston Lake – which is given grade 1 status in its own right (see OW.29).

C.44. STRUMBLE HEAD: PEN CAER-LLECHDAFAD, PEMBROKESHIRE

SM 895415–881358. 570 ha   Grade 1

These are predominantly west-facing cliffs rising to a maximum height of 137 m, but the coast is indented and all aspects from north to south also occur. The cliffs are mostly of a bevelled nature with long, vegetated slopes rising from 9 to 14 m above sea-level. This is one of the most geologically complex coasts in Britain with Cambrian and Ordovician strata and intrusive and extrusive igneous rocks. Shales, basic pillow lavas, acidic rhyolites, dolerites, sandstones, flagstones, quartzites and flaggy greywackes all occur and this complexity is matched by a highly varied flowering plant and fern flora of at least 15 species.

The vegetation shows all characteristic cliff types from exceedingly exposed grasslands and heaths to the sheltered scrubs. Notable species include *Asplenium billotii*, the dwarf form of *Chrysanthemum leucanthemum*, *Veronica spicata* ssp. *hybrida*, *Genista pilosa*, excellent growths of *Osmunda regalis* in stream sides on the cliffs, *Sedum telephium*, *Spergularia rupicola* and especially well-developed therophyte communities with *Bromus ferronii*, *Catapodium marinum*, *Cerastium atrovirens* and other species. The southern element in the flora is very well represented showing similarities to that on the Lizard peninsula. This is considered to be the best cliff vegetation site in south Wales.

The site is notable also for breeding birds including raven, chough, and two colonies of razorbill and guillemot. There is a rich littoral fauna and flora and well-developed beds of *Laminaria*. Grey seals breed here.

C.45. YNYSOEDD PRESELI, PEMBROKESHIRE

720 ha   Grade 1*

(a) Skokholm
SM 7305

(b) Skomer
SM 7209

(c) Grassholm
SM 5909

(d) Ramsey: Ynys Dewi
SM 7023

The offshore islands of Skokholm, Skomer, Grassholm and Ramsey are mostly bounded by cliffs, and Grassholm is largely a rock cone. They are famous for their breeding colonies of seabirds. On Skokholm there is a large colony of Manx shearwaters (35 000 pairs) and storm petrels (about 6000 pairs). Rabbits are abundant. Skomer has Manx shearwaters in even greater numbers (50 000–60 000 pairs) than Skokholm, another large rabbit population, and there is an interesting geographical race of the bank vole (the Skomer vole) peculiar to this island. Skomer probably has the bulk of the guillemots (3585 birds), razor-bills (1540 pairs) and kittiwakes (1630 pairs) nesting on the Ynysoedd Preseli and its bird populations are in general larger than those of Skokholm. Other breeding birds on this island include choughs, ravens, common buzzards and short-eared owls, and breeding colonies of puffins exist on both Skomer and Skokholm (*c.* 8000 pairs). On Ramsey, the first three species occur at unusually high densities. Also on Ramsey, the Atlantic grey seal has its largest known breeding colony in Wales (200 pups annually). Grassholm is famous for its large population of gannets (16 000 pairs in 1969) which forms the only colony on the west side of southern Britain. The cliff and rocky slope bird populations as a whole are the largest in the whole of western Britain south of Scotland, and these islands are currently being much used for studies of seabird ecology and population dynamics.

The vegetation of the interior of Skokholm and Skomer consists of the usual range of submaritime grassland, with moderately halophytic species, and grades into heath in places least influenced by spray. The vegetation of Grassholm over the two-thirds not occupied by the gannets consists mainly of a *Festuca rubra* sward over a hummocky layer of peat which was extensively burrowed by the once immense puffin colony. Floristically, these islands are not rich and their interest is largely faunal, though they have been much used for studies of the effects of breeding seabirds and mammals on maritime vegetation, and the character of the biotically modified vegetation is well documented. Areas strongly influenced by manuring and treading have abundance of species such as *Festuca rubra*, *Agrostis stolonifera*, *Atriplex* spp., *Cochlearia officinalis*, *C. danica*, *Holcus lanatus*, *Matricaria maritima*, *Plantago coronopus*, *Poa annua*, *Rumex acetosa*, *Sagina procumbens*, *Silene maritima*, *Stellaria media* and *Umbilicus rupestris*. The rarer plant species include *Cicendia filiformis*, *Asplenium billotii* and *Juniperus communis*.

C.46. DYFI, CARDIGANSHIRE–MERIONETH– MONTGOMERYSHIRE
SN 6391.   *c.* 2000 ha   Grade 1

Flats (1280 ha)

There is a medium-sized area of sand flat grading to silt flat up the estuary in a tidal range of 4.2 m. This is one of the most important wader and wildfowl centres in Wales with Greenland white-fronts (120 birds), wigeon (2000), pintail (150), also mallard, teal, shelduck and red-breasted merganser occur regularly. The white-fronted geese roost on the estuary but the main feeding ground is Cors Fochno (see P.29).

Marsh (440 ha)

The medium-sized marsh shows a good estuarine series from panned sandy marsh near the estuary mouth to continuous flat marsh on silted-up estuary. Pioneer *Salicornia* and *Puccinellia* are being increasingly replaced by *Spartina anglica*. The railway embankment interrupts the transition to brackish marsh (partly reclaimed), but the stratigraphic relationships to Cors Fochno are of interest. Sheep-grazing and the isolated position of these marshes have limited their floristic diversity (e.g. *Limonium vulgare* and *Halimione portulacoides*, other than experimental introductions, are absent), but much fundamental work on salt marsh ecology has been carried out here and the marshes are of special value for further study of this type.

Dune (280 ha discontinuous in two blocks of 160 ha (Aberdyfi) and 120 ha (Ynyslas))

While both these dune systems are subject to human disturbance they contain a good representative flora of lime-rich dune slack flowering plants (150+ species) and bryophytes. They are important in relation to physiographic studies on the Dyfi estuary complex as a whole and for educational use generally. Notable populations of *Dactylorchis incarnata* ssp. *coccinea* and *D. purpurella* occur at Ynyslas. The polecat is said to be common on these dunes.

Shingle (traces)

The shingle is mostly non-vegetated, but a vestigial shingle beach flora is found here and there and the lichen flora may prove to be of phytogeographic interest.

This coastal complex adjoins the large raised mire of Cors Fochno (Borth Bog) (P.29, gr. 1*), which has developed over former estuarine sediments.

C.40. SEVERN ESTUARY: ABER HAFREN (PART), MONMOUTHSHIRE   Grade 2
See under South-west England, p. 17.

C.47. KENFIG DUNES: TYWYN CYNFFIG, GLAMORGAN
SS 7981.   *c.* 640 ha   Grade 2

Flats (*c.* 160 ha)

This is a small area of high-level sand flats in a tidal range of *c.* 8 m.

Shingle (traces)

Local accumulations occur with a vestigial flora.

Dune (*c.* 480 ha)

This is a large calcareous dune system overlying Keuper Marls and boulder clay. During the thirteenth–sixteenth centuries, the dunes extended and adjacent farmland was inundated by sand. Seral stages include strandline, embryo dunes, mobile and fixed dunes with slacks, developed over a spring-fed water table which is high throughout the year. The slack vegetation is dominated by *Salix repens*. Examples of hummocks and dunes formed by the action of this plant occur frequently. The slacks are also noted for their varied flora, with disjunct populations of taxonomically interesting hybrids, e.g. *Viola tricolor*, *Mentha* spp., *Epipactis* spp. (with local forms), and the presence of species rare in Wales, e.g. *Monotropa hypopitys*, and *Pyrola rotundifolia*, as well as the nationally rare *Liparis loeselii* var. *ovata*, in substantial numbers (see also Kenfig Pool (OW.30)).

C.48. TYWYN GWENDRAETH: TOWYN BURROWS,
      CARMARTHENSHIRE

SN 3705. 1200 ha   Grade 2

Flats (610 ha)
A small area of high-level sand flats grades into silt flats
farther up the estuary.

Marsh (370 ha)
Halimione portulacoides is dominant over large areas of the
lower levels of this marsh, which exhibits a well-marked
zonation of plant communities. *Spartina anglica* is present
but restricted to the seaward edge of the marsh. In the
grazed eastern part *Puccinellia maritima* is widespread in the
upper marsh whilst *Festuca rubra* with associated *Limonium
vulgare*, *L. binervosum*, *Aster tripolium* is widespread in the
ungrazed western area. Behind Towyn Point considerable
populations of *Juncus maritimus*, *J. acutus*, and *Scirpus
maritimus* grade into a large wet slack. The marsh is the only
recorded British locality for the three species of halacarid
mites *Rhombognathus levis*, *R. uniscutatus* and *Caspihala-
carus hyrcanus*.

Dune (220 ha)
Situated at the northern end of the once extensive Pembrey
Burrows, Tywyn Gwendraeth is the only part of this dune
system that has not been planted with *Pinus nigra* var.
maritima. Wind-blown sand is rapidly accreting, forming a
200-m deep belt of *Agropyron junceiforme* embryo dunes
with associated *Salsola kali* and *Cakile maritima*. The rare
strandline beetle *Eurynebria complanata* occurs here.
Hippophaë rhamnoides scrub occurs along the older dune
ridges. The dune slack flora ranges from relatively open
associations rich in herbs, sedges and bryophytes to closed
communities dominated by *Salix repens*, *Alnus glutinosa* and
S. atrocinerea. One large slack grades into the *Juncus
maritimus* community of the upper salt marsh. The slacks
support large populations of the rare *Liparis loeselii* and
Gentianella uliginosa. Other species of interest include
Pyrola rotundifolia ssp. *maritima*, *Sisyrinchium bermudiana*,
Listera ovata, *Ophrys apifera*, *Gymnadenia conopsea*,
Anacamptis pyramidalis, *Orchis morio*, *Spiranthes spiralis*,
Epipactis palustris and many *Dactylorchis* spp. such as *D.
purpurella* here near its southern-most limit. *Centaurium
littorale* is also near its southern-most limit. The dunes also
have a colony of the marbled white butterfly.

C.49. ST DAVID'S HEAD: PENMAENDEWI,
      PEMBROKESHIRE

SM 729276–767298. 285 ha   Grade 2

Cliff (285 ha, including 180 ha of cliff top heath)
The coastline here is dominated by two north-east–south-
west orientated dolerite bands. The more northerly forms
the north-west-facing coast with near vertical cliffs rising
to 76 m. The second dolerite band lies to the south and in
parallel, outcropping to the north and south of St David's
Head. Between the two lie the Ordovician Arenig beds of
sandstones and *Tetragraptus* shales which outcrop as steeply

sloping cliffs on the south side of St David's Head. As well
as cliffs, the intrusions produce low tors standing above the
general level of the coastal plateau.

At least 150 species of flowering plants and ferns are
found on this predominantly acidic headland. Bracken and
Calluna–Erica cinerea–Ulex gallii heathland give way to
species rich *Festuca rubra* grassland in the spray zone near
the coast. Among the more notable plants are *Spergularia
rupicola*, *Scilla verna*, native chives *Allium schoenoprasum*,
fine growths of the mat-forming *Genista pilosa* spreading
over rocks, the dwarf coastal ecotype of *Chrysanthemum
leucanthemum* and extensive populations of *Anthyllis
vulneraria*, *Sedum acre*, *Armeria maritima* and *Jasione
montana*. Other south-western species such as *Sagina
subulata* occur in wet flushes. *Limonium paradoxum*,
endemic to the British Isles, is known for certain only on
basic igneous rocks on St David's Head.

Colonies of grey seals, and scattered choughs, ravens, and
common buzzards breed on this coast.

This coast is notable for its marine biological and algal
communities in a tide range of 4.5 m. The hard rocks support a good lichen flora which has yet to be fully explored.

NORTH WALES

C.50. GLANNAU HARLECH, MERIONETH   Grade 1
(a) Morfa Harlech and Traeth Bach
SH 602367–565345. c. 1170 ha

Flats (c. 380 ha)
These occupy the southern part of the Glaslyn/Dwyryd
estuary known as Traeth Bach and the western-facing sandy
beach fringing Cardigan Bay; they are sand and silt flats
low in free lime which form the source of material for
extensive dune and marsh. The Traeth Bach sector supports moderate flocks of mallard, teal, wigeon, pintail and
shelduck.

Marsh (380 ha, disjunct in blocks up to 120 ha)
There is mainly *Puccinellia maritima–Juncus maritimus*
marsh (grazing limited locally) with recent rapid extension
of *Spartina anglica* (c. 24 ha) on seaward edges. The area is
notable for *Carex punctata*, putative hybrids of *C. extensa* ×
C. distans, the very rare species *Eleocharis parvula*, and
Blysmus rufus (southern limit on west coast).

Dune (410 ha)
These form one of the larger, moderately lime-rich dune
systems in Britain, developed as northward-grown spits
enclosing dune slack areas and one small area of permanent
fresh water. The foreshore used to support one of the best
strandline floras in Britain in the 1950s, but this is a
transient feature now replaced by coast dune growth. The
dunes support relatively large populations of many local
species, e.g. *Anacamptis pyramidalis*, *Botrychium lunaria*,
Dianthus deltoides, *Hypochoeris glabra*, *Ophrys apifera*,
Viola tricolor ssp. *curtisii*, and slacks also have *Juncus acutus*
(near its northern limit), *Dactylorchis purpurella*,

D. incarnata ssp. *coccinea*, *Lycopodium selago* and *Utricularia neglecta*. The latter are rich in local bryophytes also, such as *Drepanocladus sendtneri* var. *wilsonii*, and some show an interesting hummock development. There is a great variety of invertebrates and representative populations of breeding birds. A freshwater swamp here supports a black-headed gull colony in summer and small numbers of wildfowl (up to 200) in winter including whooper swans, mallard, teal, wigeon and shoveler.

(b) Morfa Dyffryn
SH 565278–575215.　530 ha

Flats (70 ha)
This is a small area of high-level sand flats which feeds the dunes and forms their western shore. To the landward of Mochras 'Island' (a peninsula of glacial drift) lies an area of silt flats forming part of the Artro estuary and grading to salt marsh.

Marsh (10 ha)
This is a very small salt marsh with representative flora, but including several patches of *Salicornia perennis* at its north-west limit for the British Isles.

Dune (450 ha)
There is a large calcareous dune system with up to 6% free carbonate in embryo dune sand, built out (partly on shingle) from the coast between the estuary of the Ysgethin to the south and the joint Cwmnantcol/Artro estuary to the north. Dunes rise to 18 m, but ridges are now much dissected by the prevailing on-shore winds which have checked progradation and resulted in a network of dune and slack similar to that at Newborough in Anglesey. The dunes, which are very mobile, carry a representative flora with notable populations of local species (e.g. *Euphorbia paralias*).

The well-developed slack system is locally dominated by *Salix repens* and carries a very rich flora with many local species including *Juncus acutus* and *Epipactis phyllanthes* var. *pendula*. No details of the invertebrate fauna are available, but the several hundred flowering plant species present are likely to support great diversity.

C.51. NEWBOROUGH WARREN–YNYS LLANDDWYN, ANGLESEY
SH 406670–430630.　2200 ha　　　　　　　　Grade 1

Flats (660 ha, disjunct in two blocks, largest c. 400 ha)
This medium-sized area of high-level sand flats occurs in a tidal range of 7.5 m, silting at highest levels and carrying algae and with sand eels (*Ammodytes*).

Marsh (160 ha, disjunct largest unit c. 110 ha)
There is a small, ungrazed sandy-silt marsh with one of the largest continuous populations of *Juncus maritimus* in Britain, and a full range of seral stages from pioneer *Puccinellia* growths to *Salix cinerea* ssp. *atrocinerea* scrub. Although *Spartina anglica* has recently appeared, possi-

bilities of controlling it in the Braint (Traeth Melynog) estuary are good. Small natural and artificial bodies of permanent water add further to the diversity of this area. This area was until recently a regular breeding haunt of Montagu's harrier. This part of the site and the flats have some importance for wildfowl and waders, including in winter a fairly regular flock of up to about 250 pintail and over 2000 other ducks. Several hundred locally-introduced Canada and greylag geese visit the flats and marsh at times particularly in autumn while the Cob pool at Malltraeth is noted as a stopping point for migratory birds, particularly waders.

Dune (1300 ha)
Newborough Warren is the sixth largest dune system in Britain and though partly afforested contains a very fine range of *Salix repens* slacks, with an excellent population of *Epipactis dunensis*. There is a full succession from locally developed strandline flora through moderately lime-rich dunes to heather heath and incipient scrub development. Large populations of many local species (e.g. *Parnassia palustris*, *Dactylorhiza* spp., *Pinguicula vulgaris*) occur among the 560 species of flowering plants recorded, many of which have been introduced by forestry activities; and there are many local and rare bryophytes (e.g. *Drepanocladus lycopodioides* and *D. sendtneri*).

Common terns bred until recently in places and there are large numbers of dune nesting herring- and lesser black-backed gulls. A rock ridge running across the dunes and onto Ynys Llanddwyn is of high geological interest as the type area for Precambrian Gwna volcanic rocks and pillow lavas.

Shingle (60 ha)
A medium-sized area of large-pebbled shingle occurs and is mainly overlain by sand, but carries representatives of the shingle beach flora. Little terns breed here sparingly.

Cliff (20 ha)
On Ynys Llanddwyn there is a representative flora with small populations of local species (e.g. *Inula crithmoides*) on acidic volcanic rocks subject to local enrichment of lime from spray and calcareous sand. A colony of cormorants breeds on outlying rocks.

C.52. GLANNAU YNYS GYBI: HOLY ISLAND COAST, ANGLESEY
SH 224837–243795.　375 ha　　　　　　　　Grade 1

The 90–125 m cliffs of the north-west coast of Holyhead Island are composed of Precambrian rocks of the 'Mona Complex' and at South Stack the cliff section shows a classic example of folding of these rocks. The cliff ledges support the second largest breeding auk colony in west Wales with over 1000 guillemots and 400 razorbills, the main colonies being on the rock buttresses near South Stack. Puffins (50–100), fulmars, cormorants and shags also nest at suitable points along the coast. Grey seals have a small breeding colony in the caves near North Stack.

The cliff face vegetation shows a representative maritime flora, with southern species such as *Inula crithmoides* and *Spergularia rupicola*, while the submaritime cliff communities are distinguished by the presence of two rare vascular plants unknown in Britain outside north Wales, namely *Tuberaria guttata* and *Senecio integrifolius* var. *maritimus*. The ground above the cliffs has a good deal of *Calluna–Ulex gallii* heath and is rated as a grade 1 acidic heathland site (L.120). Species of oceanic distribution, such as *Scilla verna* and *Sedum anglicum*, are abundant here, and a number of Atlantic bryophytes occur, including *Dicranum scottianum*, *Frullania microphylla* and *F. germana*.

C.55. ABER DYFRDWY: DEE ESTUARY (PART), FLINTSHIRE
Grade 1*

See under Midlands (see opposite).

C.53. YNYS ENLLI & GLANNAU ABERDARON: BARDSEY ISLAND AND ABERDARON COAST, CAERNARVONSHIRE
SH 120220 and SH 182325–167264.   650 ha   Grade 2

Ynys Enlli (180 ha) is separated from the mainland by the 3 km passage of Bardsey Sound; it is partly cliff-bound, but has a grassy interior. The island's chief interest is ornithological; it lies on a migration route and an observatory has operated for a number of years. About 3000 pairs of Manx shearwaters breed on the island with small numbers of other seabirds and a few pairs of choughs. The vegetation includes maritime grassland and rough pasture and cliff top vegetation, with *Armeria maritima*, *Spergularia rupicola*, *Catapodium marinum* and *Cochlearia danica*.

The mainland opposite Ynys Enlli has a good deal of cliff and a fairly good range of coastal rock vegetation. At Pen y Cil the cliff top communities include stands of *Sarothamnus scoparius* var. *maritimus*. Choughs and small numbers of seabirds also nest at suitable places.

C.54. TYWYN ABERFFRAW, ANGLESEY
SH 3669.   355 ha   Grade 2

This is a smaller dune system 4.8 km north-west of Newborough Warren. Botanically it is notable for its damp calcareous slacks and flats where there are a number of rare bryophytes including northern species such as *Amblyodon dealbatus*, *Drepanocladus sendtneri*, *Catoscopium nigritum* and *Meesia uliginosa*, and Mediterranean species such as *Pleurochaete squarrosa*, *Southbya tophacea* and *Petalophyllum ralfsii*. Colonies of *Orchis apifera*, *Gentianella campestris*, *Spiranthes spiralis* and *Botrychium lunaria* and *Moerckia flotowiana* also occur. Merlins breed here on the marram dunes. Llyn Coron (OW.36) at the landward end of the system is a shallow base-rich lake which is one of the most important inland wildfowl waters in Wales and is linked with the wildfowl haunts in and around the NNR at Newborough. It supports mallard, teal, wigeon, shoveler, pochard, tufted duck and goldeneye and is also regularly used by the introduced Canada and greylag geese flocks numbering up to 500 birds.

MIDLANDS

C.55. DEE ESTUARY: ABER DYFRDWY, CHESHIRE–FLINTSHIRE
SJ 2380.   12 500 ha   Grade 1*

The great estuarine flats and salt marshes of the Cheshire Dee, together with the low sandstone island of Hilbre, are one of the most important winter bird haunts in Britain. Very large numbers of duck frequent the Estuary, the most notable being pintail (1000 birds) and shelduck (1500 birds). Mallard, teal, wigeon, shoveler, goldeneye, scaup, common scoter and red-breasted merganser also occur regularly in fair numbers.

The Estuary is of international importance for wading birds, especially on the lower reaches around Hilbre Island. Bar-tailed godwit, knot and oystercatcher and many other species are present each winter in enormous numbers, the average figure being in the region of 125 000 birds.

The head of the Estuary has extensive salt marshes near Connah's Quay and whilst they are in close proximity to a large steel works and are not outstanding in botanical features, they none the less provide excellent examples of salt marsh, and are an integral part of the estuarine ecosystem. *Spartina anglica* is well established and spreading here.

The presence of an isolated herd of grey seals is of interest. These haul out on to the West Hoyle Bank, at the mouth of the Estuary.

C.56. MERSEY ESTUARY, CHESHIRE–LANCASHIRE
SJ 4478.   5300 ha   Grade 2

The upper and wider part of the Mersey Estuary above Liverpool has a large area of inter-tidal mud flats. Despite the proximity of large urban–industrial complexes, the area supports very large numbers of wildfowl. In particular, pintail (1000 birds) have increased markedly there in recent years, and in 1970–71 the November and February figures were 5500. Total wildfowl numbers at that time reached 11 000. Teal (1800 birds) have also increased to about 2500 and represent the second largest gathering in the British Isles, whilst mallard, wigeon and shelduck also occur regularly in some numbers. Waders were up to 19 000 in 1970–71 (this included 13 000 dunlin).

The reclaimed and now fresh marshes to the south of the Manchester Ship Canal (which runs close to the south shore) between Ince and Frodsham are an integral part of the area from the ornithological point of view, providing refuge and feeding during high tides, and also contain uncommon plants. They are, however, affected by industrial development and agricultural improvement.

NORTH ENGLAND

C.57. AINSDALE DUNES, LANCASHIRE
SD 306134–247094.   1550 ha   Grade 1
Flats (750 ha)

This large area of high- to medium-level sand flats in a tidal range of 7.5 m is the source of sand for Ainsdale Dunes and is of physiographic and ornithological interest. There is extensive tourist use seasonally.

Dune (800 ha)

Ainsdale–Formby has the fourth largest sand-dune system in Britain on lime-rich sand not significantly grazed and with extensive dune slacks, some of which are permanently wet. Older dunes are planted with Corsican, Austrian and Scots pine. The rare *Epipactis dunensis* occurs on the dunes, and in pine plantations, where it is accompanied by *E. phyllanthes* var. *pendula*, while younger dunes carry notable populations of *Euphorbia paralias*, *E. portlandica*, *Phleum arenarium* and *Vulpia membranacea* amongst the marram. On dunes of intermediate age and in drier slacks *Hippophaë rhamnoides* has expanded in recent years, forming one of the largest continuous populations of this species in Britain.

Dune slack communities range from mixed eutrophic fen through a varied series of damp and dry types rich in herbs, sedges and bryophytes to birch scrub. There are also small areas of alder woodland. There is an abundance of a great variety of local plant species including *Dactylorhiza* spp., *Parnassia palustris* var. *condensata*, *Epipactis palustris*, *Pyrola rotundifolia* ssp. *maritima*, together with many aliens, *Montia perfoliata*, *Oenothera* spp., *Juncus tenuis* and *Schoenoplectus americanus*.

The whole area is floristically rich and typical calcicoles include *Inula conyza*, *Erigeron acer*, *Carlina vulgaris*, *Gentianella amarella*, *Monotropa hypophegea*, *Ophrys apifera*, *Saxifraga tridactylites* and *Anthyllis vulneraria*. The invertebrate fauna is equally varied and most of the usual dune breeding birds occur. In addition, there is a population of natterjack toads, and the sand lizard occurs sparingly at its most northerly British station. The woods have a colony of red squirrels and a varied bird population.

The Formby–Ainsdale dunes have retained their biological diversity despite the fact that the flora and fauna have undergone changes and become depleted in numbers of species and the abundance of many individuals during this century. Large areas of the older dunes have been planted with pines. A general trend towards drier conditions and the draining of some of the slacks has caused loss or reduction of many plants and birds which depend on wet ground, while increased human pressure in various ways has also caused losses. Some plants are now apparently extinct (e.g. *Littorella uniflora*, *Antennaria dioica* and *Corynephorus canescens*) and others survive precariously. The part of the area south of the NNR is severely affected by public pressure and coastal erosion. Reduction of rabbit-grazing following myxomatosis has resulted in increased growth of *Hippophaë rhamnoides*, *Salix repens*, birch scrub and pine regeneration in recent years.

C.58. RIBBLE ESTUARY, LANCASHIRE
SD 4326.   *c.* 8000 ha   Grade 1*

Flats (*c.* 5200 ha)

These are among the 10 largest sand–silt flats in Britain in a 6.5-m tide range and they support large populations of wildfowl and waders. In particular it is the main centre for pink-footed geese in north-west England (6000 birds), and there are considerable numbers of mallard, teal and wigeon. The numbers of waders total 95 000, with the knot and dunlin particularly numerous.

Marsh (*c.* 2800 ha)

The Ribble Estuary, mainly on the south side, has one of the largest continuous areas of salt marsh in Britain, with also very extensive reclaimed marsh behind embankments to landward. The salt marsh is an extensively sheep- and cattle-grazed *Puccinellia/Festuca rubra* marsh with areas of *Suaeda maritima*, *Atriplex littoralis*, *Cochlearia danica* and *Armeria maritima*, but *Spartina anglica* (*c.* 400 ha) is taking over locally as the pioneer species. Some 47 species of flowering plants occur on the Ribble salt marshes and 57 species on clay embankments. The reclaimed marshes also have ditches, seasonally wet depressions, pools or generally wet grassland areas which give aquatic or semi-aquatic vegetation, with species such as *Phragmites communis*, *Iris pseudacorus*, *Typha latifolia*, *Equisetum fluviatile* and *Ranunculus aquatilis*. While pollution is modifying these marshes, their carrying capacity for herbivorous wildfowl is probably extremely high. There are also considerable spring and summer breeding bird populations, including especially shelduck, redshank, lapwing, oystercatcher, skylark, black-headed gull and common tern, and this is the southernmost breeding haunt of dunlin on salt marshes in Britain nowadays.

C.59. MORECAMBE BAY (including WYRE–LUNE), LANCASHIRE
SD 3670.   *c.* 17 000 ha   Grade 1*

Flats (*c.* 15 800 ha)

The great expanse of inter-tidal sand–silt flats in Morecambe Bay between Walney Island and Fleetwood (and including the estuaries of the Kent and Leven in the north and Wyre and Lune in the south) is rich in invertebrates and supports the biggest wintering population of wading birds in Britain. On this account alone the site is of international importance: the counts made between 1967 and 1972 revealed the following maxima: oystercatcher – 45 000; ringed plover – 7000; grey plover – 150; curlew – 14 000; bar-tailed godwit – 8000; redshank – 12 000; knot – 80 000; dunlin – 44 000; sanderling – 14 000. With the numbers of the other remaining waders, these give an average total of 235 000 birds. The wildfowl are not at present of comparable interest, but there is a large roost of pink-footed geese (3000 birds) on Cockerham Sands on the Lune, and fair numbers of a wide range of other species (e.g. up to 6000 shelduck in the north of the Bay).

Marsh (*c.* 1200 ha)

These comprise a number of discontinuous saltings fringing the upper estuaries, the largest continuous area being 800 ha from Arnside Point to Warton. They are confined to the upper 2.5 m of the very large tidal range (11.5 m) and most are heavily grazed by sheep – a small area (*c.* 11 ha) near Holme Island which remains ungrazed provides an interesting exception. The long-established management of the marshes by a combination of sheep-grazing and turf-cutting has led to a dense fine sward dominated by perennial grasses and providing suitable high-tide wader roosts. The saltings are backed in places by species-rich rush-dominated communities containing both northern (e.g. *Blysmus rufus* and *Eleocharis quinqueflora*) and southern (e.g. *Centaurium pulchellum*) elements of the flora. These upper marshes are rich in *Juncus* spp. and *Carex* spp. and show transitions to freshwater marsh. The most important marshes as high-tide wader roosts are at Cockerham on the Lune in the south, Carnforth in the east, and Flookburgh–Holker in the north. The floristics of this vegetation are very similar to those described for the Solway Marshes in C.61.

Cliff and embankment (30 ha)

The head of the bay has a few rather low Carboniferous Limestone cliffs, the best example of which at Humphrey Head carries *Crithmum maritimum* but is of greater importance as a lowland calcareous rock and grassland site with a rich paramaritime flora (L.133). Stone-faced sea walls and embankments carry a limestone flora and in one area (Crag Wood) a small dune community on a former embankment contains *Allium scorodoprasum*. The Mediterranean fern *Adiantum capillus-veneris* occurs at the head of the Bay in its most northerly British station, and is an indication of the mildness of the winters here. This area should be considered in conjunction with site C.60, Walney–Sandscale.

Morecambe Bay shares with the Wash the distinction of having the largest area of inter-tidal estuarine flats in Britain, and the largest winter wader populations, though its wildfowl interest is less than that of the Wash. Careful surveys have recently been made of the wader populations, and though some parts of the Bay are clearly of greater importance to these birds than others, they are highly mobile creatures, and it has not been judged practicable to divide up the system and allocate different gradings to different parts. The whole flat system of Morecambe Bay has therefore been regarded as one very large and important area. Similarly, the fringing salt marshes, though not individually or even perhaps collectively of equivalent importance to those of the Solway or Ribble, are an integral part of this whole ecosystem, and are included within the boundaries of the grade 1 site. The Bay has recently been the subject of a feasibility study report (Water Resources Board, 1972) on the making of various types and sizes of freshwater impoundments, and on the implications of such developments for nature conservation interests, but decisions on implementation of the proposed alternative schemes are still awaited.

C.60. WALNEY AND SANDSCALE DUNES,
 LANCASHIRE
SD 220620–SD 180750. *c.* 2450 ha   Grade 1
This complex of maritime habitats consists of (1) the north end of Walney Island and the adjoining promontory of Sandscale (Roanhead) on the mainland peninsula of Furness, together with the intervening sands which spread out into the large flats at the mouth of the Duddon estuary (see C.66), and (2) the south end of Walney Island with the adjoining few small islands (notably Foulney) and the flats between Walney and Barrow-in-Furness at the western entrance to Morecambe Bay.

Flats (1300 ha – in two main blocks)
Medium-sized areas of sand flats and inter-tidal shingle occur in a tide range of 6 m. Some *Zostera* occurs in silty areas, and the winter wildfowl populations are of moderate interest. They include common scoter (1000), mallard, teal, wigeon, goldeneye, shelduck and red-breasted merganser.

Marsh (120 ha)
There is a small, representative, lightly grazed marsh on north Walney with transitions to sand and shingle with *Salicornia/Puccinellia* pioneer stages on silt (some *Spartina anglica*) and small populations of *Limonium humile*, *L. vulgare* and *Halimione portulacoides*.

Dune (550 ha in three main areas, largest of 300 ha (Sandscale Haws))
Lime-rich dunes with slacks overlying clay (Sandscale) contrast with less lime-rich dunes overlying shingle (north and south Walney Island). The south Walney dunes are locally modified by guano from the mixed ground-nesting colony of herring and lesser black-backed gulls, which is the largest in Europe and has been the subject of research in recent years. Also on south Walney there are fluctuating breeding colonies of common, Arctic, little, Sandwich and occasionally roseate terns. Some of these species breed at times on the small Foulney Island, and the colony of Sandwich terns fluctuates between Walney and the alternative haunt of Drigg Point, Ravenglass, where most of the birds have bred in recent years. Eiders also nest here in their most southern breeding station in Britain. Some 180 species of flowering plants occur on the Sandscale Haws dunes and at least 200 species in the south Walney complex of habitats. A notable plant present on north Walney is *Geranium sanguineum* var. *lancastriense*, whilst Sandscale has rich slacks with *Pyrola rotundifolia*, *Ophrys apifera* and *Epipactis palustris*.

Shingle (480 ha, disjunct with areas up to 200 ha (north Walney))
Including the shingle around Foulney the inter-tidal complex contains a total shingle area among the five largest in Britain. Northern elements (e.g. *Mertensia maritima* – last seen in 1963) combine with southern elements and aliens to provide some of the richest shingle beach floras in Britain.

Though locally modified by proximity to an industrial area and somewhat fragile as well as disjunct as a site, this diverse complex forming an arc round Barrow is of outstanding scientific and educational value.

C.61. UPPER SOLWAY FLATS AND MARSHES,
CUMBERLAND, DUMFRIES-SHIRE,
KIRKCUDBRIGHTSHIRE   Grade 1*

The sand flats of the Upper Solway Firth, above a line from
Southerness Point in Kirkcudbrightshire to Dubmill Point
in Cumberland, are probably the third largest inter-tidal
flat system in Britain, and are of international importance
for their large wintering populations of wildfowl (with
average totals exceeding 20000 birds) and waders (with
peak numbers of over 130000 birds). The whole of this
large area is regarded as a single system, of grade 1* importance, but for convenience of treatment here it has been
divided into three sections, namely: the highest section from
Rockcliffe and Burgh Marshes to a line from Bowness-on-
Solway to Dornock; a middle section extending to a line
from Skinburness to Powfoot and including Moricambe
Bay; and an outer, northern section from Powfoot to
Carsethorn and including the Lochar and Nith estuaries.
The first two sections are mainly in Cumberland but have
small northern areas in Scotland, whilst the third is wholly
in Scotland. For convenience all three are described here.

At present the middle section is the least important of the
three ornithologically. The distribution of wildfowl on the
Solway has, however, varied somewhat during this century
according to changing incidence of disturbance and protection in different parts. The outer section with the Blackshaw Bank, Carse Sands and Caerlaverock Merse is of
special importance at present, and this is evidently a reflection of the degree of sanctuary and shooting control which
have been conferred by the Caerlaverock NNR. Geese tend
at any time to use different parts of the Solway as alternative
haunts for feeding and roosting, so that ornithological
interest is inevitably rather fluid in any one part. The middle
section would almost certainly increase in value if any
extensive economic developments took place within the
uppermost sections.

(a) Sarkfoot–Bowness shore
NY 322650–230628
  Sarkfoot–Dornock shore   } *c.* 2800 ha
NY 322650–228653

  Flats (1420 ha)

These sand flats fill the upper Solway Firth and are
traversed by the Eden and Esk channels at low tide. They
are the roosting place of large numbers of wildfowl,
especially pink-footed (3600) and barnacle geese (3000;
$6\frac{1}{2}\%$ world population, 75% of the Spitsbergen population), wigeon and teal. There is also a wide variety of other
ducks and a large number of waders. Large numbers of
gulls, black-headed, common and herring, flight on to the
flats towards evening, to roost there.

  Marsh (1380+ ha)

The high-lying grass plains of the upper Solway salt
marshes (mainly Rockcliffe and Burgh Marshes, and smaller
areas of marsh near Gretna) are in contrast to the more
saline and middle-lower level marshes of south-east England. Because of the fall in sea-level relative to the land in
this area, the larger part of these marshes is flooded only by
spring tides, whilst substantial areas escape inundation
except during unusually high tides, which do not occur
every year. These sandy shores have *Puccinellia maritima*
as the main pioneer with relatively little *Salicornia* and
Spartina is so far absent. There are large areas of a tightly
consolidated *Puccinellia–Festuca rubra* sward, often coloured
pink in late spring by an abundance of flowers of *Armeria
maritima*. This passes farther inland to a sward with much
Juncus gerardii and *Agrostis stolonifera*, and locally an
abundance of *Carex flacca*, *C. panicea* and *C. nigra*. These
swards are close-grazed, and forbs are not conspicuous,
except for rosette species such as *Leontodon autumnalis* and
Crepis capillaris. Some other halophytes such as *Glaux
maritima*, *Spergularia media*, *S. marina*, *Suaeda maritima*,
Limonium vulgare, *Triglochin maritima*, *Plantago maritima*
and *P. coronopus* are locally abundant in these marsh grasslands, especially on the lower, younger areas, but larger
forbs such as *Cochlearia officinalis* and *Aster tripolium* occur
mainly in creeks, which are often deep.

Burgh Marsh shows severe marginal erosion, by under-
cutting of a brow edge during high tides, while Rockcliffe
shows a good deal of accretion.

The marshes are used as pasture for cattle (summer only)
and sheep, and the seldom-flooded inner part of Burgh
Marsh is a type of neutral grassland with much *Juncus
effusus*. The famous Solway turf is cut here; the cut-over
areas show stages in recolonisation by the sward plants.

The Solway head marshes formerly had large breeding
populations of redshank, lapwing, dunlin, oystercatcher and
skylark; numbers declined in 1963 but have shown substantial recovery on the Rockcliffe section. Rockcliffe
Marsh has colonies of common terns, lesser black-backed
and black-headed gulls, with a few pairs of great black-
backed and herring gulls. A variety of other species nest
sparingly or sporadically, e.g. Arctic tern, shoveler, ringed
plover, snipe, curlew, meadow pipit, sand martin, swallow
(under creek bridges), reed bunting, moorhen, partridge and
linnet (in gorse bushes). Shelduck feed on the sands and
nest in rabbit holes in embankments of the inner marshes
or around field edges inland, but are less numerous than
20 years ago. Now and then, unusually high spring tides
flood out virtually every nest on the marshes, but most
species soon re-lay. The marshes are sometimes used as a
feeding place by wildfowl, especially the geese and wigeon,
and they are a resting place for waders during high tides.
Flocks of lapwing, golden plover and curlew also frequent
the marshes to a variable degree in winter.

(b) Grune Point–Bowness shore
NY 144568–230628
  Powfoot–Dornock shore   } *c.* 2900 ha
NY 150657–228653

  Flats (1950 ha)

The sand flats of the middle section, including Middle

Bank, Cardurnock Flats and Moricambe Bay, are used by small flocks of greylag, pink-footed and barnacle geese. They are also used by duck and provide feeding places for waders. They have a number of boulder-strewn mussel beds.

Marsh (930 ha)

The Moricambe Bay marshes of Skinburness and Longnewton are similar in vegetation and bird populations to those of Rockcliffe and Burgh Marshes, but at present are of lesser importance ornithologically, though they were once an important wildfowl area. Longnewton Marsh has been accreting rapidly during the present century and shows good pioneer building stages at the south-west point, but elsewhere there is a good deal of marginal erosion. The strip of salt marsh along the Cardurnock–Bowness shore is generally narrow, but in recent years has shown good accretion west of the site of the old Solway viaduct. The landward fringe of salt marsh here shows interesting transitions to paramaritime grassland, and transitional communities have plants which reflect brackish conditions, such as *Oenanthe lachenalii*, *Centaurium littorale*, *Samolus valerandi*, *Carex otrubae*, *C. disticha*, *C. distans*, *C. extensa*, and *Blysmus rufus*. Species less associated with a saline influence on the rising ground include *Ononis spinosa*, *O. repens*, *Rosa pimpinellifolia* and *Blysmus compressus* (*Puccinellia distans* in driftline transition).

The Scottish shore has not been examined botanically but there is only a narrow fringe of salt marsh.

Dune (12 ha)

The protecting spit of Grune Point has a narrow and low dune ridge passing to a grassier ridge with scrub. There are good populations of *Geranium sanguineum*, *Rosa pimpinellifolia* and *Rhynchosinapis monensis*, and the site has local importance as a bird migration station.

Shingle (c. 4 ha)

The shingle beach on the open seaward side of Grune Point regularly held a breeding colony of little terns, but disturbance has recently become critical for these birds.

(c) Lochar–Nith shore

NY 150657–NX 999580. 7900 ha

Flats (6900 ha)

The flats of Priestside Bank, Blackshaw Bank and Carse Sands between the estuaries of the Nith and Lochar are among the five largest sand–silt areas in Britain at medium to high level in a big (8 m) tide range, and are of international importance as a roost for pink-footed (7500; 10% of world population), barnacle (3000; 6% of world and 75% of Svalbard populations) and greylag (1000) geese. This is the main centre for pink-footed in south-west Scotland, and outstandingly important as the principal wintering ground of the Svalbard population of barnacle geese. There are also large duck populations in winter including pintail (400), mallard (1500), teal (600), wigeon, shelduck and shoveler. The total wildfowl population averages 16000 birds annually and is the fifth largest of the separate groups identified in Britain. Some part of this total

moves between these Nith Merses and those on other parts of the Solway, notably Rockcliffe Marsh in Cumberland. The wader populations constitute an uncounted though significant fraction of the total numbers (130000) which winter on the upper Solway.

Marsh (1000 ha in two blocks of 760 ha (Caerlaverock Merse) and 240 ha (Kirkconnell Merse))

Caerlaverock Merse is one of the largest salt marsh areas in Britain of the northern type, on silt over sand and showing pioneer growth of *Puccinellia maritima* as yet undisturbed by *Spartina anglica* invasion. It is typical of the sheep- and cattle-grazed Solway marshes and notable for terraced development, the dry hinterland forming a seldom inundated grassland which has closer affinities with the neutral grasslands of reclaimed grazing marshes in southeast England. There are some of the most extensive *Blysmus rufus* populations in Britain, extensive *Juncus gerardii* communities, and good examples of transitions to brackish *Phragmites* marsh in the Nith estuary. Some wildfowl feed or rest on the marsh itself, especially barnacle geese and wigeon. The grassy merse is a breeding haunt of lapwing, redshank, dunlin, oystercatcher, lesser black-backed gull, black-headed gull, common tern and skylark, and is used by the autumn and winter wader populations as a resting place during high tides. Natterjack toads inhabit the inner edges.

C.62. HUMBER FLATS AND MARSHES, YORKSHIRE–LINCOLNSHIRE   Grade 1*

(a) Upper Humber Flats (Hull–Trent mouth)
SE 9225. c. 5000 ha
(b) Lower Humber Flats (Hull–Spurn)
TF 2517. 7600 ha

The Upper Humber Flats (5000 ha) extend from the mouth of the River Trent to the western outskirts of Hull, and are dissected by two main channels. The area contains one of the largest (discontinuous) medium- to low-level silt and sand flat systems in Britain in a tidal range of 6 m. It is of national importance as a roost for wildfowl, notably pink-footed geese (3000; 4% of the world population), mallard (3300; 1% of the UK population), teal (700), wigeon and shelduck. The site is one of the three main centres for the pink-footed goose in England and is likely to become increasingly valuable for the other species as the flats' level rises and disturbance from any impoundment activities in the Wash increases.

Marsh (200 ha)

An upper estuary sheep-grazed marsh on lime-rich silt with *Aster tripolium* or *Scirpus maritimus* as pioneer species. Extensive *Phragmites* reed-beds (30 ha) occur on the landward margins, and in association with reclaimed marsh pasture. Main marsh levels are occupied by transitional *Puccinellia maritima* to *Agrostis stolonifera* marsh. Bearded tits and reed warblers breed in the reeds and a section is kept to provide a roost for migrating swallows which are trapped and ringed.

The Lower Humber Flats, particularly the 2400 ha in the Sunk Island/Kilnsea area, are locally rich in invertebrate food resources for wildfowl and waders. About 3000 wildfowl are normally present, mainly mallard and wigeon, with smaller numbers of teal, pintail, scaup and shelduck. Average wader populations are in the order of 40000 birds.

C.63. BEMPTON/SPEETON CLIFFS, YORKSHIRE
TA 144755–233720.   c. 340 ha   Grade 1*

This is an 8 km stretch of formidable Chalk precipice facing north and rising to 120 m. The Bempton and Buckton cliffs are famous as the largest English breeding station of cliff seabirds and are the only big one on Chalk; they once held probably the largest colony of guillemots and razorbills in the British Isles. Although systematic collecting of eggs on these cliffs for food and other purposes ceased in 1954, numbers of these auks have evidently declined markedly, a recent count giving only 14300 pairs for both species together, whereas around 1900 the population may have exceeded 100000 pairs, judging by records of eggs taken annually. By contrast, kittiwakes and fulmars have increased, and the kittiwake population between Flamborough and Bempton has recently been estimated at approximately 40000 pairs. The only mainland colony of gannets in Britain (35 pairs bred in 1971) occurs here, and puffins (1000 pairs) and rock doves also breed.

The bird cliffs do not appear to have strong botanical interest, though some of the more vegetated parts of the precipice are too inaccessible to examine. The cliff top, which is mostly abrupt, has a rather narrow strip of coarse grassland soon changing to farmland, and this sward is dominated by grasses such as *Dactylis glomerata*, *Arrhenatherum elatius*, *Holcus lanatus* and *Festuca rubra*, with common forbs such as *Centaurea nigra*, *Achillea millefolium*, *Plantago lanceolata*, *Rumex acetosa*, *Melandrium rubrum*, *Heracleum sphondylium*, *Lathyrus pratensis* and *Lotus corniculatus*. Steep slopes on the upper part of the cliffs appear to have a similar community.

A further 6½ km stretch of well-vegetated undercliff (boulder clay over Chalk slipping on Jurassic clays) adjoins these cliffs towards Speeton. It contains a mosaic of hawthorn scrub, tracts of rosebay willow herb, mixed chalk grassland and open herb communities on clay. Notable populations of *Dactylorchis* spp., *Gentianella amarella* and *Parnassia palustris* occur and wooded ravines with ash and hawthorn scrub are likely to provide shelter for a rich paramaritime invertebrate fauna.

C.64. FARNE ISLANDS, NORTHUMBERLAND
NU 2337.   30 ha   Grade 1*

The 28 rocky off-shore islands of the Farnes are the most easterly outcrops of the Great Whin Sill. On the larger islands the dolerite is covered by boulder clay, and this is overlain in turn by a peaty soil. The soils are of interest and differ in structure according to the extent of exposure and degree of secondary erosion. The islands are not of great botanical interest but have long been famous as

the breeding ground of a large population of grey seals and for their nesting seabird colonies, which number at least 13 species.

The seal population, now numbering about 7000, is concentrated during the breeding season on Staple, Brownsman, and the North and South Wamses, but at other times of year they haul out on the outer islands of the group.

Inner Farne, Brownsman, and Staple provide nest sites for large numbers of kittiwakes, puffin (8000 pairs), shag, and guillemot (3000 pairs), the last being particularly numerous and densely packed on the flat-topped Pinnacles off Staple Island. About 3000 pairs of puffins nest on the East and West Wideopens where herring and lesser black-backed gulls are the other main breeding species. Colonies of cormorants breed on the Megstone and North Wamses, while the main concentrations of eiders (700 pairs), as well as of the four tern species, common, Arctic, Sandwich and roseate, nest on the Inner Farne and Brownsman.

Seabirds of several species have been studied here and an extensive ringing programme has been carried out for some years. Similarly, the seal populations have been carefully censused over a long period.

C.65. LINDISFARNE–ROSS LINKS–BUDLE BAY,
          NORTHUMBERLAND
NU 0447, NU 1636.   c. 3650 ha   Grade 1

Flats (3220 ha)

These large areas of tidal sand and silt flats carry notable populations of *Enteromorpha* and *Zostera* (c. 25 ha), including *Z. angustifolia* and *Z. noltii*, which provide food for internationally important populations of wildfowl. The most numerous species is the wigeon with numbers up to 25000 (average 11500) birds. This is one of the few sites in Britain still regularly used by pale-bellied brent geese and peak numbers of this species may reach 2500 (80% of Svalbard population) but in recent years has been from 700–1000. Some 200 whooper swans winter on the reserve which is also an important wintering ground for waders (30000 birds), particularly bar-tailed godwit, knot and dunlin.

Marsh (40 ha)

This consists partly of newly established *Spartina anglica* now threatening the wildfowl food resources to seaward. At higher levels a northern-type *Puccinellia maritima* marsh grades to sand dune or low boulder clay cliffs, and *Blysmus rufus* occurs locally in wet flushes.

Dune (325 ha, disjunct: 225 ha (Ross Links) and 100 ha (Lindisfarne))

Calcareous dunes occur on Lindisfarne, and behind the seaward fringe of marram and *Agropyron junceiforme* sandhills there are extensive slacks with a rich flora, including large orchid populations (*Dactylorhiza fuchsii*, *D. incarnata*, *D. purpurella* and *Epipactis palustris*), and a combination of southern species (*Phleum arenarium* and *Trifolium scabrum*), with a strong northern element (*Carex maritima*, *Corallorhiza trifida*, *Blysmus rufus*, *Pinguicula vulgaris*, *Equisetum vari-*

egatum and the mosses *Catoscopium nigritum* and *Amblyodon dealbatus*). Among other noteworthy species are *Pyrola rotundifolia* and *Epipactis dunensis* (otherwise known only from Anglesey and Lancashire). There is a good deal of *Salix repens*, and there are gradations to a more acidic *Agrostis stolonifera* type of slack, while the eastern end of the island has luxuriant dune meadows with a variety of grasses. Forb- and moss-rich communities are well developed in places on stable dunes. The presence of the vigorously competitive alien *Acaena anserinifolia* gives concern over the maintenance of floristic interest. *Ligusticum scoticum* reaches its southern limit on the east coast here.

Ross Links have a more distinctly acidic dune system, though the flora is again rich, and there are slacks with the very local mosses *Drepanocladus lycopodioides* and *D. sendtneri* var. *wilsonii*. *Elymus arenarius* is here especially abundant as a pioneer dune plant, and there is a small population of *Ammocalamagrostis × baltica*. In the forb–moss communities of stable dunes, noteworthy species are *Astragalus danicus*, *Cerastium arvense*, *Thalictrum minus*, *Gentianella campestris* and *Helianthemum chamaecistus*. Farther inland there is a change to an acidic dune heath of *Calluna*, *Erica cinerea* and *Rumex acetosella*, with acidophilous lichens and mosses, on leached sand, and this in turn grades into acidic grassland or bracken. The inner edge of the system is artificial, as a considerable extent has been reclaimed for agriculture.

Cliff (65 ha)

Low cliffs cut in boulder clay and the Whin Sill on Lindisfarne provide further diversity and there are fine wave-cut platforms with rock pools offshore. Fulmars breed on the cliffs.

C.55. MERSEY ESTUARY (PART), LANCASHIRE

Grade 2

See under Midlands, p. 23.

C.66. DUDDON SANDS, LANCASHIRE–CUMBERLAND
SD 2080.   3800 ha   Grade 2

This large area of sand flats which fills the estuary of the Duddon between north Walney and Haverigg Point is primarily important for its wader populations. The most numerous species are oystercatcher (10000) and dunlin (9000+). Curlew are also present (1000+) and the sands around north Walney are notable for redshank (3000). The winter of 1970–71 saw a peak wader population of 34000 birds but this was largely due to a spectacular (and unusual) influx of dunlin. It is not certain to what extent there is an interchange between the wader populations of this site and those of Morecambe Bay.

There is an interesting area of salt marsh (400 ha) flanking both sides of the estuary, and though this has not been examined in detail, it is evidently botanically similar to the Morecambe Bay marshes.

C.67. DRIGG POINT, CUMBERLAND
SD 0796.   *c.* 1300 ha   Grade 2

Flats (c. 885 ha)

Sand flats fringe the seaward shore of the dunes, and the Irt estuary behind Drigg Point.

Marsh (c. 20 ha)

A small area of pioneer marsh with *Salicornia* and *Limonium vulgare* occurs in the Irt estuary, and *Halimione portulacoides* is near its northern limit as a marsh plant here.

Dune (395 ha)

This long dune peninsula at the mouth of the River Irt is notable as the breeding place of one of the largest colonies of black-headed gulls in Britain. There are also good colonies of Sandwich, common, Arctic and little terns which formerly moved interchangeably between here and Walney Island; since the increase in herring and lesser black-backed gulls at Walney and the establishment of Drigg dunes as a Local Nature Reserve (LNR), they have remained at the latter. The locality has been a study area for important ethological research on birds in recent years. An interesting and probably unique feature is the presence of dune flats behind a series of cuspate dunes. The dunes are slightly acidic and the flora is less rich than on Walney Island; even so, there are good populations of local species such as *Geranium sanguineum*, *Carlina vulgaris*, *Gentianella campestris*, *Calystegia soldanella*, *Euphorbia portlandica* and *E. paralias*. The adder is numerous on the more stable areas of dune, and natterjack toads also occur.

Shingle

Small areas of shingle have a strand flora which includes the very local *Rhynchosinapis monensis*.

C.68. BEAST CLIFF/ROBIN HOOD'S BAY, YORKSHIRE
TA 005988–NZ 950077.   *c.* 350 ha   Grade 2

This coastal area consists of a 10.5 km stretch of spectacular slipping of Jurassic strata and has some of the highest cliffs in Britain, rising to 180 m. The undercliff is extensively wooded with oak and ash, and must be one of the most inaccessible woodlands in the country; it is rated as a separate grade 2 woodland site (see W.160).

Small pools with *Scirpus lacustris* and *Potamogeton* species occur and elsewhere there are large tracts of rosebay willow herb and bracken on mixed limestone or clay grassland. Where calcareous drainage seeps through the clay *Parnassia palustris*, *Linum catharticum* and *Triglochin palustris* are frequent. On the Jurassic sandstones as at Blea Wyke there is acidophilous vegetation dominated by *Calluna* with *Erica cinerea*, *Empetrum nigrum* and *Luzula sylvatica*.

Robin Hood's Bay contains one of the finest wave-cut platforms in Britain, and this part of the coast is of outstanding interest for its marine littoral communities of algae and invertebrates, though this habitat is excluded from the present review.

C.69. TEESMOUTH FLATS AND MARSHES,
      YORKSHIRE–DURHAM
NZ 7425. *c.* 680 ha   Grade 2

Although this estuary is of only moderate size and receives
the polluted water of the Tees from the surrounding urban–
industrial complex of Tees-side, its wader population is of
national importance (24 000 birds on average), and there is a
considerable wildfowl interest, with shelduck (2250), mallard, teal, wigeon and pintail. The estuary is undoubtedly
of importance as a staging post for wildfowl and waders on
migration and its biological significance is enhanced by the
presence of sand-dune systems at Seaton Dunes and the South
Gare, and the saltings and freshwater marsh of Cowpen.

C.70. HART WARREN–HAWTHORN DENE COAST,
      DURHAM
NZ 436476–495363. *c.* 270 ha   Grade 2

Cliff and rock shore (230 ha)

The best paramaritime Magnesian Limestone cliffs (to
50 m) in Britain occur here, though the shoreline itself is
badly polluted with colliery waste pumped directly into the
sea. Notable populations of at least eight species of orchid
occur together with other local plants such as *Botrychium
lunaria, Parnassia palustris, Pinguicula vulgaris, Primula
farinosa, Serratula tinctoria* and *Trifolium medium.*

There are vestigial shore communities on the coal waste
with depauperate *Elymus arenarius, Puccinellia distans* and
Salsola kali and these grade locally into transitional *Salix
caprea*, wych elm and ash scrub of the famous species-rich
wooded denes (including part of Castle Eden Dene – W.162)
characteristic of this coast.

Sand dune (40 ha)

A small base-rich dune system is of interest floristically,
partly because of its geographical location mid-way between
the northern and southern dune floras. The presence of the
mainly southern *Orchis ustulata* is of particular interest.

C.71. COQUET ISLAND, NORTHUMBERLAND
NU 2904. 20 ha   Grade 2

This island supports the most southerly eider colony (300
pairs), on the east coast, about 500 pairs of puffins and a
substantial ternery; breeding populations in 1972 were
Sandwich tern – 800 pairs; common tern – 1000 pairs;
Arctic tern – 500 pairs; and roseate tern – 75 pairs. There
is a colony of *c.* 600 pairs of black-headed gulls. The vegetation on thick soil covering sandstone is dominated by
grasses with *Rumex* spp. Large beds of *Urtica dioica* occur
around the lighthouse buildings.

SOUTH SCOTLAND

C.61. UPPER SOLWAY FLATS AND MARSHES (PART),
      DUMFRIES-SHIRE–KIRKCUDBRIGHTSHIRE
                                                Grade 1*

See under North England, p. 27.

C.72. TORRS WARREN, WIGTOWNSHIRE
NX 113523–171556. 800 ha   Grade 1

Flats (30 ha)

The 800 m wide strip of sand flats at the head of Luce
Bay feeds the 10 km length of dunes forming Torrs
Warren.

Dunes (770 ha)

This is a large physiographically diverse system of mainly
acidic dunes with well-developed slacks. There is a fairly
broad seaward zone of unstable marram dunes, and these
show all gradations to stabilised sand hills, though there
are also pronounced blow-outs in places. The closed
community has a rather limited flora, with prominence of
*Festuca rubra, Galium verum, Thymus drucei, Teucrium
scorodonia, Ononis repens, Veronica chamaedrys, Tortula
ruraliformis, Rhytidiadelphus triquetrus, R. squarrosus,
Rhacomitrium canescens, Pseudoscleropodium purum* and
Dicranum scoparium. Mildly basiphilous plants include
Geranium sanguineum and *Carlina vulgaris*, and the western
species *Viola curtisii* and *Sedum anglicum* are common.
Farther inland, on more leached sand, there is an acidic
dune heath of *Calluna* and *Erica cinerea*, with much *Festuca
ovina*, heath mosses and lichens such as *Parmelia physodes*
and *Cladonia impexa*. This in turn locally shows invasion by
bracken to give dense stands.

The slacks are of considerable interest, though their
vegetation is largely acidophilous. The wetter examples
have poor-fen communities with *Carex rostrata, C. nigra,
C. curta, C. echinata, Eleocharis palustris, Menyanthes trifoliata, Potentilla palustris, Hydrocotyle vulgaris, Lotus
uliginosus, Ranunculus flammula, Juncus effusus* and *J.
kochii.* Some slacks are drier, and there is local dominance of
Salix repens, Carex arenaria, or *Calluna–Erica tetralix*, and
Myrica gale is locally abundant. Colonisation by *Salix
aurita* and *S. atrocinerea* gives patches of willow scrub in
places. Interesting rarer species of slacks include *Littorella
uniflora, Pyrola minor* and *Corallorhiza trifida.* This slack
vegetation grades into a drier, dune meadow type of grassland with *Agrostis stolonifera, A. tenuis, Holcus lanatus,
Molinia caerulea, Carex arenaria, Potentilla anserina,
Ranunculus repens* and *Rumex acetosa.* At the south-western
end of Torrs Warren is a series of larger slack pools with
fringing vegetation including *Hypericum elodes* and rich-fen
species such as *Cicuta virosa, Rumex hydrolapathum* and
Carex paniculata.

Although a northern inland strip of the Warren has been
afforested, this is still the largest acidic dune system in
western Scotland, and represents an oceanic counterpart to
Tentsmuir. The area is also interesting as a northern,
Scottish example of lowland heath. The use of the area as
an experimental bombing range causes some damage to the
site but reduces other forms of human disturbance. Past
attempts to drain some of the wet slack areas behind the
foredunes have evidently had limited success and have
caused no significant loss of interest.

C.73. MULL OF GALLOWAY–CRAMMAG HEAD,
WIGTOWNSHIRE

NX 159307–089341. *c.* 265 ha   Grade 1

This cliff coast cut in Silurian greywackes and in granite has
probably the greatest diversity of interest of all the cliff
sectors of the Solway shore. There are moderate-sized
seabird colonies of guillemot, razorbill, kittiwake, shag,
cormorant and fulmar on the Mull headland, where the
cliffs rise to 87 m. The botanical interest is considerable, and
several species occur here which are quite unknown on the
coast of north-west England: *Scilla verna* and *Astragalus
danicus* are abundant in turf on top of the cliffs, while on
the rocks are *Inula crithmoides, Crithmum maritimum,
Spergularia rupicola* and *Limonium binervosum* at their
northern British limit. *Oxytropis halleri* has been recorded
here, its southernmost British station, and there are *Sedum
rosea* and *Ligusticum scoticum*, two other northern plants.

West of West Tarbert the generally more broken but
still higher (120 m on Dunman) cliffs have fewer seabirds
but even greater botanical interest. Maritime turf and rock
communities of the *Armeria–Silene maritima* and *Anthyllis–
Sedum anglicum* types are well represented, and species such
as *Carlina vulgaris, Verbascum nigrum, Ononis repens,
Pimpinella saxifraga* and *Geranium sanguineum* are locally
plentiful in forb-rich grassland on steep slopes. *Schoenus
nigricans* and *Anagallis tenella* grow in flushed places on
cliffs and slopes, and there is a colony of *Centranthus ruber*.
In places, semi-prostrate growths of juniper fringe the cliff
tops, and there is a variable development of scrub with
gorse and blackthorn. Above the cliffs in places are areas of
heavily sheep-grazed grassland with *Holcus lanatus,
Agrostis* spp. and *Festuca rubra*, and acidophilous heather
heath with variable amounts of bracken.

Shingle

Small sandy, shingle beaches formerly had *Mertensia
maritima*, and this species may still survive in the western
part of the site.

C.74. AILSA CRAIG, AYRSHIRE

NX 0199. 105 ha   Grade 1*

Cliff and rock shore

Ailsa Craig lies at the entrance to the Firth of Clyde, about
14 km from the Ayrshire mainland. The island is composed
of a fine-grained granite and is bounded by almost perpen-
dicular cliffs on its south and west sides, and the Barestack
is said to be the highest overhanging cliff in Britain, reaching
c. 190 m in height. At intervals, the columnar jointed granite
is cut by dykes of dolerite which being more readily
weathered form gullies and caves.

The vegetation is largely acidophilous though in places,
the enriching effect of the bird colonies has greatly elevated
nitrogen and phosphate levels. The summit area had mainly
Agrostis canina–Festuca ovina grassland but a large herring
gull colony has changed this to a luxuriant but open growth
of clumps of *Silene maritima* and *Rumex acetosa*, with much
bare ground and dead, grassy vegetation. Patches of grass-

land remain, and away from the bird colonies, on the lower
ground *Pteridium aquilinum–Endymion non-scriptus* and
Calluna–Erica cinerea–Teucrium scorodonia communities
occur on moderate and steep slopes respectively. A well-
developed cliff ledge and face community occurs on the
terraced sections of the south-facing Trammins; abundant
species include *Raphanus maritimus, Silene maritima,
Spergularia rupicola, Umbilicus rupestris* and *Armeria
maritima. Lavatera arborea* is also present, probably in its
most northerly native station. In some of the wetter shaded
clefts, *Cochlearia officinalis* and *Asplenium marinum* are
particularly luxuriant. Below the bird cliffs there are lush
growths of *Silene dioica, Festuca rubra* and *Cochlearia
officinalis* locally with much *Urtica dioica* and *Stellaria
media*. On the shady slopes of the north-east side there is
an abundance of *Dryopteris dilatata* and bryophytes. The
flora of the island is varied without being outstandingly rich.

Ailsa Craig is perhaps best noted for its large population
of breeding seabirds, the ancient gannetry being the fourth
largest in the British Isles, with over 13 000 pairs in 1969.
The herring gull may, however, now be the most numerous
breeding species, nesting mainly on the steep slopes above
the cliffs. The island also holds the most important colony
of razorbills (2300 pairs) and guillemots (4200 pairs) in the
Clyde area, although the numbers have severely declined
since the turn of the century, and only a few puffins now
remain. Sharing the cliff ledges with the auks is an even
larger colony of kittiwakes, and the fulmar is numerous;
other breeding species include peregrine, black guillemot,
great and lesser black-backed gulls, cormorant, shag, rock
dove, rock pipit, raven and twite.

C.75. ST ABB'S HEAD, BERWICKSHIRE

NT 850707–917677. 285 ha   Grade 1

The coast between St Abb's Head and Fast Castle has a fine
series of sea cliffs and wave-cut platforms carved out of a
sequence of Silurian and Old Red Sandstone sediments and
lava. The cliffs rise to 150 m and there are large numbers of
breeding kittiwakes (10 000 pairs), guillemots (6700 pairs),
razorbills, shags, fulmars and some puffins. The sections of
the cliffs with fewer birds have a good deal of botanical
interest, with particular abundance of *Armeria maritima*
and *Silene maritima*, and the northern *Sedum rosea* grows in
places. On steep slopes and in gullies where sheep do not
graze, there is a rich development of communities which
are usually associated with the field layer of woodland, and
may in places be relict through loss of tree and scrub
cover; the dominants include *Endymion non-scriptus, Luzula
sylvatica* and *Silene dioica*. On the cliff tops, contrasting
lime-rich and lime-poor soils give a varied maritime grassland flora (which includes *Astragalus danicus* and *Helianthemum chamaecistus*), but *Calluna* and some other species
are limited by sheep-grazing. The lichen flora is notably
rich with *Alectoria jubata* occurring unusually as a terrestrial
species among dwarf *Calluna*.

The littoral and sublittoral fauna and flora are particularly
rich because of the variety of aspects and relatively unpolluted coastal water. The tide range is 3.3 m.

C.76. FIRTH OF FORTH, FIFE, STIRLINGSHIRE, MID-, EAST AND WEST LOTHIAN
NS 925872–NT650950.   2750 ha   Grade 1*

The flats and open water of this area are important mainly as a winter wildfowl haunt. The concentrations of seaducks are outstandingly important – scaup (14000 birds; *c.* 10% of north-west European population), goldeneye (1600 birds; 20% of UK population), eider (2650) – and appear to be increasing. These large numbers of seaducks are believed to be associated with the rich marine food supply which results from the considerable amounts of sewage entering the Forth from adjoining urban areas, especially Edinburgh. Mute swan and sometimes common scoter also occur.

The flats are also of national importance for their large wader populations (34000 birds).

This area should be considered in conjunction with the sites Bass Rock (C.79) and Forth Islands (C.80).

C.77. BORGUE COAST, KIRKCUDBRIGHTSHIRE
NX 575530–665493.   1200 ha   Grade 2

There are base-rich Silurian greywacke and shale cliffs which rise to 60 m in a 6.5 m tide range, though much of this coast consists of steep grassy slopes rising above rock platforms and boulder-strewn shores. It is notable for a highly varied flora associated with the pattern of acidic and basic soils, variety of exposure and coastal flushes; for a number of sea cliff species at or near their north-west limit in Britain (e.g. *Limonium binervosum*, *Spergularia rupicola*) and for substantial populations of local species in the cliff top swards (e.g. *Antennaria dioica*, *Astragalus danicus*, *Gymnadenia conopsea* and *Scilla verna*). This site is regarded as an alternative to the Mull of Galloway botanically, but apart from herring gulls and rock doves, seabird numbers are small, though there are a few guillemots, razorbills, kittiwakes and fulmars at Meikle Ross. The area includes examples of cliff-slope woodland, though most of these have been somewhat modified, and also the Fleet Islands (accessible at low tide) with breeding common gulls and sometimes terns.

C.78. WIGTOWN BAY, KIRKCUDBRIGHTSHIRE– WIGTOWNSHIRE
NX 4654.   3300 ha   Grade 2

The fairly extensive sand flats at the head of Wigtown Bay from Innerwell Port and Ravenshall Point to Creetown are important mainly for their winter wildfowl populations. In particular, pink footed geese (2000 birds) come here in late winter, presumably from Caerlaverock. Other species include wigeon (*c.* 2000), pintail (*c.* 150), mallard, teal, shoveler, whooper swan, greylag and shelduck. There is also a moult population of up to 2000 common scoter. Wigtown Bay also has some importance as a haunt of waders.

This is one of the smaller wildfowl and wader estuaries and its importance is considerably less than that of the Upper Solway.

C.79. BASS ROCK, EAST LOTHIAN
NT 6087.   10 ha   Grade 2

This phonolitic island is flanked virtually on all sides by cliffs, rising to over 90 m, and is almost in the category of a rock stack, with a more gently conical summit. It is notable mainly as a geological feature and as the site of a large gannetry, with about 9000 pairs (1968). The Bass Rock is similar to Ailsa Craig in ornithological interest but smaller in size and in total number of seabirds, and has less ecological diversity in general. There is a colony of the rare *Lavatera arborea* which may have been introduced here. (See Appendix.)

C.80. FORTH ISLANDS, EAST AND MIDLOTHIAN
NT 207806–553870.   45 ha   Grade 2

This site comprises a group of low rocky islands – Inchmickery (Midlothian), Fidra, Eyebroughty, Lamb and Craigleith (East Lothian). All except the last named are reserves of the Royal Society for the Protection of Birds. Apart from their populations of seabirds such as shag, cormorant, fulmar and kittiwake, and the use of Fidra and Eyebroughty as a moulting station by eider, interest centres on the breeding colonies of roseate and Sandwich terns, which are among the largest in Britain. Common and Arctic terns are also present. The relative importance of the individual islands varies from year to year. The site is similar to the Farne Islands in the nature of its interest but the Forth Islands are less diverse in their other faunal interests and are fewer in number.

EAST SCOTLAND

C.81. ISLE OF MAY, FIFE
NT 6599.   55 ha   Grade 1

The main features of this NNR are its importance as a calling place for migrant birds and its large breeding population of seabirds. It is a sill of olivine–dolerite tilted eastwards, so that the west side of the island is bounded by cliffs up to 45 m high, along which the sea has eroded a striking series of rock arches, stacks and caves. The cliff ledges provide nest sites for large numbers of kittiwakes (3000 pairs), guillemots (4000 pairs), razorbills (150 pairs), shags (900 pairs) and fulmars (40 pairs). Puffins breed in large numbers (about 4000 occupied burrows) and do not appear to be decreasing, in contrast to some west coast colonies, and about 50 pairs of eider nest. Most of the grassy top of the island is now covered with a huge colony of herring gulls (15000 pairs) and lesser black-backed gulls (2000 pairs) which is increasing at an annual rate of 13%, accompanied by a progressive deterioration of the island's scientific interest (reducing the diversity of the island's flora and fauna, and causing erosion and removal of vegetation and soil). In 1946, with only 800 pairs of gulls nesting, there were 8000 pairs of four species of terns, but tern numbers declined rapidly as the gull colonies spread over available territory, and no terns have nested since 1960.

When the Reserve was declared, the island's vegetation was dominated by an extensive *Armeria maritima–Silene maritima* sward, which formed a belt encircling the island, growing on thin peaty soil. On rockier ground towards the cliff edge the same species occurred in an open community of clumps and cushions, associated with *Sedum anglicum*. Towards the centre of the island the sward merged with a submaritime grassy turf in which *Agrostis* spp. and *Festuca rubra* were important components, and other flowering plants abundant. The damp hollows and rocky cliff sections sheltered from the sea were good localities for a variety of bryophytes, in slightly base-rich conditions including the Atlantic liverwort *Frullania germana*. The rapid spread of the gull colony has resulted in the gradual disappearance of the *Armeria–Silene* sward and, in places, complete removal of vegetation and soil cover. The former mixed grassy sward is becoming dominated by *Holcus lanatus*. In de-vegetated areas where there is still adequate soil, there is dense summer growth of *Stellaria media*, *Rumex acetosa*, *Atriplex* spp. and *Cochlearia danica*.

The Isle of May is one of the 13 official Bird Observatories around the coast of Britain, and the observation and recording of bird migration has continued for nearly half a century. The island is well placed for the study of these types of migration – spring and autumn coastal movements, drift migrants from the continent, and the big arrivals in autumn of winter visitors from Scandinavia.

There is a colony of 50–60 grey seals.

C.82. TENTSMUIR POINT, FIFE
NO 5027. 505 ha   Grade 1
Flats (453 ha)

The flats (near the mouth of the Tay estuary) comprise one of the larger lime-poor sand areas in Britain, and are a source of material for the growth of the Tentsmuir dune system. The tide range is 4.5 m. The foreshore and off-shore Abertay Sands are important roosting and feeding grounds for large numbers of wildfowl and waders. The average maximum figures for pink-footed geese are 1500, with smaller numbers of greylag geese. Huge concentrations of eider build up each autumn, numbers often exceeding *c.* 15 000. Other wildfowl include mallard, wigeon, scaup, scoter, merganser and shelduck. There is a wader population of *c.* 9000, amongst which important species are: oyster-catcher, grey plover, dunlin, sanderling and little stint. The Abertay Sands are also used regularly as a haul-out for up to 150 common and grey seals.

Dune (52 ha)

Most of the dune area of this NNR is a result of remarkably rapid lateral accretion over a period of only about 40 years. (A line of coastal defence blocks erected in 1940 now lies well inland, and in places is obliterated by dunes.) The actively aggrading lime-poor dune system has full seral successions from embryo slacks and dunes to alder, birch and willow scrub. The site has the best population of *Elymus arenarius* in Britain, and notable abundance of *Astragalus danicus*, *Corallorhiza trifida*, *Empetrum nigrum* and *Juncus balticus*. Lichen-rich dwarf shrub heaths are well represented on the stable dunes. Over 400 species of

flowering plants have been recorded. The dune area is also of considerable entomological interest; the main groups have been well studied and recorded.

C.83. TAY ESTUARY, FIFE–PERTHSHIRE
NO 2823. *c.* 3000 ha   Grade 1*
Flats (c. 2200 ha)

The extensive sand flats of the Firth of Tay above Dundee, especially on the north shore, are of prime importance for the large wintering and migrant populations of geese, duck and waders. Roosting and feeding areas are extensive, particularly along the north shore of the estuary where at low tide vast banks of mud and sand stretch out from the reed-fringed shore. Large flocks of up to 3000 mallard use the lower reaches between Powgavie and Kingoodie. Large numbers of pink-footed geese (3000 birds) and smaller numbers of greylag use the central sandbanks and Mugdrum Island as a roost (and the latter island as a feeding area also). The tidal flats are the main feeding ground of the local breeding population of shelduck, and also carry large numbers of waders, with flocks of about 1000 dunlin, and flocks about half that size of redshank and curlew. Other ducks regularly recorded in the Estuary are tufted duck, teal, goldeneye, wigeon, shoveler, pochard and gadwall.

Marsh (c. 800 ha)

The north Tay marshes are notable for some of the largest continuous *Phragmites* beds in Britain, as well as locally extensive populations of *Glyceria maxima*. The salt marsh itself is one of relatively few examples of this habitat type on the east coast of Scotland, and contains dense stands of *Scirpus maritimus* and *Schoenoplectus tabernaemontani*.

The wildfowl interest of this area should be considered in conjunction with Tentsmuir Point (C.82) which lies at the mouth of the Tay on its south side.

C.84. ST CYRUS, KINCARDINESHIRE
NO 7464. 140 ha   Grade 1
Flats (52 ha)

This small area of sand flats (with little silt) lies in a 4.3 m tide range.

Marsh (12 ha)

The very small area of sandy marsh has west coast marsh type affinities and a representative flora with limited species diversity but including marsh fucoids.

Dune (40 ha)

There is a medium-sized dune system on moderately lime-rich sand consisting of coastal dunes and dune pasture (dry slack) communities, with a total of 130 species of flowering plants and ferns recorded and 23 species of bryophytes. While local species such as *Astragalus danicus*, *Atriplex laciniata*, *Botrychium lunaria*, *Dianthus deltoides* and *Vicia lathyroides* occur, this site is of more importance as a representative of dune vegetation in north-east Britain (and as part of a varied maritime complex), than for any particular richness of the dune flora alone, which is perhaps limited by the absence of significant freshwater habitats among the dunes. There is a fluctuating colony of little terns.

Cliff (36 ha)

Base-rich Old Red Sandstone lava forms cliffs and steep slopes rising to 60 m, with a strikingly rich flowering plant and fern flora of 179 species. There is also a varied crypto-gamic flora and rich invertebrate fauna. These habitats are notable for the number of species of flowering plants reaching the northern limit of their range in Britain (e.g. *Astragalus glycyphyllos*, *Trifolium scabrum*, *T. striatum*, *Silene nutans* and *Campanula glomerata*).

C.85. FOWLSHEUGH, KINCARDINESHIRE

NO 880799–880816.   120 ha.   *c.* 2 km   Grade 1*

This stretch of cliffs cut largely in basalt and andesite of Old Red Sandstone age is not particularly high (30–60 m) but the structure of the rock face, with innumerable holes and ledges, gives ideal nesting sites for cliff seabirds. There are huge colonies of kittiwakes (35 000 pairs), guillemots (32 800 pairs) and razorbills (5500 pairs), which make this one of the biggest rock seabird stations in Britain. It is comparable in many respects with Bempton/Speeton cliffs, Yorkshire, though the cliffs are lower and very different geologically. The botanical interest is limited, there being merely a rather species-poor grassland on top of the rather abrupt cliff edge.

C.86. SANDS OF FORVIE AND YTHAN ESTUARY, ABERDEENSHIRE

NK 0227.   1050 ha   Grade 1*

Flats (200 ha)

There is a small area of lime-poor sand flat with some silt in the Ythan Estuary, in a medium tide range of 3 m, important as a wildfowl roost. The Ythan is internationally important for its large winter populations of wildfowl, which average 11 000 birds, made up principally of pink-footed (7500) and greylag (2000) geese, and eiders (1000). Wigeon, mallard, shelduck, goldeneye, mute swan, whooper swan and red-breasted merganser occur regularly in smaller numbers.

Marsh (20 ha)

This rather small area in the Ythan Estuary contains a representative northern salt marsh flora.

Dune (810 ha)

These form the fifth largest, and least man-disturbed of the large sand-dune systems in Britain. Lime-deficient and locally highly mobile dunes are developed as river-mouth spits and there are open coast dunes to the south. There is an extensive development of slack communities, especially a *Salix repens–Erica tetralix–Empetrum nigrum* type, and dune dwarf-shrub–lichen heaths with *Calluna vulgaris* and *Empetrum nigrum*. This site is also regarded as an important northern example of lowland acidic heath (L.150, gr. 1). The bryophyte flora is rich and there is a strong representa-

tion of northern species, e.g. *Carex dioica*, *C. maritima*, *Goodyera repens*, *Lycopodium clavatum*, and many other local vascular plants. There are moderate colonies of breeding terns, including Sandwich terns, and the biggest colony of eiders (2000 pairs) in Britain.

Cliff (c. 20 ha)

There are andalusite schist cliffs with a representative coastal flora and notable populations of *Artemisia maritima*, *Asplenium marinum* and *Ligusticum scoticum*.

C.87. STRATHBEG, ABERDEENSHIRE

NK 0759.   *c.* 580 ha   Grade 1

Dunes (380 ha)

This is a medium-sized, lime-rich dune system with a remarkably steep seaward face at the coastal edge, characteristic of east coast dune systems with prevailing and dominant winds in opposition. There are fine transitions to salt marsh at the northern end and to freshwater marsh, boulder clay banks and shingle-bounded lagoon shores to landward. The area is lightly grazed by cattle and sheep. Probably shingle underlies much of the system and damp slacks are not extensively developed. *Ligusticum scoticum* occurs on the seaward face of the coastal dune, and other northern species include *Gentianella campestris* and *Juncus balticus* in more stable dune grassland to landward. Marsh areas carry a rich flora including *Dactylorchis incarnata* and *Parnassia palustris*.

Lagoon (200 ha)

This is probably the largest paramaritime body of water in Britain and is of considerable importance as an open water site (see OW.77, gr. 1), with a high wildfowl interest included.

Shingle (c. 4 ha)

Though only a small area, this paramaritime shingle shore along the border between the loch and the dunes carries a series of clearly zoned communities in which *Deschampsia cespitosa* and *Polygonum amphibium* are important species. These communities are of interest by comparison with those of other coastal lagoons and shingle formations, and are probably better represented at Strathbeg than anywhere else in Scotland.

C.88. MACDUFF–PENNAN HEAD, ABERDEENSHIRE–BANFFSHIRE

NJ 716650–860655.   *c.* 200 ha.   *c.* 20 km   Grade 1

This is a coastline of geological, physiographical, botanical and ornithological importance with narrow portions of dune and shingle. A fine series of precipitous headlands, rising to 150 m above sea-level, has been carved into what is a classical section in the Dalradian Schist strata of the Grampian highlands. Towards Macduff a shingle beach widens behind a fine wave-cut rock platform.

The rocks and screes of this site are locally calcareous, and support an interesting vegetation, including the only eastern coastal colonies of species such as *Saxifraga oppositi-*

folia and *S. hypnoides*. Common associated species here are *Carex flacca*, *C. panicea* and *C. pulicaris*, with *Plantago maritima*. There are also good colonies of *Helianthemum chamaecistus*, *Asplenium adiantum-nigrum* and *Vicia sylvatica*.

The cliffs of Troup Head, Lion's Head and Pennan Head support a large colony of breeding seabirds, especially kittiwakes (11 200 pairs), guillemots (9000 pairs), razorbills, puffins and fulmars.

C.89. CULBIN SANDS, MORAY–NAIRN
NJ 9561.   5050 ha   Grade 1

Flats (1500 ha with largest continuous area of about 730 ha)

This is one of the larger lime-poor sand flat areas in Britain with transitions to silt in Findhorn Bay, and lies in a medium tide range of 3.5 m. It is notable as a roosting ground for wildfowl and important as a source of material for growth of the Culbin Sands.

Marsh (200 ha with largest continuous area of about 170 ha)

A medium-sized, embayed and shingle-spit enclosed, sandy silt marsh which has a representative flora.

Dune (3180 ha)

Culbin has the largest sand-dune system in Britain and though there has been extensive afforestation, small areas still remain unplanted. The sand is lime-poor and there is extensive development of dune and slack with an acid facies flora, and transitions to marsh and shingle. It forms a significant phytogeographical boundary zone with some 43 species of flowering plants at their northern limit and only three species at their southern limit for Britain on the east coast. There are notable populations of many northern species including *Carex scandinavica*, *C. diandra*, *Listera cordata*, *Goodyera repens*, *Corallorhiza trifida*, *Antennaria dioica* and *Trientalis europaea* among the 450 species of flowering plants and ferns recorded, and also many aliens introduced by forestry activities. Sand-dune acidophilous dwarf-shrub heath communities grade to pine woodland, and dune slack communities to alder–birch–willow scrub locally. The dunes are of interest as breeding haunts of coastal birds including terns and the pinewoods have northern birds such as capercaillie and crested tit.

Shingle (170 ha with largest continuous area of 80 ha)

Small- to medium-sized shingle accumulations occur as spits and off-shore bars from the dune coast with marsh enclosed in recurves. There is a representative shingle flora.

C.90. MOUSA, SHETLAND
HU 4624.   180 ha   Grade 1

This island shows a range of flora and fauna typical of the low and grassy islands off the coast of Shetland. The *Holcus–Anthoxanthum* grassland of Haaf Gruney is less well represented but there is maritime *Calluna*-grass heath, *Plantago–Armeria* sward on the spray drenched south-west coast, species-rich *Festuca–Agrostis* grassland, acidic grassland with *Molinia* and *Potentilla erecta*, and mesotrophic marsh. The flora is considerably richer than that of Haaf Gruney. Breeding seabirds include fulmars, black guillemots, great and Arctic skuas, shags, eiders and oystercatchers, and a colony of several hundred Arctic terns. The most unusual species is the storm petrel, which nests in large numbers in the dry-stone walls, the shingle beaches, and especially within the walls of the Pictish broch. Common and grey seals frequent the shores of the island in large numbers.

C.91. NOSS, SHETLAND
HU 5540.   313 ha   Grade 1*

The island is composed entirely of red, yellow and grey sandstones of Old Red Sandstone age, weathered to form a striking coastal scenery, with cliffs up to 180 m high on the east side, which house some of the most spectacular cliff-breeding colonies of seabirds in Britain. There are about 10 000 pairs of kittiwakes, 24 000 pairs of guillemots, 4300 pairs of gannets (1969 figures), and numerous puffins, razorbills, shags and fulmars. On the plateau of the island there is a sizeable colony of breeding skuas (220 pairs of great skuas and 40 pairs of Arctic skuas).

The peaty and grassy slopes above the cliffs are much influenced by salt spray and the droppings of seabirds. On the higher parts of the interior, the prevailing plant communities are submaritime and paramaritime grasslands and grass heaths, the former with *Agrostis* spp., *Festuca rubra* and *Poa pratensis*, and the latter mainly a short *Calluna* heath with *Empetrum nigrum*, *Eriophorum angustifolium*, *Nardus stricta*, *Molinia caerulea*, *Trichophorum cespitosum* and *Potentilla erecta*. There is less mire and *Sphagnum* than on Hermaness, but a mixed *E. angustifolium–Carex nigra* community with some *Luzula sylvatica* occurs on shallow peat, and there are shallow pools and seepage channels with *S. cuspidatum* and *S. recurvum*. No montane species are recorded, but the submontane *Trientalis europaea* occurs. The lower west portion of the island carries a close-grazed turf of mixed grass and forbs, including many species which are relics of former cultivation. There is a small area of blown sand with marram.

C.92. HERMANESS, UNST, SHETLAND
HP 6016.   180 ha   Grade 1*

Marsh (20 ha)

This small loch-head salt marsh on sandy silt is the northernmost in Britain, with ecotypes of common salt marsh species, including marsh fucoids.

Cliff and boulder shore (*c.* 160 ha in continuous 24 km cliff coastline including the outlying stacks of Muckle Flugga)

There are large numbers of breeding seabirds on the cliffs and stacks, including gannets (6000 pairs in 1969), guillemots (16 000 pairs), razorbills (2000 pairs), puffins (15 000 pairs), shags, fulmars (8200 pairs) and kittiwakes (4600 pairs). This is the northernmost example in Britain of coastal cliff vegetation, modified in varying degrees by great seabird colonies. The rock is largely acidic, but the flora is varied, with populations of northern species such as *Ligusticum scoticum* and *Sedum rosea*, northern ecotypes such as *Silene dioica* ssp. *zetlandica*, and montane species near sea-level such as *S. acaulis*. The moorlands behind the cliffs have a paramaritime character, especially in the colonies of great and Arctic skuas (300 and 40–50 pairs respectively) which depend on the big gull colonies for food. Several pairs of red-throated divers also feed at sea, but breed beside dubh lochs, and the area contains nesting places of the whimbrel, one of the most noteworthy Shetland birds. Grey seals breed in the Hermaness caves. Hermaness is also a grade 1 upland site (U.78), and the blanket mires, grasslands and heaths of the interior moorland plateau are described under Upland Grasslands and Heaths.

C.93. EDEN ESTUARY, FIFE
NO 4720. 700 ha   Grade 2
The sand flats of the Eden Estuary south of and separate from the Tentsmuir dunes have an average winter wildfowl population of 10000 birds, and qualify as a grade 2 coastal site for this interest. The most numerous species are the common scoter (3000) and mallard (2350). Greylag, wigeon, teal, pintail, goldeneye, eider, long-tailed duck, red-breasted merganser, shelduck, scaup and velvet scoter occur regularly in some numbers and the estuary is also an important resort for waders. (Peak count 1970/71, 17700 birds.) There are small areas of marsh and shingle, both with a representative flora.

This is one of the smaller estuaries regarded as a key coastal site and its importance is eclipsed by that of the Tay Estuary farther north.

See also site W.188.

C.94. NORTH HOY, ORKNEY
HY 1904. 120 ha   Grade 2
The west coast of Hoy has a tremendous cliff wall stretching for 6 km and reaching 340 m at St John's Head. The Old Man of Hoy, a stack of 138 m, is a famous geomorphological feature. The cliffs have large colonies of nesting seabirds especially puffins, fulmars and rock doves; moderate numbers of kittiwakes, guillemots and razorbills; and they are the breeding place of the densest population of peregrines recorded in Britain since 1945, i.e. five to six pairs in 10 km in 1961. The nesting places in these formidable precipices are as safe as any in the country from direct interference, but even on this remote island the peregrine population has declined in recent years, and shown reduced breeding performance, evidently as a result of contamination by persistent chemical pollutants. There are nesting great skuas (23 pairs in 1969), and a very large colony of great black-backed gulls of over 1000 pairs is spread out over the moorlands behind the cliffs, but is sufficiently dense in places to have modified the vegetation, producing dense growths of *Rumex acetosa*, *Silene dioica*, *Holcus lanatus* and *Anthoxanthum odoratum*; and there is a breeding colony of Manx shearwaters on the inland scree. The ground behind

the cliffs is important for its montane dwarf-shrub heaths and lichen heaths, but these are described more fully under Upland Grasslands and Heaths (U.74). There is also a maritime heather heath along the cliff tops. Montane species such as *Salix herbacea* and *Arctous alpina* are here represented at probably their lowest elevations in Britain, in paramaritime heaths.

C.95. HAAF GRUNEY, SHETLAND
HU 6398. 18 ha   Grade 2
This is a smaller island than Mousa and more completely subject to the influence of salt spray. There is a boulder shore with a good breeding colony of black guillemots, and an abundance of the very local northern grass *Puccinellia capillaris*, and *Scilla verna*. The less halophytic sward in the middle of the island has a dominance of *Holcus lanatus*, *Agrostis stolonifera*, *A. tenuis*, *Festuca rubra*, *Poa pratensis* and *Rumex acetosa*, and is a good example of submaritime grassland. There is a breeding colony of Arctic terns and herring gulls, and several pairs of great black-backed gulls nest here.

C.96. FOULA, SHETLAND
HT 9639. 1380 ha   Grade 2
Although it has not been adequately examined during this review, the accounts of this strongly oceanic island suggest that it is in many respects comparable to St Kilda in interest. The Kame of Foula (370 m) is an Old Red Sandstone cliff almost as high as Conachair on Hirta, and there are large seabird colonies, though no gannets. The populations of guillemots, puffins and fulmars probably all number tens of thousands, and there are good numbers of kittiwakes and razorbills. Great and Arctic skuas have colonies on the moorland interior, which have paramaritime plant communities. The great skua has by far the largest colony in Britain here (1800 pairs in 1969). *Plantago* swards similar to those of St Kilda occur on the exposed cliff tops. (See Appendix.)

C.97. FAIR ISLE, SHETLAND
HZ 2172. 830 ha   Grade 2
This is another cliff-bound maritime island with numerous breeding seabirds and a largely grass and heath vegetation above the cliffs. There are large populations of guillemots (10000 pairs), razorbills (1200 pairs), puffins (15000 pairs), kittiwakes (12000 pairs) and fulmars (17300 pairs). Great skuas (10 pairs) and Arctic skuas (180 pairs) breed on the slopes above the cliffs. Fair Isle is important as a bird migration landfall, and the bird ringing station and observatory here is the northernmost of a network of key stations scattered around the coasts of Britain.

WEST SCOTLAND

C.98. SOUTH ARDNAMURCHAN COAST, ARGYLL
NM 460622–674625. 400 ha   Grade 1
Moine Schist, with locally in the west parts the Ardnamurchan igneous complex, forms the northern shore of Loch Sunart, a west coast sea loch north of the Great Glen. This

long inlet of the Atlantic is relatively sheltered, especially in its upper reaches, and the maritime zone is mostly very narrow, consisting largely of a low rocky shore of boulders and bedrock which rises quickly into a fringe of halophytic vegetation, and then a range of submaritime and para-maritime communities and habitats. This Ardnamurchan–Sunart shore with its grassy cliff terraces, coastal crags and wooded slopes, is the most westerly point on the mainland of Britain; this area has extreme oceanic features as well as a high degree of atmospheric purity. As well as constantly high atmospheric humidity, there is an extremely equable temperature regime, giving mild, generally frost-free winters. This combination of factors has allowed the survival of a lichen flora unsurpassed in Europe, and a bryophyte flora of considerable importance. These plants are associ-ated with the strongly Atlantic conditions, but many of them belong to paramaritime habitats.

The herb-rich submaritime grasslands and heaths of the steep south-facing slopes on the exposed western extremity of the peninsula have important Lepidoptera populations. There are more typical sea cliffs here but they have few sea-birds, though there is a cliff-nesting colony of herons.

The littoral zone is of marine biological interest and local species such as the free-living *Ascophyllum mackaii* occur. Vestigial salt marsh is developing locally and is a noteworthy example of the rather poorly developed salt marshes of this coast. Low rocky islands in Loch Sunart have a mainly grassy vegetation and are interesting for their fauna, which includes common gulls and Arctic terns.

See also site W.190.

C.99. LOCH GRUINART–LOCH INDAAL, ISLAY, ARGYLL

NR 290710, NR 330620.   4500 ha   Grade 1*

Flats (4140 ha)

There is a medium-sized sand flat and inter-tidal shingle area in a tidal range of 3 m (with contracted neap range) which gives way progressively to silts and acidic mud, and shingle and mud towards the head of Loch Gruinart. *Arenicola* beds are very extensive. Above high-water mark, the beaches are mainly shingle, although extensive sandy strands grading into dune systems occur on the east side of the mouth of the sea loch. At the head of the Loch the flats grade into salt marsh and then into brackish/freshwater marsh, some of which appears to be only lightly grazed.

The area is of international importance as a roost and feeding ground for Greenland white-fronted and barnacle geese. The Greenland white-fronted flock averages 1500–2000 birds, representing 15% of the world population, and 40% of the UK population, while the flock of barnacle geese numbers 15000 birds, representing a quarter of the total world population and 65% of the Greenland popula-tion. The survival of the Greenland population of barnacles and white-fronts may ultimately depend on the manage-ment of the relatively small area of central Islay including certain inland as well as coastal areas used for feeding and roosting. Other wildfowl species include scaup (600–1500 birds), greylag geese and eider.

The tidal range contrasts markedly with that at Port Ellen (south Islay) which has the smallest range in Britain and therefore is of potential marine biological interest for this contrast.

Marsh (80 ha)

Though small on a national scale this is one of the largest salt marshes in north-western Britain and is important as a wildfowl feeding and roosting area.

Dune (200 ha)

Though medium sized on the national scale, these are of interest as a relatively undisturbed 'tricorne' loch mouth system (cf. Magilligan dunes, Northern Ireland), a type rarely found in Britain.

Shingle (80 ha)

This probably consists mostly of high-level inter-tidal shingle and doubtless has importance as a wildfowl roost, but good lengths of shoreline shingle, the lighter grades of which occur, often mixed with an abundance of shell frag-ments, and northern elements of shingle beach flora are found here.

Loch Gruinart is one of the most important winter wild-fowl haunts in Britain, and the area as a whole is of particular interest as a complex of north-western coastal habitats, which need further investigation to specify their individual value. The inland roosts and feeding grounds of the geese on the Laggan peninsula (2460 ha) are regarded as part of this coastal site.

C.100. ROSS OF MULL, ARGYLL

NM 450193, NM 597247.   160 ha   Grade 1

The south-facing Tertiary basalt cliffs and slopes of this sector of the Mull coast are perhaps the best example of this characteristic Inner Hebridean habitat, though this rock formation has been incompletely surveyed.

The site comprises a succession of sheer cliffs and talus slopes in an irregular series between the cliff top and rocky shore. The cliffs are well vegetated in clefts and ledges with maritime and basiphilous communities on ranker soils, tall-herb communities in pockets of deeper soil, scrub and woodland in dispersed patches, and more extensive areas of herb-rich heath and submaritime grassland on steep unstable terraces and talus slopes. Since the cliffs and slopes mostly do not descend abruptly into the sea, and rise to about 300 m above sea-level, the bulk of the vegetation is paramaritime.

On the bare cliffs and thin ranker soils are associations of *Thymus drucei, Plantago maritima, Anthyllis vulneraria, Silene maritima* and *Armeria maritima*. The broomrape *Orobanche alba* occurs associated with *Thymus drucei*. Herb-rich *Calluna–Erica cinerea* heaths and *Festuca–Agrostis* grasslands are rich in species such as *Hypericum pulchrum, Antennaria dioica, Potentilla erecta, Lotus cornicu-latus, Hypochoeris radicata, Linum catharticum* and charac-teristic grasses such as *Koeleria gracilis* and *Sieglingia decumbens*. Invasion by *Pteridium aquilinum* occurs locally.

These grasslands support rich insect populations including the rare transparent burnet moth *Zygaena purpuralis*.

Scrub and relict woodland patches show a species composition characteristic of base-rich soils. Ash–hazel scrub is diversified with the associates aspen, blackthorn, birch, hawthorn, alder, rowan, sallows, ivy, honeysuckle and *Rosa* spp. Field layer species of scrub include *Circaea lutetiana, Brachypodium sylvaticum, Angelica sylvestris, Heracleum sphondylium, Rubus fruticosus, R. saxatilis, Hypericum androsaemum* and *Vicia cracca*, and these species also occur as tall-herb associations on ledges.

C.101. RHUM, INVERNESS-SHIRE

NM 3798. *c.* 240 ha   Grade 1*

Rhum contains a great diversity of habitat in its 48 km length of coast. The sheltered eastern inlet of Loch Scresort has shingle and boulder beaches with fucoids and intertidal mud flats providing feeding grounds for ducks, especially eider. Vestigial salt marsh is restricted to very small areas on gravelly silt deposits, but characteristic species are represented. A small sand-dune system backed by flat dune machair, grading into an alluvial marsh on the flood plain of the Kilmory River, occurs on the north coast. On sand and salt-influenced ground behind the unstable marram dunes there are areas of species-rich *Agrostis–Festuca* grasslands, with species composition typical of Hebridean machair. Associated with the grasses *A. stolonifera, A. tenuis, F. rubra, Koeleria gracilis, Sieglingia decumbens* and *Cynosurus cristatus*, the most abundant forbs are *Thymus drucei, Lotus corniculatus, Linum catharticum, Euphrasia* spp., *Galium verum* and *Plantago maritima*, but there are several otherwise sparsely occurring additional species such as *Coeloglossum viride, Botrychium lunaria, Ophioglossum vulgatum*, and *Gentianella amarella* which enrich the flora. In addition there is a submaritime heath on more acidic sand, with *Calluna, Erica cinerea* and *Empetrum nigrum*, and containing many of the above herbs. At a slightly higher level east of Kilmory mouth, is a rather different type of submaritime grassland, containing more tussocky growths of some of the machair species; and plants typical of damper ground, such as *Juncus articulatus* × *acutiflorus* and *Parnassia palustris*.

Submaritime grasslands and heaths are widely distributed elsewhere on the coast, notably on the western seaboard on cliff tops and above exposed beaches. Where these communities occur on magnesium-rich soils derived from the ultra-basic igneous rocks, they provide important floristic variants characterised by a greater abundance of *Koeleria cristata, Molinia caerulea, Carex pulicaris, C. panicea* and *Primula vulgaris*. Although they contain species such as *Plantago maritima*, these are not strictly halophytic swards. On the more poorly drained slopes the community changes to a *Schoenus nigricans–Molinia caerulea* flush-type with peat-forming tendencies. The variety of herbs in these submaritime associations is probably the reason for their rich insect fauna which includes the transparent burnet moth and strong populations of butterflies, with a handsome dark form of the dark green fritillary. A further variant of herb-rich submaritime heaths occurs on the Triassic cornstone of Monadh Dubh and contains *Dryas octopetala*. Raised beaches and wave-cut platforms are well developed on the western seaboard, and the partly vegetated storm beach at Harris has caused the formation behind it of marshy pools by impoundment.

Cliffs cover a large proportion of the coast and rise to 210 m or more at Welshman's rock, Wreck Bay and Bloodstone Hill, providing nesting sites for golden eagles. Where the cliffs drop into deep water, on the south-east sector near Dibidil there are moderate colonies of auks, kittiwakes and fulmars. Puffin and common tern colonies occur above the lower cliffs and the large colony of Manx shearwaters (about 150000 pairs) feeds at sea but breeds on the higher ultrabasic hills inland where the bird tunnels easily in the deep soils. Gullies in the sea cliffs on the shaded and sheltered north-east side at Meall a'Ghoirtein have an interesting assemblage of Atlantic ferns and bryophytes, which include *Dryopteris aemula, Hymenophyllum tunbrigense, Dicranum scottianum, Lepidozia pinnata* and *Jubula hutchinsiae*. Gullies in the broken seaward escarpment of Bloodstone Hill also have Atlantic liverworts such as *Frullania microphylla, F. germana, Drepanolejeunea hamatifolia, Radula aquilegia, Colura calyptrifolia* and *Plagiochila tridenticulata*, and the interesting moss *Myurium hebridarum* occurs on broken banks above the sea. Elsewhere, sea cliffs provide the main habitat for other non-maritime plants such as *Osmunda regalis* and *Ajuga pyramidalis*.

Rhum is also classified as a grade 1 upland site (U.71).

C.102. SOUTH UIST MACHAIR, INVERNESS-SHIRE

Grade 1

(a) Grogarry
NF 7639. 700 ha

Coastal lagoon (100 ha)

These areas of machair contain lochs which are essentially fresh-water and therefore fall properly within the wetlands habitat group; Lochs Stilligarry, a'Mhachair, Roag and Fada (OW.88) are so included. Their low-lying position near the coast and plant communities transitional to those of dune slacks, however, bring them within the paramaritime zone and they are of outstanding interest to any comparative study of the ecology of coastal lagoons.

These shallow lagoons with lime-rich sandy silt bottoms carry a submerged flora of *Myriophyllum alterniflorum, Potamogeton* spp. and *Chara* spp., grading to emergent communities of *Hippuris vulgaris, Phragmites communis*, mixed *Iris pseudacorus* marsh and, occasionally, *Salix aurita* scrub variously influenced at their edges by sheep- and cattle-grazing. Their flora is extremely varied and many of the plant and animal species are important wildfowl foods. These machair lochs and their adjoining marshes are, respectively, the characteristic feeding and breeding habitats of the red-necked phalarope. The marshes carry a higher density of breeding dunlin than any other habitat in Britain and are also the nesting place of several species of duck, and of snipe, redshank and lapwing.

Dune (600 ha)

The dune sector forms part of the most extensive machair system in Britain extending along almost the whole of the low-lying west coast of South Uist. No single site can be chosen here representing the whole range of variation from dry to wet machair, but the Grogarry section probably has the greatest all-round interest. This South Uist Machair is much disturbed by past cultivation; but Grogarry has good examples of the dry type. The constants of typical dry machair include *Festuca rubra, Holcus lanatus, Koeleria gracilis, Agrostis stolonifera, Bellis perennis, Plantago lanceolata, Ranunculus bulbosus, Senecio jacobaea, Achillea millefolium, Lotus corniculatus, Thymus drucei, Galium verum, Trifolium repens, Anthyllis vulneraria, Taraxacum officinale* agg., *Centaurea nigra, Euphrasia officinalis* agg., *Thalictrum minus, Carex flacca* and *Prunella vulgaris*. Most machair sites have a fairly uniform and distinctive floristic composition, but there are often physiognomic differences caused by the prominence of particular species in different localities, e.g. *Bellis, Senecio jacobaea, Ranunculus bulbosus*. The dry machair is the breeding habitat of oystercatchers, lapwings, skylarks and, where there is open sand, Arctic terns and ringed plover.

The machair area of Grogarry passes inland into the grade 1 open water site of Loch Druidibeg and its surrounding moorland, which are unaffected by blown sand and represent an oligotrophic ecosystem complex (see also OW.88). Based on Loch Druidibeg and its islands is the largest remaining colony of native greylag geese in the British Isles. Some 65 pairs nest there.

(b) Askernish coast

NF 7322. 650 ha

A second area of machair, farther south in South Uist than Grogarry, has been included because of the greater range of interest of its marsh and open water facies. This is the area including and surrounding Loch Hallan, near Daliburgh. Loch Hallan is a calcareous machair loch in which the depth of open water has decreased markedly by silting during the last few decades. It is fringed by a eutrophic fen community which also extends some distance north of the loch itself, and contains *Phragmites communis, Hippuris vulgaris, Potentilla palustris, Menyanthes trifoliata, Pedicularis palustris, Caltha palustris, Veronica beccabunga, Iris pseudacorus, Filipendula ulmaria* and *Eriophorum angustifolium*. There is an abundance of 'brown mosses', especially *Cratoneuron falcatum* and *C. filicinum*, while local species include *Drepanocladus lycopodioides* and *Acrocladium giganteum*. This fen community grades into tussocky marshy grassland which is an important nesting habitat of the birds of wet machair, especially dunlin which are numerous here: this vegetation has much *Agrostis stolonifera, Festuca rubra, Carex flacca, C. nigra, Potentilla anserina, Ranunculus repens* and *Leontodon autumnalis*, and *Blysmus rufus* occurs locally.

The dry machair of this section has been much affected by cultivation in the recent past, and though there is a slow recovery towards the type of vegetation associated with less

disturbance (though including grazing), this part of the area has less interest than the Grogarry section.

C.103. BALRANALD, NORTH UIST, INVERNESS-SHIRE
NF 7170. 325 ha   Grade 1

Dune (c. 245 ha)

Lagoon (c. 80 ha)

This area of calcareous machair is important for its large area of lagoon and swamp, as well as drier fringing marsh; the greater extent of wet ground makes this a more important breeding haunt of red-necked phalarope and ducks (including gadwall) than the South Uist machair. The dry machair includes a good deal of land which has been ploughed and cultivated, but there are areas of good flat machair with a typical forb-rich grassland. The swamps have very well developed 'brown moss' carpets, with mixed sedges, including *Carex paniculata, C. nigra*, and herbs of rich-fen, such as *Hippuris vulgaris, Sparganium ramosum, Caltha palustris, Mentha aquatica, Menyanthes trifoliata, Pedicularis palustris, Lychnis flos-cuculi* and *Epilobium palustre*. The less usual bryophytes include *Acrocladium giganteum, Philonotis calcarea* and sheets of *Marchantia polymorpha* var. *aquatica*. These are among the most eutrophic mire communities found in Britain and show interesting affinities with the calcareous mires on the Dalradian schist, Carboniferous Limestone and Chalk. The machair loch of Loch nam Feithean is regarded as a grade 2 lake (OW.99).

C.104. MONACH ISLES, INVERNESS-SHIRE
NF 6462. 577 ha   Grade 1

This low group of islands, lying 16 km west of North Uist, is covered mainly by machair with fringing dunes, but rather small areas of lagoon and marsh. There is less of the typical flat machair than on South Uist, and the ground tends to be gently undulating, giving the appearance of stable dune. Maritime grassland of the *Festuca rubra–Holcus lanatus* type occurs and a maritime heather heath on ground farthest from the sea. Floristically the islands are rich, but perhaps the most important feature is the large wintering flock of barnacle geese (750 birds; 3% of UK population). Good colonies of Arctic terns breed and there are small colonies of other seabirds on outlying islets. About 2000 grey seal pups are born annually.

C.105. ST KILDA, INVERNESS-SHIRE
NA 1000. 852 ha   Grade 1*

The St Kilda group, 80 km west of the Sound of Harris in the Outer Hebrides, contains the most spectacular cliff scenery in Britain, cut in gabbro, granophyre, dolerite and basalt. The main island, Hirta, rises smoothly and steeply from Village Bay to the hill of Conachair, which then falls away on its north side in a precipice almost 430 m high. The smaller islands of Boreray and Soay both have even more completely sheer walls of over 360 m, and the two great rock stacks adjoining the former, Stac an Armin (191 m) and Stac Lee (165 m), are the highest in the country.

Botanically, the most striking environmental features of the St Kilda group are, first, the prevailing high humidity, which is reflected in the generally peaty nature of the soils, and in the wide distribution of hygrophilous oceanic plants, such as *Frullania germana*; and secondly, the evidence that salt spray strongly affects the whole of these islands. On Hirta opposite Dun and on the Cambir, the occurrence of halophytic *Plantago* swards on cliff tops hundreds of metres above the sea is an indication of the spray drenching which these sites receive during storms. Halophytes such as *Asplenium marinum* and *Grimmia maritima* occur in places farthest from the sea, and much of the prevailing grassland has a submaritime character. Vast numbers of seabirds have a very marked fertilising effect on the pastures, and the enriching influence of the sea spray also helps to give swards of sufficient productivity to support a good stock of Soay sheep on Hirta and Soay, and blackface on Boreray. These flocks have been the subject of intensive research.

Away from the cliffs, Soay and Boreray are covered largely with the *Holcus lanatus*, *Agrostis stolonifera*, *A. tenuis*, *Anthoxanthum odoratum*, *Festuca rubra* type of submaritime grassland, and only Hirta has areas sufficiently free from the influence of salt water and heavy manuring by sheep and birds to carry paramaritime communities. These are mainly a range of acidic, species-poor grasslands and heaths of a submontane character, found widely on lower hills along the western Highland seaboard. A mixed *Nardus–Calluna–Rhacomitrium lanuginosum* heath is quite extensive, and the summit of Conachair has a *Luzula sylvatica* dominated grassland. There is an interesting flush community with much *Schoenus nigricans* in one place.

While St Kilda is an example of an extreme oceanic island group, there is a contrast with, for instance, the Isles of Scilly, in that the climate in this northern district is of the cool Atlantic type. This is marked by the occurrence of montane species such as *Silene acaulis* and *Saxifraga oppositifolia* on the sea cliffs. Yet the climate is still equable enough to allow the presence of some southern species, and the Mediterranean–Atlantic liverwort *Fossombronia angulosa* occurs here far beyond its next northernmost locality, in Donegal, Ireland.

Ornithologically, the St Kilda group are of first importance for their massive seabird breeding populations, which form one of the largest concentrations in the North Atlantic. The largest colony of gannets in Britain and Europe (52 000 pairs in 1969) breeds on Boreray and its stacks, and there are large numbers of guillemots (21 500 pairs), razorbills (minimum of 2500 pairs) and kittiwakes (11 500 pairs). St Kilda was once the sole British locality for the fulmar (the species has since spread all round the coasts of the British Isles) and its population is now extremely large (over 22 000 pairs). The most numerous bird until recently was the puffin, which formerly bred in prodigious numbers (estimated at two to three million pairs), especially on Dun, giving the largest colony of the species in Britain. However, the numbers on St Kilda appear to have declined alarmingly in recent years and the latest estimate of population, in 1969, is for 163 000 pairs. This is one of the very few European

breeding stations of Leach's petrel, and the almost equally local storm petrel and Manx shearwater breed too. The grass heaths of the boggy watersheds on Hirta are interesting as the site of a new colony of great skuas, and as the periodic nesting place of the northern race of the golden plover. Whimbrel also have nested on occasion. The St Kilda wren is regarded as a distinct subspecies, *Troglodytes troglodytes hirtensis*. Small flocks of grey and barnacle geese rest on the islands during migration time.

Grey seals are present in some numbers, and the other interesting mammals include a St Kilda race of the wood mouse, *Apodemus sylvaticus hirtensis*. These islands are thus notable for their examples of evolutionary divergence through isolation of small populations.

C.106. NORTH RONA AND SULA SGEIR, ROSS
HW 8132, HW 6230.   130 ha   Grade 1*

These two isolated islands have a good deal in common with the St Kilda group. Sula Sgeir is an isolated stack with a large colony of gannets (9000 pairs in 1969), from which the young are still harvested by the inhabitants of Ness in Lewis. North Rona covers a smaller area than Hirta and is much lower, so that most of its surface is covered by a submaritime grass sward which is grazed by sheep, though with a break from 1965–70. There are good colonies of guillemots, razorbills and puffins, and kittiwakes on the 110 m cliffs, fulmars nest abundantly on rocks, old houses and on the ground, and this is another of the few breeding places of Leach's petrel. A large colony of about 1000 pairs of great black-backed gulls nests on the grassland. North Rona is, however, of greatest importance as a place where grey seals land in large numbers to produce their young and it is an important research site for studies on the population biology of this species. A small number of Greenland white-fronted and barnacle geese use North Rona from time to time.

C.107. OLDSHORE–SANDWOOD COAST, SUTHERLAND
NC 225660–210570.   160 ha   Grade 1

Dune (100 ha)

The machair associated with Oldshore More and Oldshore Beg carry some 220 species of flowering plants and vascular cryptogams and for their size are among the most species-rich dune areas in Britain. They are small dune grassland plains on shell sand with damp hollows locally and carry a wealth of local species such as *Antennaria dioica*, *Botrychium lunaria*, *Carex dioica*, *Gentianella campestris*, *Pinguicula lusitanica*, *P. vulgaris*, *Trollius europaeus* and at least eight species or varieties of orchid. The larger dune system on the seaward side of Sandwood Loch, at the northern end of the site, is also floristically rich, and the calcareous shell sand there has a large colony of *Dryas octopetala*. There is a greater development of unstable marram sandhills than at Oldshore.

Cliff (60 ha)

The Lewisian Gneiss and Torridonian Sandstone cliffs between Sandwood and the mouth of Loch Inchard rise to 90 m and carry a variety of montane and northern coastal plant species as well as the usual cliff halophytes and the shores are of particular marine biological interest. Cliff vegetation here is more varied than the *Cochlearia officinalis* dominated ground of the Clo Mor bird cliffs, and has lush communities with *Sedum rosea, Luzula sylvatica, Endymion non-scriptus, Silene dioica, Athyrium filix-femina* and *Orchis mascula*. This is the coastal edge of a site also rated as grade 1 for its upland and peatland interest (see U.69 and P.97).

C.108. CAPE WRATH–AODANN MHOR, SUTHERLAND
NC 251710–407695. 2000 ha   Grade 1*

This is one of the most varied and important sections of the Scottish coast. Cape Wrath is Lewisian Gneiss, and this rock extends a few kilometres eastwards to Kearvaig Bay, where there is some blown shell sand on steep ground. From here, the cliff is cut in Torridonian Sandstone, which forms the great 4.8 km long precipice of the Clo Mor; this has cliffs reaching a vertical height of about 210 m, and also vegetated slopes of great steepness in other sections. There is here an immense seabird breeding station. The colony of puffins may perhaps have once approached that of St Kilda in size, but it appears to have recently been greatly reduced and now numbers only a few tens of thousands of pairs. The populations of guillemots, razorbills, fulmars and kittiwakes are among the biggest for these species in Britain, though the difficulties of counting are such that reliable figures are not available. Until recently golden eagles had here a coastal mainland nesting place and there were two pairs of peregrines. Great skuas are colonising the moorland. The vegetation of the bird cliffs is much modified, and in places consists largely of lush growths of *Cochlearia officinalis*. Elsewhere, the cliffs have an abundance of the common maritime plants such as *Armeria maritima, Silene maritima* and *Plantago maritima*, and there is luxuriant *Sedum rosea* in quantity. The strip above the cliff edge has a good deal of the typical submaritime short heather heath, rich in species including the montane *Salix herbacea*.

At Cape Wrath, lime-rich sand has blown over the headland to give an unusually high-lying small dune system for this windswept area. *Elymus arenarius* grows among marram at a much higher level (15–30 m) than normal. All round wind-attack on this exposed peninsula promotes remarkably conical marram hummocks liberally clothed with bryophytes on the sides exposed to moist Atlantic winds. Transitions to close-grazed *Festuca rubra* turf with occasional *Juniperus communis* ssp. *nana* and eventually to heather heath occur on the landward margins of the system inland from the coast road.

Lewisian Gneiss and Cambrian Quartzite appear again on the less precipitous coast forming the west side of the Kyle of Durness, but on the east side there is a large exposure of the Durness Limestone at Borralie. Blown shell sand here also adds considerably to the extent of calcareous habitats, and there is one of the few areas of machair-type vegetation on the mainland. Spray-influenced maritime grasslands and rocky, intermittently flushed areas are the habitat of the rare northern *Primula scotica*.

The isthmus leading to Faraidh Head north of Durness is covered with a ridge of very tall marram dunes, overlying Moine Schists and there is a good range of submaritime grassland. Faraidh Head is of interest mainly for its area of ungrazed cliff top grassland on the east side; the community is a *Festuca rubra–Agrostis stolonifera* grassland with forbs such as *Primula vulgaris, Angelica sylvestris, Rumex acetosa* and *Sedum rosea*. Breeding seabirds include a puffin colony of about 1000 pairs.

Much of the coast, including some islands just offshore, as well as the hinterland to the west of the Kyle of Durness is used as a naval bombardment range. The breeding seabirds are subjected to much disturbance and the military's bombardment of one area was the probable cause of the abandonment in about 1969 of the coast-nesting pair of golden eagles.

The montane communities of Sgribhis Bheinn above the Clo Mor and Borralie at Durness are described under Upland Grasslands and Heaths (U.68).

See also OW.89.

C.109. INVERNAVER, SUTHERLAND
NC 6961. *c.* 200 ha   Grade 1*

Flats (60 ha)

There is a small area of high-level lime-rich sand flats in a 4 m tide range.

Marsh (c. 5 ha)

This covers a very small area on sandy silt, but is of special interest for its geographical position and the dominance of *Blysmus rufus* in the Borgie estuary marsh.

Dune (100 ha)

This system is small but outstandingly interesting for its gradation from a fairly typical mobile dune front through areas of atypical blown sand on a low rocky headland to acidophilous moorland vegetation where the influence of the calcareous shell sand disappears. The unstable seaward marram dunes have a flora with many of the species constant to this habitat all round the British coast, but their northern faces have a noteworthy abundance of mosses such as *Rhytidiadelphus triquetrus* and *Hylocomium splendens*. On the western side of the area there is a patch of good machair on flatter ground, and the northern *Carex maritima* is abundant in a slack. The most distinctive and important feature is the occurrence in the higher zone of blown sand of montane dwarf-shrub communities with a great abundance of *Dryas octopetala, Arctostaphylos uva-ursi* and *Empetrum hermaphroditum*, but these have been described in greater detail under Upland Grasslands and Heaths, as Invernaver is regarded also as a grade 1 upland site (U.70).

Shingle (20 ha)

Shingle and gravel terraces near sea-level are also modified by blown sand and provide further variety in the flora, notably an abundance of the rare northern *Oxytropis halleri*.

Cliff (c. 20 ha)

Rock outcrops in the blown sand area carry montane species such as *Dryas, Saxifraga oppositifolia, Polygonum viviparum, Silene acaulis* and *Oxytropis halleri*.

C.110. LOCH FLEET, SUTHERLAND
NH 7996.   1400 ha   Grade 1

Flats (800 ha)

This is a medium-sized area of medium- to low-level sand flats in a tidal range of 3.5 m. Locally *Enteromorpha* and *Arenicola* are abundant. There is moderate wildfowl interest – regular visitors include mallard, teal, wigeon, goldeneye, eider, red-breasted merganser and shelduck.

Marsh (300 ha)

Former salt marsh has developed into a now unusual type of coastal alder–willow–birch swamp woodland as a result of the construction in the nineteenth century of a road and rail embankment, which sealed-off the upper estuary from the influence of sea water, except for a short distance above the embankment. This woodland is now the most extensive of its type in Britain, and is described as a grade 1 site (W.210) under Woodlands. Immediately landward of the embankment there is a transition from a narrow zone of relict salt marsh to freshwater flood-plain mire on this peat over sand. This ecotone is maintained by seepage of saline water through the embankment and allows *Blysmus rufus, Eleocharis uniglumis, Triglochin maritima* and *Plantago maritima* to persist side by side with typical eutrophic mire species. The saline influence disappears upriver and the sealed-off marsh grades into the swamp woodland. Only small areas of *Puccinellia* and *Festuca rubra* salt marsh occur seaward of the embankment, with *Eleocharis uniglumis, E. quinqueflora, Blysmus rufus, Sagina nodosa, Centaurium littorale* and *Euphrasia foulaensis*.

Dunes (300 ha, discontinuous)

Two small dune systems (100 and 200 ha) occur as spits (probably overlying shingle) at the estuary mouth. The northern spit is extensively afforested.

C.111. MORRICH MORE, ROSS
NH 8384.   2750 ha   Grade 1*

Flats (1620 ha)

This is a medium-sized area of mainly sand flats in a tide range of 3.5 m. The north-west shore contains a remarkable parallel series of sand ridges and hollows. There is some silt in the more sheltered bays at Inver and Tain and extensive growths of *Zostera* and *Enteromorpha* occur in Tain Bay. The flats in association with nearby Loch Eye and Nigg Bay form an important wintering ground for wildfowl, notably wigeon, mallard, pintail, scaup and greylag geese. They are of lesser importance for waders.

Salt marsh (130 ha, discontinuous)

Small areas of sandy salt marsh are developed in the Inver inlet and as transitional salt marsh to dune slack communi-ties at the north-east end of the system. *Salicornia* is the pioneer on sandy silt and *Puccinellia maritima* on damp sand. Main marsh levels are colonised by close-grazed *P. maritima, Plantago maritima, Armeria maritima* and *Festuca rubra*. Some of the most extensive populations of *Blysmus rufus* in Britain occur at the upper limits of these marshes, together with large populations of such local species as *Centaurium littorale* (in unusual variety of colour forms), distinctive *Cochlearia* spp. (cf. *C. scotica*), *Eleocharis quinque-flora* and *E. uniglumis*.

Dune (1000 ha)

Morrich More is one of the most important and distinctive dune systems in Europe. It is a very large and remarkably level, low-lying, vegetated sandy plain stretching for 4.8 km almost back to Loch Eye. Very low-lying dune ridges alternate with wide damp or flooded dune slacks. Clearly there has been very rapid progradation, which is still occurring here on to damp or just-dry sand to give an alternation of intermediate salt marsh to dune slack or low dune according to the prevailing conditions at the seaward edge at any one time. Outer dune islands colonised by marram and *Elymus arenarius* support some 300 Arctic terns. Part of the seaward area to the north-east is used as a naval bombing range, but this has not deterred a colony of Sandwich terns from nesting.

The flora of this system is exceedingly rich and contains several hundred flowering plants and ferns in the lime-rich and acid facies which occur in different parts of the area. At least 10 species of flowering plants reach their northern limit for the east coast of Britain here. Among the more notable species are *Astragalus danicus, Antennaria dioica, Carex maritima, Botrychium lunaria, Equisetum hyemale, Listera cordata, Platanthera bifolia, Gentianella septentrionalis* and *Vicia lathyroides*.

In the older parts, dune heath of heather occurs with abundant *Empetrum nigrum* and there are distinctive areas of wind-cut and grazed *Juniperus communis* scrub not known on any other British dune system. The area carries a varied lichen flora and both bryophytes and lichens form an important element in the dune and slack communities. Calcicolous dune slack mosses include *Drepanocladus lycopodioides, D. sendtneri* and *Campylium elodes*. The invertebrate fauna has not been investigated.

C.112. CROMARTY FIRTH, ROSS
NH 6667.   4000 ha   Grade 1*

The sand flats within the enclosed inlet of the Cromarty Firth are by far the most important of the wildfowl and wader haunts in north-east Scotland. Although the areas involved are only of medium size, the populations of both groups are of particular importance, the major concentra-tions being in Nigg Bay and Udale Bay. Numbers of wintering wildfowl have reached average peaks of 17000 birds, with wigeon (13800) as the most numerous species, and large numbers of goldeneye (1000; $\frac{1}{8}$ of the UK popula-tion), whooper swan (410), mute swan (500), teal (650) and pintail (225). Other well-represented species include greylag, mallard, shelduck and scaup. Recent peaks in the Firth have been lower than the levels quoted, but some species might well recover if the site is not too much disturbed. The wader populations average 8000–9000 birds with oyster-catcher (2390), redshank (1780) and knot (1500) as the most numerous species, followed closely by curlew (1040), dunlin (1020), lapwing (900) and bar-tailed godwit (750). Smaller numbers of ringed plover (160) and turnstone (40) occur.

This considerable ornithological interest is now threatened by the development of an industrial complex, including aluminium smelter, petro-chemical works, oil rig assembly yards and deep-water port facilities centred at Invergordon within the Cromarty Firth. Minor oil pollution has already occurred with some damage to wildfowl, and it remains to be seen if bird populations will be sustained in the future.

C.113. RHUNAHAORINE, ARGYLL
NR 6949. 335 ha   Grade 2

A low promontory comprising shingle beach, marsh, heath and permanent and temporary agricultural pasture (with some arable) on the western shore of Kintyre, this site is important mainly for its winter wildfowl population of 370 Greenland white-fronted geese (3% of world population, 10% of UK population). The site is used by the geese as a feeding ground only (location of roost not known) and by shore nesting seabirds in summer.

C.114. RUEL ESTUARY, ARGYLL
NS 0180. 200 ha   Grade 2

Flats (160 ha)

Broad silt and sand flats overlie gravel or shingle deposits which are revealed in estuarine creeks with cliffed edges. *Zostera noltii* is locally represented with filamentous and thalloid algae such as *Enteromorpha* spp., *Pelvetia* spp. and *Fucus spiralis*.

Marsh (40 ha)

This rather small area of estuarine salt marsh at the head of a west coast sea loch shows interesting contrasts due to variations in grazing intensity from heavily grazed *Leontodon autumnalis*-rich *Festuca rubra* grasslands to species-rich *Puccinellia maritima* and *Aster tripolium* marsh, with several species representing north-western facies of this community, such as *Blysmus rufus*, *Carum verticillatum* and *Carex vesicaria*. Both dry and damp facies are represented and transitions occur through brackish marsh, *Phragmites* reed-bed and alder–sallow carr to oak woodland beyond the maritime zone.

C.115. BARRAPOL AND BALLEVULLIN, TIREE, ARGYLL
NL 9542, NL 9647. 1500 ha   Grade 2

These two dune systems contain good representations of typical Tiree sheep-grazed machair pasture with marshy transitions to lochs on the landward side. Intensive grazing at Barrapol limits species diversity, but *Eryngium maritimum* survives and there is a typical range of machair species though *Daucus carota*, *Anthyllis vulneraria* and *Thymus drucei* are more than usually sparse and *Thalictrum minus* is

local. The marsh surrounding Loch a Phuil is rich in typical calcicolous marsh species together with some halophytes such as *Juncus gerardii* and *Plantago maritima*, while *Potentilla palustris* and *Polygonum amphibium* occur at the loch edge. The rocky headland at Ceann a Mhara is of ornithological interest for its seabird colony.

The dune system at Ballevullin is more varied with mobile and fixed dunes, rocky outcrops, machair, marsh and loch habitats. The usual range of calcicolous herbs is abundantly represented and acidophilous communities occur near the rocky outcrops. The machair pasture is mainly in the east of the site and some of it is under cultivation. The dune system to the north of Loch Bhasapoll is generally similar to that within the site but has no rock outcrops, and there are some floristic differences, notably in the increased abundance of *Thymus drucei*, *Thalictrum minus* and *Cynosurus cristatus* and a scarcity of *Leontodon autumnalis*, *Geranium molle* and *Sedum acre*.

C.116. ARDMEANACH, MULL, ARGYLL
NM 4429. *c.* 400 ha   Grade 2

The Tertiary basalt peninsula of Ardmeanach is regarded as a grade 2 upland site (U.95) and its coastal cliff and slope habitats are described there. They are essentially similar to those on the Ross of Mull and are regarded as alternative in their own right; cliff woodland and scrub are well represented, there are extensive forb-rich basic grasslands, and a basiphilous rock face flora. The invertebrate fauna is rich, especially in Lepidoptera.

C.117. MINGULAY AND BERNERAY, INVERNESS-SHIRE
NL 5683, NL 5680. 635 and 185 ha   Grade 2

These two contiguous small islands form the southernmost tip of the long island chain of the Outer Hebrides. They are composed mainly of Lewisian Gneiss and are bounded by sheer cliffs on their northern and western sides, rising to 210 m on Mingulay and 190 m on Berneray. Mingulay has a number of off-shore stacks. Ecologically these two islands are similar to Handa, with large colonies of breeding seabirds on their cliffs, and a range of maritime to para-maritime vegetation, mainly grassland and heath, on their crests and less precipitous slopes. They are rated as nationally important for the large populations of guillemots (12800 pairs), razorbills (7400 pairs), puffins (1300 pairs), kittiwakes (4000 pairs) and fulmars (7500 pairs).

C.118. BALESHARE/KIRKIBOST DUNES, NORTH UIST, INVERNESS-SHIRE
NF 7862. 1450 ha   Grade 2

This is perhaps the largest sand-dune area in western Scotland, but has little associated machair. It has yet to be adequately surveyed, but is clearly a site of importance in the national series of sand-dune systems.

C.119. NORTHTON, HARRIS, INVERNESS-SHIRE
NF 9991. 475 ha   Grade 2

This is a rather unusual zone of wet machair developed behind a fringing salt marsh. There is no machair loch, but numerous shallow pools and runnels occur. 'Brown moss' carpets and hummocks are well developed in places. A dense population of dunlin and lapwing breed here, and on low fringing dunes in one place, there is a colony of common gulls nesting in an unusual habitat.

C.120. SHIANT ISLES, ROSS
NG 4198.   225 ha   Grade 2

The Shiants, a small island group in the Minch, composed of Eilean Mhuine, Garbh Eilean and Eilean an Tighe, and about a dozen rocks and skerries, are another of the outstanding bird haunts of the Hebrides. Maximum elevation of 160 m is on Garbh Eilean and the islands are composed of columnar dolerite of Tertiary age notable for their sheer cliffs with a huge colony of puffins, now reduced but still numbering about 80 000 pairs, and the usual range of other breeding seafowl; 300–400 barnacle geese winter regularly. There is also a range of maritime grassland and heath which includes some of the types found at St Kilda. (See Appendix.)

C.121. HANDA–DUARTMORE, SUTHERLAND
NC 140480–179369.   2000 ha   Grade 2

The Torridonian Sandstone island of Handa close to the mainland coast of north-west Sutherland is another important cliff seabird breeding station, similar to the Clo Mor. Much of the island is bounded by vertical, horizontally stratified cliffs rising to 120 m, with large numbers of guillemots (*c.* 30 000 pairs), razorbills (6000 pairs), kittiwakes (8300 pairs) and fulmars (2400 pairs) but fewer puffins than the Clo Mor. Away from the sea there are submaritime grasslands and heaths of the type found on St Kilda and North Rona, and great skuas have become established here, whilst the nesting waders include golden plover and snipe.

The mainland coast is Lewisian Gneiss, and varies from cliffs to the lower, indented type of shore-line found at Inverpolly. The coast here has not been examined in detail but it links with the interesting open water, marsh and birchwood at Loch a' Mhuilinn (W.226).

C.122. FLANNAN ISLES, ROSS
NA 7246.   *c.* 80 ha   Grade 2

This remote cluster of six rocky islands 32 km west of Lewis is regarded as a site of national importance for its large breeding populations of seabirds, including guillemot (10 000 pairs), razorbill (7250 pairs) and puffin (6000 pairs). There is a small colony of gannets numbering 16 pairs in 1969 and the site is another of the breeding stations of the rare Leach's petrel.

C.123. LOWER DORNOCH FIRTH, ROSS–SUTHERLAND
NH 1586.   2000 ha   Grade 2

The system of sand flats bordering both sides of this medium-sized estuary on the north-east coast of Scotland is important for its winter wildfowl population, which on average totals 6500 birds. The most numerous species are wigeon (5250), mallard, teal, pintail, scaup, shelduck and mute swan. The wader populations are also of interest. That portion of the flats which borders the Morrich More dune system should be regarded as an integral part of that grade 1* site, but the rest of the area is regarded as a grade 2 alternative to the Cromarty Firth not far to the south. The Lower Dornoch Firth may in the future assume greater importance through the effects of industrial development now proceeding within the Cromarty Firth, and its status should be kept under careful review.

15 WOODLANDS

SOUTH-EAST ENGLAND

W.1. BLEAN WOODS, KENT
TR 1060.   305 ha   Grade 1

The Blean forms the most extensive area of nearly contin-
uous woodland on the London Clay in south-eastern
England. Within this, Blean Woods National Nature
Reserve (NNR) forms a typical example.

The whole area has a long-standing tradition of management as coppice-with-standards with sessile oak as the dominant standard. Sessile oak coppice, mixed in part with beech,
occurs in a large area on the western boundary, whilst the
latter is dominant in a very small central area of open high
forest. Hornbeam coppice dominates the northern parts and
sweet chestnut coppice dominates the south-central and
south-eastern parts and much of Crawford's Rough. Rowan
is widespread whilst wild service and aspen are becoming
increasingly common in the newly coppiced areas. Alder and
guelder rose are also widespread. Along the southern parts
of the wood the London Clay is overlain by two patches of
recent 'head gravel', part of the terrace of an ancient valley
floor of the Great Stour River. This acidic gravelly drift
supports dense chestnut coppice with a honeysuckle, bluebell and *Luzula pilosa* field layer. A small area of ash coppice
with pedunculate oak and hazel has a ground flora of *Sanicula europaea*, *Euphorbia amygdaloides* and *Ajuga reptans*.
Also in the south-east part of the wood are acidic areas with
Calluna, *Carex binervis*, *C. ovalis*, *C. demissa*, *Molinia
caerulea*, *Sieglingia decumbens* and *Dactylorchis maculata*, all
rare in north-east Kent where heathlands are scarce. The
areas of recently coppiced oak–beech–hornbeam woodland
have a rich ground flora which includes *Luzula sylvatica*,
Teucrium scorodonia, *Milium effusum*, *Melica uniflora*, *Lathyrus montanus*, *Hypericum pulchrum*, *Sarothamnus scoparius*
and *Ruscus aculeatus*. In the more dense old hornbeam
coppice *Crataegus oxyacanthoides* is an occasional associate.

The Blean has been a well-known haunt for entomologists
since the latter part of the last century. It was originally
scheduled to preserve one of the few remaining colonies of
heath fritillary *Melitaea athalia*, the larvae of which feed on
Melampyrum pratense. This plant flourishes particularly in
the light phase of coppicing and along ride margins and is
again plentiful in the Reserve. As a result, for example
during early July 1969, following coppicing, this butterfly
was a common sight in the open areas of the wood. Recent
studies in the Reserve have revealed a wealth of rare species
of a wide range of invertebrates. The wood ant *Formica
rufa* is abundant in parts of the wood and some 15 species
of myrmicophilous beetles have been found in its nests. A
number of rare staphylinid beetles have been found in the
wood including *Gyrophaena joyioides* (only known British
locality), *Borboropora kraatzi* (first British record for over
100 years) and *Staphylinus fulvipes* which is quite common
locally. *Acritus homoepathicus* (Coleoptera, Histeridae) is
abundant in fire sites in the coppiced areas. The millipede
Polyzonium germanicum, which has its British distribution
almost restricted to Kent, is common in the Reserve, as is
Choneiulus palmatus, another millipede more commonly
recorded from greenhouses and gardens. Among an impressive list of Heteroptera bugs is included *Charagochilus
weberi* (Miridae), a species new to Britain. The large area of
woodland of The Blean provides a stepping stone by which
many continental species enter the British Isles and become
established.

W.2. HAM STREET WOODS, KENT
TR 0034.   210 ha   Grade 1

These woodlands, parts of which are NNR, lie on the
plateau, slopes and valley bottoms over Lower Weald Clay.
Structurally they are coppice-with-standards throughout,
although there is a wide range of coppice types. The
standards are oak (mostly *Quercus robur*, but with about
10% *Q. petraea*) with a proportion of birch (mostly *Betula
pubescens*) which has entered as a weed species following the
cutting of the coppice. Wild service, gean and aspen also
occur as 'weed' standards.

Four types of coppice occur on the plateau areas. These,
defined by their dominant species, are clearly the product
of past management. Hornbeam coppice is the most widespread, some of the stools being massive indicators of the
long history of such coppice on at least part of the site.
Hazel coppice occurs mainly on the valley slopes. Chestnut
coppice, still actively worked, occurs mainly in the northern
block. Oak coppice occurs in Carter's Wood, but has
evidently arisen from the felling of standard oaks. Other
shrub species occur within these types, including willows
(*Salix atrocinerea* and *S. caprea*), both hawthorns and holly.
The presence of midland hawthorn as well as wild service is
circumstantial evidence that at least parts of Ham Street
Woods are primary.

The woodland is diversified by the presence of valleys and
rides. The former, which contain the richest areas floristically, have ash and alder woodland, worked as coppice, with
midland hawthorn and elder.

The ground flora develops and changes cyclically as coppicing proceeds, being least developed as the coppice becomes dense. Although the proposed future management of large areas of the woodland is of coppice-with-standards, much of the present wood is old, neglected, hornbeam coppice in which the ground flora consists of wood anemone, primrose, bluebell and honeysuckle. In the gills dog's mercury is locally dominant. Where the canopy is more open bracken and bramble are abundant. Rides in the north have heather, gorse and *Potentilla erecta*, indicating acid conditions which contrast with the base-rich nature of the valleys. The bryophyte flora, which includes such noteworthy species as *Eucalyx hyalinus*, *Rhytidiadelphus loreus* and *Hylocomium brevirostre*, supports the conclusion that woodland has been continuous on this site.

Ham Street Woods have long been famous entomologically.

W.3. ALKHAM VALLEY WOODS, KENT
TR 2644, TR 2742. 140 ha   Grade 1

Lying on steep Chalk slopes, these woods have soils 30–60 cm deep of calcareous loam with few Chalk particles and a high siliceous fraction. They consist of mixed coppice of ash and pedunculate oak with some hornbeam, hazel and field maple, and only a few poorly grown standards of pedunculate oak. Beech is rare and entirely confined to the margins. The flora is very rich. Sladden Wood, probably the best single site within the group, includes *Orchis purpurea*, *Ophrys insectifera*, *Cephalanthera damasonium*, *Neottia nidus-avis*, *Platanthera chlorantha*, *Paris quadrifolia*, *Helleborus viridis*, *Mercurialis perennis*, *Sanicula europaea*, *Adoxa moschatellina*, *Campanula trachelium*, *Ranunculus auricomus*, *Galium odoratum*, *Pimpinella major*, *Angelica sylvestris*, *Deschampsia cespitosa* and *Veronica montana*.

The significance of these sites is that almost everywhere else on Chalk scarps the woodland is dominated by beech over a thin soil: possibly the Alkham Valley Woods lie on a relict soil type.

W.4. SCORDS WOOD, KENT
TQ 4852. 340 ha   Grade 1

This site lies on a plateau of chert gravel derived from acidic Hythe Beds giving rise to a podsolised soil, falling to a valley in which first brown forest soils then calcareous soils derived from Kent ragstone and base-rich peaty soils occur in an apparent catena. Corresponding with this are four woodland types, respectively (1) sessile oak high forest and coppice over *Vaccinium myrtillus–Calluna vulgaris–Blechnum spicant*, with *Luzula sylvatica* and *Pyrola minor* locally; (2) sessile oak high forest with birch and holly with a transitional ground flora of *Endymion non-scriptus*, *Rubus fruticosus*, *Pteridium aquilinum*, *Euphorbia amygdaloides*, and *Primula vulgaris*; (3) mixed coppice and high forest of pedunculate oak, field maple, ash, hazel and wych elm with a ground flora indicative of base-rich conditions, including *Mercurialis perennis*, *Sanicula europaea*, *Galium odoratum*, *Helleborus viridis*, *Lathraea squamaria*, *Listera ovata* and *Adoxa moschatellina*; and (4) alder carr with *Chrysosplenium oppositifolium*, *C. alternifolium*, *Carex strigosa* and *Equisetum telmateia*.

With this exceptional range of habitats, the vascular flora is very rich. Both rowan and common whitebeam are present in the sessile oakwood, together with the hybrid. Numerous bryophyte and lichen species are recorded.

W.5. ASHOLT WOOD, KENT
TR 1738. 70 ha   Grade 1

Asholt Wood lies on gently undulating ground at the foot of the Chalk escarpment. Springs rising at the base of the Chalk flow through the wood. The soil, developed from Gault Clay and downwash from the Chalk, is highly calcareous but poorly drained. Its texture varies from heavy clay to clay loam, and small elevated areas appear to be neutral or mildly acid in reaction. Structurally the wood is mostly pedunculate oak standards over a range of coppice types, much neglected for the most part, but in places recently coppiced after a period of neglect. Much of the coppice is ash and hazel with some maple, dogwood and willows, but on the apparently acidic knolls, there is some hornbeam–ash coppice, and along the flood zones beside the streams a mixed coppice of alder, ash, maple and hazel has developed. The ground flora is rich, but no nationally rare species have been recorded.

This site is selected as a south-eastern counterpart of the chalky boulder clay coppices of East Anglia and the Midlands. It differs from them in having valley alder coppice, and lacking oxlip *Primula elatior* and *Geum rivale*. Other examples of this type are known, and one – Ryarsh Wood, Kent – has a richer flora, but Asholt is regarded as the best example because it has a canopy largely free of aliens, and is contiguous with a chalk grassland site (L.15).

W.6. CROOKHORN WOOD, KENT
TQ 6763. 110 ha   Grade 1

This is part of an extensive tract of woodland, scrub and grassland on the Chalk scarp and plateau of the North Downs all of which is of considerable scientific importance. Crookhorn Wood itself is a mature beechwood with ash and field maple in the canopy, and an understorey of yew. Structurally it is diverse, with a mixture of age classes, including some very old trees, forming a closed canopy. The humus lies deep over a shallow soil, and the ground flora, though sparse, includes *Cephalanthera damasonium*, *Neottia nidus-avis* and *Daphne laureola*. On the plateau over Clay-with-Flints the woodland is mainly pedunculate oak with some coppice of hazel, ash and sweet chestnut. Parts of the adjacent grassland have been invaded by scrub in which ash is (unusually) rare and the most abundant species are whitebeam, silver birch and dogwood, with patches of yew. Within this scrub *Helleborus foetidus*, *Aceras anthropophorum* and a fine colony of *Orchis purpurea* are known.

The woodlands on Wouldham–Detling Escarpment are similar but contain seral ashwood as well as the range of types present in Crookhorn Wood.

W.7. WOULDHAM–DETLING ESCARPMENT, KENT
TQ 723648–795588. 440 ha   Grade 1

The woodlands on this south-west-facing scarp slope of the North Downs are extremely variable. They include almost the entire range of types associated with the Chalk scarp and Clay-with-Flints plateau sites. On the plateau, pedunculate oak woodland is prevalent over coppice which is partly of sweet chestnut, but mostly a mixture with hazel, ash and hawthorn. The field layer includes the range of communities from *Mercurialis perennis–Sanicula europaea*, through *Endymion non-scriptus* to *Rubus fruticosus* and *Deschampsia cespitosa*. The thin rendzina soils on the slopes bear beech woodland in part, and mixtures of ash, yew and hazel, over a discontinuous field layer. At the south-eastern end on Boxley Warren, chalk scrub of yew, hawthorn, dogwood and whitebeam is developing towards woodland.

The Escarpment contains a wide range of woodland types which individually may be better represented by examples elsewhere: e.g. beechwoods at Crookhorn Wood; yew-woods at Kingley Vale; plateau woods at Box Hill. Nevertheless the woodland complex taken as a whole and in conjunction with the associated grassland and scrub qualifies for grade 1 status (see also L.10).

W.8. BIGNOR HILL, SUSSEX
SU 9713. 160 ha   Grade 1

Bignor Hill is at the southern end of extensive woodlands situated on the north- and east-facing Chalk scarp slopes. These woods are not quite continuous, and stretch in a broken chain from Duncton Down in the north to Great Bottom on the dip slope in the south. Beech is dominant, with ash as a more or less constant associate. The stand has a limited range of age, but recent thinning has facilitated some regeneration, mainly of ash. Birch and field maple are also present in the canopy, while the shrub layer of yew, whitebeam, dogwood and spindle is reasonably well developed. Ground flora communities cover the usual range from *Mercurialis perennis–Sanicula europaea* on dry, calcareous soil to *Endymion non-scriptus–Rubus fruticosus* on the deeper plateau soils. Local variations occur on Duncton Hanger where, in a valley along a springline, a wych elm woodland has developed; at Bignor Hill, where an ashwood on scree includes the only locality in the south-east for *Thelypteris robertiana*; and at Great Bottom, where on the west side there are some of the largest and possibly oldest pollarded beeches in the south-east.

There are many other stands of beechwood on the South Downs, but those at Bignor Hill are regarded as the best developed, with a number of local variations related to geological and edaphic differences.

W.9. SAXONBURY HILL/ERIDGE PARK, SUSSEX
TQ 5734. 600 ha   Grade 1*

This site comprises an ancient deer park, a more recent park now used for deer, and adjacent woodlands on Saxonbury Hill, situated in the High Weald. The parks, particularly the northern half of the Old Park, have an open woodland of ancient oaks, maple, ash and beech beneath which the ground vegetation is a mosaic of bracken, *Molinia caerulea* and heather heath, and in the lower parts on Wadhurst Clay a relatively rich woodland ground flora has developed. Small, low-lying areas are occupied by alder carrs, small areas of calcareous fen and some acidic flushes. Saxonbury Hill includes a mixture of woodland types. Mature, closed oak–beech forest occurs on plateau areas where yew and holly are also frequent. In the valley, alder occurs beside the stream, and on flushed parts of the slopes near the valley bottom. On the drier slopes woodland of oak and birch occurs locally.

Taken as a whole the site has one of the richest epiphytic lichen floras of any single park in Britain. So far 167 species have been recorded. It is the only site in south-east England where a well-developed Lobarion association occurs. Numerous species characteristic of old forests have been recorded, including *Lobaria pulmonaria*, *L. laetevirens*, *Nephroma laevigatum*, *Parmeliella plumbea*, *Leptogium lichenoides*, *L. minutissimum*, *Buellia schaereri*, *Parmelia crinita*, *Xylographa vitiligo* and *Dimerella lutea*. Bryophyte epiphytes include *Frullania fragilifolia* and *Orthotrichum stramineum*, which are otherwise unknown in south-east England. In Saxonbury Hill woods there is a small sandrock outcrop with *Dryopteris aemula* and *Hymenophyllum tunbrigense*, and a number of western bryophytes such as *Scapania gracilis* and *Bazzania trilobata*.

Although much of the central area of the Old Park has been reseeded, this site is undoubtedly one of the most important of all the ancient parklands selected, because the woodlands are diverse and the epiphyte flora is unsurpassed.

W.10. KINGLEY VALE, SUSSEX
SU 8211. 160 ha   Grade 1*

Within the general area of Kingley Vale only part of the land is occupied by woodland. This lies on the south-facing Chalk slopes and on clay in the valley bottom. Two broad woodland types occur, yew woodland on Chalk and oak on the clay, of which the former is much the more extensive. The yew woodland is almost pure in parts, but with a range of age classes. Elsewhere within the yew-wood, ash is common, and whitebeam, holly and blackthorn occur sparingly. Juniper formerly occurred there abundantly but successional changes have greatly reduced its extent. The field layer is absent, or represented by sparse development of, for example, *Fragaria vesca* and *Brachypodium sylvaticum*. The woodland on clay is dominated by pedunculate oak and ash, with an understorey of yew, holly and hawthorn.

The Kingley Vale woodland is selected as a representative of yew-dominated stands on calcareous soils. As such it is regarded as the most important site in Britain and is reputed to be the best yew-wood in Europe. Though yew woodland occurs elsewhere, e.g. Old Winchester Hill, Blackcliff, Box Hill, the stands are either less extensive or are mixed with other, taller species such as beech. A further important feature of Kingley Vale is the presence of all stages in the development from scrub on grassland to mature yew woodland.

See also L.9.

W.11. EBERNOE COMMON, SUSSEX
SU 9727.   110 ha   Grade 1

Ebernoe Common and Willand Wood together form a continuous block of woodland with a wide range of structural, floristic and soil types in the western Weald. The underlying strata range from heavy clay to sandstone and limestone, giving rise to the three main soil types of the area.

Ebernoe Common has three main woodland types. The most extensive is mature, closed beech woodland with some pedunculate oak and a dense understorey of holly with some yew. Some beech have fallen recently to produce gaps in which regeneration occurs sparingly. Along the eastern side and over base-rich soils, younger mature woodland of field maple, pedunculate oak and ash is found, with a few beech and a sparse understorey of holly. At the northern end a third type occurs, open ancient woodland of oak and beech with scattered thickets of holly. Not all the Common is wooded: large areas remain under grass and bramble, and other parts of former grassland are now occupied by scrub of gorse, blackthorn and willow with thickets of oak and birch saplings. The ground flora, virtually absent beneath the closed beech canopy, varies considerably between the *Mercurialis perennis–Primula vulgaris–Sanicula europaea* community of the base-rich soils to *Rubus fruticosus* and *Deschampsia cespitosa* on the clays. The local species include *Narcissus pseudo-narcissus*, *Ruscus aculeatus* and *Carex strigosa*. The epiphyte flora is fairly rich, but lacks a number of old forest indicators. In addition to the woods, scrub and grassland, the Common contains large ponds and marsh areas.

Willand Wood consists of coppice-with-standards typical of West Sussex, with pedunculate oak standards over mixed coppice of hornbeam, hazel and ash. The ground flora is dominated by wood anemone, bluebell and primrose.

W.12. WAKEHURST AND CHIDDINGLY WOODS, SUSSEX
TQ 3331, TQ 3432.   150 ha   Grade 1

These woods occupy the steep slopes and bottoms where the Ardingly and Cob Brooks have cut deeply incised valleys and exposed large areas of Tunbridge Wells Sandstone. At Chiddingly, the woodland on the plateau has been largely modified, consisting now in parts of scrub, coppice and planted pine with a number of exotic tree species. However, on the rocky slopes below the sandrock outcrops, a dry oak (mainly pedunculate) wood with birch, yew, holly and some beech, shades ground covered in large boulders. At points in the ravine where the soil is deep alluvium there is a local development of ash and alder woodland, grading to ash–oak on drier ground. Within this woodland there are a number of mature trees, some planted exotics and a local spread of rhododendron. The sandrock outcrops, which are the most extensive, sheltered exposures of the formation, have the richest development of the associated communities

of *Hymenophyllum tunbrigense* and suboceanic bryophytes, *Dicranum scottianum*, *Orthodontium gracile*, *Tetraphis browniana*, *Bazzania trilobata*, *Scapania gracilis*, *Pallavicinia lyellii*, *Harpanthus scutatus*, *Blepharostoma trichophyllum*, *Scapania umbrosa*, *Odontoschisma denudatum*, *Tritomaria exsectiformis* and *Lepidozia sylvatica*.

Wakehurst Woods are part of one of the most extensive stands of High Weald gill woodland with one of the largest sandrock outcrops. Much of the woodland is oak or oak–beech mixture, mature but with few really ancient trees, but along springlines alder and ash woodland occurs. Woodland types occurring in small quantity are open woodland of birch and oak, and areas of coppice, principally of sweet chestnut and hazel on lower slopes. At the higher levels bracken, bilberry, *Deschampsia flexuosa* and *Lonicera periclymenum* dominate the ground flora; whilst at lower levels on the clays, bramble, primrose, bluebell and wood anemone are prevalent, and flush communities with *Carex laevigata* and *Chrysosplenium oppositifolium* occur with the alder. The epiphytic lichen flora is moderately rich, but includes no exceptional occurrences. The ground flora includes *Dryopteris aemula* and *Wahlenbergia hederacea*. The most important feature is the community of the sandrock outcrop, second only to those in Chiddingly Wood, which includes *Hymenophyllum tunbrigense* and a number of rare bryophytes and saxicolous lichens.

At their nearest point these two woods are no more than 200 m apart. Collectively they form easily the richest of the sandrock communities. The two sites complement each other in that some of the characteristic species absent in Chiddingly are present in Wakehurst, and vice versa. In neither case are the tree and shrub strata of particular importance, except that the continuity of a substantial tract of high forest with few large clearings is essential for the continued existence of the sandrock communities.

W.13. THE MENS AND THE CUT AND BEDHAM ESCARPMENT, SUSSEX
TQ 0223.   190 ha   Grade 1

This extensive common woodland lies along the parish boundaries of Kirdford and Fittleworth from Idehurst Hurst to the Bedham Escarpment. For the most part it is on flat, low-lying ground drained by the headwaters of the River Arun, but at the south-west end it rises to a small hill. This is where the sandy Hythe Beds outcrop above Atherfield Clay, and give rise to acidic, sandy soils which are nevertheless imperfectly drained. Most of the site lies on Lower Weald Clay, but through Hammonds Wood there are numerous sandstone bands, and Paludina Limestone outcrops in a narrow band across The Cut.

The woodland is mostly high forest of sessile and pedunculate oaks, beech and locally ash, wild service and the birches. There is a tendency for beech to be dominant over a holly or yew understorey on the lighter soils, and for oaks and ash to be dominant over a mixed shrub layer on the heavy soils. A few ancient oaks are present, but most of the trees are probably less than 100 years old. Even so, the structure of the wood is one of its important features, for all stages of the regeneration cycle are well represented. The ground vegetation is limited for a site of this size, but many characteristic woodland species are present, including *Carex pendula*, *C. strigosa* and *Milium effusum*. There is a moderately rich bryophyte flora which includes, at the Bedham end, a number of local species on small boulders, *Campylostelium saxicola*, *Brachydontium trichoides*, *Marsupella emarginata* and *M. ustulata*. The epiphytic lichen flora is not fully known, but is certainly among the richest for woodland in the south-east. Recent detailed examination of the fungal flora has revealed that, in this respect, The Mens and The Cut is one of the richest woods in Britain, and may even be the richest: included in the list are three *Russula* spp. not known elsewhere in Britain, and another two known only from one or two other sites. Entomologically, this site is regarded as extremely rich, especially in the Crimbourne Wood area, with many extremely rare beetles on record and thriving populations of most of the woodland butterflies.

W.14. FAIRLIGHT, ECCLESBOURNE AND WARREN GLENS, SUSSEX
TQ 8511.   205 ha   Grade 1

The Lower Cretaceous rocks of the Weald are exposed along this stretch of coast. Magnificent cliff sections include the Fairlight Clays (type locality), Ashdown Sand and Wadhurst Clay. Considerable slipping and erosion has occurred creating a distinct undercliff zone which is heavily overgrown with scrub. Isolated boulders in this zone support a number of interesting bryophytes including *Tortula cuneifolia*, *T. marginata*, *Desmatodon convolutus* and *Lophocolea fragrans* in its only station east of Dorset.

The three glens have been cut down through the Wadhurst Clay, Ashdown Sand and in the case of Fairlight and Warren Glens through the Fairlight Clays as well. The valleys produced have steep sides covered in parts with mature woodland consisting of oak, beech, and ash with yew, holly, field maple, birch and alder which grade into a coastal scrub towards the cliff edge consisting of wind-pruned thickets of privet and blackthorn. The ground flora varies from bracken-dominated communities on the sands, to communities of *Mercurialis perennis* with *Carex pendula* and *Epipactis purpurata* on the clays. Flush communities with for example *Chrysosplenium oppositifolium* and *Allium ursinum* occur with the alder.

Floristically, Fairlight Glen is of considerable importance for the presence of the rare hepatic *Dumortiera hirsuta* and the moss *Fissidens rivularis* in their only stations east of Devon and a number of lichen species characteristic of old forest, e.g. *Normandina pulchella*, *Dimerella lutea* and *Graphina anguina*. Its coastal situation is rare in lowland English woods.

The area known as the Fire Hills was at one time covered with a low growing heath community of *Calluna vulgaris* and *Erica cinerea*; this has now been largely replaced by *Ulex europaeus*.

W.15. WORMLEY WOOD–HODDESDON PARK WOOD, HERTFORDSHIRE
TL 3306.   570 ha   Grade 1

The site is a series of contiguous woods which include in the west Wormley Wood and in the east Hoddesdon Park Wood. Much of the intervening woodland has been recently felled and replanted with conifers but broad-leaved trees and patches of broad-leaved woodland still occur throughout. Part of the outstanding interest of the area lies in its large extent, which provides for a greater variety of woodland habitats and also for areas of scrub and rough grassland.

Wormley Wood lies mainly on the London Clay but there are also gravel deposits. The varied geology and former land-use have produced a mosaic of vegetation. Sessile oak is the principal standard species over a coppice of almost pure hornbeam, but there is a proportion of other tree species including ash, pedunculate oak and birch. There are also some areas of high forest structure with standards of both oak and hornbeam. The ground flora consists largely of communities dominated by bramble, wood anemone, bluebell, *Luzula sylvatica* and *Lonicera periclymenum* with bryophyte carpets of *Dicranum majus* on fairly acid areas under standards. On more calcareous areas the field layer is richer with *Galium odoratum*, *Galeobdolon luteum*, *Mercurialis perennis* and *Carex pendula*: such areas tend to have a high proportion of ash in the canopy. Within the site there are areas of hawthorn and blackthorn scrub and birchwood on old field sites. The wood is crossed by a small stream along which alder has developed.

Hoddesdon Park Wood is mainly high forest although there are areas of coppice. The oak is well grown and there is a wide range of sizes, including oak saplings and seedlings. Indeed the abundance of oak regeneration throughout this woodland complex is one of its interesting features. The more open canopy produces a ground flora richer in species of both vascular plants and bryophytes than the dense coppice areas. There is also a good variety of epiphytic species including a community of *Dicranum* spp. (*montanum*, *flagellare* and *strictum*) which occurs on the Continent.

W.16. ELLENDEN WOOD, KENT
TR 1062.   100 ha   Grade 2

Ellenden Wood is part of the ancient Blean Woods lying on London Clay and spreads of gravel drift. Within the one block of woodland are a number of woodland types. Coppice-with-standards of sessile oak, with rowan, holly and wild service occurs over a field layer dominated by *Luzula sylvatica* and *Melampyrum pratense*. Parts have been planted with sweet chestnut, managed as coppice. A small plateau area of clays has blackthorn, hornbeam and hazel with a neutral ground flora. Hornbeam coppice with some oak standards (both species) occurs on another area of clay with a predominantly calcicolous ground flora. Valley sides have local woodland types, including high forest of oak and beech, and of small-leaved elm, ash and crab apple. Taken as a whole the flora is extremely rich, with a wide ecological range, including heather and *Galeobdolon luteum*.

This site is close to and comparable with Blean Wood.

Botanically, there is probably little to choose between the two, but Blean Wood is better known zoologically and is therefore chosen as the grade 1 site.

W.17. ASHBURNHAM PARK, SUSSEX
TQ 6914, TQ 7016.   110 ha   Grade 2

Ashburnham is a former mediaeval deer park lying on Tunbridge Wells Sandstone and Wadhurst Clay, much of which is now arable. The woodland is of two types, (1) closed, high forest of oak, beech, birch and holly with planted sweet chestnut, and (2) very old, open oak–beech woodland. Both types are overmature and contain a rich assemblage of epiphytic lichens, second only to those in Eridge Park, including species characteristically on holly which are not so well developed east of the New Forest. The ground flora is limited, but includes *Dryopteris aemula* on sandstone. In its general character and many other features this site is similar to the ancient oak–beech–holly woods of the New Forest.

W.18. PARHAM PARK, SUSSEX
TQ 0514.   280 ha   Grade 2

Parham Park lies on Folkestone Sands at the foot of the South Downs. It is a mediaeval deer park which still contains deer. Parts of the woodland comprise open forest of huge, ancient oaks, probably the best remaining stand of overmature oaks in south-east England. North Park Wood is closed canopy high forest of beech and oak with an understorey of holly. Despite the presence of sheltered valleys, the vascular flora is very limited, but the epiflora is richer than all other sites in the south-east except Eridge Park and Ashburnham Park. Among the 103 lichen species are *Thelopsis rubella* and *Ophegrapha rufescens*, known nowhere else east of the New Forest.

W.19. STAFFHURST WOOD, SURREY
TQ 4148.   50 ha   Grade 2

Staffhurst is a former common woodland lying on Weald Clay. Structurally it is very irregular coppice-with-standards in which cutting has been sporadic rather than systematic. The dominant species, pedunculate oak, beech and hornbeam, all occur as standards, but only the latter two have been coppiced. The shrub layer, in addition to the coppice species, contains holly and yew. Throughout the wood the ground flora is dominated by bramble, bracken and bluebell. Two subsidiary woodland types also occur. On the western side is a small area of open woodland of ancient oaks and yew, with a number of epiphytic lichens. On low-lying base-rich and partly flushed areas a mixed deciduous woodland with oak, hornbeam, ash, field maple and wild service occurs over a ground flora including *Brachypodium sylvaticum*, *Mercurialis perennis*, *Primula vulgaris* and *Sanicula europaea*, with the local sedge *Carex strigosa*. Marginal to the Staffhurst Common is Butcherswood Bank, a small area of hazel and hornbeam coppice with oak and birch as standards.

Taken as a whole, this wood is important as one of the few woods with a wide range of structural types and age classes, associated with a range of field layer communities.

W.20. COLYERS HANGER, SURREY
TQ 0448.   35 ha   Grade 2

This wood occupies a south-facing slope running down to the River Tillingbourne. Like Scords Wood it has a range of woodland types zoned on this slope to correspond with marked differences in soil nutrient status and water content. The highest zone over dry, sandy soil is oak woodland over a field layer dominated by bracken. The intermediate zone is mixed deciduous woodland of oak standards and hazel coppice with wych elm, ash and field maple over a basiphilous ground flora including *Mercurialis perennis*, *Adoxa moschatellina* and *Campanula trachelium*. On a springline below is alder woodland containing *Chrysosplenium oppositifolium*, *C. alternifolium*, *Equisetum telmateia* and *Cardamine amara*.

This site is selected partly to represent eutrophic alder carr in the south-east, where it is particularly characteristic of springlines and the floors of gills and valleys. It is, however, preferred to other, more extensive alder carrs in the district (e.g. at Iping) because of the diversity of woodland types present, related to geological diversity in the escarpment at different levels.

W.21. GLOVER'S WOOD, SURREY
TQ 2240.   95 ha   Grade 2

This is a substantial wood which lies on neutral and mildly acid clays across the incised valley of the Welland Gill. Two main woodland types may be distinguished. On the steep-sided gill there is hornbeam coppice with a limited proportion of ash, wych elm, maple, hazel and small-leaved lime, and a ground flora with *Galeobdolon luteum*, *Endymion non-scriptus*, *Rubus*-Section *Sylvatici* and patches of *Mercurialis perennis*. This woodland appears to be primary, and can be distinguished from the plateau woodland which has developed in the last century or more on abandoned fields. Much of the plateau woodland is of birch, hazel and pedunculate oak, but numerous other tree and shrub species are present, including hornbeam, which is now invading from the former hedgerows. The ground flora is mainly *Rubus*-Section *Sylvatici*, honeysuckle and small patches of bracken.

This site is one of many in the Weald with a mixture of primary and secondary woodland, and relatively uniform coppices. It is selected partly because of its large size and also because it has small populations of lime and wych elm which are rare in the Weald.

SOUTH ENGLAND

W.22. BRADENHAM WOODS, BUCKINGHAMSHIRE
SU 8397.   180 ha   Grade 1

The Bradenham Woods are examples of plateau and dip slope Chiltern woodlands, comprised of the three almost contiguous Naphill, Bradenham and Park Woods. As a group they are believed to be the best example of this type in the Chilterns.

Naphill Common is an oak (*Quercus robur* and *Q. petraea*)–beech woodland with some birch. Holly and cherry also reach the canopy though they are more frequently present in the understorey with elder, willow, whitebeam, rowan and yew. Bramble with wood sorrel, bracken and honeysuckle are abundant in the field layer and heather, unusual in this area, is present in the rides. Apparently in the 1890s parts of this wood were open, with gorse and juniper 4.5–6 m high.

Bradenham Wood is a well-grown dip slope beechwood north of Naphill Common with occasional sycamore, pedunculate oak and whitebeam. Both beech and oak are regenerating. One area has been clear-felled (1969) and young beech has been planted at 120 cm intervals. The ground flora is predominantly bramble–wood sorrel though much of the ground is litter covered. Many other calcifuge species are common, including heather, foxglove and *Potentilla erecta*. A dew pond at the summit and Sarsen pits add to the variety of habitat.

Park Wood lies north of Bradenham and is separated from it by an RAF housing estate. A small area of scrub grassland, managed by the Berkshire, Buckinghamshire and Oxfordshire Naturalists' Trust, is at the north-west corner. The beech woodland is richer in shrub and herbaceous species than Bradenham and regeneration of both beech and pedunculate oak is taking place. Other canopy species present are sycamore, ash and yew, The trees, at 160 years, are some of the oldest in the Chilterns. Shrub species include field maple, clematis, hazel, holly, privet, gean, willow, wayfaring tree and guelder rose. The field layer consists mainly of *Galeobdolon luteum*–*Geranium robertianum*–*Rubus fruticosus*–*Mercurialis perennis*–*Sanicula europaea* with sheets of ivy in places.

W.23. WINDSOR FOREST, BERKSHIRE
SU 9373.　710 ha　　　　　　　　　　　　　　　Grade 1

An area of 3150 ha of Windsor Forest is managed commercially by the Crown Estate. Of this, approximately 1200 ha consists mainly of oak woodland or mixed woodland in which the oak complement will be progressively enhanced by thinning. At High Standing Hill 18 ha of unmanaged woodland contain oak and overmature beech in the best surviving piece of the original Forest. This extends farther west on either side of a stream valley where remnants of old beech–oak woodland predominate with an epiphytic lichen flora of 58 species, including some old-forest relics. The ancient oaks of The Parks have a number of other lichen species. Although the ground flora tends to be poor on the Bagshot Sands such areas have proved outstanding for oak regeneration.

Windsor Forest probably ranks second only to the New Forest with regard to the richness of its insect fauna. It is particularly noted for many rare beetles associated with the old oaks and Donisthorpe (1939) published an impressive list. With more recent additions the total number of Coleoptera recorded from the forest must number close on 2000 species. Some very rare beetles are known in this country only from the Windsor and Sherwood Forests. With the destruction of most of the latter, species such as *Teredus cylindricus* and *Cryptocephalus querceti* may only be able to survive in Windsor. Although individual entomologists would probably nominate particular areas as outstanding from their particular specialist point of view, it is the size of the Forest as a whole, forming a nucleus within a much larger area of well-wooded countryside, that is of paramount importance. The maintenance of the high entomological importance of this area depends on sufficient oak and beech trees being allowed to become overmature, die, and rot *in situ*, as is the present management practice.

W.24. WYCHWOOD FOREST, OXFORDSHIRE
SP 3316.　261 ha　　　　　　　　　　　　　　　Grade 1

This large block of woodland was formerly a Royal Forest, disafforested as late as 1858. It is a complex area ecologically, this complexity arising first from the variety of soil types derived from the limestone, clays, marls, sands and siliceous drifts on which it lies, and also from differences in management. Much, if not all, of the woods were managed as coppice-with-standards but this has now largely disappeared and the old coppice boundaries have been obscured by more recent developments. Parts of the woodland are now oakwood with a proportion of ash, but large areas are dominated by hawthorn (both species and hybrids). Many other types of scrub occur, including blackthorn, willow, field maple and elder, the existence of which appears to be a direct result of different forms of management. Numerous exotic species of both soft and hard woods have been introduced in recent decades. Floristically, Wychwood is fairly rich, the variety of ground flora communities reflecting not only the variety of soils and tree cover, but also the presence of glades. It is an important site for the lichens of old woodland. The small marl ponds within the forest are given grade 2 for their open water interest (OW.11). (See Appendix.)

W.25. WATERPERRY WOOD, OXFORDSHIRE
SP 6009, SP 6008.　135 ha　　　　　　　　　　　Grade 1

Waterperry Wood is part of Bernwood Forest where extensive insect records go back for 100 years or more. Bernwood Forest is famous for its Lepidoptera, which include rarities such as the purple emperor and black hairstreak butterflies. Waterperry is a deciduous high forest lying on gently sloping land on an outcrop of Oxford Clay, and is dominated by pedunculate oak with ash, elm, aspen and birch. It is similar floristically to other clay woodlands such as Monks Wood, but it is unlikely that Monks Wood can duplicate its entomological value. Much of it has been planted with conifers although a final crop of oak is planned.

W.26. NEW FOREST, HAMPSHIRE
SU 20.　12600 ha　　　　　　　　　　　　　　　Grade 1*

This former Royal Forest lies on Tertiary sands, gravels and clays dissected by wide, shallow valleys. Its soil types encompass a considerable range from relatively base-rich brown earths to extremely acidic podsols, and from these to waterlogged clays, alluvium and acidic peats in flushed and low-lying situations. Only part of this area is wooded though the woods are extensive: within the New Forest as a whole the tracts of grassland, heathland and valley mire grade into woodland, forming a tremendous variety of transitional habitats of scientific importance. The woodlands themselves are partly unenclosed, these being known as the Ancient and Ornamental Woodlands, and managed largely for amenity and nature conservation, and partly within enclosures: the remainder, the Statutory Inclosures, are mostly managed commercially, but include a number of scientifically important sites.

The woodlands are of different types. The most extensive are mature and overmature stands of beech, pedunculate oak, sessile oak, and any combination of these (though it is rare to find both oaks together), with an understorey of holly and rarely other species such as yew and hawthorn. Structurally these are diverse, with a range of age classes from saplings to ancient, overmature trees, many of which have been pollarded. Over some sites on base-rich clays, ash and less commonly field maple are important constituents, but hazel, formerly common, is now rare within the unenclosed woodlands. The ground flora in the woodlands on acid soils is very poor, often no more than patchy *Leucobryum glaucum*, but on the deeper soils bramble and bracken may be abundant, and on base-rich clays a fairly rich basiphilous flora may develop.

Less extensive woodland types fall into four broad categories. In valley bottoms with alkaline and neutral ground water, alder carrs have developed, some with a rich, marsh flora including *Impatiens noli-tangere* and the national rarity *Ludwigia palustris*: many of these have been coppiced until recently, but there are some with a range of age classes, including very old trees. Scrub, dominated by holly, but also including yew, whitebeam and hawthorn, has developed on the better, reasonably well-drained soils, and is in many places developing into a mixed woodland with pedunculate oak dominant. Self-sown pinewoods occur on the more heathy areas and into areas of wet heath. Birch woodlands, though not uncommon, are found mainly around the margins of the larger stands of mature woodland.

The vascular flora of the New Forest woodlands is, with few exceptions, composed of widely occurring plants. Species of biogeographical interest in addition to the two species mentioned above include ferns such as *Thelypteris phegopteris* and *T. palustris* which are local in southern England. It is the cryptogamic flora of the New Forest that is extraordinarily rich. The bryophyte flora includes some rare species, e.g. *Zygodon forsteri*. In recent surveys over 180 species of epiphytic lichens have been recorded by F. Rose, including numerous species characteristic of ancient woodland (e.g. *Lobaria pulmonaria*), oceanic species reaching their eastern limit in the New Forest (e.g. *Sticta limbata*), hyper-oceanic species formerly thought to be confined to west Scotland, Wales or western Ireland (e.g. *Mycoporellum sparsellum*), boreal species not otherwise found south of north Wales, e.g. *Alectoria subcana* and

Pertusaria velata which is now apparently extinct elsewhere in Britain.

The New Forest woodlands are of international importance. In the lowland areas of north-west Europe, no area equals them in extent of old woodlands, the number of overmature trees, the relative lack of human interference over a long period, the invertebrate fauna and the epiphytic lichen flora. The woods are also an important breeding area for birds, with the honey buzzard and hobby as notable rare species. The scientific importance of the New Forest lies mainly in the unenclosed woodlands. The enclosed woodlands, with the exception of two areas enclosed early and still retaining their ancient woodland, are not so rich floristically although they have some important features (e.g. *Pulmonaria longifolia* and *Illecebrum verticillatum* in some rides). The Ancient and Ornamental Woodlands, and to a lesser but still significant extent the Statutory Inclosures, support a rich invertebrate fauna which is in many respects unique in Britain. The groups particularly well represented are the Heteroptera, Homoptera, Lepidoptera, Hymenoptera (Aculeata and Symphyta), Diptera and Coleoptera. The fauna of dead and dying wood is of especial importance. Although the greatest interest naturally attaches to the insects associated with deciduous trees, especially oak, the fauna of the conifers, particularly Scots pine, is by no means negligible. This is a famous area for Lepidoptera and contains the only British localities for the interesting insect *Cicadetta montana*.

The scientific value of the unenclosed and ancient woods results in part from their great extent and variety and therefore the selection of areas of outstanding importance within the complex must be carried out with caution. Present knowledge indicates that the biologically richer sites within the complex include Vinney Ridge, Mark Ash, Eyeworth Wood, Rufus Stone, Hollands Wood, Whitley Wood, Denny Wood, Mallerd Wood, Linwood, Bramshaw Wood, and South Bentley Inclosure.

See also L.20, OW.6, and P.3.

W.27. SELBORNE HANGER, HAMPSHIRE
SU 7333. 95 ha   Grade 1

Selborne Hanger lies on the north-east-facing Chalk scarp overlooking the western limits of the Weald. It consists of a pure beechwood on a steep east-facing Chalk slope grading to Clay-with-Flints on a plateau with a more mixed woodland. The beech is of uniform age and 30 m tall, with a poorly developed shrub layer of hazel and yew. The most abundant plants are dog's mercury, ivy and bramble, with *Sanicula europaea* and *Brachypodium sylvaticum* locally abundant. The plateau is wooded common land with oak and ash, hazel and hawthorn over a field layer of *Rubus fruticosus–Galeobdolon luteum*. (Selborne Hanger is associated with Gilbert White.)

Selborne Hanger should be considered with Noar Hill (L.50) and High Wood Hangers. These are not contiguous with Selborne but lie on the Chalk scarp about a kilometre to the south. Within this beechwood there is almost a complete range of aspects. The beech is uneven aged, but casts a dense shade which has allowed only local development of an understorey. Here yew is common, but many species are confined to the wood margin. *Mercurialis perennis, Sanicula europaea, Galium odoratum* and *Hedera helix* are the most abundant field layer species.

Noar Hill has the advantage that it is adjacent to floristically rich chalk grassland, whereas Selborne has the additional plateau woodland feature.

W.28. BURNHAM BEECHES, BUCKINGHAMSHIRE

SU 9585. 450 ha   Grade 2

This woodland occupies a low plateau intersected by shallow valleys, on coarse gravelly sands derived from Reading Beds and areas of superimposed plateau gravel. Structurally the woods are very diverse with ancient pollards, closed stands of younger but mature woodland, old coppice and scrub by open grassland. Beech is the most abundant species, with pedunculate oak, birch and holly also locally abundant. The field layer is sparse, with mainly calcifuge species such as *Deschampsia flexuosa, Luzula pilosa*, bracken and in open areas heather and other heathland species. Although it is so close to London, it retains a moderately rich epiphytic lichen flora, including *Graphis elegans* and *Thelotrema lepadinum*. The rare moss *Zygodon forsteri* is also recorded.

This wood has similarities to the New Forest, but differs structurally and is inferior in extent, diversity and floristics and so is not an alternative site.

W.29. ASTON ROWANT WOODS, BUCKINGHAMSHIRE/OXFORDSHIRE

SU 7598. 275 ha   Grade 2

Grove Wood is a scarp woodland dominated by tall vigorous beech. It appears to be even aged (123–169 years), and below gaps in the canopy there is a field layer of dog's mercury. Ash, sycamore and some beech regeneration occurs. Small groups of ash and one of common elm are present, *Salix capraea* is abundant in some wet sites and whitebeam is occasional in the canopy. Mature sycamore is absent but regeneration of this species is profuse in places. The shrub layer is not prominent and locally is lacking altogether. It consists of characteristic chalkland species such as elder, broom, buckthorn, hazel, box, field maple and whitebeam.

Upper Grove Wood lies on the plateau and, though pedunculate oak is the commonest species, the canopy contains frequent ash and beech with coppiced small-leaved lime, gean, hornbeam and hawthorn. Saplings of all these species, except oak, are present: *Paris quadrifolia* grows here.

Aston Wood forms a curving rectangular block facing north-west, to the south of and above the A40 trunk road. It is contiguous with the present NNR. Beech (90–150 years old) dominates the western two-thirds, but a number of other species share the canopy. Oak, whitebeam, sycamore and hornbeam are rare but ash and gean are locally abundant, filling in gaps left by selective felling. In addition to ash and gean, beech, sycamore and elder saplings are present, and some of the young beech is now 20–25 years old. Holly, hawthorn and elder form a sparse understorey

with rowan and hazel coppice stools in a depression at the eastern end. The eastern one-third of Aston Wood is dominated by ash, though beech occurs frequently and oak is abundant. Mixed with these are a few sycamore, gean, Norway spruce, elder, holly and large coppiced rowans. The boundary between the two parts of Aston Wood is marked by three large lime stools and a number of young trees.

On a narrow strip of sloping ground between the A40 and the old sunk way down the escarpment, lies a woodland of great ecological diversity. Beech and numerous pole ash form the canopy with some sycamore, and there is a thicket of blackthorn, a group of poorly grown larch, a group of common elm and poplar. There is some sapling horse chestnut, whitebeam and a stand of large field maple and shrubs include dogwood, wayfaring tree, hawthorn and elder.

Kingston Wood, one the largest woods in the area, extends down the scarp slope from the plateau. Beech dominates the plateau woodland but pedunculate oak is frequent and ash occasional. Regeneration of beech, ash, bird cherry and willow is taking place in the gaps. Sycamore invasion is at present being discouraged. In contrast, much of the scarp woodland is pure beech, forming large areas of unbroken canopy, therefore excluding both the shrub layer and regeneration. Crowell Hill Wood is virtually a pure beechwood and on the whole not of outstanding interest though it contains a number of chalkland herbs, notably *Ophrys insectifera* and *Epipactis purpurata*.

Crowell Wood is a large block of woodland, most of which is situated on a north-east-facing dip slope. Beech is dominant throughout but occasional ash, oak and cherry share the canopy. Drastic thinning occurred during the First World War and probably resulted in the dense growth of bramble which covers the ground and may have prevented immediate regeneration.

High Wood is another dip slope woodland dominated by beech but, unlike Crowell, bramble is rare in the ground flora and the canopy is very dense. Ash is occasional and oak occurs on the upper areas. Elder forms a sparse understorey.

See also L.21.

W.30. WINDSOR HILL, BUCKINGHAMSHIRE

SU 8202. 85 ha   Grade 2

This is a mature beechwood on the south-facing Chalk scarp about 3 km from the Bradenham Woods. It is similar to parts of the Aston Rowant Woods, but includes the only Chiltern station of *Cephalanthera rubra*, a species of biogeographical importance. Although it is clearly a separate site, it could be considered with Bradenham Woods: taken together these include most of the range of diversity in Chiltern beechwoods.

W.31. SAVERNAKE FOREST, WILTSHIRE

SU 2366. 930 ha   Grade 2

Savernake was one of the ancient Royal Forests, and is largely managed commercially. Most of the area lies on Clay-with-Flints. The woodland is open pedunculate oak, with numerous huge and ancient trees, which has recently been interplanted with oak. As in most ancient parkland woods the ground flora is limited, but the epiphytic lichen flora is outstandingly rich, over 100 species having been recorded recently by F. Rose. It includes species of a more continental distribution than are found in the more coastal New Forest, e.g. *Caloplaca herbidella*. Amongst the bryophytes are the local species *Pterogonium gracile* and *Dicranum montanum*.

Though this site is of less importance than the New Forest, the average age of its oaks is considerably greater and the epiphytes are less oceanic.

W.32. CRANBORNE CHASE, WILTSHIRE/DORSET
ST 9619. 680 ha   Grade 2

Cranborne Chase is a large wooded tract lying over Chalk along the Wiltshire–Dorset county boundary. Within this the Rushmore Park Estate comprises a large wooded plateau area and slopes leading down to chalk grassland in the valley. The woodland includes what may be the largest remaining area of worked hazel coppice, with pedunculate oak and some ash and maple standards. On the plateau Clay-with-Flints soil there is high forest of pedunculate oak and some beech. In the valley, grading into open grassland, is closed woodland of ash and field maple with some pedunculate oak, beech, yew and holly and some coppiced hazel. The ground flora throughout is rich with abundant *Mercurialis perennis*, *Sanicula europaea* and *Galium odoratum*. The ash–maple woodland is notable for epiphytes, with abundant *Viscum album* and the local cryptogams *Leptodon smithii*, *Lobaria pulmonaria* and *Sticta limbata*.

EAST ANGLIA

W.33. HINTLESHAM WOODS, SUFFOLK   Grade 1

(*a*) *Hintlesham and Ramsey Woods*
TM 0743. 80 ha
(*b*) *Wolves Wood*
TM 0544. 40 ha

These distinct woodlands are separated by less than 0.5 km of arable land and as they are complementary they have been considered as a single aggregate site. The larger wood is a complex of two ancient woods, Hintlesham and Ramsey, and secondary woodland of various dates surrounding and linking the two ancient nuclei. Wolves Wood is likewise mainly ancient woodland with some secondary extensions, which probably include the small Keeble's Grove, continuous with Wolves Wood.

These woods lie on boulder clay of a lighter and less chalky type than is found in the east Midlands and western parts of East Anglia. The clay soil is mainly neutral or mildly acidic with only small areas of a calcareous nature. Much of the woodland is the oak–hazel–birch combination with much ash on the wetter sites, but the heavier, neutral or slightly calcareous soils have relatively little birch and some maple. Other calcifuge coppice types occur, notably lime coppice in Hintlesham Wood and hornbeam coppice mainly in Wolves Wood. Part of Wolves Wood occupies a

basin situation in which the water table is high and aspen and willows are abundant in the coppice. In addition there is a series of secondary elm woodland in the Hintlesham part, and a series of elm coppice types in the ancient parts of Wolves Wood, some of which have apparently invaded other coppice types whilst others are evidently non-invasive and of local origin. There is a range of ground flora communities corresponding with the wide range of edaphic conditions, which includes a number of local woodland species such as *Paris quadrifolia* and *Helleborus viridis*.

These woods have an unusually complex system of earthworks and apparently have a good historical record. Only Ramsey is a complete ancient wood, but a substantial portion of the other ancient woods have survived. All the existing woodland is semi-natural. Many primary woods or parts thereof survive in east Suffolk, and a proportion of them have been examined in detail recently, but none has been found which surpasses these two as examples of the coppice types on the lighter glacial deposits.

W.34. STAVERTON PARK, SUFFOLK
TM 3550. 85 ha   Grade 1

This site lies on freely drained, glacial sands wholly within the boundary of a former mediaeval park. Documentary evidence suggests that this is one of the few sites on the Suffolk Sandlings which contains primary woodland. This is supported by the absence of a podsol profile in an area where such soils are widespread following woodland clearance, and by the presence of a rich assemblage of corticolous and lignicolous lichens.

The existing woods are in two parts. The Park is occupied by open woodland of ancient pollarded oaks (*Quercus robur*) and holly, with local dominance of mature birch (both species) over a poor ground flora dominated by bracken and *Holcus mollis*. The Thicks has developed from this in the last 170 years, by an upsurge of holly, which now forms an almost closed canopy with the oak, beneath which ground flora is absent. Among these are some huge hollies, reaching over 21 m in height and over 3 m in girth. Indeed, the site is remarkable for the profusion of individuals of oak, holly birch, rowan and hawthorn sharing the extreme forms adopted by these species after long and vigorous growth. The only locally rare vascular plant is *Corydalis claviculata*, but the epiphytic lichen flora includes a number of rare and Atlantic species, such as *Haematomma elatinum*, *Lecanora cinnabarina*, *Thelotrema lepadinum*, *Phaeographis ramificans*, *Stenocybe septata*, *Phlyctis agelaea* and *Opegrapha lyncea*.

In addition to the floristic and historical interest, Staverton Park and its immediate environment have a number of relatively rare birds, such as sparrowhawk and stone curlew. The invertebrate fauna is unknown in detail but on casual inspection appears to be rich.

W.35. FELSHAMHALL AND MONKS PARK WOODS, SUFFOLK
TL 9357. 70 ha   Grade 1*

These two contiguous woodlands are ancient primary woodland which has been managed as coppice and coppice-with-standards for many centuries, but unlike most other woods of similar origins in East Anglia, these have been coppiced on a commercial scale up to the present time and have thus suffered less floristic deterioration than those sites in which the coppice cycle has been discontinued. Felshamhall is almost certainly the demesne wood of Bury St Edmunds Abbey and Monks Park is likewise a park given to the Abbey in the early twelfth century.

Four main types of woodland have been distinguished: (1) the typical oak–ash–hazel–maple-type of the boulder clay woods; (2) a wet variant of this, with alder and *Salix alba* (this feature is very unusual); (3) an oak–birch woodland where the boulder clay gives way to sand and sandy gravel; and (4) secondary woodland, occupying the sites of former clearings which were the launds of the old mediaeval park. Associated with these types are distinctive ground flora communities and important transition types, including the *Primula elatior–Filipendula ulmaria–Mercurialis perennis* association widespread in these woods. In this site bluebell is unusually rare. Bracken and *Sarothamnus scoparius* occur on the sand, and a totally distinctive assemblage with *Neottia nidus-avis* marks the secondary woodland. A total of over 280 species of vascular plants has so far been recorded, including all the tree species of the primaeval mixed oak forest.

Historical evidence of woodland continuity is good. Coppicing was practised at least as early as the thirteenth century. As in many boulder clay woods, the oak standards were felled some time ago and not replaced, but unusually a good natural crop of young oaks is developing to restore the oak canopy.

The fauna is apparently unknown, though among the birds there is an obvious abundance of woodland warblers, but on botanical and historical grounds alone this site is regarded as the most important of the ancient boulder clay woods of East Anglia. Its vascular flora is already known to be richer than almost every other wood in eastern England. The record of its existence and management is unusually detailed as far back as the twelfth century. As such it is a site of both botanical and archaeological importance.

W.36. CAVENHAM–TUDDENHAM WOODS, SUFFOLK
TL 7573.   80 ha   Grade 1

Woodland forms an important component of the interesting habitat complex of this Breckland site, and shows a range of types seral to dry heath and to rich-fen. The dry parts of both heaths have a good deal of birchwood (of both birch species), varying considerably in stature and stocking density of the trees. There are dense thickets and pole stands with little but litter beneath, but more open birch growths have either bracken or heather with well-developed carpets of the common acidophilous heath and woodland mosses. On Tuddenham Heath, dense swards of *Carex arenaria* occur within the birchwoods in places. There are scattered trees of Scots pine and oak, but though oak seedlings are numerous on the heaths, few survive, perhaps as a result of roe deer browsing or unfavourable soil conditions.

Where the ground becomes damper, there is a change

beneath the birch to a field layer with *Deschampsia cespitosa, Molinia caerulea, Agrostis stolonifera* and abundant *Lonicera periclymenum*. There are ferns such as *Dryopteris austriaca, D. spinulosa, D. filix-mas* and *Athyrium filix-femina*, and mosses here include *Eurhynchium praelongum, Mnium hornum, M. undulatum* and *Aulacomnium androgynum*. In still wetter places within the birchwoods, there are transitions to fen communities with *Phragmites communis, Filipendula ulmaria, Lycopus europaeus, Mentha aquatica, Eupatorium cannabinum, Iris pseudacorus, Urtica dioica, Equisetum palustre* and *Carex acutiformis*. Ash plantation probably has less ash than formerly, as there are some large dead trees of this species, but ash and alder are mixed with birch in the damper part of this wood, which also has an abundance of *Thelypteris palustris*. Towards the River Lark (OW.19), the birchwoods give way to dense areas of willow carr, mainly of *Salix cinerea*, which grade into open fen communities.

W.37. SOTTERLEY PARK, SUFFOLK
TM 4685.   205 ha   Grade 1

This is one of the finest examples of the deer park habitat remaining in East Anglia. The park is at least of early mediaeval origin and hence may have been formed by the enclosure of more or less primary forest. The records indicate that it was even more wooded in the seventeenth and eighteenth centuries than it is today but it still contains numbers of ancient oaks and areas of old woodland.

Four main habitat types are recognised in the park:
(i) The ornamental landscaped garden area around the gardens of the Hall itself with both woodland and open parkland areas containing native trees and some exotics such as walnut.
(ii) The open parkland north-west of the Hall with avenues and groups of elms and ash trees, many of which are of great age, and also some sycamore.
(iii) The areas of very old oak woodland, or oak in open canopy in which are also old ash trees.
(iv) Areas of enclosed woodland largely oak but with beech, chestnut, hazel and other trees.
Of these four habitats the first three are most important. Many of the oaks are of huge size and great age and the epiflora is very rich. The fourth type appears less rich but needs further study.

The epiphyte flora of 89 species of lichens and 14 bryophytes is the richest known in East Anglia today for an area of comparable size. The most notable lichens are *Anaptychia ciliaris, Calicium abietinum, Chaenotheca brunneola, Normandia pulchella, Opegrapha sonedufera,* and *Ramalina fraxinea*. Other species found in abundance here include *Opegrapha lyncea, Rinodina roborus* and *Hechancha premnea*.

W.38. BURE MARSHES, NORFOLK
TG 3316.   245 ha   Grade 1

Alder occurs extensively sometimes in association with ash, pedunculate oak and birch, and the shrubs include buckthorn, alder buckthorn, guelder rose and grey sallow.

Species of *Ribes* (*R. nigrum, R. silvestre* and *R. uva-crispa*) occur and are very characteristic of this woodland type as are the climbers *Calystegia sepium, Humulus lupulus* and *Solanum dulcamara*. The field layer contains *Carex paniculata, Iris pseudacorus, Urtica dioica* and *Thelypteris palustris*.

The alder woodland here is probably the best example of its type in Britain, showing as it does a complete range of successional stages from open marsh, together with floristic richness. The site has also been given grade 1* status as a peatland (P.7).

W.39. SWANTON NOVERS WOODS, NORFOLK
TG 0131.   65 ha   Grade 1*

This wood straddles a geological boundary between glacial sands and gravels to the north and calcareous boulder clay at the southern end. Correlated with this is the boundary between two contrasting woodland types. On the acid sands and gravels, coppice-with-standards with both species of oak in intimate mixture forms a closed canopy over *Pteridium aquilinum, Lonicera periclymenum, Convallaria majalis* and *Calluna vulgaris* with *Teucrium scorodonia* along the rides. Mixed deciduous woodland grows over the mildly acid and neutral boulder clay: this is coppice-with-standards with both oak species as standards over mixed coppice of small-leaved lime, ash, maple and willow. The ground flora here comprises *Filipendula ulmaria, Geum rivale, Ranunculus repens* on the damp areas, and *Mercurialis perennis, Endymion non-scriptus* on the drier transition to the sands. In a very wet site on the western margin a third woodland type with oak, alder and bird-cherry exists. Floristically the site is exceptionally rich with at least 25 native tree and shrub species, and a number of rare and local herbs, notably *Maianthemum bifolium* in what is almost certainly a native location. Many bryophytes and epiphytic lichens have been recorded, but most of the species are common and widespread.

Swanton Novers is undoubtedly an important site, containing three woodland types, each of which on its own would have been enough to justify selection. Furthermore, the mixed coppice is still actively worked, but a small block has been felled and replanted with conifers. It is almost certainly a primary woodland site and as such constitutes an important contrast with the more widespread type of oak–ash–maple–hazel primary woodland.

W.40. HAYLEY WOOD, CAMBRIDGESHIRE
TL 2953.   50 ha   Grade 1

Hayley Wood stands on the Chalky Boulder Clay plateau on soil which is heavy and waterlogged or flooded for much of the year. Structurally it is coppice-with-standards, with both large coppice of field maple and ash and small coppice of hazel and hawthorn below a thin canopy of pedunculate oak standards. Small areas have been invaded by *Ulmus carpinifolia* over the last 200 years. The ground vegetation forms concentric zones from the wet middle and north, dominated by oxlip and *Filipendula ulmaria*, to the drier eastern, southern and western fringes dominated by dog's

mercury. The intermediate zones have the richest plant communities, with tracts of bluebell and *Galeobdolon luteum*. The coppice plots in the wetter area have luxuriant vegetation resembling fen communities, with *Cirsium palustre, Ranunculus flammula* and *Galium palustre*. A number of rare and local species occur, including *Melampyrum cristatum, Serratula tinctoria, Sedum telephium, Ophioglossum vulgatum* and *Centaurium pulchellum*. About 250 species of vascular plant have been recorded, including 29 native tree and shrub species.

Hayley is one of the largest of the boulder clay woods. It has perhaps the largest single population of oxlip, and this in a site lacking primrose. It has a rich bryophyte flora for eastern England, notable for the inclusion of *Nowellia curvifolia*. It is almost wholly an ancient wood, with a recorded history of over 700 years, embodying the typical features of other ancient coppice woods in the vicinity. Furthermore, it has been used for research and teaching for many years. It is one of a number of boulder clay coppice woods selected, which cover a range of soil types from very light (Swanton Novers Woods), light (Hintlesham Woods) to heavy (Hayley Wood) and transitional to fen carr (Felshamhall and Monks Park Woods, where there is a range of conditions, including light soils).

W.41. HOLME FEN, HUNTINGDONSHIRE
TL 2189.   260 ha   Grade 1

The NNR of Holme Fen lies partly on the site of the former Whittlesey Mere. After drainage, part of the area was used for agriculture and later abandoned. Since then, extensive birchwoods (both species) have developed, which now constitute the finest development of this type of woodland in lowland Britain. Other tree species are present (oak, alder, willow and pine) in some areas, but in general the birch woodland is remarkably pure. Another feature, which is particularly valuable for experimental research, is the fact that stands of different ages are present, covering almost the entire life span of birch.

The area is additionally interesting as a relict location of raised mire species, including *Sphagnum* sp. and *Calluna vulgaris*. A recent survey has shown that Holme Fen is exceptionally rich in fungus species, including *Naucoria langei* which has been added to the British list.

Excavations for a new pond to supplement the existing duck decoy are well advanced. When completed this will be an important feature of the reserve and of the area generally.

W.42. MONKS WOOD, HUNTINGDONSHIRE
TL 2080.   157 ha   Grade 1

Centred on the Oxford Clay dip slope on the edge of the Fens, Monks Wood embodies the typical features of ancient woodlands of the Huntingdon area. It is predominantly an ash–pedunculate oak wood with local dominance of elm. It has been managed as coppice-with-standards, but in recent decades the system fell into neglect and the big timber was largely extracted and not replaced. A wide range of tree and shrub species occurs, including maple, aspen, wild service, birch (both species), hawthorn (both species and hybrids), many willows, hazel, guelder rose, wayfaring tree, spindle, privet, blackthorn and dogwood. The ground flora is extremely rich, ranging from dog's mercury on the well-drained sites to *Filipendula ulmaria* on the waterlogged areas, and diversified by the presence of rides, streams, ponds, overgrown old fields and small glades. Oxlip is absent although primrose is common: Monks Wood is evidently just outside the tolerance of oxlip. Recently, the management has partially restored the coppicing cycle, and with it the herb richness associated with the years following cutting. In addition to its floristic richness, Monks Wood has long been famous entomologically. Among the species for which it is noted is the black hairstreak *Strymonidia pruni*, which was first collected here in Britain, but the purple emperor has not been seen for some years. In certain years there is a large breeding population of woodcock, and the wood is still a good locality for the nightingale.

W.43. BEDFORD PURLIEUS GROUP, NORTHAMPTON-
SHIRE, HUNTINGDON AND PETERBOROUGH
Grade 1

(a) *Bedford Purlieus*
TL 0499. 185 ha

(b) *Wittering Coppice*
TF 0200. 15 ha

(c) *Easton Hornstocks*
TF 0100. 50 ha

(d) *Collyweston Great Wood*
TF 0000. 145 ha

The royal forest of Rockingham once comprised an extensive tract of semi-natural coppices, some of which were in large, continuous woods many thousands of hectares in extent. These have now been fragmented by clearance and opencast mining, and most of the surviving woods have been converted to plantations. Of the remaining stands of semi-natural woodland, only the former Purlieu Woods at the north-eastern extremity of the forest are of outstanding importance. These formed one continuous woodland until the mid nineteenth century when the clearance of the western half of Thornhaw Woods cut the woods into two main blocks, Bedford Purlieus to the east and Easton Hornstocks to the west.

These woods lie mainly on Jurassic limestone covered in places by clay drift with patches of sand. Thus, although the soils tend to be calcareous and poorly drained, there are appreciable areas of freely drained soils of a variety of texture, and some tracts of acidic, sandy soils. The coppice in consequence includes a wide range of types including lime coppice on soils which are appreciably more calcareous than most of its eastern locations, ash, hazel, wych elm, maple coppice on calcareous clays, birch and poplar groves, sessile oak–hazel coppice on acidic sands, valley *Ulmus procera* woodland and extensive areas of sycamore invasion.

Bedford Purlieus is clearly the most important part of the group. Structurally it is very limited, having been clear-felled in recent decades and partly replanted. Its outstanding feature is its assemblage of herbaceous species (over 450 species of vascular plants have been recorded), which include *Euphorbia lathyrus*, a species of national rarity, *Melica nutans* at the southern edge of its range, and *E. amygdaloides* towards its northern limit. Within this wood both calcicolous and calcifuge species occur together with those found more commonly in northern and western woodlands, including *Galium odoratum*, *Melampyrum pratense*, *Platanthera chlorantha*, *Allium ursinum*, *Convallaria majalis*, *Aquilegia vulgaris*, *Ophrys insectifera*, *Blechnum spicant*, *Paris quadrifolia*, *Luzula sylvatica*, *Atropa belladonna* and *Serratula tinctoria*. On the grounds of this floristic richness, Bedford Purlieus has been described as one of the most important woods in Britain.

The fauna is also rich, and although it is still relatively unknown, it is regarded as the richest locality in this part of the east Midlands. Among the butterflies recorded are the white admiral, pearl-bordered fritillary, the silver washed fritillary, the dark green fritillary, high brown fritillary, chequered skipper, brown hairstreak, and white-letter hairstreak. Numerous local moths have been recorded here. It is an isolated east Midland locality for both the palmate newt and the adder.

Coppicing has now stopped entirely in the group. Part of Collyweston Great Wood has become a plantation whilst the centre was cleared for an RAF establishment. A large quarry occupies the centre of Easton Hornstocks. Part of Wittering Coppice has been converted to a poplar plantation. Substantial areas of Bedford Purlieus have been replanted with oak, beech and a variety of conifers, and other sections have been destroyed by quarrying and military needs in wartime. Despite all this, substantial areas of semi-natural woodland exist in all four component woods of the site.

W.44. CASTOR HANGLANDS, HUNTINGDON AND
PETERBOROUGH
TF 1101. 45 ha
Grade 1

The woodlands of Castor Hanglands NNR straddle a zone of marked geological variety in Jurassic rocks, ranging in north–south sequence from limestone to clay, cornbrash, sand and then clay again. The soils reflect this sequence with a range from calcareous loams to calcareous and neutral gleys. Most of the woodland was formerly coppice-with-standards, most of which has been removed, leaving a mixed ash–pedunculate oak woodland, with hazel, privet, dogwood and spindle. On wetter soils, large ash stools occur with hazel, willow and aspen. Part of Moore Wood, also in the reserve, is high forest pedunculate oak. Corresponding with the soil variation, a wide range of field layer types occur; *Rubus fruticosus* is locally dominant, but *Mercurialis perennis–Endymion non-scriptus* is the most widespread type, with *Primula vulgaris*, *Anemone nemorosa*, *Lonicera periclymenum* and *Euphorbia amygdaloides*. *Paris quadrifolia*, *Oxalis acetosella* and *Allium ursinum* occur on the wetter soils. The rides and clearings are kept open and this encourages the rich invertebrate fauna.

The woodlands are a good example of oak–ash woodland, but their most important feature is that they constitute part of a complex of habitats on a range of soil types in a relatively small area.

See also L.81.

W.45(i). BARDNEY FOREST (LINCOLNSHIRE LIMEWOODS), LINCOLNSHIRE   Grade 1

(a) Hatton Wood
TF 1674.   35 ha

The eastern (non-conifer) part is high forest of lime and oak of some 80–90 years' growth over a sparse shrub layer of hazel. The ground flora includes *Convallaria majalis*, *Luzula sylvatica* and *Campanula latifolia*. The eastern end is secondary oak–ash woodland, as is the northern strip beside the stream. Adjacent to the high forest is an overgrown pond with *Salix fragilis* and *S. viminalis*. A small part of the main wood is well-developed oak standards over hazel coppice.

Hatton Wood lies on heavy clay, acid or neutral at the surface, with variable quantities of sandy drift overlying this in patches. Floristically, the wood is limited, but is selected as the limewood which most closely corresponds with a high forest structure.

(b) Newball and Hardy Gang Woods
TF 0876, TF 0974.   88 ha

Newball and Hardy Gang Woods were almost continuous until the nineteenth century when the intervening Coldstead Wood was cleared. They both lie on clay with a covering of sand which varies from over 50 cm in depth to negligible. On the clay soils, most of which are gleyed, there are extensive tracts of lime coppice, whilst on the low-lying clays aspen, hazel and ash are abundant with no lime. On the deep sands, birch scrub with bracken and *Holcus mollis* is prevalent. Marginal to this, sessile oak and hazel dominate with the birches. The soils of both woods are almost entirely strongly to mildly acid, with small areas of heavy neutral soils notable for the increase in abundance of calcicoles such as field maple and dog's mercury. In Newball Wood there is a small patch of plateau alder coppice on locally waterlogged sand, which constitutes an important ecological line with the large fen-edge coppices near Woodhall Spa and Tumby. Both woods appear to have been simple coppice with only few oak standards, but the northern part of Newball has a number of oak standards. In Hardy Gang there is a small area where pedunculate oak is one of the main coppice species, with some large, ancient stools. Records to date indicate that Newball Wood alone is floristically the richest of the Lincolnshire limewoods, with Hardy Gang only slightly less rich: their flora includes many of the local woodland species. Furthermore, Newball is, on present evidence, the richest limewood entomologically.

Both sites have been partly felled and replanted with conifers. The southern part of Newball was the scene of a Forestry Commission trial, and the small control plots of untouched coppice are important remnants which indicate the nature of the coppice over much of the land now under new plantations.

(c) Stainfield and Scotgrove Woods
TF 1273, TF 1370.   87 ha

Unlike other woodlands in central Lincolnshire, the Stainfield Woods occupy a shallow basin situation. The soils vary from sand with a high water table to strongly gleyed and well-drained acid and neutral clays. Much of the woodland is lime coppice but with a variety of other species, notably the birches. The wide range of ground flora communities extends to the *Lonicera periclymenum*, *Convallaria majalis*, *Rubus*-Section *Suberecti* community on strongly acidic, organic sand, and to *Sphagnum* where similar soils have the water table permanently at or near the surface.

Within a short distance of Stainfield Woods, but separated from it by arable farmland, is Scotgrove Wood. This is a good example of lime–oak coppice derived from oak over lime coppice-with-standards, developed mainly on acid, poorly drained clays, which have an appreciable sand fraction in surface horizons at the southern end. The marginal diversity characteristic of coppice woods shows well at Scotgrove, where wild service and wych elm are confined to the woodland edge. A drainage line runs through the southern area, along which mixed coppice of ash, maple, hazel occurs over a fen-like ground flora including *Carex acutiformis*. The northern boundary is marked by a massive dyke and bank, on which calcareous clay subsoil is exposed, and a rich flora has developed, including calcareous grassland, and mixed scrub and coppice.

Both woods have been partly felled and replanted with conifers. The most important areas for conservation are the western part of Scotgrove and the sections of Stainfield known as Great South and Demerose Woods. Of these the Stainfield part is more important for its unusual edaphic conditions.

(d) Potterhanworth Wood
TF 0767.   35 ha

The western half has been converted to conifers, but the eastern half remains as coppice derived from coppice-with-standards, on a site which is known to have been continuously wooded. The relatively strong relief gives rise to both receiving sites and freely drained slopes. Much of the wood lies on clay but a substantial tract lies on sandy loam above the clay. Most soils are neutral, but the textural and drainage variety is sufficient to enable a wide range of ground flora communities to develop. Most of the coppice consists of almost pure small-leaved lime but, towards the south, lime is rare, ash, oak and birch being the most abundant. The particular features of Potterhanworth are repeated to some extent in other Lincolnshire limewoods, but in the presence of *Frangula alnus*, *Prunus avium* and *Campanula trachelium* it has affinities with woods further south and west. The Roman-built Car Dyke runs along its eastern margin.

W.45(ii). BARDNEY FOREST (LINCOLNSHIRE LIME-
WOODS), LINCOLNSHIRE   Grade 2

(a) *Great West–Cocklode–Spring Woods*
TF 1076.   37 ha

Four contiguous woods occupy a relatively low-lying area
along parish boundaries. Of these Little West, and substantial parts of Cocklode and Great West, have been felled
and replanted with conifers. The remaining areas under
lime woodland include one of the best high forest stands
(Great West); a herb-rich coppice (Spring) in which *Carex
strigosa*, *Ophioglossum vulgatum* and *Myosotis sylvatica*
occur; and an area of uniform coppice of high potential
research value (Cocklode), all on mainly neutral clay and
sandy clay soils. In Cocklode, outlying parts of the earthworks of Bullington Priory extend into the wood and offer
an opportunity to study the development of the characteristic woodland. Recently some two-thirds of Spring Wood
was cleared for arable cultivation.

(b) *Stainton–Fulnetby Woods*
TF 0778.   68 ha

Stainton, Fulnetby and Rand Woods form contiguous
stands, of which Rand has been completely felled and
replanted with conifers. Stainton is typical high forest lime
woodland in which lime is a minority element through part
of the wood. Fulnetby is the best remaining stand of
coppice-with-standards oak over lime, with spindle locally
common, but is floristically impoverished in comparison
with most other woods.

(c) *Wickenby Wood*
TF 0882.   45 ha

Uniformly wet throughout, this coppice has a variety of
woodland types, being partly dominated by lime, with
areas of ash, maple and hazel and local dominance of willow.
Wickenby is one of the richer woods floristically, and is
markedly the most alkaline of all the Lincolnshire limewoods. As such there is a case for including it as a grade 1
site, but most of its features can be found elsewhere in
grade 1 sites, even if they are less well-developed than at
Wickenby.

W.46. BENACRE PARK, SUFFOLK
TM 5084.   135 ha   Grade 2

Benacre Park contains similar areas of ancient oak with a
rich epiphytic flora as described for Sotterley Park, and
must be considered as an alternative to it though the two
areas are close together and complement each other. It too
contains species of lichen that are now extremely rare elsewhere in East Anglia.

W.47. FOXLEY WOOD, NORFOLK
TG 0524.   65 ha   Grade 2

Three broad woodland types occur in Foxley Wood. The
most widespread, on wet clay soils, is mixed deciduous in
which pedunculate oak and hazel are the most abundant,
but ash, field maple and birch are common and a number

of other tree and shrub species are present. The ground
flora here is *Filipendula ulmaria–Geum rivale* grading to
Mercurialis perennis–Endymion non-scriptus and *Convallaria
majalis* on the drier areas. The 'sacred ground' near the
wood's centre is sandy, with oak high forest over a discontinuous holly understorey and a ground flora dominated by
bracken and *Holcus lanatus*. Thirdly, a flushed tract is
occupied by alder coppice, while alder also occurs as a
constituent of coppice on the lighter soils. Floristically,
Foxley is one of the richest woods in East Anglia: though
no rare species are recorded, many are very local, notably
Myosotis sylvatica, *Sedum telephium*, *Sorbus torminalis*,
Prunus padus and *Carex strigosa*.

Though Foxley has been partly replanted with conifers,
and the remainder has been cleared of all worthwhile
timber, the site is nevertheless important. As an ancient
coppice site, it is unusual in possessing alder, and in some
respects grades into fen woodland (*Carex lepidocarpa* and
Prunus padus are present). Furthermore, this ranges through
to dry, acidophilous woodland. It is almost as important as
Swanton Novers, and in many respects is similar and is
graded as an alternative site.

W.48. WAYLAND WOOD, NORFOLK
TL 9399.   35 ha   Grade 2

Lying on wet, calcareous boulder clay, this is a coppice-
with-standards woodland. Pedunculate oak is the main
standard which with a few ash and birch forms a fairly
open canopy. The coppice layer contains a limited amount
of ash and field maple, but is mainly a hazel–bird-cherry
mixture with dogwood, willow and groups of holly. At a
point on the margin, elm has encroached into the wood. The
soil is wet throughout, and the ground flora is mainly of the
Filipendula ulmaria type with no *Mercurialis perennis*. Said
to be rich floristically, this is the only site for *Gagea lutea* in
Norfolk.

This is a good example of a coppice-with-standards woodland still managed as such. It is selected for this and the
unusual combination of coppice species otherwise unknown
in lowland England.

W.49. SEXTON WOOD, NORFOLK
TM 2991.   40 ha   Grade 2

Sexton Wood lies mostly on neutral clay soils and comprises
an almost pure stand of hornbeam coppice with oak
standards. Towards the southern end the soil is almost calcareous, and here maple is relatively abundant. Centrally
there is a small, wet basin occupied by ash and willow and a
poor-fen flora. At the north end where the soils are appreciably more sandy there is much more birch, and the oak is
dense enough to form high forest above hornbeam shrub
layer.

Sexton Wood is selected as a representative of hornbeam
coppice near its geographical limit which is still cut sporadically. Its value for conservation is unfortunately much
diminished by the state of the rides, which are all concrete
tracks. Brooke Wood, Norfolk, was an excellent example,
but it has been almost completely replanted with conifers,

and Sexton Wood may be the best remaining example. However, the woods of south-east Norfolk are insufficiently known and other, better examples may be found.

W.50. FELBRIGG WOODS, NORFOLK
TG 1940. 155 ha   Grade 2

Felbrigg Great Wood and Felbrigg Park lie on the gravels of the Cromer End Moraine. The Great Wood is ancient beech forest, closed over large areas, but opened locally to admit birch regeneration. Mixed with beech are some oak and holly and these, together with the pollarded beech, add to the similarities between this site and some of the Wealden and New Forest woods. The ground flora is largely composed of bryophytes, with *Dicranum scoparium*, *Plagiothecium undulatum*, *Polytrichum formosum* and *Leucobryum glaucum* abundant. There is a rich epiphytic flora, including *Isothecium myosuroides* and *Parmelia perlata*, both rare in Norfolk.

Felbrigg Park is ancient, open oak woodland with some old sweet chestnut and sycamore. The pasture remains unploughed. The epiphytic lichen flora is one of the richest in Norfolk, with many old-forest species.

The site is selected primarily as a representative of beechwoods at the limit of their supposed native range. It is also worthy of selection as an overmature woodland with an epiflora rich by the standards of eastern England.

W.51. KING'S AND BAKER'S WOODS, BEDFORDSHIRE
SP 9229. 230 ha   Grade 2

King's Wood, together with Baker's Wood, is the largest area of woodland in Bedfordshire. It lies on boulder clay passing to Lower Greensand. The sandy soils are covered by birch woodland with some sessile oak and Scots pine over bracken and in open areas heather. The clays on the other hand have pedunculate oak–ash woodlands in which hornbeam is co-dominant over large areas, and some stands of small-leaved lime. Here the ground flora is predominantly of *Primula vulgaris*, *Euphorbia amygdaloides*, *Mercurialis perennis*, *Galeobdolon luteum* and *Lonicera periclymenum*. The woods have a number of rare and local plant species, including *Convallaria majalis*, *Osmunda regalis*, *Luzula sylvatica* and *Vicia sylvatica*.

Although the site has been partly damaged by development and replanted with conifers, it remains a rich and diverse wood, and the damage is not irreversible. Its flora and fauna are relatively well known, and include national and regional rarities in the fungi and Hemiptera.

W.52. HALES WOOD, ESSEX
TL 5740. 8 ha   Grade 2

In east Cambridge, west Suffolk and north Essex there is a series of coppice-with-standards woodlands over an area dominated by Chalky Boulder Clay. Hales Wood is a good example of such a woodland. The canopy is dominated by pedunculate oak together with ash, field maple, elm and hornbeam, the last forming an interesting link with the concentrations of this species in the Home counties. There is a wide range of shrub species present including hazel,

hawthorn, dogwood, blackthorn, rose, wayfaring tree and guelder rose.

The most characteristic feature of the ground flora is an abundance of the true oxlip. Other species dominant in the field layer include *Mercurialis perennis*, *Fragaria vesca*, *Sanicula europaea*, *Viola* sp. and, in the wetter patches, *Filipendula ulmaria*. The dewberry is common in some parts of the wood whilst occasional small patches of *Paris quadrifolia* may be found.

W.53. CANFIELD HART WOOD, ESSEX
TL 5619. 30 ha   Grade 2

Canfield Hart Wood lies close to Hatfield Forest on calcareous till. It is transitional in character between the oak–ash coppice-with-standards type widespread in eastern England, and the derived type dominated by elm. The ground flora has abundant oxlip and where the canopy is broken patches of grass occur. Many rare and local species are present, including *Iris foetidissima*, and *Campanula glomerata*, *Anacamptis pyramidalis*, *Ophrys apifera*, more characteristic of the grassland.

The wood is selected mainly as the southernmost population of oxlip. This is a species on which much research has been carried out and whose range-determining factors are not understood. This, coupled with the wood's diversity, justifies inclusion as a grade 2.

W.54. HATFIELD FOREST, ESSEX
TL 5320. 360 ha   Grade 2

This former Royal Forest lies mainly on Chalky Boulder Clay with patches of gravel exposed near low-lying ground. Large oak, hornbeam and horse chestnut occur in the open parkland, but most of the woodland is coppice-with-standards from which many of the standards have been felled. Ash, hazel and field maple are now the most abundant species, with hornbeam and field maple standards. Within the Forest as a whole there are also ponds and streams. A wide variety of plants occur in the area, with *Epipactis purpurata* and *Paris quadrifolia* among the local species present.

The site is included as an example of eastern coppices with a composition somewhat intermediate between the hornbeam and the ash–hazel–maple coppices. It has the additional advantage that a variety of habitats occur in a single location.

W.55. EPPING FOREST, ESSEX
TQ 4298. 1150 ha   Grade 2

Epping Forest stands on London Clay overlain in places by gravel and sands, giving rise to a mosaic of neutral and acid soils with locally impeded drainage. Most of the woodland is ancient groves of pollarded beech, some of coppice origin, with some pedunculate oak, silver birch and holly. Hornbeam forms a separate woodland type with some pedunculate oak, mainly on the lower-lying clays. Throughout the Forest, birch and holly invade where there are gaps in the canopy. Although the woodland is mostly overmature, all the dominant species are regenerating sporadically, mainly on the margins of mature woodland. The ground flora is poor, often absent completely below beech and hornbeam, but along watercourses and beside ponds a marsh flora has developed. Epiphytes are much reduced by air pollution and shade.

This site represents both beech and pedunculate oak–hornbeam woodland but in view of pollution and public pressure the site is not considered to merit grade 1 status.

W.56. OVERHALL GROVE, CAMBRIDGESHIRE
TL 3363. 20 ha   Grade 2

This site lies on moderately steep slopes. The soil throughout is heavy clay, with calcareous boulder clay at high levels and neutral or mildly acidic Kimmeridge Clay at low levels. *Ulmus carpinifolia* is dominant throughout with some pedunculate oak, ash, field maple and elder. It is probable that the wood originally had a fairly conventional coppice-with-standards structure, with oak and elm over ash and maple, but in recent centuries the elm has spread vigorously. Some massive elm and oak standards remain, however, and in its present state Overhall Grove approximates to high forest closer than most woods in the east Midlands and western East Anglia. The ground flora includes a vast population of oxlip and some other woodland species, but is mostly dominated by *Urtica dioica*, *Glechoma hederacea*, *Galium aparine* and *Heracleum sphondylium*.

Other areas of small-leaved elm woodland are known in the area. This one is selected partly because of its structural maturity and oxlip population, but it also has a number of peculiar features. Within it is an extensive field monument (the Hall of the name) and associated earthworks which, with other information, indicates that the wood is ancient, secondary woodland, with no primary woodland nucleus. Its importance is increased by the selection of Hayley Wood (mainly primary with a small, recent, secondary area) and Hardwick Wood (primary and a succession of secondary, adjacent stands) on similar soils and in the same area, for Overhall is a particularly fine demonstration of the long-lasting effects of discontinuity of woodland cover on the woodland flora.

W.57. HARDWICK WOOD, CAMBRIDGESHIRE
TL 3557. 16 ha   Grade 2

This is an example of woodland on Chalky Boulder Clay, in which the ancient core is oak–ash woodland with a coppice layer of hazel, in which oak is much more abundant than ash. Surrounding this ancient core is secondary woodland arising at various dates from the sixteenth century to about 1930, which includes a variety of types with wych elm, ash and birch locally dominant. The ground flora includes abundant oxlip and, on the wood margin, *Melampyrum cristatum* and *Lathyrus sylvestris*. The bryophytes include the rare *Ptilidium pulcherrimum*.

In a general sense, this site is an alternative to Hayley Wood, but it has its own features of scientific importance. Its management history is exceptionally diverse and well documented: similar secondary woodland series occur in other woods selected, but these are comparatively recent

(e.g. Hintlesham Woods, Suffolk). Unlike other Cambridgeshire woods it has apparently never had a significant tall coppice component of ash and field maple. There is a classic primrose–oxlip hybrid situation, which can be related to the development of the wood.

W.58. KESTEVEN WOODS, LINCOLNSHIRE   Grade 2

The concentration of woods in southern Lincolnshire and Rutland is mainly dominated by pedunculate oak, ash and hazel over predominantly calcareous clay soils. Most if not all have been managed as coppice-with-standards. They mostly have a rich assemblage of subordinate native tree and shrub species, including wild service, field maple, midland hawthorn, wayfaring tree, gean and aspen. The ground flora is usually dominated by mixtures including dog's mercury, *Sanicula europaea*, primrose, bluebell, wood anemone and bramble, but a number of local species are found, including *Milium effusum*, *Sedum telephium*, *Epipactis helleborine*, *Carex strigosa* and *Dipsacus pilosus*.

As a group they have both similarities with and fundamental differences from the Bardney Forest woods (W.45). They had a similar development and their range of coppice types overlap to some extent, but the Kesteven Woods have mainly calcareous soils and, correspondingly, limewood is relatively rare and calcicolous species such as *Campanula trachelium* are more abundant. Here, as in Bardney, the full range of variation is represented in a number of small woods, the differences between which yield information on the effects of management. The Kesteven Woods are placed in grade 2, but they are not regarded as a substitute as a group for the Bardney Forest woods.

The Kesteven Woods have not been surveyed in detail and the selection within them is extremely tentative. Further survey may reveal other sites which merit grade 2 status, either in addition to those selected, or more likely as replacements for them. In particular, Tortoiseshell Wood is a good example of calcareous coppice with an excellent structure, with large numbers of well-grown standard oaks and some magnificent standard wild service trees.

(a) Dole Wood
TF 0916.   5 ha

This is a small, coppice-with-standards wood of oak, hazel and ash, with abundant midland hawthorn, and small areas of lime and elm. The ground flora ranges to mildly acid communities with *Holcus mollis*, *Teucrium scorodonia* and *Lonicera periclymenum*.

(b) Dunsby Wood
TF 0826.   60 ha

Formerly this was coppice-with-standards, but most of the oak standards have been removed and the coppice has been allowed to grow up. The canopy is now mainly ash and field maple, with birch, aspen, gean and patches of invasive English elm. In the shrub layer, hazel, midland hawthorn, crab apple, and wild service are locally abundant. The ground flora includes *Dipsacus pilosus* and *Carex strigosa*.

(c) Kirton Wood
TF 9832. 30 ha

Kirton Wood still possesses its coppice-with-standards structure, but the coppice ash has now become rather overgrown. Small-leaved lime is abundant in parts. The ground flora is predominantly calcicole, with abundant *Filipendula ulmaria*, *Geum rivale* and *Valeriana officinalis*.

(d) Sapperton–Pickworth Woods
TF 0334. 25 ha

Although formerly one wood, this has now been divided by partial clearing into three separate stands. These retain a good quality oak–ash coppice-with-standards structure with local blackthorn thickets. Parts of the wood are invaded by English elm. The ground flora includes *Campanula trachelium*.

SOUTH-WEST ENGLAND

W.59. MELBURY PARK, DORSET
ST 5706. 170 ha   Grade 1

This ancient park is, for its size, one of the richest sites for epiphytic lichens known in Britain, due largely to its freedom from air pollution and from disturbance. Interesting comparisons can be made between the lichen flora of the south-western part, where ancient trees of oak, alder, birch and willow are associated with boggy ground in the valleys, and where there are also some ancient ash and beech, and that of the northern part where many old elms and other planted trees occur. Several of the lichens of the site are not known to occur elsewhere in Britain.

W.60. BOCONNOC PARK AND WOODS, CORNWALL
SX 1460. 30 ha   Grade 1

This site lies within an enclosed area of parkland and woodland, covering some 600 ha, situated near Lostwithiel. The ancient trees support 180 epiphytic lichen species – the largest number known for an area of this size in western Europe. Many of these species are of considerable interest; at least one (*Porina hibernica*) is not known to occur anywhere else in Britain, while several are known from only one or two other localities. These include *Arthonia leucopellaea*, *Pannaria mediterranea* and *Lecanactis corticola*.

W.61. FAL ESTUARY, CORNWALL
SW 8841. 60 ha   Grade 1

This site is a complex of saltings, salt marshes, carr and woodland situated in the valleys and around the confluence of the rivers Fal and Ruan. Its particular interest lies in the transition from salt marsh through an invasive stage to tidal woodland which is rare in Britain. The history of the site is known and studies on the stratigraphy and the plant and animal communities in relation to tidal submergence have been carried out. The tidal area of woodland is dominated by *Alnus glutinosa* together with *Salix cinerea* var. *atrocinerea*, the willow in places forming a scrubby boundary to the more mature woodland and extending out into the surrounding marsh. Passing up the river valley the tidal woodland grades into a birch–oak wood. On the sides of the valley and, in many places sharply defined from the marsh by a boundary ditch or bank, is a drier acidophilous oakwood. Here sessile oak has been coppiced and some hazel, hawthorn, rowan, willow and gorse are present. The ground flora includes species such as *Calluna vulgaris*, *Vaccinium myrtillus*, *Blechnum spicant*, *Rubus* sp., *Lonicera periclymenum* and *Holcus mollis* together with bryophytes including *Thuidium tamariscinum*, *Dicranum majus* and *Hypnum cupressiforme*.

In contrast to this the alder tidal area contains *Angelica sylvestris*, *Oenanthe crocata*, *Galium palustre*, *Juncus* sp., *Caltha palustris* and *Carex* spp. as well as occasional occurrences of salt marsh species.

See also C.38.

W.62. DIZZARD–MILLOOK CLIFFS, CORNWALL
SW 1799. 60 ha   Grade 1

The cliff woodlands on this site have a north to north-easterly aspect and an altitude range from sea-level to approximately 150 m at the highest point. The area of cliff over which the woodland has developed is subject to land-slips. This, combined with a friable rock type, has given the steeply sloping cliffs a varied topography. The tree layer is exposed to strong winds from the sea and this has resulted in a tight wind-pruned canopy. As a direct consequence of the varied topography and wind-pruning the canopy height varies between 1 and 8 m, and is composed mainly of sessile oak together with some birch and rowan. Of interest is the occurrence in the canopy of wild service, a species rare in the south-west. The shrub layer is represented by hazel, hawthorn, holly, privet, gorse and spindle. The edges of the woodland both on the seaward side and near the cliff top have a scrub margin in which blackthorn is well represented. Scrubby patches are also found where recent land-slips have caused disturbance. The ground flora of the area is extremely varied for this part of the country and includes both basiphilous and acidophilous areas of vegetation. Areas on the base-rich soils support *Allium ursinum*, *Arum maculatum*, *Filipendula ulmaria*, *Fragaria vesca*, *Sanicula europaea*, *Primula vulgaris* and *Mercurialis perennis*, whilst in contrast to these may be found a ground flora dominated by *Vaccinium myrtillus*, *Calluna vulgaris*, *Deschampsia cespitosa* and *Melampyrum pratense*. *Dryopteris aemula* is also present within the woodland. This contrast of vegetation types is also reflected in the shrub layer. The epiphyte flora is well developed: *Lobaria pulmonaria* is to be seen throughout the wood and *Sticta limbata* has also been found.

W.63. BOVEY VALLEY AND YARNER WOODS, DEVON
SX 7778. 385 ha   Grade 1

This woodland complex is one of the richest and most varied remaining in the Dartmoor National Park. The many different conditions of slope, aspect, and soil, together with the Atlantic climate, support a very rich and varied flora and fauna.

The woods lie in the valleys of the River Bovey and some

of its tributary streams on the eastern fringe of Dartmoor. Included are Rudge Wood, parts of Houndtor and Hisley Woods, Water Cleave, Woodash, Wanford Cleave, Lustleigh Cleave and Neadon Cleave, all in the main Bovey Valley, and the lower slopes of the valley of the Becka Brook, together with Yarner Wood to the south and the smaller detached block of Higher Knowle Wood to the east. Considerable parts of the site are already managed as the NNRs of Yarner Wood and Bovey Valley Woodlands.

Yarner Wood includes the valleys of the Yarner and Woodcock Streams, together with the intervening spur of land, giving an altitudinal range of 240 m. The tree canopy is composed mainly of sessile oak, with birch locally on the sites of old fields. There are also plantations of Scots pine and other conifers, and much planting of oak and other hardwoods has been done since the Reserve was declared in 1951. The wood is similar in character to some of the Welsh woodlands, but is generally drier, and some of the oaks are much larger than those typical of western British woods nowadays. Holly and rowan form an understorey, which is locally dense, and the ground flora of the drier slopes is dominated by bilberry, bracken, heather and *Melampyrum pratense*. The rare *Lobelia urens* is associated with some of the old field sites.

In the valleys, on better soils, ash and alder are frequent, with hazel below, over a mesophilous ground flora including such species as *Primula vulgaris* and *Sanicula europaea*. *Osmunda regalis* and *Chrysosplenium oppositifolium* occur locally, together with good epiphyte and bryophyte floras including such sensitive species as *Hookeria lucens*.

The main block in the Bovey Valley carries a variety of woodland types, including those already described. Whereas Yarner Wood is entirely on Culm rocks, however, much of this area is on granite, giving relatively base-rich soils often littered with granite boulders. On the lower slopes, bluebell and *Holcus* may dominate the field layer, with a mixture of ferns and *Oxalis acetosella* on flushed areas. Pedunculate oak replaces sessile oak, and ash, alder, birch and beech are all frequent over a relatively calcicolous field layer. The granite boulders in and near the river and the Becka Brook carry a very rich bryophyte flora.

Higher Knowle Wood, to the east of the main block, lies on an unusual conglomerate rock which is probably related to the nearby Bovey Beds (Oligocene). Pedunculate oak is the main tree, but beech, ash and many others also occur.

The fauna of the whole complex is characteristically western, with such birds as the dipper, grey wagtail and pied flycatcher.

W.64. HOLNE CHASE, DEVON
SX 7271.   290 ha   Grade 1*

This is an extensive valley system of the rivers Dart and Webburn on the southern fringe of Dartmoor. Steep-sided valleys of nearly all aspects are present with altitude ranging from 75 to 230 m. There is a series of oakwoods, and sessile oak predominates in the area particularly on the valley

alluvial soils. The oak occurs with other species such as ash, beech, small-leaved lime, hornbeam, aspen, wych elm, holly, hazel and willow. Planted larch and Douglas fir are also present. On the richer soils a mesophilous ground flora is to be found containing species such as dog's mercury, primrose and *Sanicula europaea*. The hillsides and more acidic soils support more pure stands of sessile oak under which a field layer dominated by bilberry, bramble, *Luzula sylvatica* and *Lonicera periclymenum* is present. Throughout the area, flushes are to be found containing much *Chrysosplenium oppositifolium* under an ash and alder canopy; at their edges these merge gradually into the surrounding oak woodland. At the uppermost edges of the valleys the epiphyte flora resembles that of the woodlands higher on the Moor although the flora is less varied. A point of particular note is the presence of a rich bryophyte flora, both in the woodland and in the rivers themselves; the very rare *Fissidens polyphyllus* and *F. serrulatus* can be found in some quantity near Holne Bridge.

W.65. WISTMAN'S WOOD, DEVON
SX 6177.   4 ha   Grade 1

This is a small area sited on the west-facing side of the West Dart river valley. The wood lies between 380 and 435 m on 'clitter', a granite block scree. In contrast with many Dartmoor woodlands pedunculate as opposed to sessile oak is dominant. The trees are gnarled and twisted, many having their lower branches resting on the granite blocks which form the woodland floor. There is some rowan, a little hazel, holly and willow (*Salix aurita*). The epiphyte flora, both bryophyte and vascular, is luxuriant and epiphytic lichens are well represented. *Antitrichia curtipendula* is known to occur as are many bryophytes with a western distribution such as *Douinia ovata*. The ground flora consists of a bryophyte carpet covering the blocks, and species such as bilberry, *Luzula sylvatica*, *Holcus mollis* and bramble grow in soil-filled crevices. Ferns form an important part of the ground flora.

W.66. BLACK TOR COPSE, DEVON
SX 5689.   6 ha   Grade 1

Black Tor Copse is on the northern edge of Dartmoor but having similarities to the Wistman's Wood situation in that the area has developed over a granite clitter on the north-west-facing slope of the valley of the West Okement River. Pedunculate oak is again the dominant species but the trees are taller and it is possible to walk beneath much of the canopy. A rich and luxuriant epiphyte flora is present containing several species such as *Antitrichia curtipendula* and *Douinia ovata* which are of local, northern or western distribution. The ground flora contains acidophilous species such as bilberry together with grasses and ferns growing in crevices and on patches of soil. The majority of the granite blocks are covered with a carpet of bryophyte species such as *Rhytidiadelphus loreus*, *Thuidium tamariscinum* and *Plagiothecium undulatum*.

See also L.92, P.25 and U.1.

W.67. AXMOUTH–LYME REGIS UNDERCLIFFS, DEVON
SY 255898–333914. 320 ha   Grade 1
This site, on the south Devon coast on Lyme Bay, extends
from west of Lyme Regis to the mouth of the River Axe.

The area is of stratigraphic importance and includes outcrops of Triassic, Rhaetic and basal Lower Lias exposures
of the sub-Cretaceous unconformity, the most westerly
exposure of the Gault Clay as a distinct lithology, examples
of penecontemporaneous erosion in the Cenomanian Limestone and the most satisfactory exposure of the *planus* Zone
of the Upper Chalk in Devon. Much of the interest of the
area has arisen from a massive landslip in the mid nineteenth
century when a large field became detached from the main
cliff and moved seawards. This cliff area, now called Goat
Island, and the chasm left when it moved, have largely
become covered with woodland and scrub. A continuing
series of minor slips has given an area of varied topography
as well as exposing fresh areas for colonisation. The climate
is typically western Atlantic and the frequent damp mists
encourage a profuse, vigorous growth of ferns and climbers.

The woodland here is varied: photographic records
establish that much of it has developed since 1905, and all
ages of tree from that date are present. Some areas have
regenerated naturally, such as the chasm between Goat
Island and the mainland where ashwood has developed,
whilst others have been planted. The main species in the
planted areas include beech, ash, holm oak and Turkey oak,
silver fir and pines. Extensive areas of the reserve are
covered by a mixture of ash and field maple with a thick
understorey of hazel, dogwood, spindle, blackthorn and
other scrub species. The whole area is a mosaic of developing woodland and scrub together with abundant climbers,
traveller's joy and ivy featuring prominently.

The ground flora varies in luxuriance depending on tree
cover, ranging from areas dominated by ivy with abundant
clumps of *Phyllitis scolopendrium* to almost open grassland
where scrub is just developing. Species present in some
abundance include *Mercurialis perennis*, *Circaea lutetiana*,
Geranium robertianum, *Carex pendula*, *Rubus fruticosus* agg.,
Dryopteris filix-mas, *D. dilatata* and *Polystichum setiferum*
together with the usual mesophilous herbs. A feature of
some areas is a low scrub with much *Rubus fruticosus* agg.,
Ligustrum vulgare and *Rubia peregrina*. In proximity to this
vegetation *Lithospermum purpurocaeruleum* is found.
See also C.26.

W.68. WATERSMEET, DEVON
SS 7448. 140 ha   Grade 1
This is an extensive area of woodland occupying the hill and
valley system of the East Lyn River and its tributaries. The
most common rock types found in the area are grits, shales
and mudstones all of which yield soils poor in bases. Slopes
of all aspects are to be found in the system with an altitudinal range from near sea-level to *c.* 240 m.

The tree dominant is sessile oak, there being both high
forest and coppice woodland present. A number of rare
Sorbus spp. grow in the area and *S. subcuneata* and *S.
devoniensis* are recorded from these woodlands. The ground

flora exhibits a range of communities from the dry acidophilous facies where *Vaccinium myrtillus*, *Calluna vulgaris*,
Melampyrum pratense and *Deschampsia flexuosa* are common
to more base-rich areas with *Mercurialis perennis*, *Sanicula
europaea*, *Fragaria vesca*, *Primula vulgaris* and *Asperula
odorata*. Added variety is given to the site by the presence of
wet rock faces providing rich bryophyte habitats, as well as
flushes with much *Chrysosplenium oppositifolium*. Ferns are
frequent throughout the area; of particular note being the
abundance of *Polystichum setiferum* in some parts of the
wood and the presence of *Dryopteris aemula*. Other forbs of
particular note are *Sedum forsteranum* and *Euphorbia
hyberna*, the Irish spurge, which here grows with some
luxuriance in one of its only two localities in Britain.

W.69. HOLNICOTE AND HORNER WATER, SOMERSET
SS 8943. 405 ha   Grade 1
This area, part of an extensive complex of woodlands
owned by the National Trust, lies mainly on Lower Old
Red Sandstone which produces relatively poor soils. The
valley bottoms contain high forest of pedunculate oak
together with ash, wych elm and birch. The shrub layer in
this valley woodland contains hazel and holly with *Rosa* spp.
The field layer is dominated by bramble but species such as
Geranium robertianum, *Glechoma hederacea*, *Teucrium
scorodonia*, *Viola* spp. and *Oxalis acetosella* also occur.

Higher up the slopes the pedunculate oakwood gives way
to sessile oakwood which was formerly coppiced. The
associated species here are much more acidophilous and
include birch and rowan in the shrub layer and *Blechnum
spicant*, *Luzula pilosa*, *Holcus mollis*, bracken and bilberry in
the field layer. The acidophilous oakwood gradually merges
into moorland on its upper edge with *Calluna vulgaris*,
Erica cinerea and *Ulex* sp. The upper edge of the woodland
is particularly exposed and the wind shapes the canopy here
to near ground level.

The lichen flora is very rich both in numbers of species
(110) and in the presence of many rarities, such as *Usnea
articulata*, which are now confined to south-western England because of air pollution elsewhere. This assemblage of
species is very characteristic of ancient forest areas in north-
western Europe.

This is an extensive area of characteristic Exmoor woodland which shows the transition from moorland to valley
woodland particularly well. It is also an important wintering
area for the Exmoor red deer which form one of the three
largest concentrations of red deer in England.
See also L.107 and U.2.

W.70. AVON GORGE (LEIGH WOODS),
       GLOUCESTERSHIRE, SOMERSET
ST 5675. 105 ha   Grade 1
Leigh Woods are situated on the western side of the gorge
of the River Avon at Bristol. The area covers those woodlands on the plateau and on the gorge side.

The plateau woodland occurs on a shallow marl and a
clay soil. A mixture of sessile and pedunculate oak is present
together with ash, wych elm and small-leaved lime. Yew is

found on some of the more stony sites. Beech has been planted in the area and occasional specimens of hornbeam are to be found. An important consideration in this region is the number of rare endemic whitebeams (*Sorbus* spp.) present in the woodland. *S. wilmottiana* and *S. bristoliensis* are endemic to this area whilst *S. eminens*, *S. porrigentiformis* and *S. anglica* are all local limestone species. The ground flora contains the common species such as *Mercurialis perennis*, *Endymion non-scriptus*, *Euphorbia amygdaloides*, *Fragaria vesca*, *Viola* sp., *Anemone nemorosa* and *Rubus fruticosus* agg., as well as those of more particular note such as *Aquilegia vulgaris*, *Carex digitata*, *Neottia nidus-avis*, *Rubia peregrina*, *Orobanche hederae*, *Lathraea squamaria* and *Helleboris viridis*. Ferns include *Thelypteris phegopteris* and *Polystichum setiferum*.

The bryophytes of this area include *Dicranum montanum*, *D. strictum* and *Nowellia curvifolia*.

The scrub woodland of the gorge side, particularly near the quarry areas, is of particular conservation value as it contains a mixture of the usual calcareous scrub species, rare *Sorbus* spp. and in the associated grassy areas rare plants including *Veronica spicata* ssp. *hybrida*, *Hornungia petraea*, *Carex humilis*, *Potentilla tabernaemontani*, *Trinia glauca* and *Scilla autumnalis*.

There is an interesting list of Lepidoptera recorded. The scarce hook-tip moth was formerly found in association with the small-leaved lime.

See also L.102.

W.71. MENDIP WOODLANDS, SOMERSET Grade 1

(a) Rodney Stoke
ST 4950. 35 ha

Although five facies of ashwood and one each of oak, lime and elm have been recognised the intermediate types are so extensive that the area is best considered as a varied ashwood. These woodland types occur over Carboniferous Limestone with some areas of Dolomitic conglomerate. Pedunculate oak is an important associate and field maple, wych elm, small-leaved lime and whitebeam are of lesser importance. Other species which occur are crab apple, blackthorn, hawthorn, buckthorn, sallows, elder and wayfaring tree. Holly and yew however are rare, as are specimens of the endemic *Sorbus anglica* and of wild service.

Spurge laurel is unusually common particularly on the rockier slopes, and privet occurs extensively. Under more open conditions spindle and dogwood occur. Ivy is abundant but honeysuckle is not common and traveller's joy is rare.

The dominant species of the ground flora are dog's mercury and ivy and widespread associates include *Ranunculus ficaria*, *Anemone nemorosa*, *Endymion non-scriptus*, *Primula vulgaris*, *Galeobdolon luteum*, *Euphorbia amygdaloides*, *Campanula trachelium*, *Lithospermum purpurocaeruleum*, *Geranium robertianum*, *Viola* spp., *Colchicum autumnale* and *Phyllitis scolopendrium*.

The fauna includes a characteristic range of species with no particular rarities.

The Mendip Woodlands are an interesting and floristically rich variant of the ashwoods found throughout Britain

on Carboniferous Limestone. Rodney Stoke is the best example of the drier facies of this woodland type. The woodland interest is enhanced by the limestone grassland and abandoned agricultural land which also occur in the reserve.

(b) Asham Wood
ST 7045. 195 ha

This wood lies on a steep limestone gorge with a cliff and alluvial floor. The western area is a plateau woodland. The presence of a stream is an unusual feature of these Mendip Woodlands.

Ash is dominant but there is a very extreme variety of trees and shrubs. Small-leaved lime is common and other tree associates are wych elm, pedunculate oak, gean, birch species, alder, yew (rare), and field maple. The shrubs include dogwood, hazel, hawthorn, spindle (rare), holly (rare), crab apple, blackthorn, blackcurrant, gooseberry, sallows, whitebeam, rowan, elder, wayfaring tree and guelder rose.

The ground flora of Asham Wood contains a great variety of limestone species although it is unusual that *Daphne laureola* and *Lithospermum purpurocaeruleum* are absent. Particularly notable plants here include *Polygonatum multiflorum*, *Convallaria majalis*, *Dipsacus pilosus*, *Colchicum autumnale*, swarms of the *Geum* hybrids (*G. urbanum* × *G. rivale*), *Vicia lutea* and *V. sylvatica*.

In addition rare Diptera have been recorded as well as the wood white *Leptidea sinapis* butterfly and the rare mountain Bulin snail *Ena montana*.

The importance of this floristically outstanding Mendip ashwood has long been recognised and it represents the wetter facies of this woodland type (cf. Rodney Stoke).

(c) Ebbor Gorge
ST 5248. 45 ha

The site is on the south-west-facing slope of the Mendip hills and consists of a steep-sided gorge in Carboniferous Limestone together with an associated tributary valley. Added interest is given to the site by caves of palaeontological value. The canopy of the mature woodland is dominated by ash and pedunculate oak. Other species present are wych elm, beech and hornbeam (rare). The understorey, together with the scrub that is a feature of the area, contains a range of species and includes field maple, traveller's joy, dogwood, hazel, spindle, ivy, holly, buckthorn, small-leaved lime, wayfaring tree and guelder rose. The woodland has been managed in the past and most has been coppiced to some extent.

The ground flora is indicative of the basiphilous nature of the site, dog's mercury, wood anemone, bluebell and *Asperula odorata* being abundant together with primrose, *Sanicula europaea*, *Ajuga reptans*, *Circaea lutetiana*, *Galeobdolon luteum*, and *Viola* sp. A more mesophilous vegetation is represented by patches where bracken, *Lonicera periclymenum*, bramble and grasses are present. In the sheltered gorge a damp woodland facies is found; bryophytes are abundant as is *Phyllitis scolopendrium*. Scree areas are present within the woodland area in which scattered ash regeneration is to be found together with plants of *Geranium robertianum*.

W.72. COTSWOLD COMMONS AND BEECHWOODS, GLOUCESTERSHIRE

SO 8913–9011.   740 ha   Grade 1

Although there are many fine stands of beechwoods in the Cotswolds, the Birdlip–Painswick Woods are regarded as the finest example. The high forest beech here varies in age from about 300 years downwards, but the majority appear to be 150–160 years. The understorey of holly and yew is sparse, and only locally forms a closed canopy. Natural regeneration of beech, ash, holly and yew occurs, aided by the recent thinning of some of the canopy. The field layer consists mainly of *Oxalis acetosella*, *Mercurialis perennis*, *Anemone nemorosa*, *Sanicula europaea*, *Circaea lutetiana*, *Helleborus viridis* and *Daphne laureola*, but numerous other species have been recorded, including *Cephalanthera rubra*, *Monotropa hypophegea*, *Neottia nidus-avis*, *Pyrola minor*, *Epipactis leptochila*, *E. vectensis*, *Convallaria majalis* and *Aquilegia vulgaris*. Common rights exist over the land and this, coupled with the fact that the area carried beechwood in the fourteenth century, suggests that the woodland here is primary.

The neighbouring woods of Buckle, Witcombe, Cranham and Brockworth are also dominated by beech with an admixture of ash. Some appear to be of coppice origin. Holly forms the main understorey, but the absence of old individuals suggests that it has invaded recently. Within Cranham Wood is an open area, formerly grassland, now being invaded by a considerable variety of trees and shrubs, including beech, ash, yew, holly, hawthorn, whitebeam, hazel and oak. It appears that this is developing towards 'mixed beechwood' and constitutes an important variant of beech woodland.

The Sheepscombe Wood complex is extensive and lies on both sides and round the head of a valley above Sheepscombe. Although partly under conifers, there are substantial areas of beech woodland containing rare species. Together with Saltridge Hill Wood it is almost contiguous with the Birdlip–Painswick Woods.

The Painswick Beacon area is open grassland, scrub and small copses surrounded by extensive beech woodland which is used intensively by the public as an open space for recreation. The higher parts of the Hill, particularly the flat plateau, are used as a golf course, on which *Brachypodium pinnatum* has been controlled by mowing. Many of the grasslands accessible from the road are used as car-parks.

The lower slopes of the Hill are old quarry workings with typical Cotswold grassland species, being well-known for the abundance of musk orchids *Herminum monorchis*, pyramidal orchids *Anacamptis pyramidalis* and fragrant orchids *Gymnadenia conopsea*. Colonisation by subspontaneous Scots pine has occurred in most of the old quarries – in some places trees are 6–10 m tall. Seedlings are widespread. Grassland is of the *Brachypodium pinnatum*-

Bromus erectus type with a little *Festuca ovina*, *Koeleria gracilis* and *Briza media*. *Cirsium acaulon* is frequent, with good quantities of *Lotus corniculatus* and *Anthyllis vulneraria*. *Hieracium exotericum*, which is widespread on the open screes and quarry floors, is a feature of the Cotswolds.

Juniper is uncommon, 12 bushes being found in 1968, most of them 30–46 cm high, although three moribund 1.2–1.5 m examples were found in mixed scrub under pine.

W.73. FOREST OF DEAN, GLOUCESTERSHIRE   Grade 1

The Forest of Dean, like the New Forest, was a Royal Forest which has survived as a large area of woodland. Although it has been exploited, mainly for large timber, for centuries the woodlands have been maintained by planting and careful management. In the past few decades large areas of The Dean have been converted to conifers but existing deciduous woodland still reflects differences in the underlying rocks.

The central region lies on Coal Measures from which a clay–loam soil has developed and which carries oak (*Quercus robur*) woodland and a poor, calcifuge ground flora. Surrounding this acid area are limestone and Old Red Sandstone. These form more fertile soils which bear a variety of woodland types over a richer ground flora. Oak woodland, which is often pure but may contain birch and beech, commonly grows over a bluebell, *Holcus mollis* and bracken field layer. In the more acid areas this is replaced by bilberry, and in the more base-rich areas by *Sanicula europaea*, *Circaea lutetiana* and primrose. Woodlands on the limestone are often mixtures of oak, beech, lime, ash and a variety of shrubs.

Conservation in the Forest of Dean, like the New Forest, is best effected by a broad agreement covering the whole of the Forest. Among sites which together constitute a more or less complete range of woodland types, the following are regarded as the most important.

See also W.95.

(a) Nagshead Inclosure
SO 6008.   28 ha

This area of mature, broad-leaved woodland planted in 1814 lies on the Pennant Sandstone (Coal Measures). The main species is pedunculate oak with sweet chestnut, beech, birch and gean. The western part, which has been closed to grazing since 1947–48, has a developing and dense understorey of holly, rowan and other species and some tree regeneration, but not of oak. The eastern part remains open to grazing and has a sparse and scattered understorey of holly and rowan.

The field layer is dominated by *Holcus mollis*, *Pteridium aquilinum* and bramble with *Deschampsia flexuosa*, *Endymion non-scriptus* and *Oxalis acetosella* locally abundant.

This is a good example of the older age class of Forest of Dean oakwood on the Coal Measures. Since 1942 it has been the site of important ornithological studies mainly in connection with a series of nest boxes which totalled 238 in 1964. The four important species breeding in the boxes are pied flycatcher, redstart, blue tit and great tit. All these species nest here in some numbers and there are no other nest box areas in Britain where so many pairs of pied flycatcher and redstart breed. The study of the pied flycatcher is the most prolonged ever made and only Wytham, near Oxford, has a titmouse study of comparable size and duration. Recently a study of the wood warbler has been started and almost the whole population of adults and young have been ringed. There is nothing on a comparable scale elsewhere in Britain.

(b) Dingle Wood
SO 5611.   9 ha

This woodland lies on Carboniferous Limestone which has been quarried in the past. The result is a series of deep pits and gullies (or 'scowles') surrounded by irregular cliffs which have been abandoned for long enough to allow woodland to develop naturally. Part of the area has been planted.

The woodland consists of a great variety of species with beech and wych elm often dominant together with holly and yew in the shrub layer. Other trees present include birch, sweet chestnut, ash, oak, sycamore and rowan with a scattered shrub layer of holly and yew together with field maple, dogwood, hazel, hawthorn, willows, elder, roses and guelder rose.

The herb layer contains a rich variety of calcicolous species with *Paris quadrifolia*, *Pyrola minor*, *Colchicum autumnale* and *Neottia nidus-avis* of particular note. A good calcicolous bryophyte flora also occurs.

The woodland is particularly notable for the richness of its tree, shrub and herb layers and the scowles are floristically some of the richest areas of the Dean Forest.

(c) Speech House
SO 6212.   18 ha

An area of open woodland with very ancient oaks, beeches and hollies. The soils are poorly drained acid loams and patches of *Juncus effusus* occur. The ground flora is mostly a *Pteridium–Rubus* carpet with large areas of *Agrostis tenuis* grassland.

The combination of large trees and open conditions has perpetuated an outstandingly rich epiphytic flora and 53 epiphytic lichens and 15 epiphytic bryophytes have been recorded. The epiphytic flora is one of the richest in central lowland England and is exceeded only by that of some of the ancient parks, e.g. Moccas Park in Herefordshire. *Usnea* spp. are now rare in the forests of lowland central, north and east England but they are finely developed here. *Alectoria fuscescens* is a species of northern (boreal) distribution and the *Parmelias*, especially *P. caperata*, show a luxuriance not otherwise seen in midland England. *Pertusaria hemisphaerica* and *Thelotrema lepadinum* are probably relic species of the old forests as is *P. flavida* which is rare everywhere. Other relic species may be *Haematomma elatinum*, once thought to be confined to south-west Ireland and north-west Scotland, but now known in widely scattered areas of Britain, and *Normandina pulchella*, formerly considered as highly Atlantic.

W.74. COLLINPARK WOOD, GLOUCESTERSHIRE
SO 7528.   65 ha   Grade 1

Collinpark Wood lies on clay soils sloping gently into the alluvial plain of the River Leadon, and contains tributaries of this river. It is an overgrown coppice woodland of up to about 40 years' growth, dominated by sessile oak and small-leaved lime, with local concentrations of silver birch and a few ash and poplar. Wild service is also locally abundant and regenerating profusely. The sparse shrub layer includes hazel, broom, crab apple and willows. Soils are mostly heavy, neutral to acid. The ground flora has abundant bluebell and dog's mercury and a range of species including *Galeobdolon luteum*, *Primula vulgaris*, *Pteridium aquilinum*, *Deschampsia cespitosa*, *Carex pendula* and *Chrysosplenium oppositifolium*. Along the northern margin there is a massive causeway embankment and associated moat. The latter is filled with organic material with a fen-like flora, whilst the calcareous subsoil brought to the surface on the embankment has enabled calcicolous species such as wych elm, field maple and dog's mercury to become established.

The wood is selected as a representative of damp calcifuge lime woodland in western Britain, complementary to the Lincolnshire lime coppices, where, however, the oaks are almost entirely pedunculate.

W.75. HUDNALLS, GLOUCESTERSHIRE
SO 5404, SO 5303.   75 ha   Grade 1

The wide range of semi-natural coppice types in the lower Wye valley area includes a series on the more acidic sandstone rocks in which beech is the main constituent, even though other species are usually mixed with it. Much of this woodland occurred on the Monmouthshire side, where it has all, as far as is known, been allowed to develop to high forest or, more commonly, has been replaced by a variety of plantations. On the Gloucestershire side substantial tracts of these calcifuge coppice types survived as coppice into the present century, particularly to the north and south of the St Briavels meander, and extending north to the Staunton area. Recently, however, much has been cleared, notably at Lords Grove near Monmouth, and north from Wyegate Hill, but one group, centred on Hudnalls, remains virtually intact.

Hudnalls and adjacent woods occupy steep, north- and west-facing sandstone slopes. Much of the woodland is a mixture of beech and sessile oak over a ground flora of *Luzula sylvatica*, *Blechnum spicant*, *Lonicera periclymenum* and *Melampyrum pratense*. Part of this is a mixture which retains the small-coppice structure, but other parts on the steepest slopes are ancient beech high forest with very few oaks and a negligible field layer. Along the stream sides and in parts of the coppice, ash and small-leaved lime occur. All these are on strongly acid soils, but where streams drain down the slope and along flushed areas at the base of the slope a far richer coppice type occurs in which wych elm, ash and hazel are more abundant and the ground flora is extremely rich.

Hudnalls has a complex management history. Part was common woodland, but adjacent parts are coppice-with-standards. Structural differences coincide partly with walls within the wood and are clearly a relict of use and management, but the composition of the wood appears to be natural.

W.95. WYE GORGE (PART), GLOUCESTERSHIRE
Grade 1*

See under South Wales, p. 72.

W.76. MERTHEN WOOD, CORNWALL
SW 7226.   45 ha   Grade 2

This valley woodland sited on the northern shore of the Helford River is complementary to part of the Fal Estuary woods (W.61) but lacks the tidal alder carr found in that area. The tree layer is dominated by oak although areas of pure hazel coppice are to be found. Beech and holly are present in the canopy. In the lower parts of the wood the trees overhang a bank and then estuarine mud in which are patches of *Spartina* marsh. In the lower parts of the wood, rowan, alder buckthorn and gorse are to be found.

The ground flora in the upper parts and hazel coppice region is dominated by bluebell together with wood anemone, bramble, *Blechnum spicant* and *Lonicera periclymenum*. Near the river, bracken is frequent as are bilberry, *Luzula pilosa*, heather and *Teucrium scorodonia* illustrating a more acidophilous facies. A large active badger sett is present within this area of woodland.

W.77. NANCE WOOD, CORNWALL
SW 6645.   14 ha   Grade 2

A coppiced sessile oakwood dwarfed by exposure to the wind. In addition to oak there is beech and the shrubs include hazel, hawthorn, holly, blackthorn, sallows and gorse. The field layer is acidophilous with much *Holcus mollis*, *Digitalis purpurea*, *Calluna vulgaris*, *Blechnum spicant* and bluebell with bracken and bramble locally abundant.

The wood is notable as one of only two British localities for the Irish spurge *Euphorbia hyberna* which is plentiful here.

W.78. DRAYNES WOOD, CORNWALL
SX 2268.   40 ha   Grade 2

This is a wooded gorge which carries irregular stands of high forest. The high forest areas are characteristically pedunculate oak with ash and beech over a shrub layer of hazel. There are also patches of sessile oak which have been coppiced. The field layer is generally acidophilous with much *Luzula sylvatica*, *Vaccinium myrtillus* and *Blechnum spicant* but on the better soils bracken and bramble occur with species such as *Sanicula europaea* on the best sites.

This woodland is notable mainly for its bryophyte communities and there are some rare species. The filmy fern *Hymenophyllum tunbrigense* also occurs here in some quantity.

W.79. PILES COPSE, DEVON
SX 6361.   5 ha   Grade 2

This is a valley woodland on the southern edge of Dartmoor on the west-facing slope above the River Erme. Although strewn with boulders the woodland floor does not exhibit such extreme clitter formations as found in Wistman's Wood or Black Tor Copse. The tree layer is again dominated by pedunculate oak but the trees are less stunted and the appearance is of a more ordinary woodland. The climate appears to be milder and more humid; there is little or no *Antitrichia* or *Douinia* but *Jamesoniella autumnalis*, *Harpanthus scutatus* and *Dicranum flagellare* occur, these not having been recorded anywhere else in Devon.

W.80. DENDLES WOOD, DEVON
SX 6162.   65 ha   Grade 2

The site occupies the two arms and junction of a Y-shaped valley system on the south-west edge of Dartmoor. Sessile oak woodland is present over much of the site but on the east and south-west beech has been planted. The beech is gradually becoming dominant and a successional series is exhibited. The ground flora is for a large part a grassy sward containing species such as *Holcus mollis*, *H. lanatus*, *Anthoxanthum odoratum*, *Potentilla reptans*, *Endymion nonscriptus* and *Pteridium aquilinum*. There is a good epiphyte and bryophyte flora, the latter being particularly rich in the vicinity of the streams.

W.81. WOODY BAY, DEVON
SS 6748.   55 ha   Grade 2

A coastal woodland which has a generally north-facing aspect. The cliff slopes steeply and drops precipitously to the sea which forms one boundary, whilst on the landward side the woodland is bordered by moorland. The tree canopy is dominated by sessile oak, there being a little rowan and birch. The rare *Sorbus devoniensis* and *S. subcuneata* are found in this woodland. Other tree species include yew, holly, sallow and rose mainly as understorey species.

The ground flora is for the most part acidophilous with *Vaccinium myrtillus*, *Melampyrum pratense*, *Deschampsia flexuosa*, *Calluna vulgaris* and *Erica cinerea* being frequent. Some more base-rich areas support *Allium ursinum*, *Fragaria vesca*, *Sanicula europaea* and *Circaea lutetiana*. The fern and epiphyte floras are well developed; the ferns including *Dryopteris aemula* and *Polystichum setiferum*.

W.82. HEDDON VALLEY WOODS, DEVON
SS 6549.   165 ha   Grade 2

Heddon Valley is an unspoilt, steep-sided, straight valley leading down to the sea. The valley runs north–south and the woodland is at the landward (south) end. Included in the site is open, grassy moorland, damp meadowland on the valley floor and scree slopes at the seaward end of the valley. The woodland is dominated by sessile oak with some patches of ash. A wide range of tree and shrub species are present including alder, birch, beech, hazel, hawthorn, holly, traveller's joy and gorse. The field layer is varied and includes both basiphilous and acidophilous communities. There are areas containing dog's mercury, primrose,

Fragaria vesca, Euphorbia amygdaloides and *Sanicula europaea* which may be contrasted with areas supporting communities which include bilberry, heather, foxglove and bracken. Yet another facies represented is the damp, fern-rich woodland type with *Dryopteris* spp. abundant.

W.83. HOBBY WOODS, DEVON

SS 3323. 90 ha   Grade 2

The Hobby is an area of steep, wooded sea cliffs facing in a north-easterly direction over Barnstaple Bay on the north Devon coast. The tree dominant is sessile oak although within the woodland beech, ash and some planted conifers are present. These other species occur on the upper parts of the slopes, pure oak woodland being present on the steeper slopes close to the sea. Shrub species are represented by hazel, hawthorn, holly, blackthorn and gorse; some rhododendron is present. Large areas of the ground flora are dominated by a sward of *Luzula sylvatica*, other areas supporting a flora which includes *Ajuga reptans, Geranium robertianum, Fragaria vesca, Sanicula europaea* and *Asperula odorata*. A rich fern flora is present including *Dryopteris borreri, D. filix-mas, D. dilatata* and *D. aemula*. Epiphytes are well represented on the boles and branches of the trees, their presence emphasising the moist conditions found within this type of woodland.

W.84. HOLFORD AND HODDER'S COMBES, SOMERSET

ST 1540. 325 ha   Grade 2

The Quantock Hills consist of Devonian sandstone and grits. At the northern end two steep-sided combes above Holford are clothed for much of their lengths in sessile oak woodland of coppice origin. Other species are present in small numbers, including birch, holly, rowan and alder. Structurally the stands vary from dense, young coppice to mature, but short, high forest. Growing only 3 km from the coast at elevations up to 300 m, the more exposed portions are severely wind-pruned. The ground flora is dominated by bilberry, bracken, heather and other calcifuges, with only local development of base-rich conditions with primrose and *Chrysosplenium oppositifolium*.

The woodlands of the two combes are not quite contiguous, but are linked by heathland of *Calluna vulgaris, Ulex gallii* and *Erica cinerea*. The site extends up the combes to Bircham Wood and the Dowsborough respectively.

W.85. ASHEN COPSE, SOMERSET

ST 7942. 35 ha   Grade 2

This is a very fine example of coppice-with-standards woodland with pedunculate oak over hazel on Oxford Clay. Ash is common and other associates are field maple and alder (along the ditches). In addition to hazel the shrub layer contains hawthorn, blackthorn, sallows, guelder rose and *Rosa* spp.

The oaks are particularly well-grown here and, as the understorey has not been cut extensively for many years, an interestingly varied understorey is developing.

The field layer is characteristic of clay woodlands with species such as *Anemone nemorosa, Rubus fruticosus* agg., *Endymion non-scriptus, Viola* spp., *Brachypodium sylvaticum, Fragaria vesca, Galeobdolon luteum, Mercurialis perennis, Ajuga reptans, Allium ursinum, Carex pendula* and *C. sylvatica* and *Filipendula ulmaria*.

Ashen Copse has features resembling the eastern boulder clay coppices and is thus, like Salisbury Wood, Monmouthshire, one of the westernmost of this type. It is adjacent to Longleat Woods and Park, additional remnants of the former Selwood Forest. These woods which contrast with Ashen Copse include ancient oak–beech high forest, mature but younger high forest and old, open park woodland, which together have a very rich epiphytic lichen flora including numerous old forest relic species.

W.86. GREAT BREACH AND COPLEY WOODS, SOMERSET

ST 5031. 60 ha   Grade 2

Mainly an oak–ash woodland on wet Lower Lias clays.

The woodland is extensive and covers some 400 ha but felling and replanting with beech and conifers have taken place.

The woodland varies from almost pure oakwood in some areas, through oak–ash woodland to some stands of almost pure hornbeam and of English elm. There is a wide range of associated trees and shrubs which include field maple, sycamore, alder, sweet chestnut, beech and sallows. The shrubs include traveller's joy, dogwood, hazel, hawthorn, spindle, privet, blackthorn, elder, gorse and wayfaring tree. There are also many spruces, larches and pines.

The field layer is characteristic of the more base-rich clays with *Mercurialis perennis, Carex pendula* and *Rubus fruticosus* agg. locally abundant, and a good variety of other species.

The area forms a good example of a western oak–ash wood on clay with a wide range of associated species.

W.87. WESTON BIG WOOD, SOMERSET

ST 4575. 40 ha   Grade 2

An attractive and varied woodland, formerly coppiced, on Carboniferous Limestone.

The tree layer is dominated by pedunculate oak with small-leaved lime and wych elm locally abundant. In addition there is field maple, ash, gean, common lime and English elm. The *Sorbus* spp. are particularly interesting; *S. torminalis* occurs, as does *S. aria* and the hybrid between them. A *Sorbus* close to *S. rupicola* is also found here.

The shrub layer has abundant hazel with dogwood, hawthorn, spindle, abundant holly, privet, crab apple, currant, *Rosa* spp., wayfaring tree and guelder rose. The field layer is dominated by bramble, *Brachypodium sylvaticum* and dog's mercury but a very wide range of calcicolous species also occurs.

This is a fine example of a mixed deciduous woodland with a rich variety of plant species. The *Sorbus* spp. need further study.

SOUTH WALES

W.88. CWM CLYDACH, BRECKNOCK
SO 2112. 20 ha   Grade 1

This reserve, which is within the Brecon Beacons National Park, consists of two blocks of woodland, the upper Coed Fedw-ddu and Coed Ffyddlwn, both on the south side of the Afon Clydach ravine. The underlying Millstone Grit and Carboniferous Limestone provide both acidic and base-rich conditions. The soils are shallow, stony and boulder strewn, and podsols only lie on the gentler slopes. Litter up to 50 cm has been recorded and it decomposes rapidly, partly because of the extreme dampness at the bottom of the valley which rarely receives any sun.

Beech is dominant in the canopy throughout, and on the shallower well-drained soils sessile oak is a co-dominant with birch. Rowan, hawthorn, hazel, blackthorn and *Salix atrocinerea* are in the shrub layer.

Where the soil is wet with a deeper clay overlying limestone, wych elm is co-dominant with ash, and yew, holly, elder, as well as hazel, are in the understorey. There is a range passing through pure beechwood between these two woodland types. The poor, acidic soils characteristically have a herb layer dominated by *Deschampsia flexuosa*, accompanied by species including *Blechnum spicant*, *Dryopteris borreri*, *Luzula sylvatica* and *Athyrium filix-femina* with locally frequent *Vaccinium myrtillus* and *Pteridium aquilinum*. Where the soil is neutral, base-rich and poorly drained, *Deschampsia cespitosa* dominates the herb layer in association with *Brachypodium sylvaticum*, *Epilobium montanum*, *Mercurialis perennis*, *Mycelis muralis*, *Phyllitis scolopendrium*, *Polystichum setiferum* and *P. lobatum*. *Allium ursinum* is locally abundant. Accumulations of *Sphagnum* spp. and *Leucobryum glaucum* also occur.

Hawthorn scrub and a mixed scrub community occur on the margins and river flushes; stream-bank communities and limestone outcrops with yew add to the variety of habitats within the reserve boundary.

The trees are not markedly even-aged and regeneration appears to be successful. Although it has been recorded growing elsewhere in the locality associated with the Carboniferous Limestone, Cwm Clydach appears to be the largest and therefore the best representative area of native beech on the western fringe of its natural distribution in Britain.

W.89. PENMOELALLT, BRECKNOCK
SO 0109. 7 ha   Grade 1

This Forest Nature Reserve comprises a small strip of mixed deciduous woodland owned by the Forestry Commission overlying a narrow Carboniferous Limestone belt which forms a low escarpment. The major interest is the presence of three well-developed specimens of *Sorbus leyana*, endemic here, and the abundance of *S. porrigentiformis*. However, the Reserve bears a type of woodland now rare in Wales. On the limestone scree the tree cover is dominated by ash together with wych elm and rowan. The ground flora has much *Mercurialis perennis*, *Geranium lucidum* and

Asperula odorata, and calcicolous bryophytes are well represented on the rocks.

On deep clay soil towards the southern end of the woodland the tree cover is mixed and is dominated by pedunculate oak together with ash, elm, rowan and silver birch. Small-leaved lime is also present and hazel is frequent in the shrub layer. Abundant species of the ground flora are *Endymion non-scriptus*, *Oxalis acetosella*, *Viola riviniana* and *V. reichenbachiana*.

W.90. COED RHEIDOL, CARDIGANSHIRE
SN 7478. 75 ha   Grade 1

The Rheidol valley sides are covered in mainly oak woodland over much of their length, with the best stands immediately above and below the Rheidol Falls. At Devil's Bridge there is a confluence of twin streams which have cut deeply through Silurian sediments to form deep gorges clothed for the most part in even-aged sessile oak woodland with some birch and rowan. Beneath this on the acidic brown earth and podsol soils, the field layer is strongly calcifuge in character, i.e. of *Vaccinium myrtillus*, *Molinia caerulea*, *Deschampsia flexuosa* and *Melampyrum pratense*, with a strong bryophyte component, e.g. *Dicranum majus*, *Leucobryum glaucum* and *Bazzania trilobata*, reflecting the high humidity in the ravine. Locally in the acidophilous woods birch is dominant, but the main variation is produced by river- and streamside flushing. Here mixed deciduous woodland of sessile oak, ash, wych elm and hazel with rare small-leaved lime has developed with a basiphilous ground flora of *Circaea lutetiana*, *Sanicula europaea*, and ferns. A number of Atlantic bryophytes are present, *Jamesoniella autumnalis*, *Radula aquilegia*, *Marchesinia mackaii*, *Cephaloziella pearsonii*, *Harpalejeunea ovata*, *Scapania gracilis*, *Jubula hutchinsiae*, *Saccogyna viticulosa*, *Lepidozia pinnata* and *L. pearsonii*, and some local vascular plants, including *Trollius europaeus*, *Festuca altissima*, *Meconopsis cambrica*, *Hymenophyllum tunbrigense*, *Asplenium septentrionale* and *Dryopteris aemula*. The site extends below the Rheidol Falls to the western end of Allt Ddu where on either side of a tributary stream in sessile oak coppice woodland, ranging in age up to 150 years, there is a fine example of contrasting ground flora types on broadly east- and west-facing slopes.

W.91. COTHI TYWI, CARMARTHENSHIRE
SN 7648. 200 ha   Grade 1

This is a composite name for Allt Rhyd-y-Groes and Allt Pen-y-rhiw-iar and their surrounding upland country (see also U.6). These lie on a steep north-east-facing valley side overlooking the Afon Doethie. Silurian rocks, predominantly shales, have weathered to produce podsols and brown earths of low base-status.

Both woodlands are dominated by sessile oak, with some particularly good specimens at Allt Rhyd-y-Groes. The trees in Allt Pen-y-rhiw-iar are more closely spaced and have been subjected to coppicing in the past. Associated tree species in both woodlands include ash and alder on the damper soils with rowan and birch scattered throughout: wych elm, holly, hawthorn, crab apple and willows (*Salix cinerea* and *S. aurita*) are also present. The shrub layer is not well developed though hazel is abundant where the oaks have been coppiced. Blackthorn is marginal and honeysuckle and ivy are restricted to inaccessible rocks.

The woodland ground flora is not particularly rich and bryophytes form an important constituent. On the lower slopes of both woods, *Anthoxanthum odoratum* is abundant, replaced by *Festuca ovina* and *Deschampsia flexuosa* at the upper levels. Other flowering plants include *Vaccinium myrtillus*, *D. cespitosa*, *Oxalis acetosella*, *Endymion non-scriptus*, *Geranium robertianum*, *Filipendula ulmaria* and *Chrysosplenium oppositifolium*, illustrating the range of soil conditions. Such ferns as *Dryopteris filix-mas* and *Polypodium vulgare* are abundant, *Hymenophyllum wilsonii* and *Thelypteris dryopteris* are present. The commonest bryophytes are *Polytrichum* spp., *Dicranum majus*, *Rhytidiadelphus loreus* and a cascading stream has several oceanic bryophytes including *Jubula hutchinsiae* and *Plagiochila tridenticulata*. *Bazzania trilobata* and *Mylia taylori* are also very luxuriant. *Nowellia curvifolia* and the rare *Sphenolobus helleranus* grow on rotting logs.

W.92. COED Y CERRIG, MONMOUTHSHIRE
SO 2921.   50 ha   Grade 1

This wood lies on rocks of the Old Red Sandstone series in a secluded valley within the boundary of the Brecon Beacons National Park. Two woodland types are present, a hanging wood on steep slopes giving way to a wet wood on the valley flats. The latter is dominated by alder, with willows, blackthorn and *Rosa* spp. in the shrub layer. Herbs in abundance include *Chrysosplenium oppositifolium*, *Ranunculus repens*, *Juncus* spp. and *Filipendula ulmaria*. Both the north- and south-facing slopes, up to 300 m, are dominated by sessile oak with some good specimens. Also in the canopy and locally abundant are ash, elm and silver birch. The understorey is well developed, with field maple, rowan, crab apple, holly and hazel. Shrubs such as hawthorn and elder occur, and the moss *Cryphaea heteromalla* grows on elder. The wood is apparently ungrazed and species composition of the ground flora varies from mesophilous to base-rich types. This includes *Anemone nemorosa*, *Endymion non-scriptus*, *Viola* spp., *Brachypodium sylvaticum*, *Primula vulgaris*, *Mercurialis perennis*, *Arum maculatum*, *Orchis mascula*, *Silene dioica*, *Paris quadrifolia*, *Chrysosplenium alternifolium* and *Lysimachia nemorum*; patches of *Lathraea squamaria* are frequent. More acidic areas with *Deschampsia cespitosa*, *Digitalis purpurea*, *Galium hercynicum* and *Luzula pilosa* also occur.

W.93. SALISBURY WOOD: COED SALSBRI,
MONMOUTHSHIRE
ST 4289.   30 ha   Grade 1

Salisbury Wood lies on the steep slopes and summit of hills composed of limestone, calcareous shales and calcareous head. Much of the woodland on the slope is an intimate mixture of small-leaved lime, ash, wych elm and hazel with much gean, forming high forest derived from coppice. The

plateau areas have two types of woodland on partly drained, neutral clay: ash–gean coppice now grazed by cattle occupies the south-western arm of the wood, and coppice-with-standards pedunculate oak over small-leaved lime, ash and hazel occurs round a complex of parish boundaries and associated pollarded trees. The ground flora is predominantly calcicolous, with *Mercurialis perennis*, *Galium odoratum*, *Brachypodium sylvaticum*, *Rubus fruticosus* agg. and *Phyllitis scolopendrium* perhaps the most abundant in a rich mixture not clearly dominated by any one species.

This wood is selected as an example of mixed deciduous woodland, with a particularly rich flora. It has several other important characteristics. Both oaks and birches are completely absent from most of the wood. Structurally, the stand has a variety of types based on the coppice system, one of which, the ash–gean, is very rare. It lies on a complex of parish boundaries along which are numerous fine, ancient, pollarded trees. In management and floristic terms it appears to be closely allied to the eastern mixed deciduous coppices on calcareous soil, a type which extends along the north Cotswolds and into south Wales.

W.94. BLACKCLIFF–WYNDCLIFF–PIERCE WOODS:
CLOGWYN DU–CLOGWYN GWYN–COED PYRS,
MONMOUTHSHIRE
ST 533988–533942.   180 ha   Grade 1

This extensive stand lies on the right bank of the lower Wye and stretches from Castle Wood in the south to Blackcliff Wood in the north, and includes those woods on the Liveoaks meander which have so far been spared destruction by quarrying. The area is composed of Carboniferous strata, mostly limestone but including a small proportion of acidic rocks, and includes the two cliffs of Blackcliff and Wyndcliff and small river cliffs elsewhere, precipitous slopes along, for example, Piercefield Cliffs, and gently sloping ground in the centre of Pierce Woods. The woods cover an altitudinal range greater than 230 m and have a variety of aspects lacking only west-facing slopes. The woodland is mostly mature high forest, some of it grown up from coppice-with-standards. The principal species are beech, yew, small-leaved lime, pedunculate and sessile oaks, wych elm and ash. Although these are commonly found in intimate mixtures, one or two species assume dominance locally. This is particularly evident on the cliff faces and the scree slopes where beech and yew dominate, and on some of the lower, gentler slopes where sessile oak and lime are dominant. Structurally, there is considerable variety including nearly open scrub on the cliff faces, mixed-age woodland on Piercefield Cliffs and even-aged, former coppice-with-standards in Martridge Wood. The subordinate tree and shrub species include a variety of *Sorbus* spp. (*S. torminalis*, *S. aria*, *S. porrigentiformis*, *S. anglica* and *S. rupicola*). The ground flora is limited, partly by the heavy shade but also by the lack of surface water. Floristically, the site has a number of rare and local species, including *Geranium sylvaticum* and large-leaved lime.

These woods represent part of the range of structural and

floristic variation in the extensive Wye valley woods, particularly the lower region of limestone. These woods are chosen, rather than the woods on the left bank from Caswell Wood to Chapelhouse Wood, because they are less altered by recent forestry operations, include a greater variety of habitat and woodland types and, on available information, are floristically the richer.

W.95. WYE GORGE: HAFAN GWY, MONMOUTHSHIRE–GLOUCESTERSHIRE–HEREFORDSHIRE

SO 5414.   240 ha   Grade 1*

These woodlands lie on either side of a spectacular meandering river gorge cut through rocks of Old Red Sandstone and Carboniferous Limestone series. They extend from the area of the Far Hearkening Rock to Elliotts and Court Woods, and include Lady Park Wood and the riverside parts of Lords Wood and Mailscot Wood.

Lady Park Wood is mixed deciduous woodland of an exceptional character. It lies at the northern end of High-meadow Woods on slopes and cliffs above the River Wye on Carboniferous strata which give rise to three major soil types: shallow, stony, limestone soils, light loams derived from drift of Old Red Sandstone origin and clay loams derived from shales. This woodland is exceptionally rich in tree and shrub species, including sessile oak, beech, ash, small-leaved lime, wych elm, field maple, silver birch, whitebeam, wild service and the only stand in Britain where large-leaved lime is an appreciable constituent of the canopy. Much of the Wood has been cut over in recent decades and now constitutes coppice regrowth and saplings, but a scattering of mature trees, mainly beech, has survived. The ground flora varies with soil conditions, with much *Luzula sylvatica* on the light loams, *Deschampsia cespitosa* and *Rubus caesius* on the clays, and calcicolous communities with *Mercurialis perennis* on the limestone. Numerous rare species have been recorded, including the tree species *Tilia platyphyllos*, *Sorbus anglica* and the rare hybrid *S. torminalis × aria*.

On the opposite bank are the Seven Sisters Rocks. These limestone pillars are important refugia for certain rare grassland species including *Carex humilis*, *C. montana*, *C. digitata* and *Geranium sanguineum*. In adjacent Lords Wood a number of disused stone mines are important overwintering sites for greater horseshoe bats. Coldwell Rocks are north-facing cliffs (75 m) rich in bryophytes and ferns.

W.96. NANT IRFON, BRECKNOCK

SN 8454.   40 ha   Grade 2

The Irfon valley is narrow and steep-sided with extensive outcrops of Silurian rocks. Two blocks of north-east-facing, hanging sessile oakwoods spanning an altitude of 290–380 m lie within the boundary of the NNR. Their primary interest is the presence of breeding raptors. The site includes woodland on the opposite side of the valley.

Coed Tŷ-mawr is a steep compact area of almost pure, uncoppiced sessile oakwood. Apart from the northern,

exposed section the trees are well developed and open grown. It has a wet oakwood field layer with a rich and varied bryophyte flora, from *Polytrichum* and *Hypnum* species on dry sites through *Thuidium tamariscinum* and *Dicranella heteromalla*, to *Sphagnum palustre*, *S. papillosum* and *Fissidens taxifolius* on wet sites. Coedydd Hen-Nant & Digydd is an extended and discontinuous woodland intersected by deep cwms and is variable in breadth and density. It is predominantly sessile oak, open, uncoppiced and with well-developed crowns, with some downy birch, rowan, hazel and ash. Hawthorn and occasional beech are present. The lush ground cover is similar to Tŷ-mawr but there are patches of *Pteridium aquilinum* or of *Agrostis tenuis* and other grasses. Wet boggy flushes have *Molinia caerulea*, *Sphagnum* spp., and *Carex* spp. and there are bryophyte-covered wet, shady screes.

Coedydd Bron-gynes & Clawdd-coch lie outside the present Reserve. These are comparatively dry woodlands on shallow soils facing west-south-west. They form a low bank intersected by a few shallow cwms. Coppiced sessile oak is dominant with occasional downy birch and rowan. The ground flora is variable though grazed. Bracken is dominant in the more open areas and in other sections mosses, including *Hypnum cupressiforme* var. *ericetorum*, *Hylocomium splendens*, *Rhytidiadelphus squarrosus*, *Polytrichum commune*, *P. formosum*, *Mnium hornum* and *Atrichum undulatum*, are most abundant. The higher levels are grassy with *Agrostis tenuis* and *Anthoxanthum odoratum*. Rock outcrops bear *Calluna vulgaris* with *Festuca ovina* and *Polytrichum piliferum*.

See also U.9.

W.97. CARN GAFALLT, BRECKNOCK

SN 9464.   110 ha   Grade 2

This complex of woodlands lies south of Rhayader on the slopes of Silurian rocks above the rivers Elan and Wye. A discontinuous belt of oakwood lies around the north-west, west and south flanks of the hill, Carn Gafallt. The slopes above Elan village are block strewn, the rock being a hard grit compared to the slates nearby. Variation in form and size of the trees, due to past management, occurs throughout. Here the oaks, though short, are spreading and of good girth. Bryophyte communities are well developed on the blocks, particularly *Scapania gracilis* with *Lepidozia pinnata*, and other western species present include *Bazzania trilobata*. Bilberry is dominant locally but in places there are dense, pure carpets of moss. A small area of large oak (up to 21 m) with a more uniform field layer, dominated by bracken, lies to the west of a nearby stream. The remainder of the woods towards the south also contain oak of medium size with moss or bilberry-dominated communities.

A woodland with an intimate mixture of sites and species lies on gentler slopes to the south side of the Dulas stream, where the rock is richer in bases and numerous flushes occur. Patches are dominated by oak, ash, alder or birch or by a mixture of all four species. Wych elm is scattered throughout, hazel and hawthorn are plentiful, and rowan and holly are also present. Parts of the wood have a block-strewn floor and elsewhere a rich field layer on mull soils passes in places to flush mire under alderwood.

Some of the woodlands in this complex are perhaps as good as existing Reserves but since they duplicate the interest of these and there are no unusual associated features, a status higher than grade 2 is not considered to be justified. (See Appendix.)

The valley bottom has old pastures and hay meadows (with *Sanguisorba officinalis* abundant, *Carex hostiana*, *Equisetum sylvaticum*, *Platanthera chlorantha*, *Vicia cracca* and *V. orobus* locally common), *Juncus* marsh (with *Eleocharis palustris*, *Scutellaria galericulata*, *Sparganium ramosum* and *Triglochin palustris*) and wet heathy fields with some developing *Sphagnum* bog (with *Vaccinium oxycoccus*, *Drosera rotundifolia*, *Wahlenbergia hederacea* and in drier parts *Genista anglica*, *G. tinctoria* and *Cirsium dissectum*).

W.98. BLAENAU NEDD & MELLTE, BRECKNOCK
SN 9210.   60 ha   Grade 2

These woodlands are situated in the upper gorges of the Neath River to the north of the South Wales coalfield, and within the Brecon Beacons National Park. Outcrops of Carboniferous Limestone occur only on the higher parts of the gorge sides and its influence is localised; the river itself cuts through Millstone Grit. The composition of the woodland in these gorges varies from a grazed acidophilous sessile facies; through a more mixed deciduous type with ash, wych elm and a little small-leaved lime in the canopy with hazel, field maple and some hawthorn below; to the stream sides dominated by birch and alder. Small areas of mesophilous vegetation occur, though, in the main, a grazed acidophilous field layer is present. *Deschampsia flexuosa* is the main constituent with a ground layer of *Dicranum majus*, *Leucobryum glaucum*, *Polytrichum formosum*, *Mnium hornum* and *Diplophyllum albicans*. *Luzula sylvatica* and *Vaccinium myrtillus* are only present on inaccessible rock outcrops. The splash areas of the waterfalls and trees and rocks in the gorges have ferns and bryophytes, rare or local in south Wales, including *Hymenophyllum tunbrigense*, *H. wilsonii*, *Ptilidium pulcherrimum* and *Isopterygium pulchellum*.

W.99. DARREN FACH, BRECKNOCK
SO 0110.   12 ha   Grade 2

This west-facing site lies across the upper Taff valley, a short distance upstream from Penmoelallt, and can be considered an alternative to it. It consists of an open scrub on low limestone cliffs with screes and woodland on the gentler slopes. The latter are dominated by ash inter-mixed with wych elm together with a well-developed understorey of hazel and hawthorn. Field maple is present and a group of small-leaved lime lies at the northern end. The primary interest lies in a concentration of *Sorbus* spp. on the southern end of the Darren Fach crags. Several shrubs of *S. leyana* together with a specimen of *S. porrigentiformis* grow just below the crags together with ash, yew and holly.

The ground layer is heavily grazed and includes *Mercurialis perennis*, *Oxalis acetosella*, *Rubus fruticosus* agg.,

6

Deschampsia cespitosa, *Phyllitis scolopendrium* with some *Asperula odorata*.

W.100. GLANNAU, RADNOR
SN 9065.   25 ha   Grade 2

This site on Silurian shales and sandstones occurs on the steep slopes above the Garreg-ddu reservoir which bounds it on the east and south. The soils vary in base content and though dominated by sessile oak, three distinct blocks occur. On basic soils at the northern end a dense mixture of wych elm, oak, hazel, willow and birch grows over abundant *Mercurialis perennis* with *Circaea lutetiana* and *Geranium robertianum*. Outcrops of rocks support *Asplenium trichomanes*, *Neckera crispa*, *Tortella tortuosa*, *Bartramia halleriana*, *Brachythecium plumosum* and *Ctenidium molluscum* indicating their moderate lime content. The central area contains a less dense growth of oaks, 15–18 m in height, with a few birch and rowan over a bracken-dominated floor with patches of moss-rich grassland with *Deschampsia flexuosa*, *Digitalis purpurea*, *Galium hercynicum* and *Oxalis acetosella*. *Nowellia* and *Lepidozia reptans* cover fallen, rotting tree trunks. At the south end, sycamore and beech increase in abundance with a scattering of conifers. *Saccogyna viticulosa* and *Plagiochila spinulosa* are abundant here and other species include *Athyrium filix-femina*, *Dryopteris filix-mas*, *Blechnum spicant* and *Deschampsia cespitosa*.

W.101. COED ABER EDW, RADNOR
SO 0847.   16 ha   Grade 2

This wood lies to the south of the River Edw. The steep north-facing slopes of the valley carry both oakwood and mixed deciduous wood; the former occurring on acidic and the latter on the calcareous shaly beds of the Ludlow Group of the Silurian. Where the calcareous rock outcrops the main trees are ash, wych elm and hazel but there are some field maple and rowan and a few trees of small-leaved lime. There is also some elder and gooseberry but birch is scarce. The ground flora although sparse is species-rich and includes *Polystichum setiferum*, *Asplenium trichomanes*, *Phyllitis scolopendrium*, *Melica uniflora*, *Brachypodium sylvaticum*, *Poa nemoralis*, *Saxifraga hypnoides*, *Mycelis muralis*, *Mercurialis perennis*, *Chrysosplenium oppositifolium*, *Glechoma hederacea*, *Veronica montana*, *Hedera helix*, *Geranium robertianum*, *G. lucidum*, *Anomodon viticulosus*, *Thamnium alopecurum*, *Neckera crispa*, *N. complanata*, *Camptothecium sericeum*, *Brachythecium rutabulum*, *B. plumosum*, *Eurhynchium praelongum*, *Mnium rostratum*, *M. undulatum*, *Metzgeria furcata*, *Plagiochila asplenioides* and var. *major*, *Madotheca platyphylla*, *Marchesinia mackaii*.

In other areas oak is dominant and this dominance is clearly associated with scarcity of lime in the parent rock which in turn seems to depend on the disappearance of the calcite veins. The flora of these acidic rocks is poor and includes the common woodland bryophytes. There is a local abundance of *Vaccinium myrtillus* and grasses such as *Holcus mollis*, *Anthoxanthum*, *Festuca ovina* and *Deschampsia flexuosa*.

Presence of small amounts of lime in the generally acidic

rocks is marked by an increase in richness of the ground flora although oak remains dominant.

W.102. COOMBE WOODS: COED Y CWM, MONMOUTHSHIRE

ST 4593.   35 ha   Grade 2

This complex of woods lies on a narrow, steep-sided valley of the Cas-Troggi brook where it cuts through Carboniferous Limestone. It includes Coombe Wood itself, Common Wood on the opposite side of the valley, those parts of Llanmelin Wood which have not been replanted with conifers, and other woodlands which form a contiguous group. Almost all the woodland lies on steeply sloping ground with strongly calcareous soil in a matrix with limestone fragments, but small areas occupy gently sloping ground in both the plateau and valley-bottom situations, where the soil is heavier, less stony, less well drained and locally with impeded drainage, but still calcareous. The woodland is mixed deciduous with beech, ash, wych elm, small-leaved lime, pedunculate oak, field maple and hazel the most abundant, but with many other species present, including whitebeam. Over large areas the ground flora is dominated by dog's mercury, mixed with *Allium ursinum* at the base of the slopes, but there is a good deal of variation from this, with areas of *Convallaria majalis*.

Coombe Woods is best regarded as an alternative to the Blackcliff–Wyndcliff–Pierce Woods grade 1 site (W.94). It is similar in that much of the woodland is mature high forest derived from coppice; in the intimate mixture of the most abundant species, with only small areas of single-species dominance; and in possessing a hill fort occupied by similar mixed deciduous woodland.

NORTH WALES

W.103. COEDYDD DYFFRYN CONWY, CAERNARVONSHIRE

                                                            Grade 1

(a) Coed Dolgarrog

SH 7666.   70 ha

This wood extends for about 1.6 km along the steep western side of the Dyffryn Conwy and is bounded to the north and south by deep rocky ravines formed by streams whose flow is now somewhat reduced by the Dolgarrog Hydro-electric Scheme. The wood has a large altitudinal range from 30 m to over 300 m but, apart from the upper margin, is sheltered from the prevailing south-west winds. Rainfall is about 150 cm annually, but humidity is lower than in the adjoining gorge woodlands, such as Ceunant Dulyn. The rocks are Ordovician rhyolites and rhyolite tuffs in the south, followed in a northerly direction by a massive buttress of pumice tuff projecting into the main valley, then a concave slope of slate and finally, in the extreme north, a second but smaller buttress of pumice tuff. The pumice tuff yields soils of moderate base-status, as in Ceunant Dulyn, whilst the other rocks yield more acid soils. The underlying rocks are often masked by layers or pockets of drift particularly on the upper slopes and mixed colluvium on the lower slopes.

The dominant tree is oak, of both species as well as hybrids, though in contrast to Coed Gorswen there is a preponderance of sessile types; there is no marked association here between soil type and species of oak. However, this wood is best included in the mixed deciduous category, for there are numerous other tree species, either as scattered individuals or locally dominant. They include birch, wych elm, ash, alder, sycamore, rowan, holly, small-leaved lime and crab apple. Beech is occasional throughout the wood and a few conifers, Scots pine, Norway spruce and larch, are also present. On the more base-rich soils the flora is characterised by such species as *Brachypodium sylvaticum*, *Mercurialis perennis*, *Circaea lutetiana*, *Sanicula europaea*, *Fragaria vesca*, *Allium ursinum*, *Geranium robertianum*, *Mycelis muralis*, *Viola riviniana*, *Dryopteris filix-mas*, *Polystichum setiferum*, *Rubus fruticosus* and *Carex sylvatica*. The more acidic soils are dominated by such species as *Agrostis tenuis*, *Pteridium aquilinum*, *Festuca rubra*, *Deschampsia flexuosa*, *Anthoxanthum odoratum*, *Galium hercynicum*, *Oxalis acetosella*, *Digitalis purpurea* and *Vaccinium myrtillus* along with a range of bryophytes. Bryophytes are not conspicuous throughout most of the woods but the two ravines and some of the older trees provide a useful range of habitats. *Hylocomium brevirostre* is abundant in the west of the area. The wood includes a wide range of habitats for larger mammals and birds and is notable in having a large population of badgers.

In the south the wood extends high up the valley of the Afon Ddu which contains the Ardda Alder Wood. This is a high-level alderwood at 210–260 m, a type previously common but now extremely rare in Wales. This was part of the Cistercian monastery of Aberconwy established in the twelfth century. The survival of the alder woodland may be because of the more limited extent of sixteenth-century enclosures in this area compared to similar valleys in Snowdonia. The shrub layer is well developed in some parts of the wood but almost completely absent from others, the main species being hazel but holly and rowan are also common. Spindle occurs but is rare. The ground flora of the alderwood is extremely varied.

(b) Coed Gorswen

SH 7570.   14 ha

The wood lies on the western side of the more gently sloping lower Dyffryn Conwy at an altitude of 45–150 m. It is the driest of the base-rich series with a rainfall of about 130 cm annually. The underlying rocks are completely masked by glacial drift and colluvium of mixed composition containing acid sedimentary, acidic and basic igneous rocks, resulting in a mixture of acidic and base-rich soils. Several streams and flush lines run through the wood adding further to the base-rich influence. The result is a diverse wood consisting of oak, wych elm, alder, ash, sycamore, both birches and gean. Both sessile and pedunculate oaks and hybrids are present in the wood but pedunculate types are probably in the majority. There seems to be a characteristic distribution with pedunculate types on wetter flushed sites and sessile types on the more freely draining soils, particularly at the higher west side of the wood. There is a well-developed shrub layer, and blackthorn are locally dominant. Other species present include rowan, hawthorn, elder, crab apple and field maple. The ground flora is equally rich and five main communities have been described. On freely and imperfectly drained soils the main species are *Oxalis acetosella*, *Geranium robertianum*, *Rubus fruticosus*, *Viola riviniana*, *Veronica chamaedrys*, *Brachypodium sylvaticum*, *Geum urbanum*, *Sanicula europaea* and *Circaea lutetiana*. Less common plants include *Botrychium lunaria* and *Epipactis helleborine*. On the wetter gleyed soils, in flushes or beside streams the main species are *Ranunculus repens*, *R. flammula*, *Chrysosplenium oppositifolium*, *Mentha aquatica*, *Phalaris arundinacea*, *Carex remota*, *C. laevigata*, *C. nigra*, *Juncus effusus* and *J. acutiflorus*.

(c) Ceunant Dulyn
SH 7568. 16 ha

This site is situated in the steep-sided valley of Afon Dulyn which flows east into the River Conwy. The altitude ranges from 75–240 m. Rainfall is about 152 cm annually but with high humidity within the ravine. Flow in the river is affected by the Dolgarrog Hydro-electric Scheme. The underlying rocks are Ordovician sediments and pumice tuff which have produced acid and moderately base-rich soils respectively. The acidic soils support oak (mainly *Quercus petraea*) and birch woodland with a sparse shrub layer and a ground flora consisting of such species as *Pteridium aquilinum*, *Agrostis tenuis*, *Deschampsia flexuosa* and *Oxalis acetosella*. On the more basic soils the main species is again oak, but this time *Q. petraea*, *Q. robur* and hybrids, along with ash, wych elm, alder and sycamore. There is a well-developed shrub layer consisting mainly of hazel and a much richer ground flora including such species as *Ranunculus repens*, *Carex remota*, *Angelica sylvestris*, *Sanicula europaea*, *Mercurialis perennis*, *Brachypodium sylvaticum*, *Deschampsia cespitosa*, *Oxalis acetosella*, *Viola riviniana*, *Geranium robertianum*, *Dryopteris filix-mas* and *Rubus fruticosus* agg. The Atlantic bryophyte flora is only moderately rich.

W.104. COEDYDD ABER, CAERNARVONSHIRE
SH 6671. 165 ha   Grade 1

These woods form a somewhat dissected complex along the valley of Afon Aber, and contain at least four distinct types. In altitude they range from 30 to 210 m, and at the north end of the valley rainfall is only 114 cm annually. The parent rocks are Ordovician and Cambrian grits and shales, and the lower slopes are drift covered. The woods on the upper parts of the system on both east and west sides have typical dry oakwood of sessile oak with some birch and rowan on acidic skeletal brown earths, but these grade below into mixed deciduous woodland of ash, wych elm, oak, birch and abundant hazel on base-rich clayey soils, on both steep slopes bounding a central ravine and flatter ground to the north and south.

The oakwood has a typically acidophilous field layer with *Agrostis–Anthoxanthum* grassland, a good deal of bracken locally, and a well-developed moss layer in which Atlantic

species are not particularly well represented, probably because there are few blocks and also because of unfavourable management. The mixed woodland has the richer *Brachypodium sylvaticum* herb-rich grassland, with an abundance of basiphilous species. On the steep slopes flanking the ravine, the fern *Polystichum setiferum* is abundant, while the rock ledges have a fine colony of the very local grass *Festuca altissima*, and *Hypericum androsaemum* also grows here.

On flatter, waterlogged ground there are patches of alderwood with a swampy floor containing fairly hydrophilous species such as *Ranunculus repens* and *Chrysosplenium oppositifolium*. Where the wood thins out at the head of the valley, there is a transition to a fairly extensive area of open hawthorn scrub with some crab apple in a grassland community containing a great abundance of bluebell. This passes into the precipitous northern cliffs down which pour the Aber Falls, and the lower and more broken faces here have interesting examples of ungrazed cliff woodland with stunted oak, birch and rowan, and a luxuriant field layer of *Luzula sylvatica* (illustrating the sensitivity of this species to grazing). Atlantic bryophytes are well represented on these cliffs near the falls and include very local species such as *Adelanthus decipiens*, *Anastrepta orcadensis*, *Bazzania tricrenata* and *Hylocomium umbratum*.

The lichen epiphyte flora is one of the most interesting in north Wales. It is essentially lowland in character, consisting of a rich Lobarion community in the ravine with *Parmeliella plumbea* in its only certain recent north Welsh locality in local abundance. Great rarities here are *Arthonia cinereopruinosa* (four British localities), on an old dry bank, *Polyblastia allobata*, *Gyalidiopsis* sp. (undescribed and new to science) and *Mycoblastus fuscatus*.

Perhaps the most important feature of Coedydd Aber is the diversity of woodland types within a single complex, reflecting differences in soil conditions and management. The site is contiguous with the Carneddau part of the Eryri upland site (U.10), and can be regarded as a habitat extension of the latter. Coedydd Aber also has a particularly varied bird fauna, with strong breeding populations of wood warbler, pied flycatcher and redstart.

W.105. COED TREMADOG, CAERNARVONSHIRE
SH 5640. 24 ha   Grade 1

This woodland lies on cliff and scree at 15–150 m on the south-facing scarps of the Moel Hebog massif, overlooking the reclaimed estuary of the Afon Glaslyn (the Traeth Mawr). The site is strongly exposed to south-west onshore winds but the rainfall is lower (about 152 cm annually) than for many of the Snowdonian woodlands, and the aspect is sunny. The underlying rocks are Ordovician slates but there are several large intrusions of base-rich dolerite which form high, vertical cliffs. The steep slopes below the cliffs have a great deal of scree, varying from huge tumbled blocks in the east to much smaller material at the west end. Soils are mostly thin and skeletal, and vary from acidic to strongly basic, with fertile brown earths where there is flushing from the dolerite.

The vegetation varies from closed woodland to open cliff and scree communities. The closed woodland varies from an acidophilous type dominated by sessile oak, with some pedunculate oak, to a basiphilous ash–hazel type. Beech and sycamore are locally plentiful. The oakwood has rowan and holly in the shrub layer, and field communities have *Deschampsia flexuosa*, *Vaccinium myrtillus*, *Anthoxanthum odoratum*, *Agrostis tenuis*, *Teucrium scorodonia* and *Pteridium aquilinum*. The ashwood has a field layer with grasses such as *Brachypodium sylvaticum* and *Melica uniflora*, and forbs such as *Mercurialis perennis*, *Geum rivale*, *Epilobium montanum*, *Melandrium rubrum* and *Veronica officinalis*.

The woodland shows all degrees of opening out, to scattered growths of trees on the screes, and in places a scrubby oakwood spreads up the less precipitous cliffs. There is a variable development of tall scrub, mainly of hazel and hawthorn, with lesser amounts of privet and blackthorn. The screes locally have dense masses of bramble and there is a good deal of ivy. The flora of the more open habitats is rich and interesting, with a variety of moderately to strongly basiphilous species, including *Sedum forsteranum*, *S. telephium*, *Origanum vulgare*, *Hypericum androsaemum*, *H. hirsutum*, *Geranium lucidum*, *G. robertianum*, *Chrysanthemum leucanthemum*, *Polystichum setiferum*, *Phyllitis scolopendrium*, *Asplenium trichomanes*, *A. adiantum-nigrum*, *Pterogonium gracile* and *Marchesinia mackaii*. More acidophilous or acid-tolerant species of rocky habitats include *Sedum anglicum*, *Teucrium scorodonia*, *Hypochoeris radicata*, *Cotyledon umbilicus*, *Corydalis claviculata*, *Dryopteris filix-mas*, *Polypodium vulgare* and *Hedwigia integrifolia*.

The interest of the site is thus partly for the range of woodland features, but also for the more open scrub and rock communities which are referable to types discussed under Lowland Grasslands, Heaths and Scrub.

W.106. COED DINORWIG, CAERNARVONSHIRE
SH 5860. 50 ha   Grade 1

This wood is unusual in being an ungrazed upland sessile oakwood; fenced off from sheep by the farms above and the Dinorwig quarries to the south-east. The oaks are mostly rather small and many are grown over with ivy; there is a patchy underscrub of hazel and holly. The field communities are the most interesting feature, with dominance of *Luzula sylvatica* in the upper part, and a good deal of bilberry and bramble elsewhere. Field communities of this kind are characteristic of ungrazed hill woods on acidic to mildly basic soils, and are well represented in the oakwoods of the Loch Lomond islands (W.169), and some ravine woods. They are, however, rare in the hill woods of Wales. There are block screes and rock outcrops with some Atlantic plants, including *Hymenophyllum wilsonii*, *Plagiochila spinulosa* and *Scapania gracilis*. At the upper fringe, the wood grades into tall Callunetum on rocky bluffs, and there is a transition zone with small, stunted oaks, which are almost certainly the result of coppicing or other human disturbance.

W.107. COEDYDD DYFFRYN MAENTWROG, MERIONETH
Grade 1*

(a) Coed Camlyn–Ceunant Llennyrch
SH 6539. 119 ha

Coed Camlyn is situated on steep slopes on the south side of the Ffestiniog Valley, and the main section of the wood has a north-west aspect, but other parts face north and south-west. Altitude ranges from 15–150 m and exposure to wind, particularly on the upper slopes, is severe, the south-west winds having a more or less clear run from the sea about 8 km distant. Rainfall is about 180 cm annually. The underlying rocks are Upper Cambrian and consist mainly of acidic slates. These rocks are exposed in cliffs at the top of the slopes, whilst the lower slopes are mainly covered with scree of periglacial origin on which freely draining acidic skeletal soils are formed. In the main wood the tree layer is dominated by sessile oak whilst birch is locally co-dominant or forms an understorey in some more open areas. Holly, beech and sycamore are also present. There is a small outlying area dominated by birch and in another sweet chestnut is common. The southern end of the wood has few tall shrubs and the ground flora is almost completely dominated by bilberry, with *Deschampsia flexuosa* and *Molinia caerulea* subdominant. Bracken dominates the field layer in more open areas. In the north bilberry is less prominent, there is a sparse understorey of hazel and the ground flora is dominated by *Agrostis* spp., *Deschampsia flexuosa*, *Oxalis acetosella* and bryophytes. There were formerly several groups of conifers in the wood but these have recently been removed. *Rhododendron ponticum* is present in parts of the wood, but its spread is now largely under control.

At its south-west end, Coed Camlyn bends round into the deep wooded glen of Ceunant Llennyrch which carries the stream from the Trawsfynydd reservoir and contains one of the finest river gorges in north Wales. The rocks are mainly Cambrian slates and shales, but there are basic intrusions, and soil conditions vary from acidic to basic, giving the usual variation from sessile oak to mixed deciduous woodland. In places here, however, the oakwood has been replaced by seral birch. On the precipitous sides of the gorge, woodland species (e.g. *Luzula sylvatica* and numerous forbs) which suffer from sheep-grazing are able to flourish, but the most outstanding feature of the glen is the extremely rich Atlantic cryptogamic flora. The two ferns *Dryopteris aemula* and *Hymenophyllum tunbrigense* probably grow more abundantly here than anywhere else in Wales, and *Osmunda regalis* occurs more sparingly. The bryophyte flora compares favourably with that of Coed Ganllwyd and includes species such as *Sematophyllum demissum*, *Hylocomium umbratum*, *Hypnum callichroum*, *Adelanthus decipiens*, *Colura calyptrifolia*, *Drepanolejeunea hamatifolia*, *Harpalejeunea ovata*, *Radula voluta* and *Marchesinia mackaii*.

The gorge and its flora provide a complement to the hanging woods of Coed Camlyn, which do not have a block-strewn floor and have only the commoner species of Atlantic bryophytes. The construction of the Trawsfynydd reservoir has greatly reduced the flows of the stream through Ceunant Llennyrch, but this has apparently had no significant effect on atmospheric humidity and the richness of the hygrophilous flora.

The lichen flora shows a fine development of the lowland Lobarion community on the large sheltered oaks at the lowest part of the valley, with least rainfall and richest soil. *Rinodina isidioides* and *Pannaria sampaiana* are particularly noteworthy here; the latter species, recently described from Iberia, proves to be rare though widely scattered in western Britain from the New Forest and Devon through north Wales to western Scotland. Other rarities include *Thelopsis rubella* and *Parmelia horrescens*.

Although the upper part of the valley has a magnificent bryophyte flora, the lichen vegetation is represented by the species-poor Parmelietum laevigatae. However, there occurs an undescribed *Bacidia* sp. with an isidiate thallus which is known to be widespread but rare in old southern and western forest fragments.

Thelotrema lepadinum, a lichen which seems to be a very good indicator of ancient forest relict sites, also occurs, as does *Haematomma elatinum* and *Lecidea cinnabarinum* of similar occurrence.

The site is particularly important lichenologically because in this one forested valley there exists both the lowland type of oakwood and its typical lichen flora, and also the upland types with the zone of transition.

(b) Coedydd Maentwrog–Coed Cymerau
SH 6741, SH 6742, SH 6841, SH 6842.   147 ha

These lie on the north side of the Vale of Ffestiniog, Coed Cymerau occupying the steep slopes of the Afon Goedol ravine, whilst Coedydd Maentwrog extends 2.4 km along the main valley. At Coed Cymerau altitude ranges from 45–150 m and apart from the upper slopes on the east side of the river the wood is very sheltered. Rainfall is 200 cm annually but within the confines of the narrow valley atmospheric humidity is markedly higher than in surrounding areas. There is a rather shallow gorge with a small waterfall near which *Hymenophyllum tunbrigense* grows. The underlying rocks are Cambrian slates which weather to produce an acidic soil. On the west side of the river much of the soil is little more than stabilised scree originating from a line of cliffs above. In the east the soil is deeper in places and may be partly formed on drift but throughout the wood as a whole there are numerous areas of exposed rock or tumbled detached boulders.

The tree layer is dominated by oak *Quercus petraea* with only a small contribution of *Q. robur* types. Birch is a scattered co-dominant and becomes locally dominant. Rowan is also common usually as a subdominant and there are a few widely scattered individuals of ash, sycamore, alder, holly and crab apple. Throughout most of the wood the shrub layer is poorly developed but in some slightly flushed areas particularly in the north and west, there is a moderate density of hazel. *Molinia caerulea, Deschampsia flexuosa* and *Agrostis tenuis* are the three main ground flora dominants under closed canopy. In open areas bracken takes over. In contrast to Coed Camlyn, bilberry has a

fairly minor role here. Other common herbaceous species include *Melampyrum pratense, Oxalis acetosella, Galium hercynicum* and *Potentilla erecta*. Bryophytes dominate large areas of the wood particularly in the more rocky areas and a wide range of species has been recorded including several rare Atlantic species, though this site is less rich than some other Merioneth woodlands. Other habitats represented within the wood include several small acidic mires (with *Sphagnum imbricatum*), grassland (with *Wahlenbergia hederacea*) and a small area of open partly stabilised scree on the west side. The river traversing this glen is heavily polluted by sewage from Blaenau Ffestiniog.

Coedydd Maentwrog has an altitude range of 15–150 m. There is also a small detached area a few hundred metres from the west end of the main wood running down to Llyn Mair. The main aspect of the wood is south and it is therefore sun exposed. Rainfall is about 180 cm annually, but there is not the high atmospheric humidity associated with the ravine at Cymerau. This wood is also considerably less humid than the north-west-facing slopes of Coed Camlyn which receive little direct sunshine. The underlying rock is Upper Cambrian shale. As at Camlyn these have been frost shattered to produce extensive periglacial screes upon which acidic soils have developed, but rock weathering at Maentwrog has produced a higher proportion of finer fractions in the soil which is generally richer and more retentive than at Camlyn. The dominant species in the tree layer is sessile oak but there are a number of trees with pedunculate characters indicating some hybridisation. Birch is also common either as a scattered co-dominant or a local dominant round clearings. Other species present include rowan, ash, alder and sycamore. The shrub layer is poorly developed with only scattered hazel, and, though *Rhododendron ponticum* is common in the west end of the wood, its spread is under control. The ground flora beneath the tree canopy is dominated mainly by grasses (*Anthoxanthum odoratum, Agrostis* spp., and *Deschampsia flexuosa*) and mosses. The wood has been more disturbed in recent times than its neighbours, and large gaps are dominated by dense bracken. The oak trees of Coedydd Maentwrog have a much wider age distribution than the other woods in the Ffestiniog Valley (100–200 years) compared with 100–150 at Cymerau and about 100–120 at Camlyn. The different ages, however, tend to be in groups rather than intimately mixed as in some parts of Cymerau.

(c) Coed y Rhygen
SH 6836.   27 ha

The wood lies on the western side of Trawsfynydd Lake at an altitude of 200–260 m. Rainfall is about 200 cm annually, and the proximity of the lake may add to the local atmospheric humidity. Topography within the wood is extremely broken with ridges of rock running up the slope, and there are numerous small cliffs, slabs and block litters. The area lies at the north edge of the Harlech Dome and the underlying rocks are mainly hard Cambrian grits, acidic and resistant to weathering. Except at the north-west end of the wood where there is a deeper acidic soil on drift material, the soils are extremely shallow and skeletal (on the rock ridges) or wet and peaty (in the hollows between). The main species in the tree layer are sessile oak and birch. The most common composition is large, old oak trees set in a matrix of birch but, at the east end of the wood, birch is dominant and there has probably been selective removal of oak over a long period. Rowan is common and scattered throughout the wood and there are a few willows in the wet hollows. The shrub layer is poorly developed, being limited to a few patches of hazel in areas of slight enrichment. The ground flora is generally bryophyte-dominated although *Deschampsia flexuosa* is common throughout and both bracken and bilberry may attain local dominance. Local enrichment of soil is indicated by the local presence in the field layer of *Mercurialis perennis, Geranium robertianum, Lysimachia nemorum* and *Filipendula ulmaria*. The characteristic woodland mosses such as *Rhytidiadelphus loreus* are in profusion in rocky places but over 100 other bryophytes occur. Many species grow with a luxuriance only equalled in western Scotland, notably *Plagiochila spinulosa, Scapania gracilis, Lepidozia pinnata, Bazzania trilobata* and *Saccogyna viticulosa*. *Hymenophyllum wilsonii* is common amongst the rocks and the older trees are covered with epiphytic species including *P. punctata*. Rarer bryophytes are also present and these include *Sematophyllum demissum, Hypnum callichroum, Hylocomium umbratum, Thuidium delicatulum, Adelanthus decipiens, Harpanthus scutatus, Plagiochila tridenticulata, B. tricrenata* and *Lepidozia pearsonii*. The richness of the bryophyte flora points to Post-glacial continuity of tree cover at the site.

The epiphytic lichen flora is limited to the Parmelietum laevigatae community on highly leached acidic bark with only traces of the Lobarion community (*Pannaria pityrea, Parmeliella corallinioides, Sticta sylvatica, Dimerella lutea*) on a few more sheltered old trees. The epiflora, in fact, comprises only 39 species of lichens, a remarkably low number.

Indicators of ancient, relic woodland present are *Thelotrema lepadinum, Haematomma elatinum, Lecidea cinnabarinum*, and probably the Lobarion spp. mentioned. Of oceanic species, the wood possesses *Menegazzia terebrata* and *Cetrelia cetrarioides* as well as the common *Parmelia laevigata, Mycoblastus sanguinarius, Sphaerophorus* spp. and *Ochrolechia tartarea* of the Parmelietum laevigatae.

The rock flora is interesting and typical of highly leached acid environments with several *Cladonia* spp. and the oceanic *Alectoria bicolor*.

The larger peaty areas between the rock ridges often have no trees on them and are wet grass–heaths or even soligenous mires dominated by such species as *Myrica gale, Molinia caerulea* and *Erica tetralix*.

(d) Ceunant Cynfal
SH 7041. 10 ha

This wooded ravine below Ffestiniog is one of the finest river gorges in the whole of Britain. The Afon Cynfal has cut across the dip of acidic and mildly basic Cambrian slates to a depth of 30–45 m, and much of the gorge is flanked by sheer cliffs and interrupted by several considerable waterfalls. As such the area is of outstanding geomorphological interest.

The variety of rock types results in a mosaic of oakwood communities on the acidic sites and mixed deciduous woodland on the richer soils. The oakwood along the top of the gorge is an excellent *Quercus petraea* wood, with some birch, rowan and holly. The ground flora is grazed in parts and it is therefore predominantly grassy, except in steep, ungrazed situations where there is an abundance of *Luzula sylvatica* and *Vaccinium myrtillus*. Seepage areas within the wood are characterised by banks of *Chrysosplenium oppositifolium*, growing with *Trichocolea tomentella*.

Bryophytes are abundant in the wood in a variety of habitats, for example on the woodland floor, on blocks, on rotten logs, and as epiphytes. Atlantic species are particularly well represented with *Dicranum scottianum, Hylocomium umbratum, Lepidozia pinnata*, and *L. pearsonii*, and the filmy ferns *Hymenophyllum wilsonii* and *H. tunbrigense*. Epiphytic lichens are abundant with *Lobaria* spp., *Sticta* spp., and *Parmeliella atlantica*. Several notable bryophytes have been found in the gorge including *Jubula hutchinsiae, Metzgeria hamata, Isothecium holtii, Tetraphis browniana, Drepanolejeunea hamatifolia, Grimmia hartmanii*, and *Harpalejeunea ovata*.

The small side-stream flowing into the Afon Cynfal from Ffestiniog carries much sewage and seriously pollutes the lower kilometre of the river in the glen, but the better upper section is unaffected. There is a general similarity to the gorge of Ceunant Llennyrch, but many differences in detail, and the Afon Cynfal, unlike the other stream, is undiminished in flow through damming higher up.

(e) Ceunant Llechrwd, Gellilydan
SH 6840. 7 ha

Below the hamlet of Gellilydan and between the wooded glens of Ceunant Llennyrch and Ceunant Cynfal, a third north-west-flowing stream which feeds the Vale of Maentwrog has cut a deep ravine. This glen also is wooded, mainly with sessile oakwood, but contains fragments of mixed deciduous growth. A number of Atlantic bryophytes are represented and there is a small colony of *Osmunda regalis*. On the whole, however, this glen is less rich floristically and less spectacular in the depth and abruptness of its gorge than the other two mentioned. It is, however, an integral part of the Coedydd Dyffryn Maentwrog complex and was once continuous with the woods of the other adjacent sites.

W.108. COED GANLLWYD, MERIONETH
SH 7224. 25 ha   Grade 1*

The wood occupies a comparatively gentle slope on the east side of the Rhinog Mountains at 60–140 m, and is traversed along its north side by the rocky gorge of the Afon Gamlan with its well-known waterfall Rhaiadr-ddu. The local rainfall is about 190 cm annually and the atmospheric humidity is accentuated by the sheltered nature of the site and by river spray immediately around the falls. The underlying rocks are Cambrian grits, acidic, hard and resistant to weathering, but there are also several intrusions of base-rich dolerite outcropping in the wood. Several smaller streams run through the mid and southern sections of the wood and there are significant areas of flushing from the base-rich rocks, giving a mixture of acidic and basic soils.

The tree layer is dominated by oak (mainly *Quercus petraea* but some *Q. robur* types are present) with distinctive strips of ash along the various streams. Birch and sycamore are widely scattered throughout the wood and alder is locally dominant in wet places. Other species present include wych elm, beech, rowan and gean. Development of the shrub layer is poor, the most common species being hazel, but holly, hawthorn, blackthorn and alder buckthorn are all present in small quantities. Bracken dominates large areas of the ground flora whilst in other more shaded areas bryophytes are abundant in both number and species. In a few areas there is a true herb layer and on drier acidic soils *Agrostis* sp., *Anthoxanthum odoratum, Festuca ovina, Galium hercynicum, Endymion non-scriptus, Digitalis purpurea, Potentilla erecta* and *Melampyrum pratense* are common, whilst flushed sites contain such species as *Circaea lutetiana, Mercurialis perennis, Brachypodium sylvaticum, Geranium robertianum, Geum urbanum* and *Prunella vulgaris*. Small acidic soligenous mires occur which contain *Sphagnum imbricatum*.

The wood is famous for the presence of a wide variety of rare oceanic ferns, liverworts and mosses. Parts of the wood are strewn with boulders of coarse grit and it is in and around these that bryophyte communities are best developed, and in the actual gorge. On the shady and/or wet rocks beside the waterfalls and streamlets are species such as *Campylopus setifolius, Leptodontium recurvifolium, Hylocomium umbratum, Colura calyptrifolia, Jubula hutchinsiae, Drepanolejeunea hamatifolia, Harpalejeunea ovata, Radula voluta, R. aquilegia, Frullania microphylla, Plagiochila tridenticulata* and the ferns *Hymenophyllum wilsonii, H. tunbrigense* and *Dryopteris aemula*. On slabs and rocks in the woods and beside the stream there is a great abundance of the rare *Sematophyllum demissum*, and *S. novae-caesareae* is recorded. *Adelanthus decipiens* is locally abundant and *Mylia cuneifolia* has been found here in its only station outside Scotland. Such species require warm humid conditions and most are found in and around the main gorge of the Afon Gamlan and its tributary streams. The presence of so large an assemblage of rare and local Atlantic bryophytes is believed to indicate continuity of at least some woody cover throughout the Post-glacial Period. Although there is evidence that the present oaks were planted together during the nineteenth century, it is inconceivable that so many drought-sensitive species could have survived if the whole area had been totally cleared of woodland or scrub at any one time.

The area also contains important geological features including one of the few localities on the Harlech Dome yielding Middle Cambrian fossils.

W.109. COED CRAFNANT, MERIONETH
SH 6128.   35 ha   Grade 1*

This wood is about 1.6 km in length and occupies a north-west-facing terraced slope on the south-east side of the Afon Artro valley on the western flanks of the Rhinog massif (U.12). The wood extends from 76 to over 210 m altitude. The high annual rainfall (200 cm), the shaded aspect, the prevalence of moist sea winds and mist, and the general topographical setting results in locally humid conditions. The underlying rocks are acidic Cambrian grits of the Harlech Dome complex, but there are numerous intrusions of base-rich rocks in the area, resulting in a rich and diverse flora and vegetation. A second wood, occupying a small valley and east-facing slope to the west of the Afon Artro, is mostly on more base-rich soil than the main part to the east.

The dominant tree is oak, *Quercus petraea*, with some birch, rowan and holly (rather rare). In wet areas along streams and in flush bogs, alder is locally dominant, with willows *Salix aurita* and *S. cinerea*. The shrub layer is poorly developed with scattered hazel and some hawthorn. The ground flora on moist but well-drained sites is predominantly grassy with *Deschampsia flexuosa, Agrostis* spp., *Molinia caerulea*, and an abundance of *Potentilla erecta, Galium saxatile, Pteridium aquilinum*, and *Melampyrum pratense*. Ash and hazel are abundant in the wood west of the river, and a basiphilous field layer is well developed here.

Throughout the wood there are rock outcrops, some of which are virtually ungrazed, supporting an abundance of *Luzula sylvatica* and *Vaccinium myrtillus*, with *Rubus fruticosus* agg., *Corydalis claviculata*, and in shaded areas *Hymenophyllum wilsonii* and, more rarely, *H. tunbrigense*. These outcrops and boulders in the wood provide habitats for rare or local Atlantic bryophytes, such as *Dicranum scottianum, Lepidozia pinnata, Adelanthus decipiens, Harpanthus scutatus, Plagiochila punctata, P. tridenticulata, Jamesoniella autumnalis*, and *Bazzania trilobata*. The luxuriance of the bryophyte growth in the wood is one of its most important features, for besides the common woodland species, it supports several local species in abundance, for example *Hylocomium umbratum, Leucobryum juniperoideum* (only a few other localities in Britain) and *Lepidozia pearsonii*.

There is a good epiphytic lichen growth on the trees and rocks with *Lobaria pulmonaria, Sticta sylvatica, S. limbata, S. fuliginosa* and *Sphaerophorus melanocarpus*. The western sector with abundant ash is especially rich in lichens. Rotten logs provide specialised habitats for several interesting liverworts, such as *Tritomaria exsecta, Scapania umbrosa* and *Blepharostoma trichophyllum*.

In waterlogged areas within the wood, as on terrace flats, there is a range of interesting flush bogs with *Juncus acutiflorus, Hypericum elodes*, and *Scutellaria minor*, and a range of bryophytes including *Sphagnum imbricatum, S. contortum*, and *S. warnstorfianum*. Small rivulets flowing through the wood provide habitats for several rare hepatics, such as

Porella pinnata, Aphanolejeunea microscopica, Cephaloziella pearsonii, and *Jubula hutchinsiae.*

The principal interest of this wood is the rich and varied Atlantic bryophyte and lichen flora, and the intricate woodland mosaic related to topographical features. It provides one of the finest examples of the range of woodland bryophyte habitats in western oakwood, and in north Wales is second only to Coed Ganllwyd in this respect.

W.110. BRYN MAELGWYN & GLODDAETH, CAERNARVONSHIRE

SH 8081.   80 ha   Grade 2

This is one of a group of similar woodlands on Carboniferous Limestone close to Llandudno. It is high forest of ash, wych elm and oak, with some sycamore and yew, and a shrub layer with privet, hazel and hawthorn, over a calcicolous ground flora with *Brachypodium sylvaticum* and *Mercurialis perennis* dominant. The woodland grades through scrub of hawthorn, clematis, privet, blackthorn and bramble to limestone grassland containing the rare *Veronica spicata* ssp. *hybrida.*

Other woods in the group are Pydew Pabo, Caernarvonshire, and Bryn Euryn, Denbighshire. Whilst Pydew Pabo is regarded as marginally the best woodland in the group, Bryn Maelgwyn is chosen because it is adjacent to and grades into rich limestone grassland.

W.111. HAFOD GAREGOG, CAERNARVONSHIRE

SH 6044.   115 ha   Grade 2

This cluster of woods is situated on a number of low, rocky hills and ridges rising abruptly from the estuarine flats (now reclaimed) associated with the Afon Glaslyn. About half the area is woodland and the other half mire or lake. The tree layer consists of mainly sessile oak in mixture with birch, rowan and holly, and with a sparse shrub layer of hazel. The field layer is generally acidophilous in character, being dominated by *Anthoxanthum odoratum, Festuca ovina, Melampyrum pratense, Potentilla erecta* and *Oxalis acetosella,* with *Pteridium aquilinum* in more open areas. There are historical reasons for supposing this to be an area in which there has been a long period of continuous woodland cover. In floristics the wood is fairly typical of western sessile oakwood, but the site is unusual in being on flat or gently sloping ground, in contrast to many of the remaining hill woodlands in Wales, most of which occur on steep slopes as oak hangers.

W.112. COED MAES YR HELMAU: TORRENT WALK, MERIONETH

SH 7518.   25 ha   Grade 2

This deep rocky glen near Dolgellau has fringing woodlands with both sessile oak on acidic soils and mixed deciduous wood on basic soils. Some of the oaks in particular are tall, well-grown trees, and this site is regarded as of national importance mainly for the quality of these two contrasting types of woodland and their respective field layers. The wood is ungrazed, and the ash–wych elm–hazel woodland has fine examples of herb-dominated field communities with *Mercurialis perennis, Filipendula ulmaria, Asperula odorata* and *Brachypodium sylvaticum.* There are a few non-indigenous trees, but small-leaved lime in the glen may well be native. The gorge carries a large stream but is less deep and spectacular than the Coedydd Dyffryn Maentwrog gorges (W.107). There are block strewn areas of the woodland floor, with some moisture- and shade-loving ferns and bryophytes (e.g. *Hymenophyllum wilsonii, Scapania gracilis, Plagiochila spinulosa* and *Bazzania trilobata*) and many trees are thickly clothed with moss. On the whole though, the Atlantic element of the flora is not outstanding, and the more notable species (e.g. *Hymenophyllum tunbrigense, Isothecium holtii, Radula voluta* and *Jubula hutchinsiae*) are confined to the gorge itself.

The contrast between the Coed Maes yr Helmau and Atlantic bryophyte-rich woods such as Coed Ganllwyd appears to result not from difference in present conditions – since none is obvious – but from a different history of management. The Coed Maes yr Helmau woods appear to have been replanted after a period of clearance during which moisture-loving ferns and bryophytes disappeared, except from the actual ravine. When the wood grew up again, only the more common species were able to spread back to recolonise the suitable habitats which developed. By contrast, at Coed Ganllwyd, it would appear that there has been continuity of woody cover – if only of scrub – over at least part of the site throughout the Post-glacial Period, so that drought-sensitive species survived somewhere and spread again when high forest was restored after nineteenth-century clearance and replanting of oak and beech.

W.113. COED LLETY WALTER, MERIONETH

SH 6027.   45 ha   Grade 2

This woodland lies at 60–80 m on fairly level ground, north of the Afon Artro, and at the mouth of the valley, about 5 km from the sea. The bed rock is Cambrian grit and the rainfall about 200 cm annually. The wood is young, 30–40 years old perhaps, with a dominance of naturally regenerated oak and birch. Other species present include ash, alder, rowan and holly. A few large Scots pine and beech remain as remnants of the previous woodland. The ground flora is predominantly acidophilous but there are local occurrences of *Brachypodium sylvaticum* and *Geranium robertianum* indicating some base enrichment. The wood is notable for a wide range of habitats in the form of rock outcrops, short slopes with various aspects, streams, wet flats and glades.

W.114. COED LLECHWEDD, MERIONETH

SH 5932.   55 ha   Grade 2

The wood occupies a steep north-west-facing slope just north of Harlech, looking out over Morfa Harlech. Altitude ranges from 15–180 m and the exposure to wind is moderate to severe. The underlying rocks are Cambrian and the diverse woodland vegetation suggests the presence of base-rich rock outcrops. The tree layer is dominated by oak but a wide range of other trees are present, including less common species for this area, such as gean. There are both acidophilous and basiphilous elements in the ground flora, as indicated by the presence of heather and *Allium ursinum*. This is a good example of a hill wood with considerable ecological diversity resulting from varying base content of the soil.

MIDLANDS

W.43. BEDFORD PURLIEUS GROUP (PART), NORTHAMPTONSHIRE Grade 1

See under East Anglia, p. 57.

W.115. DERBYSHIRE DALES WOODLANDS, DERBYSHIRE/STAFFORDSHIRE Grade 1*

The Low Peak of Derbyshire contains one of the most important masses of Carboniferous Limestone in Britain. In the river valleys or Dales coming from this area are a series of ashwoods occurring on steep hillsides over a thin rendzina soil or on scree. These woodlands together with those of the Mendip Hills exhibit the best-known development of ash-wood. The areas are for the most part ungrazed and have a rich shrub and field layer. A series of woodlands is listed in order to cover the range of variation; these areas are also associated with key grassland sites. Historical documentation indicates that the bulk of the woodland in the Dales area has originated since the middle of the seventeenth century.

(a) Lathkill Dale
SK 1865. 70 ha

Lathkill Dale is orientated east–west and lies just south of Bakewell. Some woodland on the north and east end has been modified by planting but the remainder of the area contains some fine ashwood. Species found with the ash include wych elm, hazel, privet, guelder rose, field maple, elder, haw-thorn, dog rose, gooseberry and rowan. The field layer is locally dominated by *Mercurialis perennis* or *Deschampsia cespitosa* together with ferns but there is a wide variety of forbs present including much *Geum rivale, Galeobdolon luteum, Campanula trachelium, Poa nemoralis, P. trivialis, Brachypodium sylvaticum* and *Melica uniflora*. A long list of characteristic but less common species is to be found including dogwood, *Daphne mezereum, Convallaria majalis, Neottia nidus-avis, Helleborus viridis, Gagea lutea, Litho-spermum officinale, Mycelis muralis, Asperula odorata, Cirsium heterophyllum, Hypericum hirsutum, Tamus communis, Euonymus europaeus, Milium effusum, Zerna ramosa* and *Festuca gigantea*. Occasional old lead workings add interest as the spoil heaps support a rich flora with species such as *Helianthemum chamaecistus, Campanula glomerata, Orchis fuchsii, Minuartia verna* and *Briza media*.
See also L.124(i) and OW.44.

(b) Cressbrook Dale
SK 1773. 25 ha

The Dale runs in a north–south direction, is steep sided and contains some good limestone crags. The tree canopy is of ash with a little wych elm and a dense shrub layer of bird-cherry, field maple, buckthorn, guelder rose and hazel. There are patches of aspen-dominated scrub. The lower part of the Dale appears to have been disturbed to some extent and here sycamore is more abundant. There is some good cliff scrub with rowan, rock whitebeam, yew, small-leaved lime and wych elm. The field layer is dominated by *Mercurialis perennis* with patches of *Allium ursinum* and *Convallaria majalis. Melica nutans* and *Campanula latifolia* are frequent. There is an interesting juxtaposition of grass-land and woodland in the Dale as well as species-rich mine spoil heaps where *Minuartia verna* is common. The Dale also contains the only known English locality for the rare moss *Thamnium angustifolium*. It has been suggested that the presence of small-leaved lime together with *Convallaria majalis*, bird-cherry and dogwood indicates that at least a part of the area may be primary woodland.
See also L.124(i).

(c) Dove Dale Ashwood
SK 1453. 20 ha

The craggy valley of the Dove runs north–south and has good woods on both east and west aspects. Dovedale Wood itself is dominated by ash with beech, holly (very local), field maple, sycamore and pedunculate oak. It has been suggested that the wood can be regarded as intermediate between pure ashwood and the oakwoods of western Britain. There are areas of fine cliff woodland dominated by yew together with *Sorbus aucuparia, S. aria, S. rupicola, Prunus spinosa, Ribes alpinum, Rosa pimpinellifolia* and *Crataegus monogyna*. The herbaceous flora is varied; areas near the river are dominated by *Filipendula ulmaria, Phalaris arundinacea, Veronica beccabunga* and *Petasites hybridus* whilst on many of the slopes *Mercurialis perennis, Geum urbanum, Brachypodium sylvaticum, Fragaria vesca* and *Deschampsia cespitosa* are dominant. Where the ground is broken by outcrops and the canopy is more open a rich assemblage of forbs is present, at times approaching a limestone grassland sward in composition.
See also L.124(i).

W.95. WYE GORGE (PART), HEREFORDSHIRE Grade 1*
See under South Wales, p. 72.

W.116. HALESEND WOOD, HEREFORDSHIRE
SO 7449. 55 ha Grade 1

Halesend Wood lies largely on a Silurian limestone ridge near the northern end of the Malvern Hills. The woodland is coppice and coppice-with-standards in which sessile oak, hazel and common lime are the most abundant species but many other native tree and shrub species are frequent throughout the northern half of the wood, notably yew, wild service, field maple and ash. The southern end, whilst retaining the mixed deciduous character to some extent, has a high proportion of birch and ash. The ground flora is of the rich, basiphilous type, dominated by dog's mercury, bramble, wood anemone and bluebell, with local areas of *Allium ursinum*. Certain local forbs are common, including

Campanula trachelium, *Platanthera chlorantha*, *Lathraea squamaria* and *Narcissus pseudo-narcissus*.

Although hybrid lime is one of the more abundant species here, it is intimately mixed with other tree and shrub species and occurs as coppice and ancient pollards. This unusual condition, and a number of old quarries, add to Halesend Wood's value as a representative of the rich, calcicolous woodlands of the south-west Midlands.

W.117. MOCCAS PARK, HEREFORDSHIRE
SO 3442.   140 ha   Grade 1

Moccas Park is an ancient deer park lying on north-facing slopes of Old Red Sandstone, with flat ground below. The lower areas are occupied by open, ancient park woodland with pedunculate oak and sweet chestnut growing from an old grassland sward. On the higher slopes the woodland is less open and richer in species, including small-leaved lime, large-leaved lime, wych elm, field maple, holly, beech, yew and ash, with a number of ancient specimens of exotic trees, notably horse chestnut, sweet chestnut, and sycamore. The field layer, which is heavily grazed in places, has abundant bracken and other species of dry, mildly acid soils, such as foxglove, bluebell and bramble, and patches of dog's mercury. The bryophytes and epiphytic lichens are extremely rich, over 100 species of the latter having been recorded recently by F. Rose. The fauna has been relatively well studied, and is outstanding for Coleoptera, three species being known nowhere else in Britain, namely *Pyrrhidium sanguineum* (Cerambycidae), *Hypebaeus flavipes* (Malachiidae) and *Ernoporus caucasicus* (Scolytidae).

Existing information clearly suggests that Moccas is the best ancient park wood in the Midlands, but other sites have been so little studied that some may be of equal merit. Furthermore, recent ploughing and fertilising of the grassland may have damaged its ecological value. Brampton Bryan Park (W.124) is at least as rich in its lichens and can be regarded in this respect as an alternative site but its Coleoptera have not been properly studied.

W.118. HILL HOLE DINGLE, HEREFORDSHIRE
SO 5354.   40 ha   Grade 1

This is the steep-sided valley of the Humber Brook, about 1.6 km long, and cut through Old Red Sandstone. At its upper end the slopes are boulder strewn. The sides are wooded and undisturbed and a miniature alluvial plain bears ash–alder wood and willow carr. Ash is the most abundant species on the valley sides but sessile oak and elm are co-dominant in some areas. Birch, field maple and beech are also present. Shrubs include hazel, hawthorn, elder and blackthorn. The field layer illustrates the downwash of bases that has occurred; and varies from a community dominated by *Deschampsia cespitosa* with abundant primrose in upper, more open areas, through bluebell, bramble or wood anemone to dog's mercury. Flushes with *Chrysosplenium oppositifolium* and the rarer *C. alternifolium* are common. Also of great interest are large patches of *Helleborus viridis*. Bryophytes carpet tufa springs, rock outcrops

and rotting logs. Flanking the woodland are more open areas of bracken and gorse.

This has been chosen to represent a rich mixed deciduous woodland type characteristic of the west Midlands. It also has a range of wetland habitats within this small area and has the added advantage of being undisturbed. (See Appendix.)

W.119. TICK WOOD, SHROPSHIRE
SJ 6503.   55 ha   Grade 1

This is a scarp woodland, mostly north-facing, near the site of Telford New Town and overlooking the Severn Valley. It overlies Silurian rocks, predominantly calcareous shales, though a band of Wenlock Limestone occurs along the top of the ridge.

It is essentially a pedunculate oak–lime (*Tilia vulgaris*, ?*T. cordata*, ?*T. platyphyllos*) high forest with ash and some elm. The site is not managed now though hazel has been coppiced in the past. There is one area of pure cherry in all stages of development, including some very old trees. Many other native species are present in the canopy including field maple, silver birch, holly, crab apple, wild service, rowan and yew, and there are shrubs such as spindle, privet, blackthorn, dogwood and guelder rose.

The topmost part of the site has extensive scrub woodland and here the ground flora is extremely rich in herbs, with abundance of *Allium ursinum* with *Mercurialis perennis*, *Filipendula ulmaria*, *Geum rivale* and *Paris quadrifolia*. Orchids include *Listera ovata*, *Orchis mascula*, *Platanthera chlorantha* and *Epipactis helleborine*. Over the rest of the wood *Oxalis acetosella*, *Veronica montana* and *Deschampsia cespitosa* are dominant but more local species such as *Carex pendula*, *C. strigosa*, *Euphorbia amygdaloides* and *Campanula trachelium* also occur.

Tick Wood differs both pedologically and floristically from better known limestone woodlands such as those of the Derbyshire Dales and the Cotswolds. Its vegetation is typical of woods on the highly calcareous shales of this region.

W.120. LONG ITCHINGTON AND UFTON WOODS, WARWICKSHIRE
SP 3862.   80 ha   Grade 1

These woods are situated on a gentle north-east-facing slope, rising to a plateau at 90–120 m, with soils which vary from medium clay to loam. This is a fine example of oak–hazel coppice woodland that is still managed as such. There are well grown standards of pedunculate oak, open grown and up to 15 m in height; the coppice layer is dominated by vigorous hazel which is coppiced in rotation, several different age classes being present. Other shrubs are present including hawthorn, roses, wayfaring tree and dogwood.

The ground flora may be divided into two main types. The upper parts of the slope and the edge of the plateau are dominated by species such as *Rubus fruticosus* agg., *Deschampsia cespitosa* and *Carex* spp. In the damper areas and along the ditches there is an abundance of *Geum rivale*. On the lower slopes the soil is a rich loam and there is a mesophilous field layer dominated by dog's mercury, bluebell and primrose, with occasional patches of *Paris quadrifolia*. There are a number of orchids in the wood including *Listera ovata*, *Platanthera bifolia*, *Neottia nidus-avis* and *Epipactis helleborine*.

W.121. WYRE FOREST, WORCESTERSHIRE, SHROPSHIRE

SO 7576. 495 ha   Grade 1

Wyre Forest lies astride the county boundary, west of the Severn, on either side of Dowles Brook, on the varied formations of the Coal Measures, which include sandstones, marls and conglomerates. The soils are mainly freely drained and acidic, but local calcareous pockets occur.

Sessile oakwood, mainly of coppice origin, is the widespread type but in the valleys, rich mixed deciduous woodland with wild service, ash, elm, small-leaved lime and alder have developed. The field layer is predominantly calcifuge with *Pteridium aquilinum*, *Vaccinium myrtillus*, *Calluna vulgaris*, *Erica cinerea* and *Melampyrum pratense*. In the valleys, however, there is a wide variety of habitats from moderately acidic, to basic soligenous mire with *Sphagnum* spp., *Molinia caerulea* and *Eriophorum latifolium*, to communities on drier, base-rich soils with *Brachypodium sylvaticum*, *Mercurialis perennis* and *Primula vulgaris*. Within the woods many rare and local species occur, including *Cephalanthera longifolia*, *Aquilegia vulgaris*, *Carex montana*, *Convallaria majalis*, *Melica nutans*, *Geranium sylvaticum* and *G. sanguineum*. The whole area is rich in bryophytes and epiphytic lichens (by comparison with the Midlands generally), especially the Seckley Wood ravine and other valleys. Over 320 species of fungi have been recorded here.

The forest fauna is one of the richest in the Midlands. The mammals include fallow deer, otter, dormouse and several species of bat, as well as the commoner woodland species. A wide variety of woodland and water-side birds breeds and the avifauna has been extensively studied. Amongst the reptiles the adder is common. The insects are outstanding for variety and number, and include some nationally rare species. The Kentish glory and alder kitten moths are two notable examples amongst the Lepidoptera. The rare cerambycid beetle *Strangalia nigra* occurs in one of its most northerly stations, and Wyre Forest is one of the few British localities for the terrestrial caddis fly, *Enoicyla pusilla*. Rare spiders and sawflies are also recorded.

These woodlands constitute an important meeting point of a number of woodland features. The oaks, though mainly sessile, have characters intermediate with pedunculate, yet the plateau woods are structurally and floristically allied to the oak coppices of Wales. The valley woods on the other hand have the small-leaved lime and wild service characteristic of the southern Welsh borderlands. Local developments of hazel, ash and dogwood over dog's mercury and primrose on clays are reminiscent of East Anglian woods. Floristically, too, the area is intermediate, with, for example, *Melica nutans* and *Geranium sylvaticum* on the edge of their range. The forest as a whole is outstanding for invertebrates and forms one of the most important wildlife environments in the Midlands. The most important parts are Seckley Wood, Dowles Brook and its tributary stream valleys, and the coppices east of Park Brook.

W.122. CANNOCK CHASE, STAFFORDSHIRE

SJ 9818. 880 ha   Grade 2

Most of the site is covered by heather heathland, grading into valley fen and bog, but the woods occupy a substantial part of the area, particularly in the north. Four main woodland types can be recognised:

1 *Oak–birch woodland*. *Quercus petraea* and *Betula verrucosa* form a closed canopy over much of Brocton Coppice, but large clearings exist, and the margin of the wood grades into surrounding heathland. The oaks are clearly much older than the birch, perhaps 150–200 years in most cases, with a few individuals of greater age.

2 *Birch woodland*. *Betula verrucosa* woodland occurs in the vicinity of Brocton Coppice and elsewhere in small clumps.

3 *Alder coppice*. The Sherbrook valley has alder coppice along most of its length.

4 *Willow scrub*. Contrasting strongly with the Sherbrook valley, the Oldacre valley has a discontinuous line of *Salix cinerea* in the marsh of the valley bottom.

The open heath is invaded by trees and shrubs and birch woodland is the most widespread seral stage. Other species also occur, notably sycamore in the Sycamore Hill area, Scots pine and beech in the southern area, hawthorn in the vicinity of Brocton Field, pedunculate oak particularly among the birch in the Oldacre valley and gorse at various points on the heath.

Bracken is dominant over some areas and apparently on the increase in others. The heathland is a noted locality for hybrid *Vaccinium myrtillus* and *V. vitis-idaea* (*Vaccinium* × *intermedium*). *Empetrum nigrum* is also present.

There are several valley bogs, reminiscent of those in the New Forest. The best has a large expanse of *Thelypteris palustris* and *Equisetum sylvaticum*, with a rich assemblage of bog plants including *Anagallis tenella*, *Carex pulicaris*, *C. dioica*, *C. hostiana*, *Drosera rotundifolia*, *D. anglica*, *Eleocharis quinqueflora*, *Hydrocotyle vulgaris*, *Orchis fuchsii*, *Parnassia palustris*, *Pinguicula vulgaris*, *Vaccinium oxycoccus* and *Valeriana dioica*. *Narthecium ossifragum* occurs in one of the valleys.

The insect fauna of the whole area is extremely rich. Two of the most notable Lepidoptera are *Stilbia anomala* and *Enargia paleacea*.

W.123. HAMPS AND MANIFOLD VALLEYS, STAFFORDSHIRE

SK 0955. 325 ha   Grade 2

The site follows the valley of the River Manifold from Ecton southwards towards Ilam and incorporates part of the valley of the River Hamps. The valleys contain woodland and scrub as well as grassland. The woodlands are similar in many respects to the ash woodlands of the Derbyshire Dales but exhibit some unusual features. Thus old oak trees of *Quercus robur* and *Q. petraea* occur in several places;

and holly is present, both as scrub and as a component of established woodland. These features reflect some of the characteristics of woodland under more oceanic conditions and indicate a somewhat different climate on the extreme west of the Peak District.

The woodlands of the Manifold Valley show an extremely wide range of variation in canopy structure and ground flora.

The grasslands included within the site are on the whole damp and well grazed. *Agrostis* spp. are generally dominant, but variations occur according to slope and aspect. *Potentilla tabernaemontani*, *Carex pulicaris* and *Parnassia palustris* are noteworthy amongst the herbs.

Rare plant species present include *Polemonium caeruleum*, *Daphne mezereum*, *Hordelymus europaeus*, *Festuca altissima*, and *Cardamine impatiens*. *Daphne laureola*, uncommon in the Peak District, is also present.

The area is also of interest for its karst topography. During periods of dry weather the River Manifold disappears down a series of swallets just below Wettonmill and the water resurges from springs at Ilam Hall about 11 km downstream. Thors Cave is an impressive rock shelter perched on the side of the valley.

W.124. BRAMPTON BRYAN PARK, HEREFORDSHIRE
SO 3671. 60 ha   Grade 2

Brampton Bryan Park lies at the northern end of Renwordine Hill on steep east-, west- and north-facing slopes across a geological transition between Old Red Sandstone and Silurian strata. The woodland is ancient open oak parkland with sweet chestnut, beech, ash and holly, with an area of wych elm woodland above a vestigial dog's mercury field community. The ancient woodland is extremely rich in epiphytic lichens.

The biological richness of Brampton Bryan Park has been recognised only recently. It is clearly very similar to Moccas Park and its epiphyte flora is at least as rich but the invertebrate fauna has not received a similar degree of study. (See Appendix.)

W.125. DOWNTON GORGE, HEREFORDSHIRE
SO 4373. 55 ha   Grade 2

The ravine below Downton Castle is wooded for a distance of over 2.4 km. The river has cut a deep gorge through Silurian rocks leaving soils of an acid to weakly calcareous character. At higher levels the woodland is mainly dominated by sessile oak, with a field layer of *Luzula sylvatica*, but at lower levels a mixed deciduous woodland occurs with ash and wych elm dominant. There is a wide range of age classes, and one cliff has an old holly–ash–wych elm wood with a vigorous colony of *Festuca altissima*. This is a sheltered site which at lower levels is very rich in bryophytes, including *Plagiopus oederi*, *Pohlia cruda* and many oceanic and submontane species. The epiphytic lichen flora, though not inspected yet in detail, is already known to be rich, with a fine colony of *Lobaria pulmonaria*, *Graphina anguina* on holly and *Peltigera horizontalis*.

W.126. BUSHY HAZELS AND CWMMA MOORS, HEREFORDSHIRE
SO 2851. 30 ha   Grade 2

This site lies *c*. 3 km from the Radnor border on a level and damp site, with loamy soils derived from Lower Old Red Sandstone rocks. Ash is most abundant in the canopy though coppiced wych elm is often co-dominant. Pedunculate oak and birch associate with them in varying amounts though these are completely absent in some parts. A stream divides off Bushy Hazels, a pure hazel coppice in the north-eastern corner. The understorey and shrub layers are not well developed throughout but the field layer is herb rich. Beneath the hazel coppice are *Deschampsia cespitosa* and *Endymion non-scriptus* with patches of *Paris quadrifolia*. In the ash–elm woodland, *E. non-scriptus*, *Anemone nemorosa*, *Mercurialis perennis* and *D. cespitosa* are predominant with *Circaea lutetiana* and *Sanicula europaea*. Wetter patches contain *Filipendula ulmaria*, *Chrysosplenium oppositifolium* and *Carex pendula*.

This site may be considered alternative to Hill Hole Dingle, i.e. it is an example of a mixed deciduous woodland on the Welsh borders. As it has been heavily managed in the past, fewer native woody species are present and the field layer is not as herb rich. The Dingle also has more variety in its micro-habitats.

W.127. LEIGHFIELD FOREST, LEICESTERSHIRE
SK 7502. 170 ha   Grade 2

Leighfield Forest was recommended for special status in Cmd 7122 (Ministry of Town and Country Planning, 1947) and relics of this ancient woodland still remain. The site is composed of four woods (Loddington Reddish, Tugby, Tilton and Skeffington woods) grouped in the Eye Brook valley which runs through Jurassic ironstone and clays. Deposits of boulder clays and gravels have resulted in rich loamy and calcareous clay soils. The tree canopy is mainly standards of oak plus wych elm, together with ash, often coppiced. The understorey of hazel and field maple is often dense and there is a mixed association of shrubs including dogwood, Midland hawthorn, privet, sallow, elder and buckthorn.

Filipendula ulmaria and *Juncus* spp. occur extensively in the rides with *Rubus fruticosus* and *Pteridium aquilinum* locally abundant. Beneath the coppice, *Mercurialis perennis* is dominant with clumps of *Deschampsia cespitosa* and *Dryopteris filix-mas*. *Myosotis sylvatica* is abundant and the presence of *Vicia sylvatica*, *Campanula trachelium* and *Dipsacus pilosus* is of interest.

The more important Lepidoptera of the Eye Brook valley include *Cymatophorina diluta*, *Nola confusalis*, *Ladoga camilla*, *Nymphalis polychloros*, *Quercusia quercus* and *Ochlodes venata* which are rare or not present elsewhere. The list of Coleoptera from these woods includes a number of rare or localised species of which the following are the most noteworthy: *Platyrrhinus resinosus*, *Anthribus fasciatus*, *Metoecus paradoxus*, *Lissodema quadripustulata*, *Hypophloeus bicolor*, *Agapanthis villosoviridescens*, *Tetropium gabrieli*,

Pediacus dermestoides and *Nemosoma elongatum*. The woods of this area are among the most northerly known British localities for many species of Coleoptera, including some of those listed above.

The earliest record of these sites is 1235 and it is believed that they have indeed been wooded since that time. The vegetation as a whole is typical of that found on heavy boulder clay but this is already represented in the grade 1 series by Monks Wood (W.42) and Castor Hanglands (W.44), so Leighfield Forest is given grade 2 status.

W.128. PIPEWELL WOODS, NORTHAMPTONSHIRE
SP 8286. 80 ha   Grade 2

Monks Arbour and Pipewell Woods lie on deep, calcareous clay soils at the south-western extremity of Rockingham Forest and have a coppice-with-standards structure. Pedunculate oak is the main standard species, with ash, birch and a few planted beech. The coppice layer is dominated by hazel, with ash, dogwood and field maple locally abundant in Monks Arbour Wood. The field layer ranges from *Mercurialis perennis–Galeobdolon luteum* on the drier soils, to *Filipendula ulmaria–Ranunculus repens* in waterlogged patches, and *Pteridium aquilinum–Rubus fruticosus–Holcus lanatus* on the more acidic patches. The ground flora includes such local species as *Iris foetidissima* and *Campanula latifolia*. At the southern end of Pipewell Wood, English elm has invaded from the hedge to form a nearly pure community.

This is one of the Ancient Forest coppices. It is typical of such woods and has the advantage that it is not damaged by ironstone working or replanting with conifers, and indeed the coppicing continues actively. Other woods in Rockingham Forest, however, were once known to be richer faunally.

W.129. WHITTLEWOOD FOREST, NORTHAMPTONSHIRE
SP 7342. 110 ha   Grade 2

Three relics of this ancient woodland, in the south of the county, still remain. They once formed a link in the chain of woodlands which stretched across the clay belt from Oxfordshire to Huntingdon and Peterborough. Lying on calcareous clays and boulder clays they are typical examples of the woodlands on these soil types. Buckingham Thick Copse is the largest area; it contains fairly uniform oak–ash high forest. Understorey and shrub species are confined to the rides and edges; these include field maple, dogwood, Midland hawthorn and hazel. Sweet chestnut is also present. The ground flora is dominated by *Rubus fruticosus*, *Chamaenerion angustifolium* with *Deschampsia cespitosa* and *Brachypodium sylvaticum*. Patches of *Luzula multiflora* and *Carex pendula* indicate waterlogging. Say's and Smalladine Copses are similar but ash or English elm outnumber the oak in parts. The shrub layer is better developed here and is dominated by hazel. *Cornus sanguinea*, *Euonymus europaeus* and *Viburnum opulus* are common in the hedgerows.

Lichens that are absent or rare elsewhere in the county are found here; these include *Lecanora confusa*, *Usnea certatina*, *Opegrapha varia* and *Pertusaria lutescens*.

East and West Ashall's Copses consist of ash scrub and mature ash woodland and oak is only locally dominant. English elm occurs on the edge and hazel, hawthorn, field maple and Midland hawthorn are present in the understorey and shrub layers. The ground flora here is dominated by bramble interspersed with areas of *Deschampsia cespitosa*, *Oxalis acetosella* and *Glechoma hederacea*. Other plants include *Sanicula europaea*, *Epipactis helleborine*, *E. purpurata* and *Dactylorchis fuchsii*.

W.130. SHERWOOD FOREST, NOTTINGHAMSHIRE
SK 6368. 525 ha   Grade 2

The Birklands and, to a lesser extent, the Bilhaugh are fine remnants of Sherwood Forest. They lie on deep, freely drained acidic soils developed from Bunter Sandstone. The woodlands are an actively regenerating population of both oak species in more or less equal numbers, with a wide size range from saplings to some of the largest oaks in the country. Between these extremes are younger, but mature generations of the oaks. Birch (mainly *Betula pendula*) is abundant, forming groves between the oaks, but the canopy is still rather open, enabling a dense bracken field layer to develop. The flora is very poor, restricted to calcifuge species, and the epiphyte lichen flora has been largely eliminated by pollution. The beetle fauna, however, is very rich and contains some extremely rare species.

The oak population here is exceptional but public pressure and atmospheric pollution have damaged the area, hence it is accorded grade 2 status.

Immediately to the north lies Budby South Forest Heath (170 ha) on soils derived from the Bunter Sandstone at an altitude of about 60 m. The heathland area is dry heath dominated by heather and *Deschampsia flexuosa*. Much of it (c. 50%) is covered by scattered birch or birch scrub. There is some gorse scrub but this habitat is by no means abundant on the site. Bracken is only locally abundant.

The heath is at present used as a military training area but there is little apparent physical damage and the site has not been extensively burnt in recent years. Its inclusion within the grade 2 site adds interest.

W.131. HABBERLEY VALLEY, SHROPSHIRE
SJ 4104. 30 ha   Grade 2

This narrow, steep-sided valley cuts through base-rich Ordovician shales at its lower end and acidic pre-Cambrian conglomerates, which give rise to two contrasting soil types, and strong associated differences in the vegetation. The base-rich lower woodland is dominated by wych elm, large-leaved lime, ash and yew with some sessile oak: here the ground flora is a moderately rich assemblage of mainly calcicolous species, with abundant *Mercurialis perennis* and *Polystichum setiferum*, the rare *Circaea intermedia* and a range of calcicole and calcifuge bryophytes. On the acidic rocks sessile oak woodland grows over a ground flora of *Vaccinium myrtillus*, *Blechnum spicant* and *Leucobryum glaucum*, with a number of Atlantic bryophytes.

Several features have combined to justify including this site. It has good examples of two types of woodland whose distribution is clearly determined by the nature of the underlying rocks. It is one of the few sites where the native large-leaved lime occurs, and here it is locally dominant, with many fine specimens. Furthermore, the woodland is part of a complex of habitats which taken together include a rich variety of plant species.

W.132. CHADDESLEY–RANDAN WOODS, WORCESTERSHIRE
SO 9273.   170 ha   Grade 2

These woods lie on Keuper Marl from which a poorly drained, rather acidic, loamy clay soil develops, but the higher ground is capped by glacial drift of a sandy and gravelly character on which freely or excessively drained, light, strongly acidic soils have formed. The woodland is almost entirely dominated by mature oak high forest in which both native species are represented. There is a tendency for most oaks on the light soil to be *Quercus petraea* and most on heavy soils to be *Q. robur*, but this is not a particularly close relationship and mixed populations are widespread. A coppice and shrub layer is present throughout, although it is thin on the most acid soils, and consists of a mixture of species, including hazel, ash, alder and birch. A considerable number of native tree and shrub species are present in small numbers. Along the deeply incised stream lines, influenced by calcareous water, a rich alderwood has developed.

A number of local plant species are present, including *Epipactis purpurata* and *Carex strigosa*, but no nationally rare species are recorded. The fauna includes the rare terrestrial caddis fly *Enoicyla pusilla*.

The scientific interest is not confined to the woodland for a number of small herb-rich meadows and green lanes occur within the woods. One in particular, in the centre of Chaddesley Woods, occupies a receiving site on heavy clay, and has developed as a meadow/marsh in which *Serratula tinctoria*, *Silaum silaus* and various *Dactylorchis* spp. are present.

Chaddesley–Randan Woods are undoubtedly the most important to nature conservation of the group of woods which were formerly within Feckenham Forest. The others, centred on the parish of Himbledon, are much more uniform where they survive as native woodland. The richest woods in this group have recently been clear-felled, but it is doubtful whether even they were richer than Chaddesley–Randan Woods.

These woods have been included in the *Review* primarily as an extensive and rich example of the oak woodlands in the West Midlands, and are more closely related to the Wealden oak woodlands than the coppice-with-standards woods typical of much of the Midlands. In so far as they possess significant stands of sessile oak woodland on acidic, freely drained sandy soils, in association with pedunculate oak-wood in an apparently natural distribution, Chaddesley–Randan Woods are similar to Wyre Forest (W.121).

NORTH ENGLAND

W.133. BORROWDALE WOODS, CUMBERLAND   Grade 1*

(a) *Castle Head Wood*
NY 2722.   8 ha

(b) *The Ings*
NY 2622.   4 ha

(c) *Great Wood*
NY 2721.   43 ha

(d) *Lodore–Troutdale Woods*
NY 2618.   370 ha

(e) *Johnny's Wood*
NY 2514.   35 ha

(f) *Seatoller Wood*
NY 2413.   85 ha

Borrowdale probably contains a greater extent of native woodland than any other of the Lakeland valleys, and from the road it can appear that almost the whole dale is forest clad on its lower slopes – an impressive effect. Most of the woods are of the hanging type, on steep slopes ranging from *c.* 75 to 370 m, and covering all aspects, but The Ings and Castle Head Wood lie on the floor of the valley: the latter on a small hill. The parent rock is almost entirely the Borrowdale Volcanic Series, which generally gives acidic soils, but contains calcite bearing beds (and fault shatter belts) in many places, as at Lodore and in Seatoller Wood. The slopes within most woods are variably covered with block scree. These are composed of rocks of all sizes. Many woods have outcrops which vary in size from small faces to high cliffs around Lodore. These woods lie within a very sharp rainfall gradient ranging from about 178 cm annually at Castle Head Wood to about 318 cm at Seathwaite.

There are fine stands of high forest sessile oakwood in Great Wood, Johnny's Wood and Seatoller Wood, and smaller coppice in Troutdale. A shrub layer is generally absent and there are merely scattered individuals of birch, holly and rowan. Ash–hazel wood occurs in all sites except The Ings, but forms a large part of Seatoller Wood and its juxtaposition here with sessile oakwood illustrates the same kind of edaphic separation of woodland types as that found in the lowland situation with slate and limestone in Roudsea Wood. The ashwood contains a good deal of wych elm, and there is usually an understorey of hazel, plus a greater variety of shrubs such as *Prunus padus*, *P. spinosa*, *Crataegus monogyna* and *Rubus fruticosus*. The respective field communities are of *Deschampsia flexuosa–Anthoxanthum odoratum*, with sparse bilberry and much bracken on leached brown earths under oak, and *Brachypodium sylvaticum–Geranium robertianum* with numerous other basiphilous herbs on base-rich loams under ash–hazel. Rare herbs include *Festuca altissima* at Lodore and Great Wood, *Impatiens noli-tangere* in Great Wood and *Circaea alpina* in several localities; the last two species have their British headquarters in Lakeland.

Castle Head Wood differs from the others in a number of respects. It is well-developed sessile oak over hazel woodland surrounded by farmland and not open to the upland fell. This has reduced grazing pressure, which in turn has enabled some natural regeneration to take place and accounts for the relatively strong development of field and shrub layers.

By the shore of Derwentwater near Lodore, a fringe of alder, willow, reed and sedge completes the ecological zonation of the catena from the top of the hanging oakwoods to the lake shore. Alder woodland near the lake is an important feature of Great Wood and is exceptionally well-developed in The Ings. This site, although small, is ungrazed, and the good field layer varies according to the mineral/humus component of the substratum which may depend on variations in silting from the inflowing stream.

Fern communities are well developed, especially on block scree and include *Dryopteris filix-mas*, *D. dilatata*, *Athyrium filix-femina*, *Thelypteris oreopteris*, *T. phegopteris*, *T. dryopteris* and *Blechnum spicant*. The rare *Asplenium septentrionale* grows on rocks in one place. There is a general carpet of bryophytes composed of the common species appropriate to oak and ash–hazel woods, but the most important feature is the strong representation of the Atlantic element. These woods, including the famous cascade ravine of Lodore Falls, together constitute the most important locality in England for Atlantic bryophytes and in richness they rival those of north Wales and the western Highlands. The *Hymenophyllum wilsonii–Scapania gracilis–Plagiochila spinulosa* community on blocks is well developed, and there is local abundance of mosses such as *Hylocomium umbratum*, *Hypnum callichroum*, *Bartramia halleriana* and the northern *Ptilium crista-castrensis*, and *Sematophyllum novae-caesareae*. The notable hepatics include *Radula voluta*, *R. aquilegia*, *Jubula hutchinsiae*, *Colura calyptrifolia*, *Plagiochila tridenticulata*, *Frullania germana*, *F. microphylla*, *Marchesinia mackaii*, *Adelanthus decipiens*, *Sphenolobus helleranus* and *Jamesoniella autumnalis*. Borrowdale appears to be especially rich in moisture-loving species not only because of its western position and heavy rainfall, but also because of the apparent historical continuity of woodland cover in places. Seatoller Wood faces south-east and it is difficult to account for the abundance of moisture-loving bryophytes, including several species with very limited powers of spread, except in terms of continuous Post-glacial woody cover.

The Borrowdale Woods are equally important for oceanic lichens; the main interest lies in the presence of a corticolous association, characterised by the co-dominant *Parmelia laevigata* and *P. taylorensis*. A total of 111 species have been recorded from Seatoller Wood, which include species such as *Bacidia affinis*, *B. isidiacea*, *Lecides berengeriana*, *Lopadium pezizoideum*, *Micarea violacea* and *P. plumbea* which are all very rare in Britain.

Great Wood is one of the best localities in England for arboreal lichens, including large foliose species such as *Lobaria pulmonaria*, *L. laete-virens*, *Sticta sylvatica* and *S. limbata*.

The woods nearer the dale head were once, and perhaps still are, the haunt of the pine marten, and they have the red squirrel, now reduced and local. The more notable breeding birds include common buzzard, pied flycatcher, wood warbler and grey wagtail.

These Borrowdale Woods are a key station in the internationally important series of western hill woodlands with rich Atlantic floras, and as a group they are clearly in the first echelon of grade 1 sites.

W.134. KESKADALE AND BIRKRIGG OAKS, CUMBERLAND

NY 208195, NY 215205 and NY 220205. 9 ha Grade 1

These two small areas of woodland are situated on the southern slopes of two adjacent mountain ridges. The Birkrigg area extends from 350 to 430 m and the Keskadale Oaks from 300 to 460 m. A shallow acidic soil is formed by the weathering of the shaly rock of the Skiddaw Slate Group.

These woods are almost completely of sessile oak with a few scattered rowans. The oak in both areas is low and springs from multiple stems and at least in the Keskadale Wood coppicing has probably taken place. However, coppicing is not the sole reason for the growth form, as factors such as fire, grazing, disease and bruising of the tree base all contribute. The woods apparently differ in that there is much more active scree in and near the Birkrigg Oaks whilst the Keskadale Oaks have a more stable as well as more grazed appearance. Both woodlands are wind-pruned, with stature of the trees decreasing to that of scrub at the upper edges, especially in the Keskadale wood.

The field layers in both woods are similar and open as the thin fine soil layer tends to get broken and eroded. Bilberry is dominant together with bracken and heather, the heather becoming dominant where the canopy is open. Other species common in the field layer include *Blechnum spicant*, *Deschampsia flexuosa*, *Potentilla erecta*, *Agrostis canina*, *Galium saxatile*, and *Oxalis acetosella*. Bryophytes are abundant and *Dicranum scoparium*, *Hypnum cupressiforme* and *Pleurozium schreberi* occur frequently. Epiphytic bryophytes and lichens clothe most of the trunks, with *Ulota* sp. common on the upper twigs.

These woodlands represent relict fragments of high-level sessile oakwood and may be near the altitudinal limit for oak woodland in western Britain.

See also U.27.

W.135. ORTON MOSS, CUMBERLAND

NY 3454. 50 ha Grade 1

These very mixed woods are developed partly on a former peat moss, possibly of the raised mire type but probably grading into valley mire. Areas of Scots pine are periodically cut and replanted, but this tree regenerates very freely naturally. Pinewood has a typical bilberry–moss community, but *Dryopteris dilatata* is locally abundant. The pine stand felled around 1958 had a good colony of *Goodyera repens*, but this has not been found in other areas of pine. A good deal of sessile oak is scattered through the woods, usually mixed with Scots pine and birch, and birch also forms pure stands of different ages with some trees reaching a large size. There is also much rowan, hazel and holly, and more locally, alder buckthorn. In one place, old peat diggings in the original ombrotrophic peat carry an acidophilous mire vegetation with a *Sphagnum* carpet and *Myrica gale, Andromeda polifolia, Oxycoccus palustris, Carex curta* and *Osmunda regalis.*

Heathery clearings on dried out peat have gradually developed a subspontaneous growth of Scots pine and birch during recent years. The former valley mire which floods during winter has a poor-fen with a great deal of *Carex rostrata, Calamagrostis epigejos* and *Dryopteris spinulosa.* In this part of the woods there is a much mixed willow (mainly *Salix cinerea*)–alder–birch swamp woodland with a *Sphagnum recurvum–S. auriculatum* floor. *Pyrola minor* is frequent in these damper areas. While the soils are mostly acidic, a few areas of more basic loam occur on which grow herbs such as *Geum rivale, Circaea lutetiana,* and *Sanicula europaea.* Ivy and polypody commonly occur as members of the field community on dry acidic soils.

Orton Moss is especially interesting for the old hay meadows which occur around the edges, especially on the south and west sides. These unploughed and herb-rich meadows grade into the woodland, and, because of the abundance of *Succisa pratensis,* the larval food plant, are celebrated as the haunt of the marsh fritillary *Euphydryas aurinia.* The whole area is extremely rich entomologically and rates highly on this account. Ornithologically, it is important as the breeding haunt of at least three pairs of sparrowhawks, and it also contains a good range of other woodland bird species.

W.136. WHITBARROW AND WITHERSLACK WOODS, WESTMORLAND
SD 4487. 160 ha   Grade 1

The area contains two main blocks of woodland. On the west side in a slight valley, below the west-facing Carboniferous Limestone scarp of Whitbarrow Scar (see L.136), is a large stand of high forest, grading into scrub as the slope steepens. On the eastern, dip slope of Whitbarrow Scar, is a much more heterogeneous woodland with a mosaic of coppice, scrub and planted conifers on discontinuous limestone pavement.

The high forest, extending from Pool Bank to Witherslack Hall, consists of a mixed sessile oak–ash wood, becoming purer oakwood near the road, where the rock changes to Silurian slate. This wood is important for its relatively large area of tall, well-grown oak, a relatively rare feature in this district where so much of the woodland has been coppiced. Although the wood is ungrazed, the field layer is not species rich, and the influence of the limestone is not particularly obvious until the slope of the Scar is reached. *Rubus fruticosus* is dominant locally, though *R. saxatilis* is also abundant near the road. There is local abundance of *Mercurialis perennis* and *Brachypodium sylvaticum* but the herb flora is not large. *Thelypteris phegopteris* is locally luxuriant. Birch is quite abundant, there are patches of hazel thicket, and dense ash regeneration occurs in places. Wych elm is frequent and small-leaved lime occurs here in one of its northernmost localities.

On the slope falling from Whitbarrow Scar there is a belt of pure yew-wood and above this a lower growth of oak, ash and hazel, passing on the scarp to scrub with juniper, yew, hazel, birch, buckthorn and *Sorbus lancastriensis.* There are old records of *Daphne mezereum.*

To the west of the road there is a change to ashwood on and beneath a second, smaller, and east-facing limestone scarp. The flora here is richer than that of the oakwood, with most of the typical ashwood species, and more local plants such as *Ophrys insectifera,* and the shady rocks have an abundance of calcicolous bryophytes.

The native woodland on the dip slope is mainly a scrubby ash–hazel growth, grading into sessile oak locally, and the field layer contains much *Brachypodium sylvaticum* and *Sesleria caerulea,* with *Carex ornithopoda* and *Melica nutans* quite plentiful. The grikes have *Phyllitis* and *Dryopteris villarii,* and *Epipactis atrorubens* occurs in more open places, while interesting bryophytes include the northern *Rhytidium rugosum* and the southern Atlantic *Marchesinia mackaii.* There was formerly a native colony of *Allium schoenoprasum* near Rus Mickle. Basiphilous woodland herbs are well represented and there are all transitions to open pavement with its characteristic flora (see under Lowland Grasslands, Heaths and Scrub). Despite conifer planting, which clearly causes surface acidification and impoverishment of this interesting flora, it is apparent that there will always be a patchy occurrence of native scrub and associated field/ground communities on the rockier, unplantable ground, and this eastern area is included in this important grade 1 site for its great botanical interest.

W.137. BIRK FELL, WESTMORLAND
NY 4018. 100 ha   Grade 1

This is the most extensive continuous stand of juniper in Lakeland, and equals or exceeds that of Upper Teesdale in size. Unlike juniper scrub considered under the lowland calcareous habitats it grows on leached skeletal brown earths over Borrowdale Volcanic rocks and has few basiphilous associates, though there are some patches of richer soil locally. The relationship with woodland is fairly close and this juniper scrub passes below into a stand of birchwood which occupies the base of the slope. Towards the edges of the wood, the junipers are smaller, probably as a result of grazing by sheep and red deer. The individual trees of the Tynron Juniper Wood have a generally greater stature, but Tynron Wood covers a much smaller area than the Birk Fell juniper wood. In the Highlands juniper scrubs mostly occur as the shrub layer of pine and birch woods, and stands on open moorland tend to occupy damp hollows rather than dry slopes as in Lakeland.

The birchwood may be a seral derivative of sessile oakwood, for it occupies the habitat held by the latter elsewhere in the Ullswater valley. The field layer of this wood is virtually identical with that of the other Lakeland oakwoods on acidic soils, and the bryophyte communities are also typical, but with poor representation of Atlantic species. The filmy fern *Hymenophyllum wilsonii* occurs sparingly.

W.138. HELBECK AND SWINDALE WOODS, WESTMORLAND
NY 7816–8016.   135 ha   Grade 1*

This is the northernmost of the internationally important series of ashwoods on the Carboniferous Limestone and lies on the Eden valley scarp slope of the Westmorland Pennines, above Brough. Helbeck Wood is on the frontal slope which rises in ridges and tiers of limestone scar towards Little Fell at the southern end of the Cross Fell range, while Swindale is the adjoining deep and cliff-lined valley cutting this slope at the eastern end. The ashwood is fairly pure in places, but there is locally a good deal of wych elm, and towards the edges more open birchwood with hawthorn takes over. Oak is scattered and there are varying amounts of hazel, aspen, rowan, holly, gean and bird-cherry. Southern species of tall shrubs are represented: *Crataegus oxyacanthoides* occurs sparingly here, its northern limit; buckthorn is recorded; and there is a small amount of spindle. The northern willow *Salix phylicifolia* occurs alongside Swindale Beck. Non-native species such as larch, sycamore and beech are present, but in rather small quantity, and they thus add to the diversity of the woods rather than detract from their quality.

Parts of the woods are ungrazed or lightly grazed, and there is a rich development of herbaceous communities, with the usual *Allium ursinum–Mercurialis perennis* types conspicuous, but also a variety of others associated with more open conditions, especially on screes and outcrops. The more local herbs include *Myosotis sylvatica*, *Cephalanthera longifolia*, *Convallaria majalis*, *Vicia sylvatica*, *Paris quadrifolia*, *Aquilegia vulgaris*, *Campanula latifolia*, *Epipactis helleborine*, *Rubus saxatilis*, *Geranium lucidum*, *Cirsium heterophyllum* and *Polygonatum officinale*. On steep rocks are *Hippocrepis comosa* and *Carex ornithopoda*. The two rare horsetails *Equisetum pratense* and *E. hyemale* grow within the site.

Other field communities include the grassy type, dominated by *Brachypodium sylvaticum* and there are also transitions to the *Sesleria albicans* and *Festuca* grasslands of the open hillside. In places there is dominance of bluebell with bracken, especially around the lower edges of Swindale. Within Helbeck Wood is a small tarn, with fringing calcareous marsh of sedges and 'brown mosses', with an abundance of *Primula farinosa* and *Valeriana dioica*. Altogether, the diversity of habitat and floristics, and the gradation into other important upland communities, make this a most important site. It is contiguous with the Appleby Fells grade 1 upland site (U.22).

W.139. ROUDSEA WOOD, LANCASHIRE
SD 3382.   118 ha   Grade 1

This exceptionally diverse woodland lies almost at sea-level (0–20 m) on the east side of the Leven Estuary at the head of Morecambe Bay. It merges to the east into the northern end of an estuarine raised mire complex (the Holker Mosses) and to the west and north into salt marsh flanking the Leven Estuary. The wood itself covers two ridges of contrasting geology separated by a shallow valley which contains a valley mire and small tarn.

The east ridge is of Carboniferous Limestone and carries an ash–oak wood with some small-leaved lime, gean and birch. The oak is mainly pedunculate but sessile and intermediate forms occur. Characteristic limestone shrubs include purging buckthorn, spindle, blackthorn and guelder rose, and there are also hazel, holly and hawthorn. The field layer of this ash–oak wood is markedly calcicolous, with a general predominance of *Brachypodium sylvaticum* and *Mercurialis perennis*, local abundance of *Convallaria majalis*, and a wide variety of species. The more local herbs include *Allium scorodoprasum*, *Aquilegia vulgaris*, *Anacamptis pyramidalis*, *Brachypodium pinnatum*, *Campanula latifolia*, *Carex digitata*, *Hypericum montanum*, *Inula conyza*, *Lathraea squamaria*, *Lithospermum officinale*, *Neottia nidus-avis*, *Ophrys insectifera*, *Ornithogalum umbellatum*, *Rubus saxatilis* and *Sesleria albicans*.

The west ridge is composed of greywackes of the Bannisdale Slate Series, with small areas of slate, and carries a contrasting sessile oakwood with birch and some rowan and hazel. The field layer is acidophilous, with dominance of *Deschampsia flexuosa* and *Pteridium aquilinum*, or *Molinia caerulea* where there is an overlying peaty alluvium.

The valley mire between the ridges has a fairly eutrophic fen vegetation, with *Phragmites communis*, *Carex paniculata*, *C. vesicaria*, *C. diandra*, *C. disticha*, *C. pseudocyperus*, *Juncus subnodulosus*, *Calamagrostis canescens*, *Thalictrum flavum*, *Thelypteris palustris*, *Lycopus europaeus*, *Lythrum salicaria* and *Lysimachia vulgaris*. The tarn has species such as *Baldellia ranunculoides* and *Alisma plantago-aquatica*. There is a scattered growth of birch and alder on this wet ground. The greatest rarity of Roudsea Wood, *Carex flava* (here in its only known British station), occurs on the transition from dry limestone soils to peat, and flourishes along the rides in this habitat.

Where the limestone ridge passes into the raised mire system, there is a change to birchwood over peat, with rowan and some Scots pine. Where the canopy is open, there is dominance of bracken, but with deeper shade this is replaced by bilberry. Alder buckthorn is a conspicuous shrub in this transitional woodland. There is then a change to the open mire surface, somewhat dried by cutting, draining and burning, but still with characteristic plants such as *Andromeda polifolia*, *Narthecium ossifragum* and *Drosera rotundifolia*. The larger area of the adjoining Deer Dike and Stribers Mosses are a grade 1 peatland site (P.47), and form with Roudsea Wood a single composite grade 1 site.

On the western and northern side there is a transition from oakwood through alderwood to estuarine salt marsh, a sequence seen in few other places, though the oak is on higher rocky bluffs and is not a seral development from salt marsh. The brackish transition zone is marked by the presence of such plants as *Carex distans*, *C. extensa*, *C. otrubae*, *Samolus valerandi*, *Oenanthe lachenalii*, *Centaurium littorale* and *Scirpus maritimus*.

This site contains an unusual range of habitats, and the flora of the Roudsea Wood site contains at least 340 vascular species. The woodland and the adjoining mosses are also very rich in Lepidoptera, and this is a station for the rare white-marked moth *Cerastis leucographa*.

W.140. GAIT BARROWS, LANCASHIRE
SD 4877. 31 ha   Grade 1

The most important feature of this site is the massive central exposure of Carboniferous Limestone pavement, which is probably the finest example in Britain of this extremely local habitat. The vegetation of the pavement is described under lowland grasslands (L.134). There is a patchy distribution on the pavement of a tall scrub with yew, hazel, juniper and young ash, and this has associated shrubs such as purging buckthorn, spindle, dogwood, privet, holly, small-leaved lime and *Sorbus lancastriensis*. This type of scrub grades into taller woodland on more broken and dissected pavement around the edges of the central mass, and there is a general increase in stature of species such as ash and hazel on deeper soils, where pedunculate oak also appears. This rather low and open type of woodland has a rich limestone flora, with species such as *Convallaria majalis, Epipactis atrorubens, Atropa belladonna, Hypericum montanum, Rubus saxatilis, Carex digitata, Polygonatum odoratum* and *Melica nutans*.

The pavement woodland passes into a broad peripheral zone of taller forest, though this varies in height and structure according to past differences in management. In general, there is a dense coppice of hazel, with standards of pedunculate oak, ash and sycamore. There are also thickets of silver birch, and hornbeam and beech occur locally, though both were probably introduced. The drift-derived soils in this part of the wood vary from basic to moderately acidic, and there is a lesser abundance of markedly calcicolous species than in the limestone woodland. Bramble is widespread throughout the coppice, and the field layer characteristically has *Mercurialis perennis, Endymion non-scriptus, Brachypodium sylvaticum, Primula vulgaris, Sanicula europaea, Circaea lutetiana* and *Viola riviniana*.

W.141. ROEBURNDALE WOODS, LANCASHIRE
SD 6066. 35 ha   Grade 1

This has been chosen as an example of a northern mixed deciduous woodland, and lies mainly on the east side of a deep glen draining the northern side of the Bowland Fells. It lies on Carboniferous shales and sandstones which give a range of soils from highly acidic to strongly basic, and it is ungrazed. The most acidic brown earths have typical sessile oakwood with *Vaccinium myrtillus, Luzula sylvatica* and heath mosses. This grades into a mixed oak–birch wood on slightly less acidic soils, and the field layer here is of *Holcus mollis* and *Endymion non-scriptus*, with *Stellaria holostea, Athyrium filix-femina* and *Pteridium aquilinum*. On wetter ground this type changes to alder–birch wood, with *Deschampsia cespitosa, Carex remota, C. laevigata, C. sylvatica, Dryopteris spinulosa, D. austriaca* and *Ranunculus repens*. On the most basic soils there is a mixed ash–oak–wych elm–hazel wood, with grass-herb communities of the *Brachypodium sylvaticum–Deschampsia cespitosa* and *Mer-*

curialis perennis–Allium ursinum type. Species of particular interest include *Stellaria nemorum, Carex pendula, Festuca altissima, Phyllitis scolopendrium, Polystichum setiferum* and *P. lobatum*.

Although this is a woodland developed on the steep sides of a glen, it extends over more level ground on top of the east bank, and covers a larger area than many gorge woods.

W.142. RIBBLEHEAD WOODS, YORKSHIRE   Grade 1
(a) *Colt Park*
SD 7778–7776. 9 ha
(b) *Ling Gill*
SD 8078. 5 ha

These sites are regarded as fragments of a once more extensive subalpine ashwood covering much of the lower slopes of the Craven Pennines and have survived by virtue of physical features; a limestone pavement in the case of Colt Park and a steep-sided ravine at Ling Gill, both of which afford protection from grazing. Both woods are on Carboniferous Limestone; Colt Park is developed over a pavement of limestone at about 340 m whilst Ling Gill is cut into the upper part of the Great Scar limestone, at a similar elevation, 3 km to the north-east.

The tree layer in both woodlands is composed mainly of rather open and somewhat stunted ash. In Ling Gill the ash tends to be more abundant on the crags and gill sides. In both woodlands a shrub layer is present and contains hazel, hawthorn, bird-cherry and rowan. Wych elm, birch and (in Ling Gill) aspen are also to be found scattered throughout the canopy in places. Both areas have a rich flora as a result of the calcareous substratum and lack of grazing. Tall-herb communities are well developed and contain *Trollius europaeus, Geranium sylvaticum, Cirsium heterophyllum, Actaea spicata, Crepis paludosa, C. mollis, Geum rivale, Angelica sylvestris, Campanula latifolia* and *Paris quadrifolia. Gagea lutea* is less frequent. Submontane plants include *Potentilla crantzii, Galium boreale* and *Asplenium viride*. In Ling Gill podsolic soils above the rocky ravine slopes have an acidiphilous field layer with *Pteridium aquilinum, Molinia caerulea, Potentilla erecta* and *Galium hercynicum*.

The moist atmosphere and shade of Ling Gill ravine and the grikes at Colt Park have led to the occurrence of a rich bryophyte flora on the limestone.

See also OW.50 and U.23.

W.143. CONISTONE OLD PASTURE AND BASTOW WOOD, YORKSHIRE
SD 9867. 380 ha   Grade 1

The site occupies part of the Carboniferous Limestone escarpment on the eastern side of upper Wharfedale. Great Scar limestone, divided into two main blocks by a narrow gorge, outcrops as pavement, scar and associated scree. Much of the soil is thin humus-carbonate occurring in patches on the exposed limestone, but on the valley sides and in depressions a deeper clay has developed, and in some places acid, sandy loam. The more southerly of the blocks is wooded; closed woodland mainly of ash, wych elm, and hazel with calcicolous shrubs such as privet, buckthorn, and whitebeam, considerably invaded by sycamore, characterises Grass Wood, while in the contiguous Bastow Wood birch is predominant over much of the area and forms an open canopy. This difference is probably related to site history, in addition to somewhat greater elevation, for Bastow Wood overlies a Celtic field system, and the contrast is now being accentuated by re-forestation of Grass Wood, mostly on a shelter wood system, but locally by clear felling and re-planting with conifers. Dib Scar, descending steeply into the gorge drained by Dib Beck, forms the northern limit of this block, beyond which rises the complementary limestone grassland and pavement of Conistone Old Pasture, characterised by typical close-cropped species-rich swards and a grike flora. Ecologically this site belongs partly with the lowland calcareous grasslands, and gives an interesting comparison with the more distinctly montane limestone communities in Cowside valley and the higher slopes of Malham–Arncliffe (U.24).

The main feature of interest is the herbaceous flora which is outstandingly rich. The woods of the area are known as a locality for the very rare *Cypripedium calceolus*, which has been reduced almost to extinction by plant collectors. Herbs still present include *Polemonium caeruleum*, *Thalictrum minus*, *Geranium sanguineum*, *Polygonatum odoratum*, *Paris quadrifolia*, and *Origanum vulgare*. More open ground in the area has *Draba incana*, *Arabis hirsuta*, *Polygala amara*, *Saxifraga hypnoides*, and *Sedum telephium*, while flushes and damper pastures have an abundance of *Primula farinosa* and *Parnassia palustris*. The afforestation programme may ultimately reduce the variety to some extent, but most species and the general richness of the habitat are expected to survive.

W.144. RAINCLIFFE WOOD, YORKSHIRE
SE 9888. 130 ha   Grade 1

The east side of the valley has been partly felled and replanted but it still shows a fine gradation from alder in the valley bottom through ash–wych elm woodland with a basiphilous field layer to pedunculate oakwood with an acidophilous field layer near the top of the slopes. Scarwell Wood on the west side has an alder–ash woodland with willow and a very varied and well-developed field layer on the valley bottom. Above this there is ash–elm woodland with sycamore and extensive *Mercurialis perennis* and *Allium ursinum* communities. A feature of this zone are the well-developed tufa areas with a characteristic calcicolous moss flora. The upper slopes carry oak–sycamore woodland with some elm, birch, rowan and hazel over a less calcicolous field layer of *Rubus fruticosus*, *Lonicera periclymenum*, *Endymion non-scriptus*, *Anemone nemorosa*, *Oxalis acetosella*, etc., with patches of *Luzula sylvatica*.

W.145. SHIPLEY WOOD, DURHAM/YORKSHIRE
NZ 0021. 60 ha   Grade 1

These woods occupy the rocky gorge of the River Tees cut through the Carboniferous Series, 6.4 km above Barnard Castle. The lower parts of the wood are high forest of wych elm, ash, pedunculate oak and alder, with yew, hazel, holly, rowan and bird-cherry locally. There is a wide range of age classes, but some of the elm has been coppiced or pollarded. At the southern end where the wood was once cut-over, birch, hawthorn and willow dominate. These woods are on limestone, but the upper levels over acidic rocks are dominated by oak and birch. The ground flora of the lower levels is particularly rich with abundant *Myosotis sylvatica*, *Geranium sylvaticum*, *Geum rivale*, *Paris quadrifolia*, *Chrysosplenium* spp., *Allium ursinum*, *Luzula sylvatica* and numerous ferns. The bryophyte flora is quite rich, both in calcicolous elements on the damp boulders lower down, and in calcifuge species on the acid loamy soil and rocks higher up. The wood is, however, outstanding for its flora of epiphytic lichens, which includes the relict forest species *Lobaria pulmonaria*, *L. laetevirens* and *Baccidia affinis*: this is the first definite British record of the last-named lichen.

W.146. SCALES WOOD, CUMBERLAND
NY 1616. 30 ha   Grade 2

Scales Wood lies between 100 m and 250 m on a fairly steep slope of Ennerdale Granophyre facing north-east. From its position on the lower slopes of the High Stile range in the high fells of western Lakeland, the wood receives a heavy rainfall of about 203 cm annually, and the shaded aspect enhances atmospheric humidity. The parent rock gives mainly acidic soils and the lower part of the wood is a well-grown stand of high forest sessile oak with few undershrubs since there is sheep-grazing throughout, though scattered birches fulfil this role in places. The upper part of the wood consists of fairly pure birchwood, though this is probably seral as it lies well within the altitudinal range of oak. The ground is generally block littered and there is a luxuriant fern and bryophyte flora, with abundance of Atlantic species such as *Hymenophyllum wilsonii*, *Plagiochila spinulosa*, *Scapania gracilis*, *Hylocomium umbratum* and the rare moss *Sematophyllum novae-caesareae*, unknown elsewhere in England outside Borrowdale. At the upper edge of the wood the grassy field layer grades into bilberry heath with a high cover of *Sphagnum capillaceum* and *S. quinquefarium*. There is an old record of *Festuca altissima*, probably referring to the ravine of Far Ruddy Beck, where calcareous rocks bear a more varied flora.

This site could be regarded as an alternative to Johnny's Wood (W.133(e)), but is too small and limited in range of habitat, vegetation and flora to take the place of the Borrowdale Woods as a whole.

W.147. LYNE WOODS, CUMBERLAND
NY 4569. 115 ha   Grade 2

These consist of a series of ungrazed lowland gorge woodlands along the course of the River Lyne. The lowest section, near Kirklinton, has only thin fringes of ash–oak–wych elm–hazel wood, and is interesting mainly for its crags of New Red Sandstone, which is here moderately calcareous in places and supports species such as *Myosotis sylvatica*, *Carex pendula*, *Phyllitis scolopendrium*, *Polystichum lobatum* and *Equisetum hyemale*. There is a rich bryophyte flora. The section above Waingatehead is cut mainly through acidic beds of Carboniferous sandstone; it has more oakwood and is notable for the abundance of Atlantic bryophytes. There is an isolated small colony of *Hymenophyllum tunbrigense*. The basic soils have a field layer with *Mercurialis perennis*, *Primula vulgaris*, *Sanicula europaea*, *Stellaria nemorum* and *Carex sylvatica* on drier ground, and *Ranunculus repens*, *Chrysosplenium oppositifolium*, *Filipendula ulmaria* and *Carex remota* where it is wet. The acidic brown earths have an abundance of *Luzula sylvatica*, *Vaccinium myrtillus*, *Oxalis acetosella*, *Dryopteris austriaca* and *D. filix-mas*.

The upper section, below Kinkry Hill, is cut through Carboniferous sandstones and shales, and has a mixture of the acidic and basic woodland types described above. Another distinctive type on a wet river terrace here is an ungrazed alderwood, with wet mull soils carrying *Carex acutiformis*, *C. paniculata*, *Equisetum telmateia*, *Paris quadrifolia* and *Phalaris arundinacea*. Through all sections, the high flood level of the river produces a zone of enrichment which supports numerous basiphilous vascular plants and bryophytes, and these include *Trollius europaeus* and *Geranium sylvaticum* in the upper section, which is closer to the source of the river on the Bewcastle Fells of north Cumberland.

W.148. GOWBARROW PARK, CUMBERLAND
NY 4120. 85 ha Grade 2

The southern edge of Gowbarrow Park around Yew Crag consists of a mixture of woodland, grassland and heath on steep slopes and bottom lands overlooking the northern shore of Ullswater, at 150–275 m. Two distinct kinds of woodland occur. On the low-lying ground at the foot of the slopes the woodland is dominated by alder with a few ash. In Dobbins Wood and higher up the valley of the Collierhag Beck, much of the alder is open – in Dobbins Wood it was coppiced within the last decade and has been kept open by grazing – but in the area south and west of Yew Crag it mostly forms a closed canopy. The soil here is a flushed silty material with boulders at the base of the slopes, mildly acid or neutral in reaction and slightly gleyed. The ground flora is extremely rich with numerous marshland species especially in the open alder areas.

On the steep south- and east-facing slopes most watercourses and rocky bluffs are occupied by open irregular woodland in which wych elm, ash and hazel are abundant. Many other species occur there including bird cherry, yew and sessile oak. This kind of woodland is best developed on Yew Crag, whence it grades westwards into a distinct variant, resembling in some respects the woodland of calcareous soils south of the Lake District. This lies on the steep south-facing slopes immediately above the oak, and is characterised by the presence of pedunculate oak, small-leaved lime and spindle and the absence of sessile oak in the mixture which includes wych elm, ash and hazel. The soil on the craggy slope varies considerably in depth, stability,

base-status and wetness, but seems mostly to be mildly acid or neutral. The rock outcrops belong to the Borrowdale Volcanic Series and vary from strongly acidic to markedly calcareous.

The alder woods thin out below Collier Hagg to open, acidic, flushed grassland and bracken on drier areas. Between the patches of crag woodland and on the hillside above are heathland communities ranging from bracken to a mixture of *Vaccinium myrtillus*, *Calluna vulgaris*, *Erica cinerea* and *Nardus stricta*.

The lichen flora is rich, both in the lower alderwoods and on the steeper wooded slopes and cliffs. Gowbarrow supports a fine assemblage of relic forest lichen species within which *Lobaria* spp. are particularly well developed.

W.149. NADDLE LOW FOREST, WESTMORLAND
NY 5015. 110 ha Grade 2

Naddle Low Forest is situated at 200–400 m on the slope overlooking the lower end of Haweswater and on both sides of a re-entrant valley joining the main river just below the foot of the lake. The aspect is mainly north-west, but on the spur between the two main sections varies through north to east. The parent rock belongs to the Borrowdale Volcanic Series, and contains calcite in places, so that the soils vary from acidic to basic brown earths, while the slopes are generally steep and locally precipitous. The poor soils of steep ground have sessile oakwood, but birch locally replaces oak, evidently through selective extraction of the latter. Ash–hazel wood is well developed on the richer soils, and where the slope flattens to the river, beyond the dam, there is a good mixed deciduous wood, and alder–*Carex* swamp in places. The slopes are thickly strewn with blocks and here there is a profusion of ferns and bryophytes. Lightly grazed sections of the wood have herbs such as *Geranium sylvaticum* and in open places there are soligenous mires with *Juncus acutiflorus* and *Primula farinosa*.

Naddle Low Forest shows much the same range of habitat and vegetational variation as the Borrowdale Woods, but is regarded as a second choice for the following reasons.

(i) There is a much lesser representation of good oak and a correspondingly greater amount of probably seral birch.

(ii) There is a smaller extent of ash–hazel wood.

(iii) There is a lesser range of aspect.

(iv) Though luxuriant and rich, the bryophyte flora is much poorer in Atlantic species, probably because of the eastern position of Naddle Low Forest.

Naddle Low Forest has the advantage of being in two almost continuous blocks and probably contains a few herbs not present in the Borrowdale Woods.

W.150. LOW WOOD, HARTSOP, WESTMORLAND
NY 4013. 50 ha Grade 2

Low Wood is situated about half way between the Borrowdale Woods and Naddle Low Forest, on a moderate to steep and east- to south-east-facing slope of Borrowdale Volcanic rock at 150–400 m, overlooking Brothers Water. Both oakwood and ash–hazel wood on acidic and basic soils are well represented here, and many of the trees are tall and well grown. The field communities of the Borrowdale Woods are mostly represented, but the drier aspect gives a much lesser abundance of bryophytes, particularly of the moisture-loving Atlantic species.

This site has too limited a range of aspect, communities and flora to rank as an alternative to the Borrowdale Woods, but is regarded as an important example of hill oak and ash–hazel wood in Lakeland.

See also U.19.

W.151. SMARDALE WOODS, WESTMORLAND
NY 7207.   30 ha   Grade 2

This deep gill, draining through the Carboniferous Limestone belt west of Kirkby Stephen at 200–260 m, has a fairly extensive ashwood, grading to open hazel and hawthorn, with rich grasslands containing much *Sesleria caerulea*, *Helianthemum chamaecistus*, *Poterium sanguisorba* and *Geranium sanguineum*. There is, however, less diversity than in the Helbeck–Swindale Woods, and the prevailing field layer is of *Mercurialis perennis* with *Brachypodium sylvaticum*. Above the railway the wood is mostly a mixture of birch, hazel and hawthorn.

See also U.25.

W.152. LOWTHER PARK, WESTMORLAND
NY 5223.   105 ha   Grade 2

This is a park woodland of great antiquity lying on Carboniferous Limestone south of Penrith at around 230 m. The park is reputed to be over 1000 years old and was probably enclosed from the open waste. Most of the ancient trees are oaks, some very large indeed, with a number of old ash and wych elm. The former deer park stretches for several kilometres and includes ancient avenues of yew, with elm, oak, sweet chestnut, lime and other avenues of more recent date. The epiphyte lichen flora has been subject to only a cursory examination, but even this revealed 59 species, one of the richest of such assemblages in northern England. Two river valleys cross the park, and these contain woodland with a basiphilous field layer.

W.153. EAVES WOOD, LANCASHIRE
SD 4676.   50 ha   Grade 2

Eaves Wood, on the low Carboniferous Limestone hills of Silverdale, is situated over discontinuous limestone pavement. The native tree canopy has been much modified and whilst native species such as oak, ash, birch, yew and hazel are present, felling and replanting have led to the presence of considerable areas of Scots pine and larch and the spread of sycamore. Native species, particularly ash, regenerate well. The woodland is managed by the National Trust and is open to the public as an amenity area.

The main interest in the woodland lies in its floristic richness. It contains a number of rare or local herbs including *Helleborus foetidus*, *Neottia nidus-avis*, *Epipactis atrorubens*, *Carex digitata*, *Geranium sanguineum* and *Filipendula vulgaris*.

W.154. BURTON WOOD, LANCASHIRE
SD 5466.   18 ha   Grade 2

The site is on a steep slope at 15–140 m over rocks of the Bowland Series, which consist of a mixture of sandstone, mudstone and calcareous shales. The soils vary from shallow acid podsols through brown earth types on ridges to deep sandy mulls (pH 6.5) on the slopes of the two shaly ravines. The canopy, which appears to be uneven-aged, is dominated by sessile oak and ash; also present are birch, Scots pine, and gean. Wych elm and small-leaved lime are locally abundant. The shrub layer is only developed to any extent in the ravines and includes hazel, hawthorn, elder, rowan and guelder rose.

On the podsolic areas the ground flora is a *Deschampsia flexuosa–Vaccinium myrtillus* dominated community, whilst *Mercurialis perennis* takes over on the neutral mull soils. Also present in the field layer are *Endymion non-scriptus*, *Lonicera periclymenum*, *Primula vulgaris*, *Geranium robertianum*, *Oxalis acetosella*, *Holcus mollis* and *Luzula pilosa*. *Polystichum setiferum* is abundant in the ravines and the very local liverwort *Lophocolea fragrans* occurs here.

W.155. HAWKSWICK WOOD, YORKSHIRE
SD 9471.   12 ha   Grade 2

This Littondale ashwood has a rather open growth of medium-sized trees on a south-west-facing slope of Carboniferous Limestone with scree and scar at 200–300 m. There are rich brown loams, supporting a varied herbaceous field layer with mixed grasses and forbs, including *Brachypodium sylvaticum*, *Allium ursinum*, *Anemone nemorosa*, *Endymion non-scriptus* and *Mercurialis perennis* as the chief dominants. Other abundant species include *Primula vulgaris*, *Fragaria vesca*, *Potentilla sterilis*, *Viola riviniana*, *Prunella vulgaris*, *Circaea lutetiana* and, more locally, *Paris quadrifolia* and *Convallaria majalis*. This wood is evidently only lightly grazed, and is probably the best remaining limestone wood of the Wharfedale area, the rest having been ecologically degraded in recent years by felling or sheep-grazing.

W.156. SCOSKA WOOD, YORKSHIRE
SD 9172.   35 ha   Grade 2

This is a second Littondale ashwood but lies on the opposite, north-east-facing slope to Hawkswick Wood, and is more heavily grazed in places. The rock is again Carboniferous Limestone and the altitude 250–370 m. The wood also contains some sycamore, a few larch and spruce, and birch is locally abundant. The shrubs include hazel, hawthorn and willows with bird cherry and *Ribes sylvestre* in places. The middle level of the wood is broken by a line of low scar and scree, and here, since grazing is less heavy than at the margins, the field layer is very rich. A wide range of mesophilous and calcicolous species is represented and includes *Actaea spicata*, *Paris quadrifolia*, *Sesleria caerulea*, *Cirsium heterophyllum* and *Asplenium viride*. Grazing has increased within the wood in recent years and there has been modification of the field layer communities, with grasses spreading at the expense of forbs.

See also U.24.

W.157. THORNTON AND TWISLETON GLENS, YORKSHIRE

SD 6974, SD 7074.   45 ha   Grade 2

These two valleys north of Ingleton lie at 120–200 m on strongly contrasting rock types, namely Carboniferous Limestone which is confined to the western glen, and Silurian slate in the eastern and part of the western glen. The limestone woodland has pedunculate oak, wych elm, ash mixtures with a range of age classes, but over the slates sessile oak is dominant, with rowan, birch and, beside the stream, small-leaved lime. Though the vascular flora reflects the strong contrast in underlying lithology and is rich in aggregate, the site is more important for its outstanding bryophyte and lichen floras. The bryophytes include many species of calcareous habitats, but also a number of moisture-loving oceanic species surviving in an area of relatively low rainfall and calcareous rocks. After the Lodore Falls in the Borrowdale Woods (W.133), this is probably the best locality in northern England for Atlantic liverworts characteristic of damp, waterfall glens at low elevations. Some of these species are unknown elsewhere in the Pennines, for they avoid limestone. The site owes this bryological richness, unusual also in an area of relatively low rainfall, to its western position, the presence of relatively acidic rocks and the probable historical continuity of tree cover in these glens. The lichen flora includes a number of rare species of old forests, notably *Thelotrema lapadinum*, *Normandina pulchella*, *Lobaria laetevirens* and *Opegrapha rufescens*.

W.158. ASHBERRY AND REINS WOODS, YORKSHIRE

SE 5685.   80 ha   Grade 2

These form part of an extensive group of woodlands at 90–150 m on the steep sides of upper Rye Dale near Rievaulx, one of the deep glens draining the south-western part of the North York Moors.

The woods lie on the west slope of this valley and on both aspects of the ridge bounding the east side. Soil conditions range from acidic to strongly calcareous, and from dry to permanently water-logged. On the acidic soils oak and birch dominate over a field layer of *Rubus fruticosus*, *Pteridium aquilinum*, *Vaccinium myrtillus*, *Lonicera periclymenum* and *Luzula sylvatica*. On calcareous soils, mixed deciduous woodland of ash, field maple, wych elm, hazel and small-leaved lime grows over *Brachypodium sylvaticum*, *Deschampsia cespitosa* and a rich variety of herbs including *Actaea spicata* and *Ophrys insectifera*. The lower 15 m of the valley are occupied by fragments of alderwood and more extensive *Juncus–Carex* calcareous marsh and wet grassland, with an unusual number of rare and local species, notably *Primula farinosa*, *Trollius europaeus*, *Epipactis palustris*, *Schoenus nigricans* and *Carex aquatilis*. Adjacent to the mixed deciduous woodland is limestone grassland with numerous herb species (e.g. *Cirsium eriophorum*) showing invasion by hawthorn. The whole forms an important woodland–grassland–mire complex of great floristic interest.

W.159. BECKHOLE WOODS, YORKSHIRE

NZ 8202.   170 ha   Grade 2

Here there is ash–elm–small-leaved lime–oak woodland in a ravine with a very mixed field layer including acidophilous and basiphilous communities in the valley bottom. The woodland further up the slopes loses some of its diversity and consists mainly of oak over a *Vaccinium–Melampyrum–Deschampsia flexuosa* field layer.

W.160. BEAST CLIFF, YORKSHIRE

SE 998999–TA 005988.   20 ha   Grade 2

This coastal site, about 11 km north of Scarborough, is on a system of slipped Jurassic strata of considerable size and contains steep scrubbed-over areas that are accessible only with great difficulty. The area is apparently undisturbed by man and an extensive undercliff woodland complex of oak and ash within which much scrub has developed. Shrub species present include rowan, willows, hawthorn, birch, broom, gorse, rose and sycamore. The ground flora list is extensive and contains a wide range of species including those of coastal habitats. Under the best-developed woodland dog's mercury, bramble and bracken are dominant; in other flushed areas *Luzula sylvatica* and fern species form the main cover whilst some rocky outcrops are colonised by *Calluna vulgaris* and *Succisa pratensis*. Additional habitats are provided by two pools colonised by *Scirpus lacustris* and *Potamogeton* spp. surrounded by a fringe of *Salix* spp.

See also C.68.

W.161. KISDON FORCE WOODS, YORKSHIRE

NY 9000.   12 ha   Grade 2

These woods are on Carboniferous Limestone of the Yoredale Series in steep gorges associated with the west–east-flowing River Swale and its small north–south-flowing tributary, East Gill, near Keld. While forming an ecological unit, they are physically separated by a field in the angle of the junction of the rivers. The altitude is 270–350 m, so that the woods have a submontane character.

The woods are dominated by ash, particularly fine specimens occurring on the south side of the Swale. Birch is important as a constituent of the canopy toward the upper woodland edges whilst wych elm is locally abundant near the rivers and alder follows some small side streams on the south side of the Swale. Hawthorn, bird-cherry, blackthorn, and rowan are present as understorey or shrubs; hazel occurs, and is particularly well developed on some relatively open and more level ground south of the Swale. Though variable, the average height of the tree canopy is about 8 m.

The ground flora varies according to the substrata which range from limestone to acidic sandstone and, alongside East Gill, to base-rich alluvium, but in general reflects only moderately base-rich conditions. A disused lead mine tip with *Minuartia verna* forms a scree, cutting through the wood on the north side of the Swale. The range of forbs includes such species as *Brachypodium sylvaticum*, *Mercurialis perennis*, *Allium ursinum*, *Primula vulgaris*, *Sanicula europaea*, *Filipendula ulmaria* and *Viola* spp. In East Gill, *Campanula latifolia* and *Cirsium heterophyllum* also occur at lower levels and the woodland ground flora gives way to a small piece of attractive, wet, calcicolous meadow flora between wood and river. Ferns, notably *Athyrium filix-femina*, are prominent on the south side of the Swale among the bigger trees. A range of bryophyte communities is also represented.

W.162. CASTLE EDEN DENE, DURHAM
NZ 4339. 210 ha   Grade 2

This is the best remaining example of the steep-sided wooded valleys which run through boulder clay-covered Magnesian Limestone to the coast in this region.

Two main types of Magnesian Limestone of the Middle Series, Shell Limestone Reef and Bedded Limestone, are exposed in cliffs up to 30 m high. The soils are derived from variable boulder clay and are mainly alkaline but leaching of sandy soil produces acid conditions locally.

Pedunculate oak and ash occur together with some yew, elder, hawthorn, hazel, rowan and rhododendron. The field layer is composed mainly of *Pteridium aquilinum*, with *Anemone nemorosa*, *Mercurialis perennis*, *Deschampsia cespitosa*, *Holcus lanatus*, *Endymion non-scriptus* and *Blechnum spicant*. *Festuca ovina* occurs on the leached sandy soils.

Beech has been planted in some areas and sycamore has established itself. There are also a number of mixed conifer plantations and some plantations of hardwoods. *Cypripedium calceolus* and *Ophrys insectifera* formerly occurred but are now thought to be extinct. Other notable species still occurring are *Pyrola rotundifolia* and *Convallaria majalis*.

The northern brown (Castle Eden) argus butterfly *Aricia artaxerxes* occurs here.

See also C.70.

W.163. HOLYSTONE WOODS, NORTHUMBERLAND
NT 9201, NT 9301, NT 9401. 30 ha   Grade 2

This site has four separate units, three being composed principally of sessile oak woodland and the fourth a mixture of habitats including woodland and moorland in which juniper scrub is a significant feature.

The small sessile oakwoods occupy mainly the south-facing slope of a glen draining from the Carboniferous gritstone moorlands of the Harbottle Moors, south of the main Cheviot range. They are examples of this woodland type in a much drier climate than that of Lakeland or north Wales. They adjoin young conifer plantations and are now less grazed by sheep than formerly. In Holystone Burn there is open growth of medium-sized spreading oaks, some of which are large for a hill wood. North Wood consists in the main of twisted, many stemmed trees suggesting former coppicing. Underscrub is absent, and field communities are of the type found in Lakeland sessile oakwoods on acidic soils. There is an abundance of bracken in open places, and the field dominants include *Deschampsia flexuosa*, *Vaccinium myrtillus*, with much *Galium saxatile*, *Potentilla erecta* and *Melampyrum pratense*. Heath mosses cover part of the ground but Atlantic bryophytes are very few. The northern

herb *Trientalis europaea* is abundant. The steep opposite bank has birchwood with tall heather and a luxuriant carpet of heath mosses and *Sphagnum* which is the habitat of *Listera cordata*.

W.164. MONK WOOD, NORTHUMBERLAND
NY 7856. 20 ha   Grade 2

Monk Wood and its surroundings are part of the ancient Whitfield Park, lying in the sheltered valley of the River West Allen. The parkland is open, old woodland of ash, wych elm and sycamore, with the richest epiphytic lichen flora known in north-east England. The main block of woodland, estimated at 250–300 years old, is an almost pure stand of sessile oak with only occasional beech, birch and rowan. The shrub layer is not well developed except towards the foot of the slope where rhododendron is abundant and hazel and hawthorn are locally common.

Where not shaded out by rhododendron, *Luzula sylvatica* forms a continuous carpet. While the variety of field layer species is not great, the presence of *Vicia sylvatica* is noteworthy. There is a luxuriant epiphytic lichen flora in which *Lobaria pulmonaria* is locally abundant. Although the wood has not been thoroughly examined it is already known to be an important site for epiphytic species.

W.165. HESLEYSIDE PARK AND HARESHAW LINN, NORTHUMBERLAND
NY 8183, NY 8484. 45 ha   Grade 2

Two woods, Hesleyside Park and Hareshaw Linn, Northumberland, lie within 5 km of each other near Bellingham. Hesleyside is partly ancient parkland woods and partly a ravine woodland which, like Hareshaw Linn, is pedunculate oakwood over acid soils, grading to wych elm woodland on calcareous soils. The parkland area of ancient oaks and beech has a rich epiphytic lichen flora, including *Parmeliopsis hyperopta* and *Haematomma elatinum*.

Hesleyside has marginally the richer cryptogamic flora of the two sites.

W.166. BILLSMOOR PARK AND GRASSLEES WOOD, NORTHUMBERLAND
NY 9496. 175 ha   Grade 2

The site lies in a small valley fed by branches of the Grasslees Burn. The woodland, mainly on shallow peat of gleyed alluvial soils, occupies the bottom and lower slopes of the valley and extends up the tributary glens. Alderwood occupies the area near the stream and this is surrounded by oak–hazel or birchwood on the higher, better-drained slopes. The alderwood is pure and contains a good spread of age classes from old senescent trees to young regeneration stages. The oak–hazel woodland contains many old hazel shrubs carrying good epiphyte communities. The ground flora under the alder is dominated by *Juncus* spp. including *J. effusus*, *J. articulatus* and *Agrostis stolonifera*; also present are *Mentha aquatica*, *Carex pendula*, *C. remota*, *C. paniculata* and *Sphagnum* spp. A glade containing *Myrica gale*, *Eriophorum latifolium*, *Parnassia palustris*, *Angelica sylvestris* and *Viola palustris* is present. The bryophyte flora is rich and alkaline runnels contain species such as *Fissidens osmundoides*, *Bryum pallens*, *Cratoneuron commutatum*, *Ctenidium molluscum* and *Mnium punctatum*. The epiphyte flora of lichens and bryophytes is varied, because of the high humidity, and the species recorded include *Antitrichia curtipendula*, *Pyrenola* sp. and *Arthonia* spp. The area is also of ornithological interest.

See also U.28.

SOUTH SCOTLAND

W.167. TYNRON JUNIPER WOOD, DUMFRIES-SHIRE
NX 8292. 5 ha   Grade 1

This is a scrub of juniper *Juniperus communis* on a moderately steep south-east-facing slope of Silurian greywackes at *c*. 120 m, in a tributary valley of the River Nith. The junipers are tall, averaging 3–3.7 m high, and with some individuals reaching 6 m; there is a wide variety of growth forms from broad and spreading to narrow and columnar. There are a few, scattered and rather small trees of other species, mainly ash and gean, but this is essentially a tall scrub rather than a wood, and there is a variety of other shrubs amongst the dominant juniper. There are two main field communities, the first being a dry grassland of *Agrostis tenuis*, *Festuca ovina*, *Deschampsia flexuosa* and *Anthoxanthum odoratum*, mixed with varying amounts of heather; this occupies open spaces within the scrub. The second type is a mixed bracken–bramble community occurring mainly where the junipers are moderately dense. The grassland has species such as *Carex pilulifera* and *Luzula campestris* which belong to treeless ground, but there is a woodland flora including *Oxalis acetosella*, *Lonicera periclymenum* and *Veronica officinalis*, and where the shade is dense beneath the junipers a moss carpet takes over. Towards the foot of the slope there is flushed ground with a marshy vegetation. The flora is quite varied, but no really unusual species is recorded. The site is noted for several local insects including moths such as the juniper carpet *Thera juniperata* and juniper pug *Eupithecia pusillata*.

W.168. KIRKCONNELL FLOW, KIRKCUDBRIGHTSHIRE
NX 9770. 155 ha   Grade 1

This is the only reasonably intact raised mire along the north side of the Solway. The mire has been reduced in extent by peripheral cutting and reclamation but the central section (about 120 ha) of the cupola has a sufficiently high water table to maintain actively growing mire communities. The striking feature of this site is, however, the extensive colonisation by Scots pine which has almost certainly been initiated during a period when the mire water table was lowered, if only marginally, by drainage operations. Many of the pines on the central part of the mire show retarded growth as a result of the high water table but there are mature stands of pines on the drier sites. The vegetation shows two major facies, a wetter type dominated by *Sphagnum* (*S. magellanicum* and *S. rubellum*) with *Calluna* or *Erica tetralix* and *Eriophorum vaginatum* as the major vascular plant components, and a drier type with a *Calluna–Cladonia*

(*cladina*) association. Some characteristic mire species such as *Vaccinium oxycoccus* and *Andromeda polifolia* are widespread and abundant but others are very local. Almost certainly the present vegetational mosaic is a reflection of disturbance, as exemplified by the fragmented distribution of species such as *Trichophorum cespitosum*, *Rhynchospora alba*, *Sphagnum pulchrum* and *S. imbricatum*.

The site provides excellent facilities for research on the establishment and effects of pine on ombrogenous peatlands, a subject which is important in view of the close proximity of Forestry Commission conifer plantations to a number of acid peatland reserves. On Kirkconnell Flow, *Erica tetralix* seems to survive best as a pine canopy becomes established, but mature pinewood here has the typical bilberry community with hypnaceous mosses. Birch is also colonising the Flow in places and there are areas of fairly dense birchwood. The moss layer is well developed under both pine and birch, and includes the rare species *Dicranum rugosum*.

See also P.70.

W.169. LOCH LOMOND WOODS, DUNBARTONSHIRE/ STIRLINGSHIRE
NS 4090. 200 ha   Grade 1*

(*a*) *Inchcailloch*

(*b*) *Torrinch*

(*c*) *Clairinsh*

(*d*) *Creinch*

(*e*) *Aber Isle*

(*f*) *Inchlonaig*

(*g*) *Mainland Woods*

The site consists of a series of wooded islands towards the south-eastern corner of Loch Lomond together with areas of woodland on the mainland. The islands Inchcailloch, Clairinsh, Torrinch, Creinch and the Aber Isle, together with the mainland areas south-west of the River Endrick, are included within the Loch Lomond NNR. The remaining island, Inchlonaig, is 6.4 km north up the Loch. The Reserve is of geological interest in that the island chain Inchcailloch, Torrinch, and Creinch lie along the line of the Highland Boundary Fault. Lower Old Red Sandstone strata underlie the mainland area of the Reserve as well as Aber Isle and Clairinsh although it is overlain by loose rocks of other origin. The Fault itself occurs at the junction between the Sandstone and the Dolomite Fault Rock and is to be seen on Inchcailloch and Creinch. The Dolomite Fault Rock contains masses of limestone in carbonated serpentine and this has a marked effect on the local flora.

The islands, with the exception of Inchlonaig, are predominantly sessile oakwood although pedunculate oak and a wide range of tree and shrub species are present. Each has its own characteristics which are often related to past use. Inchcailloch, the largest of the Reserve islands, is mainly oakwood but wet areas contain alder coppice and its two summits are crowned with Scots pine. Ash occurs as saplings in the flush areas and as a component of the canopy especially on the north-west-facing slopes. Along the shore guelder rose, broom, gorse, alder, willow and bog myrtle are all to be found. Torrinch contains more birch and the only concentration of aspen, whilst on Clairinsh a wide range of age classes of oak ranging from 21–165 years may be found. Creinch is characterised by a number of large coppiced elms and mature ash. Aber Isle is small (0.4 ha) and has an abundance of guelder rose. Inchlonaig differs from the other islands in that it at one time supported a large deer herd. Birch has invaded the old grazing land which also contains a large number of yew trees some exceeding 300 cm in girth.

Inchmoan (36 ha), which is included within this site, gives a bonus peatland interest. Although largely well wooded with Scots pine its importance lies in its unusual raised mire bounded by rocky shores and its peatland communities.

The mainland woods south-west of the River Endrick, partly on the Loch shore, contain planted Scots pine, Norway spruce and larch as well as sessile oak. Willow carr and wet birchwood contained in Gartfairn Wood can be found associated with a fen on the mainland area (notably in the Crom Mhin). The mainland woods north of the River Endrick range from low growing alder/willow carr with a very wet ground flora to dry acidophilous oak woodland. These woods contain a heronry of 20–25 nests.

On the more acidic soils overlying the Old Red Sandstone or glacial drift, the ground flora is dominated by *Deschampsia flexuosa*, *Lonicera periclymenum*, *Calluna vulgaris* and *Vaccinium myrtillus*. The last is at its tallest and densest on Torrinch. On the deeper and less acidic soils *Rubus fruticosus*, *Dryopteris austriaca*, *Luzula sylvatica*, and *Endymion non-scriptus* are common. *Pteridium aquilinum* is locally abundant in the limited number of woodland clearings and usually has *Corydalis claviculata* twined into it. On the soils overlying the dolomitic serpentine, *Mercurialis perennis*, *Asperula odorata*, *Brachypodium sylvaticum*, and *Sanicula europaea* are abundant particularly on Creinch. These communities all represent the ungrazed facies of northern and western oakwoods and bryophytes are relatively less important than in grazed woods of this type. Each island seems to have had a different land-use history and the differences in composition of field layer and to some extent the tree layer reflect this.

Wet flushes support communities containing *Chrysosplenium oppositifolium*, *Iris pseudacorus* and *Allium ursinum*, whilst on the drier spots such as the summit of Inchcailloch, a *Calluna vulgaris–Erica cinerea* community is found. Inchlonaig is dominated by dense bracken which has invaded grazed areas as the grazing pressures have eased. The shores of the islands are a nutrient-enriched zone as a result of periodic flooding through rise of loch level during wet weather. They have a varied flora including *Carum verticillatum*, *Carex remota*, *Oenanthe crocata* and *Hypericum androsaemum*. Clairinsh has a rich shore zone with *Trollius europaeus*, *Polygonum bistorta*, *Rubus saxatilis*, *Aquilegia vulgaris*, *Listera ovata* and *Orchis mascula*. Ferns are well represented on the islands and include the Atlantic species *Dryopteris aemula* and *Hymenophyllum tunbrigense*. The serpentine exposures form the habitat for calcicolous mosses

such as *Ctenidium molluscum*, *Neckera crispa* and *Fissidens cristatus* and the western liverwort *Marchesinia mackaii*.

See also OW.60 and P.73.

W.170. AVONDALE, LANARKSHIRE
NS 7648.　115 ha　　　　　　　　　　Grade 1

This site lies in the valley of the Avon Water, draining to the Clyde. There is a gorge about 5 km long, with rather little topographical variation but soils varying from acidic to calcareous. Coal Measures outcrop at each end and there is Carboniferous Limestone in the middle. The woodland of this glen is essentially of two types, differentiated by geology and soil. On richer soils, the canopy is dominated by oak, elm and ash in more or less equal quantities. Species of local occurrence in Scotland, such as guelder rose and *Epipactis helleborine*, occur here. More acidic areas bear birch with bracken and bluebell communities. Where the gorge sides are precipitous, ferns are abundant and include *Asplenium adiantum-nigrum*, *Phyllitis scolopendrium*, *Dryopteris austriaca* and *D. filix-mas*. *Chrysosplenium alternifolium* occurs with *C. oppositifolium*. Other interesting species are *Carex pendula*, *Equisetum sylvaticum* and *E. telmateia*.

W.171. GLEN DIOMHAN, ARRAN, BUTESHIRE
NR 9246.　10 ha　　　　　　　　　　Grade 1

This is an open hill woodland extending for about 1.6 km along an upland river gorge cut through granite and schist. The chief interest of the site is the presence of the very rare endemic whitebeams, *Sorbus pseudofennica* and *S. arranensis*, which are restricted to north Arran. The main concentration of these small trees occurs at the junction of the Diomhan Burn and a larger tributary where there is also a luxuriant growth of *Juniperus communis* ssp. *nana*, *Salix aurita* and *S. atrocinerea*. The most densely wooded parts of the site are the steeper margins of the northern part of the glen. Here, however, there are relatively few endemic *Sorbus* spp., the dominant species being rowan and birch with a few holly and aspen. Juniper is fairly evenly distributed throughout the length of the site, with particularly fine specimens growing from stable rock faces at between 150 and 210 m. The larger specimens of willows (*Salix atrocinerea* and *S. aurita*) are similarly located, particularly along the margins of the largest lateral burn and some of the smaller laterals immediately to the south. Amongst other shrubs, only a very few plants of *Rosa pimpinellifolia* remain.

W.172. CHANLOCK FOOT, DUMFRIES-SHIRE
NX 8099.　12 ha　　　　　　　　　　Grade 2

This is the remaining block at the south-east end of a narrow belt of ash–oak–hazel woodland, on steep south-west-facing slopes above the Scar Water in upper Nithsdale. Much of the former wood has been clear-felled and replanted with conifers, but the site includes an interesting riverside strip of ash wood, and blocks of hazel scrub at the north-west end. Oak, birch and wych elm are scattered throughout. The Ordovician/Silurian rocks of the area give rather base-rich soil, and as the wood is mostly ungrazed, herbaceous field communities are well developed. These include fine examples of the *Mercurialis perennis* and *Allium ursinum* types, but grasses such as *Brachypodium sylvaticum*, *Zerna ramosa* and *Melica uniflora* are locally abundant. There are patches of scree and here, especially, ferns are well represented, including *Thelypteris phegopteris* and *T. dryopteris*, besides more common woodland species. The flora includes *Trollius europaeus*, *Geranium sylvaticum* and *Orchis mascula*, as well as more constant woodland basiphiles such as *Geum urbanum*, *G. rivale*, *Primula vulgaris* and *Asperula odorata*. More acidic patches of soil on the river bank strip have dominance of *Luzula sylvatica*, and *Endymion non-scriptus* and *Conopodium majus* are plentiful in places. Some older trees have lichens such as *Lobaria pulmonaria* and *Sticta sylvatica*, and the bryophyte flora is moderately rich, though not in western species. The Scotch argus butterfly occurs in the more open places and woodland edges.

W.173. STENHOUSE WOOD, DUMFRIES-SHIRE

NX 7993. 20 ha   Grade 2

This is a woodland on a north-east-facing slope above Shinnel Water, also on rather calcareous Silurian rocks. It exhibits a varied ground flora and an irregularly stratified canopy which indicates an unusual absence of grazing, trampling and intensive management. The canopy contains ash, wych elm and oak, with some beech. The scrub understorey is well developed and includes rowan, hazel, gean, bird-cherry and hawthorn as well as some younger individuals of the dominant trees. The field layer is similar to that of Chanlock Foot, with a mixture of grasses, forbs and ferns. There is an abundance of dog's mercury and other mesophilous species, with *Dryopteris filix-mas* and abundant bryophytes.

W.174. MAIDENS–HEADS OF AYR, AYRSHIRE

NS 2209–3219. 400 ha   Grade 2

This is a series of rather broken and extensively wooded coastal cliffs formed of Old Red Sandstone sediments and lavas, and is probably the best example of this habitat in Scotland. The prevailing mixed deciduous woodland has sycamore, aspen, ash, wych elm and scrub with hawthorn and blackthorn and a varied woodland herb layer and cliff edge flora including calcicolous species such as *Scabiosa columbaria* and *Vicia sylvatica*. The friable nature of the cliffs precludes much algal, lichen or spray zone flowering plant growth, but vestigial dune and shingle beach deposits add variety locally. The more exposed cliffs to the north rise to 90 m and carry paramaritime grassland or bracken on less steep but exposed slopes with incipient deciduous woodland development on boulder clay talus in hollows.

W.175. HAMILTON HIGH PARK, LANARKSHIRE

NS 7353. 75 ha   Grade 2

The eastern bank of this site is now a conifer plantation but extensive natural woodland occurs near the Leigh Quarter. Ash occurs on the valley bottom but sycamore, beech, birch, oak and hawthorn grow higher up the bank. The ground flora on the drier upper part of the slope is dominated by *Endymion non-scriptus* and *Luzula sylvatica* and there are local species such as *Equisetum sylvaticum* and *Epipactis helleborine*. Bryophytes abound in the damper valley bottom along with *Allium ursinum*, *Asperula odorata*, *Chrysosplenium oppositifolium* and *Milium effusum*. In the north-western end of the site, old, widely spaced oaks provide a habitat of exceptional entomological interest.

W.176. NETHAN GORGE, LANARKSHIRE

NS 8146. 40 ha   Grade 2

This ravine lies on the River Nethan and Craignethan Burn. The trees and shrubs are restricted to the immediate vicinity of the ravine in the upper reaches of the latter stream but the grassland here is extremely herb-rich. The canopy consists of beech, oak, wych elm with alder, along the river. The ground flora is reasonably herb-rich with *Hypericum hirsutum*, *Carex sylvatica* and *C. laevigata*. There is *Festuca altissima* which is rare in Lanarkshire, and *Equisetum telmateia*.

W.177. WOOD OF CREE, KIRKCUDBRIGHTSHIRE

NX 4971. 175 ha   Grade 2

This relatively large woodland lies on the east bank of the River Cree north of Newton Stewart. Of old coppice origin, it consists mainly of oak on the drier slopes and knolls; birch *Betula verrucosa* and willow *Salix atrocinerea* along stream sides; birch, alder with much *Sphagnum* spp. on the poorly drained top plateau; and hazel in the dry hollows towards the bottom of the wood. The lower part grades into floodplain mire along the River Cree, the transition from woodland to wetland being a narrow zone, with ash present in flushes. An acidophilous ground flora, including *Calluna vulgaris* and *Deschampsia flexuosa*, occupies the knolls, whereas basiphilous communities with *Allium ursinum* and *Asperula odorata* occur in flushed ground between and below. Primroses are abundant on the better soils.

W.178. FLEET WOODLANDS, KIRKCUDBRIGHTSHIRE

Grade 2

(*a*) *Castramont Wood*
NX 5960. 80 ha

(*b*) *Killiegowan Wood*
NX 5857. 40 ha

(*c*) *Jennoch Wood*
NX 5756. 12 ha

(*d*) *Craigy Braes Wood*
NX 5754. 18 ha

These oakwoods lie on the lower slopes of hills rising from the Water of Fleet. The main tree flora is sessile oak, much of which has been coppiced in the past. On the flatter ground at the foot of slopes, hazel occurs under the oaks and ash, while alder and wych elm line the streams. The wet areas are dominated by ash and alder or by birch. Mesophilous field layers occur most extensively but basiphilous and acidophilous communities are well represented. Castramont and Killiegowan Woods are renowned locally for their fine displays of bluebells.

Extensive areas of broad-leaved woodland are rare in Galloway, and the Fleet Woodlands and the Wood of Cree are two of the best remaining examples.

W.179. RAVENSHALL WOOD, KIRKCUDBRIGHTSHIRE
NX 5152.   18 ha   Grade 2

This occupies a narrow belt on a south-west-facing slope down to the shore line. The trees and shrubs are wind-pruned and the varied topographic conditions result in considerable diversity. Oaks are dominant in the upper part of the wood, ash and wych elm and oak over hazel in the middle zone, and, at the foot, willow with reeds merge into blackthorn just above high-water mark. Both gean and alder are locally abundant. The cliff tops and woodland field layer have a good deal of *Luzula sylvatica*, and there is much *Polystichum setiferum* on the rocks and slopes.

EAST SCOTLAND

W.180. DINNET OAKWOOD, ABERDEENSHIRE
NO 4698.   20 ha   Grade 1

This small stand of both pedunculate and sessile oaks is one of the few examples of oakwood in the eastern Highlands. Though almost certainly planted, it has the character of a semi-natural upland oakwood and differs from examples of this forest type in the west of Britain mainly in having northern field layer associates such as *Trientalis europaea*, *Pyrola minor* and *Rubus saxatilis*. The soils range from leached brown earths to more basic types with mull humus, so that the field layer is more varied than in a typical oak-dominated upland wood, and species such as *Fragaria vesca* and *Rhytidiadelphus triquetrus* are present. The field communities nevertheless show a strong resemblance to those of typical sessile oakwood, and have local dominance of bracken, bilberry and *Holcus lanatus*. Other trees represented are birch, rowan, hazel, ash, aspen and alder. The dominant oaks are mostly well-grown, tall trees over 100 years old.

W.181. CRATHIE WOOD, ABERDEENSHIRE
NO 2795.   125 ha   Grade 1

This is a mixed wood of birch (*Betula verrucosa* mainly), Scots pine and juniper, with the first species the most abundant. The birch is less even-aged than in Craigellachie birchwood, but more robust and well-grown than in the Morrone Wood. Juniper is locally dense and also grows to a much larger size than in the Morrone Wood, which lies at a higher altitude. The pines are of different ages, so that the whole wood has a rather uneven appearance, and approaches more closely than many woods to the hypothetical hetero-geneous structure of a natural woodland. The soils are derived in part from calcareous schists, and carry local abundance of species such as *Fragaria vesca*, *Veronica chamaedrys*, *Prunella vulgaris*, *Ranunculus acris*, *Cirsium heterophyllum* and *Rhytidiadelphus triquetrus*. At the top of the wood, at the west end and under more open conditions, there are *Saxifraga aizoides*, *Helianthemum chamaecistus*, *Ramischia secunda*, *Potentilla crantzii* and *Arctostaphylos*

uva-ursi. On the whole the woodland field communities are less species-rich than those of Morrone, and the most frequent types are *Agrostis–Anthoxanthum odoratum* grass-land with *Calluna vulgaris* and *Erica cinerea*, *Vaccinium myrtillus–V. vitis-idaea*-moss, or dense *Pteridium aquilinum*.

W.182. MORRONE WOOD, ABERDEENSHIRE
NO 1390.   100 ha   Grade 1

The wood at 380–600 m on the north slope of Morrone above Braemar is the best example in Britain of a subalpine woodland on basic soils. It is essentially a birchwood of downy birch with a locally dense understorey of juniper which is smaller in stature than typical lowland juniper. The underlying rock is Dalradian calcareous schist with bands of limestone, and gives fertile brown loams. The field layer, developed where juniper growth is more open, is typically grassy, with *Agrostis* spp. and *Anthoxanthum odoratum*, but grades into the *Vaccinium*–moss community characteristic of pinewoods. The pinewood species, *Ramischia secunda*, *Trientalis europaea*, *Pyrola minor*, *Linnaea borealis* and *Sphenolobus saxicolus*, are also repre-sented. An unusual feature is the presence under or amongst juniper of basiphilous montane herbs such as *Potentilla crantzii*, *Polygonum viviparum* and *Galium boreale*, as well as taller species such as *Geum rivale*, *Geranium sylvaticum*, *Cirsium heterophyllum*, *Festuca altissima*, *Melica nutans*, *Valeriana officinalis*, *Rumex acetosa* and *Mercurialis perennis*. Juniper gives protection from grazing to all these herbs.

Another important feature is the occurrence, on open places within the wood, of open calcareous flushes and soligenous mire systems of a distinctly upland type. The open flushes have *Juncus triglumis*, *Equisetum variegatum*, *J. alpinus*, *Tofieldia pusilla*, *Saxifraga aizoides* and *Eriophorum latifolium* with variable cover of 'brown mosses' and a range of very rare montane bryophytes including *Tritomaria polita*, *Leiocolea gilmanii* and *Tayloria lingulata*. The soli-genous mire grades from richer types with sedges and basi-philous mosses to poorer types with *Sphagnum* spp., *Erica tetralix* and *Calluna vulgaris*. A limestone knoll has an interesting area of species-rich montane grassland, and small wooded crags provide a refuge for species such as *Polystichum lonchitis*, *Vicia sylvatica*, *Stegonia latifolia* and *Grimmia atrofusca*.

The whole complex shows an extremely close resem-blance in physiognomy and floristics to some of the sub-alpine birchwoods in Dovre, Norway, and appears to be the only wood of its kind in Britain.

See also U.48.

W.183. AVIEMORE WOODLANDS, INVERNESS-SHIRE
Grade 1

(*a*) *Craigellachie*
NH 8812.   385 ha

This is a fairly large birchwood consisting mainly of *Betula pendula* but with some *B. pubescens*, and lies on the lower east-facing slopes of the Monadhliath, overlooking Avie-more. The trees on the more gentle lower ground are fairly tall, but stature decreases as the slope steepens into crags above. The soils are derived from Moine Schist, and are mainly acidic but have more fertile brown loams in places, and are generally richer than the granite soils of the Cairngorm pinewoods. The field layer is of the grass–moss type, but with an abundance locally of small forbs and ferns. On rocks there are local species such as *Geranium lucidum*, *Chrysosplenium alternifolium* and *Ramischia secunda*. Other tree species include rowan, aspen, hazel, oak, wych elm, bird cherry and juniper, but these are all rather sparse and scattered. Richer grasslands with *Polygonum viviparum* and *Helianthemum chamaecistus* occur within the wood, and there is soligenous mire, with *Myrica gale* and *Sphagnum* spp. A lochan has interesting aquatic communities and fringing alders.

The Craigellachie Wood is famous as the haunt of northern insects, notably extremely local moths such as the Rannoch sprawler, Kentish glory, great brocade, scarce prominent and angle-striped sallow. The cliffs within the wood are famous as the haunt of peregrines and the pair breeding here is consistently one of the most successful in Britain.

(b) Kinrara Woods (Torr Alvie)
NH 8708. 225 ha

Farther south from Craigellachie and across the road/railway, is an extension of this woodland, rising from low ground beside the River Spey to the steep sided hillock of Torr Alvie, which has north and south-east aspects. Torr Alvie has extensive birchwoods, with Scots pine abundant and locally dominant in the west. Both species of oak occur in a group at the south end, and are one of the few occurrences of oak in the middle Spey Valley. *Betula pendula* predominates, but there is a good deal of *B. pubescens*. Much of the birch is moribund or old, but in places are stands of young trees, especially on the west side. Juniper forms an open underscrub through much of the pine and birch, and other tree and shrub species include wych elm (rare), alder, rowan, aspen, gean, bird-cherry and willows (*Salix cinerea*, *S. capraea*, *S. aurita*).

The field layer varies from acidophilous *Calluna* or *Vaccinium* heath, and *Deschampsia flexuosa–Festuca ovina* grassland to basiphilous herb-rich *Agrostis–Anthoxanthum* grassland. On the steep eastern slopes basiphilous communities with *Brachypodium sylvaticum* and *Mercurialis perennis* form a mosaic with the acidophilous types, and local species include *Helianthemum chamaecistus* and *Melica nutans*. On the steep north face, *Deschampsia cespitosa* and *Cirsium heterophyllum* occur with *Brachypodium sylvaticum*. The upper part of the hill has much *Luzula sylvatica* and the widespread *Pteridium aquilinum* reaches dominance locally.

A few flushes and little marshes with *Juncus* spp., *Sphagnum* and *Myrica gale* occur, and north of Torr Alvie, an old arm of the Spey is occupied by a sizeable valley mire with large pools. This has some of the poor-fen communities, especially of *Carex*, found in the Insh Fens, and is an important bonus wetland habitat. This swamp, the fringing birch scrub, and the birch/pine woods along the railway are of high entomological interest, and are localities for several rare insects.

W.184. GLEN TARFF, INVERNESS-SHIRE
NH 3804. 580 ha   Grade 1

The deep, ravine-like course of this glen has a long fringing woodland with a mixture of dominants including downy birch, sessile oak, ash, wych elm, and alder (more locally). There is a well-developed shrub layer with hazel, bird cherry and goat willow. The glen is cut through Moine Schists which give base-rich soils in places, and a correspondingly varied flora. At the upper edge of the glen, birch is the principal tree over a herb-rich field layer. This is a woodland complex of a very local type in eastern Scotland. Glen Tarff drains into the southern end of Loch Ness and may have more in common climatically with the western end of the Great Glen than with the Cairngorm area.

W.185. PASS OF KILLIECRANKIE, PERTHSHIRE
NN 9262. 120 ha   Grade 1

The gorge of the River Garry at Killiecrankie has a mixture of woodland types on Dalradian schists. The most prominent type is sessile oakwood on acidic soils, but there is also a good deal of birch, ash, wych elm and alder, and hazel is locally plentiful as an undershrub. *Sorbus aria* agg. and guelder rose are present. The field layer varies from the *Vaccinium*–grass–moss type on poor soils to a forb-dominated *Allium ursinum–Mercurialis perennis* type on richer soils, and the flora of the area is quite rich, with *Vicia sylvatica*, *Convallaria majalis* and *Melica uniflora*. Small areas of rhododendron and sycamore occur but are not extensive enough to detract from the importance of the site, which is perhaps the best lowland deciduous wood in the region.

W.186. BLACK WOOD OF RANNOCH, PERTHSHIRE
NN 5555. 2350 ha   Grade 1

This wood, composed chiefly of Scots pine, but with much birch (both species) locally, lies on the gentle slopes to the south of Loch Rannoch. As the presence of oakwood on the opposite side of the loch shows that the area is climatically within the range of oak, the prevalence of pine here may be primarily edaphic, though it is also possible that leaching and soil acidification may be more pronounced on shady north slopes. Some of the pinewood is open, with large, spreading trees, and the prevailing vegetation of the forest floor is the western-type *Calluna vulgaris–Vaccinium* community with abundant *Sphagnum nemoreum–S. quinquefarium* in the moss carpet. More open ground with scattered trees has dry heather heath, and there are infilled tarns with *Sphagnum–Carex* swamp. Some pine regeneration is occurring and there is a mixture of age classes.

Where the shade is more dense, *Vaccinium* spp., *Deschampsia flexuosa* and hypnaceous mosses form the field layer. The pinewoods are on peaty or mor humus soils and have species such as *Trientalis europaea*, *Pyrola minor* and *Listera cordata*, but some of the birchwood is on richer soils and has herbs such as *Geum rivale*, *Geranium sylvaticum*,

Mercurialis perennis, Anemone nemorosa, Lysimachia nemorum and *Brachypodium sylvaticum*. Rowan, hazel and *Rosa canina* are scattered. Willows (*Salix aurita* and *S. cinerea*) occur in wetter places.

This wood is famous among entomologists, and is the site referred to as 'Rannoch' in the insect literature, where it is ranked along with Aviemore as the best Highland locality for certain rare and local species. The Scottish race of the crossbill breeds here in some years.

W.187. SPEYSIDE–DEESIDE PINEWOODS, INVERNESS-SHIRE–ABERDEENSHIRE Grade 1*

(*a*) *Ballochbuie Forest*
NO 2089. 1700 ha

(*b*) *Glen Tanar*
NO 4891. 2000 ha

(*c*) *Glens Quoich, Lui and Derry*
NO 0793. 530 ha

(*d*) *Rothiemurchus–Invereshie*
NH 8906. 1550 ha

(*e*) *Abernethy Forest*
NH 9318. 4250 ha

Although dissected into separate blocks, covering a large area, the pinewoods of the Spey and Dee Valleys in the central Highlands represent part of a once-continuous tract of forestland, and are best described in a single, comprehensive account. Pinewood is the most local of all the major forest types of Britain, yet these examples are among the most extensive of all areas of native British woodland, so that their national importance is considerable. These woods lie on the lower slopes of the Cairngorm (see U.44) and Lochnagar (U.57) massifs, and their presence is a significant aspect of the outstanding nature conservation interest of the first area, in particular, as a complex of submontane and montane habitats.

These pinewoods lie between 170 m and 640 m, mainly on coarse, sandy and gravelly drift soils derived from granite, with local admixture of schistose material, giving marked base-deficiency and acidity. Topography varies considerably: there are some hanging pinewoods on steep, craggy slopes, as in the Invereshie sector, whilst some of those in the Deeside glens of the Cairngorms approach gorge woodlands in character. The largest areas are, however, on rather gentle slopes or mildly undulating morainic foothill country. This irregularity of the glacial topography gives marked variations in drainage and, especially in Abernethy Forest, there are waterlogged hollows and channels among the moraines. These contain acidophilous *Sphagnum*-dominated valley and basin mires, showing variable colonisation by Scots pine, with growth usually poor and checked on the wettest ground. Though the scale is much smaller, there is some resemblance to the great forest mires of Scandinavia, and these habitats have some interest as peatlands (see P. 93).

Although there is a general appearance of naturalness, these pinewoods have been managed for commercial timber production for some time, and are largely semi-natural. Whilst many areas are left to regenerate naturally after felling, there has been a good deal of replanting. Some of the areas of open heather moor between or amongst blocks of pinewood remain relatively treeless because natural regeneration has been poor, whereas in other places, young trees grow up rapidly and abundantly on cleared ground. Natural regeneration of pine here depends on factors such as intensity of deer grazing and the coincidence of a good seed year with heather burning on a clearing, but the reasons for marked local variations in its incidence are not wholly understood. Regeneration is on the whole better in the Speyside pinewoods than those of the Dee, at least within the Cairngorm massif, probably as a result of heavier grazing on Deeside. Successful regeneration is achieved by fencing against deer in the Glen Tanar Forest.

These pinewoods together contain a complete range of variation in age class and individual growth form of trees, and in forest structure and density. Probably the finest old trees are those in the remnants of the former Forest of Mar, in the Glens Quoich, Lui and Derry, on Deeside; here there are many ancient pines, often grown in fairly open canopy, of vast girth and stately appearance. On the other hand, the best structural diversity, in varying age, height and form of the trees, and in the presence of a shrub layer of juniper, is found in Abernethy Forest in the Spey Valley. There are three main structural types of pinewood in this district: dense pole stands of uniform age; younger, fairly even-aged pines surrounding scattered, older and more spreading parent trees; and open growths of old, spreading trees, or clumps of old trees, on moorland (a pine–heath community).

Birch and juniper are widespread and locally abundant, and can occur in pure stands as well as mixed with pine. Their presence (especially birch) is probably related to better than average soil conditions, and the interesting mixed pine, birch and juniper woodland at Crathie on Deeside (W.181) is at least partly on soils derived from basic schists. There is also a good deal of rowan, some aspen and, on damp, richer soils (especially stream alluvium), an abundance of alder. While the upper limits of the pinewoods are mostly artificially depressed, a true natural altitudinal limit still occurs at 640 m on Creag Fhiaclach, a north-west spur of the Cairngorms, with a bushy stunted growth of pine mixed with juniper of similar stature, passing into heather moor above.

The associated field and ground communities of the pinewoods are mainly moss-rich heather heath in the more open stands, which passes into typical heather moor; and *Vaccinium myrtillus–V. vitis-idaea*-moss heaths of the denser pole stands, where light intensity is fairly low. A notable feature of both types is the luxuriance of the moss carpets, mainly the common woodland species, but with an unusual abundance of *Hylocomium splendens*, *Rhytidiadelphus triquetrus* and *Thuidium tamariscinum* on acidic soils. Some of the open, heathery clearings with leggy *Calluna*, and the valley mires, have an abundance of *Cladonia sylvatica* and *C. impexa*, but the lichen communities so characteristic of the continental pinewoods of Fennoscandia are not really represented in the oceanic climate of Scotland.

The central Highland pinewoods are not floristically rich but they have a very characteristic flora. Widespread woodland species such as *Deschampsia flexuosa, Luzula pilosa, Melampyrum pratense* and *Lathyrus montanus* are fairly constant, and there is a more diagnostic northern element represented widely by *Pyrola minor, Listera cordata, Trientalis europaea, Goodyera repens* and *Ptilium crista-castrensis*, and more locally by *Linnaea borealis, Ramischia secunda, Pyrola media, Moneses uniflora* and *Dicranum rugosum*. Bracken is less abundant than in western pinewoods, but there is a local abundance of other ferns such as *Thelypteris limbosperma, T. dryopteris, T. phegopteris* and *Blechnum spicant*. The pinewood flora is diversified by the addition of various upland submontane and montane plants as the forest passes into open moorland or is interrupted by other habitats, such as outcrops and streams. Species on acidic and peaty soils within the forest include *Rubus chamaemorus, Empetrum hermaphroditum, Chamaepericlymenum suecicum, Lycopodium annotinum, L. selago, L. alpinum* and *L. clavatum*. Streamside alluvium has *Alchemilla alpina*, whilst basic rocks and flushes provide habitats for *Saxifraga oppositifolia, S. aizoides, Tofieldia pusilla, Parnassia palustris* and *Juncus alpinus*.

The Cairngorm pinewoods are famous for their northern birds, which include capercaillie, black game, crossbills, siskins and crested tits. This is the only part of Scotland where the greenshank breeds in its characteristic Scandinavian habitat, in heathy clearings and open mires within the forest. Three pairs of golden eagles usually nest in open pinewood on the Cairngorm flanks, but the tree nesting habit in this species is not known to be regular anywhere else in Scotland. Good populations of buzzards and sparrowhawks breed in the woods, and elusive rarities suspected of nesting here include the goshawk and green sandpiper. Red deer frequent the forests a good deal during bad weather and through the winter, and there are good populations of roe deer. Other characteristic mammals are the wild cat, badger and red squirrel.

The invertebrate fauna of the Cairngorm pinewoods is extremely rich, ranging from frequent and widespread species such as the Scotch argus and dark green fritillary butterflies to rare and local insects such as the dragonflies *Aeshna caerulea, Somatochlora arctica* and *Coenagrion hastulatum*, which breed in the forest mires and lochans.

W.188. EARLSHALL MUIR, FIFE
NO 4822. 60 ha   Grade 2

This site, consisting of a series of ditches and open ridges, is near the Tentsmuir sand-dune and flat NNR. It consists of a mixed alder–birch wood showing increasing ageing from east to west. Willow is locally abundant around Cannel Loch and on the open ridges gorse is common. Two types of field layer occur on the dunes, one dominated by grasses, *Deschampsia cespitosa, D. flexuosa, Holcus mollis* and *H. lanatus* with *Blechnum spicant* and *Galium hercynicum* on the slopes. The damp depressions contain such species as *Juncus* spp., *Sphagnum* spp., *Cirsium palustre, Galium palustre* and *Ranunculus repens*.

See also C.93.

W.189. KELTNEY BURN, COSHIEVILLE, PERTHSHIRE
NN 7750. 30 ha   Grade 2

This site is a wooded waterfall gorge cut through Dalradian schists. The rock is calcareous and the derived soils quite rich, so that there is a mixed deciduous woodland, with ash, pedunculate oak, birch, wych elm, hazel, rowan and bird-cherry, but this is confined to the sides of the ravine and so forms only a narrow strip. The communities are similar to those of ashwood in northern England, with dog's mercury and *Allium ursinum* especially prominent, and this is a locality for the very rare tall herb *Polygonatum verticillatum*. The total species list is quite large, but the Atlantic bryophyte flora is poor compared with similar gorges in the western Highlands, and for this reason the gorge woodland of Inverneil Burn in Knapdale is preferred as an example of this type.

WEST SCOTLAND

W.190. LOCH SUNART WOODLANDS, ARGYLL
                                                                 Grade 1*

(a) Ariundle
NM 8464. 120 ha

This is a sessile oakwood on a moderately steep slope facing east-south-east above the Strontian River (OW.90). The oak varies from 40 to 150 years in age and is mostly of coppice origin, forming a fairly pure stand, though there is a little wych elm, ash and hazel on more basic soils. The field layer has the usual mixture of bracken and acidic grassland with *Deschampsia flexuosa*, but there is local dominance of *Molinia caerulea*, and *Calluna vulgaris* is abundant at the upper edge of the wood. The few patches of basic soil have basiphilous species but on the whole, the Moine rocks of the area here give a prevalence of acidic soils. The ground is block strewn over much of the woodland floor and there are small outcrops.

Ariundle is an important member in the south to north series of bryophyte-rich oakwoods in western Scotland, and both mosses and leafy liverworts are luxuriant on the woodland floor, especially where it is rocky. There is a luxuriant carpet with the common woodland mosses, including *Thuidium tamariscinum* and *T. delicatulum*, but on the blocks there are dense cushions with *Plagiochila atlantica, P. spinulosa, Scapania gracilis* and filmy fern *Hymenophyllum wilsonii*. The strongly Atlantic bryophytes of the wood include *Adelanthus decipiens, Radula aquilegia, Hylocomium umbratum, Hypnum callichroum, Plagiochila punctata* and *Frullania germana*. It is unusual for a woodland on a sun-exposed aspect to be so rich in Atlantic bryophytes, and this is probably to be explained both by the extremely high atmospheric humidity of the district, and the probable persistence of continuous woody cover at the site. Some mature oaks on wetter sites are showing incipient die-back in their crowns.

The more open tree growth between the west end of the wood and the river is extremely important for lichens with an oceanic distribution, and is included within the grade 1 site for this reason. These species seem to favour the more exposed conditions of open woodland and scattered tree growth, and the lichen flora of Ariundle Wood proper is less rich than that of this adjoining area.

(b) Salen–Strontian
NM 687647–784612.   580 ha

The slopes above the north shore of Loch Sunart have a considerable though discontinuous extent of sessile oak-wood, with variable amounts of birch, holly and rowan. The Camasine wood is a very fine example of western oakwood, with a more uneven aged structure than Ariundle, though rather similar field and ground layers; there is an altitudinal gradient in stature and form of the oaks, and the lower ground has some very large and well-grown trees. There is also a good variety of tree and shrub species. The soils are mainly leached brown earths derived from acidic Moine Schists, but in places, especially in stream ravines, such as that of the Resipol Glen, there are exposures of calcareous parent materials, which give richer soils with patches of ash–wych elm–hazel wood. Some of these woods are interesting in their own right, but their main importance is as the habitat for an extraordinarily rich assemblage of mosses, liverworts and lichens with an Atlantic distribution, as well as a profusion and luxuriance of the more wide-spread species.

The area has long been famous bryologically from the early studies of S. M. MacVicar (1926). Some rare bryo-phytes have their British headquarters here, e.g. *Semato-phyllum novae-caesareae*, *Acrobolbus wilsonii* and *Radula carringtonii*. The recent survey by the British Lichen Society has shown that the lichens have even greater im-portance, and there is probably the richest concentration of Atlantic species in Europe, including many rarities. The Camasine oakwood is an especially rich and important locality. As well as having many rare species, the woods and scattered trees have profuse growths of large lichens (*Sticta* spp. and *Lobaria* spp.) with a more widespread distribution, and the development of this Lobarion community is prob-ably unequalled in Britain. Other lichen communities such as the Graphidion alliance, and those with *Pseudocyphellaria* spp., *Parmelia laevigata* and *P. caperata-perlata*, are finely represented. The important lichen habitats include the rough bark of well-grown oaks and other trees, the smooth bark of holly and rowan, decaying logs, willows and other shrubs in boggy carr, rocks (including those within the inter-tidal and spray zones), and lead mine spoil heaps.

The particular richness of the area for these oceanic plants seems to result from an optimal combination of conditions – Loch Sunart is more sheltered than the open coast, but the area is still far enough south to experience very equable winter temperatures, and it is probably the

warmest part of the zone of extreme wetness in the western Highlands.

While this is only an interim account of the area, and woodlands are only one of the habitats involved, the area of Loch Sunart would seem to be of considerable inter-national importance botanically. The north shore of the loch from Kilchoan to near Strontian is also regarded as a grade 1 rocky coast site (C.98, gr. 1).

(c) Laudale–Glen Cripesdale
NM 760595–650588.   1010 ha

These woods occupy the slopes forming the south side of Loch Sunart, opposite the Salen–Strontian woods already described. The general steepness of slope and north to north-west aspect give shady and extremely humid con-ditions, which are still further amplified in the numerous stream ravines which cut down through the hillsides. The rock is again Moine Schist and ranges from acidic to cal-careous. The woods on this side of Loch Sunart are mainly of birch, but with scattered blocks of oak, and a good deal of ash and hazel on the richer soils.

The outstanding ecological feature is again the great profusion of Atlantic bryophytes and lichens, and on this north-facing slope the extremely humid conditions favour a general luxuriance of widespread mosses and liverworts, and abundance of rare or local species. There are several stations for *Acrobolbus wilsonii* and *Sematophyllum novae-caesareae*, and the rare *Mylia cuneifolia* is abundant on birch trunks. The rare *Lejeunea mandonii* has at least two stations in this area. Atlantic bryophytes growing in profusion on blocks, banks and tree bases include *Plagiochila spinulosa*, *P. atlantica*, *P. punctata*, *Scapania gracilis*, *Saccogyna viticulosa*, *Mylia taylorii*, *Breutelia chrysocoma* and *Hylo-comium umbratum*, while less abundant species are *Dicrano-dontium uncinatum*, *D. denudatum*, *Frullania germana*, *Bazzania tricrenata*, *B. trilobata*, *Herberta hutchinsiae*, *Douinia ovata*, *Nowellia curvifolia* and *Anastrepta orcadensis*. There is a great deal of *Sphagnum* on the blocks and ground, and the ferns *Hymenophyllum wilsonii* and *Dryopteris aemula* are plentiful in places. The lichens of these north-facing slopes and woods are also of great interest.

The field communities of these woods are of the usual *Agrostis–Anthoxanthum* type, becoming species-rich on more fertile soils and grading into soligenous mire on wetter ground.

(d) Ben Hiant
NM 5263.   40 ha

The wood at Uamha na Creadha on the steep seaward slope of Ben Hiant is of a mixed deciduous type, mainly oak, but with a good deal of ash and hazel. Some of the trees are quite tall for an exposed west coast situation. The soils are base-rich brown loams derived from the crumbly calcareous basalt of which this hill is composed. The field layer is mainly of the *Brachypodium sylvaticum* type, with an abundance of *Primula vulgaris*, *Senecio jacobaea* and *Teucrium scorodonia*. The main interest of the wood is the profusion of large corticolous lichens (the Lobarion alliance) which richly clothe the tree trunks and limbs, e.g. *Lobaria pulmonaria* and *L. laetevirens*. This is another of the important lichen-rich woods of the Ardnamurchan–Sunart area. Close to the shore are damp, rocky gullies, and cliffs with caves of an old raised beach, and here there is a more varied flora with species such as *Hypericum androsaemum*, *Polystichum aculeatum*, *Phyllitis scolopendrium*, *Hymenophyllum wilsonii* and *Marchesinia mackaii*.

W.191. CARNACH WOOD, ARGYLL
NN 0958.   110 ha   Grade 1

This is an ash–alder wood, which has developed on basic flushed soils on a steep, north-facing hillside, and represents a rare woodland type in Britain. The underlying rocks are calcareous schists and limestones which have produced a clayey, light brown loam of high base-status but low permeability to water. The tree layer is variable but dominated by an irregular mixture of alder and ash, with an abundance of hazel and hawthorn in the shrub layer. Birch and bird-cherry are scattered throughout.

The field layer is dominated by *Brachypodium sylvaticum*, *Deschampsia cespitosa*, *Prunella vulgaris*, *Oxalis acetosella* with *Circaea lutetiana*, *Geranium sylvaticum*, *Sanicula europaea* and other basiphilous herbs. It is grazed, but there are numerous small outcrops which give some protection in places. Interesting elements in the flora are *Cystopteris fragilis*, *Athyrium filix-femina*, *Carex sylvatica*, *Chrysosplenium oppositifolium* and *Saxifraga aizoides*. *Hymenophyllum wilsonii* and the oceanic bryophytes, *Hylocomium umbratum*, *Riccardia palmata*, *Nowellia curvifolia*, *Plagiochila spinulosa* and *Scapania gracilis* occur, but as Atlantic bryophytes are mostly calcifuge, this element is not well represented. Glendaruel and Glasdrum are similar woods, but are dominated by ash, with alder forming a separate woodland type on wetter ground.

W.192. DRIMNIN, ARGYLL
NM 5654.   75 ha   Grade 1

This is an extensive area of hazel-dominated deciduous woodland along the east shore of the Sound of Mull with a canopy only 2.4–3 m high in the most exposed places. Rowan, eared willow, and blackthorn occur with the hazel; occasional wind-cut oak, ash, birch and holly are also found. The field layer is basiphilous on a mull and loamy soil and includes *Sanicula europaea*, *Circaea lutetiana*, *Fragaria vesca*, *Asperula odorata* and *Allium ursinum*. The rare orchid *Cephalanthera longifolia* has been reported in the area. The woodland becomes double canopied on the less exposed slopes with intermediate stages between. Over areas of boulder scree, *Dryopteris borreri*, *Athyrium filix-femina* and mosses such as *Thuidium tamariscinum*, *Rhytidiadelphus loreus*, *Hypnum cupressiforme*, *Polytrichum formosum*, *Pleurozium schreberi* and *Dicranum majus* are dominant. In the centre of the site a wooded gorge adds diversity.

W.193. GLASDRUM WOOD, ARGYLL
NN 0545.   65 ha   Grade 1*

This wood lies on the south-east slope of Ben Churalain overlooking the head of Loch Creran and rises from sea-level to 180 m. Dalradian rocks, with calcareous beds along the lower sections passing to acidic rocks above, produce variable soil conditions. Near the road there is a flat, narrow strip of alder woodland with *Crepis paludosa* and *Carex remota* on wet mull soils. A hanging ash–hazel wood occupies the middle zone. This is broken by a line of calcareous schist outcrops drained by bryophyte-rich rills. Some ash standards reach 24 m, but patches of dense young growth also occur. Hazel forms a tall scrub layer throughout and alder occupies the damper pockets on the higher slopes. Wych elm, birch, rowan and hawthorn also occur.

The dominants of the field layer are *Brachypodium sylvaticum*, *Mercurialis perennis* and ferns (mainly *Dryopteris filix-mas*, *Thelypteris oreopteris* and *Athyrium filix-femina*), but the flora is herb rich and includes *Allium ursinum*, *Anemone nemorosa* and *Circaea lutetiana*. Grasses such as *Poa trivialis* and *Deschampsia cespitosa* are common.

Above the escarpment with its calcicolous flora, the soils are more acidic, and the prevailing woodland type is sessile oak with some birch which grades into birch scrub and moorland at about 270 m. The field layer is grassier with *Holcus lanatus*, *Melampyrum pratense* and *Potentilla erecta*. Many oceanic species of bryophytes occur on the screes, blocks and trees; these include *Adelanthus decipiens* and *Hylocomium umbratum*.

The NNR lies within a large Forestry Commission area, and, like Glen Nant, it is a good example of a north-western mixed deciduous woodland, but approaches closely to ash–hazel wood on limestone.

W.194. GLEN NANT WOODS, ARGYLL
NN 0128.   200 ha   Grade 1

This site comprises a narrow ravine in andesite and basalt lavas of Old Red Sandstone age, with drifts of glacial origin. The valley contains a north-western type of mixed deciduous woodland over a range of soils. An ash–hazel association is dominant on the calcareous volcanic rocks, with a sparse shrub layer of hawthorn, blackthorn and guelder rose. Elsewhere sessile oak and birch are most abundant with a scattering of rowan, holly and bird-cherry. Other woody species include wych elm and gean, with alder and sallows in the less steep areas. Coppicing has been widespread and large mature trees are rare. Acidophilous ground flora communities are most widespread particularly on the higher slopes. Two main types occur, a fern-dominated one with *Dryopteris borreri*, *Thelypteris oreopteris* and *Athyrium filix-femina*; and a heathy facies with *Vaccinium myrtillus*, *Calluna vulgaris*, *Pteridium aquilinum*. The basiphilous patches have an abundance of herbs including *Allium ursinum*, *Primula vulgaris* and *Fragaria vesca*, but are dominated by *Brachypodium sylvaticum* and *Deschampsia cespitosa*. Some of the flowering plants of particular interest include *Melica nutans*, *Trollius europaeus* and *Neottia nidus-avis*. There is a rich Atlantic bryophyte flora which includes *Hylocomium umbratum*, *Adelanthus decipiens*, *Plagiochila punctata* and *Herberta hutchinsiae* with the ferns *Hymenophyllum wilsonii* and *Dryopteris aemula*.

W.195. MEALL NAN GOBHAR, ARGYLL

NN 103445. 385 ha   Grade 1

Several blocks of birchwood (*Betula pubescens*) lie over granite block screes on the south-east-facing slopes above Loch Etive. There is a little sessile oak but the woods are mainly pure birch. The most notable feature is the rich development of bryophyte and fern communities on the extremely rocky floor of these woods. Ferns such as *Thelypteris limbosperma*, *T. phegopteris*, *T. dryopteris*, *Blechnum spicant* and *Hymenophyllum wilsonii* are in great abundance, and the blocks are crowned with carpets of moss and liverwort containing the common heath mosses (especially *Rhytidiadelphus loreus*), *Thuidium tamariscinum*, *Sphagnum quinquefarium*, *Hylocomium umbratum*, *Scapania gracilis* and *Plagiochila spinulosa*. The trees have an abundance of *P. punctata* and *Frullania* spp.

W.196. TAYNISH WOOD, ARGYLL

NR 7384. 330 ha   Grade 1*

There are 3 km of almost continuous deciduous woodland on the west side of Loch Sween on the Taynish Peninsula, south of Tayvallich. There is a marked north-east/south-west orientated system of ridges and hollows formed along the strike of the underlying Dalradian schists. This topographical variability results in a range of soil types, with little or no soil on sheer cliffs and steep, block-strewn hillsides, to shallow podsols on steep slopes, and basic brown earths on gentle slopes. Valley peats occur in the waterlogged hollows. Three main woodland types occur, with oak wood on block scree and well-drained slopes, mixed deciduous wood on the lower slopes near sea-level, and birchwood on the upper slopes and in exposed sites.

Oak, *Quercus petraea*, is predominant, with a fine growth up to 20 m high in favourable situations. Associated trees and shrubs include ash, hazel, birch, and rowan, and with some honeysuckle, ivy, and holly. The ground layer is dominated by bilberry on steep, broken areas, with *Deschampsia flexuosa*, *Oxalis acetosella*, and *Holcus lanatus*. Bracken predominates in more open areas. Boulders in the wood support a luxuriant growth of bryophytes, including several rare Atlantic species such as *Adelanthus decipiens*, *Harpanthus scutatus*, *Lepidozia pinnata*, and *Dicranum scottianum*. *Hymenophyllum wilsonii*, *H. tunbrigense*, *Corydalis claviculata*, *Sedum anglicum*, and *Sphaerophorus melanocarpus* are further notable species. There are several steep cliffs within the wood, and in intermittently flushed areas several local bryophytes occur, including *Radula aquilegia*, *Grimmia hartmanii*, *Harpalejeunea ovata*, and *Frullania germana*. There is a rich and luxuriant epiphyte growth of lichens on the larger trees, with *Lobaria* spp., *Sticta* spp., and several other Atlantic species such as *Microphiale lutea*, *Normandina pulchella*, and *Nephromium lusitanicum*. *Mylia cuneifolia* occurs locally.

On gentler slopes the woodland is more mixed, with oak, ash, wych elm, alder, and hazel. Basiphilous ground species include *Brachypodium sylvaticum*, *Circaea lutetiana*, and *Ajuga reptans*. Birch becomes increasingly prominent on exposed ridge sites and on north-facing slopes, with an acidophilous field layer dominated by heather, bilberry, and grasses. In wetter sites *Sphagnum palustre* and *Polytrichum commune* are prominent. Ferns such as *Dryopteris aemula*, *D. borreri*, and *Thelypteris dryopteris* are locally frequent, especially in open birchwoods, and there are extensive bryophyte communities.

The waterlogged hollows within the wood are of interest, with rich-fen communities of *Eriophorum latifolium* and *Carex hostiana*. Lochan Taynish has an extensive *C. rostrata* swamp at the southern end, and with *Juncus acutiflorus* flush bogs on shallower peat. Notable species in this area include *Fossombronia foveolata*, *Pellia neesiana*, and *Sphagnum squarrosum*.

The peninsula to the west of Taynish carries an extensive area of juniper scrub which extends the range of woodland types here and is included in the grade 1 site. This area is of outstanding floristic interest as well, with the Mediterranean–Atlantic species *Cephaloziella turneri*, *Epipterygium tozeri*, and *Targionia hypophylla* growing in or near their northernmost known localities.

The area as a whole is considered to be of outstanding ecological and floristic importance as one of the most extensive oakwoods surviving in Scotland.

W.197. MEALDARROCH POINT–SKIPNESS, ARGYLL

NR 8868–9260. 370 ha   Grade 1*

The moorlands of this part of Knapdale are bounded by an inaccessible coastline, where steep slopes are broken by numerous rock outcrops and extensive block-strewn slopes. The slopes are mainly wooded with scrubby birch (probably seral), with some oak (perhaps representing the remnants of a former cover of climax woodland), rowan, hazel, and holly. In places there are larger patches of wood, and numerous small cascading streams have cut deep ravines.

The major feature of interest of the area is the extremely rich and luxuriant development of fern- and bryophyte-dominated communities rather than the woodland itself, but the site is most suitably classified under this formation. The fern and bryophyte communities are essentially of a woodland type and are notable for the strong representation of Atlantic species. The southern Atlantic ferns *Hymenophyllum tunbrigense* and *Dryopteris aemula* probably occur here in greater quantity than anywhere in Britain, and they approach the profusion of these species characteristic of the Killarney woods in Ireland. There are large quantities of *H. wilsonii* and several other Atlantic species occur widely such as *Scapania gracilis*, *Plagiochila punctata*, *Lepidozia pinnata*, *Adelanthus decipiens*, *Dicranum scottianum*, and *Hylocomium umbratum*.

The cascading streams provide habitats for several local Atlantic species, including *Jubula hutchinsiae*, *Aphanolejeunea microscopica*, *Drepanolejeunea hamatifolia*, *Harpalejeunea ovata*, *Cephaloziella pearsonii*, *Plagiochila tridenticulata*, and *Grimmia hartmanii*. Ledges in the ravines support *Hypericum androsaemum* and a variety of basiphilous ferns and bryophytes. *Mylia cuneifolia* is locally frequent on birch trees.

Open areas with little or no tree cover are densely overgrown with bracken. Moist humus banks, largely unburnt, abound and provide habitats for several interesting bryophytes including *Harpanthus scutatus*, *Riccardia palmata*, and *Scapania umbrosa*. Shaded rocks by the sea support *Frullania microphylla*, *F. germana*, *Radula aquilegia*, and *Lophocolea fragrans*.

The area is of outstanding bryological interest, and although the tree component of the woods cannot be regarded as important in their present condition, the range and abundance of bryophyte communities are of high quality. The richness of the flora depends partly on shade and high humidity, which are conferred here by aspect and the rocky nature of the terrain. Tree cover is obviously not necessary for these plants here but, conversely, afforestation with conifers, as is so widespread in Knapdale today, would undoubtedly damage their chances of survival.

W.198. INVERNEIL BURN, ARGYLL
NR 8381.   10 ha   Grade 1*

This is a deep, wooded gorge cut through schists and epidiorites which are locally strongly calcareous. The woods on the more level ground above the ravine consist of well-grown birch and oak with a *Vaccinium*–moss-dominated field layer. On the blocks there is a good bryophyte growth, with abundant hepatics such as *Plagiochila spinulosa*, *P. punctata* and *Scapania gracilis*. Epiphytes of note include *Mylia cuneifolia* and *Aphanolejeunea microscopica*.

There is some beech (presumably planted) around the foot of the glen, but most of the steep slopes above the gorge are covered with an ash–hazel–wych elm wood with some birch, rowan, and willows. The ground cover is herb rich with *Deschampsia cespitosa*, *Filipendula ulmaria*, *Asperula odorata*, *Geranium robertianum*, *Stellaria holostea*, and *Thelypteris phegopteris*, and basiphilous bryophytes are abundant, with *Hylocomium brevirostre*, *Plagiochila asplenioides* and *Eurhynchium striatum*. There is an excellent growth of epiphytic lichens and bryophytes on the hazel and ash, with *Lobaria* spp., *Sticta* spp., *Parmeliella atlantica*, *Microphiale lutea*, *Normandina pulchella*, *Ulota vittata*, *U. phyllantha*, and *Frullania germana*. Rotting logs support a rich flora, including such rarities as *Tritomaria exsecta* and *Harpanthus scutatus*.

The ravine provides a range of moist shaded habitats and supports a rich assemblage of Atlantic bryophytes, including *Hygrohypnum eugyrium*, *Radula aquilegia*, *Plagiochila tridenticulata*, several members of the Lejeuneaceae, and *Metzgeria hamata*. Other notable species in the gorge include *Seligeria recurvata* and *Hygrobiella laxifolia*. There is an interesting north-facing basic cliff with tufaceous springs. This supports several calcicolous species, including *Rubus saxatilis*, *Asplenium viride*, *Saxifraga aizoides*, *Cololejeunea calcarea*, *Mnium marginatum* and *Gyalecta jenensis*. Similar habitats are represented in the north by Corrieshalloch, Allt nan Carnan, and Allt Mor (Rassal Ashwood) gorges, but Inverneil Burn is a more open gorge and supports a richer, more southerly flora.

The area is considered to be of outstanding interest in view not only of its rich and diverse flora but of the fine and

extensive stand of mixed deciduous woodland which is otherwise rare in south-west Scotland.

W.199. URQUHART BAY, INVERNESS-SHIRE
NH 5129.   40 ha   Grade 1

This alderwood lies on the delta of the River Enrick where it flows into Loch Ness and is subject to periodic flooding only. It is thus of a drier type than the alder swamps of the Mound, Sutherland. Ash, sycamore, bird-cherry, wych elm and *Salix alba* also occur in the canopy and shrubs include *Salix caprea*, *S. cinerea* ssp. *atrocinerea*, *S. fragilis*, rowan and blackthorn.

The field communities are similar to those of a typical northern mixed deciduous woodland and include *Mercurialis perennis*, *Filipendula ulmaria*, *Endymion nonscriptus*, *Brachypodium sylvaticum* and *Carex remota*. The northern species *Cirsium heterophyllum* and *Trollius europaeus* occur locally while in wetter places there is *Carex rostrata*, *Glyceria fluitans*, *Juncus effusus*, *Mentha aquatica* and *Myosotis sylvatica*.

W.200. LOCH MORAR ISLANDS, INVERNESS-SHIRE
NM 7091.   25 ha   Grade 1

Stands of Scots pine cover the islands in this loch. Eilean a'Phidhir is a rock island about 20 ha in extent rising to 39 m above water level and has a mor humus soil. The pine is mainly tall and well grown although some trees are stunted and wind cut. In the north-east corner the pines are mixed with common lime, sycamore and yew (probably self sown though traces of old walls indicate past human influences). In the remaining woodland, birch and rowan share the pine canopy and yew, birch, willow, rowan form an understorey. The woodland floor has abundant *Oxalis acetosella* with *Listera cordata*, *Blechnum spicant*, *Calluna vulgaris* and hypnaceous mosses. Patches of *Luzula sylvatica*, *Deschampsia flexuosa* and *Polytrichum formosum* are present. Boulders and *Sphagnum* are more abundant at the southern end.

Eilean nam Breac has pioneer pines, again surrounded by a dense stand of younger trees showing good sequences in the disappearance of heather, *Vaccinium* and mosses as the canopy thickens up. Oak and alder are present as shrubs in the more open areas.

See also OW.86.

W.201. TOKAVAIG WOOD, SKYE, INVERNESS-SHIRE
NG 6112.   85 ha   Grade 1*

Tokavaig Wood occurs on the north- and west-facing flanks of a large anticline, in the centre of which Cambrian Quartzite, Fucoid Beds, Serpulite Grit and dolomitic Durness Limestone are exposed. The southern part of the wood overlies Torridonian Sandstone. This geological diversity, combined with the extremely humid (250 cm of rain a year) and sheltered climate, results in a rich and varied woodland flora and vegetation.

Woodland dominated by downy birch with some rowan, holly and oak *Quercus petraea* occurs widely on the poor, podsolised soils overlying sandstone and quartzites. *Vaccinium myrtillus*, *Deschampsia flexuosa*, *Potentilla erecta*, and

Calluna vulgaris predominate in the field layer. Acidophilous bryophytes are abundant. Hazel, with some ash, wych elm, bird-cherry and guelder rose occur on richer sites on the limestone or on flushed areas on the sandstone. The field layer is herb-rich, with *Deschampsia cespitosa*, *Primula vulgaris*, *Endymion non-scriptus*, *Asperula odorata*, and *Anemone nemorosa*. On shallow rendzina-like soils developed around limestone outcrops, there are small stands of ash-wood, with some elm and abundant *Brachypodium sylvaticum*. Wet sites within the wood are characterised by alder thickets with *Carex remota* and *Chrysosplenium oppositifolium*.

Other species of note occurring within the wood include *Listera cordata*, *L. ovata*, *Coeloglossum viride*, *Cirsium heterophyllum* and *Carex sylvatica*.

There are abundant boulders within the wood and these support a well-developed range of bryophyte communities containing several Atlantic species, including *Adelanthus decipiens*, *Hylocomium umbratum*, *Dicranum scottianum*, *Bazzania trilobata*, and *Harpanthus scutatus*. *Hymenophyllum wilsonii* is abundant. Epiphytes are also abundant, especially on hazel, with *Ulota vittata*, *U. phyllantha*, *Lobaria* spp., *Sticta* spp., *Frullania germana*, *Aphanolejeunea microscopica* and *Mylia cuneifolia*. Rotting logs and peaty banks within the wood and along the coast provide habitats for *Tritomaria exsecta*, *Riccardia palmata*, *Lepidozia trichoclados* and *Cephalozia catenulata*.

There are two deep gorges that cut across the anticline. The limestone parts are extremely rich floristically with *Melica nutans*, *Paris quadrifolia*, *Rubus saxatilis*, *Arctostaphylos uva-ursi*, *Epipactis atrorubens*, *Phyllitis scolopendrium*, *Asplenium viride*, and *Polystichum lobatum*, and a wide variety of calcicolous bryophytes and lichens including *Gymnostomum calcareum*, *Orthothecium intricatum*, *Cololejeunea calcarea*, *Leiocolea turbinata*, *Marchesinia mackaii*, *Gyalecta jenensis*, and *Solorina saccata*. There are several large stands of ungrazed tall-herb vegetation in the ravines, with dominant *Luzula sylvatica*.

The wood is of considerable ecological interest because of the range of woodland types present and their intimate relationships to bedrocks and soils. The area is also of outstanding floristic interest, being one of the richest localities known in western Scotland for Atlantic bryophytes, including several species growing at or near their northernmost world locality. Such phytogeographically interesting species include *Jubula hutchinsiae*, *Fissidens celticus* and the fern *Hymenophyllum tunbrigense*. More widespread Atlantic cryptogams and lichens present include *Dryopteris aemula*, *Porella thuja*, *Dicranodontium uncinatum*, *Tetraphis browniana*, *Lophocolea fragrans*, *Trichostomum hibernicum*, *Grimmia hartmanii*, *Hygrohypnum eugyrium*, *Plagiochila tridenticulata*, *Fissidens curnowii*, *Radula aquilegia*, *Colura calyptrifolia*, *Drepanolejeunea hamatifolia*, *Sphaerophorus melanocarpus* and *Sticta dufourii*.

W.202. GEARY RAVINE, SKYE, INVERNESS-SHIRE
NG 2663. *c.* 2 ha   Grade 1

This is a deep, narrow east-north-east-facing wooded ravine up to 90 m deep, cut through calcareous basalts.

There are several waterfalls. It is inaccessible to grazing animals and it is difficult of access to people. The slopes of the ravine are partially wooded with birch, hazel, ash, rowan, aspen and, more rarely, holly, *Prunus padus*, *Salix capraea*, *S. aurita*, and juniper. On the north-facing slopes there are magnificent and extensive ungrazed stands of vegetation dominated by *Luzula sylvatica* and with a wide variety of tall herbs such as *Cirsium heterophyllum*, *Trollius europaeus*, *Crepis paludosa*, *Filipendula ulmaria*, *Geum rivale*, and *Valeriana officinalis* and of ferns such as *Dryopteris borreri*, *Athyrium filix-femina*, *Thelypteris phegopteris*, *T. dryopteris*, and, more rarely, *Dryopteris aemula*. Other plants of note in these stands include *Vicia sylvatica*, *Osmunda regalis*, *Listera ovata*, *Paris quadrifolia* and *Melica nutans*.

The area is of outstanding interest as one of the finest surviving examples of wooded ungrazed tall-herb vegetation in north-west Scotland, as well as supporting an extremely rich and diverse flora of both vascular plants and bryophytes.

W.203. GLEN STRATHFARRAR, INVERNESS-SHIRE
NH 2737. 3000 ha   Grade 1

Four groups of native woodland fall within this site. As the underlying Moine Gneiss and Schists have calcareous bands, the drift is more basic than at Glens Affric and Cannich. In Coille Gharbh and Inchvuilt Wood, Scots pine is the dominant species though birch occurs in extensive stands near the woodland margins. Coille Gharbh is well stocked with pine over the *Vaccinium*–moss association, including *Vaccinium myrtillus*, *V. vitis-idaea*, *Empetrum* spp. and *Deschampsia flexuosa*. In Inchvuilt Wood, the canopy is more open due, in the main, to felling (1940–45) though evidence of fire is present. The resulting field association is the *Vaccinium*–*Calluna* type which is widespread in the pine–birch and pure birch areas also. Culligran Wood is mainly birch and Uisge Misgeach is a mixture of birch and pine. More aspen is scattered through the area than is usual together with rowan, holly and juniper, the latter forming a discontinuous understorey under Coille Gharbh. There is more *Goodyera repens* here than in other northern and western pinewoods and less common species present include *Pyrola media*, *Moneses uniflora*, *Trientalis europaea* and *Lycopodium annotinum*. The Scottish race of the crossbill has nested here in some years.

W.204. GLEN AFFRIC, INVERNESS-SHIRE
NH 2424. 2000 ha   Grade 1

Most of the woods containing Scots pine are on the south side of Glen Affric and thus have a northerly aspect. They range in altitude from 180–460 m, and lie on sand and gravel glacial drift over Moine Schists.

The relative proportion of birch and Scots pine varies, as in other western pinewoods. On the better-drained soils there are well-stocked stands of pine but birch (predominantly *Betula pendula* and generally younger than the pine) seems to have spread in recent decades. Rowan is common in the birch areas and there is alder and *Salix atrocinerea* along the streams, but juniper is rare. Under the dense canopy the field layer consists of *Deschampsia flexuosa*, *Vaccinium myrtillus* and mosses, including *Hylocomium splendens*, *Pleurozium schreberi* and *Hypnum cupressiforme*. Where the pine is scattered, *Calluna vulgaris* and *Trichophorum cespitosum* predominate on knolls, and *Molinia caerulea* in the hollows, both these communities being typical of western pinewoods. As the drainage deteriorates, a *Calluna–Vaccinium–Eriophorum–Sphagnum* community covers the ground and where the peat increases in depth the trees thin out over mire communities.

Regeneration occurs in the open areas but is affected by deer browsing.

Woodlands stretch along the south side of Glen Cannich from near Strathglass in the east, where there is mainly birch, to Loch Mullardoch in the west, where there is mainly pine. The underlying rocks are again Moine Schists, but glacial drift covers the surface, which is not as hummocky or boggy as in Glen Affric. Rowan, alder, holly and low scrubby juniper are present with field communities as at Glen Affric, including *Pyrola media*, *P. minor* and *Goodyera repens*. There is better regeneration here than in Glen Affric.

This is another breeding place of crossbills in some years. See also U.83.

W.205. ALLT NAN CARNAN, ROSS
NG 8940. 7 ha   Grade 1

This is a 1.6 km long gorge which has been cut in calcareous schists. The sides are wooded and contrast markedly with the surrounding moorland. Sessile oak and birch dominate the mixed woodland but ash is locally abundant. Other species include rowan, holly, aspen and bird-cherry. The basiphilous ground flora includes *Rubus saxatilis*, *Saxifraga aizoides*, *Alchemilla alpina*, *Anemone nemorosa*, *Geum rivale*, *Fragaria vesca*, *Chrysosplenium oppositifolium*, and the moss *Orthothecium rufescens* is abundant. Atlantic bryophytes are well represented on the rocks and trees.

W.206. LOCH MAREE WOODS, ROSS   Grade 1*

(*a*) *Beinn Eighe* (*Coille na Glas-Leitire*)
NH 0046. 130 ha

The main wood, Coille na Glas-Leitire, covers the quartzitic lower slopes of Beinn Eighe on the south side of Loch Maree, and extends from the shore of the loch at 12 m up to 300 m in places. This was once amongst the finest pinewoods remaining in Scotland after the main period of forest clearance, but it was devastated by timber extraction during the two World Wars, and density of tree cover is now very variable. There are areas of continuous woodland, with both young and old trees, but much of the site has rather open pine heath, and on the damper ground many of the small trees are 'checked' in growth. Woodland cover is interrupted in places both by rocky outcrops and soligenous or valley mire. Two forest communities occur in the wood. One is dense pinewood characterised by the dominance of *Vaccinium myrtillus*, *V. vitis-idaea* and hypnaceous mosses (e.g. *Hylocomium splendens* and *Ptilium crista-castrensis*), as in the

Cairngorm pinewoods. The second community covers a much greater area and is typical of open forest throughout the west of Scotland and higher altitudes in the east of Scotland and western Norway. It is characterised by the co-dominance of tall, bushy *Calluna vulgaris* and *Vaccinium* and an abundant *Sphagnum* cover beneath these dwarf shrubs, with *S. quinquefarium*, *S. nemoreum* and *S. russowii*.

Special features of the western pinewoods are the abundance of holly, ivy and rowan, with a little oak, and a general scarcity of juniper. There is a good deal of bracken in places and this reaches dominance on open, drier ground. Where calcium-enriched drainage water seeps down from the outcropping bands of calcareous mudstones above the wood, the pinewood gives way to a wedge-shaped block of downy birch woodland, with a grassier *Agrostis–Anthoxanthum* field layer, passing to the forb-rich type in places, e.g. with *Primula vulgaris* and *Endymion non-scriptus*; or into the *Vaccinium–Hylocomium* community of the pinewood.

Both woods are extremely rich in Atlantic bryophytes, especially where the ground is rocky; the more notable species include the very rare moss *Daltonia splachnoides*, *Hylocomium umbratum*, *Hypnum callichroum*, *Dicranodontium uncinatum*, *Lepidozia pinnata*, *Frullania germana*, *Plagiochila spinulosa*, *P. punctata*, *Radula aquilegia*, *Mylia cuneifolia*, *Metzgeria hamata*, *Tritomaria exsecta* and *Colura calyptrifolia*. An interesting feature is the way in which some northern Atlantic liverworts, normally found at higher levels on treeless hills, here descend to within the upper parts of the wood, e.g. *Herberta hutchinsiae*, *Bazzania pearsonii*, *Mastigophora woodsii* and *Jamesoniella carringtonii*. These woods are also very rich in lichens, and some of the larger foliose species, such as *Lobaria pulmonaria*, grow abundantly on the pines.

There is an interesting *Sphagnum*-rich valley mire within the wood and this shows a pool and hummock pattern, and associated floristics, similar to that of the numerous patterned blanket mires of the northern and western Highlands. There are also *Carex echinata*, *Molinia*, *S. recurvum* soligenous mires, and *S. imbricatum* grows in this habitat. Richer examples contain a variety of forbs and *S. warnstorfianum*.

The wood is frequented by red deer, and there are roe deer as well. Wild cats occur, and this is a famous haunt of the pine marten. Buzzard, sparrowhawk and siskin are more notable breeding birds. The invertebrate fauna is rich, with a number of rare species not known elsewhere in the area.

(*b*) *Loch Maree Islands*
NG 9272. 220 ha

Eilean Subhainn, the largest of the islands, and Garbh Eilean nearby are well-wooded with Scots pine and well-grown juniper, perhaps the largest in western Scotland. There is a mosaic of woodland and mire on which tree growth is checked.

The flora is typical of wood and mire, but a feature of the freshwater loch shores here is the large quantity of *Lycopodium inundatum*, and the presence of *Osmunda regalis*.

(c) *Letterewe Oakwoods*
NG 9075–9867. 450 ha

These form the most northerly of the larger semi-natural sessile oakwoods in Britain, and make a valuable comparison with the pinewoods of Beinn Eighe on the opposite side of Loch Maree. The two blocks of oak woodland lie on Lewisian Gneiss and the soils derived from this hard rock vary from leached to flushed and enriched brown earths. These varied woodlands contain heathy facies with birch over *Anthoxanthum odoratum*, *Festuca ovina* and *Vaccinium*, and also floristically richer areas with ash–hazel. Small groups of pines occur on crags above or throughout the oak and birch wood and areas of alder and ash with a typical herbaceous field layer are also present. Areas of scrub or open woodland occur; many species are regenerating, including pine, oak, birch, rowan, juniper, hawthorn, hazel, bird-cherry and *Rosa* spp., but many seedlings, especially those of oak, do not survive.

See also U.64, U.90.

W.207. INVERPOLLY WOODS, ROSS
NC 1013. 315 ha   Grade 1

The Inverpolly grade 1 upland site (U.66) contains upwards of a score of separate and widely scattered birchwoods covering an altitudinal range from sea-level to 275 m, and ranging in size from a few hectares to over 70 ha; they occur on slopes of all aspects and varying steepness, from almost flat ground to precipitous. The woods in the western half of the site are on Lewisian Gneiss whereas those to the east are mainly on Torridon Sandstone. Some have block scree littered floor whereas others have little or no exposed rock, and a few are on marshy ground.

The best woods are in the north-west of the area, in Gleann an Strathain and along the south side of the Kirkaig River. These woods are all dominated by downy birch (of widely varying height), but rowan is frequent and *Salix aurita* locally plentiful, especially on damper ground. Hazel is locally abundant, alder occurs here or there on stream alluvium and bird-cherry is occasional in the area. In the woods on the islands of Loch Sionascaig (OW.92) holly is frequent and rowan is locally dominant on Eilean Mor; red deer graze on the islands and prevent regeneration of tree and tall shrub species on some. While red and roe deer, sheep and cattle graze the mainland woods, in a number of areas at the west end of the National Nature Reserve only, regeneration is widespread.

On the poorer brown earths the *Agrostis–Anthoxanthum* community is typically present, but in places, especially on the gneiss, there are more fertile loams and a much greater variety of herbs, such as *Prunella vulgaris*, *Ranunculus acris*, *Primula vulgaris*, *Viola riviniana*, *Filipendula ulmaria* and *Cirsium heterophyllum*. There is a good deal of wet grassland with *Carex panicea*, *C. pulicaris*, *C. echinata*, *Juncus kochii*, *Cirsium palustre*, *Succisa pratensis* and *Acrocladium cuspidatum* and this grades into more definite *Juncus acutiflorus* or *Carex* soligenous mire or into wet *Molinia* grassland. Rocky woods have a *Vaccinium–Oxalis* field layer and fern communities are well-developed, there being local dominance of *Pteridium aquilinum* and *Thelypteris oreopteris*. *Hymenophyllum wilsonii* is locally abundant and *Dryopteris aemula* occurs here in one of its most northerly stations. There is a general abundance of mosses such as *Thuidium tamariscinum*, *Hylocomium splendens*, *Dicranum majus* and *Sphagnum quinquefarium*, and Atlantic bryophytes are well represented, including *Hylocomium umbratum*, *Plagiochila punctata* and *Frullania germana*. In places the trees have good growths of foliose lichens, including *Sticta crocata*. The low cliffs beside the Kirkaig River are fairly basic and extend the range of habitats for herbs and bryophytes.

Although none of these woods is outstanding on its own, the whole group forms a complex representing virtually the whole field of variation in the climax birchwoods of the north-west Highlands. There are other birchwoods farther north but these differ from the Inverpolly woods only in the stronger representation of certain features, such as the greater abundance of rowan, and the more extreme development of bryophytic communities in the block-scree wood of Strathbeag. Some of the woods on Inverpolly are moribund, e.g. Na Leitrichean, and here regeneration may need encouragement.

See also P.101.

W.208. RASSAL ASHWOOD, ROSS
NG 8443. 85 ha   Grade 1

Ashwood is comparatively rare in western Scotland and this is the most northerly true ashwood in Britain. It lies on a discontinuous, driftless, Durness Limestone pavement with a west-facing gentle slope. Ridges of limestone form nodular hummocks running along the lines of strike with a heavy red clay loam lying between. The ash is widely spaced and open grown with some large trees. There is an abundance of hazel, occasional downy birch, goat willow and rowan with some blackthorn and hawthorn scrub. Sheep-grazing and heather-burning have reduced the field layer in the main to a grassy sward (mainly *Deschampsia cespitosa*, *Festuca ovina*, *F. rubra*, *Agrostis tenuis*, *A. canina*, *Cynosurus cristatus*) with much dense *Pteridium aquilinum*. A few fragments of *Brachypodium sylvaticum* community remain, characteristic woodland species (such as *Fragaria vesca*, *Potentilla sterilis*, *Sanicula europaea*, *Stachys sylvatica* and *Primula vulgaris*) being confined to crevices in the outcropping limestone, within the fenced enclosure or to the west side of the Allt Mor gorge. Here *Cirsium heterophyllum* and *Epipactis atrorubens* are abundant on the steep south-facing slope.

The lichen flora of Rassal Ashwood is of singular interest. The two dominant species are *Leptogium burgessi* and *Parmeliella plumbea*. Other very frequent species are *Sticta fuliginosa*, *S. sylvatica*, *Parmeliella atlantica*, *P. corallinoides*, *Leptogium saturninum* and *Normandina pulchella*. On rocks in the wood *Arthopyrenia conoidea*, *Porina chlorotica* var. *linearis*, *Verrucaria rupestris*, *V. coerulea* and *Bacidia cuprea* occur.

Outside the woodland and gorge three main communities can be defined. A mossy *Agrostis–Festuca* grassland with *Pteridium aquilinum*; a calcareous mire community with

Saxifraga aizoides, *Eriophorum latifolium* and *Schoenus nigricans* on irrigated ground; and the widespread association of *Calluna vulgaris* with *Molinia caerulea* and *Trichophorum cespitosum* on acid peat.

See also U.93.

W.209. CORRIESHALLOCH GORGE, ROSS
NH 2078.   5 ha   Grade 1

This is a narrow wooded gorge about 1.6 km long. The walls are 60 m sheer in places and the ravine is of outstanding geomorphological interest. There is a narrow strip of woodland along the flanks of the ravine, with birch, rowan, oak, hazel, wych elm, aspen, bird-cherry, and pine along with several non-native species. The field layer includes acidophilous heathy as well as damp base-rich facies, and woodland herbs are well represented, e.g. *Anemone nemorosa*, *Silene dioica*, *Lathyrus montanus*, *Filipendula ulmaria*, *Rubus saxatilis*, *Sanicula europaea*, *Primula vulgaris*, *Lysimachia nemorum*, *Stachys sylvatica*, *Ajuga reptans*, *Galium odoratum*, *Valeriana officinalis* and *Allium ursinum*. Upland species include *Sedum rosea*, *Oxyria digyna* and *Lycopodium selago*.

Much of the gorge is virtually inaccessible, but those parts that have been explored support a rich and varied Atlantic bryophyte flora, mainly on the walls of the gorge and on boulders in the stream bed. Species of interest include *Aphanolejeunea microscopica*, *Drepanolejeunea hamatifolia*, *Cephaloziella pearsonii*, *Hygrohypnum eugyrium*, *Radula aquilegia*, *Tetraphis browniana*, *Plagiochila punctata*, *Eremonotus myriocarpus*, and *Frullania microphylla*. On the steep slopes and on ledges in the ravine, ungrazed *Luzula sylvatica* communities predominate, and species of note include *Cephalozia catenulata* and *C. leucantha*. Rotten logs in the gorge provide habitats for such rarities as *Calypogeia suecica*, *Sphenolobus helleranus*, and *Tritomaria exsecta*.

The principal interest of the area is geomorphological, although the flora and vegetation are also of some interest, with several rare species present.

W.210. MOUND ALDERWOODS, SUTHERLAND
NH 7698.   265 ha   Grade 1

In 1816 an embankment (called the Mound) was built across the head of Loch Fleet. This sealed off an expanse of estuary which became colonised by alder and willow to form the present mixture of dense alder carr and open fen. The few ridges, which have probably always stood above the highest tides, have an open growth of Scots pine with a dry type of field layer. Apart from a few cattle and deer, little disturbance occurs. The alderwoods have dry and swamp facies and *Salix atrocinerea* is locally plentiful in both. In the former *Deschampsia cespitosa* is most abundant with *Juncus effusus* locally dominant. Other characteristic species include *Carex remota*, *Agrostis canina* and *Holcus lanatus*, but in general this type is species-poor. The swamp alderwoods have a much richer field layer with many herbs (including some hydrophytes) such as *Senecio aquaticus*, *Hydrocotyle vulgaris*, *Galium palustre* and *Filipendula ulmaria*. The vegetation of the swamps is mainly a meso-

trophic fen, dominated by *Carex nigra*, or locally by *Eleocharis palustris*, and containing an abundance of *Potentilla palustris*, *Galium palustre*, *Succisa pratensis*, *Pedicularis palustris*, *Eriophorum angustifolium* and *Juncus articulatus*. 'Brown mosses' are well represented and form a carpet in places. There are no rarities present, but *Carex serotina* is a local species. In less frequently flooded and less basic situations there is a more acidophilous mire community with *Myrica gale*, *Molinia caerulea*, *Hydrocotyle vulgaris*, *Carex echinata* and *Ranunculus flammula*.

Towards the embankment, conditions become brackish and halophytes appear in the fen vegetation, and there are a few residual patches of salt marsh just inside the Mound. The area is of ornithological interest, especially when considered in conjunction with the adjoining estuarine Loch Fleet, which is an important winter wildfowl haunt (C.110).

W.211. STRATHBEAG, SUTHERLAND
NC 3851.   70 ha   Grade 1*

This wood covers a steep north-west-facing slope, thickly littered with quartzite block scree, and has mainly brown earths despite the presence above of a band of calcareous mudstones. The altitude is 30–210 m and the slope passes above into a high cliff, so that the wood occupies a sheltered and shaded position. There is a co-dominance of downy birch and rowan, well grown and reaching 9–12 m in height, but uneven aged. The wood is dense and has an undisturbed appearance, with much dead timber and rotting fallen logs. The herbaceous communities of the discontinuous areas of deeper soils are of the *Vaccinium myrtillus–Oxalis acetosella* type, but with *Agrostis–Anthoxanthum* grassland in places. Herbs of mull soils such as *Luzula sylvatica*, *Primula vulgaris*, *Rumex acetosa*, *Ranunculus acris* and *Lysimachia nemorum* are quite plentiful. One of the most distinctive features of the wood is the luxuriance of Atlantic bryophyte communities on the blocks and in the ground layer. Large cushions of the *Hymenophyllum wilsonii–Scapania gracilis–Plagiochila spinulosa* community occur in profusion, and there is an abundance of *Hylocomium umbratum*, *Hypnum callichroum*, *Lepidozia pinnata*, *Bazzania tricrenata*, *Saccogyna viticulosa* and *Plagiochila punctata*. The Atlantic fern *Dryopteris aemula* is almost at its northern limit here.

This is the northernmost of the series of grade 1 birchwoods in the north-west Highlands, and has been chosen for its undisturbed character, the unusual abundance of rowan and the richness of its bryophyte communities. About 1 km farther up the glen, a more open birchwood fringes the stream and has a fairly heavily grazed floor; bryophyte communities are less well developed here but large foliose lichens such as *Lobaria pulmonaria*, *L. scrobiculata* and *Parmeliella plumbea* are more abundant than in the main wood. Both woods lie within the large Foinaven grade 1 upland site (U.65), but together rate as grade 1 in their own right.

W.212. COILLE ARDURA, MULL
NM 6829.   350 ha   Grade 1

On a complicated topographical pattern of valley side, corrie, and a peninsular mound rising to 210 m jutting into

Loch Spelve, the geology of the site is determined by the Tertiary igneous complex of the Mull volcano and the underlying Triassic sediments. The Triassic sandstones and marl, and the Tertiary basalt and granophyre with intrusive basic cone sheets produce a variety of mull and mor soils on which different woodland types develop.

The sessile oakwoods of An-t'Sleaghach are on acid Triassic sediments and granophyre. Height growths of up to 18 m are achieved in unusually sheltered conditions for the Hebrides and the stocking locally is high. Birch, rowan, holly and hazel occur as an understorey as well as in local patches in the absence of oak. Field layer communities which have developed under relatively low grazing regimes consist of *Sphagnum*-rich *Vaccinium–Calluna*, *Vaccinium–Molinia* and *Vaccinium*-rich *Agrostis–Anthoxanthum* grassland. Characteristic associated woodland plants include *Melampyrum pratense*, *Oxalis acetosella*, *Teucrium scorodonia* and *Blechnum spicant*. Open areas are dominated by bracken in which regeneration of oak, hazel, birch and rowan occurs.

The south facing woodlands of An Coire, with soil complexes dominated more by basic rocks, carry a more open woodland of ash and ash–oak mixtures with scattered pure oak groves, and ash–hazel scrub at higher elevations. Herb-rich *Brachypodium sylvaticum* communities or fern meadows dominated by *Thelypteris limbosperma* are common field layer communities, tending locally to the more acidophilous *Anthoxanthum–Agrostis* grassland, or to *Pteridium–Deschampsia flexuosa*, or to *Molinia* in wet flushes. Features such as the presence of *Arrhenatherum elatius*, the local abundance of *Vaccinium myrtillus* and regeneration of oak, birch and hazel illustrate the lack of grazing. Unlike most western woods a proportion of *Betula verrucosa* is present, and oceanic features in the bryophyte flora are less apparent than usual in the Hebrides, although the ferns *Dryopteris aemula* and *Hymenophyllum wilsonii* occur sparsely under heavy shade.

W.213. CHOILLE MOR, COLONSAY, ARGYLL
NR 4197.   40 ha   Grade 2

This coastal oakwood on Torridonian phyllites has a wind-sculptured canopy of broad-crowned trees with height development limited by exposure to under 6 m. Pure oak-wood is confined to the seaward strip which trends through oak–birch mixtures to pure birch scrub on higher ground. Hazel and rowan are important constituents in the canopy but grazing by cattle, sheep and goats has restricted the development of shrub and field layers. Herb-rich *Agrostis–Anthoxanthum* communities predominate under the oak-wood canopy, with *Pteridium* or *Calluna* towards open or birch dominated areas. *Sphagnum–Molinia* communities occupy flushed ground with *Myrica gale*, *Hydrocotyle vulgaris*, *Mentha aquatica*, or alternatively in heavy shade, *Chrysosplenium oppositifolium*. A fern flora in localised shaded areas is rich in species including *Dryopteris borreri*, *D. aemula*, *D. carthusiana*, *Thelypteris limbosperma* and *Athyrium filix-femina*.

W.214. CLAGGAIN–ARDMORE, ISLAY, ARGYLL
NR 4550.   1050 ha   Grade 2

Well-developed stretches of coastal scrub occur on parallel bands of Dalradian schists and slates on the island's east side. Mixed hazel scrub with birches, oak, sallow, rowan and alder lies inland from Claggain Bay. The canopy varies in height from 3–9 m and also in cover, with the more open areas occupied by grass and wet heaths, mires and rock outcrops. The soils are mainly acidic but mull conditions occur in the stream valleys resulting in a wide range of ground flora. The dominants are *Endymion non-scriptus–Poa trivialis–Athyrium filix-femina*; *Primula vulgaris–Oxalis acetosella–Pteridium aquilinum*; *Deschampsia flexuosa–Digitalis purpurea–Blechnum spicant*; *Thelypteris limbosperma–Ajuga reptans*; *Anthoxanthum odoratum–Potentilla erecta*. In the Ardmore area on dry knolls, oak is the most abundant canopy species, with hazel, birch and rowan. Alder and sallow lie on the margins. The ground flora is similar to the Claggain but base-demanding species are less abundant.

W.215. CRANNACH WOOD, ARGYLL
NN 3545.   280 ha   Grade 2

This is a native Scots pinewood with trees at least 120 years old, but with poor stocking and full canopy closure only in small patches. Regeneration of Scots pine is hindered by grazing though two fenced areas now contain trees up to 10 years old. Birch and rowan are present and there is a birch zone above the pine. The ground flora is mainly *Calluna vulgaris–Vaccinium–Deschampsia flexuosa* with *Luzula pilosa*, *Potentilla erecta* and *Sphagnum*. Railway fires often occurred in the past, but this is no longer a hazard.

W.216. DOIRE DONN, ARGYLL
NN 0570.   180 ha   Grade 2

This rich woodland, on rocky, almost precipitous slopes, has sessile oak, ash, birch, alder and wych elm in the canopy. The understorey and shrub layers, unlike many Highland woods, are well developed, with abundant hazel, rowan, holly and sallow. Occasional guelder rose, bird-cherry and hawthorn are also present. Scots pine becomes an important element in the otherwise broadleaved deciduous woodland on knolls and the higher colder slopes showing a transition towards native pinewood which occurs nearby in Conaglen. The ground flora is variable but fern dominated, with basiphilous and acidophilous facies. The higher slopes in which pine, oak and birch are present carry a more heathy ground flora of *Calluna* in varying mixtures with *Molinia*, *Pteridium* and *Vaccinium myrtillus*.

W.217. GLENDARUEL WOOD, ARGYLL
NS 0290.   55 ha   Grade 2

This oak–ash woodland has a well-developed understorey of hazel and other woody species. The field layer varies from areas of *Thelypteris oreopteris* or *Brachypodium sylvaticum* to dominance of herbs. *Carex remota* and *Juncus articulatus* predominate beneath the alder. This site adjoins limestone exposures at 180 m which have a good upland flora.

W.218. KINUACHDRACH, JURA, ARGYLL
NR 7097. 115 ha   Grade 2

On steep rocky slopes of Dalradian schist there are two blocks of mixed birch–rowan wood, with an abundance of *Dryopteris aemula*, *Hymenophyllum tunbrigense* and *H. wilsonii* and a rich Atlantic bryophyte flora which includes *Adelanthus decipiens*, *Lepidozia pinnata*, *Frullania germana*, *Plagiochila punctata*, *Harpanthus scutatus*, *Metzgeria hamata* and *Dicranum scottianum*, besides more common species. Below, there are areas of swampy alderwood with willows, *Iris pseudacorus*, *Carex paniculata*, *C. laevigata*, *Crepis paludosa* and *Lythrum salicaria*. On the raised beach cliff slopes rather stunted oak also occurs in the woods. The rocky shore has good marine algal communities.

W.219. CLAIS DHEARG, ARGYLL
NM 9331. 750 ha   Grade 2

Clais Dhearg, in the Lorne district of Argyll, lies to the south of Connel at the mouth of Loch Etive. The site occupies some 600 ha of land varying between 30 and 120 m in altitude, on an uneven plateau of Andesitic lavas and draining into the Black Lochs to the north-west.

The uniform bedrock and land-use produce a small range of floristic variation, comprising a complex of acidophilous communities including sessile oakwood amounting to about 200 ha, acid grassland and grass heath, bracken fern meadow, blanket bog, and small soligenous mires associated with the pattern of drainage.

The woodland has developed for a long period under relatively heavy grazing by cattle and sheep. Most of the area is oakwood, with trees up to 18 m in height and of small girth forming a single canopy. Hazel, rowan, hawthorn, blackthorn, and occasionally birch, introduce diversity in the canopy and sparse shrub layer but there are no young trees or shrubs. Alder and willows are of restricted distribution. The ground flora under open canopy conditions is dominated by bracken but elsewhere there are associations of *Deschampsia flexuosa*, *Oxalis acetosella*, *Anthoxanthum odoratum*, *Polytrichum formosum*, *Hylocomium splendens* and *Thuidium delicatulum*. Also abundant in these associations are *Potentilla erecta*, *Galium saxatile* and *Holcus lanatus*. Species present locally are *Vaccinium myrtillus*, *Melampyrum pratense*, *Stellaria holostea*, *Pteridium aquilinum*, and the moss *Rhytidiadelphus loreus*. Plants sensitive to grazing such as species of fern and tall herbs are absent, and *Vaccinium myrtillus*, *Luzula sylvatica*, *Primula vulgaris*, *Endymion non-scriptus* and even *Calluna vulgaris* are very local or exist in very depauperate forms. The marshy communities of damper depressions under closed canopy woodland comprise *Poa trivialis*, *Filipendula ulmaria*, *Deschampsia cespitosa* and *Oxalis acetosella*, with *Sphagnum–Polytrichum* hummocks locally.

Tree bases in closed woodland are frequently covered with epiphytic bryophytes and lichens, usually dominated by *Hypnum cupressiforme*, but the oceanic species characteristic of humid western woods appear to be restricted in abundance and variety.

W.220. LOCH NA DAL, SKYE, INVERNESS-SHIRE
NG 7115. 75 ha   Grade 2

This site lies on south-west-facing slopes on mainly acidic soils over Torridonian Sandstone with block litter. It is similar to Tokavaig Wood, in tree composition and field communities, but is more open. The main part is a mixed wood of oak, rowan, hazel, birch (*Betula pubescens*) and willow (*Salix aurita*), but this passes to open birch over a heather community to the north-west. On the higher slopes to the south-east oak is predominant with birch and rowan whilst lower down, thick birch, some good hazel stands and emergent ash are present. The south-east edge is an open hazel scrub under which the flora is herb rich. Areas containing a dry heathy facies of vegetation are also present.

The wood supports a very rich and diverse bryophyte flora, both on the floor and on blocks within the wood. Atlantic species are well represented, including *Hylocomium umbratum*, *Plagiochila spinulosa*, *P. punctata*, *P. tridenticulata*, *Adelanthus decipiens*, *Bazzania trilobata*, *Lepidozia pinnata*, and *Dicranum scottianum*. Epiphytic bryophytes and lichens are abundant with *Lobaria* spp., *Sticta* spp., *Parmeliella atlantica*, *P. plumbea*, *Sphaerophorus melanocarpus*, *Ulota vittata* and *Mylia cuneifolia*.

Ravines deeply cut into the sandstone provide further habitats for rare Atlantic cryptogams including *Hymenophyllum tunbrigense*, *Dryopteris aemula*, *Jubula hutchinsiae*, *Fissidens curnowii* and several members of the Lejeuneaceae.

There are several base-rich flushes in openings within the wood, supporting *Schoenus nigricans*, *Eriophorum latifolium*, *Pinguicula lusitanica* and *Carex hostiana*.

W.221. LOCH MOIDART, INVERNESS-SHIRE
NM 6773. 315 ha   Grade 2

On the north shore, an extensive and well-developed mixed sessile oakwood lies on steep, rocky slopes of Moine Schists. Ash is local in the canopy which is generally about 18 m in height. The understorey contains birches, rowan and wych elm; hazel, holly, willows and guelder rose are present in the shrub layer. Four types of field communities can be distinguished: *Erica cinerea–Melampyrum pratense*; *Pteridium aquilinum*–mixed grasses (*Agrostis* spp., *Holcus* spp., *Anthoxanthum odoratum*); a fern-dominated one, mainly *Dryopteris borreri* and *Thelypteris oreopteris*; and *Calluna vulgaris–Vaccinium myrtillus*.

W.222. SHIELDAIG, ROSS   Grade 2
(a) *Mheallaidh*
NG 8353. 60 ha

The steep, north-facing slopes of Ben Shieldaig carry woodland of *Betula pubescens*. Bracken is abundant near the road, but above, *Vaccinium* and bryophytes dominate the field layer. A line of rock faces breaks across the hillside and above it Scots pine is present with the birch. In the rock gullies, oak, holly, aspen, hazel, bird-cherry and wych elm occur over a ground flora which includes *Oxalis acetosella* and *Geranium sylvaticum*. (See Appendix.)

(b) *Coille Creag Loch*
NG 8252. 70 ha
On the south slopes, Coille Creag Loch woodland is principally Scots pine with some birch. In areas of open woodland *Calluna* and *Molinia* occur but where the trees are more dense the field layer is dominated more characteristically by *Vaccinium*, *Deschampsia* and mosses. The wood is also noteworthy for good pine regeneration in places.

W.223. FIONN LOCH ISLANDS, ROSS
NG 9480. 2 ha   Grade 2
These three small wooded islands composed of Lewisian Gneiss lie at 170 m and support fragments of mixed scrub woodland in which birch is only one of several tree species. Deer browse on the islands and there is evidence of past coppicing, but the vegetation nevertheless illustrates the effects of relative freedom from disturbance.

The west island has a layer of boulders, gravel and sand over the gneiss bedrock, and has mainly birchwood, with holly, rowan, alder and ash, and a group of pines. Within the wood is a mixed growth of *Luzula sylvatica*, *Lonicera periclymenum*, *Blechnum spicant* and *Dryopteris carthusiana*. Even here regeneration of the trees appears to be limited by deer grazing. The south island is of bedrock and is covered by a dense stand of large and ancient hollies 4.5–6 m high, supporting a long-established heronry. The floor of the wood is carpeted with *Luzula sylvatica*, *Dryopteris carthusiana*, *Oxalis acetosella* and *Endymion non-scriptus*. The third island, Eilean Fraoch, is boulder covered and has a low growth of alder, birch and rowan, mixed with a luxuriant growth of *Calluna*, *Empetrum*, *Sphagnum* and hypnaceous mosses.

These islands are important in indicating that the original tree and shrub composition of north-west Highland birchwoods was a good deal more varied than at present, and that their field communities are also considerably modified by grazing.

W.224. AMAT WOOD, ROSS
NH 4790. 130 ha   Grade 2
This wood lies at 105–275 m on three sides of a low spur of Moine Schist lying between two main branches of the River Carron west of Ardgay. It consists of a mixture of Scots pine and birchwood occurring over mainly fairly acidic soils, but with richer brown earths in flushed places. Most of the bigger blocks of pine have been felled in recent years, and the remaining woodland is predominantly birch. The climate in this part of east Ross is rather similar to that in the Affric–Cannich–Strathfarrar pine and birch woods, i.e. mid-way between the extreme oceanicity of Loch Maree and the more continental conditions of the Cairngorm flanks (the other two important pinewood areas). There is thus only a moderate representation of Atlantic plants.

The pinewood has a few areas of fairly old trees, and the field layer varies as usual from the *Vaccinium*–moss type where the shade is heavy, to the more prevalent *Calluna*–moss type where the canopy is more open (the moss layer may be dominated either by *Sphagnum quinquefarium* or

hypnaceous species). There are also stands of bracken and flush bogs with *Sphagnum* spp. and grasses. Pine regeneration appears to be very sparse in the older stands. The birchwood is extensive and is mostly of the type with a grass–*Vaccinium* field layer containing a moss carpet. On rocky slopes, especially with a northerly aspect, the mosses become dominant, and form luxuriant cushions, but there are fewer oceanic liverworts and ferns than in most western birchwoods, such as that at Strathbeag, Sutherland.

This wood can be regarded as an alternative to the group in Glen Strathfarrar. If regeneration restored pine to more or less its former extent, the site would increase in value.

W.225. EILEAN NA GARTAIG, CAM LOCH, SUTHERLAND
NC 2112. 3 ha   Grade 2
This is a partly wooded island lying close to the south end of the loch at an altitude of about 120 m. The geology is not recorded, but the site may be influenced by drift from the Durness limestone at Elphin. The tree and shrub layer consists of a mixture of downy birch, rowan, holly and *Salix aurita*. There is a rich and varied herbaceous field layer on fertile brown loam, containing at least 60 species, including *Allium ursinum*, *Luzula sylvatica*, *Endymion non-scriptus*, *Geum rivale*, *Cirsium heterophyllum*, *Galium boreale*, *Scrophularia nodosa*, *Dactylorchis purpurella* and *Heracleum sphondylium*, besides the more usual species of north-west Highland birchwoods on both fairly poor and base-rich soils. Part of the island was walled to keep out cattle which used to wade over and crop the herbage, including the garlic, thereby tainting their milk.

This island wood is interesting in that it is one of the few examples of ungrazed, or lightly grazed, woodland on base-rich soils in the northern Highlands, and has an exceptionally good field layer which indicates the former composition of the community on richer soils than those of the Fionn Loch Islands.

W.226. LOCH A' MHUILLIN WOOD, SCOURIE, SUTHERLAND
NC 1737. 25 ha   Grade 2
This wood lies on Lewisian Gneiss between sea-level and 36 m, and partly encloses the small loch, extending over moderate slopes and low ridges so that most aspects are represented. The trees are mostly under 12 m and besides the dominant downy birch there are scattered oaks, rowans, aspens, hazels and willows (*Salix aurita* and *S. cinerea*). The oaks are of special interest, not only in being at the virtual northern limit for this tree in Britain but also in being predominantly *Quercus robur*, a situation comparable with the upland oakwoods of Dartmoor. From their girths, the oaks are much older than the other trees, and the birch appears mostly to have invaded strongly over a limited and relatively recent period. The soils are mostly brown loams and the prevailing field community is the *Anthoxanthum–Agrostis* grassland with herbs such as *Prunella vulgaris*, *Ranunculus ficaria*, *R. acris*, *Primula vulgaris*, *Conopodium majus* and *Viola riviniana*. Bracken is also locally dominant. There are

rather few stone blocks and outcrops so that the bryophytes consist mainly of the widely distributed species of the woodland floor, such as *Thuidium tamariscinum, Hylocomium splendens, Rhytidiadelphus loreus* and *R. triquetrus.* The woods are grazed throughout so that herbaceous plants form only a low growth and tall species are cropped into dwarfed forms.

There is no facies of birchwood here which is not represented at Inverpolly, but the site contains a typical example of northern Highland birchwood, and the occurrence of the oak enhances its interest considerably.

See also C.121 and Appendix.

W.227. LEDMORE WOOD, SPINNINGDALE, SUTHERLAND

NH 6689.   85 ha   Grade 2

This is one of the most northerly oakwoods in Britain and shows many features more characteristic of native pinewood. Although hazel, holly, hawthorn and birch occur locally with the oak, under which such plants as *Deschampsia flexuosa, Molinia caerulea, Oxalis acetosella* and *Teucrium scorodonia* and even the basiphilous grass *Brachypodium sylvaticum* are common, the most common field layer vegetation types are *Calluna vulgaris* with *Vaccinium myrtillus* and *V. vitis-idaea*, or *V. myrtillus, Erica cinerea* and *Deschampsia flexuosa*. Associated with these types juniper, rowan and Scots pine occur sparsely but are widely distributed in the oak-dominated canopy.

With its full stocking, lack of canopy stratification and regular size class of narrow crowned trees, the wood gives an even-aged appearance and it is possible that it has been planted.

W.228. MIGDALE WOODS, SUTHERLAND

NH 648907, NH 6490.   65 ha   Grade 2

Dry calcareous slabby granitic rocks are covered at the base with small pine–juniper scrub, which passes to mature pinewood with some birch in patches. The ground flora is mainly *Vaccinium*–moss but is locally rich, with *Primula vulgaris, Rhytidiadelphus triquetrus, Ajuga reptans* and *Goodyera repens*. This is one of the most northerly pinewoods, though it is probably planted. The calcareous rocks above the wood have an interesting flora, with *Helianthemum chamaecistus* abundant.

W.229. ARDVAR WOODLANDS, SUTHERLAND

NC 1833.   *c.* 65 ha   Grade 2

These woodlands which include Allt a Ghamna, Gleann Ardbhair and Gleann Leireag occur on the Lewisian Gneiss at sheltered lower elevations, close to the coast of north-west Sutherland. The topography is varied and includes steep block scree, hollows, knolls, gorges and valleys. They are composed mainly of birch, with some rowan, hazel and wych elm locally and occasional aspen and oak, and survive as important relics of the north-west forests. They are comparable to the Inverpolly Woods in quality but not in size and are put forward as an alternative site.

The field layer is characteristically *Pteridium–Agrostis–Anthoxanthum* but where protected from grazing it is rich in ferns including *Thelypteris limbosperma, Dryopteris borreri, D. dilatata* and *D. aemula.*

16 LOWLAND GRASSLANDS, HEATHS AND SCRUB

SOUTH-EAST ENGLAND

L.1. ASHDOWN FOREST, SUSSEX
TQ 4531. 2600 ha   Grade 1

Ashdown Forest, about 8 km south-east of East Grinstead, rises from about 90 to nearly 210 m and covers over 2600 ha. The area contains a range of vegetation types that includes damp woodland, heath and shallow valley mire. The soils are derived from Hastings Sands of Lower Cretaceous age.

It is difficult if not impossible to select areas of Ashdown Forest as characteristic examples of the whole, the sites of greatest ecological value being dispersed throughout the area. As with the New Forest, much of the nature conservation value resides in the large area involved, and the different heaths are regarded as one aggregate key site.

Much of the heathland vegetation of Ashdown Forest is of a humid heath or wet heath type, and there are also areas of shallow valley mire apparently caused by impeded drainage and seepage on hillsides. The Chelwood area provides a range of habitats including concentrations of gorse, *Molinia* grassland, bracken, *Calluna–Erica cinerea–E. tetralix* humid heath, scattered pines and birch. *Nardus* is especially abundant near old tracks and locally *Sieglingia decumbens* is particularly abundant. The dry heath is a *Calluna–Ulex minor* type of association. Ashdown Forest has the most inland remaining site for *Genista pilosa* in Britain. In the Duddleswell area there is an interesting *Molinia–Ulex minor* association and an area of coppiced oak on a wet heath–shallow peat covered hillside. Another feature of this particular site is the presence along a rocky stream glen of several interesting bryophytes, *Nardia compressa*, *Diphyscium foliosum*, *Hyocomium flagellare* and *Tetraphis browniana*, and the ferns *Thelypteris limbosperma* and *Dryopteris aemula*.

The valley mires have not been examined in detail, but they appear to be of an oligotrophic to weakly mesotrophic type similar to those of the New Forest and Thursley and Hankley Commons. Sites of particular interest include 'Legsheath Bog' and an area near Newbridge containing an interesting assemblage of plants including *Thelypteris palustris*, *Galium uliginosum*, *Cardamine amara*, *Myosotis secunda*, *Wahlenbergia hederacea*, *Ranunculus omiophyllus*, *Carex paniculata*, *C. curta*, *Chrysosplenium oppositifolium* and *Alnus glutinosa*.

Fallow deer are present in the Forest and sheep-grazing is at present almost confined to the Gills Lap area. The rare dragonflies *Ceriagrion tenellum* and *Somatochlora metallica* occur respectively within and on the edge of Ashdown Forest.

The area is controlled and managed by the Conservators of Ashdown Forest and is locally subject to considerable public pressure. However, certain areas of great ecological significance in the Forest are not much affected by this pressure.

L.2. THURSLEY AND HANKLEY COMMONS, SURREY
SU 9041, SU 8841. 1150 ha   Grade 1

Thursley Common near Godalming is the finest remaining piece of heathland in Surrey and has been used extensively for research and teaching purposes. The heathland communities range from dry heath through humid and wet heath to mire. The area contains an extensive valley mire complex showing a good variety of mire communities and regarded as a grade 1 site in its own right (see P.2). The soils are derived from Lower Greensand, like most of the Surrey heathlands south of the Hog's Back. To the north of the Hog's Back the heathlands are on Tertiary deposits. The dry heath is dominated by heather and locally *Ulex minor* is an important component of the vegetation. *Agrostis setacea* is not an important plant in this area; one plant has been seen near Moat Pond, whereas the plant is abundant at Chobham Common. The rarer *Deschampsia setacea* is present. As on all the Surrey heathlands, birch regeneration and to some extent pine regeneration is a problem, mainly because of the lack of grazing and controlled burning of the heathlands. Areas of pine and birch wood are present and also areas of open water.

Hankley Common, almost adjacent to Thursley, contains about 325 ha of open heather heathland, not exposed to main roads like the heathland near Frensham Pond. This is a good area for reptiles and was once a stronghold of Dartford warblers. It is bounded by a heathland golf course to the north.

Hankley Common has been included in the grade 1 site, because it provides extensive open dry heath not subject to the same woodland encroachment as the heaths of Thursley Common.

L.3. WYE AND CRUNDALE DOWNS, KENT
TR 0745, TR 0847. 415 ha   Grade 1

This site, part of which is a National Nature Reserve (NNR), has a range of woodland, scrub and grassland communities characteristic of the North Downs. The grassland on the steep scarp slopes of the Devil's Kneading Trough is of the

Brachypodium pinnatum type with, locally, an understorey of *Festuca rubra*, containing a few other species. This is characteristic of much of the Kent Chalk, but in other areas *Brachypodium* grassland is replaced by a *F. ovina* type containing most of the constants of chalk grassland and in addition 17 species of orchid, including *Aceras anthropophorum*, *Orchis purpurea*, *O. ustulata*, *Ophrys fuciflora* and *O. sphegodes*. One area has grassland which contains *Polygala austriaca*, a rare continental species restricted to a few sites in Kent, and a great variety of orchids and other rare species.

The site is known to support a very large number of rare and local species of invertebrates. Among the more notable species are the moths *Pachetra sagittigera* (very local and more or less restricted to this area in Britain) and *Siona lineata*, both of which feed on grasses, and the cicadellid bug *Athysabus argentarius*, taken here during systematic sampling. The samples of Auchenorhyncha show rather poor diversity when compared with all samples from chalk grassland of the same height but are the most diverse of those taken on Kent Chalk sites. The samples from *Brachypodium* grassland are richer than those from *Brachypodium* grassland on other sites.

Woodland has developed at the bottom of the Chalk escarpment and on the valley sides adjacent to the important areas of chalk grassland. It is primarily of ash standards with coppiced hazel beneath, and is thus more comparable with ashwoods on Chalk elsewhere than the nearby beech woodlands in similar situations. Beech does occur in the Giddy Horn. Oak and whitebeam are scattered throughout the woodland. Yew is more localised along the southern boundary of Newgate Scrubs. Dense areas of privet, elder and hawthorn occur on the woodland margins where their blossom attracts many insects from woodland and downland habitats. The field layer comprises dense stands of dog's mercury, on which *Mermaeophaga mercurialis* (Coleoptera, Chrysomelidae) is locally abundant, together with bluebell and primrose. Among the woodland herbs are *Orchis purpurea* and *Ophrys insectifera*.

These woodlands complement those centred on Crookhorn Wood, where ash woodland is not represented, and are therefore considered to be a valuable bonus to the chalk grassland areas.

L.4. CASTLE HILL, SUSSEX
TQ 3707. 190 ha   Grade 1

This has a series of south- and north-facing slopes separated by dry valleys which have been grazed for the past five years (1970) by about 400 Galloway cows and calves. The valley bottoms and less steep hillsides are planted with cereal crops. Gorse scrub occupies considerable areas of the upper slopes.

The grasslands are of the *Festuca ovina–F. rubra* type with considerable amounts of *Helictotrichon pratense* and *Koeleria cristata* and the usual spectrum of chalk grassland herbs which are well represented on other grade 1 sites. The outstanding feature of this grassland is the abundance on the southern aspects of the southern oceanic species *Phyteuma*

tenerum. The site also has a large colony of *Ophrys sphegodes*, an abundance (population of thousands) of *Gymnadenia conopsea* and scattered plants of *Silene nutans* and *Geranium columbinum*. Grassland in which *Zerna erecta* and *Brachypodium pinnatum* are dominants is also represented on this site.

The botanical interest of Castle Hill is supported by an equally rich fauna, Auchenorhyncha being well represented here including *Ulopa trivia*, *Eupelix cuspidata*, *Psammotettix cephalotes* and *Dicranoneura citrinella*. The presence of colonies of *Lysandra bellargus* and *Decticus verrucivorus* increases the entomological importance of this site considerably.

L.5. MOUNT CABURN (LEWES DOWNS), SUSSEX
460 ha   Grade 1

Lewes Downs
TQ 4310

Mount Caburn
TQ 4408

This is an isolated block of Chalk forming part of the South Downs, and has a south-facing scarp slope, a feature absent from most of the South Downs which present normally a predominantly north-facing scarp. The southerly location in the British Isles of the Lewes Downs massif is reflected in the vegetation and flora of the south-facing slopes which contain a number of continental southern and oceanic southern species such as *Polygala calcarea*, *Phyteuma tenerum* and *Rosa agrestis* in good quantity.

The grassland communities of the south-facing and south-west-facing slopes are of the *Festuca ovina–Zerna erecta–Phyteuma tenerum* type with an abundance of herbs, characteristically *Anthyllis vulneraria*, *Daucus carota*, *Filipendula vulgaris*, *Hippocrepis comosa*, *Phyteuma tenerum* and *Poterium sanguisorba*. Of special interest and unknown elsewhere in such quantity in open grassland is the presence of *Origanum vulgare*, especially in the grassland west of Brigdens Shaw and in Caburn Bottom. This species is an important food plant for the adult chalk-hill blue butterfly which occurs at this site in great quantity (August 1970).

Orchis ustulata occurs in good quantity in some years on the Mount Caburn slopes, occasionally with *Ophrys sphegodes*. Of ecological interest is the scarcity (or complete absence) of *Helianthemum chamaecistus* and the local occurrence of *Sieglingia decumbens*, the latter especially at Bible Bottom.

Systematic samples of leafhoppers were well below average in terms of diversity and the numbers of species recorded. The most notable species recorded was *Ulopa trivia* but all the other species taken were the usual ones found on most chalk grassland sites. The heteropterous fauna was quite rich and includes the ant-mimicking species *Hallodapus rufescens*. The beetle fauna was also rich and varied and includes such local species as *Apion waltoni*, *A. filirostre* and *Rhynchaenus pratensis*.

This site is well-known entomologically for butterflies

and moths, all three species of forester moths (*Adscita* spp.) occurring on parts of the Downs.

L.6. LULLINGTON HEATH, SUSSEX
TQ 5401.   63 ha   Grade 1

The site, which is a NNR, contains approximately 40 ha of chalk heath on loess soils. This was largely *Erica cinerea–Festuca ovina*-dominated sward, but since the disappearance of rabbits in the late 1950s, *Calluna* has assumed greater dominance, perhaps because it was preferentially grazed by them. *F. rubra* has also increased greatly, both in extent and growth, and has markedly reduced the floristic diversity. More significantly, gorse has spread over nearly half the Reserve, so that the best remaining areas of chalk heath today are those managed by machine mowing. The chalk heath lies mainly on the plateau, but it contains large areas of open chalk grassland, largely dominated by *F. rubra* and *Zerna erecta* over rendzina soils and steeper valley slopes. Locally, there are small developments of mixed scrub.

The scrub component is also of some interest: much of it is strongly dominated by gorse, but in some parts there is a mixture in which gorse occurs sparingly and is mixed with *Viburnum lantana*, hawthorn, bramble and occasionally privet. *Rosa pimpinellifolia* is common especially on the cut rides. In the valley bottom is a denser scrub of *Crataegus*, *Sambucus* and *Acer pseudoplatanus*.

L.7. BOX HILL–HEADLEY, SURREY
570 ha   Grade 1

Box Hill
TQ 1851

Headley Heath
TQ 2053

This area of the North Downs has a wide range of communities representative of succession on the Chalk escarpment and the overlying plateau deposits. There are areas of scrub, woodland, chalk heath, acidic heath, and chalk grassland.

Chalk grassland occurs on the escarpment slopes, and the swards are very rich, with a large number of orchid species, including *Gymnadenia conopsea*, *Anacamptis pyramidalis*, *Ophrys apifera*, *Herminium monorchis* and *Spiranthes spiralis*. *Brachypodium pinnatum* dominates much of the grassland and is spreading.

There are limited areas of chalk heathland on the dip slope and soils of the acidic plateau deposits grade into those of the Chalk in catenas on the slopes of small valleys. These are of particular interest for the prominence of *Erica cinerea* rather than *Calluna* in a sward rich in chalk grassland species.

On the plateau and dip slopes about 80 ha of almost pure *Calluna* heathland occur over acidic, sandy soils with many flint pebbles derived from the plateau deposits. These deposits may be Clay-with-Flints from the Chalk or more recent strata of Tertiary age. They form a capping over the higher ground at an altitude of 150–190 m. Where the capping is thickest there is almost pure *Calluna* with areas dominated by bracken. Towards the edges of the heathland area, bracken and birch become more abundant, presumably because of thinning out of the capping layer and admixture of material from the underlying Chalk to give a more calcareous soil. The area is much used for public recreation.

An extensive area of box *Buxus sempervirens* occurs on the steep Chalk escarpment slopes above the River Mole. Here the box is mixed with yew and occasionally ash, and typical field layer species include *Gentianella amarella*, *Sedum acre*, *Mercurialis perennis* and rarely *Teucrium botrys*. Scrub of yew and juniper occurs in another area, and although there are only some 70 juniper bushes, the fauna includes the juniper scale *Carulaspis juniperi* and its predator *Aleuropteryx juniperi*, the latter known only from this site. Elsewhere areas of southern mixed scrub have a good field layer of herbs including *Helleborus foetidus*, *Inula conyza* and *Aceras anthropophorum*.

The woodland of Box Hill and White Hill comprises a wide range of characteristic chalk scarp and plateau woodland and scrub and other local types. Box Hill itself has beechwood on shallow rendzina soils with some pedunculate oak, ash and gean, which grades into beech–oak wood and locally oak–birch wood on the Clay-with-Flints plateau. On some cleared valley sites ashwood is developing. The shrub layer consists mainly of the three evergreens, holly, yew and box, the latter predominating on the thin soils on and near the scarp slopes, and the former two forming a locally continuous understorey on the plateau. Within this, there is a wide range of other shrub species and even trees such as large-leaved lime *Tilia platyphyllos* in a possibly native location. Structurally, the stands are fairly uniform, but recent forestry operations and death of mature beeches have facilitated natural regeneration of ash, birch and shrub species on the chalk soils. Similar developments on the plateau have enabled gean, oak and holly to regenerate. Beneath the closed canopy the field layer is sparse, but dog's mercury occurs on the calcareous soils and the Clay-with-Flints supports a community of honeysuckle, bracken, bramble and wood sage. Towards Headley Warren there is another area of beechwood. The whole site is rich in calcicolous herbs, *Cephalanthera damasonium*, *Aquilegia vulgaris* and *Ajuga chamaepitys* included.

The area is particularly interesting entomologically. The large heteropterous bug *Gonocerus acuteangulatus* which occurs here is not known from anywhere else in Britain. Systematic samples of grassland species contained below average numbers of species of Auchenorhyncha, probably because the areas sampled had been recently burned. The uncommon species *Ulopa trivia* however occurred in abundance, and the rare *Tottigometra impressopuncta* was taken. The silver-spotted skipper butterfly was quite abundant in 1968. The samples from the chalk grassland at Headley Warren were the richest and most diverse of the whole *Review* as far as Auchenorhyncha were concerned. The Heteroptera were almost equally rich and there are a number of uncommon species of which *Catoplatus fabricii*, *Drymus pilicornis* and *Acalypta carinata* are especially notable. The presence of *Leptopterna dolabrata* on chalk grassland is unusual. The weevil fauna contains several species of interest, such as *Apion flavimanum* and *A. filirostre*. Headley Heath is a noted site for the Duke of Burgundy butterfly *Hamearis lucina*.

L.8. HARTING DOWN, SUSSEX
SU 8018.   200 ha   Grade 1

Here there is a large juniper scrub with bushes of a wide range of sizes, and with some regeneration at the northern end. Amongst the other scrub species present, yew and hawthorn are the most prominent. A chalk heath with some *Calluna* and *Erica cinerea* occurs on the areas bearing a Clay-with-Flints capping, which contrasts strikingly with the wholly calcareous nature of the juniper scrub. Grassland is of the *Festuca ovina–F. rubra* type with some *Zerna erecta*. The samples of Auchenorhyncha from the grassland exhibited some unusual features. The presence of *Errastunus occelaris* was notable as it was recorded in only two other samples from chalk grassland during the review; it is not, however, a rare species. Although Coleoptera other than weevils have not been recorded systematically during the review the presence of extremely large numbers of *Stenus* sp. (Staphylinidae) was notable.

L.9. KINGLEY VALE, SUSSEX
SU 8210.   160 ha   Grade 1*

This site, which is a NNR, is very well known for its extensive yew woodlands. These occur in various stages of succession and some relatively young areas can be regarded as in the scrub category. The main areas of this type are on the western slopes of Kingley Bottom, and on the steep slopes of the extension towards Goosehill Camp. The former is an almost pure stand of closed canopy young yew, while the latter has older trees that are more widely separated, with dogwood, hawthorn, bramble and old man's beard in the glades. The area just below the Camp is where the largest numbers (some 70) of the remaining old juniper bushes occur, and here too is open *Festuca* grassland with many of the typical chalk herbs.

   On the plateau is a limited area of chalk heath over Clay-with-Flints. The community grades from chalk grassland dominated by *Festuca ovina*, *Helictotrichon pubescens* and *Poterium sanguisorba* with occasional *Calluna* bushes to heathy scrub with *Ulex europaeus*, *Calluna* and *Erica cinerea* interspersed with hawthorn, blackthorn, brambles and scattered *P. sanguisorba*.

   See also W.10.

L.10. WOULDHAM–DETLING ESCARPMENT, KENT
TQ 723649–794588.   440 ha   Grade 1

This is a very varied and extensive area (*c.* 13 km long) of the North Downs escarpment and has various mixtures of scrub types, mostly on abandoned fields, and nearly all with high woody species diversity. Most of the mixtures have hawthorn as the dominant woody species, but one interesting area which may have reverted from ploughed land is strongly dominated by dogwood, while in other areas *Viburnum lantana* is prominent. On Boxley Warren there is

an area of regenerating beech mixed with mainly hawthorn. It is noticeable that *Euonymus* is generally commoner than usual. *Rosa pimpinellifolia* occurs in patches, and there is a good range of species in the field layer including *Daphne laureola*, *Iris foetidissima* and *Atropa belladonna*. Among the other features of the area are extensive quarries at Bluebell Hill, various woods of yew and beech as well as hazel coppice. There are limited areas of grassland, mostly of *Zerna erecta*. One systematic sample of the Auchenorhyncha in grassland was surprisingly rich and with a very high diversity of species. It would be possible to reclaim some areas from scrub to chalk grassland to increase the diversity of the site. This area is also grade 1 on its woodland evaluation (W.7).

L.11. HALLING–TROTTISCLIFFE, KENT
TQ 705665–623600.   650 ha   Grade 1

This is another very extensive area of the North Downs with many interesting areas of scrub of the southern mixed type grading to areas dominated by hawthorn and dogwood. *Euonymus* is common in places and *Rosa pimpinellifolia* occurs occasionally. In the open scrub areas the ground flora tends to be dominated by *Brachypodium sylvaticum* and includes the usual range of herbs. In the damper areas are found *Succisa pratensis*, *Valeriana officinalis* and *Campanula trachelium*. The grasslands are not extensive, but again some reclamation from scrub could be undertaken. The entomological importance of the grassland is extremely high. The site is the only one in England today where the moth *Caloptilia leucapennella* occurs. Many other species of rare and local Lepidoptera are still found in the area. The Coleoptera are also notable, with the weevils *Apion millum* and *Ceuthorhynchus moelleri* occurring, among others. The heteropterous fauna is also rich; *Deraeocoris scutellaris*, a very uncommon species, was taken in the systematic samples. The Auchenorhyncha fauna recorded in the samples, however, was not particularly rich. The site contains woodlands of beech, oak and ash and there are also a number of quarries.

   See also W.6.

L.12. WHITE DOWNS, SURREY
TQ 1249.   225 ha   Grade 1

This large area of the escarpment of the North Downs has various scrub mixtures and different soil types. Along the main steep part of the Chalk escarpment it consists of abandoned fields in different stages of succession, and these are mostly of fairly open southern mixed scrub types with hawthorn as the commonest species. There is some light rabbit-grazing, and the field layer is fairly diverse in many places although in others the coarser grasses are commoner, and *Zerna erecta* may be dominant. Only one systematic sample of the grassland fauna was taken, and this contained below average numbers of species of Auchenorhyncha, Heteroptera and Curculionoidea. Towards the western end of the site is an interesting stand of juniper and yew. This is in a fairly advanced seral stage with high woody species diversity, and there are some very fine old juniper bushes perhaps 50–75 years of age. Although this is not a very extensive stand and shows no regeneration it is the best juniper site remaining on the North Downs, and the only one still supporting the full juniper fauna. On the Clay-with-Flints plateau the calcareous scrub grades into rough grassland with gorse as the dominant species. At the western end of the site there is a thinned ashwood together with a stand of *Sarothamnus* on the Greensand.

L.13. IPING AND AMBERSHAM COMMONS, SUSSEX
SU 8422, SU 9119.   265 ha   Grade 2

These two heathlands, on soils derived from the Lower Greensand, are situated about 3 km to the west, and about 3 km to the south-east of Midhurst. These two areas are typical of the Sussex commons, which are mainly confined to these soils.

They are both areas mainly of dry heath with some coloni-sation of birch and pine. Small areas of bog and wet heath are present, with more bog at Ambersham Common. Iping Common was the only Sussex site for *Agrostis setacea* but it is thought to have been lost by road widening. The moss *Dicranum spurium* has been recorded.

These two sites are the best remaining pieces of heathland in west Sussex and while providing good representative pieces of heathland are probably more valuable for their invertebrate fauna (including spiders) than their botanical interest.

The sites are partly complementary, Iping having prob-ably the richer dry heath fauna and Ambersham the richer wet heath and bog fauna. In recent years Ambersham has suffered more from fires, which may account for some of the differences in the dry heath fauna. Some 109 species of spiders were recorded from Iping and 84 from Ambersham, the overall total for the two sites being 122; these are high totals in view of the small amount of collecting done. Notable rarities from Iping are *Centromerus aequalis*, which was recorded here for the first time in Britain but which has since been recorded from two woodland sites, *Micaria silesiaca* and *Prosopotheca corniculans*. Rare species at Ambersham were *P. corniculans* and *Zora silvestris*, the latter being only the fourth record for Britain. Numerous characteristic heathland species were recorded, and the fauna of both sites appears to combine certain features of the Thursley region with features of parts of the New Forest. Ambersham is close to the Heyshott Down chalk grassland site (L.16) which is also notable for two very rare spiders, *Tapinocyboides pygmaea* known in Britain only from here and from near Edinburgh, and *Pelecopsis radicicola* recorded only here and from Rodney Stoke.

Archaeological excavations on a site at Iping Common have demonstrated the presence of a Maglemosian flint industry of the Mesolithic period.

L.14. CHOBHAM COMMON, SURREY
SU 9764.   680 ha   Grade 2

Chobham Common lies about 5 km north-west of Woking and is the most extensive piece of heathland on Tertiary deposits in the London Basin not occupied by the Ministry of Defence. The heathland is between about 30 and 70 m above sea-level; a central ridge running north-east to south-west crosses the area and the lower-lying regions to the north-west and south-east contain the damper parts of the site.

The areas of dry heath at Chobham bear a marked similarity to the dry heathland of Dorset and the New Forest in that *Agrostis setacea* and *Ulex minor* are important components of the vegetation. *A. setacea* is only rarely found in the Lower Greensand heathlands in Surrey and Sussex to the south of the Hog's Back. The damper valleys contain a number of bog and wet heath species including *Gentiana pneumonanthe* and *Lycopodium inundatum*, but do not approach the quality of wet heath and bog sites elsewhere.

Chobham Common has long been known as a site of outstanding faunal interest, both for birds and for a number of rare and local insects. The latter include the myrmeco-philous mirid *Myrmecoris gracilis*, the saldid *Micracanthia marginalis* and the ant *Formica rufibarbis* known elsewhere in Britain only from the Isles of Scilly.

Chobham is also well known for its spiders. The out-standing rarity is *Oxyopes heterophthalmus*, for which Chobham Common is the only known extant British locality; it was first found at Chobham Common in 1960, and has been seen on a number of subsequent occasions, mainly on the heathery slopes near Gracious Pond. Almost as rare is *Cheiracanthium pennyi*, and other notable rarities are *Uloborus walckenaerius*, *Micaria subopaca*, *Araneus alsine* and *Thomisus onustus*. Apart from the rarities, the spider fauna of Chobham Common appears to be rather different from that of Thursley Common and other heaths in that area, and shows both south-eastern and New Forest ele-ments in its fauna. It is possible that its faunal richness is partly related to its position in the London Basin, with its small climatic differences from the Greensand heaths farther south. (See Appendix.)

L.15. FOLKESTONE–ETCHINGHILL ESCARPMENT, KENT
TR 171385–231382.   205 ha   Grade 2

This long, narrow strip of a south-facing scarp is situated to the north of Hythe, and contains a variety of communities ranging from ash woodland, scrub, and rough grassland to areas of shorter *Festuca ovina* grassland. This site is a fine example of Kentish downland with a grassland rich in orchids, and it is an alternative site to Wye and Crundale Downs. Scrub on upper parts of the slopes consists mainly of gorse in *Brachypodium pinnatum* grassland.

Arpinge Down is not on record as being extensively surveyed for invertebrates. The floriferous *Festuca* grass-land was below average in diversity of Auchenorhyncha, although the *Brachypodium* grassland was about average, only six and ten species having been recorded, respectively. The weevil fauna is rich and includes *Alophus triguttatus*, a local species, and the Essex skipper butterfly was recorded.

See also W.5.

L.16. HEYSHOTT DOWN, SUSSEX
SU 8916.   40 ha   Grade 2

This is a small area of chalk grassland and scrub on the South Downs escarpment whose main interest is the abundance of mosses and liverworts in the old chalk workings and surrounding grassland, including several northern and north-western species not normally associated with the Chalk, and unknown elsewhere on the Chalk. Examples are *Hylocomium brevirostre*, *Rhytidiadelphus loreus*, *Antitrichia curtipendula*, *Rhacomitrium lanuginosum* and *Solenostoma triste*. There is a good representation of scrub species and *Rosa rubiginosa* is particularly common.

A large number of species of Auchenorhyncha has been recorded, probably owing to the intimate 'patchy' mixture of long and short grassland which occurs. The heteropterous fauna is rich, and *Cymus glandicolor* appears to breed here. This species is often abundant in marshy places feeding on *Carex* spp. but seems only recently to have colonised chalk grassland, where it probably feeds on *C. flacca*; very few other chalk grassland sites for this species are known.

L.17. PURPLE HILL AND QUEENDOWN WARREN, KENT
TQ 8162, TQ 8263.   45 ha   Grade 2

These two adjacent areas of downland with grassland of the *Festuca ovina–F. rubra* type have considerable quantities of *Carex flacca* and are well known for their variety of chalk grassland plants and especially for the abundance of orchids, 19 species of which occur here including *Orchis purpurea*, *O. ustulata*, *Ophrys sphegodes*, *Aceras anthropophorum* and *Spiranthes spiralis*.

Purple Hill and Queendown Warren scored only an average number of Auchenorhyncha in the systematic samples. *Neophilaenus campestris* (Cercopidae) occurs here but at relatively few other sites. The heteropterous fauna is particularly rich and includes the ant-mimicking mirid *Systellonotus triguttatus* (not recorded on any other chalk grassland site during the review). The weevil fauna is very varied and includes such uncommon species as *Smicronyx reichi*. The butterfly fauna is well-known, and is said to include the Adonis blue (1968 record).

L.18. THERFIELD HEATH, HERTFORDSHIRE
TL 3340.   85 ha   Grade 2

Although the greater part of this site is used as a golf course and general recreational area, parts of the Heath, notably at Church Hill, contain old chalk grassland which has claim to be one of the richest areas of chalk grassland in England, comparable in floristic composition with Knocking Hoe, yet differing in some important aspects. Unlike Knocking Hoe, *Seseli libanotis* and *Onobrychis viciifolia* are absent, while *Astragalus danicus*, *Thalictrum minus* and *Thesium humifusum* are present. *Anemone pulsatilla* is present in great quantity, with at least six species of orchid. This site is a good example of the East Anglian type of chalk grassland.

This site was not sampled zoologically for the *Review*; at one time it was a *locus classicus* for aberrations of the chalk-

hill blue butterfly, but has not otherwise been worked intensively for invertebrate animals.

L.19. FULKING ESCARPMENT/NEWTIMBER HILL, SUSSEX
TQ 209108–267114, TQ 2712.   370 ha   Grade 2

The chalk heath in this area is limited in extent and considerably overgrown. It is nevertheless particularly interesting because of the exceptionally acid deep clay soil (pH 4.3–5.1) over which it occurs and because of the evidence of interesting acidification associated with seral development to the present vegetation. The chalk heath community is now largely dominated by gorse: heather is restricted to anthills. Other species include *Betonica officinalis* but the only strongly calcicolous species present are *Helictotrichon pratense*, *Filipendula vulgaris* and *Poterium sanguisorba*. The area was heavily rabbit-grazed in the past, and at that time comprised a good sward of chalk heathland largely made up of calcicolous species with *Calluna* and other calcifuges of very limited extent. The area is thus a particularly valuable one for research on the changes following relaxation of grazing on chalk heaths, and on the tendency of these heaths to increasing acidification.

This site also has good scrub areas and on the lower slopes, near the road at Saddlescombe, is an area with some 200 junipers showing regeneration, representing the most easterly of the juniper sites on the South Downs. There is also an area in which *Viburnum lantana* is unusually common, and the plateau of the hill bears a scrub with gorse and hawthorn. The inclusion of Devil's Dyke in this site brings an interesting transition zone between the chalk scrub, on the escarpment, and the gorse on the Clay-with-Flints plateau.

SOUTH ENGLAND

L.20. NEW FOREST HEATHS, HAMPSHIRE
SU 31.   16 400 ha   Grade 1*

The New Forest is a large area, containing 37 560 ha within the New Forest perambulation, of which 27 120 ha are Crown Lands. Of these 7950 ha are Statutory Inclosures and of the unenclosable land 3640 ha are woodland and 14 370 ha are heathland, acidic grassland and valley mire. In the aggregate, this is the largest area of lowland acidic heath remaining in Britain. The New Forest lies almost entirely on Eocene and Oligocene deposits of the Hampshire Basin, but the distribution of heathland and woodland is largely related to the occurrence of different deposits. The heathland is found mainly on the deposits of Plateau Gravel, Bagshot Sands, Bracklesham Beds and Barton Sands.

The dry heathland vegetation of the New Forest is essentially a *Calluna–Ulex minor* association but variations in degrees of grazing, burning, past land-use history and edaphic factors such as soil moisture, produce a great variety of associated plant communities from dry heath including large areas of gorse, especially on old field systems, humid heath dominated by *Calluna* and *Erica tetralix* and wet heath to valley mire. Examples of these valley mires include Cranesmoor, White Moor, Denny Bog, Wilverley Bog and Hincheslea Bottom, all of which are described separately under Peatlands. *Agrostis setacea* is one of the most abundant grasses on the dry heaths. There are no plant species peculiar to the New Forest heaths, such as *E. vagans* on the Lizard or *E. ciliaris* in Dorset, although the latter may have once been present and have been lost by introgressive hybridisation into the *E. tetralix* population. Several local plants of lowland heaths are well represented in the Forest, e.g. *Gentiana pneumonanthe, Cicendia filiformis, Hammarbya paludosa* and other particularly interesting species include *Gladiolus illyricus, Ludwigia palustris, Illecebrum verticillatum* and *Galium debile*. It can be seen that the greatest interest in terms of pure floristics is found in the wetter areas but these depend very much upon the surrounding areas of acidic heathland for maintenance of their condition.

Ornithologically the dry heaths are important as the nesting habitat of Dartford warblers, nightjars and red-backed shrikes (in tall scrub), and as the hunting areas of hobbies. The sand lizard and smooth snake occur locally, but reptiles in general depend on the damp valley mires in summer and these are also important dragonfly habitats. Heaths within the open forest provide habitats for a very interesting assemblage of insects, many of which are at the northern limit of their range in Britain. The fauna is almost certainly less rich than that of the woodland but includes important species of Orthoptera, Hemiptera, Lepidoptera, Coleoptera, Hymenoptera–Aculeate and Diptera.

The great value of the New Forest is undoubtedly in its overall large size and the diversity of habitats and plant communities that it contains as a whole. Individual heathland areas of special interest have therefore not been defined, for it is felt that, as with Ashdown Forest, the area should be treated as one large conservation unit.

See also W.26, OW.6 and P.3.

L.21. ASTON ROWANT, OXFORDSHIRE
SU 7297. 130 ha   Grade 1

This site (a large part of which is a NNR), together with the leased areas of Bald Hill and the grassland between Bald Hill and Beacon Hill, is a fine example of the Chiltern scarp vegetation and includes beechwood, mixed scrub communities, juniper scrub and chalk grassland. The grassland is mostly of the *Festuca ovina–Carex flacca–Poterium sanguisorba* type in which *Helianthemum chamaecistus* and *Thymus drucei* are usually frequent. In addition to the constants of chalk grasslands, several rare species occur here, including *Iberis amara, Gentianella germanica* and the recently discovered *Nardurus maritimus*. On the north-facing slope adjacent to Beacon Hill a *Helictotrichon pubescens* grassland has developed, giving a grassland type uncommon on the Chalk. The variety of aspects found at Aston Rowant makes this an important site for research, and it is being used intensively by the Nature Conservancy for management experiments using sheep.

Aston Rowant was originally valued for its scrub interests and still retains high interest in regard to this feature. The main scrub area is on Beacon Hill where all the common woody species occur in a variety of mixtures. *Thelycrania sanguinea, Ligustrum vulgare* and *Viburnum lantana* are the commonest towards the lower part of the hill, while juniper is common over a rabbit-grazed area around the middle level. The ground flora is fairly rich and includes deadly nightshade, but invading trees are not very numerous and consist mainly of beech, ash and yew. Towards the Beacon Hill woodland, the scrub becomes taller and thicker, and beech and ash more prominent, in later successional stages. The field layer here is also coarser, with *Arrhenatherum elatius, Dactylis glomerata, Arctium minus* and *Urtica dioica*. Additional scrub of some interest occurs in the grazed parts of the dry coombes of Beacon Hill and Bald Hill, where there is some of the best juniper regeneration in the Chilterns.

As a result of recent survey Aston Rowant is known to support populations of some extremely uncommon invertebrates. The cicadellid bug *Euscelis venosus*, only very recently added to the British list, occurs here in numbers and the rare weevils *Brachysomus hirtus* and *Ceuthorhynchus moelleri* have been recorded. Both have an extremely restricted range in Britain and are almost exclusively confined to chalk grassland. Bald Hill is a locality for some uncommon lygaeid bugs. In the systematic samples taken here Auchenorhyncha, Heteroptera and Curculionoidea were all reasonably well represented but diversity was not outstandingly high and no rare species were recorded.

See also W.29.

L.22. ASTON UPTHORPE DOWN, BERKSHIRE
SU 5482. 40 ha   Grade 1

The primary interest in this site is the extensive stand of juniper (the best example left in the Berkshire Downs) on the sides of a steep side-valley which extends for about 1 km into the scarp slope. Juniper is most abundant on the northeast-facing slope but also occurs on the south-west-facing slope in a variety of forms ranging from low spreading bushes to columnar forms, 4.5 m high. On the steep west-facing slope there is a good mixed scrub with privet, wayfaring tree, dogwood, hawthorn, hazel and a little juniper. The scrub ground flora has a good range of herbs including deadly nightshade, and the juniper fauna is also interesting. The grassland is of the *Festuca ovina* type mixed with *Zerna erecta*, with a moderate number of associates, including *Filipendula vulgaris, Hippocrepis comosa, Senecio integrifolius, Scabiosa columbaria, Polygala calcarea* and *Anemone pulsatilla*. There is invasion by patches of *Brachypodium pinnatum* at the upper end of the site.

Invertebrate samples from Aston Upthorpe Down had high ratings for diversity of the Auchenorhyncha fauna, although no rarities were taken. The area is otherwise unrecorded for insects.

L.23. COMPTON DOWN, ISLE OF WIGHT, HAMPSHIRE
SZ 3685. 40 ha   Grade 1

This is the best example of chalk downland strongly influenced by maritime conditions and lies at the southern limit of the Chalk in England. The area includes a steep south-facing slope above the sea where insolation and exposure to maritime conditions are strongest. These conditions are reflected in the appearance of the grassland which is open with considerable areas of Chalk rubble similar to the structure seen on the Jurassic limestone grasslands developed on steep slopes. *Anthyllis vulneraria* and *Hippocrepis comosa* are unusually common under these conditions, with a good variety of other chalk species. Of special note is the presence of one bush of juniper, a large colony of *Gentianella anglica* and extensive patches of *Orchis morio* and *O. mascula*. On the more gently sloping areas, which are covered with superficial deposits, there is a well-developed gorse scrub with associated species.

Compton Down is well known for its numbers of uncommon Lepidoptera, some of them associated with maritime conditions. Three samples were taken, all scoring well above average in terms of species of Auchenorhyncha recorded. Some notable species of Heteroptera and Curculionoidea occurred in the samples, the rarest being the weevil *Apion millum*. A notable feature of the samples taken was the absence of the very characteristic cicadellid bug *Turrutus socialis* from the sample collected at the top of the sea cliff. This maritime influence was also shown in the occurrence of the weevil *Ceuthorhynchidius dawsonii*, associated with *Plantago coronopus*. Butterflies include chalk-hill, Adonis and small blues, dark green fritillary, with marbled white on the north face of the Downs, and Glanville fritillary on the nearby undercliff. This is a landfall area for migrant butterflies, including clouded yellow and Berger's clouded yellow *Colias australis*.

The adjacent Afton Down is a good example of maritime Chalk cliffs with a good flora and should be included in the key site. This site adjoins a grade 1 coastal site (C.10).

L.24. MARTIN DOWN, HAMPSHIRE
SU 0419.   115 ha   Grade 1

Situated on the Hampshire–Wiltshire border, this extensive area of chalk downland, heath and scrub has a combination of scientific interest not found elsewhere.

First, at least three types of chalk heath are represented here: plateau edge type, grading into stripes downslopes; coombe-bottom type and a loessic type developed on flat ground which was ploughed during the mediaeval period. These are developed on the Tertiary residues spread across the crest of the plateau, on the plateau edge, on Tertiary-derived downwash in the valley floors and on the crowns of broad-rig ploughing marks. The coombe-bottom type is characterised by dominance of *Calluna*, *Erica cinerea*, *Ulex minor* and *U. europaeus* while in grassy patches *Anthoxanthum odoratum*, *Rumex acetosella* and *Galium saxatile* form an interesting society with *Polytrichum* spp., *Dicranum scoparium*, *Cladonia rangiformis* and other *Cladonia* spp. Those associations are probably the best of their type in England, and in the interest of their species composition and structure, surpass those at Lullington Heath. The general chalk grassland area includes many exacting calcicoles, notably *Carex humilis*, *Anacamptis pyramidalis*,

Orchis ustulata, *Ophrys apifera* and *Senecio integrifolius*, and their absence from the immediately adjacent chalk heath makes the whole area very valuable for comparative study.

Secondly, the valley grassland in which *Zerna erecta* is the dominant contains a wide variety of forbs, including *Hippocrepis comosa* and *Polygala calcarea*, while locally there are large colonies of *Orchis mascula*, *O. morio* and *Dactylorchis fuchsii*.

Finally, the land-use of this area is well documented, exact dating being available for various agricultural activities, and provides a first-class opportunity for studying the influence of historical factors on the present-day vegetation.

The chalk heath contains a number of insects associated with acidophilous vegetation. Samples were taken, however, only from the chalk grassland, in which the representation of species of Auchenorhyncha was about average, no rarities being recorded. Hen harriers (in winter) and hobbies regularly hunt over the area, and Montagu's harrier appears occasionally.

There are also extensive areas of scrub, principally of hawthorn and gorse in chalk heath, but juniper is absent.

L.25. OLD WINCHESTER HILL, HAMPSHIRE
SU 6420.   80 ha   Grade 1

This site (which is also a NNR) contains all stages in the sere from open grassland through scrub to mature woodland and is important for the study of successional changes. The two south-facing slopes have a *Festuca ovina*-dominant grassland with a wide range of calcicoles, including, on the slope below the Iron Age camp, one of the best stands of *Phyteuma tenerum* in England. This species is associated here with *Anthyllis vulneraria*, *Hippocrepis comosa* and *Succisa pratensis* in addition to large colonies of *Coeloglossum viride*, *Gymnadenia conopsea* and *Platanthera chlorantha* growing in open grassland. Juniper, mixed with yew and whitebeam, is conspicuous on this slope, which contrasts strongly with the moss-rich, north-facing slope. There is also a good deal of hawthorn scrub. The small area of chalk heath developed on the Clay-with-Flints cap has additional interest.

One systematic sample from Old Winchester Hill grassland scored well above average in the number of species of Auchenorhyncha recorded and contained two species of particular interest, but very few Heteroptera or Curculionoidea were present. The second sample was from very short grassland, where very few insects occurred. A fairly good butterfly fauna has been recorded from the site.

The escarpments within the Reserve bear patches of pure yew and there is about 4 ha of mainly planted woodland dominated by beech with ash, sycamore, larch, spruce and Turkey oak. The adjacent Peake Wood lies on the west-facing slope with Clay-with-Flints and extends to the heavy clays on the floor of the Meon valley. The bulk of this woodland is old hazel coppice though there is a small area of oak plus beech with yew and Scots pine. Intermixed with the hazel are a few conifers, and larger quantities of ash, field maple, beech and oak. Other woody species include white-beam, crab apple, hawthorn and wayfaring tree, primarily in the understorey. The field layer is dominated by *Mercurialis perennis* and *Endymion non-scriptus* with *Anemone nemorosa*, *Viola* spp., *Circaea lutetiana*, *Geranium robertianum*, *Sanicula europaea*, *Arum maculatum*, *Galium odoratum* and *Listera ovata*. Rarer plant species include *Ornithogalum umbellatum* and *Ophrys insectifera*.

L.26. PEWSEY DOWNS, WILTSHIRE
SU 1163.   90 ha   Grade 1

The Chalk escarpment north of the Vale of Pewsey extends for 22 km from Beacon Hill in the west to Martinsell Camp in the east. The central part of this scarp comprising most of Milk Hill, Walkers Hill and Knap Hill and designated Pewsey Downs, is the most important (and is a NNR). The grasslands of this scarp, which is almost completely free of scrub, are of the *Festuca ovina–F. rubra* type with *Carex flacca*, *Poterium sanguisorba* and *Cirsium acaulon* as constants. There is a general abundance of *Zerna erecta* but little *Brachypodium pinnatum*. *Hippocrepis comosa* and *Anthyllis vulneraria* are frequent, but the special floristic feature of the Pewsey Downs is the presence of *Serratula tinctoria*, *Polygala calcarea*, *Orchis morio*, *Thesium humifusum* and colonies of hybrids between the rare *Cirsium tuberosum* and *C. acaulon*. This north Wiltshire type of grassland from which *Carex humilis* is absent contrasts strongly with the following group in which *C. humilis* is a constant.

The two samples taken from Pewsey Downs were remarkably poor in species of Auchenorhyncha – no obvious reason for this is apparent. The Reserve supports a number of interesting species of weevil, e.g. *Miarus graminis*, *Liophloeus nubilus* and *Strophosomus faber*, though none of these is rare. The heteropterous bug *Sehirus dubius* is notable; it is associated only with *Thesium humifusum*, a plant particularly of chalk grassland. The area has long been known for a variety of the chalk-hill blue butterfly, but this has not been seen in recent years.

At the eastern end of Pewsey Downs is a small woodland, Gopher Wood, over Clay-with-Flints on the edge of the scarp. Ash is dominant on the south-facing slope whereas pedunculate oak is most abundant as coppiced stools on the plateau. Common lime, field maple, yew and whitebeam are also present in the canopy. The shrub layer contains hazel, mainly on the plateau, with hawthorn, spindle, wayfaring tree and blackthorn predominantly on the margins. The ground flora includes *Brachypodium sylvaticum* and *Endymion non-scriptus* as dominants with *Mercurialis perennis* and *Allium ursinum* locally abundant. The herb layer is species-rich with *Filipendula ulmaria*, *Silene dioica*, *Listera ovata*, *Orchis mascula*, *Polygonatum multiflorum*, *Paris quadrifolia* and *Lathraea squamaria*.

This is a valuable area of bonus woodland, too small to be of grade 1 status in its own right, but important for pedological studies. (Like Alkham Valley Woods it has a deep soil in a situation normally possessing shallow soils.)

South-west Wiltshire Downs

To the west of Salisbury along the valleys made by the rivers Wylye and Ebble are scattered blocks of downland which are of unrivalled scientific interest to grassland ecologists. This interest stems from the presence of *Carex humilis* as the dominant or co-dominant species in the sward. *C. humilis*, placed by Matthews in the continental southern element of the flora, is restricted in England to the south-west with its main centre of distribution in Dorset and Wiltshire. On the Continent, however, it is present in xerophilous steppe grasslands with *Stipa* and no satisfactory explanation has yet been given for its absence from the more continental-like chalk grasslands in England. *C. humilis* grasslands may be one of the oldest grassland ecosystems in England, and their outstanding feature is floristic richness, 38–45 species of vascular plants and mosses per square metre being an average total. A group of species, including *Thesium humifusum*, *Serratula tinctoria*, *Hippocrepis comosa*, *Betonica officinalis* with *C. flacca* and *C. caryophyllea* form a distinct variant of chalk grassland which has yet to be described. The number of sites where *C. humilis* forms extensive stands in the British Isles is probably about 40, most of which are in Wiltshire, and nine sites have been selected which together cover the whole range of variation encountered in this grassland type.

Almost no entomological work has been done in south Wiltshire, except on the Lepidoptera, so that there is practically no information about the insects of the south-west Wiltshire Downs apart from that obtained during the review.

L.27. WYLYE DOWN, WILTSHIRE
SU 0036.   45 ha   Grade 1

An area of uniformly high-quality grassland occurs here on west- and east-facing slopes with a small amount of north-facing slope, and has been grazed for the past 25 years by Ayrshire dairy cattle. The grassland, which contains about 40–45 species per square metre, is developed over a complex of Celtic Field systems which rate highly in archaeological interest. *Carex humilis* is co-dominant with *Festuca ovina*, with lesser amounts of *C. flacca*, *C. caryophyllea*, *Briza media* and eight other grass species. The number of associated herbs is about 50, and includes species of restricted distribution such as *Thesium humifusum*, *Anthyllis vulneraria*, *Hippocrepis comosa*, *Serratula tinctoria*, *Orchis morio*, *O. mascula*, *O. ustulata*, *Coeloglossum viride*, *Ophrys apifera*, *Gymnadenia conopsea*, *Anacamptis pyramidalis* and *Saxifraga granulata*. Despite variation on a local scale, the outstanding feature of this grassland is its unusual structural and floristic uniformity over a large area.

Moribund juniper also occurs on the site, and in rough grassland the rare *Cirsium tuberosum* occurs together with hybrids with *C. acaulon*.

The sample taken from the grassland of the east-facing slope at Wylye Down was richer in species of Auchenorhyncha than that from the west-facing slope, scoring well above average. Several species of local occurrence elsewhere on the Chalk were taken. The heteropterous fauna was also rich and the weevils included *Trachyphloeus alternans*, not uncommon on the eastern Chalk, but apparently much rarer in Wiltshire.

L.28. PRESCOMBE DOWN, WILTSHIRE
ST 9825.   45 ha   Grade 1

This is a steep Chalk scarp with a wide range of aspects from east to west and with projecting spurs and deep flat-bottomed valleys of geomorphological interest. The grass-land varies in floristic composition with aspect, from the *Carex humilis–Festuca ovina* type on the south-west-facing aspects to a *F. ovina–C. flacca* type on the east-facing aspects. The variety of forbs in the grassland is high, and includes *Gentianella anglica* and *Polygala calcarea* in addi-tion to many orchids. The area is grazed by sheep, and occasionally horses. Small pockets of scrub occur in the valley bottoms and a few *Sambucus nigra* shrubs around rabbit warrens. The flora of this south-facing scarp con-trasts strikingly with the north-facing aspect running from Fovant Down to Whitesheet Hill.

The numbers of invertebrate species in the samples taken at Prescombe Down were about average and lacked any great rarities. The homopterous bug *Kelisia perspicillata* has been recorded at only a few other sites during the review.

L.29. KNIGHTON DOWNS, WILTSHIRE
SU 0524.   195 ha   Grade 1

An area of sheep- and cattle-grazed downland, fragmented into three portions by arable land, is here treated as a unit. All aspects are represented in the block, with a variety of slopes, degrees of grazing and varying botanical composi-tion. Some areas, particularly those on the north- to south-facing slopes, are especially rich in species, 38–42 per square metre being common; and in this area *Carex humilis* is the dominant, with *Festuca ovina*, and the usual wide variety of other grasses and herbs which is associated with this grass-land type. *Thesium humifusum* is unusually abundant in some areas, with *Succisa pratensis* and *Serratula tinctoria*. The variety of aspects and opportunity for adequate replication makes this site of great value for ecological research.

In samples from the Knighton Hill complex of sites an average number of species of Auchenorhyncha and Hetero-ptera was taken, but both samples were rich in species of Curculionoidea, particularly *Apion* spp. The lygaeid bug *Drymus pilicornis*, an uncommon species, was taken in one sample.

L.30. STEEPLE LANGFORD, COW DOWN AND
CLIFFORD BOTTOM, WILTSHIRE
SU 0438.   20 ha   Grade 1

This consists of south-west-, east- and north-facing slopes containing a variety of grassland types, including a *Dactylis–Arrhenatherum* grassland in the valley bottom, a dense *Festuca ovina–Helictotrichon pratense* grassland on the east-facing slope and, the outstanding feature of the site, a species-rich *Carex humilis*-type grassland on the west and south-west aspects. *Onobrychis viciifolia*, in what is probably

the native form, is abundant on the slope, with a grassland containing an unusual abundance of forbs, but particularly *Succisa pratensis*, *Serratula tinctoria*, *Betonica officinalis*, *Centaurea nigra* and *Campanula glomerata*. *Picris hieracioides* is abundant, in contrast to the more usual abundance of *Leontodon hispidus*, a feature of some ecological interest. The area is grazed by sheep and cattle, and has a noticeable absence of scrub.

The animals recorded in systematic samples included a number of characteristic and uncommon chalk grassland Heteroptera including *Campylosteira verna* and *Hallodapus rufescens*. The diversity of Auchenorhyncha in the samples was about average although the number of species recorded was above average. The faunal assemblage was a particu-larly interesting one with both *Dicranoneura citrinella* and *Dikraneura mollicula* present in good numbers. The Curculionoidea fauna was rich although no notable species were recorded.

L.31. WOODMINTON DOWN–KNOWLE HILL,
WILTSHIRE
ST 993218–SU 037225.   170 ha   Grade 1

This area is formed of a large variety of slopes, aspects and grassland types in unusual quantity. The south- and south-west-facing slopes are outstanding as an example of the *Festuca ovina–Carex humilis–C. caryophyllea* type of grass-land, with a great variety of forbs. *Scabiosa columbaria*, *Campanula rotundifolia*, *Galium verum* and *Leontodon hispidus* are unusually common in the *Carex humilis* turf. In contrast to these species-rich grasslands, there are areas of north-facing slopes with a poorer total flora, but rich in mosses, and areas of pasture with a botanical composition which suggests old, reverted arable. On the west-facing slopes of Knowle Hill, *Filipendula vulgaris* is abundant, which contrasts strongly with its almost complete absence from the adjacent Woodminton Down.

The Auchenorhyncha in systematic samples taken at Woodminton Down were above average in terms of the numbers of species taken. The outstanding total of 15 species of Heteroptera recorded included several un-common species. The Curculionoidea were also extremely varied.

L.32. KNAPP DOWN, WILTSHIRE
SU 0227.   75 ha   Grade 1

Knapp Down (with Barnett Down) is a large complex of steep-sided valleys and spurs. Again there is a variety of aspects with west, south-west and south slopes predominant, and supporting a wide range of plant communities; *Carex humilis*-dominant grassland and associates on the south-west slopes; *Festuca ovina–Carex flacca* type grassland on the west slopes; incipient scrub communities of hawthorn and rose. This area is threatened by intensive chicken-farming, but so far this has not seriously damaged the high quality of most of the Down.

Without being of particular interest the systematic samples taken at Knapp Down contained numbers of species of Auchenorhyncha, Heteroptera and Curculionoidea which were above average for short grassland of this height (5–7 cm).

L.33. STARVEALL DOWN AND STONY HILL, WILTSHIRE

ST 9939.   20 ha   Grade 1

This is a compact area of mostly south- to west-facing slopes which has an extremely uniformly grazed grassland of the *Carex humilis–Festuca ovina* type, characterised by the large number of forbs and other grasses. In some places the vegetation grades into the 'mixed grasses' type of chalk grassland. Locally, *Sieglingia decumbens* is common, growing with *Carex humilis* in unusual quantity, a type of association which is not common. *Thesium humifusum, Serratula tinctoria, Betonica officinalis, Onobrychis viciifolia* and *Euphrasia nemorosa* are all frequent at this site.

Populations of Heteroptera and Auchenorhyncha were, in general, poor in species and low in diversity although the sample taken from short grass on the site was richer and more diverse than that taken from longer grassland. On the other hand a large number of species of Curculionoidea was recorded. No uncommon species were included.

L.34. PARSONAGE DOWN, WILTSHIRE

SU 0541.   130 ha   Grade 1

This large area of high quality downland contrasts with all of the previous sites listed in that it is situated on level to gently undulating land and is 'ranched' with a mixed herd of cattle. The only other areas of chalk downland with this type of topography are within the Salisbury Plain military training area (L.41) and the Porton Down Ministry of Defence experimental area (L.36), the remainder having all been ploughed. The grassland is predominantly of the *Festuca ovina* type but considerable areas of the *Carex humilis* association exist, which suggests that at least parts of this Down have not been ploughed for centuries. Adjacent to Parsonage Down is Yarnbury Castle, which is an Iron Age camp site with double earth embankments and a rich flora, including juniper. These two areas are best considered together as one key site. There is high archaeological interest.

Although the numbers of species of Auchenorhyncha recorded in samples from Parsonage Down were slightly below average, the site is an outstanding one in other ways. The heteropterous fauna is very rich and the weevils recorded include the uncommon species *Tychius lineatulus* and *Phytonomus venustus*. The Adonis blue butterfly occurs here.

L.35. SCRATCHBURY AND COTLEY HILLS, WILTSHIRE

ST 9143.   50 ha   Grade 1

A species-rich grassland of the *Festuca ovina–F. rubra* type here is situated in the west of Wiltshire, and contains the range of species associated with the *Carex humilis* type of grassland, yet lacks this species. The Iron Age camp of Scratchbury Hill provides a variety of aspects with a uniform slope, the north and north-west aspects having unusually large amounts of *Neckera crispa* with *Succisa pratensis* and *Serratula tinctoria*. The more gently sloping, predominantly south- to south-west-facing slopes of Cotley Hill support a wide range of plants and insects, including large colonies of *Polygala calcarea, Hippocrepis comosa* and *Gentianella anglica*.

This is an outstanding entomological site. The Adonis blue butterfly is said to occur. The Auchenorhyncha fauna is rich and varied but not outstandingly so. The Heteroptera are very diverse and include *Drymus ryei, Catoplatus fabricii, Dictyonota tricornis, Hallodapus rufescens* and other uncommon species. Twenty-one species of Curculionoidea have been recorded, including several species of local occurrence.

L.36. PORTON DOWN, WILTSHIRE–HAMPSHIRE

SU 2135.   1700 ha   Grade 1

This large area of grassland, scrub and planted woodland is owned by the Ministry of Defence and is the home and testing ground of the Chemical Defence Establishment. It is of great importance as probably the largest continuous area of chalk grassland left in England. Much of the ground is known to have been arable land when Porton Down was requisitioned for military use in 1916, and the existence of historical records for land-use patterns during the previous century enable correlations to be made with the present distribution of plant communities. The area has great potential for research and, like the Stanford Practical Training Area (L.60(*a*)) in the Breckland, represents a type of once widespread ecosystem which now otherwise occurs only as scattered fragments.

The grasslands fall into four main types:

(*a*) *Festuca rubra–F. ovina–Helictotrichon pubescens–H. pratense* grasslands cover about 80% of the Porton ranges. They are remarkable for their relatively poor assemblage of forbs, which is probably a result of their recent origin and management.

(*b*) *Arrhenatherum elatius–F. rubra–H. pubescens* grassland occupy the most level areas with deeper soils which have been shown by studies of land-use history to be mostly less than 60 years old. They are floristically poor.

(*c*) *Festuca ovina–Leontodon hispidus* grassland occupies small areas at the edges of woodland and is found on the steeper slopes; it is floristically rich with an abundance of *Asperula cynanchica* and *Cirsium acaulon. Thesium humifusum, Hippocrepis comosa* and *Iberis amara* are known only from these areas on the Porton ranges.

(*d*) Lichen-rich areas occur which resemble some of the Breckland grasslands, but are unknown elsewhere on the Chalk. They consist of open, short grasslands with scattered tufts of *Festuca ovina, Trisetum flavescens* and *Koeleria cristata*, and with a variety of low-growing herbs set in a carpet of lichens, notably *Cladonia rangiformis, C. impexa* and *Peltigera rufescens*. This community is known from three areas on Porton Down and is of great interest because of its rarity, relationship with the Breckland grasslands (particularly Grassland B, see p. 175, Vol. 1) and its mode of origin.

Despite the large extent of chalk grassland within this

site, there are few rare chalk plants, probably because of the fairly recent cultivation of a large part of the area. Even some of the more widespread chalk species are very local, e.g. *Hippocrepis*. However, an outstanding feature is the presence in the short grassland of sheets of *Anthyllis vulneraria* and *Lotus corniculatus* which colour the ground yellow in mid July, and are important food plants for some of the chalk butterflies.

An extensive area of chalk heath, with *Calluna vulgaris*, *Agrostis tenuis*, *Anthoxanthum odoratum*, *Viola riviniana*, *Rumex acetosa* and *Potentilla erecta*, is known from the north-east part of Porton, together with two small areas elsewhere. The most interesting feature of this chalk heath is the presence of juniper among the *Calluna*, a community which is not known elsewhere on the Chalk, although it occurs on the northern limestones.

This extensive site is particularly interesting for its scrub communities, and the most notable feature is the occurrence of juniper in stands of different ages and with different field layers. The young stands appear to date back to the loss of rabbit-grazing (because of myxomatosis) and the bushes are about 9–15 years in age. They are found in typical chalk grassland swards, in unusual lichen-rich communities and in chalk heath vegetation with *Calluna*. The juniper in the old stands is about 60 years old and *Sambucus nigra* is a frequent associate, whilst the associated *Festuca* grassland has an abundance of *Helianthemum chamaecistus* and *Thymus drucei*. The number of juniper bushes on the site is estimated at over 14000, a considerably higher number than the 8000 found at Bulford Downs. Many other mixtures of scrub occur, large areas are dominated by hawthorn and others have *Rhamnus catharticus*, and less frequently dogwood as the commonest species. Scots pine is regenerating freely from plantations, and birch is also found in the scrub stage. The field layers have not been properly studied, but deadly nightshade is particularly common.

The planted woods of beech, oak, ash, sycamore and various conifers are important mainly for their interesting field layer species (e.g. *Monotropa hypopitys*, *Neottia nidus-avis*, *Cephalanthera damasonium*, *Epipactis helleborine*, *Helleborus foetidus* and *Atropa belladonna*) and for their fauna.

The birds and mammals have not been studied in detail but it is known that stone curlew, hobbies, sparrowhawks and kestrels nest within the Porton Down area while herds of fallow deer are commonly seen in the woods.

In general the Auchenorhyncha taken in systematic samples from well-separated sites on the Porton ranges were not especially rich in species. However, certain sites have high values of diversity, and numbers of species recorded from them were above average. One of the most interesting species was *Tettigometra impressopunctata* from one of the richest and most diverse sites. Otherwise during the review this species was recorded only from Box Hill, Surrey. No rarities among the Heteroptera were recorded but the Porton ranges are of considerable interest in supporting populations of *Cymus glandicolor*, a species normally associated with marshes, but which has recently been taken in a very few chalk grassland sites. A number of other species of Heteroptera were taken there and in general a good diversity was maintained at all the sites. The Curculionoidea recorded were not outstanding although some sites had a good diversity of species. The areas of very short vegetation associated with plentiful surface flints on the slopes to the north of Isle of Wight Hill support a relatively sparse but very interesting fauna of invertebrates and the occurrence of *Orthocerus clavicornis*, a beetle normally associated with sandy habitats, is unusual. Preliminary observations on the invertebrate fauna of the junipers show this to be of considerable interest.

The abundance of butterflies on Porton Down is one of its most spectacular features. Nearly all the chalk species are represented, and the small blue is especially abundant but the chalk-hill blue is evidently restricted to the small area of its food plant *Hippocrepis comosa* at Thorney Down. There are very large numbers of common grassland species, such as 'browns' and 'skippers', and also of local insects such as the marbled white, dark green fritillary and high brown fritillary.

There is also an abundance of the cistus forester moth, and the other interesting moths in a long species list include the pale shining brown, dusky sallow, blackneck and pine hawk.

L.37. TENNYSON DOWN, ISLE OF WIGHT, HAMPSHIRE
SZ 3285. 80 ha   Grade 1

This area has a variety of scrub, grassland and chalk heath influenced by maritime conditions. The chalk heath contains areas in which *Calluna*, *Erica* and *Potentilla erecta* are dominants; in others, gorse is the dominant. There are large colonies of *Orchis mascula*. The chalk heath grades into maritime chalk grassland with species such as *Sieglingia decumbens* and *Thesium humifusum*.

Tennyson Down is particularly important in being one of the few areas in which *Ulex europaeus* and *Prunus spinosa* are mixed with one of the more calcicolous scrub species, *Ligustrum vulgare*. *Crataegus* is common and *Clematis*, *Euonymus*, *Lonicera periclymenum* and *Cotoneaster microphyllum* are also present. The stand is very dense and the field layer extremely sparse, consisting principally of *Hedera helix*. *Iris foetidissima* occurs occasionally, while in the more open areas along the paths *Rubia peregrina* is present.

See also C.10.

L.38. ELLESBOROUGH WARREN, BUCKINGHAMSHIRE
SP 8306. 60 ha   Grade 1

The most extensive stands of box scrub in Britain occur on this site, and although the history of the area is not known in any detail the box is thought to be native. The stands are mostly fairly old and are found in three steep-sided valleys where they are often mixed with *Sambucus nigra*. Trees, especially beech and ash, occur in some areas. Shading is dense and the ground flora is limited to scrub woodland plants such as *Mercurialis perennis*, *Urtica dioica*, *Poa trivialis* and *Circaea lutetiana*. *Atropa belladonna* occurs rarely. In Happy Valley there is a particularly interesting area of young regenerating box on very open ground giving the appearance of a scree slope. Other woody plants in this scrub are *Thelycrania, Ligustrum* and *Daphne laureola*. The field layers are very sparse, but include many of the shorter chalk grassland species particularly *Festuca ovina, Hieracium pilosella, Sedum acre* and *Thymus drucei*. In the same valley, walnut *Juglans regia* is regenerating naturally from planted seed parents. There are also areas of good chalk grassland on the site.

L.39. BURGHCLERE BEACON, HAMPSHIRE
SU 4557.   125 ha   Grade 1

This site contains an extensive stand of juniper in an older seral stage than that on Bulford Downs. It covers about 20 ha on the west-facing slope of this prominent chalk hill. Juniper is the dominant or co-dominant woody species in much of the area, and is mixed with *Ligustrum, Rhamnus, Rosa, Rubus* and *Viburnum lantana. Sorbus aria* occurs as scattered bushes throughout the scrub, with a little haw-thorn in the centre section of the site. There are many fruiting juniper bushes, but little evidence of regeneration. The open grassland between the scrub is of the *Festuca ovina–F. rubra* type grading to a mixed grass type with a wide range of forbs including *Polygala calcarea* and *Gentianella amarella*.

Although nothing particularly uncommon was recorded in the systematic samples of grassland the Auchenorhyncha were outstandingly rich in species. On this criterion the site ranks equally with most grade 1 grassland sites and is better than many.

This site is of equal quality to Bulford Downs and complementary to it as it shows a later stage in the sere.

L.40. RUSHMORE DOWN, HAMPSHIRE
SU 3454.   105 ha   Grade 1

The most important feature of this site is the varied complex of scrub extending over almost the entire area. A particularly interesting stand includes some juniper perhaps some 100 years in age and up to 6 m in height. This stand is not extensive but nevertheless appears to be the oldest population of juniper on the Chalk, and could be valuable for a study of the longevity of the species. The principal accompanying woody species in this juniper stand are *Sambucus nigra, Thelycrania sanguinea* and *Rubus fruticosus* with some *Taxus*, and the field layer is of the damper, nitrophilous type dominated by *Mercurialis perennis* and *Urtica dioica*. There are various other areas of scrub on a variety of slopes and aspects including types dominated mainly by *Ligustrum* and *Thelycrania* separately, and an incipient open *Crataegus* scrub in chalk grassland of the *Zerna erecta* facies. Another area, of unknown history, has extensive areas of *Chamaenerion angustifolium* associated with mixed scrub of *Corylus, Crataegus* and *Ligustrum*.

The value of this site lies partly in its extensive area and range of seed parent species which makes it suitable for management aimed at producing successional stages in a variety of scrub types on a rotational basis. Much of the area functioned as a rabbit warren until 1939 and it is now managed primarily for game birds.

L.41. BULFORD DOWNS, WILTSHIRE
SU 2044.   560 ha   Grade 1

This site, which lies within the Salisbury Plain military training area, contains an extensive stand of young juniper, mixed with *Viburnum lantana* as the dominant woody species and with *Ligustrum vulgare* covering about 60 ha of a north-west- to north-facing slope. *Rhamnus, Rosa* sp. and *Rubus* sp. are constant members of the scrub community together with scattered bushes of *Crataegus, Sorbus aria, Betula pendula, Taxus baccata* and *Cotoneaster microphyllus*. Scots pine is invading the site on the east. Both the pyramidal and prostrate forms of juniper are present with a number of fruiting bushes, and regeneration is occurring in some areas. The bushes are mostly 0.5–1.5 m high. Since the scrub is in an early successional stage, there is the prospect of a slow development through the seral stages, and the present composition of woody species indicates a height diversity in the later stages. The grassland is of the *Festuca ovina–F. rubra* type, with a diverse dicotyledonous flora including several species of orchid and an abundance of *Polygala calcarea*. On the northern part of the site there are also good stands of both young and old juniper in spite of the greater military activity. This site and Porton Down (L.36) have the best remaining examples in England of the lowland type of juniper associated with the Chalk, and mixed with *Viburnum* and *Ligustrum*.

The samples of Heteroptera and Curculionoidea in the grassland were poor in numbers of species. *Hallodapus rufescens* (Heteroptera) and *Ulopa trivia* (Auchenorhyncha) were the only species of any note, but neither is particularly rare. The dark green fritillary butterfly occurs here.

L.42. OLDBURY CASTLE AND CHERHILL DOWNS, WILTSHIRE
SU 0569.   160 ha   Grade 1

This is part of the Pewsey Vale escarpment and linked through Tan Hill, All Cannings, Kitchen Barrow with the Pewsey Downs grade 1 site (L.26). It differs from this last area in the presence of a considerable north-facing slope and several truncated valleys on a south-west and north-east axis which provide a range of aspects and conditions reflected in the variety of plants and animals. On the north-facing slopes, *Brachypodium pinnatum* and *Zerna erecta* are common and locally dominant; in contrast, the south-facing slopes support a *Festuca ovina–Carex flacca–Helianthemum* type of association, with locally abundant species such as *Succisa pratensis, Serratula tinctoria* and *Phyteuma tenerum*. There are well-established colonies of *Cirsium tuberosum × C. acaulon* with a few plants of pure *C. tuberosum*. Juniper is scattered on the south-facing slopes.

Despite an encouraging appearance Oldbury Castle scored very poorly in the number of interesting species present in the systematic samples. Several species of Curculionoidea were recorded, but few Heteroptera. The outstanding entomological feature of the site is the occurrence of a strong colony of the very rare wartbiter *Decticus ver-rucivorus* (Orthoptera, Tettigoniidae), a species restricted to a very few sites in southern England. Several species of butterfly occurred, including the dark green fritillary.

L.43. NORTH MEADOW, CRICKLADE, WILTSHIRE
SU 0994.   40 ha   Grade 1
Neutral grassland group 7[1]

This site forms an island bounded by the River Churn to the north and the River Thames to the south, both rivers being linked by tributaries to the east and west of the meadow. Flooding occurs periodically, especially in winter.

Management is governed by legal clauses which *inter alia* stipulate that grazing by stock owned by certain inhabitants of Cricklade may take place between 12 August and 12 February. After mid February grazing ceases and the vegetation is allowed to grow for hay, sections of which are cut by any person prepared to buy the 'hay doles'. At present there are eight owners. Buying and selling of hay doles occurs from time to time along similar lines to normal land purchase. The grazing rights are granted in perpetuity to the people of Cricklade. This management system has operated for several centuries, so that the grassland is of considerable antiquity.

Botanically the meadow consists of large uniform areas differing in certain details of floristics, e.g. *Plantago lanceolata* is dominant in one section. The reason for this is not known, but may be a product of small differences in management, such as cutting time, continued over a long period. The most notable feature of the area is the mass of *Fritillaria meleagris* which occurs over most of the area. Though not as dominant or uniform as at Framsden, Suffolk, the size of area and associated flora are much greater at North Meadow, and represent the best site for *Fritillaria* in Britain which, on a 10-km square basis, has been reduced to a tenth of its pre-1930 national status.

Over much of the meadow the dominant grasses are *Anthoxanthum odoratum*, *Festuca rubra* and *Poa trivialis*. *Sanguisorba officinalis*, *Betonica officinialis*, *Trifolium pratense* and *T. repens* are common, and *Ophioglossum vulgatum* is abundant over large areas.

L.44. CLATTINGER FARM, OAKSEY, WILTSHIRE
SU 0193.   60 ha   Grade 1
Neutral grassland group 8[2]

Clattinger is owned by a farmer who has never used herbicides or applied excessive fertilisers on any of his grasslands, which are accordingly in an unusually unmodified condition. It is a reasonable prediction that this area will disappear to gravel extraction or the plough on the retirement of the present owner. The site consists of 12 meadows, some of which are normally cut for hay and the aftermath grazed. Some winter flooding occurs on some of the meadows, providing a link with alluvial meadows (Neutral grassland group 7) such as North Meadow, Cricklade, but normally this is slight.

As with all good permanent meadows, there are no real

dominant species but a well-balanced, mixed composition of grasses, in this instance consisting of *Agrostis stolonifera*, *Alopecurus pratensis*, *Dactylis glomerata*, *Festuca arundinacea*, *F. rubra*, *Holcus lanatus* and *Poa trivialis*. Slightly less frequent are *Hordeum secalinum*, *Bromus racemosus*, *Zerna erecta*, *Lolium perenne* and *Briza media*. Of the forbs, *Betonica officinalis*, *Serratula tinctoria*, *Linum catharticum*, *Lotus corniculatus*, *Sanguisorba officinalis* and *Achillea millefolium* are typical.

One of the meadows has quantities of *Fritillaria meleagris*, *Orchis morio* and *Listera ovata*, and *Colchicum autumnale* also occurs in small quantities. Of the other meadows, *Primula veris* and *Leontodon hispidus* occur in quantity in one, and *Dactylorchis fuchsii*, *Valeriana officinalis*, *Pulicaria dysenterica* and *Chrysanthemum leucanthemum* in another. *Silaum silaus* and the very local *Carex filiformis* are also present.

The hedges between the meadows are rich in species of shrub.

L.45. BRANSBURY COMMON, HAMPSHIRE
SU 4142.   160 ha   Grade 1
Neutral grassland group 3 (7)[2]

This area includes some disused water meadows to the north and south of the common proper. In the following description the term 'common' is used for an area now only partly flooded for short periods, and 'meadow' refers to the now disused water meadows.

Common

The major soil formation is of peat over gravel and the dominant plant association over the majority of the area is *Molinia caerulea–Carex paniculata*. This sward is moderately grazed by cattle and is open, allowing local dominance of *C. nigra* and *Anthoxanthum odoratum*, with *Cirsium dissectum*, *Potentilla erecta* and *Succisa pratensis*. In areas with a more silty soil a rich grass–sedge community is present with *Holcus lanatus*, *Festuca rubra*, *A. odoratum*, *Sieglingia decumbens*, *Carex flacca*, *C. panicea*, *C. echinata* and *C. pulicaris*. Other species of interest on the common include *Genista anglica*, *Menyanthes trifoliata* and *Isolepis setacea*.

Meadows

These are especially good examples of ecologically interesting disused (pre-1930) water meadows which have been well grazed and not allowed to deteriorate through undergrazing, or 'improved' by heavy nitrogen fertiliser applications and/or spraying with herbicides. The meadows are on a heavier soil than the common and are characteristically dominated by *Lolium perenne*, *Festuca pratensis*, *F. rubra*, *Holcus lanatus* and *Poa trivialis* with the hybrid *Festulolium* frequent. *Menyanthes trifoliata*, *Iris pseudacorus*, *Cardamine pratensis*, *Dactylorchis incarnata* and *Caltha palustris* are also present.

Combining the meadows and the common gives a wide variation of grassland and grass–sedge communities. On one

[1] As defined in p. 186, Vol. 1.

[2] See pp. 185–6, Vol. 1.

visit 97 species were noted, including 17 grass species and 12 sedges.

L.46. LOWER WOODFORD WATER MEADOWS, WILTSHIRE

SU 1234.   25 ha   Grade 1
Neutral grassland group 6[1]

Lolium perenne, Holcus lanatus and *Alopecurus pratensis* are co-dominants in a sward in which many grass species are present. Two of these are *Festuca pratensis* and *F. arundinacea* which, together with *L. perenne*, form the parents for the typical and characteristic feature of these meadows, namely the various *Lolium–Festuca* hybrids. The forbs are of less interest in this predominantly grass-dominated community, but include *Senecio aquaticus, Cardamine pratensis* and *Myosotis scorpioides*.

L.47. PIXEY AND YARNTON MEADS/PORT MEADOW, OXFORDSHIRE

SP 4810, SP 4908.   250 ha   Grade 1
Neutral grassland group 7 (5) (9)[1]

These alluvial meadows bordering the River Thames are classic sites for studying the effect of either cutting for hay or summer grazing, continued over many centuries, on the botanical composition of the sward. The documentation of past management is particularly good, and from the juxtaposition of the two areas this whole system gives a valuable measure of the effects of cutting compared to grazing on these types of grassland. The documentation includes a good description by Baker (1937) of the factors affecting Pixey Mead and Port Meadow and the resulting flora, as prevailed in the 1920s.

Pixey and Yarnton Meads are annually cut for hay, giving a uniform vegetation pattern in which *Sanguisorba officinalis* is outstandingly abundant. *Alopecurus pratensis, Anthoxanthum odoratum, Festuca rubra* and *Sanguisorba officinalis* are the dominant species in a grassland type similar to much of North Meadow, Cricklade (L.43). Differences from North Meadow are shown by the greater percentage of *Dactylis glomerata* and *Briza media*, and the absence of *Fritillaria meleagris*. The range of grassland types is less at Yarnton, but its greater uniformity makes this an ideal research site for comparative work between the northern and southern hay meadows.

Port Meadow is annually grazed. It exhibits three main vegetationally distinct areas in relation to height above the river. The highest section is to the north and has greatly altered since the 1920s, with the invasion and rise to dominance of *Cirsium arvense* and *Senecio jacobaea*. The middle area is *Lolium perenne–Festuca pratensis–Ranunculus acris–Trifolium repens* grassland with *Cirsium arvense* frequent over large areas. The southern section is the lowest lying and therefore the wettest and is dominated by *Glyceria fluitans* and *Poa trivialis*, with areas of *Eleocharis palustris, R. repens* and *Oenanthe fistulosa*. The presence of *Juncus compressus* adds botanical interest.

[1] See pp. 186–7, Vol. 1.

L.48. FYFIELD DOWN, WILTSHIRE

SU 1370.   305 ha   Grade 2

Although this site (the large part of which is a NNR) may merit a higher grading on account of its archaeological and geological interest, as a vegetation type and in floristic content it is rated as grade 2. Over much of the area, the grassland is of the *Festuca rubra* type with few other grasses and with a sparse list of dicotyledonous associates, *Poterium sanguisorba* being the commonest. Small areas of richer *F. ovina* grassland are found locally. The lichens and mosses associated with the Sarsen stones are also of interest.

Only two systematic invertebrate samples were taken from Fyfield Down. No Heteroptera and very few Auchenorhyncha and Curculionoidea were recorded. The only feature of interest was the presence of the rather uncommon bug *Hardya melanopsis*, otherwise recorded during the review only from chalk sites in Yorkshire and Lincolnshire. Although Fyfield Down has not been well worked entomologically, the limited information on the insect fauna supports the evidence from the vegetation that the site rates only as grade 2.

L.49 HOMINGTON, ODSTOCK AND COOMBE BISSETT DOWNS, WILTSHIRE

SU 1125, SU 1325, SU 1024.   40 ha   Grade 2
(for description see site L.53)

L.50. NOAR HILL, HAMPSHIRE

SU 7431.   10 ha   Grade 2

The grassland interest at this site lies in the old chalk quarries at the base of the hill which support a rich and varied plant life and insect fauna. In addition to the common downland plants and the presence of species of restricted distribution such as *Gentianella anglica, Arabis hirsuta, Ophioglossum vulgatum* and *Blackstonia perfoliata*, the outstanding feature is the abundance of orchids, nine species having been recorded here, including large quantities of the musk orchid *Herminium monorchis*. The woodland part of this site is rated grade 1 (W.27).

A very large number of Hemiptera–Auchenorhyncha was taken in the systematic samples from Noar Hill, but this was possibly because of the very 'patchy' nature of the vegetation. Diversity of the samples was high, but no rarities were recorded. Both the Heteroptera and Curculionoidea samples were also rich in species, but again no rarities were recorded.

L.51. THROOPE DOWN, WILTSHIRE

SU 0824.   30 ha   Grade 2

L.52. TROW DOWN, WILTSHIRE

ST 9621.   20 ha   Grade 2

L.53. WELL BOTTOM, UPTON LOVELL, WILTSHIRE

ST 9541.   16 ha   Grade 2

This group of sites in south-west Wiltshire (and L.49) has grassland of the *Carex humilis* type, smaller than the south-west Wiltshire Downs grade 1 group but contains mostly the same range of variation and aspect and could serve as a slightly inferior substitute.

L.54. STOCKBRIDGE DOWN, HAMPSHIRE
SU 3735.   60 ha   Grade 2

On the north-facing escarpment of this site there is a good mixed scrub with juniper, privet, hawthorn and *Rosa* spp. as co-dominants and a field layer of taller herbs. This area shows evidence of seral development to yew-wood and contrasts with an area of young juniper on a south-facing slope in a *Zerna erecta* grassland and probably of post-myxomatosis age. Nearby are areas of less interesting hawthorn scrub and on the clay capping of the plateau is an unusually advanced scrub of hawthorn, gorse and blackthorn. The common species of the rather monotonous field layer include *Agrostis stolonifera*, *Deschampsia cespitosa* and *Urtica dioica*. Tree species are relatively rare.

This particular juxtaposition of communities may have been common in the past, but the extensive conversion of plateau downland to arable farmland has largely destroyed the particular complex of plateau and scarp scrub communities now represented at Stockbridge Down. Interesting archaeological features here include Bronze Age round barrows and the earthworks of an early Iron Age hill fort.

L.55. IVINGHOE HILLS, STEPS HILL AND PITSTONE HILL, BUCKINGHAMSHIRE, HERTFORDSHIRE
SP 9615.   230 ha   Grade 2

The area contains a series of coombes and valleys, mostly facing north but with some indented valleys which provide other aspects with a vegetation characteristic of the eastern parts of the Chilterns. The scrub is predominantly hawthorn, although other species occur. Grazing by cattle in a Zernetum grassland maintains areas of open grassland which locally may have a rich flora, e.g. especially in old chalk pits. On the Clay-with-Flints capping mixtures of gorse, hawthorn, elder, blackthorn and pedunculate oak add variety. The grassland of the north-facing slope of Pitstone Hill is an unusual variant of the common *Festuca ovina* type, with an abundance of *Daucus carota*. *Anemone pulsatilla* occurs locally.

L.56. COOMBE HILL, WENDOVER, BUCKINGHAMSHIRE
SP 8406.   55 ha   Grade 2

Interesting juniper scrub with a high woody species diversity occurs on this site, the typical associates *Taxus*, *Viburnum* and *Sorbus aria* are present as well as all the other usual woody species of scrub. The influence of the clay capping is shown on the upper levels of the hill by the presence of blackthorn and gorse. A rare bug *Eremocoris fenestratus* has been recorded from juniper litter on this site.

L.57. BRITFORD–DOWNTON, WILTSHIRE
SU 173253–173208.   *c.* 65 ha   Grade 2
Neutral grassland group 6[1]

Holcus lanatus and *Poa trivialis* are the co-dominants in a grassland which can contain up to 30 species of Gramineae.

[1] See p. 186, Vol. 1.

These grasslands are generally poor in forbs following the physical removal of 'weeds' by the farmer. The numerous small waterways associated with the system are colonised by such aquatic species as *Butomus umbellatus*, *Nuphar lutea*, *Sagittaria sagittifolia* and *Iris pseudacorus*, and in addition provide an aquatic habitat differing in various ways from that of the river itself, e.g. in water temperature, depth of water, and rate of flow.

EAST ANGLIA

L.58. DUNWICH HEATHS AND MARSHES, SUFFOLK
TM 4874.   1900 ha   Grade 1

This is the heathland component of a composite site which contains the Dunwich Marshes flood-plain mires (P.11), and carr covers at least 400 ha, on low-lying non-calcareous sands of the glacial beds known as the East Suffolk Sandlings. The Minsmere–Westleton portion contains the large area of heathland which is, however, fairly uniform, consisting of mainly dry soils with a mixture of Callunetum and Pteridietum, with variable amounts of *Erica cinerea*, *E. tetralix*, *Carex arenaria* (locally dominant), *Ulex gallii*, *U. europaeus*, *Molinia caerulea* and *Chamaenerion angustifolium*. Much of the Callunetum is in the degenerate phase of growth. There are grassy areas, especially near tracks, with *Festuca ovina*, *Luzula campestris*, *Agrostis tenuis* and *Holcus lanatus*. Areas of scrub birch are developing locally and there is some rowan. The Walberswick–Blythburgh heathland has considerable areas of Pteridietum with low floristic interest, and is generally similar to the previous area although rarer plant species are present, e.g. *Jasione montana*, a plant that is local in East Anglia. The ornithological interest of these heathlands is high, for they are a refuge of decreasing species such as stone curlew, nightjar, red-backed shrike and woodlark.

The site also contains a variety of ornithologically interesting woodland types, ranging from alder carr, birchwoods, open coverts of mature Scots pine, and mixed deciduous, oak-dominant plantations. There is in addition a wide range of maritime habitats, described under the Dunwich Marshes (P.11).

L.59. ROYDON COMMON, NORFOLK
TF 6822.   180 ha   Grade 1

Roydon Common is a diverse heathland area about 6.5 km east-north-east of King's Lynn, and lies between 7.6 and 30 m above sea-level. The soils are derived from lower Cretaceous deposits, though valley gravels and drift deposits are present locally.

The importance of this heathland complex is greatly enhanced by the occurrence of extensive valley mires which, with the transitional wet heath and humid heath communities, are regarded and described as a grade 1 peatland site (P.16). The dry heath covers extensive areas of the lower ground around the valley mires, and becomes continuous where the eastern plain slopes up to the plateau at the western end. This is a heather-dominated dry heath with only limited areas of bracken, mainly towards the edges, and a patchy development of gorse scrub. Between the periodic fires the heather attains a considerable luxuriance and associated species are few: *Genista anglica* and *Cuscuta epithymum* occur sparingly, and the rather infrequent or local patches of bare ground have *Campylopus introflexus* and lichens such as *Cladonia impexa*, *C. coccifera*, *C. furcata* and *Parmelia physodes*. In places, the heather becomes sparse or lacking and rather bare sandy ground has *Carex arenaria*, *C. pilulifera*, *Rumex acetosella*, *Aira praecox*, *Polytrichum piliferum*, *P. juniperinum* and *Cetraria aculeata*.

Near the western edge of the Common are patches of herbaceous vegetation on more basic soil: these have *Agrostis canina*, *Festuca rubra*, *F. ovina*, *Galium verum*, *Potentilla sterilis*, *Veronica chamaedrys*, *Campanula rotundifolia*, *Viola riviniana* and *Teucrium scorodonia*. There are also patches of bramble, honeysuckle and rosebay willow herb, mostly associated with bracken. There is patchy colonisation of the dry heath by birch, mainly towards the edges of the Common, and a sparse occurrence of tall shrubs such as hawthorn and elder.

L.60. STANFORD–WRETHAM HEATHS, NORFOLK
Grade 1

(a) Stanford Practical Training Area
TL 8794. 4740 ha

The Stanford PTA is one of the most important grassland–heath units in Breckland for nature conservation because of its large size and freedom from intensive human usage, other than for military purposes. Some 2000 sheep range over the area, according to which parts are available for grazing, and at present about 1000 ha are leased for arable farming and a further 730 ha leased to the Forestry Commission. Approximately 5000 ha are now uncultivated grassland and heath.

Most of the characteristic Breckland habitats, except open dunes, are represented in the Training Area; three of the unique Breckland meres are included. The most widespread communities present are grasslands – calcareous, neutral and acidic. At the calcareous end of the series there are examples of Grassland B (see p. 175, Vol. 1), evidently of an ancient type, with characteristic species such as *Cirsium acaulon*. Elsewhere are quite large areas of breck which have the physiognomic appearance of Grasslands B–D but lack the typical floristic composition and are evidently former arable land which has reverted to breck since the area was requisitioned for military training and went out of cultivation during World War II. These recent brecks have the characteristic sparsely vegetated sandy and flint-strewn appearance of the ancient types, but their most characteristic species are *Hieracium pilosella*, *Erodium cicutarium*, *Agrostis stolonifera*, *Veronica chamaedrys* and *Lotus corniculatus*, and typical chalk grassland species are mostly lacking. On the more acidic sites, lichens are abundant but they seldom form the closed carpets which are especially characteristic of the older brecks. Rare species appear to be few, as might be expected from the small extent of ancient brecks, but the grass *Nardurus maritimus* occurs in the old chalk pits.

On the more acidic soils, communities of dense *Festuca*–*Agrostis* grassland, bracken, heather and sand sedge are all represented, the first two types extensively. There is a patchy occurrence of gorse scrub and one area of old, moribund-looking juniper. There are numerous blocks of woodland in the area, composed mainly of oak, but locally with a good deal of Scots pine, birch, sweet chestnut and beech. The field layer of these woodlands is mostly rather limited, with dominance of bracken in many places, and tall shrubs are often absent. Pine rows, clumps and woods are well represented, and there are some non-indigenous conifers such as cedar. The area also contains a range of dry to wet meadow grasslands, fens and open waters. The fens tend to be floristically rich with such species as *Dactylorchis praetermissa*, *D. traunsteineri*, *D. incarnata*, *Menyanthes trifoliata*, *Parnassia palustris*, and beds of *Carex riparia* and *Phragmites*. Stretches of open water, i.e. Stanford Water and Buckenham Tofts Water, are man-made in origin, but form important feeding and breeding grounds for waterfowl. The number of breeding gadwall estimated in 1969 was 27 pairs, of which about a half nested adjacent to Stanford Water. Similarly the number of breeding heathland species is large and under the present form of grazing management there is much suitable habitat for stone curlew, though the numbers of this species appear to be rather small.

(b) East Wretham Heath
TL 9188. 150 ha

East Wretham Heath contains the two most notable Breckland meres, Langmere and Ringmere, which are of great hydrological and biological importance. Their random fluctuations in water level remain unexplained and although they are within 1 km of each other it is not unusual to find one mere full and the other empty. The freshwater fauna and flora associated with the meres are considered under Open Waters (see site OW.14).

Floristically the heathland component of this site is interesting with large areas dominated by *Deschampsia flexuosa*. Twenty years ago this grass was very local in Breckland but it is now becoming increasingly common in acidic grassland and locally replacing *Festuca ovina* as dominant. The communities of the area belong largely to the acidic grassland and heather heath types.

Other habitats include a number of small water-filled pulk holes, in which the water level remains remarkably constant. Surrounding the largest pulk hole is an area of fen, dominated by *Juncus inflexus*, *J. effusus*, *Phalaris arundinacea* and *Typha latifolia*. Part of the southern section of the heath is birch woodland with a ground flora of *Pteridium aquilinum* and *Holcus lanatus*, while to the north of Langmere is a belt of very old Scots pine, where crossbills breed at times.

The site has considerable habitat diversity and taken in conjunction with the meres, the number of species of birds and insects is large. The rare, semi-aquatic weevil *Bagous lutulosus* is recorded.

(c) *Bridgham–Brettenham Heaths*
TL 9286. 460 ha

This is an extensive area of dry heathland straddling the A11 road. The soils are predominantly acidic sands, heavily podsolised in places, but Chalk comes near to the surface along the eastern boundary.

The communities range from heather- and bracken-dominated heath to acidic and chalk grassland although the last is very restricted in area. Birch, Scots pine and gorse are variously invading parts of the heath. Soil stripes and polygons have been described from Brettenham Heath.

See also P.19.

L.61. ICKLINGHAM HEATHS, SUFFOLK   Grade 1
(a) *Cavenham–Tuddenham Heaths*
TL 7573. 175 ha

These two areas, separated by a belt of pasture and arable land a hundred or so metres wide, contain among the best examples of the highly acidic type of Breckland heath. Heather is dominant over much of the open heathland and shows an unusually bushy growth form in places, associated with lack of burning and grazing, and perhaps resulting from the growth of individual clumps once heavily grazed by rabbits. The heather here was badly frosted and extensively killed in 1963, but has shown good regeneration subsequently. In places there is a mosaic of heather bushes and bare ground grown with lichens (e.g. *Cladonia impexa* and *Cetraria aculeata*) and *Rumex acetosella*. *Pteridium aquilinum* is invading the heather communities locally, and forms fairly extensive pure stands on Cavenham Heath. *Carex arenaria* is also locally dominant, more particularly on Tuddenham Heath. Interesting plants of the Callunetum are *Cuscuta epithymum*, *Genista anglica* and, in one place, the northern moss *Ptilium crista-castrensis*. *Calamagrostis epigejos*, *Erica tetralix*, *Deschampsia flexuosa* and *Dryopteris carthusiana* are local. *Crassula tillaea*, *Ornithopus perpusillus*, *Centaurium erythraea* and *Spergularia rubra* occur plentifully along tracks and on trodden sandy areas.

At the east side of Cavenham Heath is a rather small area of the more acidic lichen-rich Breckland *Festuca ovina* grasslands within the range of types D–G (see p. 175, Vol. 1) and on the north side there is an approach to the more basic Grassland C, with calcicoles such as *Cirsium acaulon*. In places there are areas of coarser grassland, especially with *Arrhenatherum elatius*, with much *Stellaria holostea* and more rarely *Dianthus deltoides*. There is some invasion by hawthorn and bramble to give fragments of scrub.

The dry heathland shows invasion by gorse and birch, and both Cavenham and Tuddenham Heaths contain areas of birchwood, with *Betula pendula* on drier ground and *B. pubescens* in wetter places. In places, this birchwood has an open field layer of heather and a well-developed moss ground layer composed of the common species of western woods, such as *Pleurozium schreberi*, *Hypnum cupressiforme*, *Polytrichum commune*, *Dicranum scoparium* and *Leucobryum glaucum*. Elsewhere, there is a luxuriant layer of bracken beneath birch, or simply a bare litter where the tree cover is

dense, and the *Carex arenaria* swards occur in birchwood locally. Towards the north side of Tuddenham Heath, birchwood grades into carr and there is an intermediate type with a somewhat hydrophilous field layer, containing sedges and *Phragmites*. Ferns are well represented in the woodland field layer, especially in Ash Plantation, where *Thelypteris palustris* is plentiful (see also p. 55). Towards the River Lark, which is bounded by artificial embankments, the ground becomes wetter and there is a transition to flood-plain mire, first with communities of *C. acutiformis* and *C. riparia* and then to extensive beds of *Phragmites communis*, with great abundance of *Urtica dioica*. These fen communities show extensive invasion by willows to give carr mainly of *Salix cinerea*, with a wet, mossy ground layer. *Glyceria maxima* is also locally dominant, and there are characteristic rich-fen species such as *Rumex hydrolapathum*, *Iris pseudacorus*, *Lysimachia vulgaris*, *Lythrum salicaria*, *Eupatorium cannabinum* and *Juncus subnodulosus*. This fen and carr is quite extensive along the riverside flats, and adds considerably to the interest of this extremely diverse area.

The heaths support a herd of at least 25 roe deer, and this was formerly a good area for the nightjar, which has declined appreciably. The stone curlew, red-backed shrike, whinchat and woodlark have also decreased recently. The tree pipit, linnet, reed bunting, grasshopper warbler, willow warbler and yellowhammer breed on the heathland, and the woods have lesser redpoll, woodcock, magpie, jay, greater and lesser spotted woodpeckers and green woodpecker. Both adder and grass snake occur here, and there are common lizards. The spider fauna of the fen areas is particularly rich and includes *Clubiona rosserae* (known from only one other locality in Britain) and rarities such as *Marpissa pomatia* and *Hygrolycosa rubrofasciata*. The insect fauna includes the very rare bug *Ortholomus puncticpennis*, and there are characteristic heathland Lepidoptera such as the grayling and small heath butterflies, and emperor and beautiful yellow underwing moths.

On the south and east sides of Cavenham Heath, areas of former arable land have been left fallow. There is also a disused airfield with a good deal of untilled ground, and part of this area is being worked for gravel. These areas show stages in reversion to breck, and are transient habitats of the kind which give refuge to organisms characteristic of disturbed ground though not of the older brecks. In places the ground remains open and sandy, with an abundance of small herbs such as *Sedum acre*, *Erodium cicutarium*, *Myosotis arvensis*, *Filago germanica*, *Trifolium arvense*, *T. repens*, *T. dubium*, *Medicago lupulina*, *Plantago lanceolata*, *Arenaria serpyllifolia*, *Ornithopus perpusillus*, *Cerastium arvense* and *Vulpia ambigua*. Elsewhere, dense and luxuriant growth of medium to tall forb 'weeds' has developed, with *Echium vulgare* (which dominates large areas in some years), *Silene alba*, *S. vulgaris*, *Reseda lutea*, *R. luteola*, *Linaria repens*, *Malva officinalis*, *Carduus nutans*, *Onopordum acanthium*, *Melilotus officinalis*, *M. alba*, *Verbascum nigrum*, *V. thapsus* and *Conyza canadensis*. Some of these fallow and disturbed areas have been included within the key site for the interest of their arable weed communities: with suitable management, this interest could be enhanced. Stone curlews nested here until recently but may have disappeared.

See also W.36.

(b) Icklingham Plains and Triangle
TL 7673. 160 ha

Icklingham Plains forms a natural northwards extension to Cavenham Heath. Botanically it comprises three major habitat types: *Carex arenaria*-dominated sand dunes, acidic grassland, and mixed fen in the Lark valley. The extensive system of mobile sand dunes, which supplements that lost on Lakenheath Warren, has become stabilised and today only a few blow-outs remain active. A considerable hectarage is covered by a pure sward of *C. arenaria*. The acidic grassland lies between the alluvial fenland and old sand dunes, and is dominated by *Festuca ovina* and *Agrostis* spp., with *Cladonia* and *Polytrichum* heath forming minor elements; there is virtually no *Calluna vulgaris*. Part of the alluvial fenland in the Lark valley is cattle-grazed, and dominated by *Juncus* spp. The ungrazed section ('Poor's Fen') has developed into mixed tussock sedge–*Phragmites* fen, with some willow and alder carr.

The greater expanse of open heathland has made the area attractive to stone curlew, ringed plover and wheatear, the first two species no longer breeding on Cavenham Heath. Redshank, snipe and several species of duck breed in the grazed fenland and Poor's Fen has a particularly interesting spider fauna which is similar in many ways to that of Wicken Fen.

The flora contains many of the interesting Breckland plants and there is a noteworthy abundance of *Saxifraga granulata*.

(c) Deadman's Grave
TL 7774. 105 ha

Deadman's Grave lies to the north-east of Icklingham Plains and Triangle and Cavenham Heath and is in marked contrast to them in being a predominantly dry chalk grassland. In detailed floristic composition this sward is rather different from other areas of calcareous grassland in the Breckland; it ranges from Grassland B–D (see p. 175, Vol. 1), although the last is very restricted, and a grassland approaching type A covers several hectares where there has been surface mining for flints. Grassland B is the most extensive and here the dominant grasses are *Festuca* spp., mainly *F. ovina*, *Koeleria cristata* and *Anthoxanthum odoratum*, with *Trisetum flavescens* locally frequent. Other species of calcareous grassland include *Astragalus danicus*, *Gentianella amarella*, *Cirsium acaulon*, *Thymus drucei*, *Asperula cynanchica*, *Lotus corniculatus*, *Linum catharticum* and *Sagina nodosa*. The presence of *Anacamptis pyramidalis* is unusual in Breckland, and the rare *Silene otites* is locally abundant.

Acidic sands are confined to one small area on which a mixed *Cladonia–Polytrichum* heath has developed. Heather is present, but only in small amounts, and the presence of scattered individual plants throughout Grassland B probably results from their association with pockets or bands of sandier soil formed during sorting of the till under peri-glacial conditions. Soil stripes are present but show clearly only during late spring droughts.

In addition to the calcareous grassland there are several old plantations consisting either of mixed hardwoods or mixed conifers and hardwoods. They are valuable breeding sites for nightjar, redstart, green woodpecker and kestrel and so add to the ornithological diversity. Winter grazing by sheep is the most important single factor in maintaining the floristic richness of the site, and probably accounts for its attractiveness to the stone curlew and formerly the woodlark. Gorse and broom scrub occurs in places, but not extensively.

A brief study of the invertebrate fauna during the summer of 1962 showed that some of the rare heathland species typical of the more open breck lived here. The rare spider *Oxyptila scabricula* was particularly numerous while *Argenna subnigra* and *Micaria silesiaca*, known only from Foxhole Heath in Breckland, were also taken. The very local beetle *Odontaeus armiger* occurs here.

L.62. LAKENHEATH–ELVEDEN HEATHS, SUFFOLK
Grade 1

(a) Lakenheath Warren and Eriswell High and Low Warrens
TL 7680, TL 7479, TL 7879. 537 ha

After the Stanford PTA, Lakenheath Warren is the most extensive of the remaining Breckland grass heaths. This was the main site for Watt's (1936–40) classic studies of the grass heath communities of the district, and is the only area left with all the main types (Grasslands A–G, see p. 175, Vol. 1). A large part of the Warren on the western side, including the area with mobile sand dunes, was levelled and converted into a military airfield in World War II, and this use has continued. The remaining, eastern sector is wedge shaped, tapering from a width of about 3 km along the edge of the A1065 road, to only 1 km at the easternmost end, along a length of 5 km.

Grassland A occurs mainly over a few hectares of undulating terrain west-south-west of Warren Lodge, and consists of discontinuous patches of open chalk ground in a matrix of closed Grassland B, and covers in aggregate probably no more than a hectare or so. A few other small patches of Grassland A occur elsewhere on the Warren in places where there has been disturbance of the soil. Grassland B occurs more widely but patchily and its total area is probably under 20 ha and even this is being steadily reduced through encroachment by naturally regenerating Scots pine, which seems especially to favour this community.

As a result of myxomatosis and also removal of sheep, the Warren is now little grazed and, although little change has taken place on Grasslands A and B, where the rawness of the thin chalk soil and sand probably limits plant growth, other types of grassland have shown a marked change and are now relatively luxuriant and tussocky. This has applied especially to types C and D, with dominance of *Agrostis tenuis*, *A. canina*, *Festuca ovina* and *Arrhenatherum elatius*. In places, *Deschampsia flexuosa* has appeared in considerable abundance, and there are numerous dense patches of both *Calamagrostis epigejos* and *Carex arenaria*. Bracken, often in dominant stands, covers large areas of the Warren, and there are smaller patches of rosebay willow herb. Heather communities are local, but quite extensive towards the north-western edge of the Warren, and these too have grown luxuriant through reduction of grazing. The lichen-dominated communities with sparse grasses have probably been unaffected, but these are very local and of small extent; the largest area is just north-east of the Lodge, and there is a mosaic development of lichen heath in association with some stands of Callunetum.

Gorse is almost absent from Lakenheath Warren, birch extremely sparse and scattered, and invasion by shrubs/trees is almost confined to the locally extensively colonisation by Scots pine which comes from the clump of old trees around the Lodge, older belts along the south edge, and the great expanse of planted forest which forms the straight and continuous northern boundary of the site.

The two Eriswell Warrens are fenced-off and differ from Lakenheath Warren largely in being still grazed, though cattle are involved and create problems through the effects of their treading and the provision of winter feed. The latter results in quantities of straw and other fodder lying about the ground and promotes a progressive nutrient enrichment which is beginning to affect both the calcareous grasslands and acidic grass heaths (including Callunetum) of the areas. There is also an introduction of arable weeds associated with modern agriculture. A feature of particular interest on Eriswell High Warren is the occurrence of well-developed heather lines corresponding to periglacial striping of the underlying till, and separated by broader alternating bands of grassland.

Apart from the importance of the plant communities as such, the area as a whole is of considerable floristic interest from the occurrence, in the calcareous Grasslands A and B, of *Carex ericetorum, Asperula cynanchica, Astragalus danicus, Gentianella amarella, Botrychium lunaria, Rhytidium rugosum* and several rare lichens in abundance; and of *Galium parisiense* ssp. *anglicum, Veronica verna* and *Trifolium striatum* in smaller quantity.

Stone curlews were once numerous on Lakenheath Warren, but the increased luxuriance of much of the vegetation has reduced the population to a few pairs, which nest on the short and open calcareous grasslands. Numbers are also much reduced on the still-grazed Eriswell Warrens, so that other factors may be involved in the decline. Common curlews have increased, however, for the more luxuriant grass heaths favour their nesting requirements. Once-characteristic birds such as the ringed plover, stonechat, wheatear and woodlark have almost gone. The nightjar is much scarcer, but whinchats remain and there is a large population of skylarks.

Records of Hemiptera–Auchenorhyncha from Watt's grassland types are available and include species of the difficult *Psammotettix* from Grassland A. The *Carex arenaria*-dominated communities support the notable species *Kelisia pannonica* f. *sabulicola* and *Xanthodelphax flaveolus*. The former appears to be associated specifically with *C. arenaria* and the latter is known from only two other

stations in Britain. A few notable Coleoptera have also been recorded from the Warren.

(b) Wangford Warren–Airfield Lights
TL 7484, TL 7683. 60 ha

Wangford Warren is the only surviving example of the once extensive open and mobile sand-dune system that stretched to the western part of Lakenheath Warren, before the ground was levelled and converted into an airfield. Active dune systems are now restricted to only three sites in Breckland, of which Wangford Warren is by far the largest and most important. A large blow-out still persists, and the dune system may gradually be depleted, as there is no source of new sand to replace that blown away. Floristically, the site is not rich, but there is a particularly fine colonisation sequence from open sand to acidic grass heath. The first stage is invasion by *Polytrichum piliferum* which then develops into mixed moss–lichen heath with the addition of *Cladonia sylvatica, C. uncialis* and *Cetraria aculeata*. The final stage is produced by the invasion of *Agrostis tenuis* and *Festuca ovina* to give a lichen-rich grassland. Much of the rest of the site is covered by pure stands of *Carex arenaria*. A plant species of great interest is *Corynephorus canescens*, a rare maritime grass which has at Wangford Warren its only inland station in Britain.

In addition to the dunes, and in marked contrast to them, is an area of alkaline fenland dominated by *Phragmites* and a *Salix* carr, now separated from the sandy Warren by fields.

Breeding birds formerly included wheatear, stone curlew and ringed plover. The open sandy areas maintain a habitat for the spiders *Arctosa perita, Attulus saltator* and *Steatoda albomaculatus* which have greatly declined in numbers on other Breckland heaths.

Airfield Lights is a mixed area of acidic grassland and wind-blown sand forming part of Wangford Warren but divided from the dune system by the A1065 road. *Carex arenaria* covers a large part, frequently mixed with *Calluna vulgaris*, and *Calamagrostis epigejos* is invading in one corner. There is in addition much oak and broom scrub. The adjacent roadside verge is a site for *Artemisia campestris*. Nightjars breed within the area.

(c) Wangford Carr
TL 7483. 18 ha

This area is somewhat similar to Wangford Warren in that a large part of it is covered by wind-blown sand, but the dune formation is less well represented and only a few blow-outs remain active. Much of the dune system is stabilised by *Carex arenaria* on the leeward face and *Polytrichum–Cladonia* on the windward, eroded face.

Both stone curlew and wheatear breed here.

(d) Berner's, Horn and Weather Heaths
TL 8076–7877. 331 ha

Berner's Heath lies about 2 km north-east of Deadman's Grave (L.61(c)), and although separated by arable land, the two sites are joined by a wide sheep drove, known as Seven

Tree Road. The soils are acidic sands, podsolised in places, but Chalk comes to the surface along the northern boundary of Berner's Heath, an extensive stretch of almost uniform heather which is burnt-off on a controlled basis at seven-year intervals to increase the value of the sheep-grazing. Floristically the whole area is poor, but the lichen flora, particularly in the older-aged stands of heather, possesses a variety of species not often found elsewhere. Intensive rabbit-grazing keeps the sward low on Horn Heath, and is preventing further spread of *Calluna*. Dry acidic *Festuca–Agrostis* grassland covers about 16 ha of Horn Heath.

Breeding birds include common curlew, a few stone curlew, wheatear, woodlark and whinchat.

(e) Maidscross Hill
TL 7282. 26 ha

This site consists of the top of a gravel-capped hill, once contiguous with Lakenheath Warren, but now divided from it by an airfield. Much of the area has been disturbed by gravel workings in the past, although today the pits exhibit stages in the colonisation sequence from bare sand to a close knit acidic grassland sward with *Festuca–Agrostis* dominant. Chalk comes to the surface on the southern slopes and a rich flora has developed. *Silene otites* is locally plentiful and nearby is a small colony of the lizard orchid *Himantoglossum hircinum*. The characteristic Breckland species *Veronica verna*, *Muscari atlanticum* and *Silene conica* occur and on the adjacent arable fields are *Veronica praecox* and *V. triphyllos*. Where the sandy tracks are consolidated *Crassula tillaea* is plentiful. Whinchat breed in the parts invaded by gorse.

(f) Lord's Well Field
TL 7280. 8 ha

The higher ground of this site is modified Grassland B (see p. 175, Vol. 1) with abundant *Silene otites* and *S. conica* on recently disturbed soil; *Veronica verna* is also recorded. On the lower ground, the vegetation is less luxuriant and the soil more acid. This is the habitat for *Scleranthus perennis* ssp. *prostratus* which grows in a rather open community with *Agrostis canina*, *A. tenuis*, *Koeleria cristata*, *Aira praecox*, *Hieracium pilosella*, *Hypochoeris radicata*, *Jasione montana*, *Filago minima*, *Ornithopus perpusillus* and *Teesdalia nudicaulis*.

L.63. FOXHOLE HEATH, SUFFOLK
TL 7378. 170 ha   Grade 1

The vegetation of Foxhole Heath is mixed and ranges from calcicolous grassland to Callunetum and acidophilous grass heath. The underlying soils are correspondingly varied, having developed on till, wind-blown sands, and gravels.

Where wind-blown sand occurs, *Carex arenaria* is locally dominant, but on this site many of the very sandy areas are not so covered but are stabilised by *Polytrichum–Cladonia* heath. Foxhole Heath still exhibits large areas of this type of heathland, particularly at the north end, where two fields were taken out of arable production 20 years ago. A number of rare plants are recorded, notably *Silene otites*, *Festuca glauca* var. *caesia* and *Ornithogalum umbellatum*.

Lack of intensive sheep-grazing has led, on all but the poorest sandy soil, to invasion by gorse and broom scrub although this is not yet detracting from the value of the area. *Helictotrichon pratense* and other grazing-tolerant species (*Scabiosa columbaria*, *Knautia arvensis*, *Leontodon taraxacoides*, *Medicago falcata*, *Silene otites* etc.) are components of ungrazed calcareous grassland, in marked contrast to their absence or rarity on Deadman's Grave (L.61(c)) and Weeting Heath (L.64).

The invertebrate fauna has been particularly well studied, and several species of insects and arachnids which are scarce elsewhere in Breckland still survive here. Notable species include *Diastictus vulneratus* (Coleoptera, Scarabaeidae), restricted to Breckland in Britain and taken in numbers only on this site. The fauna of ground beetles (Coleoptera, Carabidae) is rich in uncommon arenicolous species. The heath is probably the best surviving site in Breckland for species of spiders restricted to the extreme conditions of open, stony ground.

On no other Breckland heath can the following species be found together: *Steatoda albomaculatus*, *Agroeca cuprea*, *Attulus saltator*, *Micaria silesiaca*, *Arctosa perita* and *Phaulothrix hardyi*.

L.64. WEETING HEATH, NORFOLK
TL 7588. 140 ha   Grade 1

Weeting Heath is a fine example of the main type of calcareous Grassland B found in Breckland, and possesses a rich fauna and flora which include a number of national rarities.

Although chalk grassland dominates the greater part, there are in addition dense patches of bracken and rosebay willow herb with some sand sedge in the mid section of the heath, and an area of rough pasture, with neutral grassland, overlying peaty soils, where the southern boundary abuts on the River Little Ouse. A 16-ha rabbit enclosure was erected on the southern part in 1959 and by maintaining a high rabbit population a type of open, sandy and stony heathland has been restored. This is of a still more extreme type than the close-grazed lawns prevalent in Lakenheath Warren in pre-myxomatosis days. The activities of large numbers of rabbits and moles have produced a very sparse plant cover, especially of small annuals, mosses and lichens, and much of the ground is bare sand or flint. Rabbits have also increased to a high density on the northern part of the heath, and the grassland, which had become tall and tussocky, has been reduced to a close-grazed, moss and lichen-rich turf. This part was also fenced in 1971/72.

The heath forms one of the few remaining localities in Breckland for the rare and attractive *Veronica spicata* ssp. *spicata*, and *Herniaria glabra* is recorded. Other vascular species of interest include *Dianthus deltoides*, *Thymus serpyllum*, *Vulpia ambigua*, *Galium parisiense* ssp. *anglicum*, *Carex ericetorum*, *Thalictrum minus* and *Brachypodium pinnatum*, while the moss *Rhytidium rugosum* is locally in great quantity. Soil nets and stripes are well developed on some parts of the heath.

Typical Breckland birds are well represented, including

stone curlew and wheatear, which have increased significantly in recent years following the return of the rabbit and reduction in plant cover within the grassland areas. The woodlark, however, has become rare and may have disappeared. The crossbill breeds at times in the old pines of the northern sector or around the edges of the heath.

The invertebrate fauna has been well studied and the heath is the only known British station for the Mediterranean spider *Walckenaera stylifrons* and one of the very few stations for *W. incisa*. The Coleoptera include *Ocypus ophthalmicus* (Staphylinidae) and *Panagaeus bipustulatus* (Carabidae) as notable species. The cicadellid bug *Hardya melanopsis* occurs at the northern end of the heath but in reduced numbers in 1968, probably because of greatly increased grazing by rabbits compared with 1964–65. The scattered Scots pines in the northern section of the heath form one of the three British localities for *Philodromus collinus*, while the more barren parts of the heath yield the very scarce *Oxyptila scabricula*. A small enclosure nearby is managed as an arable weed reserve.

L.65. THETFORD HEATHS, SUFFOLK–NORFOLK

Grade 1

(a) *Thetford Heath*
TL 8480.   90 ha

(b) *Sketchvar Heath*
TL 8379.   20 ha

(c) *RAF Barnham*
TL 8580.   165 ha

(d) *Barnhamcross Common*
TL 8681.   80 ha

(e) *Little Heath*
TL 8578.   35 ha

Thetford Heath has a good range of the more typical dry heathland communities found in Breckland. The soils are mainly calcareous but with many flints and a good deal of sand intermixed in the surface layers. Since rabbits became scarce, the tall tussocky variants of former Grasslands B–D (see p. 175, Vol. 1) have developed over much of the area, and there is now little open ground, except for patches of flint-strewn lichen carpet. On the east and south-east sides, acidic grassland and Callunetum has developed; there are also several smaller, yet ecologically important, communities dominated respectively by *Polytrichum piliferum*, *Cladonia rangiformis* and *C. sylvatica*. Bracken grows on the Icknield Way which forms the west boundary. Plants of interest include *Medicago minima*, *Vulpia ambigua* and *Artemisia campestris*, the last-named having been transplanted from a colony at Thetford threatened by housing development. The lichen flora is rich and includes one notable rarity, *Verrucaria psammophila*, in only its second known station in the world (the other is on the border of Denmark and Germany).

One of the most prominent features of Thetford Heath is the local orientation of heather in long, curving lines. This is a reflection of the differential sorting of soil material caused by frost phenomena in a periglacial period, giving stripe features. The heather grows on a deep sandy soil midway between grass covered ridges of coarse flints and chalk. Striping is also very clearly shown in herbaceous communities on more disturbed ground near the road.

The invertebrate fauna has changed in some respects since rabbit grazing ceased to depress vegetation growth. Interesting heathland spiders include the local *Hypsosinga albovittata*, one of the smallest orb-web spinners which must have been absent or rare when rabbits were common. The rare linyphiid spider, *Walckenaera incisa*, has one of its few British stations at Thetford Heath. Other rare dry grassland species include *Centromerus incilium* and *Thanatus striatus*, the latter being more typical of coastal sand dunes.

The upsurge of vegetation growth following myxomatosis has reduced the number of breeding stone curlew and wheatear to only a few pairs. An experimental programme of sheep-grazing has recently been started in an attempt to create more favourable conditions.

Sketchvar Heath is an area of calcareous to neutral grassland (Grasslands B and C) with rather species-poor sward contiguous with Thetford Heath along its western boundary. There is also some bracken, gorse scrub and a considerable area (8 ha) of regenerating pine.

On the north side of Thetford Heath, Barnhamcross Common is an area of heath with a range of plant communities including calcicolous grassland and areas of *Carex arenaria*, broom and gorse. It is a site for several rare plants including *Artemisia campestris*, *Thymus serpyllum* ssp. *serpyllum*, *Medicago falcata*, *Galium parisiense*, *Veronica verna*, *Silene otites*, *Dianthus deltoides* and *Scleranthus perennis*. The invertebrate fauna is rich and includes the web spider *Araneus adiantus* in its most northerly station in the country. The site is too disturbed and overgrown for stone curlew and wheatear, but a few pairs of whinchat breed. It is close to Thetford town and is burned most years, so that the habitat is deteriorating.

Little Heath is a small but interesting area of open chalk grassland developed on a highly calcareous soil. Much of the surface soil was removed in 1946 and the bare Chalk has slowly been colonised to produce an open community which is in many ways similar to Grassland A. *Thymus drucei*, *Astragalus danicus*, *Botrychium lunaria*, *Cirsium acaulon*, *Linum catharticum*, *Sagina nodosa* and *Cladonia rangiformis* are all constituents of this open community. In places *Anthyllis vulneraria* is abundant, forming almost pure swards. Massive pine regeneration is threatening the northern section of the area.

L.66. RISBY WARREN, LINCOLNSHIRE

SE 9213.   170 ha

Grade 1

Risby Warren, 3 km north-east of Scunthorpe, is situated on the crest of the Lincolnshire Limestone escarpment at an altitude of between about 20 and 70 m above sea-level. The limestone is covered by wind-blown sand up to 6 or 9 m in thickness but is exposed in places. This variable thickness of 'cover sand' results in a variety of plant communities, which have been studied in detail by Davidson (1961). These range from marram dunes produced by marram grass planted during the 1920s to stabilise 'flying sands', fixed dunes essentially grassy and acid in character, 'grass heath' with heather dominant but herbs abundant, and more base-rich grassland with *Pia pratensis*, *Zerna erecta* and *Holcus lanatus*, where the cover sand thins out and the limestone comes to the surface. The area thus affords an interesting comparison with the range of acidic to calcareous heaths and grasslands found in the Breckland. There is much greater floristic variety than on the majority of East Anglian heathlands outside the Breckland, and Risby Warren bears some resemblance in this respect to some of the more acidic coastal dune systems.

Among the more noteworthy species of acidic to mildly basic sands in the area are *Carex arenaria*, *Cerastium arvense*, *Centaurium erythraea*, *Cynoglossum officinale*, *Echium vulgare*, *Myosotis ramosissima*, *Filago minima*, *F. germanica*, *Gnaphalium sylvaticum*, *Ornithopus perpusillus*, *Arenaria serpyllifolia*, *Sedum acre*, *Plantago coronopus* and *Salix repens*. *Gentiana pneumonanthe* was recorded from the area in 1961, presumably on damper ground. Where the limestone comes near the surface there are calcicoles such as *Zerna erecta*, *Carlina vulgaris*, *Astragalus danicus* and *Carduus nutans*. Old dunes grazed by rabbits have a high cover of mosses, notably *Phascum cuspidatum* and *Rhacomitrium canescens*. A small spring is present, producing a restricted area of wetter vegetation with species such as *Carex acutiformis*, *C. hirta*, *C. disticha* and *Juncus inflexus*.

Birds breeding on this site now or in the recent past include shelduck, wheatear, woodlark, short-eared and long-eared owls, hen harrier, nightjar and grasshopper warbler.

Shelter belts of conifers (mainly *Pinus nigra*) have been planted, and there are scattered birches. The area is used for shooting by the present owner and is relatively free from public pressure. Grazing by rabbits and hares is an important factor in the present ecology of the area. The most important external factors are the presence of Scunthorpe to the south-west and the open-cast workings exploiting the Frodingham Ironstone immediately to the south-west. The presence of this ironstone under the Warren and the incidence of atmospheric pollution cast doubts on the long-term viability of this area. The area is also somewhat 'unnatural', the introduction of marram having had a very marked effect on the site. The main interest in this site is the variety of plant communities. Although Risby Warren is the largest remaining area of cover sand vegetation in Lincolnshire it was once much more extensive, and represents only the drier end of a series of plant communities once present. Damper and more acidic areas occur at Messingham Heath (now much reduced in size by sand winning) and Scotton Common (a small site managed by the Lincolnshire Trust for Nature Conservation).

L.67. KNOCKING HOE, BEDFORDSHIRE
TL 1330.   9 ha   Grade 1

This is the smallest grade 1 site on the Chalk (and is also a NNR) of which 4 ha are recently reverted ploughland, the remainder being species-rich grassland. This site is placed in this grade, not as an example of a grassland type but because of the presence of a large number of uncommon species including four of high phytogeographical interest. *Seseli libanotis*, *Hypochoeris maculata*, *Senecio integrifolius* and *Anemone pulsatilla* are present in good quantity, *Seseli* being particularly abundant. The predominantly *Festuca ovina* grassland also contains *Onobrychis viciifolia* in its native form, and other species of special note are *Orchis ustulata*, *Spiranthes spiralis* and *Blackstonia perfoliata*. The topography of the Hoe, on which most of the rare species are found, suggests that this may be extremely old, undisturbed chalk grassland of great value for ecological–historical studies.

Knocking Hoe is not known to have been collected over extensively for insects by naturalists. The diversity of the one systematic sample taken here was below average for short grassland (5 cm). The Auchenorhyncha fauna was an impoverished version of that of the Barton Hills except that two common species, *Agallia venosa* and *Arocephalus punctum*, were present (recorded only as casual at the Barton Hills). The local weevil *Tychius lineatulus* has been recorded from the site, but on present information the entomological status of this site is below grade 1.

L.68. BARTON HILLS, BEDFORDSHIRE
TL 0929.   60 ha   Grade 1

There are about 45 ha of heavily grazed *Zerna erecta* chalk grassland with excellent replication of south and south-west facing slopes and with three north facing slopes. Different degrees of grazing intensity have created grassland with different structures, ranging from the very short to coarse types which are important for studies on the fauna and flora. There is a fairly diverse flora, *Anemone pulsatilla* occurs on four sites on the Hills, while *Senecio integrifolius* is widespread. Mixed scrub communities, whose history is well known, are represented on the east-facing slope, while hawthorn scrub, controlled by grazing, is scattered on the south- and north-facing slopes. The principal scrub interest of this site is the regeneration of hazel which is infrequent as an invasive scrub plant on chalk soils. The main associates in this stand are hawthorn, *Rosa* and *Rubus*, with a field layer in the more open areas of taller vegetation such as *Arrhenatherum elatius*, *Dactylis glomerata*, *Centaurea nigra* and *Heracleum sphondylium*. *Salix caprea* and *Paris quadrifolia* have been found in the damper shaded areas near the spring. Much of the rest of the area has an incipient scrub of hawthorn of about 0.5 m in height. A degenerate beechwood (Leete Wood) and a small planted conifer plantation add to the interest in this area. A stream issuing from the base of the Lower Chalk runs along the valley floor.

This is an extremely rich site entomologically, but it has been so well worked recently that it is uncertain whether it is particularly outstanding or merely well recorded. Single systematic vacuum net samples chosen at random from those taken in late summer from ungrazed grassland (to give a more meaningful comparison with data for other key sites) were above average in terms of the numbers of species of Auchenorhyncha recorded. Many rarities occur, particularly among the Coleoptera, e.g. *Odontaeus armiger*,

Porcinolus murinus, Homalopia ruricola and *Smicronyx reichi.*

This is an important research site for studies of chalk grassland management, especially the effects of grazing and cutting treatments on vegetation composition and structure, flora and fauna.

L.69. BARNACK HILLS AND HOLES, HUNTINGDON AND PETERBOROUGH   Grade 1
TF 0704.   20 ha

Barnack Hills and Holes, an area of ridges, mounds and hollows representing old workings for Jurassic limestone, has good calcareous grassland with a rich and varied flora, including a number of species of national importance. *Acerus anthropophorum* is locally abundant, *Anemone pulsatilla* occurs in great quantity, second only in Britain to Barnsley Warren, and the small patch of *Antennaria dioica*, a northern species, occurs in one of its few remaining stations in the lowlands of England. The grassland belongs to the *Brachypodium pinnatum–Zerna erecta* type, and contains the whole range of species characteristic of this association. A large number of micro-habitats are provided by the undulating nature of the terrain. There is a good deal of invasion by Turkey oak, but this is kept under control.

Compared with chalk grassland sites the numbers of species of Auchenorhyncha in systematic samples from Barnack Hills and Holes was below average, but this is probably not a reasonable comparison. The Heteroptera and Curculionoidea samples were above average, though no rarities were recorded. The site is a well-known one for the chalk-hill blue butterfly towards the northern limit of its range in Britain, but the present status of the species is uncertain.

L.70. OUSE WASHES, CAMBRIDGESHIRE–NORFOLK
TL 392750–TF 581010.   2350 ha   Grade 1*
Neutral grassland groups 4 and 5 (14)[1]

This linear series of meadows is continuously flooded from November to March, in a wet winter, but the duration of floods varies markedly according to winter rainfall. Because of the slope of ground across the short axis, flood waters vary in depth at any time, with a difference of up to 1 m between the east side (New Bedford River), e.g. 0.3 m, and the west side (Old Bedford River), e.g. 1.2 m. This factor also causes variable wetness during spring and summer, after the flood water drains away and as the ground dries out, and thus adds considerably to the diversity of conditions for flora and fauna.

The long period of inundation to which virtually all the meadows are usually subjected during winter is reflected in the species composition. The genera *Juncus, Oenanthe* and *Polygonum* are well represented, and included in the latter are *P. mite* and *P. minus* both of which appear to be decreasing nationally. Although some 32 km from the sea, relicts of former marine flooding may still occur, e.g. *Aster tripolium, Apium graveolens* and *Scirpus maritimus.* The ditches carry a great number of submerged and floating aquatics,

and of great interest is the large number (16) of species and hybrids of *Potamogeton*, making this an important locality for study of the genus. Other aquatic species include *Hydrocharis morsus-ranae, Nymphoides peltata, Sium latifolium* and the four species of *Lemna.*

In winter these Washes are the best inland area of water in Britain for populations of dabbling ducks. Numbers of pintail at times rise to a third of the estimated British population, and up to 42000 wigeon have been counted. Bewick's swans continue to increase so that this area now supports the largest flock in Britain, numbering up to 1280 birds.

The meadows are normally partly dry from April to November and the area then attracts many breeding birds, particularly snipe, lapwing and redshank. The area supports one of the very few breeding colonies of black-tailed godwits and the only known breeding ruffs in the country. Black terns have also nested in recent years. Mallard and shoveler are the commonest breeding duck and garganey, gadwall, pintail and occasionally shelduck nest. Of the passerines, skylark, reed warbler, sedge warbler, yellow wagtail and meadow pipit are numerous and up to two million sand martins are estimated to feed over the area whilst on migration. This use of the Ouse Washes by birds for feeding, whilst on migration, adds to the conservation importance of the site.

The Earith end of the Washes has not been so closely studied, but this less flooded area probably supports a greater small mammal population and their attendant birds of prey, e.g. short-eared owl, kestrel, than the remaining area, at least in winter.

Ideally the Ouse Washes should be thought of in their entirety, as a single unit extending from Earith to Denver Sluice.

See also OW.17.

L.71. THOMPSON COMMON, NORFOLK
TL 9395.   135 ha   Grade 1
Neutral grassland group 1 (3)[1]

This site lies at the northern edge of the Breckland, and has more of the character of lowland meadow than breck, though it contains examples of calcareous grassland and transitions from this to acidic heath. There are also wetlands and the area has a rich fauna, giving in total a high nature conservation interest. The wetland component consists of a number of streams, several ponds and a bigger lake, with their associated marginal fen communities, and other pockets of fen, and is regarded as having bonus interest in regard to both open waters and peatlands.

Much of the area consists of cattle-grazed neutral grassland approximating to groups 1 and 5. Species indicative of damp conditions include *Polygonum amphibium, Filipendula ulmaria, Phalaris arundinacea, Lotus pedunculatus, Ranunculus repens, Epilobium hirsutum, Mentha aquatica, Juncus inflexus, Carex otrubae* and *C. hirta*; whilst those typical of rather drier meadowland are *Lathyrus pratensis, Vicia cracca, Potentilla anserina, Plantago lanceolata, Centaurea nigra,*

[1] See pp. 185–7, Vol. 1.

Pulicaria dysenterica, Phleum pratense, Festuca rubra, Holcus lanatus, Arrhenatherum elatius, Carex flacca, and *Equisetum arvense.* This range of communities grades in many places into a poor chalk grassland. There are, however, scattered areas of better chalk grassland with *Carlina vulgaris, Cirsium acaulon, Poterium sanguisorba, Helianthemum chamaecistus, Ophrys apifera* and *Astragalus danicus,* showing invasion by blackthorn and hawthorn.

Another interesting feature of the Common is the local occurrence of dry acidic heath of *Calluna* with some *Agrostis–Festuca* grassland, much of which has been invaded by gorse and birch. Smaller areas of wet acidic heath are characterised by *Sphagnum* spp., *Eriophorum angustifolium* and *Drosera* spp.

The man-made lake, Thompson Water, is floristically similar to the Breckland meres, but the water level only fluctuates with rainfall and does not respond to changes in the ground water table as do the true meres. Around the water bodies are three distinct vegetation types: a tall-sedge community of *Carex rostrata, Potentilla palustris, Ranunculus lingua* (group 2); a dwarf sedge association of *C. panicea, Anagallis tenella* (group 3); and an alkaline fen community of *Phragmites communis, Cladium mariscus, Carex elata, C. appropinquata, C. paniculata, Iris pseudacorus* and *Polygonum amphibium.* These wetland communities have been invaded in varying degrees by alder and willows, and carr has developed with locally abundant *Thelypteris palustris.*

The invertebrate fauna has been little studied but promises to be of great interest. The spiders include several rare and local fen species including *Pirata piscatorius, Linyphia impigra, Mengea warburtoni, Walckenaera nodosa, Hillhousia misera, Philodromus caespitum* and *Theridion instabile.* The phytophagous Coleoptera, especially the weevils of aquatic–terrestrial transition habitats, are particularly rich and include such rarities as *Phytobius quadricornis.* The edible frog *Rana esculenta* was rediscovered here recently.

L.72. UPWOOD MEADOWS, HUNTINGDON AND PETERBOROUGH

TL 2582. 6 ha   Grade 1
Neutral grassland group 8[1]

Three small fields with old pasture lie on a calcareous clay with impeded drainage, and have an outstandingly rich and diverse flora. This type of pasture was once widespread in the Midland clay region but has almost disappeared as a result of ploughing, so that the few remaining areas are of the highest importance.

The main interest of this type of grassland is the balance reached, as a result of the type of management over a very long period, between various species, with the result that none is dominant. At this site, 15 grasses are present, including *Briza media, Alopecurus pratensis, Festuca rubra* and *Poa trivialis,* and the presence of *Sieglingia decumbens* in this calcicolous grassland is interesting. There are two sedges, *Carex flacca* and *C. caryophyllea,* characteristic of calcicolous grassland, and a large range of forbs is present, with *Primula veris, Centaurea nigra, Filipendula vulgaris, F.*

ulmaria, Sanguisorba officinalis, Genista tinctoria, Cirsium acaulon, and *Silaum silaus.* There are also three species now rare or local in East Anglia, *Trifolium ochroleucon, Serratula tinctoria* and *Orchis morio,* the last species being present in great numbers; 2000 plants were recorded in 1969. Altogether, 112 flowering plants have been recorded from these small fields.

This association forms a distinctive grassland type which is found only on this very limited type of old pasture and is restricted to Huntingdon and Peterborough and nearby counties.

The ridge and furrow system is of interest to the archaeologist and may provide an opportunity to study floristic composition in relation to age of pasture. Further interest is added by an unpolluted pond and the whole area is surrounded by tall thick hedges of value as an extra faunal habitat.

L.73. SIBSON–CASTOR MEADOWS, HUNTINGDON AND PETERBOROUGH   Grade 1
Neutral grassland group 7 (3)[1]

This stretch of the River Nene has good examples of alluvial meadows scattered on both sides.

(a) Sibson–Sutton
TL 1097. 35 ha

The Sibson Meadows are normally cut for hay, resulting in a tall grass–sedge community grading from *Glyceria maxima* in the wetter areas through *Phalaris arundinacea, Carex acutiformis* and *C. acuta* to *Alopecurus pratensis, C. disticha* and, in the driest areas, *Holcus lanatus* and *C. hirta* communities. A small marsh area of *C. disticha, Juncus acutiflorus* and *J. inflexus* contains large numbers of *Dactylorchis fuchsii* and *D. incarnata,* the latter being rare in the county. Similarly, this site is the only known locality in Huntingdon and Peterborough for *C. distans* and *C. paniculata.* The Sibson Meadows are also noteworthy for *Senecio aquaticus* and *C. acuta,* both rare in the county and the latter uncommon in East Anglia generally.

The Sutton Meadows, on the opposite side of the river, are, by contrast, summer grazed. The main community consists of *Poa trivialis, Deschampsia cespitosa, Agrostis stolonifera* and *Carex disticha,* with *Glyceria maxima* in the wetter areas. A pond and ditches provide a wide variety of aquatic and emergent plants including *Schoenoplectus lacustris, Veronica catenata, C. acuta, C. riparia* and *Equisetum fluviatile.*

(b) Chesterton–Castor
TL 1297. 25 ha

The Chesterton Meadows range from 'dry' *Bromus lepidus* grasslands through *Alopecurus pratensis, Holcus lanatus* and *Sanguisorba officinalis* to communities of *Carex disticha* and *Juncus articulatus* communities. Most of these meadows are cut for hay and contain a variety of herbs.

The Castor Meadows again comprise a wide variety of types from a *Festuca rubra, Anthoxanthum odoratum* and

[1] See pp. 185–6, Vol. 1.

Saxifraga granulata community, on ridge-and-furrow permanent pasture, through *Carex disticha* and *Juncus articulatus*, to *J. articulatus, C. acuta* and *Eleocharis palustris* communities. A further meadow, cut for hay, has a community with *J. inflexus, Poa trivialis, Filipendula ulmaria, Sanguisorba officinalis* and *Thalictrum flavum*.

The River Nene was not surveyed in detail but the presence of extensive stands of *Nuphar lutea, Potamogeton* spp., and other emergent aquatics, indicate some botanical interest.

The birds of the area are also of interest, with the meadows supporting such breeding species as redshank, common snipe and yellow wagtail. The river banks provide breeding areas for kingfisher and sand martin, while the tall grass and sedge swamps are the nesting place of moorhen, reed and sedge warblers. In the winter, large numbers of duck, mainly mallard and teal, utilise the flooded meadows.

L.74. MONEWDEN MEADOWS, SUFFOLK

TM 2257.   4 ha   Grade 1
Neutral grassland group 8[1]

This site consists of three old meadows in which a group of grasses, including *Alopecurus pratensis, Festuca rubra, Cynosurus cristatus* and *Holcus lanatus*, are co-dominants in the sward. A large number of forbs is present; *Colchicum autumnale* and *Orchis morio* occur in all the meadows, and in addition, there are *Fritillaria meleagris* and *Bromus commutatus*, two species which here demonstrate the affinities between neutral grassland groups 7 and 8. This situation is reversed in one of the meadows at Clattinger (L.44), Wiltshire, where *C. autumnale* and *O. morio* occur in an otherwise typical group 7 meadow. A further interest of this site is the presence of *Orchis mascula* in the grassland. This is normally a woodland species in the east but occurs in grasslands in the north and west.

L.75. HOLT LOWES, NORFOLK

TG 0837.   50 ha   Grade 2

This area of dry heathland is traversed by two relatively deep and steep-sided valleys with well-developed mires. The heath is the type in which *Calluna* and *Erica cinerea* are mixed with *Ulex europaeus* and *U. gallii*, with the gorse locally forming dense thickets. Bracken is dominant in places but has a patchy distribution and is absent from some parts of the heath. The area has been severely burned at intervals and patches of *Chamaenerion angustifolium* are frequent. Grassy patches with *Holcus mollis, Festuca ovina* and *Deschampsia flexuosa* occur here and there; *Rumex acetosella* is abundant on barer ground; and *Cuscuta epithymum* is frequent on the dwarf shrubs. The dry heathland shows variable colonisation by birch, but the periodic fires keep this succession in check.

The valley mires grade from oligotrophic to eutrophic. The former have the acidophilous *Sphagnum* spp.: *S. compactum, S. tenellum, S. rubellum, S. papillosum* and *S. magellanicum*, with vascular plants such as *Trichophorum cespitosum, Juncus squarrosus, Drosera rotundifolia* and

[1] See p. 186, Vol. 1.

Lycopodium inundatum. Hollows have *J. kochii, Potamogeton polygonifolius* and *Rhynchospora alba*. More mesotrophic conditions are indicated by a change to *Molinia caerulea, J. subnodulosus, J. conglomeratus, Cirsium dissectum, Carex echinata, Succisa pratensis, Dactylorchis ericetorum, Platanthera bifolia, Cirsium palustre, Drosera anglica, Hypericum elodes, Scutellaria minor, Anagallis tenella, Sphagnum contortum, S. palustre, S. subsecundum, S. teres, S. plumulosum, Aulacomnium palustre, Acrocladium cuspidatum*, and *Dicranum bonjeani*. The most nutrient-rich water has bryophyte patches with *Campylium stellatum, Drepanocladus revolvens, Cinclidium stygium, Camptothecium nitens, Philonotis calcarea* and the rare liverwort *Leiocolea rutheana*.

Vascular plants of this community include *Schoenus nigricans, Dactylorchis praetermissa, Carex dioica* and *C. pulicaris*. Birch–willow carr has developed in parts of the valleys and has *Sphagnum palustre–S. fimbriatum* carpets with rarer species such as *Equisetum sylvaticum, Pyrola minor* and *Hookeria lucens*.

A pond and pools in the valley mire were formerly the haunt of the local dragonflies *Anax imperator* and *Orthetrum coerulescens*.

L.76. SANDRINGHAM WARREN (DERSINGHAM BOG), NORFOLK

TF 6728.   160 ha   Grade 2

Nearer the coast of the Wash, the edge of the Cretaceous plateau passes into shallow valleys in which a substantial area of oligotrophic valley mire has formed. This mire, which is regarded as a grade 2 peatland site (P.23), passes through marginal wet and humid heath (containing the rare moss *Dicranum spurium* and *Sphagnum molle*) into dry heath with heather and bracken, though on shallower peat there is also an acidic *Molinia* grassland with partial *Sphagnum* carpet. The area is surrounded by birchwood and rhododendron thickets which are encroaching onto the open heathland in places. The area is open for recreation, but the mire and wet heath area is little disturbed.

L.77. BARNHAM HEATH, SUFFOLK

TL 8879.   80 ha   Grade 2

This is an area of mixed heath lying on river gravels and acidic sands. Cattle-grazed acidic grassland covers much of the site with, in addition, bracken, gorse and invading birch woodland. Gravel extraction has taken place in the past and where the old pits are overgrown with birch, scrub oak and pine a good habitat is afforded for woodland birds such as tree pipit and nightingale.

L.78. THETFORD WARREN, NORFOLK

TL 8383.   130 ha   Grade 2

This scenically attractive area of Breckland heath has both acidiphilous and calcicolous plant communities. On the site of old gravel workings a mixed *Cladonia–Polytrichum* community has developed which grades into acidic grassland with *Festuca–Agrostis* spp. dominant. Bracken, some heather and considerable pine regeneration form constituents of the 'roughs'. Plants of interest include *Gentianella amarella*,

Dianthus deltoides and *Silene otites*. There is a strip of alluvial fenland adjacent to the River Little Ouse, with *Carex paniculata* locally dominant, some *Glyceria–Phragmites* reed-swamp, *Molinia caerulea* fen and alder carr.

L.79. CHALK HILL, BARTON MILLS, SUFFOLK
TL 7271.   30 ha   Grade 2

This area includes an old conifer plantation, a strip of arable land used for experimental seed sowings, together with adjacent roadside verges and field margins. The latter are important sites for *Silene otites*, *S. conica* and *Veronica praecox*; *Herniaria glabra* formerly grew in this area. The plantation is of entomological interest.

L.80. HOLYWELL MOUND, LINCOLNSHIRE
TF 0016.   7 ha   Grade 2

This is an alternative site to Barnack Hills and Holes (L.69), with much less public pressure, but with a similar flora. A steep, south-west-facing area of Jurassic limestone grassland is heavily grazed by sheep and cattle, which have successfully prevented the dominance of *Brachypodium pinnatum*. Forbs are frequent, including *Thesium humifusum*, *Anthyllis vulneraria* and *Hippocrepis comosa*.

L.81 CASTOR HANGLANDS, HUNTINGDON AND PETERBOROUGH
TF 1101.   45 ha   Grade 2

This area of woodland, scrub and grassland was selected primarily as a representative of the ancient forest of Nassburgh and for its grass heath with a varied and characteristic insect fauna. The whole complex is regarded as a woodland grade 1 site, but the grassland component, reduced in area and interest through scrub invasion, is rated only as grade 2. The grassland is dominated by *Brachypodium pinnatum*, *Arrhenatherum elatius* and a mixture of *Festuca ovina* and *Agrostis canina*, and in the northern heath area there is much *Koeleria cristata*. The occurrence of a wide range of Jurassic rock types, ranging in age from the Great Oolite Limestone to the Kellaways Clay and Sands, has resulted in a series of grassland types which are invaluable for ecological studies. Forbs are rather few and relatively sparse and it is only in the small areas of old quarry workings that a characteristic calcicolous flora is to be found.

Besides woodland (W.44), there is a good, though small, example of mixed southern scrub, of interest in an area where scrub is rare through intensive cultivation. The history of the development of the scrub is partly known, much of the area being open grassland until 1945. The scrub corresponds with Salisbury's (1918) description of 'thicket scrub', a type thought to develop under a regime of intermittent grazing, burning and coppicing such as occurs on commons. A characteristic is the very dense close growth of the woody plants with little or no ground flora. An interesting feature is the good growth and large number of bushes of *Euonymus*, while privet, hawthorn, blackthorn, dogwood and wild rose are also common. Ash is invading the site. There are few species in the field layer below the dense canopy apart from dog's mercury; however, the marginal flora by the paths is good. In a damper part with more clay in the soil there is an area of hawthorn which has been invaded by *Quercus robur* oak; the marginal forbs here include *Pulicaria dysenterica*, *Torilis japonica*, *Sieglingia decumbens* and *Angelica sylvestris*.

The entomological interest of the grassland and scrub remains high. Outstandingly high numbers of species of Auchenorhyncha and Heteroptera were recorded in the grassland samples taken at Castor Hanglands. Features of the leafhopper fauna were the presence of two species of *Muellerianella* and the absence of the common calcareous grassland species *Turrutus socialis*. The fauna recorded in the systematic samples was much richer (except in species of Curculionoidea) than that at the nearby Barnack Hills and Holes. Castor Hanglands is a well known site for Lepidoptera, although most of the interest is centred on the woodland and the limestone grassland. The black hairstreak butterfly occurs in three places, and a rare dominant form of the marbled white has been found over several years. The chequered skipper also occurs here, and is not known at present in any other key sites.

L.82. FOULDEN COMMON, NORFOLK
TF 7600.   105 ha   Grade 2
Neutral grassland groups 9 and 3[1]

Foulden Common lies on the north-west edge of the Breckland, but is not a typical mixed heath–grassland site; and bears a closer resemblance to Thompson Common. There is a complex of habitats from rich-fen developed in periglacial ground-ice depressions, neutral grassland, calcareous grassland and scrub. On the west side there is a large eutrophic basin dominated by *Cladium mariscus* and *Phragmites communis*, and containing a large number of pools and wet hollows. Less common fen species include *Parnassia palustris*, *Utricularia neglecta*, *U. intermedia*, *Eleogiton fluitans*, *Epipactis palustris* and *Oenanthe lachenalii*; and the rare moss *Drepanocladus sendtneri* occurs here in pools. This rich-fen is regarded as a bonus peatland site, referable either to basin or valley mire.

Two neutral grassland types form a transition zone between the *Cladium* basin and the chalk grassland. The first of these grades from the *Cladium* fen and is dominated by *Molinia caerulea* and *Juncus subnodolosus*, *Calamagrostis canescens*, with *Cirsium dissectum*, *Carex disticha* and *Valeriana dioica* (group 3). Between this and the chalk grassland is a neutral grassland association characterised by *Briza media*, *Arrhenatherum elatius*, *Dactylis glomerata*, *Anthoxanthum odoratum*, *C. flacca*, *Galium verum*, *Silaum silaus* and *Ononis spinosa* (group 9) which passes into a chalk grassland of *Helictotrichon pratense*, *Festuca rubra*, *Sieglingia decumbens*, *Koeleria cristata*, *Cirsium acaulon*, *Asperula cynanchica*, *Campanula glomerata*, *Gymnadenia conopsea*, *Scabiosa columbaria*, *Poterium sanguisorba*, *Pimpinella saxifraga*, *Gentianella amarella* and *Filipendula vulgaris*. More local chalk species include *Helianthemum chamaecistus*, *Carex ericetorum* and *Hippocrepis comosa*. The drier ground

[1] See pp. 185–6, Vol. 1.

shows a good deal of invasion by a variety of tree and shrub species to form a patchy scrub; noteworthy species are oak, ash, birch, hawthorn, privet, guelder rose and *Rhamnus catharticus*.

The breeding birds include reed warbler, sedge warbler, grasshopper warbler and nightingale.

The invertebrate fauna is not well known except for certain groups such as the Arachnida. The species associations are particularly interesting and characterised mainly by those confined to rich-fen habitats. Three species of spider which are common on Foulden Common, *Hygrolycosa rubrofasciata*, *Maso gallica* and *Neon valentulus*, are exceedingly rare in Britain and occur only in a very few East Anglia fens such as Wicken Fen and Chippenham Fen. Other interesting fen species include *Sitticus caricis*, *Thanatus striatus*, *Araneus marmoreus* and *Notioscopus sarcinatus*. The presence of these species suggests that the site has probably not suffered major disturbance or change of land-use for a long time and enhances its ecological interest.

L.83. CALCEBY BECK, LINCOLNSHIRE
TF 3977. 4 ha   Grade 2
Neutral grassland group 1[1]

This site, which on further study may require extending, is bordered by a chalk stream on one side and ash woodland on the other.

On the marshy grassland, which is the major community, *Juncus articulatus*, *Carex disticha*, *Poa trivialis* and *Equisetum palustre* form the dominant species with *Caltha palustris*, *Lychnis flos-cuculi* and *Mentha aquatica* abundant. *Dactylorchis fuchsii*, *D. incarnata*, *Triglochin palustris* and *Valeriana dioica* are frequent. An alder–poplar carr was not surveyed.

The stream appeared to have an interesting aquatic vegetation, and requires further assessment for its value as an open running water.

L.84. BASTON FEN, LINCOLNSHIRE
TF 1317. 40 ha   Grade 2
Neutral grassland group 5[1]

This last remaining area of Cowbit Wash is the only surviving area of wash in Lincolnshire.

The area (which is not a fen in the usual sense) is bounded on the north by the River Glen and by the Counter Drain to the south. The grassland varies from a *Lolium perenne–Poa trivialis–Agropyron repens* community (evidently a reseeded area), through a *Deschampsia cespitosa–P. trivialis* type (group 12), to a typical wash area of *Alopecurus pratensis* and *Festuca arundinacea* grading to *Glyceria maxima* sward (group 4) in the wettest grassland areas. A flooded borrow pit is partly colonised by *Typha latifolia* and the main ditch is bordered by *Carex riparia* and *C. acutiformis*. *Ranunculus lingua* and *Hottonia palustris*, uncommon in Lincolnshire, also occur.

Snipe, redshank and lapwing are breeding species and various wildfowl utilise the area when it is flooded in winter. The range of wildfowl species and numbers is small.

L.85. PORT HOLME, HUNTINGDONSHIRE
TL 2370. 105 ha   Grade 2
Neutral grassland group 7[1]

This site has similar legal clauses governing management to North Meadow, Cricklade (L.43). An attempt was made to reseed part of the area but there is still a large representative area of grassland with *Sanguisorba officinalis*, *Alopecurus pratensis*, *Festuca pratensis* and *Poa trivialis*. Other species of interest include *Carex disticha*, *Trifolium fragiferum* and *Fritillaria meleagris*. The last species is very rare and in danger of extinction at this site.

The botanical interest of many of the River Ouse meadows has diminished rapidly following adverse management since 1940. Port Holme is the largest single area remaining and one of the largest Lammas meadows in the country.

L.86. BRATOFT MEADOWS, LINCOLNSHIRE
TF 4864. 4 ha   Grade 2
Neutral grassland group 8[1]

There are four small hay meadows and one grazed meadow, ranging from the *Hordeum secalinum*, *Holcus lanatus*, *Bromus mollis* sward, typical of old pastures in eastern England, to the type with *Anthoxanthum odoratum*, *Briza media*, *Cynosurus cristatus* and *Festuca* spp., characteristic of the hay meadows. There is a wide range of forbs varying somewhat in abundance between the different meadows. *Rhinanthus minor* is in one; *Primula veris* and *Orchis morio* in two; and *Sanguisorba officinalis* and *Genista tinctoria* in a fourth. Although *Betonica officinalis* is present, *Serratula tinctoria* is rare (cf. Upwood Meadows, L.72) and the hedges are of less interest than those of Upwood.

L.87. MOOR CLOSES, ANCASTER, LINCOLNSHIRE
SK 9843. 9 ha   Grade 2
Neutral grassland group 9[1]

These four meadows are situated on an alluvial coarse, sandy loam with a small stream running through the middle. The vegetation of the drier areas is typical of the group, with *Festuca rubra*, *Anthoxanthum odoratum*, *Holcus lanatus*, *Cynosurus cristatus* and *Leontodon hispidus* co-dominant. It is in these drier, well-drained areas that *Armeria maritima* ssp. *elongata* occurs; this plant is now confined to a few meadows in the Ancaster valley. The grassland passes into a *Carex nigra*, *C. disticha*, *Juncus subnodulosus* community with affinities to, as well as differences from, both group 1 (base-rich marsh) and group 3 (dwarf grass/sedge) neutral grasslands. This latter group is represented in one area, where *Dactylorchis fuchsii* is abundant in an *Anthoxanthum odoratum*, *Holcus lanatus*, *Carex nigra* community.

The site also contains species-rich hedgerows and some bramble scrub.

[1] See pp. 185–7, Vol. 1.

SOUTH-WEST ENGLAND

South Dorset Heathlands

The Isle of Purbeck and the Wareham district contain some of the finest acidic lowland heathlands in Britain, though these now consist of the much reduced and dissected remnants of a once continuous tract of this formation. In the *Review*, virtually all the remaining heathland of this district is regarded as of national importance and grouped into four main geographical units.

The south Dorset heathlands lie on extremely infertile soils, heavily podsolised and derived from Bagshot Beds (Eocene). The Bagshot Beds are made up of sands, local ironstones, gravels and ball clays. These ball clays are responsible for many of the areas of impeded drainage and are of considerable economic value. Between them the four sites provide a great range of plant communities, including sand dunes, dune heath, salt marsh transition, dry heath, humid heath, wet heath, valley mire and open water. Several plant species well represented at these sites are of great interest and some have their British headquarters here. *Erica ciliaris* has its main distribution centre on these heaths, especially Hartland Moor. *Gentiana pneumonanthe* is abundant on many damp heath areas, *Rhynchospora fusca* and *Lycopodium inundatum* are not uncommon, and *Ulex minor* and *U. gallii* are both found on these sites although *U. minor* is the more abundant. The valley mires at Hartland and Morden are fine examples of southern valley mires, but different from each other in details of floristics and structure. All the British reptiles occur here, and these are probably the best areas for the very local smooth snake and sand lizard, whilst the invertebrate fauna of this heathland complex is extremely rich and contains many rare species.

L.88. HARTLAND MOOR AND ARNE HEATHS, DORSET
SY 9585, SY 9788. 1200 ha Grade 1*

This includes the NNRs of Hartland Moor and Arne, Middlebere Heath, Slepe Heath and the whole remaining heathland of the Arne peninsula.

Hartland Moor contains a very fine valley mire system (P.26) and area of dry heath. The mire is Y-shaped, one of the arms being acidic and its water low in calcium (*c.* 3 p.p.m.), with an oligotrophic community containing much *Sphagnum pulchrum* and scattered *Schoenus nigricans*. A series of pools is present, some containing *Carex limosa*, and *Hammarbya paludosa* occurs here in several places. The other arm of the mire system has more calcium-rich water (up to 25 p.p.m.) and the vegetation is dominated by tussocky *S. nigricans*. Where the two arms meet there are intermediate conditions of base-status with *Eriophorum latifolium*, and the water again becomes more acid lower down. At the lower, seaward end of the mire system there is a transition to brackish conditions and *Spartina* marsh.

The wet heath of Hartland Moor contains some of the finest areas of *Erica ciliaris* in Britain and a complete range of *E. ciliaris–E. tetralix* hybrids can be found. As with

the other sites in this area, all the British reptiles are found.

Locally the Bagshot deposits are coarser grained and cemented with haematite, forming an ironstone more resistant to erosion and so producing higher ground. Two of these higher areas are present on Hartland. On one of these gorse scrub is present (and also along the boundary bank), providing breeding areas for Dartford warblers. Marsh harriers used to breed on the Reserve. The very local dragonflies *Ceriagrion tenellum* and *Coenagrion mercuriale* and the rare grasshopper *Stethophyma grossum* also occur in this area.

The Arne part of the site has a large area of dry heather and gorse heath, and is important for Dartford warblers. It also contains several habitats not or poorly represented in the other parts of the Dorset heathlands. There is a good representation along the Poole Harbour edge of coastal vegetation, including salt marsh and heathland running down to sandy shores, and the area includes examples of pinewood and a small amount of oakwood. *Erica ciliaris* is present in the Arne area, but not to the same extent as on Hartland Moor, and several species such as *Gentiana pneumonanthe* and *Rhynchospora fusca* appear to be absent from Arne although abundant at Hartland. *Crassula tillaea* grows on tracks and open sandy areas. *Ceriagrion tenellum* is also abundant in the Arne area, and the northern part of the Arne peninsula has a tract of heathland with water-filled bomb holes which has been valuable as a site for studying the ecology and behaviour of dragonflies. The Arne heaths are also important for sand lizards and smooth snakes.

L.89. STUDLAND AND GODLINGSTON HEATHS, DORSET
SZ 0284. 530 ha Grade 1*

The Studland peninsula (which includes the Studland Heath NNR) contains a wide variety of habitats and plant communities, ranging from foreshore and sand dunes to open water, dune heath, dry heath, wet heath, valley and open water transition mire, and a variety of woodlands. The open water, the Little Sea (OW.21), has been formed by the build up of the dune system on the eastern seaward side over the last three and a half centuries. The dunes form three ridges with intervening slacks between the beach and the Little Sea. The soil sections on the dry heath to the west of the Little Sea demonstrate a range of profiles from Bagshot Sand through a series of old buried profiles covered by increasing depths of blown sand.

The heathland vegetation includes the same range of types as on the Hartland–Arne area but plants of special interest at Studland include *Isoetes echinospora*, in the Little Sea, and fine stands of *Osmunda regalis* in the marshes around its edge and between the dune ridges. The valley mires are oligotrophic and have a high cover of *Sphagnum* in places; they are not of outstanding interest in their own right, but add a considerable bonus interest to this highly diverse site, and contain some interesting species. *Drosera anglica* is reasonably abundant in Spur Bog and *Eriophorum gracile* has been recorded from the area, though not recently.

Erica ciliaris is present but, apart from Brands Bog, only as scattered plants. It is thought that it may be increasing in the area, colonising relatively recently formed habitats. As on other heaths in this part of Dorset, *Gentiana pneumonanthe* is abundant in suitable places. The botany and entomology of the area were intensively studied by C. Diver and a large body of information is available in his published and unpublished records held at Furzebrook Research Station. Among the rarer insects are the dragonflies *Ceriagrion tenellum* and *Sympetrum sanguineum*.

Godlingston Heath is an area of heathland adjacent to Studland Heath, with the Isle of Purbeck Golf Course and Purbeck Forest on its other sides. A notable feature is the 'Agglestone', a large residual block of ironstone. The higher ground in the vicinity of the Agglestone has bilberry in the dry heath vegetation, a plant not common on these heaths. A series of long, narrow, flush mires run across the area. One of the curious features is the relative rarity of *Erica ciliaris* for adjacent areas of wet heath and mire to the west, now planted by the Forestry Commission, have the plant in abundance. This heath is particularly noted as a haunt of Dartford warblers and sand lizards.

L.90. MORDEN BOG, DORSET
SY 9190. 180 ha   Grade 1

The dry heathland of this site (which is also a NNR) supports some of the oldest Callunetum in the district, having been protected from fire by the Forestry Commission since before 1930, but much of the area was damaged by tracked vehicles during the war. Some fine areas of lichen-rich humid heath are present. Natural regeneration of *Pinus sylvestris* with scattered *P. pinaster* from surrounding plantations since *c.* 1925 has produced an area of pine scrub, whilst an area of mature pinewood is also present and there is considerable interest in the corticolous lichens. This area of heath has been used as the site for one of the experimental earthworks established by the Archaeological Research Committee of the British Association.

There are two duck decoy ponds within the Reserve; one is used by the estate for limited shooting and is surrounded by peaty communities in which *Deschampsia setacea* has been recorded, and the other is an old decoy pond with five arms. The mire has been cut for peat in the past (as have most of the valley mires in Dorset) and has a birchwood containing fine tussocks of *Carex paniculata* running down the centre from the second of the decoy ponds. Vegetation of the mire includes communities dominated by *Phragmites communis*, *Carex lasiocarpa*, *Myrica gale*, *Carex paniculata*, *Molinia caerulea* and *Sphagnum* carpet. The peat is about 2 m in depth, underlain by clay, and the mire appears to have developed from a series of pools of open water in a flat-bottomed valley. This means that the junction of the mire and heath produces a relatively sharp transition and wet heath is rather poorly represented. *Erica ciliaris*, although present, is by no means as well represented as in the heaths south of Wareham. The site is almost completely surrounded by conifer plantations.

Sika deer are now an important item of the fauna. Hobbies feed regularly over one of the ponds, and curlew nest in the Bog. The area has long been known as a site for interesting insects and several rare species are recorded from Decoy Heath, including the grasshopper *Chorthippus vagans*. Ragge (1965) refers to these Dorset Heathlands as being especially good for Orthoptera, the moths *Coscinia cribrum* and *Graphodactyla graphodactyla*, the flies *Ceropales variegata*, *Chrysops sepulchralis* and *Estheria cristata*, the wasp *Pompilus rufus*, the ants *Formica pratensis* and *F. transkaucasica*. The dragonfly *Ceriagrion tenellum* is also present. This is a good locality for sand lizard and smooth snake.

See also P.27.

L.91. AYLESBEARE COMMON, DEVON
SY 0690. 200 ha   Grade 1

Aylesbeare Common is the best example of a series of heathlands known as the East Devon or Pebble Bed Commons. The Triassic Pebble Beds overlie Permian marls and form an escarpment running south to north, with an easterly dip. The higher parts of the ridge rise to about 150 m, and Aylesbeare Common lies between 90 and 150 m.

The higher and drier areas are covered with heath dominated by *Calluna vulgaris*, *Erica cinerea*, *E. tetralix*, *Ulex gallii*, *Agrostis setacea* and *Molinia caerulea*. Locally, where burning has been most frequent, grasses are more prevalent than shrubs. In some parts bracken and gorse are abundant, whilst scattered pines and birch occur on the dry heath areas. A series of shallow valleys are cut into the dip slope and a sharp change to wet heath and then valley mire occurs from the sides to the floors of these valleys. The wet heaths and valley mires are similar to those of the New Forest, and in addition to the usual constants (e.g. *Trichophorum cespitosum*, *Narthecium ossifragum*, *Rhynchospora alba*, *E. tetralix* and *Sphagnum* spp.) are characteristic species such as *Drosera intermedia*, *Pinguicula lusitanica*, *Anagallis tenella*, *Eleocharis multicaulis*, *Lycopodium inundatum* and *Osmunda regalis*.

An interesting ecological feature (which shows a parallel with Hartland Moor and some of the New Forest and East Anglian heaths) is the occurrence locally of a mineral-rich influence in the drainage water affecting the wetter ground. The first signs of enrichment are in the wet heath, with the presence of species such as *Cirsium dissectum*, *Carex hostiana*, *C. panicea* and *Succisa pratensis*; but the more strongly basic flush influence is marked by the occurrence in the mire communities of soaks with 'brown mosses' (*Scorpidium scorpioides*, *Campylium stellatum* and *Drepanocladus revolvens*) and *Schoenus nigricans*.

Probably the most important feature of this site is the occurrence of heather–gorse heathland in a typical inland and lowland situation, as most of the other examples of this community are in coastal or upland transition sites. The diversity of edaphic conditions is also a feature of some interest and is unusual in western heathlands.

Coenagrion mercuriale occurs on the edge of this site.

South-west England 145

L.92. NORTH DARTMOOR, DEVON
SX 5708.   7400 ha   Grade 1

Dartmoor is a distinct geographical area extending about 37 km from north to south and about 32 km from east to west. It rises to 620 m on High Willhays, and includes a substantial area of upland. The central area is composed of granite, and surrounding this igneous intrusion are Carboniferous rocks (the Culm Measures) around the northern part of the Moor, and Devonian rocks around the southern part.

The heathlands of Dartmoor represent a transitional type between lowland and upland Callunetum, and those above 450 m are regarded as upland and described under Upland Grasslands and Heaths. Much of the higher ground is, moreover, a badly drained plateau, covered with a complex of blanket and soligenous mires (see also under Peatlands), and lowland heath is restricted to the steeper slopes and drier spurs around the edge of the moor at 300–460 m. The prevailing type is heather–gorse, but there is locally much bilberry, and grasses are usually present. A hypnaceous moss carpet is often well developed. Grazing and burning appear to have promoted the spread of grasses at the expense of dwarf shrubs and there is a good deal of more or less pure grassland dominated by *Agrostis setacea*, *Festuca ovina*, *Nardus stricta* and *Molinia caerulea*. *Juncus squarrosus* and *Carex binervis* are also locally abundant. On Blackdown there is a uniform short heath of mixed *Calluna vulgaris*, *Erica tetralix*, *Ulex gallii*, *Agrostis setacea*, *Trichophorum cespitosum*, *Hypnum cupressiforme*, *Rhacomitrium lanuginosum* and *Cladonia impexa*. There are areas of humid and wet heath, grading into the mire complex and mixed *Calluna–Molinia* communities are widespread. Bracken is much less widespread and extensive than on many heaths and moors.

The most important areas of dwarf-shrub heath remaining on Dartmoor are in the Okehampton military range, Bridestowe and Sourton Common, the Hamel Down and Warren House area, Combs Head Tor–Great Gnat's Head, Lee Moor and Stall Moor, and Trendlebere Down. A block containing parts of the first two areas has been chosen to represent the lowland and upland heaths and peatlands of Dartmoor. Grazing by ponies, cattle and sheep occurs over this ground and may in time reduce still further the extent of dwarf-shrub communities.

See also W.66, P.25 and U.1.

L.93. ISLES OF SCILLY, CORNWALL
SV 8816, SV 9415, SV 8715.   150 ha   Grade 1*

The heathlands of the Isles of Scilly are extremely exposed to the Atlantic, and this strong maritime influence prevents tree or scrub growth, besides imparting certain distinctive features to the vegetation. They lie on very thin peaty soils overlying granite and in places over Pleistocene gravel deposits which are of geological interest. The vegetation is heavily grazed by rabbits, which are controlled to some extent on Tresco, and the heaths are occasionally burnt, an undesirable practice on such thin soils where scrub

control is no problem. Again the heathland on Tresco has been afforded more protection and demonstrates older stages in the growth cycle.

The vegetation is a *Calluna vulgaris–Erica cinerea* association containing *Festuca ovina* and *Lotus corniculatus*, *Sedum anglicum*, *Armeria maritima*, *Plantago coronopus*, *Hypnum cupressiforme*, *Dicranum scoparium* and *Cladonia impexa*. As the heathland is so exposed to wind and salt spray, it takes on a 'wave'-like form with the plants dead and grey on the exposed side and growth taking place on the sheltered side. The effect is to produce lines or waves of vegetation at right angles to the prevailing wind. When the vegetation becomes older, as on Castle Down, Tresco, it becomes the equivalent of the degenerate phase of inland Callunetum and produces a less regular pattern in the vegetation. This 'wave-formed' heath is not developed to any extent on the smaller islands, and it is a feature characteristic mainly of high mountains in the Scottish Highlands. The absence of species such as *E. tetralix*, *Molinia caerulea* and *Agrostis setacea* is unusual in south-west England.

There are three main heathland sites in the Isles of Scilly:

Castle Down–Tresco

Here the vegetation is relatively older but probably not so extremely exposed as on the other two sites. Pleistocene gravels occur near the north end of the Down. Towards the southern end of Castle Down *Ulex europaeus* becomes dominant in association with *U. gallii*. On the east coast at the north end of Gimble Porth there is a well developed bracken community overlying head deposits. Gimble Porth is bordered by sand dunes, a zone of *Rhododendron ponticum* and a shelter belt of planted conifers.

Chapel Down–St Martin's

The heathlands on St Martin's are more exposed than on Tresco and again demonstrate the geologically interesting Pleistocene gravels. The cliff flora here includes two of the Scillies' more interesting species, *Ornithopus pinnatus* and *Lotus hispidus* (Brandy Point). The site is heavily grazed by rabbits and at the western end of the Down near bulb fields there is an abundance of gorse, possibly in old fields, and areas of heather within the gorse are sheltered and very uniform, presenting an almost mown appearance. There is a kittiwake colony on St Martin's Head.

Shipman Head and Shipman Down–Bryher

This piece of heathland is perhaps the most varied in degrees of exposure, with examples ranging from uniform Callunetum at the southern end of Shipman Down to extremely dissected 'wave-formed' heath on the summit and at the north end of Shipman Head. Above some of the coves where head deposits 3–6 m thick are exposed, grassland areas containing *Festuca ovina*, *Holcus lanatus*, *Armeria maritima*, *Lotus corniculatus* and *Sedum anglicum* occur. *Lotus hispidus* and *Ornithopus pinnatus* are also found on Shipman Down.

A fourth heathland site is Wingletang Down on St

Agnes largely covered by gorse and granite boulders but containing a site for *Ophioglossum lusitanicum*.

See also C.28.

L.94. CHAPEL PORTH–ST AGNES, CORNWALL
sw 6949. 150 ha   Grade 1

This is an area of submaritime heathland situated on the north Cornish coast near St Agnes. The ground slopes from about 100 m towards the sea where it meets and grades into the cliff vegetation at about 30 m. A steep-sided valley runs north-west from near Towan Cross down to the beach at Chapel Porth. The rocks of the area are of Devonian age (Grampound Beds) and are mostly silty and sandy shales. There are old tin and copper mine workings on the site (Wheal Charlotte and Wheal Coates). The heathland vegetation is of a *Calluna vulgaris–Erica cinerea–Ulex gallii* type. *U. gallii* is particularly well represented in the sheltered valleys. In places the heathland is extremely exposed and eroded by wind and salt action, as on the Isles of Scilly and Penrhyn Mawr (see L.120), but is much richer than these two other sites as it has a better and deeper soil. The area near the cliff top includes the following noteworthy species in the dwarf-shrub heaths: *Jasione montana, Agrostis setacea, Armeria maritima, Euphorbia portlandica, Anthyllis vulneraria* var. *coccinea, Scilla verna, Plantago maritima, P. coronopus, Genista pilosa* (abundant), *Rosa pimpinellifolia, Rubia peregrina, Asplenium marinum, Daucus carota, Betonica officinalis* and *Lonicera periclymenum*.

Some areas of *Festuca* grassland occur where conditions are more base-rich. In addition to some of the species listed above the following are found: *Poterium sanguisorba, Serratula tinctoria, Linum catharticum, Gentianella anglica* ssp. *cornubiensis, Hieracium pilosella, Geranium sanguineum, Lotus angustissimus, Hypochoeris maculata, Viola lactea* and *V. canina. Hypochoeris maculata* and *Schoenus nigricans* grow in a rather unusual situation in a dry, sandy and enclosed site. At the western end of the area plants of *Erica ciliaris* occur in the drier, Cornish type of habitat, which are different from those in Dorset. Gorse *Ulex europaeus* scrub is found in the vicinity of the main road at Towan Cross. The stretch of cliff heathland to the north at St Agnes Head is another good *Genista pilosa* site and included with Chapel Porth in the key site. The whole of this site lies within the more extensive Godrevy Point to St Agnes grade 1 coastal site (C.30).

The area is subject to fairly heavy use by the public in summer but this tends to be concentrated on the National Trust car park and beach and the abundance of *Ulex gallii* is something of a deterrent. Some parts of the area have been heavily burnt, but deliberate burning on this type of heath is probably unnecessary and undesirable, exposure being sufficient to prevent tree growth. There is considerable ecological interest in climax heathland of this type, where climatic factors are so important in maintaining continuity of dwarf-shrub heath.

L.95. THE LIZARD, CORNWALL
sw 7018. 1600 ha   Grade 1*

The coastal serpentine peninsula of the Lizard has a complex of dry to wet heathland communities unique in Britain. In their extensive studies of this vegetation Coombe & Frost (1956) distinguish four main heath communities.

(i) '*Rock heath*'. *Festuca ovina–Calluna* heath with 73 species of vascular plants in shallow soil pockets over serpentine humus-rich brown earths, well drained and severely exposed.

(ii) '*Mixed heath*'. *Erica vagans–Ulex europaeus* heath (77 species in typical stands) on well-drained brown earth soils.

(iii) '*Tall heath*'. *Erica vagans–Schoenus* heath (43 species) in shallow valleys and depressions, on poorly drained gleyed soils.

(iv) '*Short heath*'. *Agrostis setacea* heath (24 species) raised areas with *Calluna, Erica cinerea, E. tetralix, Molinia* and *Ulex gallii*. This community on the Lizard heathlands is related to the distribution of loess soils of granite origin, and has close association with *Calluna–Ulex gallii* heathland elsewhere in south-western Britain especially where burning has been frequent and caused an increase in *Agrostis setacea*.

The important areas of heathland and associated vegetation on the Lizard are described below.

The West Lizard

This area includes sites over serpentine with soils which are consequently rich in magnesium: Kynance Cove, Kynance Cliff, Gew Graze Cove, Vellan Head and Lizard Downs. The vegetation types include wind-pruned heath (cf. Chapel Porth and Isles of Scilly) and secondary heath over old ridge and furrow cultivation. Lizard Downs carry tall and short heath on unenclosed land overlying virgin soils. *Juncus mutabilis* is locally abundant on cart tracks and in cattle-poached areas, and associated with many rare or uncommon plants, e.g. *Ranunculus tripartitus, Cicendia filiformis, Pilularia globulifera, Anagallis minima, Nitella opaca* and *Chara fragifera*. Kynance Cove, Gew Graze Cove and Lower Predannack Cliff are sites for rarities such as *Trifolium strictum, T. bocconei, T. occidentale, J. capitatus, Minuartia verna, Herniaria ciliolata, Lotus hispidus, Isoetes histrix, Genista pilosa, Scilla autumnalis, Hypochoeris maculata, Orobanche alba* and *Bromus ferronii*.

Many plants occur here as genetically prostrate or dwarf populations, some of which have been given taxonomic recognition, e.g. *Asparagus officinalis* ssp. *prostratus, Genista tinctoria* var. *prostrata* and *Sarothamnus scoparius* ssp. *maritimus*, while others are unnamed, e.g. the distinctive population of prostrate *Juniperus communis* at Gew Graze, the prostrate *Ligustrum vulgare* on Vellan Head and elsewhere, and the dwarf populations of such species as *Succisa pratensis, Serratula tinctoria, Betonica officinalis, Centaurea nigra* and *Chrysanthemum leucanthemum*. Polymorphism is shown by a number of species, including *Erica vagans*, with at least six colour variants, and *Anthyllis vulneraria*, which varies greatly in both flower colour and indumentum. Some plants are known to be cytologically peculiar, e.g. the Gew Graze–Kynance *Campanula rotundifolia* which was the first population in Britain shown to be hexaploid.

The site is also exceptionally rich in rare bryophytes, e.g. *Gongylanthus ericetorum*, *Colura calyptrifolia*, *Harpalejeunea ovata*, *Lejeunea mandonii*, *Marchesinia mackaii*, *Riccia bifurca*, *R. nigrella*, *R. crozalsii* (also the commoner *R. sorocarpa* and *R. beyrichiana*), *Fossombronia husnotii*, *F. angulosa* (also the commoner *F. wondraczeki*), and various species of *Grimmia*, *Frullania*, *Cephaloziella* and *Ephemerum*, many of them rare and local. In contrast, many calcifuge species are scarce or absent, e.g. *Pleurozium schreberi*.

The streams running over serpentine at Kynance Cove have mire communities containing *Cladium mariscus*, *Phragmites communis*, *Schoenus nigricans*, *Molinia caerulea*, *Juncus maritimus*, *Osmunda regalis* and *Pinguicula lusitanica*. *Oenanthe crocata* is abundant in their sluggish headwaters on the Lizard Downs. The Gew Graze stream is similar.

Caerthillian Cove is mainly on hornblende-schists (with generally more acidic soils than on the serpentine, and no *Erica vagans*), with mica schists to the south and the serpentine junction to the north. Most of the area has been heavily cattle-grazed in the past, and the natural wind-swept grassland of the cliffs merges into biotically controlled grassland interspersed with *Ulex europaeus* and relict *Calluna*. *Trifolium molinerii* occurs mainly in the natural grassland near the exposed cliffs, with *T. occidentale*, *Herniaria ciliolata*, and *Bromus ferronii*. *T. bocconei* and *T. strictum*, as well as a large number of other annual *Trifolium* spp. (e.g. *T. subterraneum*, *T. scabrum*, *T. striatum*, *T. micranthum* and *T. ornithopodioides*) occur mainly on the steep south-facing slopes among wind-pruned gorse, where a combination of intense insolation, periodic drought, severe exposure to westerly gales and heavy poaching by cattle combine to keep the vegetation open. This is the only place where *Isoetes histrix* occurs on schist. To the north, the serpentine again supports *Minuartia verna*, *Juncus capitatus* and *Allium schoenoprasum*. *Parentucellia viscosa* is often present in moist pastures. Notable bryophytes include *Pleurochaete squarrosa* (on south-facing slopes), *Saccogyna viticulosa* (on north-facing slopes), *Fossombronia angulosa* (very fine on loamy stream banks), and several of the rare *Riccia* spp.

Except for the patches of rock heath and wind-pruned heather along the cliffs, all the heaths have been burnt frequently and sometimes severely, reducing sensitive species such as *Juniperus communis*, but favouring others, e.g. *Filipendula vulgaris*, *Anagallis tenella*, *Agrostis setacea*, *Erodium maritimum*, *Lotus hispidus*, *Lepidium heterophyllum*, *Briza minor*, *Scilla verna* and even *Trifolium strictum* and *T. bocconei*.

Goonhilly Downs and Brays Cot

Goonhilly Downs are broadly similar to Lizard Downs, but there is more extensive tall and short heath, and better representation of some communities and species, e.g. of an acidic wet heath with *Narthecium ossifragum*, and the occurrence of *Drosera rotundifolia* on small residual patches of acidic peat. Mixed heath is present, especially on the steeper slopes and around tors of serpentine. The Downs are notable for the occurrence at altitudes of around 100 m of *Juncus maritimus* and *Plantago maritima*. Other predominantly coastal species also occur, e.g. *Scilla verna*, *J. capitatus* and *Allium schoenoprasum*. *Viola lactea* and its hybrids with *V. riviniana* are widespread and often abundant, and *Lycopodium selago* and *L. inundatum* formerly occurred. The exceedingly rare hybrid *Erica vagans* × *E. tetralix* (*E.* × *williamsii*) has occurred, and the rare *E. ciliaris* is present in two abandoned enclosures.

Mire communities include *Cladium mariscus* by the Poltesco stream and a rich flora on the margins of the shallow pools which in mediaeval times were used for watering cattle and the famous Goonhilly horses. The numerous mediaeval (and probably prehistoric) cart tracks supported small populations of *Juncus mutabilis* until about 1960; these are never used now and are overgrown with *Schoenus*, *Molinia*, and *Erica vagans*. Grazing has entirely ceased. Serpentine is still quarried on a large scale in the north corner of this site. The floor of this quarry recently had one of the few patches of *Deschampsia flexuosa* in the area.

Traboe Downs

Although the stretches of tall and short heath are similar to those above, there is one unique feature: the occurrence of short heath on loess over hornblende schist (or a mixture of serpentine and hornblende schist at the junction of the two rocks). Also interesting is the occurrence here in 1968 and 1969 of *Juncus mutabilis*.

Crousa Downs

Gabbro underlies the whole site, but only outcrops as a very few small, deeply weathered tors. The superficial geology is complex and variable: rounded quartzite pebbles of allegedly Pliocene age on the watershed, often overlain by loess-like material of Hercynian granite origin; deeply weathered yellow soils of gabbroic origin, overlain by large angular fresh blocks of gabbro, or by patches of granitic loess; and inorganic alluvium in the broad shallow valleys. The cryptogamic flora of the gabbro rocks has little in common with that of the serpentine; thus *Hedwigia ciliata*, *Ptychomitrium polyphyllum* and *Sphaerophorus* sp. are characteristic of the gabbro. The heaths are similar to those described above, but with some additional species, e.g. *Platanthera bifolia*, *Carex hostiana*, and a large population of *Pinguicula vulgaris* in its only locality in Cornwall. *Ranunculus tripartitus* is found in small pools, *Juncus mutabilis* on two cart tracks. The bryophyte flora of the heaths is richer than on the serpentine, with such notable species as *Breutelia chrysocoma* and *Scorpidium scorpioides*. *Erica* × *williamsii* has twice been found in this general area.

Repeated pH measurements at this site emphasise the ecological heterogeneity in the heaths and related communities. The range is from 3.5 in a *Breutelia* tussock, through neutral on *Campylium stellatum* in tall heath, to 10.0 in shallow pools when the aquatics are photosynthesising.

Main Dale

The western half of this dale is strewn with large gabbro blocks, the heaths being mainly the gabbroic variant of tall and short, relatively rich in bryophytes. Peat to a depth of about 1 m occurs in the eastern half, with a good growth of hummock-forming *Sphagnum* spp.; *Cladium mariscus, Schoenus nigricans, Molinia caerulea, Phragmites communis, Pinguicula lusitanica* and *Drosera rotundifolia* are also present.

The site also includes *Salix cinerea* carr rich in epiphytic bryophytes.

Coverack Cliffs, including the Grove

Apart from the sites of geological importance in Coverack Cove, the slopes north-east of Coverack offer a great diversity of habitat from dry gabbro cliffs with an analogue of rock heath, many undescribed variants of mixed and tall heath, including a remarkable community in which gorse grows on the tops of *Schoenus nigricans* tussocks, to hazel scrub with abundant *Melittis melissophyllum*, and sheltered *Salix cinerea* carr by the rocky stream, both trees and boulders being clothed with bryophytes. *Cryphaea heteromalla* is frequent, as is *Cololejeunea minutissima*; *Fissidens rivularis* occurs on wet rocks.

Mullion Cliffs

These have good rock heath, including *Genista pilosa*, on serpentine, and good mixed heath with associated *Allium schoenoprasum* pans, and grassy patches with *Isoetes histrix*.

Hayle Kimbro Pool

The heaths are not unusual, but the pool itself is important bryologically (e.g. for *Drepanocladus lycopodioides*), and north of the pool, at Ponson Joppa, is the only Lizard patch of *Myrica gale*.

Ruan Pool

This has excellent short heath to the west, and an old cart track, not now used, on which *Juncus mutabilis* occurred until ten years ago. Other species here include *Cicendia filiformis, Pilularia globulifera, Ranunculus tripartitus*; *Colura calyptrifolia* grows on gorse here.

South and East Lizard

Although of great importance for plants not included in the preceding sites (e.g. *Poa infirma, Tortula stanfordensis*), the cliff slopes have little heath vegetation except for patches of wind-pruned Callunetum in the most exposed places. Little serpentine reaches the coast, except at Enys Head, where there is a little mixed heath. The wood of *Ulmus carpinifolia* and *U. × hollandica* at Cadgwith is also important.

Kennack to Black Head Cliffs

This fine stretch of serpentine coast has excellent rock and mixed heath in many places, and patches of atypical tall heath on relatively steep but wet slopes. *Trifolium bocconei,*

Juncus capitatus and *Gongylanthus ericetorum* occur in many places in good years (e.g. 1968). The heaths were exceptionally severely burnt in the summer of 1959; soil erosion was pronounced in many places, and in some the heaths have not fully recovered. *Isoetes histrix* occurs at Black Head, and there are a few notable species not known elsewhere in the peninsula (e.g. *Sedum telephium, Tortula canescens*).

All the separate areas described above are regarded as essential components of an aggregate grade 1 site covering the Lizard heathlands.

See also C.27.

L.96. EGGARDON HILL, HAYDON AND ASKERSWELL DOWNS, DORSET
SY 540950–545920.   140 ha   Grade 1

This is an extensive area of chalk downland on three adjacent areas with the full range of aspects, variation in slope and soil types. The site has one of the characteristic western variants of the *Festuca ovina* grassland type, with an abundance of *Succisa pratensis* and *Betonica officinalis* on south-west-facing slopes and a notable absence of *Helianthemum* from much of the area, although locally it is present in small amounts. The south facing embankments of the Iron Age fort site of Eggardon Hill support a rich community in which *Leontodon hispidus* is abundant.

The number of species of Auchenorhyncha in one of two samples from Eggardon Hill was well below average, those in the other sample just above average. On the other hand the weevil fauna was rich, 14 species being recorded from the two samples. No uncommon species were noted, but the chalk-hill and Adonis blue butterflies were present. More information is needed to determine whether this is an important entomological site.

L.97. HOD AND HAMBLEDON HILLS, DORSET
ST 8510, ST 8412.   120 ha   Grade 1

These two hills are treated as one site for the purpose of the *Review* and are well known, both botanically and entomologically. The grassland of the embankments of the two Iron Age camp sites, which exhibit all aspects, is varied and floristically rich, the south and south-west aspects being of the *Carex humilis* variety, with a rich assemblage of other species. Archaeologically it is of great interest with a Roman camp superimposed on the original earthworks. The western position of the site in relation to the Chalk as a whole makes it of high importance for studying geographical distributions of plants and animals associated with the Chalk.

All the samples taken at Hod and Hambledon Hills had more species of Auchenorhyncha than average. A large number of species of Heteroptera was recorded, and *Berytinus signoreti* was very numerous. The Curculionoidea were rich in species. In all three groups a number of uncommon species was recorded. Hod Hill is a famous entomological site.

L.98. BOXWELL, GLOUCESTERSHIRE
ST 8192.   5 ha   Grade 1

This site has a small area of almost pure box on a Jurassic limestone slope, the best example of this tall scrub-woodland type in Britain, though this area is much smaller than at Ellesborough Warren (L.38). Other species such as ash and sycamore occur scattered throughout the area but are more common along the top edge.

The heavy shade cast by box inhibits the development of a field layer over much of the area but *Mercurialis perennis*, *Urtica dioica* and *Chamaenerion angustifolium* are locally abundant. Many mosses occur including *Cirriphyllum piliferum*, *Thuidium tamariscinum*, *Mnium undulatum* and *Eurhynchium praelongum*.

This is one of the largest areas of box in the country with a documented history.

L.99. BARNSLEY WARREN, GLOUCESTERSHIRE
SP 0506.   250 ha   Grade 1

This is the most oustanding grassland site on Jurassic limestone in England. It consists of a series of valleys running north-west to south-east with secondary spurs running north-east to south-west giving a variety of aspects which support rich and varied plant and animal communities. The grassland is of the *Festuca ovina* type with locally sparse areas of *Zerna erecta*, mixed with a large number of herbs. Each valley has its own distinctive character: thus on one, *Genista tinctoria* is abundant with *Thesium humifusum*; on another slope *Trifolium pratense* is present in unusual quantity; on yet another slope the largest concentration of *Anemone pulsatilla* in Britain (in excess of 30000 plants) is found. Other species of interest include *Astragalus danicus*, *Coeloglossum viride*, *Senecio integrifolius*, *Onobrychis viciifolia*, *Cuscuta epithymum* and *Sieglingia decumbens*.

The site is used extensively by the Royal Agricultural College, Cirencester, for ecological studies and for teaching purposes, and is of exceptional importance because of its excellent condition, wealth of species and variety of aspects.

The leafhopper fauna (Hemiptera–Auchenorhyncha) is a typical lowland grassland one which includes such species as *Eupelix cuspidata*, *Batracomorphus irroratus* and *Kelisia perspicillata* on the short turf and *Deltocephalus coronifer*, *Dicranoneura citrinella* and *Laodelphax elegantulus* on the taller grassland. Several species of Heteroptera of particular interest occur, *Sehirus dubius* feeding on *Thesium humifusum*, *Hoplomachus thunbergi* feeding on *Hieracium pilosella*, and *Ceratocombus coleoptratus* which occurs in the very longest grassland. The butterfly fauna is rich and populations of small blue have been studied in relation to competition, both intra- and interspecific, and the effects of management. There is a rich fauna of phytophagous Coleoptera although the weevils consist almost entirely of *Apion* spp. and *Sitona* spp. The number of species of *Apion* recorded in particular was large.

L.100. RODBOROUGH COMMON, GLOUCESTERSHIRE
SO 8503.   110 ha   Grade 1

This site is situated in an area of about 400 ha of common land with a great variety of habitat (grassland, scrub, woodland) and aspects. The Jurassic limestone grasslands are a good example of the *Brachypodium pinnatum* type, intermingled with *Zerna erecta–Festuca ovina* which is maintained in an open condition by annual burning. The floristic composition of these grasslands, which are characteristic of the Cotswolds as a whole, is remarkably constant, with a good range of grasses and dicotyledons, including some nationally local species such as *Anemone pulsatilla* and *Astragalus danicus*. Orchids, particularly *Orchis mascula*, *O. morio*, *Gymnadenia conopsea* and *Anacamptis pyramidalis*, are usually common.

The systematic faunal samples taken at Rodborough Common were uniformly poor, no doubt because of the annual burning of the grassland.

L.101. CLEEVE HILL, GLOUCESTERSHIRE
SO 9925.   510 ha   Grade 1

This is an area of common land with a variety of habitats including Jurassic limestone scree communities with species such as *Thelypteris robertiana*, limestone heath communities with heather and bracken, and old spoil heaps with *Arabis hirsuta*, *Erophila verna* and *Thlaspi perfoliatum*. On the steeper slopes the grassland communities are similar to others on Oolitic limestone but on the higher ground surface leaching has given rise to areas dominated by gorse and heather. The site is geologically important. Parts of the Common are used as a public open space and golf course.

L.102. AVON GORGE, GLOUCESTERSHIRE–SOMERSET
ST 5674.   105 ha   Grade 1

The Avon Gorge, with its variety of habitat, ranging from Carboniferous Limestone scree communities to mixed deciduous wood and scrub, has been known since the time of the artist William Turner (1510–1568) as a site where an unusual number of rare species occur. The spring flowering crucifers, *Hornungia petraea* and *Arabis stricta*, together with *Potentilla verna* are the earliest of the rarities to flower on the limestone screes. Later in the year, on inaccessible ledges, *Carex humilis* flowers, often associated with *Trinia glauca* and *Cerastium pumilum*. In the enclaves of longer grass, *Allium sphaerocephalum*, one of the rarest of British plants, grows with *Veronica spicata* ssp. *hybrida*, *Scilla autumnalis* and *Geranium sanguineum*.

Although the scrub proper, as opposed to woodland scrub, on this site is limited to small areas on the steep rocky slopes, it shows a particularly high woody species diversity. Most of the trees found in the Avon Gorge occur as young bushes, including species such as *Carpinus*, *Quercus ilex* and *Q. cerris* as well as the rare endemic species of *Sorbus*, *S. bristoliensis* and *S. wilmottiana*, and *Tilia cordata*. There are also bushes of dogwood, wayfaring tree and privet, as well as holly, hawthorn, *Rubus*, and *Ulex gallii*. The field layer is extremely variable owing to the rocky terrain and the different degrees of shading under the trees and bushes. The commoner grasses are *Festuca ovina*, *F. rubra*, *Zerna erecta* and *Brachypodium sylvaticum*, while there is also a good range of the more widespread limestone species including *Rubia peregrina*.

On the Leigh Woods side of the gorge, native *Tilia cordata* occurs in some quantity, in association with the rare *Carex digitata*. Floristically, the Avon Gorge can be considered as unique in the British Isles and as the most important lowland Carboniferous Limestone site.

See also W.70.

L.103. CHEDDAR GORGE, SOMERSET
ST 4754.   255 ha   Grade 1

This is a deep Carboniferous Limestone gorge, lined by vertical cliffs up to 120 m high and extending for about 2.4 km, with a great variety of aspects, soil depths and vegetation types. Scrub grades into an ash woodland, with open grassland communities on rock ledges and on areas of shallow limestone soil. The outstanding interest is floristic, and some of the rare species found at the Cheddar Gorge are not found at the Avon Gorge. The Cheddar pink *Dianthus gratianopolitanus* is the best known rarity, only occurring at this site in the British Isles. The rare *Prunella laciniata* also occurs in some quantity.

The northern *Saxifraga hypnoides* here reaches its southern limit in the British Isles, and grows in some quantity on the limestone screes with *Geranium lucidum*, *G. robertianum* and *Thelypteris robertiana*. *Meconopsis cambrica*, *Thalictrum minus*, *Cerastium pumilum*, *Geranium sanguineum* and *G. purpureum* also occur in the Gorge.

Cheddar Gorge has a very good range of scrub communities of the western type. On the screes and rocky outcrops typical of Carboniferous Limestone there are mixed open areas, scrub areas and trees, and here yew, dogwood, wayfaring tree, *Sorbus aria*, *S. anglica*, *S. porrigentiformis*, holly and hawthorn are found. Ash is the commonest tree. The field layer shows an interesting variety of species including *Rubia peregrina*, *Sedum telephium*, *Thalictrum minus* and other rarer species. Ivy is abundant. In other areas, closed scrub communities of hawthorn and privet have developed and these have more limited field layer species, the commonest being *Brachypodium sylvaticum* and *Fragaria vesca* with species typical of the damper areas, such as *Iris foetidissima*, *Valeriana officinalis*, and *Arum maculatum*. Bryophytes and ferns are well represented.

Amongst the other scrub communities at Cheddar are areas of limestone heath with *Ulex gallii* and *Calluna vulgaris* in abandoned fields on the tops of the cliffs. The field layer has a curious mixture of species with *Pteridium aquilinum*, *Briza media*, *Sieglingia decumbens*, *Luzula campestris*, *Galium verum*, *Helianthemum chamaecistus*, *Potentilla erecta*, and *Thymus drucei*.

L.104. BREAN DOWN AND UPHILL CLIFF, SOMERSET
ST 2958.   145 ha   Grade 1

This coastal headland is a long, east–west projection of Carboniferous Limestone into the Bristol Channel, and has a vegetation strongly influenced by oceanic conditions, though its strictly maritime vegetation is of minor interest compared with its calcicolous communities. The open grassland communities of the steep, craggy, south-facing slope provide most of the unusual plant communities. *Koeleria vallesiana*, a member of Matthews' oceanic southern element, occurs in great quantity on the south-facing slopes, in a community containing *Helianthemum apenninum*, *Carex humilis*, *Festuca ovina* ssp. *glauca* and *Cerastium pumilum*. The maritime element, represented by species such as *Bromus ferronii*, *Armeria maritima*, *Plantago coronopus* and *Cochlearia danica*, is scattered in the *K. vallesiana–H. apenninum* community. Although this type of community is also found at Berry Head, Devon, on Devonian limestone, it is there not so well developed and the Brean Down community is unique in Britain.

Adjacent to, but separated from, Brean Down by the River Axe, is a small area (*c.* 2 ha) alternatively called Walborough Down or Uphill Cliffs containing many of the Brean Down rarities, and also a small colony of *Aster linosyris*, which is not found on Brean Down. Additionally, Uphill Cliffs is outstanding entomologically and is therefore included in the grade 1 site.

The systematic invertebrate samples taken at Brean Down had rather low values for diversity but included some particularly interesting species. Among the Heteroptera, *Chorosoma schillingi*, usually associated with sandhills, was taken and also the local weevil *Smicronyx reichi*. Other weevils of local distribution found during non-systematic collecting were *Apion sedi* and *Mecinus circulatus*. A very distinctive species of lygaeid bug has recently been discovered at Brean Down where it is associated with *Helianthemum apenninum*. It also occurs at Dolebury Warren. The small area of grassland at Uphill Cliffs supports some notable Curculionoidea, e.g. *Apion stolidum*, *A. schönherri*, *A. urticarium* and *Trachyphloeus alternans*.

L.105. BERRY HEAD, DEVON
SX 9456.   30 ha   Grade 1

This site contains a wide range of habitats and is the largest area of Devonian limestone exposed in England. On the broken limestone cliffs, which form a series of slopes and ledges down to the sea, open grassland communities are found with, locally, good amounts of *Helianthemum apenninum*, *Sedum album*, *S. acre* and *S. forsteranum*. The range of communities is large, ranging from a closed grassland with typical calcicoles, and including *Scilla autumnalis*, to open, rocky communities in which *Euphorbia paralias* is prominent. The flat plateau above the cliffs in places supports an acidophilous community of *Ulex europaeus*, *Calluna vulgaris*, and *Erica cinerea* which contrasts strikingly with areas of plateau limestone pavement carrying an extremely short turf, with *Trinia glauca*, *Bupleurum baldense*, *Helianthemum apenninum* and other rare species. *Aster linosyris* grows on one area on the cliffs, while nearby, *Orobanche hederae* and *Rubia peregrina* are present in some quantity.

Although both Berry Head and Brean Down have many rare species in common, there are differences in other rarities and in their total floras which give both grade 1 status in the series of lowland calcareous key sites. As at Brean Down, the strictly maritime flora is of only minor interest.

Berry Head is important for bats and nesting seabirds – the steeper cliffs have one of the few auk colonies on the south coast of England.

L.106. CREECH–GRANGE–POVINGTON HEATHS, DORSET
SY 8983. 1100 ha   Grade 2

These heathlands include Creech, Stoborough, Grange and Povington Heaths, lying to the west and south-west of the Hartland–Arne area and crossed by two roads and a railway. The large expanse has been much disturbed in various ways and burning at frequent intervals has produced areas where *Calluna–Agrostis* heathland (or even grass heath) predominate.

Much of the eastern block of heath, especially that south of the railway, has been extensively worked for ball clay and the ground in the south-western sector is still used for the storage, weathering etc. of clay. As a result of this clay extraction a series of old clay pits have provided pools of open water with a wide range of water conditions. These range from acidic waters from heathland drainage to more base-rich conditions where some drainage is derived from the Chalk.

These pools are especially well developed in the south-eastern sector along with plant communities ranging from dry heath and mire to scrub, pinewood and oakwood. This area also provides a range of rough grassy habitats that are good for Orthoptera. Extensive areas of gorse scrub are also present. The whole block of heath is just outside the area where *Erica ciliaris* is abundant and it is likely that the suitable habitats, being recent in origin are slowly being recolonised, the species being found mainly in small areas or as isolated plants.

The Grange and Povington Heaths, forming the western block, are the largest continuous area of heathland remaining in Dorset and are protected to some extent by their use as a military training area. The area has the form of a shallow bowl, with a wet inner centre containing much damp heath with *Molinia* especially abundant, and the outer zone covered with dry heath containing much gorse. The elevation is over the range 15–60 m. The heaths show much of the range of floristic composition found in those nearer Poole Harbour, but *Erica ciliaris* is either absent or very rare. The characteristic heathland fauna is also well represented and the notable species include the Dartford warbler, sand lizard, silver-studded blue butterfly and dragonfly *Ceriagrion tenellum*. There are several good ponds with a representative aquatic fauna.

Though less valuable than the Hartland and Arne (L.88) and Studland and Godlingston (L.89) Heaths, this complex of heathland is important for its large size.

L.107. DUNKERY BEACON, SOMERSET
SS 8943. 2700 ha   Grade 2

Exmoor rises to a height of 522 m on Dunkery Beacon but descends to sea-level in the north. The area is unglaciated and the soils are derived from sedimentary rocks of Old Red Sandstone age. When compared with the parts of Dartmoor overlying granite it produces steeper-sided valleys, less extensive peatland areas and a greater range of soil types. The rocky outcrops characteristic of Dartmoor are also absent. Much of Exmoor is enclosed and open moorland is rapidly diminishing. The Chains area of Exmoor is covered by blanket mire but has relatively low ecological interest. Other peatland interests tend to be restricted to soligenous mires on the sides of valleys or in valley bottoms.

The vegetation of the open moorland is dominated by heather, bilberry and *Ulex gallii*, though *Agrostis setacea* is locally abundant. *U. gallii* is an important constituent of the vegetation to a height of about 360–390 m, the actual upper limits being somewhat related to aspect. Above this level is a *Calluna–Vaccinium* community. *Empetrum nigrum* is present on the higher ground, but fruits only sparingly. *Vaccinium vitis-idaea* is absent from Exmoor and Dartmoor but found within one restricted area on the Quantock Hills east of Exmoor. *Lycopodium selago* may be extinct but *L. clavatum* perhaps still occurs rarely on Dunkery and Winsford Hill. *Vaccinium oxycoccus* occurs here in one of its three known sites in the south-west of England. The Exmoor heaths differ from those of Dartmoor in the greater abundance of bilberry, bracken, and perhaps dry Callunetum.

Like Dartmoor, Exmoor has a range of heath vegetation showing the transition from lowland to upland, and Dunkery Beacon has also been regarded as a grade 2 upland site (U.2), though it is not an alternative site to North Dartmoor as the differences are too great.

Lowland–upland complexes of these heathland communities are widespread in the hills of Wales, northern England and southern Scotland, though *Ulex gallii* is found mainly in the west and *Agrostis setacea* is confined to southern England.

Dunkery Beacon adjoins the important grade 1 oakwoods of the Holnicote and Horner Water (W.69), and the two formations represent the range of characteristic types of Exmoor vegetation from hill-top moorland to valley-bottom woodland.

L.108. PARK BOTTOM, HIGHER HOUGHTON, DORSET
ST 8004. 30 ha   Grade 2

This is of high botanical interest, with north- and south-facing slopes, and a flat plateau grassland which bears a varied and characteristic chalk grassland flora. Of special interest is the abundance of *Helianthemum chamaecistus* and the presence of *Festuca arundinacea* and *Succisa pratensis* on the south-facing slope. *Gentianella anglica* is present in some quantity. In addition to the high botanical interest of the site, there is considerable archaeological interest which could easily be destroyed by ploughing. This site is placed in Bowen's (1970) list of important archaeological sites in Dorset.

L.109. BRASSEY, GLOUCESTERSHIRE
SP 1322.   20 ha   Grade 2
Neutral grassland group 1[1]

This small area of rough Jurassic limestone grassland slopes steeply to the River Windrush, with a freshwater marsh formed by springs arising at the junction of the Inferior Oolite and on an impervious stratum which could be Lias Clay or possibly Cotswold Sand with sufficient clay to make it impermeable.

There are a number of well-defined plant societies within the small area of marsh, the most striking being dominated by *Carex rostrata*, *Juncus subnodulosus*, *Mentha aquatica* and *Carex paniculata*. Of particular interest are the range of species and hybrids of *Dactylorchis*, and the presence of *Molinia caerulea*, *Parnassia palustris* and *C. dioica*. In Gloucestershire this last species is known only at this site and is rare in southern Britain following increased drainage which destroys its habitat. The dry grassland is dominated by *Brachypodium pinnatum* and *Zerna erecta*, a characteristic combination on the Cotswold grassland, but with a good range of herbs, including unusually large quantities of *Astragalus danicus*. Additional interest is supplied by the presence of *Thlaspi perfoliatum* on the limestone screes on the eastern edge of the site. This species is almost confined to the north Cotswold grasslands in Britain.

L.110. HORNSLEASOW ROUGHS, GLOUCESTERSHIRE
SP 1132.   30 ha   Grade 2

These are old Jurassic limestone workings which have become vegetated and colonised by scrub but which are maintained mostly as a short, springy turf by heavy sheep-grazing. This area is the site of a large number of local and rare plants including *Anemone pulsatilla*, *Thlaspi perfoliatum*, *Polygala calcarea*, *Cerastium pumilum*, *C. semidecandrum*, *Minuartia hybrida*, *Astragalus danicus*, *Hippocrepis comosa*, *Saxifraga granulata*, *S. tridactylites*, *Gentianella anglica*, *Senecio integrifolius* and four species of orchid.

L.111. MINCHINHAMPTON COMMON, GLOUCESTERSHIRE
SO 8601.   215 ha   Grade 2

This large common on Jurassic limestone is used as a public open space and golf course. It is a flat, steep-sided plateau cut by small valleys of varying aspect, containing pockets of woodland and scrub with considerable areas of *Festuca ovina–F. rubra* grassland, interspersed with a *Brachypodium pinnatum–Zerna erecta* type. This site is near to Rodborough Common and contains almost the same range of plant communities and species, so that it is regarded as an alternative site.

L.112. CROOK PEAK, SOMERSET
ST 3855.   90 ha   Grade 2

Forming part of the Carboniferous Limestone outcrop in Somerset, this massive hill is predominantly south-west facing but also has north-west and west aspects and a flat plateau which supports heath communities. The soils are shallow, mostly red-brown rendzinas with limestone rubble on the surface preventing the formation of a continuous turf. Under these conditions the grassland is of the *Festuca ovina–Helictotrichon pratense* type with *Poterium*, *Thymus drucei* and *Asperula cynanchica* the commonest forbs. Locally, especially on the south-western aspects, small communities of *Koeleria vallesiana*, *Trinia glauca* with annuals such as *Bromus thominii* and *Linum catharticum* are scattered among the limestone rubble. The presence of these species, together with others such as *Cotoneaster microphyllus*, links this site with other areas of similar limestone in Wales and elsewhere. In addition, there is a well-developed limestone heath containing *Erica cinerea*, *Ulex gallii* and *U. europaeus*, in association with *Filipendula vulgaris*, a community which closely resembles that of the chalk heaths of southern England.

L.113. DOLEBURY WARREN, SOMERSET
ST 4559.   115 ha   Grade 2

This Iron Age camp site supports open Carboniferous Limestone grassland on the south-facing embankments below the camp; this grassland consists of *Festuca ovina* sward in which herbs are plentiful and lichens common. However, the main interest here is the extensive stand of *Calluna*, occupying some 4 ha on the west and north-west aspects below the camp. *Erica cinerea* and *Ulex gallii* form local societies with the Callunetum and the presence of *Vaccinium myrtillus* is of special interest. The presence of calcareous material near to the surface is indicated by occasional shrubs of *Sorbus aria*, but the top layers of soil are distinctly acidic and support a *Festuca ovina* grassland with acidophilous species such as *Galium saxatile*, *Agrostis tenuis*, *Potentilla erecta* and *Teucrium scorodonia*.

No systematic invertebrate sampling was done at Dolebury Warren but the fauna appeared to be much richer than that at Crook Peak, for instance. The newly discovered lygaeid bug taken at Brean Down also occurs here, where it presumably is associated with *Helianthemum chamaecistus*. The weevils *Sitona waterhousei* and *Gymnetron melanarium* were taken by vacuum sampling in May 1968.

L.114. COOMBE HILL CANAL, GLOUCESTERSHIRE
SO 8726.   145 ha   Grade 2
Neutral grassland group 5 (7)[1]

The disused canal runs due east from the River Severn to Coombe Hill. The alluvial meadows are on both sides, the more extensive being to the north. Most of the meadows belong to the *Alopecurus–Glyceria–Polygonum* community (group 5) with small localised areas dominated by *Carex acutiformis*. Group 7 is well represented by two small

[1] See pp. 185–6, Vol. 1.

meadows where *Anthoxanthum odoratum*, *Festuca rubra*, *Cynosurus cristatus* and *Briza media* are co-dominant with *Filipendula ulmaria*, *Sanguisorba officinalis* and *Silaum silaus*. There are a number of uncommon species including *Oenanthe lachenalii* and *Polygonum mite*. Agricultural 'improvements' have been and are being made to several of these meadows, resulting in a loss of botanical interest.

An area of open water known as Long Pool attracts wild-fowl in the winter when flooding occurs.

SOUTH WALES

L.115. GLYN PERFEDD, BRECKNOCK
SN 9509. 3 ha   Grade 1
Neutral grassland group 3 (1 and 10)[1]

This grass–sedge meadow is situated on Carboniferous Limestone but has a soil rich in organic matter and a high water table. It is floristically very rich and although mainly of group 3 there is gradation to both groups 1 and 10. This is well illustrated by the various species of orchid which include *Platanthera chlorantha* in the drier areas (group 10); *Dactylorchis incarnata* (group 3) and *Epipactis palustris* (group 1). The co-dominants are *Molinia caerulea*, *Anthoxanthum odoratum*, *Festuca rubra*, *Carex hostiana*, *C. panicea* and *C. nigra*, whilst the herbs include *Serratula tinctoria*, *Trollius europaeus*, *Pinguicula vulgaris*, *Cirsium dissectum* and *Pedicularis palustris*.

A late hay crop is traditionally taken from this area and, as is very typical of mid Welsh valley farming, the drier land immediately above this grass–sedge complex is also utilised for hay. These drier meadows have been ploughed and reseeded but, owing to the subsequent non-intensive management, they are showing signs of recolonisation from the unploughed margins. Such species as *Leontodon hispidus*, *Plantago lanceolata* and *Centaurea nigra* have already recolonised and *Platanthera chlorantha* still occurs in the margins.

The grade 1 site is restricted to the 3 ha referred to above but the meadows between it and the Nant Cadlan to the north (some 8 ha) should also be considered in any long-term conservation policy. Included in this extended area is a strip of unenclosed rough moorland by the side of the Nant Cadlan with such characteristic species as *Narthecium ossifragum*, *Drosera rotundifolia* and *Dactylorchis ericetorum* – in marked contrast to the meadows on the other side of the wall.

L.116. PEN YR HEN ALLT, BRECKNOCK
SO 2339. 4 ha   Grade 1
Neutral grassland group 10[1]

Three meadows are included in this site, one of which has an abundance of *Trollius europaeus*, *Alchemilla xanthochlora* and *Lathyrus montanus*. The other constants of this group, *Cirsium heterophyllum* and *Geranium sylvaticum*, are, however, absent. The remaining two meadows are either managed as hay meadows or for late summer grazing because of the presence of *Colchicum autumnale*. All meadows have the normal mixture of grasses together with

Carex pallescens and several orchid species including *Listera ovata*, *Gymnadenia conopsea* and *Platanthera chlorantha*.

L.117. BANNAU PRESELI & CHOMIN CARNINGLI, PEMBROKESHIRE
SN 1033, SN 0436. 3250 ha   Grade 2

This includes two areas of *Calluna vulgaris* heathland varying from 120–530 m in altitude. *Erica cinerea*, *Ulex gallii* and *Vaccinium myrtillus* are commonly associated with the *Calluna*. Several of the numerous species-rich soligenous mires of the northern slopes support *Lycopodium inundatum* and *Pinguicula lusitanica*. Some of the higher summits have more diverse ericaceous communities with areas of grassland dominated by *Agrostis tenuis*, *A. canina*, *Festuca ovina* and *Nardus stricta*. The site is of geomorphological interest for the numerous tors, one of which, Carn Meini, is of spotted dolerite used in the Blue Stone Circle of Stonehenge.

L.118. DROSTRE BANK: CEFN TROS DRE, BRECKNOCK
SO 0931. 5 ha   Grade 2
Neutral grassland group 3[1]

This meadow has a grass–sedge community of *Anthoxanthum odoratum*, *Molinia caerulea*, *Holcus lanatus*, *Carex nigra*, *C. panicea* and *C. hostiana* supporting a rich flora including *Cirsium dissectum*, *Valeriana dioica*, *Anagallis tenella*, *Dactylorchis incarnata*, *D. praetermissa*, *D. fuchsii* and a number of *Dactylorchis* hybrids. The whole area is surrounded by a varied scrub woodland containing oak, ash, hazel and *Viburnum opulus*.

See also U.8.

L.119. BOXBUSH, BRECKNOCK
SO 2431. 2 ha   Grade 2
Neutral grassland group 10[1]

These two herb-rich hay meadows in the Black Mountains have the typical co-dominant grasses of *Festuca rubra*, *Anthoxanthum odoratum*, *Holcus lanatus*, *Agrostis stolonifera* and *Cynosurus cristatus*, plus most of the characteristic species of group 10, namely *Trisetum flavescens*, *Platanthera chlorantha*, *Alchemilla* spp., *Trifolium medium*, *Sanguisorba officinalis*, *Lathyrus montanus* and *Geranium sylvaticum*. This last species, very characteristic of northern England hay meadows, had not been recorded in Wales since 1930.

See also U.8.

NORTH WALES

L.120. GLANNAU YNYS GYBI: HOLY ISLAND COAST, ANGLESEY
SH 2181. 375 ha   Grade 1

The heathland at Penrhyn Mawr on the Glannau Ynys Gybi lies on cliff tops at about 40 m and is exposed to the Irish Sea on the west. The soils are of variable thickness overlying quartzite, exposed in places among the 'wave-formed' heathland vegetation. The 'wave-cut' heathland is comparable with that found in the Isles of Scilly and at

[1] See pp. 185–7, Vol. 1.

Chapel Porth on the north Cornwall coast. The dry heath at Penrhyn Mawr is dominated by *Calluna vulgaris*, *Erica cinerea* and *Ulex gallii*, but it tends to the species-rich maritime type, with its characteristic associates, e.g. *Salix repens*, *Pedicularis sylvatica* and *Succisa pratensis*. Locally, *Sieglingia decumbens* and *Polytrichum commune* are abundant in the heathland vegetation, and other noteworthy species include *Hypochoeris radicata*, *Daucus carota*, *Plantago coronopus*, *Tripleurospermum maritimum*, *Centaurium erythraea*, *Scilla verna* and *Jasione montana*. Running across the dry heath are areas of damper heath and small soligenous mires containing species such as *Carex demissa*, *Trichophorum cespitosum*, *E. tetralix*, *Isolepis cernua*, *Narthecium ossifragum*, *Potamogeton polygonifolius*, *Anagallis tenella*, *Eleocharis palustris*, *Molinia caerulea*, *Eriophorum angustifolium*, *Hypericum elodes*, *Juncus bulbosus*, *Hydrocotyle vulgaris*, *Scorpidium scorpioides* and *Sphagnum recurvum*.

The heathland at Penrhyn Mawr is part of the Glannau Ynys Gybi coastland grade 1 site (C.52) extending to the north and to the east. The area to the north includes South Stack (a site for *Tuberaria guttata* var. *breweri*, and *Senecio integrifolius*) and Holyhead Mountain (Mynydd Twr). This ground consists of cliff heathland and rocky heath rising to 220 m at Caer y Twr, an ancient monument. Near the summit, species such as *Hedera helix*, *Sedum anglicum*, *Pteridium aquilinum*, *Blechnum spicant*, *Vaccinium myrtillus*, *Deschampsia flexuosa* and *Teucrium scorodonia* are found along with *Calluna vulgaris* amongst the rocks. *Ulex gallii* is present at the foot of Mynydd Twr, but does not reach the summit.

The silver-studded blue butterfly occurs within this site.

L.121. GREAT ORMES HEAD: PEN Y GOGARTH, CAERNARVONSHIRE
SH 7683.   345 ha   Grade 1

This Carboniferous Limestone headland reaches a height of 207 m and presents high tiered cliffs to the sea. There is a maritime element in the flora, but the Great Orme is noted for its assemblage of rare calcicoles, and extensive area of limestone grassland, which is, however, heavily grazed by sheep. This is the only British station for the only native *Cotoneaster*, *C. integerrimus*, which grows with the other wind-pruned shrubs such as juniper, privet and hawthorn on the steep rocks. The four disjunct species *Helianthemum canum*, *Aster linosyris*, *Hypochoeris maculata* and *Veronica spicata* ssp. *hybrida* all grow here, and there is an abundance of *Scilla verna*, *Potentilla tabernaemontani*, *Hornungia petraea* and *Geranium sanguineum*. A northern element is represented by *Antennaria dioica*, *Minuartia verna* and *Epipactis atrorubens*.

Many of these species are confined to steep, open rocks, and the grassland communities are not unusually rich. It is, however, one of the most important coastal limestone sites in Britain. The butterflies include dwarf forms of grayling and silver-studded blue.

The Great Ormes Head also has some importance as a coastal site. There are moderate breeding colonies of cliff seabirds, including guillemots, razorbills, kittiwakes and fulmars, and the rocks carry a good range of maritime vegetation.

L.122. YR EIFL, CAERNARVONSHIRE
SH 3645.   350 ha   Grade 2

The lowland heaths of this coastal massif grade into submontane types and are described under Uplands (U.15).

MIDLANDS

L.123. STIPERSTONES, SHROPSHIRE
SO 3799.   540 ha   Grade 1

The Stiperstones is a range of hills about 16 km south-west of Shrewsbury rising from about 240 to 530 m. The crest is composed of Stiperstones Quartzite, with Tremadoc Shales and Mytton Flags on the east and west flanks respectively. The hills run north-north-east to south-south-west and the area under consideration is about 3 km long and about 1–1.6 km wide. A series of dingles or valleys occur on the western side of the main ridge, and show interesting differences in the vegetation according to aspect. The vegetation as a whole is regarded as a northern example of lowland acidic heath with transitions to distinctly upland equivalents.

The north-facing slopes of the valleys carry *Calluna vulgaris*–*Vaccinium myrtillus* communities and the south-facing slopes are characterised by a *Calluna vulgaris*–*Erica cinerea*–*Ulex gallii* community. Because of the continuously curving shape of the dingles it is possible to follow the transition from one of these vegetation types to the other with the gradual change of aspect. With increasing altitude *Ulex gallii* disappears and there is a change to a *Calluna*–*Vaccinium*–*Empetrum nigrum* association containing both *V. myrtillus* and *V. vitis-idaea* towards the summit, the higher-level heaths being of a distinctly northern and submontane type which could be regarded as upland, i.e. the area has bonus upland interest. The abundance of *Vaccinium vitis-idaea* is a striking feature of the site.

The heaths also contain a good deal of *Deschampsia flexuosa*, and below screes on the west side there are large patches dominated by this grass. Bracken is locally plentiful, and *Nardus stricta* more patchy. Low on the west side there are patches of basic soil which give a species-rich grassland with *Festuca rubra*, *F. ovina*, *Dactylis glomerata*, *Agrostis tenuis*, *Lotus corniculatus*, *Trifolium repens*, *Bellis perennis*, *Campanula rotundifolia*, *Hieracium pilosella* and *Viola lutea*. This forms patches within the acidic heath, and grades into the latter through a transitional basic heath, in which *Calluna* is associated with *Lathyrus pratensis*, *Achillea millefolium*, *Cirsium palustre*, *Potentilla erecta*, *Galium saxatile* and *Deschampsia cespitosa*.

On the higher parts of the Stiperstones there are tors of quartzite and massive fields of quartzite boulders. In places these boulders represent fossil stone stripes and networks, and they also provide habitats for upland lichens such as *Parmelia incurva*.

A few relics of dry peat can be found on the summit, and a few peaty pools containing *Sphagnum subsecundum* var. *auriculatum*. Small acidic soligenous mires are present on the eastern slopes below Cranberry Rock and contain *S. recurvum, Eriophorum angustifolium, Juncus acutiflorus, J. bulbosus, J. conglomeratus, Narthecium ossifragum, Molinia caerulea, Nardus stricta, Viola palustris* and *Polytrichum commune.* Areas of *Ulex europaeus, Sarothamnus scoparius* and patchy birch scrub occur on the lower slopes. The site includes an area to the north called The Hollies which provides a bonus woodland interest.

L.124(i). DERBYSHIRE DALES GRASSLANDS, DERBYSHIRE–STAFFORDSHIRE   Grade 1

Five sites have been chosen to represent the range of variation in Carboniferous Limestone grasslands and woodlands found in the Derbyshire Dales (which, it should be noted, extend into Staffordshire) and these should be regarded as a single aggregate geographical unit. A second group of three other sites is included to provide alternatives.

(a) Dove Valley and Biggin Dale
SK 1454.   540 ha

The most important vegetational feature of Dovedale is the ashwood; although limestone grassland is extensive, it is less varied and species-rich than in some of the other dales. However, the adjoining Biggin Dale has a wider range of grassland, including the three types of *Helictotrichon pratense–Carex flacca* grassland recognised by Shimwell (1968) as characteristic of the Derbyshire limestone. The very local type with much *Carex pulicaris* is better represented here than anywhere else, and is important in demonstrating the connections with Pennine limestone grasslands. The more typical community has an abundance of *Briza media, Koeleria cristata, Helianthemum chamaecistus, Thymus drucei* and *Anthyllis vulneraria.* On more leached, deeper soils of the upper slopes this grades into a less calcareous third type, with *Anthoxanthum, Trisetum flavescens, Holcus lanatus* and *Trifolium repens,* and containing fewer strict calcicoles.

Open screes have stands of a widespread *Arrhenatherum elatius–Mercurialis perennis* community, and in this habitat there is a good deal of the very rare *Galeopsis angustifolia.* Other species of rocky situations or open grassland include *Epipactis atrorubens, Hornungia petraea, Hypericum montanum, Arabis hirsuta, Centaurea scabiosa, Allium oleraceum* and *Silene nutans,* the last three occurring especially along cliff tops.

The northern part of this dale system, Wolfscote Dale, extends the range of grassland types. The *Helictotrichon–Carex flacca* grassland here has abundant *Cirsium acaulon* and *Zerna erecta,* with *Festuca arundinacea* and *Silene nutans* quite plentiful. On the Staffordshire side there is *Filipendula ulmaria–Arrhenatherum* forb-rich grassland, with *Saxifraga hypnoides, Angelica sylvestris, Valeriana officinalis* and *Pimpinella saxifraga.*

Biggin Dale also contains good areas of scrub, both of *Ulex europaeus–Crataegus* type which is periodically burned, and the hazel-dominated type, here retrogressive and containing *Crataegus, Prunus spinosa, Brachypodium sylvaticum, Geranium sanguineum, Epipactis helleborine, Tamus com-*

munis, *Origanum vulgare* and many species of the calcareous grasslands.

See also W.115.

(b) Lathkill Dale
SK 1865.   142 ha

The grasslands of this dale contain virtually the whole range of variation to be seen in the Derbyshire Dales. The dry calcareous *Helictotrichon–Carex flacca* grasslands are especially fine in the upper reaches of the Dale on the south-facing slopes. A burned facies of this association is rich in *Allium oleraceum* and poor in mosses, and some stands are rich in *Potentilla tabernaemontani.* Good examples of tall-herb *Centaurea nigra–Arrhenatherum* grassland occur locally on south-facing slopes amongst hawthorn scrub, and contain much *Dactylis glomerata, Origanum vulgare, Clinopodium vulgare, Agrimonia eupatoria* and *Knautia arvensis.* By contrast, northern slopes have damper tall-herb grasslands, with *Filipendula–Arrhenatherum* well developed and containing in one place probably the largest colony of *Polemonium caeruleum* in Britain. This damp grassland on mull rendzinas also contains *Geum rivale, Scrophularia nodosa, Heracleum sphondylium, Galium cruciata, Mercurialis perennis* and *Hypericum hirsutum,* besides the species mentioned for Biggin Dale.

On the gently sloping upper slopes of Lathkill Dale, and on the plateau above, these calcareous grasslands grade into acidic grassland, with *Deschampsia flexuosa, D. cespitosa, Nardus stricta, Holcus lanatus, Agrostis stolonifera, Galium saxatile, Potentilla erecta, Lathyrus montanus* and patchy *Calluna vulgaris.* Limestone scree communities have *Draba muralis, Cardamine impatiens* and *Thelypteris robertiana,* whilst rock outcrops have *Arabidopsis thaliana, Arabis hirsuta, Minuartia hybrida, Arenaria leptoclados, Valerianella locusta, V. carinata* and *Ceterach officinarum.*

The woods of the Dale are probably the finest semi-natural ashwoods of the district, and are described under Woodlands (W.115(a)). There is a very rich bryophyte flora, especially on the north-facing slopes and rocks.

See also OW.44.

(c) Cressbrook Dale
SK 1773.   132 ha

The range of calcicolous communities in this dale is perhaps the finest in the whole of the Derbyshire Dales district, and grassland types are very well represented. *Helictotrichon–Carex flacca* grassland is extensive on steep slopes and grades into the less rich *Holcus–Trifolium* type on gentler slopes. The grasslands of Cressbrook Dale are distinguished by the presence in places of *C. ornithopoda, Brachypodium pinnatum* and *Cirsium acaulon,* the last two being characteristic chalk species here near their northern limits. In places, the grasslands are remarkable for their extreme richness in forbs such as *Gymnadenia conopsea, Thalictrum minus, Leontodon hispidus, Pimpinella major, P. saxifraga, Scabiosa columbaria, Carlina vulgaris, Origanum vulgare, Geranium sanguineum, Viola hirta, Convallaria majalis, Anthyllis vulneraria, Acinos arvensis, Epipactis atrorubens, Plantago media, Rubus saxatilis, Vicia sepium* and *Hypericum hirsutum.* Grasses such as *Koeleria cristata, Trisetum flavescens* and *Briza media* are plentiful, and there is some *Melica nutans. Helianthemum chamaecistus* and *Poterium sanguisorba* are constant species.

This community is evidently maintained by light grazing, and although there is colonisation locally by shrubs, mainly hazel and aspen, some of the hazel scrub is degenerating. In the scrub are also hawthorn, ash, dogwood and black-thorn, and there are affinities with some of the mixed scrubs on southern Chalk. The hazel scrub is mainly of the *Geranium sanguineum* type, and is among the most extensive examples in the country. In places there is a transitional community between dry grassland and scrub, and this is a tall-herb grassland with *Cirsium heterophyllum, Trollius europaeus, Campanula trachelium, Filipendula ulmaria, Urtica dioica, Arctium lappa, Origanum vulgare, Deschampsia cespitosa, Brachypodium sylvaticum, Melica uniflora* and *Zerna ramosa.*

See also W.115.

(d) Monk's Dale
SK 1374.   66 ha

The grasslands of this dale are the *Helictotrichon–Carex flacca* community of dry, heavily grazed ground, here with local abundance of *Bromus erectus*, a rare grass in Derbyshire; and the *Arrhenatherum* group in which the thermophilous type with *Centaurea scabiosa, C. nigra, Silene nutans, Geranium sanguineum, Carduus nutans* and *Pimpinella major* prevails on dry sunny aspects and is replaced by the damper type with *Filipendula ulmaria* on damper, shaded slopes. There is a well-developed hazel scrub, with the same shrub associates as in Cressbrook Dale, and tall-herb communities, and an area of woodland is dominated by ash, with smaller amounts of wych elm, hazel, bird cherry, hawthorn and blackthorn. Rock outcrops and screes are frequent, and these more open habitats are the main niche of *Potentilla tabernaemontani, Hypericum montanum, Trifolium medium* and *Epipactis atrorubens. Cirsium heterophyllum* is plentiful in places among the taller grassland.

A noteworthy feature of this dale is the occurrence of a range of spring and flush sites with tufa-forming bryophyte communities, and a calcareous stream in the valley bottom. This affords interesting comparison with other calcareous wet ground complexes, such as those at Malham and Sunbiggin, farther north on the Carboniferous Limestone.

(e) Long Dale and Gratton Dale
SK 2059.   80 ha

This pair of dales forms a continuous unit, but with their axes at right angles, so that together they give four aspects, north-east, south-east, south-west and north-west, and allow interesting comparisons to be made. The grasslands of these dales approach more closely to chalk grassland than any of those in other Derbyshire Dales, notably through the abundance of the characteristic chalk species *Cirsium acaulon* and *Filipendula vulgaris*. There is a wide range of grasslands, from typical *Helictotrichon–Carex flacca* to less calcicolous types usually associated with cattle meadows (i.e. an abundance of *Ranunculus acris, Rumex acetosa, Cirsium arvense, Trifolium repens, Holcus lanatus, Centaurea nigra* and *Senecio jacobaea*) and also to a heath–grassland mosaic with *Calluna vulgaris, Ulex gallii, Vaccinium myrtillus, Festuca ovina, Agrostis* spp., *Lathyrus montanus, Campanula rotundifolia, Carex flacca, Filipendula vulgaris, Lotus corniculatus, Thymus drucei* and *Hypochoeris radicata.* This last type is a Derbyshire equivalent to southern chalk heath, and it grades into a scrub of tall *U. gallii*, with a mainly calcifuge or indifferent flora. *Viola lutea* is abundant in some of the communities transitional between calcicolous and acidophilous.

While there are obvious differences in grazing pressure within the area, some of these vegetational differences are evidently related to an interesting range of variation in soil type, which possibly has resulted partly from a variable deposition of Triassic clays and sands. There is a variable representation of red limestone soils in the area, and it has been suggested that some soil differences are the result of variable release of iron during the process which led to dolomitisation of the limestone in parts of the valley. Lead was mined in the valley leading from Long Dale to Pike Hall, and on the old spoil heaps is an abundance of *Minuartia verna, Thlaspi alpestre, Viola lutea* and *Thymus drucei.*

Gratton Dale has a developing scrub of hawthorn and elder, and around this is an extremely luxuriant growth of *Filipendula vulgaris.* An interesting feature of this dale is the occurrence, on north-west-facing screes, of *Asplenium viride, Saxifraga hypnoides* and *Cystopteris fragilis.*

L.125. MARSTON MEADOWS, STAFFORDSHIRE
SJ 8413.   30 ha   Grade 1
Neutral grassland group 7 (3 and 9)[1]

This area consists of a number of poorly drained meadows liable to flooding from the Marston Brook, which forms the northern boundary to the site. The individual meadows show a range of grassland types from the drier *Conopodium majus–Festuca rubra–Anthoxanthum odoratum* community (group 9) at the eastern end, to the wetter *Sanguisorba officinalis–Alopecurus pratensis–Filipendula ulmaria* type (group 7) at the western end. One meadow in the central area is dominated in mid June by *Lychnis flos-cuculi, Trifolium pratense* and *Cirsium dissectum* with colonies of *Eriophorum angustifolium* and *Dactylorchis praetermissa* (group 3). The whole shows a rich mixture of forbs. In addition, *Fritillaria meleagris* occurs here in its most northerly native site in the British Isles and one of the only six sites now extant outside the Thames basin. A change from hay cutting to late spring grazing over the last 20 years has seriously reduced this species.

[1] See pp. 185–7, Vol. I.

L.126. FOSTER'S GREEN MEADOWS, WORCESTERSHIRE
SO 9864. 9 ha   Grade 1
Neutral grassland group 8[1]

The largest of these three meadows, Eades Meadow, is all that now remains of the once extensive *Colchicum* meadows in this area – the remainder having been either ploughed or agriculturally improved. It is typical of meadows which, although on a damp base-rich clay, are well drained. Floristically it fits into those meadows, noted by Butcher (1954) in the *Biological Flora* account of *Colchicum autumnale*, which have a wide range of grasses subdominant with *Plantago lanceolata* – the latter apparently a feature of continuous cutting for hay on damp but well-drained soils. The associated herbs at Foster's Green are typical of species-rich southern hay meadows and include *Orchis morio*, *Primula veris* and *Silaum silaus*. This similarity with other meadows such as Upwood, Huntingdon, and Monewden, Suffolk, together with the contrast resulting from an abundance of *Plantago lanceolata* and *Colchicum autumnale* makes Eades Meadow of great interest in any overall ecological study of meadows.

At the western end of the meadow are two areas of ridge-and-furrow running at right angles to each other, and a few scattered trees of oak and ash grow in the meadow.

Two further small meadows on the same farm have had a spring/summer grazing policy for at least 60 years, compared with the hay cutting of the *Colchicum* meadow. As is to be expected in a summer grazed meadow, *Colchicum* is absent and other botanical differences are apparent: *Carex caryophyllea* is more abundant and the orchid species are very rare.

These meadows owe their existence to the way they are farmed. They are either cut for hay and the aftermath grazed, or are simply summer grazed. Farmyard manure is applied in the winter; no artificial manures or herbicides are used.

L.127. BREDON HILL, WORCESTERSHIRE
SO 9540. 125 ha   Grade 2

Bredon Hill is an outlier of the Cotswold Hills with exposures of the Inferior Oolite and Upper Lias Series of the Jurassic system. On the north-facing escarpment there is calcicolous scrub, principally of *Sambucus nigra* and *Crataegus monogyna* with *Mercurialis perennis*, *Urtica dioica*, *Arum maculatum* and *Circaea lutetiana*. Badger setts are unusually abundant. An interesting ecological feature is that many of the single old hawthorns are surrounded by circles of elder. The west-facing slopes have a scrub mostly of hawthorn, but including *Fraxinus*, *Salix caprea* and *Clematis vitalba*. *Viscum album* is common on the hawthorn. There are also areas of floristically rich grassland in some old quarry workings and on the west-facing slopes.

[1] See p. 186, Vol. 1.

L.124(ii). DERBYSHIRE DALES GRASSLANDS,
          DERBYSHIRE   Grade 2

The following three Derbyshire Dales are considered in conjunction with site W.123 and form an alternative group to site L.124(i) above.

(*a*) *Coombs Dale*
SK 2274. 65 ha

Two types of *Helictotrichon–Carex flacca* grassland are represented here, and an unusual feature is the local abundance of *Festuca arundinacea*. Certain calcicoles are well represented, e.g. *Thelypteris robertiana* and *Cirsium eriophorum*, but probably the most important feature is the range of scrub types. Both advancing and degenerating hazel scrub are well represented, and have typically herb-rich field communities, with abundance of *Geranium sanguineum*, *Convallaria majalis*, *Geum rivale*, *Rubus saxatilis*, *Mercurialis perennis*, *Leontodon hispidus*, *Campanula trachelium*, *Poterium sanguisorba*, *Melica nutans*, *M. uniflora* and *Brachypodium pinnatum*. The seral hazel grades locally into ashwood with rich herbaceous communities.

On the podsolised soils in one place there is a dense gorse scrub, and, towards the top of the dale sides, an acidophilous heath with *Deschampsia flexuosa*, *Agrostis* spp., bilberry and heather is well represented. Lead mine spoil shows interesting stages in colonisation.

(*b*) *Miller's Dale*
SK 1573. 120 ha

There are good examples of *Helictotrichon–Carex flacca* grassland and species-rich hazel scrub, but Miller's Dale is especially noted for its interesting flora. *Carex ornithopoda* occurs on cliffs and in grassland, and other rock species include *Draba incana*, *Hornungia petraea*, *Silene nutans*, *Thelypteris robertiana* and *Epipactis atrorubens*. Woodland and scrub field communities contain *Pyrola minor*, abundant *Viola reichenbachiana*, *Melica nutans*, *Cirsium heterophyllum* and *Trollius europaeus*. Lead mine spoil vegetation is also well represented.

(*c*) *Topley Pike and Deep Dale*
SK 0971. 50 ha

Typical *Helictotrichon–Carex flacca* grassland is well represented in both localities, and there is good development of mixed hazel scrub and scrubby ashwood, with *Geranium sanguineum*, *Convallaria majalis*, *Epipactis helleborine*, *Rubus saxatilis* and *Melica nutans*. Herb-rich *Deschampsia cespitosa* grassland has *Trollius europaeus*, *Cirsium heterophyllum*, *Sanguisorba officinalis* and *Geum rivale*; and another type with co-dominant *Arrhenatherum* and *Holcus mollis* has a great deal of *Pimpinella major*. Cliffs and scree slopes have a rich flora, with *Sorbus aria*, *Thelypteris robertiana*, *Hornungia petraea*, *Draba incana*, *Potentilla tabernaemontani*, *Polygonatum odoratum*, *Hippocrepis comosa*, *Silene nutans* and *Saxifraga hypnoides*. Interesting mosses include the northern *Rhytidium rugosum* and the oceanic *Breutelia chrysocoma* and *Rhacomitrium lanuginosum*.

Topley Pike is much affected by limestone quarry dust, but Deep Dale is relatively free from this influence.

L.128. CRIBB'S LODGE MEADOW, LEICESTERSHIRE

SK 8918.   4 ha   Grade 2

Neutral grassland group 8/9[1]

This small ridge and furrow meadow has a typical grass flora of *Festuca rubra*, *Cynosurus cristatus*, *Holcus lanatus*, *Anthoxanthum odoratum* and *Briza media* but the presence of *Galium verum*, *Pimpinella saxifraga* and *Conopodium majus* shows some affinities with the lighter soils of group 9.

The numbers and densities of species are not as great as on grade 1 sites but include *Orchis morio*, *Dactylorchis fuchsii*, *Ophioglossum vulgatum* and *Silaum silaus*.

NORTH ENGLAND

L.129. SKIPWITH COMMON, YORKSHIRE

SE 6537.   315 ha   Grade 1

This is an extensive tract of heathland which lies at a height of 9 m on a slight spur of glacial sands forming the watershed between the lower Derwent and the Ouse valleys, in the Vale of York. It is an extremely varied area containing large tracts of wet heath merging into poor-fen swamp communities probably best regarded as valley mire. Restricted areas of dry heather heath with birch and pine colonisation, and dry woodland on sand dominated by oak and birch, also occur.

The wet heath represents the largest single tract of this vegetation type in the north of England. It is rather poor floristically and lacks some of the characterisitic bryophytes of southern wet heath, e.g. *Sphagnum compactum*. The major dominant is *Erica tetralix* with abundant *Molinia caerulea*. *Gentiana pneumonanthe* is locally abundant indicating affinities with the southern heaths. *Trichophorum cespitosum* and *Juncus squarrosus* are present but never form a major component of the vegetation. One of the abundant bryophytes is *S. fimbriatum* which forms a fairly continuous cover under birch but is also abundant within the open wet heath together with *Polytrichum* spp.

The area is important as a peatland site mainly for its extent of poor-fen communities which have developed in areas which must have originated as peat-cuttings in former valley mire. It was one of the last known stations for the northern mire moss *Paludella squarrosa* which is apparently now extinct in Britain. Poor-fen communities consist mainly of *Juncus effusus*, *J. articulatus*, *Potentilla palustris*, *Sphagnum recurvum*, *S. palustre*, *S. squarrosum* with *Carex echinata*, *C. nigra*, *Anagallis tenella*, *Eleocharis palustris*, *Galium palustre*, *Dryopteris carthusiana*, *Hydrocotyle vulgaris*. Locally, there are areas of slight base enrichment where *Lotus pedunculatus*, *Pedicularis palustris*, *Triglochin palustris*, *Lysimachia vulgaris*, *Stellaria palustris*, *Cirsium dissectum* and *Scutellaria minor* are present, and some ponds have *Phragmites communis*. *Frangula alnus* occurs locally.

The area is a diverse heathland complex which is probably most important on ornithological and entomological grounds.

[1] See pp. 186–7, Vol. 1.

The number of bird species breeding on the area is outstanding (nearly 80 species during the past 10 years) including nightjar, sparrowhawk, water rail, reed warbler and a large population of willow tit. The entomological interest is very high. A total of 306 species of Macrolepidoptera, out of a national total of 900 species, has been recorded and this includes a number of species found elsewhere in Britain only in the Cambridgeshire–Huntingdon Fens and a few localities in the vales of York and Trent (e.g. *Diarsia florida*).

L.130. WATERDALE, YORKSHIRE

SE 8261.   45 ha   Grade 1

This is probably the most important site in the Yorkshire Wolds, consisting of a long, deep valley on a north-east to south-west axis which provides a variety of aspects and slopes which are differentially grazed by cattle. As a result the grassland types are very variable, and the following communities are recognised: (i) the 'mixed grasses' community which grades into the neutral grassland type; (ii) an area of *Brachypodium pinnatum* grassland; (iii) areas of *Zerna erecta* grassland; (iv) areas of species-rich *Festuca ovina* grassland. Species of special interest noted by J. F. Hope-Simpson (unpublished) are *Arabis hirsuta*, *Cardamine pratensis* (only other record from chalk grassland is in Sussex), *Conopodium majus* (typical of Wolds), *Hypochoeris radicata* (unusual in southern Chalk), *Knautia arvensis* (unusual in southern Chalk), *Silaum silaus* (never found on southern Downs). Additionally, there is a large number of characteristic chalk species, including many mosses.

A few systematic samples which were taken from this large site contained a better than average number of leafhopper species for grassland 10 cm high. The presence of the uncommon *Hardya melanopsis* was notable. This species has not been found on the Chalk except for two sites in Wiltshire and Lincolnshire and two in the Yorkshire Wolds (here and Duggleby High Barn Wold), but it occurs on the calcareous grasslands of Weeting Heath. The occurrence of all three British species of *Streptanus* is also of interest, as is the presence of *Batracomorphus irroratus*. In the Heteroptera the occurrence of both British species of *Mecomma* is remarkable. The weevil *Sitona lineellus* (= *decipiens*), which has a distinctly northern distribution, was found at all three Wolds sites, but not on the Chalk elsewhere.

L.131. DUGGLEBY HIGH BARN WOLD, YORKSHIRE

SE 8668.   55 ha   Grade 1

Basically this is a grassland of the southern chalk type with northern floristic elements and is therefore of great interest. The grassland is of the *Festuca ovina–Poterium* type with good quantities of *Carex flacca* and *C. caryophyllea*, with local patches of *Brachypodium pinnatum* and *Zerna erecta*. Hawthorn scrub is scattered along the slopes. The outstanding floristic interest of this Wold is the presence of good quantities of *Linum anglicum* and *Geranium sanguineum*, unknown together in open grassland elsewhere on the

Chalk. In addition, there is abundance of *Betonica officinalis*, *Serratula tinctoria*, *Succisa pratensis*, *Orchis mascula* and *Filipendula vulgaris* which link this site with the south-westerly elements of the chalk association.

This is an outstanding site entomologically. The number of species recorded in systematic samples is well above average and the numbers of individuals among the highest recorded at any site. On the south-facing slope of the site, *Turrutus socialis* occurred in very high numbers, a maximum of $263/m^2$ being recorded. The *Brachypodium pinnatum* grassland on the north-facing slope is characterised by an abundance of *Adarrus multinotatus*, which appears to be associated with this grass. This site was the only one in the Wolds at which *Agallia consobrina*, *Arocephalus punctum* and *Laodelphax elegantulus* occurred. Generally on chalk grassland the heteropterous bug *Stenodema calcaratum* is uncommon, preferring damper grasslands, but at Duggleby it occurred in abundance. The weevil fauna was rich, *Apion atomarium* being recorded for the first time during the review from as far north as Yorkshire both from Duggleby and from East Dale.

L.132. EAST DALE, YORKSHIRE
TR 0575.   12 ha   Grade 1

East Dale has a uniform, steep, south-facing slope with a grassland similar in floristic composition and structure to the southern Chalk and appears generally to have a greater faunal affinity with this than the other Wolds sites. Gorse scrub with a little hawthorn occurs on the Clay-with-Flints capping at the top of the slope. Forbs, especially *Leontodon hispidus*, *Trifolium pratense*, *Campanula glomerata*, *Plantago media* and *P. lanceolata*, are unusually abundant. Of special interest in the predominantly *Festuca ovina* type of grassland, is the abundance of *Astragalus danicus*, a species rare on the southern Chalk.

The numbers of species recorded in the samples of Auchenorhyncha were above the general average and some notable species were included, particularly *Agallia brachyptera*, which has been taken at only two other chalk sites during the course of the review. The heteropterous fauna was poor, but the weevils quite rich in species.

The complementary nature of the three Yorkshire Wolds sites chosen as grade 1 is immediately apparent on tabulating the records of Auchenorhyncha. Together the three sites form an area with a particularly interesting fauna composed of rather few species, but containing many of special importance and some unusual associations.

L.133. HUMPHREY HEAD, LANCASHIRE
SD 3974.   30 ha   Grade 1

This rather small, narrow Carboniferous Limestone promontory lies on the Morecambe Bay coast, at the western side of the mouth of the Kent estuary, and is surrounded by tidal sand flats with their fringing salt marshes. Humphrey Head reaches 52 m – the west side is more or less sheer cliff and below these on the landward end is a scrub containing deadly nightshade. The east side is mainly a terraced descent to a boulder-strewn shore and has a rocky

calcareous grassland and mixed deciduous wood which complements the scrub on the steep, exposed west face. This is a floristically rich site, though most of the notable species are associated with rock ledges or steep, open slopes rather than with grassland. This is the northernmost station for the characteristic group of rarities consisting of *Veronica spicata* ssp. *hybrida*, *Helianthemum canum*, *Hypochoeris maculata* and *Aster linosyris*, which are found in scattered localities on the western Carboniferous Limestone. Other species of note include *Geranium sanguineum*, *Astragalus glycyphyllos* and *Potentilla tabernaemontani*, and there was formerly a colony of *Adiantum capillus-veneris* indicating the mildness of the climate at sea-level in this area.

See also C.59.

L.134. GAIT BARROWS, LANCASHIRE
SD 4877.   70 ha   Grade 1

This site contains the most important single example in Britain of Carboniferous Limestone pavement with clint and grike structure, and is surpassed only by the more extensive pavements of the Burren in Ireland. An important feature is the range of surface structure in the Gait Barrows pavement, which in the centre consists of massive, flat, tabular limestone with few and infrequently intersecting vertical fissures. To the east and west the surface becomes undulating and the fissures more frequently intersecting, though the clints are still large. Away from the central area, the clints become smaller, with many loose blocks and numerous, deep fissures, and the marginal areas show dissected pavement, with blocks moved from their original position and bedded in glacial boulder clay. The pavement lies at the unusually low elevation of 45 m and is only 3 km from the Kent estuary.

Over an area of at least 12 ha the pavement is largely open, though with a patchy development of scrub nuclei, but with increasing distance from the centre the scrub thickens into continuous woodland (see W.140) over the more fragmented pavement, and there is a change in associated floristics. There is little grassland on the open pavement, and the vegetation is mainly an open rupestral type of scrub with a field layer. The crevices have an abundance of *Phyllitis scolopendrium* and *Polystichum aculeatum*, and the rarer ferns include *Dryopteris villarii* and *Ceterach officinarum*. *Polygonatum odoratum*, *Hypericum androsaemum*, *Geranium sanguineum*, *Eupatorium cannabinum*, *Serratula tinctoria* and *Galium boreale* grow on the pavement or in its crevices. The northern grass *Sesleria albicans* is locally abundant.

There is a very good development of patchwork of scrub composed of yew, hazel, small ash and oak, with locally also juniper, holly, privet, dogwood, buckthorn, small-leaved lime, spindle and the rare endemic rowan *Sorbus lancastriensis* which is confined to the Morecambe Bay area, where it takes the place of the southern *S. aria*.

This is a scrub type very similar to that of the Chalk, and is especially interesting as the most northerly example in which dogwood, spindle, buckthorn, privet and small-leaved lime may be found growing together, for these shrubs are all here near their northern limit as natives. Associated with this scrub is a rich herbaceous flora including *Convallaria majalis, Atropa belladonna, Geranium sanguineum, Hypericum montanum, Melica nutans, Epipactis atrorubens, Rubus saxatilis* and *Carex digitata*. This rich assemblage of local and rare species is a relict community probably indicating a woodland ecosystem which has remained relatively undisturbed by human influence right through the Post-glacial Period.

Together with the surrounding woodlands and the wetland types at Hawes Water (see OW.53), this limestone pavement area forms one of the most important habitat complexes in northern Britain.

L.135. HUTTON ROOF CRAGS AND FARLETON KNOTT, WESTMORLAND
SD 5578, SD 5480.   630 ha   Grade 1

These two massive areas of Carboniferous Limestone pavement form a single geographical and ecological unit. They lie 10 km east of Arnside and at an elevation of 150–275 m, thus occupying a position intermediate between the low-lying coastal pavement of Gait Barrows and the inland and submontane examples at Orton and on Ingleborough (the last two are described under Upland Grasslands and Heaths). In surface structure, Hutton Roof Crags show a great range of variation, but there is more of the dissected, heavily fissured and loose pavement than at Gait Barrows. This gives an abundance of plant habitats, and the pavements here are notable for their quantity of *Phyllitis scolopendrium, Mycelis muralis, Geranium lucidum, Dryopteris villarii, Epipactis atrorubens, Filipendula vulgaris* and *Polystichum aculeatum*. More sparingly or locally are *Thalictrum minus, Galium sterneri, Hypericum montanum, Thelypteris robertiana, Asplenium viride, Hippocrepis comosa, Geranium sanguineum, Minuartia verna, Asperula cynanchica, Polygonatum odoratum, Melica nutans, Rubus saxatilis, Rosa pimpinellifolia, Cynoglossum officinale, Helianthemum chamaecistus, Convallaria majalis, Carlina vulgaris, Arabis hirsuta, Potentilla tabernaemontani, Ophrys insectifera, Carex ornithopoda* and *Rhytidium rugosum*.

The bare pavement communities show all stages in the transition to closed grassland, dominated by *Sesleria albicans* or by a mixture of grasses, including *Anthoxanthum odoratum, Helictotrichon pratense* and *Agrostis* spp. These grasslands grade into acidic heath with *Calluna vulgaris, Vaccinium myrtillus, Potentilla erecta* and *Deschampsia flexuosa* on leached drift soils, and patches of an intermediate limestone heath may be found. Gorse forms dense stands locally. There is a good deal of patchy scrub, composed of ash, hazel, rowan, guelder rose, yew, juniper, blackthorn, hawthorn, sycamore, wych elm, holly, and *Sorbus lancastriensis*. The more southern shrubs which are so notable at Gait Barrows are less represented here, though buckthorn and spindle occur sparingly. *Cirsium heterophyllum* is one of the tall herbs associated with this scrub.

On the east slope is a wood which should be regarded as a bonus habitat. It is a mixed wood containing ash, oak

and a variety of shrubs, especially hazel as coppice. The lower part of the wood is heavily grazed by sheep and lacks regeneration, but the upper part lies on limestone pavement and here the sheep have less influence. The shrubs include hawthorn, holly, rowan, gean, bird cherry, blackthorn, rose, elder and guelder rose. The ground flora is forb-rich and contains species such as *Anemone nemorosa, Endymion non-scriptus, Allium ursinum, Fragaria vesca, Mercurialis perennis* and *Primula vulgaris* as well as species of a more restricted distribution, e.g. *Paris quadrifolia*.

Farleton Knott has been greatly despoiled by the removal of surface limestone, and much of the pavement has been ruined, though there are still good areas at the north end. The flora is less rich than on Hutton Roof Crags and there is less scrub, but deep grikes have a striking quantity of *Dryopteris villarii*, and the montane fern *Polystichum lonchitis* is recorded from here. Farleton Knott also has limestone scar and scree on the scarp slope beneath its plateau, and so increases the range of habitats found within the whole area. It is regarded as an integral part of this aggregate grade 1 site.

L.136. WHITBARROW SCAR, WESTMORLAND
SD 4487.   1000 ha   Grade 1

See under next site description.

L.137. SCOUT AND CUNSWICK SCARS, WESTMORLAND
SD 4890, SD 4993.   215 ha   Grade 1

Whitbarrow Scar is a long, low, Carboniferous Limestone hill reaching 215 m, while Scout and Cunswick Scars are the two extremities of a similar hill reaching 217 m, 5–6.5 km to the north-east. These two hills lie just to the west of Kendal and on the north side of Morecambe Bay; both are about 6.5 km long in a north–south direction, and both show a western scarp slope and eastern dip slope. The scarps have lines of limestone cliff which on Whitbarrow are quite high, and these pass to scree or grassland and then woodland below. Limestone pavement is not well developed on the plateaux, and there is a good deal of flat scree, with loose, thin limestone slabs, which here and there hold many of the interesting pavement species, but in far lesser abundance than on Hutton Roof Crags. The summits are thus covered mainly with a mixture of *Sesleria albicans* grassland, poorer *Agrostis* grassland and grass heath of *Calluna vulgaris, Nardus stricta, Agrostis tenuis, Anthoxanthum odoratum, Potentilla erecta, Viola riviniana* and *Lotus corniculatus*. The flat scree and fragmentary pavement have *Oxalis acetosella, Geranium robertianum, Asplenium trichomanes, A. ruta-muraria, A. viride* and occasional prostrate patches of privet. The summit of Whitbarrow has much dead and dying juniper and yew, evidently as a result of burning.

The west-facing cliffs of both hills have locally an abundance of *Helianthemum canum, Hippocrepis comosa, Scabiosa columbaria, Thalictrum minus, Inula conyza,* and there is some *Sorbus rupicola, Polygonatum odoratum, Epipactis atrorubens* and *Geranium sanguineum*. In various limestone habitats are *Minuartia verna, Asperula cynanchica,*

Hypericum montanum, Carex ornithopoda, C. digitata, Rubus saxatilis, Filipendula vulgaris, Potentilla tabernaemontani, Rosa pimpinellifolia, Galium sterneri, Carlina vulgaris, Melica nutans, Ceterach officinarum, Dryopteris villarii and *Thelypteris robertiana*, the last occurring in great quantity on the screes under the western cliffs of Scout Scar. The varied bryophyte flora includes *Homomallium incurvatum, Rhytidium rugosum, Campylium calcareum, Amblystegiella sprucei, A. confervoides, Isopterygium depressum, Isothecium striatulum, Brachythecium glareosum, Thuidium philiberti, Entodon orthocarpus, Tortella nitida, Funaria meuhlenbergii* and *Marchesinia mackaii*.

The western slopes of both hills have a good deal of scrub and woodland, and that beneath Whitbarrow Scar passes into the extensive Whitbarrow–Witherslack Woods complex which has been identified as a woodlands grade 1 site and described separately (W.136). Cunswick, Barrowfield and Brigsteer Woods beneath the other hill have been more severely modified, though they are still of considerable floristic interest, and the same is true of the scattered woods on the dip slope of Whitbarrow Scar. The scrub of both scarps is similar to that of Gait Barrows, but is on steep rock and scree instead of level pavement, and includes yew, hazel, ash, holly, guelder rose, wych elm, birch, buckthorn and *Sorbus lancastriensis*. The woods and scrub on these two hills were formerly noted for their rare plants including *Cypripedium calceolus, Cephalanthera longifolia, Daphne mezereum, Allium schoenoprasum, Monotropa hypopitys* and *Polygonatum odoratum*, some of which may have been lost through disturbance. More common species such as *Convallaria majalis, Paris quadrifolia, Neottia nidus-avis* and *Platanthera chlorantha* are still present. The small lake, Cunswick Tarn, below Cunswick Scar is one of the few eutrophic water-bodies in north-west England and has fen communities with *Cladium mariscus, Schoenus nigricans* and *Epipactis palustris*.

Although these two hills have basic similarities, there are many differences of detail.

L.138. THRISLINGTON PLANTATION, DURHAM

NZ 3132.   20 ha   Grade 1

This is considered to be the best example of Magnesian Limestone grassland extant. The grassland is a species-rich *Seslaria albicans* type, with co-dominance of *Festuca ovina*, and locally *Antennaria dioica, Aquilegia vulgaris, Arabis hirsuta, Linum anglicum, Primula farinosa* and *Epipactis atrorubens* all occurring in some quantity, four of these being northern species which mix here with the southern elements in the calcicolous flora. Scrub of *Crataegus, Acer pseudoplatanus* and *Rosa pimpinellifolia* is relatively extensive. Although this site is mostly flat, there are gentle slopes which provide a variety of aspects. The area is scheduled for mining within the next 50 years.

The entomological samples from Thrislington Plantation were not particularly rich but had some interesting features. The uncommon cicadellid bug *Hardya melanopsis* was present and another species, *Dicranoneura citrinella*, occurred in large numbers and, unusually, predominated in the Auchenorhyncha fauna. *Cyrtorhinus caricis* was an interesting heteropterous bug recorded.

L.139. ORTON MEADOWS, WESTMORLAND

NY 6209.   25 ha   Grade 1

Neutral grassland groups 10 and 11[1]

This area contains very good examples of wet pastures and hay meadows on Carboniferous Limestone drift soils.

The wet pasture, famous for *Bartsia alpina*, has undergone some change in management, including some drainage by open guttering. There has been a decline in the quantity of *Bartsia* present and *Primula farinosa* is less luxuriant than formerly. A small stream runs through this *Bartsia* field, and on its banks is an abundance of *Carex ornithopoda*, an unusual habitat for this species of dry limestone pavement and grassland.

The hay meadows contain all the characteristic plants of such areas in northern England – *Geranium sylvaticum, Trollius europaeus, Cirsium heterophyllum* and *Alchemilla vulgaris* agg., together with *Serratula tinctoria, Betonica officinalis* and *Dactylorchis purpurella. Serratula* and *Betonica* are approaching the northern limit of their distribution here and are of particular interest as typical components of southern hay meadows.

The grazed grasslands are basically of *Festuca rubra, Anthoxanthum odoratum* and *Holcus lanatus* with *Blysmus compressus* and *Bartsia alpina* in those areas affected by cattle treading. *Primula farinosa* is abundant in the short, grazed turf by the stream side and *Pinguicula vulgaris, Valeriana dioica* and *Parnassia palustris* are frequent together with a small colony of *Antennaria dioica*.

See also L.140, P.53, OW.54 and U.25.

L.140. CROSBY GILL, WESTMORLAND

NY 6111.   150 ha   Grade 1

Neutral grassland group 11[1]

This is a large, enclosed area of mainly cattle-grazed pasture on Carboniferous Limestone at 230–320 m in the Shap Fells. The area forms the head of a valley and is drained by the twin headstreams of Crosby Gill. It consists of a mixture of dry grassland and a damper type with numerous calcareous flushes, and there are interesting patches of woodland and scrub. The dry pasture varies from a fairly typical limestone grassland community with *Festuca rubra, Sesleria albicans, Briza media, Poterium sanguisorba* and *Helianthemum chamaecistus* to a more acidophilous sward with much *Conopodium majus* and *Potentilla erecta*. There is a local abundance of forbs such as *Sanguisorba officinalis, Betonica officinalis, Geranium sylvaticum, Serratula tinctoria, Geum rivale, Trifolium medium, Leontodon hispidus, Orchis mascula* and *Salix repens. Polygonum viviparum* is frequent in places and *Silaum silaus* occasional. The marshy pastures have vast quantities of *Primula farinosa*, and other notable species of this habitat are *Dactylorchis purpurella, D. incarnata, Pinguicula vulgaris, Valeriana dioica* and *Blysmus compressus*. More open flushes have *Carex lepidocarpa, Saxifraga aizoides*, and *Schoenus nigricans*, and the hum-

[1] See p. 187, Vol. 1.

mocks of cattle-trodden sites have the rare *Bartsia alpina* and *Carex capillaris*.

The western gill has a good bonus fragment of ash–birch wood in a rocky glen. It contains a good deal of hawthorn and hazel and is rather open, except for one good stand of ash. The most interesting feature is the lightly grazed field layer, which has a profusion of medium to tall herbs, with *Geum rivale*, *Geranium sylvaticum*, *Serratula tinctoria*, *Crepis paludosa*, *Allium ursinum*, *Filipendula ulmaria*, *Orchis mascula*, *Galium odoratum*, *Polystichum aculeatum* and *Melica nutans*. The grasses *Dactylis glomerata* and *Brachypodium sylvaticum* are locally abundant but never really dominant in this field layer, in contrast to the situation in many limestone woods. Well-grown hawthorns are scattered over the slopes outside the wood. Buckthorn has been recorded, and is almost at its northernmost British limits here.

This grassland to woodland complex is in marked contrast to the sheep-grazed *Festuca–Sesleria* grassland and *Calluna* communities of the adjacent moorland. The presence of at least four montane species indicates the upland affinities of this meadow system.

See also L.139, P.53, OW.54 and U.25.

L.141. WINTRINGHAM MARSH, YORKSHIRE
SE 8773.   8 ha   Grade 1
Neutral grassland group 1 (3)[1]

This area shows a uniform gradation from dry pasture containing *Festuca rubra*, *Lolium perenne*, *Briza media*, *Linum catharticum* and *Campanula rotundifolia*, to a *Glyceria maxima*-dominated stream side. In between are two clearly defined areas: one containing *F. rubra*, *Anthoxanthum odoratum* and *Molinia caerulea* grassland and the other dominated by *Juncus subnodulosus*. Over 100 species were recorded, including *Pinguicula vulgaris*, *Epipactis palustris*, *Parnassia palustris*, *Blysmus compressus*, *Schoenus nigricans* and 10 species of *Carex*, including *C. hostiana*, *C. lepidocarpa* and *C. rostrata* and seven species of *Juncus*. Many of these species are rare in the county and some such as *Blysmus compressus* have rapidly declined on a national scale with increased drainage and land reclamation since 1940.

L.142. DERWENT INGS, YORKSHIRE   Grade 1*
(*a*) SE 7043
(*b*) SE 6941
(*c*) SE 6938 } 300 ha
(*d*) SE 6937
(*e*) SE 7036
Neutral grassland groups 4, 5 (3 and 7)[1]

There are five sites between Wheldrake and Bubwith, which between them combine an excellent range of alluvial grassland groups, coupled with a high ornithological interest. The sites are described separately but together form an aggregate grade 1 site.

(*a*) Much of this area is flooded for up to eight weeks at a time. This intensity of flooding is intermediate between

[1] See pp. 185–7, Vol. 1.

that obtaining on the Ouse Washes (L.70) and some of the alluvial meadows such as those at North Meadow (L.43) and Sibson Meadows (L.73). Large areas of *Glyceria maxima* (group 4) cover the area of maximum flooding grading through *Alopecurus geniculatus*, *Glyceria fluitans*, *Oenanthe fistulosa* (group 5) to *Alopecurus pratensis*, *Filipendula ulmaria*, *Oenanthe silaifolia*, *Sanguisorba officinalis* and *Silaum silaus* (group 7).

(*b*) This area is less flooded than (*a*) and a flora of the group 5 type has developed, encouraged by the hay-cutting which is the traditional management over much of this part of the Derwent valley.

(*c*) This area contains more grassland groups than the other four areas but is chosen mainly to represent the grazed grassland of the higher, and therefore drier, parts of this valley. The flora of these grazed areas is not outstanding, and consists of *Lolium perenne*, *Cynosurus cristatus*, *Poa trivialis*, *Cirsium arvense* and few other species (group 14). There is also a good example of the grass–sedge communities of group 3 with *Carex disticha*, *C. flacca*, *C. panicea*, *C. nigra* and *Alopecurus pratensis*, *Anthoxanthum odoratum*, *Festuca rubra* and *Holcus lanatus*. Among the numerous forbs are *Caltha palustris* and *Dactylorchis purpurella*; the latter is at the south-eastern limit of its range in Britain and is a species rare in east Yorkshire generally.

(*d*) These low lying carrs are excellent examples of group 4, being dominated by *Glyceria maxima* and *Phalaris arundinacea*, with *Stellaria palustris* as one of the few species which can compete successfully in this community. This area, and area (*a*), form the main wildfowl areas.

(*e*) The rich flora over much of this area suggests that it has common land status similar to North Meadow (L.43) and Port Holme (L.85). It is the best example of group 7 seen in the north. The grasses are a good mixture of *Anthoxanthum odoratum*, *Cynosurus cristatus*, *Festuca rubra*, *F. pratensis* and *Holcus lanatus* with many herbs including *Silaum silaus*, *Sanguisorba officinalis*, *Filipendula ulmaria* and *Thalictrum flavum*.

The whole section of the Derwent valley between Wheldrake and Bubwith, from which these five areas have been chosen, is a noted wildfowl site during winter and early spring. Populations include Bewick's swan (170 birds), wigeon (2500), teal (660) and mallard and pintail.

L.143. GOWK BANK, CUMBERLAND
NY 6773.   7 ha   Grade 1
Neutral grassland group 10

This site flanks an upper reach of the River Irthing, where the alluvial river banks rise into steep morainic banks some 6–24 m high, standing back from the river. The alluvium and drift are derived from the Scottish Calciferous Sandstone (Carboniferous) so that base-status is generally high, and there is a moist calcareous clay in places. The ground of particular interest is a grassland, rich in tall forbs, that forms part of a hay meadow system which is fenced against nearby pasture. The flatter parts of the area are cut for hay, but the steep drift banks and associated narrow strip of alluvial river bank are never cut. Grazing of the whole area would appear to be limited to late summer and winter, after the hay has been cut, and mainly by cattle.

The uncut areas of this meadow system have some of the finest examples of northern tall-herb communities now to be found in Britain. *Cirsium heterophyllum, Geranium sylvaticum, Crepis paludosa, Galium boreale* and *Geum rivale* occur in great quantity, and there are good patches of *Trollius europaeus*. The orchids are represented by *Dactylorchis purpurella, D. incarnata, D. fuchsii, Orchis mascula, Coeloglossum viride, Gymnadenia conopsea* and *Listera ovata*; and other herbs of interest include *Parnassia palustris, Valeriana dioica, Pedicularis palustris, Sagina nodosa, Anthyllis vulneraria, Trifolium medium, Sanguisorba officinalis, Knautia arvensis, Pimpinella saxifraga, Leontodon hispidus* and *Galium verum*. There is a local abundance of *Filipendula ulmaria, Centaurea nigra* and *Stachys sylvatica*.

The abundant grasses of the site are *Molinia caerulea, Anthoxanthum odoratum, Briza media, Holcus lanatus* and *Dactylis glomerata*. On damp parts of the river banks *Carex acutiformis* is locally dominant, and there is abundant *C. disticha*. The steep, uncut banks have a patchy growth of alder and willows, mainly *Salix cinerea*, but with some *S. aurita* and *S. pentandra*.

The mown parts of the meadow are much less rich in tall herbs, but have an abundance of herbs which give a distinctly northern character, notably *Rhinanthus minor* and *Euphrasia montana*, while *Gentianella campestris* occurs more sparingly.

The bryophyte flora is richer than in more southern meadows and the clubmoss *Selaginella selaginoides* occurs plentifully.

L.144. UPPER TEESDALE MEADOWS, DURHAM–YORKSHIRE
NY 8728, NY 8529, NY 8330, NY 8629. 75 ha Grade 1
Neutral grassland groups 10 and 11[1]

These four areas, three on the Durham side and one on the Yorkshire side of the River Tees, form a representative selection of Pennine dales meadows, although the pastures outnumber the traditional hay meadows. The soils are of drift and alluvium containing material from the 'sugar' limestone of the Carboniferous Series in Upper Teesdale.

All four areas contain a flush system dominated by *Juncus articulatus* and *Carex panicea*. The grassland above the flush area is composed of *Festuca rubra, Anthoxanthum odoratum, Cynosurus cristatus* and *Conopodium majus*, and is generally less species rich than that below. The more interesting hay meadows have *J. articulatus, Carex panicea, C. nigra* and *Festuca rubra* with *Cirsium heterophyllum, Caltha palustris* and *Trollius europaeus* in some quantity. The presence of quantities of *Caltha* and *Juncus* suggests a wetter meadow than at Orton. Between the flush areas and the drier grasslands, *Primula farinosa* is abundant in a sward of *Carex panicea* and *Molinia caerulea*.

Of the four areas, perhaps that at NY 8330 is the best. The flush area here extends down to the River Tees and has *Caltha palustris* and *Carex nigra* dominant with *Potentilla*

[1] See p. 187, Vol. 1.

palustris, while in the higher reaches of this flush are *Bartsia alpina* and *Parnassia palustris*. The best area for *Primula farinosa* is NY 8529, whilst NY 8728 has the only record for *Ophioglossum vulgatum* var. *ambiguum* in northern England. This area also contains the best herb meadow *per se*.

The fourth meadow, on the Yorkshire side and below Cronkley Farm, has quite a large area of *Trollius, Cirsium heterophyllum* and *Geranium sylvaticum* and is one of the best examples of an old hay meadow in the district. This type has diminished greatly in the last three decades through change in management, usually involving heavier grazing and application of artificial fertiliser. Good examples were once widespread in the Pennines but are now relatively few.

See also U.21.

L.145. STRENSALL COMMON, YORKSHIRE
SE 6459. 690 ha Grade 2

Strensall Common is a northern example of acidic heathland in the Vale of York, and lies on a complex sequence of aeolian sands above lacustrine sands and clays which in turn overlie boulder clay. Compared with Skipwith Common 24 km to the south, Strensall Common has less wetland and woodland habitat, but a marginally richer flora. Earlier drainage operations and a long period of military use have reduced the wetness of this area, and prevented more than limited invasion by trees and tall shrubs.

The dry heather heath with local abundance of bracken is extensive, and the flora includes *Genista anglica* and *Ornithopus perpusillus* in sandy places. Humid heath is well represented, with a good deal of *Molinia caerulea* and *Erica tetralix* and this is a noted northern locality for *Gentiana pneumonanthe*. Other species here include *Anagallis tenella, Dactylorchis fuchsii, Carex hostiana* and *Dryopteris carthusiana*. The permanent pools and marshy area have a diverse wetland flora with *Potentilla palustris, Menyanthes trifoliata, Oenanthe fistulosa, Baldellia ranunculoides, Utricularia* spp., *Stellaria palustris* and *Apium inundatum*.

Woodland with oak, birch, Scots pine and larch is represented, and there is a little regeneration of birch and pine on the Common, but repeated fires have maintained the heath communities over most of the area.

L.146. LAZONBY AND WAN FELLS, CUMBERLAND
NY 5241, NY 5139, NY 5236. 250 ha Grade 2

These form part of a chain of low New Red Sandstone hills, north of Penrith and forming the western flank of the Eden valley. There are a few small outcrops and patches of scree, and the sandstone has been quarried in places for flagstones. The vegetation is a range of dry Callunetum, Vaccinetum and acidophilous valley mire, with intermediate types in places. The heaths here have affinities with southern lowland heaths, and contain (albeit sparingly) characteristic species such as *Ulex gallii, Genista anglica* and *Hypnum imponens*. Local species recorded here include *Carum verticillatum, Cryptogramma crispa, Listera cordata* and *Antennaria dioica*. The heaths are moss rich or lichen rich where not recently burned, and in this respect and, in the local abundance of *Vaccinium vitis-idaea* and *Empetrum nigrum*, they approach the upland Calluneta. Locally there is invasion by birch and Scots pine, to form rather open woodland, and on Lazonby Fell there has recently been a good deal of coniferous afforestation.

The valley mires are of a northern type, with *Carex rostrata*, *C. curta*, *C. nigra*, *C. lasiocarpa*, *C. echinata*, *Trichophorum cespitosum*, *Eriophorum vaginatum*, *E. angustifolium*, *Narthecium ossifragum*, *Rhynchospora alba*, *Vaccinium oxycoccus*, *Menyanthes trifoliata*, *Sphagnum papillosum*, *S. magellanicum*, *S. rubellum*, *S. recurvum*, *S. cuspidatum*, *S. compactum*, *Aulacomnium palustre* and *Drepanocladus exannulatus*. The affinities with upland heather moor are strong; parts of the area are managed as grouse-moor, and the merlin was formerly among the breeding birds.

L.147. ARNSIDE KNOTT AND WARTON CRAG, WESTMORLAND–LANCASHIRE
SD 4577, SD 4973. 180 ha   Grade 2

These two Carboniferous Limestone hills lie close to the coast at Arnside and Silverdale. They cannot be regarded as alternative sites to Gait Barrows (L.134), or Hutton Roof Crags and Farleton Knott (L.135), as they have relatively little pavement. Both are complexes of limestone grassland, with scree and fragmentary pavement, and a good deal of scrub and woodland. Floristically they are rich, and most of the communities and species of the grade 1 pavement sites are represented. In particular, Arnside Knott has much *Epipactis atrorubens*, the third British station for *Viola rupestris*, a patch of the very rare fern *Adiantum capillus-veneris*, *Orchis ustulata*, *Carex digitata*, *Potentilla tabernaemontani*, *Asperula cynanchica* and one of the two northern England colonies of the Scotch argus butterfly. However, most of the habitat types of Arnside Knott are so heterogeneous and disturbed that they cannot be regarded as more than grade 2.

L.148. CASSOP VALE, DURHAM
NZ 3338. 80 ha   Grade 2

This complex site on Magnesian Limestone has been mined, quarried and partly used as a sewage works, but still maintains a high scientific interest. The full successional sequence from grassland to scrub and then to secondary woodland is seen on the site, together with a valley bottom containing a ground water gley and alluvium with a well-developed pond. The north-facing slopes support a grassland of the damp, tall-herb type in which *Sesleria albicans* is co-dominant with *Carex pulicaris* and *Sieglingia decumbens*, and contains good quantities of *Helictotrichon pubescens*.

Gorse scrub has encroached onto much of this grassland, but the southern slopes still retain their essentially open character, with a wide variety of calcicolous plants. Of special interest is the occurrence of *Trollius europaeus*, *Primula farinosa* and *Pinguicula vulgaris* in one of their last remaining lowland stations in this district. Other species of special note include *Astragalus danicus*, *Botrychium lunaria*, *Ophioglossum vulgatum*, *Plantago maritima* and *Preissia quadrata*.

At both Cassop and Thrislington (L.138) 12 species of *Rosa* have been recorded, which further enhances the importance of these sites.

SOUTH SCOTLAND

L.149. KEN–DEE MARSHES, KIRKCUDBRIGHTSHIRE
NX 7167. 1500 ha   Grade 1
Neutral grassland group 2 (7)[1]

This area consists of alluvial and permanent meadows, freshwater marshes and flood-plain mire on both sides of the lake-like course of the combined rivers Ken and Dee between the Loch Ken viaduct and Netherhall.

The alluvial meadows are mainly of the *Cynosurus cristatus*, *Ranunculus acris*, *Trifolium repens* type (group 14) but some contain *Juncus acutiflorus* and *Achillea ptarmica* showing affinities with group 2. The meadows seen are not of national importance.

It is the freshwater marshes which have the main botanical interest, showing a wide range of communities within the base-poor marsh group (group 2). Certain of these are transitional between base-poor and base-rich such as *Phalaris arundinacea/Lysimachia vulgaris* but the dominant poor-fen community has *Molinia caerulea* and *Juncus acutiflorus*, with *Menyanthes trifoliata*, *Potentilla palustris* and *Carex lasiocarpa*. On the drier areas there are *Myrica gale–Molinia caerulea* communities. The western umbellifer *Carum verticillatum* is abundant in this area.

A good example of flood-plain mire is by Round Loch where the mud flats are colonised by *Carex vesicaria*, *Hippuris vulgaris* and *Potentilla palustris*.

This system is of great importance for its winter populations of wildfowl. Loch Ken and Dee barrage contains Greenland white-fronted (450) geese and greylag, mallard, teal, wigeon, pintail, shoveler, pochard, tufted duck, goldeneye, goosander, mute swan and whooper swan occur regularly. The majority of the birds are usually located on the southern half below the inflow of the Dee. Threave and Netherhall Marshes contain bean geese (60; over 30% of UK population); Greenland white-fronted (200; 6% of UK population) and greylag occur regularly.

EAST SCOTLAND

L.150. SANDS OF FORVIE, ABERDEENSHIRE
NK 0227. 1300 ha   Grade 1

The area is primarily a coastal site containing a complex of mobile and fixed dunes, but in addition to the coastal interest the Sands of Forvie have great value as the best northern example of lowland heathland. The vegetation and physiography of the area have been described by Landsberg (1955) and the site has also been described by much other published research work.

There are three main series of plant communities:

1 Those of the more or less unstable dunes, principally in the southern parts of the NNR.

2 Those of the dry, fixed dunes principally in the north.

[1] See pp. 185–6, Vol. 1.

3 Those of the wet dune plains.

The soils are mostly derived from non-calcareous wind-blown sand. The most noticeable and striking feature of the heath communities is the important role that *Empetrum nigrum* plays in the vegetation. The vegetation types of the stable dunes include a sequence of seral stages leading to the development of a mature, closed, dwarf-shrub heath. The earliest stage consists of an open lichen-rich *Empetrum* heath in which there is some *Calluna* and many sand colonisers such as *Ammophila arenaria* and *Carex arenaria*. This passes to a closed community in which *Empetrum* is still dominant and there is a larger number of grasses, forbs, bryophytes and lichens. The final stage shows dominance of *Calluna*, though *Empetrum* remains abundant, and the numbers of associates are reduced by competition with the dwarf shrubs; species such as *Agrostis tenuis*, *Festuca ovina*, *Campanula rotundifolia*, pleurocarpous heath mosses and lichens remain abundant, to give a community resembling the maritime heather heaths so widespread on rocky western coasts.

A variety of communities occurs with increasing soil moisture. These include areas of damp *Calluna–Empetrum* heath with *Erica tetralix*, *Salix repens*, *Juncus effusus*, *J. squarrosus*, *Potentilla erecta*, *Hylocomium splendens*, *Pleurozium schreberi* and *Rhytidiadelphus squarrosus*. Other areas are grassier, with *Nardus stricta* dominant and associates such as *Salix repens*, *Carex arenaria*, *Deschampsia cespitosa*, *Hydrocotyle vulgaris*, *Juncus* spp. and *Molinia caerulea*, *Trichophorum cespitosum*, *Aulacomnium palustre* and *Polytri-*

chum commune. Wetter areas dominated by *Salix repens* occur with *Carex rostrata*, *C. nigra* and many of the species listed above.

A series of dune slack communities is also present in addition to open water, coastal rocks and steep grassy cliffs. See also C.86.

WEST SCOTLAND

L.151. OYKELL MARSHES, ROSS–SUTHERLAND
NH 5198.   285 ha   Grade 1
Neutral grassland group 2 (5, 12 and 13)[1]

The wide alluvial flood plain built up by the lower reach of the River Oykell has an extensive area of vegetation ranging from dry alluvial grassland to freshwater marsh.

The drier areas have a good deal of *Deschampsia cespitosa* grassland (group 12) together with *Holcus lanatus*, *Juncus effusus* and *Ranunculus acris* (group 13).

The wetter parts have areas of sedge fen varying between oligotrophic and mesotrophic and containing *Carex rostrata*, *Hydrocotyle vulgaris*, *Juncus acutiflorus*, *Potentilla palustris* and *Viola palustris*. There is an abundance of forbs such as *Ranunculus flammula*, *Filipendula ulmaria*, *Lychnis flos-cuculi* and *Iris pseudacorus* which are typical species of valley grasslands. The complex would seem to be a northern equivalent to that of the Sibson Meadows in Huntingdon and Peterborough (L.73), though the site has not yet been surveyed in detail.

[1] See pp. 185–7, Vol. 1.

17 OPEN WATERS

SOUTH-EAST ENGLAND

OW.1. OPPEN PITS, KENT
TR 0718. 2 ha   Grade 1

The Oppen Pits consists of a series of four small water-bodies situated on the accreted shingle beach at Dungeness, where they are thought to have originated from brackish lagoons. They exhibit some of the best examples of unspoilt marginal vegetation in south-east England. The largest pit is fringed at its northern end by a willow carr and the remainder of the pond is edged by a floating mat of *Typha angustifolia* with zones of *Iris pseudacorus*, *Potentilla palustris* and *Rumex hydrolapathum* on the landward side. *Cladium mariscus*, which is rare in the south-east, also occurs here. The smaller of the ponds have advanced to a late hydroseral stage, and are infilled with organic mud over which willow carr has developed, and in some there is incipient bog formation with *Sphagnum* spp., but there is surprisingly little submerged vegetation.

The pools are fed by ground water and are chemically very similar. They have a high alkalinity of 70–80 p.p.m. $CaCO_3$ and a relatively high sodium level because of their situation close to the sea, but they are poor in other nutrients with very low nitrate levels. The bottom of the ponds is covered by a layer of organic mud overlying the shingle. The invertebrate fauna is largely typical of eutrophic conditions and includes three species of triclad, nine species of gastropod and two species of *Asellus*. In addition, a few species which are found in coastal areas, such as the Hemiptera species *Sigara concinna* and *Notonecta viridis*, are present. The dragonflies *Aeshna mixta* and *Lestes dryas* occur and a rather uncommon corixid *Corixa panzeri*. There is a small but varied breeding and wintering wildfowl population.

OW.2. PEVENSEY LEVELS, SUSSEX
TQ 6508   Grade 1

Where the clay vales of the Weald reach the sea coast at Romney Marsh and Pevensey they once formed extensive salt marshes protected by a shingle spit. These areas have been drained by a series of dykes which now intersect flat, rich-grazing meadows. On the Pevensey Levels most of the dykes are 2–3 m wide and little more than 1 m maximum depth. They are steep-sided and the water level in some lies more than a metre below the surrounding grassland. In the summer there is no visible flow in most smaller dykes but one or two larger channels have a slow current. The water is moderately base-rich and, especially in dykes near the sea, sodium content is higher than in most fresh waters.

The main drains are kept free of weed by dredging but some smaller drains are completely overgrown with reeds. The dykes are rich in species of aquatic plants, the communities present varying from dyke to dyke and apparently related to the stage in succession reached since the last dredging. The possible succession following dredging is from floating-leaved co munities of *Lemna minor*, *Riccia fluitans* and *Azolla filiculoides* or communities of *Potamogeton* spp., especially *P. lucens*, to *Typha angustifolia* or more commonly *Sparganium erectum* and finally a dense bed of *Phragmites communis*. The local *Ranunculus tripartitus* occurs here.

The very rich invertebrate fauna contains many species associated with the vegetation of base-rich ponds and the slow-flowing stretches of rivers. Nineteen species of mollusc occur but Ephemeroptera and Trichoptera are poorly represented; the weed-dwelling *Holocentropus picicornis* was the only caddis collected. Large numbers of parasitic Sciomyzidae occur in association with the rich molluscan fauna. The beetle fauna is outstanding and contains several species at the edge of their range in south-east England, including *Ilybius fenestratus*, *Ochthebius nanus*, *O. exaratus*, *Bidessus unistriatus* and *Laccophilus variegatus*. This is the only known locality in Britain for the last-named species. The larger dykes contain fish, and the marsh frog *Rana ridibunda* has been successfully introduced. Compared to Romney Marsh, which is structurally similar, the Pevensey Levels have a more diverse fauna and are more intact.

OW.3. TRING RESERVOIRS, HERTFORDSHIRE
SP 9013. 110 ha   Grade 1

The four reservoirs of the Tring group which form this site lie at the foot of the Chalk escarpment of the Chilterns. Only the largest, Wilstone Reservoir, has been surveyed limnologically. It is a shallow marl lake with a maximum depth of 6 m and is used as a header reservoir for the Grand Union Canal. Its catchment is largely of arable land. The nitrogen, calcium and sodium contents of the water are all relatively high, but the phosphorus content, as is typical in marl lakes, is relatively low and the water is extremely clear. Half of the margin of the reservoir consists of concrete embankment and half is reed-swamp. One shallow section of the reservoir partially separated by a causeway has a complete cover of submerged plants of which *Ceratophyllum demersum*,

Elodea canadensis and *Myriophyllum spicatum* are dominant. In the main reservoir, where a drawdown of up to 2 m may occur, submerged plants are less abundant and in deeper water a bare clay forms the bottom substrate. The invertebrate fauna is very diverse, species typical of the sublittoral zone of eutrophic lakes being particularly well represented. Thirteen species of gastropod, seven species of leech and seven species of corixid are recorded. The limited species composition of the profundal benthic fauna suggests that thermal stratification may occur in the summer. *Sigara concinna* and *Notonecta viridis*, both of which are generally associated with coastal habitats, were both recorded, possibly associated with the high ionic content of the water draining the Chalk. Wilstone and the other reservoirs have a varied population of coarse fish species and are used by numerous water birds as nesting sites. They also hold a variety of wintering wildfowl including mallard, teal, wigeon, shoveler, pochard, tufted duck, goosander and mute swan, and at time of drawdown the reservoirs are important for waders on passage.

Rushy Meadow is a site of some 1+ ha, adjacent to Wilstone Reservoir, and is well named, having *Juncus subnodulosus* dominant over much of the area. The drier areas have a *Carex panicea*, *Holcus lanatus*, *Briza media*, *Valeriana dioica* association with *Geranium pratense* locally abundant over one area. The absence of species like *Cirsium dissectum* is of ecological interest and may be related to sporadic attempts at reclamation in the past. Many wetland species which are rare in the county, and becoming so in eastern England in general, are present and include *Anagallis tenella*, *Dactylorchis incarnata*, *D. praetermissa*, *Valeriana dioica*, *Juncus subnodulosus* and several *Carex* spp. including *C. lepidocarpa*, *C. disticha* and *C. distans*.

OW.4. ROMNEY MARSH, KENT
TR 0629   Grade 2

Structurally this site is similar to the Pevensey Levels, but it is more extensive and slightly more brackish in places with *Enteromorpha* in a number of ditches. Many of the dykes are less intact than those of Pevensey as the vegetation is regularly controlled by herbicides, and much of the grazing land has been converted to arable with a subsequent drop in the water table. The flora is rich in the smaller drains, with many species common to Pevensey. The invertebrate fauna is less diverse, but marsh frogs abound. Dragonflies present include *Lestes dryas*, *Platycnemis pennipes*, *Erythromma najas* and *Sympetrum sanguineum*. This is an alternative site to Pevensey Levels (OW.2).

SOUTH ENGLAND

OW.5. RIVER AVON SYSTEM, HAMPSHIRE/WILTSHIRE
SU 207602–156934   Grade 1*

The sources of the main river arise on the clay of the Vale of Pewsey and pass across the Chalk of the Hampshire Downs upon which the major part of this river system lies. The Wylye also rises on clay but the other major tributaries are chalk streams throughout their length. The lower part

of the river, below Fordingbridge, and the tributary streams running in from the New Forest run over Tertiary gravels. Apart from the last-mentioned tributaries, the Avon System has all the characteristics of a chalk stream and is highly alkaline. It is rich in plant nutrients throughout its length with particularly high levels of phosphorus, nitrate, organic nitrogen and silica. The total altitudinal range is about 167 m.

The Avon is at no point a rapid river and the current varies from fast to sluggish. The substrate of the source streams on the Vale of Pewsey is chiefly clay overlying gravel but once the rivers enter the Chalk the bottom consists of gravel, sand and silt in varying proportions. This favours the growth of higher aquatic plants which cover much of the bed during the summer months. *Callitriche stagnalis*, *Myriophyllum* spp., *Potamogeton perfoliatus*, *P. lucens*, *Rorippa nasturtium-aquaticum*, *Ranunculus penicillatus*, *Sagittaria sagittifolia*, *Oenanthe fluviatilis*, *Elodea canadensis*, *Phalaris arundinacea*, *Phragmites communis* and *Glyceria maxima* are dominant in various parts while the filamentous alga *Cladophora* coats the bottom and the angiosperms in some places. A wide range of plant species typical of chalk river systems occurs, including the very local *Ranunculus tripartitus* and *Potamogeton nodosus*.

From Netheravon to Amesbury, where the surrounding land is chiefly sheep-grazed, the main river is intensively managed for brown trout and is an outstanding chalk stream fishery. From Salisbury to Ringwood the flood plain of the river becomes much broader and the flat ground is intersected by the channels of old water meadows most of which have now gone over to intensive grazing. Downstream of Salisbury there is little management of the fishery but the weed is cut twice a year for land drainage purposes.

The river system has one of the most diverse fish faunas of any British river, with at least 24 species. Brown trout are found throughout the whole system, and are in many places artificially maintained, whereas the migratory sea trout is restricted to the lower stretches, spawning in the acid New Forest streams. There are large populations of grayling in the chalk streams above Salisbury but these do not occur in the New Forest streams. Dace is possibly the most abundant fish species; pike, eel, perch, roach, minnow, gudgeon, bullhead, three-spined stickleback and lamprey *Lampetra planeri* occur. *L. fluviatilis* is found throughout the chalk stream system. Bleak occur in the tidal stretch and chub, barbel and salmon are found up to Salisbury, a few of the last penetrating into the Nadder and the Wylye. The New Forest tributaries have a relatively limited fish fauna of brown trout, salmon, minnow, bullhead, eel, stone loach, and lamprey *L. planeri.*. Brown trout, minnow and bullhead are the most productive fish in these tributaries.

The invertebrate fauna of the Avon is extremely rich and contains most of the species associated with chalk streams. In the upper stretches where it flows over the clay of the Vale of Pewsey, the fauna is much poorer than in the lower stretches. With the exception of *Potamopyrgus jenkinsi* there are few gastropods in this section and *Baetis bioculatus*, which is the most abundant mayfly in the summer lower down the river, is absent. On the other hand *Polycelis felina* is more or less restricted to the upper Avon and the upper parts of the tributaries, and is replaced by *Dugesia lugubris* lower down. The middle reaches of the Avon have the most diverse fauna, especially mayflies and molluscs, and the rather rare *Baetis atrebatinus* occurs here. Of the commoner mayflies *B. vernus* and *B. rhodani* occur throughout the river system, but *B. buceratus* is found only in the middle and lower sections, while *Ephemerella ignita* is absent from the slower-flowing lower stretch. Recently *B. digitatus*, a species new to Britain, was recorded from the Avon and a few other chalk streams. Caddises are rather poorly represented both in number and variety. *Polycentropus flavomaculatus* is the most widespread species, while *Hydropsyche* spp. are found mainly in the lower reaches and *Agapetus fuscipes* in the faster areas. Another tributary, the Bourne which has higher nitrate levels than any other tributary, is the best example in the Avon System of a winterbourne and dries out for many kilometres in its upper reaches in summer.

The Avon System as a whole shows a greater range of habitat diversity and a more diverse flora and fauna than any other chalk river in Britain. Long continued practices of management in the interests of angling and the working of water meadows help to maintain this diversity. The former can be relied on to continue, but water-meadows have all but disappeared and examples of the few remaining should be safeguarded. The Avon was also the site of much research on freshwater fisheries in the 1930s and this adds to its scientific value.

The wildfowl interest of the Avon valley includes European white-fronted geese (900 birds; 11% of UK population). Mallard, teal, wigeon, pochard and tufted duck also occur regularly.

OW.6. OBERWATER, HAMPSHIRE
SU 214066–290040   Grade 1

Within the New Forest there are a number of base-poor streams draining the Tertiary sands. Some of these, such as the Dockens Water, drain westwards into the River Avon and are included within that grade 1 site. Other large streams such as the Oberwater, Avon Water, Black Water and Highland Water drain eastwards and form the Lymington River. Of these the Oberwater is believed to be the best example floristically.

The Oberwater is a mostly moderate-flowing river with a gravel bed which reaches a maximum width of up to 20 m in its lower stretches. It consists mainly of shallow runs intersected by occasional deeper pools, 1 m or more deep, in which silt, mud and leaves are deposited over the gravel. Throughout much of its length it is overhung by trees; the shading possibly restricts the growth of aquatic plants. There is a considerable range of water level and gravel banks are thrown up along the margins in many places. Chemically it is mesotrophic with an alkalinity of about 16 p.p.m. $CaCO_3$ and is slightly peat-stained. The largely non-agricultural catchment is reflected in the relatively low nitrogen and phosphorus levels. The stream is not dredged and weed growths are insufficient to obstruct drainage, covering less than 10% of the bottom. The flora contains most of the species characteristic of slow- to moderate-flowing base-poor rivers in upland areas in the north and west of Britain, together with species more often associated with eutrophic rivers in the lowlands such as *Typha latifolia*, *Alisma plantago-aquatica*, *Apium nodiflorum* and *Sparganium erectum*. In the upper stretches *Glyceria fluitans* is the most abundant plant with *Potamogeton polygonifolius* in shallow water at the margins. An algal slime covers most of the stones and in places *Cladophora* is present. The invertebrate fauna is very typical of gravelly base-poor streams and contrasts strongly with the nearby chalk streams. The crustacean *Niphargus aquilex* lives in the interstices of the gravel beds. Certain species of mayfly and stonefly, e.g. *Paraleptophlebia submarginata*, *Ecdyonurus dispar*, *Nemoura erratica* and *Leuctra inermis* which are common in upland streams, are found here as rather isolated populations. A number of uncommon, southern, riverine dragonflies have been recorded and trout, bullheads, sticklebacks and minnows are plentiful.

Oberwater has been selected as the best example of a lowland base-poor stream, which as a type is very restricted in Britain and differs biologically from its upland counterparts.

OW.7. WOOLMER POND, HAMPSHIRE
SU 7832.   75 ha   Grade 1

This is a very shallow dystrophic lake lying on the Lower Greensand of east Hampshire. Although the water area is 25 ha, the depth nowhere exceeds 50 cm. The pond is surrounded by sandy heathland and apparently fed from ground water poor in mineral nutrients, except ammonia which is relatively high (total conductivity = 51 μmhos). The bottom of the pond consists of firm peat overlying sand, on which a dense mat of *Drepanocladus fluitans* and *Sphagnum subsecundum* up to 15 cm thick grows. At the margins of the pond and in a broad band down the middle, a poor-fen community has *Eleocharis palustris*, *Potentilla palustris*, *Juncus effusus*, *Hydrocotyle vulgaris* and *Molinia caerulea* as the dominant species. *Molinia* also occurs as isolated tussocks in the middle of open water. The most common groups in the benthic fauna are chironomids, corixids, Hydracarina and the water spider *Argyroneta aquatica*. Of the corixids recorded *Sigara scotti* and *Hesperocorixa castanea* are typical of base-poor conditions, but *Hesperocorixa linnei*, *Sigara (Vermicorixa) lateralis* and *Callicorixa praeusta* are usually associated with rich or polluted waters. The moss-dwelling dipteran *Phalacrocera replicata* and the caddis *Holocentropus dubius*, which lives in thick mats of submerged vegetation, also occur and common newts are abundant. The pond was formerly the location of the rare water beetles *Graphoderus cinereus* and *Hygrotus novemlineatus*, but insecticide spraying in 1960, to control mosquitoes, may have eliminated these species.

Although this site, which may have originated as a peat cutting, has maintained the same area of open water since at least 1770 there have been certain changes in its depth and character since then. In 1855 the pond was described as a large sandy bottomed lake, possibly similar to Hatchet

Pond at the present day, but by 1938 a serious drop in water level had occurred and the pond largely dried out in summer. By this time peat development had started and *Sphagnum* was actively growing in those parts which remained wet throughout the year. Since that time the water level has once more stabilised although the lake is now so shallow that continued peat development and encroachment by poor-fen communities, especially *Potentilla palustris*, are likely to reduce the area of open water in the future.

It is unusual to find dystrophic lakes of such a size in southern Britain. The site has certain affinities to the Gull Pool on Abbots Moss (Cheshire) which also has thick mats of *Drepanocladus* covering a peaty bottom and a similar invertebrate fauna. Woolmer Pond is larger, shallower, and less subject to disturbance and is isolated from other dystrophic waters. (See Appendix.)

OW.8. MOORS RIVER, HAMPSHIRE/DORSET
SU 029156–SZ 127970   Grade 1

This tributary of the River Stour rises as a chalk stream winterbourne on Cranborne Chase where it is known as the River Crane, and flows on to base-poor Tertiary sands from which drain a number of tributaries including the Uddens Water. The land surrounding the lower stretches, on the sand, consists mainly of New Forest-type heathland and coniferous plantations. In these sections the river consists of a meandering channel 2–3 m deep and up to 5 m wide which has been dredged twice in the last 25 years and which is cleared of weeds annually. The bottom consists of a firm clay which, despite the slow current in summer, is free from sedimented organic mud. In summer, when most of the drainage is from the Chalk, the lower river is base-rich with an alkalinity of 80–90 p.p.m. $CaCO_3$, but in winter, when the contribution to the total flow from streams draining the sands is higher, the alkalinity falls and the stream may become base-poor. Drainage from agricultural land and a certain amount of treated sewage effluent enters the river and this is reflected in relatively high nutrient levels (average nitrogen level = 2.0 p.p.m. NO_3 and dissolved phosphorus (12 September 1968) = 0.175 p.p.m.), but the river is not organically polluted and retains a high oxygen concentration and low suspended solids level.

The aquatic vegetation is both luxuriant and remarkable in diversity and contains species typical of chalk streams, e.g. *Callitriche platycarpa*, *Ranunculus penicillatus*, *Apium nodiflorum*, *Potamogeton lucens* and *Sagittaria sagittifolia*, alongside species of base-poor waters such as *Potamogeton polygonifolius* and *Menyanthes trifoliata*. Along the margins in places there is a floating mat of various reed species, particularly *Phalaris arundinacea*, *Glyceria maxima* and *Sparganium erectum* which supports a rich herb community.

The outstanding feature of the invertebrate fauna is the large number of dragonfly species recorded which include rarities such as *Libellula fulva* and *Oxygastra curtisii*. For the latter species, which is at the northerly edge of its range in Britain, this is the only definite locality in which breeding has occurred, but the colony may now be extinct. The remaining invertebrate fauna is largely typical of chalk

streams, with eleven species of gastropod recorded, and mayflies abundant. Among the latter, *Paraleptophlebia tumida* is a rare species confined to heavily weeded streams in the south of England, and the bug *Notonecta maculata*, a Mediterranean species on the edge of its range in Britain, is also present. A very varied fish population includes salmonids and species of the chub zone of rivers.

This stream is particularly important on account of its intermediate character between chalk streams and the base-poor streams of the New Forest. In view of the relatively large population living within the catchment particular control must be exercised over effluent discharge quality if the river is to retain its character.

OW.9. COTSWOLD WATER PARK, WILTSHIRE/GLOUCESTERSHIRE
SU 0596.   1200 ha   Grade 1

Large scale extraction of fluvial gravel derived from Jurassic limestones is being carried out in the upper Thames valley and will result in the creation of about 1450 ha of open water. The gravel is highly calcareous and existing pits form the largest marl lakes in Britain. The older examples already have a diverse flora, and despite disturbance on most of the pits the area is a regionally important wintering site for wildfowl.

Most of the lakes are to be zoned for recreation, but one lake of approximately 100 ha extent and a number of much smaller bordering lakes have been proposed as an aquatic nature reserve. Only part of one possible area for the reserve has so far been excavated, so the opportunity exists for the lakes to be shaped and contoured according to a detailed design which has already been prepared to take into account the requirements of different forms of aquatic wildlife. Access to the larger lake would be restricted to a number of hides, but the smaller lakes would be available for educational purposes and as areas for research. The larger lake would provide a variety of aquatic habitats including an extensive area of reed-bed which could grade into an existing damp woodland in which there is a heronry. It is bounded on two sides by floristically rich streams, and plants from these sources are already colonising the reserve area.

Neighbouring lakes are typical marl lakes and have a profusion of submerged aquatic plants which have been controlled in some lakes by herbicides. Untreated examples, some of which have existed for over 20 years, have considerable floristic diversity and show the potential of the nature reserve area. In deeper water the bottom is carpeted with *Chara* spp. and in shallower water there are many angiosperms including *Groenlandia densa*, *Myriophyllum spicatum*, *Apium inundatum*, several species of *Potamogeton* and *Ranunculus trichophyllus*. Surprisingly *P. natans* is the only plant with floating leaves which has so far colonised the Water Park. The margins, which are usually steep, offer only a narrow step where a band of emergent vegetation can develop, usually initially *Epilobium hirsutum* and *Juncus inflexus*. *Typha latifolia*, *Phragmites communis* and *Equisetum aquatilis* come in at a later stage or at an early stage where there are silty patches from gravel washings. In the reserve lake, however, the margins would be graded and a more extensive area would therefore be available for plant colonisation. The phytoplankton and zooplankton is sparse and low in species as is typical of marl lakes, but benthic invertebrate fauna is quite varied and contains most of the species associated with eutrophic conditions in southern England. The pits attract over 800 pochard (2% of UK population) in the winter, and a number of pairs of little ringed plover breed.

The site is selected for its potential as the largest marl lake in Britain in an area where natural standing waters are non-existent.

OW.10. HATCHET POND, HAMPSHIRE
SU 3601.   15 ha   Grade 2

Hatchet Pond is a shallow mesotrophic lake which may be of ancient artificial origin, lying within the New Forest. Its main interest is its isolation from other water bodies of similar trophic status, which are found chiefly in northern and western Britain, by the mainly calcareous rocks of the intervening lowlands. Isolated populations of the northern species *Hammarbya paludosa* and *Sparganium angustifolium* occur here, alongside rare southern species such as *Galium debile*, *Cicendia filiformis* and *Ludwigia palustris*. The latter is found in a small pond alongside the main lake and this is now its only known British locality. Heavy grazing pressure has prevented the growth of reed-swamp and the shorelines consist mostly of gravel covered in places by a short sward of *Littorella uniflora* and *Pilularia globulifera*, both characteristic of mesotrophic conditions. The invertebrate fauna is poor in species but contains species such as *Sympetrum scoticum* and *Sigara scotti* characteristic of base-poor conditions. The introduced North American triclad *Dugesia tigrina* is abundant and the duck mussel *Anodonta anatina* occurs here in an unusually calcium-poor site for this species.

OW.11. WYCHWOOD PONDS, OXFORDSHIRE
SP 3417.   1 ha   Grade 2

These comprise four small artificial marl ponds lying within the Wychwood NNR which are spring fed from underlying Jurassic limestone. They are shallow and highly calcareous (alkalinity = 119–220 p.p.m. CaCO$_3$) and have the characteristic clear water of marl lakes. The aquatic flora of the ponds is both abundant and diverse and includes a number of calcicoles such as *Potamogeton lucens*, *Hippuris vulgaris* and *Chara* spp. A varied invertebrate fauna, typical of rich ponds, is present including the crayfish *Astacus pallipes*, and the fish fauna includes trout, ten-spined sticklebacks *Pungitius pungitius*, and bullheads, the latter being more usually a stream species. The inflow streams are good examples of small lowland limestone streams and their spring sources contain a typical cold-water fauna including *Crenobia alpina*, various stoneflies and *Helodes* spp.

EAST ANGLIA

OW.12. HICKLING BROAD AND HORSEY MERE, NORFOLK
TG 4121, TG 4422.   155 ha   Grade 1*

Hickling Broad is a large, shallow lake (average depth about 1.5 m) which is one of the oldest and most extensive areas of open water in south-east England. It is connected to the sea by the rivers Thurne and Bure and shows very slight tidal fluctuations in water level. The open water is surrounded by c. 400 ha of *Phragmites* beds and fen, and the bottom substrate is peat. The water is base-rich (alkalinity = 110–120 p.p.m. CaCO$_3$) and slightly saline (surface sodium content in July 1968 being 840 p.p.m.), but there is little evidence of artificial enrichment from agricultural fertilisers, as nitrate and phosphate levels are low compared to other broads, and there is very little inflow into the broad except from the surrounding fen and the tidal effect.

A major interest of Hickling is its breeding and over-wintering birds. The fenland harbours many rare breeding marshland birds including bitterns, marsh and Montagu's harriers and bearded tits, and the broad is an important wildfowl wintering area particularly for teal (1300), mute swan, mallard, wigeon, shoveler (700), pochard, tufted duck and goldeneye. Hickling Broad was the main locality for the aquatic plant *Najas marina*, which only occurs in the Broads, but this species has gone into decline on Hickling and is now more abundant in Upton Broad. The submerged macrophytic flora is rich and plentiful in Hickling, in contrast to many of the other broads which are now devoid of vegetation. The principal species are *Chara* sp., *Nitellopsis obtusa*, *Potamogeton pectinatus*, *Ceratophyllum demersum*, *Myriophyllum verticillatum* and *Utricularia vulgaris*. Dense growth of *Cladophora* previously occurred in late summer but these have recently disappeared. The benthic fauna is a mixture of brackish and eutrophic water species. *Neomysis integer*, *Gammarus duebeni* and *Sphaeroma hookeri* are abundant while leeches are absent, although common in the less saline broads. Seven species of gastropods were found in collections made in Hickling and this is the only broad from which the mayfly *Caenis robusta* has been recently recorded. Bream, roach, rudd, tench and eels occur, and Hickling is famous for its pike fishing. The zooplankton is dominated by the brackish water copepod *Eurytemora velox*.

Horsey Mere is also distinctly saline (sodium = 1470 p.p.m.) and has an exceptionally high calcium level (450 p.p.m.). It is 34 ha in extent with a mean depth of 1 m and is connected with Hickling Broad by a navigable channel via Heigham Sound and White Slea. Both the latter have extensive growths of *Hippurus vulgaris* and are at times covered with a mat of *Azolla filiculoides*. To the north and east of the mere is an extensive area of open fen, known as Breydon Marshes, and the remainder of the Broad is bounded by a narrow fringe of reed-swamp which is separated from grazing marshland by the flood-bank surrounding the mere. The bottom of the mere is formed of a grey mud, coated with *Cladophora*. Compared with Hickling Broad it has more extensive submerged vegetation although less rich in species; *Potamogeton pectinatus*, a broad-leaved *Potamogeton* sp., *Myriophyllum verticillatum* and *Chara* sp. all occur in spite of motor launches, and a band of *H. vulgaris* about 20 m broad surrounds the open water. Occasionally when exceptionally high tides coincide with warm weather there are outbreaks of the alga *Prymnesium parvum* which is toxic and causes severe fish kills. There is an enormous population of the gastropod *Potamopyrgus jenkinsi* (450 000 individuals/m²), among the *Cladophora*, almost to the exclusion of any other species of macrobenthos. Other species include the brackish water coelenterate *Cordylophora lacustris*, *Sphaeroma hookeri*, *Corophium* sp., *Gammarus duebeni*, *Ischnura elegans* and *Enallagma cyathigerum*. Hickling Broad, Horsey Mere and the Heigham Sound which lies between them form one grade 1* open water site which is surrounded by a large area of fen of international value as a peatland (P.6).

OW.13. ABBERTON RESERVOIR, ESSEX
TL 9718. 1200 ha   Grade 1

This large pump storage reservoir is divided into three sections by roadways. The largest section to the north-east is entirely surrounded by a concrete apron, and is very artificial, but the two smaller sections have natural shore-lines and well-developed marginal vegetation. Vegetation is particularly abundant in the smallest section to the south-west, which is fed by a small stream and is not subject to excessive drawdown. The vegetation is in well-marked zones down the shoreline starting on the landward side with *Phalaris arundinacea* followed by *Eleocharis palustris*, *Typha latifolia*, *Scirpus maritimus*, *Apium inundatum*, *Polygonum amphibium* and submerged *Potamogeton pectinatus* and *P. pusillus*. The reservoir is highly eutrophic and subject to algal blooms and in the more natural sections has a fairly typical invertebrate fauna for a eutrophic lake. A varied coarse-fish population is present.

The main interest of the site and the major reason for its selection is its national importance as a wildfowl wintering site. The more important concentrations of wildfowl which occur regularly are 2250 teal (2¼% of north-west European population), 4500 mallard (1½% of UK population), 1200 pochard (3% of UK population), 240 shoveler, 20 smew, 340 goldeneye and 25 gadwall. Wigeon, pintail, tufted duck, goosander and mute swan are also present. This site is also important as the main wildfowl ringing station in Britain. Since 1949, *c.* 60 000 ducks have been caught, ringed and released.

OW.14. BRECKLAND MERES, NORFOLK   Grade 1

These are a series of small, shallow water-bodies lying in the glacial sands and gravels of southern Norfolk. Although often leached at the surface, these sands and gravels are derived from a chalky till, which itself overlies Chalk; thus the meres are base-rich. They have no inflow and outflow and are fed by ground water. The most characteristic feature of the meres, which makes them unique in the British Isles, is the wide fluctuation in water level from year to year and season to season, which cannot be related

directly to the precipitation. All of them at least occasionally dry out in the summer months, and this impermanence has a profound effect upon the fauna.

The hydrology of the Breckland meres could be seriously affected by the abstraction of large quantities of water from the Chalk underlying not only Breckland but a large part of central and southern Norfolk. The meres as a whole are important as the main breeding centre for the gadwall in Britain, and they lie within the important Stanford–Wretham heathland site (L.60).

(a) Lang Mere
TL 9088. 3 ha

The water of this small shallow mere is very clear and base-rich (alkalinity = 40–50 p.p.m. $CaCO_3$) but low in phosphorus, nitrate and ammonia, the total conductivity being 135 μmhos. The mere is bounded by beds of *Phalaris arundinacea* and submerged and floating attached vegetation of *Potamogeton lucens*, *P. gramineus*, *P. pectinatus* and *Polygonum amphibium* growing from a thin layer of organic mud on firm sand that covers most of the bottom. The fauna includes seven species of corixid including *Sigara lateralis* which is more often associated with brackish conditions. The amphibious snail *Succinea pfeifferi* is abundant, the leech *Dina lineata* occurs, which in the south of the British Isles is confined to temporary waters, and the ephemeropteran *Cloeon dipterum* is extremely abundant in the weed-beds. No Malacostraca were found in this or any of the other meres; presumably they are not resistant to periodic desiccation. Most species found in the mere are either resistant to drying up or have a winged adult stage.

(b) Ring Mere
TL 9087. 3 ha

Ring Mere, about 0.5 km south of Lang Mere, is similar in area, depth and water chemistry, except that its soluble phosphate concentration and total alkalinity are nearly four times higher. It too fluctuates widely in depth, but independently of Lang Mere. In Ring Mere the surrounding *Phalaris* reed-swamp is more extensive, forming a band 15 m wide with dense growths of *Lemna trisulca* below the water surface. *Potamogeton lucens* occurs in the open water. The fauna of the open water was not adequately sampled and the collections are accordingly poorer in species than at Lang Mere. *Planorbis laevis* and the leech *Glossiphonia heteroclita* are recorded; the only corixid found is *Cymatia bonsdorffi*.

(c) Fowl Mere
TL 8789. 12 ha

Fowl Mere, which lies just inside the Stanford Practical Training Area (PTA), is situated about 2.5 km east-north-east of Ring Mere and Lang Mere. Except that Fowl Mere is larger, it is both physically and chemically similar to Lang Mere. Fowl Mere has 100% cover of aquatic plants starting with *Phalaris* at the outside, then a belt of *Eleocharis palustris* and *Polygonum amphibium* and finally the central area is choked with *Potamogeton lucens* and *Acrocladium* sp. The fauna of the mere is typical of a weedy pond with

Cloeon dipterum, *Valvata cristata* and *Haliplus obliquus* abundant and *Callicorixa praeusta* present. Fowl Mere is linked with Lang Mere and Ring Mere as one key site, the three meres showing different stages of hydrosere development with Fowl Mere being the most advanced.

OW.15. UPTON BROAD, NORFOLK
TG 3913.   105 ha   Grade 1

This is a small Broad about 500 m long, maximum depth 1.7 m, which lies in the Bure valley to the east of the Bure Marshes NNR. It is not tidal and is separated from the River Bure by a sluice. It is completely surrounded by open reed fen which grades into carr, and the catchment area is half carr and half arable land. The shore substrate consists of peaty and muddy areas, while away from the shore the bottom is a soft yellow-brown mud, composed of the faecal pellets of invertebrates, in which algal cells are preserved free from decay. Such muds have been recorded only very infrequently in any part of the world and are of importance geologically as indicators of the conditions under which certain fossiliferous shales have formed. The water is base-rich (alkalinity = 150–160 p.p.m. $CaCO_3$), has a high conductivity (720 μmhos) and a relatively high salinity of 48 p.p.m. of sodium. Compared with other Norfolk Broads the phosphate and nitrate levels are fairly low and the water is very clear. Since the aquatic plant *Najas marinas* has declined in Hickling Broad, this is now the main site for this species for which the Broads are the only British locality. Together with *Chara hispida* × *contraria* (?) and *Zannichellia palustris* it covers about 50% of the bottom of the broad. The surrounding *Phragmites* reed-beds are unusual for the Norfolk Broads in being rich in *Cladium mariscus*, in having both species of *Typha*, and unusually large amounts of *Schoenoplectus lacustris*. There is a small quantity of floating, attached vegetation, *Nymphaea alba* and *Nuphar lutea* being co-dominant. The zooplankton is rich in species; in late September *Ceriodaphnia pulchella* and *Cyclops vicinus* were most abundant, and *Diaphanosoma brachyurum* was also present. The macrobenthos is also rich in species and covers a wide range of aquatic groups. Eighteen species of gastropod are recorded including *Viviparus fasciatus* and *Valvata macrostoma* which are both of restricted distribution, and the amphibious species *Succinea putris*. *Crangonyx pseudogracilis*, which only occurs in this and the Ormesby–Filby complex of Broads, two species of *Asellus* and four species of triclad are present. Those species of Ephemeroptera, Trichoptera, Coleoptera and Odonata which are associated with weedy conditions are plentiful but corixids, which are normally abundant in reedbeds and among dense weeds, were not taken in any of the collections from vegetation at Upton Broad. The Broad is known to contain perch.

This Broad probably represents the type of condition which existed in many other Broads prior to the decline in submerged vegetation and associated fauna noted elsewhere. It is therefore of very high conservation value. The vegetation is typical of more saline conditions than that in Calthorpe Broad and the two sites can be considered as complementary. (See Appendix.)

OW.16. CALTHORPE BROAD, NORFOLK
TG 4125.   2 ha   Grade 1

This is a small isolated Broad about 300 m long and 0.5 m maximum depth which is separated from the adjoining dyke system by a sluice; it is therefore fed only by direct precipitation and occasional inflow from drainage dykes. It is very sheltered and entirely enclosed by alder–willow–birch carr in which nuclei of acidophilous Sphagnetum, unusual for the Broads, are present. The shore substrate is derived from the surrounding fen peat and the bottom is covered by a fine black mud.

In 1969 this was the only Broad known to contain the characteristic aquatic plant species which formerly occurred in all the freshwater Broads. A wide range of species including *Stratiotes aloides*, *Ceratophyllum demersum*, *Potamogeton friesii*, *Hydrocharis morsus-ranae*, *Luronium natans*, *Sparganium minimum* and *Nuphar lutea* occupied the entire open water area. Associated with this vegetation was a varied benthic invertebrate community which included eight species of gastropod, the swan mussel *Anodonta cygnea*, the mayfly *Cloeon dipterum* and dragonfly *Erythromma najas* and a number of water bug species.

In 1970, however, drastic changes occurred in the Broad which resulted in the loss of most of the submerged plants and invertebrates and a complete kill of the fish. In the summer of that year the water level in the inflow dykes was lowered so that the Broad became perched above the surrounding water table, and owing to seepage and a broken sluice the water level within the Broad itself and in the surrounding carr dropped. Under these conditions the usually waterlogged peat became oxidised and ferrous sulphide was converted to ferric sulphate. In the autumn there followed a period of heavy rain which leached the products of oxidation from the peat and hydrolysed the ferric sulphate to produce sulphuric acid and ferric hydroxide. The latter was precipitated on the bottom of the Broad, while in the absence of sufficient buffering cations in the rain water the acid reduced the pH of the water of the Broad to 3.0–3.6. Continued high water levels in 1971, however, resulted in a rise in pH to near neutrality and a slight recovery in the vegetation and invertebrate fauna.

The Broad appears to have experienced, in these last few years, the change which has been assumed to take place over a very long period in basin mires which become isolated from ground water by the growth of peat. It has now reached the point of balance between being eutrophic and dystrophic. Pumping alkaline water from the surrounding dykes into the Broad may restore it to its previous state, although lost species would have to be reintroduced, or alternatively the site could be sealed from any inflow of alkaline water and the growth of a ombrogenous basin mire encouraged. In the latter case the colony of coypu, which is enclosed in the Broad and is the subject of a research project, would have to be controlled to allow the spread of invasive acidophilous vegetation such as *Potentilla palustris*, *Menyanthes trifoliata* and *Sphagnum* spp., which are present in the surrounding carr. Whichever course of action is taken, the Broad would represent a type of habitat not now found elsewhere in Broadland.

See also P.10.

OW.17. OUSE WASHES, CAMBRIDGESHIRE/NORFOLK
TL 3975–5801. 2500 ha Grade 1

This is an area of flat land about 22 km long by 1 km wide lying between the canalised sections of the River Ouse known as the Old and New Bedford Rivers, which were constructed in the seventeenth century when the surrounding fens were drained. The two river courses are raised on embankments above the low-lying washes which act as a reservoir for excess flood water in winter. In the summer time the Washes mostly dry out to form meadows which are cattle-grazed or mown and which are an important botanical and ornithological site (L.70, gr. 1*). The Washes are scientifically important in that they form the largest area of regularly flooded freshwater grazing marshland left in Britain.

The marshes are rich botanically and 260 species of higher plant have been recorded. Aquatic species are mainly confined to the drains which run in a rectangular pattern across the grazing land, and which are cleaned out periodically with draglines. This encourages a wide range of aquatics, including 16 species and hybrids of *Potamogeton* and all four species of *Lemna*. The rare *Potamogeton* × *fluitans* (*P. lucens* × *P. natans*) is present. Emergent species include *Acorus calamus*, *Butomus umbellatus* and *Scirpus maritimus* which is a remnant of the once brackish water flora of the area. The water analysis of two of the drains in the summer showed a relatively high sodium level of 53 p.p.m. The latter is reflected by the presence of *Enteromorpha intestinalis* and represents the influence of tidal water backing up the main rivers from the Wash. The fauna of the dykes is rich in invertebrates particularly Crustacea, Hemiptera, Coleoptera and Mollusca, one dyke alone having over 16 species of mollusc. *Asellus aquaticus* and the mayfly *Cloeon dipterum* are abundant and the brackish water *Gammarus zaddachi* is present. The ten-spined stickleback is the only fish species collected from the dykes. Most of the fauna retreats to, or survives in, the dykes during the summer when the meadows are drained. A shallow pool in the meadows examined in September had a very limited fauna of Chironomidae, Hemiptera, Oligochaeta, Hirudinea and two species of Mollusca.

During the winter the pools are enlarged by the release of flood water from the Bedford River and on occasions the whole area between the Old and New Bedford Rivers is flooded. This new water area is colonised from the ditches but does not become as diverse in species. In particular only a few of the snail species regularly spread over the flooded area, *Planorbis spirorbis*, a species typical of marshes and ponds which dry up, and resistant to desiccation, being the most abundant. The corixid *Sigara lateralis* is also widespread. Surprisingly *Asellus aquaticus* and *Crangonyx pseudogracilis* were only found in small numbers in the Washes although plentiful in the ditches and both are species which colonise new water-bodies readily.

The Washes are of outstanding importance as the largest inland gathering ground for wildfowl in Britain. Since 1969, the wintering populations have reached an average peak of 34 000 wigeon (7% of north-west European population), 1100 pintail (2% of north-west European population), 1200 Bewick's swan (20% of north-west European population), *c.* 2000 pochard, 3000 teal, 340 shoveler, 4000 mallard, 300 mute swan and less important concentrations of tufted duck, gadwall and whooper swan. Among the breeding species are mallard, gadwall, teal, garganey, pintail, shoveler and tufted duck.

The limnological interest of the Ouse Washes is further diversified by the Old Bedford River and the River Delph, both good examples of base-rich, sluggish, lowland rivers. The latter has much higher dissolved nitrogen than the neighbouring waters. The Old Bedford River was exceptionally clear when visited in September 1969 and has a zonation of submerged plants with depth. A continuous cover of *Ranunculus circinatus* is present from the margin to the maximum depth of 1.5 m, with *Nuphar lutea* forming a band from the peaty banks to 0.5 m and below that a rich and diverse flora of *Sagittaria sagittifolia* and *Potamogeton praelongus* as dominants, with *Hippuris vulgaris*, *Hottonia palustris*, *Potamogeton perfoliatus*, *Elodea canadensis* and *Oenanthe fluviatilis*. The fauna is rich in molluscs although a number of species such as *Planorbis planorbis*, *P. (Anisus) vortex*, *P. (Hippeutis) complanatus*, *P. (Bathyomphalus) contortus*, *P. (Armiger) crista*, *P. spirorbis*, *Valvata cristata* and *V. (Tropidina) macrostoma* which are present in the dykes, were absent. Most of these species are typically found in small ponds or running water with thick plant growth. On the other hand, *Valvata* was represented by *V. piscinalis* in the larger rivers. The most abundant gastropod in the Old Bedford River was *Potamopyrgus jenkinsi*, which coated the vegetation. This species was not found in the dykes and only shells of it were found in the River Delph. *Bithynia tentaculata* and *B. leachii* were also extremely common in the Old Bedford River, and the mussels *Unio pictorum* and *Dreissena polymorpha* were also recorded. Both rivers contain cyprinid fish including roach, bream, rudd, as well as dace, eels and perch.

OW.18. RIVER GREAT EAU, LINCOLNSHIRE
TF 344762–468905 Grade 1

A number of streams and small rivers drain the Chalk of the Lincolnshire Wold and then flow eastwards across the coastal fringe of the Fenlands into the North Sea. Of these the Great Eau is one of the largest. It rises as a small ditch-like stream flowing through pasture land at the foot of a low ridge of Chalk hills, the highest sources being only about 70 m above sea-level. In these upper stretches it nowhere exceeds 2 m in width and has a mean depth of about 15 cm. The bottom is predominantly of gravel and sand and the current varies from fast, to sluggish in one or two deeper pools. Lower down, below the village of Aby, the stream widens out and becomes a typical chalk stream up to 10 m wide. Here the current is moderate to slow and the bottom consists of stones, gravel, sand and silt in roughly equal proportions with aquatic vegetation covering about 25%. In its lower stretches the river becomes a sluggish Fenland drain about 1 m deep which has been practically straightened and is contained within flood levées. The bottom of the dyke, which must be periodically dredged, consists of clay, and submerged plants cover 70% of the bottom. The surrounding fen has been completely converted to arable land, and this is reflected in the exceptionally high nitrogen levels recorded ($NO_3 + NO_2$ = from 7.2 to 9.1 p.p.m.). The dissolved phosphate concentrations are also high, particularly in the lower stretches where a concentration of 0.85 p.p.m. was found, but its source is obscure since there is only a small population living within the catchment. As would be expected of a stream draining Chalk it is very base-rich with an alkalinity ranging from 180–240 p.p.m. $CaCO_3$.

Despite the high nutrient levels the water is clear throughout and the flora and fauna are rich and diverse. In the upper reaches there is little submerged vegetation but a band of marginal plants includes *Sparganium erectum*, *S. emersum*, *Rorippa* sp., *Veronica beccabunga* and dense *Epilobium hirsutum*. In the middle sections some of the typical chalk stream plants occur, with *Zannichellia palustris* dominant and *Potamogeton crispus* and *Ranunculus aquatilis* abundant. It is in the lower section, however, that aquatic plants reach their greatest variety, 16 species of submerged plant being recorded from one short stretch. *P. pectinatus* is the dominant and *Sagittaria sagittifolia*, *Groenlandia densa*, *P. friesii* and *Oenanthe fluviatilis* are among the other typical chalk stream species but there is little in the way of marginal vegetation as the banks shelve in steeply.

The invertebrate fauna is also very rich, particularly in the lower section where there is an abundance of gastropods belonging to 13 species. Beetles, mayflies, triclads, oligochaetes, corixids and crustaceans typical of base-rich sluggish rivers are abundant. In the middle section the fauna is somewhat poorer both in biomass and variety but a few species characteristic of faster currents appear, including *Simulium ornatum*, *Ephemerella ignita*, *Hydropsyche instabilis* and *Rhyacophila dorsalis*. *Polycelis felina* is the most abundant triclad in this section and is joined by *Crenobia alpina* in the upper reaches. Here the fauna is even more restricted and only two species of gastropod are recorded. The stoneflies *Isoperla grammatica* and *Nemoura* spp., which we have not found in southern chalk streams, are present and species typical of small stony streams, such as *Gammarus pulex*, *Dicranota*, Helmidae, *Oreodytes rivalis*, *Baetis rhodani* and *Ephemerella ignita*, are abundant. Little is known about the fish populations.

The river as a whole shows an exceptional range of habitat diversity within a comparatively short stretch. It has features not found in the key chalk stream of southern England, the Hampshire Avon.

OW.19. RIVER LARK, CAMBRIDGESHIRE/SUFFOLK
TL 850597–573844   Grade 2

The Lark rises as a number of small streams draining low Chalk hills which are thickly covered with glacial till. These streams are not typical chalk streams, flow only intermittently in the summer, and have a rather poor flora and fauna.

The most interesting section is downstream of Bury St Edmunds where the river has been canalised by dredging and by the construction of locks. These are now disused and no boat traffic uses the river which in the slower sections has become silted by the accumulation of a deep deposit of organic mud. The river receives drainage from agricultural land and some sewage effluent and has extremely high nutrient levels and inexplicably high sodium and chloride contents for a site so far inland.

Submerged aquatic vegetation is dense and includes a large number of chalk stream species, but *Callitriche* spp. and *Ranunculus* spp. are not as abundant as in the chalk streams of southern England. *Potamogeton lucens* and *P. pectinatus* are the most abundant species, the latter having increased since the 1930s. Several lacustrine invertebrates are present together with typical chalk stream species, such as *Gammarus pulex*, *Baetis vernus*, *B. bioculatus*, *Ephemerella ignita* and *Leuctra inermis*. Brown and rainbow trout are present together with a wide range of coarse fish species.

In the lowermost sections, the Lark is a slow-flowing Fenland drain, lacking the abundance and diversity of vegetation found in the River Great Eau, and having a mostly lacustrine fauna. The Lark is an example of an East Anglian river intermediate in character between the chalk streams of southern England and the Fenland drains. The work of Butcher, Pentelow & Woodley (1931) on this river in the 1930s gives additional interest to the site.

OW.20. TRIBUTARY OF RIVER WISSEY, NORFOLK
TL 926976–833953   Grade 2

Practically the entire length and most of the catchment of this small chalk stream lies within the Stanford PTA Breckland site (L.60(*a*)). The stream rises on the valley mire, Thompson Common (L.71), and has a number of spring sources lower downstream. It has been impounded at two points to form two large shallow areas of standing water, Thompson Water and Stanford Water, which are important breeding areas for gadwall.

The principal interest of this stream is that, as it lies within a largely non-agricultural catchment, it is the only known chalk stream in Britain which is free from nutrient enrichment. Nitrate and phosphate concentrations are significantly lower than other East Anglian streams.

The submerged vegetation is rather limited in variety, but a diverse marginal community is present. The typical chalk stream invertebrate fauna is rich and abundant and includes the rare gastropod *Planorbis* (*Anisus*) *vorticulus*, *Simulium* (*Eusimulium*) *subexcisum*, associated with the outflow of Stanford Water, and the stoneflies *Leuctra nigra* and *Nemoura* sp. There is a varied fish population which includes trout and coarse-fish species.

SOUTH-WEST ENGLAND

OW.8. MOORS RIVER (PART), DORSET   Grade 1
See under South England, p. 169.

OW.21. LITTLE SEA MERE, DORSET
SZ 0384. 20 ha   Grade 1

Little Sea Mere was formed from a coastal lagoon which was eventually isolated from the sea by a sand bar, the history of this change being well documented. The mere lies within the Studland–Godlingston Heaths grade 1* site (L.89), an area of base-poor heathland growing on blown sand overlying Bagshot Beds. The water is now completely fresh and mesotrophic in status with an alkalinity of about 13 p.p.m. $CaCO_3$. The concentrations of dissolved phosphorus and sodium are relatively high for mesotrophic conditions (0.035 p.p.m. and 37 p.p.m., respectively), but nitrogen levels are low.

The lake is entirely fringed by *Phragmites communis*-dominated reed-swamp which contains large quantities of *Osmunda regalis*. Within the reed-swamp ombrotrophic *Sphagnum*-dominated communities are developing above the water table of the mere, and locally birch–willow carr has formed. The *Phragmites* was formerly more extensive but has recently undergone a recession, the causes of which are unknown. The submerged vegetation is plentiful and covers about 90% of the bottom, the lake having a maximum depth of only 2.5 m. The species present are characteristic of a poor mesotrophic environment and include *Isoetes echinospora*, *Littorella uniflora*, *Nitella* sp., *Potamogeton obtusifolius*, *P. perfoliatus*, *Elatine hexandra*, *Myriophyllum alterniflorum* and *Eleogiton fluitans*. The zooplankton consists almost entirely of the copepod *Cyclops strenuus* and no typically planktonic Cladocera have been found. Only two species of gastropod, *Lymnaea (Radix) pereger* and *Acroloxus lacustris*, both tolerant of low calcium concentration, are present and no leeches have been found. *Asellus meridianus* and its predator *Polycelis nigra* are both abundant, and the abundant corixid fauna contains both heath and moorland species and species characteristic of thick weed-beds. The Trichoptera likewise include several species such as *Holocentropus picicornis* and *Neuriclepsis bimaculata* associated with dense growths of submerged macrophytes. Twenty-two species of dragonfly have been recorded from Studland Heath including several restricted in Britain to the south of England, and many of these breed in the mere. Ten-spined sticklebacks and eels are the only fish.

OW.22. SLAPTON LEY, DEVON
SX 8244. 245 ha   Grade 1

Slapton Ley is a large eutrophic freshwater shingle bar lagoon (alkalinity = 60–80 p.p.m. $CaCO_3$), formed in Postglacial times by the damming of a marine bay by shingle derived from a submerged bank. To the north of the main Ley, separated from it by a causeway, is an area of rich-fen, the Higher Ley, through which the main inflow, the Gara River, flows. The outflow is via a small channel at the south end of the Ley, and possibly by percolation through the shingle bar. The maximum depth is 3.1 m and the annual fluctuation in water level is *c.* 1–2 m. The catchment area of 47 km² consists mainly of mixed, undulating farmland with arable on the steep surrounding slopes of the Ley, and nutrient concentrations in the water are high. The water of the Ley is fresh but occasionally some sea water comes over the shingle bar and spray must frequently do so. Chloride contents measured by Benson-Evans *et al.* (1964–68) varied from 29–5200 p.p.m. in 1962–64. The net phytoplankton is typical of a rich lake with diatoms such as *Asterionella formosa*, *Tabellaria fenestrata*, *Melosira* spp. and *Fragilaria capucina* predominating from October–April, with Chlorophyceae and some desmids in May–July, and Cyanophyceae (*Microcystis aeruginosa*, *Anabaena flos-aquae* and *Gleotrichia echinulata*) and diatoms in August–September. The reed-swamp communities which fringe about 65% of the shoreline are dominated by *Phragmites* with associated *Sparganium erectum*, *Typha angustifolia*, *Phalaris arundinacea*, *Schoenoplectus lacustris* and *S. tabernaemontani*. There are beds of *Polygonum amphibium* and *Nymphaea alba* and swards of *Littorella uniflora*, while in deeper water *Myriophyllum spicatum*, *Elodea canadensis* and *Potamogeton crispus* occur. Areas of shingle and angular slate form the unvegetated sections of the shoreline. Twelve species of gastropod are recorded, including the brackish water *Amnicola confusa*, the rare *Segmentina nitida* and the rather uncommon *Planorbis laevis*. Eleven species of leech and eight species of Hemiptera have been recorded from the Ley, but surprisingly no maritime species have been found. There is a rich triclad fauna and two species of *Asellus*, and *Gammarus pulex* occur. Six species of Ephemeroptera, including the silt-dwelling *Ephemera danica*, and species typical of sandy and weedy conditions are present. The Ley has a rich coarse-fish population and seven species have been recorded including rudd and dace. A little angling takes place, and the Ley is much used for educational and research purposes by the Field Studies Centre at Slapton. The site has some wildfowl interest – mallard, wigeon, pochard, tufted duck and goldeneye occurring regularly.

Shingle (20 ha)

There is a mainly unvegetated, small-pebble shingle beach with a tidal range of 2.5 m which gives a coastal bonus interest to the site. This is subject to tourist trampling, but is important as the most south-westerly area (other than fragments) of shingle in Britain. Notable populations of *Polygonum raii*, *Raphanus maritimus*, *Glaucium flavum* and *Rumex rupestris* occur.

The site, which includes an area (150 ha) of woodland and reed-bed, is also noted for its fungi which include several species that are either new (1972) to science or extremely rare. Some 225 species of lichens have been recorded, the largest number known from any site of its size in Britain; this includes new combinations and rare species.

OW.9. COTSWOLD WATER PARK (PART),
GLOUCESTERSHIRE   Grade 1

See under South England, p. 169.

OW.26. RIVER WYE (PART), GLOUCESTERSHIRE
Grade 1

See under South Wales, opposite.

OW.23. CHEW VALLEY AND BLAGDON RESERVOIRS,
SOMERSET

ST 5760, ST 5159.   690 ha   Grade 2

These two large reservoirs lie 2.5 km apart at the foot of the limestone slopes of the Mendips. Both are highly eutrophic, alkalinities ranging from 150–195 p.p.m. CaCO$_3$, but Chew Valley has consistently higher nutrient levels, particularly phosphate, which reaches concentrations as high as 1.0 p.p.m. on occasions. The origin of this phosphate is obscure since the catchment is entirely agricultural with a low human population. Both lakes stratify intermittently in the summer and, in Chew Valley Reservoir, dense algal crops lead to the deoxygenation of the hypolimnion, while Blagdon which has much clearer water remains well oxygenated. The minute xanthophycean alga *Monodus* has caused the most serious algal blooms in Chew Valley Reservoir, this being attributed to the temporary absence of the main phytoplankton grazer, *Daphnia hyalina*.

Submerged macrophytic vegetation is far more abundant in Blagdon than in Chew, but little is known of the species composition. In Chew the main submerged species are *Potamogeton pectinatus*, *P. pusillus* (?), *Groenlandia densa* and *Ranunculus* sp. The benthic invertebrate fauna of Blagdon is more diverse than that of Chew and includes a large number of gastropod and water beetle species, and species associated with vegetation, such as *Ilyocoris cimicoides* and baetid mayflies, which have not been recorded from Chew. The profundal benthos of Chew Valley Reservoir is particularly poor in species and consists almost exclusively of large numbers of tubificid worms which are characteristic of low oxygen tensions. *Asellus meridianus* occurs in Blagdon but this genus is represented by *A. aquaticus* in Chew.

Both reservoirs are renowned for their trout fishing and are heavily stocked with mature brown and rainbow trout. In addition Chew has three-spined sticklebacks, eels, roach and perch, while Blagdon lacks the last two species but has gudgeon. Chew Valley is a more important wildfowl site than Blagdon, wintering flocks comprising 680 pochard, 700 teal, 130 shoveler and less important concentrations of mallard, wigeon, pintail, gadwall, tufted duck, goldeneye, Bewick's swan and mute swan. Breeding species include mallard, tufted duck, shoveler, mute swan, shelduck, garganey, gadwall and occasionally pochard.

OW.24. SWILDONS HOLE, PRIDDY CAVES AND
PRIDDY POOL, SOMERSET

ST 5351   Grade 2

A small spating stream runs through this cave system which consists of many passages and chambers ending in a series of sumps. The total length of passages exceeds 5200 m and the maximum depth is about 140 m.

The aquatic component of the cave fauna is basically similar to that of the Ogof Ffynnon Ddu complex in south Wales except that *Crangonyx subterraneus* has not been found. *Niphargus kochianus* is present in addition to *N. fontanus* and the triclads *Crenobia alpina* and *Polycelis felina* are recorded together with a wide range of stream species, especially beetles. The cave is situated close to the International Biological Programme's (IBP) open water research site, Priddy Pool, and the two features are included within the one site.

OW.25. PRIDHAMSLEIGH CAVE, DEVON

SX 7568   Grade 2

The endemic crustacean *Niphargus glennei* is abundant in this cave and replaces *N. fontanus* which is generally the most abundant species in other caves. The site is far south of the limits of glaciation and *N. glennei* may be a preglacial relict.

SOUTH WALES

OW.26. RIVER WYE: AFON GWY, GLOUCESTERSHIRE,
MONMOUTHSHIRE, HEREFORDSHIRE, RADNOR,
BRECKNOCK, MONTGOMERYSHIRE

SN 8087–ST 5394   Grade 1

The Wye rises on the slopes of Plynlimon close to the source of the River Severn at an altitude of 680 m. The hill is composed of Ordovician shales, the catchment is of closely grazed upland grassland and the stream is a typical upland base-poor type. The water is very deficient in minerals with a conductivity of 26 μmhos and has low nitrogen and phosphorus levels. In this upper stretch the stream is moderate- to fast-flowing with a predominantly stone and gravel bed. It very rapidly becomes a moderate-sized, downcutting, base-poor river and remains as such until about 8 km downstream of Builth Wells where it leaves the upland Ordovician and Silurian rocks and enters lowland country, composed of Old Red Sandstone, through which it meanders in a broad flood plain. In its downcutting base-poor section the river alternates between moderately flowing runs with a stony and gravelly bed, where the river is up to 30 m wide and about 50 cm deep, and sections where the river is contained within a narrow bedrock and boulder strewn channel with a rapid to fast current. There are a few deeper pools, and in some restricted areas silt and filamentous algae accumulate over the stony bottom in the summer months. The water shows a steady increase in dissolved mineral content as one progresses downstream but even in the lower reaches of this section it is still nutrient-poor.

Macrophytic vegetation is very restricted in these upper

reaches. In the stream section this is confined to epilithic bryophytes and marginal *Juncus effusus*, but lower down submerged angiosperm species such as *Callitriche hamulata* and *Ranunculus aquatilis* appear as isolated clumps in areas of slower currents, together with the bryophytes. The density of invertebrates in this section is only about half that of the section downstream on the Old Red Sandstone, the biomass increasing gradually as one moves downstream in the upper sections, and then increasing sharply as the river meets the nutrient-rich rock. Similarly the variety of species is about half that of the lower section, only 39 identified taxa being taken, compared to 80 on the sandstone. The fauna is characteristic of base-poor rivers with mayflies (especially *Baetis scambus* and *Ephemerella ignita*), stoneflies, caseless caddises, *Simulium variegatum*, *S. reptans* and Chironomidae predominating. The usual fish species of the trout zone, including grayling, are found in this stretch of river.

The meandering 'sandstone' section of the river extends as far downstream as Ross-on-Wye where it enters a gorge in the Carboniferous Limestone of the Forest of Dean. The river meanders across a flood plain up to 2 km wide through rich agricultural land and has a mostly gravelly bed with currents ranging from fast in shallow runs to sluggish in the deeper pools. The river is broad and fairly shallow, with a width near Hereford of about 40 m and a mean depth of about 1 m in summer. Despite the agricultural catchment, nutrient levels are fairly low with a mean value for nitrate, below Hereford, of 1.0 p.p.m. This is sufficient, however, to sustain a dense phytoplankton consisting mostly of *Scenedesmus* which extends throughout most of the lowland section. The major source of pollution on the Wye is the town of Hereford whose sewage works is badly overloaded. As a result both raw sewage and treated effluent enter the river. This raises the phosphate concentration and causes silting for a short distance downstream, due to the settling out of suspended solids, which affects the flora and fauna locally.

Submerged macrophytes cover up to 30% of the bottom and in the section just downstream of Hereford filamentous algae cover the stones and gravel. The most abundant macrophytes are *Ranunculus aquatilis*, *Potamogeton perfoliatus*, *Myriophyllum spicatum* and, in shallow water at the margins, *Polygonum amphibium*. With increasing nutrient content of the river as one moves downstream the invertebrates change, stoneflies become less important and, in the lower regions, only small numbers of *Leuctra geniculata* and *L. inermis* survive. Molluscs are found in increasing numbers and variety, among them *Anodonta* spp. and *Unio pictorum*. *Gammarus pulex*, *Asellus* spp., leeches and the triclad *Dugesia lugubris* are among the species of eutrophic waters which appear in this section of the river but are absent upstream. The rather uncommon *Baetis buceratus* is one of the most abundant mayflies, and enormous numbers of the black-fly larvae *Simulium* (*Wilhelmia*) *equinum*, *S.* (*Wilhelmia*) *salopiensis* and *S. reptans* are found attached to the vegetation and stones. In the section affected by the effluent from Hereford, tubificids and

chironomids are found in increasing numbers, while *Hydropsyche* spp. and *Gammarus pulex* decrease, and *Simulium* spp. apparently disappear. This is the chub zone of the river, although trout are still plentiful and even estuarine species such as flounder may penetrate as far up river as this. Allis shad *Alosa alosa*, which is now very restricted in Britain because of pollution in the estuaries of most of our large lowland rivers, migrates from the sea into this stretch of river in order to spawn.

In its lower reaches the Wye flows in a series of meanders through a steep-sided limestone gorge, where it is deep and slow flowing, and there are large boulders within the river in places. Much of the catchment in this section consists of deciduous woodland including high grade sites, such as Lady Park Wood (see W.95, gr. 1).

On entering the gorge the calcium content of the water rises from 20 p.p.m. to 45 p.p.m. and the nutrient content also continues to rise steadily. Macrophytic vegetation is still relatively abundant, but limited to shallow water because of limited light penetration. Species such as *Potamogeton pectinatus* and *P. crispus* appear. There is a significant increase in the density of invertebrates, gastropods in particular becoming more abundant. On the other hand, species associated with eroding conditions such as *Baetis* spp., Ecdyonuridae, *Ephemerella ignita*, *Simulium* spp. and stoneflies disappear. *Procloeon pseudorufulum*, *Centroptilum luteolum* and *Cloeon dipterum* are the most abundant mayflies and the rare *Ephemera lineata*, *Brachycercus harisella* and *Potamanthus luteus* are present.

In the lower parts of the gorge section the river becomes tidal and brackish and there is a gradual transition to estuarine conditions. In these lower stretches the bottom of the river is covered with a thick deposit of soft silt and mud. In the freshwater tidal stretches there is little change in the fauna except that some species, such as some gastropods and triclads, requiring a firm substrate, disappear, but when the effect of sea water is felt there is a change in fauna from a freshwater to a brackish water fauna. The first brackish water species, *Gammarus zaddachi*, and an increase in the numbers of *Potamopyrgus jenkinsi*, occur in almost fresh water alongside a typical riverine fauna. With increasing salinity more brackish and marine species such as *Amnicola confusa*, *Sphaeroma rugicauda*, *Eurytemora affinis* and *Gammarus marinus* appear together with large numbers of oligochaetes, while insects disappear.

OW.27. OGOF FFYNNON DDU, BRECKNOCK
SN 8615   Grade 1*

This is by far the largest and biologically the best-studied cave system in Britain consisting of many large caverns connected by stream passages with an altitudinal range of 308 m. The main streamway shows a wide range of features including waterfalls, cascades, potholes, sumps, oxbows and downcut trenches. Only one surface stream enters the system, draining from upland grassland and resurging at the lower end of the system. The water of the resurgence stream has a surprisingly low alkalinity. Much work has been done on the microbiology of the system and among the organisms described are nitrogen fixers and autotrophs and other bacteria which form growths over the cave walls; one species, *Macromonas bipunctata*, possibly in association with an alga, is responsible for the deposition of a marl-like calcium carbonate substance known as 'moon milk'. The aquatic cave fauna is very diverse and includes *Crangonyx subterraneus* and the ostracod *Cypridopsis subterranea* both of which have very restricted distributions in Britain. The commonest species, *Niphargus fontanus* and *Asellus cavaticus*, occur along with a number of stream invertebrates usually found above ground. The aquatic fauna of these caves shows affinities to that of the Mendip caves, but, because of the extensive research carried out here and its richer fauna, this site has a higher value. This site is also of international geological importance.

Associated with the cave system is the ash-dominated woodland of Craig y Rhiwarth which extends for about 1.5 km along the steep-facing escarpment of Avonian limestone and provides a bonus interest. Deposits of boulder clay in the north result in less steep slopes and deeper soils. Here the canopy is mixed silver birch, ash, oak and rowan over hazel and hawthorn. The field layer is luxuriant and includes *Oxalis acetosella*, *Fragaria vesca*, *Geranium robertianum* and patches of bracken. This section grades into a birch-dominated zone with a dense undershrub of hazel. Here, as in the rest of the wood, the gradients are more severe, the screes more extensive and the soils thinner than in the northern zone. The field layer is dominated by *Mercurialis perennis* and includes *Convallaria majalis* and *Epipactis helleborine*. The ashwood itself lies between screes and a cliff face and has remained unaffected by man and sheep. Yew, rowan and hazel occur on the cliff top and screes with *Sorbus porrigentiformis* scattered in the overhang. On stable screes, ferns such as *Thelypteris oreopteris*, *Dryopteris dilatata*, *Asplenium viride*, *A. trichomanes* and *A. ruta-muraria* occur.

OW.28. LLYN SYFADDAN: LLANGORSE LAKE, BRECKNOCK

SO 1326. 220 ha   Grade 1

This is a large shallow eutrophic kettle-hole lake of mean depth 2–3 m which lies on Old Red Sandstone drift within the Brecon Beacons National Park. The catchment area is small for such a large lake and, compared to other eutrophic waters, the human population and intensity of agriculture within the catchment is low. Chemically the lake is base-rich (alkalinity = 140–150 p.p.m. $CaCO_3$) and fairly rich in plant nutrients, but the water is relatively clear for a eutrophic lake with dense algal concentrations at times. The planktonic algae reported in 1966–67 by K. Benson-Evans (unpublished) included *Anabaena flos-aquae*, *Microcystis*, *Oscillatoria limosa*, *Asterionella gracillina*, *Fragilaria* spp. and *Melosira* spp. which are typical of eutrophic conditions. The vegetation of the lake is both abundant and rich in species. Mixed stands of *Phragmites communis* and *Typha latifolia*, with other reed-swamp associates, fringe most of the lake, beyond which is a belt of floating-leaved plants including *Nymphaea alba*, *Nuphar lutea*, *Nymphoides*

peltata, *Polygonum amphibium* and *Menyanthes trifoliata*. At the west end of the lake there are dense beds of *Potamogeton pectinatus* and elsewhere more scattered growths of *P. perfoliatus*, *P. pusillus*, *P. crispus*, *Ceratophyllum demersum*, *Myriophyllum spicatum* and *Elodea canadensis* occur at depths down to 2 m. The zooplankton is dense and includes species such as *Daphnia hyalina*, *Cyclops vicinus* and *Bosmina longirostris*, typical of the conditions. The benthic invertebrate fauna contains 15 species of gastropod and seven of leech, including the now very restricted *Hirudo medicinalis*. Some groups, e.g. *Asellus* spp. for which the conditions appear ideal, have not been recorded, however, and the only Ephemeroptera present are *Caenis moesta* and *C. horaria*, while Baetidae are absent. On the sandy, gently shelving beaches unionid mussels are extremely abundant, *Anodonta anatina* and *A. cygnea*, and *Unio pictorum* being recorded. In the deeper water, below the limit of plant growth, the bottom consists of a reddish brown clay in which the only macro-invertebrates found are large red *Chironomus* spp. and tubificid worms, both of which occurred in large numbers (10 000/m²). The lake has a typical eutrophic fish fauna including roach, perch, pike and eels.

This lake is subject to intense recreational pressures, part of the shoreline is common land, and there is unrestricted public access for boating. Maintenance of the scientific interest of Llyn Syfaddan will depend on the introduction of measures to reduce mechanical and chemical damage caused by these pressures.

OW.29. BOSHERSTON LAKE: LLYN BOSIER, PEMBROKESHIRE

SR 9794. 80 ha   Grade 1

This is a drowned river valley on Carboniferous Limestone which once entered the sea by way of a narrow gorge through limestone cliffs, but has now been isolated by sand dunes which have filled the mouth of the gorge. It is a shallow marl lake (maximum depth 3 m) which consists of three limbs partially separated by artificial causeways. Although most of the catchment is of arable land, the lake is fringed for most of its perimeter by planted deciduous woodland which shelves steeply down to the lake and at the northern end of the eastern limb there is extensive *Phragmites* reed-swamp around the main inflow. As well as inflow streams the lake is also fed by submerged springs. The water is highly calcareous (alkalinity = 80–115 p.p.m. $CaCO_3$) and has a relatively high sodium content (26 p.p.m.) because of the influence of sea spray, but the sand-dune barrier is sufficiently high to prevent direct entry of sea water. The dissolved nitrate levels are high but the water is clear with the bottom visible all over. Even though the lake is shallow, thermal stratification with oxygen depletion at 2 m is reported especially in areas where plant growth is thick, although generally the lake is holomictic. There are dense and vigorous growths of submerged macrophytes which reach the surface over a large proportion of the area of the lake. In the eastern limb *Potamogeton crispus* and *Elodea canadensis* are dominant, together with *P. pectinatus* and *Myriophyllum spicatum*, whereas in the other limbs the bottom is carpeted with *Chara hispida*. The macrophytes are heavily encrusted with marl deposits. Major constituents of the zooplankton include *Bosmina coregoni, Ceriodaphnia quadrangula, Cyclops (Megacyclops) viridis* and *C. (Macrocyclops) fuscus* which is characteristic of clear weedy lakes. There is a rich and diverse benthic invertebrate fauna, the most abundant numerically being Chironomidae, oligochaetes, Corixidae and *Caenis moesta*. Among the Hemiptera the southern species *Ranatra linearis, Micronecta scholtzi* and *Cymatia coleoptrata* and the rare *Corixa affinis* are found. Twelve species of gastropod are recorded including three amphibious species, *Vertigo* sp., *Succinea* sp., and *Lymnaea (Galba) truncatula*, presumably living on the submerged weed mats at the surface of the water. Two species of *Caenis* and two of *Cloeon* are present and the fauna also includes large numbers of Zygoptera and water beetles. *Gammarus* is surprisingly scarce and *Asellus* appears to be absent, though its predator the triclad *Dendrocoelium lacteum* is recorded. The sponge-dwelling caddis *Ecnomus tenellus* also occurs. There is a high population density of small roach in the lake and large perch, tench and pike are present.

The site differs from all other lakes formed by coastal processes, which have been examined, in that it is a limestone lake with marl formation. Its most striking feature is the prolific growth of submerged macrophytes which carpet most of the bottom and reach to the water's surface. The lake is used for angling but recreational pressures on the lake are at present slight. The whole of the site lies within the Pembrokeshire Coast National Park and is within 5 km of the Field Studies Council centre at Orielton.

See also C.43.

OW.30. KENFIG POOL, GLAMORGAN
SS 7981. 30 ha   Grade 2

This dune slack pool, of maximum depth 3 m, is surrounded mainly by dune heath, with a caravan site to one side. The shore substrate consists almost entirely of sand, with reed-swamp fringing 70% of the perimeter and in deeper water the bottom is covered by a fine black mud. The water of the pool is very clear and is moderately base-rich, with an alkalinity of 60–70 p.p.m. $CaCO_3$, but nutrient levels are relatively low for a eutrophic water-body.

The aquatic flora is very diverse. The marginal communities include a small, species-rich fen (2 ha) which is seasonally inundated and grazed by cattle. *Oenanthe fistulosa, Lysimachia vulgaris, Lythrum salicaria* and *Berula erecta* are among the species present. Patches of scrub carr/woodland (*Alnus glutinosa, Betula pubescens* and *Salix* spp.) occur to the south while a band of *Scirpus maritimus* and *Phragmites communis*, followed by a zone of *Equisetum fluviatile*, and in deeper water *Schoenoplectus tabernaemontani* surrounds almost the entire pool. The floating-leaved community is not so well represented, *Polygonum amphibium* being the only abundant species, but submerged vegetation covers the entire bottom down to the maximum depth. Among the submerged species are *Chara aspera*, four species of *Potamogeton*, of which *P. pusillus* is the most abundant,

Myriophyllum spicatum, Ceratophyllum demersum and, in deeper water, *Isoetes echinospora*. This is an unusually rich site for the last species, and its occurrence alongside *Ceratophyllum* is most unusual.

The benthic invertebrate fauna is very abundant and diverse and the following are all present in very large numbers: *Asellus meridianus, Pisidium* spp., *Polycelis tenuis/nigra*, Tubificidae, *Helobdella stagnalis, Glossiphonia complanata, Caenis horaria, C. moesta, Cloeon simile, Mystacides longicornis*, Corixidae and Chironomidae. Eleven species of gastropod are recorded. Roach, rudd, pike and tench are said to be present in the pool, which has also been stocked with rainbow trout. Common frogs breed here.

Although the dunes and pool are much used for recreation, trampling of the margins is restricted to two small areas and elsewhere the vegetation is virtually intact. Except for disturbance to wildfowl, the flora and fauna have not suffered from the recreational activities.

See also C.47.

OW.31. LLYN Y FAN FAWR, BRECKNOCK
SN 8321. 16 ha   Grade 2

This lake is situated at an altitude of 610 m below an escarpment of Old Red Sandstone, and has a maximum depth of 18 m and a mean depth of over 5 m. The water is poor in dissolved salts, with a specific conductivity of 50 μmhos, but has a relatively high nitrogen level (0.16 p.p.m. NO_3) and is very transparent. The shoreline is chiefly of stones with a little sand and gravel and this grades into sand in deeper water. The west side below the escarpment shelves steeply into deep water and has *Fontinalis antipyretica* growing on the stones but the littoral zone of the east side shelves gently, with *Littorella uniflora* and *Isoetes lacustris* growing on the sand.

The zooplankton is typical of poor upland lakes with *Diaptomus gracilis* predominating. The diverse benthic fauna includes species typical of sandy substrates and wave-washed shores, such as the mayflies *Ecdyonurus* sp., *Caenis moesta*; five stonefly species; *Molanna angustata, Polycentropus flavomaculatus, Sericostoma personatum* and *Ancylus fluviatilis*. It is noteworthy that the leech *Erpobdella octoculata* was conspicuous and a number were seen swimming in open water. Brown trout were introduced in the past but are said not to have survived.

Llyn y Fan Fawr is a good example of a richer corrie lake and is probably the best example of this type of lake in south Wales and the most southerly in Britain.

See also U.7.

NORTH WALES

OW.26. RIVER WYE (PART), MONTGOMERYSHIRE
                                                          Grade 1

See under South Wales, p. 176.

OW.32. LLYN TEGID: BALA LAKE, MERIONETH

SH 9134.   435 ha   Grade 1

This classical glacially cut basin is occupied by the largest naturally formed lake in Wales, lying at an altitude of 163 m in a catchment predominantly used as upland grazing. The underlying rocks are mainly acidic sandstones and shales, but there is a little limestone at the head of the catchment which gives the water an alkalinity of from 3–6.5 p.p.m. $CaCO_3$. The maximum depth is 42 m and in summer a thermocline develops at about 15–20 m, but stratification is sometimes upset by wind action even in mid-summer. Oxygen values in the hypolimnion are always above 70% saturation even after prolonged stratification. Most of the shoreline is exposed and rocky, shelving steeply down to 20 m, but at either end of the lake, in more sheltered bays, mud and silt have accumulated and beds of *Juncus* sp., *Potamogeton natans* and *Nuphar lutea* occur. Around the rest of the shore vegetation is restricted to *Littorella uniflora* and *Isoetes lacustris* swards and in places a band of *Callitriche* sp. in 1.5–2 m of water. The invertebrate fauna is characteristic of this type of lake and is similar to that of Windermere and Loch Lomond. The eight species of gastropod occurring are all typical of oligotrophic conditions except the rather rare *Myxas glutinosa* which is also recorded from Windermere. *Asellus meridianus* occurs here at the lower end of its range of tolerance to calcium content, and *Gammarus pulex* is common on the stony shores. Plecoptera and Ephemeroptera are well represented and the Trichoptera fauna is predominantly of species associated with exposed wave-washed shores. The typical profundal community of *Pisidium*, Tubificidae and Chironomidae has as its two most abundant species *Limnodrilus hoffmeisteri* and *Chironomus anthracinus* both of which are associated with increasing eutrophication in lakes of this type.

The fish populations of the lake, which have been intensively studied from Liverpool University, include the gwyniad *Coregonus clupeoides pennanti* (= *laveratus* – the European whitefish). Brown trout, grayling, perch, pike and roach also occur, grayling being seldom found in lakes in Britain. The absence of charr, which are present in other similar Welsh lakes, is notable.

Although the outflow is now controlled by a small dam, for river regulation purposes, this is still an outstanding site on the grounds of the research already invested in it.

OW.33. LLYN IDWAL, CAERNARVONSHIRE

SH 6459.   12 ha   Grade 1

This small corrie lake lies, at an altitude of 380 m, below the steep crags of the Cwm Idwal NNR which are composed of Ordovician lavas, tuffs and sediments of both acidic and calcareous character. The alkalinity of the lake is relatively high (8 p.p.m. $CaCO_3$) but the concentration of calcium and plant nutrients is very low, the specific conductivity being less than 30 μmhos. For a corrie lake it is surprisingly shallow, the mean depth being only 3.4 m. At the southern end the bottom consists of a peaty mud while the rest of

the lake has shores of stones and gravel derived from lateral moraines which flank the corrie.

The main interest of the site is its submerged aquatic flora which is rich in plants associated with base-poor conditions. Especially at the shallow southern end there are extensive beds of *Pilularia globulifera*, *Subularia aquatica*, *Littorella uniflora*, *Isoetes lacustris*, *Juncus bulbosus*, *Callitriche hermaphroditica*, *Lobelia dortmanna*, *Myriophyllum alterniflorum* and *Sparganium angustifolium*. Emergent vegetation in contrast is limited to a few restricted stands of *Carex rostrata* and *Phragmites communis* but the presence of reeds in a corrie lake is most unusual. The zooplankton contains species typical of oligotrophic lakes, but Daphniidae are absent. The benthic fauna consists mainly of taxa associated with poor stony shores such as Plecoptera, and the mayflies *Baetis* spp., *Ephemerella ignita* and *Siphlonurus lacustris*. *Ancylus fluviatilis* and *Lymnaea* (*Radix*) *peregra* are the only gastropods recorded, *Erpobdella octoculata* is the only leech and this is one of the more southerly sites for *Gammarus lacustris*. The caddis larvae *Cyrnus flavidus* and *C. trimaculata* are found among the submerged macrophytes. There is a large population of minnows in the lake. Among the series of corrie lakes chosen, Llyn Idwal is biologically the richest.

See also U.10.

OW.34. LLYN CWELLYN, CAERNARVONSHIRE

SH 5655.   80 ha   Grade 2

This large, relatively deep (mean depth 22.6 m), oligotrophic glacial lake lies in a largely unpopulated catchment of upland grassland. Geologically the catchment consists primarily of slate which forms loose unstable shingle beaches round most of the perimeter of the lake. The alkalinity is 3–4 p.p.m. $CaCO_3$, and the water is very clear, but concentrations of dissolved plant nutrients are relatively high. Emergent vegetation is almost non-existent, but submerged plants, which occur in a narrow band below 2 m on the steeply shelving shorelines, include *Myriophyllum alterniflorum*, *Callitriche intermedia*, *Eleogiton fluitans*, *Lobelia dortmanna*, *Isoetes lacustris*, and *Subularia aquatica*, the last being a northern plant of restricted distribution in Wales.

The invertebrate fauna of the slate shorelines is very sparse, but includes *Asellus meridianus* in a surprisingly poor habitat for this species. In the zone of macrophyte growth the fauna is more plentiful and diverse and includes *Polycelis tenuis*, *Lymnaea* (*Radix*) *peregra*, *Cloeon simile* and *Cyrnus flavidus*. The fish population includes trout and the Welsh race of the charr for which there are only three localities. Compared to the other large glacial lake in Wales containing charr, Llyn Padarn, Llyn Cwellyn is less modified and is under less threat and is therefore to be preferred. It is, however, likely to be used in the future for water abstraction, but the proposed scheme may have only slight effects on the lake.

OW.35. LLYN GLASLYN, CAERNARVONSHIRE

SH 6154.   9 ha   Grade 2

This deep (maximum depth 39 m) oligotrophic corrie lake lies at an altitude of 601 m on the east side of Y Wyddfa. The shorelines are of stones and boulders, except in two bays where storm beaches of flat slate have been thrown up, and shelve steeply, giving way to a white sand below about 2 m. An unidentified leafy liverwort is the only macrophyte recorded and the invertebrate fauna is extremely sparse. The zooplankton consists of relatively few individuals of *Alonopsis elongata*, a species found in other high altitude lakes, and the benthic fauna of the shoreline includes upland species such as *Diura bicaudata* and *Plectrocnemia geniculata*. This paucity is possibly caused by pollution from an old copper mine on the north side of the corrie, but the gravel shores are very unstable, and would not be likely to support a rich fauna. This is the only lake seen in Wales which approaches the Arctic–alpine condition of the Cairngorm corrie lakes.

See also U.10.

OW.36. LLYN CORON AND AFON FFRAW, ANGLESEY

SH 3770.   25 ha   Grade 2

Llyn Coron is an extremely shallow eutrophic lake with a mean depth of about 1.2 m which was formed behind coastal sand dunes. Much of the shoreline and the bottom is sand which is brought into suspension during storms and reduces the transparency of the water so that a Secchi disc may disappear at 25 cm. High nutrient levels are recorded, algal blooms occur frequently and submerged macrophytes appear to be limited to areas of less than 1 m in depth. *Potamogeton trichoides*, *Ranunculus circinatus*, *P. perfoliatus*, *Myriophyllum spicatum* and *Callitriche hermaphroditica* are recorded, the last species in one of its most southerly British sites. *P. pectinatus* is notably absent as are *Chara* spp. which are, however, present in the outflow. There is very little development of marginal vegetation which at its most developed, on the sandy southern side, consists of a narrow band of *Schoenoplectus tabernaemontani* and *Eleocharis palustris* followed by a fringe of *Polygonum amphibium*.

The zooplankton is extremely dense, and includes *Leptodora kindti*, but *Daphnia* spp. are absent. The benthic fauna is characterised by the preponderance of Mollusca (10 species of gastropod) and leeches (6 species) and includes a wide range of other species associated with weedy eutrophic conditions.

The Llyn is also of value as a site for wintering wildfowl which include mallard, teal, wigeon, shoveler, pochard, tufted duck and goldeneye.

The outflow of the Llyn, the Afon Ffraw, is included within the site as an example of a base-rich sluggish lowland stream. It is a short stream about 3 km in length from the Llyn to the sea, nowhere exceeding 4 m in width, and is mostly about 1 m deep. It has a diverse flora, although submerged aquatic plants are found in abundance only in the upper shallower reaches, where *Ranunculus aquatilis* is dominant together with *Potamogeton crispus*, *P. per-*

foliatus and *Chara* sp. The marginal communities are varied with *Sparganium erectum* and *Schoenoplectus tabernaemontani* abundant in the upper and middle reaches, and *Scirpus maritimus* nearer the sea. A floating-leaved community of *P. natans* and *Polygonum amphibium* covers up to 60% of the water surface in places. The invertebrate fauna is principally a lacustrine one, stream species only being found on the faster flowing riffles where *Simulium equinum*, *Baetis rhodani*, *Ephemerella ignita*, *Hydropsyche instabilis*, *Rhyacophila dorsalis*, *Leuctra fusca* and large numbers of Helmidae are found. The fauna of the rest of the stream is very similar to that of the Llyn, and includes the rather uncommon caddis *Polycentropus irroratus* and the riverine dragonfly *Agrion splendens*. In the lower sections the brackish water crustacean *Gammarus duebeni* is abundant.

See also C.54.

OW.37. LLYN YR WYTH EIDION, ANGLESEY

SH 4781.   2 ha   Grade 2

This is a small circular pool lying within the grade 1 calcareous valley mire site of Cors Erddreiniog (P.35), and is a relatively deep (maximum depth = 8 m) remnant of a formerly much more extensive lake whose shallower regions have been invaded by fen. The valley mire is bounded by a limestone escarpment and the lake is consequently a highly calcareous marl lake (alkalinity = 240–250 p.p.m. CaCO$_3$), but is only moderately rich in plant nutrients. Because of its depth, sheltered nature and relatively turbid water for a marl pool, it almost certainly stratifies in summer, when the bottom deposits consist of a fine black sulphide mud, suggesting that at least partial deoxygenation of the hypolimnion occurs.

The pool is entirely surrounded by reed-swamp consisting predominantly of *Phragmites communis* on organic mud and lacustrine shell marl, with *Schoenoplectus lacustris* growing beyond this down to 1.5 m. *Cladium mariscus*, *Carex elata* and *Iris pseudacorus* are also widespread in the *Phragmites* zone, beyond which is a narrow zone of *Nymphaea alba* and *Nuphar lutea*. The only submerged macrophytes are *Chara rudis*, *C. acculeolata* and *Sparganium minimum*, all in restricted areas.

The shallow water benthic invertebrate fauna is rich in gastropods and leeches, seven species of snail being collected and five of leech, including *Glossiphonia heteroclita*, a species typical of eutrophic conditions. *Asellus meridianus* and *Gammarus lacustris* are both present, the latter being near the southern limit of its range in Britain here. The profundal fauna consists entirely of forms, such as *Chaoborus flavicans*, Tubificidae, Chironomidae and *Pisidium* sp., tolerant of low oxygen tensions.

MIDLANDS

OW.26. RIVER WYE (PART), HEREFORDSHIRE   Grade 1
See under South Wales, p. 176.

OW.38. ROSTHERNE MERE, CHESHIRE
SJ 7384.   153 ha   Grade 1*

This is the largest and the deepest of the Cheshire/ Shropshire meres (maximum depth 30 m), which lies in thick deposits of glacial drift overlying Triassic marls and salt-beds. Its mode of origin is unknown, but was probably a combination of subsidence following solution of the salt beds and kettle-hole formation. The catchment consists mostly of undulating arable and permanent pasture.

The bottom substrate of the mere consists of a fine black ooze, except at the northern end where submerged peat deposits occur at depths down to 4 m. Chemically the water is base-rich (alkalinity = 70–80 p.p.m. $CaCO_3$) and has high concentrations of dissolved phosphate, nitrate and ammonia due to enrichment from the droppings of large numbers of birds. The mere stratifies in summer, the hypolimnion becoming completely deoxygenated during this period so that there is no permanent profundal fauna below 23 m. The phytoplankton is typical of lowland eutrophic lakes with blue-green algae and *Ceratium hirundinella* dominant. There is no submerged vegetation, but small beds of *Nuphar lutea* and *Nymphaea alba* occur. In the reed-beds *Phragmites* is dominant, but several other species are locally abundant. Apart from its absence from the deeper parts of the mere, the invertebrate fauna is typical of such a lowland base-rich lake, 14 species of gastropod and four species of leech having been recorded.

The mere was once the only inland locality in Britain for the smelt *Osmerus eperlanus* but this species is now thought to have become extinct here, although there are still a number of coarse-fish species and trout. Rostherne is a regional wildfowl refuge holding an average of 3000 mallard plus smaller numbers of shoveler and pochard in winter, and up to 2000 teal. It is also an important gull roost where up to 20000 gulls have been counted on occasions. The mere is close to several centres of research, and work has been published on its chemistry, phytoplankton, vascular plants, zooplankton, fish and benthos. It is thus one of the most thoroughly studied of the British lowland lakes.

OW.39. CROSE MERE AND SWEAT MERE, SHROPSHIRE
SJ 4330.   60 ha   Grade 1

Crose Mere (15.4 ha) is a moderate-sized Shropshire mere, with a maximum depth of 9 m, which occupies a kettle-hole and lies in an area of undulating glacial drift, now rich farmland. Unlike most other Shropshire meres, few trees surround the lake and the zone of marginal vegetation is narrow except at the western end, where there is a small area of carr with *Carex paniculata* and *Alnus*. About three-quarters of the shoreline is fringed by a belt of reed-swamp, including *Cladium mariscus* and the maritime species *Schoenoplectus tabernaemontani* and the rest of the shore consists of gravel and sand beaches. Aquatic flowering plants occur particularly at the western end and include *Nuphar lutea*, *Nymphaea alba* and *Potamogeton crispus*. The mere is eutrophic (alkalinity = 170–180 p.p.m. $CaCO_3$) but phos-

phate and nitrate are lower than in the neighbouring Sweat Mere. Thermal stratification takes place in summer.

The phytoplankton contains *Cryptomonas* and *Aphanizomenon*, both typical of rich conditions. The zooplankter *Leptodora kindti*, which is rare in south and east England, is present and two species of *Gammarus*, *G. pulex* and *G. lacustris* (here at the southern end of its range in Britain), and two species of *Asellus*, *A. meridianus* and *A. aquaticus*, have been recorded. The rest of the invertebrate fauna is typical of eutrophic conditions with leeches, snails and tubificids being plentiful. This is a good example of a natural, lowland, eutrophic shallow lake with an interesting relict fauna and flora.

Sweat Mere is a small water-body with an open water area of about 0.5 ha lying about 200 m east of Crose Mere, to which it is connected by an artificially constructed channel. The principal interest of the site is extensive hydrosere development which grades from open water, through reed-swamp, to a *schwingmoor*, then carr and finally to damp woodland. Most of the open water is now covered by *Nuphar lutea* which is rapidly encroaching. Surrounding the open water is a floating mat of *Typha latifolia* and *T. angustifolia* with a little *Phragmites* grading into a zone of *Carex paniculata* tussocks which support saplings of *Salix cinerea* and then *Alnus* as one progresses from the open water. The more open communities nearest the water's edge contain *C. pseudocyperus*, *Equisetum fluviatile*, *Iris pseudacorus*, *Lythrum salicaria*, *Ranunculus lingua* and *Sparganium erectum* whilst the closed canopy carr includes *Agrostis canina*, *Caltha palustris*, *Carex acutiformis*, *C. remota*, *Dryopteris spinulosa*, *Lycopus europaeus*, *Thelypteris palustris* and *Urtica dioica*. Damp woodland with oak, alder and birch occurs on firm peat over sand surrounding the mire. The water is extremely turbid and dark brown in colour, and chemically eutrophic with high concentrations of plant nutrients, particularly nitrogen ($NO_3 + NO_2 = 2.01$ p.p.m.). The mean depth of the pond is about 1.2 m and the bottom substrate is a loose organic gyttja. The invertebrate fauna is typical of rich eutrophic conditions with leeches, gastropods, tubificids and chironomids abundant, but neither *Asellus meridianus* nor *Gammarus lacustris* appears to have colonised this mere from Crose Mere though *G. pulex* and *A. aquaticus* are present. Alternatively they may have died out with the intrusion of the *schwingmoor*. The main interest of the site is that the *schwingmoor* and the water of the mere are both eutrophic in character. Peat borings through the *schwingmoor* have shown, however, that the site was once isolated from the ground water and developed an acidophilous *Sphagnum*-dominated community, and that the present unusual condition results from the influence of water entering via the drains from Crose Mere and Whattall Moss.

Sweat Mere is a classic site described by Tansley (1949) and both meres have great research potential, considerable limnological work having been conducted on Crose Mere already. The basin mire surrounding Sweat Mere is also of interest in the peatland context.

OW.40. CLAREPOOL MOSS, SHROPSHIRE

SJ 4334.   0.4 ha   Grade 1

This small pool lies near the eastern edge of a basin mire (P.43) which is now largely covered by birch and pine, growing on a *Sphagnum recurvum* lawn. Although the mire itself has become isolated from the ground water and is markedly oligotrophic, the pool is still subject to alkaline influence (alkalinity = 10–20 p.p.m. $CaCO_3$) but is dystrophic and very peat stained. For a mire pool the water is unusually rich in nutrients with high phosphate, nitrate and ammonia levels (dissolved phosphorus = 0.3–0.6 p.p.m., total nitrogen = 2–3 p.p.m.), and a calcium concentration of 22 p.p.m. The pool is surrounded on its east side by a poor-fen community, with *Juncus effusus* and *Potentilla palustris* grading into alder–birch carr with *Molinia* and some *Sphagnum*, and on the west side with *Carex paniculata* tussocks and *S. recurvum* lawn. The mean depth is only 1.5 m and the bottom relatively level and covered with a fine organic mud which does not support submerged vegetation. The invertebrate fauna consists mainly of species typical of base-rich weedy, or fen habitats, such as *Asellus meridianus*, *Cloeon dipterum*, *Holocentropus picicornis* and the corixids *Sigara dorsalis*, *Callicorixa praeusta*, *Hesperocorixa linnei*, *H. sahlbergi* and *Corixa punctata*. The gastropod *Planorbis (Gyraulus) albus* occurs here as well as several species of dragonfly, including *Erythromma najas*, and water beetles, including the rare *Acilius sulcatus*. The zooplankton consists almost entirely of *Daphnia pulex* and the profundal mud fauna of Tubificidae, *Chaoborus flavicans* and *C. crystallinus*. To the south of the mire site is a small pool about 4 m across where the water is extremely peat-stained (Secchi disc transparency 10 cm) but also base-rich (alkalinity = 40–50 p.p.m. $CaCO_3$). *Lemna minor* and *Callitriche hermaphroditica* grow in this pool but the fauna is similar to that of the main pool.

OW.41. SHROPSHIRE UNION CANAL, PREES BRANCH,
          SHROPSHIRE

SJ 4933.   4 ha   Grade 1

The branch of the canal which runs for 3 km from the main Shropshire Union Canal shows a good succession of aquatic plants from closed to open communities. At the south-east end is a dense stand of *Glyceria maxima*, with some *Sparganium erectum* and *Rumex hydrolapathum*. North-westwards towards the main canal this gives way to a community dominated by *Hydrocharis morsus-ranae* and *Ceratophyllum demersum*, which chokes the canal, and in turn gives way to more open communities with *Nuphar lutea*, *Elodea canadensis*, *Myriophyllum spicatum* and six species of *Potamogeton*. In the more open reaches, where the water may be up to 2 m deep, the communities have been maintained by cutting. The nutrient level of the water at the south-east end is very much higher than that towards the main canal as exemplified by the conductivities of 522 and 131 μmhos, respectively, and this may influence the vegetational composition at different points. In the

Hydrocharis/Ceratophyllum zone the alkalinity is 210–220 p.p.m. $CaCO_3$.

There is a rich benthic fauna with a large number of gastropod species. Typical canal species such as *Sphaerium transversum*, *Crangonyx pseudogracilis* and the dragonfly *Erythromma najas* occur, and the introduced and very local bitterling is plentiful, as are roach. Smooth newt and the common frog are present.

OW.42. CHARTLEY MOSS, STAFFORDSHIRE

SK 0228.   1 ha   Grade 1

Two pools lying within this grade 1 peatland site (P.42) have been selected as representatives of lowland dystrophic peat pools whose invertebrate fauna is of particular interest on account of the caddis species recorded.

One small pool (area = 0.25 ha) at 023283 is thought to have formed by the collapse of a *schwingmoor*. It is surrounded by a *Sphagnum recurvum* raft from which pine and birch grow and several dead pines lie at an angle in the pool where the raft has collapsed. There is a fringe of *Juncus effusus*, with *Carex acuta* and *C. elata*, and the soft bottom of the pool is composed of fragments of peat on which *S. recurvum* grows down to a depth of 0.5 m. Beyond this there is no vegetation; the maximum depth of the pool is about 5 m. The water is stained dark brown and is very acid (pH 3.8) and the specific conductivity of the pool (144 μmhos) is high.

At 023281 the *schwingmoor* has not completely grown over, leaving a pool 0.3 ha in area with a maximum depth of 1 m. It is more open than the previous pool and the surrounding pines do not approach the water's edge where *Eriophorum vaginatum* and *Molinia* are growing as emergents. About half the bottom is covered with *Sphagnum* and the rest is peat. The peat-stained water is extremely acidic (pH < 3.6) and again the specific conductivity is exceptionally high (260 μmhos).

The fauna of both pools is very similar. Chironomidae are abundant and several species of Hemiptera and Odonata are present including the rare corixid *Hesperocorixa moesta*. This is one of the few known localities in Britain for the caddises *Oligotrichia ruficrus* and *O. clathrata*, and is also a site for the local *Stenophylax alpestris* and *Micropterna lateralis*.

OW.43. OAK MERE, CHESHIRE

SJ 5767.   45 ha   Grade 1

Oak Mere, the only oligotrophic large Shropshire–Cheshire mere, is a shallow lake of 5.5 m maximum depth formed as three confluent kettle-holes which have peat bottoms, separated by submerged sandy ridges. The surrounding ground is heath and woodland with some cultivated land at the southern end, and at the north-west end is a small fen/carr. The alkalinity is less than 2 p.p.m. $CaCO_3$ and the pH normally ranges between 5 and 6. Although poor in the number of plant species it is exceptionally interesting on account of its curious flora. It is one of the few lakes in Britain where very large populations of *Botriococcus braunii* develop and on occasions the water is coloured orange by blooms of this alga. The shoreline flora consists of *Juncus effusus*, *Hydrocotyle vulgaris*, *Eleocharis palustris*, *Typha latifolia* and *Molinia*, with floating mats of *Sphagnum subsecundum*, and this lake is one of the best sites for the rare *Calamagrostis neglecta*. There is little submerged vegetation, only *Littorella uniflora*, *Callitriche* sp. and *Nuphar lutea* being found. The most abundant member of the zooplankton is the rare *Ceriodaphnia dubia*, which occurs with the ubiquitous *Diaptomus gracilis* and *Chydorus sphaericus*. No mollusca are present but the presence of both the mayflies, *Cloeon simile* and *C. dipterum*, is interesting in view of the small amounts of submerged vegetation. *Asellus meridianus* is abundant and caddis are reasonably well represented. There is a big perch population but roach, which were formerly present, have not been seen in recent years.

Base-rich borehole water has been pumped into the mere on three separate occasions in the past and on each occasion striking changes in the composition of the phytoplankton were recorded with species typical of eutrophic conditions appearing. It is unlikely that this event will recur, however.

OW.44. LATHKILL DALE, DERBYSHIRE
SK 170659–220646   Grade 1

The Derbyshire Dales, forming a southern extension of the Pennine Carboniferous Limestone, are drained by a number of eutrophic rivers and streams, mostly slower flowing than the limestone streams of the Malham area and intermediate in character between them and the chalk streams of southern England. Many of these streams have been greatly modified for angling, but the River Lathkill flowing through the grade 1 calcareous grassland and woodland site of Lathkill Dale (see L.124(i) and W.115) is fairly intact.

The water of the stream is highly calcareous (alkalinity = 210–230 p.p.m. $CaCO_3$), and nutrient levels are high with nitrate concentrations ranging from 2.0 to 3.4 p.p.m. and phosphorus levels from 1.7 to 2.7 p.p.m. Most of this phosphorus is in an insoluble form however and may consist of calcium salts derived from the limestone. There is a wide range of habitat conditions within a short length of river. The upper parts are a winterbourne, and in summer the stream issues from a small spring lower down the valley. Lower downstream there are alternating moderately flowing gravelly sections and silted pools, some formed by natural tufa dams and others artificially. There is also a short underground section and a stretch where the stream percolates through a bed of *Phalaris arundinacea*. In the pools there are abundant growths of submerged plants including *Ranunculus aquatilis*, *Rorippa* sp., *Apium nodiflorum* and *Potamogeton natans*, while the faster sections and tufa dams are carpeted with bryophytes including *Cinclidotus fontinaloides* and *Scapania undulata*.

The invertebrate fauna contains upland species together with those found in lowland chalk streams. Among the former are caddises such as *Plectrocnemia conspersa* and *Wormaldia occipitalis*, and the stonefly *Diura bicaudata*. *Gammarus pulex* is abundant throughout the system, as is *Agapetus fuscipes* in the lower section. The mayfly *Baetis*

vernus is extremely plentiful and was surprisingly the only *Baetis* sp. found, and there were also unexpectedly few gastropods, only three species, *Lymnaea* (*Radix*) *pereger*, *L.* (*Galba*) *palustris* and *Ancylus fluviatilis*, being taken. The rather local caddis *Rhyacophila septentrionalis*, characteristic of limestone streams, is present. Brown trout are frequent; bullhead have also been recorded.

OW.45. BROWN MOSS, SHROPSHIRE
SJ 5639.   30 ha   Grade 2

This site consists of a series of shallow pools fed by ground water which lie in an area of glacial sands and gravel, with remnants of the peat which originally covered the site. There is a gradation of nutrient status from dystrophic pools (pH 6.4, alkalinity = 20 p.p.m. $CaCO_3$) to eutrophic waters (pH 7.8, alkalinity = 190 p.p.m. $CaCO_3$), and in places there is slight organic pollution with organic nitrogen levels as high as 6.3 p.p.m. In places *Sphagnum* spp. grow down to the water's edge and at one point the succession of vegetation has progressed to the development of a small *schwingmoor*, about 40 m in diameter, with an outer zone of *Juncus effusus* and *S. cuspidatum* and within this a lawn of *S. recurvum* with patches of *Eriophorum angustifolium* and *Aulacomnium palustre*. There is a wide variety of emergent vegetation such as *Juncus effusus*, *Typha latifolia*, *Eleocharis palustris*, *Potentilla palustris*, *Galium palustre*, *Carex rostrata*, *C. pseudocyperus*, *Sparganium erectum*, *Alisma plantago-aquatica*, *Menyanthes trifoliata*, *Baldellia ranunculoides* and *Oenanthe fistulosa*. The composition of the emergents varies from pool to pool as does their extent, some of the smaller pools being completely overgrown, whereas others have several hectares of open water. The sheltered conditions provide protection for considerable development of free-floating species, such as *Lemna minor*, *L. trisulca*, *Riccia fluitans* and the local *Luronium natans*, but there are relatively few submerged aquatic plants, *Hottonia palustris*, *Potamogeton obtusifolius*, *Pilularia globulifera*, *Nitella* sp. and *Fontinalis antipyretica* being recorded.

The benthic fauna contains species associated with both eutrophic and dystrophic conditions and varies in composition from pool to pool. *Crangonyx pseudogracilis* and *Polycelis tenuis/nigra* only occur in the largest pool while the more acid pools have a wide range of corixids. There is a varied fish fauna which includes carp, tench and pike. Great crested grebe have attempted to nest and little grebe, mute swan, mallard, tufted duck, moorhen and coot nest by or on the pools.

OW.46. ABBOTS MOSS, CHESHIRE
SJ 5968.   2 ha   Grade 2

Adjacent to the oligotrophic basin mire site (P.46) are a number of dystrophic pools, of which the Gull Pool is the largest (area = 2 ha) with a mean depth of about 1 m. It lies near the edge of the moss and is bordered by *Sphagnum* spp., birch and a fringe of *Juncus squarrosus* growing along the water's edge, with a thick carpet of *Drepanocladus fluitans* overlying soft peat within the pool. The water is very acid (pH 3.9) and somewhat peat-stained. A small pool to the south of the moss approximately 7 × 5 m in area and 1 m in depth is bordered by actively growing *Sphagnum* peat and about 40% of the peaty bottom of the pool is covered with *Utricularia minor*. The water is similar chemically to that in the Gull Pool but has a relatively high conductivity of 160–200 μmhos. The zooplankton consists of the small surface-dwelling cladoceran *Scapholeberis mucronata* and the carnivore *Chaoborus obscuripes*.

The benthic fauna of the two pools is similar and typical of lowland dystrophic waters. Hemiptera are prominent; nine species, including *Hesperocorixa castanea*, *H. sahlbergi* and *Gerris odontogaster*, are present and other characteristic species are the water spider *Argyroneta aquatica*, the moss-dwelling tipulid *Phalacrocera replicata*, the dragonflies *Libellula depressa* and *Leucorrhinia dubia* and the caddises *Holocentropus dubius* and *Phryganea* spp.

NORTH ENGLAND

OW.47. MALHAM–ARNCLIFFE, YORKSHIRE
SD 8966.   65 ha   Grade 1*

(a) *Malham Tarn*

(b) *Outflow of Malham Tarn*

(c) *Gordale Beck*

(d) *Cowside Beck*

This area of Carboniferous Limestone, which is separately graded as an upland site (U.24, gr. 1), contains a large marl lake, Malham Tarn, and three outstanding upland streams, the Cowside Beck, Gordale Beck and the outflow of Malham which are together classed as one composite key open water site.

The tarn is the highest marl lake in Britain and lies at an altitude of 380 m in a basin which consists mostly of grazed calcareous grassland with a little afforestation. The area of the tarn is 62 ha but the maximum depth only 4.4 m, and the shoreline is mostly of algal- and bryophyte-covered limestone boulders, with a peat bank up to 5 m high formed by the erosion of a raised bog, along the western side. The shore slopes gently to a depth of about 1 m and then shelves more steeply down to about 2–3 m where the substrate consists of a black calcareous organic mud formed by the decomposition of macrophytes. The water is very clear and calcareous (alkalinity = 62–142 p.p.m. $CaCO_3$), but poor in plant nutrients, and the tarn is exposed on all sides except the north, so thermal stratification has never been recorded.

Phytoplankton production is low but the species are those usually associated with eutrophic conditions, *Asterionella*, *Cryptomonas*, *Anabaena* and *Dinobryon* being the dominant genera. Malham Tarn is one of the few known British localities for *Cladophora sauteri* which forms unattached balls on the bottom of the lake. (This species is also recorded from Loch Watten and Loch Harray.) The macrophytic production is very high, in contrast to that of the phytoplankton, there being almost a complete cover of submerged plants. The distribution and abundance of the macrophytes varies considerably from year to year but *Chara delicatula* and *Potamogeton lucens* are the dominant

species over most of the tarn with occasional beds of *P. berchtoldii* and *P. perfoliatus*. *Chara aspera* and *Fontinalis antipyretica* are dominant in the shallower water, and *Chara* can even be seen growing on the peat bank of the western shore. The zooplankton is productive but with few species, *Diaptomus gracilis*, *Daphnia hyalina* var. *lacustris* and *Bosmina longirostris* being dominant. The invertebrate benthic fauna contains many species typical of a base-rich weedy lake including 14 species of gastropod and 10 lamellibranchs. Both *Gammarus lacustris* and *G. pulex* occur, but with the exception of *Caenis horaria* there are few Ephemeroptera. On the stony shores *Ancylus fluviatilis*, *Micronecta poweri*, *Polycentropus* spp., *Ecdyonurus* sp. and *Astacus pallipes* (here towards the northern end of its range in Britain) are the most abundant species. The peat shore-line supports very little fauna. This is the only UK locality for the unusual caddis *Agrypnetes crassicornis* which is otherwise only known from Scandinavia, eastern Europe and Asia. Perch, bullheads, stoneloach, minnows, three-spined sticklebacks and trout all occur, the last showing remarkably good growth.

The Field Studies Council have a centre on the banks of the tarn which is consequently the best studied marl lake in Britain. The raised bog and fen associated with the tarn are outstanding mire sites (P.52, gr. 1) and this most unusual association of acidic peat bog and highly calcareous lake promotes a great variety of plants and animals.

Of the three streams in the upland area of Malham–Arncliffe the outflow of the tarn is the slowest-flowing stream of the series. It flows out of the tarn via a sluice and disappears underground about 1 km south, the exact point of the water sink being variable and dependent upon the level of the tarn. Four metres at its widest, the stream is mostly shallow with a stone and gravel bottom, but in its upper reaches there are silted pools up to 40 cm deep. Chemically the water is much less calcareous than the other streams (alkalinity = 70–80 p.p.m. $CaCO_3$), and the dissolved nitrogen levels are also much lower than the other streams ($NO_3 + NO_2 = 0.02$ p.p.m.), possibly because of uptake within the tarn by plants. The tarn has a regulating effect on the stream flow so that spating does not occur and consequently many stones are covered with filamentous algae and silt, and this is the only stream of the series with appreciable amounts of aquatic vegetation. In the faster sections, *Fontinalis antipyretica* is the only macrophyte but the slower sections have beds of *Groenlandia densa*, *Potamogeton berchtoldii* and *Rorippa nasturtium-aquaticum*. At the margins areas of *P. polygonifolius* occur, which is most unusual for such an alkaline stream. The invertebrate fauna is more characteristic of silted and weedy conditions than is that of the other streams. More molluscs are recorded including *Sphaerium corneum*, *Potamopyrgus jenkinsi* and *Bithynia tentaculata* and this is the only stream in which *Erpobdella octoculata*, *Sialis lutaria* and the mayfly *Procloeon pseudorufulum* have been recorded. Some groups, such as Ecdyonuridae and Glossosomatidae, found in the other streams and typical of faster currents, are absent. The cold water flatworm *Crenobia alpina* is also absent.

The Gordale Beck rises as a large spring pool within the soligenous Great Close Mire and another tributary rises above Malham Tarn at 442 m. It then flows through upland grassland before plunging about 60 m over Gordale Scar in a spectacular series of waterfalls passing through natural rock arches. Except for the waterfall section, the flow is moderate to fast throughout and the bottom consists mainly of stones and gravel. The waterfall section is of bedrock, and for a short distance downstream the bed is littered with large boulders. It is a slightly larger stream than the outflow of Malham Tarn with a maximum width of up to 8 m and it is shallow with a maximum depth of about 40 cm. This is a richer stream than the Malham outflow (alkalinity = 130–210 p.p.m. CaCO₃) but the nitrate levels are reasonably low (0.34–0.54 p.p.m.) so that there is little indication of enrichment from the surrounding grassland. This stream does not appear to experience wide ranges in water level and the stones are covered with globular marl-impregnated colonies of the algae *Rivularia* and *Phormidium*. In the lower stretches the stones are covered with bryophytes such as *Cinclodotus fontinaloides* intermixed with filamentous algae, and a small amount of *Chara* sp. is found growing on gravel. The fauna of this stream is intermediate in character between that of the Malham stream and the Cowside Beck containing animals of silted conditions such as *Bithynia tentaculata* and *Caenis horaria* and species associated with faster currents such as *Agapetus fuscipes*, *Dinocras cephalotes* and *Heptagenia lateralis*. *Gammarus pulex* is at its most abundant in this stream and *Crenobia alpina* and *Polycelis felina* are found in the upper sections and in springs lower down. Upland species are represented by *Philopotamus montanus* and *Simulium monticola*. This is an intermediate type of limestone stream with one of the finest limestone waterfalls in Britain.

The Cowside Beck is the fastest flowing of the three streams and spates heavily, the water level rising by at least 1.5 m. The upper stretches and the tributaries, the Darnwood Beck and Tennant Gill, are dry for most of the year and flow only in the winter and in summer floods. The substrate in the upper sections, where the current is rapid to fast, consists of boulders and stones, with boulders carried down by floods littering the dry watercourses and the banks of the main stream. Lower down the stream enters a steep-sided limestone valley (almost a gorge) about 150 m deep. Here, as well as fast shallow stretches up to 10 m across, there are sluggish pools 1.5 m deep containing large trout. The bottom still consists largely of boulders and stones with a little gravel and in the pools a fine covering of silt. Below the gorge, before entering the River Skirfare, the stream consists of one long fast-to-rapid stony run. In the lower sections the stones are covered with marl encrustations and *Rivularia*, but in the upper parts the stones are clean and macrophytic vegetation is restricted to a few scattered patches of bryophytes. Chemically this stream is very similar to the Gordale Beck, but the nitrate levels are a little higher. The fauna is characteristic of faster conditions than that of the other streams, the only gastropods being *Ancylus fluviatilis* and *Lymnaea pereger*, which are restricted to the lower stretches. *Ecdyonurus venosus*, *Rhithrogena semicolorata*, *Perla bipunctata* and *Glossosoma conformis* only occur in the Cowside Beck and *Simulium monticola* and *S. variegatum* are more abundant than in the other streams. The Cowside Beck is a good example of a torrential upland limestone stream, comparable to parts of the Knock Ore Gill on the Moor House NNR, which is, however, peat-stained in contrast to the clear-watered Malham streams.

OW.48. ESTHWAITE WATER, LANCASHIRE

SD 3696, 3797. 195 ha   Grade 1*

This, the richest of the Lake District lakes (alkalinity = 15–22 p.p.m. CaCO₃), is a mesotrophic lake of mean depth 6.8 m in which thermal stratification and deoxygenation of the hypolimnion take place during the summer and also under ice cover in winter. The lake is gradually becoming more eutrophic because of increasing amounts of inorganic fertilisers entering from farmland in the catchment and sewage effluent from the village of Hawkshead. The shore substrate is mainly gravel with a fen at the north end which is a NNR. The aquatic transition communities here are well developed and show a succession from floating macrophytes through reed-swamp with *Phragmites communis*, *Typha latifolia* and *Schoenoplectus lacustris*; sedge-swamp dominated by *Carex elata* with *C. vesicaria*, *C. rostrata* and *C. paniculata*; grading into a carr community with a varied ground flora. Moderately acidophilous communities typical of flushed oligotrophic conditions and dominated by *Molinia caerulea* and *Myrica gale* are well developed. The hydroseral communities have been mapped on a number of occasions since 1914 so that the general trends in succession are known. The intrinsic scientific interest of this very small area (only 1.6 ha) is high but it is convenient to treat this as a bonus within the open water site.

The phytoplankton is dominated by diatoms, blue-green algae, and the flagellate *Ceratium*. *Diaptomus gracilis*, *Bosmina longirostris*, *B. coregoni* and *Daphnia hyalina* are the predominant species in the zooplankton. *B. longirostris* first appeared in lake sediments laid down 1000 years ago in Esthwaite together with other characteristic species of eutrophic conditions including *Ceriodaphnia pulchella*, *C. quadrangula* and *Chironomus* spp. Although seven species of gastropod are recorded from the lake, none of these are indicative of base-rich conditions. However, the tubificid *Potamothrix hammoniensis*, the two leeches *Glossiphonia heteroclita*, *Hemiclepsis marginata*, and the crustacean *Asellus aquaticus* which are typical of eutrophic conditions are already present. Extensive unpublished work on the invertebrates particularly the chironomids has been carried out by J. H. Mundie. Esthwaite is one of the few localities for *Najas flexilis*. Trout are now rare in the lake and have been replaced recently by roach and rudd. Perch, pike, eels and stone loach are also present, the last being unusual in the Lake District. Feral greylag and Canada geese nest but it is not otherwise an important wildfowl resort. Priest's Pot, a small pond at the north end of the fen, is interesting as it is a eutrophic pond enriched by farm drainage, with an alkalinity of about 30 p.p.m. $CaCO_3$. Work on the phytoplankton of this pond is being carried out from the Freshwater Biological Association (FBA).

A number of interesting artificial tarns on Claife Heights lie within the catchment of Esthwaite Water. Hodson's Tarn, Wise Een, Three Dubs Tarn and Scale Tarn have been studied extensively by the FBA and some have been manipulated experimentally to observe the effects of the fish stock on the food organisms of the fish.

Esthwaite Water, Priest's Pot, part of the Blackbeck and the tarns and becks on Claife Heights are regarded as one grade 1 key open water site. Not only are the water-bodies interesting in their own right but the amount of information that is now available on them makes them of exceptional value. The fen famous for W. H. Pearsall's pioneering work also lies within this area.

OW.49. HORNSEA MERE, YORKSHIRE
TA 1847. 230 ha   Grade 1

This is a large shallow eutrophic lake (maximum depth 3.4 m) formed as a kettle-hole in rich agricultural land. Most of the mere is surrounded by reed-beds (*Phragmites*) growing on sand and in one section along the southern shore there is a floristically rich fen community with *Pedicularis palustris*, *Carex flacca*, *C. panicea*, *Cirsium palustre*, *Cardamine pratensis*, *Iris pseudacorus*, *Myosotis scorpioides*, *Climacium dendroides* and *Acrocladium cuspidatum*. At the western end there are extensive hydroseral communities which are rapidly invading the open water, *Carex acutiformis*, *C. riparia*, *Typha angustifolia* and *Phragmites communis* being the main constituents. The mere is highly eutrophic with very high phosphate concentrations (0.75 p.p.m.), and dense algal crops occur. In some years extensive growths of *Cladophora* cover the bottom, but so far macrophytes appear to be competing well with algae. Extensive growths of *Elodea canadensis* and smaller quantities of *Potamogeton pusillus*, *P. pectinatus* and *Ceratophyllum demersum* are present in the open water.

The invertebrate fauna is rich in flatworms, leeches, snails and crustacea, but with the exception of Corixidae and Trichoptera the insects are very poorly represented and in spite of extensive collections along the shoreline and among the reed-beds, no Ephemeroptera have been taken. This sparsity of insect species may be an indication of the beginning of changes in the fauna similar to those which have taken place at Loch Leven (OW.67).

The main biological interest of the mire is its bird populations (most of the site is a reserve of the Royal Society for the Protection of Birds) which includes wintering flocks of 3000 mallard (1% of UK population), 1450 pochard (3½% of UK population), 870 teal, 500 tufted duck, 285 goldeneye, 1000 wigeon and smaller numbers of shoveler, gadwall, goosander and mute swan. Coot and mallard are the most abundant breeding species which also include shoveler, gadwall, pochard, tufted duck and a large population of reed warblers near the north-eastern limits of their range in Britain.

The lake is subject to some disturbance from angling and sailing, and on limnological grounds alone is not of national importance since it has suffered some modification as a result of eutrophication. In view of its overall interest including its national importance for wildfowl, however, it is given grade 1 status.

OW.50. INGLEBOROUGH CAVE SYSTEMS, YORKSHIRE
SD 7673   Grade 1

The Ingleborough Carboniferous Limestone massif grade 1 upland site (U.23) contains many pot-holes and caves. None of these has been examined during the review, but judging from faunal records collected by the Caves Research Group they are distinct from the other English cave systems. The cave-dwelling malacostracans found in the Ogof Ffynnon Ddu system and the Cheddar caves are absent, but the primitive syncarid crustacean *Bathynella natans* has been recorded from the White Scar Cave and Great Douk Cave. No other aquatic invertebrates which are restricted to subterranean habitats have been found, but a number of species such as *Canthocamptus praegeri*, *Cyclops fimbriatus*, *C. viridis* and *Crenobia alpina*, which are characteristic of caves but also found above ground, have been recorded. In addition several typical stream invertebrates such as *Gammarus pulex*, oligochaetes, stonefly and caddis larvae and the beetle *Agabus guttatus* have penetrated into the caves.

See also W.142.

OW.51. SEMER WATER, YORKSHIRE
SD 9187. 80 ha   Grade 1

This upland Pennine lake lies in a glaciated limestone valley and is retained by a terminal moraine through which the outflow now passes in a steep-sided channel. It is fed by fast-flowing precipitous streams and is subject to large fluctuations in water level following flash floods. The maximum depth is about 10 m at times of normal water level. The shoreline is mainly of stones and gravel with a large area of gravel exposed at the head of the lake left following the lowering of the water level by 55 cm in 1937. A small fen of *Phragmites* sp. and *Carex* spp. is formed on this gravel, but other emergent and submerged vegetation is apparently sparse.

It is a moderately eutrophic lake (alkalinity = 60–70 p.p.m. $CaCO_3$) with relatively high nutrient levels for an upland site and has a phytoplankton dominated by *Asterionella*, *Ceratium* and *Pediastrum* characteristic of rich waters. The outstanding feature of the benthos is the large number of mayfly species present including several stream species, such as *Baetis rhodani*, *B. scambus/bioculatus*, *Procloeon pseudorufulum*, *Paraleptophlebia cincta* and *Habrophlebia fusca* which have not been recorded from other lakes in Britain. *Astacus pallipes*, here at its northern extreme in Britain, and *Gammarus pulex* are also recorded. There is some indication that this lake was once more eutrophic than at present, since several gastropod species which are now absent, and which are typical of rich weedy conditions, have been recorded from Quaternary deposits taken from the lake bed. Brown trout, rudd, bream, perch, bullhead, three-spined sticklebacks and minnows occur. The ornithological interest is probably decreased by water skiing, and this activity is in general incompatible with the maintenance of its conservation value.

OW.52. BLELHAM TARN, LANCASHIRE
NY 3600.   50 ha   Grade 1

This tarn of mean depth of 6.75 m and maximum depth 13.5 m is surrounded mainly by grazing land and has been receiving increasing amounts of artificial fertilisers since the 1950s. On its north side it is fringed by the NNR of Blelham Bog which is not now ranked highly as a peatland but can be included within the site for its bonus interest. Along this northern shore the substrate is of peat, but elsewhere, except near the inflow and outflow where bare stones are exposed, the shores consist of stones covered by a thick deposit of organic mud on which grows a marginal belt of *Phragmites*. Chemically the tarn was formerly oligotrophic but because of drainage from agricultural land and from a small domestic sewage plant it has become enriched and is now mesotrophic. Maximum dissolved phosphorus concentrations now reach 0.01 p.p.m. and nitrogen levels are 1.2 p.p.m. NO_3. The retention time for water in the tarn is about six weeks and it regularly stratifies in summer, the hypolimnion becoming nearly completely deoxygenated.

There is relatively little submerged vegetation since the margins slope steeply, *Potamogeton alpinus* being the only species recorded, but there is a marginal band of *Nuphar lutea* in places. The phytoplankton was formerly similar to that of the oligotrophic north basin of Windermere in which diatoms such as *Asterionella formosa*, *Cyclotella glomerata* and *Fragillaria crotonensis* predominate. Since eutrophication set in, the algal crops have steadily increased with large spring diatom peaks, and species such as *Aphanizomenon flos-aquae*, *Melosira italica* and Chlorococcales, which are typical of more eutrophic conditions, have partly replaced the former flora. The zooplankter *Holopedium gibberum*, which is characteristic of extremely oligotrophic lakes, has similarly disappeared since sewage effluent started to enter the tarn. Little has been published on the invertebrates but what information there is would suggest that it has a fauna typical of a mesotrophic lake.

The research effort on the lake by the FBA has been extensive and of long duration, and it is one of the most important sites in the world for the study of lake enrichment. Weekly analyses of the phytoplankton crop, and concentrations of the three major algal nutrients, nitrogen, phosphorus and silicon, have been carried out for 27 years, and detailed temperature and oxygen concentration measurements have also been taken over an extended period of years. Thus the history of eutrophication is better documented here than in any lake in Britain. The tarn has also been the site of major limnological experiments involving artificial manipulation of parts of the lake.

Although far from intact, and to some extent artificially manipulated, this site is of grade 1 status purely as a research site. Without the research effort put into it, and the eutrophication taking place there, it would be of little value

as it is a small base-poor lake, and these lakes are widely represented as bonus interest on existing upland reserves. The tarn and part of the catchment is owned by the National Trust.

OW.53. HAWES WATER, SILVERDALE, LANCASHIRE
SD 4776.   6 ha   Grade 1

This lake, of maximum depth 12.2 m, has existed since Late-glacial times and lies upon deep lacustrine shell marl deposits up to 7.5 m in depth which are covered in places by peat. From the extent of these deposits it is obvious that Hawes Water is now only a remnant of a much larger water-body. The Post-glacial deposits overlie Carboniferous Limestone which supports mixed deciduous woodland on the surrounding hillsides. A mixed reed-swamp surrounds the lake with *Phragmites* dominant grading into willow/alder carr or into rich sedge fen with local species such as *Carex pseudocyperus*, *C. vesicaria*, *Schoenus nigricans*, *Juncus subnodulosus*, *Cladium mariscus* and *Epipactis palustris*. On one side there is a sloping edge with calcareous soligenous mire containing other *Carex* spp. The water is highly calcareous (alkalinity = 190 p.p.m. $CaCO_3$), but low in other nutrients and thermal stratification occurs in summer, the thermocline forming at about 5 m. *Oscillatoria* agg., *Asterionella*, *Peridinium* and *Ceratium* have been recorded in the phytoplankton. The extent of submerged aquatic macrophytes is unknown, but *Potamogeton lucens*, *P. friesii*, *P. obtusifolius*, *Chara aculeolata*, *Utricularia vulgaris* and *Lemna trisulca* occur, and a peripheral band of floating attached vegetation comprises *Nymphaea alba*, *Nuphar lutea* and *P. natans*. The benthic fauna is rich in species indicative of eutrophic conditions, including seven species of gastropod, *Asellus meridianus* and *Glossiphonia heteroclita*. Among the eight species of Ephemeroptera recorded from this locality is *Caenis robusta* which has previously only been found in the south of England. Perch, rudd and pike are present, the perch having an exceptionally high growth rate.

Hawes Water has great research potential both for limnological work and Quaternary studies as it is close to several research centres. It forms part of the limestone complex of open water, fen, meadow, pavement (Gait Barrows) and woodland which forms a composite grade 1 site.

See also W.140 and L.134.

OW.54. SUNBIGGIN TARN, WESTMORLAND
NY 6707.   6 ha   Grade 1

Sunbiggin is a small upland marl lake lying on the Carboniferous Limestone. Although the maximum depth is *c*. 9 m, the slope is gradual down to a depth of 1 m, and about half of the tarn is less than this depth. The bottom of the shallow eastern half is sandy and is covered with a growth of *Chara*, whereas, in the deeper water, flowering plants predominate, *Potamogeton crispus* being by far the most abundant species. Three-quarters of the shore is bounded by reed-swamp and fen, which extends to the smaller Cow Dub Tarn, 200 m south of Sunbiggin. The rich-fen is important botanically and is independently rated as a grade 1 peatland site (P.53).

The zooplankton is very dense, *Daphnia hyalina* var. *lacustris* accounting for over 80% of the individuals and *Diaptomus gracilis* and *Cyclops strenuus* making up the remainder. The macrobenthos is rich and fairly diverse and includes six species of gastropod, five species of leech (including *Glossiphonia heteroclita* and *Erpobdella testacea*), abundant *Gammarus pulex*, the mayflies *Cloeon simile* and *Caenis horaria* and corixids typical of base-rich and moorland habitats. Surprisingly, no caddis larvae have been taken.

On the fen between Cow Dub and Sunbiggin Tarns there is a large black-headed gull colony which has enriched parts of the fen and the small Cow Dub Tarn which is surrounded by fen and is quite shallow. Its bottom consists of mud and organic matter on top of sand, and no submerged or floating macrophytes are present. The soluble phosphate level was nine times that recorded in Sunbiggin Tarn, and ammonia and soluble nitrate levels were also higher, presumably due to the enrichment from gull droppings. The macrobenthos is expectedly poorer than that of the main tarn, only one species of snail, *Planorbis crista*, no Ephemeroptera and only one species of caddis larva, *Holocentropus picicornis*, being found. The ectoproct *Cristatella* was plentiful in the small tarn, possibly because of increased suspended matter in the water.

Sunbiggin and Cow Dub Tarns, together with the surrounding rich-fen, form an outstanding wetland area of biological interest which merits grade 1 status. These places are part of the larger limestone complex, Orton Fells, which is rated as a grade 1 upland site (U.25) and includes meadow grassland, limestone pavement and calcareous soligenous mire.

See also L.139 and L.140.

OW.55. KNOCK ORE GILL, WESTMORLAND
NY 716312–695300   Grade 1

A number of precipitous streams flow westwards down the limestone scarp of the Pennines into the River Eden. The largest of these, lying completely within the Moor House NNR, is the Knock Ore Gill, which is probably representative. It rises at 750 m as a precipitous boulder- and stone-strewn stream about 1 m wide, running down a 40° slope. The stones are covered with a dense growth of bryophytes typical of these situations. Chemically, the stream is moderately base-rich (alkalinity = 70–80 p.p.m. $CaCO_3$) and the soluble nitrogen ($NO_3 + NO_2$ = 0.48–0.55 p.p.m.) and particulate phosphorus (total phosphorus = 0.07–0.10 p.p.m.) are extremely high for such an upland situation. The fauna is abundant, consisting primarily of montane species such as *Crenobia alpina*, *Simulium monticola*, *Protonemura montana*, and *Diura bicaudata*. Chironomids and *Protonemura* are the most abundant, and *Gammarus pulex*, *Dicranota* and Empidae are also present.

Downstream the channel widens and becomes less precipitous so that at the lower end of the Reserve it is 3 m wide with alternating rapid torrents and moderately flowing pools up to 1 m deep. Here it runs in a steep-sided limestone

valley and resembles the Cowside Beck, Malham. Bryophytes are still the only aquatic plants, covering about 40% of the bottom which consists of boulders, stones and gravel in roughly equal proportions. There is little difference chemically between the water here and at the source, except that there is possibly a slight rise in phosphorus concentration, and the water is very slightly peat-stained. The fauna is more diverse, but some of the montane genera such as *Crenobia* and *Protonemura* persist. *Simulium monticola* is replaced by *S. dunfellense* and there is a wider range of Ephemeroptera and Trichoptera typical of small stony streams. The beetles *Helmis maugei*, *Esolus parallelopipedus*, *Latelmis volkmari*, *Hydraena* sp. and *Oreodytes rivalis* and molluscs such as *Pisidium* spp., *Potamopyrgus jenkinsi* and *Ancylus fluviatilis* are found.

This is one of the highest and most precipitous of limestone streams in Britain, and as such complements the lower-lying streams at Malham (OW.47).

See also P.50 and U.20.

OW.56. WASTWATER, CUMBERLAND
NY 1605.   290 ha   Grade 1

In many respects this is the least productive of the English Lake District lakes. With the exception of Thirlmere, which is now a reservoir, it is the only one of the larger lakes which lies wholly on the very insoluble Borrowdale Volcanic rocks, and the catchment, consisting largely of rugged upland grassland and rock, has the lowest percentage of cultivated land for any of the Lake District lakes. It is the deepest of the lakes with a maximum depth of 78.6 m and a mean depth of 41.0 m and has the clearest water which is extremely poor in dissolved minerals. Most of the shoreline is of stones and boulders, with the extensive talus shoots of the Wasdale Screes (U.18, gr. 1) flanking the south-east shore.

The phytoplankton is dominated by small Chlorophyceae such as *Chlorella*, *Ankistrodesmus*, *Raphidonema* and *Oocystis*, and by Chrysophyceae. Desmids, although prominent in the net phytoplankton, do not constitute a large proportion of the total biomass. Blue-green algae are mostly absent and *Cyclotella comensis* is the characteristic diatom. Submerged macrophytic communities typical of oligotrophic lakes, with species such as *Juncus bulbosus*, *Isoetes lacustris* and *Nitella* spp., occur. The zooplankton is also fairly typical of the oligotrophic condition, but *Holopedium gibberum* is absent, and this is one of the two Lake District lakes in which *Daphnia hyalina* has not been found.

Wastwater has the sparsest littoral fauna of any of the lakes, both numerically and in terms of diversity. The only gastropods recorded are *Lymnaea* (*Radix*) *peregra* and *Ancylus fluviatilis*; *Erpobdella octoculata* is the only leech and *Polycelis nigra* the only triclad, the remaining littoral fauna consisting of a few species of caddis, mayfly and stonefly. Deeper-water communities consist of chironomids, oligochaetes and *Pisidium*. The only fish species present are brown trout, charr, eels and a few salmon which pass through the lake to their spawning streams.

The only other Lake District lake which approaches such

oligotrophic conditions as Wastwater is Ennerdale, but this site is now less intact than Wastwater. A small quantity of water (18 million litres per day) is taken from Wastwater but this does not involve regulation of the water level and thus has little effect on the lake. Buttermere is the next most oligotrophic lake in the series, but is much shallower, smaller, is richer chemically and has a more varied fauna. As it does not show the extreme oligotrophy of Wastwater it cannot be considered an alternative, but is grade 2 in its own right.

OW.62. RIVER TWEED (PART), NORTHUMBERLAND
Grade 1

See under South Scotland, p. 191.

OW.57. TARN DUB, YORKSHIRE
NY 8528. 1 ha   Grade 2

Tarn Dub is a small upland eutrophic pool lying on a moraine at the foot of the Whin Sill scar of Cronkley Fell on the Upper Teesdale NNR (U.21). The water level in the tarn varies seasonally, and in dry summers it practically dries out. This impermanence has a profound effect on the composition of the flora and fauna. *Littorella uniflora* covers the bottom in shallower areas and is exposed in summer, while the deeper more permanent parts of the tarn have abundant *Chara* sp., *Fontinalis antipyretica*, *Glyceria fluitans*, *Ranunculus aquatilis* and *Oenanthe fistulosa*.

The invertebrate fauna is characterised by gastropods such as *Lymnaea glabra*, *L. truncatulata*, *Planorbis spirorbis*, the leech *Dina lineata*, the beetle *Agabus labiatus* and the stonefly *Nemoura cinerea* which are adapted to surviving periods of desiccation, but certain groups such as mayflies, triclads and Malacostraca are absent. Invertebrate species characteristic of both upland and lowland situations occur, the former including *Callicorixa wollastoni* and *Agabus arcticus* while lowland species include *Corixa punctata*, *Callicorixa praeusta*, *Hesperocorixa sahlbergi* and the dragon-fly *Aeshna grandis*. There are no fish, but common newts and frogs breed abundantly. The tarn has been the site of research into the mechanisms of adaptation by freshwater invertebrates to life in impermanent waters and is the best example of an upland impermanent pool known in Britain.

OW.58. BLEA WATER, WESTMORLAND
NY 4410. 110 ha   Grade 2

This small extremely oligotrophic corrie lake at an altitude of 490 m is surrounded on the north, west and south sides by steep crags going up to 830 m. For its area, it is exceptionally deep (maximum depth 68 m) and the water is very clear. The boulder and stone shorelines shelve steeply and, down to a depth of 30 m, the maximum depth to which it has been examined, the bottom consists of a silvery sand interspersed with rock.

A narrow band of *Callitriche hermaphroditica* surrounds the tarn, and *Littorella uniflora* is present. The zooplankton includes *Holopedium gibberum*, which is characteristic of very pure waters, and *Alonopsis elongata* which is often found in high-altitude lakes in Britain. Except that it is very sparse, little is known about the invertebrate fauna.

The tarn is used as a header reservoir for the Haweswater reservoir and a small dam is present at the outflow, but is not thought to affect the tarn seriously since drawdown does not take place. Blea Water is a corrie lake intermediate in character between the Arctic–alpine lakes of the Cairngorms and lower altitude richer corries such as Llyn Idwal.

OW.59. BUTTERMERE, CUMBERLAND
NY 1815. 95 ha   Grade 2

This is the third most unproductive of the Lake District lakes, although chemically it is very similar to Wastwater, the poorest. Like Wastwater most of its catchment is of Borrowdale Volcanic rocks, but Buttermere itself lies on Skiddaw Slate. It is a smaller, shallower lake than Wastwater with a mean depth of only 16.6 m and occupies the same glacial trough as Crummock Water from which it is separated by a fluvio-glacial outwash fan, 1 km wide. More research work has been carried out on it than on Wastwater and it is potentially of greater value for experimental work on similar lines to that previously and currently carried out on Blelham Tarn.

In terms of its phytoplanktonic and macrophytic flora it is very similar to Wastwater. Its zooplankton differs in that *Daphnia hyalina* is present, but *Holopedium gibberum* is absent, as in Wastwater. The littoral benthic invertebrate fauna is richer both numerically and in variety. Two additional species of triclad, *Polycelis tenuis* and *Planaria torva*, three additional leech species, including *Glossiphonia heteroclita*, and one additional gastropod, *Planorbis contortus*, have been recorded, and *Gammarus pulex* is present in small numbers. The fish fauna includes perch, pike and three-spined stickleback in addition to those species recorded from Wastwater.

Buttermere is one of the most intact of the Lake District lakes with very few people living in its catchment and only a negligible amount of water abstraction. It is bounded on its northern side by the grade 2 upland site, Buttermere Fells (U.27).

SOUTH SCOTLAND

OW.60. LOCH LOMOND, DUNBARTONSHIRE/
STIRLINGSHIRE
NS 3598. 7100 ha   Grade 1*

This loch has the largest surface area of any freshwater lake in mainland Britain. The northern end is oligotrophic in character (8 p.p.m. of calcium) and the southern end meso-trophic, owing to the difference in the catchments of these two areas. That of the northern end is essentially Highland in character, with steep hills forming the sides of the glaciated valley in which it is situated, and the streams and rivers feeding this section are nutrient-poor. This end is much deeper (maximum depth = 198 m) than the southern end (maximum depth = 23 m) which widens out south of the Highland Boundary Fault and has a more irregular shoreline and many islands. The major tributary entering the southern section is the River Endrick, which for the lower part of its course runs through agricultural land and is moderately eutrophic. Throughout the loch, depending on the degree of exposure to wave action, the shoreline varies from gravel to boulders. Thermal stratification is set up every summer in the northern end, but does not occur every year in the southern end.

Macrophyte communities typical of oligotrophic lakes occur with *Nitella opaca* growing down to about 4 m depth. *Rumex aquaticus* occurs here in its only British locality and the rare *Elatine hydropiper* is found on exposed sandy beaches. The zooplankton is dominated by *Daphnia hyalina* with some *Cyclops strenuus*, *C. leuckarti*, *Leptodora kindti* and *Bythotrephes longimanus*. The major components of the shoreline benthos are *Gammarus pulex*, and *Ancylus fluviatilis* with some stoneflies. In the weeded areas the gastropods *Physa fontinalis*, *Lymnaea pereger* and *Valvata piscinalis* are plentiful, with the mayflies *Leptophlebia vespertina* and *L. marginata* in the shallower areas and *Asellus aquaticus* and *Cyrnus flavidus* in the deeper zones. *Ephemera danica*, which is limited in distribution in Scotland, is characteristic of the sandy areas inshore of the weedbeds. The deeper-water fauna is dominated by tubificids, *Pisidium* spp., including *P. conventus*, a glacial relict, and chironomid larvae, mainly *Chironomus sergentia* and *Tanytarsus* spp. The naidid worm *Arcteonais lomondi* was named from this loch and has been found elsewhere in Britain only in Loch Morar. There are 16 species of fish, an unusually high number for a Scottish loch, including powan *Coregonus lavaretus* which is of very limited distribution in Britain. As well as this species, salmon, sea trout and brown trout are widespread throughout the loch, and roach and perch live in the southern end. For the size of the loch the populations of aquatic breeding birds are rather small. The Endrick mouth area is, however, an important winter haunt of wildfowl, notably greylag geese, mallard, teal, wigeon, shoveler, tufted duck and goldeneye and small numbers of Greenland white-fronted geese, pochard, mute and whooper swans also occur regularly. The River Endrick itself is a grade 2 open water site (OW.66).

Biological research has been carried out from the field station of the University of Glasgow since 1946 which enhances the conservation value of the loch. This work is continuing and the Clyde River Purification Board now has a research boat on the loch. Part of the loch is a NNR and the whole is given grade 1* status for its unusual trophic diversity and research value. The islands of the loch also have the same status for their woodland interest (W.169).

See also P.73.

OW.61. MILL LOCH, LOCHMABEN, DUMFRIES-SHIRE
NY 0783.   12 ha   Grade 1

The Mill Loch is the deepest of a group of kettle-holes in the vicinity of Lochmaben, lying in an area of undulating permanent pasture. The larger Castle Loch nearby is a Local Nature Reserve with some wildfowl interest but more subject to disturbance and pollution than the Mill Loch. The banks shelve steeply on the south and west

shores down to the maximum depth of 16.8 m, but the northern end of the loch where two small inflow ditches are situated is relatively shallow and there is an extensive *Phragmites* bed with *Menyanthes trifoliata*, *Polygonum amphibium*, *Nymphaea alba* and *Eleocharis palustris*. Elsewhere the shoreline is bare and stony. *Potamogeton obtusifolius* covers most of the sublittoral region down to a depth of about 2 m and in the deeper water a fine organic mud covers the bottom. The loch is eutrophic (alkalinity = 50–60 p.p.m. $CaCO_3$) and the nitrogen levels are high (0.50 p.p.m. NO_3), probably owing to enrichment from artificial fertilisers. A bloom of the blue-green alga *Microcystis* sp. was present when the loch was visited in October 1968.

The zooplankton is dominated by *Diaptomus gracilis* and *Ceriodaphnia pulchella*, the latter being indicative of rich conditions and rare in the north of the British Isles. The benthic fauna is typical of moderately eutrophic conditions with nine species of gastropods and five species of leech recorded. The trichopteran *Cyrnus flavidus* and five species of Ephemeroptera, including *Caenis horaria* and *Cloeon simile*, are abundant in the littoral region and the corixid fauna is one typical of base-rich weedy conditions. The larvae of *Chaoborus flavicans* are dominant in the profundal fauna. The outstanding interest of this site in 1969 was the presence of the last remaining population of a distinct race of the vendace, *Coregonus albula*. This is now, however, thought to be extinct here, as in Castle Loch. Recent attempts have been made to establish this species in other lochs in south-west Scotland as at present it is rather vulnerable to continued eutrophication or accidental pollution. The loch also contains trout, perch and pike, and there is angling and a little water skiing. The outflow is controlled by a small dam, but this causes no deleterious effect as little drawdown is ever achieved. The loch is of interest not only because of its fish populations but also as an example of a moderately deep eutrophic lake, which is relatively rare in Britain. It most probably stratifies in the summer and the composition of the benthic community suggests that low oxygen tensions are reached in the hypolimnion.

OW.62. RIVER TWEED, BERWICKSHIRE/PEEBLES-
        SHIRE/SELKIRKSHIRE/ROXBURGHSHIRE/
        NORTHUMBERLAND
NT 053141–NU 005522   Grade 1

The Tweed system is eutrophic throughout its length. The upper stretches and tributaries drain Ordovician and Silurian greywackes and shales while the lower reaches and tributaries such as the Teviot drain somewhat richer Old Red Sandstone and Carboniferous rocks and are richer chemically. The Tweed itself shows a regular transition from a small upland stream to a large meandering silted lowland river, with more moderately flowing gravelly sections between. The upper sections have typically calcifuge plant species such as *Potamogeton polygonifolius*, *Carex rostrata* and *Potentilla palustris* in the slower sections, but in the areas of rapid current, macrophytes are restricted to sparse growths of bryophytes. A typical upland stream invertebrate fauna is present with abundant Ecdyonuridae, *Baetis rhodani*, helmid beetles, stoneflies and *Gammarus pulex* and characteristic *Simulium* spp. including *S. brevicaule*, *S. monticola* and *S. variegatum*, but leeches and gastropods are absent.

In the moderately flowing somewhat richer middle sections macrophytic vegetation is more abundant. Emergent vegetation is represented by a narrow fringe of *Phalaris arundinacea*, while submerged plants cover up to 20% of the bottom, bryophytes dominating in the faster stretches and *Potamogeton crispus*, *Myriophyllum alterniflorum*, *Ranunculus aquatilis* and *Elodea canadensis* in the more moderately flowing sections. The fauna of this section is more diverse than that of the upper stretches. Oligochaetes, leeches and molluscs increase in abundance, *Ancylus fluviatilis* being the characteristic mollusc which is joined by other species as one moves downstream. Stoneflies and mayflies are still plentiful, *Leuctra fusca* is the most abundant stonefly in summer, and *Ephemerella ignita* the most abundant mayfly. *Baetis bioculatus/scambus* joins *B. rhodani* as the most abundant baetid, while *Rhithrogena semicolorata* disappears. Caseless caddises of the families Hydropsychidae, Glossosomatidae and Rhyacophilidae achieve their maximum numbers in this stretch, the latter particularly associated with the bryophytes, while helmid beetles are numerous in the gravel. The characteristic *Simulium* species are *S. equinum*, *S. reptans* and *S. ornatum* which occur in enormous numbers among the vegetation.

From the confluence of the Teviot downstream the Tweed becomes a deeper, depositing, and more slowly flowing river, running through good grazing land in a broad valley. Macrophytic vegetation increases in variety but not in abundance, possibly being limited by light penetration. Species such as *Potamogeton pectinatus*, *P. lucens*, *Ranunculus circinatus* and *Myriophyllum spicatum* which are characteristic of eutrophic waters are among the species found. Several species of riverine invertebrate are absent from these lower reaches; the only stonefly species found are *Leuctra fusca* and *L. geniculata* and several mayflies, particularly Ecdyonuridae, are absent. The commonest of the mayflies is *Baetis bioculatus/scambus* which occurs together with *Caenis rivulorum* and *Procloeon pseudorufulum*. Snails and helmid beetles are very abundant, but many of the riverine caddis species are absent or present only in small numbers and the *Simulium* spp. are not as numerous as upstream. In the lowermost, tidal stretches, brackish water species such as *Gammarus duebeni*, *G. zaddachi* and *Potamopyrgus jenkinsi* appear.

Certain of the tributaries differ from the corresponding sections of the main river in their physical characteristics and flora and fauna. The upper reaches of the Teviot differ in being more alkaline (alkalinity = 110–120 p.p.m. $CaCO_3$), and in having a bed consisting of unstable flat slate shingle. Aquatic vegetation is absent but the invertebrate fauna is much more numerous and varied. Several stoneflies, *Rhithrogena semicolorata*, and a number of caddis species are all abundant, and leeches and the mollusc *Potamopyrgus jenkinsi* are present in small numbers. Species

such as the mayfly *Caenis rivulorum* and the stonefly *Amphinemura sulcicollis* are associated with the silted conditions of some of the pools, but *Simulium* spp. are absent even from the runs.

The lower reaches of the Teviot are extremely slow flowing with a mud and silt bottom, and are chemically rich. The river is bounded by a fringe of *Sparganium erectum* and the bottom covered with *Cladophora*. Species associated with silted conditions such as Tubificidae, Chironomidae, *Pisidium* spp. and the gastropods *Lymnaea peregra* and *Valvata piscinalis* abound, but stream species are absent.

The Yarrow Water which forms the outflow of St Mary's Loch enters the middle reaches of the Tweed. It is similar to the main river but is faster flowing and subject to a greater range in water level. Consequently it has a somewhat poorer fauna and submerged vegetation is very sparse; the stony bottom is however covered by a dense mat of the filamentous diatom *Gomphonema*.

OW.63. GLADHOUSE RESERVOIR, MIDLOTHIAN
NT 2953.   305 ha   Grade 1

This is a relatively shallow mesotrophic water supply reservoir of complex shape, with three islands, which lies at the foot of the Moorfoot Hills. It is fed directly by streams and has a drawdown of up to *c.* 3 m. There is very little marginal vegetation, except for swards of *Littorella uniflora* and some *Polygonum amphibium*.

It has been selected on account of its wildfowl interest. The autumn populations of geese in the Lothians, Peeblesshire and Berwickshire total *c.* 10000 pink-footed and 2600 greylag geese. Gladhouse holds both species including 7300 pink-footed ($9\frac{1}{2}$% of world population) and substantial numbers of ducks.

OW.64. WHITE LOCH, LOCHINCH, WIGTOWNSHIRE
NX 1060.   60 ha   Grade 2

This is a large shallow eutrophic loch formed in a kettle-hole in glacial gravels. It is moderately base-rich and nutrient levels are fairly high, causing blooms of blue-green algae including *Microcystis*. Marginal communities grading into fen are well developed along the eastern shore and submerged angiosperms cover the bottom down to at least 2 m. The rare *Elatine hexandra* is recorded from exposed shorelines, while in deeper water *Potamogeton lucens* is dominant, this being one of its few Scottish localities. A rich and diverse invertebrate fauna characteristic of eutrophic lakes is present.

This is the headquarters of the Solway greylag geese, holding about 4000 wintering birds (5% of north-west European population). About 2000 wigeon are also present as well as mallard, teal, shoveler, tufted duck and goldeneye.

OW.65. DUDDINGSTON LOCH, MIDLOTHIAN
NT 2872.   8 ha   Grade 2

This is a small eutrophic water-body which in recent years has developed intense algal blooms during the summer. Nutrient levels are relatively high, but their source is obscure. The loch is surrounded by extensive, species-poor,

Phragmites beds, but submerged vegetation is apparently absent. This site is selected for its wildfowl interest which includes pochard (4800 wintering birds; 2 % of north-west European population), tufted duck (460), mallard and shoveler.

OW.66. RIVER ENDRICK, DUNBARTONSHIRE/ STIRLINGSHIRE
NS 678915-425896   Grade 2

In the upper reaches of the River Endrick the substrate is mainly peat near the source, followed by bare rock and boulders further downstream. The river here is small and the gradient is steep (about 1 in 25). Much of the river at this point is above 300 m and the dissolved salt content of the water is poor (calcium being about 2 p.p.m.). Trout is the only species of fish and bryophytes are the only macrophytes, and the invertebrate fauna is poor in the total number of species present, though several are restricted to this stretch, e.g. *Ameletus inopinatus*, *Leuctra nigra* and *Plectrocnemia conspersa*. Other common invertebrate species in the upper reaches are *Ecdyonurus torrentis*, *Baetis pumilus*, *Protonemura meyeri*, *Chloroperla torrentium*, *Dinocras cephalotes* and *Hydraena gracilis*, but these also occur further downstream, in the middle reaches of the river, where the main substrate gradually changes from boulders to stones, and thereafter from stones to gravel. The river in these middle reaches is larger but the gradient becomes much less steep (about 1 in 100). Much of it flows at altitudes below 150 m, and the dissolved salt content of the water is moderate (calcium being about 8 p.p.m.). The dominant macrophyte here is *Fontinalis antipyretica* but *Myriophyllum alterniflorum* also occurs. Whilst the invertebrate fauna is rich in total number of species, only a few of these are restricted to this zone, e.g. *Chloroperla tripunctata*, *Tinodes waeneri* and *Simulium variegatum*. No fish are restricted to this part of the river, but salmon, trout, minnows, stone loach and three-spined sticklebacks occur both here and in the lower reaches, as do several invertebrates – *Helobdella stagnalis*, *Leuctra geniculata*, *L. moselyi*, *Simulium reptans* and *Orectochilus villosus*.

In the lower reaches the substrate of coarse gravel gives way to sand and eventually to fine silt near the mouth. Here the river is large and the gradient slight (about 1 in 3000) whilst the dissolved salt content is relatively high (calcium being about 15 p.p.m.), and the entire river flows at altitudes less than 20 m. The number of species, both of plants and animals, which occur here is high, and many of them are characteristic of standing waters, e.g. *Potamogeton natans*, *P. crispus*, *Nuphar lutea*, *Polycelis nigra*, *P. tenuis*, *Nymphula nymphaeata*, plus many species of Oligochaeta, Hirudinea, Hemiptera and Mollusca which do not occur further upstream. Pike, perch and roach are typical fish of this part of the river.

The total number of animal species occurring in the River Endrick is probably about 300. In the middle reaches, the invertebrate fauna of the dominant substrate (stones) has an average standing crop of some 16 g wet weight/m², whilst an equivalent figure for the dominant substrate of the lower reaches (sand) is about 8 g wet weight/m² (Maitland, 1966).

EAST SCOTLAND

OW.67. LOCH LEVEN, KINROSS
NO 1501.   1597 ha   Grade 1*

Loch Leven is the largest natural eutrophic lake in Britain, but is relatively shallow (mean depth 3.9 m, maximum depth 25 m). Its islands give it an additional bonus interest. It lies on the rich agricultural land of the plain of Kinross, composed of glacial drift overlying Old Red Sandstone, and is extremely exposed to wind action. Thermal stratification is therefore seldom set up, even in the two deep regions, and is then of short duration. The shoreline is sand or small stones, and extensive areas of sand cover about 40 % of the lake, down to about a water depth of 3 m, below which the sediment is mud. Since the 1950s increasing use of nitrate fertilisers on the surrounding farmland has contributed greatly to the artificial eutrophication of the lake, where concentrations of up to 1 p.p.m. NO_3 occur regularly. High phosphate levels are maintained by sewage from the townships of Kinross and Milnathort. Over the same period there have been striking changes in the flora and fauna of the loch, including the loss of a great number of species, and the abundance and composition of the animal and plant communities has varied irregularly from year to year.

At the beginning of the century there were extensive reed-beds along the north-east shore, but now only scattered beds of *Phragmites communis* and *Phalaris arundinacea* remain. Similarly there were dense beds of *Chara* sp. and *Elodea canadensis* and eight species of *Potamogeton* were recorded, but by 1966 these had virtually disappeared. Since then some submerged vegetation has increased, *P. pectinatus*, a new species for the loch, being dominant.

There have also been striking changes in the phytoplankton community. The loch formerly had clear water, but in the 1960s prolonged and dense algal blooms occurred, often with small species of blue-green algae (e.g. *Synechococcus*) and diatoms (e.g. *Cyclotella pseudostelligera* and *Stephanodiscus astraea* var. *minitula*) predominating. These dense algal crops followed the disappearance of *Daphnia hyalina* from the zooplankton, but this species returned in 1970 and in 1971 algal crops were much reduced and consisted mainly of large species (e.g. *Asterionella formosa*).

The benthic invertebrate fauna is now very impoverished, groups such as Ephemeroptera, Trichoptera, Odonata, Coleoptera and Gastropoda being absent or represented by very few species. In the shallow sandy zone oligochaetes (mainly Naididae), chironomids (particularly *Stictochironomus*), Nematoda, *Valvata piscinalis*, *Pisidium* and *Anodonta anatina* predominate, while in deeper water tubificids (mainly *Potamothrix hammoniensis*) and chironomids (particularly Chironominae including *Chironomus plumosus* and *C. anthracinus*) are the most abundant.

Brown trout, perch, pike, sticklebacks and brook lamprey occur, and recently one or two roach have been caught. The loch is renowned for its trout fishing, approximately 17000 kg of brown trout being caught by anglers annually, and is famous for its wildfowl. Loch Leven holds the largest population of breeding ducks of any site in Britain. In 1967 the numbers of nesting pairs were tufted duck 500–600, wigeon 35, mute swan 8–10, mallard 400–450, shoveler 10, gadwall 48 and shelduck 5. It is an important moulting refuge, particularly for tufted duck (1000 birds). Winter populations include a peak of 10000–12000 pink-footed and 4400 greylag geese, up to 4000 tufted, 1000 pochard, 225 whooper swan, 2700 mallard, 725 teal, 200 shoveler, 300 goldeneye and wigeon. The loch is one of the main autumn arrival points for pink-footed geese, very large numbers remaining only a short while before moving on to other resorts in central and south-east Scotland.

The loch has been the site of a main IBP project, investigating the three food chains to brown trout, perch and tufted ducks. As a result, it is becoming one of the best-known lakes in Britain in terms of biology, chemistry and hydrography.

OW.68. CAIRNGORM LOCHS, ABERDEENSHIRE/INVERNESS-SHIRE/ BANFFSHIRE Grade 1*

These are the highest standing waters in Britain and are of an Arctic–alpine character, having a continuous ice cover from December to May in most winters. The highest examples, with the exception of the small, very shallow, Lochan Buidhe, are all corrie lakes, while larger glacial lakes such as Loch Einich and Loch Avon occupy the lower glens. The underlying rock is granite and all these lochs are extremely oligotrophic. Their shorelines consist mainly of ice polished boulders; their flora and fauna are very impoverished, and no fish occur in those lying above 900 m. Specialised winter populations of both phytoplankton and zooplankton develop below the ice and the diatom outbreak is delayed until after ice melt.

Only Loch Etchachan and Loch Einich have been examined biologically during this survey and are reported on fully below. The other lochs have been assessed primarily upon their physical characteristics.

See also U.44.

(a) Loch Etchachan
NJ 0101.   23 ha

Loch Etchachan is the largest of the corrie lakes lying at an altitude of 930 m in a north facing corrie, bounded by steep granite crags on the south and west, beneath the summit of Ben Macdhui. The shoreline consists mainly of boulders, up to 6 m across, with smaller stones in less exposed parts and a little bedrock along the western flank. In the littoral zone the boulders and stone are free of encrusting algae and bryophytes owing to the action of ice scour and wave action due to the violent down-draughts of wind to which the lake is exposed on all sides. Although no soundings have been taken, the maximum depth, as judged by the aspect of the shoreline, is likely to be at least 20 m. The water is extremely poor in dissolved salts, the alkalinity being

0.7 p.p.m. $CaCO_3$ and the specific conductivity about 37 μmhos. The phytoplankton consists mainly of desmids, such as *Cosmarium*, *Euastrum*, *Penium* and *Tetnemorus*, typical of very poor waters.

No submerged angiosperms have been found but extensive growths of *Jungermannia* sp. are found on sheltered stones by the shore and in deeper water, and *Fontinalis antipyretica* occurs in the small gravelly pool at the outflow. The zooplankton is very sparse consisting only of a few individuals of the alpine species *Alonopsis elongata* together with *Bosmina coregoni*. The benthos contains several insects characteristic of high altitudes in Britain such as the mayfly *Ameletus inopinatus*, the caddis *Plectrocnemia conspersa* and the stonefly *Capnia atra*. The rest of the invertebrate fauna consists of insects typical of exposed stony shores and ubiquitous and successful species of Chironomidae and the beetle *Agabus bipustulatus*. A pair each of common gulls, dippers and common sandpipers breed by the loch, and brown trout have been introduced in the past but recent attempts to catch any have failed.

Loch Etchachan is an extreme example of an Arctic–alpine corrie lake, very similar to Loch Coire an Lochain.

(b) Loch Coire an Lochain
NH 9400.   6 ha

This corrie lake lies at an altitude of 995 m and is closely hemmed in on the south side by the cliffs of the 1300 m massif of Braeriach. Apart from its smaller size and higher altitude it is very similar to Loch Etchachan.

(c) Lochan Uaine, Ben Macdhui
NO 0098.   3 ha

This loch lies at an altitude of 956 m but unlike all the other main corrie lochs in the Cairngorms is open to the south-east and therefore has higher summer water temperatures and earlier ice melt. It is surrounded by crags, boulders and granite debris and has a stone and gravel shoreline.

(d) Loch Einich
NN 9199.   60 ha

Loch Einich is a large glacial trough lake lying at a much lower altitude (503 m) occupying a steep-sided valley. It is relatively deep (maximum depth = 47 m), extremely oligotrophic (alkalinity = 3 p.p.m. $CaCO_3$) and exposed to violent winds which have resulted in the formation of a large gravel storm beach at the northern end. The rest of the shoreline is mainly stones, gravel and boulders with a few sheltered bays along the east side with sand and peat deposits.

The loch has a more diverse flora and fauna than the higher altitude lochs. In sheltered conditions in shallow water *Littorella uniflora*, *Elatine hexandra*, *Nitella* spp., *Fontinalis antipyretica*, *Juncus bulbosus* and *Ranunculus flammula* occur, but the flora of the deeper waters has not been sampled. The zooplankton must be very sparse since zooplankton net tows taken in July at the outflow contained no planktonic animals. The benthos of the shoreline is extremely sparse, the greatest abundance of animals being found in the sheltered bays on the east side where Tubificidae, Naididae, Chironomidae, *Tipula* sp. and *Pisidium* occur. The only mayfly found on the sandy shores is the stream species *Baetis rhodani*. Caseless caddis, stoneflies and beetles occur, the latter including the northern *Oreodytes septentrionalis*, while the only gastropod recorded is *Lymnaea pereger*. Charr, brown trout, salmon and sea trout occur, but the loch is too exposed to support a waterfowl population.

(e) Loch Avon
NO 0102.   43 ha

Loch Avon (altitude 686 m, maximum depth 31 m) is the largest lake above 600 m in Britain. It is orientated south-west/north-east and is enclosed by crags on three sides and open to a U-shaped valley at the north-east end. It is a good example of a high altitude glacial trough lake, and is probably similar biologically to Loch Einich.

OW.69. DUPPLIN LOCHS, PERTHSHIRE
NO 0320.   265 ha   Grade 1

These are two small (25 ha and 6 ha) artificially constructed shallow eutrophic lakes sheltered by trees. The larger loch which has a maximum depth of only just over a metre has very turbid water with exceptionally high phosphate levels (0.8–0.9 p.p.m.) which may be due to enrichment from bird droppings. Periodic algal blooms occur and submerged vegetation is very sparse, but *Phragmites communis* is rapidly invading the open water. Leeches and molluscs are plentiful, but the variety of insects is poor, and the invertebrate fauna generally lacks diversity.

This site is of outstanding importance as a roost for very large numbers of pink-footed geese – up to 12000 birds occur throughout the winter (17% of world population). Greylag number *c.* 1000, but little information is available on other wintering species. The wildfowl breeding population is believed to be large and varied.

OW.70. CARSEBRECK LOCHS, PERTHSHIRE
NN 8609.   340 ha   Grade 1

These are another two artificially constructed shallow eutrophic lochs situated about 20 km south-west of Dupplin Lochs. They are an important site for wintering wildfowl which include 4000 greylag (5% of north-west European population), 3500 pink-footed (4½% of world population), 1600 mallard and smaller numbers of teal, wigeon and tufted duck.

OW.71. LOCH LAIDON, PERTHSHIRE/ARGYLL
NN 3955.   460 ha   Grade 1

Loch Laidon is a narrow lake occupying a glacially excavated basin and lying at the edge of the Rannoch Moor NNR (see P.85) in a catchment which consists largely of blanket mire and peaty moorland. The water of the loch is consequently dystrophic, with a pH of 5.1 and an alkalinity of < 2 p.p.m. $CaCO_3$, and this is the largest loch of this type known in Britain. The soluble phosphate concentration is, however, surprisingly high (0.018–0.030 p.p.m.). The shoreline, which shelves steeply in most places, consists mostly of

coarse-grained granite boulders and stones with a few sheltered bays where sand and/or peat debris accumulate and where species such as *Juncus bulbosus*, *Eleogiton fluitans*, *Isoetes lacustris*, *Utricularia intermedia*, *Lobelia dortmanna* and *Nitella* sp. are found. The islands have bonus woodland interest.

The zooplankton of the loch is very sparse, only *Bosmina coregoni* var. *obtusirostris* occurring in any numbers, but *Daphnia hyalina*, *Cyclops* sp. and *Diaptomus gracilis* are also recorded in very small numbers. The macrobenthos of the deeper water, in which the bottom consists of a dark brown peaty *dy*, is also extremely sparse, only Chironomidae and *Cyrnus flavidus* being found, with a total population density of about 40 organisms/m². In the littoral, Chironomidae and Naididae predominate, the remaining sparse fauna consisting largely of species typical of wave-washed shores such as the trichopterans *Sericostoma personatum* and *Polycentropus kingi*, the stoneflies *Nemoura erratica*, *Leuctra fusca* and *Diura bicaudata* and the water beetles *Hygrotus* (*Coelambus*) *novemlineatus* and *Platambus maculatus*. It is somewhat surprising to find the gastropod *Lymnaea* (*Radix*) *peregra* in such an acidic loch. The larvae of *Tipula montium* and Ceratopogonidae are found in peaty deposits in sheltered bays. The loch contains brown trout, including 'ferox' specimens, and a few perch and minnows, but few waterfowl are found here.

OW.72. TAY–ISLA VALLEY, PERTHSHIRE
1100 ha   Grade 1

(a) Monk Myre
NO 2142
(b) Stormont Loch
NO 1942
(c) Meikleour
NO 1439
(d) Loch of Clunie
NO 1144

For convenience this is treated as an open water site, although it includes three areas of open water, alluvial meadows and freshwater marsh. Its main importance is for the wintering populations of greylag geese. These are the largest in Britain at all stages of the winter, except possibly in March. The four sites listed are used regularly, and each is known to have held over 10000 roosting greylags during recent winters.

Other species present include shoveler (85), mallard, teal, wigeon, pochard, tufted duck and goldeneye.

OW.73. RIVER SPEY, INVERNESS-SHIRE
NN 709980–NH 835055   Grade 1

Compared to the Dee this is a somewhat richer chemically and less actively eroding river system. Most of the features by which it differs from the Dee are represented in the section from Newtonmore to Loch Insh. This section can be considered in isolation, without reference to the catchment upstream, as the human population there is very small and the terrain is such that developments which are likely to have deleterious effects on the river are improbable.

In the upper parts of this 15 km section of river, which lies at an altitude of 230 m, it is mainly fast to moderate flowing, with a stone and gravel bed. Lower down, as the river approaches Loch Insh, it is ponded back by the loch and becomes extremely slow flowing. In this section within the Loch Insh Fens, the river has been partially embanked and is deep and canal-like. The short section downstream of Loch Insh to Kincraig bridge is once more moderately flowing.

Most of the catchment is of various schists vegetated by unproductive deer forest, but locally calcareous pockets occur and this section of river is mesotrophic with an alkalinity ranging from 10–26 p.p.m. $CaCO_3$. The water is low in nitrogen and phosphorus and is somewhat peat-staired. Treated sewage effluents from the towns of Newtonmore and Kingussie enter the river, but they cause little pollution. In the upper, fast-flowing stretch the river is up to 40 m wide, but mainly shallow with alternating riffles and pools. Submerged vegetation covers about 15% of the bottom, *Myriophyllum alterniflorum* being the dominant species. The fauna is characterised by the large numbers of caddis larvae including Glossosomatidae, *Brachycentrus subnubilus*, Hydropsychidae, Polycentropidae, Hydroptilidae, *Athripsodes* spp. and Rhyacophilidae. Five species of riverine mayfly are recorded, including large numbers of *Baetis bioculatus/scambus* among the *Myriophyllum*. The oligochaetes, stoneflies, beetles, Diptera larvae and molluscs typical of fast-flowing, gravelly rivers are also present and among the Diptera are *Simulium monticola*, *S. retans* and *S. ornatum*. In the slower stretches downstream the river is over 2 m in depth and the bottom probably consists of peat debris overlying stones. Submerged vegetation is restricted by the limited light penetration to a narrow band along the margins, where *Callitriche stagnalis* is dominant. There is also a marginal plant community of emergent species such as *Carex rostrata*, *C. aquatilis*, *Sparganium angustifolium* and *Myosotis* sp. The invertebrate fauna is entirely lacustrine and no typical stream species have been found. The fauna includes burrowing species, such as large numbers of *Pisidium* and *Sialis lutaria*, associated with the soft sediments, free-swimming species, such as Hydroporini, Haliplidae and Corixidae, and species associated with vegetation, such as large numbers of the worm *Stylaria lacustris*, the mayflies *Centroptilum luteolum* and *Cloeon simile*, and the caddises *Cyrnus flavidus* and *Anabolia nervosa*. The only species present which are generally associated with stony conditions are small numbers of helmid beetles, and the stonefly species *Nemoura erratica* and *Leuctra fusca*.

The fish species in this section of the Spey are salmon, brown trout, sea trout, minnows, perch, pike and eels plus charr, which run up from Loch Insh to spawn in the tributaries running into the Spey from the north side.

Slow-flowing large rivers at such an altitude have not been found elsewhere in Britain so that the lower section represents a unique habitat. The faster-flowing sections upstream are intermediate in character between the River Dee and parts of the Rivers Wye or Tweed although the abundance and variety of caddis species is striking. The river is within the composite site which includes the Loch Insh Fens (P.87, gr. 1*) and Loch Insh itself which is a grade 1 lake (see below).

OW.74. LOCH INSH, INVERNESS-SHIRE
NH 8304.   110 ha   Grade 1

This loch lies within the extensive morainic deposits of the Spey Valley and forms an expansion of the River Spey with a depth of 30.5 m. From the subaquatic contours it is evident that the river is slowly filling the loch basin with deposited silt. The loch receives the water from the entire upper Spey Valley, an area of 819 km², which consists mostly of schists and granite vegetated by upland grassland and dwarf-shrub heath. The loch has a very short mean retention time, 16.9 days, but it is likely to be much less than this in periods of spate. Chemically, the loch is mesotrophic with an alkalinity of 12 p.p.m. $CaCO_3$ but the concentration of dissolved nutrients is low. About 60% of the shoreline is of exposed wave-washed stones and boulders, but the shore is sandy along the southern end where the loch grades into fen and along the west side where there are sheltered bays with deciduous woodland coming down to the water's edge. Submerged macrophytic growth is abundant in the shallower regions of the loch where *Myriophyllum alterniflorum*, *Littorella uniflora* and *Juncus bulbosus* are the most abundant species. The following species of *Potamogeton* are also recorded: *P. praelongus*, *P. perfoliatus*, *P. praelongus* × *perfoliatus*, *P. filiformis* and *P. obtusifolius*, and in deeper water *Isoetes lacustris* and *Nitella* sp. are found. About 50% of the shoreline is fringed with emergent vegetation with *Carex aquatilis* and *C. nigra* dominant at the south end, and *C. rostrata* at the north end. The zooplankton is very sparse (*Diaptomus gracilis* is the only species recorded) presumably because of the very short retention time. The shallow water benthic fauna is entirely typical of the trophic status of the loch and its predominantly wave-washed shores. The most abundant species are Chironomidae, which occur in all habitats, the oligochaete *Stylaria lacustris* and the mayfly *Centroptilum luteolum*, on vegetation and sand, and the trichopteran *Tinodes waeneri* on stones. Ephemeroptera, Trichoptera, Plecoptera and water beetles are each represented by several species, but the only gastropods found are *Lymnaea (Radix) peregra* and *Planorbis contorta*. The loch contains salmon, brown trout, pike and a race of charr which run several kilometres up the River Spey to spawn, this being the only site in Scotland where this fish is known to spawn in streams.

Loch Insh has associated with it a large *Carex*-dominated poor-fen, which has been assessed as a grade 1 site of peatland interest (P.87) and the section of the River Spey running through the Loch Insh Fens as far up as Newtonmore is a grade 1 open water site (OW.73).

OW.75. RIVER DEE,
ABERDEENSHIRE/KINCARDINESHIRE
NN 988993–NJ 892018   Grade 1

The River Dee rises as a large number of streams draining the east central Highlands of Scotland, some of which form the outflows of high altitude lochs such as Loch Etchachan and Loch Muick, and the highest sources are found on the slopes of Ben Macdhui within the Cairngorms NNR. Compared to the streams of the Spey watershed, within the Cairngorms, those of the Dee are more precipitous and streams, such as the Allt a'Choire Mhoir, after rising on a gently sloping boulder field at 1220 m then plunge 600 m down the 40° slopes of the Lairig Ghru. In its uppermost sections the substrate of this stream consists of granite gravel and stones, but on the steep slopes the stream cascades over bedrock and large boulders. In both sections most of the rock surfaces are covered in quite dense growths of bryophytes such as *Scapania undulata*, *Jungermannia cordifolia* and *Marsupella emarginata*. The maximum width is about 3 m and the greatest depth only 20 cm in this stretch and the water is extremely deficient in dissolved minerals, the conductivity being one of the lowest measured in this survey (12–19 μmhos), but the nitrate levels are fairly high (0.24–0.25 p.p.m. NO_3) and the pH low (5.1). For most of the year the flow consists largely of snow-melt and even in late summer the temperature does not rise much above 5 °C. The invertebrate fauna comprises those species of Simuliidae, Plecoptera, Tricladida, caddis, Diptera and oligochaetes typical of Arctic–alpine streams, with the larvae of orthoclad chironomids predominating numerically. There are no fish or aquatic angiosperms at these altitudes.

Lower down, in the main glens of the Cairngorms, the Arctic–alpine streams converge to form small fast-flowing rivers which are prone to heavy spating. Among these rivers are the Dee itself, the Geldie Burn, the Lui Beg and the Quoich Water. All are characterised by their clear waters and their unstable shingle beds, interrupted at some points by areas of smooth flat bedrock. The water is extremely poor in nutrients but is less acid than higher up. Higher aquatic vegetation is completely absent and the stones are virtually free of epilithic algae. The invertebrate fauna is extremely sparse, and, after a period of flooding, large areas of the bed are virtually devoid of animals although remnants of the fauna are found isolated in oxbows. The fauna still contains a large Arctic–alpine element, but some species characteristic of lower elevations, such as the caddis *Polycentropus flavomaculatus*, the alderfly *Sialis fuliginosa*, the stonefly *Taeniopteryx nebulosa* and *Gerris costai*, are also present. These rivers are the spawning grounds of many of the Dee salmon.

Below the falls known as the Linn of Dee the river becomes broader and is moderate to fast flowing with a more stable bed consisting of stones and gravel with a few boulders and a little sand. It remains very similar throughout almost its entire length downstream, gradually increasing in size so that at Cults just upstream of Aberdeen it is up to 60 m wide. The dissolved nutrient content of the water also increases downstream as the river enters farmland and leaves the hills, and at Peterculter the river is mesotrophic (alkalinity = 16 p.p.m. $CaCO_3$) but nitrogen levels are still relatively low (average = 0.5 p.p.m. NO_3). In its lower reaches the water is less clear and in August 1970 the river was slightly discoloured by the phytoplankter *Gleotrichia echinulata* derived from the Loch of Skene, which drains into the river. Macrophytic vegetation is virtually absent throughout the river, only a few clumps of bryophytes being found.

Associated with the increasing nutrient content there is an increase in the biomass and variety of benthic invertebrates as one moves downstream. A number of montane species such as *Simulium (Odagmia) monticola*, *Protonemura montana*, *Diura bicaudata* and *Crenobia alpina* disappear and in the lower mesotrophic sections the fauna is augmented by *Polycelis tenuis/nigra*, *Gammarus pulex*, *Simulium reptans*, *Baetis pumilus*, *Ephemerella ignita*, a number of caddis species and a few gastropods, all of which appear in increasing numbers downstream.

The fish fauna is dominated by salmonids especially salmon and in the lower stretches pike and minnows are also found. Very few aquatic birds are associated with the Dee, but dippers, herons, common sandpiper, goosander, common tern (and possibly kingfisher) are breeding species. In times of severe freezing, the lower stretches are particularly important for wintering duck such as goldeneye.

The Dee is one of the most famous salmon rivers in Britain and is virtually intact from pollution and nutrient enrichment except in its lowermost sections, a large proportion of its catchment consisting of exposed upland country. It is one of the few large rivers in Scotland unaffected by hydro-electric schemes and it also shows the greatest altitudinal range of any river in Britain, making it the finest example of a large oligotrophic river.

OW.76. LOCH KINORD, ABERDEENSHIRE
NO 4499.   20 ha   Grade 1

Lochs Davan and Kinord lie on the Moor of Dinnet upland/peatland site (U.46, P.88), but biological information is only available for Kinord. Both lochs are extensive shallow kettle-holes, Loch Kinord being a relatively rich oligotrophic lake (alkalinity = 10 p.p.m. $CaCO_3$) with a maximum depth of 4 m. The main inflow stream flows off *Calluna* moorland but the loch is surrounded by a fringe of open *Betula* woodland for much of its perimeter. At the western end of the loch where the inflow enters there is extensive marginal vegetation with communities of *Nymphaea alba*, *Nuphar lutea* and *Menyanthes trifoliata* grading into a fen dominated by *Schoenoplectus lacustris*, *Phragmites communis*, *Typha latifolia* and *Carex rostrata*. Reed-swamp, growing on organic mud, fringes about 75% of the shoreline, and elsewhere, in more exposed situations, the shoreline consists of stones and sand with *Littorella uniflora* and *Lobelia dortmanna*. In the shallower open water, *Potamogeton obtusifolius*, *P. berchtoldii*, *P. perfoliatus*, *Juncus bulbosus* and *Myriophyllum alterniflorum* are the most abundant species, while in deep water, where the substrate consists of a black organic mud with light brown ferric granules, plant communities are dominated by *Nitella translucens* and *Isoetes lacustris* which do not extend below 3 m. The benthic invertebrate fauna is typical of mesotrophic conditions. Three species of gastropod, all tolerant of low calcium concentrations, are recorded and a fourth, *Lymnaea (Radix) peregra*, is almost certainly present. Four species of leech and the malacostracans *Gammarus (Gammaracanthus) lacustris* and *Asellus meridianus* also occur, together with the triclad *Polycelis tenuis*. The Trichoptera fauna includes several species associated with weedy conditions and wave-washed stony shores, and the corixids consist mostly of species found in base-poor moorland lochs and the fen species *Callicorixa praeusta*. Great crested grebe and wigeon breed and there is a colony of several hundred black-headed gulls in the fen. This loch is somewhat unusual in that it is considerably poorer than most kettle-holes in Scotland, this being no doubt because of the drift in which it lies having derived from the extremely insoluble granite of the Cairngorm massif. The loch differs from most shallow Highland lochs where extensive fen development seldom occurs and the diverse aquatic flora of Kinord, including species such as *Typha latifolia*, usually only found in rich waters, makes this an interesting site.

OW.77. LOCH OF STRATHBEG, ABERDEENSHIRE
NK 0759.   200 ha   Grade 1

This, the largest dune slack pool in Britain, lies in an extremely exposed position at Rattray Head and is separated from the sea by a dune system about 0.5–1 km in width. The dunes are calcareous and the loch is eutrophic (alkalinity = 70–80 p.p.m. $CaCO_3$), with a high sodium level (110–123 p.p.m.) owing to its proximity to the sea. It is fed by streams which drain mainly from farmland, and fairly high levels of nutrients are recorded. The loch is extremely shallow for its size with a mean depth of 1.5 m, and in periods of strong winds the sand which forms the bottom over most of the loch is brought into suspension making the water turbid. The shores consist of alternating areas of sand and stones lying on gravel with limited emergent vegetation comprising a narrow band of *Eleocharis palustris*, sometimes accompanied by *Polygonum amphibium*. At the north-west end, however, there are extensive beds of *Phragmites*. The submerged vegetation of the sandy beaches consists of *Chara aspera*, *Potamogeton filiformis* and *Littorella uniflora*, with *P. pectinatus*, *P. perfoliatus* and *Cladophora* in deeper water. The zooplankton community consists of the common association of *Daphnia hyalina*, *Cyclops* (?)*strenuus* and *Diaptomus gracilis*. As in many other maritime lakes, the gastropod *Potamopyrgus jenkinsi* is extremely abundant and the other snails present are species tolerant of a wide range of conditions. The fauna contains *Gammarus (Rivulogammarus) duebeni* and *Sigara selecta* which are characteristic of slightly brackish conditions, and the rest of the invertebrates recorded are either species characteristic of a sandy substrate (e.g. *Caenis moesta*, *Arctocorixa germari* and *Sigara dorsalis*), wave-washed shores (e.g. *Tinodes waeneri* and *Oreodytes rivalis*) or weed-beds in eutrophic conditions (e.g. *Cloeon simile*, Lepto-

ceridae, *Sigara falleni* and *Callicorixa praeusta*). Three-spined sticklebacks, eels and brown trout are present in this loch.

This site is of international importance as a wintering ground for wildfowl especially pink-footed (2500; *c.* 3% of world population) and greylag (2200; *c.* 3% of north-west European population) geese, whooper swan (300; 10% of UK population), mallard (3600), pochard (1650), tufted duck (600), mute swan (250) and smaller numbers of wigeon, teal, goosander, goldeneye and Bewick's swans. The associated dune system is a grade 1 coastal site (C.87).

OW.78. LOCHS OF HARRAY AND STENNESS, ORKNEY
HY 2915.   1400 ha   Grade 1

These two water-bodies show a gradation from a salinity close to that of sea water to eutrophic freshwater, and are unique in the British Isles. Stenness is a shallow sea loch (mean depth 3.2 m) connected to both the sea by a narrow tidal channel, and to Harray by culverts. The sodium content ranges from 6.0% near the channel connecting with the sea to 5.6% near the inflow from Loch Harray, but is possibly somewhat lower in the isolated northern arm. Both lochs are extremely exposed and their shorelines consist mainly of stones.

The only aquatic angiosperms recorded in Loch Stenness are *Potamogeton pectinatus*, *Ruppia maritima* and the rare *R. spiralis*: otherwise the benthic flora consists entirely of inter-tidal seaweeds. The invertebrate fauna consists largely of marine organisms especially polychaetes, crustaceans, triclads and molluscans, the latter including dense beds of edible mussel *Mytilus edulis*. The only freshwater and brackish species present are Tubificidae, Chironomidae, *Gammarus (Rivulogammarus) duebeni*, *Potamopyrgus jenkinsi* and the zooplankter *Acartia* sp. Fish populations include marine genera and salmonids, and grey seals occur occasionally.

Loch of Harray shows a salinity gradient from the south to north (conductivity = 2800–644 μmhos; sodium level = 167–63 p.p.m.) but calcium, phosphate and nitrogen concentrations are similar at both ends, the alkalinity being 140–150 p.p.m. $CaCO_3$ at the freshwater end. The distribution of some organisms is governed by the salinity gradient. Brackish waters species such as the algae *Enteromorpha intestinalis*, the triclad *Procerodes littoralis* and the crustacean *Jaera* sp. are restricted to the outflow and *Neomysis integer* and *Potamopyrgus jenkinsi* are more abundant there. The gastropod *Theodoxus fluviatilis*, mostly confined to streams in southern Britain, is found near the outflow in its only Scottish locality. In the fresher parts of Loch Harray the flora and fauna is fairly typical of eutrophic conditions. Six species of *Potamogeton* are recorded, of which *P. crispus*, *P. gramineus* and *P. perfoliatus* are most abundant, while in deeper water *Chara baltica* and *C. aspera* occur. The unusual alga *Cladophora sauteri* occurs here and is piled in drifts along lee shores. Hirudinea, Gastropoda, Tubificidae, Chironomidae, Trichoptera and *Gammarus duebeni* are fairly abundant and the rather rare *Diaptomus laticeps* is the dominant zooplankter. Salmon, trout, sticklebacks and eels are the only fish present and considerable kills have been caused in the past by the alga *Prymnesium parvum* producing toxin during periods of exceptionally high salinity. Further outbreaks will be controlled by the installation of sluices at the connection between the two lochs which will allow only a limited inflow of saline water into Loch Harray.

Both lochs are important sites for wintering wildfowl, 750 pochard occurring on Harray and a total of 860 tufted duck and smaller numbers of mallard, teal, wigeon, goldeneye, mute and whooper swans on both lochs. In addition Stenness has considerable numbers of seaduck including scaup, long-tailed duck and red-breasted merganser.

OW.79. KILCONQUHAR LOCH, FIFE
NO 4801.   55 ha   Grade 2

This shallow eutrophic kettle-hole with mainly sandy shores has very high nutrient levels, possibly deriving from farmland and an adjacent village, and experiences heavy algal growths of *Aphanizomenon* and *Enteromorpha intestinalis* among others. The submerged vegetation appears to have been reduced in diversity compared with the large number of species recorded by West (1910); *Zannichellia palustris* is now the most widespread and the only other species found are *Potamogeton pectinatus* and *P. pusillus*. There is still a diverse emergent vegetation dominated by *Phragmites*, but the invertebrate fauna is rather limited in species composition, the most abundant being chironomids, oligochaetes, *Asellus meridianus*, *Gammarus* (*Gammaracanthus*) *lacustris* and a variety of molluscs including the rather uncommon introduced species *Physa acuta*. Insects are particularly poorly represented, no caddis larvae, mayflies, dragonflies or stoneflies having been recorded. *Daphnia magna* is the dominant zooplankter, here at one of its most northerly localities in Britain. Three-spined sticklebacks were taken in the collections, but the status of perch and pike, which used to occur in the loch, is doubtful.

The main interest is the wildfowl, with wintering populations of 1050 pochard (2½% of UK population), 740 tufted duck (2% of UK population), 120 shoveler, and mallard, teal, goldeneye and greylag. Breeding species include mallard, teal, pochard, tufted duck, gadwall, shoveler, mute swan and black-necked grebe. Large numbers of little gulls (up to 500) occur on passage in late summer.

OW.80. DRUMMOND POND, PERTHSHIRE
NN 8518.   135 ha   Grade 2

Very little is known about this small (27 ha) eutrophic loch which is the main centre for greylags in upper Strathearn, holding 8000 birds (10% of north-west European population) in winter, and smaller numbers of mallard, wigeon, teal, tufted duck, pochard and goosander.

OW.81. LOCHS RESCOBIE AND BALGAVIES, ANGUS
NO 5151–5350.   215 ha   Grade 2

These lochs, which are interconnected, are eutrophic kettle-holes which now have very high nutrient levels and ex-

perience dense algal crops including *Asterionella* and *Anabaena*. There has been a reduction in the extent and variety of submerged angiosperms in recent years, but rich marginal communities, including local species such as *Lysimachia thyrsiflora* and *Cicuta virosa*, are present. The benthic invertebrate fauna is rich and includes at least 10 species of gastropod and an abundance of Trichoptera.

The limnological interest is assessed as grade 3, but in view of the high value of the site for wildfowl and botanically, an overall grading of 2 is considered appropriate. A roost of pink-footed geese holds 1800 birds (2½% of world population). Mallard, teal, wigeon, shoveler, pochard, tufted duck, goldeneye, greylag geese, whooper and mute swans also occur regularly.

OW.82. LOCH OF KINNORDY, ANGUS
NO 3654.   65 ha   Grade 2

This shallow eutrophic lake was partially drained last century and now only a small area of permanent open water remains. There are extensive areas of seasonally inundated rich-fen, however, which include *Phragmites communis*, *Typha latifolia*, *Sparganium erectum*, *Carex rostrata*, *Hippuris vulgaris*, *Menyanthes trifoliata* and *Ranunculus lingua*.

It is used by 2400 greylags (3% of north-west European population) as an alternative roost to Lintrathen Loch, and other wintering wildfowl include mallard, teal, wigeon, tufted duck, shoveler and whooper swan. It is probably also an important wildfowl breeding site.

OW.83. LOCH OF LINTRATHEN, ANGUS
NO 2855.   220 ha   Grade 2

This is a large, rather deep loch, occupying a glacial basin which has been deepened through being dammed artificially. It is used as a water supply reservoir by Dundee Corporation and is probably mesotrophic. There is little information available on limnological interest, but its value for wildfowl is high. Populations include greylag (2450; 3% of north-west European population), mallard (3200; 1% of UK population) and tufted duck (370). Teal, wigeon, goosander and whooper swan also occur regularly.

OW.84. LOCH SPYNIE, MORAYSHIRE
NJ 2366.   70 ha   Grade 2

This formerly more extensive shallow eutrophic loch, which has been partially drained by a canal, has a fairly diverse submerged flora and extensive marginal communities including *Typha latifolia* and *Hippuris vulgaris*, the former in one of its most northerly stations. The invertebrate fauna is typical of eutrophic conditions and includes *Asellus meridianus* and several species of gastropods. It is important for its wintering wildfowl populations, particularly greylag (1350; 2½% of UK population). Mallard, teal, wigeon, pochard, tufted duck, and mute swan also occur regularly.

OW.85. LOCHS OF SPIGGIE AND BROW, SHETLAND
HU 3716.   150 ha   Grade 2

These two eutrophic lochs were formed by the damming of a shallow bay by coastal sand dunes, and are separated by a narrow spit of marshy land about 300 m wide. Loch of Spiggie, the larger of the two lochs, is nearer the sea, being separated at its outflow by less than 100 m, and has a relatively high sodium content (59 p.p.m.). They are both shallow and extremely exposed to most winds so that the shorelines are very barren, with stones and gravel predominating, and reed-swamp is very limited in extent.

Where aquatic marginal vegetation is found, it consists of a sparse community of *Juncus articulatus*, *Iris pseudacorus* and *Ranunculus flammula*, growing on a wave-cut platform, with *Littorella uniflora* in deeper water. A number of other submerged aquatic plants are found, but, with the exception of *Chara aspera* and *Potamogeton filiformis*, none of the species are typical eutrophic lake species, and most are widespread species characteristic of a wide range of trophic conditions.

The zooplankton of Loch of Spiggie includes the rather rare *Diaptomus wierzejskii*. The slight saline influence in both lochs is indicated by the presence of the brackish water crustaceans, *Neomysis integer* and *Gammarus (Rivulogammarus) duebeni*, and the abundance of *Potamopyrgus jenkinsi*. For eutrophic lakes the fauna is somewhat poor in species, and most of those present are tolerant of a wide range of trophic conditions. The low temperatures at this latitude are indicated by the presence of the cold-water triclad *Crenobia alpina* in Loch of Brow.

The Lochs of Spiggie and Brow are important as a wildfowl site, particularly for whooper swans of which 150 birds (5% of UK population) occur regularly together with less important concentrations of mallard, pochard, tufted duck and goldeneye.

WEST SCOTLAND

OW.86. LOCH MORAR, INVERNESS-SHIRE
NM 8090.   3350 ha   Grade 1*

This is an excellent example of an extreme oligotrophic fjord lake lying in a glacial trough directed east and west and dammed by a rock threshold. The water is extremely poor in nutrients (conductivity 42 μmhos) and exceptionally clear (Secchi disc transparency 30 m). It is the deepest lake in Britain, reaching a maximum depth of 310 m with an average depth of 87 m, and the shorelines shelve steeply into deep water. Along its length it is exposed to the westerly winds, and in many places long shingle storm beaches are thrown up. Mineral deposits with a high proportion of sand extend to depths of over 30 m. The outflow river flows only about 0.5 km to the sea and the lake level is only 10 m above sea-level. Thermal stratification takes place in the summer with a thermocline at *c.* 25 m and the hypolimnion remains at 5 °C throughout the year. The phytoplankton is rich in desmids but the zooplankton is extremely sparse. No *Daphnia* have been recorded and typical species are *Diaptomus gracilis*, *Bosmina coregoni* var. *longispina*, *Holopedium gibberum*, *Bythotrephes longimanus* and *Leptodora kindti*. The macrobenthos of the shoreline is typical of that of exposed stony shores with mayfly species such as

Ecdyonurus dispar and *Ephemerella ignita*, stoneflies and caseless caddis. The benthos of the sublittoral is extremely sparse. Salmon, sea trout, brown trout, charr, eels and sticklebacks occur in the loch. In sheltered areas there is a zonation of rooted vegetation, starting with *Myriophyllum alterniflorum* at 1 m depth, then *Littorella uniflora*, *Lobelia dortmanna* and *Eleogiton fluitans* followed by a dense sward of *Isoetes lacustris* down to a depth of at least 5 m.

Future developments in the catchment area are unlikely to threaten its conservation seriously as this is relatively small, rugged and mountainous. A hydro-electric dam on the outflow river has a negligible effect upon the loch, and there is a small sailing school at the west end which is unlikely to be deleterious. The islands at the west end are graded 1 for their scrub woodland (W.200).

See also P.103.

OW.87. LOCH AN DUIN, NORTH UIST, INVERNESS-SHIRE
NF 8974.   245 ha   Grade 1*

This is a complex much dissected shallow sea loch with many small islands and a tidal range of 3.5 m at its seaward end. It is divided into five basins, the inner two with a salinity of about 4‰, the middle basin ranging in salinity from *c.* 9‰ at its inner end to about 26‰ at the outer end and two outer basins with salinities about 34‰.

The outer basins are silted except at the gravelly outlets to the sea where there are many large stones covered with *Fucus serratus* and stunted *Laminaria saccharina*. In the silted areas *Akera bullata* is abundant along with *Chironomus aprilinus* larvae and *Corophium volutator* while at the outlets the fauna is very different being similar to that of the inter-tidal zone of a rocky sea shore.

The southern and eastern shores of the middle basin are of rock covered with *Fucus vesiculosus*, *F. serratus*, *Cladophora rupestris* and *Chondrus crispus* while the western shore consists mostly of shallow sandy bays carpeted by *Ruppia maritima* and *F. vesiculosus* and *Zostera marina*. In the fresher water bays *F. ceranoides* and *Enteromorpha intestinalis* occur. The fauna consists entirely of brackish water forms and the lagoon cockle *Cerastoderma glaucum* appears here.

The shores of the inner basins are rocky, alternating with sandy bays. The only plants are *Potamogeton pectinatus*, *Chara* sp. and in the fresher parts *Myriophyllum alterniflorum*. In the slightly brackish waters *Neomysis integer* and *Gammarus (Rivulogammarus) duebeni* occur and in the most fresh regions they are joined by freshwater groups such as dragonflies and water beetles.

Associated with the loch are much dissected areas of salt marsh little more than 1 ha in maximum extent which comprise a complex of *Puccinellia maritima–Plantago coronopus–Armeria maritima* on silt to sandy silt, which grade to blanket bog (locally cliffed) via an *Empetrum nigrum* fringe. The boulder and undeveloped cliff line bordering much of the loch has a notable lichen flora yet to be described.

The fish populations include both salmonids and sticklebacks and marine genera and large numbers of mute and whooper swans occur in winter. A few pairs of greylag geese nest nearby.

OW.88. GROGARRY LOCHS, SOUTH UIST, INVERNESS-SHIRE   Grade 1*

Three distinct loch types are present in this area of South Uist where much of the land surface is covered by open water. Those lochs nearest the sea and having direct connection with it (e.g. Lochs Roag and Fada) are brackish, while others including Loch a'Mhachair and Loch Stilligarry are situated on the shell sands or machair of the raised beach and are eutrophic. As the influence of blown shell sand fades with distance inland there is a transition from calcareous machair (which runs for about 2 km inland) to acidic heath and blanket mire on which shallow oligotrophic lochs such as Druidibeg are situated. Because of their proximity to the sea and extreme exposure all the lochs in this area are, however, distinctly maritime.

See also C.102.

(a) Loch Druidibeg
NF 7937.   320 ha

This, the largest of South Uist oligotrophic lochs, with an alkalinity of 3.4 p.p.m. $CaCO_3$, is extremely shallow (mean depth = c. 1.5 m) with a stony bottom, complex shape and many islands. It has a relatively high sodium and chloride level and a few brackish water species such as Gammarus (Rivulogammarus) duebeni and Neomysis integer, the numbers of these declining from the western to the eastern end. The aquatic fauna and flora are generally sparse, Lobelia dortmanna and Eleogiton fluitans being among the few submerged plant species present. The littoral fauna is sparse and lacking in diversity compared to the machair lochs; only three species of gastropod are recorded, but Plecoptera are plentiful.

The loch supports the largest breeding colony of greylag geese in Britain (65 pairs). The breeding biology of this colony and the impact of the geese upon the crofters' crops are being studied. There is also a breeding colony of herons on one of the islands, which are themselves of interest for their scrub vegetation.

(b) Loch a'Mhachair and Loch Stilligarry
NF 7639.   83 ha

These are shallow base-rich lochs (both of the same area) which were originally formed as dune slacks behind the windblown calcareous shell sands on the machair. Their alkalinities range from 85–90 p.p.m. $CaCO_3$ and, being closer to the sea, the salinities are slightly higher than those of Druidibeg. There are extensive weed-beds of Potamogeton spp., Myriophyllum sp., Chara sp., Hippuris vulgaris, Eleocharis palustris and Phragmites communis. There is a rich zooplankton and benthos, the latter being typical of eutrophic conditions, with Mollusca well represented both in quantity and in range of species. Elements of the brackish water fauna (Neomysis integer, Gammarus (Rivulogammarus)

duebeni and Potamopyrgus jenkinsi) are plentiful. The greylag geese which nest on Loch Druidibeg bring their young to the rich machair grassland to rear them, and during this period the lochs are used as a roost. The trout are fast growing, specimens over 1 kg being recorded, but the only other fish present are sticklebacks and eels.

(c) Howmore Estuary, Loch Roag and Loch Fada
NF 7535.   47 ha

These two lochs and the short estuary of the River Howmore are situated on the machair just south of the Loch Druidibeg NNR. The Howmore River and Loch Roag are both under tidal influence and have a brackish fauna and flora. In the river the stones are coated with Enteromorpha intestinalis and Fucus ceranoides and the latter is the main alga in Loch Roag. Common constituents of the invertebrate fauna are Potamopyrgus jenkinsi, Limnephilus sp., chironomid species, Crangon sp., Neomysis integer, Gammarus zaddachi and the isopod Jaera albifrons. Of these Crangon does not extend into Loch Roag. Salmon, trout, eel, flounder, sand goby and three-spined stickleback are present in both these brackish situations. In the south-west corner of Loch Roag, by the inflow from Loch Fada, freshwater plants, Eleocharis, Littorella uniflora and Potamogeton sp., are present with water beetles, chironomid larvae and dragonflies.

Loch Fada shows a range of salinity from 400 to 850 p.p.m. sodium but is low in plant nutrients and has an alkalinity of only 40–50 p.p.m. $CaCO_3$. The shoreline is characterised by a mixture of sand and stones with large swards of Littorella uniflora developed in 0.5–10 cm of water. The rest of the flora is of freshwater species typical of base-poor conditions, such as Lobelia dortmanna, Myriophyllum alterniflorum and Eleogiton fluitans, but Potamogeton pectinatus which in Scotland is associated with coastal habitats is also present. The only brackish water invertebrates found are Neomysis integer, Gammarus (Rivulogammarus) duebeni and Potamopyrgus jenkinsi and these are more numerous at the northern end being replaced at the southern end by a freshwater fauna comprising a wide range of Ephemeroptera, Trichoptera, Corixidae, Coleoptera and Hirudinea species. Eels, three-spined sticklebacks, salmon, brown trout and sea trout occur in the loch.

The transition of this series of river and lochs runs further into freshwater than for the Loch an Duin complex on North Uist.

OW.89. DURNESS LOCHS AND STREAMS, SUTHERLAND
NC 3967.   140 ha   Grade 1*

This site comprises four marl lochs (Lochs Lanlish, Croispol, Borralie and Caladail) and the streams forming the inflow and outflow of Loch Croispol, all of which lie on the Durness Limestone.

The lochs are shallow, except Borralie which has one area of 20 m depth, and being very exposed have stony shorelines with very little marginal vegetation. The water is extremely clear with very low nitrate concentrations (0.003–0.013 p.p.m.) and phytoplankton production is low. In contrast there are extensive growths of submerged macrophytes including seven species of *Potamogeton* and three of *Chara*. The diversity of the invertebrate fauna is low, presumably because of the isolation from other base-rich water-bodies, and Mollusca are relatively poorly represented. However, those taxa which are present, especially those associated with the macrophytes, such as the mayfly *Cloeon simile* and several caddis flies belonging to the Phryganeidae, Limnephilidae, Leptoceridae, Polycentropidae and Hydroptilidae, are present in very large numbers. *Micronecta poweri*, *Lymnaea (Radix) peregra*, and *Gammarus (Gammaracanthus) lacustris* are plentiful along the shoreline and *Caenis horaria* and chironomids in the marl. Sticklebacks are abundant and brown trout numbers are maintained by stocking. Large trout up to 6.8 kg have been caught in the past, particularly in Borralie and Lanlish. Borralie is the only marl lake in Britain with a population of charr and these grow to a larger size than in most other British lakes. The island in Loch Borralie gives the site a bonus interest.

The streams associated with Loch Croispol show many of the features of chalk streams and have abundant vegetation including *Chara* sp., *Rorippa nasturtium-aquaticum*, *Veronica anagallis-aquatica*, *Callitriche stagnalis*, *Ranunculus aquatilis* agg. and *Myriophyllum spicatum*. The invertebrate fauna is characterised by the abundance of mayflies, stoneflies and caddises, the latter occurring in great variety including *Rhyacophila obliterata*, characteristic of high altitudes in Britain. The cold-water triclad *Crenobia alpina* is present in the inflow stream, but *Gammarus (Rivulogammarus) pulex* is notably absent. This species does not extend this far north-west in Britain, and its place is taken by *G. (R.) lacustris*, small numbers of which are present in the outflow burn.

See also C.108 and U.68.

OW.90. RIVER STRONTIAN, ARGYLL
NM 895653–814617   Grade 1

This is a good example of a short, west-coast, spating oligotrophic river. It rises as a number of streams, the highest at about 650 m, and flows for about 10 km, eventually into the sea at Loch Sunart by the village of Strontian. The catchment consists mainly of upland grassland but along its north side it is flanked by Arriundle oakwood (see W.190). The trees do not, however, come down to the water's edge and the river is mostly unshaded, and except for a few deep pools in the lower reaches it is fast flowing and eroding throughout, with a stone-and-gravel bed. The river is subject to a rise in water level of up to 1 m following heavy rain and the water is clear and fairly low in dissolved nutrients.

Aquatic angiosperms are completely absent, but there are small quantities of bryophytes attached to some of the stones where the rather unusual alga *Lemanea* also occurs. The invertebrate fauna is generally very sparse, though varied in species composition. Seven species each of stonefly and mayfly are recorded, and caddises, and helmid and helodid beetles are well represented. *Simulium (Odagmia) monticola* is a characteristic species in the upper

reaches, being replaced by *S. tuberosum* and *S. reptans* lower down. In sluggish pools the fauna is more abundant and species associated with slower-flowing water, such as the mayfly *Centroptilum luteolum*, the beetle *Deronectes depressus* and the caddis *Anabolia nervosa*, appear together with the gastropods *Lymnaea peregra* and *Ancylus fluviatilis*. Salmon, sea trout, brown trout, eels, lampreys and possibly minnows are the only fish species present.

OW.71. LOCH LAIDON (PART), ARGYLL   Grade 1
See under East Scotland, p. 195.

OW.91. LOCH EYE, ROSS
NH 8379.   360 ha   Grade 1

Loch Eye is a large, very shallow waterbody (mean depth = 1.2 m), situated in sands and gravels on a raised beach overlying Old Red Sandstone. Most of the drainage comes from the non-arable land, and, although moderately eutrophic with an alkalinity varying from about 30–50 p.p.m. $CaCO_3$, nutrient levels are relatively low. The loch is fairly exposed from all directions and most of the shoreline consists of stones and gravel, with a little sand and mud at the east end where there is a small reed-swamp and fen community with *Polygonum amphibium*, *Eleocharis palustris*, *Potentilla palustris*, *Potamogeton polygonifolius*, and various carices.

About 90% of the bottom of the loch is covered with submerged macrophytic plants showing an exceptional species diversity. A few species associated with oligotrophic conditions are found, including *Lobelia dortmanna*, *Subularia aquatica*, *Isoetes lacustris*, *Myriophyllum alterniflorum* and in deeper water *Nitella opaca*. These occur alongside a wide range of species, including some, such as *Chara delicatula*, *Potamogeton filiformis*, *P. pectinatus* and *P. berchtoldii*, which are more normally associated with eutrophic conditions. In all, 14 species of *Potamogeton* have been recorded including *P. rutilus*, a northern European species previously only known in Britain from Shetland and the Outer Hebrides. The diverse macrobenthos consists mostly of species found in weedy eutrophic conditions with four species of gastropod including *Potamopyrgus jenkinsi* and *Planorbis (Gyraulus) laevis*, the former being extremely abundant in the *Nitella* zone. *Cloeon simile* and two species of *Caenis* are very common among the weeds, together with leptocerid Trichoptera such as *Mystacides azurea*. The stony shores support species associated with exposed conditions such as the stoneflies *Leuctra hippopus* and *Diura bicaudata* and the caddis *Tinodes waeneri*. *Gammarus (Rivulogammarus) lacustris* has been recorded from this loch, but is surprisingly somewhat scarce.

The loch contains a population of fast-growing brown trout and is locally important as a wintering ground for geese and ducks lying between the Lower Dornoch Firth (C.123, gr. 2) and Cromarty Firth (C.112, gr. 1*).

OW.92. LOCH SIONASCAIG, ROSS
NC 1214.   620 ha   Grade 1

This large irregular-shaped oligotrophic loch lies in an area of Lewisian Gneiss and Torridonian Sandstone intensely eroded by glacial action, which has resulted in a landscape with a greater proportion of open water-bodies than any other area on the mainland of Britain. Of the many lochs in this area Sionascaig is one of the largest and deepest, with a mean depth of 18.4 m and a maximum depth of 65.5 m. Very little glacial deposition occurred around the loch and 70% of the shoreline is composed of solid bedrock with finer deposits of stones and gravel in a few sheltered bays. In deeper water considerable areas of the bottom consist of gneiss bedrock without any covering of subaquatic sediment such as is usually found in the deep profundal of lakes, but at the southern end of the loch, where the bedrock is of sandstone, there are deposits of organic mud up to 5.5 m deep overlying glacial deposits of clay and sand. The loch is now oligotrophic (alkalinity = 6 p.p.m. $CaCO_3$, pH 6.4–6.6) and low in nutrients with a conductivity of 62 μmhos but there is some evidence from the composition of the diatom flora of deep mud cores that the loch was once more eutrophic than it is at present. The loch is extremely exposed to wind action from all directions and is surrounded by moorland and blanket mire. The islands of the loch have bonus woodland interest.

A submerged flora, comprising *Subularia aquatica*, *Lobelia dortmanna*, *Eleogiton fluitans*, *Isoetes lacustris*, *Littorella uniflora* and *Myriophyllum alterniflorum*, is present in sheltered areas but there is apparently no emergent or floating-leaved vegetation. The zooplankton consists mostly of the infrequently occurring northern species *Diaptomus laciniatus* together with smaller numbers of more common species. The nature of the shore substrate makes collecting of invertebrates very difficult, and the largest numbers of animals are recorded among the submerged vegetation. The most abundant organisms are Chironomidae, Tipulidae and the mayfly *Ephemerella ignita*. Five other species of mayfly are recorded and four of Trichoptera (two polycentropids and two leptocerids). The only gastropod is *Lymnaea* (*Radix*) *peregra*. In the deep-water sediments the fauna is very sparse, only small numbers of Chironomidae being recorded. The loch contains populations of brown trout and charr.

The entire catchment of the loch lies within the Inverpolly NNR and it is therefore unlikely to be affected by enrichment from fertilisers in the future.

The stratigraphy of the bottom deposits is currently being investigated by the FBA and shows interesting features not yet found elsewhere.

See also W.207, P.101 and U.66.

OW.93. LOCH WATTEN, CAITHNESS
ND 2356.   375 ha   Grade 1

This is the largest of a series of extremely exposed eutrophic kettle-hole lochs situated on undulating drift overlying Old Red Sandstone on the Caithness plain. Much of the catchment is non-agricultural land, so that despite its high alkalinity (60–110 p.p.m. $CaCO_3$) nutrient levels are relatively low and the water is clear. For its size it is extremely shallow (mean depth = 3.5 m) and the shorelines

consist mainly of flat slabs of sandstone but there are also sheltered bays with extensive marginal vegetation. Typically this consists of *Phalaris arundinacea*, *Iris pseudacorus* and *Equisetum fluviatile* in an outer band followed by *Sparganium erectum*, *Carex aquatilis* and *Eleocharis palustris* then *Polygonum amphibium*, *Menyanthes trifoliata* and *Potamogeton natans* leading on to submerged communities of *P. pectinatus*, *P. filiformis*, *P. praelongus*, *Myriophyllum spicatum*, *Chara aspera* and *C. delicatula*. *Cladophora sauteri* occurs in great profusion and large piles composed of the spherical balls of this alga are washed up on lee shores.

The benthos is rich in species, and includes species characteristic of stony shores, such as *Gammarus* (*Rivulogammarus*) *lacustris*, the mayflies *Ecdyonurus dispar* and *Ephemerella ignita*, the stonefly *Diura bicaudata*, the caddises *Tinodes waeneri* and *Polycentropus flavomaculatus*, and the helmid *Limnius tuberculatus*, and species associated with the weed-beds such as the mayfly *Cloeon simile*, corixids and leptocerid caddises. The snail *Potamopyrgus jenkinsi* is abundant in the beds of *Chara*. The loch supports a thriving brown trout fishery and three-spined sticklebacks are abundant amongst the weeds.

OW.94. LISMORE LOCHS, ARGYLL
NM 8339, 8037, 8239, 8542.   55 ha   Grade 2

Three marl lochs of similar size are situated on metamorphic Dalradian Limestone on the island of Lismore. Loch Baile a-Ghobhainn (mean depth 11.9 m) is slightly deeper than Loch Fiart and Loch Kilcheran, average depth 7 and 6.4 m, respectively. Chemically all the lochs are similar, the alkalinity varying between 120–160 p.p.m. $CaCO_3$, but nutrient levels are low and the water is extremely clear. There is a wave-cut terrace of variable width extending down to a depth of about 1 m, beyond which the bottom plunges into deeper water. A band of *Schoenoplectus lacustris* grows just beyond the terrace where the water depth increases rapidly, and between this and the shore there is little or no emergent vegetation but in places there are extensive growths of *Chara aculeolata* and *Littorella uniflora*. At the ends of each loch are rich-fens with similar floristics. The fauna is typical of that of marl lakes, nine species of gastropods, *Asellus aquaticus*, *A. meridianus* and *Gammarus pulex* being recorded. The very local leech *Hirudo medicinalis* is found in Loch Baile a-Ghobhainn.

OW.95. LOCH SHIEL, ARGYLL/INVERNESS-SHIRE
NM 8072.   1600 ha   Grade 2

This is a good example of a large, deep, oligotrophic glacial loch which has been very little affected by human activities and is regarded as an alternative to Loch Morar. In all respects, however, it is a less extreme case of oligotrophy, being shallower (maximum depth only 128 m), chemically somewhat richer (conductivity 47 μmhos), and more sheltered, and having water which is a great deal less clear. The loch lies only 3.5 m above sea-level and Post-glacial marine sediments have been found on its bed. It is now entirely fresh water but seals frequently travel up the short length of river from the sea into the loch.

Emergent vegetation is virtually absent, but submerged macrophyte communities typical of oligotrophic waters occur, especially in more sheltered bays. A fairly varied littoral benthic fauna is recorded including a number of Trichoptera species of which *Hydroptila* sp. is abundant, but stoneflies and mayflies are poorly represented and only one gastropod (*Lymnaea* (*Radix*) *peregra*) and one leech (*Helobdella stagnalis*) have been found. The profundal benthos is extremely sparse, only chironomids and tubificids being recorded, with a standing crop of about 120 organisms/m². Fish species include brown trout, sea trout, salmon, eels and three-spined sticklebacks, but significantly no charr.

See also P.94.

OW.96. LOCH MHAOLACH-COIRE AND RIVER TRALIGILL, SUTHERLAND   Grade 2

(a) *Loch Mhaolach-coire*
NC 2719.   8 ha

This is a small very shallow loch (mean depth 1.5 m) lying on the Inchnadamph NNR (see U.67), in a catchment consisting mainly of Durness Limestone which in places is thickly covered with blanket peat. Thus the loch is eutrophic (alkalinity = 70 p.p.m. CaCO₃) but also peat-stained. Being very isolated from other eutrophic lakes, the flora and fauna contain very few species characteristic of such waters, *Potamogeton praelongus* and large numbers of *Gammarus* (*Rivulogammarus*) *lacustris* being the only exceptions. A variety of adaptable submerged macrophyte species grow in abundance over most of the lake-bed, but emergent vegetation is surprisingly scarce for a eutrophic lake, being confined to a few stands of *Carex rostrata* near the inflow. The zooplankton is characterised by the predominance of the rather uncommon *Diaptomus wierzejskii*. The *Bosmina* sp. present is *B. coregoni* var. *obtusirostris* and not the species typical of eutrophic habitats, *B. longirostris*. No triclads are recorded and only two adaptable species of gastropod and one of leech, but mayflies, caddises and stoneflies are well represented. The loch contains a population of fast-growing brown trout which are said to be mollusc feeders and are known locally as Gillaroo trout.

(b) *River Traligill*
NC 277197–257218

This short upland limestone river system includes the out-flow of Loch Mhaolach-coire, and is fast flowing, and subject to spates throughout its length. Many karst features are present including swallow holes, resurgences, a downcut trench forming a flood-water channel and caves in which Pleistocene animal remains have been found. However, no typically cavernicolous freshwater organisms have been recorded. The alkalinity measured at time of spate is unusually low for a limestone stream (12 p.p.m. CaCO₃), but the phosphorus concentration is high. Aquatic vegeta-

tion is limited to a coating of filamentous algae, such as *Oscillatoria* and *Gomphonema*, and scattered bryophytes, such as *Eurynchium riparoides*, attached to the stones. With the exception of stoneflies, of which 10 species are recorded, the fauna is very limited in variety, notable absentees from the fauna being helmid beetles, triclads, *Ancylus fluviatilis* and *Gammarus* (*Rivulogammarus*) *pulex*, their absence being possibly associated with the severe spating. Four species of mayfly (predominantly *Baetis rhodani* and *Rhithrogena semicolorata*), three species of caddis (*Glossosoma conformis*, *Rhyacophila dorsalis* and a limnephilid), chironomids, *Dicranota* and Simuliidae are the only insects. Four species of montane Simuliidae occur in the upper stretches, including *Prosimulium hirtipes* and *P. inflatum*.

OW.97. LOCH STACK AND RIVER LAXFORD, SUTHERLAND
NC 2943.   255 ha   Grade 2

Loch Stack is a relatively rich oligotrophic loch (alkalinity = 7 p.p.m. CaCO₃) which occupies two parallel glacial troughs gouged out of the Lewisian Gneiss and separated by a shallow ridge of granite, the maximum depth being 33 m.

Marginal and submerged macrophytic communities typical of oligotrophic lochs are present, the latter including the northern *Subularia aquatica*. At the inflow there is a poor-fen community of *Phragmites communis* and *Equisetum fluviatile* grading through to open water communities including *Potamogeton natans*, *Nymphaea alba* and *Schoeno-plectus lacustris*.

The zooplankton is diverse, but not very prolific, and includes the northern species *Diaptomus laciniatus*. The benthic invertebrate fauna, particularly that of the sub-littoral zone, is fairly diverse for an oligotrophic lake. On the predominantly stone and boulder shorelines the mayfly *Ecdyonurus dispar*, a few stonefly species, oligochaetes, helmid and haliplid beetles and *Oreodytes rivalis* predomin-ate, while among the vegetation of the sublittoral zone these are joined by *Cloeon simile*, *Centroptilum luteolum*, *Lepto-phlebia* spp. and *Siphonurus lacustris*, seven species of caddis (of which *Polycentropus flavomaculatus* is the most abundant), and hydroporine and agabine water beetles. *Gammarus* (*Rivulogammarus*) *lacustris* is found in small numbers, but the only gastropod recorded is *Lymnaea* (*Radix*) *peregra*, although *Ancylus fluviatilis* is almost certainly present.

The fish present are mainly salmonids – salmon, charr, sea and brown trout – but eels and sticklebacks also occur and perhaps lampreys; these are the only species recorded from freshwater habitats at this latitude in Britain.

A section of the outflow of Loch Stack, the Laxford River, is included within the site boundary as an example of a naturally regulated base-poor river. These open waters border the important upland grade 1* site of Foinaven–Meall Horn (U.65).

OW.98. BURN OF LATHERONWHEEL, CAITHNESS
ND 164392–191321   Grade 2

This is a good example of the many eutrophic upland streams lying on the Old Red Sandstone of Caithness. The highest tributary rises at 260 m above sea-level and the stream runs for a distance of 8 km to the sea. In its upper reaches it is a typical upland stream and in the lower parts becomes rich in nutrients, and the biomass of invertebrates per unit area is high for a site north of the Highland Boundary Fault. Here the substrate is predominantly sandstone, with most of the bottom covered by stones, 5–30 cm across, with a coating of moss and seasonally of algae. The lower section is bordered by deciduous trees and the leaf-fall contributes to the food supply for invertebrates.

It is rich in invertebrate species. The stonefly *Amphinemura sulcicollis* is an important component of the spring fauna as are *Hydropsyche* spp. and the small chironomid *Corynoneura*. *Baetis rhodani*, *B. pumilus* and Helmidae are plentiful at all times but there are very few *Simulium* larvae.

OW.99. LOCH NAM FEITHEAN, BALRANALD,
        NORTH UIST, INVERNESS-SHIRE
NF 7170.   50 ha   Grade 2

This shallow eutrophic lake is situated on the machair of North Uist and is largely overgrown with emergent vegetation including *Schoenoplectus tabernaemontani*, *Iris pseudacorus*, *Hippuris vulgaris* and *Polygonum amphibium* with dense beds of *Chara* spp. and *Myriophyllum alterniflorum* covering the bottom in deeper water. The benthic invertebrate fauna is abundant with particularly high numbers of molluscs, but the number of species is rather limited for such a eutrophic situation. The considerable saline influence (sodium level = 46 p.p.m.) is indicated by the presence of *Gammarus (Rivulogammarus) duebeni*, *Corixa affinis* and *Potamopyrgus jenkinsi*. The fish fauna consists of eels, three-spined sticklebacks, ten-spined sticklebacks and brown trout, the latter growing up to 2 kg weight. It is an important ornithological site, particularly on account of the nesting red-necked phalarope and is an RSPB reserve. On open water grounds it is an alternative for the grade 1 Loch Stilligarry and Loch a'Mhachair within the Druidibeg NNR, but is much smaller.

See also C.103.

18 PEATLANDS

SOUTH-EAST ENGLAND

P.1. STODMARSH, KENT

TR 2261. 375 ha Grade 1

This mire contains extensive but uniform beds of *Phragmites communis* together with periodically inundated meadows, developed on ground flooded by colliery subsidence. The dykes have a rich flora and include the following species: *Ranunculus lingua, Utricularia vulgaris, Stellaria palustris* (only three other Kent localities), *Thalictrum flavum, Potentilla palustris, Menyanthes trifoliata, Rumex hydrolapathum, Glyceria maxima, Juncus subnodulosus, Hydrocharis morsus-ranae, Wolffia arrhiza, Oenanthe fistulosa, Veronica catenata, Ceratophyllum submersum, Ranunculus sardous, Rorippa palustris, Triglochin palustris, Scirpus tabernaemontani.* It is particularly important as an ornithological site, but the vegetation is a good example of southern eutrophic flood-plain mire. There is here an outpost of the Norfolk Broads avifauna, with marsh harrier, bittern, bearded tit, garganey, gadwall and water rail, and one species, Savi's warbler, formerly found in the Broads. Reed warblers breed in large numbers in the *Phragmites*-beds. There is a large winter population of mallard (1800), and teal, wigeon, shoveler and pochard occur regularly. Summer breeding birds include garganey, shoveler and pochard.

P.2. THURSLEY COMMON, SURREY

SU 9141. 640 ha Grade 1

This site consists of an extensive area of wet heath and valley mire, through which protrude gentle knolls of the underlying Folkestone Sands with dry heath or pine woodland. A range of mire communities is represented, including some expanses of intact Sphagnetum, similar to the *Sphagnum* lawn communities of certain New Forest valley mires. Other areas show relative base enrichment along more typical axial valley mires which have peripheral zones of *Sphagnum*-dominated vegetation. Some Sphagneta appear to have developed over shallow areas of open water, possibly following colonisation by a mat of *Eriophorum angustifolium* or sedges, for nuclei of *Sphagnum* spp. can be seen in some such swamp communities in certain areas.

Although there are several important areas of acidophilous mire vegetation, Ockley Bog is perhaps the most interesting in that it shows a remarkable similarity with *Sphagnum*-dominated raised mire. There is an extensive and continuous *Sphagnum* carpet, largely of *S. papillosum* and *S. magellanicum*, with a field layer consisting of *Erica tetralix, Molinia*, and a remarkable abundance of *Narthecium ossifragum*. Associated species are *Eleocharis multicaulis, Eriophorum angustifolium, Sphagnum recurvum, S. cuspidatum* and *S. tenellum* in the hollows whilst *Calluna* and *S. rubellum* are scattered throughout and *Vaccinium oxycoccus* is locally abundant on the *Sphagnum* hummocks; the last species is extremely local in southern England. This vegetation can be regarded as a flushed oligotrophic type which is gradually growing above the ground water influence. A marginal *Molinia–Narthecium* lagg community is present.

Extensive areas of wet heath occur with carpets of *Sphagnum compactum* or *S. tenellum* associated with *Narthecium, Erica tetralix, Eriophorum angustifolium* and *Trichophorum. E. vaginatum* is surprisingly scarce. In such areas *Drosera intermedia* is locally abundant, colonising shallow peaty bottomed hollows along with *Zygogonium ericetorum. Lycopodium inundatum* occurs on similar bare peat surfaces, especially along paths. The presence of a pronounced and clearly zoned valley mire, with relatively high nutrient status along the central water course, adds to the interest of the mire systems on Thursley Common. In addition there are a number of areas which have clearly been open water until recently and are now colonised by *Carex rostrata–Menyanthes trifoliata* swamp communities, in which *Utricularia minor* and *Hypericum elodes* are present.

The area has a considerable importance as a breeding ground for heathland birds and, perhaps more important, a remarkably large proportion of British dragonflies is known to occur including several rare species, e.g. *Leucorrhinia dubia, Somatochlora metallica* and *Ceriagrion tenellum*. Thursley and Hankley Commons are also rated as a grade 1 lowland heath site (L.2).

SOUTH ENGLAND

P.3. NEW FOREST VALLEY MIRES, HAMPSHIRE

Grade 1*

(a) Cranesmoor

SU 1903. 95 ha

This most outstanding of the mire systems in the New Forest is divided into two parts. There is a mesotrophic valley mire with central swamp communities dominated by *Molinia, Myrica, Erica tetralix* and *Schoenus nigricans*, with wetter areas of *Hypericum elodes* and *Potamogeton polygonifolius*. Lateral to this is a gently sloping, more acidic surface which has distinct affinities with the northern, patterned blanket mires, both in structure and floristics. Over most of this oligotrophic area *Sphagnum magellanicum* and *S. papillosum* are the dominant species of the ground layer, with *Eriophorum angustifolium*, *Rhynchospora alba*, *Erica tetralix*, *Narthecium*, *Molinia* and *Trichophorum* forming the major components of the field layer. *Calluna* is frequent and *Sphagnum tenellum* locally abundant. Aligned pool systems, remarkably similar to those of the Silver Flowe, though on a much smaller scale, are present and elsewhere the peat surface shows distinct furrows and ridges where the community is dominated by *Myrica*, *Schoenus*, *Molinia* and *Erica tetralix*. This type of peat surface is a major feature of British mires and has affinities with some Scandinavian patterned mires. The southern oceanic element in the flora is well represented, with *Drosera intermedia*, *Hypericum elodes* and *Scutellaria minor*, and *Lycopodium inundatum* is locally abundant.

(b) Denny Bog and White Moor
SU 345052–320080. *c.* 140 ha

Denny Bog is an unusual development of *Sphagnum*-rich valley mire with an extensive semi-floating oligotrophic vegetation raft, dominated by *Sphagnum magellanicum*, merging into a central swamp community with *Potentilla palustris*, *Molinia*, *Hypericum elodes*, *Myrica gale* and *Potamogeton polygonifolius*. A carr has developed down the centre of the site but the marginal communities appear to have been affected by a rising water table possibly caused by the mire being dammed up by the railway embankment. The floating *Sphagnum* carpet is mainly dominated by *S. papillosum* and *S. magellanicum* with a field layer of *Molinia*, *Juncus acutiflorus* and *Myrica*. *Rhynchospora alba* is locally abundant in distinct *Sphagnum* lawns with *S. papillosum*, *S. cuspidatum*, *Narthecium*, *Eriophorum angustifolium*, *Erica tetralix* and *Myrica*. The range of communities is of considerable interest, but recent drainage operations may have severely affected the scientific interest.

White Moor is a series of small valley mires which exhibits vegetation zones similar to those of Wilverley and Holmsley but with a well-developed carr along the drainage axis of each valley. The range of communities between dry heath and valley mire is better displayed than at Wilverley. The carr is dominated by *Alnus glutinosa* and *Salix atrocinerea*, with a field layer of *Carex paniculata*. A marginal *Phragmites–Sphagnum* swamp occurs in which *Hypericum elodes* is locally dominant. The *Sphagnum* lawn communities are less extensive and poorer in species than at Wilverley. However, this area shows many features seen elsewhere in the New Forest but not usually found in combination in such a small area.

(c) Wilverley, Holmsley and Thorney Hill
SZ 255996–215996. 115 ha

Wilverley and Holmsley consist of an oligotrophic valley mire system which shows the typical vegetation zones very clearly. In addition it has a rich flora, especially in the Wilverley section. The upper limbs are floristically poor with communities dominated by *Molinia–Myrica* and *Erica tetralix*, with *Schoenus nigricans* co-dominant in one limb (233014). In the Wilverley section a number of vegetation zones can be recognised including a central alder carr modified by deepening and straightening of the central stream, alongside which is a *Phragmites–Juncus acutiflorus–Sphagnum* swamp community with abundance of *S. subsecundum* and *S. contortum*. The most extensive zone is a *Sphagnum* lawn in which *S. papillosum*, *S. magellanicum* and *S. rubellum* are dominant. *Erica tetralix*, *Calluna*, *Molinia* and *Myrica* are major components together with lesser amounts of species such as *Narthecium*, *Rhynchospora alba*, *Drosera rotundifolia*, *Cirsium dissectum* and *Eleocharis multicaulis*. A number of rare and local bog species occur, including *Hammarbya paludosa*, *Eriophorum gracile*, *Rhynchospora fusca*, *Carex limosa*, *C. lasiocarpa*, *Drosera anglica*, *D. intermedia* and *Pinguicula lusitanica*. Hollows within the *Sphagnum* lawn contain *Scorpidium scorpioides*. Along the edge of the valley the *Sphagnum* lawn grades into wet heath with *Erica tetralix*, *Trichophorum*, *Eriophorum vaginatum*, *S. tenellum* and *S. compactum*. The importance of this system lies in its length and the unusual quality of the *Sphagnum*-dominated communities.

Thorney Hill is unusual in being a eutrophic valley mire (lying on the calcareous Headon Beds). It forms part of the same system as Wilverley–Holmsley but provides a considerable contrast, having abundant *Schoenus nigricans*, *Philonotis calcarea* and a number of local fen species including *Eriophorum latifolium* and *E. gracile*. In the central water track the pH is 7.6 and here a number of fen bryophytes are encrusted in tufa. These include *Cratoneuron falcatum*, *Drepanocladus intermedius*, *Fissidens adianthoides* and *Ctenidium molluscum*. *Preissia quadrata*, a calcicolous hepatic, is present in one of its few lowland localities.

(d) Hincheslea Bottom
SU 2602. 90 ha

This fourth example of New Forest valley mire is a good representative site: it does not have any special additional features or unusual floristic composition.

The central drainage axis has a mixture of acidophilous hummocks and flushed oligotrophic vegetation. *Molinia caerulea*, *Myrica gale*, *Erica tetralix* and *Eriophorum angustifolium* are the major dominants with nuclei of *Sphagnum*-rich hummocks including *S. papillosum*, *S. plumulosum*, *S. rubellum*, *Drosera rotundifolia* and *Narthecium ossifragum*. Soligenous tracts contain *Sphagnum subsecundum* var. *auriculatum*, *Equisetum limosum* and *Eleocharis multicaulis*, *Cirsium dissectum* and *Succisa pratensis*.

Locally, carr with peripheral *Phragmites* is developed along the central drainage axis and *Hypericum elodes* swamp communities are also present in places. Along the edges of the mire are wet heath communities with *Sphagnum tenellum*, *S. compactum*, *Erica tetralix*, *J. squarrosus*, *Calluna* and *Trichophorum*. Within this zone are local flushed areas with *Carex echinata*, *Potentilla palustris*, *Juncus bulbosus*, *Anagallis tenella* and *Drosera intermedia*.

See also W.26 and L.20.

P.4. COTHILL FEN AND PARSONAGE MOOR, BERKSHIRE

SU 4699.   9 ha   Grade 1

This is a small area of calcareous (eutrophic) valley head mire developed over Jurassic calcareous grits. Although the total extent of mire vegetation is less than 8 ha there is a wide range of vegetation types and the area is extremely rich in basiphilous plant species. A number of pockets of mire are separated by drier mineral ground. The flora and fauna of the part known as the 'Ruskin Plot' (0.7 ha) are well documented and it is clear that the area has lost a good deal of its floristic richness during this century. The most important vegetation in this area is a semi-floating *Juncus subnodulosus–Schoenus nigricans* mire community with which are associated *Molinia caerulea, Lycopus europaeus, Valeriana dioica, Carex lepidocarpa, Oenanthe lachenalii, Cirsium palustre, Philonotis calcarea* and *Campylium stellatum*. Other communities include small areas of tall-herb communities with *Eupatorium cannabinum, Filipendula ulmaria* and *Calamagrostis epigejos* and there is open water with *Potamogeton coloratus* and the freshwater crayfish *Astacus*.

Along the east side of the present National Nature Reserve (NNR) is a zone of alder carr with *Carex paniculata* and *Daphne laureola* to the east of which is the open area of calcareous mire known as Parsonage Moor. This is the most important section of the site. It is outstanding as an example of a bryophyte-rich mire with a variety of communities. These include *Phragmites–Campylium stellatum* (the mosses being encrusted in tufa), a short herb *Carex–Schoenus nigricans* association again rich in bryophytes and tall-herb fen communities containing *Filipendula* and *Eupatorium cannabinum*. Species present include *Schoenus nigricans, Phragmites communis, Campylium stellatum, Drepanocladus revolvens, Eriophorum latifolium, Pedicularis palustris, Valeriana dioica, Cirsium dissectum, Carex disticha, C. flacca, C. hostiana, C. lepidocarpa, Dactylorchis incarnata, D. praetermissa, Gymnadenia conopsea, Epipactis palustris, Equisetum fluviatile, Pinguicula vulgaris, Listera ovata, Drosera rotundifolia, Sphagnum plumulosum* and *Briza media*. The population of the scarlet tiger moth *Panaxia dominula* has been studied for many years by Oxford University.

The mire communities grade into drier areas of calcareous grassland. Similarities exist between this site and certain of the Anglesey and Norfolk fens.

P.5. GREYWELL FEN, HAMPSHIRE

SU 7251.   35 ha   Grade 2

Greywell Fen is a calcareous valley mire, dominated by alder carr with *Carex paniculata*, which extends for *c.* 2 km along the headwaters of the River Whitewater. Although the site is composed predominantly of carr there are locally extensive areas of grazed fen meadow, *Phragmites*-beds and restricted areas of open-fen communities containing *Phragmites, Lychnis flos-cuculi, C. flacca, C. lepidocarpa, C. hostiana, C. diandra, Galium uliginosum, Menyanthes trifoliata, Cirsium palustre, Mentha aquatica, Dactylorchis praetermissa, Pedicularis palustris, Epipactis palustris, Eriophorum latifolium* and the rare *E. gracile*. The carr contains abundant *Thelypteris palustris*.

The course of the Whitewater, which is a chalk stream of considerable scientific interest in its own right, has been modified to produce a series of ponds above the water mill and these are now subject to colonisation by hydroseral communities. The site has not been investigated fully but it is clearly of national importance as an example of alder carr and rich valley fen in the headwaters of a chalk stream.

EAST ANGLIA

P.6. HICKLING AND HORSEY AREA, NORFOLK

TG 4121, TG 4522.   750 ha   Grade 1*

Hickling Broad, Heigham Sound and Horsey Mere on the Thurne river system contain a rich variety of Broadland habitats. Several major differences exist between this and the next three sites. A good deal of the area is alluvial marshland with extensive and often rather uniform tracts of reed-swamp and sedge-beds from which a harvest is still obtained. The area lies within 3 km of the coast and is influenced by salt water seepage producing slightly brackish conditions which are reflected in the limnology. Furthermore, because the tidal influence is very small there is an insignificant diurnal fluctuation of the fen water table with the result that acidophilous communities have become established locally above the influence of ground water. This contrasts with the strongly tidal Yare valley, where the considerable fluctuation of the fen water table inhibits the development of such communities.

Commercial sedge-beds, although dominated by *Cladium mariscus*, contain a variety of tall herbs and other mixed-fen species including *Phragmites communis, Schoenus nigricans, Valeriana officinalis, Eupatorium cannabinum, Peucedanum palustre, Rumex hydrolapathum, Galium palustre* and *Lythrum salicaria*. Elsewhere there are various fen and marsh communities including some floristically rich mowing and grazing marshes. The acidophilous communities include species such as *Juncus acutiflorus, Sphagnum subsecundum* var. *inundatum, S. plumulosum, Potentilla palustris, P. erecta, Carex echinata, C. curta, Calluna vulgaris, Genista anglica, Erica tetralix, Agrostis stolonifera* and *Menyanthes trifoliata*.

Several rare plants are abundant in this area. *Pyrola rotundifolia*, a rare fen species *Sonchus palustris*, which occurs in few localities outside Broadland in Britain, and *Peucedanum palustre*, which is mainly restricted to East Anglia and even then is rare outside the Broads, are examples. The latter species, which is abundant in fen communities throughout Broadland, is important as the main food plant of the larvae of the swallowtail butterfly *Papilio machaon*. In addition there is a rich fauna of marshland insects including the rare dragonflies *Aeshna isosceles* and *Libellula fulva*.

Above all this area has outstanding importance since it contains populations of characteristic marshland birds, some of which are now very rare in Britain and have their headquarters in Broadland. The extensive areas of reed-swamp and sedge-bed provide the necessary habitat for a large population of bearded tits, whilst the bittern breeds in reasonable numbers and in some years several pairs of marsh harrier have bred. Montagu's harrier hunts in the area and in recent years has bred in the vicinity. Other wetland species such as water rail, kingfisher and garganey also breed in the area. In addition the grazing marshes and large areas of open water are important for migratory and overwintering species of waders and wildfowl.

Hickling Broad and Horsey Mere are regarded as grade 1 open water sites, and are described under Open Waters, though the separation from the surrounding mire is entirely artificial.

P.7. BURE MARSHES, NORFOLK

TG 3316. 412 ha Grade 1*

The upper section of the River Bure including Hoveton Great Broad, Woodbastwick Marshes and Ranworth Broad is probably the most representative section of flood-plain mire in the Ant and Bure river systems. In this area much of the research was carried out to determine the origin of the Broads and their associated vegetation complexes. This consisted of numerous stratigraphical investigations, detailed examination of the vegetation succession and correlation of both these with documentary evidence of land-use history; the area is thus very well documented and its developmental history is reasonably well understood.

It is known that in 1845 much of the area consisted of open mowing marsh, sedge-bed or shallow turf ponds. Since then there has been a relatively rapid colonisation of turf ponds followed by succession to alder carr throughout a whole range of communities. Much of the carr development has taken place over the past 20 years with the result that only a relatively small proportion of the open fen communities remains. Of about 365 ha of carr and fenland, only about 80 ha are now relatively open reed- and sedge-bed and even this is substantially colonised by woody species, so that much of the scientific interest will be lost unless extensive areas are managed to maintain open conditions.

Abandoned sedge-beds contain *Cladium mariscus* as the dominant species, together with varying amounts of *Phragmites communis*, *Myrica gale*, *Juncus subnodulosus* and *Molinia caerulea*. Associated herbs such as *Peucedanum palustre* and *Cicuta virosa* are present but there is not the same degree of floristic richness as is found in the Yare fens. Elsewhere a number of open fen species such as *Carex appropinquata* and *Lathyrus palustris* occur frequently along the edges of dykes where they are not shaded out by alder.

In contrast to the Yare system, alder is commonly found colonising abandoned sedge-beds direct, together with *Frangula alnus*, whilst *Salix cinerea* is relatively insignificant here in the succession to carr. Where *Carex paniculata* has followed the initial reed-swamp phase in the colonisation of turf ponds the succeeding stages of colonisation by tree species result in the development of 'swamp carr', an unusual community abounding in dead and moribund trees which have been sunk by their own weight. *Osmunda regalis* is frequent and *Thelypteris palustris* locally abundant in the carr communities, together with a

variety of shrubs such as *Prunus padus*, *Ribes sylvestre*, *R. nigrum*, *Rubus idaeus* and several climbing plants including *Humulus lupulus*. *Carex pseudocyperus*, which is a rather local species, occurs around the margins of the Broads.

Ranworth and Cockshoot Broads form an important refuge for overwintering ducks and geese. These include shoveler (125 at Ranworth), mallard, teal, wigeon, pochard, and greylag geese. The breeding population is also important. The swallowtail butterfly occurs here but less abundantly than at Hickling.

See also W.38.

P.8. SURLINGHAM MARSHES, WHEATFEN AND ROCKLAND BROAD, NORFOLK

TG 3305. 305 ha Grade 1*

This area of fen, carr and broad along the south side of the River Yare is one of the most important areas in Broadland since it exhibits extensive open mixed-fen communities. These communities, which are so very restricted elsewhere in the Broads because of succession to carr, contain a rich assemblage of animal and plant species many of which have a restricted distribution in Britain. In the Surlingham Marshes these fens show a clear zonation of plant associations related to decreasing inundation with distance from the river and its interconnected dyke system. Superimposed on this basic zonation is a patchwork of community structures resulting from past land-use practices.

Most characteristic of the area is the dominance of *Glyceria maxima* as the primary coloniser of open water. The species is dominant along certain reaches of the Yare and, more especially, there are extensive and uniform stands where the species has colonised broads and turf ponds by spreading across as a floating raft. In addition *Glyceria* occurs throughout the fens adjacent to the dykes which connect with the river system. This species is insignificant elsewhere in the Broads and it has been suggested that its dominance on the Yare is a response to the strong tidal influence with consequent increased water movement and greater availability of nutrients. *Glyceria* stands are remarkably poor in associated species; *Epilobium hirsutum*, *Urtica dioica*, *Solanum dulcamara*, *Phalaris arundinacea* and *Caltha palustris* being the few which occur regularly.

Mowing marsh which previously occupied much of this area has now reverted to secondary fen. Stands of *Phalaris arundinacea* and *Phragmites communis*, with associates, dominate the regularly inundated areas whilst variable tall-herb and sedge communities, rich in species, predominate over the slightly higher parts. The following species occur in one such community: *Filipendula ulmaria*, *Eupatorium cannabinum*, *Thalictrum flavum*, *Iris pseudacorus*, *Epilobium palustre*, *Carex paniculata*, *C. appropinquata*, *Rumex hydrolapathum*, *Potentilla palustris*, *Peucedanum palustre*, *Equisetum fluviatile*, *Oenanthe fistulosa* and *Myosotis scorpioides*. Such areas are devoid of fen bryophytes.

Elsewhere, in some of the mowing marshes most isolated from tidal influence, *Juncus subnodulosus* is co-dominant with *Phragmites*, again with a tall-herb community rich in species, in which the only bryophytes are occasional patches of *Acrocladium cuspidatum*. *Carex appropinquata* is abundant and *Dactylorchis praetermissa* is present in such communities. Further diversification is afforded locally by communities dominated by *Cladium mariscus* and *Myrica gale*, again with a rich associated flora including several rare and local species such as *Ranunculus lingua*, *Scrophularia umbrosa*, *Cicuta virosa*, *Sium latifolium*, *Lathyrus palustris* and *Stellaria palustris*.

Although large areas of open fen remain, colonisation by *Salix cinerea*, *Viburnum opulus* and *Ligustrum vulgare* is widespread and considerable areas of *Salix* carr have developed over the mowing marshes. Several areas of pure alder carr and damp alder–ash–oak woodland are present, and the very rare fern *Dryopteris cristata* is present in one of its few remaining localities in Britain.

This is one of the most intensively investigated areas of fenland in Britain, owing to the energy of E. A. Ellis who owns a good deal of the area which he manages as a nature reserve. Many of the more difficult plant and animal groups have been investigated by Ellis (1965) and other specialists, and the area is particularly renowned for its extraordinary fungal flora.

P.9. SUTTON BROAD, NORFOLK
TG 3723. 170 ha   Grade 1

Sutton Broad is at present one of the richest areas of vegetation in Broadland. At the beginning of this century the broad was almost entirely open water and there was in fact a Sutton Broad Freshwater Laboratory but rapid hydroseral succession has resulted in most of the Broad being colonised by fen vegetation. A narrow navigable channel extends through the centre. To the north and south of this channel the vegetation shows a distinct zonation from tall mixed reed-swamp in the centre through herb-rich fen to lower sedge and bryophyte communities adjacent to the narrow zone of carr which forms the boundary of the site. The reed-swamp is dominated by *Schoenoplectus lacustris*, *Phragmites* and *Typha angustifolia* and this grades into a mixed-fen community very rich in species, dominated by *Phragmites* and *Juncus subnodulosus* with abundant *Ranunculus lingua*, *Sium latifolium*, *Carex pseudocyperus*, and *Cicuta virosa*. This again grades into sedge-dominated communities in which over 50 species of angiosperms occur. Many of these are rare or local fen species including *Schoenus nigricans*, *Epipactis palustris*, *Liparis loeselii*, *Pyrola rotundifolia*, *Carex lasiocarpa*, *C. dioica*, *C. limosa*, *C. appropinquata* and the ferns *Dryopteris cristata* and *Thelypteris palustris*.

The latter areas are obviously long established and relatively stable communities, but those of the central areas are liable to considerable change. Since most of the Broadland fens are now progressing to alder carr this site offers opportunities for retaining the earlier stages of hydroseral succession which are becoming unavailable elsewhere.

P.10. CALTHORPE BROAD, NORFOLK
TG 4125. 45 ha   Grade 1

This Broad and its surrounding carr lie a considerable distance away from the main river systems and are sluiced.

Until 1970 there was species-rich aquatic vegetation in the Broad, including *Stratiotes aloides*, *Nymphaea alba* and *Nuphar lutea*, but this has since largely disappeared. Primary hydroseral communities which are restricted in extent and rather fragmentary include swamp with *Phragmites communis*, *Calamagrostis canescens*, *Carex acutiformis*, *C. riparia* and *Acorus calamus*. *Pyrola rotundifolia* is recorded. The greater part of the area consists of alder, common sallow and downy birch carr with some secondary planted woodland dominated by the last-named species. Patches of acidophilous (pH 5.6) vegetation, including *Eriophorum angustifolium* and *Sphagnum molle*, are present within the carr.

The Broad itself is regarded as a grade 1 open water site, and the recent hydrological changes which have resulted in virtual disappearance of aquatic macrophytes are described under the site description (OW.16).

P.11. DUNWICH HEATHS AND MARSHES, SUFFOLK
(a) Minsmere   Grade 1*
TM 4667. 850 ha

(b) Walberswick
TM 4774. 1050 ha

This composite site, which abuts the Suffolk coast on either side of Dunwich, contains a number of habitats including flood-plain mire with reed-beds, mixed and carr woodland, acidic heathland, coast shingle and mud flats.

The peatland component consists of two shallow river valleys draining to the sea, Minsmere Level and Walberswick Marshes, which were embanked, drained and reclaimed as damp grazing pasture during the eighteenth century. These were flooded in 1940 by impounding the rivers, as a wartime defence measure. Following further sea water flooding in 1953 the shore embankments of shingle and sand were repaired. As a result, the marshes which have developed are almost fresh, except for a little halophytic vegetation where there is sea water seepage at the seaward end. Both the Minsmere and Walberswick marshes consist mainly of *Phragmites communis* and form the two largest continuous stands of this species in Britain. Both marshes contain shallow pools of open water with some as large as 4 ha. The landward end of both marshes is subject to invasion by willows and alder. This is particularly so at Walberswick where Fen Covert adjoins the marsh. On drier parts of the flood plains there is a change to seasonally wet grassland used as grazing marsh. The marsh flora is not as rich as that of the Norfolk Broads mires, but the area contains a large population of *Sonchus palustris*.

Both valleys are extremely important as breeding places for marsh and fenland birds and as roosting and recuperation areas during migration, though Minsmere is the better known, as it has been a reserve of the Royal Society for the Protection of Birds (RSPB) for some time. There are large populations of reed warbler, sedge warbler and bearded tit. Other notable breeding species include marsh harrier, bittern, Savi's warbler and water rail. The lagoon at Minsmere first attracted avocets back to breed in Britain after the war, though Havergate Island subsequently became the more favoured haunt of this bird. Wildfowl occurring in winter at Minsmere include shoveler (150), gadwall (70), teal (650), Bewick's swan (65); mallard, wigeon, mute swan and shelduck also occur regularly. Of these, gadwall, shoveler, teal, mallard, garganey and shelduck regularly breed. There is no information on the numbers present at Walberswick but they are thought to be similar to those at Minsmere.

The white-mantled wainscot *Archanara neurica* is among the most notable moths taken from Walberswick Marshes, together with *Senta flammea, Chilodes maritima, Arenostola phragmites* and *A. brevilinea*.

See also L.58.

The composite site also includes the Blyth Estuary which is composed of the River Blyth, Bulcamp Marshes, Sandpit Covert Marshes and Angel Marshes all formerly reclaimed as damp meadow and subsequently flooded. At low tide it presents a considerable area of mud flats which constitute an important feeding ground for wildfowl and waders, especially in the winter and during migration. Large numbers of redshank and dunlin are often present together with small numbers of other waders, and there is a spring (March/April) flock of up to 250 black-tailed godwits. A few hundred wigeon and shelduck also occur. Redshank, oystercatcher and common tern are among those known to breed on the saltings and riverbanks. The estuary is fringed with *Halimione* salt marsh together with *Spartina anglica, Limonium vulare* and *Aster tripolium*. On more elevated areas *Juncus maritimus, Puccinellia maritima, Atriplex patula* and *Glaux maritima* occur. There is a small area of *Phragmites* reed-bed which supports a small population of bearded tit as well as reed and sedge warblers.

The shingle beach which stretches from Walberswick to Sizewell is subject to erosion and disturbance by the public. Nevertheless it supports a shingle flora with *Lathyrus japonicus* and *Silene maritima* well represented, together with small populations of other shingle species including *Crambe maritima* and *Glaucium flavum*.

P.12. WOODWALTON FEN, HUNTINGDON AND
       PETERBOROUGH
TL 2384. 205 ha   Grade 1

Woodwalton Fen is a rectangular block of relict peatland which lies close to the south-western margin of the Fenland. Most of the area has been cut for peat, the maximum depth of which is now 3.5 m, and the area is divided into numerous compartments by dykes which connect with the raised dykes in the surrounding Fenland. Stratigraphical studies have shown that acidophilous raised mire vegetation succeeded the fen communities but most of the acidic peat has been removed by cutting during the last hundred years. The present surface vegetation has therefore developed over an almost entirely artificial surface. Differences in vegetation can be related to differences in nature of the surface peat. Two main seral communities are recognised, a *Molinia*-dominated type developed over acidic peat and a community characterised by *Calamagrostis epigejos* which is developed

over *Glyceria* peat. *Cladium–Molinia* stands are developed locally and acidophilous vegetation (including *Calluna vulgaris, Erica tetralix, Potentilla erecta* and *Myrica gale*) occurs within an area dominated mainly by *Molinia caerulea*.

Mixed fen which is floristically rich covers a large proportion of the areas cleared of carr. *Calamagrostis canescens* is dominant whilst *Thalictrum flavum, Phragmites communis* and *Calamagrostis epigejos* are frequent. Rare fen species, e.g. *Peucedanum palustre, Luzula pallescens* and *Viola stagnina*, also occur in this habitat.

Carr covers over half of the mire surface and is varied in composition, with common sallow, blackthorn, buckthorn, downy birch, silver birch, guelder rose and creeping willow. Alder buckthorn is surprisingly almost totally absent and alder forms mature stands only locally.

The whole is a patchwork of communities considerably inferior to the Broadland fens in terms of the intrinsic scientific interest of the vegetation. The degree to which the invertebrate populations have been studied and the outstanding representation of numerous rare and local invertebrate species compensates for the relatively low quality of the vegetation. In the mixed fen, plant communities rich in species ensure a varied and abundant fauna of phytophagous insects, many of which are restricted to East Anglia. In 1927 the Dutch form of the large copper butterfly *Lycaena dispar batavus*, which differs only slightly from the extinct British subspecies *dispar*, was introduced, and a population has been maintained by careful management.

Woodwalton has been a nature reserve (Society for the Promotion of Nature Reserves) since 1919, a factor which is probably responsible for the unusual degree of investigation to which the site has been subjected.

P.13. CHIPPENHAM FEN, CAMBRIDGESHIRE
TL 6469. 115 ha   Grade 1

This site is important for its ecological diversity, for it contains not only areas of characteristic eutrophic sedge fen, but also damp meadow grassland, carr and taller woodland. The north-eastern part and several smaller areas represent old planted woodland, dating from the attempted drainage of this fen at the end of the eighteenth century, and there are all stages in the subsequent colonisation of the open fen. There are areas of alder and willow carr, and also older woodland with ash, sycamore, birch and a variable shrub layer. The western end has a 'Poor's Fen' with a history of peat digging and this area is lower and wetter than the other parts, containing eutrophic, tall, fen communities with *Molinia, Phragmites, Cladium, Eupatorium cannabinum* and *Filipendula ulmaria*. There are also lower communities with *Schoenus nigricans, Juncus subnodulosus, Epipactis palustris, Serratula tinctoria* and *Cirsium dissectum*. The fen meadow communities are less wet, and have an abundance of grasses, including *Molinia* and *Deschampsia cespitosa*, with *Carex flacca, C. hostiana, Serratula, Briza media, Dactylorchis praetermissa* and *Gymnadenia conopsea*. The flora is notable for the abundance of the very rare umbellifer *Selinum carvifolia* and for the presence of local rarities such as *Menyanthes trifoliata, Parnassia palustris, Pinguicula vulgaris* and *Aquilegia vulgaris.*

Chippenham Fen is also famous for its rich fauna, especially of invertebrates, an effect partly associated with its position on the transitional zone between the Fenland and the Breckland. Birds such as the water rail and stone curlew here breed close together, as representatives of fen and grass-heath habitats. The known insect fauna amounts to a very long list, and includes the celebrated fenland moth, the silver barred *Deltote bankiana.*

Chippenham Fen is fed by springs and its water regime could therefore be damaged by schemes involving the abstraction of ground water.

P.14. WICKEN FEN, CAMBRIDGESHIRE
TL 5570.   305 ha   Grade 1

This is a marginal remnant of the original peat fens of the East Anglian basin basically under control of rising sea-level and inflow from rivers draining a large calcareous catchment area. It has been preserved as a floor catchment area and its water level (about +2 m) is controlled by sluice gates at Upware. The peat is 3–3.6 m in depth formed in *Cladium–Alnus* fen over a basal oak forest. The vegetation has a strongly mosaic character associated with past multiple ownership in strips with different systems of crop exploitation and with extensive peat-cutting. Large areas of Cladietum (sedge) were cut at intervals of about four years, and of Cladio–Molinetum yearly for litter, and both communities, as well as a big length of drove and path, are maintained by a sustained cutting regime. The 'sedge' is characterised by such tall species as *Lysimachia vulgaris, Angelica sylvestris, Lythrum salicaria, Peucedanum palustre,* the host plant of the swallowtail butterfly, together with *Salix repens* var. *fusca* and *Lathyrus palustris,* the marsh pea. The areas cut more often support a far greater variety of species including many sedges, rushes, spike rushes, marsh orchids etc., and a corresponding wealth of insect life. In the absence of repeated mowing the vegetation is invaded by bushes, at first common sallow and alder buckthorn, so that closed *Frangula* carr results, to be transformed by natural succession to buckthorn carr, and locally into fen woodland with pedunculate oak or ash. The dykes, abandoned clay pits and the main lode carry a great wealth of aquatic angiosperms, many, such as *Ranunculus lingua, Baldellia ranunculoides* and *Oenanthe aquatica,* now far from common elsewhere. There is a long history of recording of the flora and many intensive studies have been published on the ecology of the plant communities, on which indeed experimentation is still continuing.

The rich, invertebrate populations have long attracted collectors, professional and amateur, so that the documentation for many groups is extremely thorough, and here again investigation is constantly expanding. The local management committee of the National Trust, to whom most of the Fen belongs, publish general or detailed guides to the area and are exercising a policy of active management that includes excavation of a large mere for waterfowl, control of water levels in species areas of wetland and sustained crop-taking and bush clearance. Wildfowl interest includes mallard, teal, wigeon, shoveler, pochard and tufted duck.

P.15. SMALLBURGH FEN, NORFOLK
TG 3224.   7 ha   Grade 1

The vegetation of this calcareous valley mire bordering a tributary of the River Ant in many ways resembles that of Scarning Fen, though it lacks the more distinct zonation of plant communities shown by that site. The vegetation consists largely of *Alnus–Salix* carr with a variable ground flora; *Phragmites* beds of limited extent; and an extensive bryophyte-rich fen within which the field layer components show local variation from low sward to tall-herb communities. Many of the hollows within the fen area contain *Chara* spp. whilst elsewhere an almost continuous carpet of *Campylium stellatum, Drepanocladus revolvens, Acrocladium cuspidatum* and *Lophocolea bidentata* is present, though locally *Sphagnum palustre* forms extensive patches. Vascular plants include *Salix repens, Valeriana dioica, Parnassia palustris, Menyanthes trifoliata, Anagallis tenella, Hydrocotyle vulgaris, Carex flacca, C. dioica* and *Epipactis palustris* whilst the taller communities also have *Thelypteris palustris, Juncus subnodulosus, Eupatorium cannabinum, Phragmites communis,* and locally *Schoenus nigricans.* Along the stream margin are also found *Lycopus europaeus, Phalaris arundinacea* and *Valeriana officinalis.* The alder–willow carr contains extensive patches of *Carex acutiformis,* together with *C. remota, Dryopteris dilatata, Lonicera periclymenum* and *Solanum dulcamara.*

Little recent information is available as to the status of rare species but it is the only known Norfolk station of *Brachythecium mildeanum,* and earlier records exist for *Camptothecium nitens.* This site appears less vulnerable to external disturbance than other similar bryophyte-rich valley mires in East Anglia, particularly Scarning Fen, with which it has close affinities. No examination has been made of the hydrological regime but it appears from the extremely high concentration of calcium carbonate that the area is spring fed and therefore differs from most fenland areas in the Norfolk Broads. In position it can be regarded as a valley mire rather than the usual flood-plain mire of this area. (See Appendix.)

P.16. ROYDON COMMON, NORFOLK
TF 6822.   40 ha   Grade 1*

Roydon Common consists of a complex of dry heath grading into peatland, and lies over Greensand in the north-west of Norfolk. The dry heath, dominated largely by heather, is rated as a grade 1 heathland site (L.59). The important peatland area is a diffuse system of shallow valley mires which forms a substantial part of the site. This is the best example in Britain of a lowland mixed valley mire. It exhibits a clear zonation of communities parallel to the two main drainage axes and parts of the mires show an intimate mixture of contrasting communities due to the development of acidophilous nuclei within a relatively base-enriched soligenous tract.

Dry heath on sand grades into a wet heath community

along the flanks of the mire. This is dominated by *Erica tetralix* with abundant *Molinia caerulea*, *Eriophorum angustifolium* and *Trichophorum cespitosum*; *Sphagnum compactum* and *S. tenellum* are widespread and locally dominant in this zone. *Juncus squarrosus* and *Carex panicea* occur less plentifully, and the rare moss *Dicranum spurium* is recorded. Between this and the communities occupying the central drainage axes is a *Sphagnum*-rich zone with an ill-defined hummock–hollow morphology. This is similar to the equivalent development in the New Forest valley mires. Most of the zone is dominated by *S. recurvum* with *S. subsecundum* var. *auriculatum* and *S. cuspidatum* in hollows whilst *S. papillosum* and, locally, *Polytrichum commune* and *Aulacomnium palustre* form low hummocks. Associated vascular plants are *Narthecium ossifragum*, *Eriophorum angustifolium*, *E. vaginatum* (locally), *Drosera rotundifolia*, *Vaccinium oxycoccus* and *Molinia caerulea*. The marginal communities around pools or in shallow hollows contain a *S. recurvum*, *S. papillosum*, *Rhynchospora alba*, *Juncus kochii*, *Drosera intermedia* association. This community grades into the next as the ground water becomes more base-rich.

Along either side of the drainage axis is a mixed mire, in which *Phragmites communis*, *Schoenus nigricans*, *Juncus subnodulosus*, *Molinia caerulea*, *Succisa pratensis*, *Myrica gale*, *Erica tetralix*, *Sphagnum subsecundum* var. *inundatum*, *S. plumulosum* and *Narthecium ossifragum* are the major constituents. An important community developed locally in depressions includes *Schoenus nigricans*, *Scorpidium scorpioides*, *Campylium stellatum*, *Drepanocladus revolvens*, *Ctenidium molluscum*, *Riccardia pinguis*, *Pellia epiphylla*, *Carex pulicaris*, *C. lepidocarpa*, *Pedicularis palustris*, *Anagallis tenella*, *Dactylorchis praetermissa*, *Drosera anglica*, *Pinguicula vulgaris*, *Sphagnum subsecundum* var. *auriculatum* and *S. contortum*. *Hammarbya paludosa* occurs sparingly here. Bryophytes of rich-fen are well represented, and in addition to species mentioned above include *Drepanocladus lycopodioides*, *D. aduncus*, *Camptothecium nitens* and *Philonotis calcarea*. Other local vascular plants of the swamps are *Utricularia intermedia*, *U. minor*, *Eleogiton fluitans*, *Eleocharis quinqueflora*, *E. uniglumis*, *E. multicaulis*, *Isolepis setacea*. Towards the central drainage axis *Molinia* and *Myrica* become dominant and there is an abundance of *Cirsium dissectum* and *Dactylorchis maculata* var. *ericetorum*. Acidophilous nuclei composed of the wet heath *Sphagnum* community described above are frequent within this mixed mire complex.

Carr is developed along the central axis. At the upper end of the system this consists of incipient carr and there is a marked gradation along the drainage axis to true carr at the lower end. This consists of alder *Frangula alnus* and willow *Salix aurita* with an understorey of *Carex paniculata*, *Caltha palustris*, *Thelypteris palustris* and *Myosotis palustris*. Other species occurring locally along the zone of carr communities are *Parnassia palustris*, *Osmunda regalis* and *Eriophorum latifolium*. *Cladium mariscus* forms a local dominant along the central watercourse within the carr at the lower end of the system.

This mire is the best example in Britain of a valley mire exhibiting progressive base-enrichment from highly acidic heath to calcareous fen. The only comparable sites are Buxton Heath and Holt Lowes (both in Norfolk) – see under Lowland Grasslands, Heaths and Scrub – but neither of these is of such high quality.

P.17. SCARNING FEN, NORFOLK
TF 9812.   4 ha   Grade 1

This is a small calcareous valley mire consisting of several distinct community types including: extensive 'brown moss' carpets with a low sward and varied field layer, beds of *Phragmites communis*, restricted areas of tall-herb and sedge communities, and alder–willow carr with a varied ground flora.

The bryophyte-dominated communities, which are extremely rich in plant species, are unusually extensive and these communities give the site its grade 1 status. Whilst similar communities exist at other sites (e.g. Cothill Fen, Berkshire, and Smallburgh Fen, Norfolk) they are nowhere so well developed as at Scarning Fen. Not surprisingly, since this community type is rare in Britain, many of the component species are also rare or local. It can be argued this this type of stable community has formed a 'reservoir' from which various species have, in the past, colonised seral communities such as are found in the Broads.

Along the southern margin of the mire these communities are clearly zoned. Although *Juncus subnodulosus* and *Schoenus nigricans* are present throughout the low-sward communities, *J. subnodulosus* is dominant in the slightly drier marginal areas along with various herbs such as *Valeriana dioica*, *Lotus pedunculatus* and *Lychnis flos-cuculi*. *S. nigricans* is dominant in the lower bryophyte-rich areas where the water table is slightly higher. In the lowest parts of the mire *Phragmites communis* is dominant.

In the bryophyte carpets the following species form an almost continuous carpet: *Drepanocladus revolvens*, *Campylium stellatum*, *Ctenidium molluscum* and the rare *Leiocolea rutheana*. Less abundant species include *Drepanocladus lycopodioides*, *Campylium elodes* and *Brachythecium salebrosum*. In addition there is a rich assemblage of vascular plants including *Pedicularis palustris*, *Utricularia minor*, *Carex lepidocarpa*, *C. flacca*, *C. dioica*, *C. pulicaris*, *Drosera anglica*, *Pinguicula vulgaris*, *Anagallis tenella*, *Parnassia palustris*, *Epipactis palustris*, *Gymnadenia conopsea*, *Dactylorchis praetermissa*, *D. incarnata*, *D. fuchsii*, *Menyanthes trifoliata*, *Triglochin palustris*, *Isolepis cernua*, *Eleocharis quinqueflora* and *Salix repens*. Higher-sward communities include species such as *Valeriana officinalis*, *Angelica sylvestris*, *Cirsium palustre* and *Filipendula ulmaria*. Damp alder carr contains *Thelypteris palustris*, *Carex acutiformis*, *Mnium pseudopunctatum*, *Sphagnum squarrosum* and *Listera ovata*.

The mire lies along one side of a shallow valley and is bounded at the lowest point by a stream, the course of which has been modified artificially in places. A public footpath crosses the mire along a raised bank and the site lies very close to a new housing development. The resultant public pressure does not yet, however, appear to have caused deterioration except very locally.

P.18. REDGRAVE–SOUTH LOPHAM FEN, NORFOLK–SUFFOLK

TM 0579. 130 ha   Grade 1

At Redgrave on the borders of Norfolk and Suffolk 8 km west of Diss, two rivers rise on either side of a watershed consisting of a low sand ridge (at 26 m) and flow in opposite directions, the Waveney to the east and the Little Ouse to the west. Each river has a system of calcareous valley head mire, Redgrave–South Lopham Fen on the Waveney being the more extensive, with a length of 2.4 km along the valley and a width of 0.4 to 0.8 km.

Redgrave–South Lopham Fen consists essentially of a large tract of rather uniform high-sward fen communities dominated by *Phragmites communis* and *Molinia caerulea* with abundant *Filipendula ulmaria*, *Eupatorium cannabinum* and *Valeriana officinalis*. Some degree of zonation can be recognised in that *Molinia* is more dominant along the drainage axis (which is artificially maintained) whilst tall-herb communities are best developed towards the margins where the water table is lower. The stratigraphy shows that this mire developed in a lake basin and the present surface morphology and vegetation are clearly a result of many attempts to drain the mire. Peat-cuttings are now colonised by a low-sward *Schoenus nigricans* community containing *Valeriana dioica*, *Thalictrum flavum*, *Angelica sylvestris* and *Galium uliginosum*, whilst in other parts of the system *Cladium mariscus* is locally dominant. This is a locality for the rare fen orchid *Liparis loeselii*. Sandy ridges protrude through the mire and locally bear a mixture of acidophilous, basiphilous and intermediate vegetation types. Species present in these areas include *Calluna vulgaris*, *Erica tetralix*, *Drosera rotundifolia*, *Sphagnum girgensohnii*, *S. fimbriatum* and *Juncus subnodulosus*. The insect and spider fauna is of considerable importance and probably of greater account than the botanical interest.

P.19. CRANBERRY ROUGH, NORFOLK

TL 9393. 55 ha   Grade 2

This basin mire has a rich-fen vegetation complex representing various stages of hydroseral development on a former lake (Hockham Mere), of interest as a Quaternary site with a classic sequence of deposits going back to the beginning of the Late-glacial Period, but was drained during the eighteenth century. Four main communities may be recognised, the first being a rather open low- to tall-herb sward with abundant *Carex appropinquata*, *Menyanthes trifoliata*, *Potentilla palustris*, *Oenanthe fistulosa*, *Bidens cernua*, *Cicuta virosa*, *Ranunculus lingua*, *Dactylorchis praetermissa* and the very rare grass *Calamagrostis stricta*. This is bordered by a *Phragmites* swamp with *Eupatorium cannabinum*, *Peucedanum palustre*, *Lythrum salicaria*, *Carex appropinquata* and *C. paniculata*. These communities are variably invaded by alder and willow (mainly *Salix cinerea*) to give carr, that with alders being locally of a swamp type with *C. pseudocyperus*, *C. elata*, *C. acutiformis* and *Hottonia*

palustris (in dykes). *Thelypteris palustris* is locally plentiful in both types of carr, and *Myosotis sylvatica* occurs in damp woodland.

This range of eutrophic fen communities gives an outpost of the characteristic Norfolk Broads hydrosere. The invertebrate fauna is imperfectly known, but at least 61 species of spider are recorded.

See also L.60 and OW.14.

P.20. BARTON BROAD AND REEDHAM MARSH, NORFOLK

TG 3521. 445 ha   Grade 2

This large area contains a wide variety of broadland habitats including a greater amount of open fen communities than the Bure Marshes. It has extensive areas managed for commercial reed and sedge harvesting and other areas previously managed for reed, sedge and marsh hay are now progressing towards carr and in places alder carr is established. This site forms an alternative to the Bure Marshes grade 1* site (P.7). (See Appendix.)

P.21. THELNETHAM AND BLO' NORTON FENS, SUFFOLK

TM 0178. 20 ha   Grade 2

At Thelnetham, near the head of the west-flowing Little Ouse, a second calcareous mire system has developed, only just over a mile from Redgrave–South Lopham Fen, but quite separate from it. Two small areas of herb-rich fen at Thelnetham have a greater intrinsic botanical interest than the larger Redgrave–Lopham Fens. The western area consists of a tall-herb community in which *Schoenus nigricans*, *Phragmites communis*, *Eupatorium cannabinum* and *Filipendula ulmaria* are co-dominant, but a large number of other species are abundant including: *Sanguisorba officinalis*, *Vicia cracca*, *Succisa pratensis*, *Dactylorchis praetermissa*, *Epipactis palustris*, *Oenanthe lachenalii* and *Cirsium dissectum*. A discontinuous ground layer of bryophytes includes *Drepanocladus revolvens*, *Campylium stellatum*, *Acrocladium giganteum* and *Fissidens adianthoides*. Wetter areas contain *Carex diandra*, *Typha angustifolia*, *Mentha aquatica*, *Campylium stellatum*, *Mnium seligeri*, *Riccardia pinguis* and *Marchantia polymorpha*. Other species present include *Rumex hydrolapathum*, *Cladium mariscus*, *Oenanthe fistulosa* and *Lythrum salicaria*. This community is similar to that developed over abandoned mowing marshes in the Surlingham–Rockland area of the Broads.

The second area at Thelnetham is more varied than any other part of the Waveney–Ouse fens. It consists of a strikingly zoned spring-fed fen including an acidophilous vegetation at one side which grades into a rich, sedge-grown, 'brown moss' carpet. Tall-herb communities, reed-beds and carr cover most of the remaining area. The sedge–bryophyte community is very similar in floristics to that at Scarning Fen (Norfolk) but is much more restricted. Where it grades into more acidophilous communities the following species are present: *Sphagnum plumulosum*, *Drosera rotundifolia*, *Carex pulicaris*, *Genista anglica*, *Potentilla erecta* and *Luzula multiflora*, all of which occur on the hummocks whilst the following occur in the intervening calcicolous fen community: *Schoenus nigricans*, *Anagallis tenella*, *Pedicularis palustris*, *Epipactis palustris*, *Ctenidium molluscum*, *Campylium stellatum*, *Carex lepidocarpa*, *C. flacca*, *Eriophorum latifolium* and the rare fen orchid *Liparis loeselii*. Tall-herb communities are similar to those of the western site but have a more continuous bryophyte layer and are rather more varied. Development of alder carr is taking place rapidly.

This area of valley-head calcareous mires was until recently one of the most important in Britain but drainage operations in the headwaters of the Little Ouse have caused a lowering of the water table threatening the viability of the Fens. In addition a recent severe fire has probably caused irreversible damage to the bryophyte-dominated communities. Despite these problems the area may retain its scientific value and the aggregate site is considered to merit grade 2 status.

P.22. BUXTON HEATH, NORFOLK

TG 1721.   65 ha   Grade 2

The common land known as Buxton Heath consists mainly of dry heath which surrounds a small but unusual valley mire system containing a remarkable variety of plant associations. This variation is a response to differences in ground-water chemistry within quite small areas. A moderately rich fen occupies part of the valley bottom where there is a supply of relatively base-rich water, whereas the valley sides support acidophilous communities, the springline here being in glacial sands and the water oligotrophic. In some areas the boundary between these communities is very distinct but in others there is an intimate mixture of fen and bog elements. The following is a floristic list for a 1-m quadrat in such an area: *Juncus subnodulosus*, *Valeriana dioica*, *Briza media*, *Epipactis palustris*, *Schoenus nigricans*, *Cirsium palustre*, *Climacium dendroides*, *Philonotis calcarea*, *Cinclidium stygium*, *Eriophorum latifolium*, *Ranunculus acris*, *Pinguicula vulgaris*, *Succisa pratensis*, *Drosera rotundifolia*, *Erica tetralix*, *Molinia caerulea*, *Anagallis tenella*, *Sphagnum plumulosum*, *S. recurvum* and *S. palustre*.

More distinctly acidic areas have an abundance of *Potentilla palustris*, *Molinia caerulea*, *Erica tetralix*, *P. erecta* and *Genista anglica*, whilst the pronounced fen areas contain species such as *Carex disticha*, *Dactylorchis praetermissa*, *Parnassia palustris*, *Lotus pedunculatus*, *Sphagnum contortum*, *S. subsecundum*, *S. squarrosum* and *S. fimbriatum*, *Filipendula ulmaria* and *Thelypteris palustris*. *Listera ovata* is abundant in the birch–willow carr developed locally along the drainage axis. In addition to the remarkable mixed-mire community, Buxton Heath is notable for the rich bryophyte flora including the extremely rare hepatic *Leiocolea rutheana*, and local mosses such as *Cinclidium stygium*, *Camptothecium nitens*, *Drepanocladus vernicosus*, *Philonotis calcarea* and *Acrocladium giganteum*.

The site has been subject to considerable modification, especially as a result of moss-gathering. In spite of this the intrinsic scientific interest of the intact central communities

of the valley mire, with their assemblage of rare and local species, is sufficient to give the site national importance, though there are other comparable mire systems of even higher quality.

The wet heathland adjoining the valley mire includes a good representation of typical wet heath species. *Sphagnum* spp. include *S. papillosum*, *S. magellanicum*, *S. compactum*, *S. tenellum*, and *S. rubellum*, and there are species of wet hollows such as *Rhynchospora alba*, *Drosera intermedia* and *Eleocharis multicaulis*. *Lycopodium inundatum* is of very local occurrence and *Gentiana pneumonanthe* is almost entirely confined to a track crossing the wet heath where the vegetation is kept low and in an open condition. Management treatments within this particular habitat could probably increase the numbers of this species in a region where it is by no means common. The dry heathland component at Buxton Heath has another important feature in the abundance of *Ulex gallii*, which is essentially a species with a western distribution but is also found in some heathlands in East Anglia especially those to the north of Norwich. The dry heath is in danger of being over-run by birch and in places by bracken, bramble and rosebay willow herb but with management it could be kept as a valuable dry heathland site essential for the viability of the peatland system that it contains.

P.23. SANDRINGHAM WARREN (DERSINGHAM BOG), NORFOLK

TF 6829.   160 ha   Grade 2

North of King's Lynn a steep scarp face of Greensand extends for several km, and along its base an acidic valley mire has developed. This is a very shallow peat deposit, nowhere more than 1 m deep, which shows a distinct zonation outwards from the scarp face. The high water table is clearly maintained by seepage from the Greensand, but the communities are markedly oligotrophic. A *Sphagnum*-rich zone occurs immediately adjacent to the scarp face and this zone is locally more extensive especially at the southern end of the mire. *S. recurvum*, *S. rubellum*, *Rhynchospora alba*, *Narthecium ossifragum* and *Vaccinium oxycoccus* are the main species in this zone which includes a number of other *Sphagnum* spp. and a large number of leafy liverworts. Occasional hollows in the *Sphagnum* carpet contain *Drepanocladus revolvens*, the most basiphilous species present. Further out from the scarp *Eriophorum angustifolium* and *S. recurvum* are dominant along with *Calluna* and *Erica tetralix*. In some areas an unusual erosion surface has developed. The thin peat cover (20–30 cm) has been removed to form shallow pools which dry out seasonally, and *Eriophorum angustifolium* is growing on the exposed mineral ground which has the remarkably low pH of 2.7–4.0.

The mire has affinities with the New Forest valley mires but is more allied to the northern mire element in its floristics. It is not of grade 1 quality but is nationally important in that it exhibits an interesting form of mire development unusual in Britain. Dersingham Bog is part of Sandringham Warren grade 2 heathland site and shows a good transition from mire communities through marginal wet heath and humid heath (containing the rare moss *Dicranum spurium*, *Campylopus brevipilus* and *Sphagnum molle*) into dry heath with heather and bracken; though on shallower peat there is also an acidic *Molinia* grassland with partial *Sphagnum* carpet. The area is surrounded by birch-woods and rhododendron thickets which are encroaching onto the open heathland and in places onto the mire communities.

P.60. THORNE AND CROWLE WASTE (PART), LINCOLNSHIRE   Grade 2

See under North England, p. 230.

SOUTH-WEST ENGLAND

P.24. SHAPWICK HEATH AND ADJACENT AREAS, SOMERSET

ST 4340, ST 4543, ST 4639.   460 ha   Grade 1

In historic times the Somerset Levels consisted of a series of raised mires with intervening areas of marsh and fen. Most of the region has now been drained and peat has been cut extensively on a commercial scale. The remaining areas of scientific interest are now isolated blocks, analogous to those of the Cambridgeshire Fens, the conservation of which presents considerable problems. Nevertheless these areas are still sufficiently important to merit grade 1 status in view of the variety of communities present and the richness of flora and fauna.

No areas of undamaged raised mire remain but one section at Westhay Moor provides the nearest approach to this type of vegetation. Old peat-cuttings now support communities remarkably similar to those of raised mire. Other small remnants of the original surface occur elsewhere. Most of the semi-natural vegetation elsewhere in the Levels consists of stages in succession from poor-fen through *Myrica*-dominated communities to birch carr. All these are developed on cut-over areas. Some of the richest communities are the fen-meadows which are maintained either by grazing or mowing. Some of these have oligotrophic associations without counterpart in the British Isles except in meadows adjacent to central Ireland raised mires. Many plant species in this area have a limited distribution in Britain, e.g. *Rumex hydrolapathum*, *Thelypteris palustris*, *Peucedanum palustre* and *Lathyrus palustris* which are all associated with base-rich fens; also *Wahlenbergia hederacea* which is a Lusitanian species of oligotrophic habitats.

The Somerset Levels have long been known to have a high entomological value which may well outweigh the botanical interest. In addition the area forms a classic locality where archaeological and botanical studies of peat stratigraphy have been carried out.

P.25. NORTH DARTMOOR, DEVON

SX 5786.   1350 ha   Grade 1

Blanket mire covers a good deal of the northern plateau of Dartmoor between 520 and 580 m. In the region of East Dart Head two types can be recognised, distinguished by

differences in vegetation and geomorphological position. Blanket mire, with peat rarely more than 2 m thick, extends over the watersheds and is generally eroded to some extent. The vegetation of such areas consists predominantly of vascular plants. In contrast the valley-side terraces, well developed along the west side of East Dart, have deeper peat which is usually more intact with a high water table and a continuous cover of *Sphagnum*. These two hydromorphological types are analogous to the valley side flows and watershed flows of Sutherland.

Valley-side terraces exhibit extensive flat or very gently sloping mire surfaces dominated by *Sphagnum papillosum*, non-tussocky *Molinia caerulea* and *Eriophorum angustifolium*. *Trichophorum* and *Calluna* occur throughout these level surfaces, in which hummock centres are rarely developed. *Narthecium ossifragum* and *Erica tetralix* are frequent and *Polygala serpyllifolia* is remarkably abundant; occasional hollows are colonised by *Sphagnum subsecundum* var. *auriculatum* and *Zygogonium ericetorum* with marginal *Narthecium*. Low hummocks or 'flats' of *S. rubellum* or *S. capillaceum* are frequent whilst *Leucobryum glaucum* forms occasional taller hummocks. Eroded areas whilst not usually severely hagged are extensively dissected by shallow gullies. *Molinia* and *Calluna* predominate on the ridges, where *Rhacomitrium lanuginosum* is generally abundant, and locally this species is dominant over more severely hagged areas. *Eriophorum vaginatum* is present though not with a high cover, and *Juncus squarrosus* is locally abundant. *Vaccinium myrtillus* is also locally abundant, but *Empetrum nigrum* absent.

These communities belong to the western Trichophoreto–Eriophoretum type but represent a *Molinia*-rich facies similar to that of the Galloway blanket mire. Absence of northern oceanic species such as *Pleurozia purpurea* and *Drosera anglica* is of interest and *Sphagnum imbricatum* is known in southern England only in a similar community at Tor Royal Mire south of Princetown.

Dartmoor blanket mire represents one end of an ecological gradient and as such merits a place in the grade 1 mire series. The area around East Dart Head is considered to be most suitable in view of the range of communities present. Whilst a number of high-quality blanket mire areas occur on the southern plateau of Dartmoor (e.g. Cater's Beam) the overall quality of the vegetation in that area is lower. In addition to the blanket mire, the lowland heath communities and upland habitats of the northern plateau have been recognised as of grade 1 status, and are described under the appropriate chapters.

P.26. HARTLAND MOOR, DORSET

SY 9485.   180 ha   Grade 1

One of the main features of this grade 1* lowland acidic heathland area is the presence of an important valley mire system. This consists of two limbs with differences in ground-water chemistry. One limb of the system is relatively calcium rich and mesotrophic with vegetation dominated by tussocky *Schoenus nigricans*, whilst the other limb is distinctly oligotrophic with an acidophilous vegetation containing much *Sphagnum pulchrum* and only scattered *Schoenus nigricans*. Bog pools are present along this second limb of the system, and some of these contain *Carex limosa*. The very local *Rhynchospora fusca* is present and *Hammarbya paludosa*, another rather rare bog species, also occurs. Where the two limbs meet, intermediate conditions are produced and *Eriophorum latifolium* is present. Below this, more acid conditions prevail. *Molinia*-rich facies and other areas with *Molinia–Myrica–Sphagnum* associations are present. Within the acidophilous communities, *Drosera anglica* is present and *Narthecium ossifragum* abundant whilst *Osmunda regalis* occurs locally. The oligotrophic communities associated with the mire pools are unusual in a lowland context, those of nearest similarity being found on Cranesmoor in the New Forest. In both these sites the vegetation has affinities with northern mire communities.

Insect populations of the area are outstanding. Of the species found in the mire communities, the two rare dragonflies, *Ceriagrion tenellum* and *Coenagrion mercuriale*, are especially noteworthy.

P.27. MORDEN BOG, DORSET
SY 9192.   180 ha   Grade 1

Morden Bog is a valley mire *c.* 2 km in length, lying over Bagshot Beds to the north-west of Poole Harbour. In size it compares favourably with some of the larger New Forest valley mire systems. The vegetation is, however, very different, consisting essentially of flushed oligotrophic communities including *Molinia–Myrica–Sphagnum* associations, *Carex lasiocarpa*, extensive areas of *Phragmites* (in association with acidophilous species) and *Sphagnum*-rich mire communities with *S. magellanicum* and *S. papillosum* which are, however, rather poorly developed in comparison with that facies of the New Forest valley mires. The rare *S. pulchrum* is locally abundant. In addition there is a carr of downy birch over *C. paniculata* following a section of the drainage axis.

The mire is shallow, with 2 m depth of peat in general, and has been subject to peat-cutting. It lies within a relatively dry area of heathland, much of which is under Forestry Commission plantations, so that the catchment is unusually free from disturbance. The site therefore provides good opportunities for research into the water regime of a valley mire.

The insect fauna of this area is outstanding, and includes several very rare species, some of which are unknown elsewhere in Britain. Among the dragonflies is the rare *Ceriagrion tenellum*. Furthermore the dry heath and pine colonised heathland are important habitats in their own right, and the area rates as a grade 1 lowland heath (L.90).

P.28. CATER'S BEAM, DARTMOOR, DEVON
SX 6269.   800 ha   Grade 2

On the southern plateau of Dartmoor at about 460 m there is an extensive area of blanket mire some of which, particularly on the saddles, is of high quality. At Cater's Beam is an extensive *Sphagnum*-rich area with a slight hummock-

hollow mosaic. *Molinia* dominates except in the sometimes extensive lawns of *S. papillosum*, *Eriophorum angustifolium*, *Erica tetralix* and *Narthecium ossifragum*. *Trichophorum* is abundant throughout and both this species and *Eriophorum vaginatum* frequently form tussocks. *S. magellanicum* is locally abundant and hummocks of *S. rubellum*, *Molinia* and *Trichophorum* are frequent. Peripheral areas are subject to severe modification possibly due to grazing. *Juncus squarrosus* and *Carex panicea* are both present in a more disturbed community containing abundant tussocky *E. vaginatum*. Some peat-cutting has occurred in the past at the north end of the saddle. Eroded blanket mire similar to that of the northern plateau covers the plateau to the east of Cater's Beam.

This area contains sufficient high-quality blanket mire to merit at least grade 2 status and can be regarded as an alternative to the northern plateau though it does not exhibit the well-defined morphological mire types found in that area.

SOUTH WALES

P.29. CORS FOCHNO (BORTH BOG), CARDIGANSHIRE
SN 6391.   550 ha   Grade 1*

Cors Fochno is an estuarine raised mire lying on the south side of the Dyfi estuary. The viable raised mire surface is now reduced to about one third of the total area of mire vegetation, since extensive areas have been severely modified in various ways (including agricultural reclamation and extensive peripheral peat-cuttings). Nevertheless the central area contains the most extensive tract of unmodified raised mire vegetation in Britain. It is effectively buffered by the surrounding areas of modified raised mire communities dominated particularly by a *Molinia caerulea–Myrica gale* association. A lagg community with *Salix cinerea* carr is developed along the eastern margin and an important gradation from raised mire to salt marsh communities is present along the western margin adjacent to the tidal Afon Leri.

The intact central communities have a low-amplitude hummock–hollow mosaic in which broad, shallow *Sphagnum*-dominated hollows alternate with slightly higher areas in which vascular plants predominate and the *Sphagnum* cover is discontinuous. Hollows generally have a *S. pulchrum–Rhynchospora alba–Andromeda polifolia* association but *S. cuspidatum* and *Eriophorum angustifolium* form the main association of more pronounced pools in which *Menyanthes trifoliata* is present. Large areas are dominated by a relatively level *Sphagnum* lawn containing *S. pulchrum*, *S. tenellum*, *Rhynchospora alba*, *Erica tetralix*, *Eriophorum angustifolium*, *Narthecium ossifragum*, *Drosera rotundifolia* and *D. anglica*. Hummock-forming *Sphagnum* spp. are relatively unimportant, but *S. papillosum*, *S. rubellum* and *S. magellanicum* occur in association with *Calluna vulgaris* and *Cladonia impexa*, forming slight ridges. *S. imbricatum* is present very locally and *S. fuscum* is frequent in this association, both of these being very local species in southern Britain. *Myrica gale* is present throughout on the slightly higher hummocks.

The marginal *Salix cinerea* carr has a ground flora dominated by either *Carex paniculata* or *Phragmites communis*, with the following species: *Osmunda regalis, Dactylorchis incarnata, Potentilla palustris, Menyanthes trifoliata, Viola palustris, C. curta, Iris pseudacorus, Lycopus europaeus, Eupatorium cannabinum, Sphagnum subsecundum* and *S. fimbriatum*. In the gradation from raised mire to brackish conditions there is an association of *Myrica gale* with *Juncus maritimus*, and *Schoenus nigricans* occurs locally. Compared with more northerly raised mire systems, there is a richer flora, resulting mainly from the stronger marginal influence of ground water, giving weakly mesotrophic conditions. Some northern species here approach their most southern British limits, e.g. *Andromeda polifolia, Vaccinium oxycoccus, Sphagnum imbricatum* and *S. fuscum*.

The rosy marsh moth *Eugraphe subrosea*, extinct for a century in its only other British locality in the Fenland, has recently been found here. Polecats frequent the area.

The mire is an important site for stratigraphical studies of raised mire development, since the deposits on which it has developed are continuous with those of the present estuary and the developmental sequence is well displayed. See also C.46.

P.30. CORS GOCH GLAN TEIFI, CARDIGANSHIRE
SN 6964. 800 ha   Grade 1

Cors Goch glan Teifi is a very extensive raised mire system developed over a Late-glacial lake which once occupied the broad valley of the Teifi in mid Wales. The raised mires lie at an altitude of about 160 m. They extend for 4 km along the valley and reach 2 km in width. Several distinct mires are separated either by the River Teifi or by lagg streams which join the Teifi; the largest single expanse lies to the west of the river. This mire was the first true raised mire to be described in detail in Britain, by Godwin & Conway (1939), and is regarded as a classical site where the developmental sequence from aquatic conditions through flood-plain mire to an ombrogenous mire surface is well demonstrated in the stratigraphy.

The vegetation of the mire expanse shows an unusually wide range of variation including *Sphagnum*-rich vegetation (exhibiting a small scale hummock–hollow topography), Callunetum and areas in which both *Molinia caerulea* and *Trichophorum cespitosum* are major components. This variation may be caused by disturbance (by grazing and burning) rather than by differences in vegetational succession in different parts of the mire. However, there is a relationship between the distribution of these communities and the profile of the mire surface, and in this respect the variation in communities is important.

The intact *Sphagnum*-rich communities contain *S. papillosum, S. pulchrum, S. cuspidatum* and *S. tenellum* with *Calluna vulgaris, Eriophorum vaginatum, E. angustifolium, Erica tetralix, Trichophorum cespitosum* and *Rhynchospora alba* in varying degrees of abundance. Numerous shallow mud-bottomed hollows occur which contain *Zygogonium ericetorum* and often *Drosera intermedia*. Although *Narthecium ossifragum* and *Andromeda polifolia* are fairly abundant

they do not form major components as they do at Cors Fochno, and *Myrica gale* is completely absent, even in the *Molinia*-dominated rand. Other differences in floristics include a greater development of *Cladonia, Cladina* agg. on hummocks and an abundance of *Empetrum nigrum* here, reflecting the most fundamental difference between the two mires, namely, that the water table is very much closer to the surface on Cors Fochno. Moreover, there is a much gentler micro-topography at Borth, which exhibits greater areas of tall hummock communities.

River terraces which are regularly flooded show a zonation of communities parallel to the river. *Phalaris arundinacea* and *Deschampsia cespitosa* occur along the river edge and a broad zone of *Juncus effusus* with incipient carr formation occurs between this and a *Molinia*-rich lagg community. A wide rand is present which is mainly dominated by vascular plants with a discontinuous *Sphagnum* carpet.

This is the most southerly locality in Britain for the large heath butterfly.

P.31. RHOS GOCH, RADNOR
SO 1948. 60 ha   Grade 1

Rhos Goch consists of a variety of mire communities lying at 250 m on a flat valley floor in central Radnor. Essentially it is a confined raised mire with a well-developed carr along the lagg streams around the upper margins and an extensive tract of poor-fen swamp communities occupying the full width of the valley below the raised mire. The site is particularly notable for the well-developed hummock–hollow network on the raised mire surface. This is of a type known elsewhere in Britain only at Wem Moss (P.40) in Shropshire. It consists of numerous wet hollows or pools separated by drier ridges dominated mainly by vascular plants (e.g. *Molinia caerulea, Calluna vulgaris, Eriophorum vaginatum, Vaccinium myrtillus* and *Erica tetralix*) but with some hummocks of *Pleurozium schreberi* and *Polytrichum alpestre* and areas of *Cladonia impexa*. Hollows are very varied but are often colonised by *Sphagnum subsecundum* var. *inundatum, Potamogeton polygonifolius* and *Equisetum fluviatile* or by *S. cuspidatum, Menyanthes trifoliata* and *Eriophorum angustifolium*. Around the pool margins, *Narthecium ossifragum, Erica tetralix, Molinia caerulea, S. papillosum* and *S. tenellum* form a frequent association. Birch is rapidly colonising the dry ridges of this mire surface. Around the margins of the raised mire adjacent to the carr a distinct community occurs which reflects increasing base status in the presence of *Scorpidium scorpioides, Cirsium dissectum, Cardamine pratensis* and *Aulacomnium palustre*. *Ulex gallii* and *Genista anglica* occur along with more acidophilous species on the drier ridges.

The carr consists of downy birch or common sallow as the main tree species with guelder rose, rowan and pedunculate oak present. The ground flora is locally dominated by *Carex paniculata* or *Phragmites communis* and elsewhere consists of a mixed community including *C. acutiformis, Listera ovata, Apium inundatum, Potentilla palustris, Eupatorium cannabinum, Valeriana dioica, Thelypteris palustris* and an unusually large amount of *Osmunda regalis* which also occurs throughout the open mire surface.

The large extent of poor-fen swamp in the lower part of the valley is an important additional facet. This is dominated by *Juncus–Carex* associations containing *Juncus acutiflorus, J. effusus, C. paniculata, C. nigra, C. rostrata, C. vesicaria, Equisetum fluviatile, Lychnis flos-cuculi, Lycopus europaeus, Menyanthes trifoliata, Veronica scutellata, Scutellaria minor* and *Ranunculus lingua.*

The importance of this site lies in the wide variety of mire communities represented, including the classic representation of wooded lagg communities marginal to the raised mire. The intrinsic scientific interest of the central raised mire surface is not as high as that of Wem Moss.

P.32. OXWICH, GLAMORGAN

SS 5087.   60 ha   Grade 1

An area of aquatic transition mire is developed within the sand dune system of Oxwich on the Gower coast (C.41). This consists of extensive *Phragmites* beds, mixed fen and areas of open water with a good aquatic flora. Low sward fen associations include areas which are floristically very rich, with *Equisetum fluviatile, Menyanthes trifoliata, Lychnis flos-cuculi, Potentilla palustris, Iris pseudacorus, Hydrocotyle vulgaris, Carex flacca, C. panicea, C. nigra, C. otrubae, Lycopus europaeus, Triglochin palustre, Dactylorchis praetermissa, Rumex hydrolapathum, Listera ovata, Philonotis fontana* and *Climacium dendroides.* Well-developed carr is dominated by alder and common sallow, whilst mixed-fen communities composed of sedges and tall herbs occupy an extensive area. These communities contain a variety of vascular plants, the dominant species being *Carex nigra, Achillea millefolium* and *Galium palustre*, and associates include *Pedicularis palustris, C. riparia, C. otrubae, Eleocharis palustris, Epilobium obscurum, Lotus pedunculatus, Oenanthe lachenalii, Butomus umbellatus, Scutellaria galericulata, Typha latifolia* and *T. angustifolia.* A maritime influence is indicated by presence of *Schoenoplectus tabernaemontani* and *Hippophäe rhamnoides.*

The area is potentially a good ornithological habitat owing to the extent of reed-beds (*c.* 2 km in length), but is particularly outstanding as an educational site since there is a wide range of maritime habitats represented in the area in addition to the mire communities, all of which are easily accessible.

P.33. LLYN, RADNOR

SO 0155.   15 ha   Grade 1*

This is a small composite basin mire lying in an irregular glacial hollow of about 0.4 km in length. The developmental history of the two main basins which underlie the present mire vegetation was rather different. In both cases there is a substantial depth of Late-glacial sediments, followed by organic silts indicating an open water body with aquatic macrophytes. In the northern basin this was followed by establishment of reed-swamp and carr, whilst a thin (1 m) floating raft of acidic peat was developed over the southern basin. Substantial sections of the mire have

been cut for peat in the past, especially around the northern margins, but this does not seem to have occurred in the southern basin. Old peat-cuttings are now colonised by an association of *Eriophorum angustifolium, Sphagnum recurvum* and *Vaccinium oxycoccus*, and the intervening baulks support mature Scots pine. Most of the northern basin is now covered by a poor-fen community in the form of a floating vegetation raft consisting of *Eriophorum angustifolium, S. recurvum, Potentilla palustris, Carex rostrata* and *V. oxycoccus,* which has developed relatively recently across open water which was almost certainly an area of flooded peat-cuttings. This is being invaded by species from the *Sphagnum* lawn to the south, e.g. *Drosera rotundifolia, Narthecium ossifragum* and *Rhynchospora alba.*

The most interesting feature of the site is the acid *schwingmoor* which is mainly composed of a gently undulating *Sphagnum* lawn, dominated by *S. papillosum, S. cuspidatum, S. recurvum, Rhynchospora alba, Narthecium ossifragum, Vaccinium oxycoccus* and *Erica tetralix.* Hummocks support *Calluna vulgaris, Molinia caerulea, Trichophorum cespitosum, Empetrum nigrum, Eriophorum vaginatum, Cladonia impexa, S. plumulosum* and *S. rubellum.* This area is most comparable with Moorthwaite Moss (P.56), Cumberland. It is one of the few basin mires which is not becoming dominated entirely by a *S. recurvum–V. oxycoccus* community. Relatively dry areas surrounding this *Sphagnum* lawn have a ground flora of *Eriophorum vaginatum, V. myrtillus, Calluna vulgaris, Pleurozium schreberi* and *Empetrum nigrum.*

The southern oligotrophic mire surface is not subject to inflow of run-off water from surrounding agricultural land because this drains peripherally along a lagg area in which downy birch dominates a carr community containing *Filipendula ulmaria, Molinia caerulea* and locally *Juncus effusus.* There is a rich epiphytic lichen flora associated with birch, amongst which *Cetraria sepincola* is notable as a scarce species with a disjunct distribution in Britain. This carr is separated from surrounding pasture by a fence.

P.34. CORS GOCH, RADNOR

SN 8963.   125 ha   Grade 2

Whilst a good deal of the blanket mire on the central Welsh plateau is rather degraded there are local patches of a higher quality which usually occur where the topographic conditions maintain a high water table. Cors Goch is one such area, lying in a shallow depression on a wide spur between the Elan and Claerwen valleys at an altitude of 430 m.

The central part of this blanket mire is strongly eroded and represents the site of a previous pool–hummock complex, with *Rhacomitrium lanuginosum* abundant as a hummock-forming species where the erosion has resulted in severe desiccation. Surrounding this central erosion complex is a remarkably intact *Sphagnum*-rich blanket mire with an unusual development of flushed communities on one side where the mire receives inflow of drainage water from a second section of the site. The intact mire communities are dominated by *Calluna vulgaris, Trichophorum cespitosum* and *Eriophorum vaginatum* together with a virtually continuous ground layer of *Sphagnum* moss, *S. papillosum, S. cuspidatum, S. subsecundum* var. *auriculatum, S. rubellum* and *S. plumulosum*. Other important constituents include *Narthecium ossifragum, Erica tetralix, Eriophorum angustifolium, Cladonia uncialis, Vaccinium oxycoccus, Molinia caerulea* and rather depauperate but frequent plants of *Andromeda polifolia*, this being its most southerly locality in Britain. *Empetrum nigrum* and *Pleurozium schreberi* are present.

Flush communities containing *Carex lasiocarpa, C. nigra, C. rostrata, Scorpidium scorpioides, Potamogeton polygonifolius, Sphagnum subsecundum* var. *auriculatum* and *Menyanthes trifoliata* are developed in a series of soaks between islands of more oligotrophic vegetation dominated by *S. papillosum, Narthecium ossifragum* and *Molinia caerulea*. These occur over an area of several hundred metres and add considerably to the scientific interest of this area of blanket mire.

The vegetation of the site as a whole is a facies of Trichophoreto–Eriophoretum, most similar perhaps to the example of this vegetation type on Dartmoor, but with considerably less *Molinia*. This is the best example of actively growing blanket mire yet seen in Wales, but is not of sufficient national importance to merit grade 1 status.

NORTH WALES

P.35. CORS ERDDREINIOG, ANGLESEY
SH 4780.   125 ha   Grade 1

Cors Erddreiniog is an area of calcareous valley mire extending over a distance of 2.4 km along the floor of a shallow valley adjacent to an outcrop of Carboniferous Limestone. The mire appears to have developed over a shallow Postglacial lake. In places the peat, which is generally only 0.9–1.2 m thick, overlies *Chara* marl.

The dominant associations are similar to those of Cors Goch (Anglesey) which lies about 1.6 km to the north-east. *Cladium mariscus, Schoenus nigricans* and *Juncus subnodulosus* are all locally dominant and tall-herb, mixed fen communities are widespread. As in the case of Cors Goch there is a mixture of northern and southern floristic elements. *Carex elata, Cladium mariscus, Dactylorchis traunsteineri, Epipactis palustris, Serratula tinctoria* and *Ophrys insectifera* are characteristic southern species, whilst *Carex hostiana, C. lasiocarpa, Dactylorchis purpurella* and *Selaginella selaginoides* have a northern distribution in Britain.

An important area of Cors Erddreiniog is a section of the mire in which acidophilous nuclei are well developed, forming an incipient acidic mire surface. Towards the northern end of the site is a small lake where an aquatic transition community is well developed, including *Hippuris vulgaris* and *Potamogeton coloratus* and stands of mixed reed-swamp. *Sparganium minimum* occurs in the open water.

Although Cors Goch (Anglesey) and Cors Erddreiniog are separate and rather similar sites, calcareous mire is so rare in western Britain that both are rated as grade 1 in

order to include an adequate *area* of this type in the highest category, and there are good reasons for regarding the two as parts of a single complex.

See also OW.37.

P.36. CORS GOCH, ANGLESEY
SH 4981.   40 ha   Grade 1

This is a highly calcareous valley mire developed in a depression originally occupied by a shallow lake in a strike valley within the outcrop of Carboniferous Limestone. It lies only about 1.6 km away from another rich calcareous mire, Cors Erddreiniog, with which the drainage was once continuous.

The mire is almost divided into two sections by a transverse ridge of limestone and is bounded on the east side by a steep limestone scarp. In the eastern section the main communities show a zonation from areas of standing water in the centre towards the drier margins. Stands of *Phragmites communis* occur in the centre and elsewhere rich-fen communities dominated by *Cladium mariscus* or *Juncus subnodulosus* are extensive. Locally small areas of willow carr are developed but the bulk of the vegetation is open fen. *Schoenus nigricans* forms a distinctive marginal zone in association with 'brown mosses' and drier areas have a *Molinia–Myrica* association where more acidic conditions are developing.

The calcareous fen has peat with a pH ranging from 6.0 to 7.5. This area is floristically very rich and is comparable with the Norfolk–Suffolk valley fens. Presence of a northern and western element in the flora (e.g. *Carex limosa, C. lasiocarpa, C. rostrata, Dactylorchis purpurella, Selaginella selaginoides* and *Littorella uniflora*) distinguishes this vegetation from the East Anglian facies of calcareous mire. The Anglesey fens are intermediate in type between those of Norfolk and the northern type represented by Newham Fen (Northumberland) and the Whitlaw Mosses (Selkirk). Other noteworthy species present include *D. incarnata, Parnassia palustris, C. diandra, C. lepidocarpa, Pedicularis palustris, Thelypteris palustris, Osmunda regalis, Sphagnum contortum, Campylium elodes, C. stellatum, Drepanocladus revolvens* and *Scorpidium scorpioides*.

The western section of the site is more dissected but is notable for the presence of an area of open water and more pronounced development of aquatic transition communities.

P.37. CORS BODEILIO & CORS Y FARL, ANGLESEY
SH 4977, SH 4978.   80 ha   Grade 2

These are two calcareous valley mires lying in depressions in the Carboniferous Limestone of eastern Anglesey. Together they contain a wide variety of plant communities and as a combined grade 2 site they can be regarded as an alternative to Cors Goch (Anglesey) or Cors Erddreiniog.

Cors Bodeilio lies at about 30 m and occupies a shallow valley extending for about 1.2 km in length and 0.8 km wide. It is surrounded by limestone and the pH of the peat associated with *Schoenus nigricans* is 7.5–8.0. The vegetation includes *Cladium mariscus, S. nigricans, Phragmites communis, Juncus subnodulosus* and *Molinia caerulea*, all of which attain dominance. The pattern of communities is largely determined by past and present management, especially mowing and drainage. Low-sward herb-rich fen communities are particularly outstanding for the number of members of the Orchidaceae represented which include *Gymnadenia conopsea, Epipactis palustris, Ophrys insectifera, Dactylorchis fuchsii, D. incarnata, D. traunsteineri, D. ericetorum, Platanthera bifolia* and *Coeloglossum viride.* The vegetation does not have such a natural character as that of the 'brown moss' associations of Cors Erddreiniog and Cors Goch.

Cors y Farl lies in an enclosed hollow again surrounded by limestone. As in the other Anglesey fens, *Cladium mariscus, Juncus subnodulosus* and *Schoenus nigricans* form the dominant associations. Areas of mixed herb-rich fen also occur which include numerous rare and local fen species such as *Ranunculus lingua, Oenanthe lachenalii, Eleocharis quinqueflora* (here at the southern limit of its range), *Carex elata, C. disticha, C. diandra, C. acuta* and *Eriophorum latifolium.* Although small (400 m in diameter) this mire is floristically very rich.

The two sites lie within 0.8 km of each other and together provide an outstanding example of calcareous mire in Anglesey, equalling the grade 1 sites in intrinsic quality but lacking the degree of structural isolation which makes Cors Goch and Cors Erddreiniog better conservation units.

P.38. CORS Y SARNAU, MERIONETH
SH 9739. 14 ha   Grade 2

Cors y Sarnau is a valley mire with extensive mesotrophic fen communities, areas of carr and incipient development of acidophilous vegetation. Swamp communities dominated by *Potentilla palustris, Hypericum elodes, Menyanthes trifoliata, Potamogeton polygonifolius, Hydrocotyle vulgaris, Carex rostrata, C. nigra, C. panicea* and *Lychnis flos-cuculi* are widespread. In places carr has developed over such associations, but elsewhere a true fen carr is present, dominated by *Alnus glutinosa* with a ground flora including *C. paniculata, Filipendula ulmaria, Caltha palustris, Ranunculus flammula, Valeriana officinalis, Potentilla palustris, Acrocladium giganteum* and various epiphytic lichens and bryophytes.

Acidophilous vegetation is widespread and includes the following species: *Erica tetralix, Narthecium ossifragum, Vaccinium oxycoccus, Sphagnum palustre, S. plumulosum, S. rubellum* and *Drosera rotundifolia.*

The site is a good example of a mesotrophic to oligotrophic valley mire exhibiting a range of habitats and plant associations related to seral succession from a shallow lake to an alder carr and acidic mire surface. It is similar in type to Caw Lough in Northumberland.

P.39. CORS GRAIANOG, CAERNARVONSHIRE
SH 4945. 35 ha   Grade 2

This area of acidophilous mire is developed within an enclosed basin. The present surface, lying at *c.* 170 m, is partially developed over old peat-cuttings and includes open raised mire vegetation, poor-fen swamp, willow carr, and

peripheral acid flushes. A stream drains across the mire from the north-east.

Part of the mire is enclosed by a dry stone wall, within which the communities are dominated by *Molinia, Eriophorum vaginatum, Erica tetralix* and *Sphagnum* spp. Elsewhere the mire surface is wetter and shallow pools or wet hollows are scattered throughout the open mire surface. These contain lawns of *S. cuspidatum* or *S. recurvum* locally with *Carex limosa. Utricularia intermedia* occurs in some of the pools. Most of the area is dominated by *Molinia* and *Eriophorum* spp. with abundant *Sphagnum* (mainly *S. papillosum, S. magellanicum, S. rubellum* and *S. plumulosum*). *Trichophorum cespitosum, Drosera rotundifolia* and *Vaccinium oxycoccus* are also abundant. Drier hummocks support *Calluna, Empetrum nigrum, Pleurozium schreberi* and *Hylocomium splendens.* To the south the mire is considerably wetter with oligotrophic swamp communities of *Potamogeton polygonifolius* and *Potentilla palustris.* Other species present in the wetter parts include *Hypericum elodes, Eleogiton fluitans* and *Scutellaria minor.* There is an abrupt transition between this area and common sallow carr which is extremely dense and supports epiphytic lichens.

Marginal acidic flushes are of considerable interest. These are dominated by *Erica tetralix* and *Molinia caerulea* with an open bryophyte surface including *Sphagnum subsecundum* and *Campylopus atrovirens.* Other species include *Drosera intermedia, Rhynchospora alba, Pinguicula vulgaris, Eleocharis multicaulis* and *Narthecium ossifragum.*

Despite the fact that it has been considerably modified by peat-cutting this site is considered to merit grade 2 since it has considerable importance as a southern example of oceanic mire vegetation. The flush associations in particular are characteristic of mires in north-western districts but there is also a southern element in the flora.

MIDLANDS

P.40. WEM MOSS, SHROPSHIRE
SJ 4734. 30 ha   Grade 1

Wem Moss is a lowland raised mire now reduced in extent through partial reclamation. Although small it is a viable mire system and has considerable importance as an extreme form of raised mire development in Britain. The climatic regime of the area (76 cm rainfall per annum and long summer droughts) is such that the vegetation is predominantly of a dry facies but the mire surface exhibits a remarkable high amplitude pool-and-ridge network which is evidently a reflection of this climatic regime. The general surface is dominated by *Calluna vulgaris* and *Erica tetralix* with some *Cladonia impexa* and *Molinia caerulea.* Within this are many elongated steep-edged hollows dominated by *Sphagnum cuspidatum, Eriophorum angustifolium* and *Rhynchospora alba* with a marginal zone of *S. papillosum* and *Drosera rotundifolia.* These hollows have an artificial appearance owing to the steep edges but their natural origin is indicated by extreme regularity of the system and similarity of the spatial pattern to that developed extensively on oceanic raised mires. The only site where a similar type of pattern is developed is Rhos Goch (Radnor) where the acidic surface is more extensive but the intrinsic vegetational quality is not so high as on Wem Moss. The difference between these two sites in terms of the vegetation facies represented is, however, sufficient for both to be considered grade 1 sites.

The raised mire surface contains a number of local species including ·Sphagnum pulchrum, Drosera anglica, Drosera intermedia, Eleocharis multicaulis, Andromeda polifolia and Osmunda regalis in addition to characteristic species of raised mire such as Narthecium ossifragum and Vaccinium oxycoccus. The mire is divided into two parts by a lagg dominated by Molinia caerulea and Myrica gale with robust Narthecium abundant. Species present in this lagg include Carex lasiocarpa, Osmunda regalis, Dactylorchis incarnata, Cirsium dissectum, Platanthera bifolia, Ranunculus flammula and Caltha palustris.

Although Wem Moss merits grade 1 status in its own right, in view of its proximity to the north Shropshire area of meres and mosses (including Crose Mere, Sweat Mere and Clarepool Moss), it should be considered with these other grade 1 sites.

P.41. KINDER-BLEAKLOW, DERBYSHIRE/YORKSHIRE
SK 0994.   4500 ha   Grade 1

The High Peak is one of the most notable upland districts in Britain for development of blanket mire and a representative area of this formation has high claims for grade 1 status. The area chosen as containing the best examples of blanket mire also has a range of dry upland communities regarded as grade 1 in their own right (see U.16).

Blanket mire in the southern Pennines consists mainly of a dry facies of Calluneto-Eriophoretum in which Sphagnum and often Calluna vulgaris are entirely absent, the vegetation being dominated either by Vaccinium myrtillus and Empetrum nigrum or Eriophorum vaginatum. Peat erosion occurs on a very large scale producing many square km of a characteristic hagg and gully topography.

The plateaux of Kinder Scout (636 m) and Bleaklow Hill (628 m) are covered by blanket mire showing an extreme erosion facies. All stages can be seen in erosion of peat from small gullies with intact intervening surfaces, through a phase of large gullies with mineral ground exposed and vegetation restricted to the hagg tops, to the extreme case where total removal of all vegetation has occurred except for rounded knolls or eroding peat islands within areas of bared sand, gravel or stones. In addition there is some re-colonisation of denuded mineral ground by Juncus squarrosus, Nardus stricta, Deschampsia flexuosa and Vaccinium myrtillus, as on Far Moss north of Bleaklow Hill. The vegetation of residual and more intact peat surfaces consists of dense V. myrtillus and Empetrum nigrum with Eriophorum angustifolium constant and E. vaginatum locally abundant to dominant. The abundance of Empetrum nigrum, both in uneroded Eriophorum vaginatum mire, and on severely hagged peat, has no parallel in Britain outside the southern Pennines. Rubus chamaemorus is locally abundant whilst E. angustifolium and D. flexuosa

are frequent associates. Blanket mire peat deeper than about 2.7 m is usually eroding, and the same is true on Moor House in the northern Pennines. It is probable that the more compact, shallow peat dominated by E. vaginatum is to a large extent a climatic type since there is stratigraphical evidence that Sphagnum has never been more than a minor constituent. In the deeper peat now eroding there are abundant remains of S. acutifolium agg., S. imbricatum and Rhacomitrium lanuginosum indicating the former presence of a hummock–hollow system. Degeneration of the peat to an erosion complex may well have been accelerated by anthropogenic factors, especially fire and grazing.

One of the notable factors affecting the blanket mires of this district has been the extremely heavy pollution fall-out, both of solid particles and volatile soluble pollutants (especially sulphur dioxide); this is believed to have killed off the Sphagnum component and may have affected the vegetation otherwise. Smoke abatement schemes have, however, greatly reduced atmospheric pollution, especially of solid fall-out, during the last two decades. The great extent and depth of blanket mires on these High Peak moorlands suggests a high precipitation/evapotranspiration ratio, in the past if not in the present. Mean annual number of wet days now exceeds 180, but it is not clear whether this level of wetness is adequate to account for the past scale of peat formation in this district.

P.42. CHARTLEY MOSS, STAFFORDSHIRE
SK 0228.   40 ha   Grade 1

Chartley Moss is a large basin mire roughly triangular in shape (with each side about 0.8 km long) situated in a deep basin (16 m) in glacial deposits overlying Keuper Marl. The central part of this moss is a floating peat raft or schwingmoor overlying a reservoir of water at least 9 m deep, but around the margins the peat is continuous above the basin floor.

The vegetation of the peat raft is predominantly composed of Sphagnum recurvum-Eriophorum angustifolium-Vaccinium oxycoccus with certain regularly associated species such as Erica tetralix, Drosera rotundifolia and Andromeda polifolia. Other less abundant species are Calluna, Eriophorum vaginatum and Empetrum nigrum. Locally the level of the S. recurvum lawn is broken by hummocks of S. papillosum frequently accompanied by S. capillaceum and Aulacomnium palustre (occasionally with S. magellanicum). V. oxycoccus, Andromeda polifolia and Erica tetralix tend to be more vigorous on these hummocks.

Scots pine forms localised stands and is abundant as seedlings or 'checked' and moribund trees in the Sphagnum lawn. Some areas show Empetrum nigrum dominance over pine needles below older pines, and there is evidence of lateral spread of S. recurvum from adjacent Sphagnum lawns into some such areas.

Within this floating raft are two large pools which may be continuous with the reservoir below, and are described as an example of this type under Open Waters. In places these pools show colonisation by Sphagnum recurvum and Eriophorum angustifolium. One area towards the margin of the mire has a base-rich influence, for there is a patch of rich fen vegetation consisting of a canopy of *Alnus glutinosa* and *Sorbus aucuparia* together with a ground flora including *Calamagrostis canescens*, *Carex paniculata*, *Cladium mariscus*, *Valeriana dioica*, *Scutellaria galericulata* and *Thelypteris palustris*.

This moss is the largest basin mire in Britain and fully merits grade 1 status as a structural type despite the somewhat uniform surface vegetation.

P.43. CLAREPOOL MOSS, SHROPSHIRE
SJ 4334. 16 ha   Grade 1

This is an elongated basin mire occupying a series of hollows in glacial drift. The vegetation is predominantly acidophilous and as in the case of Wybunbury Moss a recent drainage phase accompanied by birch and particularly pine colonisation has been followed by a recurrence of *Sphagnum*-dominated communities. Much of the surface now supports *Pinus–Sphagnum* or *Pinus–Empetrum nigrum* communities but open areas occur where old peat-cuttings now recolonised still have a water table too high for pine establishment. There is a limited area of *Sphagnum* lawn bordering an extensive pool at the north-eastern margin of the Moss. This pool is described as a grade 1 open water (OW.40), and is bordered by an alder, downy birch, common sallow carr containing *Osmunda regalis*. Tussocks of *Carex paniculata* form a fringe adjacent to the *Sphagnum* lawn in which region there is a pronounced gradient of pH and base-status.

The *Sphagnum* lawn consists predominantly of *S. recurvum* with abundant *S. rubellum* and *S. cuspidatum*. *Eriophorum angustifolium*, *Drosera rotundifolia*, *Calluna vulgaris*, *Andromeda polifolia*, *Empetrum nigrum* and *Vaccinium oxycoccus* are locally abundant. The rare moss *Dicranum undulatum* is present and *Carex limosa* occurs as a relict poor-fen species in a *S. recurvum* association which forms a small discrete *schwingmoor* in one place. Remains of *Scheuchzeria palustris* are abundant only 50 cm below the surface in many places (this species is now restricted in Britain to one area – Rannoch Moor in Argyll–Perthshire). The communities occupying old peat-cuttings have a remarkably natural appearance and include a *Sphagnum cuspidatum–Rhynchospora alba* association, containing *Andromeda*, *Drosera anglica* and *V. oxycoccus*. One of the most important communities, although derived, is the *Pinus–Empetrum* woodland rich in bryophytes and lichens. This community is not as well developed in any other basin mires in the Midlands, but is equally well represented in Cliburn Moss, Westmorland.

See also OW.40.

P.44. WYBUNBURY MOSS, CHESHIRE
SJ 6950. 14 ha   Grade 1

Wybunbury Moss is a basin mire which occupies a small but deep hollow in glacial drift of the Cheshire Plain. The present surface consists predominantly of a central oligotrophic vegetation dominated by *Sphagnum recurvum* (which is being colonised by birch and pine) and includes also *Pinus–Molinia–Betula* woodland and a marginal

eutrophic fen community. This combination of such contrasting vegetation types adds considerably to the scientific interest of the area. The mire is particularly important as a structural type. It consists of a floating raft of peat, nowhere more than 4.5 m thick, overlying 14 m of water below which are further deposits of peat on the floor of the basin. In this case, however, there is some doubt as to the exact mode of formation of the raft, and there is evidence that it may have formed secondarily by subsidence of the basin and splitting of a previously formed peat-body.

The central *Sphagnum* lawn is dominated by a *S. recurvum–Eriophorum angustifolium–Vaccinium oxycoccus–Erica tetralix* community in which occur slightly higher hummocks of *S. rubellum* and *S. papillosum*. *Eriophorum vaginatum* occurs throughout, though in a sparse form. Scots pine is colonising the area but rarely grows above 3 m in height. Elongated hollows within the *Sphagnum* lawn contain *Drepanocladus fluitans* and *Cladopodiella fluitans* whilst the rare moss *Dicranum undulatum* occurs in association with *S. rubellum*. A small pool in one area contains *Carex limosa*, *C. rostrata* and *C. curta*, representing a relict poor-fen association.

The marginal mesotrophic fen community contains *Carex paniculata*, *C. pseudocyperus*, *Typha latifolia*, *T. angustifolia*, *Thelypteris palustris*, *Phragmites communis*, *Menyanthes trifoliata*, *Salix* spp. and locally *Cladium mariscus*. It appears that this rich fen community is dependent on a lateral movement of relatively base enriched water flowing into the basin. There has been a slight rise in the water table of the basin during recent years, but the central acidophilous communities appear to be unaffected. Nevertheless the area is very vulnerable to any changes on the adjacent land which might affect the quantity or quality of water entering the basin.

P.45. CRANBERRY BOG, STAFFORDSHIRE
SJ 7450. 2 ha   Grade 2

This is a very small basin mire not more than 90 m across which is, however, outstanding in that it shows a clearly defined central oligotrophic surface surrounded by a fen lagg containing a large number of species characteristic of eutrophic conditions. The central section is an open *Sphagnum* lawn with an undulating surface in which distinct hummocks are numerous. These are often capped by *Aulacomnium palustre*. *S. rubellum* and *S. recurvum* are the main components of this surface together with *Eriophorum angustifolium*, *Erica tetralix* and *Vaccinium oxycoccus*, the latter two species being particularly abundant on the hummocks. *Narthecium ossifragum* is locally abundant and *Drosera rotundifolia* is widespread. *Molinia caerulea* and *Eriophorum vaginatum* are abundant near to the margin of the lawn. Pines have invaded this surface but many are dead.

The lagg communities are severely modified but several important species are present including *Alnus glutinosa*, *Angelica sylvestris*, *Carex elata*, *C. paniculata*, *C. pseudocyperus*, *Cicuta virosa*, *Dryopteris spinulosa*, *Frangula alnus, Hottonia palustris, Lycopus europaeus, Lythrum salicaria, Oenanthe aquatica, Osmunda regalis* and *Rumex hydrolapathum*, giving a rich-fen community which contrasts strongly with the central acidic surface.

Because of its size and situation the site presents difficulties in regard to conservation, since it will probably be easily affected by external phenomena, especially inflow of agricultural chemicals from surrounding farmland. The intrinsic scientific interest is, however, sufficient for the site to be rated grade 2.

P.46. ABBOTS MOSS, CHESHIRE
SJ 6069.   45 ha   Grade 2

This is a complex of mire sites within an area of glacial sands on the Cheshire plain. It includes two major basins at slightly different levels, one draining into the other, and several smaller hollows showing various stages of colonisation of open water by oligotrophic vegetation. All these occur in an area of semi-natural vegetation surrounded by forestry plantations on what was until recently heathland.

Both of the major basin mires are characterised by an almost level expanse of oligotrophic mire vegetation dominated by *Sphagnum recurvum, Vaccinium oxycoccus* and *Eriophorum angustifolium*. The upper basin (Abbots Moss) is more varied than the lower one in that distinct wetter and drier areas can be recognised which are almost certainly overgrown peat-cuttings. On the firmer ridges *Calluna vulgaris* and *S. papillosum* are present and locally there are hummocks of *S. rubellum* with *Erica tetralix* and *Aulacomnium palustre*. *Drosera rotundifolia* is locally very abundant on *S. recurvum–V. oxycoccus* communities and *Andromeda polifolia*, though frequent throughout the mire, is also most abundant in such communities. Where the water level is highest *S. recurvum* is dominant, with a very sparse growth of *Eriophorum angustifolium* and little else. Colonisation of open pools by *S. recurvum* and *E. angustifolium* stems is well displayed. These pools are described in greater detail under the Open Waters. In one section of the basin there is a source of base-enriched water reflected in the development of a stand of *Typha latifolia* and localised carr communities containing alder, *S. fimbriatum* and *S. squarrosum*. Much of the mire surface is being colonised by Scots pine and birch. The lower basin (Shemmy Moss) receives run-off water from the upper one by a drainage channel. This mire surface is much more open, with less tree growth, and consists of a remarkably level expanse of *S. recurvum–V. oxycoccus–E. angustifolium* with *Andromeda polifolia* scattered throughout and local patches of *Calluna–Erica tetralix–V. oxycoccus* forming loose hummocks sometimes with a remarkably robust shrubby growth of *A. polifolia*.

Although these mires are extraordinarily poor in plant species they are intact units which provide ideal facilities for the study of hydrological aspects of basin mire ecology, especially in view of the nature of the catchment. The vegetation is comparable with that which dominates Chartley Moss but the two sites differ considerably in

structure. Chartley Moss is more varied, but is less suitable for studies of the mire water regime.

See also OW.46.

NORTH ENGLAND

P.41. KINDER–BLEAKLOW (PART), YORKSHIRE   Grade 1
See under Midlands, p. 222.

P.47. ROUDSEA MOSSES AND STRIBERS MOSS, LANCASHIRE
SD 3382, SD 3480.   100 ha   Grade 1

The series of estuarine raised mires along the east side of the Leven estuary consists of a number of severely modified units, none of which contains sufficient scientific interest on vegetational grounds to warrant a grading higher than 3. However, these mosses have long been recognised as having exceptional entomological importance. As a result of a recent survey of Macrolepidoptera it is known that a high proportion of the British species occur here (314 species out of a British total of about 900) and these form a very high proportion of the total (about 500) for the Lake District as a whole. One of the features of the area is the occurrence of a number of rather local species together. The most important of these are *Coenonympha tullia* ssp. *davus, Odontosia carmelita, Diacrisia sannio, Celaena haworthii, Eustrotia uncula, Hypenodes turfosalis, Idaea muricata* and *Carsia sororiata*. These mosses adjoin Roudsea Wood (W.139) and are regarded with this as forming a composite grade 1 site.

P.48. GLASSON MOSS, CUMBERLAND
NY 2360.   250 ha   Grade 1

Glasson Moss forms a small part (about 2.5 km²) of a once extensive tract of raised mire along the south side of the Solway Firth. Several patches of viable raised mire still exist in this area and of these Glasson now contains the largest area of relatively undamaged vegetation. A good deal of the southern part of the mire has been cut commercially for peat, resulting in a dry surface with dominant *Calluna*, but the northern section has only been cut insignificantly around the margins. The continuous Sphagnetum of the northern section had recovered well after a fire in 1956, but was again burnt over almost the whole surface in 1971. It is essential to maintenance of the scientific interest of the site that no more fires on this scale occur. (See Appendix.)

This northern area, which measures about 0.8 by 1.2 km, has a high water table throughout. The vegetation is *Sphagnum*-dominated and the mire surface forms a gently undulating hummock–hollow mosaic (as on Cors Fochno) with shallow *Sphagnum*-filled hollows and low-amplitude hummocks. The hollows contain the characteristic *S. pulchrum–Rhynchospora alba–Andromeda polifolia* association, and *S. cuspidatum* is dominant along with *Eriophorum angustifolium* in the centre of many of these hollows. The slightly higher areas are dominated by *S. magellanicum* with associated *Vaccinium oxycoccus, Erica tetralix* and lesser amounts of *Calluna, Eriophorum vaginatum* and *E. angusti-*

folium. The gentle hummocks have an association of *C. vulgaris*, *Empetrum nigrum*, *S. rubellum* and *Pleurozium schreberi* with many other characteristic raised mire bryophytes. A feature of the vegetation as a whole is the relative insignificance of *S. papillosum*, and corresponding prominence of *S. magellanicum*.

Other features of importance are the extreme abundance of *Andromeda polifolia* and *Rhynchospora alba*, and the presence of certain local and rare species such as *Sphagnum imbricatum*, *S. fuscum*, *Drosera anglica*, *D. intermedia* and the rare mire moss *Dicranum undulatum* which is locally abundant. *Myrica gale* becomes abundant towards the edges of the Sphagnetum. The margins of this site are mostly modified by cutting and burning. Where the surface has become partly dried there is an abundance of *Campylopus brevipilus*, *S. compactum*, *S. tenellum* and, more locally, *S. molle*. At the edges there is local invasion by downy birch to form thickets, and *Dryopteris austriaca* and *Polytrichum commune* become abundant in places. Some marginal peat-cuttings which hold water have developed spongy lawns of *S. recurvum* with *Molinia*, *Carex nigra* and *Dryopteris spinulosa*, all these being absent from the central Sphagnetum. On the north side there is a patchy development of a lagg, with *Salix cinerea* thicket over *Sphagnum* swamp with *S. palustre*, *S. fimbriatum*, *S. squarrosum* and *S. recurvum*. A few more basiphilous species such as *Lychnis flos-cuculi* are represented.

The ornithological interest of this site has declined in recent years, as on others of these coastal Solway peat mosses. Grouse have become extremely few, merlin and twite seldom if ever breed now, and former colonies of great black-backed, lesser black-backed and black-headed gulls have disappeared. This and adjoining raised mires are, however, an important haunt of the ssp. *tullia* of the large heath butterfly.

P.49. IRTHINGHEAD MIRES, CUMBERLAND/NORTHUMBERLAND Grade 1*

Afforestation and the construction of a rocket-testing site have destroyed large tracts of the former vast expanse of blanket mire on the moorlands drained by the rivers Irthing and North Tyne, while sheep-grazing and moor-burning have modified much of the rest. Throughout this area there nevertheless remain numerous discrete patches of high-quality blanket mire occupying various topographical situations including extensive valley-side flows, 'flat' blanket mires lying on saddles and convex blanket mires on the gently sloping watersheds. The undamaged state of many of these mires, together with the remarkable range of vegetation and morphological mire types within a very small area, makes this an outstanding complex, not only because of the high intrinsic scientific interest of the mires but also because of the potential which the area has for research into the relationship between vegetation, hydrology and mire dynamics. Although many high-quality mires exist in this area the range of vegetational and morphological types can be represented by the following five sites, which occur in a variety of topographical condi-

tions over an altitudinal range of 230–300 m, within the Irthing catchment. These sites all lie within a circle of 4-km radius, and as they are part of the same expanse of moorland (though now dissected somewhat by afforestation) they are regarded as component parts of a single aggregate site.

(a) Butterburn Flow
NY 6776. 325 ha

Butterburn Flow is the most important *Sphagnum*-rich blanket mire outside Scotland. It occupies a wide gently sloping valley side spur, which falls only 15 m over 2.4 km, and the mire surface covers about 325 ha making it by far the largest of the five sites. The greater part of the surface is dominated by a *Sphagnum*-rich facies (*S. magellanicum*–*S. papillosum*–*Erica tetralix*–*Vaccinium oxycoccus* constant) of Calluneto–Eriophoretum with a low amplitude hummock–hollow mosaic. A number of local and rare mire species are present, notably *Carex paupercula*, *C. limosa*, *C. pauciflora*, *S. pulchrum*, *S. imbricatum*, *S. fuscum*, *Dicranum undulatum* and *Drosera anglica*. In addition *Andromeda polifolia* is abundant and the vegetation has certain affinities with that of the Solway raised mires in the presence of an association of *S. pulchrum*–*Rhynchospora alba* and *A. polifolia*. In places, there are drier patches with a more tussocky growth of typical blanket mire vascular plants such as *Calluna*, *Eriophorum vaginatum*, *E. angustifolium* and *Trichophorum cespitosum*, and the *Sphagnum* carpet has a more hummocky form. Drier hummocks have *Empetrum nigrum* and *Cladonia sylvatica*. *Rubus chamaemorus* occurs here at an unusually low elevation (270 m) for England. The Flow contains one of the most extensive undamaged Sphagneta in Britain, of a type once widespread in the Scottish Borders and the Pennines, but now rare and still diminishing.

(b) Haining Head Moss
NY 7175. 30 ha

Haining Head Moss is the next most important, and forms the flat floor of an elongated valley head or col at about 260 m between the Irthing and North Tyne catchments. It is floristically extremely rich and characterised by a level *Sphagnum*-dominated mire surface extending along the valley for over 1 km. The dominant *Sphagnum* spp. are *S. magellanicum*, *S. papillosum*, *S. cuspidatum* and *S. tenellum* which form an unusually level surface in which pool–hummock development is negligible. *Drosera anglica* is especially abundant and both *Andromeda polifolia* and *Carex pauciflora* are frequent. Other major components of the vegetation are *Erica tetralix*, *Eriophorum angustifolium*, *Vaccinium oxycoccus*, *Narthecium ossifragum*, *Trichophorum cespitosum*, *S. rubellum*, *Polytrichum alpestre* and *D. rotundifolia*, together with a rich assemblage of leafy liverworts (eight species). In addition, hummocks of *S. imbricatum* and *S. fuscum* are present. The site is remarkably free from damage by fire or drainage, except for a section of the south side which has been drained adjacent to Forestry Commission plantations.

(c) Hummel Knowe Moss
NY 7071. 60 ha

Hummel Knowe Moss occurs on a col at a lower level than Haining Head and although it is of the same topographic type the vegetation differs considerably. Again the mire surface is level with remarkably little development of hummock-forming vascular plants but here by contrast *Sphagnum papillosum* is dominant throughout and the main vascular plants are *Eriophorum angustifolium, E. vaginatum* and *Erica tetralix. Andromeda polifolia* is remarkably abundant but there is not the same degree of floristic richness as at Haining Head. These two sites are the only known areas of 'flat' *Sphagnum*-rich blanket mire in northern England.

(d) Coom Rigg Moss and Felecia Moss
NY 6979, 7277. 35 ha, 35 ha

Coom Rigg Moss and Felecia Moss both lie at a higher level on plateaux and are dominated by *Calluna–Sphagnum–Erica tetralix* communities in which *Calluna* and *Eriophorum vaginatum* may be locally dominant as on large areas of Coom Rigg or a hummock–hollow mosaic may develop as on Felecia Moss, which is floristically the richer site. The stratigraphy of Coom Rigg has been intensively investigated and the site has been the subject of hydrological studies. It represents the drier end-point of the series. Both sites are now almost entirely surrounded by conifer plantations, but their surfaces are undamaged and are, in fact, protected against fire and sheep-grazing.

The vegetation of these five sites is clearly intermediate between oceanic Trichophoreto–Eriophoretum and upland Calluneto–Eriophoretum. Moreover the *Sphagnum* facies has close affinities with lowland raised mire vegetation. Certain species characteristic of the oceanic type are absent or very insignificant, such as *Molinia caerulea* (abundant on surrounding drier, modified moorland), *Myrica gale, Pleurozia purpurea* and *Rhacomitrium lanuginosum* and there is a similar scarcity of characteristic upland species such as *Vaccinium vitis-idaea, Plagiothecium undulatum, Rubus chamaemorus* and *S. capillaceum.*

P.50. MOOR HOUSE–CROSS FELL,
WESTMORLAND/CUMBERLAND/DURHAM
NY 7233. 6600 ha   Grade 1*

The existing Moor House NNR covers an area of about 4000 ha of moorland drained by the headwaters of the Tees. Over half of this is covered by blanket mire, much of which is severely eroded and exhibits a characteristic peat–hagg topography similar to that widespread farther south in the Pennines and Forest of Bowland. The vegetation of the intact mire surfaces (and intervening surfaces where the peat is eroding) is, however, generally much less modified on Moor House than on most of the Pennine blanket mire south of Stainmore. Calluneto–Eriophoretum is the most widespread community, occurring on gently sloping surfaces throughout the area. It is characterised by co-

dominance of *Calluna vulgaris* and *Eriophorum vaginatum* with associates such as *Rubus chamaemorus* and *Sphagnum rubellum,* and hypnaceous mosses, whilst undamaged areas have a good deal of *S. magellanicum.* An *Empetrum nigrum* facies of this vegetation is present locally in which *S. capillaceum* and *Vaccinium myrtillus* are abundant. Although a constant species, *R. chamaemorus* is rarely found in such abundance as in the similar vegetation on the Burnhope Seat ridge north-east of the Alston–Middleton road.

Trichophoreto–Eriophoretum occurs on flatter areas often over deeper peat. In general the water table is consistently higher than in Calluneto–Eriophoretum, and areas with a *Sphagnum*-rich hummock–hollow morphology are present. Within these communities various species attain physiognomic dominance including *Calluna, E. angustifolium, Erica tetralix* and *Trichophorum cespitosum* along with a ground layer of *S. papillosum, S. cuspidatum, S. tenellum* and *S. rubellum. Narthecium ossifragum* and *Drosera rotundifolia* are abundant. Affinity with western Scottish blanket mire vegetation is recognisable but there is (as in the case of the Irthinghead Mires (P.49)) a striking absence of certain characteristic oceanic species, some of which are diagnostic constants in west Highland Trichophoreto–Eriophoretum, e.g. *Myrica gale* and *Molinia caerulea,* and this Moor House community is an intermediate geographical type. Where vegetation of this type is subject to erosion a *Rhacomitrium* facies has developed locally in response to a lowered water table, as in many blanket mires of western Scotland, but at high levels, as on Knock Fell, the eroding Calluneto–Eriophoretum is rich in lichens, giving a continental facies of blanket mire.

The existing Reserve has been intensively investigated and is now the best-documented area of upland peat in Britain. The large grade 1 upland site (U.20) of which Moor House is a part has been extended to include not only Cross Fell but also the north-easterly area containing Bellbeaver Rigg, Yad Moss and Burnhope Seat (on the Tees–Wear watershed) since the mire communities in these areas include a high-level Calluneto–Eriophoretum extremely rich in *Rubus chamaemorus* and local areas of Trichophoreto–Eriophoretum flow containing *Sphagnum imbricatum, S. fuscum* and *Carex paupercula.* None of these facies is represented to the same extent on the present Reserve. Moreover, the second type compensates for the loss of an interesting blanket mire on Widdybank Fell, and a mixed mire with a large population of *C. paupercula* on the opposite bank of the Tees, both drowned by the new Cow Green reservoir.

Also on the high plateaux of Knock Fell and the approaches to Cross Fell summit are areas of either pure or mixed *Eriophorum vaginatum, E. angustifolium* and *Juncus squarrosus* on shallow peat, accompanied locally by rather low *Sphagnum* cover. Small peaty tarns and pools have developed in places amongst the eroding high level mires, notably on Knock Fell. Knock-Ore Gill (OW.55) is an upland limestone stream lying within this area which is a grade 1 open water site in its own right.

P.51. LEIGHTON MOSS, LANCASHIRE
SD 4875. 135 ha   Grade 1

Leighton Moss (Storrs Moss on 1 in. OS map) is a flood-plain mire which has developed after flooding the valley between Warton Crag and Silverdale, on the eastern side of Morecambe Bay, at some time during or soon after the First World War. Its most obvious feature is a large and dense stand of *Phragmites communis*, but around the margins there are areas of fen vegetation and there is also a considerable development of willow carr. The reed-beds are important as a northern outpost of a Broadland-type breeding avifauna, with several pairs of bittern (breeding regularly), a large population of reed warblers (one of the most northerly colonies in Britain), garganey, water rail, grasshopper warbler and spotted crake. This type of habitat is rare in northern Britain and Leighton Moss is regarded as having considerable national importance. Subsidiary wildfowl interest includes a winter population of shoveler (135), mallard, teal, pintail, tufted duck, gadwall and mute swan. The area is managed as a nature reserve by the RSPB.

P.52. TARN FEN, MALHAM, WEST YORKSHIRE
SD 8866. 100 ha   Grade 1

A remarkable complex of mire communities occurs in the vicinity of Malham Tarn on a broad limestone platform at about 380 m in the Craven Pennines. The Tarn itself lies over Silurian shales covered with boulder clay. To the west is an area of eutrophic mire alongside the main inflow stream to the Tarn, south of which is a small raised mire, Tarn Moss. On the flanks of the limestone scarp north-east of the tarn are extensive areas of grazed soligenous mire with numerous springs and seepage channels (see U.24).

The presence of these areas of impeded drainage within the extensive tract of limestone upland is most unusual. A comparable situation occurs at Sunbiggin Tarn in Westmorland but in the Malham mire complex a greater range of mire types is represented. In the combination of strongly calcicolous fen and soligenous mire communities with the acidophilous types of the raised mire there is a range of mire vegetation unparalleled elsewhere in Britain in areas of similar size. The fen communities and soligenous mire are particularly important, both meriting grade 1 in their own right, whilst Tarn Moss is of importance within the mire complex as an upland raised mire, although the present vegetation is severely modified.

Fen communities along the inflow stream include sedge swamp, herb-rich fen and closed carr. Community structure is related to past disturbance, especially peat-cuttings now recolonised by essentially natural hydroseral communities. *Carex rostrata, C. lasiocarpa, Equisetum fluviatile, Potentilla palustris, Mentha aquatica, Sparganium erectum* and locally *Phragmites communis* occur in the swamp communities (pH 7–8). The herb-rich fen is dominated by carices especially *C. appropinquata, C. rostrata* and *C. diandra* with characteristic associates, e.g. *Caltha palustris, Pedicularis palustris, Cardamine pratensis, Valeriana dioica, Lychnis flos-cuculi, Angelica sylvestris, Lotus pedunculatus* and

Galium palustre. A discontinuous bryophyte layer is present, including *Mnium pseudopunctatum, Scorpidium scorpioides, Acrocladium giganteum, Campylium stellatum, Chiloscyphus pallescens* and *Marchantia polymorpha.* Carr communities include a field layer under dense carr of *Caltha palustris, Myosotis scorpioides* and *Crepis paludosa*, whilst *Carex appropinquata* forms the sole dominant in some open areas. Ten *Salix* spp. are thought to be native here, including *S. phylicifolia, S. pentandra* and *S. nigricans*. The fen and carr contain a number of rare and local species notably *Primula farinosa, Carex flava* (but probably a hybrid population), *C. appropinquata, Calamagrostis stricta, Cinclidium stygium, Sparganium minimum, Camptothecium nitens* and *Barbilophozia kunzeana.* Because the site has been protected as a Field Studies Council reserve the communities are remarkably free from disturbance.

See also OW.47.

P.53. SUNBIGGIN TARN FEN, WESTMORLAND
NY 6707. 160 ha   Grade 1

Areas of rich-fen vegetation adjacent to Sunbiggin Tarn (OW.54) (the pH of which is 8.0–8.5) include *Carex rostrata* swamp, drier mixed-fen again with *C. rostrata* the main dominant, reed-swamp *Phragmites communis* mainly fringing the tarn and other more restricted fen communities dominated by either *C. elata, Potentilla palustris* or *Filipendula ulmaria. Cladium mariscus* is locally dominant in its highest known station in Britain. The *Carex rostrata* swamps include *C. lasiocarpa, C. paniculata, Utricularia vulgaris, Eleocharis palustris, Menyanthes trifoliata, Phragmites communis* and *Sparganium erectum. Potentilla palustris* swamp communities include *C. diandra*, whilst the herb-rich mixed fen (pH 7.0–7.5) contains a variety of species of which the most abundant are *C. rostrata, C. lasiocarpa, Agrostis stolonifera, C. nigra, E. palustris, Equisetum fluviatile, Menyanthes trifoliata, Stellaria alsine* and *Scorpidium scorpioides*. Other mixed-fen associations include a facies dominated by *C. elata* (a very local and mainly eastern species in Britain) and tussocky surfaces lying about 10–20 cm above the dry weather water table which are only intermittently flooded. These have a very rich flora but *C. nigra, C. rostrata, Filipendula ulmaria, Caltha palustris* and *Galium palustre* are constant associates.

On the fen between Sunbiggin Tarn and Cow Dub Tarn there is a large breeding colony of black-headed gulls, which has caused nutrient enrichment of the peatland, some of the drier surrounds, and the smaller tarn.

Sunbiggin Tarn Fen forms part of the important limestone complex of the Orton Fells grade 1 upland site (U.25), which includes also the open water of the Tarn itself (OW.54), the soligenous mire system of the adjoining Tarn Moor, the limestone pavements of Great Asby Scar, and a range of limestone grasslands and heather moor.

P.54. NEWHAM FEN, NORTHUMBERLAND
NU 1629. 14 ha   Grade 1

This is a small, eutrophic basin mire which occupies a deep basin (maximum 13 m) in glacial deposits adjacent to an esker overlying Carboniferous Limestone. Although at one time slightly more extensive, the mire communities now occupy a small area which is separated from surrounding pasture by a fence. The mire is spring fed (by ground water of pH 7.8), a feature of considerable significance to the conservation management since such a site is unlikely to pose difficulties associated with run-off of agricultural fertilisers.

Much of the mire is occupied by a floristically rich carr composed of birch and willow with an understorey of *Carex* spp. and *Phragmites*. In one part of the site is an open community dominated by carices and 'brown mosses' with *Schoenus nigricans* locally dominant and many local and some rare fen species present. Within this area is an association dominated by *C. lasiocarpa*, whilst adjacent areas have an association characterised by *C. lepidocarpa* with bryophytes such as *Scorpidium scorpioides* and *Cratoneuron commutatum* var. *falcatum*. In addition a further community characterised by *Carex panicea*, *Salix repens* and *Briza media* includes facies dominated by either *Cratoneuron commutatum* var. *falcatum* or *Campylium stellatum* and locally contains *Camptothecium nitens* in abundance.

The degree of floristic richness of the site is indicated by the occurrence of 16 species of *Carex*, and the following rare or local mire species: *Corallorhiza trifida, Dactylorchis incarnata, D. purpurella, Parnassia palustris, Pinguicula vulgaris, Platanthera bifolia, Potamogeton coloratus, Pyrola rotundifolia, Ranunculus lingua, Salix nigricans* and *S. pentandra*. In addition, certain fen species are here close to their northern limit in eastern Britain or become very local further north, e.g. *Lycopus europaeus, Lythrum salicaria, Valeriana dioica* and *Oenanthe lachenalii*.

This is one of the best examples of calcareous lowland fen now known in Britain. It should be compared with some of the southern calcareous valley mires, e.g. Scarning Fen (P.17), Norfolk, and Cothill Fen (P.4), Berkshire.

P.55. TARN MOSS, TROUTBECK, CUMBERLAND
NY 4027.   18 ha   Grade 1

This basin mire lies in a shallow, but apparently quite enclosed, elongated hollow in acidic glacial drift immediately north of Great Mell Fell, and is surrounded by poor-quality upland pastures. The vegetation is mostly oligotrophic and the main interest of the site is the predominant poor-fen which forms a good example of this north British vegetation type. Very few true basin mires exhibit this type of vegetation and it is significant that here it is associated with a patchy development of acidophilous vegetation representing the initiation of still more oligotrophic surface.

The central section of the mire is mostly dominated by *Sphagnum*–sedge communities of which the following are important constituents: *S. recurvum, S. palustre, S. subsecundum* varieties *inundatum* and *auriculatum, S. teres, Carex nigra, C. echinata, C. rostrata, C. curta* and *C. lasiocarpa*. The very local northern *Carex paupercula* is plentiful in association with *Sphagnum* spp. and *C. limosa* is also present where there is some degree of base enrichment. Other characteristic species are *Potentilla palustris, Epilobium palustre, Galium palustre, Ranunculus flammula, Hydrocotyle vulgaris, Equisetum fluviatile, Vaccinium oxycoccus, Utricularia minor, Dryopteris spinulosa, Acrocladium stramineum* and *Aulacomnium palustre*.

Acidophilous nuclei are widespread, in places merging to produce an acidic mire surface characterised by the following species: *Calluna vulgaris, Erica tetralix, Empetrum nigrum, Andromeda polifolia, Eriophorum vaginatum, E. angustifolium, Trichophorum cespitosum, Drosera rotundifolia, Narthecium ossifragum, Sphagnum papillosum, S. capillaceum* and *Polytrichum alpestre*. Locally, there occur areas in which the ground water is of a slightly higher trophic status than throughout most of the mire. Here there is a richer vegetation (weakly mesotrophic) including *Carex demissa, Pedicularis palustris, Lychnis flos-cuculi, Caltha palustris* and locally *Carex paniculata*.

The mire has affinities with Heart Moss, Kirkcudbrightshire, and Cliburn Moss, Westmorland, which both form alternatives for this site, as examples of poor-fen.

P.56. MOORTHWAITE MOSS, CUMBERLAND
NY 5151.   10 ha   Grade 1

This basin mire lies in a glacial hollow within the undulating drumlin landscape of the Cumberland Plain east of Carlisle. It is small but has a high water table throughout, the drainage being internal and impeded. The whole Moss has been affected by peat-cutting but has been allowed to regenerate and, despite the development of the present surface in response to intense disturbance, it is a most important example of lowland acidophilous Sphagnetum.

There is now a healthy, actively growing association of dominant *Sphagnum magellanicum* with great abundance of *Vaccinium oxycoccus* and *Andromeda polifolia*, which has a gentle hummock–hollow relief and forms the dominant vegetation type of the wetter facies. This is the only British lowland basin mire dominated by *S. magellanicum* and it is one of the few basin mires where the less acidophilous *S. recurvum–Eriophorum angustifolium* association (which indicates some process of artificial base enrichment) is not now dominant. A wide range of species representative of lowland acidic peat is present, including local abundance of very luxuriant *Narthecium ossifragum, Rhynchospora alba* and *Platanthera bifolia*. An interesting feature of the site is that the margins and drier areas, representing old uncut surfaces, are dominated by *Pinus sylvestris–Empetrum nigrum* woodland with the result that seedling pines occur in all but the wettest areas, though many of the saplings are checked or moribund. This feature, which is shared by acidic mires of other types, is reminiscent of the vast Fennoscandian pine-grown *Sphagnum* mires. There is a lesser amount of birch, and associated with both tree species are robust growths of *Pyrola minor* and *Listera cordata*. A fragment of poor-fen is present in one peripheral region, where there is lateral seepage at the surface, and has species such as *Carex rostrata, C. curta* and *Potamogeton polygonifolius*.

The basin is an important Quaternary site in which Late-glacial deposits are represented. As the basin is entirely surrounded by farmland, there is potentially a danger that lateral seepage of nutrients will here cause the same kind of mild eutrophication which has been affecting several Midland basin mires, and may well be responsible for the general dominance there of *Sphagnum recurvum*.

P.57. CUMWHITTON MOSS, CUMBERLAND
NY 5151. 45 ha   Grade 1

Although it lies only 1 km from Moorthwaite Moss, this site shows certain contrasting features which result from differences in hydrology of the two sites. Moorthwaite Moss is a basin mire with internal drainage and a largely acidic surface, whereas Cumwhitton Moss is partly a valley mire and has a surface varying between acidic and mesotrophic. Like Moorthwaite, Cumwhitton Moss has been subjected to intensive interference in the past by peat-cutting and it is now difficult to interpret its original morphology. The glacial hollow has two arms which converge to give a Y-shape; one arm is drained by a small stream and is best regarded as valley mire, while the other has a dried out ombrogenous mire which may occupy a basin or simply a second valley.

The Moss as a whole shows a great diversity of vegetation types and a rich flora. The dried ombrogenous surface at the eastern side is periodically burned and is covered mainly with dry heather heath with a good deal of *Erica tetralix*, but contains numerous peat-cuttings in which have developed spongy *Sphagnum* carpets, mainly of *S. recurvum*, with some *S. magellanicum*. *Vaccinium oxycoccus* occurs here in profusion, but *Andromeda polifolia* is rare, in contrast to its great abundance in Moorthwaite Moss. A wetter part of the general mire surface has a colony of *V. uliginosum*, normally a montane plant of high altitudes in the Highlands. Fringing and colonising birch occurs, and much of the remaining area of the Moss is covered with mixtures of woodland dominated either by birch or Scots pine on acidophilous peat. The pines are of all sizes and native status seems possible here in view of the presence of a relict pinewood flora with *V. vitis-idaea*, *Goodyera repens*, *Pyrola minor*, *Listera cordata*, *Ptilium crista-castrensis* and *Dicranum rugosum*.

Both types of woodland are interspersed with water-filled peat-cuttings containing large tussocks of *Carex paniculata*, and along the valley mire arm there is a more general development of vegetation showing the influence of base-rich water. Much of this area has a rather open growth of willow carr with *Salix cinerea* and *S. pentandra*, and there is a mesophilous fen community containing *Menyanthes trifoliata*, *C. diandra*, *Eriophorum latifolium* and *Dactylorchis fuchsii*. The most interesting community is, however, a *Sphagnum warnstorfianum–S. teres* carpet containing *Camptothecium nitens* and *Aulacomnium palustre*, representing a characteristic but very local northern type of weakly mesophilous mire vegetation. Also present on other parts of the Moss are more usual poor-fen *S. recurvum* lawns with *Carex echinata*, *C. nigra*, *C. curta*, *Potentilla palustris* and *Vaccinium oxycoccus*.

The invertebrate fauna is rich and includes the rare dragonfly *Leucorrhinia dubia*.

While the degree of modification of this mire system might otherwise preclude its selection as grade 1, the presence of the unusual transition mire communities and the great diversity of vegetational features give Cumwhitton Moss a high scientific value. Moreover, it is so close to the very different Moorthwaite Moss that the two could almost be regarded as forming a single complex, and they are important as a contrasting pair.

P.58. MUCKLE MOSS, NORTHUMBERLAND
NY 7966. 45 ha   Grade 1

This is an oligotrophic valley mire occupying a narrow strike vale at 210 m in the steeply dipping Lower Carboniferous south of Hadrian's Wall. A number of distinctive communities are present, the most important of which is a central *Sphagnum–Eriophorum–Carex* soak. A surface pattern is developed here which is unique in British peatlands, but bears a strong resemblance to certain patterned topogenous fens in Scandinavia. This consists of a series of large crescentic pools and intervening ridges partially colonised by Scots pine.

Marginal vegetation consists of a *Calluna vulgaris–Eriophorum angustifolium–Erica tetralix* community which grades into a *Sphagnum*-rich community occupying the bulk of the site. *S. magellanicum*, *S. papillosum*, *E. tetralix* and *Eriophorum angustifolium* are dominant with *Calluna vulgaris*, *Vaccinium oxycoccus*, *Andromeda polifolia* and *S. recurvum* abundant. Two species conspicuously absent are *Narthecium ossifragum* and *Trichophorum cespitosum*. In the central patterned soak, *S. recurvum* and *S. cuspidatum* are dominant in hollows along with *E. angustifolium*, *Carex curta*, *C. paupercula*, *A. polifolia* and *V. oxycoccus*. Intervening ridges are dominated by drier and more acid communities with *Empetrum nigrum*, *Calluna vulgaris*, *E. vaginatum*, *S. papillosum* and *V. oxycoccus*. *Polytrichum commune* is a major component which may indicate disturbance. Unfortunately the lower section of this mire has been planted with conifers but the extensive upper section described above is relatively undisturbed.

The site is important as a structural type, the stratigraphy showing that it has developed by succession from a richer type of mire, filling a lake basin, to oligotrophic valley mire. A wide range of *Sphagnum* spp. is represented including the rare *S. riparium* and *S. balticum*, and the site is the only known British station for *S. dusenii* (a species related to *S. cuspidatum*) which is common in Scandinavian mires.

P.59. FEN BOGS, NORTH YORKSHIRE
SE 8597. 60 ha   Grade 1

Fen Bogs is an oligotrophic valley mire lying in Newtondale, a deep glacial spillway in the north Yorkshire moors. It is separated into two parts by the railway which follows the valley but this has not detracted greatly from the scientific interest. The mire surface has suffered to some extent from burning and is still subject to a detrimental amount of grazing by sheep.

The peat deposit is known to be very deep (locally 18 m) and although it is now covered with acidophilous mire vegetation, it probably originated as a mesotrophic mire. The communities present include an acidic surface in which the following are abundant: *Sphagnum papillosum*, *S. rubellum*, *Eriophorum angustifolium*, *Trichophorum cespitosum*, *Vaccinium oxycoccus*, *Molinia caerulea*, *Erica tetralix*, *Myrica gale*, *Drosera rotundifolia*, *Potentilla erecta* and *Polygala serpyllifolia*. *Rhynchospora alba* is locally abundant. Higher hummocks are dominated by *Myrica*, *S. magellanicum* and *S. papillosum* whilst *Calluna vulgaris*, *E. tetralix* and *Eriophorum vaginatum* are locally dominant. These acidophilous communities have been rather damaged locally by burning but the extent of this surface (*c.* 1 km) is such that local reduction of quality is relatively insignificant.

The most important feature of this site is the development of lateral water tracks containing a plant association more usually characteristic of valley mires in oceanic regions. A number of species occurring in these communities at Fen Bogs do not occur elsewhere in north-east England and are very locally distributed outside western districts. This soligenous mire association includes *Sphagnum subsecundum* var. *auriculatum*, *S. recurvum*, *Carex rostrata*, *C. limosa*, *C. echinata*, *C. dioica*, *Potamogeton polygonifolius*, *Eleocharis multicaulis* and *Menyanthes trifoliata*. Within these soaks occur acidic nuclei dominated by *S. plumulosum*, *Myrica gale*, *Eriophorum angustifolium* and *Drosera rotundifolia*. Other species locally abundant in this community are *C. nigra*, *C. panicea*, *C. echinata*, *C. lasiocarpa*, *C. lepidocarpa*, *C. pauciflora*, *C. pulicaris*, *C. pallescens*, *C. flacca*, *C. binervis*, *Equisetum palustre*, *Narthecium ossifragum*, *Potentilla palustris*, *Phragmites communis*, *Typha latifolia*, *Schoenus nigricans*, *Scorpidium scorpioides*, *Drepanocladus revolvens* and *Sphagnum recurvum*. Some of these clearly show the influence of quite base-rich water.

Although somewhat fragmented (and lacking certain species characteristic of the valley mires in oceanic areas, e.g. *Drosera anglica*) this mire is nevertheless the best example in Britain of an upland mixed valley mire with both ombrogenous and soligenous facies. The remarkably easterly position, considerably isolated from similar sites, adds significantly to its importance.

P.60. THORNE AND CROWLE WASTE, WEST YORKSHIRE, LINCOLNSHIRE

SE 7315.   2000 ha   Grade 2

At one time the raised mire between the Aire and the Trent must have been one of the most extensive in Britain. Even today there is a vast block of semi-natural vegetation totalling 2630 ha in this area. The original character of the vegetation has, however, largely been lost. The raised mire was almost entirely cut over for peat during the last century but owing to the method of cutting, a wide variety of new artificial habitats was produced, some of which now have considerable value. The individual cuttings contain species-poor oligotrophic swamp communities largely dominated by *Juncus effusus* or *Eriophorum angustifolium* but locally there is a development of *Sphagnum* carpets with *Vaccinium oxycoccus*. The original mire surface between the cuttings is dominated by downy birch, bracken, heather and *Eriophorum vaginatum*. Other habitats, notably the extensive series of canals linking the cuttings, contain a much wider range of plant species including some elements of the original raised mire, e.g. *Andromeda polifolia*, but also a number of species characteristic of fen conditions which become more abundant towards the margins of the site. Many of the species which occur here have a very limited distribution in Britain, e.g. *Viola stagnina*, *Calamagrostis stricta* and *Lathyrus palustris*. The same applies to many invertebrates recorded from the area. In many respects the present ecological conditions and the conservation problems which these pose are similar to those of the cut-over raised mires in the Somerset Levels.

Despite the fact that the present condition of Thorne and Crowle Waste is a direct result of past exploitation it is felt that the area has considerable value especially in view of its very large size and the variety of habitats which have developed. It provides an ideal situation for investigating vegetation succession in oligotrophic sites, so necessary for conservation management.

P.61. BOWNESS COMMON, CUMBERLAND

NY 2060.   600 ha   Grade 2

This is a very extensive area of modified raised mire within which a number of relatively small patches of viable mire surface survive. In view of the rate at which peat of this type is now being exploited this site must be considered nationally important though not of grade 1 status since other comparable sites are of higher quality. (See Appendix.) Where unaffected by cutting the vegetation is similar to that of Glasson Moss (P.48) but the communities are more fragmented and much of the area has been severely modified by burning. Some of the older peat-cuttings are now *Sphagnum*-filled and the intervening baulks have an interesting vegetation of rank *Calluna* and a robust growth of *Andromeda polifolia*, which seems at first to benefit from drying of the peat. *Drosera anglica*, *D. intermedia*, *Dicranum undulatum* and *D. rugosum* still occur locally. The mire has numerous small clumps of colonising birchwood often carrying a profusion of lichens (especially *Usnea* spp.), and these are sometimes associated with dominance of large hummocks of *Polytrichum commune* and *Sphagnum palustre*, with *Vaccinium oxycoccus* and *Empetrum nigrum*. Wet heath communities near the edges of the mire have an abundance of *Dactylorchis maculata* ssp. *ericetorum*. There are also a few pines, and a small wood on the edge of the Common, near Bowness village, has a great abundance of *Sorbus intermedia*. A bracken area amongst birchwood at the eastern end has an outlying colony of *Trientalis europaea*.

P.62. WEDHOLME FLOW, CUMBERLAND

NY 2151.   270 ha   Grade 2

Wedholme Flow lies about 8 km south of Glasson Moss and forms a single extensive raised mire unit, but is severely modified and, though it covers a total area of *c.* 8 km², only a very limited section of the mire system is now viable. A great deal of the eastern part of the Flow is now being cut for peat commercially whilst areas in the northern half were so cut many years ago. The area of intact *Sphagnum*-rich raised mire vegetation is now reduced by cutting and by recent fires to a section about 0.4 km long by only 90–180 m wide. Despite this the site merits considerable conservation effort in view of the high quality of this remaining Sphagnetum and the rarity of such vegetation nationally. It differs in detail from Glasson Moss (P.48) in that the surface is an almost level spongy carpet with fewer wet hollows. *Andromeda, Rhynchospora alba, Eriophorum angustifolium* and *Erica tetralix* are abundant in a continuous carpet of *S. papillosum, S. tenellum* and *S. rubellum* in which *S. magellanicum* is relatively insignificant. Areas which have been modified by burning some time ago now have a derived, drier vegetation containing much *Sphagnum molle* and *Drosera intermedia*.

On the southern side there is a transition to a lower, wet fringing wood of birch and willow with alder buckthorn and carices; this evidently represents a remnant of the former lagg on this side. There is also some colonising Scots pine on this side of the Flow. (See Appendix.)

P.63. FALSTONE MOSS, NORTHUMBERLAND
NY 7086.   25 ha   Grade 2

This is a small isolated area of blanket mire lying on a gently sloping col at 243–260 m and completely surrounded by conifers of the Kielder Forest within the North Tyne catchment. The vegetation consists of a combination of an almost continuous ground layer of *Sphagnum magellanicum* and *Vaccinium oxycoccus* (with associated leafy liverworts and vascular plants such as *Erica tetralix* and *Trichophorum cespitosum*) over which occurs a discontinuous sward of leggy heather, 30–45 cm in height. Although the site is not of sufficient importance to merit grade 1 status, nevertheless it is nationally important as a restricted type of blanket mire vegetation clearly related to that of the Irthinghead Mires (P.49) in the same district.

P.64. GOWANY KNOWE MOSS, NORTHUMBERLAND
NY 7378.   20 ha   Grade 2

This site is an alternative to Felecia Moss in the Irthinghead Mires and lies within the North Tyne catchment. It is surrounded by conifer plantations and has an open blanket mire community dominated by *Calluna vulgaris, Eriophorum vaginatum, Trichophorum cespitosum, Erica tetralix, Vaccinium oxycoccus, Sphagnum papillosum, S. rubellum, S. magellanicum* and *S. recurvum*. *Eriophorum angustifolium* is locally co-dominant in *Sphagnum*-rich areas. There is a gentle hummock–hollow surface which is generally intact and rich in plant species, but without the floristic richness of Felecia Moss.

P.65. NEWTON REIGNY MOSS, CUMBERLAND
NY 4730.   12 ha   Grade 2

This eutrophic basin mire occupies a hollow in glacial drift of the Eden Valley 3 km west of Penrith, and is bordered by pasture and arable land from which it is fenced. As with Newham Fen (P.54), the mire is spring fed from either calcareous drift or direct from the underlying Carboniferous

Limestone. The Moss has undergone intense modification, having been cut extensively for peat at some time in the past so that the surface (now recolonised) shows regular alternating areas of swamp and carr. A main ditch cut during 1939–45 has resulted in significant lowering of the water table during the past 25 years, and the Moss has dried out considerably in consequence. The peat cuttings now provide the only true swamp conditions since most of the original mire surface is rapidly changing to carr, but usually the only open water is the stream in the main ditch.

The carr consists mainly of thickets of willow which are densest round the periphery of the Moss; *Salix cinerea* and *S. pentandra* are the most plentiful species, but the northern willows *S. phylicifolia* and *S. nigricans* occur.

The wetter parts of the fen interior consist of sedge-swamp dominated largely by *Carex lasiocarpa* or *C. rostrata*, with local abundance of *C. disticha* and *C. diandra*. The sedge-swamp gives way in places to dominance of *Menyanthes trifoliata, Potentilla palustris* or *Eriophorum angustifolium* which form local societies. Species of general abundance in the swamp are *Valeriana officinalis, Galium palustre, Epilobium palustre, Agrostis stolonifera* and *Lychnis flos-cuculi*. More local though still plentiful are *Ranunculus lingua, Caltha palustris, Carex limosa, C. panicea, Salix repens, Equisetum fluviatile, E. palustre, Molinia caerulea, Solanum dulcamara, Hydrocotyle vulgaris, Succisa pratensis* and *Mentha aquatica*.

Much of the swamp has a carpet of 'brown moss', variously dominated by *Acrocladium cuspidatum, A. giganteum, A. cordifolium, Drepanocladus aduncus, D. revolvens, Climacium dendroides, Mnium seligeri* and *Campylium stellatum*, either singly or in mixtures. Less common species are *Bryum pseudotriquetrum, Scorpidium scorpioides, Cinclidium stygium* and *Campylium elodes*. Other important species present are *Schoenus nigricans* and *Cladium mariscus*, both of which are rather restricted and are decreasing here. *Epipactis palustris* was once well known but has not been seen for some years, and species of open, wet habitats, such as *Primula farinosa* and *Utricularia vulgaris*, seem to have disappeared entirely. The site forms a drier alternative to Newham Fen, which does not have the same problems of desiccation.

P.66. CLIBURN MOSS, WESTMORLAND
NY 5725.   40 ha   Grade 2

Cliburn Moss is a much modified basin mire occupying a hollow in glacial drift of the Eden valley north west of Appleby. A good deal of the site is covered by Scots pine on peat with a ground flora of *Empetrum nigrum*, lichens and mosses (e.g. *Leucobryum glaucum*). The most important section of the site is however an area now reverting from previous intensive peat-cuttings. The surface was obviously cut many years ago and the cuttings are now colonised by poor-fen swamp communities with *Carex lasiocarpa, Menyanthes trifoliata* and locally *Potentilla palustris* and *C. rostrata* as dominants, and *Scorpidium scorpioides, Potamogeton polygonifolius, C. diandra, C. limosa, C. vesicaria, Dactylorchis purpurella, D. incarnata, Catabrosa aquatica,*

Eleogiton fluitans, Eleocharis multicaulis, Utricularia minor, Sparganium minimum, Sphagnum subsecundum var. *auriculatum* and *Acrocladium giganteum* in 'water tracks'. *Carex pseudocyperus* is recorded. Acidophilous vegetation on the intervening uncut ridges includes *Narthecium ossifragum, S. papillosum, S. imbricatum, S. magellanicum, Vaccinium oxycoccus, Erica tetralix, Rhynchospora alba, Andromeda polifolia, Trichophorum cespitosum, Eriophorum angustifolium* and *E. vaginatum*, the last occurring on the highest hummocks along with *Calluna vulgaris* and *Pleurozium schreberi*. The rare northern dwarf shrub *Vaccinium uliginosum* occurs sparingly, *Genista anglica* grows around the edge of the Moss, and *Hypnum imponens* is recorded. Self-sown pine occurs throughout on the firm baulks of peat together with abundant *Salix* spp., and there is some *Myrica gale*.

Cliburn Moss is a most unusual basin mire which has affinities with Heart Moss, Cumwhitton Moss and Tarn Moss, Troutbeck. It contains an interesting range of plant communities and species, and should be considered for possible upgrading in the light of fuller knowledge of the group of mixed mires to which it belongs.

P.67. HALLSENNA MOOR, CUMBERLAND
NY o6oo. 30 ha   Grade 2

This is a complex of dry to wet heath and oligotrophic basin mire. Extensive *Sphagnum* lawns in the mire are dominated by *S. recurvum, Vaccinium oxycoccus, Eriophorum angustifolium, Carex curta* and *Drosera rotundifolia* with abundant *Narthecium ossifragum*. Areas with a still higher water table have oligotrophic swamp communities composed of *C. rostrata, Menyanthes trifoliata, Eriophorum angustifolium, Potentilla palustris, Caltha palustris, Hypericum elodes* and *Vaccinium oxycoccus*. Distinctly acidophilous communities containing *S. papillosum, S. rubellum* and *S. recurvum* with *E. vaginatum* and *Calluna vulgaris* are frequent. *Osmunda regalis* occurs frequently and there is a large colony of *Dactylorchis maculata* var. *ericetorum* with numerous hybrids. Birch–willow (*Salix cinerea*) carr has developed on one part of the mire. The heath is dominated by *Calluna* and *Erica tetralix* and in damper places has much *Sphagnum compactum* and *S. tenellum*, with lesser amounts of *S. molle*. The poor-fen part of Hallsenna Moor may be best compared with Tarn Moss, Troutbeck (P.55).

P.68. CAW LOUGH, NORTHUMBERLAND
NY 7668. 30 ha   Grade 2

This basin mire has developed relatively recently in a hollow previously occupied by a lake, in one of the narrow valleys developed along shale-bands in the steeply dipping Lower Carboniferous, north of Hadrian's Wall. Along the southern margin the mire is spring fed from limestone and a rich-fen meadow is present along this zone. Most of the mire is separated from surrounding pasture by a wall.

The vegetation is mainly a swamp carr with open areas of reed-swamp (*Phragmites communis*) and poor-fen swamp communities. Where the calcium-rich water produces local base enrichment there is a very rich flora both in the marginal flushes and within the carr. Poor-fen communities are

dominated by *Carex rostrata, Potentilla palustris, Equisetum fluviatile* and *Juncus effusus*, with *Caltha palustris, Eleocharis palustris* and *Phragmites* locally abundant. Areas with some base enrichment contain *Menyanthes trifoliata, Hippuris vulgaris, Galium palustre, Mentha aquatica, Ranunculus flammula* and *Lychnis flos-cuculi*. The carr is composed of *Salix atrocinerea* and other *Salix* spp. with a ground flora of *Carex paniculata, Phragmites* and locally tall-herb or sedge-dominated communities including *Filipendula ulmaria, Lycopus europaeus, Scutellaria galericulata, C. disticha, Angelica sylvestris, Crepis paludosa* and *Pedicularis palustris*.

The calcareous flushes along the southern margin have herb-rich sedge–bryophyte communities which add to the interest of this site. The whole mire has a very intact structure and forms a good conservation unit. There are similarities between the vegetation of this site and that of the Tarn Fen, Malham, but the mire structure is quite different and the Malham vegetation a good deal more diverse. The calcicolous bryophyte communities link with those at Newham Fen, but on the whole the vegetation ranges from oligotrophic to mesotrophic fen, and is of a type represented in various northern basin, valley and flood-plain mires.

P.69. BIGLANDS BOG, CUMBERLAND
NY 2553. 18 ha   Grade 2

Biglands Bog is a small area of both eutrophic and oligotrophic mire lying in a shallow valley in the drift cover of the Cumberland Plain. Although small it is a most unusual site since it contains a sharply defined acidophilous *Sphagnum* carpet on one edge of the eutrophic fen. In places there are transitions from fen to wet meadow grassland around the edges.

The fen communities include fairly pure stands of *Phalaris arundinacea* or a mixed sedge-swamp with *Carex rostrata, C. lasiocarpa, C. nigra, C. disticha, C. diandra, Menyanthes trifoliata, Pedicularis palustris, Ranunculus flammula, Acrocladium cordifolium* and locally *Typha latifolia*. Much of the fen has now developed into *Salix* carr with *S. atrocinerea, S. pentandra* and *Frangula alnus*. Base-tolerant *Sphagnum* spp. (*S. teres* and *S. contortum*) are present, and *Acrocladium cordifolium* is abundant in the carr. The sluggish course of Bampton Beck traverses the middle of the fen and is fringed or overgrown with dense tussocks of *Carex paniculata*.

The acidic surface is sharply defined. It consists of a level *Sphagnum* lawn in which occur *S. rubellum, S. capillaceum, S. magellanicum, S. tenellum, S. recurvum* and *S. cuspidatum*. *Dicranum undulatum* is frequent in this carpet and *S. pulchrum* formerly occurred. Major vascular plants are *Calluna vulgaris, Erica tetralix, Vaccinium oxycoccus, Eriophorum angustifolium* and *Narthecium ossifragum* but *Andromeda polifolia, Rhynchospora alba* and *E. vaginatum* are abundant. *Carex limosa* occurs sparingly and *Drosera anglica* is present around the edges of shallow pools, which until recently (1954) contained 'brown moss' carpets and *Pinguicula vulgaris*.

Since 1954, however, seepage of water polluted by

sewage, probably from adjoining farms, has killed the 'brown mosses' in the pools and led to a spread of *Utricularia vulgaris*. In the *Sphagnum* carpet, *S. pulchrum* has disappeared whilst *Aulacomnium palustre* has increased markedly – a change which suggests that there may also be enrichment by run-off of fertiliser from surrounding fields. In spite of these changes, the site is of considerable importance as an example of a mixed mire with a pronounced pH and base-status gradient between the two contrasting vegetation types.

SOUTH SCOTLAND

P.70. KIRKCONNELL FLOW, KIRKCUDBRIGHTSHIRE
NX 9769. 155 ha   Grade 1

This is the only reasonably intact raised mire along the north side of the Solway. The mire has been reduced in extent by peripheral cutting and reclamation but the central section (about 120 ha) of the cupola has a sufficiently high water table to maintain actively growing mire communities. The striking feature of this site is, however, the extensive colonisation by Scots pine which has almost certainly been initiated during a period when the mire water table was lowered, if only marginally, by drainage operations. Apart from this the vegetation shows two major facies, a wetter type dominated by *Sphagnum* (*S. magellanicum* and *S. rubellum*) with *Calluna* or *Erica tetralix* and *Eriophorum vaginatum* as the major vascular plant components, and a drier type with a *Calluna–Cladonia* (*cladina*) association. Some characteristic mire species such as *Vaccinium oxycoccus* and *Andromeda polifolia* are widespread and abundant but others are very local. Almost certainly the present vegetational mosaic is a reflection of disturbance, as exemplified by the fragmented distribution of species such as *Trichophorum cespitosum*, *Rhynchospora alba*, *S. pulchrum* and *S. imbricatum*.

The site provides excellent facilities for research on the establishment and effects of pine on ombrogenous peatlands, a subject which is important in view of the close proximity of Forestry Commission conifer plantations to a number of acidic peatland reserves. On Kirkconnell Flow, *Erica tetralix* seems to survive best as a pine canopy becomes established, but mature pinewood here has the typical bilberry community with hypnaceous mosses and is of some value as an example of this woodland type (W.168). Birch is also colonising the Flow in places and there are areas of fairly dense birchwood. The moss layer is well-developed under both pine and birch, and includes the rare species *Dicranum rugosum*.

P.71. SILVER FLOWE, KIRKCUDBRIGHTSHIRE
NX 4782. 190 ha   Grade 1*

The series of patterned blanket mires forming the Silver Flowe constitutes the least disturbed and most varied extent of acidic peatland in southern Scotland, and is one of the most important systems of blanket mire in Britain. These mires, which have developed on the floor of a broad glacial valley in the Galloway hills, exhibit a complete gradation from discrete mires along the valley bottom which, in their external features, have obvious affinities with raised mire topography to others at the head of the valley which are indisputably blanket mire. These latter areas are similar to the more extensive watershed flows of north Scotland, both in the development of extensive pool networks and in the relative importance of hummock-forming *Sphagnum* spp. and vascular plants as opposed to the more hydrophilous *Sphagnum* spp. A notable difference is the absence of 'peat alpines' such as *Arctostaphylos uva-ursi*, and other species such as *Carex limosa*, and the scarcity of *C. pauciflora*.

Whilst the lowest mires of the series show distinct resemblance to the valley side blanket mires of Sutherland, there is a greater representation of *Sphagnum papillosum* and the present development of *S. imbricatum* and *S. fuscum* is less marked on the Silver Flowe, though both are present and locally abundant. Presence of the *S. pulchrum–Andromeda polifolia–Rhynchospora alba* association in one mire reflects the intimate floristic relationship between the flatter-lying blanket mire and lowland raised mire, but the scarcity of *Vaccinium oxycoccus* on the Flowe is surprising.

The series has one of the best developments of aligned hummock–hollow systems in Britain. The considerable variety of surface patterns, which is equalled elsewhere only in the Strathy River series of blanket mires in Sutherland, is remarkable especially in view of the relatively small total extent of the series. The dominant vegetation type is Trichophoreto–Eriophoretum, of a *Molinia*-rich type, with an oceanic element indicated by abundance of *Sphagnum plumulosum*, *Drosera anglica*, *Pleurozia purpurea* and *Campylopus atrovirens*. In addition there is a *Rhacomitrium* hummock facies, similar to that of Claish Moss, Argyll, especially on the upper mires. This is the most southerly development of the characteristic oceanic blanket mire vegetation so widespread in north-west Scotland, some of the characteristic plant species being absent further south. Abundance of *Molinia* in the upper mires of the series produces a vegetation remarkably similar to that of the blanket mire on Dartmoor but the surface morphology is quite different.

The major part of the western catchment, which is remarkably small, falls within the Merrick–Kells grade 1 upland massif (U.35). Safeguarding of the whole catchment is highly desirable as a conservation principle and in this case such a procedure is simplified by the size and nature of the catchment.

P.72. MOORFOOT HILLS, PEEBLES-SHIRE/
MIDLOTHIAN/SELKIRKSHIRE
NT 3646. 710 ha   Grade 1

On the watershed plateaux of the Moorfoot Hills at an altitude of between 520 and 610 m are quite extensive areas of blanket mire of the upland Calluneto–Eriophoretum type, rich in *Rubus chamaemorus*. The quality of this blanket mire varies considerably and though there are patches with severe erosion, areas of intact blanket mire are well represented, and occur on the saddles and flatter spurs (e.g. Deaf Heights and Pringles Green). The vegetation is obviously more disturbed where sheep-grazing is heavy, as on the west side of the fence along Eastside Height. *Calluna, Eriophorum vaginatum, E. angustifolium* and *Empetrum nigrum* are present in varying amounts here and, whilst *Sphagnum* spp. occur throughout, there are areas which are more *Sphagnum*-rich where *S. papillosum, S. magellanicum, S. rubellum, S. capillaceum, S. fuscum, S. tenellum* and *S. cuspidatum* attain dominance. Throughout these communities, which exhibit a gentle hummock–hollow mosaic, *Rubus chamaemorus* is abundant. Other abundant species are *Plagiothecium undulatum, Hypnum cupressiforme, Cladonia sylvatica, C. uncialis, Pleurozium schreberi* and *Polytrichum alpestre* which all occur on the relatively dry hummocks. The lichen-rich facies of Calluneto–Eriophoretum occurs in patches. In many areas there is evidence of recolonisation of erosion gullies especially by *Sphagnum cuspidatum* and in some places on the flatter areas there are linear pools filled with *S. cuspidatum.* Seepage channels and small soligenous mires typically show dominance of *S. recurvum.* Where erosion is severe, an *Empetrum nigrum* facies occurs on the haggs as in the Derbyshire development of this type of mire, and *Nardus stricta* grows luxuriantly in some of the drier gullies and ground affected by downwashed peat.

The Moorfoot Hills are also regarded as an important upland site (see U.37).

P.73. ABER BOGS AND LOCH LOMOND MARSHES, STIRLINGSHIRE/DUNBARTONSHIRE
NS 4389, NS 4387.   310 ha   Grade 1

On both sides of the River Endrick where it joins Loch Lomond are areas of flood-plain mire. These are of two types. Inundated mineral marshes, including reed-beds and rough grassland with *Juncus* spp. together with stretches of common sallow carr and other damp woodland, occur on the north bank of the Endrick forming the Crom Mhin. On the south side of the river, similar but smaller areas occur close to the water but there is a tract of flood-plain mire consisting mainly of eutrophic–mesotrophic swamp communities farther from the river, known as the Aber Bogs.

The Aber Bogs consist of a patchwork of swamp and mixed-fen communities with small areas of willow carr and four or five scattered pools of open water. The mire is underlain by deep deposits of fluvio-glacial clays and silts and now shows a parallel rather than radial zonation as a result of years of attempted drainage for hay cutting and grazing. Earlier pools are often grown over with *Hippuris vulgaris, Equisetum fluviatile* and *Lysimachia thyrsiflora* and may give way to floating mats of *Menyanthes trifoliata, Bidens cernua, B. tripartita, Cicuta virosa* and *Typha latifolia.* The edges of the drainage channels are lined with almost pure stands of *Phalaris arundinacea.* The mixed swamp contains varying amounts of *Iris pseudacorus, Scutellaria galericulata, Lysimachia vulgaris, Mentha aquatica, Epilobium palustre, Myosotis palustris, Lythrum salicaria, Carex vesicaria* and *Caltha palustris.* These communities

are often inundated during the winter by inflowing streams or by the backing up effect of Loch Lomond into the drainage ditches. Where the water table is further below the surface there are less hydrophytic herbaceous communities composed of *Juncus acutiflorus, Filipendula ulmaria, Angelica sylvestris, Cardamine pratensis, Ranunculus repens, Hydrocotyle vulgaris* and *Solanum dulcamara.* Acidophilous communities containing *Sphagnum* spp., *Eriophorum vaginatum, E. angustifolium, Vaccinium oxycoccus* and *Drosera rotundifolia* have developed close to the much more eutrophic Aber Bogs. This adds considerably to the range of vegetation types represented in the area. The mire system fully merits grade 1 status on its own merits, but the additional interest of the marshlands along the Endrick mouth, which are of considerable ornithological interest, makes this a site of high national importance. The adjoining Loch Lomond is itself regarded as a grade 1 open water site (OW.60).

See also W.169.

P.74. ADDERSTONLEE MOSS, ROXBURGHSHIRE
NT 5312.   15 ha   Grade 1

Adderstonlee is a basin mire lying in a shallow valley at an altitude of *c.* 240 m in the eastern Southern Uplands. It is surrounded by pasture from which most of the site is separated by a fence. The main vegetation type is a *Betula–Sphagnum* carr which is very rich in *Sphagnum* spp. Surrounding this are mesotrophic to eutrophic swamp communities, also some tall-herb communities, patches of acidophilous vegetation and small areas of rich-fen.

The mesotrophic swamp and herb-rich communities contain *Menyanthes trifoliata, Carex rostrata, Juncus acutiflorus, J. articulatus, Phragmites communis, Equisetum fluviatile, Potentilla palustris, Lychnis flos-cuculi, Angelica sylvestris* and *Filipendula ulmaria.* Richer associations occur around the outflow area and here *Campylium stellatum, Scorpidium scorpioides* and *Dactylorchis purpurella* are present.

The central carr has not been investigated in detail but there is an outstanding variety of basiphilous *Sphagnum* spp. forming an almost continuous cover along with various carices (e.g. *Carex echinata, C. diandra, C. acutiformis*) under a closed canopy of silver birch. This community type is very local in Britain and though examples are present elsewhere (e.g. Flitwick Moor, Bedfordshire) none has the degree of floristic richness exhibited by Adderstonlee Moss.

P.75. WHITLAW MOSSES, SELKIRKSHIRE/ROXBURGH-SHIRE   Grade 1

(a) *Beanrig Moss*
NT 5129.   2 ha

(b) *Blackpool Moss*
NT 5128.   4 ha

(c) *Murder Moss*
NT 5028.   10 ha

(d) Nether Whitlaw Moss
NT 5029.   4 ha

These four separate mire systems lie within 1 km of each other, occupying shallow valleys or basins in glacial drift overlying Silurian shales. The three southern mires, Murder Moss, Blackpool Moss and Beanrig Moss, are fed by base-rich ground water and have a considerable range of rich-fen communities from closed *Salix cinerea* carr to open bryophyte-rich carpets and tall-herb communities. The fourth site, Nether Whitlaw Moss, has less intrinsic scientific interest than any of the other three but has a more uniform mesotrophic community with local patches of rich-fen vegetation. All four mires merit inclusion in an aggregate grade 1 site.

Succession to undisturbed *Salix cinerea* carr is shown well by Blackpool Moss. This has a rich ground flora of vascular plants and bryophytes including *Angelica sylvestris*, *Caltha palustris*, *Geum rivale*, *Crepis paludosa*, *Pyrola rotundifolia*, *Carex paniculata*, *Climacium dendroides*, *Acrocladium cuspidatum* and *Cinclidium stygium*. The rare northern orchid *Corallorhiza trifida* is present.

Swamp communities and tall-herb fen communities are well developed at Murder Moss which also has both calcareous flushes, rich in calcicolous bryophytes, and willow carr. The swamp communities contain *Menyanthes trifoliata*, *Utricularia vulgaris*, *Hippuris vulgaris*, *Sparganium ramosum*, *S. minimum*, *Carex rostrata*, *C. lasiocarpa*, *Potentilla palustris*, *Ranunculus lingua* and *Cicuta virosa*.

Beanrig Moss, though a very small basin mire, is extremely important since it shows a range of communities from rich calcicolous bryophyte–sedge communities containing *Parnassia palustris*, *Scorpidium scorpioides*, *Cratoneuron filicinum*, *Camptothecium nitens*, *Campylium stellatum*, *Drepanocladus revolvens*, *Carex flacca*, *C. lepidocarpa* and *C. pulicaris* through tall-herb communities to willow carr and, most significant, the development of open mesotrophic communities with *Sphagnum contortum*, *S. warnstorfianum* and *C. limosa* in which occur oligotrophic nuclei with *Vaccinium oxycoccus*, *Erica tetralix*, *Calluna vulgaris*, *Dactylorchis maculata* ssp. *ericetorum*, *Drosera rotundifolia* and *Carex curta*. It is also of considerable importance as a stratigraphical site since the underlying clays and solifluction deposits show a good Late-glacial sequence (which includes layers rich in subfossil bryophytes).

This group of mires forms a northern example of rich calcicolous fen which has southern equivalents in Anglesey, Berkshire and Norfolk. The presence of the northern floristic element, e.g. *Carex rostrata*, *C. limosa*, *Dactylorchis purpurella* and *Corallorhiza trifida*, and the absence of the southern *Schoenus nigricans–Cladium mariscus* association are noteworthy.

P.76. BLAWHORN MOSS, WEST LOTHIAN
NS 8868.   125 ha   Grade 2

Although many areas of raised mire have developed in the central Lowlands of Scotland most of these have been exploited in some way or other and few examples remain undamaged. Dogden Moss (within Greenlaw Moor (P.78)) is one, and Blawhorn Moss is selected as a second example of the unusual confined raised mires developed in this area. It is difficult to decide whether this site should be categorised as blanket or raised mire. It lies at 220 m in a slight depression, is slightly domed, and merges into more typical blanket mire on one side.

The vegetation shows a gentle hummock and hollow relief with few distinct pools. The dominant plants are *Calluna*, *Empetrum nigrum*, *Eriophorum vaginatum* and *Erica tetralix* forming hummocks, with *Vaccinium oxycoccus*, *Eriophorum angustifolium*, *Sphagnum papillosum*, *S. magellanicum* and *S. recurvum* in the hollows. The abundance of *Empetrum nigrum* is unusual but shows affinities with the areas of blanket mire in the southern Pennines which have been subject to modification through atmospheric pollution. The presence of a relatively undamaged *Sphagnum*-rich blanket mire within the industrial belt of the central Lowlands affords opportunities for research into the effects of atmospheric pollution on bog vegetation.

P.77. MOCHRUM LOCHS, WIGTOWNSHIRE
NX 2953,   500 ha   Grade 2

Nearly all the low-level, peat-covered moors of southern Wigtownshire are now being afforested by the Forestry Commission. Of the remaining areas one is considered to contain the range of blanket mire vegetation characteristic of this district. This is the area adjacent to Mochrum Lochs. The blanket mire lies between 75 and 100 m and is a type intermediate between western Scottish blanket mire and more southerly raised mires.

The mire surface does not have a pronounced hummock–hollow pattern but there is a variation from drier to wetter areas on a broad scale. In places *Sphagnum* communities are dominant especially *S. tenellum*, *S. papillosum* and *S. magellanicum* along with *Andromeda polifolia*, *Rhynchospora alba*, *Trichophorum cespitosum* and *Myrica gale*. The major species in slightly drier areas are *Vaccinium oxycoccus*, *S. rubellum*, *Molinia caerulea*, *Calluna vulgaris*, *Eriophorum vaginatum* and *Erica tetralix*. Some particularly dry areas have a growth of lichens, especially *Cladonia impexa*, in association with *Hypnum cupressiforme*, *Calluna* and *Rhacomitrium lanuginosum*. Hummocks of *S. imbricatum* occur locally.

There is a close resemblance between this and Kilquhockadale Flow (P.79). This type of blanket mire with a mixture of oceanic and southern elements is comparable with that of the Irthinghead Mires (P.49) but shows a greater influence of oceanicity. Despite their intermediate position in the vegetational gradient this site and Kilquhockadale Flow are considered to merit only grade 2 status.

P.78. GREENLAW MOOR, BERWICKSHIRE
NT 7050.   1200 ha   Grade 2

This is an area of moorland varying in altitude from 180–270 m on the southern flanks of the Lammermuir Hills. Several different habitat types are represented including a raised mire (Dogden Moss), areas of heather moorland and small areas of woodland. In addition the site includes the Bedshiel Kame which is a physiographic feature of considerable importance, and Hule Moss which is important for wildfowl.

Dogden Moss is a large raised mire, over one mile in extent, lying on a terrace at about 210 m. The moss itself has been subject to burning, grazing and draining in the past. Aerial photographs show many old drains and there is a patchwork of communities. At present, however, the water table is high and although the moss is heavily grazed there is no severe development of anthropogenic vegetation which often occurs under such conditions. In the more intact areas *Sphagnum cuspidatum* forms the dominant ground layer with *S. papillosum*, *S. rubellum*, *Eriophorum vaginatum*, *E. angustifolium*, *Erica tetralix* on the flatter parts in which hummocks of *S. papillosum*, *S. magellanicum*, *E. vaginatum*, *Calluna*, *Vaccinium oxycoccus* and *Aulacomnium palustre* occur. *S. imbricatum* is present locally in its most easterly outpost in south Scotland.

This site is considered to merit grade 2 status since it is the best example of the 'confined' raised mires which are particularly abundant in south Scotland. Although the vegetation is considerably modified, the high water table ensures that the system is viable and the site appears to have a good chance of regaining an actively growing raised mire vegetation cover.

Hule Moss is of special importance as an outlying centre for pink-footed geese (2500 birds; 3% of world population). Mallard, goldeneye, pochard and shoveler also occur regularly in winter.

P.79. KILQUHOCKADALE FLOW, WIGTOWNSHIRE
NX 2769.   180 ha   Grade 2

The flows of northern Wigtownshire were once an important tract of rather low-lying blanket mires on gently sloping watersheds at an altitude of between 120 and 210 m. Many of these have been severely modified by burning and others are now afforested or will soon become so. The best remaining example in this area is Kilquhockadale Flow.

The vegetation consists of Trichophoreto–Eriophoretum with areas rich in *Sphagnum* spp. especially *S. papillosum*, *S. tenellum*, *S. magellanicum* and *S. rubellum*. *Vaccinium oxycoccus* is abundant and *Andromeda polifolia* frequent. Major vascular plant components are *Calluna*, *Erica tetralix*, *Eriophorum vaginatum*, *E. angustifolium*, *Trichophorum cespitosum* and *Narthecium ossifragum*, with *Empetrum nigrum* locally abundant in association with *C. vulgaris* and hummocks of *Pleurozium schreberi* and *Hylocomium splendens*. *S. imbricatum* and *S. fuscum* are present locally, and some areas are dominated by a *Molinia*-rich facies.

The vegetation is most comparable with some of the Irthinghead Mires (P.49) in Cumberland and Northumberland and contrasts strongly with the blanket mire of the Silver Flowe (P.71). The absence of any distinct surface pattern other than a gently undulating hummock–hollow mosaic and the absence also of a *Rhacomitrium* facies adds

to this similarity to the Irthinghead Mires. There are a few peaty lochs with marginal *Carex rostrata* and *Juncus effusus* swamp.

P.80. FALA FLOW, MIDLOTHIAN
NT 4258.   535 ha   Grade 2

Vegetationally this site has no outstanding features but the area has considerable ornithological importance as the wintering haunt of a large flock of pink-footed geese, numbering up to 7300 birds (9% of the world population). These geese have an alternative roosting site at Gladhouse Reservoir (OW.63).

P.81. BARMUFFLOCK DAM, RENFREWSHIRE
NS 3664.   6 ha   Grade 2

This basin mire has developed by hydroseral succession across a small reservoir impounded by a dam built around 1800. Pollen analysis has shown, however, that a mire has existed on the site prior to the construction of a reservoir, the basal peat being Zone VIIa. In spite of its artificial nature the site has considerable ecological interest, and the very fact that the outflow is restricted to a single channel makes the site an ideal unit for hydrological studies.

The present vegetation consists of soaks or water tracks leading into the mire (from a rather small catchment) which exhibit a variety of associations with *Menyanthes trifoliata*, *Carex limosa*, *C. rostrata*, *C. demissa*, *C. diandra*, *Narthecium ossifragum*, *Carum verticillatum*, *Molinia caerulea*, *Scorpidium scorpioides*, *Campylium stellatum*, *Drepanocladus revolvens*, *Sphagnum recurvum* and *S. palustre*. An open community dominated by *Carex rostrata* and *C. diandra* occupies the site of the former reservoir, and *C. aquatilis* is locally abundant around the inflow. The greater part of the mire surface is occupied by *Betula–Molinia–Sphagnum* communities with some limited open areas of *S. palustre*, *S. plumulosum* and *S. recurvum*. Most of the western half has been drained and planted with *Picea abies*.

This site does not merit grade 1 since the communities are fragmented and the whole site is severely modified. However, it does have considerable value as a research site and the vegetation is representative of a northern element in the mesotrophic mire series.

P.82. DUNHOG MOSS, SELKIRKSHIRE
NT 4724.   2 ha   Grade 2

Dunhog Moss is a good example of the valley mires widely developed in the eastern Southern Uplands. It lies in a narrow elongated valley at an altitude of about 275 m. The mire shows an excellent zonation, having a willow carr along the central axis and mesotrophic sedge–bryophyte communities along either side. At the upper end of the system the central carr is replaced by open acidophilous communities including *Calluna*, *Erica tetralix* and *Molinia* with a variety of *Sphagnum* spp. The lateral communities vary from bryophyte rich low-sward types to *Carex rostrata* and *Potentilla palustris* swamp, infilling areas of open water. *Carex paniculata*, local in southern Scotland, is present. This is a nationally important site as a northern example of an upland valley mire but it does not compare in quality with the Tarn Fen (P.52) at Malham, Yorkshire, which includes similar communities.

P.83. HEART MOSS, KIRKCUDBRIGHTSHIRE
NX 7748. 20 ha   Grade 2

This mire, about 0.8 km long, occupies a shallow valley in Silurian shales at 120 m near the southern coast of Galloway. The main habitats are an extensive and undisturbed *Salix cinerea* carr with a rich flora of bryophytes and vascular plants along the full length of the eastern side, a central tract of swamp communities with a mixture of oligotrophic and mesotrophic elements and a western zone of mixed herb-rich fen and grazed fen meadow. In addition acidophilous vegetation is widespread along the western margin and is locally extensive.

The zonation of communities and the range of plant associations is outstanding. In particular the central swamp communities are important. These have extensive areas of sinuous channels colonised by *Carex rostrata* and *C. lasiocarpa* separated by ridges supporting an oligotrophic vegetation including *Molinia*, *Myrica*, *Sphagnum plumulosum*, *Erica tetralix* and *Narthecium ossifragum*. Where there is a more eutrophic influence, fen communities are developed which include *C. lepidocarpa*, *Scorpidium scorpioides*, *Filipendula ulmaria*, *Epilobium palustre*, *Cirsium palustre*, *Angelica sylvestris* and *Lychnis flos-cuculi*. There are similarities between this site and Tarn Moss (P.55), Cumberland; Cliburn Moss (P.66), Westmorland; and Morden Bog (P.27), Dorset.

EAST SCOTLAND

P.84. DUN MOSS, PERTHSHIRE
NO 1756. 185 ha   Grade 1

Dun Moss is a small confined raised mire lying on a saddle at 350 m in the gently rolling hills of the Forest of Alyth. This mire forms the main research site in a fundamental investigation of peat hydrology being carried out by the University of Dundee. Certain features of the stratigraphy have been investigated and it is known that the mire began as an open water-body, succeeded by a *Paludella squarrosa* mire, which was superseded by a *Camptothecium nitens-Betula* community, and this eventually gave way to an ombrogenous mire surface. There is striking similarity between this sequence and that described for certain other upland raised mires, e.g. parts of Tarn Moss, Malham (see P.52).

The vegetation is partially modified by burning, but where undisturbed it is of a high quality and represents a type which has a very restricted distribution in Britain. This is a *Calluna-Eriophorum vaginatum-Sphagnum* community, rich in lichens and with a pronounced *Sphagnum*-rich hummock–hollow mosaic, in places dominated by *S. fuscum* and *S. imbricatum*, but more generally by *S. papillosum*, *S. magellanicum* and *S. capillaceum*. Tall leggy *C. vulgaris* occurs throughout unburnt areas and lichens such as *Cladonia rangiferina* and *C. impexa* are locally

dominant. *Empetrum hermaphroditum* is abundant on hummocks whilst *Trichophorum cespitosum*, *Narthecium ossifragum*, *S. cuspidatum* and *Erica tetralix* are locally abundant in hollows.

The ombrogenous mire surface is bounded by a distinct poor-fen lagg containing *Carex rostrata*, *Juncus effusus*, *Sphagnum palustre* and *S. recurvum* around the eastern side and is separated from mineral ground elsewhere by a narrow poor-fen soak.

The high quality and unusual character of the vegetation together with the fact that this represents a type of mire which is extremely rare in Britain provide adequate basis for regarding this as a grade 1 site. The fact that it is being intensively investigated provides considerable additional support.

P.85. RANNOCH MOOR, ARGYLL/PERTHSHIRE
NN 3652. 10 300 ha   Grade 1*

The Rannoch Moor is an extensive tract (over 250 km^2) of relatively gentle terrain, occupying a high-level depression, at about 360 m, between the western end of the Breadalbane range and the mountains of Glen Coe and Black Mount. Intense glaciation has resulted in a confused relief (not unlike the Lewisian Gneiss country of north-west Scotland) characterised by morainic and granitic bed-rock knolls, gentle peat-filled depressions, areas of flow, and numerous lochs of varying size. The blanket mire, though discontinuous, is developed on gentle slopes and broad flats, the intervening valleys being occupied by oligotrophic soligenous mires, while the definite depressions show various types of topogenous mire, often associated with lochans. The whole area is important since it exhibits a diverse complex of northern oligotrophic mire types. The blanket mire may be referred to Trichophoreto–Eriophoretum, for characteristic western species such as *Molinia caerulea*, *Myrica gale*, *Drosera anglica*, *Pleurozia purpurea* and *Rhacomitrium lanuginosum* are all abundant. There are areas of undamaged Sphagnetum with an abundance of *S. imbricatum* and *S. fuscum*, and well-developed pool–hummock systems occur locally. A notable feature is the occurrence of *Scheuchzeria palustris*, Rannoch Moor being the only remaining British locality known for this characteristic species of north European mires. *Betula nana* occurs in various places, both in wet Sphagnetum and in drier Trichophoreto–Callunetum. Local erosion of the peat reveals the buried remains of ancient Scots pines.

The soligenous mires may be regarded as the northern equivalent of the typical southern valley mires, usually merging into blanket mire instead of into wet and then dry heath. Similar examples occur widely in north-west Scotland, but on Rannoch Moor they are particularly numerous and well developed. They are characterised by a central soakway of *Carex–Sphagnum* associations (with *S. subsecundum* var. *auriculatum*, *C. limosa*, *C. lasiocarpa*, *C. rostrata*, *Eleocharis multicaulis*, *Utricularia vulgaris*, *U. intermedia*, *U. minor* and *Equisetum fluviatile*) with marginal areas of blanket mire vegetation. A few small hollows filled with peat, and the swamps surrounding small lochans, have the character of basin mires. They are mostly filled with a vegetation varying between poor-fen and acidophilous Sphagnetum, i.e. there is a carpet of *Sphagnum*, usually with carices, including *C. rostrata*, *C. lasiocarpa*, *C. curta* and *C. paupercula*, and still more acidophilous nuclei, in which *Sphagnum* hummocks have *Calluna* and *Erica tetralix*.

Rannoch Moor has long been noted as a rich haunt of moorland insects, e.g. of local northern dragonflies such as *Aeshna caerulea* and *Somatochlora arctica*. There is, however, a considerable unevenness in knowledge of insect distribution on the Scottish moorlands, and Rannoch Moor may appear at present to be a richer area than it is in reality. Greenshanks breed here and the area is notable for its moorland birds, including those of open water.

Rannoch Moor is bounded along its north-east side by the grade 1 open water site of Loch Laidon, and it has a large number of moorland tarns of varying size, and streams, which are all of considerable interest. The Perthshire portion is already a NNR, but some of the Argyll sector is of great interest and is included within the grade 1 site.

P.86. CARN NAN TRI-TIGHEARNAN, NAIRN/INVERNESS-SHIRE

NH 8239.   4350 ha   Grade 1

Blanket mire is developed extensively on this gently domed massif on the northern fringe of the eastern Highlands, and the summit plateau between 550 and 610 m is of particular scientific interest. The most impressive feature of this area is the dominance of lichens, especially *Cladonia arbuscula*, *C. impexa* and *C. rangiferina*, which give the ground a greyish-white appearance. Vascular plants are subordinate to this continuous lichen cover, but include *Calluna vulgaris*, *Eriophorum vaginatum*, *Erica tetralix*, *Vaccinium myrtillus*, *V. microcarpum* and *Empetrum hermaphroditum*. *Sphagnum* spp. are plentiful, mainly *S. capillaceum*, but with a good deal of *S. fuscum* and occasional hummocks of *S. imbricatum* and *S. magellanicum*. *Rubus chamaemorus* is locally abundant on the highest ground whilst *Trichophorum cespitosum* is dominant on the shallower peat at low levels around the plateau. *Rhacomitrium lanuginosum* is quite plentiful, especially on the edges of peat haggs and on some tall hummocks, but does not form the extensive cover so characteristic of this species in the peat haggs of more oceanic districts. The vegetation of the plateau is a lichen-rich facies of the eastern Calluneto–Eriophoretum blanket mire vegetation, the normal facies of which is so extensive in the eastern Highlands. This is the most extensive development of the lichen-rich facies in Britain, though there are other good examples on the Ladder Hills and A'Mhoine in Sutherland. Over much of the plateau the blanket mire is extensively eroded by gullying, giving haggs up to 3.6 m deep exposing numerous large pine stumps, up to at least 590 m. There are a few bog pools and tarns, but the watershed mire here is in contrast to that on Knockfin Heights (Caithness–Sutherland) where pools and dubh lochans are numerous.

On the highest ground the peat thins out and there is a lichen-rich short (but not prostrate) Callunetum. On the steep slopes above the Findhorn there are areas of *Arctostaphylos–Calluna* heath, locally of the species-rich kind. These communities of dry ground are mostly widespread submontane types and give only bonus upland interest.

P.87. LOCH INSH FENS, INVERNESS-SHIRE

NH 8103.   1000 ha   Grade 1*

Along the flat valley floor of the River Spey between Kingussie and Kincraig (in a section where the river falls only 15 m over 18 km) is an extensive tract of flood-plain mire. Although the vegetation has a natural character, consisting essentially of oligotrophic, northern poor-fen, the mire owes its existence to the presence of artificial embankments which extend along the Spey for several kilometres, effectively impeding the drainage of the valley floor on either side. The total extent of this mire system, excluding Loch Insh itself, covers an area nearly 5 km long and up to 1.6 km wide. It is therefore comparable in extent with some of the largest flood-plain mires in Broadland and is certainly the most important tract of flood-plain mire in northern Britain.

The vegetation consists mainly of sedge-dominated poor-fen communities but areas of reed-swamp, herb-rich fen and common sallow carr are locally extensive. Within the communities dominated by *Carex*, the most important species are *C. aquatilis* and *C. rostrata*, but *C. vesicaria*, *C. lasiocarpa* and *C. nigra* are all locally dominant. Although sedges are completely dominant in places, the community is usually two-layered, consisting of tall sedges and a lower growth of dicotyledons, notably *Potentilla palustris*, *Caltha palustris*, *Menyanthes trifoliata*, *Equisetum fluviatile*, *Galium palustre*, *Epilobium palustre*, *Ranunculus flammula*, *Veronica scutellata* and *Scutellaria galericulata*. Reed beds consist of dense *Phragmites* or *Phalaris arundinacea*, usually with few other species, and the herb-rich communities which occur where the water table is lower include *Carex nigra*, *C. echinata*, *Deschampsia cespitosa*, *Juncus effusus*, *Eriophorum angustifolium*, *Potentilla palustris*, *Galium palustre*, *Pedicularis palustris*, *Filipendula ulmaria* and *Lychnis flos-cuculi*.

Although a depth of at least 7 m of peat has been found under central parts of the fens, some of the drier edges have been drained, and at the Newtonmore end the system passes into damp pastures with neutral grasslands. The seasonal flooding of the fens excludes bryophytes from much of the vegetation but, on slightly higher ground below Insh village, this effect disappears, and there is a change to oligotrophic vegetation of the kind often found in valley mires, with *Calluna vulgaris*, *Erica tetralix*, *Trichophorum cespitosum*, *Narthecium ossifragum* and *Sphagnum papillosum*. Intermediate communities include a *Molinia caerulea–Myrica gale* type with abundant *Eriophorum angustifolium*, and a sedge mire which shows a slightly mesotrophic influence, with *Carex nigra*, *C. demissa*, *C. hostiana*, *C. panicea*, *Nardus stricta*, *Juncus squarrosus* and base-tolerant *Sphagnum* spp. such as *S. contortum*, *S. teres*, *S. squarrosum* and *S. palustre*. The rarer *S. imbricatum* and *S. strictum* also occur in this area.

There is a pronounced difference between this vegetation and that of most flood-plain mires in England. The northern floristic element is well represented and there is an extraordinary quantity of *Carex aquatilis*, a very local northern species.

One of the most important features of this area is the rich assemblage of wetland birds, both breeding species and migrants. The Spey Valley is a very important migration route and this results in large concentrations of birds using the Insh Fens in spring and autumn. Breeding species include many species of waders and duck including some which are local or rare as breeding species elsewhere in Britain.

The associated slow-running reach of the Spey, and Loch Insh into which the river flows, are regarded as grade 1 open water habitats representative of their type, and the whole complex is one of outstanding importance.

P.88. MOOR OF DINNET, ABERDEENSHIRE

NO 4399. 1600 ha Grade 1

The Moor of Dinnet is a composite site in which heather moorland, birch woodland, open water, transition and flood-plain mire form an interesting ecological complex.

The two lochs, Davan and Kinord (OW.76), have fringing communities of *Phragmites communis* and *Schoenoplectus lacustris* in places, and these pass into marginal poor-fens which vary from a markedly acidic type with *Myrica gale*, *Erica tetralix*, *Molinia caerulea*, *Narthecium ossifragum* and *Sphagnum auriculatum* to a weakly mesotrophic type with *Carex rostrata*, *C. vesicaria*, *Potentilla palustris*, *Menyanthes trifoliata*, *S. squarrosum* and *S. plumulosum*. The most important valley mires are Ordie Moss and Black Moss to the east of Loch Davan. Here, there is a mixture of the same mire communities, and also extensive stands of the *C. rostrata*, *Eriophorum angustifolium–S. recurvum* community so typical of northern poor-fens. There is also a great deal of *C. lasiocarpa*, *C. curta*, *C. nigra*, *C. diandra*, *C. aquatilis*, *C. echinata*, *Epilobium palustre*, *Galium palustre*, *Acrocladium cuspidatum* and *Marchantia polymorpha* var. *aquatica*. *Myrica* is locally abundant and there is some invasion by *Salix cinerea* to form willow carr. The area has not been examined thoroughly, but strongly mesotrophic mire would appear to be either absent or represented only by fragments.

A large breeding colony of black-headed gulls occurs in the swamps.

See also U.46.

P.89. EAST FLANDERS MOSS, PERTHSHIRE

NS 6398. 245 ha Grade 2

A series of raised mires, collectively known as Flanders Moss, in the upper part of the Forth valley, is by far the most extensive development of raised mire in Britain. This series extend for 11 km along the valley, the largest single unit, East Flanders Moss, being 3 km wide and over 5 km long. At one time the mires extended eastwards almost to Stirling, but at the eastern end the peat was removed and the underlying marine clay reclaimed for agriculture. The group of mosses to the west of the Menteith moraine is now afforested and so the best remaining example of the series is now East Flanders Moss.

Despite the size of this moss, the vegetation has been substantially altered through past efforts to improve the ground by drainage and burning. Birch scrub is present in places across the whole expanse of the moss, especially along old drainage lines where it may now be held in check by the high water table. The open moss vegetation is largely dominated by vascular plants, with a discontinuous *Sphagnum* carpet. The least modified raised mire vegetation lies to the west of the small burn which dissects the Moss, but even here the dominance of *Sphagnum* spp. is local and patchy. Even though there is now a high water table, much of the surface has *Calluna vulgaris*, *Erica tetralix* and rather tussocky *Eriophorum vaginatum* as co-dominants, with rather a low *Sphagnum* cover (mainly *S. tenellum*). Where the surface is *Sphagnum*-dominated the most important species are *S. magellanicum* and *S. papillosum*. *S. rubellum*, *S. cuspidatum*, *S. recurvum* and *S. tenellum* are sparse, whilst *S. imbricatum*, *S. fuscum* and *S. molle* are rare. *Erica tetralix*, *Andromeda polifolia*, *Narthecium ossifragum*, *Vaccinium oxycoccus*, *Eriophorum angustifolium* and *Rhynchospora alba* are generally abundant in these areas. Towards the edges of the mire expanse *Myrica gale*, *Trichophorum cespitosum* and *Cladonia impexa* become locally dominant. In places *Polytrichum commune* is dominant, probably because of disturbance. The present vegetation of the central mire surface thus forms a patchwork of communities related to past disturbance, especially drainage and burning. Under suitable management, the central vegetation complex might recover its former high *Sphagnum* cover, and the site could possibly merit upgrading under these circumstances.

The margins of the Moss are mostly grown with downy birch, and the ground here is relatively dry, with much *Dryopteris dilatata*, *D. carthusiana*, *Polytrichum commune*, *Sphagnum palustre* and *S. fimbriatum*, *Molinia caerulea* is locally abundant and *Narthecium* forms tall growths at the edge of the wooded ground. *Myrica* also grows taller near the drier margin.

Botanically, East Flanders Moss is famous as the locality for the rare northern acidophilous mire plant *Ledum groenlandicum*, which grows locally in the centre of the Moss. The area is important ornithologically since it acts as a roosting area for overwintering flocks of up to 2500 pink-footed geese.

P.90. LADDER HILLS, ABERDEENSHIRE/BANFFSHIRE

NJ 2513. 485 ha Grade 2

The Ladder Hills may be compared with the Moffat and Tweedsmuir Hills (in the Southern Uplands) in topography and altitude. They are a range of smooth, fairly steep-sided hills with broad, rounded summits which exceed 760 m in several places. The watershed plateaux have quite extensive areas of eastern Calluneto–Eriophoretum which is here distinguished by a general abundance, or local dominance, of lichens of the reindeer moss group (*Cladonia sylvatica*, *C. impexa* and *C. rangiferina*). *Rubus chamaemorus* occurs in great quantity and there is often a high cover of *Sphagnum* spp. including especially *S. capillaceum* and *S. fuscum*. The blanket mire grades on more exposed and better drained ground into lichen-rich dwarf Callunetum, and on steeper, more sheltered slopes into snow-bed bilberry heath.

See also U.59.

P.91. GULL NEST, MORAY
NJ 2250.   255 ha   Grade 2

The upland area north-west of the River Spey in Morayshire has extensive tracts of blanket mire, certain areas of which show morphological features similar to those of the Caithness watershed flows. Gull Nest is one such area where undamaged blanket mire with a hummocky *Sphagnum*-rich surface covers about 2.5 km². The vegetation has affinities with Calluneto–Eriophoretum, but in parts there are pool complexes with an abundance of *Trichophorum cespitosum* and *Narthecium ossifragum*, which together with the presence of the oceanic species *Drosera anglica* in one of its few eastern outposts, indicate affinities with the lowland and western Trichophoreto–Eriophoretum.

P.92. WARTLE MOSS, ABERDEENSHIRE
NJ 7232.   65 ha   Grade 2

This mire occupies a basin at 116 m within an agricultural district. The catchment area is partly underlain by base-rich igneous rocks, which have influenced the overlying drift. The peat is shallow because of extensive cutting.

The present surface is mostly mesotrophic mire, with local oligotrophic nuclei which may be remnants of the former peat cover although no peat facies are visible. Small areas of *Salix atrocinerea* carr have developed, with stunted trees festooned in *Parmelia* spp. At the north end, birch woodland covers a small area of drier ground.

The mesotrophic mire is mainly dominated by *Carex rostrata*, with much *Angelica sylvestris*, *Caltha palustris*, *Dactylorchis purpurella*, *Filipendula ulmaria*, *Lychnis flos-cuculi*, *Menyanthes trifoliata*, *Pedicularis palustris*, *Potentilla palustris*, and *Senecio aquaticus*. A central area has shorter vegetation with scattered pools and *Carex curta*, *C. demissa*, *C. diandra*, *C. pulicaris*, *Eleocharis palustris* and *Parnassia palustris*. There are also areas with large tussocks of *Deschampsia cespitosa*, and fragmentary stands of *Juncus acutiflorus*, *Phalaris arundinacea* and *Phragmites communis*.

A typical fauna occurs with roe deer, mallard, redpoll, reed bunting, sedge warbler, short-eared owl, teal and whinchat. There are many butterflies and moths including orange-tip *Anthocharis cardamines*, wood tiger *Parasemia plantaginis* and small pearl-bordered fritillary *Boloria selene* which is abundant.

Although no nationally rare species have yet been found the site has value because of its relatively large extent and undisturbed nature, as a northern example of mesotrophic mire in a basin situation.

P.93. ABERNETHY FOREST MIRES, INVERNESS-SHIRE
NH 9618.   20 ha   Grade 2

A series of oligotrophic to mesotrophic valley mires occupies a system of glacial drift hollows and channels to the west of Loch Garten. Where water movement is negligible and base status low there is a *Sphagnum*-dominated *Calluna–Eriophorum vaginatum* community, with an abundance of *Erica tetralix*, *Narthecium ossifragum* and *Carex pauciflora*. In places there are systems of long, aligned pools filled with aquatic *Sphagnum* spp. This vegetation resembles that of some blanket mires, but locally there is a soligenous influence, revealed by the presence of poor-fen communities with *C. rostrata*, *C. lasiocarpa*, *C. nigra*, *C. echinata*, *Menyanthes trifoliata*, *Potentilla palustris*, *Utricularia intermedia*, *Potamogeton polygonifolius* and carpets of *S. recurvum*, passing into open water swamp. In one area, mineral charged water emerges to give a patchy occurrence of the mesotrophic *Carex rostrata*–'brown moss' community, showing some development of a hummock–hollow surface pattern.

There is a rather complex mosaic of the three main vegetation types, i.e. acidophilous (ombrogenous) mire, poor-fen and rich-fen, so that the hydrology of the system is evidently complex. This mire system was, until recently, surrounded by pine forest, but this has now been felled. Numerous pine seedlings have grown on the wet mire surface but many of these remain checked or become moribund.

See also W.187.

WEST SCOTLAND

P.85. RANNOCH MOOR (PART), ARGYLL   Grade 1*
See under East Scotland, p. 237.

P.94. CLAISH MOSS, ARGYLL
NM 7168.   485 ha   Grade 1*

Claish Moss consists of an extensive, linear series of strikingly patterned raised mires, eccentrically domed, lying along the south side of Loch Shiel almost at sea-level. Streams draining northwards from the uplands separate the individual units of the series which vary in length from several hundred metres to over 1.6 km. The total extent of the series is nearly 5 km and other similar mires occur at Kentra Moss (grade 2) immediately west of Acharacle.

Each mire unit has a pronounced surface pattern consisting of linear ridges following the contours of the mire surface which form successive terraces each of which has its own water table. The large amplitude and total scale of the pattern is however unparalleled in Britain and these mires are more closely allied to Scandinavian patterned mires than anything else in Britain.

Stratigraphical studies show that the mires developed over an extensive area of almost level ground, possibly a raised beach terrace, at about 8 m but there is no evidence of any widespread development of fen conditions at the onset of mire formation. The vegetation is very similar to that of western Scottish blanket mire (Trichophoreto–Eriophoretum) but certain unusual floristic elements are well developed. Numerous hummocks of *Rhacomitrium lanuginosum* occur, especially on islands. Suitable conditions appear to be produced by the local lowering of the water table caused by down-slope coalescing of pool systems.

This *Rhacomitrium* facies is not only a surface phenomenon but also occurs extensively at depth in the peat. Abundance of *Sphagnum pulchrum* indicates affinities with the southern raised mires and *Rhynchospora fusca*, which has a very restricted distribution in Britain, is plentiful in pools and hollows on some of the mires of the series. Otherwise, most of the plants are characteristic of western blanket mire including *Molinia caerulea*, *Trichophorum cespitosum*, *Calluna vulgaris*, *Pleurozia purpurea*, *Campylopus atrovirens*, *Eleocharis multicaulis*, *Carex limosa*, *Drosera anglica* and *Myrica gale*. Alga-covered peat surfaces, frequently covered by water, are abundant and these areas show little *Sphagnum* growth. Around pool margins, *Sphagnum* cover is more continuous including *S. papillosum*, *S. cuspidatum*, *S. pulchrum*, *S. magellanicum* and *S. plumulosum*. Hummock-forming *Sphagnum* spp. are scarce relative to more southerly raised mires but *S. imbricatum* and *S. fuscum* occur frequently. Even in the centre of the pool networks the vegetation is heavily grazed by deer and this may well explain the widespread lack of *Sphagnum* cover.

Claish Moss adjoins the grade 2 open water lake of Loch Shiel (OW.95).

P.95. BLAR NAM FAOILEAG, CAITHNESS
ND 1444. 4600 ha   Grade 1*

The eastern type of blanket mire vegetation in northern Scotland is represented by numerous extensive watershed flows in Caithness. Of these the most outstanding is Blar nam Faoileag, a large tract of actively growing blanket mire occupying a gently domed watershed, at a maximum elevation of just over 150 m. The mire surface, which extends over 6.5 km north–south and about 5 km east–west, is bounded by tributaries of the River Thurso, and is broken only by the numerous and varied pool systems characteristic of these flows. There are no significant areas of erosion or peat-cutting, and little evidence of burning.

The vegetation is a northern shrub-rich and lichen-rich facies of the upland Calluneto–Eriophoretum type of blanket mire vegetation. *Calluna vulgaris*, *Eriophorum vaginatum*, *Arctostaphylos uva-ursi*, *Sphagnum rubellum*, *S. capillaceum*, *Hylocomium splendens*, *Pleurozium schreberi* and lichens of the *Cladonia* (*Cladina*) group attain varying degrees of dominance. *S. imbricatum* and *S. fuscum* are frequent but not as abundant as in the Strathy River Bogs. A bryophyte ground layer is continuous except in the lichen-rich facies. Extensive steep-edged irregular pool networks have developed on the flatter expanses. Absence of *Molinia caerulea* and relative insignificance of *Trichophorum cespitosum* and *Rhacomitrium lanuginosum* together with the development of shrub-rich and lichen-rich facies distinguish this from the western type of blanket mire vegetation.

In addition to the usual birds of such mires, a few pairs of Arctic skuas nest on this great flow.

This area is of outstanding importance as an undamaged example of a regional type of blanket mire and probably represents the largest continuous expanse of actively growing mire remaining in Britain.

P.96. STRATHY RIVER BOGS, SUTHERLAND
NC 7955. 950 ha   Grade 1*

Four relatively undisturbed examples of valley-side flow occur in this area, which is otherwise predominantly covered by rather modified (heavily grazed and burned) blanket mire vegetation covering the watersheds. The four sites, one of which is the existing Strathy Bog NNR, lie alongside the River Strathy or its tributaries (at 802530, 795558, 794535 and 775566) and they show well-developed but differing forms of surface topography related to the geomorphological position in which they have arisen. A *Sphagnum*-rich facies is well developed, including *S. papillosum*, *S. rubellum* and *S. fuscum* on the ridges and *S. cuspidatum* or *S. subsecundum* var. *inundatum* in the pools and linear hollows. *S. imbricatum*, which seldom attains a high cover on British mires, occurs here as a major constituent of a characteristic marginal hummock–hollow mosaic. A northern 'peat alpine' element is present in *Arctostaphylos uva-ursi* and *Betula nana*, but the presence of *Molinia caerulea*, *Myrica gale*, *Carex limosa*, *Drosera anglica* and *Pleurozia purpurea* together with abundance of *Trichophorum cespitosum* indicates that the vegetation belongs essentially to the western Trichophoreto–Eriophoretum.

No other area of similar size in this central district of north Sutherland is comparable in terms of quality of vegetation and variety of structural types of mire represented. The valley-side flows are particularly important since they are generally more modified elsewhere in this district.

P.97. SOUTHERN PARPHE, SUTHERLAND
NC 2563. 1350 ha   Grade 1

Flat-lying land in north-west Sutherland is mostly covered by blanket mire of an extreme western, oceanic type, one of the best examples being an area south west of Strath Shinary in the southern part of the Parphe (the area of moorland forming the north-western extremity of Sutherland). Here the blanket mire is developed over a fairly level area of Torridonian Sandstone. Within an area of some 1335 ha there is a wide range of morphological mire types showing a variety of surface patterns. These types include a number of watershed flows with differences in surface features, a small valley-side flow, remarkably similar to Strathy Bog in structure but having a more distinctly oceanic vegetation, several areas of sloping blanket mire with pronounced linear patterns, and, in addition, an important area of valley mire above Sandwood Loch.

Blanket mire vegetation in this area is characterised by relative insignificance of *Sphagnum*, and is generally dominated by vascular plants together with certain mosses and liverworts such as *Pleurozia purpurea*, *Campylopus atrovirens* and *Rhacomitrium lanuginosum*, which form a discontinuous plant cover on the peat surface. Indeed, much of the mire surface between the vascular plant components consists of a layer of gelatinous and filamentous algae, e.g. *Zygogonium*. Physiognomic dominants are *Trichophorum cespitosum*, *Calluna vulgaris*, *Eriophorum angustifolium* and

E. vaginatum with frequent discrete hummocks of *Sphagnum rubellum* and *S. fuscum* with which is associated *Empetrum nigrum*. *Arctostaphylos uva-ursi* is dominant in some areas whilst *Erica tetralix* is generally absent. The small valley-side flow is comparatively rich in *Sphagnum* (including *S. magellanicum*, *S. papillosum*, *S. cuspidatum* and *S. subsecundum* var. *auriculatum*) together with a remarkable abundance of *Carex limosa* and *Eleocharis multicaulis* in the numerous linear hollows. A feature of the blanket mire vegetation in this area is the abundance of *Drosera anglica*.

The valley mire at Sandwood includes communities typical of north-west Scottish valley mires, species such as *Carex limosa*, *C. lasiocarpa*, *Schoenus nigricans*, *Myrica gale*, *Sphagnum subsecundum* var. *auriculatum* and *Scorpidium scorpioides* being abundant. Depauperate stands of *Phragmites communis* are also extensive.

See also C.107 and U.69.

P.98. KNOCKFIN HEIGHTS, SUTHERLAND/CAITHNESS

NC 9134. 3950 ha   Grade 1

Blanket mire of a most unusual type covers an extensive plateau of Moine Schists and granitic rocks which extends for over 13 km along the Caithness/Sutherland border. The central section of this plateau between 380 and 440 m in height is the area of greatest interest. Throughout this area pools have developed on the peat, as they have on many of the lower level watershed flows, but here they have subsequently expanded considerably by lateral erosion of peat so that many of them have eventually coalesced. A number of the larger lochans are over 0.5 km in length and many of the pool systems are several hundred metres long.

Many areas still have a high water table and intact communities on the mire surface between the pools. Other areas, where peripheral erosion has extended into inter-linked pool networks, exhibit widespread drainage of the pools and lowering of the peat water table in the immediate vicinity. Erosion of peat below pools and bare hollows (previously occupied by pools) down to the mineral ground is common. In some cases recolonisation of exposed mineral ground occurs. This area of eroded peat is most unusual and forms the extreme end-point in the development of pool-dominated blanket mire in northern Scotland. The pattern of erosion is quite different from that of the Pennine blanket mires, although the scale of erosion is similar.

Where the vegetation is intact it consists of Trichophoreto–Eriophoretum of the less oceanic type, in which *Calluna vulgaris*, *Eriophorum vaginatum*, *Sphagnum papillosum*, *S. rubellum*, *S. tenellum*, *Trichophorum cespitosum*, *Eriophorum angustifolium*, *Rhacomitrium lanuginosum*, *Pleurozia purpurea*, *Cladonia impexa* and *C. uncialis* attain varying degrees of dominance locally. Areas of intact mire vegetation with a high water table frequently lie close to areas of severe erosion, so that the site provides an extremely good example of the restricted hydrological effect of drainage in peat of this type.

P.99. BEN WYVIS, ROSS AND CROMARTY

NH 4869. 5350 ha   Grade 1

The eastern and upland type of blanket mire vegetation which is so extensive on the plateaux of the eastern Highlands is represented locally in northern Scotland by a shrub-rich and lichen-rich facies containing a northern floristic element. This type of blanket mire is well developed on Ben Wyvis and here contains abundant *Arctous alpinus* and *Betula nana* but contrasts with other northern shrub-rich examples of Calluneto–Eriophoretum in the absence of *Arctostaphylos uva-ursi*. *Empetrum hermaphroditum*, *Vaccinium vitis-idaea*, *V. myrtillus*, *Carex bigelowii* and *Rubus chamaemorus* are all abundant and the luxuriant development of these species is associated with a reduced cover of *Calluna vulgaris* and *Eriophorum vaginatum*. Hummocks of *Sphagnum capillaceum* and *S. fuscum* are frequent and there are facies with an abundance of hypnaceous mosses, *Rhacomitrium lanuginosum* and lichens. The shrub-rich facies of blanket mire is particularly sensitive to burning and grazing, and was once widespread but is now very restricted in its distribution. The examples on Ben Wyvis are remarkably undisturbed, and add to the interest of this grade 1* upland site. There are also patches of lichen-rich Trichophoreto–Callunetum with *B. nana*. Some of the blanket mires on this hill show considerable dissection by gullying of the peat.   See also U.63.

P.100. MONADH MOR, ROSS AND CROMARTY

NH 5853. 160 ha   Grade 1

The Monadh Mor originated as a zone of glacial deposition which developed numerous deep channels. The area now supports a complex of pine woodland, mires and large oligotrophic ponds more akin to the Scandinavian wooded bogs than anything else in Britain. Most of the mire communities are associated with the valleys within which local conditions depend on the extent of hydroseral succession. Some of the deeper channels retain open water but most are now dominated by oligotrophic swamp communities. The site includes a pine-grown raised-mire with *Sphagnum* filled hollows set in a dry facies of raised mire vegetation dominated by lichens.

The gentle morainic ridges are largely covered by Scots pine, with a ground layer of *Vaccinium myrtillus*, *Calluna*, *Empetrum nigrum*, and a fairly continuous and varied bryophyte carpet including *Sphagnum rubellum*, *Pleurozium schreberi*, *Hylocomium splendens*, *Hypnum cupressiforme* and *Aulacomnium palustre*. Lichens, especially *Cladonia impexa*, are also abundant.

Several species of duck breed in the area, besides waders such as curlew and redshank. The woodland avifauna includes crested tit and capercaillie, and roe deer are numerous.

P.101. INVERPOLLY VALLEY MIRE, ROSS

NC 1014. 6 ha   Grade 1

Much of the gneiss topography along the north-west Scottish seaboard shows peat-filled depressions which merge locally into more extensive flats of blanket mire. Some of the valleys show a distinct form of mire development with strongly soligenous tracts. A small valley mire west of Loch Sionascaig is of this type, forming a discrete unit bounded by steep rocky slopes except for a narrow defile at the lower end of the valley. It is about 230 m long by 90 m wide and the peat has a maximum depth of slightly over 9 m.

The vegetation consists of a mixture of poor-fen and blanket mire elements. A good deal of the surface is influenced by seepage of water from the surrounding mineral ground. These soligenous tracts are locally dominated by *Carex lasiocarpa* but usually have an open semi-floating mat of *Potamogeton polygonifolius*, *Sphagnum subsecundum* (vars. *auriculatum* and *subsecundum*) and *Schoenus nigricans*. Acidophilous hummocks of *Sphagnum* often capped by *Rhacomitrium lanuginosum* occur throughout this zone. The oceanic species *Pinguicula lusitanica* occurs on the margins of these hummocks. Away from the soligenous influence the vegetation is essentially that of oceanic blanket mire with *Rhynchospora alba*, *Myrica gale*, *Erica tetralix*, *Drosera anglica* and *Pleurozia purpurea* all abundant. Distinct pools within this vegetation contain *C. limosa*, *Eleocharis multicaulis* and *Utricularia minor*.

This is the best-known example of oceanic valley mire. It shows a rather wider range of vegetation than the similar valley mire at Little Loch Roag on Lewis. Despite its small size this section of the Inverpolly grade 1 upland site (U.66) merits grade 1 status in its own right.

See also W.207 and OW.92.

P.102. KENTRA MOSS, ARGYLL

NM 6668.   95 ha   Grade 2

Kentra Moss is the name given to several raised mires occupying the low lying coastal flats between Kentra Bay and the River Shiel. They form part of the extensive raised mire complex which has developed adjacent to Loch Shiel, of which Claish Moss is the more important section.

Much of Kentra Moss has been damaged by drainage and localised peat cutting, but one section to the south-east of Arevegaig is almost undamaged. It has a variety of features which together make the site an important conservation unit. The vegetation and surface features are similar to parts of Claish Moss but there are differences in detail. The most fundamental difference is that this site lies in a slight depression bounded by rocky knolls. The peat surface slopes very gently from east to west and there is a very pronounced surface pattern of linear pools and ridges associated with this gradient. The peat is generally shallower than on Claish Moss, averaging 3 m. The main difference in surface pattern is one of scale, the ridges and hollows being much narrower on Kentra Moss with fewer deep pools. A pool system with *Rhacomitrium* islands is, however, developed where the surface is almost level. Because the amplitude of pools and ridges is less than on Claish Moss the vegetation is rather different. Most of the pools are shallow, often with bare peat supporting *Zygogonium* with an abundance of *Drosera intermedia*, *Carex limosa* and

Rhynchospora fusca. The dominant plants of the ridges are *Trichophorum cespitosum*, *Molinia caerulea*, *Myrica gale* and *R. alba* together with a large number of *Sphagnum* spp. and many leafy liverworts. All the major hummock-forming *Sphagnum* spp. are present and locally abundant but *Rhacomitrium* is not well developed on this site.

One value which this site has above others is its ease of access, which gives it considerable potential for research purposes.

P.103. BLAR NA CAILLICH BUIDHE, INVERNESS-SHIRE

NM 6890.   255 ha   Grade 2

This raised mire has developed on low ground adjacent to Loch Morar grade 1 open water site (OW.86). It is bounded by well-defined lagg streams and has a steeply sloping rand round the entire site. The centre is almost level and has a strongly patterned surface. There is, however, considerable variation in the form of pattern. In places extensive pool networks with deep pools and numerous *Rhacomitrium*-dominated islands are developed whilst other sectors show narrow linear pools which have more complete vegetation cover. In this respect the site is intermediate between Kentra Moss and Claish Moss, but has suffered more from burning and drainage.

This site represents the most northerly development of the *Rhynchospora fusca*–*Sphagnum pulchrum* assemblage which characterises the coastal raised mires of western Scotland. The vegetation of ridges and hummocks is essentially similar to that of Claish. Lagg communities are dominated by *Molinia* and *Myrica* but local enrichment gives rise to more mesotrophic communities with *Parnassia palustris*, *Triglochin palustris*, *Filipendula ulmaria* and *Eriophorum latifolium*.

P.104. DUBH LOCHS OF SHIELTON AND THE FLOWS, CAITHNESS

ND 2048.   1100 ha   Grade 2

An extensive area of blanket mire occurs at a height of 90–107 m on the watershed immediately east of Blar nam Faoileag (P.95) in Caithness. This site is relatively small (only 3 km in length) but the vegetation is very similar in type and quality to that of the other preferred site, for which this can be regarded as a straightforward alternative. There is a generally high cover of *Sphagnum*, and the systems of pools contain hollows many of which are infilled with this moss. Noteworthy features of this area are the presence of several very large pools (dubh lochans) with a marginal *Juncus effusus*–*S. recurvum* association and abundant *Menyanthes trifoliata*, and the presence of several pairs of Arctic skuas breeding on the flow. Plants of interest include *Dicranum bergeri*, *S. imbricatum*, *S. fuscum* and *Vaccinium microcarpum*. This site is of particular interest for the very well-developed surface patterns that are characteristic of watershed mires, but it does not exhibit the same degree of variation in surface patterns as Blar nam Faoileag, and the shrub-rich facies of the prevailing Calluneto-Eriophoretum is less well represented.

P.105. FORSINARD–BADANLOCH FLOWS, SUTHERLAND

NC 8745, NC 7737. 1650 ha   Grade 2

Several areas of intact blanket mire occur on the gentle spurs (between 150 and 180 m) north-west of Forsinard between the Halladale River and the River Dyke. These mires are of the watershed flow type, but the vegetation is of considerably higher quality than the corresponding, much modified type in the Strathy River Bogs (P.96). There are, however, none of the high quality Strathy valley-side flows in the Forsinard area. The vegetation is intermediate between the western and eastern blanket mire types as befits the rather eastern position of the site. It is a 'dry' type with *Calluna vulgaris* and *Eriophorum vaginatum* dominant, but many of the oceanic indicator species which are absent on the east Caithness flows are still present here. In particular *Sphagnum imbricatum*, *Myrica gale* and *Pleurozia purpurea* are abundant. There is also a patchy occurrence of *Betula nana* and *Arctostaphylos uva-ursi*.

In the vicinity of Loch Badanloch are two important areas of blanket mire which together merit grade 2 status. One of these is a valley-side flow about 1 km in length which is bounded by pronounced marginal laggs except on the upslope side. The mire surface has a well-developed linear pattern of pools and hummocks and it is this feature which is of greatest interest. The vegetation is that characteristic of western blanket mire and includes abundant *Myrica gale* and *Trichophorum cespitosum*.

The second area lies on a gently sloping spur to the north of Loch nan Clar, between the Allt na Cailbhe Mor and the Feith a'Chreagain. The vegetation has not been investigated in detail, but the variety of surface pool and hummock patterns in this relatively small area is outstanding. These areas of mire lie on either side of the grade 2 upland site of Ben Griam More and Ben Griam Beag (U.97), and the whole is best regarded as forming a single complex.

P.106. A'MHOINE, SUTHERLAND

NC 5465. 2550 ha   Grade 2

The peninsula between the Kyle of Tongue and Loch Eriboll is mostly covered by blanket mire with the exception of sharply protruding low hills such as Ben Hutig. The importance of blanket mire in this area lies chiefly in the extensive occurrence of a lichen-dominated facies in which vascular plants are subordinate to reindeer moss lichens of the genus *Cladonia* (especially *C. sylvatica*). In addition a shrub-rich facies is present, containing much *Arctostaphylos uva-ursi* and *Arctous alpinus* but without *Betula nana*. Such vegetation is developed locally throughout the peninsula and forms an unusual facies of northern Scottish blanket mire vegetation. It is much more closely allied to the

Calluneto–Eriophoretum of the eastern Highlands (as on Carn nan tri-tighearnan (P.86)) than to the usual development of blanket mire in north-west Scotland. There are also areas of patterned watershed mire, and some of the pools are of the large dubh lochan type while others show a terraced appearance. The typical western Trichophoreto–Eriophoretum is well represented besides the other mire communities.

Ben Hutig is a low Moine Schist hill (408 m) with a series of wind-swept ridges which carry fine examples of *Loiseleuria–Arctous*–dwarf *Calluna* heath at lower elevations than usual, and with both lichen and *Rhacomitrium*-rich facies represented. The northern boundary of this site is abruptly delineated by the tremendous range of sea cliffs east of Whiten Head, giving a bonus example of this coastal habitat.

P.107. LITTLE LOCH ROAG VALLEY MIRE, LEWIS, INVERNESS-SHIRE

NB 1424. 20 ha   Grade 2

Several good examples of oceanic valley mire vegetation occur on Lewis. All of these are rather small sites which do not merit grade 1 status as single isolated units. The best example of this type of mire occurs in a small rock-bounded depression east of Little Loch Roag.

The mire surface consists of a floating vegetation mat composed of two distinct vegetational components. There are soligenous tracts dominated by sedges and base-tolerant *Sphagnum* spp. within which occurs the second type, which consists of more acidophilous nuclei composed of hummock-forming *Sphagnum* spp. and a variety of vascular plants. The *Carex–Sphagnum* flats in the central area include the following species as dominants: *C. limosa*, *C. lasiocarpa*, *S. subsecundum* var. *auriculatum*, *Eleocharis multicaulis*, *Menyanthes trifoliata* and *Potamogeton polygonifolius*. *Drosera anglica* is very abundant throughout and all the above species occur within a muddy iron-stained matrix.

Acidophilous nuclei are dominated by *Sphagnum papillosum*, *S. rubellum*, *Calluna vulgaris*, *Narthecium ossifragum* and *Trichophorum cespitosum*. *Schoenus nigricans* is dominant around the margins of these nuclei. Along the edge of the system the acidophilous hummocks are more extensive, eventually merging to form a marginal community indistinguishable from blanket mire.

Other species which are abundant in this mire system include *Utricularia minor*, *Carex rostrata*, *C. dioica*, *C. nigra*, *Pinguicula vulgaris*, *Molinia caerulea* and *Pedicularis sylvatica*. Mires of this type are widespread in the western Highlands and are adequately represented on the Rannoch Moor grade 1 complex (P.85), and by the Inverpolly Valley Mire (P.101).

19 UPLAND GRASSLANDS AND HEATHS

SOUTH-WEST ENGLAND

U.1. NORTH DARTMOOR, DEVON
SX 5786. 7400 ha   Grade 1

On Dartmoor it is difficult, if not impossible, to find one area of reasonable size which contains the full range of ecological diversity; the best heather heaths are in the north-east around Headland Warren, and good blanket mire occurs on Cater's Beam on southern Dartmoor. Another area centred on Fur Tor (571 m) and Cranmere Pool, extending west to Tavy Cleave and north-west to Kitty Tor, has been chosen as containing the greatest range of vegetation; this includes much of the highest granite ground of northern Dartmoor and some of the peripheral Culm Measures to the west. These two rocks give almost exclusively base-deficient soils and calcicolous plants are virtually absent from the area.

The granite plateau is largely covered with *Molinia*-rich blanket mire which is somewhat degraded in places, but still regarded as nationally important (see Peatlands). This forms the breeding place of a few golden plover and dunlin. Below 460 m, or on sloping ground, blanket mire gives way to dwarf-shrub heath, locally of heather and bilberry, but often showing replacement by acidic grassland in which *Agrostis setacea* is dominant rather than the usual *A. canina* and *Festuca ovina*. *Calluna–Molinia* mixtures are quite frequent on damper soils and shallow peat. Bracken stands occur on some of the drier slopes, and *Nardus stricta* and *Juncus squarrosus* are plentiful on damper ground. On the lower western side of the area, extending onto the Culm Measures, there is a good deal of *Calluna–Ulex gallii* heath (see Lowland Grasslands, Heaths and Scrub).

Large flushes and soligenous mires are very characteristic of Dartmoor. There are examples of *Juncus effusus–Sphagnum recurvum* mire with *S. palustre* and *Polytrichum commune*, and these grade on very wet ground into the type in which *Carex rostrata* replaces *J. effusus* and *S. cuspidatum* is abundant. Perhaps the most widespread type of soligenous mire on Dartmoor is one which has floristic affinities with blanket mire, and contains *Eriophorum vaginatum*, *E. angustifolium*, *Molinia caerulea*, *Erica tetralix*, *Calluna vulgaris*, *Potamogeton polygonifolius*, *S. papillosum*, *S. recurvum*, *S. cuspidatum* and *S. auriculatum*. This grades into stands with abundant *J. effusus* and/or *J. acutiflorus*, and also into flushes dominated by *S. auriculatum*. There are also transitions to wet grass heath, with *Nardus stricta*,

J. squarrosus, *Carex binervis*, *M. caerulea* and *Calluna*. *Molinia* becomes dominant and tussocky in some seepage tracks, but *Myrica gale*, which commonly occurs as a co-dominant in such situations in the western Highlands, is very local on Dartmoor. Floristically, these flush mires are rather poor, but *Hypericum elodes* and *Wahlenbergia hederacea* are widespread species.

In the oceanic climate of Dartmoor there is a profusion of common mosses and liverworts, and Atlantic species are well represented especially in the crevices of block screes on shaded slopes. Here both filmy ferns *Hymenophyllum* spp. occur also, and Kitty Tor is the southernmost station for the northern hepatic *Anastrepta orcadensis*. The granite appears to be an especially favourable substratum for lichens and a large number of species occur. The vegetation complex of Dartmoor bears a strong resemblance to that of the granite uplands of Galloway, particularly in the abundance of *Molinia* and the large extent of strongly acidic soligenous mire.

The vegetation of this Dartmoor site belongs to the lowland heath type at the lower levels, and even the highest parts are only submontane. Montane plants are absent and only a very few submontane species (e.g. *Lycopodium selago*) have been found.

An important oakwood, Black Tor Copse (W.66 gr. 1), is included within this site.

See also L.92 and P.25.

U.2. DUNKERY BEACON, SOMERSET
SS 8943. 2700 ha   Grade 2

This has greater affinities with lowland acidic heath and is described under Lowland Grasslands, Heaths and Scrub (L.107).

See also W.69.

SOUTH WALES

U.3. CRAIG Y CILIAU AND MYNYDD LLANGATWG, BRECKNOCK
SN 1915. 1500 ha   Grade 1

The existing National Nature Reserve (NNR) of Craig y Ciliau includes one of the biggest exposures of upland limestone in south Wales, consisting of a shallow north-facing scarp of tiered cliffs and steep slopes with a good deal of scree, at an altitude of 275–460 m. There are extensive calcareous grasslands of the herb and moss-rich *Festuca–Agrostis* type, and below the main cliff is a dense, tall, hawthorn scrub. The cliffs are famous as the refuge of the rare whitebeams, *Sorbus minima*, *S. leptophylla*, *S. anglica* and *S. porrigentiformis*, and there are scattered small trees of native beech at an unusually high altitude. The slopes and rocks support a rich calcicolous flora of herbs and ferns, including *Polygonatum odoratum*, *Circaea alpina*, *Saxifraga hypnoides*, *Melica nutans*, *Asplenium viride* and *Thelypteris robertiana*. There is a small mire of raised mire type in a hollow beneath the cliffs, and the geomorphological and geological interest of the site includes the extensive cave system known as Agen Allwedd.

Above the limestone escarpment is the gritstone plateau of Mynydd Llangatwg with a contrasting complex of acidophilous moorland vegetation. There is a patchy occurrence of Callunetum, but the most interesting community is a dwarf-shrub heath in which *Empetrum nigrum* is co-dominant with *Vaccinium myrtillus*, and approaches complete dominance in places. This grades into shallow *Eriophorum vaginatum* blanket mire on more poorly drained ground, and into mixed *Nardus–Juncus squarrosus* grassland, where grazing and burning have been more intense. By the inclusion of some of this gritstone moorland with the limestone area, the single site encompasses the total significant range of vegetation variation of the Carboniferous block. The vegetation is essentially of a submontane character. The whole area is of great geological and geomorphological importance.

U.4. PEN Y FAN (including CRAIG CERRIG GLEISIAD), BRECKNOCK
SO 0121.   5750 ha   Grade 1

The existing NNR covers a pair of low hills just topping 610 m on the west side of the Brecon Beacons. There are two precipitous corries, facing east and west, though the main cliffs in both face north. The area was chosen as a representative example of the Brecon Beacons Old Red Sandstone upland ecosystem. Craig Cerrig Gleisiad, rising from 460–610 m, is a tiered escarpment, with many scattered small trees, mainly rowan, growing up to near its summit. The intervening accessible ledges are mostly covered with bilberry or grasses, but on the ungrazed rocks and ledges are rare and local plants such as *Saxifraga oppositifolia*, *S. hypnoides*, *Asplenium viride*, *Hymenophyllum wilsonii*, *Thalictrum minus* and *Trollius europaeus*. The lower-lying cliffs in the other corrie, Cwm Du, have fewer alpines, and the bigger ledges are distinguished by luxuriant growths of *Luzula sylvatica*. The rest of the NNR has a largely submontane complex of heather and bilberry heath, evidently representing remnants of more extensive communities now largely converted to the prevailing acidic grasslands dominated by *Molinia*, *Agrostis–Festuca*, *Nardus* and *Juncus squarrosus*. The summit plateau has a small area of *Eriophorum vaginatum* mire.

The inclusion of high ground of the main Brecon Beacons ridge, Pen y Fan (886 m) and its subsidiary ridges, completes the range of variation and makes this a fully representative site for this area. Although the ridges are so narrow that the area of ground over 760 m is small, this area includes a significant extent of montane *Festuca–Agrostis* grassland, with *Salix herbacea* in its southernmost British station. The extensive escarpments of the north-facing corries give a rich rock ledge flora at a higher elevation than in the existing NNR, and better examples of herb-rich grasslands below the cliffs. The area is of considerable geomorphological interest for its well-developed glacial features. Cwm Sere, the valley running north from Pen y Fan, has an interesting example of woodland which is included in the site for its bonus value. The woodland drops steeply down to the stream and is very damp with numerous seepages and boggy patches. Alder is dominant with abundant ash. Rowan, holly and field maple are frequent with a few sessile oak. Large downy birch trees occur on the margins but the woodland becomes alder–hawthorn scrub on the upper edge. Hazel forms the shrub layer throughout. The area is heavily grazed so that the open areas are grassy, but the wet flushes are forb rich, while ferns form an important component of the field layer.

U.5. CWM YSTWYTH, CARDIGANSHIRE
SN 8071.   6850 ha   Grade 1

This upland area lies in Cardiganshire, on the south side of the River Ystwyth, and rises at first with fairly steep slopes bearing patchy oakwood to a moorland plateau reaching 593 m on Trawsallt, whence the headstreams of the Elan and Claerwen valleys drain eastwards into Radnor. There is a transition from *Molinia–Eriophorum* communities in the wet bottom of Cwm Ystwyth, through bracken infested *Festuca–Agrostis* grassland on the dry lower slopes, which also have patches of oakwood, to *Nardus* grassland on the higher slopes. Heather and bilberry dwarf-shrub heaths are now only sparsely represented. The moorland plateau carries a good deal of blanket mire, though this is rather dissected, owing to the unevenness of the terrain. Most of this vegetation approximates to Calluneto–Eriophoretum with variable *Sphagnum* cover, but *M. caerulea* and *Trichophorum cespitosum* are locally abundant, giving affinities with western Trichophoreto–Eriophoretum. The area of greatest interest is a patch of pool and hummock mire, Gors Lŵyd, at the north-eastern edge of the site on a col between Afon Elan and Afon Ystwyth. This ground has locally a high cover of *Sphagnum*, and there are local species such as *Andromeda polifolia*, *Drosera anglica* and *Rhynchospora alba*. A drier facies has numerous *Rhacomitrium lanuginosum* hummocks, and there are transitions to soligenous mire. There are extensive systems of soligenous mire within the site as a whole, and clusters of moorland tarns including the Teifi Pools.

Floristic interest is much lower than in the other grade 1 sites of the region and the Cwm Ystwyth site is regarded more as a typical example of the slate uplands of south-central Wales. The special importance of the site is ornithological, as it is a breeding and feeding haunt of upland birds. The area is geomorphologically interesting for its river braiding and stratified screes. The inclusion of the disused Cwm Ystwyth lead mine and its spoil heaps adds another habitat not represented in Welsh upland key sites.

U.6. COTHI TYWI, CARMARTHENSHIRE

SN 7547. 3650 ha   Grade 1

This site contains a complex of habitats characteristic of the uplands and valleys in the 'slate' hill country of south-central Wales. It includes the Royal Society for the Protection of Birds' (RSPB) Gwenffrwd reserve which is based on a hill sheep farm, with its range of grasslands from the walled and hedged fields and meadows of the valley bottom, through the improved pastures of the 'fridd' where sheep are folded, especially during winter, to the unimproved grasslands above the limits of enclosed land. These last range from the species-poor *Festuca–Agrostis* grasslands of steep ground, which are as usual densely invaded by bracken in places, to *Nardus* and *Molinia* types prevalent on the damper, peaty soils, especially on the plateaux above the steep valley sides. Bilberry heath occurs patchily, but Callunetum is very sparse, and mainly on the rockier hillsides. There are a number of hanging oakwoods within the site, including the fine example at Allt Rhyd y Groes (see W.91), which rates as a grade 1 woodland in its own right. The area also contains a number of streams, which vary from the cascading ravine type to the valley type with broad alluvial flats.

This area is a classic haunt of the red kite which has maintained a precarious foothold among the wooded hills of this part of Wales after its spectacular nineteenth-century decline and disappearance from other parts of Britain where it was once numerous. This raptor has tended usually to show a close association with man and its survival in this district may be connected with the persistence of a rather primitive kind of rural economy in these uplands. The kite breeds in the hillside woods but feeds mainly on the surrounding open land, both enclosed and unenclosed, where sheep carrion is an important item of its diet. Its feeding habits overlap with those of the raven and buzzard which also breed in the woods as well as on the rocky outcrops, and whose high density in south and central Wales is also related to management of the uplands for sheep. A wide range of smaller hill birds is represented in the area.

U.7. MYNYDD DU: BLACK MOUNTAIN, BRECKNOCK–CARMARTHENSHIRE

SN 8221. 6700 ha   Grade 2

The massif containing Fan Brycheiniog (802 m) is similar in physical features and vegetation to the Brecon Beacons massif containing Pen y Fan, and on biological grounds could be regarded as an alternative to that grade 1 site. The highest ground is about 90 m lower than Pen y Fan, but the summit ground covers a larger area. The vegetation of the summit is mainly a *Nardus stricta* grassland whilst the lower western slopes support large areas of *Calluna–Empetrum nigrum* heath, blanket mires with *Molinia*, *Eriophorum angustifolium* and *E. vaginatum*, as well as *Festuca–Agrostis* grassland. The extensive northern and eastern escarpments are again calcareous and support such species as *Asplenium viride*, *Galium boreale*, *Hymenophyllum*

wilsonii, *Salix herbacea*, *Saxifraga hypnoides*, *Sedum fosteranum*, *S. rosea*, *Silene maritima*, *Thalictrum minus* and *Vaccinium vitis-idaea*. These cliffs form the walls of corries containing two tarns, one of which, Llyn y Fan Fawr, is regarded as a grade 2 example of a corrie lake in its own right. In the southern part of the site, the Old Red Sandstone gives way upwards through basement conglomerate to Carboniferous Limestone which forms a karst area with scars, pavements, sink-holes, pot-holes and caves; this area is of great geological interest and has a fairly rich calcicolous flora, though herb-rich *Festuca–Agrostis* grassland is the main community.

See OW.31.

U.8. MYNYDD DU: BLACK MOUNTAINS, BRECKNOCK–MONMOUTHSHIRE

SO 2132. 2000 ha   Grade 2

This massif has deep and steep-sided valleys, bounded by cliffs in places, but is generally less rugged than the other Old Red Sandstone ranges, and lacks their clearly defined corries. The ridges above the steep-sided valleys are broad and plateau-like, giving rise to extensive moors at over 610 m and culminating in the flat top of Waun Fach at 790 m. This upland massif lies on the south-eastern borders of Wales and the climate is less oceanic than farther west. The higher ground has extensive Molinietum and *Calluna–Eriophorum vaginatum* blanket mire, with a good deal of *Vaccinium vitis-idaea* and *Empetrum nigrum*, but a rather low cover of *Sphagnum* and locally severe erosion or sheep-induced modification. There are large areas of heather and bilberry heath, and these moors hold fair stocks of red grouse.

The long lines of broken cliff facing north-east on the steep slopes below have a number of interesting features; the most noteworthy is Tarren yr Esgob, where a band of outcropping calcareous cornstone provides extensive calcareous habitats. There are species-rich *Festuca–Agrostis* grasslands on the slopes below the cliffs, tufaceous *Cratoneuron commutatum* springs and banks, and a calcicolous rock flora which includes *Saxifraga hypnoides*, *Asplenium viride* and *Geranium sylvaticum* in its southernmost British station. The most interesting ecological feature, however, is an open scrub growth on the escarpment, composed of a mixture of birch, willow, ash, rowan, elder, hawthorn and the endemic *Sorbus porrigentiformis*. This high level remnant of woodland reaches fully 610 m at the top of the cliffs (which otherwise have a mixture of rich grassland, heather and bilberry) and indicates the submontane character of these derived grasslands. This elevated tree line is probably a reflection of a relatively warm and continental climate, compared with the oceanic mountains of, for example, Snowdonia. Its survival here is also related to the rugged nature of the ground, which restricts grazing and allows regeneration of the species concerned.

This massif thus inclines towards a Pennine character, and in the rest of Wales it compares most closely with Y Berwyn in the north.

See L.119.

U.9. NANT IRFON, BRECKNOCK

SN 8556. 2000 ha   Grade 2

The steep sides of Nant Irfon are covered partly by sessile oakwood, but acidic grassland prevails over most of the area, and extends from the valley bottom to the highest ground at 645 m on Drygarn Fawr. *Molinia caerulea* grassland covers large areas at all levels where drainage is impeded, and there is also a good deal of *Nardus stricta* on damper slopes and summits. *Festuca–Agrostis* grassland prevails where the ground is steep and dry, but there has been a good deal of invasion by bracken on the lower slopes. On the higher plateau bilberry is locally abundant, but there is now little heather as the area is heavily grazed by sheep. Small areas of blanket mire have *Eriophorum vaginatum*, and there are flush mires with *Juncus effusus* and *Sphagnum*. The area is ornithologically interesting, and is now one of the few Welsh breeding haunts of the golden plover. A few red grouse also remain.

See W.96.

NORTH WALES

U.10. ERYRI: MOUNTAINS OF SNOWDONIA,
        CAERNARVONSHIRE. 13400 ha   Grade 1*

(a) *Y Wyddfa: Snowdon*
SH 6253

(b) *Glyder*
SH 6558

(c) *Carneddau*
SH 6864

The three adjoining massifs dominated by Y Wyddfa (1086 m), Glyder Fawr (999 m) and Carnedd Llewelyn (1062 m) contain the highest mountains south of the Highlands and are separated by the spectacular glaciated valleys of Llanberis and Nant Ffrancon. The area is geologically complex, with a mixture of igneous and sedimentary rocks, but ecologically the important distinction is between the prevailing acidic slates, grits, rhyolite and granite, and the substantial occurrences of calcareous pumice tuff and dolerite. All three massifs have numerous glacial features, including magnificent corries, corrie lakes and arêtes. There is quite a large area above 760 m, especially on the Carneddau, where solifluction features (both active and fossil), including terraces, stone nets and stripes, and soil hummocks, are well represented. This is one of the heaviest rainfall areas in Britain, and the upper parts of Snowdon receive a mean annual total exceeding 430 cm, though there is a sharp gradient, declining to around 115 cm in the adjoining coastal lowlands barely 15 km distant.

These mountains are heavily grazed by sheep and their prevailing vegetation is the submontane acidic grassland complex, with *Festuca–Agrostis* on dry, mainly steep ground (densely invaded by bracken in places on lower slopes), *Nardus stricta* on damper soils and *Juncus squarrosus* over shallow peat (a mixture of all three types is widespread). Bilberry heath is locally quite extensive, especially on the Carneddau, but Callunetum is patchy and still dwindling,

with scattered occurrences on rocky slopes and escarpments where the parent material is strongly acidic. Extensive screes show pioneer colonisation stages with a great abundance of *Cryptogramma crispa*, but only in a few places is it apparent that seral development can restore a closed community again. Blanket mire occurs on some of the gentler lower slopes of the Carneddau, and is essentially of the *Calluna–Eriophorum* type, though in places heather is replaced by bilberry and *Sphagnum* cover reduced, through burning and grazing. *Juncus squarrosus* blanket mire with abundant *Sphagnum* occurs on some of the high watersheds, and grades into the *Eriophorum* type.

On steep well-drained slopes where the soil is derived from pumice tuff or dolerite, or periodically flushed by water from these rocks, there is a close cropped *Festuca–Agrostis* sward with an abundance of small forbs, on base-rich brown soils. These nutritious swards are grazed preferentially by sheep and have a much higher carrying capacity than the acidophilous grasslands and heaths on the leached podsolic soils. They usually have an abundance of earthworms, and are inhabited by moles up to levels around 910 m.

Soligenous mires are well represented throughout the area, and include both oligotrophic and mesotrophic types. In particular the massif of the Carneddau contains one of the most varied complexes of soligenous mire in the southern British mountains. The best examples are alongside the three north-west-draining streams of Afon Llafar, Caseg and Berthen, and the east-draining Afon Dulyn and Porth Llwyd, where glacial drift deposits along the valley floors are associated with markedly impeded drainage. The commonest type is the *Juncus effusus–Sphagnum recurvum–Polytrichum commune* mire which occurs through almost the whole of upland Britain, except parts of the western Highlands. This is well represented here, and grades into *Carex rostrata–S. recurvum* communities where drainage is still more impeded. With approach to ombrogenous conditions there is an *Eriophorum vaginatum–Erica tetralix–S. recurvum* community which grades into typical *Calluna–Eriophorum* blanket mire. In the other direction, with increasing base-status of the drainage water there is a change to *Juncus acutiflorus* mire with numerous herbs such as *Leontodon autumnalis*, *Ranunculus acris*, *R. flammula*, *Epilobium palustre*, *Myosotis secunda*, and Bryalean mosses instead of *Sphagnum* spp. On each side of the Afon Porth Llwyd there are communities containing much *Molinia caerulea* with *Myrica gale* locally abundant, and associated species such as *Salix aurita*, *Menyanthes trifoliata*, *Scutellaria minor*, *Pedicularis palustris* and *Potamogeton polygonifolius*. These are similar to soligenous mires wide-spread in the western Highlands. Acidic bryophyte springs at higher levels have *Drepanocladus exannulatus*, *Dicranella squarrosa*, *Philonotis fontana*, *Scapania undulata*, *Bryum weigelii* and *Saxifraga stellaris*.

Although Y Wyddfa reaches 1086 m, the higher levels are mostly narrow ridges and precipitous slopes, so that the area of montane grassland and heath is small, but there is one large stand with *Juniperus communis* ssp. *nana*. The

Glyder (999 m) have much larger summits, but here much of the ground is extremely uneven and rocky. Only on the more massive high watersheds and plateaux of the Carneddau (1062 m) is there an extensive occurrence of such montane communities as *Rhacomitrium lanuginosum* heath with *Salix herbacea* and *Carex bigelowii*, and *Vaccinium–Empetrum hermaphroditum* heath. Some of the montane grasslands here have large quantities of the three club-mosses *Lycopodium clavatum*, *L. selago* and *L. alpinum*.

On Y Wyddfa and in Cwm Idwal the highly calcareous pumice tuff is extensively exposed as large cliffs and numerous smaller outcrops, which provide a refuge for many calcicolous Arctic–alpines, including *Saxifraga oppositifolia*, *S. nivalis*, *S. cespitosa*, *S. hypnoides*, *Minuartia verna*, *Galium boreale*, *Dryas octopetala*, *Silene acaulis*, *Poa alpina*, *P. glauca*, *Carex atrata*, *C. capillaris*, *Juncus triglumis*, *Draba incana*, *Potentilla crantzii*, *Polystichum lonchitis*, *Woodsia alpina* and *W. ilvensis*. The disjunct *Lloydia serotina* occurs on several cliffs, and is otherwise unknown in Britain outside Snowdonia. Three other montane species *Cardaminopsis petraea*, *Deschampsia alpina* and *Cerastium arcticum* occur here but are otherwise confined to Scotland. Some of these calcicoles occur on dolerite cliffs in the Carneddau, and *Cerastium alpinum* has its only Welsh station on Carnedd Llewelyn. Where sheep cannot graze, the bigger ledges with deeper soils have luxuriant growths of tall herbs, including *Sedum rosea*, *Thalictrum minus*, *Oxyria digyna*, *Saussurea alpina*, *Trollius europaeus* and *Meconopsis cambrica*. On steep, grazed slopes where the soil is derived from pumice tuff or flushed by water from this material, there is close cropped *Festuca–Agrostis* grassland rich in small herbs. The whole area contains 41 of the 43 montane vascular plants known to occur in north Wales. There is also a rich assemblage of montane bryophytes in various habitats, including *Orthothecium rufescens*, *Encalypta alpina*, *Rhytidium rugosum*, *Arctoa fulvella*, *Dicranum falcatum*, *D. blyttii*, *Hypnum hamulosum*, *Pseudoleskea catenulata*.

The northern Atlantic bryophyte flora is well represented, with *Leptodontium recurvifolium*, *Campylopus setifolius*, *Scapania nimbosa*, *S. ornithopodioides*, *Herberta hutchinsiae* and *H. adunca*. The lower slopes and glens also have southern Atlantic species, including *Adelanthus decipiens*, *Jubula hutchinsiae*, *Marchesinia mackaii* and the fern *Hymenophyllum tunbrigense*. More widespread oceanic bryophytes are well represented and there is an abundance of *Hymenophyllum wilsonii*.

Y Wyddfa has numerous seams of copper-bearing rock, with which the moss *Grimmia atrata* is especially associated, and the old copper mines and spoil heaps are a habitat not represented on other Welsh upland grade 1 sites.

Zoologically these three massifs are probably most important for their invertebrate fauna, which includes a relict Arctic–alpine element. The vertebrates are rather limited, but include raven, common buzzard and formerly peregrine; choughs nest in old copper mines, pine martens still occur and there are herds of feral goats. The endemic moths, Ashworth's rustic *Xestia ashworthii* and the very local Weaver's wave *Idaea contiguaria*, both occur in the

area and are unknown outside north Wales, and there is a rare beetle *Chrysolina cerealis*.

This mountain system contains a large number of corrie lakes and streams, and two of the former, Llyn Idwal on the Glyder and Glaslyn on Y Wyddfa, have been identified as grade 1 and 2 open water sites in their own right. Llyn Cwellyn at the western foot of Y Wyddfa is regarded as grade 2. The grade 1 woodland site of Coedydd Aber is contiguous with the Carneddau sector on its northern side, below the Aber Falls.

Y Wyddfa and the Glyder annually draw large numbers of walkers and climbers, but the Carneddau are much less popular, for they are less spectacular mountains and their most imposing features are remoter from roads. From the conservation and research viewpoint, this lower pressure from man is an advantageous feature.

These three massifs together contain virtually all the major types of upland vegetation represented in Snowdonia proper. The Moel Siabod massif has a much greater extent of *Molinia* grassland and soligenous mire, and some of the lower foothills have a better development of *Calluna–Ulex gallii* heath.

U.11. CADER IDRIS, MERIONETH
SH 7213. 1350 ha   Grade 1

This fine mountain range rises above the south side of the Mawddach estuary in a tremendous north-facing escarpment, indented by a series of corries. There is a relatively narrow summit ridge, rising to the highest peak, Pen y Gadair (893 m), and south of this is Cwm Cau, one of the finest corries in Britain, with 300 m cliffs. There is a range of plant communities closely resembling those of the Carneddau in Caernarvonshire, for this is also an area of sheep-walk. *Festuca–Agrostis*, *Nardus* and *Juncus squarrosus* grasslands prevail, bilberry heath is quite extensive but heather heath is patchy and diminishing. There are montane *Festuca–Vaccinium* heaths and the summits have *Festuca–Rhacomitrium* communities. Small areas of *Calluna–Eriophorum* blanket mire occur and there are well-developed acidic soligenous mires, including the *Juncus effusus–Sphagnum recurvum* type.

Whilst acidic rocks with the usual range of upland podsolic soils prevail, the geology of the mountain is complex and though calcareous rocks are much less extensive than on Y Wyddfa, there is a moderately rich flora, with *Saxifraga oppositifolia*, *S. hypnoides*, *Minuartia verna*, *Sedum rosea*, *Oxyria digyna*, *Cochlearia alpina*, *Asplenium viride*, *Thalictrum minus*, *Melica nutans*, *Trollius europaeus*, *Meconopsis cambrica* and *Rubus saxatilis*. Several montane vascular species, such as *Silene acaulis*, *Saussurea alpina*, *Woodsia ilvensis*, *Empetrum hermaphroditum*, and the northern Atlantic bryophytes *Leptodontium recurvifolium*, *Scapania ornithopodiodes*, *Herberta adunca* and *H. hutchinsiae* here reach their southern British limits. There is an isolated, northernmost British population of *Genista pilosa* on one of the lower spurs, and the rare fern *Asplenium septentrionale* is recorded from acidic rocks. The outlying hill, Tir Stent, has basic rocks which give richer grasslands and an interesting complex of soligenous mires and flushes which include calcareous types rich in herbs and bryophytes.

Some of the streams draining from the high ground have cut deep waterfall gorges along their lower courses, on the partly wooded lower slopes of the mountain. These gorge woodlands are, like those of the Rhinog north of the Mawddach, extremely rich in oceanic bryophytes and ferns, such as *Polystichum setiferum*, *Hymenophyllum tunbrigense*, *H. wilsonii*, *Jubula hutchinsiae*, *Radula voluta*, *Adelanthus decipiens*, *Plagiochila tridenticulata* and *Marchesinia mackaii*. Only the ravine of Afon Cau is actually included within the grade 1 site, but the grade 2 gorge woodland of Coed Maes yr Helmau (W.112) is along the course of a stream draining eastwards from Cader Idris, and the northern slopes of the massif have several ravines and associated woodlands of some importance. Afon Cau is flanked by an area of oak and mixed deciduous woodland which has bonus value.

The similarity of Cader Idris to Eryri raises slight doubt about its qualification for inclusion in the grade 1 series of upland sites. Nevertheless it is a site of considerable importance, and from long continued studies has become a classic area for training students in upland ecology. The close geographical association between thermophilous oceanic plants on the lower slopes and Arctic–alpines on the high ground is nowhere better shown, and the great geological diversity has much value in itself. On the whole, therefore, it seems best to include Cader Idris in the national series of key upland sites.

U.12. RHINOG, MERIONETH

SH 6530. 3350 ha   Grade 1

Lying between Snowdonia proper and Cader Idris, in Merioneth, this upland massif has no close counterpart either in Wales or in the rest of Britain, though it interests relatively few tourists. It is composed of hard acidic Cambrian grits of the Harlech Dome and these give an extremely rugged topography consisting of block-littered slopes, numerous scarps and outcrops and the two rocky summits of Rhinog Fawr (720 m) and Rhinog Fach (711 m). The combination of unsuitable terrain and peaty soils of low fertility has led to a very low grazing pressure and infrequent burning, reflected in turn by an unusual extent and luxuriance of heather, which matures to rank, leggy growths and then regenerates naturally beneath. There are often luxuriant bryophyte carpets beneath the heather, and northern species such as *Ptilium crista-castrensis*, *Herberta hutchinsiae*, *Anastrepta orcadensis* and *Bazzania tricrenata* are present. Callunetum covers most of the area; there is rather little bilberry and bracken, and grassland appears mainly on the higher hills.

This rugged massif has numerous broad terraces and watersheds where waterlogging has allowed the development of blanket mire, albeit in a dissected pattern, because of the irregularity of the terrain. The vegetation has features of both the lower level and western Trichophoreto–Eriophoretum and the higher level and eastern Calluneto–Eriophoretum. There is a good deal of Molinietum locally with much *Myrica gale*, and *Sphagnum imbricatum* is quite

frequent. There are all degrees of transition to soligenous mires, and the mire vegetation of the area is generally rather heterogeneous.

The highest summits show the nearest approach to a dwarf, montane Callunetum still to be found in Wales. The vascular flora is rather limited, but the Rhinog, together with some of the woods and ravines on their lower flanks, form one of the richest areas in Britain for Atlantic bryophytes and have important lichen communities. *Hymenophyllum tunbrigense* grows in block screes up to 400 m, *H. wilsonii* is common at all levels, and the area has long been famous as the locality for such rare bryophytes as *Bartramidula wilsonii*, *Leptodontium recurvifolium* and *Gymnocolea acutiloba*. *Sphagnum strictum* occurs here in its southernmost British station.

Uplands receiving so low a level of exploitation as grazing land are most unusual anywhere in Britain, and although the original forest cover has been extensively lost, this area would seem to offer a good deal of scope for study of an ecosystem which has been less degraded than those represented on most British mountains today. The Rhinogau have probably the most extensive development of Callunetum found in any of the western, oceanic mountain systems of Britain. Among remaining sessile oakwoods on the lower flanks, those in Cwm Bychan can conveniently be included within the grade 1 upland site as a bonus but the larger Coed Crafnant lower down the Artro valley is regarded as a separate, though contiguous grade 1 woodland site (W.109).

U.13. Y BERWYN, MERIONETH–DENBIGHSHIRE–MONTGOMERYSHIRE

SJ 0631. 3900 ha   Grade 1

Y Berwyn, reaching 827 m on Moel Sych, are the preferred alternative area to Mynydd Du (Brecknock–Monmouth) as an eastern upland grade 1 site in Wales. They lie in a district climatically rather more continental than Snowdonia, and are managed both as grouse-moor and sheep-walk. The lower slopes have extensive dry Calluneta, with areas of Vaccinetum and Pteridetum, though at higher levels these grade into the usual complex of acidic grasslands and montane *Vaccinium–Festuca* heath. The broad ridges and spurs of this upland massif have quite extensive development of blanket mire, which shows variations according to position and altitude. There is a good deal of the characteristic Pennine blanket mire (Calluneto–Eriophoretum) with locally abundant *Rubus chamaemorus* (at its southernmost limits and unknown in Wales outside this area) and *Listera cordata*. Hummock–hollow surfaces occur on flat areas and saddles, with a good deal of *Rhacomitrium lanuginosum* on the hummocks, giving a connection with western Trichophoreto–Eriophoretum, though markedly western species are absent. *Sphagnum* cover is locally high and there is generally little erosion of the blanket mire. Above 700 m, the peat becomes shallower and both *Juncus squarrosus* and bilberry more prominent in the mire vegetation, evidently in response to heavy biotic pressure. The blanket mire vegetation on Y Berwyn is not regarded as nationally important on its own, but nevertheless provides an interesting contrast with that of the High Peak in a climatically similar district, but one subject to much heavier atmospheric pollution.

The rocks and soils of the area are almost entirely base-deficient, so that calcicolous vegetation is lacking, and the broken crags of the shallow eastern corries of Moel Sych have a poor, calcifuge flora. Y Berwyn are regarded as a typical area representing the less heavily exploited acidic mountains formed of sedimentary rocks in Wales, and they show a distinct resemblance in many ecological features to Skiddaw Forest in Lakeland and the sedimentary mountains of the Southern Uplands (especially the Tweedsmuir Hills). This area is one of the few present-day breeding haunts of the golden plover in Wales, and has other moorland birds such as the merlin and ring ouzel.

U.14. MYNYDD EGLWYSEG, DENBIGHSHIRE
SJ 2246. 490 ha   Grade 2

Mynydd Eglwyseg in Denbighshire is unique in Wales, but compares very closely in physiography and botanical interest with a number of Carboniferous Limestone hills in northern England. There is no clint and grike structure on the flat top and terraces of the hill and the limestone is exposed mainly as free faces or scars girdling the hill on its western side and breaking down into scree which litters the slopes below. The range of soil types is particularly interesting and throws light on the geomorphological history of the site. There is a fairly rich calcicolous flora, including such limestone plants as *Dryopteris villarii*, *Thelypteris robertiana*, *Cardamine impatiens*, *Sorbus rupicola* and *S. anglica*, but *Sesleria albicans*, so characteristic of the northern England limestone, is absent. The calcicolous bryophytes include *Tortula princeps*, *Grimmia orbicularis*, *Bryum canariense* and *Scapania aspera*.

An especially interesting ecological feature is the contrasting alternation between acidophilous vegetation with heather, bilberry, bracken and *Nardus* on the poor soils of the upper terraces and summit, with rich *Festuca–Agrostis* grasslands on calcareous soils on the steep slopes below. As the altitudinal range is from 245–430 m, montane plants are extremely few, and the flora has more in common with lowland limestone outcrops. Several limestone pavement and scar areas around Kendal–Silverdale and in the Craven Pennines are superior to Mynydd Eglwyseg in conservation value, but this site is important from its geographical and ecological position, intermediate between lowland and upland, as well as southern and northern Carboniferous Limestone sites. Perhaps because of the very heavy grazing, many of the more interesting calcicolous plants are extremely sparse.

U.15. YR EIFL, CAERNARVONSHIRE
SH 3645. 350 ha   Grade 2

The coastal range of Yr Eifl (the Rivals – 564 m) in Lleyn is different from any other upland massif in Wales; the three peaks of this small but spectacular intrusive granite and felsite mass are covered with dry heather heath (with varying amounts of *Ulex gallii*) on well-drained ground, and damp heath, in which *Calluna* is mixed with *Erica tetralix*, *Trichophorum*, *Molinia* and *Sphagnum* spp., on wetter ground. Callunetum also grades into *Nardus* and *Festuca* grasslands. The rocks and soils are mostly acidic, but there are a few *Carex demissa–Drepanocladus revolvens* flushes, indicating a richer drainage water than the more prevalent *Campylopus atrovirens–Sphagnum auriculatum* type. This range of dry to wet heath shows transitions from distinctly lowland and maritime types to more obviously upland examples. The higher slopes have extensive networks of block scree and the seaward face is a vast, gullied precipice, hundreds of metres high with, in places, steep block-littered slopes below. Yr Eifl supports a colony of choughs and a small herd of feral goats, and on the seaward aspect are a number of interesting oceanic plants, including the ferns *Asplenium obovatum* and *Dryopteris aemula*, and bryophytes such as *Frullania germana* and *Campylopus setifolius*. The cliffs are set back a little from the sea, except at the Bird Rock, so that they mostly lack the usual maritime communities, though there are rocky slopes below which run into the sea and have a halophytic grassy sward.

See also L.122.

MIDLANDS

U.16. KINDER–BLEAKLOW, DERBYSHIRE–YORKSHIRE
SK 0994. 11750 ha   Grade 1

An area including the 610 m plateaux of Kinder Scout and Bleaklow Hill forms an appropriate grade 1 site for the High Peak moorland ecosystem on Millstone Grit. The lower moors of the more peripheral areas locally have larger areas of heather, but on the whole show less diversity than the central tract described.

The prevailing vegetation is of the submontane acidic grassland and dwarf-shrub heath complex, with extensive blanket mires, which are often severely hagged by erosion. Where grazing has been heavy the steeper slopes have a *Deschampsia flexuosa*-rich facies of the usual *Festuca–Agrostis* grassland, with varying amounts of bracken and short bilberry. On damper ground, especially that affected by down-washed peat, *Nardus* grassland is usual. Callunetum is now rather local, having lost ground during the present century but heaths dominated by bilberry are locally extensive. In a few places, there are stands of completely dominant *Vaccinium vitis-idaea*, a most unusual condition in Britain, and this species may also be co-dominant with *Calluna*. The blanket mires are regarded as grade 1 in their own right and described in detail under Peatlands. *Empetrum nigrum* grows in this habitat in exceptional quantity and luxuriance, and the only truly montane plant of the Peak, *Rubus chamaemorus*, is locally plentiful.

Outcropping gritstone edges have a poor flora but there is geomorphological interest in these features, the scattered gritstone tors and the landslip feature of Alport Castles.

The moors of the High Peak formerly supported extremely dense populations of red grouse, but since 1950 there has been an evident decline, though grouse numbers are still high by normal standards. Golden plover have also declined, but this district is still the most southerly part of Britain where the species breeds in good numbers. There are also other northern species breeding, including merlin, dunlin and ring ouzel, and the curlew seems to have increased in recent years.

NORTH ENGLAND

U.16. KINDER–BLEAKLOW (PART), YORKSHIRE
Grade 1

See under Midlands, above.

U.17. SKIDDAW FOREST, CUMBERLAND
NY 3030.   4750 ha   Grade 1

This moorland basin, rising from about 275 to 930 m on the summit of Skiddaw and 868 m on Blencathra, gives an unusually clear demonstration of contrasting land-use effects, the catchment north and west of the Caldew having long been managed as grouse-moor and the Blencathra area to the south and east as sheep walk. The grouse-moor management has maintained a cover predominantly of dwarf-shrub heath up to 610 m, with extensive dry-to-moist Callunetum and rather less Vaccinetum, whereas the heavier stocking of sheep on the other sector has almost eradicated dwarf-shrub heath, and produced an acidic grassland complex, with bracken on dry ground. The sharpness of the contrast is drawn by the clear-cut dividing line which the River Caldew makes between the two areas. There is also a good patch of juniper scrub on the rocky south front of Carrock Fell, but only scattered bushes on the Bowscale Fell side of the river. While this is now a largely treeless 'forest', the steep-sided little valley of Burdle Gill within the grouse-moor sector has an open stream fringe of birch and rowan.

There is a parallel difference in faunal richness between the two sectors. The Ericaceous grouse-moor communities provide a breeding habitat not only for red grouse, but also for merlin, and they are the habitat of a rich insect fauna, including day-flying moths such as the emperor, northern eggar, fox, scarce silver Y, pale oak eggar and beautiful yellow underwing. The montane northern dart moth has also been taken on Skiddaw. The *Festuca–Agrostis*, *Nardus* and *Juncus squarrosus* grasslands of the Blencathra sheep-walk sector lack most if not all of these species.

Since 1945, a reduced interest in grouse has led to heavier stocking of sheep on the dwarf-shrub heaths of the grouse-moor sector; the result has been to threaten the botanical and faunal interest of this area by causing incipient retreat of the once-dominant dwarf shrubs in favour of grasses. Skiddaw Forest will continue to decline in nature conservation value unless this process of deterioration is arrested.

Several rounded or flat spurs at about 610 m have areas of *Eriophorum vaginatum* blanket mire, and *Rubus chamaemorus* occurs here, along with golden plover, both being otherwise very rare in Lakeland. Heather is abundant in the blanket mires of the grouse-moor sector but has been lost from those on the Blencathra sector. Submontane *Carex–Sphagnum* soligenous mires are well represented, and there are many acidophilous bryophyte springs with *Saxifraga stellaris*. The higher slopes have a good deal of lichen-rich *Vaccinium–Festuca* montane heath, and on Skiddaw itself *Rhacomitrium–Festuca* heath is probably better represented than anywhere else in the district, with the possible exception of Grasmoor; *Salix herbacea*, *Carex bigelowii*, *Lycopodium alpinum*, *L. selago* and *Vaccinium vitis-idaea* are locally plentiful in these montane communities.

Apart from the particular faunal interest of the grouse-moor sector, Skiddaw Forest is one of the best areas for upland birds in Lakeland, the crag, moorland and stream-side species being well represented. As the parent materials are largely acidic, the flora is rather poor, and the only other noteworthy species are *Listera cordata*, *Antennaria dioica*, *Carex pauciflora*, *Saxifraga aizoides* (Brandygill), and a few uncommon bryophytes such as *Grimmia montana*, *G. elongata*, *G. incurva*, *Coscinodon cribrosus* and *Scapania paludosa*. Geomorphologically it is notable for its glacial features (especially the tarns and ridges on the Blencathra section), and for its various solifluctional forms on the higher ground. Geologically it is famous for the igneous intrusions of gabbro, granophyre and granite into the Skiddaw Slates, and for the outstanding richness of the mineral veins associated with these intrusions. Many rare minerals from the Brandygill and Roughtengill mines are to be found in collections all over the world.

U.18. WASDALE SCREES, CUMBERLAND
NY 1505.   425 ha   Grade 1

In south-west Lakeland, Wastwater is overlooked on the south side by the precipitous front of a whaleback mountain reaching 603 m on Illgill Head. Although relatively low at its summit, this north-west-facing escarpment rises for 460 m above the lake and is one of the most spectacular features of the district. It is important geomorphologically as a classic example of the active disintegration of cliff into unstable talus, and of gully erosion along planes of weakness. An immense rock fall occurred here in the eighteenth century, and several thousand tons collapsed from the upper cliffs in 1967. The upper part of the face consists of a long line of cliffs up to 180 m high, riven by great chasms of equal depth, feeding the unstable scree fans below. Except for the crumbling granite ravine of Hall Gill at the south-west end, the escarpment is formed of Borrowdale Volcanic rocks; these are mainly acidic but the fault breccia of the shatter belts contains considerable amounts of calcite (and ferric oxide), especially where chasms have formed.

On the more stable, vegetated slopes below the cliffs there is a patchy *Festuca–Agrostis* grassland, passing to dense bracken in places, and with *Rubus fruticosus* abundant near the lake shore. The less precipitous parts of the cliff range have a good deal of *Calluna* heath, with much *Erica cinerea*, and common plants of the rocky slopes include *Teucrium scorodonia*, *Digitalis purpurea* and *Solidago virgaurea*. The broad crest of the mountain above the cliffs has extensive damp *Nardus* grassland grading into small soligenous *Sphagnum* bogs, with some peaty pools.

Although the whole of Wasdale Screes lies within the submontane zone, tree and tall-shrub growth is extremely sparse. There are scattered hawthorns and sycamores close to the lake shore, and occasional yews, aspens, rowans and stunted oaks on the cliffs. The most interesting ecological feature is the occurrence of a fairly rich montane flora on the escarpment, overlapping with a rather curious mixture of lowland species. Some of the abundant montane species descend to the shore of Wastwater at only 60 m, e.g. *Alchemilla alpina, Saxifraga aizoides, Cryptogramma crispa* and *Lycopodium alpinum*. There are good populations of *Saxifraga oppositifolia, S. hypnoides, Silene maritima, Sedum rosea, Oxyria digyna* and *Thalictrum minus*, and the rare *Potentilla fruticosa* has two colonies on damp, calcerous rocks. Some species are sparser, e.g. *Galium boreale, Antennaria dioica, Asplenium viride* and *Melica nutans*, whilst others are very rare, e.g. *Asplenium septentrionale, Arctostaphylos uva-ursi*, and *Dryas octopetala* (a single inaccessible patch). The interesting lowland element, ascending to varying elevations, is provided by *Osmunda regalis, Hypericum androsaemum, Arabis hirsuta, Anthyllis vulneraria, Sedum anglicum, S. telephium, Carlina vulgaris, Orchis mascula, Teesdalia nudicaulis, Senecio sylvaticus, Jasione montana, Aquilegia vulgaris* and *Vicia orobus*. There are several strongly Atlantic bryophytes, especially in damp, sheltered ravines, and a few montane species, including *Hypnum hamulosum* and *Dicranum blyttii*. At least 22 species of fern grow on Wasdale Screes.

Wastwater itself, bounding the Screes along their base, is rated as an open water grade 1 site (OW.56).

U.19. HELVELLYN AND FAIRFIELD, WESTMORLAND
NY 3512.   2400 ha   Grade 1

Helvellyn (950 m) is the highest summit in the long north–south mountain ridge lying between Thirlmere and the head of Ullswater in central Lakeland. Fairfield (872 m) is a distinct summit at the southern end of this massif. The western side of this range rises in steep, mainly smooth slopes to the rounded summits, but the eastern aspect has been carved by ice into a series of well-marked corries bounded by high cliffs facing from east to north. Helvellyn has the largest continuous area above 760 m in Lakeland, and the corrie below the main summit contains the high-lying Red Tarn at 718 m. The rock belongs entirely to the Borrowdale Volcanic Series, which varies from highly acidic to strongly calcareous.

The area has been very heavily grazed by sheep for a long time, and the predominantly podsolic soils are covered mainly with the 'grazing climax' of hill vegetation, i.e. *Festuca–Agrostis* grasslands on dry ground (extensively invaded on the lower slopes by bracken), with *Nardus* grassland and *Juncus squarrosus* heath on the damper soils. In places, bilberry is still abundant, especially as a depauperate form, but heather heath is found mainly as fragments in rocky situations, as is the montane dwarf-shrub *Empetrum hermaphroditum*. Patches of species-rich

Festuca–Agrostis grassland occur, especially where there is intermittent flushing from calcareous rocks. The summit areas evidently once had a considerable extent of *Rhacomitrium* heath, but through sheep influence this moss has been largely replaced by *F. vivipara, F. ovina* and *Deschampsia flexuosa* to give a species-poor montane grassland. The two characteristic montane species, *Carex bigelowii* and *Salix herbacea*, still remain abundant on the high tops, the latter especially on stony ground. Solifluction features such as small scale stone stripes and soil hummocks occur in places along the high watershed. Some of the high-lying *Nardus* communities may be snow-influenced, but sub-alpine Nardetum is so extensive that there is no clear pattern.

The most important biological feature of the Helvellyn–Fairfield range is the relict calcicolous montane flora. In the eastern corries, calcareous rock outcrops more extensively at high elevations (i.e. above 600 m) than anywhere else in Lakeland. In consequence, this area is the chief station among the Lake fells for montane calcicoles, which have found refuge on the open faces, rock ledges and in the stony flushes of these elevated corries. Altogether there are 43 montane vascular plants, including 12 not found in the Pennines. *Alchemilla alpina* is extremely abundant on many cliffs and in rocky grassland below, and *Cryptogramma crispa* occurs in profusion, especially on the extensive screes. On the bigger ledges with moist basic soils are well-developed tall-herb woodland or northern meadow communities with *Geum rivale, Angelica sylvestris, Heracleum sphondylium, Geranium sylvaticum, Luzula sylvatica* and *Silene dioica*. In these communities, but also on bare rocks, there are montane or northern plants such as *Sedum rosea, Oxyria digyna, Cochlearia alpina, Thalictrum minus, Galium boreale* and, more rarely, *Trollius europaeus, Rubus saxatilis* and *Saussurea alpina*. Rocky habitats locally have a good deal of *Saxifraga aizoides, S. hypnoides, S. oppositifolia, Silene acaulis* and *Minuartia verna*. Wet rocks, flushed ground and springs frequently have *Saxifraga stellaris, Thalictrum alpinum* and *Juncus triglumis*. A number of montane species occur in very small quantity, and evidently represent the last remnants of populations which have declined gradually through the Post-glacial Period; they include *Dryas octopetala, S. nivalis, Cerastium alpinum, Potentilla crantzii, Poa alpina, P. glauca, Carex atrata, Draba incana, Thlaspi alpestre, Salix lapponum, Polystichum lonchitis* and *Polygonum viviparum*. Species once seen, but not lately, include *Cystopteris montana, Woodsia ilvensis, Sagina saginoides* and *Phleum alpinum*, and it is probable that *Potentilla fruticosa* has become extinct.

There is a good bryophyte flora with such notable species as *Hypnum hamulosum, Pseudoleskea catenulata, Oncophorus virens, Dicranum blyttii, D. falcatum, D. starkei, Plagiopus oederi, Hygrohypnum dilatatum, Leptodontium recurvifolium, Dicranoweissia crispula, Bryum weigelii* and *Scapania ornithopodioides*.

The *Nardus* grasslands are, very locally, the haunt of the mountain ringlet butterfly.

See also W.150.

U.20. MOOR HOUSE AND CROSS FELL, WESTMORLAND–CUMBERLAND–DURHAM

NY 7233.   6600 ha   Grade 1*

This area contains the most elevated part of the whole Carboniferous Pennine mountain system. The main watershed is crowned by the large summit plateau of Cross Fell (893 m) with the twin peaks of Little and Great Dun Fells (842 and 847 m), and then the lower plateaux of Knock Fell (793 m) and Meldon Hill (762 m) to the south-east. The Tees–Tyne moorlands of the gentle dip slopes have been managed as grouse-moor, with some sheep, and are mostly blanket mire, but the Eden valley scarp slopes of the Cross Fell range have long been sheep-walk, and are covered mainly by the acidic grassland complex found so widely on the Lake fells. *Festuca–Agrostis* grasslands occur on steep ground, with some bracken on the lower slopes, but there are large areas of peaty podsolic soils with dominance of *Nardus* and/or *Juncus squarrosus*. Some bilberry heath remains, but typical heather heath has virtually disappeared.

In places, these grasslands extend with little change, other than the appearance of *Carex bigelowii* above 550 m, up to the highest ground. However, on the broad ridge running north-east from Cross Fell to Melmerby Fell (711 m), are interesting montane heath communities on dry, stony flats. On Stony Rigg at 655–700 m are patches of a prostrate *Calluna–Empetrum nigrum* community mixed with a unique bilberry lichen heath dominated by *Cetraria islandica* and *Cladonia sylvatica*. This passes on Green Fell and Skirwith Fell to *Festuca–Vaccinium* heath with less lichen and more *Rhacomitrium lanuginosum*, and on Cross Fell summit there is the largest area of *Rhacomitrium–Carex bigelowii* heath in northern England, though it is the *Festuca*-rich facies.

Cross Fell summit plateau has very finely developed periglacial forms, mainly small scale fossil polygons, soil hummocks, and large scale stone-nets and stripes. The summit cap is sharply defined on all sides by steep block screes, and there are numerous gritstone stone-beds and block screes at intervals along the ridge and Eden slopes. The slopes below Cross Fell summit cap, on both north and west sides, consistently hold the longest lasting snow-beds occurring south of Scotland, though sheep grazing has largely destroyed any original associated vegetational pattern. The Eden slopes have a few minor Whin Sill exposures, but this, and the more extensive Cross Fell inlier along the lower ground, yield acidic soils. More important ecologically are the exposures of limestone which occur as scars, screes, and pot-holes, or a covering of base-rich brown earth, up to 760 m.

While the Dun Fells and Knock Fell have less varied montane acidophilous vegetation than Cross Fell–Melmerby Fell, they have the more important exposures of limestone, especially around the head of Knock Ore Gill. Species-rich *Festuca–Agrostis* grasslands with abundant *Minuartia verna* and *Saxifraga hypnoides* occur here. The high limestone outcrops and grasslands of the Cross Fell range have several noteworthy montane and submontane species,

though some are in very small quantity; they include *Sedum rosea*, *Draba incana*, *Phleum alpinum*, *Potentilla crantzii*, *Galium boreale*, *Antennaria dioica*, *Viola lutea*, *Asplenium viride*, *Polygonum viviparum*, *Polystichum lonchitis*, *Myosotis alpestris* and *Alchemilla wichurae*. Outlying limestone turf on Bellbeaver Rigg adds *Gentiana verna* and *Carex capillaris*, as well as lichen-rich short Callunetum and *Festuca* grassland on gritstone. *Sesleria caerulea* is abundant on limestone at all levels. Uncommon bryophytes of the limestone include *Pseudoleskea catenulata*, *Encalypta rhabdocarpa*, *Rhytidium rugosum*, *Distichium inclinatum*, *Mnium orthorhynchum*, *Entodon orthocorpus* and *Lophozia lycopodiodes*. The old lead mine spoil heaps in this area are often floristically interesting, those near Moor House having an abundance of *Minuartia verna*, *Thlaspi alpestre*, *Cochlearia alpina* and *Gentianella amarella*.

The extensive blanket mires (see P.50) and acidic grasslands are interrupted by various types of soligenous mire. On the lower ground the *Juncus effusus–Sphagnum recurvum* type is represented, but *Carex rostrata–S. recurvum* mires are more characteristic of this area, and there are many small flush mires with mixed *Sphagnum* carpet and variety of sedges (mainly *C. nigra*, *C. curta* and *C. echinata*). Soligenous tracks in the blanket mire locally contain *C. paupercula*, and a spongy mire on the summit plateau of Cross Fell has an *Eriophorum angustifolium–Sphagnum auriculatum* community. The higher level examples grade into spring and rill communities of bryophytes which include *S. auriculatum* and *Philonotis fontana*; these are the habitat of montane species such as *Saxifraga stellaris*, *Epilobium anagallidifolium*, *E. alsinifolium*, *Myosotis breviflora* and the rare *Alopecurus alpinus*. The rare moss *Haplodon wormskjoldii* grows on animal remains in both wet and dry places.

Where the drainage water is influenced by underlying limestone, mesotrophic to eutrophic flush mires are developed. Mostly these are of the *Carex*–herb–brown moss type, with *C. nigra*, *C. demissa*, *C. hostiana*, *C. pulicaris*, *C. dioica*, *C. panicea*, *Equisetum palustre*, *Selaginella selaginoides*, *Leontodon autumnalis*, *Ranunculus acris*, *Prunella vulgaris*, *Parnassia palustris*, and often a carpet of 'brown mosses', such as *Drepanocladus intermedius*, *Campylium stellatum*, *Cratoneuron commutatum* and *Scorpidium scorpioides*. Rare plants of these rich soligenous mires include *Saxifraga hirculus*, *Sedum villosum*, *Juncus triglumis*, *Cinclidium stygium*, *Oncophorus virens* and *Meesia uliginosa*. The richer mires grade into calcareous flushes and springs in places, and a complex with all three types is finely developed at the head of Knock Ore Gill at 670–760 m. In a few places there is a patchy occurrence of an intermediate type in which basiphilous *Sphagnum* spp. replace the 'brown mosses', and *Camptothecium nitens* occurs (rarely) in this community.

Wading birds are numerous and several species nest here at record elevations in Britain, e.g. lapwing (880 m), curlew (790 m), snipe (790 m) and redshank (730 m). Golden plover and dunlin breed to within a short distance of the summit cairn on Cross Fell (893 m), but occur in varying density, reaching probably their greatest numbers on

Bellbeaver Rigg, which also carries the highest density of grouse. The northern dart and red carpet are montane moths which occur in the area.

There are numerous streams, including the headwaters of the River Tees itself, and Knock-Ore Gill (OW.55), draining the Eden slope of the range, has been identified as a key example of a limestone stream also affected by peat water.

U.21. UPPER TEESDALE, DURHAM–YORKSHIRE
NY 8427. 3500 ha   Grade 1*

This is another tract of Carboniferous Pennine upland, similar in many respects to the Cross Fell–Moor House area higher up the Tees, but reaching a lower elevation – 790 m on Mickle Fell. The Tees is here a much bigger river with greater development of alluvial banks, but the most important difference, compared with adjoining areas, is the extensive exposure on Cronkley Fell (S. of the Tees) and Widdybank Fell (N. of the Tees) of 'sugar' limestone, metamorphosed by contact with the intrusive Whin Sill. The crumbling exposures of this rare type of rock, with their close-grazed and open grassy swards and extensive systems of open, calcareous flushes and mires, have an extraordinary number and abundance of rare or local montane plants, notably *Gentiana verna*, *Kobresia simpliciuscula*, *Carex capillaris*, *Minuartia stricta*, *Tofieldia pusilla*, *Bartsia alpina*, *Juncus alpinus*, *Polygala amara*, *Dryas octopetala* and *Viola rupestris*. Not the least interesting feature is the low altitude (300–535 m) at which most of these species grow. There are, besides, interesting high-level occurrences of southern species such as *Hippocrepis comosa*, *Helianthemum canum* and *Carex ericetorum*. Some of these plants grow in rare communities which appear to be confined to the area. There are numerous patches of a dry sward dominated by *Festuca ovina* and a small form of *Sesleria caerulea*, and containing species such as *Gentiana verna*, *V. rupestris*, *Potentilla crantzii*, *C. capillaris*, *C. ericetorum*, *Helianthemum canum*, *Draba incana* and *Rhytidium rugosum*. Calcareous springs and open gravelly flushes, which occur in unusual abundance, have *Cratoneuron commutatum* hummocks, and smaller cushions of other mosses such as *Catoscopium nigritum*, *Meesia uliginosa*, *Amblyodon dealbatus*, *Gymnostomum aeruginosum* and *G. recurvirostrum*. These are the habitat for *Minuartia stricta*, which is known only on Widdybank Fell in Britain. *Saxifraga aizoides*, *Juncus triglumis*, *J. alpinus* and *Equisetum variegatum* are plentiful in some flushes. These habitats grade into calcareous soligenous *Carex* mires with 'brown mosses' and a rich flora, including a profusion of *Primula farinosa*, with other calcicoles such as *Parnassia palustris*, *Selaginella selaginoides* and the moss *Cinclidium stygium*. The rare *Bartsia alpina* grows especially where such mires are hummocky through cattle poaching. An unusual variant of this soligenous mire has *Kobresia* as a dominant; this rare sedge ally has several Highland stations but appears to be sparse in most of these. Important examples of all these main communities have recently been destroyed by the making of the Cow Green reservoir.

These calcicolous communities are set in a typical complex of heather moor, blanket mire and acidic grasslands similar to those of Moor House, and there is a good deal of an unusual transitional herb-rich Callunetum on the ground with 'sugar' limestone turf. Dry heather heath is more extensive than in the Moor House area, and some screes and crags above the Tees have patches of *Arctostaphylos uva-ursi*. At intervals on the slopes rising to Mickle Fell, are areas of *Festuca–Agrostis–Sesleria* grassland on unaltered limestone, some with species such as *Gentiana verna*, *Draba incana*, *Minuartia verna* and *Saxifraga hypnoides*, and *Myosotis alpestris* grows in one of the highest-lying examples.

Although blanket mire is very extensive on the gently sloping plateau between the Tees and the escarpment of the Westmorland Pennines it is generally rather more dissected than on Moor House. Certain areas of considerable importance occur on Cronkley Fell and Widdybank Fell where a *Sphagnum*-rich facies is well developed locally. This is intermediate in type between typical Calluneto–Eriophoretum and the *Sphagnum*-rich blanket mires of the Irthinghead Mires (P.49). The mires occur on terraces and have a high water table throughout, with abundance of *S. papillosum*, *Calluna*, *Eriophorum angustifolium*, *E. vaginatum* and *Trichophorum* together with local occurrence of *Rubus chamaemorus*, *S. fuscum*, *S. imbricatum* and *Rhacomitrium lanuginosum*. *Betula nana* occurs here in its most southerly British station, and the rare moss *Haplodon wormskjoldii* grows on animal remains in peat haggs.

Lower down the Tees, mainly on the river banks, are extensive thickets of the low shrub *Potentilla fruticosa* and of the taller juniper, and on the ungrazed river banks and adjoining hay meadows are luxuriant communities of tall herbs such as *Geranium sylvaticum*, *Cirsium heterophyllum*, *Trollius europaeus*, *Angelica sylvestris*, *Alchemilla vulgaris* agg. (including some rare segregates), *Filipendula ulmaria* and *Geum rivale* (see L.144). These last represent the field layer of former subalpine birchwood, fragments of which still remain close to the river. The river banks and damp pastures also have much *Primula farinosa* and some flush species such as *Eriophorum latifolium*, and there is an abundance of local plants such as *Polygonum viviparum*, *Plantago maritima*, *Antennaria dioica*, *Parnassia palustris* and *Viola lutea*. The total list of vascular plants is unusually large for an upland area.

The 'sugar' limestone and associated exposures of Whin Sill at Cauldron Snout, Falcon Clints, Cronkley Scars, White Force and High Force are geologically famous. Ornithologically this is one of the richer moorland areas in northern England, and the waders are especially well represented, there being a dense breeding population of golden plover, greater than average number of snipe and redshank, and lapwing, curlew, oystercatcher, sandpiper and dunlin. The area is managed as grouse-moor and sheep-walk, and on the Cronkley Fell 'sugar' limestone grasslands there are indications that the combined grazing pressure of sheep and rabbits is now critically high for survival of some of the rarer plants. Unlike Y Wyddfa and Helvellyn, where most of the rarer montane species grow on steep cliffs, the majority of important plants in Upper Teesdale are at risk to disturbing influences. However, the only recorded species which seems to have disappeared is the cliff-dwelling *Woodsia ilvensis* which was collected out by thoughtless fern hunters. *Polystichum lonchitis* is much reduced and *Gentiana verna* is said to be less profuse than formerly.

Although the Cow Green reservoir has reduced the area of some important communities and depleted the populations of a few species, the Upper Teesdale NNR remains one of the most outstanding upland areas in Britain. The whole area is of international importance for its unique combination of different phytogeographical elements, including Arctic, Alpine, Arctic–alpine, continental and northern montane.

At its nearest point, the boundary of this site lies only 2 km from the Moor House NNR. A large pool, Tarn Dub, on the lower terrace of Cronkley Fell is regarded as important as an open water body (OW.57), and described in the appropriate section.

U.22. APPLEBY FELLS, WESTMORLAND
NY 7426, NY 7720.   2800 ha   Grade 1

In the part of the Carboniferous Cross Fell range overlooking the Eden valley between Appleby and Brough are several places of outstanding interest, separated by ground of value as a more typical upland ecosystem. These important places are Helbeck Scars–Roman Fell, Scordale, Little Fell, High Cup Scars and Maizebeck Scars. This area is contiguous with the grade 1 Helbeck–Swindale Woods (W.138) and with it forms a composite grade 1 site.

Helbeck Scars form the tiered limestone escarpment with scree, grass slopes and some pavement, rising above Brough. The flora is of especial interest, and contains *Carex ornithopoda*, *Hippocrepis comosa*, *Epipactis atrorubens* and a very rare *Senecio* is recorded which appears to be intermediate between *S. integrifolius* vars. *integrifolius* and *maritimus*. The grasslands contain great quantities of *Sesleria caerulea*. The limestone scars rise gradually in a north-westerly direction and reach almost 610 m on Long Fell, one of the three British stations for *Viola rupestris*. The gritstone plateau of Roman Fell farther west is unusual in showing clint-and-grike-type structure in rock of this character.

Scordale is the deep valley drained by Hilton Beck. It is geologically famous and was formerly extensively worked for lead, barytes and a yellow form of fluorspar. The limestone scars and screes have a rich flora which includes *Dryopteris villarii* and *Thelypteris robertiana*, and there is much dry limestone grassland. The southern musk thistle *Carduus nutans* occurs here. Above Scordale to the east there is a stretch of acidic grassland, bilberry heath and *Eriophorum* blanket mire rising to the limestone summit plateau of Little Fell (746 m). This hill has probably the finest example of Pennine mountain top limestone grassland. The whole summit is girdled at 700–730 m with dry stony slopes of species-rich *Festuca–Agrostis* turf containing a profusion of the rare *Myosotis alpestris* and also *Minuartia verna*, with much lesser abundance of *Gentiana verna* and

Draba incana. In the scree crevices, *Asplenium viride* and *Saxifraga hypnoides* are abundant. The limestone extends onto the summit plateau and is exposed as fragmentary pavement with small crevices containing tall herbs.

High Cup Scars are the classic exposure of the intrusive Whin Sill at the head of a long dale facing Appleby. The Scars are striking in the complete evenness of the upper rim of the crags, which extends in a horse-shoe round the dale head. The subcolumnar structure gives rise, through weathering, to rock pinnacles and needles standing out from the cliffs, and eventually feeding the great block screes below. The overlying beds of limestone lead to a calcareous flushing of the otherwise acidic Whin Sill, which supports several interesting plants, including *Saxifraga nivalis* in its only Pennine station, *Sedum rosea*, *Thlaspi alpestre*, *Carex capillaris* and *Draba incana*. *Sibbaldia procumbens* reputedly grows above the cliffs, and is otherwise unknown south of the Highlands. Tall-herb ledges have *Heracleum sphondylium*, *Anthriscus sylvestris*, *Crepis paludosa*, *Silene dioica* and *Alchemilla glabra*. The lower part of High Cup Dale has extensive systems of calcareous springs, flushes and soligenous mires, and interesting communities include tufa-forming *Cratoneuron commutatum* carpets, *Carex*–'brown moss' and herb-rich *Juncus acutiflorus* mires. *Primula farinosa* is abundant and *Eriophorum latifolium* frequent. The northern willow *Salix nigricans* is recorded here, and *Polygonum viviparum* occurs in grassland.

Maizebeck Scars lie only about 1 km beyond High Cup Nick, but within the catchment of the Tees. They form a limestone ravine with plants such as *Sorbus rupicola*, *Prunus padus*, *Potentilla crantzii*, *Poa alpina*, *Galium boreale* and *Sedum villosum*. There are adjoining areas of limestone pavement, flushes and damp basic grassland which add to the variety of habitat and vegetation and which are included in the grade 1 site.

Basic flushes and small soligenous mires are frequent on the higher ground, below the summit slopes of Little Fell and beyond the head of High Cup Nick, and their flora includes *Thalictrum alpinum*, *Epilobium alsinifolium*, *E. anagallidifolium*, *Myosotis brevifolia*, *Juncus triglumis*, *Saxifraga hirculus*, *Equisetum variegatum* and the rare moss *Splachnum vasculosum*.

U.23. INGLEBOROUGH, YORKSHIRE
SD 7673.   4750 ha   Grade 1*

Ingleborough forms a single well-defined massif on the western side of the central Pennines (Craven) and reaches 723 m. It is geologically famous as a classic karst area, and has extensive limestone scars and scree on the steep lower slopes, passing to a flatter terrace, at 365–455 m, with large areas of clint and grike pavement, sink-holes, caves and pot-holes with enormous underground caverns. From this terrace, the higher part of Ingleborough rises steeply, with more scars of limestone and gritstone, flattening into the level summit and the larger but lower plateau of Simon Fell (637 m).

While limestone pavement covers a large total area, it varies in quality, and the best examples are at Scar Close,

Moughton Fell and above Raven Scars. Along with Gait Barrows in Silverdale, the Scar Close pavements are possibly the finest example of this geomorphological feature in Britain in showing wide diversity of physical structure. There is a patchy development of calcicolous grass–forb communities and, interestingly, of an acidophilous heath with *Calluna vulgaris*, *Vaccinium myrtillus*, *Potentilla erecta*, *Teucrium scorodonia* and *Succisa pratensis* on acidic drift with mor humus, over the limestone pavements. A fragmentary scrub of ash, hazel, sycamore, willow, rowan, hawthorn, blackthorn, bird-cherry and oak has developed and represents a transitional stage to the open ashwood on limestone pavement in Colt Park Wood (see W.142) which lies within the Ingleborough site. The Scar Close pavements are ungrazed, so that the herbaceous vegetation on the surface of the clints grows fairly tall. The grasses include *Sesleria caerulea*, *Festuca ovina*, *Briza media*, *Helictotrichon pratense*, *Molinia caerulea*, *Arrhenatherum elatius*, *Anthoxanthum odoratum* and *Agrostis canina*; and among the more notable forbs are *Geranium sanguineum*, *Convallaria majalis*, *Serratula tinctoria*, *Thalictrum minus*, *Cirsium heterophyllum*, *Trollius europaeus*, *Mycelis muralis*, *Trifolium medium* and *Arabis hirsuta*, as well as a large number of more common species typical of basic woodland and lowland grassland. The grikes contain luxuriant growths of herbs and ferns, especially *Phyllitis scolopendrium*, *Polystichum aculeatum*, *Dryopteris filix-mas*, *Mercurialis perennis*, and the rare *Actaea spicata* occurs more sparingly. The clint and grike flora includes a submontane/montane element with *Potentilla crantzii*, *Sedum villosum*, *Galium boreale*, *Primula farinosa*, *Minuartia verna*, *Rubus saxatilis*, *Melica nutans*, *Asplenium viride* and *Rhytidium rugosum* as a reflection of the moderate elevation. The bryophyte flora is rich and contains most of the common calcicoles and a number of rarer species.

Much of the limestone pavement elsewhere on Ingleborough is grazed by sheep, so that grasses rather than forbs are more prominent in the surface (clint) vegetation. The deeper grikes, which are very well developed, give protection from grazing and contain luxuriant fern and forb communities including many of the Scar Close species. The limestone screes and scars of the steeper ground also provide habitats for many species. There is a notable abundance locally of the two rare ferns *Dryopteris villarii* and *Thelypteris robertiana*. The montane fern *Polystichum lonchitis* grows in pavement, and on the higher limestone scars at about 600 m is a good montane cliff flora with *Saxifraga oppositifolia*, *S. aizoides*, *S. hypnoides*, *Sedum rosea*, *Poa alpina*, *Encalypta alpina*, *Pseudoleskea catenulata* and *Myurella julacea*. *Saussurea alpina* grows on other rocks.

The lower grasslands are species-rich, with an abundance of such typical calcicoles as *Helianthemum chamaecistus* and *Poterium sanguisorba*. Ingleborough has the only British locality for *Arenaria norvegica* ssp. *anglica* which grows here on open limestone soils at rather low elevations. Floristically, the area is very rich, both in vascular plants and bryophytes, and is regarded by botanists as one of the most important sites in northern England. Acidophilous vegetation is well

represented on the Yoredale rocks of the middle and upper elevations and includes widespread *Agrostis–Festuca* and *Nardus* grasslands, *Juncus squarrosus* communities and soligenous *Sphagnum* mire. On Moughton Fell, there is an area of juniper scrub, once fine but now moribund, and an ombrogenous mire, Thieves' Moss, over limestone.

The very local least minor moth *Photedes captiuncula* occurs in the area.

The extensive cave systems are of great physiographic importance, and the waters draining them are rated as grade 1 for the interesting aquatic fauna (see OW.50).

U.24. MALHAM–ARNCLIFFE, YORKSHIRE
SD 9267.   4600 ha   Grade 1

This area has a great diversity of limestone features and, like Ingleborough, is an important karst area with recession of fault scarps, dry valleys, disappearing streams and underground caves. Malham Cove, Kilnsey Crag and the gorge of Gordale Scar are spectacular examples of limestone cliffs, and there is also a good deal of scar overlooking Arncliffe, and in Cowside Beck and Cote Gill. Limestone pavement is extensive, but is of a lower quality than that on Ingleborough. It is a relatively low-lying area, reaching only 538 m at the highest, but has several montane plants, including three colonies of *Dryas octopetala*, *Potentilla crantzii*, *Bartsia alpina*, *Draba incana*, *Minuartia verna*, *Carex capillaris*, and *Asplenium viride*. There are other northern plants, including *Polemonium caeruleum*, *Epipactis atrorubens*, *Polygala amara*, *Hornungia petraea*, *Dryopteris villarii*, *Thelypteris robertiana* and a profusion of *Primula farinosa*. The limestone pastures have an abundance of *Sesleria caerulea*, *Helianthemum chamaecistus* and *Poterium sanguisorba* and this northern type of calcareous grassland covers large areas. Other widespread calcicoles include *Thalictrum minus*, *Arabis hirsuta*, *Scabiosa columbaria*, *Parnassia palustris*, *Cystopteris fragilis* and *Pimpinella saxifraga*. Transitions to acidic *Festuca*, *Nardus* and *Juncus squarrosus* grassland and heath communities are well represented and there is a wide range of soil types. There are fragments of ash–hazel wood, and *Sorbus rupicola* and *Taxus baccata* grow on the limestone scars. Notable bryophytes of the limestone rocks include *Orthothecium rufescens*, *Zygodon gracilis*, *Seligeria* spp. and *Pedinophyllum interruptum*.

Great Close Mire and Ha Mire are highly calcareous soligenous mire systems with vegetation often encrusted in tufa. The surface consists of hummocks bearing a *Carex–Festuca ovina* sward rich in flowering plants between which occur muddy soaks (pH 8.0) with a restricted flora including *C. lepidocarpa*, *Eleocharis quinqueflora* and *Triglochin palustris*. Acidic hummocks with *Sphagnum papillosum*, *Eriophorum angustifolium*, *C. nigra* and *C. panicea* are frequent. *Primula farinosa* and *Pinguicula vulgaris* are abundant and a number of rare or local northern species are present including: *Equisetum variegatum*, *Rhinanthus spadiceus*, *Bartsia alpina*, *Eriophorum latifolium*, *C. capillaris*, *Polygala amara*, *Potentilla tabernaemontani*, *Cinclidium stygium*, *Camptothecium nitens* and *Amblyodon dealbatus*.

The calcareous flush and mire system at Malham shows

affinities with those at Sunbiggin Tarn and Tarn Moor, Upper Teesdale, and Tulach Hill in Perthshire, as well as with lowland base-rich mires. The related rich fen communities surrounding Malham Tarn are described under Peatlands (P.52), and the Tarn itself, Cowside Beck, Gordale Beck and Malham Water are treated as a grade 1 open water site (OW.47). These wetland features contribute strongly to the outstanding scientific value of the whole Malham–Arncliffe upland site. This area is an important educational site much used by the Malham Field Centre.

The total number of vascular plant species and bryophytes for the whole site is very large. The area is rich in molluscs and the least minor moth is among the more notable insects.

U.25. ORTON FELLS, WESTMORLAND

NY 6610. 745 ha   Grade 1

The complex of Carboniferous Limestone habitats on the low range of hills around Orton in Westmorland makes an interesting comparison with that at Malham. The area reaches only 412 m at its highest so that it is only submontane, and some of the most important vegetation types have marked affinities with lowland grasslands. The most interesting areas consist of scattered units separated by less valuable ground, and it is probably best to regard this as an aggregate site. Five separated sites have been selected to represent the major formations found in the area.

The sites are

Great Asby Scar, NY 6509	Upland grassland
Sunbiggin Tarn Moor, NY 6707	Upland grassland and heath, peatland (P.53) and open water (OW.54)
Crosby Gill, NY 6111	Northern neutral and calcareous grassland (L.140)
Smardale Gill, NY 7207	Northern calcareous grassland, woodland (W.151)
Orton Meadows, NY 6209	Northern neutral grassland (L.139)

Essentially there is a combination of limestone pavement and hill grassland, calcareous flushes, soligenous mires, open water and associated fen, herb-rich upland neutral grassland, and a range of acidic heather moor and acidic grassland. The pavements, grasslands, heaths and soligenous mires of the open fell on Great Asby Scar and Sunbiggin Tarn Moor are described here. The neutral grasslands belong to enclosed meadows separated from these main areas and are described under Lowland Grasslands, Heaths and Scrub (L.139 and L.140), and the wooded portions of Smardale Gill are discussed under the name Smardale Woods (W.151), whilst Sunbiggin Tarn and its associated rich-fen are described under Open Waters (OW.54) and Peatlands (P.53), respectively.

Many of the extensive limestone pavements in the area have been ruined by stone working, but there are still fine examples on Great Asby Scar, with an abundance of calcicolous herbs and ferns such as *Mycelis muralis, Thalictrum minus, Melica nutans, Dryopteris villarii, Thelypteris robertiana, Polystichum lobatum, Phyllitis scolopendrium, Cystopteris fragilis* and *Asplenium viride* in a typical grike flora. There is no juniper and only occasional stunted hazel in crevices, so that these pavements lack the vegetational diversity of those on which scrub and acidophilous heath have developed. The pavements thin out and pass into limestone grassland, of the species-rich *Festuca–Agrostis* type but locally with much *Sesleria caerulea*. An *Empetrum nigrum* facies of this sward occurs, and *Carex ornithopoda* is quite plentiful. Rare species of the area include *Hornungia petraea* and *Polygala amara*, whilst more widespread vascular plants are *Rosa pimpinellifolia, Antennaria dioica, Carlina vulgaris* and *Arabis hirsuta*.

On more acidic drift soils there is a good deal of heather heath ranging from the drier hypnaceous moss facies to the damper *Sphagnum*-rich type. On Tarn Moor are good stands of the very local herb-rich Callunetum (cf. Upper Teesdale), with *Anemone nemorosa, Poterium sanguisorba, Galium verum, G. boreale, Lathyrus montanus* and *Lotus corniculatus* (the northern equivalent of chalk heath). *Nardus* grassland is also well represented, and passes into *Molinia caerulea* and *Trichophorum cespitosum* communities. There are also patches of an unusual mixed *Erica tetralix–Empetrum nigrum*–grass community.

Where the drift cover of Tarn Moor at 240–270 m has developed a surface drainage system, the influence of calcareous water (pH 7.5–8.5) is shown by the occurrence of calcareous soligenous mires, flushes and springs. These range from tufa-forming *Cratoneuron commutatum* mounds, to open *Schoenus nigricans–Scorpidium scorpioides* flushes to mixed *Carex* 'brown moss' mires with *C. lepidocarpa, C. hostiana, C. nigra, C. flacca, C. dioica, Eleocharis quinqueflora* and *Eriophorum latifolium*. There is a profusion of *Primula farinosa* in these wet pastures, and other characteristic vascular species include *Parnassia palustris, Blysmus compressus, Pinguicula vulgaris, Valeriana dioica, Pedicularis palustris, Dactylorchis purpurella* and *D. incarnata*. The montane sedge *C. capillaris* occurs sparingly. In places, the calcareous seepage hollows are separated by acidophilous hummocks, with *Sphagnum rubellum, S. fuscum, Erica tetralix, Succisa pratensis* and *Drosera rotundifolia*. The marked vertical gradient of pH (7.6–3.4) in the taller hummocks is striking.

The wet calcareous habitats grade into forb-rich calcareous grassland as the influence of calcareous drainage water decreases, and into related rich-fen communities as waterlogging increases by the edge of Sunbiggin Tarn and along Tarn Sike.

U.26. MALLERSTANG–SWALEDALE HEAD, WESTMORLAND–YORKSHIRE

SD 8000. 2150 ha   Grade 1

This area of Carboniferous Pennine upland on the borders of Westmorland and Yorkshire is not particularly high (the summits are High Seat, 710 m and Great Shunner Fell,

713 m) but contains vegetational and other features not otherwise represented on key sites in northern England. At the northern end, Tailbridge Hill (533 m) is composed of limestone and has a summit plateau descending on the north-east side into a craggy gill with an interesting flora, including *Potentilla crantzii, Saxifraga aizoides, S. hypnoides, Cochlearia alpina, Draba incana, Primula farinosa, Valeriana dioica, Pinguicula vulgaris, Orchis mascula, Viola lutea, Myosotis sylvatica, Hippocrepis comosa, Rosa pimpinellifolia, Melica nutans* and *Orthothecium rufescens*; and extensive areas of *Sesleria caerulea* grassland. The limestone plateau consists largely of a regularly hummocky *Festuca ovina* turf, with areas of rather open pavement and a number of pot-holes. The hummocks are interesting in mostly having a 'crown' of lichens (*Cladonia impexa, C. arbuscula, C. rangiferina*) whereas the intervening hollows are grass dominated. This sward is the unusual nesting habitat of golden plover and dunlin, and the population of breeding lapwings reaches a high level in some years. The heavily grazed turf has an abundance of *Sesleria* and small herbs which include *Polygonum viviparum, Antennaria dioica, Draba incana, Saxifraga hypnoides, Minuartia verna* and *V. lutea*. The pot-holes have tall, ungrazed growths of forbs such as *Urtica dioica, Mercurialis perennis* and *Chamaenerion angustifolium*, and ferns such as *Polystichum lobatum* and *Asplenium viride*.

Farther south there is a change to gritstone and shale, with mainly acidic soils and a poorer flora. Steep slopes have *Festuca–Agrostis* grassland, with *Lycopodium alpinum, L. clavatum* and *L. selago* on Fair Hill, whilst *Nardus* and *Juncus squarrosus* communities are well represented on damper ground. Blanket mire is extensive, but as usual in the Askrigg Block, is mostly severely modified. The typical *Calluna–Eriophorum vaginatum* community is represented, but heather has often been replaced by bilberry and in places dwarf shrubs have been lost altogether, leaving *Eriophorum* dominant. Erosion by hagging is widespread, and a most interesting feature is the extensive recolonisation of residual soil and stones after sheet erosion has completely removed the peat mantle. This cycle is especially well shown on the plateaux of Lodge Edge–Lodge Haggs and Knoutberry Currack, where numerous and steadily dwindling peat islands indicate that much of the ground once had a deep cover of blanket mire which has mostly disappeared. All stages of recolonisation of the bared ground occur, with *Festuca ovina, Deschampsia flexuosa, Nardus stricta, Juncus squarrosus* and even *Eriophorum* spp., but the most unusual is one dominated by *Polytrichum juniperinum. Campylopus flexuosus* is another but less widespread colonising moss. This peat erosion–recolonisation cycle is characteristic of many Irish mountains, but is a more unusual feature in Britain. In places, secondary cycles of erosion and re-deposition of mineral soil may be observed, as on some of the summits of the northern Highlands.

Ordinary heather heath has largely disappeared, but on dry plateau ground at 640 m are good patches of a dwarf *Calluna–Empetrum nigrum* heath seen elsewhere in England

only on Melmerby Fell (Cross Fell range). These may also represent recolonisation stages after peat erosion. On the spurs of Great Shunner Fell are stands of a lichen-rich *Vaccinium–E. nigrum* montane heath. Acidic soligenous mires are well represented, the *Carex rostrata–Sphagnum recurvum* type being extensive on Shunner Fell, and there is here one basic 'brown moss' flush containing *Saxifraga hirculus. Sphagnum* pools of varying size occur, and in places the wastage of blanket mire has left small, shallow peaty tarns. Mallerstang Edge has an extensive escarpment of gritstone scars with great boulder screes below; the flora is mainly acidophilous, with an abundance of *Luzula sylvatica, Dryopteris dilatata* and *Lathyrus montanus* on the ledges.

Within the whole site moorland birds such as golden plover, red grouse, dunlin, lapwing, snipe, ring ouzel and black-headed gull are well represented.

U.27. BUTTERMERE FELLS, CUMBERLAND
NY 1919. 3700 ha   Grade 2

These fells, including Grasmoor (851 m), Hobcarton Pike (770 m), Robinson (737 m) and Hindscarth (727 m), are composed entirely of Skiddaw Slate. They are too steep to have been managed as grouse-moor (though there are a few grouse) and the whole area is run as sheep-walk, so that *Festuca–Agrostis* and *Nardus* grasslands prevail. Nevertheless, the Buttermere Fells still have quite large areas of heather and bilberry communities and on the western slope of Grasmoor is a good stand of a *Juniperus–Calluna–Arctostaphylos uva-ursi* community. *J. communis* approaching ssp. *nana* is quite abundant on Whiteside, and on the other fells there are good examples of montane *Vaccinium–Empetrum nigrum* heath rich in lichens. Grasmoor summit plateau has an extensive *Festuca–Rhacomitrium* heath, and both Robinson and Hindscarth have an interesting range of montane grass-heath at a rather low elevation (670–730 m), containing *Salix herbacea* and *Carex bigelowii*, and with well-developed solifluction features, especially terraces. Hobcarton Crag is one of the two British stations for *Lychnis alpina*, a montane plant of particular interest because of its peculiar mineral requirements. *Alchemilla alpina* is abundant on the north side of Grasmoor but is otherwise rare on the Skiddaw Slate. Rare mosses include *Grimmia elongata* and *G. atrata*. Although the Buttermere Fells show many of the same vegetational features, they are less rich faunally than Skiddaw Forest and cannot be regarded as an alternative site. This area adjoins the grade 2 open water site of Buttermere (OW.59).

See also W.134.

U.28. SIMONSIDE HILLS, NORTHUMBERLAND
NY 9797. 1900 ha   Grade 2

This moorland massif of Carboniferous gritstone rises to 441 m on Tosson Hill. Its chief value lies in its large and continuous area of Callunetum, for this type of vegetation is dwindling in extent in most upland areas not managed mainly for grouse, and could in time disappear from uplands south of Scotland. Its survival as an extensive community on at least three moorland areas of Northumberland is probably partly due to the low productivity of the grit-stone soils, which has discouraged heavy stocking with sheep. The heather is very luxuriant in places and contains *Listera cordata*. There is relatively little bracken and bilberry heath on the Simonsides, but an interesting feature is the dominance of *Erica tetralix* as a seral stage after burning of damp heather moor.

On wet ground there is a change to blanket mire, and the flow of Boddle Moss is in itself a valuable bonus peatland site, with an undamaged hummocky surface, dominated by *Sphagnum*. It is similar in type to the Irthinghead Mires (P.49) in that the vegetation is intermediate between Calluneto–Eriophoretum and western blanket mire but is not as floristically rich as Butterburn Flow or Haining Head Moss, and the dominant *Sphagnum* sp. is *S. papillosum* rather than *S. magellanicum*. There are numerous low-amplitude hollows with *S. pulchrum*, and both *Andromeda polifolia* and *Vaccinium oxycoccus* are abundant. Small base-poor soligenous mires with *S. recurvum* are frequent. Darden Lough is a small tarn set in rather dry moorland and lacks marginal swamp. On the Darden Burn and in Billsmoor Park and Grasslees Wood there are interesting remnants of upland birch and alder wood, on moist clayey soils, regarded as a grade 2 woodland (W.166). There are basiphilous herbs here, such as *Valeriana officinalis*, *V. dioica*, *Ajuga reptans* and *Crepis paludosa*, and this community passes into soligenous mires with *Juncus acutiflorus* and *Myrica gale*. On the higher ground the substrata are entirely acidic, and the flora is thus calcifuge and poor. *Arctostaphylos uva-ursi* grows sparingly on gritstone outcrops and appears to be the only montane plant.

There are small but steep gritstone scars, but these are now so regularly climbed upon that crag-nesting birds are discouraged by disturbance. Merlin probably still breed on the heather slopes and golden plover, curlew and dunlin occur sparingly.

U.29. ARMBOTH FELLS, CUMBERLAND
NY 2916, NY 3011.   1600 ha   Grade 2

This is an upland area composed of andesitic rocks of the Borrowdale Volcanic Series, and consists of a broad ridge between Thirlmere and Borrowdale lying at a general level of 460 m with gently rounded hills rising to nearly 610 m. The more important mires developed on this ridge are soligenous though there are substantial areas of blanket mire. The habitats are varied and range from open pools amongst blanket mire on watershed, to more typical soligenous tracks, and a valley mire (the Bog, on Wythburn Beck). The *Carex rostrata–Sphagnum recurvum* mire is well represented, but of greater interest are communities transitional between this type and acidophilous blanket mire. There is a wide variety of sedges, including *C. lasiocarpa*, *C. curta*, *C. echinata*, *C. nigra*, *C. pauciflora*, *C. limosa* and *C. paupercula* (which locally grows in great luxuriance). *Vaccinium oxycoccus* is widespread and *Andromeda polifolia* plentiful at up to 460 m, being here especially associated with water seepage. At the head of Launchy Gill are a few

base rich open flushes with *Saxifraga aizoides* and *Eriophorum latifolium*.

Most of the communities and species of these mires are well represented elsewhere, but here they form an interesting complex, of considerable importance on the national scale. A branch of Launchy Gill widens out into a large pool (Launchy Tarn) and the site boundary is extended downwards to the shore of Thirlmere to include the waterfall ravine of this stream, with its rich bryophyte and vascular flora. This part has some interesting gorge woodland, though the growth of trees (mainly oak, birch, ash, rowan) is rather sparse.

U.30. HARBOTTLE MOORS, NORTHUMBERLAND
NT 9004.   1300 ha   Grade 2

Only 10 km to the north of the Simonside Hills is a similar area of heather-clad moorland on Carboniferous rocks above Harbottle. The maximum elevation here is lower at 361 m. Apart from the dense continuous Callunetum, again with only local bilberry and bracken, the area is notable for the several pockets of mire which are of the basin mire type, with an essentially acidophilous vegetation, including a high cover of *Sphagnum* and a hummock–hollow surface structure of large vertical amplitude, with marked vegetational zonation. There are also a number of soligenous *Sphagnum* mires, with local abundance of *Myrica gale*, and these are transitional to *Calluna–Eriophorum–Trichophorum* blanket mire on the high ground.

There are patches of woodland, especially as fringing growths of alder, ash, birch, oak, willow, hazel, hawthorn and rowan. Good examples on the Barrow Burn have basic areas with *Allium ursinum*, *Mercurialis perennis*, *Geranium sylvaticum* and *Geum urbanum* on drier ground, and *Crepis paludosa*, *Carex paniculata* and *C. remota* in wetter places. This woodland grades into open moorland and the willow thickets pass into soligenous mires either of the acidophilous *C. echinata*, *C. rostrata*, *Myrica*, *Molinia*, *Sphagnum* type, or basic examples with *C. lepidocarpa*, *Parnassia palustris*, *Valeriana dioica*, *Pinguicula vulgaris* and *Myosotis secunda*.

There are a few small gritstone outcrops, and on north aspects these have western bryophytes such as *Lepidozia pinnata* and *Bazzania trilobata*.

U.31. KIELDERHEAD MOORS, NORTHUMBERLAND/ ROXBURGHSHIRE
NT 6501.   1750 ha   Grade 2

This third area of Carboniferous rocks in Northumberland is different in some respects from both the Simonside Hills and Harbottle Moors. The maximum elevation is greater, reaching 602 m on Peel Fell, and there is an extensive development of *Calluna–Eriophorum vaginatum* blanket mire, locally with abundant *Rubus chamaemorus* and *Trichophorum cespitosum*, along the main watersheds.

Callunetum is again extensive and continuous over much of the area, and the damp facies with cloudberry and *Listera cordata* is well represented. Bilberry heath is well developed and *Empetrum nigrum* is abundant in the area. There are areas of grassland and basic flush, evidently associated with thin bands of limestone or calcareous shale, so that the total flora is quite varied. Montane calcicoles are lacking, but calcareous flushes and marshes have species such as *Eriophorum latifolium, Parnassia palustris, Carex lepidocarpa, Galium sterneri, Amblyodon dealbatus* and *Sphagnum warnstorfianum* as well as more common herbs and bryophytes. A patchy fringe of willow scrub occurs on flats and banks beside Scaup Burn, and there are birches and a few Scots pines along some stream sides, but remnants of woodland are less well represented here than on the other two above-named sites.

Kielderhead bears some resemblance to Skiddaw Forest, as it used to be, but lacks the montane vegetation associated with the higher elevations reached in that area. Moorland birds, including the merlin, are well represented and there is a herd of feral goats. There are a few small outcrops and boulder screes, and an interesting geological feature is the huge detached block known as the Kielder Stone, *c.* 8 m high and estimated to weigh 1.4 Mkg.

U.32. CAUDBECK FLOW, CUMBERLAND
NY 5872. 300 ha   Grade 2

This site lies near the western edge of the large expanse of boggy moorland known as Spadeadam Waste (now partly occupied by a rocket testing site) on the Bewcastle–Irthinghead Fells. The Caud Beck, draining sluggishly to the King Water, arises as soligenous tracks and associated flushes in an area of somewhat disturbed blanket mire which still has a good deal of *Sphagnum*, including *S. magellanicum* and *S. papillosum* and *Andromeda polifolia*. There is a transition from this mire through communities in which *Eriophorum vaginatum, E. angustifolium, Molinia caerulea, Narthecium ossifragum* and *Erica tetralix* remain abundant, to more typical poor-fen with *Juncus acutiflorus, J. effusus, Carex echinata, C. rostrata, C. curta, C. panicea, Oxycoccus palustris, S. recurvum, S. palustre, S. squarrosum, S. plumulosum* and *Aulacomnium palustre. C. lasiocarpa* is occasional. Increasing base content of water is matched by the appearance of *C. hostiana, C. demissa, S. teres, S. subsecundum, Drepanocladus revolvens, Scorpidium scorpioides* and *Mnium seligeri*.

These richer soligenous mires change in places to still more localised calcareous flushes, with a more open vegetation cover including some of the above plants, with stricter calcicoles such as *Parnassia palustris, Eriophorum latifolium, Eleocharis quinqueflora, Isolepis setacea, Briza media, Carex flacca, C. dioica, Campylium stellatum* and *Cratoneuron commutatum*. These calcareous flushes are especially well developed, often showing tufa formation, on Green Knowe and the more sloping ground of Low Park draining westwards to the River Lyne.

This range of communities shows considerable similarity to those developed over Carboniferous Limestone in the Pennines, but montane vascular plants are entirely lacking. Although the thin limestone and calcareous shale beds of the Carboniferous rocks locally increase the calcium con-

tent of the water, the altitude of the Caud Beck area is too low (230–300 m) for montane species.

U.33. THE CHEVIOT, NORTHUMBERLAND
NT 9121. 3050 ha   Grade 2

This hill reaches 815 m, the highest point in the range bearing its name, and has a massive summit plateau above 730 m. The rock is igneous, mainly andesite and granite, and the Cheviot has the only large crags in the whole range, in the twin glens of Henhole and the Bizzle. Heather heath is now only sparingly represented, but there are large areas of bilberry heath, which is probably in places the snow-bed community, as it contains several colonies of the indicator species *Chamaepericlymenum suecicum*, in one of its very few English stations. There is a considerable extent of acidic grassland, locally with much *Deschampsia cespitosa* and *Anthoxanthum odoratum*, and some of the high-level Nardetum is probably associated with late snow-beds. The summit plateau is covered with a large expanse of blanket mire, mainly of the *Calluna–Eriophorum vaginatum* type, with abundant *Rubus chamaemorus*, and some *Sphagnum fuscum* though *Sphagnum* cover is not high. The *Vaccinium–Empetrum* facies is also represented, and there is moderate erosion by gullying locally.

The Cheviot has several rare or local montane plants, mostly species which grow in wet bryophyte springs and rills, including *Epilobium anagallidifolium, E. alsinifolium, Sedum villosum, Saxifraga stellaris* and *Splachnum vasculosum*. Markedly calcareous rocks are few, but one small outcrop has *Sedum rosea* and *Saussurea alpina. Vaccinium uliginosum* grows sparingly in the summit mires. The Bizzle glen has a number of rare or local bryophytes, including the only locality for *Chandonanthus setiformis* outside the Highlands, and there are basic rocks with *Saxifraga hypnoides, Asplenium viride, Geranium sylvaticum* and *Trollius europaeus*.

Upland birds are well represented, and include golden plover and dunlin on the peaty summit plateau; and feral goats frequent the area.

The Cheviot bears some resemblance to the northern Pennines and to the Moffat–Tweedsmuir Hills, but has certain features lacking in these other areas. Geologically it is quite different, and there are several conspicuous tors, a feature not noted in either the northern Pennines or Southern Uplands. The similarities to related grade 1 sites of higher interest are, however, sufficiently close to suggest that grade 2 is the appropriate status for the Cheviot.

SOUTH SCOTLAND

U.34. CAIRNSMORE OF FLEET, KIRKCUDBRIGHTSHIRE
NX 5266. 2850 ha   Grade 1

This has been chosen as the most representative of the granite uplands of Galloway, and is now the only hill massif in this district where there is continuity between unafforested moorland extending down to low levels (90 m) and montane ground well above the potential woodland limit. Virtually the whole area is Caledonian granite, forming the broad whaleback ridge of Cairnsmore (710 m), with high cliffs, slabs and screes along its flanks and spurs, and areas of pavement with perched blocks along the watershed of the northern top, Craignelder.

The lower ground on the eastern and southern sides is rather gently contoured moorland with a prevalence of peaty gleys and blanket peat of varying thickness. This carries large areas of species poor *Molinia caerulea* grassland between 90 and 245 m, which grades into soligenous mire with abundant *Myrica gale*, *Juncus acutiflorus* and *Sphagnum* spp. At slightly higher levels, and on much-burned ground, there is extensive *Calluna–Trichophorum* vegetation, also with *Sphagnum*-rich facies, and this passes in places to the western *Trichophorum–Eriophorum* blanket mire, with *Molinia* and locally high cover of *Sphagnum*, especially *S. papillosum* and *S. rubellum*. Characteristic species such as *Drosera anglica*, *Carex pauciflora*, and *Pleurozia purpurea* occur sparingly. Pools and channels in the blanket mire have *S. cuspidatum–Eriophorum angustifolium* communities, and grade into acidic *Carex–Sphagnum* soligenous mires. Only a few species associated with even mildly basic conditions are represented in these habitats of wet ground, e.g. *C. hostiana*, *C. dioica* and *Pinguicula lusitanica*.

Areas of dry heather heath are rather limited, and are found mainly on rockier ground below or on escarpments. The eastern corrie of Cairnsmore has a good deal of submontane bilberry heath, but the moderately steep western slopes are covered mainly with mixtures of *Calluna*, *Vaccinium*, *Molinia*, *Trichophorum*, *Nardus* and *Juncus squarrosus*. An interesting feature is that above the Door of Cairnsmore, *Calluna* decreases in stature until at around 640 m there are examples of a community approaching the dwarf, prostrate montane Callunetum of the Highlands. This passes on the highest ground to montane *Festuca–Vaccinium* and *Festuca–Rhacomitrium* heath with *Carex bigelowii* and *Salix herbacea*. These montane communities occur here at a rather low elevation, probably reflecting the wind-exposed position of this isolated granite mountain close to the western seaboard. Calcicolous plants of rocky ground are very few, but include *Saxifraga hypnoides* and *Asplenium viride*.

Cairnsmore of Fleet is particularly important for its characteristic upland fauna, which includes breeding birds such as golden eagle, peregrine, merlin, raven; mammals such as mountain hare, fox, red deer and a large herd of feral goats; reptiles such as the adder and common lizard; and invertebrates such as *Coenonympha tullia*, *Saturnia pavonia*, and *Carabus nitens*. Although the area is now managed as sheep-walk, the lower slopes are former grouse-moor, and grouse at times reach high numbers (as during the 1960s) though they are now (1972) at a low ebb. The afforestation of almost the whole of the extensive moorlands to the east of Cairnsmore is causing a steady change in fauna. There are initially beneficial effects in encouraging species such as hen harrier, short-eared owl and black grouse but these are ephemeral, and as the tree canopy closes, the moorland birds disappear and are replaced by woodland species. Even where the cliffs and higher ground remain unplanted there are changes, particularly through the removal of sheep, which provided the staple diet for certain carrion-feeding predators. Afforestation in the Cairnsmore massif has been associated with decline of the breeding population of ravens from seven pairs to two pairs, though competition with golden eagles could also be involved.

Cairnsmore of Fleet is thus important not only in its own right, as an example of Galloway granite upland, but also as an area against which the effects of afforestation on wildlife can be measured and assessed.

U.35. MERRICK–KELLS, KIRKCUDBRIGHTSHIRE
NX 4682. 2910 ha   Grade 1

This site lies about 16 km north of Cairnsmore of Fleet, and consists of two parts separated by an expanse of afforested upland. The larger western part is another granite mass, lower than Cairnsmore, but still more rugged, with several moorland lochs; and this rises to the higher but more rounded hills of Ordovician rock containing the Merrick (842 m), the highest summit in the Southern Uplands. The eastern part contains the main summits of the almost equally high Kells range, again of Ordovician rock, the Corserine (814 m) and Carlin's Cairn (808 m). The ground above 670 m is included in the grade 1 site, and the boundary descends lower to include the magnificent eastern corrie with Loch Dungeon. The whole area has long been managed as sheep-walk.

Craignaw and the Dungeon Hill in the granite mass form the main catchment to the Silver Flowe NNR (see P.71), which lies along the eastern edge of the western part of the site, so that control over management here is important in order to protect this unique series of mires from disturbance. The east slopes of Craignaw and Dungeon Hill rising above the Silver Flowe have a similar range of submontane vegetation to Cairnsmore, including especially Molinietum and damp Callunetum. The slopes steepen into massive granite slabs and crags with heather, bilberry, small juniper and *Luzula sylvatica* and several Atlantic bryophytes. Craignaw is geomorphologically interesting for its glaciated terrain and extent of bare granite; on the summit are granite pavements, unfissured and with numerous perched blocks. Beyond to the west is a stretch of wild, rugged and boggy moorland covered with wet heath and shallow blanket mire, and containing several tarns. This rises steeply for 300 m westwards above Loch Enoch to the Merrick, which has largely grassy slopes with much *Nardus* and *Juncus squarrosus*, but good *Rhacomitrium* heath on its summit plateau. Being composed of grits and shales, this hill has less bare rock than Craignaw and the Dungeon but there are some basic patches in its extensive north-facing cliffs, which support several montane species, such as *Saussurea alpina*, *Saxifraga stellaris*, *S. hypnoides*, *Salix lapponum*, *Sedum rosea*, *Thalictrum alpinum* and *Polygonum viviparum*, and the mountain form of *Armeria maritima*. *Saxifraga oppositifolia* has recently been recorded in basic flushes.

The Corserine and Carlin's Cairn have good *Rhacomitrium* heath containing *Salix herbacea* and *Carex bigelowii*. The rocks here are mainly acidic and have few montane plants of note, but the rare hawkweed *Hieracium holosericeum* is recorded. The area as a whole has a number of Atlantic bryophytes, including *Herberta hutchinsiae, Campylopus setifolius, Dicranodontium uncinatum, Pleurozia purpurea, Anastrepta orcadensis* and *Bazzania tricrenata*, and *Hymenophyllum wilsonii* occurs quite widely.

Within the site there is a fauna similar to that of Cairnsmore of Fleet, with herds of feral goats and red deer, but no golden eagles and few grouse. Animals associated with blanket mire, streams and lochs are better represented and the boreo–Alpine dragonfly *Aeshna caerulea* breeds here in its only British station outside the Highlands.

The Merrick–Kells grade 1 site is regarded as complementary to Cairnsmore of Fleet in representing the fuller range of ecological variation found in the Galloway uplands. The higher hills of this site afford an interesting comparison with the other high sedimentary massifs of the Southern Uplands (the Moffat and Tweedsmuir Hills) farther east, and show more oceanic features.

U.36. MOFFAT HILLS, DUMFRIES-SHIRE
NT 1614.   2800 ha   Grade 1

This massif of Silurian greywackes and shales is the most rugged area of the Southern Uplands outside Galloway, though the summits are mainly flat or rounded. The rocky ground lies mostly within the valley of Moffat Water, which, with its subsidiary glens, shows much evidence of glaciation, with classic U-shape, corrie formation, and a fine hanging valley above one of the biggest waterfalls in Britain, the 60 m Grey Mare's Tail. There are extensive broken escarpments within the glens of Black's Hope, Carrifran and the Tail–Midlaw, and a spectacular gorge at the Grey Mare's Tail. Several of the subsidiary streams have cut deep and picturesque ravines along their lower courses, and these contain relict fragments of woodland, notably on Black's Hope, which has a good example of oak–ash–wych elm–hazel wood, with a rich herbaceous field layer on basic soils. Where the slopes are not broken by crags, they are impressive in their smooth steepness. The Moffat Hills form a high watershed between the rivers Tweed and Annan, with several plateau summits above 760 m, and reach 821 m on the White Coomb.

The area is managed as sheep-walk, and the steep slopes have extensive areas of *Festuca–Agrostis* grassland and bilberry heath. Callunetum is patchy and dwindling, and best developed on rocky escarpments. *Nardus* and *Juncus squarrosus* communities are widespread on damper, peaty soils, and there are good examples of *Calluna–Eriophorum* blanket mire with much *Rubus chamaemorus* especially in the Tail catchment, and up to 760 m on high watersheds. The rock is calcareous in many places, and rich drainage water gives numerous basic springs, rills, open and closed flushes, and soligenous mires. *Cratoneuron commutatum* springs are finely developed but *Saxifraga aizoides* is absent. Herb-rich *Festuca–Agrostis, Agrostis–Anthoxanthum*, and

Nardus grasslands are well represented, and *Molinia* grasslands occur here in flushed situations. On the higher slopes are examples of snow-bed *Vaccinium–Empetrum hermaphroditum* heath and Nardetum, patches of Callunetum resembling the dwarf montane type, and the extensive summit plateaux have *Festuca–Rhacomitrium* heath on solifluction hummock ground. There are high-level oligotrophic to mesotrophic *Carex* soligenous mires, and fine examples of bryophyte springs with *Philonotis fontana, Bryum weigelii, Splachnum vasculosum*, and *Saxifraga stellaris* occur on White Coomb.

The most important botanical feature of the area is its floristic richness. There is a concentration of cliffs, strongly calcareous in places, which has provided a refuge for the richest assemblage of montane and submontane plants in the Southern Uplands. Some species are in very small quantity, with only one or two stations, but others are plentiful. Thirty-seven vascular species are represented, and among the most notable are *Woodsia ilvensis, Polystichum lonchitis, Saxifraga nivalis, S. oppositifolia, S. hypnoides, Ajuga pyramidalis, Cerastium alpinum, Salix lapponum, Thalictrum alpinum, Saussurea alpina, Potentilla crantzii, Orthilia secunda, Carex capillaris* and *C. atrata*. Tall-herb ledge communities with *Geranium sylvaticum, Trollius europaeus, Sedum rosea, Oxyra digyna, Cochlearia alpina* and *Thalictrum minus* are well represented in places. The high springs, rills and soligenous mires have *Alopecurus alpinus, Epilobium alsinifolium, E. anagallidifolium, Myosotis brevifolia, S. villosum* and *Carex vaginata*, and the calcifuge montane species of various habitats include *Vaccinium uliginosum, Arctostaphylos uva-ursi, Chamaepericlymenum suecicum, Salix herbacea* and *Carex bigelowii*. Interesting bryophytes include *Dicranum falcatum, Arctoa fulvella, Grimmia atrata, G. funalis, G. torquata, Oedipodium griffithianum, Sphagnum fuscum, S. warnstorfianum* and *Gymnomitrion concinnatum*; there are a few Atlantic species and the filmy fern *Hymenophyllum wilsonii* is frequent.

The area contains the high-lying Loch Skene, once the nesting place of the sea eagle, recently colonised by common gulls and long celebrated for its trout. Moffat Water has long been a haunt of peregrines and ravens and there is a large herd of feral goats. The Arctic–alpine moth *Anarta melanopa* is common on the higher ground in early summer, and is here in one of its southernmost British stations. The area is geologically important especially for the classic fossiliferous locality of Dobb's Linn, which gave the key to interpreting the structure of the Silurian rocks of south Scotland and correlating their graptolitic facies internationally.

U.37. MOORFOOT HILLS, MIDLOTHIAN-
PEEBLES-SHIRE-SELKIRKSHIRE
NT 3744.   3250 ha   Grade 1

This well-defined massif consists of rounded and mainly steep-sided hills drained and dissected by deeply incised valleys; cliffs are almost entirely absent, but there are a number of minor stream ravines with small cascades. There are two extensive, broad watersheds, rising from a prevailing level at around 460–580 m to 659 m on Windlestraw Law in the east and 651 m on Blackhope Scar in the west. These high ridges are covered with good examples of *Calluna–Eriophorum* blanket mire, which is described under Peatlands (P.72, gr. 1). The drier ground is covered largely by Callunetum, but this is a wetter grouse-moor area than some in eastern Britain and there is a good deal of damp heather moor transitional to blanket mire. The heather is carefully managed by rotational burning, though where sheep-grazing has been heavy there has been conversion to the usual range of derived communities from *Vaccinium* heath to *Nardus*, *Juncus squarrosus* and *Festuca–Agrostis* grasslands. Management here is for both grouse and sheep, and though most of the area is covered by peat or podsolic type soils, areas of rich *Festuca–Agrostis* sward on stream alluvium and intermittently flushed ground indicate the relatively high base content of the underlying Silurian rocks.

Some of the steep, rocky-sided glens carry relict fringes of tree growth, with a variety of species including rowan, birch, wych elm, aspen, blackthorn, *Salix cinerea*, *S. aurita* and *S. capraea*. These 'cleughs' often have pockets of quite base-rich soil, with a fairly rich herbaceous flora, especially woodland species and including northerners such as *Geranium sylvaticum*, *Rubus saxatilis* and *Crepis paludosa*. Ferns are well represented, with at least 13 species present, and particularly fine growths of *Dryopteris borreri*.

This area is not rich in montane species, *Rubus chamaemorus* and *Sedum villosum* being the only ones noted, though the former is very abundant. It is, however, faunally one of the richest moorland areas in Britain, and particularly notable for its large breeding population of golden plover. There are in most years large stocks of red grouse, and a very high density of mountain hares. Other moorland birds, e.g. ring ouzel, merlin, dunlin, snipe, curlew, skylark and meadow pipit, are well represented. The breeding success of most of these birds is high, as predators of nests, such as crows and gulls, are eliminated by keepering. It would be desirable to know to what extent moorland species such as the golden plover depend on the presence of richer feeding places, particularly grasslands and including hill farms, away from the actual nesting grounds.

U.38. LANGHOLM–NEWCASTLETON HILLS, DUMFRIES-SHIRE–ROXBURGHSHIRE

NY 4290. 7350 ha   Grade 1

Both the Southern Uplands and the Cheviots along the Scottish Borders contain large tracts of relatively low-lying and unspectacular hill country, and the range of such uplands characteristic of both districts is well represented in the hill area forming the catchment of the Tarras Water near Langholm. The southern part of the area is composed of Carboniferous rocks, mainly sandstones, while the northern part is Silurian grits and shales, with an interesting exposure of Old Red Sandstone and a few small igneous intrusions. The range of soils and their plant communities developed on this variety of parent rocks is of special interest, and shows well the influence of varying base-status. The terrain varies from gently undulating moorland to steep, smooth sided hills deeply dissected by numerous water-worn glens. There are few cliffs, but some streams have cut ravines with small crags and waterfalls, and two deep gorges in the Old Red Sandstone at Mosspeeble Linns are of particular interest. The highest point is Roan Fell (568 m), but Arkleton Hill (521 m) forms a distinctive peak.

The moorlands of Tarras Water were once famous grouse-moors, but heavy sheep-grazing and burning have reduced the extent of heather in the upper reaches, and the population of grouse is much less than formerly. There is, however, quite an extensive tract of Callunetum along the lower, southern reach of Tarras. Bilberry heath is well represented but much of the area is covered with grassland of the *Festuca–Agrostis*, *Nardus* and *Molinia* types. There is a good deal of base-rich soil, especially on the Silurian, so that herb-rich grasslands and soligenous mires with 'brown mosses' are well represented. The higher watersheds have well-developed areas of blanket mire, mainly of the Pennine *Calluna–Eriophorum* type. This is perhaps more disturbed than on the Moorfoot Hills, but has great quantities of *Rubus chamaemorus*. *Andromeda polifolia* occurs locally.

Some of the stream-sides, and especially the rocky glens, have fringes of woodland, especially of alder, birch, hazel, willow and rowan. A strip of birchwood near Tarras Lodge passes into an area of planted tall old Scots pines. In some of the rocky glens are rich communities of basiphilous woodland herbs, and in a few places ungrazed rock ledges have luxuriant growths of such species as *Geranium sylvaticum*, *Crepis paludosa*, *Geum rivale*, *Alchemilla glabra*, *Silene dioica*, *Valeriana officinalis* and *Luzula sylvatica* (the 'tall-herb nodum'). The hills are not high enough for truly montane species (except *Rubus chamaemorus*), but northern plants are represented on rocky ground by *Asplenium viride*, *R. saxatilis*, *Saxifraga hypnoides*, *Orthilia secunda*, and *Antennaria dioica*; whilst *Parnassia palustris* and *Selaginella selaginoides* are common on flushed slopes and *Eriophorum latifolium* is present. The area has a rich bryophyte flora, the sandstone rocks being an especially favourable substratum, and the Black Burn above Newcastleton is one of the two known British stations for *Trochobryum carniolicum*.

There is a varied moorland avifauna and whilst some species, such as the golden plover, are less abundant than on the Moorfoot Hills, the predators are better represented. The Tarras Water becomes a sizeable river along its lower reaches, and there are nesting goosanders. A herd of feral goats frequents the head of this valley, and mountain hares still occur.

U.31. KIELDERHEAD MOORS (PART), ROXBURGHSHIRE   Grade 2

See under North England, p. 260.

U.39. TWEEDSMUIR HILLS, PEEBLES-SHIRE–SELKIRKSHIRE

NT 1725. 5350 ha   Grade 2

A few kilometres north of the Moffat Hills, forming a high watershed between the Meggat Water and certain head-streams of the Tweed, is another range of rounded Silurian hills with Broad Law (840 m), Cramalt Craig (830 m) and

Dollar Law (817 m). These hills differ in having very few cliffs and thus a much more limited montane flora, most of the species in this class being associated with flushes and rills, e.g. *Alopecurus alpinus*, *Thalictrum alpinum* and *Myosotis brevifolia*. There are, however, good examples of hummocky *Festuca–Rhacomitrium*, montane *Festuca–Vaccinium*, and snow-bed bilberry heaths, the last with *Chamaepericlymenum suecicum*. Heather heath is better represented than on the Moffat Hills and there are patches approaching the montane dwarf type at high levels. The *Calluna–Eriophorum* blanket mire has much *Rubus chamaemorus* and is locally rich in both *Sphagnum* and lichens. *Salix herbacea* occurs and there are montane bryophytes such as *Dicranum falcatum*, *D. blyttii*, *Splachnum vasculosum*, *Meesia uliginosa*, *Oedipodium griffithianum* and *Gymnomitrion concinnatum*. In many respects the area is a more elevated example of the Moorfoot Hills vegetationally, but lacks the high population density of moorland birds and mountain hares.

EASTERN HIGHLANDS

U.40. BEINN LAOIGH (BEN LUI),
       PERTHSHIRE–ARGYLL
NN 2626.   798 ha   Grade 1

Beinn Laoigh (1130 m) occurs at the western and oceanic end of the Ben Lawers Schist, on the borders of Argyll and Perthshire. Its northern cliffs have an extremely rich calcicolous montane flora, occurring at a lower elevation (460–600 m) than anywhere else along the Dalradian tract. The typical montane calcicolous vascular plants and bryophytes of Breadalbane are mostly well represented and there is a notable abundance of *Dryas octopetala*, *Salix arbuscula*, *Cystopteris montana*, *Draba norvegica*, *Bartsia alpina* and *Orthothecium rufescens*. A few species occur here but not farther east in Breadalbane, e.g. *Cardaminopsis petraea* and certain Atlantic bryophytes. Some of the rarer Breadalbane species, such as *Kobresia simpliciuscula*, *S. reticulata*, *S. myrsinites* and *Woodsia alpina*, are present rather sparingly and several of the Ben Lawers rarities are absent. In places, curtains of vegetation cover almost vertical faces, and there is a fine development of tall-herb ledges of the type with *Sedum rosea*, *Oxyria digyna*, *Saussurea alpina*, *Pyrola rotundifolia* and *Trollius europaeus*. There are banks of *Saxifraga aizoides*, *S. oppositifolia* and *S. hypnoides* and on some steep dry ledges are fragmentary examples of a moss-rich *Dryas* heath.

On the slope below and around the rich cliffs, other communities, including forb-rich *Deschampsia cespitosa*, *Juncus squarrosus*, *Nardus* and *Festuca–Agrostis* grasslands, *Silene acaulis* swards and open *Saxifraga aizoides–Carex* calcareous flushes are well developed, but some of the Ben Lawers types such as *C. saxatilis* and *Carex* 'brown moss' mires are less strongly represented, for the range of topographic diversity is less, with a prevalence of steep slopes, crags and screes. The lower slopes, away from the calcareous outcrops, have a largely acidophilous vegetation, with *Festuca–Agrostis*, *Nardus* and *J. squarrosus* grasslands and

a good deal of soligenous *Carex–Sphagnum* and *J. acutiflorus* mire. The morainic ground has a good deal of *Molinia* and *Trichophorum* wet heath. Heather is very sparse in the area, evidently as a result of heavy grazing and burning, and although there is some submontane bilberry heath on dry slopes, this is usually grassy. Some of the lowest crags have open growths of birch and rowan.

The outcropping schist appears to become steadily less calcareous above about 760 m, so that the strongly calcicolous vegetation occupies the middle level of the mountain, and at higher levels the vegetation becomes increasingly acidophilous. Ben Lui is a rather sharply peaked mountain with a small summit area, so that montane communities of exposed upper slopes and flats are rather poorly represented, but there is a good deal of the western *Alchemilla–Festuca vivipara* grassland with much *Vaccinium myrtillus*, *Rhacomitrium lanuginosum* and *Salix herbacea*. There is, however, a good range of late snow-bed vegetation, though some types are not extensive.

Alpine *Nardus* grassland, *Rhytidiadelphus* moss heath, *Alchemilla alpina–Sibbaldia procumbens* patches, *Cryptogramma crispa–Athyrium alpestre* fern beds in scree, *Gymnomitrion–Salix herbacea* patches, mixed *Rhacomitrium* and *Dicranum starkei* moss heath all occur. There is at least one example of the *Pohlia albicans* var. *glacialis* flush, and the more widespread *Anthelia–Scapania* types are frequent. The upper level of the mountain, especially in the northeast corrie, has a great deal of bryophyte-dominated vegetation, and species associated with late snow-lie are well represented.

U.41. BEN LAWERS–MEALL NAN TARMACHAN,
       PERTHSHIRE
NN 6442, NN 5838.   5600 ha   Grade 1*

This famous massif, reaching 1214 m on Ben Lawers, is the highest part of Breadalbane and has long been regarded as the richest of all British mountains for Arctic–alpine plants. A total of 75 species of montane vascular plant occurs within the grade 1* site. A large number of calcicolous plants are common to all or nearly all the main outcrops of the Ben Lawers Schist, from Beinn Laoigh in the west to Caenlochan in the east. Some are restricted to the open habitats of steep cliffs, but others grow on the dry soils of slopes and summits where grazing animals roam, and still others occur mainly in wet flushes and soligenous mires. The constants of this flora include *Sedum rosea*, *Oxyria digyna*, *Saussurea alpina*, *Dryas octopetala*, *Saxifraga aizoides*, *S. hypnoides*, *S. oppositifolia*, *S. nivalis*, *Silene acaulis*, *Cherleria sedoides*, *Cerastium alpinum*, *Sagina saginoides*, *Salix myrsinites*, *S. lapponum*, *S. arbuscula*, *S. reticulata*, *Draba incana*, *Polystichum lonchitis*, *Asplenium viride*, *Woodsia alpina*, *Cystopteris montana*, *Galium boreale*, *Polygonum viviparum*, *Veronica fruticans*, *Potentilla crantzii*, *Thalictrum alpinum*, *Tofieldia pusilla*, *Poa alpina*, *P. glauca*, *Phleum alpinum*, *Juncus triglumis*, *J. castaneus*, *Carex capillaris*, *C. rupestris*, *C. atrata* and *C. saxatilis*. Most of these are plentiful in suitable habitats along the whole range of calcareous Dalradian hills, and the main variations between different hills are in the varying presence and abundance of certain species which are not constant in the calcicolous flora.

The pre-eminence of Ben Lawers among the Breadalbane Hills is largely the result of its greater elevation, giving a larger extent of favourable montane plant habitat and, consequently, a richer flora than the other hills. Several species occur here which are either absent or sparingly represented on the other hills of the district; they include *Saxifraga cernua, S. rivularis, Sagina intermedia, Draba norvegica, Minuartia rubella, Erigeron borealis, Myosotis alpestris, Gentiana nivalis, Juncus biglumis, Agropyron donianum, Carex microglochin* and *C. atrofusca*. The montane bryophyte flora is also extraordinarily rich, though several rare species have in recent years been found to have a wider distribution in the southern Highlands; notable species include *Ctenidium procerrimum, Hypnum bambergeri, H. revolutum, H. vaucheri, Hygrohypnum smithii, Plagiothecium piliferum, Campylium halleri, Scorpidium turgescens, Timmia norvegica, T. austriaca, Blindia caespiticia, Grimmia agassizii, Tortula norvegica, Ptychodium plicatum, Barbula icmadophila, Tayloria lingulata, Plagiobryum demissum, Bryum arcticum, Mnium lycopodioides, M. spinosum, Myurella tenerrima, Lescuraea striata, Leskea nervosa, Brachythecium starkei, Cirriphyllum cirrosum, Lophozia quadriloba, Solenostoma schiffneri, Plectocolea subelliptica, Scapania calcicola* and *S. degenii*. Several northern Atlantic bryophytes (e.g. *Leptodontium recurvifolium*) occur here in their easternmost British locality.

The chief habitats of this spectacular montane flora are the faces and ledges of the extensive, high-lying cliffs of mica-schist which flank the Lawers range. Some species belong especially to grassland and dwarf forb communities on the high slopes, and there are fine examples of *Alchemilla alpina* and *Silene acaulis–Cherleria sedoides* swards, with *Sibbaldia procumbens, Cerastium alpinum, Polygonum viviparum, Thalictrum alpinum* and *Carex capillaris*. Wet ground affected by lateral water movement also forms another important habitat complex for montane plants.

This massif contains probably the most extensive development of base-rich, montane soligenous mire in Britain. There are two main types, the first being alpine *Carex–Hypnum* mire with *Carex nigra, C. panicea, C. pulicaris, Eriophorum angustifolium, Leontodon autumnalis, Polygonum viviparum, Thalictrum alpinum, Selaginella selaginoides,* and a wide variety of basiphilous mosses that locally include *Camptothecium nitens* and *Cinclidium stygium*. In less wet places, *Nardus stricta* or *Juncus squarrosus* largely replace the Carices, but the community otherwise remains much the same in floristics. All these types grade into oligotrophic soligenous mire such as the *Carex echinata–Sphagnum* type through transitional types with basiphilous *Sphagnum* spp., e.g. *S. warnstorfianum* and *S. contortum*.

The second type of mire is dominated by *Carex saxatilis* and confined to high levels (mainly above 760 m) where snow lies late. Many species of the *Carex–Hypnum* mire still occur, and there are montane species such as *Juncus castaneus, J. triglumis, Saxifraga aizoides, Epilobium anagallidifolium* and *Carex bigelowii*. The soils are less rich than those of the *Carex panicea–Campylium stellatum* mire, which also occurs in the area and appears to be the lower-level equivalent of *Carex saxatilis* mire. Both types are often associated with open *Carex demissa–Saxifraga aizoides* flushes, which at high levels have rare montane species such as *Juncus biglumis, Carex atrofusca, C. microglochin* and *Scorpidium turgescens*.

On the south side of Beinn nan Eachan, a small basin contains a good stand of the *Carex rostrata*-brown moss mire, over 'Hypnum peat-moor' (Kubiena), while nearby is an example of the more mesophilous *Carex rostrata–Sphagnum warnstorfianum* mire, a very local northern type. Elsewhere on the Lawers–Tarmachan range there is a wide range of the widespread acidophilous types of soligenous mire and flush met with in a great many parts of the central Highlands.

From the large area above 900 m late snow-bed *Nardus* grasslands and *Dicranum starkei* bryophyte heaths are well represented. The high summit areas tend to be sloping and narrow, so that *Rhacomitrium* heath is not extensive, and there is a variety of montane communities of unstable ground, especially rich in bryophytes and lichens, including *Gymnomitrion* crust. The lower slopes have large areas of grassland, dwarf-shrub heath with *Calluna* having been much reduced by heavy sheep-grazing, and there are acidophilous sub-montane *Nardus* and *Juncus squarrosus* communities, as well as the species-rich facies. Sub-montane soligenous mires show a similar range of variation. There are also limited areas of *Calluna–Eriophorum* blanket mire with *Rubus chamaemorus*.

Situated immediately west of Ben Lawers and Ben Ghlas, Meall nan Tarmachan (1042 m) has always been regarded by botanists as an offshoot of the parent mountain, and as equally important in its flora – notably on its long eastern cliff, Creag an Lochain, where the wealth of montane plants and the luxuriance of the tall herb ledges is unsurpassed anywhere in Britain. Some species, such as *Dryas* and *Woodsia alpina*, occur here more plentifully than on Ben Lawers itself. Herb-rich *Deschampsia cespitosa* grassland is extensive below the cliffs. This is now the most easily accessible of the floristically rich Breadalbane cliffs, and while it is valuable as an educational site, the problem of plant collecting (which is the only threat to many cliff-dwelling rarities) is especially sharply focussed here. Tarmachan has also an extremely wide range of calcicolous and species-rich montane vegetation including grasslands, dwarf herb swards, soligenous mires and flushes, and there are other cliffs with good assemblages of rock plants. Craig na Chaillaich, another famous botanical locality at the west end of the range, is an outlier of the Tarmachan part of the massif and is included within the grade 1 site.

From the occurrence of calcareous rocks at elevations up to nearly 1220 m, Ben Lawers is famed among zoologists for its rich mollusc fauna, which includes montane species and lowland types occurring at unusually high levels. The insect fauna is rich, and includes the mountain ringlet butterfly, which has its Scottish headquarters on the Breadalbane Mountains.

U.42. CAENLOCHAN–CLOVA, ANGUS–PERTHSHIRE–ABERDEENSHIRE
NO 2070. 6100 ha Grade 1

East of the Devil's Elbow road there is an important exposure of calcareous Dalradian rocks, in the corries at the head of Glen Isla and Glen Clova. The geology here is complex, and some of the rock types are not calcareous or only slightly so. The highest hill, Glas Maol (1068 m), stands at the head of Caenlochan Glen, where calcareous rocks outcrop up to 945 m, and there is here probably a larger number (67) of montane vascular plant species than in any other single corrie in Britain. Most of the Breadalbane species are represented, including all the British montane willows, along with *Dryas octopetala, Gentiana nivalis, Erigeron borealis, Veronica fruticans, Carex rupestris, Woodsia alpina, Cystopteris montana* and a large number of other more widespread calcicoles, including all the species listed in the site account for Ben Lawers–Meall nan Tarmachan (U.41), para 1. The more acidic rocks give in addition a few rare calcifuge or indifferent species, such as *Cicerbita alpina, Veronica alpina, Cerastium arcticum* and *Gnaphalium norvegicum*. There is also a large number of rare bryophytes, including some of notable Breadalbane species such as *Hypnum bambergeri, Ptychodium plicatum, Campylium halleri, Grimmia trichodon, G. borealis, Plagiobryum demissum, Bryum arcticum, Mnium lycopodioides, M. spinosum, Myurella tenerrima, Plagiothecium piliferum, Hygrohypnum smithii, Tayloria lingulata* and *Timmia austriaca*.

In Glen Clova, the twin corries of Glen Doll and Corrie Fee have extensive outcrops of calcareous hornblende schist at rather lower elevations, with many of the Caenlochan plants and others such as *Oxytropis campestris, Astragalus alpinus, Carex norvegica, C. stenolepis* and the moss *Saelania glaucescens*. One high precipitous slope has the best surviving British example of montane willow scrub with *Salix lanata* and *S. lapponum* which is so characteristic of the Norwegian mountains. This part of the NNR contains *Homogyne alpina* in perhaps its only native British station. Both Caenlochan and Glen Clova have fine tall-herb ledges on the cliffs, and in the latter, the slopes below have a mixture of Callunetum, rich grassland and tall herbs which have benefited from a rather low grazing pressure in recent years. This area offers good opportunities for restoring, by means of fencing, examples of natural tall-herb and scrub vegetation on hill slopes which everywhere now carry biotically derived communities.

The high ground above the cliffs bears a wide range of oligotrophic alpine vegetation characteristic of the eastern Highlands. There are extensive high-level blanket mires, locally much dissected by erosion, and with abundance of dwarf shrubs such as *Empetrum hermaphroditum* and *Vaccinium uliginosum*. In this eastern district, lichen heaths dominated by *Cladonia sylvatica* and *C. rangiferina* are more extensive than *Rhacomitrium* heath on the high plateaux, and there are large areas of *Carex bigelowii* communities. A wide range of late snow-bed vegetation, from Vaccinetum to *Dicranum starkei–Polytrichum norvegicum* moss heath, occurs, especially in the Glas Maol area. On the plateau of Meikle Kilrannoch at 820 m is an area of serpentine debris and outcrop, with an interesting flora which includes the second British colony of *Lychnis alpina*.

There is a wide range of soligenous mire. On the Glen Shee side are good examples of *Carex panicea–Campylium stellatum* mire (in one place with a great abundance of *Eriophorum latifolium*) and *Carex–Hypnum* mire (one stand containing much *Camptothecium nitens*). These are on calcareous schist and are associated with open *Saxifraga aizoides* flushes. Other examples of these types occur in Glen Clova. There are high-level facies of these types but these are less distinctive floristically than on Ben Lawers, and although *Carex saxatilis* occurs in Caenlochan, it is rather rare and does not reach dominance anywhere. Of greater interest here are the less base-rich soligenous mires. The *C. rostrata–Sphagnum warnstorfianum* type occurs in places, and on the high, broad ridges are many montane *Carex–Sphagnum* mires, locally with an abundance of the rare species *S. lindbergii* and *S. riparium*. The most distinctive high-level mire is a type with abundance of a small, montane form of *C. aquatilis* and the rare eastern sedge *C. rariflora*; these are usually mixed with other sedges but form a distinctive community in wet hollows on the high watershed between Glas Maol and Cairn of Claise. Rills and springs with their associated mires draining into the head of Caenlochan have the montane grasses *Alopecurus alpinus* and *Phleum alpinum* in places.

This area is one of the most outstandingly valuable upland sites in the whole country in its vegetational diversity and floristic richness. A little to the north, there is another extensive exposure of calcareous rocks at the head of Glen Callater and in Coire Kander. The flora here is similar to, but rather less rich than, that of Caenlochan–Clova, though it includes the rare mosses *Mielichhoferia elongata* and *Grimmia atrata* (on an outcrop of acid pyritic rock) not found in the latter. The most notable vascular plants are *Cicerbita alpina, Carex norvegica, C. rupestris, Cystopteris montana* and *Salix reticulata*. This area is included in the grade 1 site, with a small but important outcrop of 'sugar' limestone with *Dryas–Empetrum hermaphroditum* heath on the outlying hill, the Cairnwell (932 m) just west of the Devil's Elbow.

The site as a whole contains at least 79 out of the 118 British montane vascular plant species listed in Table 27, and so is by a narrow margin the richest site in Britain for this element in our flora. The Cairngorms have 77 and Ben Lawers–Meall nan Tarmachan 75 species.

The total area has an interesting fauna: golden eagles breed, there is a large population of ptarmigan, and dotterel, golden plover and dunlin nest along the high watersheds. There is also a very large herd of red deer.

U.43. TULACH HILL, PERTHSHIRE
NN 8663. 1050 ha Grade 1

This rather low-lying area, at 300–460 m is important for its exposures of 'sugar' limestone which resemble those of

Upper Teesdale and give a range of habitat from dry outcrops to wet mire and open flush. The dry ridges of Tulach Hill and another low hill Meall na h'Imrich have a grass heath with *Arctostaphylos uva-ursi, Helianthemum chamaecistus, Festuca ovina, Helictotrichon pratense, Koeleria gracilis* and *Rhytidium rugosum*; this community appears to be unique in Britain. There are associated herb-rich grasslands, locally with much *Saxifraga aizoides*, but in places the limestone is drift covered and has acidophilous grassland and heath.

Above Ardtulichan is a system of open calcareous flushes (Cariceto–Saxifragetum aizoidis) with rarer species which include *Carex capillaris, Tofieldia pusilla, Equisetum hyemale, Juncus alpinus, Catoscopium nigritum* and *Orthothecium rufescens*. These grade into a closed mixed sedge sward with *Carex hostiana, C. panicea, C. flacca, C. demissa* and *C. pulicaris*, and a large number of basiphilous species, especially *Campylium stellatum*. Separating these damp, flushed habitats are mounds and ridges with an acidophilous moorland vegetation of a type akin to ombrogenous mire, with *Calluna, Erica tetralix, Trichophorum cespitosum, Molinia caerulea, Eriophorum angustifolium, Cladonia impexa* and pleurocarpous heath mosses; there are also the rarer mosses *Sphagnum imbricatum* and *Dicranum undulatum* growing in dense cushions.

Above Creag Odhar, a hollow receiving calcareous drainage has zones of marsh surrounding a central open pool and almost qualifies as a basin mire. There is a central swamp with 'brown moss' carpet grown with *Carex rostrata* and *C. lepidocarpa*. This is surrounded by a zone of *C. panicea–Campylium stellatum* mire, with several open *Saxifraga aizoides* flushes, while beyond this is an outer zone of a mire with *Erica tetralix, Molinia caerulea* and hypnaceous mosses which is transitional to acidophilous Callunetum over podsolised drift on the surrounding moorland.

Nearer the top of Tulach Hill are other mire areas, one being of particular interest in having pools and infilled hollows with mesotrophic and eutrophic vegetation and hummocks with oligotrophic communities. The pools have *Hippuris vulgaris, Utricularia intermedia, U. vulgaris* and *Chara* sp., while the infilled hollows have 'brown moss' carpets with *Carex rostrata, C. lepidocarpa, C. panicea, C. nigra* and *C. pulicaris*. The intervening hummocks are mainly of acidophilous *Sphagnum* spp. (*S. papillosum, S. nemoreum* and *S. fuscum*), but in the intermediate zone between hummock and hollow are species such as *S. auriculatum, Aulacomnium palustre* and *Drepanocladus fluitans*.

Together with the dry 'sugar' limestone outcrops, and their associated rich *Festuca–Agrostis* grassland and *Arctostaphylos* grass-heath, these wetland areas form a complex of considerable ecological interest, and one which has no real counterpart elsewhere in the Highlands. The nearest equivalent area is around Sunbiggin Tarn and Tarn Moor in the Orton Fells, but Tulach Hill is sufficiently different to rate as a separate grade 1 site.

U.44. CAIRNGORMS, INVERNESS-SHIRE–ABERDEENSHIRE–BANFFSHIRE

NJ 0101.   39 200 ha   Grade 1*

In contrast to Breadalbane–Clova, the prevailing rock here is acidic, base-poor granite which gives land of extremely low fertility, managed mostly as deer forest and grousemoor, with sheep only a minor interest. There is thus a prevalence of dwarf-shrub heaths within their climatic zone, and grasslands occupy a subsidiary role, mainly as 'natural' montane types. The lower hillsides are largely heather moor, but bear in places the largest native forests, of Scots pine, remaining in Britain. The greatest importance of the Cairngorms is, however, that they are by far the largest mass of really high land in this country, with four summits rising above 1220 m (Ben Macdhui, 1309 m; Braeriach, 1296 m; Cairn Toul, 1291 m and Cairngorm, 1245 m) and two eastern tops only just below this level (Beinn a'Bhuird, 1196 m and Ben Avon, 1171 m). Moreover, the mountain forms are massive, with large summit plateaux and broad watersheds, giving, altogether, a considerable area above 1100 m. The generally high elevation and relatively continental position of the Cairngorms make low winter temperature a notable feature of the environment and this may be regarded as the most 'arctic' area in Britain. There is, in addition, a fine series of corries, with tremendous ranges of cliff, and of mountain lakes and streams highly valued in their own right (OW.68 and OW.75).

The lower, drift-covered slopes have large areas of dry heather moor grading through open pine heath into pinewood, and passing on wetter ground to *Calluna–Trichophorum* communities. Callunetum extends to a higher elevation here than anywhere in Britain, but changes with altitude to the prostrate montane form, rich in *Arctostaphylos uva-ursi* and *Loiseleuria procumbens*, and finally peters out at about 1000 m. Where snow cover is greater than average, *Vaccinium myrtillus, Vaccinium–Empetrum hermaphroditum* and *Nardus stricta–Trichophorum cespitosum* communities are well developed. Peat alpines such as *Lycopodium annotinum, Chamaepericlymenum suecicum, V. uliginosum, Trientalis europaea* and *Rubus chamaemorus* are abundant in these montane heaths, and *Betula nana* occurs locally in blanket mire.

The Cairngorms have three main types of blanket mire vegetation. On the lower slopes and valley floors there is a prevalence of Trichophoreto–Callunetum, varying from a drier facies in well-drained or much disturbed situations to a *Sphagnum*-rich facies where the water table is high. On the high watersheds this type passes into Calluneto–Eriophoretum, and at elevations above about 850 m the disappearance of *Calluna* gives the montane Empetreto–Eriophoretum. Both of the high-level types are rather local, perhaps because of the porosity of the granite soils, but blanket mire probably occurs at a higher elevation (at least 1000 m) than in any other mountain range in Britain. Above Glen Feshie, Moine Mhor is probably the highest area of blanket mire in Britain, set amongst large areas of chionophilous Nardetum and *Carex bigelowii* communities, at over 900 m. Submontane *Carex–Sphagnum* soligenous mires are frequent, and are replaced at higher elevations by montane examples.

Prostrate Callunetum, often of the 'wave' variety, is extensive at around 900 m and very fine lichen heath facies of this community occur on the western spurs and ridges above Glen Feshie. It here passes at a higher level into extensive *Rhacomitrium lanuginosum* heath, but farther east in the Cairngorms this community becomes more patchy, and the most characteristic vegetation type of the high fell-fields on the Cairngorm plateau is *Juncus trifidus* heath. No other massif in Britain has a comparable extent of *J. trifidus* communities, which vary from types in which this rush is co-dominant with *Rhacomitrium lanuginosum* to an open tussocky growth in which lichens are the main associates. The porous gravelly soils at over 1100 m mostly have a very discontinuous vegetation cover, but where snow lies a little deeper there are beds of dense, short *Nardus* with a few lichens.

Snow cover is a factor of great importance in the Cairngorms, and there is a greater range and extent of late snow-influenced vegetation than in any other mountain system; in particular, the *Alchemilla alpina–Sibbaldia procumbens* communities, *Cryptogramma crispa–Athyrium alpestre* fern-beds, *Dicranum starkei–Polytrichum norvegicum*, mixed *Rhacomitrium* and *Gymnomitrion varians–Salix herbacea* heaths, and associated bryophyte spring communities of the longest-lasting snow-beds are finely developed. Reliable snow cover also seems to be the reason for the survival here of several northern Atlantic bryophytes, e.g. *Scapania nimbosa*, *S. ornithopodioides*, *Anastrophyllum donianum* and *Jamesoniella carringtonii*, although the heavy precipitation also favours these plants. This is the richest area for montane calcifuge or tolerant vascular plants such as *Luzula arcuata*, *Saxifraga rivularis*, *Cardaminopsis petraea*, *Cerastium arcticum*, *Veronica alpina*, *Carex lachenalii*, *C. rariflora*, *Alopecurus alpinus* and *Cerastium cerastoides*, and a number of snow-bed and spring bryophytes, e.g. *Polytrichum norvegicum*, *Dicranum glaciale*, *D. starkei*, *D. falcatum*, *Hygrohypnum molle*, *Andreaea nivalis*, *Moerckia blyttii*, *Haplomitrium hookeri*, *Gymnomitrion apiculatum*, *G. varians*, *Nardia breidleri*, *Cephalozia ambigua*, *Pleuroclada albescens*, and various *Marsupella* spp., including *M. condensata*.

The Glen Feshie sector on the western side of the Cairngorms includes another major geological system, the Moine Schist, which contrasts with the granite in giving soils of higher base-status and fertility. The schistose rocks of Coire Garbhlach and those flanking the main glen compare quite favourably in their calcicolous montane flora with the Breadalbane–Clova Hills. Most of the widespread species occur and there are many local or rare species such as *Dryas octopetala*, *Salix reticulata*, *S. myrsinites*, *S. lanata*, *S. lapponum*, *Draba norvegica*, *Cardaminopsis petraea*, *Saxifraga nivalis*, *Potentilla crantzii*, *Cerastium alpinum*, *Veronica fruticans*, *Carex rupestris*, *C. capillaris*, *C. atrata*, *C. vaginata*, *Poa alpina* and *Cystopteris montana*. The calcicolous bryophyte flora of this area is also rich and includes *Saelania glaucescens*, *Ctenidium procerrimum*,

Hypnum bambergeri, *Pseudoleskea patens*, *P. catenulata*, *Hylocomium pyrenaicum*, *Rhytidium rugosum*, *Encalypta alpina*, *Orthothecium rufescens*, *Grimmia trichodon*, *Mnium spinosum* and *Aulacomnium turgidum*; two species *G. atrofusca* and *Weissia wimmerana* are unknown elsewhere in Britain. Contact zones between the schist and granite are also quite calcareous and rich floristically, as at the head of Glen Einich, where there is an abundance of *Saxifraga oppositifolia*, *Saussurea alpina*, *Salix myrsinites*, *S. lapponum* and *Carex atrata*. Glen Feshie also has the largest area of submontane grassland, for its relative fertility has sustained a higher grazing pressure by deer and sheep than most parts of the Cairngorms.

The central Cairngorms, with Braeriach, Cairn Toul and Ben Macdhui, contain the most important area of high montane habitat. However, the two easterly mountains, Beinn a'Bhuird and Ben Avon, have a large area of high plateau and snow-bed habitat, and since they are more sequestered hills than the central Cairngorms, these tops may become increasingly important as refuges for species such as dotterel, and as research areas, as tourist pressure in the district increases. Ben Avon, in particular, is important for its numerous projecting tors, which give its summit area a striking appearance, and both hills have in their corries crushed zones of granite impregnated with epidote, giving scattered occurrences of a rich flora which includes the rare *Saxifraga cespitosa*. The lower ground of Inchrory immediately to the east has much limestone and shows a fine example of river diversion by glacial breaching. South of Ben Avon, the lower, isolated hill, Creag an Dail Bheag (862 m), is famous for its calcicolous flora on calcareous schists, in flushes, grasslands and on cliffs. This has a station for the very rare *Astragalus alpinus*, and there are noteworthy plants such as *Dryas octopetala*, *Carex rupestris*, *Salix myrsinites* and *Potentilla crantzii*, in addition to most of the widespread calcicoles; it is also the haunt of the very rare mountain burnet moth *Zygaena exulans*.

This is the second richest site in Britain for montane vascular plants, with 77 species out of a possible 118. Some of the characteristic Breadalbane species are sparse (e.g. *Carex saxatilis*) or unknown, probably because of the small extent of calcareous rock. Species lists for the separate hills and corries are given by MacGillivray (1855), but new species have been found within the last few years and there may be others. An interesting feature of the district is that montane plants on the Cairngorms, such as *Silene acaulis* and *Cardaminopsis petraea*, sometimes appear at low levels on gravel and alluvium of the Spey and Dee, having become established from downwashed seed.

The fauna, both vertebrate and invertebrate, is of considerable importance, and this is a famous area for montane or northern birds such as golden eagle, greenshank, ptarmigan, dotterel and snow bunting. It contains the main breeding places known for the last species in Britain today. There are large numbers of red deer and the area is a notable refuge of the wild cat. Geologically and geomorphologically, the Cairngorms are also an important area, with classic glacial and periglacial land forms.

U.45. DRUMOCHTER HILLS, INVERNESS-SHIRE–PERTHSHIRE
NN 6374.   8900 ha   Grade 1

The steep-sided but flat-topped Moine Schist hills lying on either side of the Pass of Drumochter are lower (reaching 1010 m on Beinn Udlamain) than many other ranges, but they are biologically important. There is a high-level and eastern outlier of western type blanket mire, on wet ground at 460 m in the actual Pass. This Trichophoreto–Eriophoretum has characteristic species such as *Myrica gale*, *Sphagnum imbricatum* and *Pleurozia purpurea*. Above this there is extensive Callunetum on drier moraine ground and lower slopes, carrying a good stock of grouse. Snow-bed Vaccinetum is well developed, and the Sow of Atholl contains the rare dwarf shrub *Phyllodoce caerulea*. On windswept spurs above 760 m dwarf Callunetum with abundant *Loiseleuria procumbens* is usual, and often shows wave patterns, with bare strips. Some calcareous outcrops on the slopes give a moderately good flora, with *Dryas octopetala*, *Carex atrata*, *C. rupestris*, *Salix myrsinites* and *S. arbuscula* and calcicolous grassland below. *S. lapponum* scrub occurs along one rocky stream-side. The *Rhacomitrium* heaths on some of the high plateaux show transitions to high-level blanket mire of the *Calluna–Eriophorum* type, including the montane *Empetrum hermaphroditum* facies. *Nardus* grasslands occur on some hills and there are montane springs, flushes and soligenous mires with species such as *Alopecurus alpinus*, *Carex rariflora* and *Sphagnum lindbergii* on the high ground. The large flat summits have probably the biggest area of species-poor *Rhacomitrium–C. bigelowii* heath in Britain, with the exception of Ben Wyvis in Ross.

The Drumochter Hills are a breeding haunt of dotterel, ptarmigan occur at high density, and where the ground is peatier, especially east of the Pass, golden plover and dunlin breed in company with these other birds at around 900 m. Greenshank nest on the lower morainic slopes in the Pass of Drumochter. Grouse are numerous up to 760 m and this is a good example of high-altitude grouse-moor. These hills are particularly vulnerable to tourist development, from their proximity to the main Perth–Inverness road, but their accessibility also gives them valuable research potential.

U.46. MOOR OF DINNET, ABERDEENSHIRE
NO 4399.   1600 ha   Grade 1

The Moor of Dinnet is an interesting ecological complex containing open water (OW.76), mire (P.88), woodland and heather moor.

Typical Callunetum is extensive on the higher ground to the west but over much of the moor *Calluna* shares dominance with *Arctostaphylos uva-ursi* in a distinctive community confined to the central and eastern Highlands. This community has a flora richer than that of the typical Callunetum, and includes *Thymus drucei*, *Viola riviniana*, *Pyrola media*, *Lathyrus montanus*, *Genista anglica*, *Campanula rotundifolia*, *Listera cordata* and an abundance of *Erica cinerea*. The community is extremely rich in lichens and mosses, including the very local *Dicranum spurium*.

Scots pine and more widely silver birch show stages in colonisation of the moor, giving a vegetational succession of considerable interest. This site could be considered as a northern equivalent to the complexes of heath, wetland and woodland found at Thursley and Hankley Commons (L.2) in Surrey and Cavenham–Tuddenham Heaths (L.61(a)) in Suffolk. The Moor of Dinnet has well-developed glacial and periglacial features, including eskers, kames, kettle-holes and terraces.

U.47. HILL OF TOWANREEF, ABERDEENSHIRE
NJ 4424.   2150 ha   Grade 1

This rather low-lying hill area at 380–530 m has been chosen as a representative of the north-east Highland serpentine outcrops. It is a dolomitic serpentine, and as such gives base-rich soils in which magnesium exceeds calcium as the chief exchangeable cation. These soils are unfavourable for strict calcicoles and have a limited though distinctive flora, including *Minuartia verna*, *Armeria maritima*, *Cochlearia officinalis* agg. and *Asplenium viride* and *A. cuneifolium*. The very rare moss *Grimmia alpestris* is quite abundant. The serpentine is exposed as outcrops varying from fairly massive to friable and as spreads of gravel, and has flushes with abundance of *Campylium polygamum*.

The site chosen also contains the Buck (721 m). Callunetum is extensive on both hills, and on the latter there is Calluneto–Eriophoretum. Stands of Nardetum, and *Carex–Juncus* soligenous mire are scattered over the lower ground, some being base-rich with much *Parnassia palustris*. *Chamaepericlymenum suecicum*, *Saxifraga hirculus* and *Sedum villosum* occur. To the north, an area of norite on Turf Hill and White Hill of Bogs is included, bearing a species-rich grass heath, locally of the *Arctostaphylos–Calluna* type.

U.48. MORRONE, ABERDEENSHIRE
NO 1390.   230 ha   Grade 1

The north side of this hill, above Braemar, is important chiefly because of its unusual high level birch–juniper wood, but within the wood are open areas with interesting upland flush and soligenous mire communities, and above it there is a range of montane dwarf-shrub heath. The wood and lower ground are on calcareous schist, and the flushes are of the rich type with *Saxifraga aizoides*, *Juncus alpinus* and *Tofieldia pusilla*. There is a variety of herbs protected from grazing under and between the juniper bushes, and these include montane species such as *Potentilla crantzii* and *Polygonum viviparum*. The whole complex closely resembles that found in subalpine birch–juniper woods in Dovre, Norway. Rich limestone swards occur in dry places and outcrops of schist have species such as *Polystichum lonchitis* which are sensitive to grazing.

The wood passes above into Callunetum, with patches of snow-bed Vaccinetum, and changes near the summit to wind-flattened prostrate *Calluna* showing wave erosion and containing montane species such as *Loiseleuria procumbens* and *Luzula spicata*.

See also W.182.

U.49. CREAG MHOR AND BEN HEASGARNICH,
       PERTHSHIRE
NN 4137. 3900 ha   Grade 2

These two contiguous hills lie near the western end of the
Breadalbane range and form the watershed between the head
of Glens Lyon and Lochay. They are composed of Dalradian schist and as this is generally calcareous there is a
large extent of calcicolous vegetation and a rich flora with
many of the Ben Lawers–Ben Lui species. Ben Heasgarnich
(1076 m) is the higher and probably has the greater extent
of snow-influenced vegetation, but Creag Mhor (1032 m)
probably has the more spectacular cliff and ledge flora. Both
hills are heavily grazed by sheep and there is rather little
heather, except as an associate of *Eriophorum vaginatum* in
blanket mire on the eastern side of Ben Heasgarnich.

The lower slopes, which are heavily seamed by gullies,
have a good deal of acidic grassland (*Agrostis–Anthoxanthum,
Nardus, Juncus squarrosus*) and soligenous mire (*J. acutiflorus, Carex, Molinia, Sphagnum*) and at higher levels there
is much of the montane *Festuca–Vaccinium* grassland with
Alchemilla alpina. These are replaced locally by calcicolous
counterparts, e.g. forb-rich *Agrostis, Nardus, J. squarrosus*
and *Carex* communities. *C. saxatilis* mires and open *Carex–
Saxifraga aizoides* flushes are well developed, and there are
patches of *C. rostrata–Sphagnum warnstorfianum* mire. Rare
plants of these wet habitats include *C. atrofusca, Kobresia
simpliciuscula* and *J. biglumis*.

The south-facing cliffs of Creag Mhor are broken, and
form fine 'hanging gardens' with montane communities
from the tall-herb ledge to steep-face and crevice types.
There is a notable abundance of *Dryas octopetala, Salix
reticulata, Vaccinium uliginosum* and *Potentilla crantzii*,
which remain abundant, along with other montane calcicoles, in the rich grasslands adjoining the cliffs. Ben
Heasgarnich has a large extent of damp, flushed ground in
the northern corrie with a heterogeneous mixture of grassland and soligenous mire; species such as *Saxifraga
aizoides* and *S. oppositifolia* are in profusion. There is also a
fine development of late snow-bed communities on rich
soil with *Sibbaldia procumbens–Alchemilla alpina* patches
and a much more unusual herb-rich moss heath with an
abundance of *Rhytidiadelphus triquetrus*. Montane dwarf
forb dominated swards with *Silene acaulis* occur locally and
both summits, especially that of Ben Heasgarnich, have
areas of the north-west Highland *Rhacomitrium lanuginosum*
heath with abundance of *Silene acaulis, Cherleria sedoides*
and *Polygonum viviparum*.

The total montane flora of the area is large and, in
addition to rare species mentioned, there are stations for
Carex norvegica, Cystopteris montana and *Woodsia alpina*.
The bryophyte flora is extremely rich and Ben Heasgarnich
is the only known British locality for the liverwort *Odontoschisma macounii*.

U.50. MEALL GHAORDIE, PERTHSHIRE
NN 5139. 1650 ha   Grade 2

This hill (1038 m) differs from most of the Breadalbane
range in having a large extent of acidophilous vegetation.
The southern side appears to be formed of base-poor rocks
from base to summit, and the main communities are
Calluna heath (patchy and up to 760 m), *Nardus* and/or *Juncus squarrosus* grassland, *Calluna–Eriophorum vaginatum*
blanket mire (local, mainly on the south-east spur), *Calluna–
Trichophorum* wet heath and species-poor *Rhacomitrium
lanuginosum* heath on the summit area. The dry lower
slopes up to 460 m have much bracken, but in damp places
there is a good deal of base-poor soligenous mire, especially
the *Carex echinata–Sphagnum recurvum* type. An unusual
Calluna–Juncus squarrosus community occurs on shallow
blanket peat at high levels. There is a patchy development
of the montane acidophilous communities characteristic of
both dry and wet ground in the central Highlands, including
types of moderately late snow-beds.

This vegetation complex is, however, of secondary
interest compared with the contrasting calcicolous complex
so well represented on the extensive bands of calcareous
Dalradian schist and limestone which outcrop on the
northern face. There are extensive broken cliffs here with a
rich ledge flora which includes species such as *Salix
reticulata, S. arbuscula, Sesleria caerulea, Carex atrata,
Saxifraga nivalis* and *Cystopteris montana*. There are fine
banks of *S. aizoides* and *Silene acaulis*, and a general profusion of the more widespread Scottish montane calcicoles.
Tall-herb ledges with *Saussurea alpina, Sedum rosea* and
Polystichum lonchitis are also well developed. The cliff communities grade into herb-rich grasslands on the adjoining
slopes. These grasslands include extensive areas of a damp
type with *Nardus, Juncus squarrosus* and *Deschampsia
cespitosa*, and there is a good representation of *Carex
saxatilis* mire and open calcareous flushes with *Saxifraga
oppositifolia, S. aizoides, Juncus castaneus, J. triglumis*, and
Acrocladium trifarium.

U.51. MEALL NA SAMHNA, PERTHSHIRE
NN 4833. 3150 ha   Grade 2

This is the eastern part of the relatively low (*c.* 900 m)
massif to the south of Glen Lochay in Breadalbane. The
lower slopes mostly have rather ordinary acidophilous moorland communities, ranging from dry and damp *Calluna*
heath, through wet *Calluna–Trichophorum* heath to
Calluna–Eriophorum vaginatum blanket mire, with numerous *Juncus–Carex–Sphagnum* soligenous mires. These grade
at higher levels into various types of flushed grassland, with
Nardus, Anthoxanthum, J. squarrosus and *Trichophorum*,
becoming forb-rich where there is soil enrichment by water
from calcareous rocks.

The most important features are, however, the high-lying
crags of calcareous Dalradian schist and limestone, especially
those on the north aspects. Here there is a rich flora, with
virtually all the widespread Breadalbane species and
several which are rare or local. In particular, there is a

colony of *Salix lanata*, growing with *S. lapponum*, and *S. arbuscula* is abundant. Good examples of the *S. reticulata–Dryas octopetala* community occur, and other noteworthy species include *Bartsia alpina*, *Draba rupestris*, *Saxifraga nivalis* and *Carex atrata*. There is a striking abundance of the local moss *Orthothecium rufescens*, imparting a reddish colour to the rocks in places, and *Cystopteris montana* occurs on another part of the range. Beneath the crags there is rich grassland of *Nardus* and *Deschampsia cespitosa*, with an abundance of forbs including *Silene acaulis*. These pass in places into calcareous soligenous mires with an abundance of sedges, forbs and bryophytes.

U.52. CARN GORM AND MEALL GARBH, PERTHSHIRE

NN 6550. 2150 ha   Grade 2

These two hills, which reach 1027 and 960 m respectively, lie immediately to the north of Ben Lawers in the massif forming the watershed between Glen Lyon and Loch Rannoch. They are formed of Dalradian schist, which is highly calcareous locally, and their vegetation has a wide range of both acidophilous and calcicolous types. On the lower southern slopes there is a complex of heather heath, grassland (variably invaded by bracken) and soligenous mire. The Callunetum appears to be retreating under the influence of fire and heavy grazing, with its place being taken by grasses and bracken. An interesting feature is that on base-rich soils there are examples of species-rich Callunetum with various grasses, forbs (e.g. *Polygonum viviparum*, *Prunella vulgaris*, *Achillea millefolium*) and other dwarf shrubs (e.g. *Helianthemum chamaecistus*, *Thymus drucei*). These give way to related species-rich grassland. The soligenous mires include poor *Carex–Sphagnum*, *Erica tetralix–Trichophorum* and *Myrica–Molinia* types, grading into richer *Juncus acutiflorus* communities with numerous forbs and bryophytes.

On higher ground there are both rich and poor *Nardus*, *Juncus squarrosus*, *Deschampsia cespitosa* and *Carex* communities according to the varying influence of the calcareous schists. The richer types grade into the typical calcicolous Breadalbane crag face and ledge flora where cliffs break the upper slopes, and there are also many open calcareous flushes. The rocks have a number of distinctive species, such as *Dryas octopetala*, *Potentilla crantzii*, *Salix reticulata*, *S. myrsinites* (dominant on some ledges), *Saxifraga nivalis*, *C. atrata*, *C. vaginata*, *J. biglumis*, and the rare *Erigeron borealis*. There are fine banks of *S. aizoides*, *S. oppositifolia* and *Silene acaulis*.

The upper slopes have a range of grass heaths with varying proportions of *Festuca vivipara*, *Agrostis* spp., *Vaccinium myrtillus*, *V. vitis-idaea* and *Alchemilla alpina*, with rich and poor facies. Snow-bed communities include *Nardus* grasslands, *Rhytidiadelphus loreus* and *Alchemilla–Sibbaldia* patches. On exposed higher slopes *Calluna* heath is patchy, and there is relatively little of the wind-pruned type, but *Vaccinium–Empetrum* heath is well represented, and is lichen-rich locally. This grades on the summit areas into *Rhacomitrium–Carex bigelowii* heath which is generally

species-poor, though locally with much *A. alpina*, a very abundant plant on this range.

U.53. BEN MORE AND STOBINIAN, PERTHSHIRE

NN 4122. 2650 ha   Grade 2

These two high hills (reaching 1174 and 1165 m, respectively), with the neighbouring Cruach Ardrain (1045 m), are composed of Dalradian schists, which are calcareous in places. Whilst their flora is less rich than that of the main Breadalbane key sites to the north and west, these are the most southerly mountains in the Highlands exceeding 1070 m and they possess many features of ecological interest.

Sheep-grazing and moor-burning have severely reduced the extent of *Calluna* heath on the lower slopes, and there is a prevalence of acidic grasslands, including both species-poor and species-rich *Agrostis–Festuca* types (showing invasion by bracken locally), *Nardus*, *Juncus squarrosus*, *Molinia* and *Trichophorum* communities. There are complexes of soligenous mire, with *Juncus acutiflorus*, *Molinia*, *Myrica gale*, *Carex* spp. and *Sphagnum* spp., but more base-rich types with forbs and hypnaceous mosses occur in places, and open calcareous flushes have *Saxifraga aizoides*. The higher slopes have a range of montane grasslands, including the *Festuca–Vaccinium* type with *Alchemilla alpina*, and late snow-influenced vegetation with *V. myrtillus* and *Nardus* patches. Species-poor *Rhacomitrium* heath with *C. bigelowii* and *Salix herbacea* occurs on the high ridges, and in places there are finely developed solifluction terraces, and here there is an open *Juncus trifidus* community with *Alchemilla alpina* and *Festuca vivipara*.

Some of the high-lying crags are of calcareous mica-schist, and here there is a varied montane calcicolous flora. Nearly all the widespread Breadalbane species are present, many in abundance, and the more local alpines include *Draba norvegica*, *Saxifraga nivalis*, *Woodsia alpina*, *Poa alpina*, *Salix arbuscula*, *Tofieldia pusilla*, *Draba incana*, *Cherleria sedoides* and *Carex vaginata*. Calcifuge and indifferent species are also well represented and include *Gnaphalium supinum*, *Sibbaldia procumbens*, *Luzula spicata*, *Deschampsia alpina*, *Epilobium anagallidifolium*, *Vaccinium uliginosum* and *Rubus chamaemorus*. Tall-herb ledge communities with *Sedum rosea*, *Saussurea alpina*, *Trollius europaeus*, *Rumex acetosa* and *Luzula sylvatica* occur on the basic cliffs.

U.54. BEN CHONZIE, PERTHSHIRE

NN 7731. 1600 ha   Grade 2

This hill is the highest summit (929 m) in the massif of the south-eastern Highlands between Strath Earn and Glen Almond. Ben Chonzie has not been fully surveyed, but is regarded as important for its outcrops of calcareous Dalradian schist, which give an outlying occurrence of the rich Breadalbane montane calcicolous flora. The east-facing cliffs at the head of Glen Turret are especially productive, though they are rather dry and there is a lesser development of the wet ledge and flush communities than on some of the other Perthshire hills. Tall-herb ledge communities of the type with *Trollius europaeus*, *Geranium sylvaticum*, *Geum rivale*, *Angelica sylvestris*, *Valeriana officinalis* and *Filipendula ulmaria* are, however, finely developed. Most of the more widespread montane calcicoles of open rocks are well represented, and there is a particular abundance of *Potentilla crantzii*, *Viola lutea*, *Draba incana* and *Polystichum lonchitis*. Other plentiful species include *Saxifraga oppositifolia*, *S. aizoides*, *S. hypnoides*, *Silene acaulis*, *Galium boreale*, *Alchemilla alpina*, *Oxyria digyna*, *Sedum rosea* and *Asplenium viride*. There is less of *Cerastium alpinum*, *Juncus triglumis*, *Thalictrum alpinum* and *Poa alpina* (the non-viviparous form), and some of the montane species are local or rare, namely *Carex atrata*, *C. capillaris*, *C. vaginata*, *Saussurea alpina*, *Salix lapponum*, *S. arbuscula*, and *Tofieldia pusilla*. Some of the ascending lowland calcicoles occur, such as *Arabis hirsuta*, *Anthyllis vulneraria*, *Geranium lucidum*, *Galium pumilum* and *Helictotrichon pratense*. The most unusual plant of this hill is the rare *Oxytropis halleri*, which has a colony on a somewhat acidic igneous dyke. Rarer mosses include *Orthothecium rufescens*, *Leucodon sciuroides* var. *morensis* and *Sphagnum riparium*.

Acidophilous communities are extensive in the area, ranging from *Calluna* moor and acidophilous grasslands, *Vaccinium* and *Vaccinium–Empetrum* heaths to *Calluna–Eriophorum vaginatum* blanket mire with abundant *Rubus chamaemorus*, soligenous *Carex echinata–C. nigra–Sphagnum* mires, and grassy *Rhacomitrium lanuginosum* heath on the summit. Calcareous flushes and small soligenous mires occur in places, and here there are species such as *Saxifraga aizoides* and the rarer *Sedum villosum*. Herb-rich grasslands occur beneath the rich cliffs and the *Alchemilla alpina–Thymus* type occurs in places. Sheep density is high and mountain hares are numerous. Heavy grazing is probably responsible for the abundance of grasses and bilberry in certain montane communities – a condition which gives a resemblance to some Southern Upland hills.

U.55. BEINN A'GHLO, PERTHSHIRE

NN 9572. 6700 ha   Grade 2

South-east of Glen Tilt in the Forest of Atholl, this twin-peaked hill rises steeply to reach 1119 m. This is a massif of Dalradian rocks, with schist and quartzite forming the higher levels above a massive lower platform of limestone, which is extensively exposed as crags in Glen Tilt and above Loch Loch to the north-east of Beinn a'Ghlo. The vegetation of the more acidic soils above the limestone has a fairly typical range of central Highland montane communities, with dwarf Callunetum, *Vaccinium–Empetrum* heath (lichen-rich in places), *Vaccinium myrtillus* and *Nardus* snow-beds, *Alchemilla alpina* grassland, and *Rhacomitrium* heath on the exposed summits. *Juncus trifidus* heath is patchily developed on the quartzite summit ridges. The latest snow-bed communities are hardly represented, there being only a fragment of the *Dicranum starkei* type in the north-east corrie, but the *Alchemilla alpina–Sibbaldia procumbens* type is found, and a patchy development of *Gymnomitrion* crust with *Salix herbacea* occurs on more exposed ground. There are also oligotrophic springs, flushes and flush mires and incipient blanket mire on the higher ground.

The limestone terrain, which reaches only about 690 m, provides a very marked contrast, with a rich flora, though because the altitude is rather low, the calcicolous high montane element of Breadalbane is hardly represented. There are extensive species-rich *Festuca–Agrostis* grasslands on dry slopes, with an abundance of *Alchemilla alpina*, *A. vulgaris* agg., *Polygonum viviparum*, *Campanula rotundifolia* and *Helictotrichon pratense*. There is a local abundance of *Saxifraga aizoides*, *S. oppositifolia*, *S. hypnoides*, *Potentilla crantzii*, *Galium boreale*, *Carex capillaris*, *Helianthemum chamaecistus* and *Gentianella campestris* in these grazed grasslands. The outlying and much lower hills of Meall Breac and Sron na h-Innearach have outcrops of 'sugar' limestone resembling that of Upper Teesdale, and this rich turf with montane species is well developed there. This calcicolous sward grades on soils of intermediate calcium status to both herb-rich heather heath and *Alchemilla alpina–Thymus drucei* grassland, and then into poor Callunetum and bilberry heath or poor *Festuca–Agrostis* grassland on podsolised soils.

The crags above Loch Loch are famous for the large colony of the very rare *Oxytropis campestris*, which seeds freely into the grassland below. There are also *Veronica fruticans*, *Carex rupestris*, *Draba incana*, *Polystichum lonchitis* and *Asplenium viride* on the rocks as well as the more widespread montane species of the grasslands. *Dryas octopetala* is recorded from Glen Tilt but appears to be rare in this area. The limestone crags are mostly within the forest zone, as indicated by their scattered growths of birch and rowan, and the calcareous grasslands are evidently derived from a subalpine woodland field layer, for they contain an abundance of dog's mercury, raspberry and *Geum rivale*. Common whitebeam grows on the limestone crags in Glen Tilt but its status here is not known.

Calcareous springs, flushes and soligenous *Carex* mires are very finely developed on this limestone, though they are essentially similar to those on Tulach Hill. Tufa-forming mounds of *Cratoneuron commutatum* are frequent, and the flush flora includes *Juncus alpinus*, *J. triglumis*, *Tofieldia pusilla*, *Equisetum variegatum*, *Armeria maritima*, *Orthothecium rufescens*, *Catoscopium nigritum*, *Meesia palustris* and *Amblyodon dealbatus*.

Glen Tilt has a stream section of international geological importance.

U.56. BEN VRACKIE, PERTHSHIRE

NN 9563. 2700 ha   Grade 2

This relatively low (840 m) outlying hill towards the southern fringe of the Highlands has long been noted for its rich flora. There is a mixture of acidic and strongly calcareous Dalradian schists, and these are exposed as broken crags on various aspects of the hill. The influence of the basic rocks soon fades, away from the outcrops, except where there is flushing, and the predominant submontane vegetation is that of grouse-moor, from dry Callunetum to *Calluna–Eriophorum* blanket mire, with a good deal of *Vaccinium–Empetrum* heath on the upper slopes. The outcrops of calcareous schist have widespread calcicoles such as *Saxifraga oppositifolia*, *Cerastium alpinum*, *Salix myrsinties*, *Potentilla crantzii*, *Saussurea alpina*, *Draba incana* and *Polystichum lonchitis*, whilst the rarities include *Oxytropis halleri*, *Astragalus alpinus* and *Carex rupestris*. Calcareous open flushes have *Saxifraga aizoides*, *Juncus alpinus*, *Tofieldia pusilla* and are sometimes associated with *Cratoneuron commutatum* springs. Intermittently flushed patches of ground sometimes have a great abundance of *Saxifraga aizoides*, with *Polygonum viviparum* and other small forbs and these pass into calcareous *Carex* marshes with *C. panicea*, *C. demissa*, *C. nigra*, *C. pulicaris* and *C. dioica*.

Soligenous mires range from extensive oligotrophic types with *Sphagnum recurvum*, through more localised mesotrophic types with basiphilous *Sphagnum* spp. (especially *S. warnstorfianum*, *S. teres* and *S. contortum*), to calcicolous 'brown moss'-dominated carpets. *Carex rostrata* is abundant to dominant in all three, but *Juncus effusus* belongs to the more acidic types, and the flora of the calcicolous mire communities is much richer. An interesting hollow on the north side has a mixture of all three mire types. The bryophyte flora of these habitats includes the local species *Camptothecium nitens* and *Cinclidium stygium*. The summit area of Ben Vrackie is rather small and uneven, and montane communities show only a limited development. *Vaccinium myrtillus* and *Nardus* snow-bed communities are patchy but there is a good deal of *Alchemilla alpina* at high levels, and *Sibbaldia procumbens* occurs in intermittent flushes. High-level Callunetum is very sparingly represented.

The very rare *Schoenus ferrugineus* was transplanted into this area from its only known station beside Loch Tummel to avoid the total destruction of the plant as a result of hydro-electric developments.

Ben Vrackie is of some interest for its moorland birds, which include species such as the hen harrier and short-eared owl.

U.57. LOCHNAGAR, ABERDEENSHIRE
NO 2584. 3700 ha   Grade 2

This granite mountain (1155 m) combines many vegetational features of the Cairngorms (U.44) to the north and the Caenlochan–Clova hills (U.42) to the south, but lacks the extent and diversity of the former and the rich calcicolous flora of the latter. Lochnagar and Caenlochan–Clova are in fact the northern and southern parts of a single massif, joined along the high watershed of Glens Clova and Callater, where elevation only just falls below 910 m.

The acidophilous plant communities characteristic of this district of the Highlands are mostly well represented. Callunetum is extensive on the lower slopes and grades into the dwarf, montane type with *Arctostaphylos uva-ursi* and *Loiseleuria procumbens* at high levels. *Vaccinium–Empetrum* heath is finely developed and lichen-rich facies occur on the outlying spurs of White Mounth and Cairn Bannoch. Exposed ground on the high plateaux has a range of communities from typical closed *Rhacomitrium–Carex bigelowii* heath to open *Juncus trifidus*–lichen heath, and intermediate types are extensive. There is a good deal of vegetation influenced by the late snow cover, with widespread *Vac-*

cinium myrtillus, *Nardus stricta* and *Trichophorum cespitosum* communities, and more local occurrence of those characterising ground where the snow lies longest, namely, the *Cryptogramma crispa–Athyrium alpestre* type on block screes, with *Gnaphalium supinum–Sibbaldia procumbens* and *Polytrichum norvegicum–Dicranum starkei* patches in elevated hollows. On the highest plateaux there are substantial areas of dominant *Carex bigelowii* with associated *Dicranum fuscescens*, *Polytrichum alpinum* or lichens. On poorly drained ground there is a good deal of *Calluna–Trichophorum* mire, grading to the typical *Calluna–Eriophorum* blanket mire. High-level examples of the latter, with high cover of other dwarf shrubs, are extensive at the head of Glen Muick. Subalpine and alpine *Carex–Sphagnum* soligenous mires are well represented and there are numerous oligotrophic springs and flushes in the high corries.

The most famous feature of Lochnagar is the magnificent north-east corrie, with its 240 m, gully-riven granite cliffs. Broad, sloping ledges, inaccessible to sheep and deer, are the classic locality for the very rare alpine tall herb *Cicerbita alpina*, which is accompanied by mildly base-demanding plants such as *Sedum rosea*, *Oxyria digyna*, *Cochlearia alpina*, *Cirsium heterophyllum*, *Trollius europaeus* and *Geranium sylvaticum*. In places below the cliffs is a species-poor *Deschampsia cespitosa* grassland evidently derived by grazing from the tall-herb ledge vegetation. In addition to the usual snow-influenced communities, there are springs and flushes with mosses such as *Pohlia ludwigii* and *P. albicans* var. *glacialis*. Enrichment of the generally poor soil occurs locally from lime-bearing pockets in veins and crushed zones in the granite, but the effect is not strong, and the flora of Lochnagar is lacking in stricter calcicoles. Most of the noteworthy alpines are calcifuge or indifferent to base–status and many belong to damp or wet ground; in addition to species mentioned above they include *Gnaphalium norvegicum*, *Saxifraga rivularis*, *Veronica alpina*, *V. serpyllifolia* ssp. *humifusa*, *Cerastium alpinum*, *Salix lapponum*, *Alchemilla alpina*, *Epilobium alsinifolium*, *E. anagallidifolium*, *Lycopodium annotinum*, *Betula nana*, *Carex lachenalii*, *C. rariflora*, *C. pauciflora*, *Alopecurus alpinus*, *Phleum alpinum*, *Poa flexuosa* and *Sphagnum lindbergii*. The cliffs are another famous locality for alpine forms of hawkweed *Hieracium* spp. Lochnagar is the only known locality in Britain for the liverwort *Marsupella sparsifolia*, and bryophytes associated with prolonged snow cover are well represented.

See also W.187.

U.58. MONADHLIATH, INVERNESS-SHIRE
NH 6201. 9700 ha   Grade 2

The vast tableland of the Monadhliath, north of the Drumochter Hills, is still largely unexplored, but an area has been selected which contains the highest tops and appears to be representative of the range of variation. A great area above 600 m is covered largely with blanket mire, showing considerable erosion by gullying. Up to 760 m it has mainly the *Calluna–Eriophorum vaginatum* community, but above this level, *Empetrum hermaphroditum* and *Vac-*

cinium spp. replace *Calluna* as the dwarf shrubs in this mire community. *Betula nana* occurs locally in this vegetation and *Rubus chamaemorus* is abundant. The steeper lower slopes have a mixture of Callunetum (including the species-rich *Arctostaphylos* type), snow-bed *Vaccinium* heath and acidic grasslands, with numerous soligenous mires varying from base-poor to base-rich. An interesting feature at high levels is the occurrence of lichen-rich *Vaccinium–Empetrum* heath and extensive *Rhacomitrium* heath (i.e. a mixture of continental and oceanic types) on the same ground. *Rhacomitrium* heath covers large areas above 820 m, and is the most montane vegetation of the area, which reaches only 940 m at its highest. Dwarf Callunetum occurs on upper spurs and lower tops, and outside the site, above Aviemore, it shows local dominance of lichens. There is a wide range of moderately late snow-bed communities, especially Nardetum, and associated springs and flushes. The montane flora of the area is not rich, and most of the few cliffs are acidic. One glen has extensive exposures of calcareous rock with a large colony of *Polystichum lonchitis* and abundance of *Saxifraga aizoides* and *S. oppositifolia*, and there are good patches of *Salix lapponum* on at least one cliff.

U.59. LADDER HILLS, ABERDEENSHIRE–BANFFSHIRE
NJ 2513. 2100 ha   Grade 2

The flat-topped hills on either side of Lecht summit (Meikle Corr Riabhach, 787 m; Beinn a'Chruinnich, 776 m) have a good deal of *Calluna–Eriophorum* blanket mire with a high cover of lichens. The total area of this vegetation is far less than on Carn nan Tri-tighearnan (P.86), but the mire is less eroded, and *Rubus chamaemorus* has a higher cover. There is also a wider range of other communities due to the steeper slopes, the greater altitude and the occurrence on the summits of areas of better-drained soil. These carry moss heaths and lichen-rich dwarf Callunetum. On the slopes there are extensive stands of wet Callunetum, Juncetum squarrosi, Vaccineto–Callunetum and Vaccinetum chionophilum.

See also P.90.

U.60. COYLES OF MUICK, ABERDEENSHIRE
NO 3391. 370 ha   Grade 2

This relatively low (601 m) hill lies in the north-eastern foothills of Lochnagar, and is famous for its outcrops of serpentine near the summit. The serpentine is more calcareous and less toxic to plants than some of the other Aberdeenshire occurrences of this rock, such as that at Towanreef (U.47) and it lies at a higher elevation. The eastern slopes have been afforested with conifers to an elevation of 530 m, but the western slopes pass into heather moor and grassland. The rock outcrops amongst rather ordinary grasslands, and the distinctive flora belongs largely to the open serpentine habitats. The more notable species include strict calcicoles such as *Saxifraga aizoides* and *Potentilla crantzii*, but are mainly plants which can grow on a variety of base-rich rocks such as *Cerastium alpinum*,

Cardaminopsis petraea, *S. hypnoides*, *Asplenium viride*, *A. trichomanes*, *A. ruta-muraria*, *Anthyllis vulneraria*, *Gentianella campestris*, *Armeria maritima* and *Silene maritima*. Some of the characteristic species of the Towanreef serpentine are absent.

WESTERN HIGHLANDS

U.61. BEN ALDER AND AONACH MOR, INVERNESS-SHIRE
NN 4974. 4950 ha   Grade 1

This is a massif formed of rocks of the Moine Series and lying in a remote area between Lochs Ericht and Laggan. Ben Alder (1147 m) lies to the south and is separated from Aonach Mor (1128 m) by a deep col; both hills have large summit plateaux with a good deal of ground above 970 m. The rock is mainly acidic schists and grits approaching quartzite in places, but in one area there is a band of limestone which outcrops at 900–1000 m, with spectacular effects on the vegetation and flora. The area as a whole is important as the most varied mountain system in the western Grampians.

These hills have suffered less from heavy grazing and burning than many of the high hill ranges of western Inverness-shire, and their lower slopes have a good deal of heather heath, grading on the north-east side into *Calluna–Eriophorum* blanket mire. Windswept moraines and upper spurs have montane dwarf Callunetum, including types with *Arctostaphylos uva-ursi* and *Rhacomitrium lanuginosum*. Higher slopes have extensive *Empetrum–Vaccinium* heaths which grade into the types with *Rhacomitrium* and *Nardus* or *Alchemilla alpina*. Grasslands of *Nardus* and *Deschampsia cespitosa* are also extensive and there is a good deal of *Trichophorum cespitosum*. The high ground, on the upper slopes and plateaux, has a fine range of late snow-bed vegetation, including *Athyrium alpestre–Cryptogramma crispa* growths on block screes, *Alchemilla alpina* and *Sibbaldia procumbens* in association with *Rhacomitrium canescens*, *Gymnomitrion* crust with *Salix herbacea*, *Polytrichum norvegicum–Dicranum starkei* moss heaths, and springs dominated by *Pohlia albicans* var. *glacialis*, *P. ludwigii*, *Anthelia* spp. and other bryophytes.

The plateau of Ben Alder has a mixture of *Rhacomitrium lanuginosum–Carex bigelowii* heath with varying amounts of *Juncus trifidus*, *C. bigelowii* mixed with *Dicranum fuscescens*, *Polytrichum alpinum* or lichens, and *Deschampsia cespitosa* and *Nardus* grasslands. There are acidophilous *Carex–Sphagnum* soligenous mires and *C. saxatilis* grows in the poorer snow-bed flushes. The summit of Aonach Mor is still more varied, with most of these high-level communities but a greater variety of snow-bed types in hollows on the actual plateau, and *J. trifidus* heath on quartzite. *C. bigelowii* is often associated with *Festuca vivipara* and *D. flexuosa* and there is an abundance of *Salix herbacea* and *Luzula spicata*. *Cherleria sedoides* occurs in patches and there is a little *Armeria maritima*. Solifluction forms include vegetated hummock–hollow and open stone-net systems.

The outcrops of limestone are small and localised but

support an interesting assemblage of rare and local calcicoles, including *Saxifraga cespitosa*, *S. nivalis*, *Salix lanata*, *Draba norvegica*, *Minuartia rubella*, *Dryas octopetala*, *Carex atrata*, *Poa alpina*, *Campylium halleri*, *Hypnum bambergeri*, *Ptychodium plicatum*, *Blindia caespiticia*, *Timmia norvegica*, *Encalypta alpina*, *Orthothecium rufescens*, *Mnium spinosum* and *Hylocomium pyrenaicum*.

In one locality, copious flushing with calcareous water draining from this limestone has enriched the slopes below, giving fine examples of dwarf-forb swards with *Silene acaulis*, *Sibbaldia procumbens*, *Alchemilla alpina*, *A. vulgaris* agg., *Saxifraga oppositifolia*, *S. hypnoides*, *S. aizoides*, *Thalictrum alpinum*, *Polygonum viviparum*, *Carex capillaris* and *Oncophorus virens*. The base-rich water also emerges to give springs, flushes and soligenous mires; there are banks of *Cratoneuron commutatum*, *S. aizoides* flushes with an abundance of the very rare *Carex atrofusca*, and *C. saxatilis* mires. The flora of these habitats is rich and includes *Armeria maritima*, *Juncus castaneus*, *J. alpinus*, *J. triglumis*, *Tofieldia pusilla*, *Equisetum hyemale* and *Acrocladium trifarium*.

Basic schist outcrops elsewhere have *Cerastium arcticum* and *Cystopteris montana*, and species associated with mildly basic conditions include *Salix lapponum*, *Veronica alpina* and *Phleum alpinum*. The total montane vascular flora is large, and includes most of the widespread species. The calcifuges are well represented and include *Cerastium cerastoides*, *Carex lachenalii*, *Deschampsia alpina*, *Athyrium flexile* and *Phyllodoce caerulea*, the last two being very rare species. Bryophytes associated with prolonged snow cover are well represented, and in addition to species mentioned there are *Andreaea nivalis*, *Conostomum tetragonum*, *Gymnomitrion varians*, *Pleuroclada albescens* and *Moerckia blyttii*. Some of the northern Atlantic liverworts have eastern outposts here, namely, *Scapania nimbosa*, *S. ornithopodioides*, *Anastrophyllum donianum* and *Herberta adunca*.

U.62. BEINN DEARG AND SEANA BHRAIGH, ROSS
NH 2781. 13 600 ha   Grade 1*

The large massif, lying east of the head of Loch Broom, has Beinn Dearg (1084 m) as its highest point and contains several summits over 900 m, including Am Faochagach (954 m) to the east and Seana Bhraigh (927 m) to the north. This is the most northerly hill area in Britain with ground reaching 1070 m, and has more massive, rounded summits and broad watershed plateaux than many of the western Highland mountain systems. It is less exposed to extreme Atlantic influences than some ranges in the region, but must nevertheless be regarded as a strongly oceanic area, and contrasts in this respect with Ben Wyvis only 24 km to the south-east. The rock is entirely of the Moine Series, but varies from hard siliceous granulite to soft, calcareous mica-schist, giving a wide range of soil fertility.

After the Cairngorms (U.44) and Ben Lawers–Meall nan Tarmachan (U.41), this is regarded from a botanical viewpoint as the most important mountain system in Britain. In the diversity of its montane vegetation (which includes

certain types hardly if at all represented south of the Great Glen) and the richness of its flora, the Beinn Dearg area is unsurpassed in the northern Highlands. It lacks a few communities, such as the dwarf juniper scrub of the quartzite and native woodland on the lower slopes, and Atlantic bryophyte communities are better represented elsewhere, but no other area is quite so varied.

There is a wide range of submontane grassland, dwarf-shrub heath and mire on the lower ground. *Calluna–Molinia* and *Calluna–Trichophorum* wet heath are extensive, but drier Callunetum is rather patchy, though the now rare type with tall forbs occurs on the west side of Beinn Enaiglair. *Agrostis–Anthoxanthum* grassland is present locally, as on stream alluvium, and submontane *Nardus* and *Juncus squarrosus* communities are represented. There are complete mixtures of these heaths and grasslands on some slopes. The valley floor around Loch a'Gharbhrain has a limited extent of the western *Trichophorum–Eriophorum* blanket mire, but the gentler slopes above 460 m have a larger area of *Calluna–Eriophorum* mire, locally with much *Betula nana* and *Arctous alpina*. Soligenous *Carex–Sphagnum* mires are well represented and *B. nana* also occurs in these and in *Calluna–Trichophorum* vegetation. On high plateaux and watersheds above 760 m, the blanket mire approaches the high-level *Empetrum–Eriophorum* type, and in places shows a good deal of erosion by hagging. The desolate plateau south and east of Seana Bhraigh has a complex of eroding blanket mire, with heterogeneous spring and soligenous mires on denuded ground, and there are rare plants such as *Deschampsia alpina* and *Sphagnum lindbergii* here.

On wind-exposed moraines and dry spurs there are good examples of prostrate montane Callunetum, with three facies, rich in *Rhacomitrium lanuginosum*, lichens, or other dwarf shrubs such as *Arctous alpina*, *Arctostaphylos uva-ursi*, *Loiseleuria procumbens* and *Empetrum hermaphroditum*. At around 730–760 m this usually passes into *Rhacomitrium* heath, which on these hills is mostly of the north-western type rich in the cushion herbs, *Silene acaulis*, *Cherleria sedoides* and *Armeria maritima*. On intermittently flushed ground, with richer soil large patches of *Silene* and *Cherleria* occur, with a variety of small forbs such as *Polygonum viviparum*, *Thalictrum alpinum*, *Sibbaldia procumbens* and *Alchemilla alpina*; *Rhacomitrium* cover is reduced but there is a larger number of other species, including the rare but characteristic mosses *Hypnum hamulosum* and *Aulacomnium turgidum*. The high summits and ridges of this massif have good solifluction features, with stone nets and stripes on Beinn Dearg. On Am Faochagach and its spurs, in particular, there is a good deal of spectacular and still active terracing, and extensive ablation surfaces which give deposition to the leeward followed in turn by variable secondary erosion. A characteristic community of the bare stony Hamada soils of these terraces and ablation surfaces has a sparse growth of *Juncus trifidus*, *Festuca vivipara*, *Luzula spicata*, *Alchemilla alpina*, *S. procumbens*, *Gnaphalium supinum*, *Salix herbacea*, *Antennaria dioica* and small tufts of the cushion herbs. There is often a patchy liverwort crust of *Gymnomitrion concinnatum*, and the moss *Cono-*

stomum tetragonum and lichen *Solorina crocea* are characteristic.

Snow lies late on Beinn Dearg and Am Faochagach, and the complete range of snow-bed communities of the northern Highlands is represented. Pure *Vaccinium* or *Vaccinium–Empetrum* heath is sparse, but mixed *Nardus–Vaccinium–Empetrum–Rhacomitrium* stands are extensive. There are *Nardus*–hypnaceous moss and *Nardus–Rhacomitrium* communities and good areas of *Rhytidiadelphus* moss heath on the upper slopes. The corries have well-developed *Deschampsia cespitosa* grassland, with *Cryptogramma crispa–Athyrium alpestre* fern beds in block scree. The highest north- and east-facing hollows have *Alchemilla alpina–Sibbaldia procumbens* patches grading into mixed *Rhacomitrium* carpets with much *Gnaphalium supinum*, and there are good examples of the *Polytrichum norvegicum–Dicranum starkei* moss heath. A variety of acidic snow-bed springs occurs, including the type dominated by *Pohlia albicans* var. *glacialis*. The bryophytes of late snow areas are well represented, with the other species including *Moerckia blyttii*, *Pleuroclada albescens*, *Andreaea nivalis* and *Dicranum falcatum*, and this is the only known British locality for *Hygrohypnum polare*. *Philonotis fontana–Saxifraga stellaris* springs are frequent at various levels, and there are fine *Sphagnum auriculatum* springs.

Many of the elevated cliffs of Beinn Dearg and Seana Bhraigh are strongly calcareous, and have a rich flora. Most of the widespread montane calcicoles are present, together with a number of much more local species such as *Salix reticulata*, *Dryas octopetala*, *Saxifraga rivularis*, *S. nivalis*, *Cerastium alpinum*, *C. arcticum*, *Sagina saginoides*, *Draba norvegica*, *Cardaminopsis petraea*, *Potentilla crantzii*, *Carex saxatilis*, *C. atrata*, *C. capillaris*, *Juncus biglumis*, *J. castaneus*, *Phleum alpinum*, *Poa alpina*, *P. glauca* and *P. balfourii*. There are fine examples of tall-herb vegetation, often mixed with *Salix lapponum*, on the bigger ledges, and on flushed ground below the cliffs is a variety of species-rich grasslands and dwarf-forb communities, including the type with carpets of *Silene acaulis*. Where the flush influence disappears, there is sometimes a change to *Festuca–Vaccinium* grass heath with *Alchemilla alpina* and *Rhacomitrium*, and on rocky ground, such as block screes, dry cliff tops and ledges, there are good examples of *Empetrum*–moss heath, with *Rhacomitrium* or hypnaceous species. Open calcareous flushes occur at all levels, and their flora includes *Saxifraga aizoides*, *S. oppositifolia*, *Tofieldia pusilla*, *Juncus triglumis*, and *Acrocladium trifarium*. They grade in places into species-rich *Carex* mires.

The total montane vascular flora numbers at least 66 species, though this includes high-level calcifuges such as *Cerastium cerastoides*, *Gnaphalium norvegicum* and the very rare *Artemisia norvegica*. The northern Atlantic bryophyte flora is rich, and includes *Leptodontium recurvifolium*, *Herberta adunca*, *Scapania nimbosa* and *Anastrophyllum joergensenii* as well as the more constant species. Calcicolous montane bryophytes include *Rhytidium rugosum*, *Meesia uliginosa* and the very rare *Cirriphyllum cirrosum* but this element does not appear to be particularly rich. The general abundance of common mosses, especially *Rhacomitrium lanuginosum*, in these north-western mountains is a striking feature.

There are large numbers of red deer on these hills, and the area is the haunt of both wild cat and pine marten. The bird fauna contains most of the breeding species typical of the treeless hills of the northern Highlands.

U.63. BEN WYVIS, ROSS
NH 4869. 5350 ha   Grade 1*

This massive hill of Moine pelitic gneiss in east Ross is the only really high hill (1046 m) on the eastern side of the northern Highlands, but is still only 24 km north of Inverness. It is also only 24 km south-east of Beinn Dearg (U.62), but experiences a distinctly less oceanic climate, illustrating the steepness of the west to east climatic gradient in this region. Ben Wyvis forms a long south-west to north-east ridge, with spurs branching off on the south-east face and enclosing two deep, rocky corries. The most distinctive topographic feature, however, is the broadness of the high spurs and summit ridge, giving a flat-topped appearance to the mountain, and a large area above 760 m. In this respect, Ben Wyvis contrasts with the general tendency to peaked summits and narrow ridges in the northern Highlands.

The lower slopes are mostly gentle and have a large extent of *Calluna–Trichophorum* and *Calluna–Eriophorum* wet heath and blanket mire, with oligotrophic *Carex–Sphagnum*, *Juncus effusus* and *J. squarrosus* soligenous mires. Fragments of western *Molinia*- and *Myrica*-rich communities also occur. There is extensive heather heath of both the dry and moist facies on steeper ground; the dry type has *Arctostaphylos uva-ursi* locally. There is also dry to wet acidic grassland, with the *Agrostis–Anthoxanthum*, *Nardus* and *Juncus squarrosus* types. Part of the ground with this submontane complex has been recently afforested, but this is the least important area on Ben Wyvis.

Above 600 m on dry ground is Callunetum of montane type, and this grades on windswept moraines and spurs into the prostrate community, which occurs up to 760 m, and shows facies rich in dwarf shrubs (*Loiseleuria procumbens* and *Arctous alpina*), *Rhacomitrium lanuginosum* and lichens. The montane heather heaths pass on badly drained ground to extensive blanket mire of the *Calluna–Eriophorum vaginatum* type with abundance of *Rubus chamaemorus*, and this shows considerable dissection by erosion gullies locally. There are, nevertheless, very good examples of the undisturbed northern facies rich in dwarf shrubs such as *Betula nana*, *Arctous alpina*, *Empetrum hermaphroditum* and *Vaccinium vitis-idaea*, and with abundance of lichens, *Sphagnum rubellum* and *S. fuscum* (see P.99). At about 760 m, *Empetrum* takes over from *Calluna* in this mire.

On dry ground where snow lies late, the higher level heather heaths give way to a variety of chionophilous vegetation. The central Highland bilberry community is well represented, there are patches of the later *Nardus–Pleurozium* type, and on high, sheltered slopes are large areas of the western *Rhytidiadelphus* moss heath. On the long, steep and smooth north-west slope of Ben Wyvis, Callunetum gives out at about 600 m (though it rises higher on the windswept spur of An Cabar), and is replaced above by mixtures of these chionophilous communities. First is a zone of moss-rich and rather grassy *Vaccinium–Empetrum* heath, showing various transitions to the *Agrostis, Nardus* and *Juncus squarrosus* grassland series. Higher up this grades into a *Rhacomitrium*-rich *Vaccinium–Rhytidiadelphus* community, and this is replaced above about 820 m by *Rhacomitrium* heath. On wind-exposed spurs *Rhacomitrium* heath takes over from dwarf Callunetum at about 760 m, sometimes through a mosaic transition.

The most outstanding vegetational feature of Ben Wyvis is the vast extent of species-poor *Rhacomitrium lanuginosum–Carex bigelowii* heath, which covers the high windswept plateaux above 760–820 m in an almost continuous carpet. In places *Vaccinium myrtillus* and *C. bigelowii* separately reach a fairly high cover, but over several kilometres along the summit ridge this moss heath shows little variation. On the highest summit there is a patch of the eastern and central Highland *C. bigelowii–Dicranum fuscescens* heath. Vegetated solifluction hummocks and ridges are well developed in places, but there is little terracing, ablation surface or exposed stone. *Juncus trifidus* is rather uncommon, and cushion-herbs almost absent. This is in marked contrast to the summit areas of the Beinn Dearg massif not far to the west.

The corries have areas of species-poor *Deschampsia cespitosa* grassland, probably derived from tall-herb communities with species such as *Caltha palustris, Geum rivale, Trollius europaeus* and *Cochlearia alpina* which occur on ungrazed cliff ledges. There is also a *Luzula sylvatica–Rumex acetosa* ledge community and fragments of *Salix lapponum* scrub. Richer ledge communities with *Sedum rosea* and *Oxyria digyna* are poorly represented. Block screes have *Cryptogramma crispa–Athyrium alpestre* fern beds associated with prolonged snow cover, and the latest snow hollows have good examples of the *Alchemilla alpina–Sibbaldia procumbens, Gymnomitrion–Salix herbacea* and *Dicranum starkei–Polytrichum norvegicum* communities. The high corries and slopes also have extensive systems of oligotrophic bryophytes and mire communities, with *Philonotis fontana, Scapania undulata, Acrocladium sarmentosum, Sphagnum auriculatum, Bryum weigelii, Pohlia ludwigii,* and vascular plants such as *Saxifraga stellaris, Epilobium anagallidifolium, Veronica serpyllifolia* ssp. *humifusa. Alopecurus alpinus, Sphagnum lindbergii* and *S. riparium* occur more locally in these habitats.

The rock of Ben Wyvis appears to be largely non-calcareous, and only very limited representation of calcicolous vegetation and species has been found on localised outcrops of richer parent material. Small areas of *Alchemilla alpina–Thymus drucei* grassland, and open *Scorpidium–Carex panicea* flushes occur, and there are a few of the more widespread montane calcicoles such as *Saxifraga oppositifolia, S. aizoides, Thalictrum alpinum* and *Saussurea alpina.* Ben Wyvis is, however, rich in peat alpines and calcifuge species of rocky or other open ground, including bryophytes.

Gnaphalium norvegicum has been recorded from the corries. Hepatic-rich vegetation is evidently absent, and only a few of the more common northern oceanic liverworts occur, but there is a good representation of the bryophytes characteristic of late snow-beds with *Moerckia blyttii, Haplomitrium hookeri, Nardia breidleri, Pleuroclada albescens* and *Marsupella varians.*

Ben Wyvis is rated as grade 1* from its ecological position as the most continental mountain of the northern Highlands, and the particularly fine and complete range of acidophilous vegetation types which reflect this feature. The Affric–Cannich Hills (U.83) are similar in some respects, but are more oceanic and have a smaller area of the species-poor *Rhacomitrium* heath.

U.64. BEINN EIGHE AND LIATHACH, ROSS
NG 9862, NG 9358.   8050 ha   Grade 1*

The rugged mountain range of Beinn Eighe to the south of Loch Maree reaches 1010 m on Ruadh Stac Mor. The geology of the area has been complicated by folding, thrust planes and faults, but the rocks are all ancient; Cambrian Quartzite forms most of the eastern sector but farther west there are massive exposures of Torridonian Sandstone, and there are limited occurrences of Lewisian Gneiss and bands of calcareous Serpulite Grit and Fucoid Beds. Coire Mhic Fhearchair at the western end is one of the most spectacular corries in Britain, with a 300 m cliff of quartzite and sandstone, and this is a heavily glaciated massif with summits consisting of narrow ridges and rather sharp peaks. Climatically the area lies in the zone of maximum humidity in Britain, with an annual number of wet days exceeding 220. The area also has a number of cascading streams and small tarns.

The quartzite and sandstone give extremely base-poor soils, and the quartzite sector has a great deal of bare rock, both outcrop and scree, with only the sparsest vegetation. The north-east slopes above Loch Maree carry the Beinn Eighe pinewood (W.206(a)), but the tree limit is relatively low, and in places the wood itself is very open, passing into the prevailing Trichophoreto–Callunetum and damp Callunetum of the lower morainic slopes. On wet ground at the foot of the mountain these wet heaths pass into small areas of western Trichophoreto–Eriophoretum, and within the wood is a *Sphagnum*-rich example best regarded as a valley mire. *Molinia–Myrica* and *Carex–Sphagnum* soligenous mires are well represented. Atlantic bryophytes of these communities include *S. strictum, S. imbricatum, Campylopus shawii, C. atrovirens* and *Pleurozia purpurea.*

On windswept stony moraines of the mid-altitude (400–600 m) north-east slopes are good examples of the two types of montane dwarf-shrub heath virtually confined to the northern Highlands. The first has co-dominance of dwarfed *Calluna, Juniperus communis* ssp. *nana* and *Arctostaphylos uva-ursi,* and contains masses of a large and conspicuous leafy liverwort, *Herberta borealis,* described in 1970 as a new species, and known elsewhere in the world only in western Norway. The second is the mixed *Calluna, Arctous alpina, Arctostaphylos uva-ursi, Loiseleuria pro-*

cumbens, *Empetrum hermaphroditum* type, with an abundance of lichens, including the local *Alectoria sarmentosa* and *Platysma lacunosa*. Both are extremely sensitive to fire and have been eradicated on many hills by burning. Where the soils are enriched by drainage from basic rocks, there are areas of herb-rich *Festuca–Agrostis* and *Deschampsia cespitosa* grassland, including a montane type of the former with *Alchemilla alpina* and *Carex bigelowii*, and there is an interesting damp herb community with much *Thalictrum alpinum* and *C. pulicaris* in one area.

The higher ground of Beinn Eighe has only moderately late snow-beds, but these areas have examples of the *Nardus stricta*, *Deschampsia cespitosa*, *Athyrium alpestre* and *Alchemilla alpina–Sibbaldia procumbens* communities. The montane zone is more interesting in the occurrence of limited areas of the calcareous mudstones, which give deep, base-rich brown soils and a varied calcicolous flora contrasting sharply with that of the quartzite and sandstone. The most extensive occurrence is on Ruadh Stac Beag, where the gentle summit slope is much affected by downward creep under frost–thaw movement. The vegetation is a species-rich moss heath in which *Rhacomitrium lanuginosum* is mixed with hypnaceous mosses, and there is an abundance of montane forbs such as *Silene acaulis*, *Saussurea alpina*, *Thalictrum alpinum*, *Sibbaldia procumbens*, *Sedum rosea*, *Cerastium arcticum*, *Saxifraga hypnoides* and *Cochlearia micacea*. There is also a sparse summit vegetation of erosion surfaces, with an abundance of *Festuca vivipara*, *Juncus trifidus*, *Salix herbacea*, *Cardaminopsis petraea*, *Armeria maritima*, *Sagina saginoides* and *Luzula spicata*. Typical *Rhacomitrium* heath is only patchy, and a mixed *Nardus–Rhacomitrium* community is more widespread. The bigger ledges of cliffs formed of both mudstones and sandstone (which has thin beds of more basic shale in places) have good examples of tall-herb communities with *Trollius europaeus*, *Cirsium heterophyllum*, *Saussurea alpina*, *Sedum rosea*, *Oxyria digyna*, *Geum rivale*, *Angelica sylvestris* and *Luzula sylvatica*. Mudstone crags have calcicolous montane species such as *Saxifraga oppositifolia*, *Silene acaulis* and *Polystichum lonchitis*. The montane flora is less rich than that of the Beinn Dearg/Seana Bhraigh massif farther north, but includes the local *Ajuga pyramidalis* and *Saxifraga rivularis*.

The magnificent Torridonian Sandstone mountain Liathach (1053 m) lies next to Beinn Eighe and rises above Glen Torridon in a great sweep of tiered escarpment, whilst the north face is carved into several corries with high cliffs. In many places, especially on the north face, the cliffs have numerous large ledges, with moist, basic soils, and these have a fine development of tall-herb communities. Some of the other characteristic vegetation types of Beinn Eighe are represented, but there is less diversity of habitat. The montane flora is more limited, but includes characteristic north-western species such as *Cardaminopsis petraea*, *Cerastium arcticum* and *Deschampsia alpina*. On north-facing rocks and steep slopes there are especially fine and luxuriant examples of the communities of northern Atlantic hepatics such as *Herberta hutchinsiae*, *Bazzania pearsonii*,

B. tricrenata, *Mastigophora woodsii*, *Scapania nimbosa*, *S. ornithopodioides*, *Jamesoniella carringtonii*, *Anastrophyllum donianum* and *Anastrepta orcadensis*. Mosses of similar ecological/geographical affinities include *Dicranodontium uncinatum*, *Campylopus setifolius* and *Leptodontium recurvifolium* (on more basic rocks); and *Hymenophyllum wilsonii* is abundant, behaving as a bryophyte. These oceanic plants are also well represented on Beinn Eighe.

Both mountains are managed mainly as deer forest, though their carrying capacity is low. The fauna includes some of the characteristic north-west Highland species, notably the pine marten, which ranges beyond the woods over the treeless, rocky hillsides.

U.65. FOINAVEN AND MEALL HORN, SUTHERLAND
NC 3250.   13 300 ha   Grade 1*

The long ridge of Foinaven (908 m) and the adjoining hill, Arkle (786 m), form the other important group of quartzite mountains, lying 97 km north of Beinn Eighe. Also forming part of the site, the neighbouring hill of Moine Schists, Meall Horn and its spurs, is similar in many respects to Beinn Dearg in Ross. Both the quartzite and Moine areas show even more marked altitudinal descent of vegetation, compared with their Ross counterparts, with still lower limits of certain montane communities. Snow-lie on the high ground is here of shorter duration, however, and associated vegetation accordingly less well represented. The north-western part of the area has a rugged and undulating low-level gneiss topography, with numerous rock bosses and moorland lochs, at 60–300 m, and this resembles the gneiss country of the Inverpolly grade 1 site (U.66).

On the lower ground, *Calluna–Trichophorum* and *Calluna–Molinia* wet heath is extensive, and there are numerous occurrences of western *Trichophorum–Eriophorum* blanket mire. Strath Dionard and the area near Gualin show an interesting range of patterned pool and hummock blanket mire, and a discontinuous chain of these systems occurs as a series of valley-side mires in hollows and on flats alongside the River Dionard. In situation, structure and floristics, the whole mire complex of the area shows a general similarity to and affords an interesting comparison with the Silver Flowe (P.71), Claish Moss (P.94) and patterned mires elsewhere in Sutherland and Caithness. Most of these patterned mires have deep enlarged pools (sometimes forming dubh lochans), a reduced *Sphagnum* cover and much *Rhacomitrium lanuginosum*. On sloping ground east of Loch Tarbhaidh there are good examples of the 'step-ladder' arrangement of mire pools.

On steep ground at lower levels there are examples of both dry and moist Callunetum, including at least one good unburned example of the second type rich in northern Atlantic liverworts. Quartzite scree has the only substantial occurrence of dwarf juniper heath after that on Beinn Eighe and windswept spurs have good examples of *Rhacomitrium*-rich *Arctous–Arctostaphylos* heath. There is a short *Calluna–Empetrum–Rhacomitrium* community on less exposed ground at higher levels and this shows transitions to *Calluna–Eriophorum vaginatum* or *Juncus squarrosus* blanket bog. There is patchy *Vaccinium–Empetrum* and *Empetrum–Rhacomitrium* heath on rocky ground, but the snow-influenced vegetation appears to be limited to these species in varying mixture with *Nardus stricta*, and *Rhytidiadelphus* moss heath on the high slopes. *Deschampsia cespitosa* grassland occurs in the corries and there are examples of *Anthoxanthum–Agrostis* grassland. *J. effusus* flush mires occur on the lower ground and there is a variety of *Carex–Sphagnum* acidophilous types, and bryophyte flush and spring communities.

The summit areas have a good extent of *Rhacomitrium* heath with abundance of *Armeria maritima*, *Silene acaulis* and *Cherleria sedoides*, and the richer type with *Polygonum viviparum*, *Alchemilla alpina* and *Achillea millefolium* occurs in places. *Juncus trifidus* is locally plentiful, both in closed *Rhacomitrium* heath and the open communities of stony ablation surfaces. The narrow quartzite ridges and vast screes forming the northern part of Foinaven have little vegetation, but an interesting plant of this area is *Luzula arcuata*.

The high Moine Schist cliffs in the north-east corries of Meall Horn are calcareous, and their base is traversed by thick bands of calcareous Serpulite Grit and Fucoid Beds. There is a rich cliff flora here, with a profusion of the more widespread montane calcicoles, such as *Saxifraga oppositifolia*, *Silene acaulis* and *Polystichum lonchitis*, and several rarer species such as *Saxifraga nivalis*, *Draba norvegica* and *Poa glauca*. The moss *Orthothecium rufescens* is abundant, in addition to many more common species. There are fine examples of tall-herb ledges with a notable abundance of *Sedum rosea* and *Trollius europaeus*. The area as a whole has a rich representation of northern Atlantic bryophytes, with all the notable Scottish species, including *Anastrophyllum joergensenii*, *Scapania nimbosa*, *Leptodontium recurvifolium* and *Herberta adunca*; in places, both on steep rocky ground and beneath dwarf shrubs, the characteristic liverwort community is well developed.

The River Dionard is itself a good salmon river and on the lower moors of the gneiss country there are numerous open water bodies, ranging from dubh lochans to quite large lochs. Along the south-western boundary, the large Loch Stack and its outflow stream, the Laxford River, are famous salmon and sea trout waters, and are regarded as a grade 2 open water system. In Strathbeag, there is an important example of northern Highland birchwood (W.211) covering a block-littered quartzite slope and extending up the steep ledges of a large cliff.

Most animals and birds of the north-west Highlands are represented including red-throated and black-throated divers, golden eagle, greenshank, golden plover, dunlin, common sandpiper, ring ouzel, merlin, teal, red-breasted merganser, pine marten, otter and badger. There is a large herd of red deer, notwithstanding the generally low productivity of the area.

Geologically and geomorphologically the area is important, showing the marked unconformity of quartzite over Lewisian Gneiss, a classic series of truncated spurs rivalling those of Bidean nam Bian in Argyll, hanging valleys, corries,

frost shattered summit debris and scree. Scenically, Strath Dionard is one of the most spectacular glens in Scotland, and near its head is Creag Dionard, a 300 m precipice of quartzite. The north end of the area has a large extent of the low-level, rugged, undulating country typical of the Lewisian Gneiss. Base-poor open water-bodies are well represented.

See also W.211 and OW.97

U.66. INVERPOLLY AND KNOCKAN, ROSS
NC 1312. 10856 ha   Grade 1

This large NNR consists of two contrasting parts, belonging essentially to two different geological formations. On the seaward side the ground is a rather low but rugged area of moorland on Lewisian Gneiss, containing the large Loch Sionascaig (OW.92, gr. 1) with its wooded islands, and a number of smaller lochs. The northern boundary here follows the turbulent Kirkaig River, and the area is drained by many streams. There are numerous patches of birchwood (see W. 207), and a wide range of western Highland wet heath and mire communities (see P.101).

This undulating Lewisian Gneiss area has a complex of wet heath (mainly Trichophoreto–Callunetum and Molinieto–Callunetum) on the drier morainic ground, and blanket mire with Trichophoreto–Eriophoretum (many pockets have well-developed pool and hummock systems) on wet flows and in waterlogged hollows. This is a complex similar to that on Rannoch Moor (but with more wet heath and less blanket mire) and contains a similar range of soligenous mire communities. *Molinia–Myrica* mires are widespread here and in places there are extensive *Schoenus* soaks with pools; these areas have a mixture of species including *Rhynchospora alba*, *Drosera anglica*, *Menyanthes trifoliata*, *Utricularia intermedia*, *Pinguicula vulgaris*, *Selaginella selaginoides*, *Campylium stellatum*, *Scorpidium scorpioides* and *Drepanocladus revolvens*. There are related soligenous mire communities with an abundance of *Carex lasiocarpa*, *C. limosa* and *Utricularia intermedia* (in shallow pools). These communities grade into typical Trichophoreto–Eriophoretum blanket mire. This area is a good example of this kind of submontane moorland and wetland complex so characteristic of west Ross and west Sutherland, and is similar to that below the north end of Foinaven (U.65). The gneiss area is bounded to the west by the sea, and provides a rocky coast section of considerable interest in its own right.

The landward part is dominated by the twin sandstone mountains Cul Mor (849 m) and Cul Beag (769 m) which are steep and rocky on all sides. These hills have typical western Highland montane communities such as *Nardus–Rhacomitrium* heath and summit erosion surfaces with *Juncus trifidus*, and they have one of the few British colonies of the disjunct *Artemisia norvegica*. Northern Atlantic bryophytes are also well represented. However, they have rather undistinguished corries, a relatively low elevation, limited development of tall-herb communities and a rather restricted vascular flora, and in most respects are inferior to sandstone mountains such as Liathach and Beinn Bhan.

They nevertheless add considerably to the overall diversity of this most varied and important upland area which so well represents the typical upland complex of the north-west Highlands.

The important limestone area of Knockan cliff is also included in this site. Geologically, the junction here between the Moine and Cambrian rocks (Moine Thrust Plane) is a classic section and a site of international importance, not only for the phenomena it displays but also because of the role it has played in the development of geology. The main cliff of Durness Limestone, on the Sutherland side of the border, is floristically rich and the knolls above the cliff are notable for their fine examples of *Dryas octopetala–Carex rupestris* heath. Golden plover are noticeably more numerous in association with this limestone ground than on the extensive acidic moorlands which prevail in this region.

The area supports a characteristic west Highland predator fauna, with golden eagle, peregrine, raven, pine marten, wild cat, otter and badger. Greenshank and black-throated diver breed on these lower moorlands and their lochs.

U.67. INCHNADAMPH, SUTHERLAND
NC 2719. 1300 ha   Grade 1

The outcrop at the head of Loch Assynt contains the largest exposures of the Durness Limestone, and reaches the greatest altitude (*c.* 520 m). There are large limestone cliffs, steep slopes with scree, and fragmentary pavements or outcrops on the plateau behind. Geologically this is a famous area, with classic thrust planes, caves in which bones of numerous prehistoric animals were found, and underground streams. It is one of the very few parts of Scotland showing any resemblance to the Carboniferous Limestone areas of the Craven Pennines.

Floristically, the Inchnadamph NNR is rich, although high montane species are absent, as the limestone is mainly at low levels. There is great abundance of *Dryas octopetala*, *Polystichum lonchitis*, and common calcicoles, and rarities include *Arenaria norvegica*, *Agropyron donianum*, *Carex rupestris* and *Epipactis atrorubens*. The bryophyte flora is rich and includes rare submontane calcicoles such as *Tortula princeps*, *Amblystegium compactum*, *Seligeria trifaria*, *Grimmia trichodon* and *G. apocarpa* var. *homodictyon*. On the plateau above is a patchy willow scrub with the largest colony of *Salix myrsinites* in Britain. Species-rich grasslands are extensive, and the presence of numerous tall herbs in grazed-down form suggests that these are derived from submontane woodland and scrub. Fencing experiments have demonstrated the possibility of restoring these communities to a more original state. The plateau is also variably covered with peat, giving calcifuge elements of flora with typical peat alpines which contrast with the limestone species. There is a fairly extensive occurrence of Calluneto–Eriophoretum developed over limestone. The presence of this vegetation type in a rather low-lying western situation is interesting, as it is more characteristically found at higher levels and in eastern districts. The lower ground has numerous calcareous flushes and marshes, but there are also examples of more acidic mire.

Golden plover occur on the plateau at higher density than usual in the north-west Highlands, and the limestone ground has a rich invertebrate fauna, including molluscs.

The peaty but eutrophic Loch Mhaolach-coire and the limestone stream of the Traligill River are regarded as grade 2 in quality as an open water system, although they lie within the Inchnadamph site. The adjoining higher ground of Breabag, Conival and Ben More Assynt is regarded as a separate grade 2 upland site (U.91), as its significant features duplicate those well represented on other north-west Highland grade 1 mountain systems.

U.68. DURNESS, SUTHERLAND
NC 3768. 1300 ha   Grade 1*

On either side of the Kyle of Durness there are areas of contrasting lithology and vegetation which illustrate the importance of available lime as an ecological factor. To the east is a low-lying tract (0–60 m) where the dolomitic Durness Limestone outcrops as fragmentary pavement and low scarps, and gives extensive areas of brown calcareous loams (covered with grass heath) which merge at the sea-ward side with ground extensively influenced by blown shell sand. This area of calcareous soils contains the best *Dryas octopetala* heaths in Britain, and the only ones which rival those of the Burren, County Clare (Ireland), in the high cover of this characteristic Arctic–alpine dwarf shrub. *Dryas* is abundant or even dominant on the limestone and shell sand soils, in a community which otherwise has much in common with the characteristic herb-rich *Festuca–Agrostis* grasslands of northern limestone. This relationship is demonstrated by peripheral areas of the grassland which have lost their *Dryas* through heavy sheep-grazing.

The *Dryas* grass heaths here are the extreme northern equivalents to *Helianthemum* grass heaths of the southern chalk and limestone, and they still contain constants or characteristic species of the southern community, such as *Festuca rubra*, *Carex flacca*, *Lotus corniculatus*, *Plantago lanceolata*, *Koeleria gracilis* and *Orchis mascula*. There are, however, other montane species such as *Polygonum viviparum*, *Saxifraga aizoides*, *Draba incana*, *C. capillaris* and *C. rupestris*.

In many places the *Dryas* heaths and grasslands grade into Callunetum which is either the typical dry acidic heath or calcareous heath in which heather is mixed with somewhat basiphilous herbs and *Salix repens*. There are also patches of shallow *Eriophorum vaginatum* mire. The pavements have grikes with a relict woodland flora, and colonies of *Phyllitis scolopendrium*, while the scars have fragments of birch and hazel scrub with typical field communities containing *Allium ursinum*, *Valeriana officinalis* and *Heracleum sphondylium*. The area contains the limestone open waters, Lochs Borralie, Croispol, Lanlish and Caladail, and their associated streams, which are regarded as a grade 1 complex in their own right (see Open Waters). There are also wet hollows with calcareous soligenous mires dominated by *Schoenus nigricans*, and containing an abundance of vascular marsh plants and bryophytes. The shell sand approaches true machair in places and is one of the few examples of this habitat on the Scottish mainland. Towards the sea, the vegetation comes increasingly under the influence of salt spray, and species such as *Plantago maritima* appear. These slightly saline damp soils are the main habitat for *Primula scotica* in this area.

The area has a large population of twites, corncrakes are still to be heard, buzzards nest on the scarps and an unusually large colony of common gulls nests on the island in Loch Borralie, where Arctic terns, tufted duck and red-breasted merganser also breed.

West of the Kyle of Durness there is an area of barren moorland, on Torridonian Sandstone and Lewisian Gneiss, stretching away to Cape Wrath. Much of the ground has been heavily burned and has dull *Trichophorum–Calluna* wet heath, but the hill of Sgribhis Bheinn (370 m) has an interesting range of montane heaths at an unusually low elevation. At the top of the steep south slope is an area of good *Juniperus communis* ssp. *nana*–dwarf *Calluna* heath with *Arctostaphylos uva-ursi*, *Arctous alpina* and lichens, while the windswept plateau has areas of wave-eroded dwarf Callunetum with *Loiseleuria procumbens*, passing to *Rhacomitrium–Carex bigelowii* heath with *Nardus*. There are patches of shallow blanket mire of the high-level type with *Juncus squarrosus*, *Calluna*, *Empetrum nigrum*, *Eriophorum angustifolium*, *Sphagnum* spp. and hypnaceous mosses. Ptarmigan breed here at low levels, whilst great skuas are attempting to establish a foothold – one of the few on the Scottish mainland.

These two contrasting lithologies, the limestone and the sandstone/gneiss, thus both illustrate admirably the general phenomenon of low-level occurrence of true montane vegetation on this extremely exposed north-west coast of Scotland.

The sandstone part of the area also illustrates another important ecological principle – the richness of the sea. There could be no more striking contrast than that between the sterile moorlands with their extremely sparse vertebrate populations, and the great sea cliffs of the Clo Mor, with their myriads of breeding seafowl. This line of 150–210 m sandstone precipice, which forms the abrupt northern face of Sgribhis Bheinn and the other coastal habitats such as sand dunes, are described under Coastlands as a grade 1 site (C.108).

U.69. SOUTHERN PARPHE, SUTHERLAND
NC 2563.   5300 ha   Grade 1

This wild area of acidic Torridonian Sandstone upland has a range of oceanic montane communities which complement those of Sgribhis Bheinn (U.68) to the north-east and the area of blanket mire to the south-west which forms the western end of the series of pool and hummock systems recognised in northern Scotland.

These hills are not high, Creag Rhiabhach (485 m) being the highest point, but the altitudinal depression of vegetation zones characteristic of this corner of north-west Sutherland gives occurrences of montane communities and species well below this level. Morainic ground below 300 m has a good deal of *Calluna–Trichophorum* heath of the

heavily burned type, but at higher levels on windswept ground there is *Rhacomitrium*-rich dwarf Callunetum, usually in 'wave erosion' form. There is a good deal of *Alchemilla alpina* and *Plantago maritima* in this open vegetation, and both *Lycopodium alpinum* and *L. selago* are abundant. *Empetrum hermaphroditum* is plentiful, but other montane dwarf shrubs more sparse (*Juniperus communis* ssp. *nana*, *Arctous alpina*, *Arctostaphylos uva-ursi*, *Loiseleuria procumbens* and *Salix herbacea*). *Rhacomitrium–Nardus* communities are well developed on the highest ground, and there is some bare scree and ablation surface, with much *Antennaria dioica* and a little *Juncus trifidus*.

These are mostly communities of dry ground, but there is a good deal of shallow peat with an oceanic wet grass heath characteristic of hills along the north-west seaboard and the Hebrides; it is composed of a mixture of *Calluna*, *Nardus* and *Juncus squarrosus*, with a high cover of *Rhacomitrium lanuginosum*. This grades into more definite blanket bog with *Eriophorum vaginatum*, *Sphagnum papilosum* and *S. nemoreum* on wetter ground. The north-east face of Creag Rhiabhach has high cliffs which have some of the more common ledge plants such as *Sedum rosea*, and a mixture of tall herb and *Vaccinium myrtillus–Luzula sylvatica* communities. Some of the northern Atlantic bryophytes are represented.

The blanket mire system south of Strath Shinary is described under Peatlands (P.97), along with the valley mire at Lon Mor, while Sandwood Loch and the associated sand dunes are mentioned under Coastlands (see C.107).

U.70. INVERNAVER, SUTHERLAND
NC 6960.   552 ha   Grade 1

This is one of the most important botanical sites in Scotland, with unusual plant communities and a rich flora, which both illustrate interesting ecological features. The extreme wind exposure on this north Scottish coast has virtually extinguished tree growth even at low levels in places, and only a few patches of hazel–birch scrub are found in sheltered hollows on the slopes facing the sea. On the projecting spur of Moine Schists forming a low headland, strong winds have caused the widespread deposition of sand, blown inland from the seashore. This sand contains a moderate amount of calcium carbonate in the form of comminuted shell fragments, and its deposition substantially enriches what would otherwise be base-poor soils overlying the hard, non-calcareous bedrock and drift. With distance from the sea this enriching effect fades as the amount of blown sand decreases, and there is a gradual transition to the acidic podsolic and peat soils of ordinary moorland.

There is a seaward zone of essentially maritime habitats, with sandbank foreshore, and a line of mossy marram-grown dunes, with one good area of machair, and small slacks. Above this level the blown sand banked up on bedrock is characterised by a profusion of *Dryas octopetala* and other dwarf shrubs, notably *Empetrum hermaphroditum*, *Arctostaphylos uva-ursi*, *Salix repens* and *Juniperus* approaching ssp. *nana*, and there are more stable areas of these mixed heaths on machair-like ground. These are typically montane communities here growing almost at sea-level in response to the severity of the climate which inhibits the growth of more luxuriant and competitive life forms. It is the classic example in Britain of altitudinal descent of montane vegetation with increasing latitude and oceanicity.

The importance of available calcium to the floristic richness of the area is shown by the transition from *Dryas* and other dwarf-shrub heath to heather–juniper heath, poorer heather heath, and then to ordinary acidic wet moorland communities. Calcareous flushes and marshes are well represented where water drains from ground influenced by blown sand, and include patches of *Schoenus nigricans* mire, and carpets of 'brown mosses' (e.g. *Scorpidium scorpioides*) with calcicolous sedges. There is a range of open rock habitats, including low cliffs and rocky knolls and slopes with wet flushes. Several small tarns have water of different base-status, and show corresponding vegetational variations.

In the zone between the outer dunes and the acidic moorland, soil conditions are so variable, in regard to both lime and moisture content, that plant species occur in such a multiplicity of combinations as to make the recognition of particular communities difficult.

Invernaver is famous besides for its aggregation of rare plants, which include *Oxytropis halleri*, *Carex maritima* and *Primula scotica*; and more widespread montane species such as *Polygonum viviparum*, *Silene acaulis*, *Saxifraga aizoides* and *S. oppositifolia* are abundant. Coastal species such as *Armeria maritima*, *Plantago maritima* and *Silene maritima* also contribute to the floristic diversity. This is the only known British locality for the moss *Brachythecium erythrorrhizon*, and the rich bryophyte flora includes both southern species such as *Entodon orthocarpus* and northerners such as *Catoscopium nigritum*.

Invernaver is also regarded as a grade 1 coastal site for its maritime features.

See also C.109.

U.71. RHUM, INVERNESS-SHIRE

NM 3798.   10684 ha   Grade 1

The island of Rhum has a long and mainly rocky coastline, but the interior is almost entirely a mountain and moorland complex with numerous streams and small lakes. There is some planted woodland, but most of the area is treeless upland, with fragments of woodland and scrub only in a few rocky places. Geology is complex, but ecologically there are three main rock groups: acidic Torridonian Sandstone and granophyre giving the usual base poor soils, calcareous basalt and Triassic limestone giving local areas of lime-rich soil, and gabbro, peridotite and other ultra-basic materials giving soils rich in magnesium. The sandstone is mostly on low-lying ground and has a rather poor flora, though round the coast there are a number of interesting plants, including *Ajuga pyramidalis*, and *Vicia orobus* grows in several places inland. The calcareous rocks cover a small area and do not rise above 580 m; they nevertheless have quite a rich montane cliff flora, with *Dryas octopetala*, *Saxifraga nivalis*, *Poa alpina*, *P. glauca* and *Thlaspi alpestre*. Extensive herb-rich grasslands cover the slopes below the cliffs, and on the north coast is a maritime herb-rich Callunetum, containing *Dryas* in one place.

The basic and ultra-basic igneous rocks form the highest range of hills, with Askival (811 m). These have a few rare montane plants, such as *Arenaria norvegica* and *Juncus biglumis*, and there is a great quantity of *Cardaminopsis petraea*. The submontane fern *Asplenium septentrionale* has been found recently. The soils of these magnesium-rich rocks are, however, perhaps more interesting than their flora. Deep weathering gives friable brown soils of unusual depth and there is a general instability of the surface, with frequent redistribution by wind and water, so that a good deal of the ground is very open, with only a sparse vegetation. On the steep slopes of Askival, Hallival and Ruinsival is a large colony of Manx shearwaters which are able to burrow deeply into the loose textured soils, and which, by their manuring, produce a rich grassy sward. The granophyre forming the southern high mountains with Sgurr nan Gillean (763 m) is hard and acidic, and gives shallow soils with a more typical western Highland vegetation complex, including poor *Rhacomitrium* heath. On the lower moorlands there is a large area of western type wet heath and blanket mire, notably of *Calluna–Trichophorum* and *Calluna–Molinia* communities on shallow peat, and *Trichophorum–Eriophorum* mire with abundant *Molinia* on deeper peat. Shallow pools occur in some patches of blanket mire, and their flora includes *Drosera intermedia*, *Utricularia intermedia* and *Rhynchospora fusca* in its northernmost British station.

Rhum contains most types of submontane soligenous mire characteristic of the western Highlands. These include the *Carex panicea–C. echinata* facies of Trichophoreto-Eriophoretum; tussocky *Molinia caerulea* mires of the type which usually contain *Myrica gale* (a very rare species on Rhum); oligotrophic *Carex–Sphagnum subsecundum* var. *auriculatum* mire with *C. echinata*, *C. demissa*, *Eleocharis multicaulis* and *Ranunculus flammula*; *Juncus effusus–S. recurvum* mire; mesotrophic mires dominated by an apparent hybrid *J. articulatus × J. acutiflorus*, with species such as *Parnassia palustris*, *Prunella vulgaris* and *Succisa pratensis*; another mesotrophic type with *C. panicea*, *C. flacca*, *C. nigra*, *C. pulicaris*, *Leontodon autumnalis*, *Parnassia*, *Eleocharis quinqueflora*, *Selaginella selaginoides* and *Drepanocladus revolvens*; and calcareous mire of the *C. panicea–Campylium stellatum* type.

In addition, especially on peridotite in the Harris area there is a great abundance of *Schoenus nigricans* in a range of communities influenced by lateral water seepage. These vary from open flushes with a variety of species to communities with little but large tussocks of *Schoenus*, growing in open base-rich soils in which magnesium is the predominant cation. There are transitions to the *Molinia* and *Juncus articulatus × acutiflorus* communities and *Schoenus* also occurs in seepage areas as the vegetation passes into ombrogenous mire; and in places the widespread Trichophoreto-Eriophoretum of the badly drained lower ground contains a sparse growth of *Schoenus*. This is the nearest equivalent found in Britain to the characteristic *Schoenus*-rich ombrogenous mires of western Ireland.

Rhum has an extremely wide range of soil conditions and vegetation types, especially in the series from submontane grassland to dwarf-shrub heath and from these to both soligenous and blanket mire. Relatively large areas of fertile pasture are associated with both basic rocks or drift deposits and maritime influence. Montane vegetation is not particularly well represented by mainland Highland standards, but the oceanic flora is rich, especially in Atlantic bryophytes, which include rare northern species such as *Myurium hebridarum*, *Campylopus shawii*, *Trichostomum hibernicum*; and southern species such as *Jubula hutchinsiae* and the ferns *Dryopteris aemula* and *Hymenophyllum tunbrigense*, here in one of their northernmost outposts. A number of plant species once recorded as native were judged to be introduced, but have evidently disappeared or are in such small quantity that no biogeographical confusion has been created: it is quite clear which are the native species of the island.

The bird fauna is quite varied and rich for a Hebridean island, and includes a resident population of three to four pairs of golden eagles, peregrines, merlins, ravens, twites, red-throated divers, corncrakes and golden plover. The insect fauna is very rich, especially the Lepidoptera, which include Hebridean forms of some species such as the dark green fritillary and rarities such as the transparent burnet.

While the vegetation, flora and fauna are diverse and important in themselves, and there is a representative range of Hebridean ecosystems, the greatest value of Rhum is probably as an area for research and development of conservation techniques, for it has the advantages which an island gives to this kind of work. A great deal of work has been done on red deer, which can here be studied as a single unit, without problems of movement into and from the study area, and with complete freedom from disturbance. The herd of feral goats offers similar opportunities, and there is scope for studying the effects of absences of certain species or, conversely, of introductions. The very marked differences in productivity on different parts of the island give especially good opportunities for determining relationships between herbivores, fodder plants and soils. The coast of the island, with its wide range of habitats, is regarded as a grade 1 coastal site in its own right.

See also C.101.

U.72. TROTTERNISH RIDGE, SKYE, INVERNESS-SHIRE
NG 4569, NG 4954, NG 4562. 3250 ha   Grade 1

The Trotternish peninsula of northern Skye is formed for most of its length by the impressive basalt plateau which reaches 720 m at The Storr, and gradually descends to 540 m at Meall nan Suireamach in the north. The eastern face of this ridge has the most extensive inland cliff system in Britain, with several buttresses over 150 m high, screes and gullies. Rotational slipping has caused extensive landslips, producing a mass of collapsed basalt columns, tumbled rocks, block-litters, and detached pinnacles that extend for some considerable distance (2130 m at The Quirang) away from

the cliffs. By contrast the western slopes are gentler and largely follow the low westward dip of the basalt lavas. The slopes are dissected by consequent streams rising in the high ground and flowing sinuously through open alluvial valleys into Loch Snizort. The area is thus of considerable geomorphological interest, as it contains the largest landslip system in Britain.

The basalt is strongly calcareous in parts and this, coupled with the wide variety of habitats and aspects, results in the richest assemblage of montane plants anywhere in the Hebrides. The Storr and The Quirang are particularly rich, although Beinn Edra and Sgurr Mor also support several interesting species not known elsewhere on Skye. Many of the cliffs are unstable and rapidly weather to produce a fine-grained reddish lithosol. The larger, more stable cliffs, generally of north or east aspect, support fine examples of tall-herb communities with *Alchemilla glabra*, *Salix myrsinites*, *Saussurea alpina*, *Saxifraga hypnoides*, *Sedum rosea*, *Herberta adunca*, and *Leptodontium recurvifolium*. Fern-rich crevice communities with *Asplenium viride*, *Cystopteris fragilis*, *Polystichum lonchitis*, *Mnium orthorhynchum*, *Orthothecium rufescens*, and *Pohlia cruda* occur locally on shaded cliffs and *Saxifraga aizoides* banks are rather rare.

Dry, sun-exposed rock outcrops support a rich and diverse flora including *Draba incana*, *Poa balfourii*, *P. glauca* (locally abundant), *Saxifraga oppositifolia*, *Encalypta ciliata*, *E. rhabdocarpa*, *Grimmia funalis*, *G. torquata*, *Reboulia hemisphaerica*, and more locally *Dryas octopetala*, *Barbula icmadophila*, *Grimmia apocarpa* var. *homodictyon*, *Anomobryum concinnatum*, *Pterygynandrum filiforme*, and *Myurella julacea*.

Damp rocks or bare soil on shaded cliffs and in gullies also support a rich assemblage of montane plants including *Cerastium arcticum*, *Poa alpina*, *Rhinanthus borealis*, *Saxifraga nivalis*, *Ditrichum lineare*, *Hylocomium pyrenaicum*, *Pohlia polymorpha*, *Eremonotus myriocarpus*, *Marsupella alpina*, *Plectocolea subelliptica*, *Scapania calcicola*, *S. gymnostomophila* and *Solenostoma oblongifolium*. This assemblage of hepatics is otherwise characteristic of the schists of Breadalbane and Caenlochan.

On the steep slopes below the cliffs, very fine *Alchemilla*-rich *Agrostis*–*Festuca* grasslands occur, with an abundance of *Alchemilla alpina* and with *A. wichurae*. Other species of interest include *Cherleria sedoides*, *Sibbaldia procumbens*, *Aulacomnium turgidum*, *Entodon concinnus*, *Barbilophozia lycopodioides*, *Lophozia obtusa*, and *Mastigophora woodsii*. Dwarf-shrub heaths are rare, probably because of the high grazing pressure this area sustains. Basalt screes are relatively common, either in unstable sites or in over-grazed areas, and they support *Cardaminopsis petraea*, *Koenigia islandica*, *Luzula spicata* and *Sagina saginoides*. Areas of block-litters, such as at Carn Liath, provide specialised habitats for *Cryptogramma crispa* and a variety of rare saxicolous bryophytes including *Dicranoweisia crispula*, *Glyphomitrium daviesii*, *Grimmia ovalis* and *Marsupella stableri*, as well as many of the commoner species of Atlantic mosses and liverworts.

The summit vegetation is predominantly species-rich *Rhacomitrium* heath, with an abundance of cushion-herbs, and of *Antitrichia curtipendula* and *Aulacomnium turgidum*. Small areas of chionophilous *Nardus stricta* vegetation occur locally, and shallow blanket bog with *Juncus squarrosus* is frequent in waterlogged hollows. On The Storr, Beinn Edra, and, more rarely, Sgurr Mor, are several high-altitude spring and open flush communities. These are of varying base-status and water temperature and they support an extremely rich assemblage of species, such as *Euphrasia frigida*, *J. biglumis*, *J. triglumis*, *Koenigia islandica*, *Acrocladium trifarium*, *Cinclidium stygium*, *Oncophorus virens*, *Scapania paludosa*, *S. uliginosa* and *Tritomaria polita*.

On the lower slopes of the eastern side there is an abundance of *Juncus acutiflorus* and *J. articulatus* flush mires with a rich herbaceous assemblage.

Besides being one of the three British localities for the Arctic–subarctic *Koenigia islandica*, the area is of outstanding geological, floristic and vegetational interest. The flora, both of vascular plants and bryophytes, and the range of montane communities are remarkable considering the relatively low altitude of The Storr. The area as a whole is particularly important, as it represents an intermediate area between Scottish montane vegetation and the vegetation of the basalts of Iceland and The Faeroes. The bryophyte flora is unique in north-west Scotland, with several rare species otherwise known only in the central Highlands, as well as many Atlantic species.

U.73. STRATH SUARDAL, SKYE, INVERNESS-SHIRE
NG 6020. 1750 ha   Grade 1

The southernmost exposure of the Durness Limestone occupies several square kilometres from Strath Suardal southwards, and forms a low range of hills reaching *c.* 290 m.

Although much of the area is covered with acidic drift, there is a wide range of limestone habitats which include small but fine examples of clint and grike pavement, a ravine, and a calcareous tarn with adjoining soligenous mire system. Part of the north slope of the Strath is covered by birch–ash–hazel wood, and the western edge of the site is bounded by the sea, so that the whole area is one of exceptional ecological diversity and interest. The area has considerable geological interest, and these are amongst the best pavement exposures of the Durness Limestone.

Amidst the peat-covered slopes of Ben Suardal there is a mosaic of open limestone pavement, *Dryas octopetala* heath and species-rich *Festuca–Agrostis* grasslands, with noteworthy plants such as *Alchemilla alpina*, *Thalictrum alpinum*, *Saxifraga aizoides*, *Arctostaphylos uva-ursi*, *Epipactis atrorubens*, *Polygonum viviparum*, *Asplenium viride* and *Polystichum lonchitis*. The grike flora is remarkably similar to that of the Carboniferous Limestone pavements in northern England, with woodland species such as *Paris quadrifolia*, *Hypericum androsaemum*, *Polystichum aculeatum*, *Phyllitis scolopendrium*, *Rubus saxatilis*, *Sanicula europaea* and *Allium ursinum*. *Cratoneuron commutatum* springs occur locally, and grade into open *Eriophorum latifolium–Carex hostiana* gravel flushes.

Coille Gaireallach is primarily a birch–hazel wood with heavily grazed field layer of *Agrostis–Anthoxanthum* grassland, grading to a forb-rich type. Small areas of ashwood with *Brachypodium sylvaticum* grassland occur around outcrops of limestone pavement, and there is an unusual feature in *Dryas* growing under trees in places. On ledges of a limestone gorge, some of the woodland forbs such as *Cirsium heterophyllum*, *Trollius europaeus*, *Crepis paludosa*, *Listera ovata*, *Geum rivale* and *Galium odoratum* grow ungrazed, and there are northern species such as *G. boreale*, *Melica nutans* and *Orthothecium rufescens*. On the granite of Beinn an Dubhaich there is a sudden change to birchwood with bilberry and heather communities, while non-wooded areas have a good deal of *Trichophorum cespitosum–Calluna* wet heath and mire, with oceanic mosses such as *Campylopus shawii* well represented.

The calcareous tarn, Loch Cill Chriosd, has stony margins with *Littorella uniflora*, *Baldellia ranunculoides*, *Myriophyllum alterniflorum*, *Potamogeton coloratus*, *P. gramineus* and *P. natans*. *Carex rostrata–Menyanthes trifoliata* stands form a marginal swamp in shallow water on deep organic muds, and there are small areas of mud-bottom communities with *C. lasiocarpa*, *C. limosa*, *C. rostrata*, *Sparganium minimum*, *Acrocladium giganteum* and *Scorpidium scorpioides*. In deeper water there are beds of *Phragmites communis* with *Nymphaea alba*, and *Schoenoplectus lacustris* with *Potamogeton lucens* forming an outer zone in deeper water. Extensive fen has developed around the main inflow at the western end of the loch, and consists largely of *C. rostrata*, *C. dioica* and *Eleocharis quinqueflora* with carpets of *Scorpidium scorpioides*, *Campylium stellatum*, *Drepanocladus revolvens* and *Sphagnum contortum*. This passes into soligenous soaks with *Schoenus nigricans*, *Eriophorum latifolium* and *Drosera anglica*, and one area poached by cattle has the characteristic open mud and gravel, with tufa and residual hummocks carrying a rich flora, e.g. *Carex lepidocarpa*, *Thalictrum alpinum* and *Dactylorchis purpurella*. This soligenous complex is remarkably similar to Great Close Mire at Malham, and some of the examples on 'sugar' limestone in Teesdale.

The rare lichen *Sticta canariensis* occurs on acidic rocks within the area.

U.74. NORTH HOY, ORKNEY
HY 2101. 2600 ha   Grade 1

The two adjacent hills, Ward Hill (479 m) and Cuilags (433 m), are composed of Old Red Sandstone, which varies from non-calcareous to strongly calcareous. There is a remarkable diversity of vegetation and flora for so limited an area. The coast bounding Cuilags on the west and north is a tremendous rampart of vertical cliff, with the great outlying stack, the Old Man of Hoy (137 m). The cliffs rise to one of the highest headlands in Britain at St John's Head (338 m). Vegetationally, the moorland above the cliffs is remarkable for the quality and extent of lichen heath, dominated by *Cladonias* of the reindeer moss group, and montane dwarf-shrub heath with *Calluna vulgaris*, *Loiseleuria procumbens*, *Arctostaphylos uva-ursi*, *Arctous alpina*,

Empetrum nigrum and *Salix herbacea*. The lichen heath is not only a particularly good example of this very local community, but is remarkable as a notably oceanic occurrence of an otherwise essentially continental vegetation type. Both communities occur also at unusually low elevations.

There are also low-level occurrences of well-developed ablation surface, and solifluction terraces with a very sparse plant cover, while gully formation is well shown on the north face. There is a patchy occurrence of species-poor *Rhacomitrium* heath and many communities here have *Rhacomitrium*-rich facies. Oceanic conditions are indicated even more strongly by the presence on steep, north-facing slopes of Callunetum with an abundance of montane Atlantic hepatics in the bryophyte layer such as *Herberta hutchinsiae*, *Jamesoniella carringtonii* and *Scapania ornithopodioides*. There is also fairly extensive blanket mire both at the foot of the hills and on the watershed plateaux.

On the north-east face of Ward Hill, the crags and screes are calcareous and carry a rich calcicolous montane flora, with *Dryas*, *Poa alpina*, *Polystichum lonchitis* and *Salix myrsinites*. Some species, e.g. *Saussurea alpina* and *Saxifraga aizoides*, are in great abundance. Several of these plants are here in their most northerly British stations. Yet the climate is still sufficiently mild to give an outpost for the thermophilous *Dryopteris aemula*.

The deep valley of Berriedale contains Orkney's only indigenous woodland, with willow, downy birch, aspen and rowan, all of which are regenerating well in the absence of heavy grazing pressure. There are several species of *Rosa* here, and also honeysuckle, and a number of fern species (notably the filmy fern) and a variety of oceanic liverworts. The ground flora of the wood is mainly bracken, *Calluna* and *Vaccinium*.

The long line of coastal cliff carries the densest breeding population of the peregrine now remaining in Britain, and there are considerable numbers of seabirds such as puffins, fulmars and rock doves, and this section is a grade 2 coastland site (C.94). The moorlands have colonies of great skuas (23 pairs) and great black-backed gulls (over 1000 pairs).

U.75. MILLDOE AND STARLING HILL, ORKNEY
HY 3523.   1800 ha   Grade 1

This typical area of Orkney moorland lies on the Mainland and forms the watershed for streams flowing both east and west. The hills are gently contoured and low, reaching only 221 m on Mid Tooin, and the valleys are wide, so that the underlying Old Red Sandstone is little exposed, except along stream sides. The vegetation is entirely submontane in character and very few alpine plants occur here, in contrast to the hills of North Hoy (U.74). There is a range of acidophilous types from dry heath and grassland, through wet heath to blanket mire, with slightly richer soligenous mires and flushes developed on ground affected by lateral water seepage.

The area is much modified by fire, grazing and peat-cutting, so that the vegetation has a rather heterogeneous

character. Typical dry Callunetum is rather sparse, but there are mixed heaths with *Calluna*, *Erica cinerea*, *Empetrum nigrum* and *Potentilla erecta*, and extensive mixtures of *Calluna* with *Trichophorum cespitosum* or *Eriophorum vaginatum*. The blanket mire is essentially the *Calluna–Eriophorum* type, but much modified, with local abundance or dominance of species such as *Sphagnum* spp., *Narthecium ossifragum*, *E. angustifolium*, *Juncus squarrosus*, *Nardus stricta*, *Rhacomitrium lanuginosum*, other mosses, and lichens. In one place the vegetation has been modified by a gull colony and includes species such as *Rumex acetosa* and *J. conglomeratus*. The watershed has a number of pools, up to 90 m across, and there is a large colony of *Carex limosa* in the Bog of Surtan.

Soligenous mire communities include base-poor types with *Juncus* spp., *Carex rostrata*, *C. nigra*, *C. echinata*, *Hydrocotyle vulgaris*, *Potentilla palustris*, and *Sphagnum* carpets, and these occur on some of the ground affected by peat-cutting. In the Dale of Cottascarth there are calcareous flushes showing a little tufa formation and containing species such as *Thalictrum alpinum*, *Schoenus nigricans*, *Eleocharis quinqueflora*, *C. hostiana*, *C. dioica* and 'brown mosses'. Some of the adjoining mires show the influence of this richer water. A distinctive feature of the damper ground is the occurrence of a patchy willow scrub, mainly of *Salix cinerea* and *S. aurita*. The rocky sides of the cascading streams have in places a luxuriant vegetation of tall herbs and ferns, including *Valeriana officinalis*, *Geum rivale*, *Chamaenerion angustifolium*, *Dryopteris filix-mas* and *D. dilatata*. The flora of the area includes local Orkney plants such as *Botrychium lunaria*, *Listera ovata* and *L. cordata*.

These Orkney moorlands are famous for their birds of prey. This is still a stronghold of hen harrier, which during the earlier part of this century was almost confined to Orkney and the Outer Hebrides in Britain, and the merlin is probably now as numerous here as anywhere in the country. Orkney is the only part of Britain where kestrels regularly nest on the ground, and it is a celebrated area for short-eared owls. All four species are represented within the site. There are other typical moorland birds such as golden plover, stonechat and red-throated divers on the dubh lochans, and a colony of black-headed gulls.

U.76. KEEN OF HAMAR, UNST, SHETLAND
HP 6409.   420 ha   Grade 1

This hill is famous botanically, and makes an interesting contrast with the other major outcrop of serpentine in the extreme south of England, on the Lizard, and with the more limited exposures inland in Aberdeenshire. There are two main types of serpentine vegetation here: first, a closed heath of short heather, grasses and small herbs, generally species rich, but with few or no montane plants; secondly, a fell-field type of open community on bare serpentine debris, locally flushed with water. Montane species are conspicuous and include *Silene acaulis*, *Cardaminopsis petraea*, *Arenaria norvegica* and *Cerastium edmondstonii*. Part of the fell-field community has recently been converted to a grass sward by application of fertilisers and seeds mixture in an attempt at agricultural improvement. The success of this treatment suggests that the open nature of the debris results largely from a nutrient deficiency. The closed serpentine heath is interesting floristically, as a variant of the local northern species-rich Callunetum on basic soils. It contains a large number of species including *Antennaria dioica*, *Potentilla erecta*, *Lotus corniculatus*, *Thymus drucei*, *Agrostis canina*, *Festuca vivipara*, *F. ovina*, *Plantago lanceolata*, *P. maritima*, *Carex flacca*, *C. pulicaris*, *Anthyllis vulneraria*, *Gentianella campestris*, *Thalictrum alpinum*, *Scilla verna*, *Selaginella selaginoides* and *Succisa pratensis*. There are some wet gravelly flushed areas with *Schoenus nigricans*, *C. demissa*, *Armeria maritima*, *Molinia caerulea* and *Eleocharis quinqueflora*.

The serpentine of adjacent areas has a different appearance, and instead of bare debris there are numerous outcrops, exposed bosses of bedrock, and embedded blocks. The ground between mostly has a closed community, but the serpentine grass heath here often has fewer basiphilous species than on the Keen of Hamar, and a greater abundance of plants such as *Narthecium ossifragum*. Some of this ground on Muckle Heog is included in the grade 1 site.

U.77. NORTH FETLAR, SHETLAND

HU 6293. 1800 ha   Grade 1

This island contains the second main area of serpentine in Shetland, and the northern part is regarded as an alternative botanical site to the Keen of Hamar, though it lacks the open debris with a rich flora, and the vegetation consists mainly of closed grass heath. On ornithological grounds, however, it is rated as a grade 1 site in its own right. The area has become famous from 1967 onwards as the first and only breeding place of the snowy owl in Britain. There are also tarns and associated mires with fairly base-rich water, and these are the main British breeding haunt of the red-necked phalarope. Fetlar is an important nesting place of whimbrel, great skua (200–300 pairs), Arctic skua (200+ pairs – the largest British colony), puffin (thousands of pairs) and fulmar (13 000 pairs for the whole island). Other breeding birds of note include peregrine, twite, corncrake, black guillemot, storm petrel and Manx shearwater.

U.78. HERMANESS, UNST, SHETLAND

HP 6016. 964 ha   Grade 1

There is maritime grassland along the cliff tops, but most of the peninsula is covered with acidic grassland (mainly *Nardus* and *Juncus squarrosus*), dry dwarf-shrub heath (*Calluna* and *Vaccinium*, with grasses), damp heath and blanket mire, fairly typical of Shetland. The blanket mire has an abundance of hummocks of *Sphagnum nemoreum* and *S. papillosum*; *Molinia* and *Trichophorum* are less abundant than in most western Highland blanket mires, but there is more *Eriophorum angustifolium*. *Rhacomitrium lanuginosum* dominance is characteristic of much of the Shetland blanket mire and wet heath, but is less marked on Hermaness than in many other areas. *Rubus chamaemorus* does not occur, and on the whole, the Shetland mires and heaths are poor

in peat alpines. Base-poor soligenous mires and flushes with *Sphagnum* carpets are frequent.

The cliff-bound west coast and its stacks are important breeding haunts of gannets, shags, guillemots, razorbills, puffins, kittiwakes and fulmars, whilst the moorlands above have colonies of great skuas (300 pairs) and Arctic skuas (40–50 pairs), and several pairs of red-throated divers. Other breeding birds include whimbrel, Shetland wren, twite, golden plover and dunlin. Shetland is noted for the occurrence of local dark forms of certain widespread moths, and many of these occur on Hermaness. They include the northern rustic *Standfussiana lucernea*, autumnal rustic *Paradiarsia glareosa* var. *edda*, square-spot rustic *Xestia xanthographa*, and the rarer Arctic northern arches *Apamea exulis*.

See also C.92.

U.79. BEN NEVIS, INVERNESS-SHIRE

NN 1970. 6150 ha   Grade 2

This massif lies at the western edge of the Grampians, immediately south of the Great Glen. Ben Nevis, a mountain of granite and andesite, is the highest ground in Britain (1344 m), has the tallest cliffs (600 m in Coire Leis) and carries the only semi-permanent snow-beds outside the Cairngorms. It shows important glacial erosion features and the summit might be described as a site of climatological importance, in view of the unique series of recordings made by the former Meteorological Observatory. Ben Nevis and its eastern neighbours, Aonach Mor (1220 m) and Aonach Beag (1236 m), are also the only *c.* 1220 m peaks outside the Cairngorms. Aonach Mor and Aonach Beag are composed of rocks of the Moine Series, in which bands of calcareous schist outcrop quite extensively at high levels. There are also highly localised occurrences of calcareous rock in the predominantly acidic mass of Ben Nevis itself.

The lower slopes of these hills have been heavily grazed and burned, so that *Calluna* heaths and other dwarf-shrub communities have largely been replaced by swards of *Molinia* and *Trichophorum*. The terrain is mostly too steep for blanket mire, but there is a wide range of soligenous mires. The summit of Ben Nevis is rather small and covered largely with boulder fields, whilst the upper levels are mostly block scree or cliff; this gives a rather limited range of montane vegetation though *Nardus stricta*, *Rhacomitrium lanuginosum*, *Vaccinium* spp. and *Empetrum hermaphroditum* are prominent in various mixtures. Some of the snow-bed communities, including the *Rhytidiadelphus–Deschampsia cespitosa* and very late *Polytrichum norvegicum–Dicranum starkei* type, are well represented. The high montane plants of poor soils in the Cairngorms mostly occur here, e.g. *Luzula arcuata*, *Poa flexuosa*, *Carex lachenalii*, *Deschampsia alpina*, *Cerastium cerastoides*, *Veronica alpina* and *Saxifraga rivularis*. Late snow-bed bryophytes (see p. 269 for list) are well represented and include the very rare *Marsupella boeckii*.

The summits of Aonach Mor and Aonach Beag are also rather small in area, but there is *Rhacomitrium lanuginosum* heath which shows an interesting variant dominated by *R. canescens* in one place where there is heavy wind deposition of soil particles. Where seepage from the calcareous schists influences the upper slopes there are good examples of calcicolous communities characteristic of the Breadalbane range, such as dwarf swards with carpets of *Silene acaulis*, *Carex saxatilis* marshes and open flushes with *Juncus biglumis*. Most of the widespread montane calcicoles of Breadalbane occur within the site, and the total flora is rich. Some of the rare species are scattered, and they include *Saxifraga cernua*, *S. cespitosa* (both growing with *S. rivularis* in one place), *Myosotis alpestris*, *Cystopteris montana*, *Salix reticulata* and *Dryas octopetala*. The bryophyte flora is rich, including northern Atlantic species, and both calcifuge and calcicole elements in the high montane group.

U.80. CREAG MEAGAIDH, INVERNESS-SHIRE
NN 4187. 7250 ha   Grade 2

Creag Meagaidh (1128 m) is the highest point of a massif lying immediately north of Loch Laggan and is famous for its magnificent north-eastern corrie, Coire Ardair, walled with 300 m gullied cliffs. It is formed of rocks of the Moine Series, which are here mainly acidic schists and granulites with only moderately calcareous beds locally. The vegetation is very similar to that of the Ben Alder and Aonach Mor massif (U.61) about 16 km to the south, but there is less dwarf-shrub heath at the lower levels, and the calcicolous flora is less rich.

Patchy birchwood and some plantations of Scots pine occur on the southern slopes, which appear to have been heavily grazed and burned, giving a rather limited and patchy distribution of heather communities. There is a considerable extent of submontane grassland of very varied character, from *Agrostis–Festuca* on well-drained slopes, through *Nardus* and *Juncus squarrosus* types to *Molinia* and *Trichophorum* communities which grade into both *Carex* soligenous and *Eriophorum* blanket mire. The influence of base-rich flush water is apparent in many places, giving forb-rich facies of these grasslands and soligenous mires, and there are open *Saxifraga aizoides* flushes locally. Late-snow areas have montane *Nardus* and *Juncus squarrosus* communities, and *Deschampsia cespitosa* grasslands are extensive on the high corrie slopes. *Vaccinium myrtillus* and *Vaccinium–Empetrum* communities are well represented at higher levels, and on steep ground there is a good deal of *Vaccinium–Empetrum* heath with much *Rhacomitrium lanuginosum* and *Alchemilla alpina*.

Dwarf Callunetum is represented rather locally on windswept upper spurs mainly at the Carn Liath end of the range (east) and there grades either into somewhat eroded high level *Eriophorum vaginatum* bog or into extensive, species-poor *Rhacomitrium–Carex bigelowii* heath on hummocky ground. Creag Meagaidh has a broad summit plateau with a large area above 970 m, but this is covered mainly with *Carex bigelowii* sward with much *Dicranum fuscescens* and *Polytrichum alpinum*, or by short *Deschampsia cespitosa* grassland, and there is little *Rhacomitrium* or *Juncus trifidus* heath here. *J. trifidus* communities are better developed on lower ground to the north of the main summit.

A high col at 1036 m has a pocket of blanket mire at an unusual altitude. A notable feature of this range is the good representation of late-snow communities, including the late *Alchemilla–Sibbaldia* and *P. norvegicum–Dicranum starkei* types, and even more the associated spring and flush bryophyte carpets with numerous species. Carpets of *Pohlia albicans* var. *glacialis* occur, and the flora of these habitats includes *Cerastium cerastoides*, *Deschampsia alpina*, *Alopecurus alpinus* and *Sphagnum lindbergii*.

Where there are base-rich rocks in the corries, the cliffs and slopes have some of the widespread calcicolous communities and species. The ungrazed ledges have good tall-herb stands with the usual species, and similar communities at lower levels have *Vicia sylvatica* and *Cirsium heterophyllum*. *Salix lapponum* ledges are well developed in one corrie. There are forb-rich *Deschampsia cespitosa* grasslands beneath the cliffs, and *Carex saxatilis* flushes with *Juncus castaneus* and *Phleum alpinum* occur in at least one place. The basic rocks have many of the more widespread montane calcicoles, and there are local species such as *Saxifraga nivalis*, *C. atrata*, *C. vaginata*, *Poa alpina* (non-viviparous), *P. glauca*, *P. balfourii*, *Cerastium alpinum* and *Tofieldia pusilla*. Acidic rocks in one place have *Gnaphalium norvegicum*, and *Veronica alpina* is apparently indifferent to base-status.

U.81. BIDEAN NAM BIAN, ARGYLL
NN 1555. 1750 ha   Grade 2

This mountain (1141 m), forming the southern side of Glen Coe, is scenically magnificent and geomorphologically classic, with abrupt truncated spurs separated by hanging valleys which drain from the high corries. It is formed largely of lavas and agglomerates of Old Red Sandstone age, but they vary greatly in lithology. The great cliffs of these spurs are of hard, acidic rhyolite and are much frequented by climbers, but there are numerous outcrops of calcareous andesite, which give a rich flora. Some of the lower ledges and ravine sides have vestiges of birch and rowan wood, but all the more accessible lower slopes have been heavily grazed by sheep and are covered with grassland mixtures of *Festuca–Agrostis* and *Nardus*. Locally there is much bracken and *Trichophorum*, *Molinia*, *Sphagnum* and *Potentilla erecta* on damper ground. *Calluna* and *Vaccinium myrtillus* are generally poor but grow luxuriantly on ungrazed ledges. In places there is species-rich *Festuca–Agrostis* grassland, and the 'Lost Valley' has much *Festuca–Thymus* grassland with *Rhacomitrium canescens* on alluvial soils.

Higher on the slopes this submontane complex passes to good *Vaccinium–Empetrum* heath, and on the ridges of the Three Sisters there is a great deal of the western variant of this type, in which the dwarf shrubs share dominance with *Nardus* and *Rhacomitrium lanuginosum*. Steep ground has the alpine *Festuca–Vaccinium* grass heath with *Alchemilla alpina* and *Rhacomitrium*, and this merges with patchy *Rhacomitrium* heath on the upper ridges. The summit areas are too small to have an extensive development of this last community.

The high corries have a great deal of species-poor *Deschampsia cespitosa* grassland, and there are both *Nardus* and *Nardus–Trichophorum* snow-bed grasslands in more definite hollows. Other late snow communities include the *Cryptogramma–Athyrium, Sibbaldia–Alchemilla, Rhytidiadelphus–Deschampsia* and *Rhacomitrium–Dicranum starkei* types and in the highest corrie, rocky hollows and gullies with late snow cover have much mixed bryophyte-dominated vegetation from dry to spring and flush types.

The calcareous cliffs, which occur from near the foot of the mountain to the actual summit, have a rich montane flora with most of the widespread calcicoles characteristic of Breadalbane mica-schist hills, together with a number of rare and local species, notably *Saxifraga cernua, S. rivularis, S. nivalis, Draba norvegica, Cystopteris montana, Juncus biglumis, Cerastium arcticum, C. alpinum* and *Poa alpina*. Many of the more common species are in profusion and tall herb communities are well represented. *Deschampsia alpina* is common on both acidic and basic rocks and many calcifuge alpines are abundant. From its western position this mountain has a large number of oceanic bryophytes, and some of the lower ledges have good fragments of the northern Atlantic liverwort community so widespread in the north-west Highlands. The deep, block-filled stream ravine of Allt Coire Ghabhail provides a wide range of bryophyte and fern habitats, and there are fine growths of *Hymenophyllum wilsonii*.

The adjacent but much lower hill Meall Mor (675 m) has extensive outcrops of Dalradian limestone, with an abundance of calcicoles, including *Dryas, Salix myrsinites* and *Thalictrum minus*, and there is a large area of rich grassland. These two hills are complementary ecologically and have been treated as a single area.

U.82. DUN BAN, KINTYRE, ARGYLL
NR 5915.   90 ha   Grade 2

This site is of considerable interest for its flora and is the most southerly place in Britain where a group of montane species may be seen growing close to sea-level. This rugged coast shows precipitous outcrops of calcareous Dalradian rocks rising up to 150 m or more above the sea. The calcicoles include *Dryas octopetala, Anthyllis vulneraria, Saxifraga oppositifolia, Sedum rosea* and an *Oxytropis* which appears to be intermediate between *O. halleri* and *O. campestris*. Other interesting species occurring in tall-herb cliff ledge associations are *Vicia sylvatica, Solanum dulcamara, Phyllitis scolopendrium* and *Saxifraga aizoides*. There is also an abundance of sea cliff halophytes such as *Silene maritima, Tripleurospermum maritimum* and *Asplenium marinum*. Probably the extreme wind exposure of this coast has, by preventing the formation of closed woodland, provided a low-lying refugium for these competition-sensitive plants. This coast also has the most southerly sea cliff nesting pairs of the golden eagle, also a somewhat montane species in Britain, but this bird probably owes its presence to the large expanses of moorland hunting grounds which extend back for several kilometres from the top of the cliffs.

U.83. AFFRIC–CANNICH HILLS, INVERNESS-SHIRE–ROSS
NH 1630.   17 000 ha   Grade 2

This area contains the highest hills north of the Great Glen, namely, Carn Eige (1182 m) and Mam Soul (1177 m) forming the high ridge between Glens Affric and Cannich, and Sgurr na Lapaich (1150 m) north of Cannich. These two groups are both formed of rocks of the Moine Series and are so similar that they are best described together. Climatically and vegetationally, the area is intermediate between the Beinn Dearg-Seana Bhraigh massif (U.62) and either the western Grampians or the Cairngorms (U.44). It is less oceanic than the extreme western ranges of the northern Highlands, such as Beinn Eighe–Liathach (U.64), but more oceanic than Ben Wyvis (U.63). Although of considerable importance for its full and representative range of vegetation, it has few if any features not represented on one or other of the grade 1 sites mentioned.

The lower slopes have a typical complex of western Highland submontane dry heath to blanket mire with Callunetum, *Trichophorum–Calluna* and *Molinia–Calluna* wet heath, *Eriophorum–Trichophorum* mire, and soligenous mires of the *Molinia–Myrica, Carex–Sphagnum* and *Juncus effusus* types. Examples of base-rich grassland, soligenous mire and open flush occur in various places. Higher up, on windswept shoulders and lower summits there are extensive areas of montane dwarf Callunetum of the shrub, lichen and *Rhacomitrium* rich facies, showing a good deal of the wave-eroded form. These pass into blanket mires of the *Calluna–Eriophorum vaginatum* type, and at over 760 m the *Empetrum–Vaccinium* facies of this community is represented. *Empetrum–Vaccinium* heaths occur, but there is a greater extent of the mixed type in which these species share dominance with *Nardus* and *Rhacomitrium lanuginosum*. *Rhacomitrium–Empetrum* communities also occur on rocky ground. There are patches of *Vaccinium–Alchemilla* grassland, and in the high corries *Deschampsia cespitosa* grassland is locally extensive.

These hills carry a great deal of long-lasting snow, and the communities of the latest snow-beds are finely developed. On the high slopes there is a large extent of mixed *Nardus*-rich vegetation and the western *Rhytidiadelphus–Deschampsia cespitosa* type, whilst the corries have very good examples of *Cryptogramma crispa–Athyrium alpestre* fern beds, *Sibbaldia procumbens–Alchemilla alpina* patches with various *Rhacomitrium* spp. and *Gnaphalium supinum, Dicranum starkei–Polytrichum norvegicum* moss heath, and spring communities with *Pohlia albicans* var. *glacialis, Anthelia* spp. and mixed bryophytes. High montane calcifuge and indifferent species, especially those associated with prolonged snow cover, are well represented in this area, e.g. vascular plants such as *Gnaphalium norvegicum, Luzula arcuata, Cerastium cerastoides, Carex saxatilis, Deschampsia alpina*, and bryophytes such as *Moerckia blyttii, Pleuroclada albescens, Dicranum falcatum, Conostomum tetragonum, Sphagnum lindbergii* and *S. riparium*. Northern Atlantic liverworts are quite abundant, with most of the distinctive species, but the community with all these plants growing luxuriantly together is less well represented here than on many western hills.

By contrast, since only very limited exposures of calcareous rock have been found, the montane calcicole flora is much less rich, and does not compare with that of Beinn Dearg, farther north. Many of the more widespread species occur, and there are a few more local ones, such as *Phleum alpinum*, *Salix lapponum*, *Draba incana* and *Juncus castaneus*. Similarly, the high summits and ridges do not cover a large area, and whilst species-rich *Rhacomitrium* heath is better developed than in most districts to the south, it is not as fine or extensive as on other hills farther north in Ross and Sutherland. Some of the *Rhacomitrium* heath is the species-poor *Carex bigelowii* type, but *Silene acaulis* and *Armeria maritima* are locally abundant. There is a good deal of stony ablation surface and solifluction terracing on the high tops, and a species-poor facies of the very open *J. trifidus* heath occurs here. Accumulations of deep, sandy soil to the leeward have a mossy *Nardus–Deschampsia cespitosa* community, but show secondary erosion.

See also W.204.

U.84. FANNICH HILLS, ROSS
NH 2271. 9550 ha — Grade 2

This massif lies immediately to the south of Beinn Dearg–Seana Bhraigh, and could be regarded as an alternative site. The rock again belongs wholly to the Moine Series, and varies from acidic to calcareous. The highest summit, Sgurr Mor Fannich (1109 m), slightly exceeds Beinn Dearg in altitude, but the high ridges are narrower and the summits more peaked, lacking the broad plateaux, compared with the neighbouring massif, so that some montane communities are less well developed. The flora also appears to be less rich in calcicoles.

The lower ground has much the same range of submontane heath and mire communities as the Beinn Dearg area, with some *Calluna* heath, but larger areas where heather is co-dominant with *Trichophorum*. There are tracts of *Trichophorum–Eriophorum* and *Calluna–Eriophorum* blanket mire, with much *Rhacomitrium lanuginosum* and local abundance of *Betula nana*. There is a more patchy distribution of *Agrostis–Anthoxanthum*, *Nardus*, *Juncus squarrosus*, and *Carex–Sphagnum* communities, but some parts of the Fannichs have a good deal of this grassland complex. Dwarf Callunetum with *Arctous alpina* and other montane dwarf shrubs occurs on the higher moraines, and *Rhacomitrium–Empetrum* heath is luxuriant on cliff tops. *Vaccinium–Empetrum* heath occurs mainly on block strewn slopes, but the mixed community with these species, *Nardus* and *Rhacomitrium* is widespread, and there are good *Nardus* patches. *Deschampsia cespitosa* grassland is well developed in the corries, and there is a fairly full range of late snow-bed communities, with extensive *Rhytidiadelphus* moss heath, and more patchy occurrence of *Alchemilla–Sibbaldia*, *Cryptogramma–Athyrium* and *Polytrichum norvegicum–Dicranum starkei* communities, with associated bryophyte springs and flushes.

On the high watersheds there is a great deal of species-rich *Rhacomitrium* heath with great profusion of *Silene acaulis*, and much *Cherleria sedoides* and *Armeria maritima*. Flushed areas here have a still greater variety of small forbs and mosses, e.g. *Sibbaldia*, *Polygonum viviparum* and *Aulacomnium turgidum*. There are fine systems of solifluction terraces in places, such as the summit slopes of Sgurr Mor Fannich, and these have the open *Juncus trifidus*–herb community which also occurs on more extensive ablation surfaces along the high ridges.

The cliffs have some of the more widespread montane calcicoles, and there is a variable development of tall herb communities with *Trollius europaeus* on the bigger ledges. The flora has not been examined fully, but the more notable species are known to include *Gnaphalium norvegicum*, *Carex saxatilis*, *C. atrata* and *Juncus castaneus*. All the northern Atlantic hepatics of the western Highlands occur here, and they are present locally as a carpet in association with other communities, such as *Vaccinium–Empetrum* heath. Bryophytes of late snow-beds are also well represented.

U.85. MONAR FOREST, ROSS
NH 1345. 5500 ha — Grade 2

This site includes the part of the extensive ranges of Moine Schist hills south of Strath Carron containing Sgurr a'Chaorachain (1052 m) and Maoile Lunndaidh (1007 m). The lower slopes of these hills have little dwarf-shrub heath and are covered mainly with a complex of acidic grassland and soligenous mire, including types with *Agrostis–Anthoxanthum*, *Nardus*, *Juncus squarrosus*, *Trichophorum*, *Molinia* and *Carex echinata–C. nigra*. The higher slopes and corries have extensive *Deschampsia cespitosa* grasslands. There are occurrences of montane dwarf Callunetum with both *Rhacomitrium* and *Loiseleuria–Arctous* facies, and of both *Calluna* and *Vaccinium–Empetrum* heath rich in northern Atlantic liverworts. There is one example of bilberry snow-bed heath, but the mixed type with this species, *Empetrum*, *Nardus* and *Rhacomitrium*, is much more extensive, and on rocky ground is good *Rhacomitrium–Empetrum* heath.

Virtually the full range of late snow-bed communities is represented, though the latest types are fragmentary, e.g. *Cryptogramma–Athyrium*, *Dicranum starkei–Polytrichum norvegicum* and *Pohlia albicans* var. *glacialis* communities. *Rhytidiadelphus* moss heath is extensive and there are good examples of *Alchemilla–Sibbaldia* patches in the high corries. Some of the cliffs are moderately basic, and there are good tall-herb ledge communities with *Cirsium heterophyllum*, *Sedum rosea* and *Saussurea alpina*. Forb-rich grasslands occur on grazed ground below the cliffs.

The most important vegetational feature of the area is the extensive occurrence on the high summits and spurs of species-rich *Rhacomitrium lanuginosum* heath. In places this has a high cover of *Silene acaulis* and *Armeria maritima*, with an abundance of other forbs such as *Polygonum viviparum*, *Alchemilla alpina*, *Sibbaldia procumbens*, *Thalictrum alpinum*, *Saussurea alpina*, *Achillea millefolium*,

Ranunculus acris; *Thymus drucei*, grasses, and mosses, including *Hypnum hamulosum* and *Aulacomnium turgidum*. This approaches the dwarf-herb swards of intermittently flushed ground locally, and there are transitions also to rich *Rhytidiadelphus* moss heath, mixed *Saxifraga oppositifolia–S. aizoides* banks and open flushes with these species. On drier and more wide exposed flats there are also transitions to open stony ablation surfaces, with a mixture of a species-rich *Juncus trifidus* open community and the *Salix herbacea–Gymnomitrion concinnatum* crust. There are examples of solifluction hummocks and ridges, and in places, deep brown soils have formed through deposition of eroded material.

The flora of this area is not rich compared with that of Beinn Dearg (U.62) to the north, but there is at least one notable species in *Luzula arcuata*, and *Deschampsia alpina* and *Carex saxatilis* are represented. The area has not, however, been fully explored botanically.

U.86. BEN HOPE, SUTHERLAND
NC 4849.   2700 ha   Grade 2

Ben Hope (927 m) is an isolated mountain of Moine Schist and granulite rising abruptly from the low moorlands of northern Sutherland. Its western base, at the south end of Loch Hope, rises almost from sea-level in a steep slope partly covered with birchwood and breaking out into high cliffs. Above this is a platform with a tarn at about 300 m, and then the main mass of the hill rises in a tremendous escarpment right to the summit. On the east side are two rocky corries, sloping away below more gradually into the boggy moorlands towards A'Mhoine and the Kyle of Tongue.

On the lower western slopes, burning and grazing have greatly reduced the heather and so the vegetation is largely a mixture of modified *Trichophorum* and *Molinia* communities with soligenous mire. On really wet ground up to 300 m or so there is the western *Eriophorum–Trichophorum* blanket mire, but at higher levels this is replaced by the *Calluna–Eriophorum* community. On the middle level slopes on the north east side of Ben Hope Callunetum is more extensive, occurring up to 685 m, and there are examples of the montane prostrate type with other dwarf shrubs and *Rhacomitrium lanuginosum* on severely wind-swept ground. This passes in the corries to *Empetrum–Vaccinium* and *Rhacomitrium–Empetrum* heaths, which have great quantities of the usual northern Atlantic hepatics on shady aspects. There are transitions from these communities to the mixed type also containing abundant *Nardus*, and *Deschampsia cespitosa* is also abundant on flushed ground. The latest snow-bed communities do not occur on Ben Hope, but there is a good representation of *Rhytidiadelphus–Deschampsia*, *Nardus* and *Nardus–Rhacomitrium* types in these corries and on the upper slopes.

The sloping summit and tops of the upper spurs have a great deal of bare, stony ablation surface indicating extreme wind exposure, and bearing an extremely sparse vegetation with *Juncus trifidus* and *Arctous alpina*. There are patches of species-poor *Rhacomitrium* heath, but despite the local

abundance of *Silene acaulis*, *Cherleria sedoides* and *Armeria maritima* in mixed moss–*Empetrum* heath along the crest of the western escarpment, there is no significant occurrence of the species-rich facies on the summit areas.

The most important ecological feature of Ben Hope is the occurrence of a thick horizontal band of calcareous hornblende–schist which traverses the predominantly granulite western escarpment at mid level (*c.* 600 m). The exposures of this rock give the second richest assemblage of montane calcicoles in the northern Highlands (after Beinn Dearg–Seana Bhraigh), and the downwash of bases produces relatively rich swards on the steep slopes and ledges below. On parts of the escarpment accessible to deer and sheep, there is a large extent of a herb-rich *Deschampsia cespitosa* grassland containing numerous grazed-down plants such as *Angelica sylvestris*, *Geum rivale*, *Ranunculus acris* and *Trollius europaeus* which suggests a derivation from tall-herb ledge communities. There are transitions from this grassland to a *Vaccinium myrtillus–Luzula sylvatica* community with fewer species as the flush influence wanes. Examples of moss- or herb-rich *Anthoxanthum–Agrostis* grassland are also represented.

The calcareous schist is a soft, crumbling rock and perhaps because of surface leaching, the outcrops have an unusual mixture of species. In places, a mat of *Empetrum hermaphroditum*, short *Calluna*, *Rhacomitrium lanuginosum* and hypnaceous mosses is mixed with an abundance of *Dryas octopetala*, *Silene acaulis* and *Saxifraga oppositifolia*. On steeper and barer faces calcicoles take over, and most of the widespread montane species are present. The more notable plants include *Draba rupestris*, *S. nivalis*, *Cerastium alpinum*, *Salix reticulata*, *S. lapponum*, *Potentilla crantzii*, *Cardaminopsis petraea*, *Polystichum lonchitis*, and the mosses *Orthothecium rufescens*, *Rhytidium rugosum* and *Pseudoleskea catenulata*. There is an old record for *Minuartia rubella*. Several of these species are here in their northern-most British stations. Tall-herb communities of ungrazed ledges are less luxuriant and rather more mixed than those of Meall Horn (U.65) to the west.

U.87. BEN KLIBRECK, SUTHERLAND
NC 6029.   11 000 ha   Grade 2

This isolated mountain of Moine Schist rises abruptly from the great expanses of blanket mire at the head of Strath Naver, north of Lairg, and its conical summit reaches 961 m. Vegetationally it is similar to Ben Wyvis (U.63), but with a slightly more oceanic character, and a lesser development of high-level montane vegetation. There are corries on the south-east side of the long spine of the mountain but their cliffs are not particularly lime-rich and the flora is rather limited.

The lower blanket mires are the western *Eriophorum–Trichophorum–Molinia* type, changing to *Calluna–Trichophorum* on less wet ground and at higher levels *Calluna–E. vaginatum*, with much *Rubus chamaemorus* and, more locally, *Betula nana* and *Arctous alpina*. Dry ground has *Calluna* heath, with some bilberry in sheltered places, and this changes to prostrate *Calluna* mat on windswept moraines and shoulders above 460 m reaching a variable upper limit at 670–780 m. There are good examples here of the mixed dwarf-shrub heath with *Arctous, Loiseleuria procumbens* and abundant lichens. *Rhacomitrium* heath is well represented on dry exposed ground above 670 m, and varies from an *Empetrum hermaphroditum*-rich type on the south top, through the typical community with *Carex bigelowii* to a *Cherleria sedoides* facies on the main summit.

There is extensive solifluction terracing on the summit slopes, and the *Juncus trifidus–Festuca vivipara* community of erosion surfaces is well represented. Solifluction hummocks and ridges, with associated vegetation patterns, also occur in places.

Moss heaths of the latest snow-beds are apparently lacking, but there are examples of *Hylocomium* moss heath, *Alchemilla alpina–Sibbaldia procumbens* patches, *Nardus* and *Empetrum*-hypnaceous moss communities. The western *Nardus–Rhacomitrium* and mixed *Nardus–Vaccinium–Empetrum–Rhacomitrium* (or hypnaceous moss) communities are well developed. Shallow blanket mire extends well up the slopes and is mixed in high corries with more soligenous *Sphagnum* communities and acidic bryophyte springs. *Juncus squarrosus* is locally abundant in many of the wetter areas, and the peat alpines include *Vaccinium uliginosum* and *Chamaepericlymenum suecicum*.

Basic rocks have some of the more widespread calcicolous alpines such as *Saxifraga oppositifolia, S. aizoides, Saussurea alpina, Sedum rosea, Juncus triglumis* and *Thalictrum alpinum*. Tall-herb communities with *Trollius europaeus* occur on the richer cliff ledges. The bryophyte flora is only moderately rich and some of western species are apparently absent or scarce, but species such as *Pleurozia purpurea, Sphagnum strictum* and *S. imbricatum* are well represented in the lower blanket mires and wet heaths.

U.88. BEINN BHAN, APPLECROSS, ROSS
NG 8045. 4200 ha   Grade 2

The massif of Beinn Bhan (895 m) with its outlier, Sgurr a'Chaorachain (776 m), is a spectacular Torridonian Sandstone mountain group, with several deep corries and high cliffs. The general range of vegetation is similar to that of Liathach (U.64) to the north but, although Beinn Bhan is lower, its larger summit area gives a better representation of montane communities of exposed ground compared with most of the sharp-ridged Torridon hills.

The lower slopes have a highly modified complex of the usual western *Calluna–Trichophorum* and *Calluna–Molinia* communities, and there is little of particular importance until the corries are reached. The most interesting feature, in Coire na Poite, is a huge sloping corrie ledge measuring about 229 × 45 m and sealed-off from grazing animals by cliff above and below. This ledge carries a remnant of completely original, unmodified vegetation, consisting of dense and luxuriant sheets of ferns which give way to equally profuse growths of tall herbs in streaks and patches, where downward seepage of water produces soil enrichment. The fern community is dominated in places by

Athyrium alpestre, and other abundant species include *Thelypteris oreopteris, Dryopteris austriaca, D. abbreviata, Blechnum spicant* and *Rumex acetosa*. This community is reminiscent of the field layer of birchwoods on base-poor soils in oceanic parts of south-west Norway. The tall-herb stands on the flushed soils have *Ranunculus acris, Caltha palustris, Trollius europaeus, Rumex acetosa, Geum rivale, Crepis paludosa, Alchemilla glabra, Valeriana officinalis, Filipendula ulmaria, Angelica sylvestris, Sedum rosea, Saussurea alpina* and *Rubus saxatilis*. In places the fern-beds have patches of a subordinate *Vaccinium myrtillus–Luzula sylvatica* community with very fine *Chamaepericlymenum suecicum*.

In contrast to the luxuriant ledge vegetation, the corrie slopes below the cliffs are mostly scree, with patchy development of herb-poor and herb-rich facies of *Deschampsia cespitosa* grassland, which obviously correspond to the fern and tall-herb communities and suggest that these grassland types are biotic derivatives. Elsewhere, shady block screes and rocky slopes have good examples of *Calluna–Vaccinium* and *Vaccinium–Empetrum* heath with profuse development of the northern Atlantic liverwort mats described for Liathach (U.64) and containing all the characteristic species. There are extensive areas of mixed *Nardus–Vaccinium–Empetrum–Rhacomitrium* grass heath on the upper slopes, and *Rhacomitrium* heath occurs on the summits. *Cryptogramma crispa* is plentiful on screes and not confined to areas of late snow-lie – a feature probably reflecting proximity to the west coast. The Torridonian Sandstone of Beinn Bhan appears to have more strongly calcareous beds than is usual on this formation and the cliff flora appears to be at least as rich as that of Liathach, though it is incompletely studied. Basiphilous mosses are well represented, including the strongly Atlantic *Leptodontium recurvifolium*.

U.89. AN TEALLACH, ROSS
NH 0785. 5050 ha   Grade 2

Scenically, the heavily glaciated Torridonian Sandstone mass of An Teallach (1062 m) above Dundonnell is one of the finest mountains in Britain. The spectacular geological features include deep corries lined by cliffs up to 300 m high, and narrow, jagged summit ridges. In vegetational features, An Teallach is rather similar to Liathach (U.64) farther south. The summit areas are small, so that only a limited range of high-level vegetation is present. The approaches have *Calluna–Trichophorum* heath on drier moraines and *Trichophorum–Eriophorum* blanket mire on wetter ground. The dry and rocky lower slopes have mixtures of ericaceous heath, with *Calluna, Vaccinium–Empetrum* or *Vaccinium* alone, or with all three types intergrading. *Rhacomitrium lanuginosum* is abundant and in places, especially in bilberry heath, there is much *Chamaepericlymenum suecicum*. Heather heath extends to 760 m, but above this level is replaced by a mixed *Rhacomitrium–Nardus–Empetrum–Vaccinium* community.

Steep north-facing rocky slopes and cliffs in the corries have fine development of northern Atlantic liverwort communities with all the characteristic species (see list on p. 279), especially in association with dwarf shrubs, but in places under the cliffs there is a species-poor *Nardus–Deschampsia cespitosa* or *Agrostis–Festuca* grassland. The cliffs themselves appear to be generally less basic than those of some Torridonian Sandstone mountains. There is only a moderate development of tall herb ledges, with species such as *Saussurea alpina*, *Sedum rosea* and *Cochlearia alpina*, and the poorer ledge community with *Luzula sylvatica*, *Angelica sylvestris* and *D. cespitosa* is more prevalent. Feral goats graze on the cliffs, however, and may have reduced the richness of the ledge vegetation. A remarkable recent botanical discovery was *Saxifraga cespitosa*, otherwise unknown north of the Great Glen, and confined in its other British stations to highly calcareous rocks. *S. rivularis* also grows here, and *Poa glauca* occurs on the cliffs. Species characteristic of high summit areas in the northern Highlands are sparse, but there is an abundance of *Salix herbacea*.

U.90. LETTEREWE FOREST, ROSS

NG 9873. 7300 ha   Grade 2

North of Loch Maree, a magnificently rugged group of mountains including Beinn Lair (859 m), Beinn Airidh Charr (790 m), A'Mhaighdean (975 m) and Mullach Coire Mhic Fhearchair (1019 m) surrounds the head of the Fionn Loch and Lochan Fada. All four are composed largely or entirely of Lewisian Gneiss, which is exposed in great precipices, but the last hill is capped by quartzite and has a western outlier, Beinn Tarsuinn (869 m), formed of Torridonian Sandstone. The summit of A'Mhaighdean is also composed partly of the sandstone. The vegetation includes many of the types characteristic of the north-west Highlands, but there is a less varied range of dwarf shrub-heath than on Beinn Eighe (U.64) just to the south, and a lesser development of high montane communities than on Beinn Dearg (U.62) to the north.

The lower ground has the usual complex of western *Calluna–Trichophorum* and *Calluna–Molinia* wet heath grading to blanket mire. Short *Calluna* heath with *Empetrum hermaphroditum* is patchy on higher and drier slopes, whilst windswept moraines and shoulders have a rather fragmentary development of prostrate *Calluna* heath rich in *Rhacomitrium lanuginosum*, with variable occurrence of dwarf shrubs such as *Arctous alpina*, *Arctostaphylos uva-ursi*, *Loiseleuria procumbens* and *Juniperus communis* ssp. *nana*. Some middle-level slopes, as on A'Mhaighdean, have extensive grasslands with *Nardus*, *Juncus squarrosus*, *Trichophorum* and *Deschampsia cespitosa*. *Vaccinium–Empetrum* and *Empetrum–Rhacomitrium* heath are local, but mixtures of these three species and *Nardus* are widespread. *Festuca–Vaccinium* grass heath with *Alchemilla alpina* and *Rhacomitrium* occurs on upper slopes and grades on the summits into *Rhacomitrium–Carex bigelowii* heath with an abundance of *Silene acaulis*, *Cherleria sedoides* and *Armeria maritima* in places. Windswept ablation surfaces have the characteristic species-rich *Juncus trifidus–Festuca vivipara* community, this type being extensive on the summit plateau of Beinn Lair.

Late snow-bed vegetation is represented by *Nardus*, *Rhytidiadelphus–Deschampsia cespitosa*, *Alchemilla–Sibbaldia* and *Cryptogramma–Athyrium* communities, but these hills do not carry really long-lasting snow-beds, so that certain extreme types are lacking. In places there is a fine development of northern Atlantic liverwort communities, especially amongst dwarf-shrub heath on north-facing slopes, and *Scapania nimbosa* is unusually luxuriant.

The Lewisian Gneiss of these hills is quite strongly calcareous in many places and on Mullach Coire Mhic Fhearchair there are also small exposures of the calcareous Serpulite Grits and Fucoid Beds. These give species-rich communities and a varied calcicolous montane flora which exceeds that of Beinn Eighe in number of species, but is less varied than that of Beinn Dearg and Seana Bhraigh. Open calcareous flushes of the type with *Saxifraga aizoides*, *S. oppositifolia* and *Juncus triglumis* are locally frequent, especially on Beinn Lair, and there are good examples of rich flushed *Agrostis–Festuca* grassland, with *Thalictrum alpinum* in damp places, and *Alchemilla alpina* and *Thymus drucei* on dry ground. The flora of the calcareous crags and flushes includes virtually all the more widespread montane calcicoles and indifferent species of the region, with the following as the more notable species: *Draba norvegica*, *Cerastium arcticum*, *Cardaminopsis petraea*, *Hieracium holosericeum*, *Tofieldia pusilla*, *Carex atrata*, *C. capillaris*, *Poa glauca*, *Deschampsia alpina* and *Polystichum lonchitis*. Tall-herb ledge communities of a fairly rich type are represented, but the acidophilous examples with *Vaccinium* spp., *Empetrum hermaphroditum*, *Luzula sylvatica* and ferns are prevalent.

The site also includes a small outcrop of Durness Limestone forming a shore promontory at the foot of Lochan Fada at 300 m. This limestone has a colony of *Dryas octopetala* and some of the more widespread calcicoles.

The Letterewe Oakwoods (W.206(*c*)) lie on the lower slopes of Beinn Airidh Charr and Beinn Lair above Loch Maree, and add greatly to the ecological importance of this area.

U.91. BEN MORE ASSYNT AND BREABAG, SUTHERLAND

NC 3117. 7050 ha   Grade 2

The site consists of the horse-shoe of ridges bounding the head of the River Oykell and lying immediately east of the Inchnadamph limestone (U.67). The western half of this watershed, from Creag Liath (814 m) to Conival (986 m), is largely quartzite, whilst the eastern half, from Meall an Aonaich (715 m) to Ben More Assynt (998 m), is composed largely of Lewisian Gneiss. The Lewisian Series, which reaches its greatest elevation in Britain on Ben More Assynt, is in this area markedly calcareous, resulting in the presence of a rich montane flora and a heavy grazing pressure from sheep and deer. This last factor is probably responsible for the extensive and heterogeneous assemblage of grassland types in the area. On the whole, the vegetation is similar to that of Beinn Dearg–Seana Bhraigh (U.62), but more modified by human influences and with a lesser development of certain montane types.

The lower ground of the quartzite area has a good deal of *Calluna–Trichophorum* wet heath and *Calluna–Eriophorum* blanket mire, but this is considerably degraded in places, with loss of *Calluna* and erosion of peat. Callunetum rich in the usual northern Atlantic liverworts was obviously once well developed under the east- and north-facing cliffs of Breabag and Creag Liath, but has been severely modified and fragmented by burning. On the western side of this broad ridge there are patches of dwarf Callunetum with abundant *Rhacomitrium lanuginosum* on dry, windswept places, but *Rhacomitrium* heath is extensive above 640 m and has great quantities of *Armeria maritima* and *Cherleria sedoides* at the higher levels, though *Silene acaulis* is less abundant. Limited outcrops of mudstones on this range have a *Rhytidiadelphus loreus–Saxifraga hypnoides* herb-rich moss heath, and other communities include *Rhacomitrium–Empetrum* and *Rhacomitrium–Nardus* types.

The south-western slopes of Ben More Assynt have a great deal of mixed grassland and soligenous mire of a mesotrophic character. There are *Agrostis–Anthoxanthum*, *Alchemilla alpina–Thymus*, *Nardus*, *Juncus squarrosus* and *Molinia* types, and some of these are rich in forbs. Soligenous *Carex* mires with both *Sphagnum* spp. and hypnaceous mosses occur and there are open *Saxifraga aizoides–Juncus triglumis* flushes. The drier grasslands grade at higher levels to types with abundant *Vaccinium myrtillus*, *Alchemilla alpina* and *Rhacomitrium lanuginosum*. These pass on the summit ridges to mixtures of *Festuca–Vaccinium*, *Rhacomitrium* heath with cushion herbs, *Rhytidiadelphus* moss heath and *Nardus* communities. On Carn nan Conbhairean there are good solifluction terraces with alternating *Juncus trifidus* ablation surface and *Rhacomitrium* heath rich in dwarf forbs.

The south-western side of Ben More Assynt has extensive escarpments of Lewisian Gneiss, in two main tiers, and the eastern aspect has two rather shallow corries lined by rather broken cliffs. These places have a rich calcicolous flora with most of the widespread montane species, and a good development of tall-herb ledges. The more notable plants include *Draba norvegica*, *D. incana*, *Saxifraga nivalis*, *Cerastium alpinum*, *Juncus biglumis*, *J. castaneus*, *Deschampsia alpina*, *Poa alpina* and *Polystichum lonchitis*. In the corries, there are complexes of flush and soligenous mire, with an abundance of bryophytes, including one *Pohlia albicans* var. *glacialis* spring, and a patchy development of *Carex saxatilis* mire. Moss heaths associated with the longest-lasting snow-beds appear to be absent, but there are patchy *Athyrium alpestre* growths in scree, good *Alchemilla–Sibbaldia* patches, *Rhytidiadelphus* moss heath (including the rich facies) and montane *D. cespitosa* grassland. *Silene acaulis* mats with abundance of small forbs are well developed on intermittently flushed ground. The northern Atlantic liverworts are well represented, but not in good communities. The bryophyte flora is rich, and the rarer species include *Leptodontium recurvifolium*, *Oncophorus virens*, *Splachnum vasculosum*, *Aulacomnium turgidum*, *Acrocladium*

trifarium, *Hylocomium pyrenaicum*, *Hypnum hamulosum*, *Orthothecium rufescens*, *Scapania nimbosa* and *Anastrophyllum joergensenii*.

The quartzite of Conival has a more limited and largely acidophilous range of vegetation, with extensive development of the mixed western *Nardus–Vaccinium–Empetrum–Rhacomitrium* community, *Nardus–Rhacomitrium*, poor *Deschampsia cespitosa* grassland, *Philonotis–Sphagnum* springs and *Carex–Sphagnum* mires. *Cerastium arcticum* occurs here and was not seen on the Lewisian.

U.92. NORTH HARRIS, INVERNESS-SHIRE
NB 0012, NB 0711, NB 0906. 12 700 ha   Grade 2

The strongly oceanic mountains of Harris are composed entirely of Lewisian Gneiss and are among the rockiest hills in Britain. Clisham is the highest point at 799 m. The gneiss is here mainly non-calcareous and the montane flora is poor, though a few cliffs have some of the more common calcicoles. Floristically, the outstanding feature is the abundance in wet heaths of the large endemic moss *Campylopus shawii*, though other northern Atlantic bryophytes are well represented. The range of vegetation is more limited than on the high mainland hills, montane dwarf-shrub heath and chionophilous vegetation being poorly represented, but there is a great deal of grass heath with an abundance of *Rhacomitrium lanuginosum*. In particular, a mixed *Calluna*, *Nardus*, *Juncus squarrosus* community with abundant *Rhacomitrium* occurs extensively. Many of the cliff ledges have luxuriant growths of *Luzula sylvatica*. In many features, this upland massif is intermediate between the Lewisian or Moine hills of the mainland and St Kilda. North Harris is regarded as a representative example of an ecosystem associated with a particular geological and climatic combination. Strone Ulladale, within this area, is the most spectacular overhanging cliff in Britain. Song thrushes here replace the ring ouzel as the mountain *Turdus* sp. and occur high up on treeless mountains.

U.93. GLAS CNOC, ROSS
NG 8744. 740 ha   Grade 2

Together with those in Strath Suardal in the south of Skye, the exposures of Durness Limestone at Kishorn are the major outcrops of this rock formation towards its southern limits. The Rassal Ashwood NNR stands on a low-level exposure, but at about 300 m on the slopes above are limestone scarps and screes with montane plants such as *Dryas*, *Carex rupestris* and *Salix myrsinites*, and their more common calcicolous associates. This area of calcareous habitat and its vegetation are not sufficiently different from those at Inchnadamph, Knockan and Durness to merit grade 1 status, but they are nevertheless important as one of the few occurrences of this ecosystem. (See Appendix.)

U.94. BEN LOYAL, SUTHERLAND
NC 5847. 4250 ha   Grade 2

This isolated mass of syenite rises steeply from the boggy moorlands south of Tongue to a height of 763 m. It forms a north–south ridge with several distinct summits, rather shallow corries on the western side, and extensive cliffs on the northern and western flanks. The summit ridge has pronounced tors. The rock is mainly acidic and the flora rather restricted, whilst the range of montane vegetation is rather limited. Ben Loyal nevertheless has several interesting vegetational features and is rather atypical among the mountains of northern Scotland.

There is good birchwood on the north-west slope and above Loch an Dherue, and in blanket mire below the mountain is a presumed hybrid population of *Betula pubescens* × *nana*. The lower slopes in places have a good deal of heather heath, which is often of a mossy facies and grades into a dwarf, montane type with *Loiseleuria procumbens* on the windswept upper slopes. The most extensive and distinctive community is, however, one dominated by bilberry and *Luzula sylvatica*, with a great abundance of hypnaceous mosses. This extends to at least 600 m and there grades into types with *Vaccinium myrtillus*, *Empetrum hermaphroditum* and *Rhacomitrium lanuginosum* in varying combinations. Species-poor *Rhacomitrium–Carex bigelowii* heath with *Armeria maritima* as the only cushion-herb is well developed along the summit ridge, and on ablation surfaces on the south top shows an open facies with much *Alchemilla alpina*, *Festuca vivipara* and *Salix herbacea*. There are small areas of *Hylocomium* moss heath with *Deschampsia cespitosa*, but late snow communities are not strongly represented. Damper ground has *Nardus* and *Juncus squarrosus* communities, grading in places into *Calluna–Eriophorum vaginatum* mire. The lower-level blanket mires surrounding Ben Loyal are of the western *Eriophorum–Trichophorum–Molinia* type, locally with pool and hummock systems.

Local occurrences of lime-bearing rock on the western crags have *Saxifraga oppositifolia*, *S. hypnoides*, *Silene acaulis*, *Sedum rosea*, *Draba incana* and *Thalictrum alpinum*, and there are a few tall-herb ledges. One of the most distinctive botanical features of Ben Loyal is the general profusion and luxuriance of lichens, mainly fairly common species, on rocks everywhere, and the strong development in various communities of a hypnaceous moss carpet which includes, unusually, an abundance of *Antitrichia curtipendula*.

U.95. ARDMEANACH, MULL, ARGYLL

NM 4402. 3300 ha   Grade 2

The Ardmeanach peninsula lies on the area of Tertiary basalt which forms a large part of Mull. It consists of a range of rather low hills reaching 519 m on Beinn na Sreine, and showing quite large areas of bare, gravelly debris in places on the higher ground. There are numerous small outcrops, and on the western and north-western sides of the peninsula there is a tremendous line of cliff and scree falling precipitously to the sea. This escarpment has relics of woodland with hazel, oak, aspen, wych elm, ash, blackthorn, hawthorn, willows and ivy, with a tall-herb field layer containing *Filipendula ulmaria*, *Solidago virgaurea*, *Eupatorium cannabinum*, *Teucrium scorodonia*, *Hypericum androsaemum*, *H. tetrapterum*, *Deschampsia cespitosa*, *Dac-*

tylis glomerata and *Brachypodium sylvaticum*. The very local northern whitebeam *Sorbus rupicola* occurs here.

Calcicolous grasslands beneath the basalt cliffs are rather similar to the species-rich *Agrostis–Festuca* coastal grasslands on Rhum, both in flora and fauna. Among the characteristic plants are *Koeleria cristata*, *Thymus drucei*, *Linum catharticum*, *Galium verum*, *Hieracium pilosella*, *Hypochaeris radicata*, *Euphrasia officinalis* agg. and *Plantago maritima*. The rare *Orobanche alba* occurs as a parasite on *Thymus*. On these pastures there is an abundance of butterflies such as the small heath, common blue, meadow brown, grayling and dark green fritillary, and the day-flying five spot burnet and transparent burnet moths.

The higher ground has a moderately rich montane flora, mainly associated with open habitats. *Dryas octopetala* and *Orthothecium rufescens* occur in places on the coastal escarpment, and *Saussurea alpina*, *Sedum rosea*, *Oxyria digyna* and *Polystichum lonchitis* are other noteworthy cliff plants. The most interesting species is, however, *Koenigia islandica*, here in one of its three British localities, growing abundantly in the bare gravel spreads at the north-east end of the range. Other plants of this ground include *Cherleria sedoides*, *Juncus triglumis*, *Galium boreale* and *Sedum villosum*. There is a good deal of acidic grassland, especially *Nardus* types, of a submontane character.

The area contains the famous geological feature of McCulloch's Tree, a fossil tree embedded in columnar basalt lava.

See also C.116.

U.96. BEINN IADAIN AND BEINN NA H-UAMHA, ARGYLL

NM 6954. 1650 ha   Grade 2

These two Tertiary basalt capped hills in Morvern reach 571 and 464 m, respectively. The interesting ground lies above 300 m, and consists of crags, screes and rocky slopes of calcareous basalt, which have provided a refugium for a rich calcicolous montane flora in an area which lacks high mountains, and has a good deal of rather dull acidophilous moorland. The more noteworthy species include the very rare *Arenaria norvegica*, *Dryas octopetala*, *Cardaminopsis petraea* var. *grandiflora*, *Saxifraga nivalis*, *S. oppositifolia*, *S. hypnoides*, *S. aizoides*, *Silene acaulis*, *S. maritima*, *Sedum rosea*, *Polystichum lonchitis*, *Orthothecium rufescens* and *Rhytidium rugosum*. Rich swards on steep slopes below the cliffs are mainly the *Alchemilla alpina* type of *Festuca–Agrostis* grassland on the sun exposed slopes, and a mossy facies on shaded north slopes. There are patches of a species-rich *Juncus squarrosus* community with *Thalictrum alpinum*. Most of the surrounding moorland is covered with *Trichophorum–Calluna* or *Molinia–Calluna* communities on shallow peat.

U.97. BEN GRIAM MORE AND BEN GRIAM BEAG, SUTHERLAND

NC 7939, NC 8441. 3250 ha   Grade 2

The Old Red Sandstone of north-east Scotland does not form high mountains, and the only hills of any significance are a few small though steep-sided peaks which rise from the great blanket mire plains of east Sutherland and Caithness. The Bens Griam west of Forsinard are examples of calcareous sandstone hills (in part), with summits reaching 590 and 580 m. The higher ground has examples of montane dwarf Callunetum, of the shrub-rich type with *Arctous alpina, Loiseleuria procumbens* and lichens in places. On wetter ground there is a transition to *Calluna–Eriophorum vaginatum* blanket mire with *Rubus chamaemorus*, but at lower levels this is replaced by the western community with abundant *Molinia caerulea, Myrica gale, Trichophorum cespitosum* and *Pleurozia purpurea*, and vegetation of this type covers great areas of the flows around the foot of these hills. There are soligenous mires on the lower slopes, varying from acidic to basic, and the south slope of Ben Griam More has a species-rich intermittently flushed *Festuca–Agrostis* grassland with abundant *Alchemilla alpina, Thalictrum alpinum* and *Ctenidium molluscum*.

Dry slopes have a moss-rich *Calluna–Empetrum* heath, changing on richer soils below cliffs to mossy, herb-rich grassland. Bigger cliff ledges have a *Vaccinium myrtillus–Luzula sylvatica* community, grading into tall-herb growths with *Trollius europaeus, Succisa pratensis, Geum rivale* and *Filipendula ulmaria*, and both of these types are rich in hypnaceous mosses. The most interesting feature is the occurrence on the steeper calcareous cliffs of both hills of a rich calcicolous montane flora with *Dryas octopetala, Saxifraga oppositifolia, Silene acaulis, Cerastium alpinum, Potentilla crantzii, Cardaminopsis petraea, Polystichum lonchitis, Draba incana, Saussurea alpina, Sedum rosea, Oxyria digyna* and *Galium boreale*. These crags are a particularly good example of an Arctic–alpine plant refugium for they lie far from the nearest localities for these species, and are surrounded by a very large area of unsuitable terrain, covered almost entirely by blanket mire. The mire between Ben Griam Beag and Forsinard, and two other mires near Loch Badanloch are of considerable interest (P.105, gr. 2) for their patterned areas and are described under Peatlands.

U.98. MORVEN AND SCARABENS, CAITHNESS
ND 0427.   3300 ha   Grade 2
These hills are complementary to the Bens Griam, in being composed largely of acidic Old Red Sandstone and Moinian Quartzite, and are interesting mainly for their range of dwarf-shrub heath. They rise steeply from a large expanse of low-lying moorland with extensive blanket mire and wet heath of a rather eastern type, with much *Calluna–Trichophorum* vegetation. This passes to *Calluna–Eriophorum vaginatum* bog at higher levels, and as the ground steepens into the main peaks, some form of *Calluna* heath takes over. Morven (705 m) is a pronounced cone, but has on its upper slopes an interesting area of lichen-rich dwarf Callunetum and an *Empetrum hermaphroditum* heath with high moss cover. The broader quartzite ridge of the Scarabens (626 m) has a good deal of species-poor *Rhacomitrium–Carex bigelowii* heath. An interesting feature is the relatively low elevation at which these montane communities occur. As

the rock is mainly acidic, the montane flora consists mainly of calcifuge species such as *Empetrum hermaphroditum, Rubus chamaemorus, Arctous alpina, Loiseleuria procumbens* and *C. bigelowii*, but the calcicolous *Draba norvegica* is recorded from the area. Some patches of basic soil on Smean have grassland of various kinds, with some forbs, but much *Nardus, Juncus squarrosus* and hypnaceous mosses, and there are basic moss and *Carex* flushes in a few places. The area is interesting geomorphologically for the pronounced tors of sandstone which crown the summits or spurs of several of these hills.

U.99. LAXFORD MOORS, SUTHERLAND
NC 2342.   445 ha   Grade 2
The moorlands of the undulating Lewisian Gneiss country south of Laxford Bridge have numerous lochans of varying size, morainic knolls with wet heath (Trichophoreto–Callunetum and Molinieto–Callunetum) and areas of wet ground with blanket mire (Trichophoreto–Eriophoretum). In the area just north of Allt an Riabhach there are, however, areas of moorland which show the emergence of base-rich seepage water – perhaps from calcareous beds of gneiss, and these have systems of soligenous mire and flush. The most noteworthy feature is the abundance of *Schoenus nigricans*, which grows in a range of communities varying from open, stony flushes with *Saxifraga aizoides, Eriophorum latifolium* and *Scorpidium scorpioides*, through soligenous tracks in Trichophoreto–Eriophoretum to blanket mire with pools containing *E. angustifolium, Juncus kochii, Potamogeton polygonifolius, Carex limosa, Utricularia vulgaris, S. scorpioides* and *Acrocladium trifarium. Schoenus* appears here always to be associated with lateral water seepage; it is most luxuriant where this influence is strong and becomes sparser as the flush influence fades and the mire becomes ombrogenous.

The *Schoenus* communities of this area bear some resemblance to those on Rhum, but are less extensive. They are included as one of the few mainland occurrences of such communities in an area of acidic moorland and blanket mire.

U.100. RONAS HILL, SHETLAND
HU 3184.   3600 ha   Grade 2
This hill, the highest point in Shetland (450 m), is composed of granite rocks, and its soils are almost entirely base-poor. There is a large area of *Rhacomitrium* heath, at the unusually low elevation of 270–300 m, but much of it is sparsely grown with *Nardus*, so that it is not quite the same as the *Carex bigelowii–Rhacomitrium* heath of mainland Highland summits. Solifluction terraces and ablation surfaces are well developed at very low altitudes, providing important examples of these phenomena. The associated vegetation communities are floristically poor compared with those of the Beinn Dearg massif. The summit consists of bare granite gravel and boulder field even more sparsely vegetated than the high Cairngorm tops at 1220 m, but there are scattered rosettes of *Saussurea alpina* (in an unusual habitat), *Plantago maritima, Antennaria dioica* and *Alchemilla alpina*. On more stable ground below the top is a

Rhacomitrium rich dwarf-shrub heath with much *Arctous alpina*, *Lycopodium alpinum* and *Vaccinium uliginosum*, and showing a 'wave-like' form in places. Northern Atlantic hepatics are well represented in number of species, but are poorly developed as a community, as the north-facing slopes are not steep enough to give the required amount of shade. There are mixed *Calluna–Nardus–Trichophorum* heaths and areas of shallow blanket mire on the north side, and many small- to medium-sized tarns. The seaward slope has much broken cliff and the granite sea cliffs have an unusual development of landslips within which deep fissures provide habitats for bryophytes and ferns.

The montane area of Ronas Hill is in some respects inferior to that of North Hoy (U.74) with which it is most closely comparable. It does not have as wide a range of vegetation types, lichen heath and calcicolous communities being absent, and the dwarf-shrub heaths are not so well developed. Solifluction terraces and ablation surfaces are, however, very well developed and provide better examples than those of North Hoy. (See Appendix.)

APPENDIX: SITE ACCOUNTS

C.11. NORTH SOLENT MARSHES, HAMPSHIRE Regraded 1

C.124. BERROW MARSH, SOMERSET
ST 2952–2250.   *c.* 80 ha   Grade 1

The marsh at Berrow on the north side of Bridgwater Bay started to grow earlier this century to seaward of a sand-dune system. Subsequently a new line of dunes developed to seaward so that the site is now almost enclosed by dunes although several small breaches in the seaward dune ridge allow tidal flooding to occur, albeit infrequently. This seaward dune ridge is densely covered along much of its length by *Hippophäe rhamnoides* which would appear to have spread considerably since 1960.

The marsh itself is covered largely with tall-growing vegetation, the major species being *Spartina anglica, Agropyron pungens, Scirpus maritimus, Phragmites communis* with locally *Typha latifolia, Juncus maritimus* and *J. gerardii*. The marsh is the only known site in the British Isles for *J. subulatus* which occurs over a limited area of the northern part. The *Juncus* would seem to have increased since 1960 and occurs as open clones mixed with *Scirpus*.

At the southern end of the marsh some alder and *Hippophäe* bushes occur in dense *Phragmites*. Elsewhere the subsidiary flora includes *Berula erecta, Apium graveolens, Oenanthe lachenalii, Lycopus europaeus, Carex extensa, C. distans, C. otrubae, Sonchus arvensis, Rumex crispus, Melilotus altissima, Iris pseudacorus* and *Catabrosa aquatica. Agrostis stolonifera* and *Hydrocotyle vulgaris* are curiously rare considering their abundance in brackish habitats elsewhere. The bryophyte flora is poor in comparison with that of dune slacks; the major species being *Cratoneuron filicinum, Leptodictyon riparium, Eurynchium praelongum* and *Acroladium cuspidatum*.

Along the western edge of the marsh, in contact with the dune ridge, is a narrow zone of shorter vegetation in which *Festuca rubra, Parapholis strigosa, Plantago coronopus, Centaurium pulchellum, C. erythrea, Trifolium repens* and *T. fragiferum* occur with locally *Limonium binervosum* and *Artemisia maritima*. The occurrence of *L. binervosum* is of interest as the only site known on the west coast where this species occurs in a dune salt marsh transition which is its common habitat in East Anglia.

Along the eastern (landward) side of the marsh there are signs of a *Festuca arundinacea*-dominated zone but in August 1974 there had obviously been some encroachment with fresh, newly dug mounds of soil in places along the marshy edge. To seaward of the dune ridge a new marsh is forming.

Older records mention a dune marsh at Berrow which obviously had some similarity with the present marsh. This old marsh, notable for the occurrence of the very rare *Holoschoenus vulgaris*, was reclaimed in the construction of the golf course which borders the marsh to the east although the *Holoschoenus* just hangs on.

The importance of this site can be judged in at least three ways: its intrinsic floristic interest, notably the presence of *Juncus subulatus*; as an example of a brackish marsh, transitional in many ways between a dune slack and a salt marsh; and as a site which demonstrates the interaction between vegetation and physiography and illustrates the dynamic nature of coastal plant communities. In addition to the published accounts detailed unpublished records exist of the changes at this site going back to before the Second World War, so that the historical record of salt marsh development here gives an excellent basis for study of future changes in the existing marsh and of the marsh developing to seaward of the dunes.

The site should be regarded as an extension to the Bridgwater Bay complex (C.34).

C.125. CARMARTHEN BAY, CARMARTHEN/GLAMORGAN/
            PEMBROKE
SN 3003.   *c.* 20 000 ha   Grade 1

Large numbers of common scoter winter here and some remain throughout the year. The population may move widely between Saundersfoot and Worms Head. Counts from the shore in the Pembrey–Cefn Sidan area in 1974 included at least 5000 in February, 6000 in June, 16 000 in August and 10 000–12 000 in September. In March 1974 a traverse across the bay and back gave an estimate of 25 000 scoters. Even at a more conservative average level of 5000 + the wintering population is acknowledged to be of international importance.

C.79. BASS ROCK, EAST LOTHIAN   Regraded 1

C.126. MARWICK HEAD, ORKNEY
HY 2225.   25 ha   Grade 1

This Old Red Sandstone headland on the west side of Mainland Orkney reaches a height of only 75 m and extends along only 3 km of coast, but its vertical cliffs have an abundance of good ledges of the kind favoured by breeding seafowl, and support the second largest concentration of guillemots and kittiwakes in Orkney. Because of the difficulty of viewing all the cliffs from the land, the populations have not been counted accurately, but for both these species are estimated to be Order 5 (tens of thousands of pairs). There are also large numbers of razorbills and fulmars, but only a few puffins.

The uncultivated maritime heaths and grasslands above the cliffs have not been examined for botanical interest, but the flora is not known to include any species of particular note.

C.127. WESTRAY AND PAPA WESTRAY, ORKNEY

Grade 1*

This composite grade 1 site includes the cliff coast and parts of the western hills of Westray together with North Hill, Papa Westray. These areas have a range of northern maritime vegetation types and some of the largest seabird breeding colonies in Britain.

West Westray

HY 4247. 380 ha

The 8 km stretch of Old Red Sandstone cliffs between Noup Head and Inga Ness supports an immense colony of cliff nesting seabirds. Although the cliffs reach only about 75 m, the horizontal strata give a fine development of the ledges needed for nesting by these seafowl. There are probably the largest colonies of guillemots and kittiwakes in the British Isles, both estimated at a minimum of 60000–70000 pairs each, and concentrated at Noup Head. The number of guillemots and kittiwakes in this single area exceeds the total for all the colonies in Shetland. There are also large numbers of razorbills (Order 4), fulmars (3000+ pairs), and shags (Order 4), but puffins are less abundant (400 pairs).

The vegetation of the Westray Hills includes good examples of maritime sedge heath within which occur ablation surfaces and soligenous tracts. This sedge heath is very rich in species, and in addition to ericaceous plants such as *Calluna vulgaris*, *Erica cinerea* and *Empetrum nigrum* includes several maritime species, e.g. *Plantago maritima*, *Scilla verna* and *Primula scotica*. Rock outcrops on the Westray Hills have well-developed fern communities including *Asplenium adiantum-nigrum*, *A. ruta-muraria*, *A. marinum*, *A. trichomanes*, *Polypodium vulgare*, *Cystopteris fragilis* and *Athyrium filix-femina*. Some of the wet rock ledges have *Silene acaulis*, *Thalictrum alpinum* and in places flushes include *Anagallis tenella*, *Parnassia palustris*, *Selaginella selaginoides* and *Pinguicula vulgaris*. Dry, east-facing outcrops have *Galium sterneri*, *Draba incana* and *Arabidopsis thaliana*.

North Hill, Papa Westray

HY 5055. 200 ha

The main ornithological interest of this area is the very large colony of Arctic terns (about 8000 pairs) and a colony of 90 pairs of Arctic skuas. In addition there are cliff nesting seabirds, but these colonies are not as large as those of Westray and Marwick Head. There are about 8000 pairs of kittiwakes and 3000 pairs of guillemots. This island was the last known breeding station of the great auk.

The vegetation of North Hill is comparable with that of the hills of Westray, maritime sedge heath being the dominant vegetation. In places soligenous tracts dominated by *Schoenus nigricans* are extensive. In exposed places around the cliff coast there are well-developed ablation phenomena and there is a gradation from strongly halophytic vegetation of cliff tops to maritime sedge heath away from the direct influence of sea spray. The vegetation is however strongly maritime in character throughout the whole area, and is the best example of this type of vegetation in northern Scotland.

C.96. FOULA, SHETLAND

HT 9639. 1380 ha

Regraded 1*

Recent botanical and ornithological surveys allow a fuller account to be given of the biological interest of this oceanic island.

Foula is an Old Red Sandstone island forming the most westerly of the Shetland group, and is the most isolated inhabited island in Britain. The eastern side is mostly low lying, but rises steeply into a central ridge, reaching a height of 418 m at the Sneug, and terminating abruptly on the western side of the island in the tremendous coastal precipice of the Kame (370 m).

Under the cool oceanic climate, peat formation has been extensive on the gentler slopes, and there is a range of bog vegetation. Peat has been extensively cut, but on uncut areas below 240 m there is a widespread *Eriophorum vaginatum–Empetrum nigrum* blanket mire of somewhat montane character, with *Vaccinium uliginosum* and *Carex bigelowii*. *Calluna-Trichophorum cespitosum* and *Calluna–Eriophorum vaginatum* communities on shallow peat occur locally. On cut-over peat areas there is a good deal of *Calluna–Erica tetralix* heath rich in *Empetrum nigrum*. Acidic grasslands include subalpine *Nardus* and *Festuca–Deschampsia flexuosa* types, and there are swards of *Juncus squarrosus*. A submaritime *Luzula sylvatica* community occurs on the highest ground, as on St Kilda. Montane species of the high ground include *Salix herbacea*, *Polygonum viviparum* and *Chamaepericlymenum suecicum*. Cliffs tops drenched by sea spray during storms have swards of *Plantago maritima*, *P. coronopus* and *Armeria maritima*. *Hymenophyllum wilsonii* occurs abundantly in a variety of communities as an indicator of the extremely humid climate, and the bryophyte flora is quite rich.

The outstanding wildlife feature of Foula is, however, its large and varied breeding population of seabirds. The great size and inaccessibility of the cliffs has so far prevented an accurate count of the cliff-nesting species, but it seems clear that there are over 10000 pairs each of guillemot, puffin and fulmar, several thousand pairs of kittiwakes and at least several hundred pairs of razorbills. The colony of shags (Order 4) is also one of the biggest in Britain, and the black guillemot is well represented. The colony of 1800 pairs (in 1969–70) of great skuas, scattered over the interior moorlands, is by far the largest in Britain; and the Arctic skua nests in smaller numbers. All the British gulls except the black-headed do so. The total confirmed number of species of nesting seabirds is 16. Manx shearwaters and stormy petrels breed in small numbers, and Leach's petrels may well do so.

This is, in aggregate, one of the most outstanding breeding stations for seabirds in the North Atlantic, and is regarded as internationally important.

C.120. SHIANT ISLES, ROSS

Regraded 1

C.128. WICK RIVER MARSHES, CAITHNESS

ND 3052–3551. *c.* 240 ha

Grade 1

The lower course of the Wick River is bordered by alluvial marshes and fens. These marshes extend from Wick towards Loch Watten and are of considerable extent although in places they have been reclaimed for agriculture. The river appears to be tidal as far as 2.4 km inland from Wick. However, although saline water might reach some of the marshes on extremely high spring tides, the presence of a weir in Wick probably prevents seawater penetrating far up the river on most tides. The rise of the water level below the weir will pond back fresh water above the weir so producing freshwater tides. In many estuaries the freshwater tidal zone coincides with the lowest crossing point of the river so that in many places the vegetation of the zone has been destroyed by urban development. The Wick River Marshes represent the largest area of freshwater inter-tidal marsh known in Britain.

Immediately inland of the weir in Wick the emergent vegetation consists of *Eleocharis palustris*, *Carex aquatilis*, *C. aquatilis × recta*, *Scheonoplectus lacustris* and locally *S. tabernaemontani*. Around the weir a limited halophytic element occurs (including *Juncus gerardii*, *Plantago maritima*, *Triglochin maritimum* and *Cochlearia officinalis*).

A few hundred metres from the weir a *Filipendula–Phalaris* marsh develops on the northern bank of the river and farther inland occurs on both banks. Backwaters of the river in this marsh support dense stands of *Carex aquatilis*, *Schoenoplectus lacustris* and *S. tabernaemontani* with *Equisetum fluviatile*, *Sparganium erectum* and *Alisma plantago-aquatica*. Open water in these backwaters contains *Potamogeton natans*, *P. perfoliatus*, *P. crispus* and *P. berchtoldii*.

Within the *Phalaris–Filipendula* marsh there are areas dominated by *Iris pseudacorus*, *Carex aquatilis* and locally *C. recta*. *Phalaris*-dominated areas occur near the river but elsewhere in the marsh *Filipendula* is more important and locally dominant.

On the northern bank of the river opposite Fairy Hillock about 2 km inland from Wick, the emergent vegetation of the river is *Schoenoplectus lacustris* with *Carex aquatilis* and some *C. rostrata*. The marsh is dominated by *Phalaris* and *Filipendula* but with a number of tall herbs. Within the marsh a number of patches of *C. aquatilis*, *C. recta* and hybrids between the two occur.

C.129. BERRIEDALE CLIFFS, CAITHNESS

ND 0617–1324.   *c.* 200 ha   Grade 1

This long section is bounded along most of its length by cliffs of Old Red Sandstone reaching a height of 150 m or more. Its most important feature is the large population of breeding seabirds. The south-west end, at the Ord of Caithness, has the largest colony of cormorants in Britain, with approximately 450 pairs. There are huge concentrations of guillemots (31 000 pairs), razorbills (8000 pairs), kittiwakes (15 500 pairs) and fulmars (6000 pairs); especially in the north-east sector, at Inver Hill at An Dun and Coan Dubh; these are minimum figures, for the colonies are extremely difficult to count, some sections of cliff being unviewable from land. Shags are numerous and well distributed along the cliffs.

Except for the short section north-east of Berriedale, where there are fields, the cliff tops run into open moorland (of *Calluna* in dry places) with increasing amount of *Trichophorum cespitosum* and *Sphagnum* spp. as the ground becomes damper. The rock is acidic and the flora predominantly calcifuge, but on the cliff tops and slopes there is greater variety of species, including some mildly basiphilous types. Small shrubs include *Empetrum nigrum*, *Arctostaphylos uva-ursi*, *Erica cinerea*, *Salix repens*, *S. aurita* and small forms of *Juniperus communis* (on the cliff edge). A miscellaneous selection of herbs, in grassland and on rocks has *Lotus corniculatus*, *Anthyllis vulneraria*, *Lathyrus montanus*, *Orchis mascula*, *Teucrium scorodonia*, *Hieracium pilosella*, *Hypericum pulchrum*, *Eupatorium cannabinum*, *Saxifraga hypnoides* and the rare northern *Ajuga pyramidalis*, locally in great luxuriance. The sea cliffs have an abundance of maritime species such as *Cochlearia officinalis*, *Armeria maritima*, *Silene maritima* and *Tripleurospermum maritimum*. In places, the cliff top appears to be enriched by upward washing, presumably under storm conditions, of guano from the faces below, giving a fairly rich grassland with *Festuca rubra*, *Agrostis* spp., *Anthoxanthum*

odoratum and *Holcus lanatus*. This is much favoured as pasturage by red deer.

The site also has considerable importance for its geological features.

C.130. MONTROSE BASIN, ANGUS

ND 6858.   1125 ha   Grade 2

Montrose Basin is a large, almost circular, enclosed estuarine basin of the River South Esk, exposing extensive mud flats at low tide (nearly 800 ha). It is situated some distance from the other east coast estuaries of ornithological importance (96 km north of the Tay, 185 km south of the Ythan). The Basin supports very large numbers of roosting and feeding wildfowl and waders (in relation to its size especially), mainly in autumn and winter. At one time an important goose roost (4000–5000 pink-footed, 1000–2000 greylag) and the most important wildfowl resort in the district, numbers have decreased in recent decades due to excessive shooting disturbance. However, the Basin is still a major roost and feeding ground for up to 2000 wigeon (1 % of the UK population) and supports good numbers of pintail, teal, eider, tufted duck, mallard, goldeneye and shelduck, as well as mergansers and goosanders. The inter-tidal fauna is dominated by *Hydrobia* in great abundance, and this together with mussel beds and *Zostera* spp. constitute important components of the wildfowl food supply in the Basin. The rich feeding grounds also contribute to the Basin's wader population, which reaches peaks of over 20000 (fifth largest on the Scottish list) making the site of national importance for waders alone. The main feature of the wader population is the mid-winter peak of knot (about 10000) and the early autumn peaks of oystercatchers and curlews; there are high counts of dunlin and redshank, and good numbers of bar-tailed godwits, golden and ringed plovers, and many other species. There is a large autumn roost of up to 10000 terns (common, Arctic and Sandwich) as well as a small breeding colony at the edge of the Basin. Apart from the extensive *Enteromorpha* and *Zostera* beds, there are interesting areas of salt marsh at the western end of the Basin, and the entire Basin is of considerable geomorphological importance.

C.131. BUCHAN CLIFFS, ABERDEENSHIRE   Grade 2
Collieston–Whinnyfold
NK 0428–0833.   115 ha

Bullers of Buchan–Boddam
NK 0935–1341.   160 ha

These two cliff-bound sections of the Aberdeenshire coast lie between the Sands of Forvie (C.86, gr. 1) and Peterhead, and are separated in the middle by the low sandy shores of Cruden Bay which is not included in the site. The Collieston–Whinnyfold section is composed of Dalradian schists, and shows many phenomena of importance in structural geology; whilst the second section is formed of granite and has fine examples of coastal erosion features such as caves, arches and blowholes. The cliffs, which lie mostly between 30 and 60 m in height, are important for their large colonies of breeding seabirds. These are well scattered along the two lengths, and consist mainly of kittiwakes (10000 pairs) and guillemots (3000 + pairs), with smaller numbers of razorbills, puffins, fulmars and shags.

This coast has a good deal of interest in its cliff face and cliff top vegetation, though the latter occupies only a narrow zone and passes fairly quickly into enclosed farmland. The flora is quite varied, and includes local species such as *Juniperus communis*, *Scilla verna*, *Ligusticum scoticum*, *Rubus saxatilis* and *Sedum rosea*.

C.132. COPINSAY, ORKNEY
HY 6001. 150 ha   Grade 2

The small Old Red Sandstone island of Copinsay rises from a low rocky shore to 1.5 km of sheer cliffs reaching over 60 m on the south-east face. The precipices are the breeding station of a large seabird colony, with guillemots (9000 pairs), kittiwakes (10200 pairs), and smaller numbers of razorbills (300 pairs), puffins (50 pairs), black guillemots (65 pairs), fulmars (580 pairs), shags (84 pairs), cormorants (16 pairs) and great black-backed gulls (230 pairs). Other breeding birds include the lesser black-backed gull, Arctic tern, rock dove and rock pipit.

The island away from the cliffs is covered largely by a maritime to submaritime range of sheep-grazed swards, varying from an *Armeria maritima–Plantago coronopus* community along the crest of the cliffs to *Holcus lanatus*, *Festuca rubra* and *Deschampsia cespitosa* grasslands. The rocky north coast with its stacks, geos and promontories has an abundance of *Aster tripolium* growing luxuriantly, and other plants of note include *Sagina maritima* and *Spergularia salina* in quantity, *Puccinellia maritima* and *Asplenium marinum*. *Mertensia maritima* has a fine colony on the adjoining little island of Corn Holm which is connected to Copinsay by a storm beach exposed at low water.

C.133. SULE SKERRY AND SULE STACK (STACK SKERRY), ORKNEY
HX 6224, HX 5618. *c.* 1 ha   Grade 2

These two small oceanic islands lying off the north coast of Sutherland are important breeding places of seabirds. The larger and lower Sule Skerry has a mantle of soil and vegetation in which breeds a great colony of puffins, numbering around 60000 pairs. The ground is much affected by the combination of salt spray and bird droppings, and the flora is very limited. The central area is dominated by waist-high *Tripleurospermum maritimum* beneath which are the puffin burrows. On the more exposed rocky areas with little soil *Puccinellia maritima* and *Cochlearia* spp. are dominant.

Sule Stack is a rocky cone occupied largely by 4000 pairs of gannets, with smaller numbers of guillemots, razorbills, kittiwakes and fulmars.

C.134. DUNNET HEAD, CAITHNESS
ND 1973–2077. 55 ha   Grade 2

The vertical Old Red Sandstone cliffs of Dunnet Head reach a height of almost 120 m near the lighthouse, and support large breeding populations of seafowl, including guillemots (6000+ pairs), razorbills (Order 4), puffins (Order 5), kittiwakes (15000 pairs) and fulmars (5000 pairs).

The cliff tops pass quickly into uncultivated and acidic moorland which has been heavily burned and grazed, and has *Calluna* and *Calluna–Trichophorum–Eriophorum vaginatum* communities, with small peaty lochans. Northern dwarf shrubs are well represented, with an abundance of *Empetrum nigrum* and *Arctostaphylos uva–ursi*, and an example of montane heath with *Arctous alpina* and *Salix herbacea* occurring at an unusually low level. Ground on the cliff top influenced by salt spray has *Primula scotica* and *Scilla verna*, and the northern *Saussurea alpina*, *Sedum rosea* and *Ligusticum scoticum* occur on the cliffs.

C.135. DUNCANSBY HEAD, CAITHNESS
ND 3968–4073. 40 ha   Grade 2

The 80 m Old Red Sandstone precipices and adjacent stacks of this north-eastern tip of the Scottish mainland have another important concentration of breeding seabirds, with guillemots (7500 pairs), razorbills (2300 pairs), puffins (Order 4), kittiwakes (6800 pairs) and fulmars (2500 pairs).

The acidic moorland abutting the cliff tops is floristically poor, and has *Calluna* heath, passing to boggy ground with much *Trichophorum* and *Eriophorum vaginatum*. Noteworthy species of the area include *Scilla verna* and *Ligusticum scoticum*.

W.24. WYCHWOOD FOREST, OXFORDSHIRE
SP 3316. 240 ha   Grade 1 (Extension)

The description of the grade 1 site given earlier referred to that portion of this woodland complex established as a NNR. Further survey has revealed the high quality of the remaining compartments outside, covering an equivalent area, and these are now described as an extension to the site.

Wychwood as a whole is an oak–ash forest with an understorey of hawthorn, hazel and field maple, and a field layer generally dominated by dog's mercury. This applies equally to the additional compartments, though in many areas these have a woodland structure more varied and uneven-aged than that within the NNR. Besides the dominant oak and ash are elm, hornbeam, Turkey oak, field maple and sycamore; and there is a stand of beech high forest. The shrub layer is mainly hazel and hawthorn (both species), with sallow, privet, spindle, buckthorn, blackthorn, wild cherry, dogwood, and occasional rowan, crab apple, guelder rose and holly. The climbing shrubs honeysuckle and traveller's joy are widespread. Several rare or local species of vascular plant are recorded from the field layer, notably *Aquilegia vulgaris*, *Platanthera chlorantha*, *Orchis mascula*, *Lathraea squamaria*, *Ribes uva-crispa*, *R. sylvestre*, *Euphorbia amygdaloides*, *Colchicum autumnale* and *Ophioglossum vulgatum*.

The additional area has received similar management to the Reserve itself, and contains a network of wide, mown rides. These often contain isolated trees and as they cross a wide range of soil types they support a diversity of herbaceous communities, and are likely to be of considerable value for fallow deer, birds and insects. There is also an area of limestone grassland sloping down to a pond, and this has characteristic calcicoles such as *Brachypodium pinnatum*, *Inula conyza*, *Dactylorchis fuchsii*, *Anacamptis pyramidalis*, *Campanula glomerata*, *Cirsium acaulon*, *C. eriophorum*, *Astragalus glycyphyllos*, *Clinopodium vulgare*, *Helianthemum chamaecistus*, *Hippocrepis comosa*, *Origanum vulgare* and *Viola hirta*. Old overgrown limestone quarries have growths of yew, dogwood and privet, and their flora includes *Polystichum aculeatum*, *Helleborus foetidus* and *Atropa belladonna*. These habitats have long been noted for their population of the Roman snail *Helix pomatia*.

W.230. STANNER ROCKS, RADNOR
SO 2658. 5 ha   Grade 1

This small area of open mixed deciduous woodland with some grassland on doleritic cliffs is of exceptional botanical interest. Facing south-east at only 230–300 m, the cliffs are subject to summer drought, maintaining open communities of plants of base-rich and base-poor soils. The flora contains a distinctive basiphilous element characteristic of open rock and scree habitats within woodland in continental Europe. Of particular note in the drier open area are *Scleranthus perennis* in its only Welsh locality, *Veronica spicata* ssp. *hybrida*, *Festuca longifolia*, *Lychnis viscaria*, *Sedum fosteranum*, *Geranium sanguineum* and *Helianthemum chamaecistus*. Representing a calcifuge element on leached habitats are *Teesdalia nudicaulis*, *Umbilicus rupestris* and *Jasione montana*. The moss *Bartramia stricta*, a Mediterranean species with only two or three localities in mainland Britain, occurs here and other interesting bryophytes of rocks and open soil include *Grimmia decipiens*, *G. commutata*, *G. stirtonii*, *G. subsquarrosa*, *Tortella nitida*, and *Riccia nigrella*. *Tortula canescens* recorded from this site has not been seen recently. The mixed deciduous woodland has sessile oak, occasional ash and wych elm with hazel and some elder as a shrub layer. *Targionia hypophylla*, an uncommon liverwort usually of exposed rocks, is common on shaded rocks in the wooded areas.

After the partial destruction by quarrying of the Breidden Hill farther north in the Welsh borders, this is probably the best example in Britain of a base-rich igneous outcrop with an interesting flora, including continental European and Mediterranean elements, and containing several species of highly localised British distribution. The site is an important one, posing intriguing problems for the ecologist, plant geographer and phytosociologist. It is classified here as woodland, but also has distinct grassland affinities.

W.231. TYCANOL WOOD, PEMBROKESHIRE
SN 0936.   30 ha   Grade 1

This woodland lies between 100–180 m on the exposed north and west slopes of a spur of the Bannau Preseli within 8 km of the sea. The site is noteworthy for its rich cryptogamic flora, particularly the lichens and ferns, which contain many old-forest indicator species. The topographic and geological variation within the wood is largely responsible for its wide range of habitats.

The northern and lowest parts on ashy shales of Ordovician age support a ground flora typical of base-rich woodlands. Ash and sessile oak dominate the canopy with sallow and alder in the wetter areas. The southern and central parts of the wood lie on dolerite. Erosion by marginal meltwater during the retreat of the Irish Sea ice is thought to have been responsible for the many deep rocky gullies with cliff-like walls, found in these parts of the site. The two filmy ferns (*Hymenophyllum wilsonii* and *H. tunbrigense*) and the hay-scented fern (*Dryopteris aemula*) occur in these rocky gullies which are also rich in bryophytes. Towards the southern end of the Wood the canopy is dominated by oaks which become smaller and more stunted and very reminiscent of those in Wistman's Wood, Dartmoor. At the tor-like summit of the dolerite crags, the oak trees are only a metre or so high and almost prostrate in form, resembling subalpine woodland such as is seen near the tree-line in other parts of Britain at higher elevations. The ground flora is largely limited to bilberry and heather, whilst the boulders and gnarled trunks support abundant bryophytes and lichens.

Of the 103 species of bryophytes recorded, those of oceanic distribution are most noteworthy. The lichen flora is, however, the outstanding feature. Of the *c*. 170 species recorded, over 100 are epiphytic, and the following seven are not recorded elsewhere in south Wales: *Arthonia stellaris*, *Bacidia leprosula*, *Melaspilea ochrothalamia*, *Nephroma parile*, *Ochrolechia tartarea*, *Parmelia endochlora* and *P. taylorensis*. Species of old-forest recorded are *Lobaria pulmonaria*, *Sticta*

fuliginosa, *S. limbata*, *S. sylvatica*, *Parmelia crinita*, and *P. reddenda*. Oceanic lichens of note are *Pannaria mediterranea*, *Parmelia cetrarioides*, *P. laevigata*, *Sphaerophorus globosus* and *S. melanocarpus*. This site is now one of the most northerly locations on the mainland of Britain for *Usnea articulata*, a large beard lichen, very sensitive to air pollution.

W.124. BRAMPTON BRYAN PARK, HEREFORDSHIRE
                                                            Regraded 1

W.222. OB MHEALLAIDH, SHIELDAIG, ROSS
NG 8353.   60 ha   Regraded 1 (Extension)

This is an extensive and well-developed example of a bryophyte-rich birchwood characteristic of much of north-west Scotland. The wood occupies a steep (10–30°) block-strewn slope and there are large rock outcrops of mildly basic Torridonian sandstone in the upper part of the wood. The wood runs from near sea-level to about 180 m altitude. The canopy is dominated by downy birch, with some rowan, pine, and holly. Ivy, aspen, and honeysuckle occur occasionally. The understorey consists largely of bilberry and heather. The blocks in the wood are densely clothed with bryophyte mats with a range of Atlantic and Sub-atlantic species such as *Sphagnum quinquefarium*, *Thuidium delicatulum*, *Hylocomium brevirostre*, *H. umbratum*, *Dicranodontium denudatum*, *Scapania gracilis*, *Plagiochila spinulosa*, *P. punctata*, *Mylia taylori*, *Herberta hutchinsiae*, *Bazzania tricrenata*, *Douinia ovata*, *Saccogyna viticulosa*, *Lepidozia pinnata*, and *Anastrepta orcadensis*. *Ptilium crista-castrensis*, and *Hymenophyllum wilsonii* are locally abundant, and *Dryopteris aemula*, *Dicranum scottianum*, *Dicranodontium uncinatum*, *Harpalejeunea ovata*, and *Sphaerophorus melanocarpus* occur more rarely. Damp flushed boulders in the cascading stream at the east end of the wood, and rocks in small rivulets and in flushed areas on and near the rock outcrops support *Hypericum androsaemum*, *Ulota americana*, *Hypnum callichroum*, *Trichostomum tenuirostre*, *Heterocladium heteropterum*, and *Sematophyllum novae-caesareae*. Rotten logs and damp humus-banks provide habitats for *Nowellia curvifolia*, *Scapania umbrosa*, and *Riccardia palmata*. Epiphytic growth is rather limited, but *Mylia cuneifolia*, *Plagiochila tridenticulata*, *Lobaria* spp. and *Ulota phyllantha* occur locally on trunks of birch and oak. Base-rich flushes within the wood support *Sphagnum warnstorfianum* and *S. contortum*.

The most notable feature of this extensive birchwood is the luxuriance and richness of the bryophyte cover. It is one of the finest bryophyte-rich birchwoods known in north-west Scotland. Its ecological relationships to the pine-dominated woods on the nearby south-west-facing slopes at Coille Creag-loch in Shieldaig are obscure, and warrant further research.

W.226. LOCH A' MHUILLIN WOOD, SUTHERLAND
                                                            Regraded 1

W.232. HANLEY DINGLE, HEREFORDSHIRE
SO 6866.   10 ha   Grade 2

The Teme Valley between Newnham Bridge and Martley has its sides cut by a number of wooded, narrow stream-ravines. Some of these have been modified by reafforestation, but several remain in a semi-natural condition, the finest example being Hanley Dingle.

The deep, steep-sided ravine is cut through Devonian rocks and is lined by wych elm and ash, with a scattering of several other native trees and shrubs, including oak and yew. The ground flora is very rich and luxuriant and is basiphilous in character. The base-rich flushes and marshy areas are particularly rich, the latter supporting both *Chrysosplenium oppositifolium* and *C. alternifolium*. Other notable herbs are *Allium ursinum*, *Campanula trachelium*, *Carex strigosa*, *Colchicum autumnale*, *Euphorbia amygdaloides*, *Ophioglossum vulgatum*, *Paris quadrifolia* and *Ranunculus auricomus*.

The Dingle is particularly noted for its rich and abundant fern flora. This includes *Athyrium filix-femina*, *Dryopteris borreri*, *D. filix-mas*, *Phyllitis scolopendrium* and *Polystichum setiferum*, the latter two being locally abundant on steep slopes.

The bryophyte flora is also rich and includes *Cratoneuron commutatum*, *Dicranum montanum*, *Lejeunea cavifolia* and *Mnium stellare*. The lichen flora is rather limited because of the heavy shade, but several interesting species occur, including the old-forest indicator *Thelotrema lepadinum*.

W.118. HILL HOLE DINGLE, HEREFORDSHIRE

Regraded 2

W.233. SWITHLAND WOOD, LEICESTERSHIRE
SK 5412.   60 ha   Grade 2

Swithland wood occupies a gentle east-facing slope on Triassic marls and sands which overlie the pre-Cambrian rocks of Charnwood Forest. The soils are mostly acidic, and range from clay loam to sandy loam.

Most of the woodland is dominated by oak *Quercus petraea*, birch and small-leaved lime in various proportions. The birch predominates on the highest, most acid soils, and lime is most abundant on the more basic soils. Over most of the wood, however, oak is the main tree species. In a valley which cuts through to heavier soils, alder and hazel are abundant, and pedunculate oak and ash replace sessile oak and birch in the canopy. Field layer communities typically are dominated by *Holcus mollis*, *Pteridium aquilinum*, *Deschampsia cespitosa*, *Rubus fruticosus*, *Luzula sylvatica* and *Deschampsia flexuosa*, whilst in the valley *Carex pendula* and *Dryopteris austriaca* are locally abundant. Some 230 species of vascular plants have been recorded including many characteristic of ancient woodland in the Midlands, e.g. *Melampyrum pratense*, *Luzula pilosa*, and *Lysimachia nemorum*. An ancient meadow within the woodland area supports a number of local species, including *Serratula tinctoria*, *Betonica officinalis* and *Ophioglossum vulgatum*. An adjacent area of sessile oak woodland and heathland, The Brand, has a rich lichen flora, including species extinct elsewhere in the east Midlands, and a *Leprania* sp. new to science.

Swithland appears to be an ancient wood formerly managed as coppice, but it has been allowed to develop towards high forest for over 100 years. It exhibits a considerable variety of habitat over woodland structure, coupled with a rich complement of rare and local species. Such woods are rare in the east Midlands, and at Swithland these assets are associated with exposures of pre-Cambrian rocks.

W.234. FINGLANDRIGG WOODS, CUMBERLAND
NY 2757.   125 ha   Grade 2

This area of mixed woodland lies to the west of Carlisle on the Solway Plain and is similar in overall character to Orton Woods (W.135). The main woodland types are of Scots pine and downy birch, either in pure or mixed stands, though in places there is scattered sessile oak and rowan. The soils are mainly base-poor, and part if not all of the woodland lies on

former peat-moss (raised bog). The field layer is acidophilous, with a prevalence of species such as *Dryopteris austriaca*, *D. spinulosa*, *Rubus fruticosus* agg., *Lonicera periclymenum*, *Holcus mollis*, *Polytrichum commune*, *Sphagnum palustre* and *S. fimbriatum*. One especially wet area south of the road is dominated by willows, *Salix cinerea*, with *Deschampsia cespitosa*, *Agrostis stolonifera* and *Angelica sylvestris*.

Adjoining the woods and forming part of the interesting complex are wet heaths and meadows. The heaths have *Calluna*, *Erica tetralix*, *Narthecium ossifragum*, *Molinia*, *Myrica*, *Trichophorum*, *Eriophorum angustifolium*, *Sphagnum compactum*, *Hypnum imponens*, and a remarkable outlying colony of the southern dwarf gorse *Ulex minor*. The meadows have a slightly acidophilous grassland with such species as *Cardamine pratensis*, *Pedicularis sylvatica* and *Succisa pratensis*, and were until recently a haunt of the marsh fritillary butterfly, *Euphydryas aurinia*.

L.14. CHOBHAM AND PIRBRIGHT COMPLEX, SURREY
SU 9254, SU 9159, SU 9764.   *c.* 1450 ha   Regraded 1

This large heathland complex, which is an extension and upgrading of the grade 2 site L.14, consists of three approximately equal-sized tracts of heathland which stretch for 16 km north-east of Aldershot. The Pirbright and Bisley sections are military training areas closed to the public, but Chobham Common has free access and is more disturbed. These heaths lie on the Bagshot, Bracklesham and Barton sands and gravels of the Tertiary deposits of the London Basin, and on plateau gravels on high ground, at altitudes of 30–120 m. The topography, which shows the greatest relief on Pirbright Common (the southern block), is undulating with valleys leading into ranges of low, flat-topped hills.

The open dry heath of the complex is characterised by extensive even-aged stands of heather, mostly maintained by accidental fires. Management otherwise is minimal and invasion of the open communities by bracken, birch and Scots pine, from the open woodland and copses of Scots pine and birch which are widely distributed over the whole complex, is advanced in many areas. There are also areas of old oak woodland with bluebell, and an alder carr. Wet heath communities with *Erica tetralix*, *Trichophorum cespitosum*, *Sphagnum compactum* and *S. tenellum*, dominated in parts by *Molinia caerulea*, are widespread; and in the valley bottom and around pools there are peat bog communities with good cover and representation of mesotrophic and oligotrophic *Sphagnum* spp.

At Chobham Common (the most northerly area) there is a marked similarity of the dry heathland communities to those of Dorset and the New Forest in that *Agrostis setacea* and *Ulex minor* are important components of the vegetation; the former being in its most easterly station in the British Isles.

The wet heath communities contain a number of locally distributed species, including at Chobham *Gentiana pneumonanthe* and *Lycopodium inundatum*; and the peat bog communities are also rich in rare species. Colony Bog, in the central block (Westend Common), is the only Surrey locality for *Schoenus nigricans* and *Eleocharis quinqueflora*, and contains two of the three colonies in the county of *Thelypteris palustris*, and one of only three localities for *Eriophorum vaginatum*. *Carex pulicaris*, *C. dioica*, and *Dactylorchis incarnata*, including an albino form, are also present. This bog also has bryophytes rare in Surrey such as *Scorpidium scorpioides*, *Drepanocladus revolvens*, *Climacium dendroides*, and *Riccardia pinguis*. Peat Moor Pond, on Pirbright Common, is important for the presence in an oligotrophic hydrosere of *Eriophorum gracile*.

There are notable breeding populations of such heathland birds as hobby, nightjar, whinchat, stonechat, and woodlark on the commons of this complex; red-backed shrike and other now very localised species also occur. Sparrowhawk and redstart breed in some numbers.

Chobham Common has long been known as a site of outstanding interest for its invertebrate fauna. A number of rare and local insects have been recorded from the area including a myrmecophilous mirid *Myrmecoris gracilis*, the saladid *Micracanthia marginalis*, and the ant *Formica rufibarbis* known elsewhere in Britain only from the Isles of Scilly.

Chobham is also well known for its spiders. The outstanding rarity is *Oxopes heterophthalmus*, for which Chobham Common is the only known British locality, apart from an old record from the New Forest. It was first found at Chobham Common in 1960, and has been seen on a number of subsequent occasions, mainly on the heathery slopes near Gracious Pond. Almost as rare is *Cheiracanthium pennyi*, which apart from Chobham Common has been recorded once recently from the New Forest and once a hundred years ago from near Wokingham. Other notable rarities present are *Uloborus walckenaerius*, which is almost confined to a few localities in the New Forest and Surrey, *Micaria subopaca*, which occurs on pine trunks only in Surrey and Sussex, *Araneus alsine*, a very local species with few British records, and *Thomisus onustus*, which is locally abundant on heathland but very restricted in distribution.

Apart from the rarities, the spider fauna of Chobham Common appears to be rather different from that of Thursley Common and other heaths in that area, and shows both south-eastern and New Forest elements in its fauna. It is possible that its faunal richness is partly related to its position in the London Basin, with its small climatic differences from Greensand Heaths farther south.

L.152. WOOLMER POND AND FOREST, HAMPSHIRE
SU 8032. *c.* 225 ha   Grade 1 (Extension)

This is a large but isolated tract of acidic heath and mixed wood lying between the major heathland complexes of the New Forest and Surrey, and lies over sands of the Folkestone beds. It contains the important open water site of Woolmer Pond (OW.7) which is rated as grade 1 in its own right.

There is a large extent of dry *Calluna* heath which has been little affected by fire in recent years, and shows an uneven age structure in places. *Erica cinerea* is locally abundant, and a good range of heathland *Cladonia* lichens is present, in sufficient density to give a lichen heath in places. Acidic valley mires with *Sphagnum* spp. are well developed, and there are characteristic species such as *Eriophorum vaginatum* and *Rhynchospora alba*. The heath shows variable colonisation by trees to give patches of woodland. Birch is the most abundant species, but there is some Scots pine and oak locally. Carr woodland on damp ground has the saprophytic liverwort *Cryptothallus mirabilis*. The very local orchid *Cephalanthera longifolia* also occurs, under oak and pine on apparently acidic soil.

Characteristic heathland birds and reptiles are well represented.

L.26. PEWSEY DOWNS, WILTSHIRE   Grade 1 (Extension)

L.153. CARN GAFALLT MEADOWS, BRECKNOCK
Regraded 1 (Extension)

(*a*) SN 952632. 4 ha

(*b*) SN 934637. 6 ha

(*c*) SN 933644. 2 ha
Neutral grassland group 10[1]

These six upland meadows are geographically grouped into three sites (*a*), (*b*) and (*c*) situated in the Dulas valley at the foot of the Carn Gafallt woodlands (W.97, gr. 2). The management of these meadows centres on early spring grazing followed by a hay cut in late July/August, though occasionally one or two may be summer grazed when fodder is in short supply.

Site (*a*) consists of two meadows; the hedge dividing the two is discontinuous and for management purposes the area is treated as one unit. The site, although heavily grazed in summer 1972, is normally cut for hay in late summer. Much of the slope is gentle which makes cutting possible but there are small steep banks and a wet area which are not cut and management consists of aftermath grazing only, to which the site as a whole is regularly subjected. The grassland is of the *Festuca rubra*, *Agrostis tenuis*, *A. stolonifera*, *Anthoxanthum odoratum*, *Holcus lanatus* type with a rich blend of grasses and sedges, 17 species having been recorded. Over 50 herb species were recorded including the typical meadow species of herb rich swards in mid Wales, *Platanthera chlorantha*, *Lathyrus montanus* and *Ophioglossum vulgatum*.

Site (*b*) consists of three meadows, two on the south side of the track and one on the north side. All three meadows are *Anthoxanthum odoratum*, *Cynosurus cristatus*, *Holcus lanatus*, *Agrostis tenuis* herb-rich grasslands. Included in the 50 or so herbs recorded were *Platanthera chlorantha*, *Lathyrus montanus*, *Leontodon hispidus*, *L. autumnalis*, *Sanguisorba officinalis* and *Vicia orobus*. Of the two southern meadows one is a small narrow field with a steep slope at one end, the other is the finest herb-rich meadow seen in the valley. It is outstanding for the abundance of *V. orobus*, a plant mainly confined to Welsh valleys and with only a very scattered westerly occurrence outside Wales. Its botanical diversity is increased by having a strip of wetter ground along the eastern border. This is a *Molinia–Carex* zone with *Viola palustris*, *Pedicularis sylvatica* and *Narthecium ossifragum*.

The northern meadow is less herb-rich than the other two and the virtual absence of *Sanguisorba officinalis* may indicate that this meadow has been summer grazed more often.

Site (*c*), unlike (*a*) and (*b*), is much less uniform, showing three characteristic habitat types: grassland, heath and marsh. The grassland is similar to the other sites and includes a few plants of *V. orobus*. The heath is characterised by *Anthoxanthum* and *Molinia* with small patches of *Erica tetralix*, *Galium saxatile* and *Vaccinium myrtillus*. The marsh is a *Molinia–Carex* community with *Lotus pedunculatus*, *Lychnis flos-cuculi*, *Viola palustris*, *Dactylorchis ericetorum* and a few plants of *Trollius europaeus*.

L.154. CLEHONGER MEADOW, HEREFORDSHIRE
SO 4436. 1 ha   Grade 1
Neutral grassland group 8[1]

This small meadow is an excellent example of 'unimproved' permanent grassland on a heavy loam soil in the west Mid-
[1] See pp. 186–7, vol. 1.

lands. The vegetation comprises a typical grass association in which *Agrostis stolonifera, Anthoxanthum odoratum, Cynosurus cristatus, Festuca rubra* and *Holcus lanatus* are co-dominant, with a further 10 grass species recorded. Although *Carex flacca* and *C. caryophyllea* are present, the sedges, together with *Rhinanthus minor*, are rare; which is unusual in this group. The herbaceous component of the sward is particularly rich and includes five orchid species of which *Coeloglossum viride* is of particular interest. A total of 66 species has so far been recorded, but does not include the large number of hedgerow plants enclosing the meadow. Hazel is abundant with hawthorn, blackthorn, oak, field maple, ash and holly frequent.

Other grassland examples of this type are rare in the country, Foster's Green, Worcestershire, being the nearest geographically and Monewden, Suffolk, having similar botanical characteristics – *Orchis morio, O. mascula* and *Colchicum autumnale* being typical.

Clehonger differs from Foster's Green and Monewden, in the former instance by the absence (i.e. unrecorded) of *Conopodium majus*, a characteristic species of somewhat lighter soils than those occurring at Clehonger, and from the latter by the absence of *Genista tinctoria*.

L.155. PARLEY COMMON, DORSET
SZ 0999.   100 ha   Grade 2

Parley Common, 6.4 km north of Bournemouth near Hurn airport, lies at about 15–20 m above sea-level. The site forms a strip, about 2 km in length and at the most 800 m in width, bounded by Ferndown Golf Course, a caravan site and residential development on the west and assorted dwellings, caravans and rubbish dumping to the east. There is agricultural land to the south and new housing development to the north. The common is a remnant of a once much larger area, but the shape of the site and nature of the surrounding area means that there is increasing disturbance to the remaining heathland area.

The site contains a reasonable selection of heathland communities but is perhaps best known for its entomological interests. In particular the site has a very diverse spider fauna, including a wide range of dry heath species as well as some fen types. The site appears to be intermediate between the New Forest and Purbeck heathlands in its spiders, but has more species in common with the former area. Among the more notable species are *Ero aphana*, new to Britain here, *Maro subestus* and *Xysticus robustus*.

L.156. HORTON COMMON, DORSET
SU 0707.   130 ha   Grade 2

Horton Common, 6.4 km east of Ringwood, lies between about 40 and 75 m above sea-level. There are areas of open dry heathland (*Calluna–Ulex minor*) on stony and gravelly soils, and areas of impeded drainage with humid and wet heath. Whilst there appears to be no immediate threat to these areas of open heath from scrub invasion there are considerable areas of gorse scrub and some areas where Scots pine is becoming established. The area is considered to be an important site for the Dartford warbler.

L.157. HOLT HEATH, DORSET
SU 0604.   385 ha   Grade 2

This area of heathland *c.* 1.6 km to the south of Horton Common is crossed by a road running east to west. The higher ground (up to 57 m) to the north of this road (Bull Barrow and Crooked Withies) is similar to Horton Common, containing open areas of dry *Calluna–Ulex minor* heath and areas of impeded drainage containing damper heathland communities. There are extensive areas of gorse scrub and the area is considered to be a most important Dartford warbler site. This particular area has also been listed as a Sand Lizard Conservation site by the British Herpetological Society. The area to the south of the road is more extensive (*c.* 300 ha) and contains a good range of heathland communities, including peatland areas in the lower south eastern parts.

L.158. DRYSLWYN MEADOWS, CARMARTHENSHIRE
SN 5720.   250 ha   Grade 2

A flock of European white-fronted geese has wintered in the meadows alongside Afon Tywi near Dryslwyn for over 30 years. Numbers have increased in the last decade from *c.* 500 in the early 1960s to a peak count of 2500 in 1971. At this time it was the second or third largest concentration of this goose in Britain. The last few years have shown a decrease to 520 in 1972, 1250 in 1973 and 1000 in 1974, perhaps associated with milder winters.

The birds do not appear in any number until late December even in 'good' years and they depart in late February–early March.

The main feeding area lies between Cilsan and Dryslwyn bridges. In the 1950s many of the geese used to flight to roost in the Loughor estuary, but in recent winters the actual roosting area has not been located. It has been suggested they may roost at sea farther out in Carmarthen Bay.

L.159. DRAYCOTE MEADOWS, WARWICKSHIRE
SP 4570.   5 ha   Grade 2
Neutral grassland group 8[1]

Two meadows, both on ridge and furrow, constitute the site. The most northerly field is normally cut for hay, the other usually being summer grazed by cattle.

Both meadows have a co-dominance of *Agrostis stolonifera, Anthoxanthum odoratum, Cynosurus cristatus* and *Festuca rubra* with nine further grass species having been recorded, including *Briza media* and *Trisetum flavescens*. The normal herb species for this group are present – *Chrysanthemum leucanthemum, Primula veris, Silaum silaus, Ophioglossum vulgatum* plus *Orchis morio* and *Botrychium lunaria*, an unusual species in neutral grasslands and uncommon in this region.

There is a species-rich hedge along the north-western boundary.

P.108. UPTON BROAD, NORFOLK
TM 3913.   105 ha   Grade 1 (Extension)

The Broad itself, a grade 1 open water site (OW.15), is surrounded by a large area of fen, fen carr and woodland, all on peat. These habitats are complementary to the Broad and the whole area should be regarded as a unit of grade 1 interest.

The largest area of open fen is on solid peat and is dominated by *Cladium mariscus* and *Schoenus nigricans* and contains a wide range of tall herbs including *Ranunculus lingua, Peucedanum palustre, Thelypteris palustris, Calamagrostis canescens, Salix repens, Carex elata* and *Carex lasiocarpa*. A contrasting area on lake muds overlain by peat is dominated by *Phragmites communis* and *Typha angustifolia*. This community contains *Cicuta virosa, Lathyrus palustris, Carex*

[1] See p. 186, vol. 1

appropinquata, C. paniculata and *C. pseudocyperus.* Where paths are cut, a wide range of species appears, including *C. flacca, C. disticha, C. diandra, C. lepidocarpa, Epipactis palustris, Dactylorhiza praetermissa, D. incarnata, Valeriana dioica, Pedicularis palustris* and at least five *Sphagnum* spp. In the more wooded areas there is a complex network of paths which have been regularly mown for a very long time, and these support a rich flora which includes *Pyrola rotundifolia, Platanthera bifolia, Parnassia palustris* and *Anagallis tenella.*

The fen carr and woodland are old and well developed. There is a wide range of shrubs including *Frangula alnus, Viburnum opulus, Rhamnus catharticus, Myrica gale, Thelycrania sanguinea* and *Prunus padus.* In several places there are many old oaks which add to the entomological and ornithological interest of the site, and give a woodland character to these parts of the site.

Breeding birds include sparrowhawk, heron, woodcock, water rail and great and lesser spotted woodpeckers. There is a very strong population of grass snakes, and otters also frequent the area. The open areas support a strong population of the swallowtail butterfly, and there is a rich and very important Odonata fauna which includes the rare *Aeshna isosceles,* confined to the Norfolk Broads. Lepidoptera are well represented, with strong colonies of white admiral and comma butterflies.

P.20. ANT MARSHES, NORFOLK
TG 3620.   500 ha   Regraded 1 (Extension)

The site includes the fen and fen carr around Barton Broad and a large area of fenland either side of the River Ant, downstream from the broad. The broad and associated waterways formerly supported a very rich fauna and flora but aquatic conditions have deteriorated markedly in the last two decades, and there are now dense algal blooms every year. Nevertheless the fen and fen carr habitats are of a very high quality.

Part of the site is managed for commercial reed and sedge harvesting, and there are extensive areas formerly managed for reed, sedge or marsh hay. There are examples of fen carr in all stages of development but in other areas the high water table has impeded invasion by scrub. The variation in management, substrate and water level has led to a very wide range of fen types. *Phragmites communis, Cladium mariscus, Schoenus nigricans, Juncus subnodulosus, Typha angustifolia, Molinia caerulea* and *Calamogrostis canescens* provide the dominant or co-dominant species.

The most floristically interesting area is cut on a three to four year rotation for sedge (*Cladium*). This is an outstanding example of a 'sump' type rich-fen in which a high water level is maintained throughout the year with standing water even in late summer. The cutting of the sedge every three to four years is clearly beneficial in allowing a wide range of fen herbs to survive. These include *Cicuta virosa, Peucedanum palustre, Ranunculus lingua, Baldellia ranunculoides, Drosera anglica, Parnassia palustris, Hypericum elodes, Ophioglossum vulgatum, Liparis loeselii, Epipactis palustris, Dactylorhiza traunsteineri, Dactylorhiza incarnata, Carex limosa, C. lasiocarpa, C. approinquata, C. diandra* and the mosses *Cinclidium stygium, Drepanoclalus revolvens, Scorpidium scorpioides, Campylium stellatum* and *Mnium seligeri.* Proof of the permanently high water table is afforded by the presence of *Utricularia vulgaris, U. intermedia* and *Potamogeton coloratus* growing on the fen surface.

Around the margins of this latter area there has been en-

croachment by scrub, primarily *Myrica gale* and *Betula pubescens* but with some *Salix cinerea* and *Alnus glutinosa.* Locally on the perimeter of the open area surface acidification has enabled *Sphagnum fimbriatum* and *S. teres* to develop, and in these areas *Dryopteris cristata, Osmunda regalis* and *Pyrola rotundifolia* are present. *Pyrola* persists well into the birch scrub in the *Sphagnum* carpet along with *Drosera rotundifolia. Calluna vulgaris* is also locally present in this habitat.

Another interesting habitat is a high water level reed-swamp in which *Phragmites* is dominant and *Typha angustifolia* locally co-dominant. The other constituents of this community are *Sium latifolium* (abundant), *Peucedanum palustre, Oenanthe fistulosa, Lycopus europaeus, Potentilla palustris, Stellaria palustris, Mentha aquatica* and *Carex pseudocyperus.*

Near Barton Broad there are areas of tussock fen slowly developing into swamp carr. These areas, dominated by *Carex paniculata* but also containing *C. approinquata* and *C. elata* provide quite a different habitat type and support a contrasting flora and fauna. The diversity of the site is also enhanced by several shallow pools and a system of dykes and banks. *Sonchus palustris* is present on some of the banks.

The site supports diverse bird populations including bearded tit, bittern, water rail and several species of wildfowl. It is also an important stronghold for the swallowtail butterfly.

P.61. BOWNESS COMMON, CUMBERLAND   Regraded 1

P.62. WEDHOLME FLOW, CUMBERLAND   Regraded 1

P.109. DEE OF DIRKADALE AND GLIMS MOSS, ORKNEY
HY 3124.   210 ha   Grade 1

This area includes several different types of mire in a valley within Old Red Sandstone rocks. Glims Moss is an area of raised-mire which grades into oligotrophic swamps on surrounding poorly drained land and into blanket mire on the surrounding hills. The oligotrophic swamps occur in the head of a shallow valley through which flows the Burn of Hillside. The lower part of this valley is occupied by an extensive calcareous valley mire known as the Dee of Dirkadale. In this mire the dominant vegetation is a sedge–bryophyte community dominated by *Carex diandra, C. paniculata, C. flacca, C. dioica, Lychnis flos-cuculi, Succisa pratensis, Sagina nodosa, Angelica sylvestris, Rhinanthus minor, Anagallis tenella, Schoenus nigricans, Parnassia palustris* and extensive carpets of bryophytes such as *Mnium punctatum, Acrocladium cuspidatum, A. giganteum, Bryum pseudotriquetrum* and *Trichocolea tomentella.* In places there are low clumps of willow scrub composed of *Salix aurita* and occasionally *S. phylicifolia.* Soligenous tracts have more extensive calcicolous bryophyte carpets and there are large areas of swamp vegetation dominated by *Equisetum fluviatile, Menyanthes trifoliata, Potentilla palustris, Carex rostrata, C. limosa* and *Triglochin maritima,* the latter indicating the proximity to the sea.

This is the most northerly example of calcareous valley mire in Britain and is the best example of this habitat on the Old Red Sandstone of northern Scotland.

Glims Moss is less important but is included in the grade 1 site in view of the complete gradation from acid to alkaline conditions which this area displays. Though the raised mire surface has been severely altered by drainage, it is still dominated by raised-mire vegetation with the exception of a poor-fen flora in the drainage channels and hollows. Most of the surface is dominated by *Calluna vulgaris, Empetrum nigrum, Deschampsia flexuosa, Eriophorum vaginatum.* There is relatively little *Sphagnum* cover and other mosses such as *Hylocomium splendens, Pleurozium schreberi*, and *Plagiothecium undulatum* are abundant.

P.110. LOCH TALLANT, ISLAY, ARGYLL
NR 3358.   *c.* 80 ha   Grade 1

There is an extensive area of mire vegetation developed in a large basin at the east and south-east ends of Loch Tallant. In the loch there is an extensive *Phragmites communis* reed-swamp with *Carex rostrata, Schoenoplectus lacustris, Cladium mariscus, Eleocharis palustris, Nymphaea alba*, and *Potamogeton natans*. This merges into the main area of fen which is dominated by *Phragmites* but with an almost continuous *Carex rostrata*–'brown moss' rich-fen vegetation as an under-storey. This understorey is dominated by *Carex rostrata, C. limosa, C. nigra, C. lasiocarpa*, and *Menyanthes trifoliata*, with *Potentilla palustris, Hypericum elodes, Utricularia minor, Potamogeton polygonifolius, C. diandra, C. lepidocarpa, Eleocharis quinqueflora*, and *Drosera anglica*. 'Brown mosses' are locally abundant with *Scorpidium scorpioides, Drepanocladus revolvens, Campylium stellatum*, and *Acrocladium giganteum*. Other bryophytes of note in this fen include *Cinclidium stygium, Sphagnum contortum*, and *S. warnstorfianum*.

Within this rich-fen there are large hummocks of *Molinia caerulea* with *Carex echinata, C. pulicaris, Myrica gale, Narthecium ossifragum, Platanthera chlorantha, Dactylorchis purpurella, Salix aurita*, and *Dicranum bonjeani*. In drier areas there are large stands of willow carr dominated by *Salix cinerea, S. aurita*, and *S. phylicifolia*. Birch and alder occur more rarely but are locally prominent in the transition to the oakwood on the north side of the fen. Within the carr *Dryopteris spinulosa, D. dilatata, Carex paniculata, Caltha palustris, Angelica sylvestris, Filipendula ulmaria, Cirsium palustre, Valeriana officinalis, Sphagnum teres, S. squarrosum, Acrocladium stramineum, Climacium dendroides*, and *Mnium seligeri* are frequent. *Thelypteris palustris* occurs rarely in the carr.

There is a well-developed transitional zone between the fen and the surrounding bog dominated by *Molinia caerulea* associated with *Carex rostrata, C. nigra, C. distans, Myrica gale, Deschampsia flexuosa, Anagallis tenella, Sphagnum palustre, S. plumulosum*, and *Erica tetralix*.

The fen is virtually unique in its floristic composition and ecological situation but it has some similarities with Malham North Fen, differing in the excellent development of rich-fen vegetation growing under *Phragmites communis*.

P.111. PITMADUTHY MOSS, ROSS
NH 7777.   90 ha   Grade 1

This is an unusual type of mire which has characteristics of both raised and valley mire. It is developed in a valley system within glacial sands and gravels. The raised mire occupies a slight col at the head of two valleys and merges into oligo-trophic mire communities within each of these valleys. It is bounded on each side by gently sloping mineral ground covered by woodland of Scots pine and birch and there is a gradual transition from the open raised mire with stunted pines to closed canopy pinewood.

The vegetation of the open raised mire is predominantly a dry facies composed of dwarf shrubs and lichens with numerous stunted pines. Within this relatively level surface there are many small hollows which have steep edges and a carpet of *Sphagnum*. The surfaces of such hollows generally lie about 20 cm below the level of the mire surface. Within the dry facies of the mire expanse the dominant species are *Calluna vulgaris, Erica tetralix, Eriophorum vaginatum, Cladonia impexa, Hypnum cupressiforme* and *Parmelia physodes*, whilst others such as *Drosera rotundifolia, Eriophorum angustifolium, Narthecium ossifragum, S. rubellum* and *S. tenellum* are abundant. *S. fuscum* is present locally. Within this vegetation there are also many species of liverwort. These are particularly abundant on the steep edges of the hollows. Over 20 species of liverworts have been found within the open raised mire which is an unusually large number. The vegetation of the hollows is, in contrast, very uniform. *S. cuspidatum* or *Zygogonium* are the dominant species and many hollows have dense carpets of *Drosera anglica* and *Rhynchospora alba*.

This type of raised mire seems to be confined to north-east Scotland the only other example known being the Monadh Mor on the Black Isle. In both areas the climate is very dry. There are close similarities between this type of mire and the 'stunted pine' raised mires around the southern Baltic.

Pine woodland around the margin of the raised mire supports siskin and crested tit.

P.112. CNOC NA MOINE, SUTHERLAND
NC 6352.   500 ha   Grade 1

This interesting stretch of moorland, east of Loch Craggie, near Tongue, has unusual habitat and mire features and a considerable ornithological interest. It contains the small, elongated Loch na Moine, a dystrophic lochan which is clearly the remnant of a larger tarn tapped some decades ago by cutting a drain through the naturally low and narrow retaining bank on the south edge. This attempt to drain the loch was only partly successful, and has produced a smaller area of open water surrounded on all but its north-eastern side by a treacherous swamp, the result of plant colonisation of the former lake-bed.

The western edge of the loch has open luxuriant tussocks of common rush *Juncus effusus* growing in varying density in peaty mud. Beyond the rushes is a zone of deep spongy *Sphagnum* swamp (*S. papillosum, S. palustre, S. recurvum, S. cuspidatum, S. auriculatum*) with a tussocky growth of vascular plants such as *Eriophorum angustifolium, E. vaginatum, Carex nigra, Molinia caerulea* and forbs such as *Ranunculus flammula* and *Viola palustris*. This passes into a drier *Molinia, Calluna, Myrica* and *Erica tetralix* community, still with abundant *Sphagnum*, and much *Nardus* and *Juncus squarrosus* where the peat is shallower. An outermost, stony zone with the last two species, *Calluna, Carex panicea, Pinguicula vulgaris, Drosera anglica* and *Rhacomitrium lanuginosum* marks the original margin of the former lake. Higher and drier ground has patches of gorse.

In places, the loch edge communities are separated from the surrounding moorland by a low peat face, and above this the ground rises gently into the fairly uniform mantle of blanket mire extending over Cnoc na Moine, the semi-circular spur containing the loch. Though not completely flat, this mire has the character of typical Sutherland flow; there are numerous pools, some quite large, and the general surface has the usual *Trichophorum–Eriophorum–Molinia–Sphagnum* community. There are domed hummocks of *S. imbricatum* and *S. fuscum*, and an abundance of *Pleurozia purpurea* and *Rhacomitrium lanuginosum*.

The breeding bird population is varied and includes many of the characteristic northern Scottish wetland species. A moderate-sized (200–300 pairs) colony of black-headed gulls nests in the *Juncus* tussock swamp, and both black-throated and red-throated divers breed here. Greylag geese are sometimes seen on the loch and may nest in the vicinity. Mallard, wigeon and several pairs of teal nest around the drier edges, and there are reed buntings here. Waders are especially well represented, though they breed mainly on the surrounding flow; they include greenshank, redshank, golden plover, dunlin, snipe, curlew and lapwing. Woodcock nest in the birchwood on Sron Ruadh overlooking Loch na Moine to the south, and sandpipers along the adjacent shores of Lochs Craggie and Loyal.

P.15. SMALLBURGH FEN, NORFOLK   Regraded 2

P.113. CORS GEIRCH, CAERNARVONSHIRE
SH 3136.   140 ha   Grade 2

Cors Geirch is a valley mire situated about 3 km south of Nefyn in the Lleyn Peninsula. The mire occupies a shallow valley over a distance of 5 km and has apparently developed over the site of a glacial lake dammed by moraines. The drainage water from surrounding hills is in places strongly calcareous and the mire vegetation consists of a mosaic of communities of contrasting nutrient status. The wide range of vegetation communities and transition zones is one of the most important features of this site, but it is also outstanding on account of the large number of rare and local species of mire plants which occur. Herb-rich fen associations dominated by *Schoenus nigricans*, *Cladium mariscus*, *Phragmites communis*, *Juncus subnodulosus*, *Molinea caerulea* and *Myrica gale* are extensive. These include a very large number of herbs and over 18 species of sedge, including *Carex diandra*, *C. lasiocarpa*, *C. lepidocarpa*, *C. flacca* and *C. stellulata*. Other important species in this community are *Dactylorchis traunsteineri*, *Eriophorum gracile* and *Utricularia intermedia*. In places there are bryophyte carpets composed of *Campylium stellatum*, *Acrocladium giganteum*, *A. cordifolium* and locally the rare mosses *Camptothecium nitens* and *Bryum neodamense*. In predominantly base-poor conditions there are poor-fen swamps dominated by *Carex lasiocarpa* and *C. rostrata* which grade into bog communities which include *Vaccinium oxycoccus*, *Platanthera bifolia* and *Narthecium ossifragum*. Drier areas of heath support *Genista anglica* and *Ulex gallii*.

P.114. DRUMBURGH MOSS, CUMBERLAND
NY 2558.   140 ha   Grade 2

This is one of the four remaining areas of raised mire in north-west Cumberland. The vegetation is a similar type to that of the grade 1 raised mires in this area. This site has been affected by several severe fires over recent years but still has good examples of raised mire plant communities. The structure of the mire is less affected by artificial drainage than any of the other sites in this area, but the margins have in the past been subject to localised peat-cutting for domestic fuel.

The vegetation of the central cupola is dominated by *Erica tetralix*, *Calluna vulgaris*, *Eriophorum angustifolium*, *E. vaginatum*, *Andromeda polifolia*, *Sphagnum cuspidatum*, *S. tenellum* and *S. magellanicum*. There is a slight development of hummocks and hollows on the surface but much of the mire expanse is occupied by a fairly uniform vegetation in which species normally associated with wet hollows are very abundant. The mire surface has a very high water table and it seems that the communities damaged by fire are likely to revert to the more normal raised mire vegetation. The

lack of artificial drainage makes this site an important example of lowland raised mire since most other examples have been considerably affected by shrinkage and desiccation resulting from drainage schemes. In this case the mire is virtually intact as a hydrological unit. Certain species of undamaged raised mire, such as *Sphagnum pulchrum* and *Dicranum bergeri*, were once present and may have disappeared as a result of fire. Small patches of colonising birchwood occur along the southern edge of the Moss.

P.115. AUSTWICK MOSS, YORKSHIRE
SD 7666.   30 ha   Grade 2

This is a small area of raised mire in the valley of the River Wenning. The present surface of the moss is entirely modified by past peat-cutting but the site has retained a considerable diversity of plant and animal species characteristic of raised mire. Through peat-cutting the depth of peat has been reduced to only 1–2 m and the central part of the moss has many pools or wet hollows, some of which extend down to the underlying shell marl. There is therefore a mixture of poor-fen vegetation and truly ombrotrophic vegetation in close proximity. Many of the hollows are dominated by *Sphagnum*, either *S. cuspidatum* or *S. recurvum*, and *Vaccinium oxycoccus* is often dominant in these *Sphagnum* lawns. The water level in the hollows is about 25–30 cm below the general surface of the moss which is comparatively firm and dry. This dry surface has become colonised by *Betula pubescens* but *Calluna vulgaris*, *Eriophorum vaginatum*, *Erica tetralix*, *Vaccinium myrtillus*, *Pleurozium schreber* and *S. rubellum* are locally dominant. In places the pools have a wider diversity of plant species including *Andromeda polifolia*, *S. papillosum*, *S. magellanicum*, *Drosera rotundifolia* and *Drepanocladus* sp. One section of the central area is dominated by a 1.5 m high stand of *Myrica gale*. Towards the edge of the moss there is a gradation to poor-fen vegetation through *Betula–S. palustre* carr, and this grades into a species-rich *Molinia* grassland around the margin of the Moss.

Austwick Moss is well known as an important locality for rare and local species of insects and spiders.

P.116. DERGOALS FLOW, WIGTOWNSHIRE
NX 2458.   160 ha   Grade 2

This is an example of a type of mire, intermediate between raised and blanket mire, which is widespread in Wigtownshire. At the lower margin there is a distinct rand and the bog extends upslope over a gently sloping watershed. The highest part of the flow forms an extensive flat or gently sloping mire surface. In places hummocks of mineral ground protrude through the peat. The vegetation has a small-scale microtopography produced by hummocks of ericaceous plants within a predominantly level surface. There are no pools and few wet hollows, and *Sphagnum*, though abundant throughout, does not form a continuous ground layer. The dominant species are *Calluna vulgaris*, *Erica tetralix*, *Eriophorum angustifolium*, *Sphagnum rubellum* and *Sphagnum tenellum* with abundant *Andromeda polifolia*, *Eriophorum vaginatum*, *Myrica gale*, *S. papillosum* and *Hypnum cupressiforme*. Other species present include *Drosera rotundifolia* and *Drosera anglica*, *Rhynchospora alba*, *Vaccinium oxycoccus*, *Trichophorum cespitosum* and *Cladonia* spp. especially *C. impexa* and *C. uncialis*. *S. magellanicum* and *S. cuspidatum* are abundant in the wetter areas and there are occasional hummocks of *S. imbricatum* and *S. fuscum*. The vegetation has close affinities with that of the Irthinghead Mires.

Most of the mires of this type in Wigtownshire have been afforested in recent years and Dergoals Flow is one of the best remaining areas.

U.93. GLAS CNOC, ROSS   Regraded 1

U.100. RONAS HILL AND NORTH ROE, SHETLAND
HU 3387.   7200 ha   Regraded 1 (Extension)

Ronas Hill and the moorland area to the north, known as North Roe, contain an unusual range of upland and peatland habitats. Ronas Hill (450 m) which is the highest point in Shetland is composed of granitic rocks whilst the area to the north is composed of orthogneiss. Throughout the whole area the soils are base-poor but there is a wide range of habitats resulting from the action of frost, severe wind exposure and variations in topography. Ronas Hill is particularly important for the range of patterned ground conditions resulting from frost and wind action. The vegetation in such areas is very similar to the Faeroese fell-field. Patterns include turf-banked terraces, wind stripes and hill dunes, all of which include vegetated and bare ground. *Rhacomitrium* heath is an important component of this vegetation together with *Calluna* and *Empetrum nigrum*. Many alpine species occur in this vegetation including *Carex bigelowii*, *Juncus trifidus*, *J. triglumis*, *Loiseleuria procumbens*, *Luzula spicata*, *Salix herbacea*, *Festuca vivipara*, *Lycopodium alpinum*, *Saussurea alpina*, *Antennaria dioica*, *Alchemilla alpina* and, at lower levels, *Vaccinium uliginosum* and *Arctous alpina*. Northern Atlantic hepatics are well represented in number of species, but are poorly developed as a community, as the north-facing slopes are not steep enough to give the required amount of shade. The seaward slope of Ronas Hill has much broken cliff and the granite sea cliffs have an unusual development of landslips within which deep fissures provide habitats for bryophytes and ferns.

The solifluction terraces and ablation surfaces are developed at unusually low altitudes and the interaction between the effects of frost and wind is seen more clearly on Ronas Hill than on any other upland area in Britain.

North Roe is an area of depressions and rocky knolls resulting from ice action. Many of the hollows are occupied by mire communities and there are numerous small lakes. Some of these lakes have important relict scrub communities on fringing cliffs and on islands. These include *Salix aurita*, *S. lapponum* and *Populus tremula*. An important feature of North Roe is the development of an unusual vegetation type probably associated with wind action. This takes the form of numerous separate mounds which are composed entirely of peat and are dominated by ericaceous species. Such peat mounds also occur on high ground on Hoy (Orkney) but are not known elsewhere in Britain. The cliff coast of North Roe is important for the range of geomorphological features and this area supports about 30% of the grey seal population of Shetland. Seabird colonies are not particularly important but inland there is a high population of great skuas often associated with areas of peat mounds which provide nest sites.

U.101. GELTSDALE–TINDALE FELLS, CUMBERLAND
NY 6054.   6000 ha   Grade 1

This area forms the northernmost extremity of the Pennine Chain, overlooking the Tyne Gap, and ranges from fell-bottom meadows to elevated moorland reaching 627 m on Cold Fell. The small lake of Tindale Tarn lies at the foot of the steep slope of Tindale Fell, and gives an additional open

water interest. Carboniferous rocks underlie the whole area, but the limestone beds are only thin and most of the area is formed of acidic sandstone and shales. Coal Measures occur on the lower ground and have been sporadically mined on a small scale, and there is an exposure of Whin Sill along the glen of the Black Burn in the north-east, and this has been quarried on the hillside. Sandstone has also been quarried near Forest Head and Hallbankgate. The moorland area is managed both as grouse-moor and sheep-walk.

Most of the higher moorland is covered by typical Pennine *Calluna vulgaris–Eriophorum vaginatum* blanket bog, somewhat modified by burning and grazing, and showing local erosion by gullying. *Empetrum nigrum*, *Vaccinium vitis-idaea*, *V. oxycoccus* and *Rubus chamaemorus* are locally abundant. *Sphagnum* cover is generally not high, and there are rather few pools and wet hollows, but *S. fuscum* still occurs. Dry heather moor occurs on better-drained ground, and there is local dominance of bilberry and bracken. Acidic grassland is well represented, mainly of the *Nardus stricta* and *Festuca–Agrostis* type, but there are only rather small patches of basic grassland with a typical limestone flora. Both acidic and calcareous moss springs and flushes occur widely. The marshy meadows around Tindale Tarn and Coalfell Beck have been variously improved and drained, and have variable amounts of *Juncus effusus*. The 5-km stretch of the Gelt Valley above Greenwell has several blocks of fringing woodland, and this varies from ash–wych elm–oak–hazel on dry basic soils to birch–hazel on more acidic sites, and varying amounts of alder as drainage deteriorates. The main oakwoods lie farther down the Gelt, but this tree is well represented within the site. Other frequent species include rowan and hawthorn, and there are introduced species such as beech and sycamore, as well as small blocks of planted conifers, mainly larch and spruce. The lower woods are fenced and ungrazed, but the upper ones are open to the hillside and are heavily grazed. Attenuated fringes of woodland, especially of birch, occur along some streams, notably the Black Burn and Old Water. Compared with the Cross Fell and Upper Teesdale areas farther south, the area is not distinguished botanically, and montane/submontane species are few; in addition to those mentioned, there are *Cochlearia alpina*, *Sedum villosum* and *Saxifraga stellaris*. *Primula farinosa* occurred formerly.

The main interest of the area is ornithological, for it supports a particularly large and diverse breeding bird population when the woods and enclosed marginal lands are taken together with the open moorlands. The meadows and marshy pastures around the northern fringe of the area and the lower moors have good numbers of lapwing, snipe, redshank, curlew, stonechat, whinchat and reed bunting. The population of curlews is especially dense, there being an estimated 120–140 breeding pairs. Good numbers of dippers and grey wagtails breed along the streams, and the numerous ring ouzels are mainly along the watercourses. Wheatears and skylarks breed widely, but the most abundant species are the meadow pipit and red grouse. In high vole years, up to 20 or even more pairs of kestrels breed, in the small streamside crags and old carrion crow nests in trees. Merlins nest in smaller numbers, and one pair of ravens sometimes breeds. Short-eared owls appear to be sporadic nesters. Some species have declined over the last few decades, mainly the golden plover, dunlin, sandpiper and black grouse. Golden plover still nest widely on the blanket bogs, but are patchily distributed and less numerous than in some parts of the Pennines farther south. The woodlands have a wide variety of breeding birds, including a recent colonist – the goosander – pied flycatcher, redstart, wood warbler, garden warbler, blackcap, goldfinch, redpoll, willow tit, marsh tit, goldcrest, tree pipit, green woodpecker, greater spotted woodpecker, woodcock, tawny owl and sparrowhawk. Altogether, at least 81 species have been known to nest recently within the area.

Tindale Tarn has local interest as an autumn and winter haunt of wildfowl, including mallard, tufted duck, pochard, goldeneye and whooper swan. Breeding species include great crested grebe, sedge warbler, coot and common sandpiper.

SITE INDEX